U0585858

荆楚文庫編纂出版委員會
武漢大學出版社

馮漢驥集

FENG HAN JI JI

圖書在版編目(CIP)數據

馮漢驥集/馮漢驥著.
—武漢:武漢大學出版社,2021.12
ISBN 978-7-307-19033-7
Ⅰ.馮…
Ⅱ.馮…
Ⅲ.社會科學—文集
Ⅳ.C53
中國版本圖書館 CIP 數據核字(2016)第 315563 號

責任編輯:詹　蜜　韓秋婷
整體設計:范漢成　曾顯惠　思　蒙
責任校對:汪欣怡
出版發行:武漢大學出版社
地址:武昌珞珈山
電話:(027)87215822　　郵政編碼:430072
録排:衆欣圖文設計室
印刷:湖北新華印務有限公司
開本:720mm×1000mm　1/16
印張:59.75　插頁:16
字數:828 千字
版次:2021 年 12 月第 1 版　2021 年 12 月第 1 次印刷
定價:178.00 元(全二册)

出版説明

湖北乃九省通衢，北學南學交會融通之地，文明昌盛，歷代文獻豐厚。守望傳統，編纂荆楚文獻，湖北淵源有自。清同治年間設立官書局，以整理鄉邦文獻爲旨趣。光緒年間張之洞督鄂後，以崇文書局推進典籍集成，湖北鄉賢身體力行之，編纂《湖北文徵》，集元明清三代湖北先哲遺作，收兩千七百餘作者文八千餘篇，洋洋六百萬言。盧氏兄弟輯録湖北先賢之作而成《湖北先正遺書》。至當代，武漢多所大學、圖書館在鄉邦典籍整理方面亦多所用力。爲傳承和弘揚優秀傳統文化，湖北省委、省政府決定編纂大型歷史文獻叢書《荆楚文庫》。

《荆楚文庫》以“搶救、保護、整理、出版”湖北文獻爲宗旨，分三編集藏。

甲、文獻編。收録歷代鄂籍人士著述，長期寓居湖北人士著述，省外人士探究湖北著述。包括傳世文獻、出土文獻和民間文獻。

乙、方志編。收録歷代省志、府縣志等。

丙、研究編。收録今人研究評述荆楚人物、史地、風物的學術著作和工具書及圖册。

文獻編、方志編録籍以 1949 年爲下限。

研究編簡體横排，文獻編繁體横排，方志編影印或點校出版。

《荆楚文庫》編纂出版委員會

2015 年 11 月

馮漢驥（1899.11—1977.3）

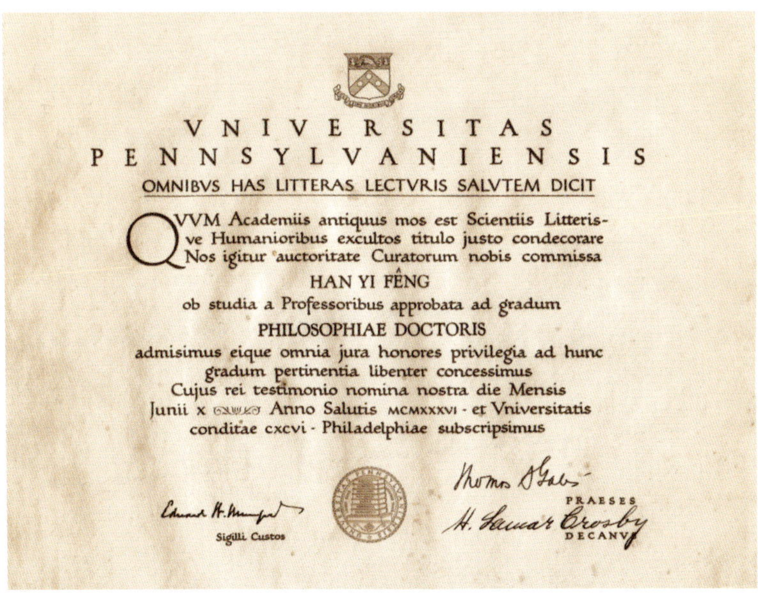

VNIVERSITAS
PENNSYLVANIENSIS
OMNIBVS HAS LITTERAS LECTVRIS SALVTEM DICIT

QVVM Academiis antiquus mos est Scientiis Litteris-ve Humanioribus excultos titulo justo condecorare Nos igitur auctoritate Curatorum nobis commissa

HAN YI FÊNG

ob studia a Professoribus approbata ad gradum

PHILOSOPHIAE DOCTORIS

admisimus eique omnia jura honores privilegia ad hunc gradum pertinentia libenter concessimus Cujus rei testimonio nomina nostra die Mensis Junii x Anno Salutis MCMXXXVI - et Vniversitatis conditae CXCVI - Philadelphiae subscripsimus

Sigilli Custos

PRAESES

DECANVS

1936年獲賓夕法尼亞大學人類學哲學博士學位

STUDENTS, BOONE LIBRARY SCHOOL, WUCHANG

Some of the future librarians of the new public libraries which will be established in China in the years to come. The Americans in the front row are: (left to right) Miss Wood, Bishop and Mrs. Gilman

参加武昌文華圖書館專科學校研究會會議（後排右二爲馮漢驥）

考古工作中（左四爲馮漢驥）

馮漢驥與家人

前　　言

一、成長經歷

馮漢驥，字伯良，湖北宜昌人，1899 年 11 月 21 日出生於宜昌杜林鄉馮家灣農家。曾一度在家務農，能掌犁耕田。入私塾發蒙後，因父親馮藝林在武昌武益堂(武昌文華附屬中學)任教，故進入宜昌美華中學附屬小學上學。後考入安慶聖保羅高等學校讀至大學預科，以第一名的優異成績畢業後，於 1919 年按校際合同規定直接升入武昌文華大學文科就讀，兼修圖書館科，1923 年畢業。1923—1931 年，先後擔任厦門大學圖書館襄理、主任，湖北省圖書館館長，浙江大學文理學院圖書館主任，與魯迅、顧頡剛、秉志、錢寶琮、貝時璋等相識，對人類學、歷史學和考古學產生了興趣。1931—1933 年，以數年工作積存的薪金 4000 銀元赴美國波士頓，留學於哈佛大學研究院人類學系，深受狄克遜(R. B. Dixon)文化進化論的影響。1933 年，因與公派至紐約哥倫比亞大學研讀學前教育的陸秀結婚，轉入賓夕法尼亞大學人類學系研讀，師從哈羅威爾(Hallowell)學習文化心理學，從布朗(N. Brown)和斯賓塞爾(Spencer)學習亞洲考古。留學期間，除有一年時間的半官費資助之外，完全靠自己打工的收入解決費用。1936 年夏獲賓夕法尼亞大學人類學哲學博士學位，當年即受聘於哈佛大學任教并兼任哈佛大學漢和圖書館主任。1936 年末，中央博物院籌備處主任李濟訪美，專程前往波士頓邀馮漢驥回國共同創辦人類學研究所。哈佛大學校方聞訊後，曾許以工作兩年後破格晉升終身教授的優厚待遇相挽留，馮漢驥出於愛國熱忱，婉然謝絶，於 1937 年春啓程經歐洲回國服務。因“八一三”淞滬抗日軍興，中央研究院輾轉搬遷，博物院無力再建新所，遂於是年 11 月應四川大學之聘任史學系教職，爲該校七名中英庚款講座教授之一，講授人類學、先史考古學、人生地理學課程。1939 年秋，因簽名反對教育部任命國民黨黨棍程天放做四川大學校長，并拒絶加入三青團、國民黨，離開四川大學。經蒙文通之推薦，受四川省教育廳郭有守之聘籌建四川博物館，於 1941 年春建成後對外開放展覽。此後，本擬應邀前往雲南大學或浙江大學任教，適逢成都修建防空工程挖掘出“撫琴臺”古代大墓部分室壁，馮漢驥認證其爲前蜀皇帝王建永陵，有很大的學術價值，遂應郭有守之請，留在四川省博物館進行發掘研究。1942 年應聘任華西大學社會學系教授，後任系主任。1944—1949 年，在徐中舒的一再邀請下，馮漢驥又回到四川大學。在此期間，仍兼任四川省博物館館長。1946 年和 1948 年，曾兩次受邀到聯合國教科文組織任職，但因相繼回湖北老家奔父、母之喪而未能成行。1950—1956 年，任西南博物院副院長。自 1956 年至 1977 年 3 月辭世，任四川省博物館館長，兼任四川大學歷史系教授、考古教研室主任。

馮漢驥一生受家庭教育影響甚深。父親早年參加同盟會，家中無一人參加教會、袍哥和黨團組織。馮漢驥秉承“不愛錢，不置産，待人恕，律己嚴，行爲正派”的家訓，從小養成堅毅正直的獨立性格，苦讀成學，從不依附權貴、阿世媚俗、屈服於反動政治勢力。在 1949 年中華人民共和國成立之前，大學中同事多爲國民黨或青年黨成員，時來相邀加入組織，均遭拒絶，除參加中國科學社、中國民族學會、中國博物學會等純學術團體外，從未加入任何政黨。“雖有相熟之人，當其一人政界，就等於斷絶來往了”。除裘開明、徐中舒、蒙文通、任乃强和朱光潛、聞在宥、楊人楩、胡鑑民等學者而外，很少與人交往。一生以追求真理、獻身祖國科學事業爲宗旨，潛心學術研究，淡泊名利。馮漢驥治學嚴謹，從不寫應酬作品。他曾多次告誡學生，文章寫成之後，一定要放上一段時間再看更多的材料，經過反復檢驗訂正，萬勿輕易寄出發表，誤人誤己。他倡導勤奮好學之風，極富學術民主精神，虛懷若谷，愛惜人才，不遺餘力，在四川省博物館多年，凡有一技之長者，莫不受其器重。他雖不喜社會活動，不好交遊，但對朋友、對下屬，却能坦誠相見，助人爲樂，對後生青年，誨人不倦，愛護備至，道德文章，深受大家的愛戴。

二、在考古學上的學術特點和貢獻

馮漢驥不僅是考古學家，同時也是人類學家和民族學家。馮漢驥早年在國内攻讀文科并兼修圖書館專業，打下了堅實的中國傳統國學基礎，具有深厚的古代歷史文獻功底。後來留學美國攻讀人類學，接受嚴格的近代西方學術有關理論和技能的科學訓練，按其學制，除體質人類學、文化人類學課程之外，同時修讀社會學、民俗學、民族學、考古學、歷史學等多種相互關聯的課程，參加田野實習。在美留學期間，曾到南美洲進行瑪雅遺址的考古發掘，從事理論研究實踐，發表著作多種。1937年學成歸國後，馮漢驥最初是人類學、民族學、考古學三者并治而以人類學與民族學爲主；自1942年發掘王建墓以來，逐漸把研究重點轉向考古；1949年以後，更是把大部分精力集中到了這一方面，在很大程度上將人類學、民族學理論知識融入考古研究之中。馮漢驥的學術經歷，決定了他的學術成就和治學特點。

馮漢驥之治考古，博大精深，從理論、方法、技能、知識結構到具體的研究實踐，形成了具有鮮明特點的學術體系。在理論方面，力主考古學是歷史科學的一個組成部分。他編寫的《考古學通論》油印講義明確提出：考古學在本質上“始終是歷史科學”。“研究古物不是本來目的。只有把這些古物當做歷史研究的材料時，它們才有科學價值”。他多次教導學生：“從事現代考古工作，必須親自參加田野發掘，不能只是坐在家中搞沙發考古。但一個考古學家首先必須是一個歷史學家，否則便只能成爲考古匠。”按照他的觀點，田野考古是現代考古學的基礎，不懂得田野考古，整個考古研究也就無從談起。但考古學家不應“把自己的工作局限於從表面上描述獲得的物品，確定其年代、日常用途、製造技術、屬於某一部落，等等。這當然是研究的必要準備階段，但是考古學如果只限於此，就没有權利考下去。在研究物品的時候……應以闡明根據該史料可以探索出來的人們之間的關係爲主要目的。決不能局限於只登記事實，而必須力求歷史地説明它們”。

基於上述理論思想，在考古學研究方法方面，强調歷史事物之間的相互聯繫、縱橫貫通，是馮漢驥治學最大的特點。從横向而言，一是多種不同學科知識的融會貫通，與人類學(文化人類學與體質人類學)、社會學、民族學、民俗學材料相結合，研究歷史考古材料，特别强調古代文獻材料的廣泛運用；二是中學和西學的融會貫通。從縱向而言，則是時間上的上下貫通，溯源尋流，以觀事物的來龍去脈和發展變化規律。馮漢驥的考古研究領域至爲廣博，從史前的舊石器、新石器到歷史時期的商周、兩漢、南北朝、唐五代以至於明，從墓葬遺存到青銅器、陶器、造像、畫像石刻，從工農業生産技術以至社會組織結構、名物制度、宗教、藝術、文明起源等，均有不同數量的專題研究論著問世，有許多獨到的見解。

馮漢驥是中國近代考古學的奠基者之一，對西南地區考古的貢獻尤爲卓越。20世紀30年代末至60年代初，四川和重慶地區一系列重要田野考古調查發掘和研究，大部分都是由他主持或親手完成的。

三、在人類學、民族史、民俗學上的貢獻

馮漢驥作爲人類學家，運用西方現代人類學的理論方法研究古代文獻記載的中國親屬制材料，“在繼承摩爾根研究成果的基礎上進一步發展了關於中國親屬制的理論”。自20世紀30年代以來，馮漢驥在國内外先後發表了《作爲中國親屬制構成部分的從子女稱》《由中國親屬名詞上

所見之中國古代婚姻制》等論文。其中最具代表性的是其博士學位論文《中國親屬制》(*The Chinese Kinship System*)，1937年馮漢驥用英文在美國《哈佛亞洲研究》(*Harvard Journal of Asiatic Studies*)上發表之後，有評論説：該文"不僅研究中國親屬制，具有開拓性的意義，在世界人類學研究方面也具有很高的學術價值"。此後，又於1948年和1967年兩次以單行本的形式在國外重印，在學術界産生了巨大的影響。時隔五十多年，1989年該文由徐志成以《中國親屬稱謂指南》的書名譯成中文，由上海文藝出版社首次在國内出版發行。譯者在"譯後記"中説："在《中國親屬制度》中，他運用現代人類學把親屬制分爲'描寫式親屬制'和'類分式親屬制'的原理，通過分析親屬制的表層結構——親屬稱謂入手，探討了中國親屬制與婚姻制、宗法制的關係，闡述了中國親屬制的發展軌迹，在當時的學術界産生了較大的影響。"寫於30年代的"這部舊著至今仍然是此項研究中最系統、最深入的一部。因此，它的出版現在仍然具有重要意義"。

在民族學研究方面，馮漢驥早在留學美國賓夕法尼亞大學期間就完成了題爲《中國倮儸的歷史與文化》(*The Lolo of China*：*Their History and Cultural Relations*)的碩士論文，1938年又與J. K. Shryock合作撰寫*The Historical Origins of the Lolo*(《彝族的歷史起源》)一文在《哈佛亞洲研究》上發表。歸國以後，馮漢驥着手對西南民族做全面系統的深入研究。從1938年開始，他親至原西康松、理、茂等地做實地考察，同時又組織人力對西南方志及其他文獻進行廣泛系統的清理，將其中有關西南民族的材料收集起來。雖然後來貯存的幾大箱材料在50年代初不幸散失，這項工作未能完成，但就已做的工作而言，也是成績斐然。《雜説月刊》編者在發表《倮儸與東爨》一文時所加的按語説："馮漢驥先生是國内知名的人類學、民族學專家……最近對西南民族問題曾作系統的研究，《倮儸與東爨》是當中的一小部分，極富學術的價值。吾人希望因此而引起國内學術界對此問題之密切注視和深刻研究。"馮漢驥撰成的大量有關論著，由於衆所周知的原因，除20世紀40年代發表的《倮儸與東爨》與《彝族的歷史起源》兩篇文章之外，絶大部分都没能發表。他的遺稿，如《西康民族總論》《倮儸與夜郎》《黑夷與白夷》《倮儸與水田》《筆摩之祖師比什姆拉子》《筆摩之方術》《番族文化總説》《西藏帝系譜》《西藏六十年大事記》等，數量不少。所論包括彝族、羌族、藏族（番族）以及苗族、瑶族、侗族、傣族等族在内，有關“農業”“畜牧”“飲食”“屋宇”“陳設用具”“衣飾”“社會生活”“階級制度”“奴隸制度”“家庭組織”（“農民之家庭”“貴族之家庭”“商人之家庭”等）、“文字”“宗教與神話”“器用”“飲食”“社會階級”“宗族及家庭”“婦女之地位”“婚姻”“生育風俗”“節令”“娱樂”“喪葬”等諸多方面的内容，材料豐富翔實，有不少獨到的見解。

在民俗學方面，馮漢驥也曾做過專門的田野調查，并有論著問世，如1935年在國外與J. K. Shryock合作發表題爲《以蠱著稱的中國黑巫術》（*The Black Magic in China Known as Ku*）的論文，1950年又用英文發表《宜昌附近的婚姻習俗》，即係其中的部分成果。1948年在巴黎召開國際民俗學會，他被推選爲終身會員，并特函邀赴會，後因故未能成行。

鑒於馮漢驥在人類學、考古學等多方面所取得的成就和貢獻，1950年曾被法國科學院推選爲外籍院士（因戰争而未與其保持聯繫），1957年受聘爲中國科學院考古研究所學術委員。

四、在圖書館學上的貢獻

馮漢驥於1928年9月任湖北省圖書館館長，1929年1月參加中華圖書館協會第一次年會，主持編撰了《湖北省圖書館圖書目録（第一期）》。1943年，馮漢驥與裘開明、于震寰合作編寫了《漢和圖書分類法》（*A Classification Scheme for Chinese and Japanese Books*），首次發表於Commuttees on Far Eastern Studies（American Council of Learned Societies, Washington, D. C.）。《漢和圖書分類法》曾被北美和諸多東亞圖書館以及燕京大學圖書館等20餘家圖書館採用，有着重要的學術和實用價值。

主要參考文獻

馮漢驥：《馮漢驥自傳（手稿）》，1952.

馮漢驥：《馮漢驥考古學論文集》，文物出版社，1985.

四川大學歷史文化學院考古學係編：《四川大學考古專業創建四十周年暨馮漢驥教授百年誕辰紀念文集》，四川大學出版社，2001.

張勛燎，白彬編：《川大史學・馮漢驥卷》，四川大學出版社，2006.

馮士美：《先父馮漢驥與四川大學》，參見党躍武，姚樂野主編：《毛坤先生紀念文集》，四川大學出版社，2010.

張勛燎

（重慶江津人。四川大學考古學係教授。主治漢唐考古、道教考古，係馮漢驥生前助教。）

（原文載于《20世紀中國知名科學家學術成就概覽・考古學卷》（第一分册），科學出版社2015年出版，收入本集時，編者有修改。）

總 目 録

中文論文篇

目　　録

《藏书绝句》的著者

民國十六年冬，余閱《中華圖書館協會會報》第三卷第二期，見其“新書介紹”欄内有《藏書絶句》一卷一册，楊守敬著，上海中國書店排印本。因亟購而讀之，讀既竟，深怪其不類楊氏生平之所作之文字，而後序默庵識語亦有：“《藏書絶句》一卷，乃同里趙森甫世丈自楊惺吾先生手稿迻録者。光緒季年，趙丈在鄂任編譯館事，與先生朝夕見。一日，先生示以此稿，因録附本還之。置篋中有年。及先生遺書多刊行，而此稿獨否，意謂失之。頃偶於丈之案上見及，詢其端委，因付剞氏，以公諸世。案先生自定年譜，謂平日不工詩，今觀此稿，筆致樸茂，信乎爲學者之詩，而非詩人之詩也。”等語。不意默庵亦疑楊氏平日不工詩而有此也。然予初不敢疑此非惺吾先生之著作，因私意非先生不能爲此詩也。然恍忽之間，曾於何處見之，但一時亦不能憶及。及民國十七年秋，余返鄂，長湖北省立圖書館(該館爲張文襄督鄂時所創辦，當時有“天下奇書，爲文襄所收盡”之語。但民國以來，迭經兵燹，多所失散，然收集餘燼，亦尚有十余萬本)。因檢查舊籍，見有《文史雜誌》，因翻而閱之。見其第二期内亦有《藏書絶句》三十二首，署爲王葆心。因急讀之，而與中國書店出版之《藏書絶句》一字不異，至是心始恍然。

案《文史雜誌》爲民國二年時文史社所編輯。而該社則爲前武昌存古學堂學生張仲炘等所創辦。是時適值姚彦長氏爲湖北教育司，姚氏曾任存古學堂教習，故該雜誌之略例内有：“本雜誌經發起人籌足三年資本，並由教育司撥款補助，經費充足，不募外捐”云云。但姚氏於是年冬去職，而文史社亦因而停頓。故《文史雜誌》亦祇出至第八期而停版。當《文史雜誌》出版之初，該社曾向王葆心先生徵稿，先生即以所著之《歷朝經學變遷史》《藏書絶句》《天完徐氏國史》《近世事箋》等稿以應之。而《藏書絶句》即登載於該雜誌之第二、第三、第五等期。第一期衹登其敘文，及詩四首，署曰晦堂。晦堂爲先生之别號，其所著書稱曰《晦堂叢書》。第三期詩八首，第五期詩七首，後因該雜誌停版，故未登完。

王葆心先生，字季香，湖北之羅田人。於學無所不窺，平生著作等身，而尤以《古文辭通義》一書爲海内所推崇，林琴南稱爲"百年來無此作"，王葵園謂爲"今日確不可少之書"。是書爲先生教授各學校時所編之講義，初未有印本，前清宣統二年時，上海商務印書館曾欲以是書，及先生所著之《歷朝經學變遷史》壽諸梨棗，而以版權未諧而罷。後是書乃排印於湖南官書報局。

至《藏書絶句》三十二首，爲先生於前清光緒二十四年(戊戌)王勝之同愈學使視學湖北時所作。當王氏勝之下車之初，即出題以觀風，凡經史詩賦均出有題，而《藏書絶句》即其題中之一也。是時先生爲鍾祥博通書院院長，見此題，遂成三十二首。是年冬，先生返里，其同宗某，倩先生代筆，先生即録此稿與之。及榜發之日，則列爲第一，且於其下批云："此題非楊惺吾不能作，今作者有此詩，楊氏後第一人也。"並賞銀十兩，書一部，以旌之。此或誤爲楊惺吾先生所作原因之一也。此詩曾膾炙一時，今之稍知當時典故者，類能道之。案是時王季香先生共代人作六題，而六題皆居第一。時先生之友人等笑謂先生曰："此後先生可稱六一居士矣。"其後或楊惺吾先生將此詩抄置案頭，而不知者見之，則以爲惺吾先生之所作也。不然何先生没後，其遺書多刊行，而此詩獨否也。案《文史雜誌》出版之日，據惺吾先生自定《鄰蘇老人年譜》，是時適寓上海，而"文史雜誌"四字，即爲其所題簽，其於該雜誌必定見之，而王季香先生豈敢於是時攘其著作爲己有乎?

余曾於武漢大學遇王季香先生(先生現爲該校國學教授)，而以《藏書絶句》詢之。先生曰："惺吾先生精於金石目録之學，書賈不過假其名以射利耳，亦何足深怪。古今來文人著作之張冠李戴者，豈止此數十首詩而已哉!"然終不可不辨也。

(原載《武昌文華圖書科季刊》一九二九年第一卷第一号)

彝族的歷史起源

彝族爲中國西南重要的少數民族。他們在其居住之地區世代相傳，名稱多變，距今已近兩千年。其現在之人數不詳，有學者估計總數約三百萬①。四川之彝族估計約有一百萬，居住在一萬一千平方英里的土地之上。看來上述人數估計均偏高，其總數可能僅一百萬左右。

彝族散居于雲南山區及四川西南部。其分佈西延至湄公河谷，在歷史上東邊曾達貴州西部。越南北部邊境地區亦有小群彝族居住。

在東北方，彝族沿着與東北向流之金沙江平行的大凉山向北深入，直達大渡河以南之嘉定、雅州。此一狹長地帶約 150 英里長，不到 100 英里寬。山地崎嶇，乃彝族獨立生存之鄉。其西部有藏、西番和么些諸部落。北鄰西番，東南方則有分散的撣、苗部落。

彝族居住之地區，乃西藏高原之東南邊緣。長江上游及其支流横貫其間。水流湍急，不能航行。氣候温和，然冬季酷冷。

彝族聚居之地理位置，不僅對其本身重要，且扼亞洲東南各族移徙

---

① 此數爲 Terrien de Lacouperie 所估計，見 *The Language of China before the Chinese*, Trans. Philological Soc. 1885－1886, p. 479. Frederick Stan 引此數字，見 *Lolo Objects in the Public Museum, Milwaukee*, Bull., 1911, Vol. 1, Pt. 2, pp. 209-220. E. Pittard, in Les Races et L'histoire, 1924, p. 495. 又引用 Stan 所使用之資料。楊成志在《羅羅説略》中重述 Pittard 之所引，見《嶺南學報》第一卷第三期，第 134-152 頁。儘管此數目出現在最近的論文中，却只不過是 Lacouperie 之猜測而已。《科學》雜誌編者在 1934 年第 18 卷第 1672 頁中估計，四川境内之彝族大致一百萬；然此數僅據 W. R. Morse. *The Nosu Tribes of Western Szechwan* Chin. Med. Jour., March, 1933. 這些數字均非出自計算，言過其實。“中國西部科學院”之調查表明，四川之黑彝不足二十萬，白彝未逾八十萬，見《特刊》1935 年第 1 卷。此數可信。調查者在凉山地區實地計算了彝族家庭成員。

之關隘。彝族雖有文字①，但就目前所知，並无歷史文獻。現在有關其歷史之原始資料，僅有内容貧乏而經常記載不確的漢文史書。

“羅羅”之稱，始于元朝，亦即此名稱，已有八百年之歷史。人們以爲“羅羅”乃盧鹿；盧鹿者，公元五至九世紀東爨土著部落之名也②。“羅羅”是否即盧鹿，實難判定。然元朝確在建川河谷之北，設有行政區羅羅斯宣慰司③。

今彝族各部落對自己之稱呼，相異頗大，詞首之輔音極少用“L”，元音又各不一致；第二音節通常用“so”或“su”，有時又略去第二音節④。外國調查者對彝族之稱謂，變化多端，其理論並无多大助益⑤

---

① 彝文乃一種象形文字，略仿漢字。漢文資料指出，此種彝文爲名叫阿比之彝人在公元550年所創。彝文之創造，彝族中傳説有三。阿比稱其所創文字爲“文書”，即標準文字也；漢族稱之爲爨文。彝文主要用于宗教文件，惟“畢摩”(“白馬”)能讀釋。然畢摩僅能讀懂自己部族之文字。丁文江在《漫遊散記》中對此有述，見《獨立評論》1933年第35卷第13頁，及第42卷第19~20頁，D'Ollone在In Forbidden China第106-107頁，亦有所述。今已有涉及彝文之大量文獻。丁文江做了全新及廣泛的工作，見1936年《爨文叢刊》；亦見楊成志《羅羅之字體和文書》，1935年。

② 《炎徼紀聞》4，17a：“羅羅本盧鹿而訛”。亦見Pelliot. *Deux itinéeraires de Chine en Inde*(《從印度到中國之兩次行》)，BEFEO4，1904(137)。

③ 參見《新元史》卷二四八。

④ 此中一些差異是：Mo—su，Mou—su，Ngo—su，Ne—su，Nei—su，No—su，No，Na，以及Leisu。在四川，他們被稱爲“蠻子”，或“蠻家”，後者爲較禮貌之稱呼。在滇南，擺族稱其爲“蒙”。

⑤ Lacouperie，op. cit. pp. 480-481，稱“羅羅”源于“盧鹿”，而“盧鹿”又源于“羅鬼”(Lo—Kuei)。“羅鬼”之説實誤，乃貶義綽號，此爲近稱，既非“羅羅”，又非“盧鹿”。

Paul Vial在“Les Lolos”(《羅羅各部》，1898)中解釋，漢族以其音而重譯此音。此亦非也。較早之漢文書籍將其寫爲盧鹿人，後又縮寫之，倘此名爲盧應寫爲盧人。

Lietard認爲“Lolo”係“No—so”之誤，“No—so”爲“羅羅”人自稱，見(*Au Yunnan*，*Les Lo—lo* P，o，1913)。然Shirokogoroff在*Phoneetic Notes on a Lolo Dialect and the Cosonant L*，(Academia Sinica，Bull. Vol. 1，No. 2，p. 183)中認爲，音節“No”與“so”，其義在彝族中極爲不同，任何語源學的派生均不可靠；此使Liltard之解釋失去意義。Shirokogoroff乃作出若干假設，謂“羅羅”或許有政治原因，如“滿洲”之稱，或則鄰居對其之特定稱呼，如通古斯之稱；亦或從古迹中鈔録者。

S. C. Clarke在*Among the Tribes of Southwest China*文中從傳教士C. C. Hicks之説(The Nou Su，Chinese Recorder，41，p. 211ff)，即“羅羅”之名爲彝族祭祀祖先所用竹制小籮籮得名。Clarke謂，漢族據此諢稱之。此極不可信。

C. E. Jamieson. *The Aborigines of Westrn China*(China Journal of Artand Science l，p. 376ff)引用十九世紀中國作者張寅之説，即“羅羅”爲“科羅”(kolo)類人猿之後裔，“科羅”衍變“羅羅”。此全然與歷史事實不符。

“羅羅”一詞係八百年前之漢語音譯。譯時或許即欠準確，亦或該詞乃地方方言。可能數百年來，漢語、彝語之語音均有變化。以我等現今之知識，欲定其名稱之起源及含義，必將造成錯誤，因其中未知之因素過多。我們當前所能判斷者，僅知此詞非始于外國，但其語源則不詳。

“羅羅”一詞雖元朝即已産生，然直至明朝，方始廣泛采用。《南詔野史》記載了臣屬于南詔撣國之十一個彝族部落①。此等部落之名稱，並非由于其種族之不同，大部分係因特殊之文化，如衣着、職業、風俗之不同而異。有時，即簡單地采用了統治家族之名稱。隨着部落遷徙，家族滅絶，某一名稱亦隨之消失，但這並非意味着一個部族集團之消失。在獨立之彝族部落中，據説有黑彝二十六部，白彝三十部，混合部落三個，奴隸部落兩個②。早期之漢文書籍，亦有相同之記載。

在中國西南各族中，廣泛流行黑、白之稱，但其含義則各不相同。有時，此稱呼代表服裝之顔色，如黑苗、白苗即是一例③。在湘南，某一部族被稱之黑苗，則因其開化程度不如靠近漢族之苗人④。生息在湄公河上游、與彝族緣近之傈傈族，其黑傈傈、白傈傈之稱，亦同出一因⑤。通常這些民族自己並不如此稱呼，以黑、白區分之者乃漢族。

然而彝族却與此不同，他們自己劃分成黑白兩部。一些西方觀察者完全混淆這種區别⑥。在雲南，黑彝由統治家族搆成；所有居其下者，

---

① 《南詔野史》（卷二）。Lietard（前引）稱，此大多數名稱爲漢族虚構。此爲矛盾之説。他本人列數二十以上之部落名稱，其中大多數與《南詔野史》所列相同。

② Lietard（前引）。其資料爲第二手，且未進一步解釋。d' Ollone 于 1908—1909 年遍訪彝區，謂各部族佔據之地域相互妥訂，侵犯了令人忿恨，故而行中不得不經常更换向導。

③ Clark, op. cit. p. 371.

④ Jamieson, op. cit. pp. 381-382.

⑤ A. Rose and J. C. Brown. “Li－su (Yawyin) Tribes of the Burma—China Frontier”, Memoirs, Asiatic Society of Bengal, Vol. Ⅲ, 1910—1914, pp. 249-276.

⑥ Jamieson, op. cit. p. 381. 他稱：黑色一詞源于皮膚之顔色。Buxton 在 *The Peoptes of Asia* p. 156 中重復此説。事實上，彝族之膚色較大多數土著居民爲淺。許多觀察家均有記載。一些觀察家甚而稱“羅羅”之膚色比南歐人還白皙。倘黑彝之稱因膚色之故，則白彝以何謂之？Lietard 以爲“Lolo”之名係從“No—so”演變而來，又因“諾”（No）含黑色之意，漢文按 Lolo 音譯乃誤。此假設前已提及。

皆爲白彝。在四川，黑彝則居多數。

彝族中黑彝、白彝之分，早已有之。《蠻書》《新唐書》即有黑蠻、白蠻之記載①。此種區分或許意味着種族之差異，至少確切地表明兩者語言之不同②。

今之彝族中，黑彝、白彝體格有别。黑彝身材高大，有的報告謂其身材較歐洲人還高，鷹鈎鼻、高鼻梁，總體觀之，與蒙古人種顯然有異③。白彝多似蒙古人種，體格較差，頭部指數亦與黑彝略别④。

雲南之黑彝構成統治階級，四川之黑彝還統治了黔西之苗族。黑乃顯貴之標誌，黑彝只在其内部通婚。雲南之黑彝時有將其女兒嫁給漢族官吏之子或高貴漢族世家⑤。而四川之黑彝則嚴格實行族内婚。

此種情况可能解釋爲：黑彝或許源于一個單獨族係之征服集團，而白彝則是被征服之另一些種族集團，以後逐漸接受了征服者之語言。此過程在四川之彝族中仍在進行。在雲南，黑彝或在戰争中被漢族統治者殺戮，或向北退却。故而雲南所謂之彝族之大多數，屬于較低下之白彝；少數統治家族仍居原地，接受了漢族統治者所授官職。

儘管彝族在很早以前即爲漢族所知，然在漢文資料中涉及彝族者極少。又因其他部族之存在，實情常被弄混。某些記載中之部落，要確定其是否爲彝族，殊感困難。在本文的歷史研究中，我們可以從黔西北水西⑥地區開始，此地爲彝族頭人安氏⑦大家族統治之地區。

---

① 在《新唐書》(卷二二二)提到諸如烏蠻：東爨(羅羅)、哀牢、南詔、施蠻、順蠻、裸蠻，等等；及白蠻：西爨、弄棟蠻、青蛉蠻。

② 《蠻書》卷八："言語音，白蠻最正，蒙舍蠻次之，諸部落不如也。"

③ 從馬哥·波羅到今之旅行家，均記下其詳細特徵，E. C. Baber謂"他們較歐洲人高"，此似夸大之詞。d'Ollone，op. cit. p. 51，稱：彝人无亞洲人特點，非黄色皮膚，呈黝黑色，如南歐人之膚色，其目深而大，弓眉護之，鷹鈎鼻，口正。"

④ Cf. A. Legender. "Far west Chinois", Tp, 1909, tab. A—CDixon, Racial History of Man, p. 281，作了分析。亦見丁文江《漫遊散記》。

⑤ 關于此一婚俗，見J. K. Shryock, "ch"en Ting's Account of the Marriage Customs of Chief of Yunnan and Kueichou", Amer. Anthro. 36, No. 4, Oct. —Dec. 1934.

⑥ 水西，今大定、黔西附近。水西之名，始于明朝。其界域時有變化。

⑦ 安氏家庭自稱其祖先乃公元第三世紀之濟火，然在明朝之前安氏之名不見使用。

在周朝，水西爲牂牁①、且蘭②所轄。約在公元前四世紀末，被楚將莊蹻所征服。而在公元前 316 年，與楚敵對之秦，派司馬錯佔領其地。彼時此地居民之情况，我們一无所知。

西漢前期，水西屬夜郎③國之域。時夜郎爲中國西南最大、最强之國家。當代學者王静如從語言學角度論定夜郎居民乃彝族之祖先④。此説可得到歷史依據之印證。

東漢後期，此地區據説爲水西彝族安氏家族之祖先所統治。《讀史方輿紀要》對水西安氏家族有如下記載：

> 水西宣慰司⑤在貴陽府西北三百里。土酋安氏，世守其地。其先濟火⑥之後也。蜀漢建興三年(公元 226 年)，諸葛武侯南征，牂柯帥濟火積糧，通道以迎。武侯表封羅甸國王⑦。居普里，即今普定衛⑧。
>
> 俗尚鬼號，正祭者爲鬼主。唐開成初(836 年)，鬼主阿風内附。會昌中(841—846 年)，封羅甸王。後唐天成二年(927 年)，羅甸王普露請率九部入貢。宋開寶間(968—975 年)，有普貴者納土歸附，仍襲王爵，自濟火至普貴，凡三十六世矣。時有宋景陽者，真定人⑨，奉詔平定諸蠻。因析置大萬谷落總管府授之。元開置安撫、長官分授諸酋長。明朝洪武四年(1372 年)，有靄翠⑩、宋欽及

---

① 一説牂牁者，係船之樁也，莊蹻遠征時人們設想其船隊停靠于此地，故名。然鄭珍謂，在莊蹻遠征之很久以前，牂牁之名即有之，見《巢經巢文集・牂牁考》。此地之寬度不明。

② 且蘭，一小國，漢武帝併之，其地今貴州之平越。

③ Han shu, Tung—wên ed., ch. 95. p. 1：“南夷君長以十數，夜郎最大。”

④ 王静如：“A Comparative Linguistic study on the Songs of Bair—Long Tribe”, Acdademia sinica, Nat. Res. Inst. of History and philology, mon. 8, Hsi—hsia yen—chiu, pp. 15-54.

⑤ 水西宣慰司，明朝首建。

⑥ 濟火，《明史》稱火濟。

⑦ 羅甸在東漢之後靠近牂牁地區。羅甸一詞可能與“羅羅”有些聯繫，因“甸”有領地或國家之意。

⑧ 普定衛，在安順縣北約 22.5 公里處。在宋朝，此處稱爲普里蠻部。元時，此地稱普定路，雲南轄屬。明朝，更名爲今安順地區之普定衛。民國又改爲定南汎。

⑨ 真定，今之正定。

⑩ 靄翠在元朝身兼四川行省左丞、順元宜慰史之職。見《炎徼紀聞》卷三。

土人安沙溪等歸附。詔以靄翠爲貴州宣慰使，欽與沙溪等俱同知；皆設治于會城内，仍各統所部，居水西，而靄翠最强。靄翠死，弟安的①襲職，因爲安氏。安氏領羅夷民四十八部，部長曰頭目。宋氏世居衛城側，領夷民十二部，部長曰馬頭。同知安氏領夷民一部，部長亦曰頭目。

安氏世據水西之地，南逾陸廣②，東接遵義③，西連赤水④，北抵永寧⑤，延袤數百里，山險箐深，有水西、大方⑥、織金⑦、火灼諸城堡⑧，而大方尤爲險固；役屬部落，日以富强。

萬曆中(1573—1619年)，安疆臣潜與播酋⑨相結，繼而朝廷赫然，誅播⑩，懼禍及，遂悉力深入，播平；朝廷嘉其功，不問也。

天啓初(1621年)，疆臣死，子安位幼弱，土目安邦彦挾之以叛。時永寧賊奢崇明⑪者亦倡亂，與邦彦相結。朝廷討之，崇明敗，歸邦彦。又，烏撒土目安效良⑫，霑益⑬土目李賢等皆叛應邦彦。邦

① 田汝成《炎徼紀聞》謂，靄翠由其妻繼承，後靄翠幼弟安勻繼承之，並未提及安的。此處恐顧祖禹有誤。

② 陸廣，陸廣河岸一城鎮，在貴州修文地區。陸廣河爲水西最大之河流。它起自普定東，流經修文，匯入烏江。

③ 遵義，清朝名。

④ 赤水，今畢節縣，明時稱爲赤水衛。

⑤ 永寧，今四川敘永地區，元朝稱永寧路，明朝稱永寧衛。

⑥ 大方地，在今大定地區，時在水西之西部，靠近畢節衛。

⑦ 織金城，水西之西北地帶。

⑧ 火灼城，今黔西縣之北，亦稱火灼堡，或火著。

⑨ 播酋，即楊應龍，公元1595—1601年率部反叛。唐時，楊的祖先始爲播州首領，奪取南詔領土。楊應龍已是第二十九代首領。從其始祖至楊應龍，統治已近八百年。見《明史》卷三二一。

⑩ 明朝廷震怒，遣遠征軍征之，擊敗楊，并誅之。

⑪ 明朝時期，奢氏家庭爲川黔邊境一大彝族家族。永寧在今關嶺縣境。

⑫ 烏撒，靠近雲南鎮雄、貴州威寧。《元史・地理志》"烏撒者，蠻名也。其部在中慶東北七百五十里，舊名巴凡兀始，今曰巴的甸，自昔烏雜蠻居之。今所轄部六，曰烏撒部、阿頭部、易溪部、易娘部、烏蒙部、閟畔部。其東西又有芒布、阿晟二部。後烏蠻之裔折怒始强大，盡得其地。因取遠祖烏撒爲部名。憲宗征大理，累招不降，至元十年(1273年)始附，十三年立烏撒路。"烏撒是彝族。隨安疆臣反叛者安效良。

⑬ 霑益，雲南東，唐時爲播、剌部落占，此部可能操撣語。南詔治下，此地爲摩彌部落所占，摩彌可能與彝族同源。與這次反叛有關的頭目乃李賢。

彦縱横滇黔之交，南犯會城，東襲偏沅①，洪邊②土司宋萬化及東西諸苗悉叛，應之。官軍四面攻討未克。

天啓四年(1624年)督臣朱燮元議以滇兵出霑益，遏烏撒應援，而别布天生橋③、尋甸④，以絶其走。蜀軍臨畢節⑤，扼其交通四出之路，而别出龍場⑥、巖頭，以奪其險。黔兵由普定⑦渡思臘河徑趨邦彦巢，而陸廣、鴨池⑧搗其虚。粤西出泗城⑨，分兵策應。然後率大軍由遵義鼓行而進。燮元旋以憂去。

崇禎二年(1629年)燮元復督川湖雲貴廣五省之兵，再涖黔。乃檄滇兵下烏撒，蜀兵出永寧、畢節，扼其各要害，而自帥大軍駐陸廣，逼大方。會邦彦與奢崇明犯赤水，深入永寧。乃遣官軍一從三岔⑩入，一從陸廣入，一從遵義入，復以奇兵繞其後，賊不能支，遂大潰，斬邦彦等。圍安位于大方，賊窘，請削水外六目地及開畢節等驛路以降，許之。燮元又遣兵誅擺金、兩江、巴鄉、狼狽、火烘五崗叛苗⑪，以孤其勢。位尋死，其族黨争納土歸附。燮元因請分水西之壤授諸渠長及有功漢人，使勢少力分，易以制馭。

于是水西復定。(卷一二三，貴州，四)

在上述之部落諸頭人中，安氏和奢氏家族確係彝族，而宋、李二氏，則難判定其是否彝族。可斷定者，彝族頭人轄下之諸多部落，並非彝族。

---

① 偏沅，沅州、偏橋關之合稱。明朝，偏沅巡撫受命管理苗族事務，在沅州、偏橋關駐留各半年。清朝廢之。明時它爲中國西南最重要地區之一。

② 洪邊，元朝首次建立，貴陽以北約4公里處。反叛首領名宋萬化。

③ 天生橋，貴州安順縣西北，乃戰略要地。

④ 尋甸，在雲南。明時，稱爲尋甸軍民府，後稱尋甸府。

⑤ 畢節，貴州西北、川滇黔間之重要商業中心。

⑥ 龍場，今貴州之修文縣。

⑦ 普定，貴州安順地區屬地。

⑧ 鴨池河，爲陸廣河上游一支流。

⑨ 泗城，今廣西凌雲地區。民國廢之。

⑩ 三岔，即三岔寨，普定北。

⑪ 此五部今不能判定，似爲地名。

通過這段記載我們可以看出明代爲平定彝族付出了何等巨大的努力——以督臣率五省兵力，始獲成功。此在多大程度導致其最後垮臺，難以確評；然 1644 年明朝之覆滅，此乃爲一大因素无疑。

清朝治下，水西安氏彝族仍然强大。康熙三年(1665 年)，吳三桂征服安坤①，將其領地劃分五府。安坤之妻逃至烏蠻，生一子名安世宗②。後清廷決定不以朝官治理，安世宗于 1683 年被委任爲宣慰使。1792 年，總督王繼文上奏，稱安世宗理政不善，當應革除。故而安世宗之職被奪，其轄地復爲朝廷官員控制。

《炎徼紀聞》對水西地區之彝族，描述極佳。此爲田汝成于 1560 年所撰。田汝成乃中國西南一位高級官吏，有十餘年處理土著部落事務之經驗。該書爲後代研究者廣泛引用；然書中所述彝族史實，則常被人忽視。

> 羅羅本盧鹿而訛爲今稱。有二種。居水西、十二營③、寧谷④、馬場⑤、漕溪者爲黑羅羅，亦曰烏蠻。居慕役者爲白羅羅⑥，亦曰白蠻。風俗略同，而黑者爲大姓。羅俗尚鬼，鼓又曰羅鬼。
>
> 蜀漢時有火濟者，從丞相亮破孟獲有功，封羅甸國王，即今宣慰使安氏遠祖也。自羅甸東西，若自杞、夜郎、牂牁，則以國名；若特磨⑦、白衣、九道，則以道名，皆羅羅之種也。羅羅之俗，愚而戀主，即虐之赤族，猶舉其子姓，若妻妾戴之，不以爲讐。故自火濟至今，千有餘年，世長其土。勒四十八部，部之長曰頭目。其人深目長身，黑而白齒，椎結跣蹻，荷氈戴笠⑧而行，腰束葦索，左肩拖羊皮一方，佩長刀箭菔。富者以金釧約臂。悍而喜鬥，修習

① 《清史稿·土司傳》。
② 《清史稿·土司傳》。
③ 十二營，貴州鎮寧北 15 公里，清朝廢之。
④ 寧谷，貴州安順西南 15 公里，清朝廢之。
⑤ 馬場，貴州平越沿馬場河之一地名。
⑥ 慕役，關嶺南約 30 公里，元時爲一寨子，明清時爲長官司。
⑦ 特磨，雲南之廣南地區屬，宋朝稱特磨道。
⑧ 竹絲編制之錐形帽。

攻擊，雄尚氣力。寬則以漁獵、伐木爲業，急則屠戮相尋，故其兵常爲諸苗冠。諺云："水西羅鬼，斷頭掉尾。"言其相應若率然也。

亦有文字，類蒙古書者。坐无几席，與人食，飯一盤，水一盂，匕一枚，抄飯哺客，摶之若丸，以匕躍口，食已，必滌臊刷齒以爲潔。作酒盎而不縮，以葦管啐飲之。男子則薙髮而留髯。婦人束髮，纏以青帶。烝極旁通，醜不恧也。父死收其後母，兄弟死則妻其妻。新婦見舅姑不拜，裸而進盥，謂之奉堂。男女居室，不同帷第，潛合如奔狠。而多疑忌，相賊也。白羅羅之俗略同。而飲食惡草，盛无盤杯，爨以三足釜，灼毛醋血。无論鼠雀省蚳蝝蠕動之物，攫而燔之，攢食若彘。不通文字，結繩刻木爲信。女子以善淫名者，則人争取之，以爲美也。人死以牛馬革裹而焚之。居普定者爲阿和，俗同白羅，以販茶爲業。(《炎徼紀聞》卷四)

有關唐以前之黔西、滇東北之記載，頗爲不足。此乃多山、偏僻之地，漢族之影響幾未越出犍爲、朱提①(今宜賓)之西南境外。從唐至今，川滇主要通道沿此地區以東，經敘永、畢節、霑益而昆明②。《蠻書》稱之爲北路。自晉代開始(公元 265 年)，此地之居民被稱之爲爨。"當天寶中，東北自曲靖州③，西南至宣城，邑落相望，牛馬被野，在石城、昆州、曲軛、晉寧、喻獻、安寧至龍和城，謂之西爨。在曲靖州、彌鹿川、昇麻川、南至步頭，謂之東爨"④。

據《蠻書》所載，石城⑤爲味縣故地，距今曲靖 15 英里。龍和城位于

① 朱提，朱讀如殊，提，上支反。

② 此爲《蠻書》所定之地名，尚待考訂。然該書卷一稱，沿此路所居者，盧鹿，及與羅羅有關之部落。例如："過魯望第七程至竹子嶺，嶺東有暴蠻部落，嶺西有盧鹿蠻部落。第六程至生蠻磨彌殿部落。此等部落，皆東爨烏蠻也。男則髮髻，女則散髮。見人无禮節拜跪，三譯四譯乃與華通，大部落則有鬼主……"

③ 唐朝无曲靖之名。此處應讀爲曲州、靖州。曲州，靠近今慶符；靖州位于四川舊敘永。

④ 《蠻書》(卷四)。

⑤ 《蠻書》(卷二)："石城川，味縣故地也。貞觀中爲爲郎州。開元初改爲南寧州。州城即諸葛亮戰處故地也。"

大理以東。故而西爨所據之地，約從今之曲靖向西至大理。唐之曲州、靖州，與今四川之慶符、長寧南緊連。彌鹿大致相當于今之瀘西縣。昇麻位近今之曲靖。步頭无確考，似在今紅河畔之建水縣南①。故而東爨之域，爲長江以南宜賓南至越南邊境之廣闊地區。

人們通常視爨爲彝族。東爨乃彝族无疑。《蠻書》所述可證之。而西爨則不然。他們屬于白蠻，其語言、文化均不同于東爨。唐朝後期，東爨、西爨均爲南詔國轄屬。南詔王閣羅鳳(748—749年)迫西爨兩萬家族遷居永昌地區。東爨則散逃山區，以免遭西爨之命運。後東爨擴及西爨故地②。

爨之起源，尚待研究。西爨自稱其祖先晉時居山西安邑地區③。此傳説與事實不符，從公元三世紀起，爨爲雲貴統治家族之一。諸葛亮遣軍征戰雲南，移黑羌萬户入川，而將其羸弱者分配給大姓爲部曲，爨即爲此種大姓之一④。或許因此大姓日益强大，漢族乃以其名稱呼其治下所有之部族。爨之統治家族是否爲漢族之後裔，難以論定，因此傳説包涵之内容極少。唐朝以後，不復使用爨之稱呼。

論者常以雲南之彝族爲爨。中國古書稱彝文爲爨文，然視所有之爨均爲彝族，則不甚確切。爨爲公元四至十世紀常用之政治名稱。在此期間，爨或許指許多極不相同之土著落族。東爨名爲南詔所轄，實有頗大之獨立性。

明朝期間東爨在四川所佔據之地，唐時分屬四個軍民府，即烏蒙、

① 建水縣，即舊臨安府。有關步頭之考證，見 Pelliot. “Deuxitinéraires de Chine en lnde”, BEFEO4, 138.

② 《蠻書》(卷四)：“閣羅鳳遣昆川城者楊牟利以兵圍脅西爨，徙二十餘萬户于永昌城。烏蠻以言語不通，多散林谷，故得不徙……烏蠻種類，稍稍復振，後徙西爨故地。”

亦見《新唐書・南蠻》(下)：“閣羅鳳遣昆川城使楊牟利以兵脅西爨，徙户二十餘萬于永昌城。東爨以語言不通，多散依林谷，得不徙……烏蠻種復振，徙居西爨故地。”

③ 《新唐書・南蠻》(下)：“西爨自云本安邑人，七世祖晉南寧太守，中國亂，遂王蠻中。”《雲南廳志》(卷一八九)稱：晉時南寧太守之職。南寧在齊、梁時方設，然長官爲刺史，非太守也。

④ 《華陽國志》(卷四)：“(諸葛亮)……移南中勁卒青羌萬餘家于蜀，爲五部。所當无前，軍號正……分其羸弱配大姓焦雍婁爨孟量毛李爲部曲。”

烏撒、東川、鎮雄是也。據《明史》[1]，此地之居民乃唐時稱爲烏蠻之"羅羅"後裔。歷史記載亦表明。宋時一彝族頭人獲烏蠻王頭銜，元朝授與此地區頭人爲宣慰使銜。其中最重要者爲烏撒，故有一專門官吏留駐其間。明初，此地區爲漢族征占，然極不成功，叛亂時部民常助其水西之親屬。

吳三桂爲滿族人佔據了此地。後吳又反叛，清廷不得不再度征服之。雍正年間(1723—1735年)總督鄂爾泰[2]奏請廢土司之地方自治政權，爾後由流官取代之。故所有土司起而反叛。統治者以血腥屠殺鎮壓叛亂，大批彝族被殺。今此地幾无彝族餘存，蓋因于此。

最後，大凉山西北之建昌河谷，乃僅存之獨立之彝族聚居地。漢朝時期，此河谷之北部稱邛都。元鼎六年(公元前111年)，此地開爲越嶲郡。後漢、晉、劉宋和齊朝，沿襲稱之。後周改其名爲西寧州，繼而名爲嚴州。咸通三年(公元863年)，此地爲南詔所並，南詔始稱其爲建昌，引黑蠻、白蠻入。但黑蠻、白蠻是否爲彝族，實不可知。在宋朝，承繼南詔之大理國，對此地失去控制，故此地内亂頻繁。蒙古族征服雲南，土司均投降。明朝並此地，更名爲建昌衛[3]。

沿建昌河谷爲一通往中國西南及其以遠區域之主要通道。此即諸葛亮遠征之路。歷朝均盡力使之暢通，然成功之時甚少，即使唐朝時也僅能在短期内維持此道。此地河谷、山麓之彝族，爲漢族統治者所屈服，並在其地設治。

有關大凉山彝族之資料甚少。可能直至清末此地之彝族仍保持了獨立。在雍正(1723—1735年)、嘉慶(1796—1820年)年間，數次力圖降服此地彝族，但顯然没有成功。彝族各部不斷襲擊漢族統治者，擄去不少漢族人丁充當奴隸。約在1869年(同治三年)，貴州提督周達武率部

---

① 《明史》(卷三一一)："東川芒部諸夷，種類皆出于玀玀。厥後子孫蕃衍，各立疆埸，乃異其名曰東川、烏撒、烏蒙、芒部、禄肇、水西。无事則互起争端，有事則相爲救援。"

② 《清史稿》(卷五一四)。

③ 朝代更换，地名隨之而變者，常也。新名爲建昌衛。

入大凉山核心地區，釋放成千之漢族俘虜。20 世紀初，趙爾豐奏請清廷，欲徹底征服山區之彝族，旋因 1908 年光緒去世而擱置。此後不久，彝族殺死一英國傳教士，趙爾豐乃從東北、西南兩路，夾攻其地。兩軍匯聚山區，趙爾豐乃得以辟一通道，横貫此地，沿途要塞駐扎軍隊。趙爾豐禁止黑彝畜奴，廢土司制，建立漢族統治。所以臨近清朝覆亡之際，因巴貝爾(Baber)、多隆(Dollone)之介紹而聞名于世的“獨立儸羅區”，最後屈服了①。

彝族所居三個重要地區之歷史梗概，從漢文資料中所能窺其貌者，大致如是。關于彝族文化之特殊表規，下略述之。

除頭人家族外，彝族與其鄰居相比，物質文化較爲落後。他們爲半畜牧民族，然並不擠奶飲用。凡有奴隸之地農業即爲奴隸所事，而奴隸者幾不能以彝族稱之。彝族之房屋，乃竹籬板舍。他們幾无傢具可言，僅有之器皿，惟幾只略事加工之木碗、竹簍和鐵鍋。

彝族所知之調味品僅鹽一種，此乃昂貴之奢侈品。其僅有之紡織品，乃粗制原始之麻織品，及用作大氅之粗氈。彝族既无貨幣，亦无度量衡。他們没有陶器，這一特點與古代當地之居民相似。《蠻書》稱，南詔无陶器，所用則金銀器皿及竹單②。

彝族之羊毛氈氅，爲其獨有。氈質粗糙而不均匀，其色有褐、藍或羊毛本色。彝族男女，冬夏皆不離身。氈氅又是床墊、毯子，乃至充作屋頂。此物在《蠻書》中即有記載：

> 其蠻丈夫一切披氈，其餘衣服略與漢同，唯頭囊特異耳。南詔以紅綾，其餘向下皆以皂綾絹。其制度，取一幅物，近邊撮縫爲角，制木如樗蒲。頭實角中，總發于腦後，爲一髻，即取頭囊都包裹，頭髻上結之羽儀。已下及諸動有一切房甄别者，然後得頭囊，若子

---

① 《清史稿》(卷五一四)。

② 《蠻書》(卷八)：“南詔家食用金銀，其餘官將用竹單。貴者飯以筋，不匙。賤者，摶之而食。”

弟及四軍羅苴已下則當額絡爲髻，不得戴囊角，當頂撮鑿髻。披氈皮，俗皆跣足。（武英殿聚珍版）

唐朝之南詔，口操儸語。今之儸族，一般不用氈子，尤不使用氈氅。

彝族著名之"天菩薩"，乃髮式之一種。其法係將頭髮前梳，編織纏繞于前額，使其突出成角狀。中國西南各族，均无以此方式梳髮者。《蠻書》載，南詔之低級官員、武士乃着此飾。此可能因南詔大多數軍士係由彝族組成。

在印度曼尼普爾（ManiPur）之那加諸部落中，有一部落之髮式與彝族相同①。由于亞洲其他民族无此髮式，故兩者之巧合，絶非偶然。據説有一種彝族傳説，其祖先來自該地區，但此説尚難肯定。

彝族文化之另外兩個特徵，即葬禮和祭祀，亦應作一簡單介紹。

概而論之，所有的民族之宗教信仰都是守舊的，其中尤以喪禮爲最。彝族周圍均爲信佛教的民族，然這些民族之信仰、行爲對他們毫无影響。基督教傳教士之努力，亦未能起作用。彝族因長期抵制外來影響，其葬禮頗具古代遺風。彝族行火葬，此與中國之其他土著截然不同。早在唐朝，漢文史書即有此記載。《蠻書》謂：

蒙舍及諸烏蠻不墓葬。凡死後三日焚屍，其餘灰燼掩以土壤，唯收兩耳。南詔家則貯以金瓶，又重以銀，爲函盛之，深藏別室，四時將出祭之。其餘家或銅瓶、鐵瓶盛耳藏之也。②

烏蠻包括彝族之祖先東爨。彝族不保存雙耳，惟行火葬，此爲訪問過這個地區的馬哥·波羅所證實："人民焚其屍，取其骨置盒中，懸于

① T. C. Hodson, *The*, *Naga Tribes of Manipur*, 1911, pp. 29-30. See also the plate facing p. 21. 然如纏繞之髮乃辮之，則北方諸民皆尚此，Cf. Kurakichi Shiratori. *The Queue among the Peoples of North Asia*, Mem. Tōyō Bunko, No. 4.

② 《蠻書》（卷八）。

崖穴内，避人畜及之也。”①

人們多認爲南詔即“擺”，然“擺”爲語言集團，非種族集團也。今之擺族不火葬死者，儘管在佛教及印度教影響之下，他們仍行土葬，此可能表明，在文化上南詔與彝族之關係，較今自稱南詔是其祖先之擺族，更爲密切。或則説明南詔之大部分臣民，均係彝族。《蠻書》又稱：

> 白爨及白蠻，死後三日埋殯，依漢法爲墓，稍富室，廣栽杉松。②

此亦黑、白蠻在文化上之差異。

《新唐書》稱：

> 夷人尚鬼(祖先？—作者)，謂主祭者爲鬼主，每歲户出一牛或一羊，就其家祭之。送鬼迎鬼必有兵，因以復仇云。③

上述各種歷史、傳説上之史料，均與彝族起源之理論有關。拉古柏裏(Lacouperie)立論最早④，謂彝族乃古代西藏東北之民族向東南擴張而來。拉古柏裏氏把中國古書上之氐羌與彝族相連。然其並未出據支持此論。故待討論丁文江氏之理論時再述。

維爾(Vial)及其他學者，試圖從語言學角度論證彝族與藏族有關。可惜此種立論的根據，全在于仰賴精選有限之詞彙進行比較。根據我們對藏族的語言原則的瞭解，這兩種不同的語言，是很難精確地概括在一

① E. C. Baber. *China in Some of Its Physical and Social Aspects*, Proceedings of the Royal Geographic Society, n. s., V, 1883, pp. 445-448, identifies the Coloman of marco polo with the Lolo, in which he is probably correct. 巴貝爾視馬哥・波羅所説之“科羅人”乃“羅羅”，此説可能正確。

② 《蠻書》(卷八)。

③ 見《新唐書・南蠻》(下)。同樣之習俗以前雅庫特人亦有。見 W. Jochelson. *kumiss Feslivals of the yakut*, Boas Aniversary Volume, 1906, p. 263.

④ Op. cit., pp. 480-81. Vial, Les Lolos, 1898. 亦見 J. Deniker. *Races of Man*, 1900, pp. 381-382, and H. R. Davies, yunnan, p. 337.

起的。

丁文江氏乃第一個實地調查者。他將自己的理論奠基于體質及歷史的事實之上[①]。他在雲南旅行時曾測量了許多彝族居民，所獲得的大部頭部指數乃長頭型。丁氏斷定："在歷史上，儸羅與羌族結合，在四川西北、青海、南疆，形成一重要之部族。在南疆，他們與名爲月支的伊朗族通婚。伊朗血統又通過羌族而影響了儸羅。"丁氏所用伊朗一詞，似與裹普利(Ripley)之觀念相同。

丁氏在其後來著作中宣稱，他測量之彝人，多係白彝。是以丁氏之發現，乃不足爲奇[②]。長頭型的因素與狄克森(Dixon)之裹海型相一致[③]，此種因素在白彝中占第二位。由于白彝乃是臣服于黑彝之民族集團，故長頭因素或許體現了古老的孟—高棉族之血緣[④]。狄克森以吕真達(Legendre)之測量爲其分析之基礎，然此測量表明占優勢者乃短頭型。丁氏，吕真達調查彝民之數目均有限，不足以證明其推論。

將假定的彝族的某些高加索特徵，歸之于通過月氏傳入的伊朗血緣，實爲牽强附會。實則，月氏之族屬至今尚无定論，但大多數人均認爲他們乃印度一斯基泰人[⑤]。《前漢書》中之片斷材料記載[⑥]，月氏爲敦煌、祁連間一遊牧民族，約在公元前三世紀末被匈奴打敗，其中之大部分向西遷徙，征服了曾經推翻希臘人巴克特利亞王國(大夏)之塞種人。在公元初，月氏人征服印度西北，後在此建貴霜帝國。少數未西遷之月支氏，則向西南移動，與羌族混居；漢族將匈奴逐出今新疆東部後，小月氏被勸重歸故地。

人們常將此期間中亞之一切事情，皆與月氏聯繫。事實上，月氏是

---

① 丁文江：《雲南之土著部落》，《中國醫學雜誌》，1921年，3月號。

② 見《漫遊散記(雲南之行)》，《獨立評論》1933年，34-36號。

③ R. B. Dixon, *Racial History of Man*, p. 281. L. Kilborn and R. morse 兩人最近測量了彝人，其結果尚未公諸于世。

④ Dixon, op. cit. p. 276：普儂、摩伊、卡及其他孟—高棉語族人，有明顯的長頭特徵。

⑤ 此論近有探討。見 Sten Konow. *Kharoshthi Inscriptions*, *Corpus Inscriptionum Indicarum*2, Pt. Ⅰ, 1929, pp. 510-522.

⑥ 《前漢書》(卷九十五)。

否曾到達四川，殊難肯定。歷史上彝族有向北遷徙之舉，假若夜郎爲彝族之祖先，則月氏遷徙之時，他們早已定居于南方。

巴克斯頓(Buxton)之理論[①]，基于丁文江氏的測量及詹彌森(Jamieson)提供的資料。詹彌森堅持彝族來自藏緬邊界，因爲他們是中國西南惟一畜馬之人[②]。故而巴克斯頓把彝族與他的黑亞細亞族相聯，此即埃利奧特·史密斯(Elliot smith)之褐色種族，他們曾横跨西亞到達地中海。此論與丁文江之理論不同，因巴克斯頓係將彝族與南方喜馬拉亞山麓之民族相聯繫。儘管吕達真之測量較丁氏所測重要，然丁文江、巴克斯頓均未重視他的結果，而巴克斯頓則對所研究對象的歷史事實不甚熟悉。

彝族傳説，謂其起源于藏緬邊境，其先民與漢族首次接觸之地係在雲南東北部。近有關于這一地區的有趣報導。昭通地區平原上有許多引人注意的土丘，“其中一些已被發掘，土丘之内，有粗糙而未經加工之石頭，顯然作門框之用。又有燒制之特大磚塊，上有特殊之花紋”[③]。以此推論它與彝族之起源有何關係，爲時尚早。但此地之彝族流傳，土丘乃彝族到此之前濮人所築。後濮人爲彝族所併。

彝族傳説，他們並非大凉山之土著。在漢族奪其富裕河谷之後，方陸續逃至山區，此過程持續到1727年。此傳説雖不可全信，然彝族非當前所居之地的土著，似无疑義[④]。

黑、白之分，也許與所論之問題有些關聯。用黑色一詞表示高貴血統，在東北亞各族中普遍存在。耶律大石所建西遼國，自稱黑契丹，此暗示百姓臣民乃原始契丹人。蒙古人自始就分黑白，成吉斯汗及其文武大臣，均屬黑蒙古人。這可能説明彝族與北方文化有聯繫。彝族使用氈子、古代爨人之鬼魂祭祀，均説明同一問題。至于彝族火葬之來源，尚

---

① Buxton. *The Peoples of Asia*, pp. 156-157.

② Jamieson. The *Aborigines of Western China*, *China Journal of Art and Science* 1, p. 381.

③ C. C. Hicks. *The Nou Su*, *Chinese Recorder* 41, p. 211.

④ E. C. Baber, *Travels and Researches in the Interior of China*, *Royal Geographic Society*, *Supplementary. Papers*, Ⅰ, p. 121. D'Ollone, op. cit. p. 107.

難以推測。此不能歸之于佛教或印度教之影響，而在驅邪典禮上用火，却是一廣泛存在的習俗。

彝族缺陶器，亦表明與北方有關。因歷史上只有少數幾個民族不用陶器，其中就有蒙古人。意味深長的是，儘管彝族周圍之民族均用陶器，而彝族獨无。

然彝族又如漢族，非飲用奶品之民族。亞洲的民族可分成比鄰而居的兩大集團。即食奶者與不食奶者。東北亞之通古斯人，蒙古人，土耳其人，藏族，伊朗人，近東各族及部分原始亞洲人，屬食奶民族。漢族，日本人，撣族，彝族以及大多數孟—高棉人，均不食奶。在此情況下，彝族之不食奶，絶非偶然。他們擁有牧群，然並不擠奶。倘彝族爲原始牧民，失此重要文化特徵，極不可能①。此亦不能視爲受漢族之影響，因彝族一貫反感外來影響。

彝族之另一些特徵，又表明與南方有關，如赤足行走，使用毒箭，頭上之“天菩薩”。然東南亞之典型武器弩，彝族中却未發現。

以上之討論，使我們難于下一肯定之結論。一些事實表明某一傾向，另一些事實則截然相悖。現今之一些理論，僅據其中某一事實而得出。如果考慮到東南亞少數民族之複雜性，以及缺乏由訓練有素之調查者作出的報導，很顯然，必須先作大量的工作，方能得出準確的分類。

（本文與J. K. 希沃古合著，見《哈佛亞細亞研究》(*Harvard Journal of Asiatic Studies*)，一九三八年第三卷二期，劉達永譯）

① 雅庫特人在最不利環境下仍保留牧群。見Jochelson，op. cit. pp. 257-271.

由中國親屬名詞上所見之中國古代婚姻制

近來研究中國古代社會進化者，莫不以莫爾根(L. H. Morgan)之社會進化階段爲其立論根據。但莫爾根之社會進化思想，特其表現于《古代社會》一書之中者，多與近來新發現之事實不合，故現在研究人類之社會進化者，即根本否認普遍之社會的進化有同一固定之程序，有如莫爾根及其他十九世紀中諸社會進化論者所主張者。不過從學術之發展上視之，莫爾根之所以爲十九世紀偉大社會學家之一者，並不在其社會進化階段之劃分，而在其發現親屬名詞與社會制度之關係；並不在其《古代社會》一書，而在《人類中之血族與姻族之系統》一書①。不過後者之篇帙繁重，措詞專門，不爲學者所習知耳。

《人類中之血族與姻族之系統》一書，出版于1871年，當是時麥克令南曾力加以反駁②，彼以爲親屬名詞與社會組織无甚重大之關係，不過爲一種“稱呼詞”而已。但平心論之，莫爾根之論證可議之處固甚多，究不失爲社會學上一極重大之發現。麥克令南係一業律師出身之社會學家，長于辯才，其對于莫爾根之攻擊，每多過分之處。故

① Systems of Consanguinity and Affinity of the Human Family. 1871. 莫爾根氏在此書中收集世界各民族之親屬名詞，而加以分析。其性質固瑕瑜互見，但其收集之數量則至爲可驚。其《古代社會》中之社會進化理論，即根據于此書之所得。世人只知其《古代社會》而不知有此書，固莫由窺莫爾根學説之真諦也

② J. F. Mclennan：Studies in Ancient History. 1876. 莫爾根在其《古代社會》附録中有所答辯，可參見楊東蓴、張栗原譯本，925-961 面。楊張二氏之漢譯，竟將書名譯錯，可知其未見麥克令南之原書也。

一般學者，多左麥克令南而右莫爾根。自是之後，莫爾根所謂之“類分式的(classificatory)”親屬制，及“敘述式的(descriptive)”親屬制遂成社會學中之口頭術語矣。

但親屬制度研究上之争論，並不自此而終止。如克洛伯于 1909 年在其最著名之《類分式的親屬制》一文中[①]，又舊事重提，以爲親屬名詞，不過爲一種語言上及心理上之現象，與社會組織，无任何關係。克洛伯並詳論親屬制之分爲“類分式的”及“敘述式的”之不當。因莫爾根所認爲“敘述式的”親屬制中，亦有“類分式”之名詞，而“類分式”的親屬制中，亦有“敘述式”之名詞也。自克洛伯此文發表之後，瑞弗斯乃根據其在海洋洲所得之親屬制度資料，對克洛伯加以反駁[②]。瑞弗斯以爲莫爾根之推論，誠多有錯誤，但彼爲此問題研究之開始者，篳路藍縷，其開創之功，自不可没，况其在大端上，尚不失爲極重要之發現乎？吾人自不能因其小疵而棄其大醇也。瑞弗斯所著之《親屬與社會組織》一書，爲其精心之作，論親屬制度之書中，現在尚无出其右者。瑞弗斯在此書中暢論親屬名詞與婚姻制度之關係，于“交表婚姻制”論列尤詳，爲後來之研究婚姻制度者，辟一新途徑。

論中國親屬稱謂與婚姻之關係者，在歐西則有格蘭内[③]、施愛客[④]等，但皆偶一及之，詞意閃鑠，未能得其詳也。國人著述中亦稍稍有及之者，如郭沫若之《中國古代社會研究》及陳顧遠之《中國婚姻史》中，均以“諸父”“諸母”“兄弟”“亞壻”“娣姒”等稱，以推論古代“群婚”之制。

---

① A. L. Kroeber：Classificatory Systems of Relationship，Journal，Royal Anthropological Institute. 1909，39：77-84. 克洛伯此文之真供獻，並非在其批評“類分式的”一名詞之不當，而在其親屬名詞中 categories 之鑒定，爲後來之研究親屬制度者另創一新工具。

② W. H. R. Rivers：Kinship and Social Organization(《親屬與社會組織》)，1914.

③ M. Granet：La Civilization Chinois，1929. 此書之引證事實，可謂亟牽强附會之能事，然彼亦自有其立場也。

④ J. K. Shryock and T. S. Chen：Chinese Relationship Terms，American Anthropologist，34：4，623-669，其他如 H. P. Wilkinson 之 The Chinese Family Nomenclature，New China Review 1921，159-191，則更卑卑不足道矣。

然皆囿于見聞，絀于方法，不能脱出莫爾根之圈套①。再者，“群婚”之俗，是否真有其事，亦爲現在之人類學者所否認。

婚姻制度之最能與親屬名詞發生關係者，莫過于交表婚、姊妹同婚及收繼婚三種。人類學者于研究親屬名詞之特徵時，或推衍特種婚姻制度之實在性與普遍性時，往往將二者互爲利用，交相解釋。因親屬名詞之形式爲語言現象，而語言爲事實之表徵。又語言之變演，每較其所表現之事實爲緩。往往一事物早歸淘汰，然其表現于語言名詞上者，獨立存在，或稍變其義以名其他後起或相類似之事物。故研究古代制度者，時時利用語言之現象，以推求古代之事物，所謂“語言的古生物學(linguistic paleontology)”，蓋實有其事也。

交表婚姻制

何謂交表親屬(cross-cousin)？“交表親屬”爲人類學上研究親屬制度之術語，其意義仍係對平表親屬(parallel-cousin)而言②，姑母之子女，舅父之子女，與己身(ego)爲交表親屬，因姑母與父爲異性，而舅父與母亦爲異性也。伯叔父之子女，及姨母之子女，與己身爲平表親屬，因伯叔父與父爲同性，而姨母與母亦爲同性也。但交表親屬與平表親屬在婚姻上之意義，並不由于其親屬“所自來”性别上之分，而在其在於宗族制度中親屬分配之不同。如在母系制度之下，姨母之子女與己身同屬于一宗族之内，在宗族外婚制之下，故不能互爲婚姻。在父系制度中，父之

---

① 莫爾根之學説，已成爲學術史上之陳迹，其在現在學術上之地位，可參考 B. J. Stern: Lewis Henry Morgan, Social Evolutionist, 1931. 當莫爾根之著作發表之初，即爲馬克思及昂格斯所採用，故後之崇共産主義者，因欲尊馬克思，故亦奉莫爾根之《古代社會》爲天經地義，莫之或易。彼等固不得不如此者，因若否認莫爾根之説，即否認馬克思學説之根據也。郭沫若之《中國古代社會研究》一書，並非能以實事求是之精神以研究中國古代社會者，不過欲借中國之資料，以證明古代之原始共産社會而已。其盲從主義，昧於學術之進展，自屬幼稚，然彼亦自有其立場也。若陳顧遠之《中國婚姻史》，亦拾莫爾根、郭沫若之餘唾，可謂不知所從矣。

② “交表”亦有作中表者。但俗所謂“中表”之涵義，亦有將姨母之子包括在内者，與人類學上所用之 cross-cousin 不合，故不用。

兄弟之子女，與己身屬于同一宗族之内，在宗族外婚制之下，亦不得互爲婚姻。舅父之子女，與姑母之子女，不拘其係在父系或母系制度之下，均與己身所屬之宗族不同，故不受外婚制之影響，而可互爲婚姻。

交表婚姻，又分二種。在若干原始民族中，有只能與舅父之子女爲婚，而不能與姑母之子女爲婚者；又有只能與姑母之子女爲婚，而不能與舅父之子女爲婚者。此種婚俗，稱之曰“單系的”交表婚。再在許多民族中，舅父之子女及姑母之子女，與己身均可互爲婚姻，此種制度，稱之曰“雙系的”交表婚。

在人類學上之所謂交表婚姻，並非如現行之所謂“中表婚”，其執行爲兩造父母或本人之自由意志而定。此處之所謂交表婚姻者，乃係一種有“優先權的(preferential)”“指定性的”或“强迫性的”婚制。例如本身爲男子，而姑母有女，本身至少與姑母之女有結婚之優先權。若姑母之女欲與他人結婚者，至少須得本身之許可，或須給相當之補償，甚至非與之結婚不可。如《貴州通志》所言清江黑苗之婚嫁風俗：

> 姑之女定爲舅媳，倘舅无子，必獻重金于舅，謂之外甥錢，否則終身不得嫁。

漢族在古時有无此種“指定的”交表婚姻，載籍之中，未曾明言，其曾存在與否，須由他方證驗之推斷。在推論之先，可先論交表婚姻在我國現在之情形如何。

所謂交表婚姻，記載中之實例，自周秦以來，不勝枚舉。現在各地之風俗中，亦多有行之者。不過在理論上則爲所不許，在法律上，亦爲所禁止。如《白虎通》(卷十九)：

> 外屬小功以上，亦不得娶也。是以春秋傳曰：譏娶母黨也。①

---

① 此篇所引之卷數，爲淮南書局刻陳立《白虎通疏證》本。

又《通典》(卷六十)引晉袁準内表不可爲婚議:

> 曰:今之人外内相婚,禮歟?曰:中外之親,近于同姓,同姓且猶不可,而况中外之親乎?古人以爲无疑,故不制也。今以古之不言,因謂之可婚,此不知禮者也。

袁準此論,引申過甚,不免有曲解之嫌。細考言禮者之所以反對交表婚姻者,並非由其血統之太近,而實由于其不合乎禮。其不合乎禮之處,即爲雙重親屬在喪服上所發生之糾紛是也。何以言之?例如姑之女與己之兄結婚,倘其亡故時,以叔嫂論則无服,以表姊弟論則有服。此問題在唐以前之論禮著作中,討論綦多,又均各執己見,不肯相下。故最簡便之解决方法,莫若以此種婚姻爲根本不合乎禮,則服制問題,當然不解决而自行解决矣。

在法律上之禁止,説者以爲始于唐律,如《唐律議疏·户婚》:

> 其父母之姑舅兩姨姊妹……並不得爲婚……

洪邁《容齋續筆》(卷八),曾記在宋時即有據此文以禁止中表爲婚者,其言曰:

> 姑舅兄弟爲婚,在禮法不禁,而世俗不曉。案《刑統·户婚律》云①:父母之姑舅兩姨姊妹,及姨,若堂姨;母之姑,堂姑;己之堂姨,及再從姨,堂外甥女,女婿姊妹,並不得爲婚。議曰:父母姑舅兩姨姊妹,于身无服,乃是父母緦麻,據身是尊,故不合娶。及姨又是父母大功尊,若堂姨雖于父母无服,亦是尊屬。母之姑,堂姑,並是母小功以上尊。己之堂姨,及再從姨,堂外甥女,亦謂

① 《刑統》係謂《宋刑統》。此律文係全襲《唐律議疏》。

> 堂姊妹所生者，女婿姊妹，於身雖並无服，據理不可爲婚。並爲尊卑混亂，人倫失序之故。然則中表兄弟姊妹，正是一等，其於婚姻，了无所妨……今州縣官書判至有將姑舅兄弟成婚而斷離之者，皆失於不能細讀律令也。

洪氏所言良是，唐律所禁者，(《宋刑統》此條乃全據《唐律議疏》之文)爲尊卑(即不同輩分者)爲婚，而非中表爲婚也。不過洪氏言爲“禮法所不禁”，似未深考，法雖不禁，而在禮則所不許也①。

律例中之明文禁止中表爲婚姻者，則爲明律。《明律集解·户婚》：

> 若娶己之姑舅兩姨姊妹者，杖八十，並離異。

清律全襲其文，不過法律自法律，風俗自風俗，若盡執法以繩，則杖不勝杖，離不勝離矣。故《清律例》在此律文後《條例》中則言：“其姑舅兩姨姊妹爲婚者，聽從民便。”

中國歷來法律之矛盾，大牴如是。

交表婚姻，在現在中國之社會中，爲一種矛盾的現象，一方面爲禮法所不許，而民間行之者甚多。但在古代，交表婚姻，不只爲禮法所許，而爲一種“强制的”婚俗，此種現象，在中國古代之親屬名詞上，即可見之。

記載古代親屬名詞之最完備者，當推《爾雅·釋親》及《儀禮·喪服傳》。二書之時代，以其所載之親屬名詞推之，《釋親》當較早，《喪服傳》較晚，但均不得晚于西漢。换言之，即公元以前之物也。作親屬名詞上之推論者，若能知其時代之大概，即已足用，因親屬名詞之變演，爲時甚緩，非一朝一夕之可能就，常需經過數十年或數百年之間也。本篇所引之親屬名詞，多以《爾雅》爲主，再攙以他書，而用《喪服傳》以補

---

① 如《通典》(卷九五)：“大唐之制，兩姨姑舅姊妹並不得通婚。”此乃據禮言之，而非據律言之也。至於西魏文帝時禁中外及從母兄弟姊妹爲婚，周武帝曾下詔不得娶母同姓以爲妻妾，宣帝又詔母族絶服外者聽婚等等，皆係外族之婚制，又當别論也。

其不足。

《爾雅・釋親》(《喪服傳》同)所載之親屬名詞，有數種特徵，與現行之親屬名詞不同，歷來之説經者，均陳陳相因，不得其解。如《釋親》：

> 母之晜弟爲舅。
> 婦稱夫之父曰舅。
> 妻之父爲外舅。
> 父之姊妹爲姑。
> 夫之母爲姑。
> 妻之母爲外姑。

是“舅”之一名詞，包括母之兄弟、夫之父及妻之父。“姑”則包括母之姊妹、夫之母及妻之母。如此複雜之親屬關係，而以兩名詞統括之，自非偶然，其中必有重大之原因在也。解經者之説，如《白虎通》：

> 稱夫之父母爲舅姑何？尊如父而非父者，舅也。親如母而非母者，姑也。故稱夫之父母爲舅姑也。

又如《釋名》：

> 妻之父曰外舅，母曰外姑，言妻從外來，謂至己家爲歸，故反此義以稱之，夫婦匹敵之義也。

以上之解釋，讀之仍令人茫然。如“尊如父而非父者”，何必爲舅？伯叔父豈不是一樣？“親如母而非母者”，何必曰姑？姨母豈不較姑更爲親似？至于《釋名》，則只解釋“外”字，而並未解釋“舅”與“姑”字也①。然

① 陳顧遠《中國婚姻史》，87 面及 207 面，以爲舅姑之義，爲交换婚之遺，真不自知其所云爲何也。

舅姑二名詞所含之意義，從交表婚姻制觀之，則甚爲明瞭，不必作種種之臆測也。

如己身(女)與母之昆弟之子結婚，則母之昆弟(舅)與夫之父爲一人，以“舅”一名詞統之，固屬自然。再如己身(女)與父之姊妹之子結婚，則父之姊妹(姑)與夫之母又爲一人，以“姑”一名詞統之，亦屬自然也。吾人當知，在親屬關係增加之程序上，舅(母之昆弟)姑(父之姊妹)之關係在先，舅(夫之父)姑(夫之母)之關係在後，以先有之名詞，加諸後來增加之關係上，在語言上固屬自然之趨勢也。

反之，己身(男)若與母之昆弟之女結婚，則母之昆弟(舅)與妻之父爲一人。又如己身(男)與父之姊妹之女結婚，則父之姊妹(姑)與妻之母同爲一人。以同上之理由，舅姑之名，亦可加之於妻之父母也。

舅姑二名詞所表現者，爲“雙系的”交表婚姻制，即己身能與舅姑之子女互爲婚姻是也。但《爾雅》所載親屬名詞之特徵，並不只此，又如，《釋親·妻黨》：

> 姑之子爲甥，舅之子爲甥，妻之昆弟爲甥，姊妹之夫爲甥。

以“甥”之一名詞，統括四種不同之親屬，最爲奇特。歷來之解經者，均以郭注爲主：

> 四人體敵，故更相爲甥。甥，猶生也。

“體敵”爲相等之義，但如何爲“體敵”？從未有人能作明白之解釋者。如俞樾之“姑之子爲甥，舅之子爲甥，妻之昆弟爲甥，姊妹之夫爲甥解”①，洋洋數百言，仍不能説出體敵之義何在也。如姑舅之子體敵，而從母(姨母)之子如何不能敵體？再者妻之昆弟爲姻族親屬(affinal

① 見《詁經精舍自課文》，《春在堂全書》本。

relatives)，姑舅之子爲血族親屬(consanguineal relatives)，其性質迥然不同，而彼此何能“敵體”？諸如此類，皆必須明白之解釋者也。

《釋名》曾將“妻之昆弟爲甥”加以解釋云：

> 妻之昆弟曰外甥，其姊妹女也，來歸己内爲妻，故其男爲外姓之甥。甥者，生也。他姓子本生于外，不得如其女來在己内也。

此乃望文生義之臆説，不足爲據。然則，“甥”一名詞將作何詮釋乎？曰：此亦交表婚姻及姊妹交换婚(sister exchange)之表現也。何以言之？

若己身(男)與姑之女結婚，則姑之子與妻之昆弟同爲一人。又如己身(男)與舅之女爲婚，則舅之子與妻之昆弟，又同爲一人。在雙系的交表婚姻制之下，己身若不與舅之女爲婚，即與姑之女爲婚。故姑之子，舅之子，妻之昆弟，實際上實屬相等，故可以一名詞統之也。又若在雙系的交表婚姻制之下，姑之子，或舅之子，娶己身之姊妹爲妻(彼等均系交表親屬，故可爲婚。如是則爲互相交换姊妹爲妻矣)，則己身姊妹之夫，與姑之子，舅之子，妻之昆弟亦屬相等，故皆可以“甥”名之也。

如此，則歷來經師所不能明者，可以一旦冰釋。而同時“甥”之義，與“姑”“舅”之義相輔而行，均爲交表婚姻制之表現。又交换姊妹爲婚，常與交表婚姻制並行，因己身及己身之姊妹，與姑之子女，舅之子女，互爲交表親屬，故可互爲婚姻①，此在原始民族中爲例固甚多也。

由上之親屬名詞觀之，雙系的交表婚在中國古代之存在，可无疑義。但何以知其爲一種“强制性”的婚俗？此亦至易明瞭。如婚姻可以自由選擇，則舅之子不一定娶姑之女，而姑之女亦不一定爲舅之媳。若此則《爾雅》中所言“姑”“舅”“甥”之義與親屬之實際不合，則无由發生矣。换言之，婚俗當有多少之“强制性”始能影響到親屬名詞也。

---

① 經籍中每以“婚媾”二字並用。據許氏《説文》：“媾，重婚也。”段注：“重婚者，重叠交互爲婚也。”是“媾”之一詞，似與將姊妹互相交换爲之婚俗上，亦不無關係也。

姊妹同婚

姊妹同婚(sororate)者，爲姊妹同嫁一夫之謂。然其方式，亦稍有不同。例如己身娶一女子爲妻，則妻之姊妹，亦得有娶之之權利。如妻之姊妹欲另嫁時，須得己身之許可，或給相當之贖償，再者如妻不育或亡故時，妻族須另備一女子，以補妻之缺。此女子必爲妻之姊妹，如无姊妹，妻之兄弟之女(即内姪女)亦可。後者稱爲“内姪女婚”，爲姊妹同婚之引申。因妻之兄弟之女，爲妻之姊妹最好之代替人也。原始民族中多有行此種婚俗者，如北美印第安人中之 Miwok 及 Omaha 族，即其例也。

姊妹同婚，在周時頗爲盛行，而特以統治階級爲尤甚①。古代親屬名詞中，亦稍有具此俗之表徵者，如《爾雅・釋親》：

> 女子謂姊妹之夫爲私。

又《詩・碩人》：

> 譚公維私。

傳統的詮釋，如《釋名》所言：

> 姊妹互相謂夫爲私，言于其夫兄弟中，此人與己姊妹有恩私也。

此説亦稍覺牽强。果如是，則男子亦可稱姊妹之夫爲私，何以“私”之名詞，只限於女子間之互稱也。與其間接的言於己之姊妹有恩私，不如直接的釋爲與己有恩私也。如是則“私”當爲姊妹同婚之表現。不過此種推論，尚欠明瞭。《爾雅》又謂：

---

① 可參見 M. Granet：La polygyanie sororale et le sororat dans la Chine féodale，1920. 格蘭内之解説，多不可憑信，不過其收集之材料，尚爲豐富。

> 母之姊妹爲從母。

從母之義，以其爲從母而來，以作父妾，後雖不來，亦得以從母呼之也①。如此義，則“從母”之名，亦當爲姊妹同婚之遺也。不過“從母”亦可謂爲“從父”之對稱②，不必一定爲姊妹同婚之表現。

在周時貴族中盛行一種姊妹同婚及内姪女婚，經傳中稱之曰媵。《公羊傳》(莊公十九年)：

> 媵者何？諸侯娶一國，二國往媵之，以姪娣從。姪者何？兄之子也。娣者何？弟也。

媵婚之制，共爲九女，所謂“諸侯一聘九女”是也。此九女共分三組，一爲諸侯所聘之正妻(夫人)，及其一姪一娣。再爲二國來伴嫁之媵，稱爲左媵右媵，媵各一姪一娣。共三組，合爲九女。來媵者，必與所聘之正妻同姓，《左傳》(成公十八年)：

> 衛人來媵共姬，禮也。凡諸侯嫁女，同姓媵之，異姓則否。

媵妾之必爲同姓者，取其可爲姊妹(娣)及兄弟之女(姪)，亦即姊妹同婚及内姪女婚之遺意也。前人不察，以爲无甚意義，則過矣。但媵妾之來，在理論上不可以强求，須出自來媵者之自願。《公羊傳》(莊公十九年)，何休注：

> 言往媵之者禮，君不求媵，二國自往媵夫人，所以一夫人之尊。

---

① 《釋名·釋親屬》：“母之姊妹……禮謂之從母，爲娣而來，則從母列也。”故雖不來，猶以此名之也。

② 《爾雅義疏》：“從母者，猶宗族中之有從父，言從母而得尊稱也。”

其用意雖爲“所以一夫人之尊”，此或者出於往媵者之意，而在於嫁女者方面，亦爲不欲“求人爲賤”之義。《白虎通》(卷下)：

> 所以不聘妾者，何？人有子孫，欲尊之義，義不可求人爲賤也……妾雖賢不得爲嫡。

媵婚制度之意義何在？當以《白虎通》所言者，爲最詳盡：

> 天子諸侯一娶九女者何？重國廣繼嗣也①。
>
> 大夫成功受封，得備八妾者，重國廣嗣也②。
>
> 不娶兩娣何？博異氣也。娶三國女何？廣異類也。恐一國血脈相似，以无子也③。
>
> 備姪娣從者，爲其必不相嫉妒也。一人有子，三人共之，若己生之也④。

媵婚之制，可謂周詳。而其原始姊妹同婚之痕迹，則至爲明顯。前已言之，在姊妹同婚制下，若妻不育時，得收妻之姊妹或姪女爲妻妾，以期其有子。不過在媵婚制度之下，組織較爲完密，不論妻之育與不育，諸侯大夫爲“重國廣嗣”計得收妻之姪娣，先備媵妾。至于“備姪娣從者”之意，“爲其必不相嫉妒”，在事實上或不盡然，但亦與原始民族之有姊妹同婚制者之解釋，爲同一説法也。

此爲媵婚制之大概，他如媵婚制下之“諸侯不再娶”⑤，媵妾不得稱

---

① 《白虎通疏證》(卷十)，頁 11。
② 《白虎通疏證》(卷十)，頁 13。
③ 《白虎通疏證》(卷十)，頁 11。
④ 《白虎通疏證》(卷十)，頁 11。又《公羊傳》(莊公十九年)，何休注：“必以姪娣從之者，欲使一人有子，二人喜也。所以防嫉妒，令重繼嗣也。因以備尊尊親親也。”
⑤ 《公羊傳》(莊公十九年)：“諸侯一聘九女，諸侯不再娶。”

夫人①，媵妾幼可以“待年父母之國”②等，乃爲媵婚制中後起之枝節，然不能掩蓋姊妹同婚之原來面目也。

關于媵婚再有一問題，即“娣”之是否爲夫人或媵之同母之妹是也。毛際盛以爲凡媵婚中之娣，均爲媵妾之子。《説文解字述誼》(卷二)：

> 古不以同母妹爲娣，宣姜二女一爲宋桓夫人，一爲許穆夫人。莊姜同母姊妹一適荆，一適譚可證也。且夫人所出，恆爲夫人，娣之所出，恆爲娣，所謂貴賤有常也。

毛氏之論，自有根據，不過娣之是否爲夫人之親妹，並不關重要。因在原始姊妹同婚之俗中，名詞至關重要，只需有姊妹之名，不拘其爲正出或庶出，均得以姊妹視之。且“娣”爲媵婚制中之專名，其他之含義，多爲引申或備用。以前之解釋“娣”在親屬上之意義者，多離開媵婚而言，故不能得其真諦③。

“姪”之義表現内姪女婚更爲明顯。“姪”在《爾雅》中爲女子呼兄弟之子女之專稱。《釋親·妻黨》：

> 女子謂晜弟之子爲姪。

男子則呼姊妹之子爲“出”。姪與姑爲對稱詞④，《儀禮·喪服》：

> 傳曰：姪者，何也？謂吾姑者，吾謂之姪。

---

① 《左傳》(隱公元年)：“孟子卒，繼室以聲子。”杜注：“諸侯始娶，則同姓之國以姪娣媵，元妃死則次妃攝治内事，猶不得稱夫人，謂之繼室。”此不過在理論上如此，事實上亦有不盡然者。

② 《公羊傳》(隱公七年)：“叔姬歸于紀。”注：“叔姬者，伯姬之媵也。”至是乃歸者，待年父母之國也。

③ 如鄭珍《巢經巢文集·娣似篇》即其一例也。

④ 對稱詞(reciprocity)之定義，參見拙著之《中國親屬制》(*The Chinese Kinship System*)，170-171面。

至於男子呼兄弟之子爲姪則爲媵婚停止後，字義上之轉變（semantic change），其時約在魏晉之世[①]，姪爲姪女婚中之特别名詞，觀乎姪之原來解釋，即可知之。《左傳》（僖公十五年）：

姪其從姑。

雖姪可兼通男女[②]，則皆言從姑而嫁也。又《釋名》所言，更爲明顯：

姑謂兄弟之女爲姪。姪，迭也。共行事夫，更迭進御也。

從現在之倫理觀念視之，此乃何等荒謬之解釋，劉熙若無所本，何敢出此讕言，淆亂尊卑，以致人倫失序。但自距劉熙不遠之媵婚觀之，此自爲正當之詮釋，與當時之倫常觀念，固無所觝觸也。

古代親屬名詞中尚有一特徵，可與内姪女婚相印證，即以前所論之“甥”是也。“甥”字之意義，除《爾雅》所言之姑之子，舅之子，妻之昆弟，及姊妹之夫外，《儀禮·喪服》言：

甥者，何也？謂吾舅者，無謂之甥。[③]

此乃言姊妹之子，而謂之曰甥。《孟子》又稱女之夫曰甥。

---

① 《顏氏家訓（卷二）·風操篇》：“兄弟之子已孤，與他人言對孤者前呼爲兄子弟子，頗爲不忍，北土人多呼爲姪。案《爾雅·喪服經》《左傳》姪名雖通男女，並是對姑之稱，晉世以來，始呼叔姪。今呼爲姪，於理爲勝也。”

② 此爲兩對稱詞中之特徵。如“姑”對於所稱親屬之性别，則指示明白，而對於稱呼者（speaker）之性别，則無所知也。“姪”則對於所稱親屬之性别，無所指示，而對於稱呼者之性别，則曾明白指示也。故此兩對稱詞之涵義中，每一詞含有一種類别（category），而爲其對面之詞所無者。

③ 《爾雅·釋親》亦言：“謂我舅者，吾謂之甥也。”但附於《婚姻》類之最末，可謂極無倫次，與《釋親》之分類不合。其爲後來誤入之衍文，則可無疑。

> 舜尚見帝，帝館甥于貳室……

姊妹之子也，女之夫也，均與姑之子，舅之子，姊妹之夫，妻之昆弟，不僅行輩不同，且亦戚屬各異，而一皆稱之曰甥，其中必有大原因在也。

歷來之注釋家，均避開此問題，即有釋之者，亦不得其要領。如郝懿行之《爾雅義疏》：

> 男子謂姊妹之子爲出，又謂甥者，甥之言生，與出同義。故《釋名》云："舅謂姊妹之子爲甥，甥亦生也。"出配他男而生，故其制字，男旁作生。按上文云舅姑之子，妻之昆弟，姊妹之夫，俱謂之甥。彼謂敵體，此則同名而實異也。

"甥"一名詞中各種意義之構成，並非由字義或字形可得解釋，其後必有社會制度之背景。縱認"甥"與"出"之義同，而姊妹之子之"甥"，與"甥"之其他意義，尚須説明。郝氏不得已，乃以"同名而實異"含糊了之，而不能得其"同名"之所以然也。

案"出"爲男子呼姊妹之子之原名，壻爲女之夫之原名(《爾雅》："女子子之夫爲壻。")，"甥"者乃在内姪女婚制影響下所引申而來之新名。蓋甥之本義爲舅之子、姑之子，姊妹之夫及妻之兄弟。其姊妹之子，女之夫亦曰甥者，乃其後來之引申也。請詳言之。在交表婚、姊妹交换婚及内姪女婚制之下，姊妹之子可與己之女爲婚(交表婚)，姊妹之夫亦可與己身之女爲婚(内姪女婚)，如是則姊妹之夫，姊妹之子，女之夫，在親屬關係上，實屬相等。又如，舅之子與己身之姊妹爲婚(交表婚)，則亦可與己身之女爲婚(内姪女婚)。故舅之子，姊妹之夫，女之夫，在親屬關係上亦屬相等。綜合言之，則舅之子，姑之子，姊妹之夫，婦之兄弟，姊妹之子，女之夫，在親屬上均爲相等之關係。故用"甥"一名詞以統之，亦無不可也。

由此可見姊妹同婚中之内姪女婚，表現于"姪""娣"及"甥"之名詞上者，至爲明顯。不過以近代之倫理眼光視之，則似覺可駭，故宋人直有以媵婚之俗實無其事，不過爲漢儒所臆造者。但吾人自不能以現代之倫理觀念繩古代之風俗，婚姻中之行輩限制，自魏晉以後始盛，魏晉以前，則無所拘也①。自人類社會學上視之，内姪女婚之俗，則更不足爲怪，不只我國古時有之，現代之民族中，亦常見不鮮也。

收 繼 婚

收繼婚(levirate)之本義，爲夫之兄弟婚。不過其在各民族中之變式，頗有不同。廣泛之收繼婚，兄死可以收嫂，弟亡可以娶弟婦；引申之，父死可以妻群母(生母除外)，甚至祖亡亦可娶祖父之妻妾。狹義的而較普遍的收繼婚，爲夫亡時只可與夫之弟結婚，即俗所謂叔接嫂或轉房是也，在人類學上則稱曰 Junior levirate。叔嫂婚之俗，在亞洲分布甚廣，如印度、東北亞洲及中國境内之土著民族中，多有之。漢族之下級社會中亦有行之者，但不甚普遍耳。

本義的收繼婚，在分布上，多與姊妹同婚並行。即一民族中之有姊妹同婚者，多有收繼婚；反之，有收繼婚者，亦多有姊妹同婚之俗也。從現有之證據及親屬名詞上觀之，中國古時確有姊妹同婚之俗，再者，接近中國之各民族中，亦多有行叔嫂婚姻者，但在中國古時有無叔嫂婚姻之習，乃尚須研究之問題也。

格蘭内即爲主張中國古代有叔嫂婚姻者②，其所援之證據，如《左傳》(莊公二十八年)：

① 不同行輩之親屬婚姻(inter-generation marriages)，典籍所載，在魏晉以前，爲例特多。如梁玉繩《瞥記》(卷二)所言："楚成王取文芈二女(《左》僖廿二)，晉文公納嬴氏(僖廿四)，皆以甥爲妻者，可謂無別矣。"嗣後妻甥者，漢孝惠取張敖女，章帝取竇勛女，吳孫休取朱據女，俱楚頵晉重作之俑也。梁氏不明倫常觀念進化之跡，故有是嘆。此種不同行輩之婚姻，不只不爲當時禮法所不禁，而言禮者，亦公開討論。如《通典》(卷九五)所載族父是姨弟爲服議，及娶同堂姊之女爲妻，姊亡服議等是也。及至唐時，尚有行之者，如中宗娶其表姑爲妻，《唐書》(卷一六)："中宗和思順聖皇后趙……父環，尚高祖常樂公主，帝爲英王，聘后爲妃。"而在當時亦未有非議之者。

② 參考 M. Granet：La civilization chinois，424-425 頁。

> 楚令尹子元欲蠱文夫人，爲館於其宫側而振萬焉。夫人聞之泣曰：先君以是舞也，習戎備也，令尹不尋諸仇讐，而於未亡人之側，不亦異乎！

又(定公十九年)：

> 敝無存之父將室之，辭之以與其弟，曰：此役也，不死，反必娶於高國。

格蘭内之援用此類證據，直等於無證據。子元之蠱息嬀，不過爲貪其色，並無娶嫂之義務，更非娶其嫂後，始能得其兄之權力，而掌楚之國政也。至於敝無存之辭婚與弟，實因其心目中另有所屬，欲娶於高氏國氏。其所辭之女，既非其妻，而其弟更非兄亡而收嫂，可謂與收繼婚毫無關係。

格蘭内又舉喪服叔嫂无服爲證，彼以爲叔嫂無服，自然可以互爲婚姻。不過服制一項，不能用作婚姻限制之標準，特别爲小功以下之服，於婚姻無大阻礙，所謂"緦麻之服，不禁嫁娶"是也。

格蘭内之必欲證中國中古有收繼婚及姊妹同婚者，因彼以爲收繼婚及姊妹同婚爲原始的群婚，即一群兄弟與一群姊妹結爲婚姻之變相的遺留(survival)。如能證明收繼婚及姊妹同婚之存在，則群婚制在中國古代之存在，可不證自明。格蘭内之此種理論的推測，自高出國人之研究古代群婚及母系社會者一等，但其根據，亦援用莫爾根、泰洛耳(E. B. Tylor)，及弗内色(Sir James Frazer)諸人之説，亦無所謂創見也。但以收繼婚及姊妹同婚爲群婚之遺，早爲現在一般人類學者所否認。至于群婚一説，亦爲有實地經驗之人類學家所摒棄也。

施、陳二氏所著之《中國親屬名詞》一文中①，曾言"伯"一名詞爲收

① J. K. Shryock and T. S. Chen：Chinese Relationship Terms，American Anthropologist，34：4，623-669，其他如H. P. Wilkinson之The Cinese Family Nomenclature，New China Review 1921，159-191，則更卑卑不足道矣。

繼婚之表現，因伯有“夫之兄”之義，而又有“丈夫”之義也。夫與夫之兄同統於一親屬名詞之下，是夫之兄亦有作已身（女）丈夫之可能性（potential husband）也。考以“伯”作夫之義，則爲《詩經·伯兮》：

> 伯兮朅兮，邦之桀兮；伯也執殳，爲王前趨。自伯之東，首如飛蓬，豈無膏沐？誰適爲容。

此處之“伯”，係指女子之夫而言。但“伯”之義，抑爲稱夫之親屬名詞乎？夫之官爵乎？或呼夫之美稱乎？均不甚明瞭。即使“伯”爲稱夫之親屬名詞，亦不能用作爲收繼婚之證。因呼夫之兄爲伯，最早亦不過起於五代之時也。

《爾雅》稱夫之兄爲兄公。公亦作伀，或作妐，讀如鍾。《釋名》則作爲兄章。章或作偉，或嫜。稱夫之兄爲伯，蓋始于五代之時。陶岳《五代史補》（卷五）：

> （李）濤爲人不拘禮法，與弟澣雖甚雍睦，然聚話之際，不典之言，往往間作。澣娶禮部尚書竇寧固之女，年甲稍高，成婚之夕，竇氏出參濤，輒望塵下拜。澣驚曰：“大哥風狂耶？新婦參阿伯，豈有答禮儀？”濤應曰：“我不風，只將謂是親家母。”

自是之後，以“伯”稱夫之兄之用漸廣，及至現代，則蔚爲通稱。兄公、兄章之名，則鮮有知之者矣。由此可知以伯稱夫，及以伯稱夫之兄，不惟不同時，而且相距至少有一千餘年之遠，用之以作收繼婚之證驗，自屬不當。

收繼婚在禮法上之禁止，爲時甚早，亦且甚嚴厲。古代與漢族接觸之民族有此俗者，亦早知之。史家每引爲異俗，而不齒其於人類。如《史記·匈奴列傳》所記之：

> 父死妻其後母，兄弟死皆取其妻妻之。

是也。至於法律之禁，唐以前不可知，現在所存最早之完全法典《唐律疏議》户婚條下：

諸嘗爲袒免親而嫁娶者，各杖一百。緦麻及舅甥妻，徒一年。小功以上以姦論。妾各減二等，並離之。

在此律令之下，各種之收繼婚，自屬不可能，而其罰亦不可謂不重，所謂姦者，即 incest 之謂也。至於明律，則更爲明白嚴厲，《明律集解》户婚：

若收祖父妾及伯叔母者，各斬。兄亡收嫂，弟亡收弟婦者，各絞。

清律亦全與此相同。間嘗推之，明律之所以特別標明者，大概係由於元人收繼婚傳入中國後之一種反響，亦未可知。

春秋時代及春秋以後，史籍所載之上烝下報之事，爲例甚多，然皆不能視爲收繼婚之遺，乃爲例外之事也。因其大都皆出於貪慕女子之色，而非出於娶之之義務也。正當之收繼婚俗，如兄没之後，不管嫂之有色與否，或己身已娶與否，均須收嫂爲妻，不然者，則无以對亡兄，對寡嫂，對親戚，而將爲社會所不齒。再者，或視女子爲財產，防其外溢，則惟有收繼之一途。細考典籍中所載，均無此類觀念之遺留或表現。若爲一時財色所驅使，則隨時隨地均可發生，不必爲收繼婚俗之表現也。

結　　論

由以上所論之各點觀之，中國古代婚俗之表現在親屬名詞上者，以交表婚姻爲最肯定，姊妹同婚及内姪女婚次之，至於收繼婚則全无徵驗①。媵婚(即姊妹同婚及其引伸之内姪女婚)隨封建制度以俱去，秦漢

① 中國現代下層社會中所行之少數叔嫂婚，大概係受外族之影響。可參見：China Review, 10, 71, 1881—1882, The levirate in China; P. G. von Mollondorff, The Family Law of The Chinese, 1896；黄華節，《叔接嫂》，《東方雜誌》，31, 1934, 7；及李魯人，《元代蒙古收繼婚俗傳入内地之影響》，《大公報・史地週刊》，廿五年四月十日，第八期。

以後則無聞。經典中對於此婚俗之記載雖多，但以其制度之奇特，後之學者對之疑信參半，鮮有能明瞭其真實意義者。今得親屬名詞上之徵驗，其在中國古代婚制中之重要意義，則可以概見矣。

交表婚姻，自秦漢而後，行之者頗多，普通稱爲“中表婚”。但爲一種“許可式”的，而非“指定式”的婚俗，故於現代之親屬名詞中，則無所表現。交表婚制之失掉其“强制性”，大概在春秋以前，或在殷周之際。因至秦漢之時，《爾雅》中所釋“舅”“姑”“甥”之義，已與當時親屬關係之實際不合，而需要新興名詞以代之。如妐(夫之父)見《吕氏春秋》①，尊章(夫之父)見《漢書》及《釋名》②，中表③、内兄弟④、外兄弟⑤、婦公⑥等名詞均始於漢。至魏晉以後新起之名詞代替“舅”“姑”“甥”之各種意義者更繁，而交表婚姻，亦已開始爲禮法所禁止矣。

(見《齊魯學報》一九四一年第一期)

---

① 《吕氏春秋(卷一四)·慎人篇》：“姑妐知之，曰：‘爲我婦而有外心。’”

② 《漢書(卷五三)·廣川王去傳》：“背尊章嫖以忽。”師古曰：”尊章，猶言舅姑也。今關中俗婦呼舅爲鍾。鍾者，尊聲之轉也。”《釋名·釋親屬》：“俗或謂舅曰章，又曰妐。”

③ 《後漢書·鄭太傳》：“公業懼，乃詭詞更對曰……又名公將帥，皆中表腹心。”

④ 《儀禮·喪服》：“舅之子。”鄭注：“内兄弟也。”

⑤ 《儀禮·喪服》：“姑之子。”鄭注：“外兄弟也。”

⑥ 《後漢書(卷七十一)·第五倫傳》：“帝戲謂倫曰：‘聞鄉爲吏，篣婦公，不過從兄飯，寧有之耶?’倫對曰：‘臣三娶妻皆無父。’”

倮儸與東爨

倮儸文舊稱爨文，故倮儸亦有稱之作爨人者，但倮儸是否爨人，或與爨人之關係如何？兹爲略論之。

“爨”一字之最早見者，則爲《華陽國志》。其中之《南中志》言“諸葛亮平南中，移南中勁卒青羌萬餘家于蜀……分其羸弱配大姓焦、雍、婁、爨、孟、量、毛、李，爲部曲”，又言亮收其俊傑建寧爨習、朱提孟琰及獲爲官。《南中志》又言“建寧郡之同樂縣大姓爨氏”。是知爨乃當時之大姓，既非種名，亦非國號也。現在所保存之大小爨碑，爨龍顔碑在陸凉，爨寶子碑在曲靖，均在雲南境。前者作于劉宋大明二年，後者作于晉安帝義熙元年。二碑均用漢文，而爨龍顔碑之書者爲爨道慶。是知爨姓不一定爲夷姓，亦可爲漢姓，至少其漢化之程度實甚深也。

爨之成爲一種民族稱號，或國號，約在隋唐之際。隋唐時其中又分東西，故有東西兩爨蠻之稱。《新唐書》言“西爨自言本安邑人，七世祖晉南寧太守，中國亂，遂王蠻中”。故有人以爲倮儸原爲來自西北，而西歐學者如 Terriende Dacoupepie 輩，更張大其詞，以爲中國境内民族向西南遷移之張本。《雲南通志》則駁《新唐書》之在晉時无南寧之名，南寧于齊梁時始有之，而官階又非太守而爲刺史。

爨人所居之地，爲現在之四川南部、貴州之西部以及雲南。《蠻書》言：“西爨，白蠻也。東爨，烏蠻也。當天寶中，東北自曲靖州，西南至宣城，邑落相望，牛馬被野。在石城、昆川、曲軛、晉寧、喻獻、安寧至龍和城，謂之西爨。在曲靖州、彌鹿川、昇麻川南至步頭，謂之東爨。”

據《蠻書》，“石城川，味縣故地也。貞觀中有郎州，開元初改爲南寧州，州城即諸葛亮戰處故地也”。其地距今曲靖 22.5 公里，龍和城在今大理以東。故西爨所居之地，約在今曲靖以西至大理之間。曲靖州在唐時，當爲曲州、靖州，自今四川之慶符、長寧以南之地，皆爲唐時之曲州、靖州。彌鹿約當現在之瀘西縣，昇麻亦在曲靖以東。步頭在于何地，頗不易言。據《讀史方輿紀要》及法人伯希和之考證，當爲現今之建水縣境（見馮承鈞譯伯希和著之《交廣印度兩道考》）。故東爨所居之地，約爲自四川敘府以南至越南之邊境。

現在均以爨人爲倮儸，但實有不盡然者，因東爨固屬倮儸，而西爨則非也。西爨在語言文化上均與東爨不同，而類分上亦異。東爨爲烏蠻，西爨爲白蠻，樊綽早已明言之矣。西爨爲何種民族？據其自言，則爲漢人，此言當不甚可靠。西歐學者則以西爨爲現在居于緬甸之克倫（Karen）民族。如《蠻書》言“閣羅鳳遣昆川城使楊牟利以兵圍脅西爨，徙二十萬户于永昌城。烏蠻以言語不通，多散林谷，故得不徙。……烏蠻種類，稍稍復振，後徙居西爨故地”。説者以爲克倫族南移之先聲，因克倫族亦自言係來自北方也。此雖可爲一種解釋，但无法證明。

東爨之爲倮儸，似可无疑義，《蠻書》所載極爲明顯。“過魯望七程至竹子嶺，嶺東有暴蠻部落。嶺西有盧鹿蠻部落。第六程至生蠻磨彌殿部落。此等部落皆東爨烏蠻也。男則髮髻，女則散髮。見人无禮節拜跪，三譯四譯乃與華通，大部落則有大鬼主”。此爲盧鹿之最早見，亦即“倮儸”爲其訛音。其所言鬼主之事，亦與後來言倮儸者相因。盧鹿大概本爲一强大部落之名，後乃用爲倮儸之總稱。

此處所言之魯望、竹子嶺等地名，均不可考。按自漢以來，由蜀通雲南之道，大約有二。一爲自雅安滎經越大相嶺經西昌而入雲南，此即所謂司馬相如所開，武侯南征之路也。按諸葛亮南征之路綫，説者頗多。《華陽國志》有言自安上縣由水道入越巂之語。安上今不可考，又自蜀无水道可入越巂者，去夏在康定晤任曉莊先生談及此事，任君言安上應爲現在之沈村及冷磧，清時冷邊及沈邊土司駐牧地也，因自滎經以西皆係崇山峻嶺，无處可設縣，果如是，則武侯南征，並未經大相嶺，乃係自滎經由小路出化林坪下之龍壩鋪，以達大渡河邊之冷邊及沈邊。此路較之大相嶺爲平坦，且較捷(冷磧與沈村，在瀘定下10餘公里，雖沿大渡河可通漢源之富林，但不能行船，且全程不過50多公里)，此爲入南中之主要路綫，亦即《蠻書》所稱之南路也。再爲由戎州(敘府)渡江南行，經慶符、筠連、曲靖等處而至昆明，《蠻書》所謂之北路是也。大概樊綽所稱之南路與北路，係從雲南方面視之，不然一在西南，一在東南均南路也，何有南北之分。不過北路崎嶇險阻，且生夷爲患，梗阻之時多而通時少。所謂魯望、竹子嶺等地，即在此道之中，自唐以來此道沿途，即爲倮儸活動之地。《明史·土司傳》載明太祖遣傅友德、沐英等平雲南而敕之曰："東川芒部諸夷，種類皆出于倮儸，厥後子孫蕃衍，各立疆場，乃易其名曰東川(雲南會澤縣境)、烏撒(雲南鎮雄、貴州威寧境)、烏蒙(雲南昭通境)、芒部(雲南鎮雄縣境，烏蒙子芒部居此，故號)、祿肇、水西(貴州境)，无事則互起争端，有事則相救援。"關于烏撒等源流，《元史·地理志》言"烏撒烏蒙宣慰司，在本部巴的甸。烏撒者蠻名也，其部在中慶(今昆明治)東北七百五十里，舊名巴凡兀姑，今曰巴的甸。自昔烏蠻雜居之，今所轄部六，曰烏撒部、阿頭部、易溪部、易娘部、烏蒙部、閟畔部。其東西有芒布、阿晟二部，後烏蠻之裔折怒始强大，盡得其地。國取遠祖烏撒爲部名。憲宗征大理，屢招不降，至元十年始附。十三年立烏撒路。十五年爲軍民總管府。二十一年改軍民宣撫司。二十四年昇烏撒烏蠻宣慰司。"明平其地爲烏蒙、烏撒、東川及鎮雄四軍民府。故以地望而言，隋唐時東爨所處之地，亦即後來倮儸活動之中心區域也。

爨人在隋時爲文帝所滅，唐時臣服於南詔。但西爨爲白蠻，爲南詔所賤視，東爨爲倮儸，與南詔爲互爲婚姻之族。大概倮儸在西南民族中世爲統治階級，故雖臣于南詔，而尚能與之互爲婚姻約(近凌純聲先生在《人類學集刊》上著有《唐代的烏蠻白蠻考》一文，言南詔屬倮儸族，其言甚辯，當另爲文以論之)。倮儸與南詔之關係，在當時頗爲密切，南詔中之勁旅，亦多倮儸爲之。《蠻書》言"羅苴(音斜)子皆于鄉兵中試入，故稱四軍苴子。戴光兜鍪，負犀皮銅鼓排，跣足，歷險如飛，每百人羅苴佐一人管之。”又言“負排又從羅苴中揀入，无員數，南詔及諸鎮下將軍起坐不相離捍蔽者，皆負排也。”由此可見羅苴子在南詔軍旅中之重要。羅苴與倮儸自稱之曰“羅蘇”，極爲相近。其所言之裝束及跣足、歷險如飛等語，又與現在之言倮儸者，甚爲相似也。

由此可見“爨”，在初並非一國號，亦非一種名，而爲當時之一大姓，及至今日在宜賓一帶尚有姓爨者。爨姓之爲夷姓或爲漢姓，今尚不甚了，不過在春秋時，土士亦有姓爨者。而在唐時西南民族中實少有用姓之習，如南詔命名，則爲“父子以名相屬”，即子名之首一字連父名之末一字，而不用姓，倮儸至今尚有沿此習者。論者以此爲南詔屬倮儸族之證，然實不足爲據。《唐書》所載“父子以名相屬”爲緬甸民族之特徵，南詔、倮儸，或得之于彼等。又倮儸受南詔之統治，倮儸中此種命名之俗，或爲轉得之于南詔，亦未可知。如元人統治西南未久，而倮儸酋豪中，即有“蒙古語式”之命名者，月魯帖木耳是也。又倮儸酋豪中之有姓氏，始于明初，水西安氏是也。故從唐宋以前，西南民族中无姓氏之習推之，爨亦可爲漢姓，或漢化之夷姓，不過彼自言爲安邑人，則未可爲典據也。但无論如何，自魏晉而後，中原擾攘，爨氏以西南豪族而徵服其他各民族，遂據有雲貴，中土之人遂以爨人呼之而爨則由族姓而變爲國號而兼種號，此等現象，在西南民族中，實不乏實例。故爨人中所包括之民族，想至爲複雜，倮儸不過爲其中之一種，東爨是也。

（原載《雜説月刊》一九四二年第一期）

中國文化發展的南向與北向説的新論

近來研究中國文化問題的，有時注意到中國文化發展中方向，即向南與向北發展的問題。此一問題在中國文化的教育及構成上，自然有相當的重要性，因爲在一種文化發展的方向中，實包括環境的變遷，民族的接觸以及文化的交流等等問題，因而影響整個文化的内容與結構。現在這個問題的研究，可以説剛在萌芽之中，文獻並不甚多，其中比較有價值的要以日人桑原鷺藏的《由歷史上觀察的中國南北文化》(楊筠如譯，國立武漢大學《文哲季刊》一卷三號)，張振之的《中國文化之南向開展》(《新亞細亞雜誌》一卷三期)，梁東園的《現代中國的北方與南方》(《新生命》三卷十二期)及陳序經的《南北文化的真諦》(見陳氏所著《中國文化的出路》第七章)。

以上各論文的大意，均以爲中國文化在歷史上的發展，係由北而南，特别自永嘉亂後，其南趨的動向，較前尤爲加速。但自海通以後，中國之文化發展的動向，則完全掉轉來變爲由南而北。他們在各方面舉出若干事實，以爲左證，不過我們在此處不必一一加以闡述，因本文的目的，並不在闡明或推翻此種學説，而本文所要研求的是中國文化發展中之所以動向及其轉變的原因，所以注重在原理闡述，而不在事實蒐集。

中國文化的發展先由北而南，現在則爲南而北的原因，在上面所舉的論文中，亦稍有論及者，如梁東園氏以爲中國文化的發展在歷史上有北而南的原因，是屬於經濟的，這當然我們不能完全否認，否過未離地理環境論的窠臼，實不足以解釋中國文化之動向也。陳序經氏則以爲北方文化，是中國固有的文化，而南方文化則是西洋的文化，中國固有文化的發展，係由北而南，而西洋文化的傳來，則係由南而北。陳氏似乎明白一點其中的道理，而實際上實不能捉摸其所謂動向的“真諦”何在也。

研究文化發展的動向，並不是一種新的探討，特別在地理環境論中此説爲最早，文化向冷的方向移動，在歐洲即早有此説，例如以歐洲文化的發展史上觀之，則發源皆於温暖的南方，逐漸向寒冷的北方移動。如埃及、蘇墨爲西歐文明進步之最早者，埃及、蘇墨衰，巴比侖，克里特，腓力基，亞敘利亞等繼之而起，巴比侖等之文化衰，則有西臘、羅馬，西臘、羅馬之文化衰，現代之北歐文明乃繼之而興。故從整個文化發展史上觀之，文化的動向，是朝北冷的方向走的，在歐西文化的進展整個歷史中自然亦不乏例外，而向南游移，但均爲暫時的，與當文化衰落之際，倘若文化繼續向前進步，則仍然轉而向北移動，此時我們若試問歐西文化的發展，爲什麽總是向北方推進，根據此説的解答，其原因完全爲氣候(即環境)。因爲文化進步，對於環境的管制愈趨嚴密，以前所謂寒冷地帶，不適於文化的發展者，現在因爲文化的進步變爲最宜於文化發展的地帶。所以説文化愈爲進步，則愈向寒冷的地帶進展。

此説在驟然間視之，頗覺動聽，不過文化的發展，決不是如此簡單，完全受環境的支配的。環境當然是文化發展最重要因子之一，但不是惟一的因子。文化的動向與進展，其中尚有其他的成分，是不受環境決定的。此處自不是詳細批評此説的地方，不過藉以指出研究文化問題上一種趨向而已。

在世界文化的進展上，歐西的文化，是向寒冷的北方發展，東方的中國文化，是向温暖南方發展。這種相反的動向，自不是環境一項可以説明的了，我們要解釋這個問題需要將舊大陸(包括亞非歐)整個文化的傳播問題加以檢討，方可明瞭，因爲這個問題，根本是一個文化的傳播問題，與民族之遷徙問題，而地理環境不過其背景之一而已。

我們知道一種文化的生長與增加繁富，十九是依靠傳播。一種文化中的各種特徵(Traits) 其爲本文化中所發明者，十常不得一二。例如以我們中國文化而言，我們若將我們之文化中的成分詳細加以分析而溯其來源，恐怕很少是我們中國人自己發明的。我們可將現代從歐輸入的各種機械文化，撇開不説，只以所謂中國固有的文化而言，即可以明瞭了。以中國的食物(一種文化的經濟基礎)而言，例如米，是我們南方重要的食品，而米是我們中國的發現嗎？不是的，米的最早的種植大概是在印度或巴比倫，在新石器時代始傳至中國(以現在考古學上所知，在新石器時代末期在河南仰韶已知種稻)。玉蜀黍與蕃薯，是美洲印第安人的農作物，至明代始入中國，這是有記載可稽的，然而這不是中國若干地方的主要食物嗎？再進一步，我們若將中國其他主要農作品(所謂五穀)一一追溯其來源，其中恐怕没有一種是原在中國地方種植的，或最早爲中國人種植的。然而我們豈不是常常自傲地説，我們是以農立國嗎？我們文化的基本特性是農業嗎？簡而言之，我們若將我們文化中的成分，自外面傳入者提出，自己發明者留下，我想我們將要回返到原始的舊石器時代了，這並不是過言，而是事實。所以説一種文化倘不受外界傳播的影響，不止其内容無從增加豐富，亦無從生長，根本就不肯進步，現在地球上各邊遠地帶文化落後民族，並非他們創造文化的能力不如其他高級文化的民族，實是因爲他們處於邊遠地帶，外面的發明傳播不到他們當中罷了。

中國文化南進的問題，亦是一個文化傳播的問題。中國文化爲什麽要先南進而後變爲北進？此問題的解答及總括言之，不過是世界文化傳播的路線轉變而已。我們若問，文化傳播的路線爲什麽要轉變？講起來這也很簡單，這是文化自身發展的結果。自新石器時代以來，舊大陸的文化的重心，是埃及，兩河間，印度斯河及黄河流域。這四處的文化，在傳播上，是互相的影響，又均建築在一共同的原始文化基礎之上。再者，這四處文化在其傳播上即互相影響上，均以中亞爲其交通的孔道。例如中國自新石器以來以至海道未開以前，泰半之文化上的傳播，均來自從中亞而來的西方；而西方的兩河間及埃及則反是。民族上的遷徙，亦復如是。此在歷史上考古學上，可以找出充分的證據，此處因爲限於篇幅，不能詳細地討論了。

然而，文化傳播，並不是單方面的，隨便哪一種文化，都是一方面接受外來的文化特徵，又一方面將已有的文化特徵，傳播出去，中國文化當然亦是如此，例如中國文化中的特徵，在早如絲，在後如紙張印刷，火藥，指南針等，均係由中亞而傳往西方。

現在我們既説明文化的生長，主要是靠傳播，而舊世界的文化重心間的主要傳播方向及路綫，亦已稍爲説明，現在我們可以討論文化重心之移動方向了。

歷史常常告訴我們，世界上的文化重心，時時在那裏移動，往往一種文化在某一地發展至相當時間之後，又移往他處。這種現象，不只舊世界是如此，新世界的高級文化，亦復如是，如瑪雅(Maya)及亞茲特克(Aztec)等文化是也。文化重心之移動的動向，(一)靠文化傳播的方向；(二)民族移動的方向，(三)地理的背影。明乎此三者，文化發展的動向，可得其大半了。現在我們可先討論中國文化爲什麽要向東南發展?

前已言過，中國文化在傳播上所得各種文化的新特徵，係由中亞這一條交通大道，换言之，即由西至東。此並非説從東南一方而中國文化毫未得到新的文化特徵，實際上中國文化包含東南文化的成分，亦復不少，此不過講中國文化所受之主要的影響，是從西北而已。文化上自西至東的這種傳播方向，不只在物質方面是如此，在文化的其他各方面，亦莫不是如此。以宗教而言，如佛教，早期耶教，回教等，均自西北陸路以入中國。

自民族之遷徙上言之，其主要方向，亦爲自西北而向東南，在歷史前如羅底克人(Nordic)及亞爾班人(Alpine)中各混合種之東向遷徙，波南尼西亞人之南入太平洋。其路綫皆必需經過東亞者。在歷史期間，舉其最著者而言，如秦漢間之匈奴，兩晉六朝之五胡，唐之突厥，宋之遼金元，其壓力的方向，均係自西或北，以向東或南。當漢族的抵抗力量强盛時，當然他們不能越雷池一步，但是當漢族衰弱的時候那就不能不被迫南遷，東晉與南宋就是當中最好的例子，當然，民族的遷徙，其中亦當然包括文化的移動了。

文化與民族的發展動向，前已言之，地理的環境，亦爲當中的因子之一。我們若把亞洲的地形一看，横斷東亞中部的，爲一廣大的沙漠。我從歷史上面看，知道沙漠是文化與民族移動上的大障礙。甚至於現代高度機械化的文化中，通過廣大的沙漠，有時亦非易事，其在以前爲人類交通上阻礙力之大，是可想而知的。沙漠當中，除了少數沃原(Oasis)，或緣邊的草原地帶可以存留少數的遊牧民族而外，是不能發生高級文化的。所以在傳播上自西而東的中國的文化，北方有沙漠的大阻礙，除了向東向南發展以外，實别無其他的途徑。實際上，中國文化發展途徑，亦只有這兩種方向。中國比較早期的文化發展是在山西、陝西、河南一帶，其後逐漸向東發展，其前哨實達於高麗、日本，此在近代的考古上已得充實的證明。然而中國文化根本爲大陸文化，不慣利用海洋交通的機會，故其對海洋，不只不能視爲一種便利，反而爲一種阻礙，那末它最易發展的方向，爲折而向南。再者中國文化爲一種高級農業文化，而南方熱濕肥沃，兼有長江及珠江流域的冲積平原，其土壤之肥沃，氣候之宜於農業，實駕乎黄河流域而上之，故中國文化之向南發展自爲自然之趨勢了。加以世界文化傳播的動向，民族流動的壓力，欲求中國文化之北移，實不可得也。

中國文化的南向發展，既然是如此，那末，自明清以後爲什麽掉轉頭來由南而北呢？這個問題的解答，驟然視之，頗爲矛盾，其實亦頗簡單，即世界文化傳播的路徑及方向轉變了是也。自從十五世紀之末，科侖布發現新大陸而後，探險之風大行，其後造船航海等術進步，海洋交通益行發達。從前西方文化由中亞而傳至中國西北者，現在則由海道而先至東南，俟東南接受以後，再傳播到西北。從前中國與西方的交通孔道中央亞細亞，自明清而後，幾完全蔽塞，甚而有人不知有此一回事者，從前的東南是中國文化的尾巴，現在則西北變成中國文化的尾巴了。再者中國自秦漢而後，文化的重心漸向東南移動，其結果，至明清之時，東南的文化，實高於西北的文化。文化的傳播，雖爲交互的，低級文化自高級文化接受文化的特徵，而高級文化，亦自低級文化吸收其所無。但文化之傳播，亦猶水然，每從高而就下，此不過譬而言之；即低者從高者接受較多是也。所以從世界文化傳播路綫上的轉變上而看，及從中國文化本身發展上而看，雖然地理的環境無殊於前，而文化發展的動向，實不能不掉轉過頭來了。

（見《學思》一九四三年三卷第六期）

禹生石紐辨

大禹的生地一問題，自陳志良君作《禹生石紐考》一文載《禹貢》月刊後，後來之談到此問題者，幾无不以禹生於四川的汶川縣，因而牽引到禹是羌人，禹是四川人，以及夏民族發祥於岷江流域等問題。但是把他們所舉出來的證據稍爲仔細檢查一下，實爲微弱，不只不能證明禹生于四川的汶川縣石紐鄉刳兒坪，連這種傳説亦根本爲後起的附會，而无事實的根據。在檢討此問題之前，我們不妨先將明陸深的《蜀都雜抄》中的一段，抄在這裏，作爲楔子。

成都學宫前綽楔題曰"神禹鄉邦"，予始至視學，見而疑之。昔堯舜禹嗣興冀爲中州兩河之間，聲教暨焉，而輿地尚未拓也。後千餘年而周始有江漢之化。至秦盛强，蜀始通焉。彼所謂蠶叢、魚鳧、鱉靈、望帝者，文物未備，且在衰周之世，蜀之先可知也。禹都在今之安邑。鯀實四嶽，封爲崇伯，崇，今之鄠縣。其地遼絶，何得禹生于此乎？新志亦以此爲疑，問之人士，皆曰禹生于汶川之石紐村，禹穴在焉。檢舊志稱唐《元和志》廣柔縣有石紐村，禹所生也，以六月六日爲降誕云，是蓋幾於巫覡之談。至宋計有功作禹廟碑，始大書曰崇伯得有莘氏女，治水行天下，而禹生于此。其言頗爲无據，有莘氏于鯀亦不經見。按莘今之陳留，與崇近，鯀娶當或有之。鯀爲諸侯，厥有封守，九載弗績，多在河北，今諸處之鯀城是已，安得治水行天下乎？又安得以室家自隨荒裔之地如石紐者乎？予益疑之。雖有功亦曰稽諸人事，理或宜然，蓋疑詞也。此必承《元和志》之誤，而後説益紛紛矣。此雖於事无所損益，而蜀故不可以不辨。按揚雄《蜀都賦》止云禹治其江，左思《三都》所賦人物，奇若相如、君平，文若王褒、揚雄，怪若萇弘、杜宇，僭若公孫、劉璋皆列，獨不及禹生耶？至宋王騰不平左詞，作賦致辨，頗極辭鋒，亦云岷山導江，歷經營于禹蹟。其後云鯀爲父而禹子，此概人倫之辨爾，亦不言禹所生也。又按《華陽國志》載禹治水，命巴蜀以屬梁州；禹娶于涂山，辛壬癸甲而去，生子啓，呱呱啼，不及視，三過其門而不入室，務在救時，今江州之塗山是也，帝禹之廟銘存焉。志作于晉常璩，可謂博雅矣，况留意蜀之材賢，然亦不云禹所生也。今徒以石紐有禹穴二字證之，又安知非後人所爲耶？禹穴實在今會稽，窆石在焉。古稱穴居，衆詞也。禹平水土，時已爲司空，恐不穴居，今言穴蓋葬處，非生處也。《古今集記》則云岷山水源分二派，正南入溢村，至石紐過汶川，則禹之所導江也。由是言之，石紐蓋禹蹟之始，而非謂禹所生也。又按塗山亦有數説，江州今重慶之巴縣，有山曰塗；鳳陽之懷遠，古鍾離也，亦有涂山，啓母石在焉，江州治水所經，鍾離帝都爲近，未知孰是。蘇鶚又云，涂山有四，皆禹蹟也，並指會稽與當涂云。宋景濂游山記甚詳，然亦不能决。孔安國曰塗山國名，非山也。《史記》所載，啓，禹之子，其母塗山氏之女，又似姓氏，猶今司馬氏、歐陽氏之謂，恐亦非國名也。聊附所疑於此。

陸子淵並不是考據家，且其中亦頗有謬誤，不過其見解實高出近人一等，故爲標出，以明在數百年前已有人懷疑禹生於石紐之非，且能舉出相當的證據。

一、禹生石紐説起何時

細考禹生石紐説之起，實源于“禹興於西羌”一語，按最早之作此説者，莫過於陸賈與司馬遷。

陸賈《新語·術事篇》：“文王生於東夷，大禹出於西羌，世殊而地絶，法合而度同，故聖賢與道合。”

《史記·六國年表序》：“夫作事者必於東南，收功實者常於西北。故禹興於西羌，湯起于亳，周之王也以豐鎬。”

關于《新語》，我們可以斷定陸賈在那裏杜撰事實。因爲无論如何將“地方搬家”，決不能使文王生于東夷。我們倘若以“文王生於東夷”係杜撰，那麽，我們還能接受他的“大禹出於西羌”的話嗎？陸賈根本爲一辯士，而辯士的論證，是不很講究史實的。又《新語》一書，有根本疑其爲依託者。至于司馬遷，亦不過爲要證明其“收功實者常於西北”一原則，亦不妨暫把禹變作西羌。不然者，何以他寫《夏本紀》時，禹興于西羌的話，一字不提，難道他忘掉了嗎？其實，因爲他寫《夏本紀》，是在寫歷史，不能隨便杜撰，或采風聞，而作《六國年表序》一類的議論文章，亦不妨隨便一點。太史公的良史才，亦實在乎此，而我們不察，竟把他的議論，當爲史實一樣看待，實在是曲解太史公了。再者，若以禹生於汶川之石紐，以關中及中原言之，太史公當言“西南”，不當言“西北”。而《史記》中之汶山郡冉駹夷，亦實列在西南夷之中了。

有人説“禹生于石紐”之傳説，在戰國時已有之，舉《史記集解》(《六國年表序》)“皇甫謐曰，《孟子》稱禹生石紐，西夷人也，”以爲證驗。此文不見今本《孟子》，而《孟子》一書，脱簡甚少，又何來此逸文？其可信之程度，自屬有限。縱使《孟子》有此語，亦不可過於深信，因孟子亦爲一辯士，曾自言“盡信書不如无書”，故凡辯證至緊要關頭時，不妨杜撰史實以實之，《孟子》七篇之中，此類杜撰之故事寓言，隨處可見，而况此言不見《孟子》本文乎！

由此我們可以知道“禹興于西羌”的傳説，是起於“以客從高祖定天下，名爲有口辯士，居左右，常使諸侯”的辯士陸賈之口。其《新語》一書，即使非僞託，亦爲説高祖之書，而高祖乃係“迺公居馬上而得之，安事詩書”的雄主，陸賈自可盡量的杜撰，不怕露馬脚了。司馬遷亦知此説之不可靠，故只在議論中偶一及之。然而三人成虎，其後之議論文字中，亦時相引用。如桓寬《鹽鐵論》之《國病篇》言："禹出西羌，文王生北夷。"由"文王生北夷"一語，即可知"禹出西羌"之不可靠。因爲文王的生地，史曾明言，不可隨便胡說。此則偏言其"生北夷"。不過要與"西羌"相對，亦不妨把文王由"西夷"暫變成"北夷"了。又如《後漢書·戴良傳》："同郡謝季孝問曰：子自視天下，孰可爲比？良曰：我若仲尼長東魯，大禹出西羌，獨步天下，誰與爲侶？"這根本是狂妄！自不得據爲"禹出西羌"之史實？其用意亦不過用西羌與東魯相對而已。

後來因漢初有禹興于西羌的傳説，竟而附會到禹生於廣柔的石紐。禹生石紐之主要證據，不外後列四家：

> 揚雄《蜀王本紀》："禹本汶山郡廣柔縣人也，生於石紐。"(見張守節《史記正義》所引)
>
> 譙周《蜀本紀》："禹本汶山廣柔人也，生於石紐，其地名刳兒坪。"(見《三國志·秦泌傳》注所引)
>
> 《三國志·秦泌傳》：秦泌對夏侯纂曰："禹生石紐，今之汶山郡是也。"
>
> 《華陽國志·蜀志》：譔曰："五嶽則華山表其陽，四瀆則汶江出其徼，故上聖則大禹生其鄉，媾姻則皇帝婚其女。"

此四種證據，嚴格講來，均爲後起的傳説，不能成爲有力證據。揚雄本文人，其《蜀王本紀》，有根本疑其爲僞者。彼在《蜀都賦》中，對于蜀事及人物，均特爲鋪張，何以獨不言禹爲蜀人？或禹之生地？此自是可疑了。秦泌辯士，往往曲解詩傳，信口杜撰，如天有頭，有耳，有足，有姓之類。其言自不足信，况此爲其對夏侯纂夸張之語乎？譙周亦文人，况其《蜀本紀》已爲逸書，斷簡零篇，不知其下文何如也，充其量亦不過文人慣技，抄襲當時之傳説而已。至于《華陽國志》之文，則頗有語病。《禹貢》"華陽黑水惟梁州"，巴蜀在華山之陽，非華山在巴蜀之陽也。因"五嶽則華山表其陽"之語欠通，後人有爲之曲解者。然此實不明行文之過，常氏不過欲求對仗之工，並非不明地理之方位也。其言禹當亦係如此，不然者，彼在《巴志》《蜀志》之中，敘述巴蜀之先，遠溯人皇黄帝，何以獨不及禹？想常氏亦有自知其非史實，但不關史實之論贊中，因行文之便，需此一句，亦不妨湊上。如其隨後又言："顯族大賢彭祖育其山，列仙王喬昇其崗"，此則全爲神話了。或者曰，此實不然，常璩言禹生蜀，實不止此。例如劉昭《續後漢書・郡國志》引《華陽國志》："汶川石紐山中，夷人以其爲禹生處，共營其地，方百里内，今猶不敢牧。"此不是明明言禹生於汶川嗎？此文不見今本《華陽國志》，但《國志》汶山條下本有脱簡，此條是否《國志》之文，不得而知，但此語實出自緯書，倘《國志》縱有此文，常氏亦不過採述傳説，以廣異聞而已。不然，如范蔚宗《後漢書》對于汶山郡之冉駹及羌人，記載最詳，何以獨不及禹生地？

以上所論，在事實上實均不關重要，其緊要之點，實爲在揚、譙、秦、常四人，生於禹後二千餘年，何以能知禹生於四川之汶山郡廣柔縣石紐鄉刳兒坪？又何以如此其詳且細？陸賈、司馬遷不過言"禹興于西羌"而已。何以司馬遷所不言者，彼三人知之？豈非神話傳説，愈傳而附會愈多，愈加詳細麼？此神話之發展原因，仔細推之，亦頗自然。西漢之初，既有"禹興西羌"之説，其後武帝開冉駹置汶山郡，羌人每來蜀爲傭，蜀人對于汶山郡之羌人，知之漸稔。禹既有興於西羌之説，而汶川有羌人，禹即可以生於汶山郡了，稍爲富於想象力者，便可及之。又因《淮南子・修務訓》有"禹生於石"及《焦氏易林》有禹生石夷的説法，因而又附會到"石紐"了。由此以後，愈傳愈真，愈傳愈詳密了。我們把現代謡言的傳播現象，稍爲注意一下，即可以知之，最初不過有人隨便説了一句話，本來是没有什麽用意的，但愈傳愈廣，愈傳愈僞，若干不相關的事實，也附會上去，恍若真有其事了。禹生石紐的事，也不過是如此而已。

有人説："不然！揚、譙、秦、常皆蜀人，以蜀人言蜀事，自較信確。"然正因渠等爲蜀人，知其言之不可靠。何以言之？中國人之鄉土觀念極重，誰都想挪幾個先聖先賢，爲他的家鄉生色。現在我們可以以李冰爲例，便可以知道了。李冰之地望，史籍未曾明言，兩千年以來亦未有人能言之或知之者，作者近來時與蜀中友人之諳于掌故者閒談，詢以李冰爲何許人？皆答是“四川人”。再問其何所根據？則皆答“我們是四川人也”。此雖然是戲言，然是實情。揚、譙、秦、常言之禹爲蜀人者，正因爲他們是蜀人也，再如李冰之地望，二千年來既无人知之，但至清中葉劉沅作《李公父子治水記》則言：“公本猶龍族子，隱居岷峨，與鬼谷子交，張儀築城不就，兼苦水灾，乃強薦公于秦而任之，治龜城，立星橋，通地脈，功業非一。”這真是滿紙荒唐，二千年來所不知者，至止塘先生忽然知其與老子同宗，隱居岷峨了，豈非異事？此不過只言其隱居岷峨而已，不一定是四川人也。至姜蘊剛先生，則李冰實非四川人不可了(見其所著《治水及其人物》載《説文月刊》)。倘再過兩千年後，考據家亦將根據劉、姜二氏，言李冰是四川人了。而劉、姜二氏之出此言，亦何嘗有所依據！實際上，在文翁守蜀以前，實未有蜀人作蜀守者，何者？文教未興故也，常璩已慨乎言之。禹生石紐，當亦不外此例。最初司馬遷不過因議論之便，言禹興西羌，而蜀有羌，蜀人便言生于蜀了；再後，不只生于蜀，而生于蜀之某一郡，某一縣，某一鄉，某一山之某一點，都可以指出來了；至最近，夏民族亦因而產生，而搬進古代的四川來了的。試問何以二千年以前的人不知道，而生于禹後四千多年的人反而知道？

由上面所論，我們可以知道在傳説中的禹二千多年以後，約其當西漢初年，至早在戰國末年，發生了“禹興于西羌”的傳説。發生的原因，大概係由于當時的遊説之士，假託先王以實其論證的慣技。此時不過只言“興”而並未言“生”也。又過了幾百年，因爲蜀土有羌，蜀人就説禹“生”于蜀了，於是乎四川的先聖先賢之中，又添了一位神話人物。有人説，這是一個很美麗的神話，何必將它揭穿。然而美麗的神話，終要被醜陋的事實所擊破。當然，若是只當它作神話看待，自無不可，無奈現在一般人竟當它作史實，那就不能不辨了。

二、石紐在何處?

石紐山，或石紐鄉或村，究在何處? 古今來亦言人人殊，未有一定地方。但由此亦可知其非實有其處，好事者隨便指點而已。例如，《路史》言石紐鄉在僰道，然僰道在今宜賓境，離汶川境千有餘里。又理番縣通化上(在岷江之支流理番河上，理番河亦稱沱江)亦石紐山刳兒坪。著者於民國 27 年(1938 年)考察羌族，宿通化，晨起見西南之高峰上，有廟高聳雲霄，似甚狀偉，詢之故老。則言禹廟也，上爲石紐山刳兒坪。因往返需二日程，又須繞出大道，因是時目的在研究羌人，故未往探訪，至今尤覺悵然。

記載中均言石紐在汶山郡廣柔縣，但廣柔在于何地? 亦无人能確指其處。《四川通志》言在汶川縣西北七十二里，但汶川西北百里以内，皆萬山重叠，且少居人，實無可置縣之處。《通志》想係襲《括地志》之誤，因《括地志》言在縣西七十二里故也。現在之汶川縣，漢時爲綿虒縣，晉改汶山，梁、周時改汶川，因縣西有汶水故名。故城在現在之威州城(唐時維州)，南山腰半平坦口，俗稱古城坪。明宣德中，因威州數罹番害，遂遷州治於汶川縣城，而移縣城於南四十里之寒水驛，即今之縣城。現在一般所知之刳兒坪，即在今縣城南又十里。

漢之廣柔，多認爲係唐時之石泉，故《唐書・地理志》言:“石泉縣有石紐山。”而石紐之得名，乃係由兩石相結紐而生。《四川通志》引舊志以爲“刳兒坪在(石泉縣)九龍山第五峰下，地稍平闊，石上有迹儼如人坐卧狀，相傳即聖母生禹遺蹟”。《錦里新編》(卷十四)言:“刳兒坪在石泉縣南石紐山下，山絶壁上有禹穴二字，大徑八尺，係太白書。坪下近江處，白石纍累，俱有血點侵入，刮之不去。相傳鯀納有莘氏，胸臆折而生禹，石上皆血濺之迹，土人云取石潤水，可治難産。”他如李蕃之《禹穴辨》，姜炳章之《禹穴考》，均以石紐山刳兒坪在石泉，而不在汶川。石泉爲今之北川縣，石泉縣之江爲嘉陵江之支流，而非岷江。北川縣雖與茂縣接境，但離汶川縣則甚遥。

以前之地志中，甚少言石紐在汶川縣者。有之，則爲《括地志》與《寰宇記》。但其所言之方位，與現在所言汶川縣與刳兒坪之方位不合。《括地志》言“石紐山在汶川縣西”，《寰宇記》言“石紐村在汶川縣西一百四十里”。現在所稱之刳兒坪，在現在汶川縣南約十里，在明以前之汶川縣城南約五十里，但亦無所謂石紐山(兩山相紐狀)。大概《括地志》與《寰宇記》均誤汶江爲汶川。因石泉在漢時爲汶江縣屬故也。

現在之談此問題的，竟將石泉縣的石紐忘掉了，在汶川縣另創了一種新神話，其實汶川縣並無所謂石紐山，或石紐鄉，或石紐村。刳兒坪之名，亦十分可疑(其地之羌人並不知刳兒坪之名)。討論此問題者十九均未到過汶川縣，所以不妨談談此刳兒坪是一個什麽樣的所在。

汶川縣南約十里岷江東傍旁有一石岬突入河中，將河阻而向西折流。又因岷江上游山峯高，而河谷低，正午以後，上下氣壓變殊故，河谷中每逢晴日午後必大風，風行至此，爲突出河心之石岬所阻，乃折而上昇，風急則帶有細砂石，故俗謂飛沙射人，午後每爲行旅所戒，因曰飛沙關，關頗險要。其下流水迂迴，相傳爲楊貴妃洗手處。往汶川者，至此即可望見縣城，亦至此始可見兩岸羌寨，不復爲漢地景象矣。

關之上約二里許，有一小斜坡，廣約三四畝，此即近來所稱爲禹所生的刳兒坪了。坪上一小廟，名東嶽廟。予至其地時，廟祝爲一老道士，既聾且瞎，答亦非所問。坪中種玉麥(蜀謂玉蜀黍之稱)，此外别無所有。在明代時，大路則繞道坪上，相傳有禹母啓聖祠，但因過于陡險，後乃改道山脚，啓聖祠亦移建山下路旁之崖壁上。現爲小小板壁廟一間，香火頗盛，但爲觀音大士，而非禹母也。

刳兒坪(當地漢人呼爲撻兒坪)乃漢人名稱，羌人並无所知。石紐之名，即漢人亦不知道了。予在飛沙關附近及對河各羌寨曾調查數日，在縣城時又召羌中老人熟於往事者詢問，他們並不知道禹或關于禹的傳説，間有一二狡黠者，從漢人聽得下雨王(夏禹王)名字，編一點故事以迎合“自稱爲專家”的考察家的心情，但稍具現代民族學調查方法與經驗者，一見即可知道他們在編故事了。近人又將酈氏《水經注》沬水條下所言之禁忌搬到汶川縣。酈氏之言曰："縣(廣柔)有石紐鄉，禹所生也，今夷人共營之，地方百里，不敢居牧，有罪逃野，捕之者不逼，能藏三年，則共原之，言大禹之神所佑也。"我們且先放下此故事之真實性不言，看《水經》所言之沫水在什麼地方。《水經》："沫水出廣柔徼外(上所引之故事注於此句下)，東南過牦牛縣北，又東至越嶲靈道縣，出蒙山南，東北與青衣水合。"由《水經》所言，沫水所經過之地方而言，故多以沫水即現在之青衣江(俗稱雅河，以其出雅州，又稱平羌江)。而《雅安縣志》直以青衣水之支流長濆江當之，因其發源於大相嶺下青溪縣北(牦牛縣)，出蒙山(俗稱周公山)之東北，與青衣江合，亦頗近是。但无論如何，絶不能誤沫水爲江水也。倘以沫水爲青衣江，或長濆江，是則沫水上游之廣柔，與江水上游之汶川，實隔千里而遥，而近人引用，竟將其移至汶川縣，豈非大謬！且酈氏亦不免錯誤，《水經》在此處所言之廣柔，與北川縣之廣柔，是否異地同名，實不得而知，而酈氏妄加徵引，亦屬謬誤。《水經》沫水條所言，以古今之地望考之，尚屬可通。而酈氏之注，則根本不通。酈氏對於西南諸水，每多如此，亦不獨以沫水爲然也。

以上所言，乃地理方位上引用之錯誤與矛盾，而此故事之本身，亦頗乖情理。所謂"地方百里，不敢居牧"者，仔細計算起來，則現在之整個汶川縣"不敢居牧"了，有是理乎。現代居其地之羌人不止毫无此類信仰，連大禹爲何人，亦毫不知道，尚有人談"這個信仰，全體羌人都崇奉着，到現在還没有改變"。真是痴人説夢，欺人之談。

汶志又載刳兒坪下巖壁上有"禹穴"二字，予在其處搜尋累日，不得其處，遍詢當地居人，亦無有知者。憶予在其處荆棘中爬尋時，不只衣襟皮膚爲荆棘所傷，在巖壁間將余所帶之攝影機，亦跌壞一架，而嚮導亦幾跌至巖下也。前人作書，每多耳食，自不足責，而今人亦往往受其欺，是可深慨！

禹娶塗山之説，古來聚訟紛紜，莫知其在於何地。此問題本與禹生石紐之説無關，但因爲現在汶川縣西北約十里許亦有涂禹山之名，故説者用以作爲生汶川之旁證。按古今來之言塗山者，或言在當塗，或言在江州(今巴縣)，或言其爲國名，或言其爲姓氏，要之均爲附會之説，不能證明，亦無法否認；但無論如何，從未有言其在汶川縣者。其言在汶川者，實始於《汶川縣志》，因俗有銅鈴山之名，銅鈴與塗禹音近，故《汶志》從而附會之。按銅鈴山爲瓦寺土司駐牧之地，爲一山岬，將岷江阻而東流，可上下遠眺，頗爲險要。其名自明中葉瓦寺土司駐牧其地後，始見於記載，與禹娶涂山之説，可謂全無關係，今人又反從而附會之，可見其穿鑿。

三、禹與羌人

因爲有“禹興西羌”之説，後來又有“禹生石紐”之附會，石紐又附會在羌地，故推想到禹爲羌人。主此説者之主要證據，以爲禹是中國神話中之治水者，而羌人亦善治水，舉成都市上掛“包打水井”牌子的羌人來作證明。然而此類證據，直等於无證據，因爲同具一種技能者，不一定爲同一民族，其理甚明。不然者，英人與日人均擅海軍，豈可謂其同族乎？況且禹之治水(指所鑿所導之河而言)，自地質學上言之，爲不可能之事。而傳説中之堯時洪水，經鯀治九年，禹治十三年，共二十二年，經如許久之時間，縱不治也要平息了。禹所能作者，充其極不過挖幾條小小灌溉溝渠而已，因其爲其所處之時代及工具所限故也。

至於羌人之善曉水性，亦完全是神話，而非事實。成都市上之羌傭，在漢時已有之，《後漢書》汶山郡冉駹夷傳言“土氣多寒，在盛夏冰猶不釋，故夷人冬則避寒入蜀爲傭，夏則違暑返其邑……又土地剛鹵，不生穀粟麻菽……”《華陽國志》汶山郡條下言：“土地剛鹵，不宜五穀，惟種麥，而冰多寒，盛夏凝凍不釋，故夷人冬則避寒入蜀，傭賃自食，夏則避暑返落，歲以爲常，故蜀人謂之作五百石子也。”“五百石子”之義，遍詢之蜀人，均不得其解。清嘉慶間張澍作《蜀典》(卷五)言：“按今其俗猶然，男則負棗核桃椒鬻於市，女爲人家供薪汲，呼爲播羅子，亦呼二姐子也。”對于“五百石子”一詞，猶未説明。不過歷來之紀載羌傭者甚多，只言其地寒土鹵，冬季至蜀傭工自給，不言其能打水井。案羌人之在成都打井，係起於近代，亦爲一種不得已之工作，並非其長於爲此也。按成都之淘井挖井工作，必在冬季，因是水位下落，方可挖淘。但冬季天寒，漢人視爲畏途，而羌人生長寒地，其視成都冬季之天氣，有如其夏秋，故不怕冷而可工作。余每見羌人淘井，先飲酒一二兩，再脱衣入井挖淘，每十數分鐘後必出井取暖，但仍不勝其縮瑟之狀也。羌人生長寒地尚如此，漢人當然不願作了。此乃淘舊井。至於掘新井，羌人只能挖一深坑(成都之井，最深無過兩丈者，因入地六七尺即及泉故也)。而嵌石砌磚，需漢人爲之，羌人不能爲，亦無此技能也。余親見成都某機關欲掘一井，先以爲羌人係打井專家也，雇羌人掘之，議定深一丈五尺，但掘坑至一丈深時，即遇河沙，羌人無法再往下掘，因河沙無黏性，再往下挖掘四壁即隨之崩塌故也。某機關因其與議定之深度不够，不肯付錢，遂與夷人發生争執。但井淺則水不清，某機關不得已乃再僱漢人掘之，由此可見羌人掘井，只能掘坑，不能起井，甚至于掘井坑，亦不如漢人高明，如此尚能稱爲“水利專家”乎？至於打井掘坑，至愚之人，亦可爲之，與治水无關。淘井掘坑，漢人視爲苦役，羌人恃其不怕冷，蠻幹而已。余曾遍遊羌地，無有掘井者，又山皆巖石，亦無法掘井。其來成都掘井，不過充當漢人掘井工人之“下手”而已，實無專門掘井之知識也。再有以灌縣修堰時兼僱羌人，便以其能治水。予亦曾往其處調查數次，其僱羌人所作之工作，爲起“竹落”時入水取石，漢人視爲苦役而不作者。歷來哪有羌人作工頭計劃治水者乎？總之，羌人爲生活所迫，來蜀傭工，因其性耐寒，故凡冬日入水，漢人之視爲畏途者，皆令羌人爲之，彼豈得已哉？

羌人雖住岷江兩岸及其支流，但對于水力，則完全不知利用，引水灌溉，爲絶無之事，連水磨水碾亦無之，而漢人至其地者，則皆有之。羌人無舟楫，連康藏皮船亦無之，如此尚可説他們習知水性乎？

禹爲羌人之主要證據既不存在，禹是羌人之説，自可不攻自破了。

四、夏民族與岷江流域

因爲説禹是羌人，又説他生于汶川，所以又因此而聯想到夏民族發源於岷江流域了。作此説者，以羅君香林的《夏民族發祥於岷江流域説》一文最爲代表(見《説文月刊》三卷九期)。羅先生這篇文章，可以説是“考據八股”中的十足代表。不問材料之真僞，不問時代之先後，凡有一字一音一義之相似者，都揉雜在一起，驟看起來，似乎博洽非常，但如此作文，何事不可證明！不只可以證明禹是羌人，夏民族發祥於岷江流域，而利用同樣的材料，亦可證明禹是太平洋島中吃人的黑人，夏民族發祥於新幾内亞了。

這類的文章，本來無討論的必要，但其有時附會現代科學，不知者以爲得着科學上的證明，爲其所惑，所以有幾點不得不爲指出，以免科學爲人所誤會。例如羅氏解釋岷江之水患有言：“以巫山崩墜，致江水涌滯逆行，影響岷江宣泄，自必變成水灾。巫山以地層關係，既崩墜于漢晉，未必不崩墜于遠古，此即構成鯀禹時代洪水横流之一重要原因。”隨即引謝家榮、趙亞曾二氏之湖北宜昌、興山、秭歸、巴東等縣地質礦産中之論述以實之。謝、趙二氏爲地質學家，其所論述，係完全有地質學上之原則，以解釋峽谷與灘險之構成。而地質學家則從不相信禹疏河開峽之説，因自地質學上之原則律之，爲不可能故也。羅氏在此處之錯誤，即未將巫山峽谷之海拔，與岷江流域之海拔比較一下，即使將巫山峽谷壅塞至山巔，不過上流數百里内發生水害而已，絶不能影響岷江之宣泄，而使發生水灾也。又巫山崩墜，與傳説中鯀禹所治之中原水灾有何關係？

羅氏之利用現代考古學上的材料，亦多牽强。例如羅氏把夏民族與西北的彩陶文化相聯繫，此不啻羅氏自駁其説。因爲彩陶文化，根本爲一種西北文化，其分佈爲河南、山西、陝西、甘肅、新疆等地，再西與中亞、印度西北、俄國南部，以及近東的彩陶文化相連，與岷江流域實毫無關係。所以羅氏若認彩陶是夏民族的東西，那麼即根本將其夏民族發祥於岷江流域説自行全部推翻了。因爲依照羅氏之説，岷江流域既爲夏民族發祥之地（自宜賓以上以至茂縣、松潘），就應該發現大量的彩陶，其奈此區域内無彩陶何！再者若以中國西北的彩陶爲夏民族遺物，那麽，中亞與夫近東的彩陶，亦是屬於夏民族的嗎？

因在考古學上有彩陶與黑陶之發現，故一般人多以黑陶屬殷民族，彩陶屬之夏民族。此種説法，實欠精密。黑陶固爲殷人在一時期中所採用，但其在前亦很可能曾採用彩陶，特别以河南爲然。若言殷人只用黑陶而不用彩陶，以現有之證據言之，似尚不足。至於彩陶問題，則更爲複雜。彩陶之早者，可早過夏以前。而在甘肅、青海一帶，至秦漢時尚有用之者。歷時如此長久的一文化特徵，其採用當然不只限於一民族，或限於一地域了。再者普通一般人利用考古學上的證據，以爲一文化特徵，被採用之後，就永遠地採用它，永遠不變换；考古學言某一種文化，以爲就代表某一種民族，這實是大謬。一民族對於同一需要，在先後可採用不同樣的文化特徵以滿足之。例如漢族，對於陶器一項在最早可採用粗糙的灰陶，以後再採用彩陶，再黑陶，再有彩釉陶器，再瓷器，其後在不同時代或不同地域中採用不同窑口之瓷器到現在甚至可採用玻璃。然而皆爲同一漢族也，而所用之陶器，則隨時在轉變中。我們若以某一種文化特徵，與某一民族永遠的相聯繫，是相當危險的事。因爲文化特徵可以離開民族而獨立傳播，所以考古學上言某一種文化，並不一定指某一種民族而言。

近來之談中國古史的，多侈言夏民族、殷民族或周民族等，但自文獻上言之，及自考古學上言之，此種説法，實有未妥。載籍中只言夏、商、周三代，且其在初均婚姻相通，世系相承，充其極亦不過部落之不同，似非民族上之有異也。

所以説，近人時常所言的夏民族、殷民族、周民族等，无論其自哪一方面講，都是没有充分的證據的。而羅君香林所言的夏民族更是渺茫。根據其説，好似禹所領導的夏民族，數十年之間，走遍了全中國。當然，民族的遷徙，爲古今之常，但在古時，没有火車輪船，移動不是像這樣想象中的容易。又如羅君以爲夏民族祀雷，故其發祥之地，有以雷名地者，舉峨眉山之雷洞坪爲證。而羅君恐未到過峨眉山，不知雷洞坪在於何處，按雷洞坪在峨眉山中弓背山之上，懸崖陡壁，明以前爲人迹不到之處。因明以前之朝峨眉者，至華岩頂即止，再上則无路。雷洞坪之名，大概自明中葉以後始有之。試問與禹或夏民族何關？中國地名中以雷字名，而見諸記載者，不下四十餘處，豈可盡附會之與夏民族之祀雷有關乎？羅君又言夏民族初以龍蛇爲圖騰祖，但他對圖騰在人類學上之含義，實未明瞭。現在國内之一般談圖騰者，以爲凡與禽獸有關者，必爲圖騰，有圖騰必爲祖，而必加以崇拜。此實不然。民族學上之圖騰概念，雖不是什麼神秘東西，却亦不如此簡單。實際上言之，各民族中實未有將圖騰加以崇拜者，“圖騰崇拜”一詞，實乃法國沙發椅上的社會學家所發明的一種錯誤，人類學中並無此種概念也。自民族學上言之，現在亞洲境内的各原始民族，均很少有圖騰的迹象(有以傜人之祀槃瓠爲圖騰者，實與人類學上之圖騰概念不合)，他們在古代有無圖騰，是很有問題的。亞洲其他民族，既無圖騰痕迹，而漢族爲其中之一，在古代時有無圖騰，自大是問題了。

五、羌人什麼時候纔到汶川縣

從前面的討論，我們可以看出禹生石紐的傳説，全係出於附會，而附會之者，又多爲蜀人，其中之作祟者，實鄉土一觀念誤之也。現在我們可從汶川的實在情况，來考察此問題。自揚雄、譙周輩言禹生汶山郡廣柔之石紐後，廣柔並不指現代的汶川縣。其究指何處，恐怕揚、譙輩亦不自知。但自隋唐以來，多謂川西北的石泉縣(今北川縣，傍嘉陵江支流)。故北川縣的石紐，特爲以前言此問題者所稱道。最近言汶川之刳兒坪爲禹生地者，實皆爲莊君學本的遊記所誤。現在既大家誤傳汶川的刳兒坪爲禹之生地，我們可先看汶川縣的自然環境如何？是否宜於初民的居住？

汶川縣羌地之山窮水惡，他處實罕其匹。自灌縣而上，即無平地。

清末時有灌縣人名董玉書(號湘琴)者，平日以戎馬書生自負，後入松潘總兵夏毓琇幕，作《松遊小唱》一詞，詞雖不甚工，但頗能描寫，淋漓盡致。例如其寫岷江沿河風景一段云："松潘西望路漫漫，風景漸難看。河在中間，山在兩邊，九曲羊腸，偏生跨在山腰畔。抬頭一綫天，低頭一匹練，灘聲響似百萬鳴蟬，纏綿不斷。最可厭，一山纔斷一山連，面目無更換，總是司空見慣。問蠶叢開國幾經年？這滄桑如何不變？"此並非時人過甚之詞，而實際情形實有更甚於此者。例如"九曲羊腸"不只"跨在山腰畔"，而路之上下，多爲絶壁，仰首不見山巔，俯首則峭岩千尺，稍一失足，不知身歸何處！又因山勢過陡，一有風吹草動，或禽獸過處，則飛石擊人，憶予至映秀灣時，前有一揹子爲飛石將他的腦袋打得不知去向了，所以走此路的人，言爲"飛石打死"，爲最傷心咒語。

汶川的俗語説汶川的地方是"九石一土"，意思説是九分石一分土。但據實際的情形説，簡直是"有石无土"，所以在前清時有汶川縣的知縣名宋廷真者，曾説它"士無兩榜，財無三萬，男無才子，女無佳人"。其貧瘠之況，由此可以推知了，至于汶川縣城，其範圍直等于外面的一個么店子，所謂"大堂打板子，四門都聽見"的一小小山縣。實際上汶川縣並无四門，只有兩道城門，居民數十家，多在北關外。因爲土地剛鹵，羌人專靠種植與牧畜(主要爲山羊)是不能生活的，所以他們自漢以來，每屆冬令，即紛紛入蜀爲傭以自給，在他們實爲生活上被迫不得已的一種辦法，並非樂於爲傭也。例如抗戰軍興，國府西移後，因種種關係，他們在裏面掙錢稍爲容易，所以近來亦少出來傭工，成都市上的包打水井的羌人，亦少看見了。

這樣貧瘠險惡的地方，當然爲初民所避免了。除非經人口過多的壓迫，是很少向這些地方移動的。我們退一步講，假設禹實有其人，那末他約當於什麽時代？自考古學上言之，殷周爲中國之銅器時代，則傳説中的大禹之時代，至多不過銅器時代之初期，或新石器時代之末期。當此時期中，地球上除數處文化較高，人口集中而外，其他多爲地曠人稀之境，那時候的山窮水惡的汶川，想亦是人迹罕到之區。此不一定言在當時汶川縣没有居人，不過説，當人類初期農業時期，无金屬工具時，不易到此種區域中罷了，縱然到了，亦不容易生活。所以在松、理、茂、汶發現之古物，到現在爲止，均係秦漢或秦漢以後之物，即是爲此種道理。或者有人要説，我們對於邊區的考古，歸是極端的幼稚，現在所未發現者，並不能决定其將來没有。此固然是事實，不過汶川的考古調查，是比較容易的，因其地適宜於人類居住之地有限，現代之村落，亦即古代之村落，故古物之暴露，自比較易於發現了。

所以説，當堯舜之世(公元前二十四世紀)，中國文化極幼稚之時，汶川縣的景况，是可想而知的。而事迹功業都在中州的鯀，而能生禹於當時人迹罕到的汶川，自是不可思議之事了。

這不過是自然環境的背景，而不是直接的證據。討論此問題的，豈不都是説禹之生於汶川縣者，是因爲他與羌人的關係嗎！我們現在可以討論羌人什麽時候纔來到汶川縣。

羌人什麽時候來到現在的松、理、茂、汶等地，據記載，據羌人自己的傳説以及考古學上的證據，都指明羌人之來到汶川等地，是在戰國末年，及西漢初年。據《後漢書》所載，羌人自無弋爰劍後，始向西南遷徙，是則在秦穆公以後。而汶川、理番及茂縣的羌人自己的傳説，亦講當他們的祖先初來到此地的時候，其地爲另一種民族所據，羌人稱此民族曰“戈”。在初羌人與戈人雜居，雙方時相戰鬥，最後戈人爲羌人所滅。羌人對于此類戰争之故事，尚津津樂道，現在羌人每届舊歷十月初一日過年還願中，端公所誦之經咒，其中有一折係完全講述其祖先與戈人争鬥之情形者。戈人的墳墓，羌人尚能指出，現在羌地凡有黄土地帶，用石塊所起之墓，即是此類。墓中所出銅器，多與長城地帶者相似，其中出一種特别的陶器，即黑色大耳，飾以旋紋，有似西臘之 amphora 陶罐是也。予曾在汶川縣之小岩子，親自發掘一墓，其中出一銅股排、銅劍、鐵劍、銅斧、鐵斧、秦戈與各種小銅器、金項帶、珠飾及文帝四銖半兩錢三百枚，其他各種佩飾，不類漢人，亦不類羌人。例如金項帶一項而言，質極薄，其形製與銅器時代歐洲愛爾蘭所出之金 Lunul 相似。

羌人言此即戈人之墓也。

但有人或疑此得非羌人祖先之墓，而彼等自行忘之者乎？是不然，因爲羌人歷來均舉行火葬，而不行穴葬，所以《吕氏春秋》譏笑他們説："氐羌之民其虜也，不憂其係累，而憂其死不焚也。"(見《義賞編》)此雖是輕侮之詞，亦可見羌人對火葬儀式的舉行，在他們觀念中的重要。在近三十年前，羌人尚均舉行火葬，現羌寨中每一姓均各有其火墳，爲每姓焚尸之所，絶不相亂。不過近來羌人亦多染漢化，惑於風水之説，多舉行穴葬，而少行焚屍。但據其故老傳言，三十年前無有行穴葬者。現在羌人所指點之戈人墓，均係穴葬，屍骨完整，未經焚燒，且其中所出殉葬物品，與羌人者不類，故可知其絶非羌人祖先之墓也。或者又可問此得非漢人之墓乎？此固有其可能，不過予在理蕃縣東門外所發現之東漢初年漢墓，其中所出之銅器與陶器，與川中所出之漢器相同，而與戈人墓中者絶異，是又可斷其非漢人墓了。

此類之戈人墓，自汶川縣沿岷江上至茂縣，西至理蕃，爲數至多。凡兩岸高處之着土地帶，莫不洞穴纍累，皆戈人墓也。其中所出之銅器與陶器，現頗流布成都市上，四川博物館及華西大學博物館收集頗多，雖形製特異，但皆秦漢間物。戈人墓既爲秦漢間物，而戈人爲羌人以前之民族，故羌人之達到岷江流域，最早亦不能早過春秋戰國之間，由此可以知當禹之時，岷江流域或根本無羌人，禹則無從生於汶川的刳兒坪，禹與汶川羌人之關係，亦化爲子虚烏有了。

六、餘　　論

我們若細考傳説中的堯、舜、鯀、禹事迹，多在黄河中游河北、河南、山西、陝西毗連之區，此亦是爲當時的時代及文化水準所限，個人的能力，是無法超過的。在事實上，我們縱然承認堯、舜、鯀、禹確有其人，以當時之文化水準推之，亦不過爲比較有勢力之大酋長，其影響所及，亦不過其四周數百里内之小部落，絶不能像儒家所渲染的那樣偉大熱烈。我們若打開《史記》的《五帝本紀》及夏、商、周等本紀一看，他們在計算祖先時，無不追溯到黄帝。所以有人因此致疑，以爲事實没有這樣的巧合。但以現代的民族學知識視之，反爲極可能之事。因在部落組織中，酋長之子女，只可與酋長之子女通婚，此在我國西南邊疆之土司中，尚保存此種情况。黄帝既爲一比較有勢力之酋長，其妻妾必多，其子女亦必多(在若干原始社會中，亦只有酋長可以多妻)。又在氏族組織不十分完密，親屬計算方式未十分固定之時，祖先的計算，可時而父方，時而母方，總以將最偉大先祖之包括在内爲榮。如此，在酋長中人人皆可以黄帝爲祖先了。此種親屬計算方法，在現在之西南民族中，尚有如此者。由此可證明鯀、禹在親屬上與堯、舜與商、周之接近，其通婚實限於比較小區域内之酋長間，亦可反證鯀、禹不會至與中原隔絶之四川邊徼了。

我們退一步講，縱然承認陸賈、司馬遷"禹興於西羌"的話有所根據，那不一定説禹就生於西羌，或禹是羌人。例如漢高祖興於巴蜀，那末漢高祖就生於巴蜀，及是巴蜀之人嗎？這種錯誤是極顯而易見的。"禹興於西羌"一語，即使其有事實上之根據，充其量也不過説禹之興起與羌人有點關係而已。不過我們雖知，在秦漢以前，羌人的分布，是在河南西部，陝西西南，甘肅東南等地，與中原關中密邇，漢人之活動，幾無時不與羌人接觸，甲骨文中多言周之母族爲姜。姜亦羌，而此等之羌，並非指四川邊徼之羌，實指鄰近中原之羌而言。縱然説禹與羌有關係的話，亦不過指與中原附近之羌人而言，不必遠到四川邊徼來找關係了。

(原載《説文月刊》一九四四年第四卷合刊本)

明皇幸蜀與天回鎮

誰道君王行路難，六龍西幸萬人歡，地轉錦江成渭水，天迴玉壘作長安。

秦開蜀道置金牛，漢水元通星漢流，天子一行留聖跡，錦城長作帝王州。

——李白

二十九年冬，聞成都北天回鎮有唐碑，因往訪之。既聞其地之耆老言：鎮名天回者，蓋因唐明皇幸蜀，並未至成都，乘輿至此時，聞兩京收復，遽爾回鑾，故曰“天回”。當時以爲齊東野語，不足徵信；後偶檢通志及縣志，亦均作此語，如清雍正十三年所修《四川通志》(卷二十二)言：

天回山在縣北三十里，舊名天隳，唐明皇幸蜀至此，及聞長安平，車駕乃回，因更名，下有天回鎮。

其後嘉慶二十年所修通志及同治十二年成都縣志所載與此略同，知其致誤，蓋已久矣。邇來寒窗無事，因略爲正之，亦有關乎地方之小掌故也。

按天回鎮之名，實本於天回山，天回亦名天隳，《蜀本記》曰：

杜宇自天而降，爲蜀人主，稱望帝，號曰天隳，言自天而隳也，今成都北三十里天回山是其處。

更名之説，明以前無可考，曹學《蜀中廣記》於蜀中掌故，蒐羅至富，亦衹言隳、回音近而訛。楊升菴言天隳山，亦不過引揚雄《蜀本記》言"有王曰杜宇，出於天隳山，有朱提氏女，爲杜宇妻，號曰望帝。"云云，未及明皇至此更名之事，通志此説，實不知何所本，又按明皇幸蜀之事，當時頗有記載，如《蜀中廣記》(卷九十二)《著作記》中載：

> 明皇幸蜀記三卷。唐李匡文、宋臣周、宋居白撰。初，匡文記盡明皇崩，臣周記止於歸長安，敍事互有詳略，居白合此記，以宋爲本，析李爲注，取二序冠篇，復撰遺事增廣焉。

此書今雖佚，但可知當時記載頗詳，且有軼聞遺事流傳於後也。幸蜀之事，畫家亦有以之爲題材者，如宋葉夢得《避蜀録話》(卷下)：

> 明皇幸蜀圖，李思訓畫，藏宗室汝南郡王仲忽家。余嘗見其摹本，廣不滿二尺，而山川雲物車輦人畜，草木禽鳥，無一不具。峯嶺重複，徑路隱顯，渺然有數百里之勢，想見其爲天下名筆。宣和間，内府求畫甚急，以其名不佳，獨不敢進，明皇作騎馬像，前後宦官宫女，導從略備，道傍瓜圃，宫女有即圃採瓜者，或諱之爲摘瓜圖。而議者疑元稹《望雲騅歌》，有騎騾幸蜀之語，謂倉猝不應儀物猷若是盛，遂以爲非幸蜀時事者，終不能改也。山谷間民皆冠白巾，以爲蜀人爲諸葛孔明服，所居深遠者，後遂不除。然不見他書。

葉氏言或以爲此畫所繪之騎從猶盛，以爲非畫幸蜀之事者，是亦未深考。《舊唐書》明言明皇抵成都，時扈從官吏軍士尚有千三百人，宫女二十四人，雖非後宫二千盡室而行，而自非措大之所能想見也。近來外間人入蜀，見蜀中男女多頭纏白巾，每引以爲怪，或謔爲爲孔明服孝，知此語唐宋時已有之矣。

明皇幸蜀之事，據新舊兩《唐書》所載，安禄山於天寶十四年(公元九五五年)冬，反於范陽，明皇於十五年(公元九五六年)六月十三日(乙未)凌晨出延秋門西奔，次日(十四日丙申)次馬嵬驛，十七日(己亥)次扶風郡。《舊唐書》載此時：“軍士各懷去就，咸出醜言，陳元禮不能制。會益州上春綵十萬疋，上悉命置於庭，召諸將諭之曰：卿等國家功臣，陳力久矣……朕須幸蜀，路險狹，人若多往，恐難供承。今有此綵，卿等即宜分取。如圖去就，朕自有子弟中官相隨，便與卿等永訣。衆咸俯伏涕泣曰：死生願隨陛下……”七月十日(壬戌)，渡吉柏江，有雙魚夾舟而躍，議者以爲龍……”二十八日(庚辰)“車駕至蜀郡，扈從官吏軍士到者一千三百人，宫女二十四人而已。”次年(肅宗至德二年，公元七五七年)郭子儀收復兩京，肅宗遣中使啖廷瑶奉迎，十月廿三日(丁卯)上皇發自蜀郡，十二月四日(丁未)至京師。以時計之，玄宗幸蜀，來程共行四十五日，歸程共行四十一日，在成都共駐一年兩月另二十四天。安有行至天回鎮即聞收復兩京而回長安，未至成都之事乎！

玄宗之幸蜀，雖事起倉卒，但楊國忠於成都，實早有準備。《舊唐書·楊國忠傳》：

> 自禄山兵起，國忠以身領劍南節制，乃布置腹心於梁益之間，爲自全之計。

唐姚汝能撰《安禄山事蹟》(卷下)：

> 先是國忠樂於蜀地，爲自全計，於天下之兵，頗置心腹於梁益之間，卒行其志。

《舊唐書·崔圓傳》：

> ……幸臣楊國忠遥制劍南節度使，引圓佐理。乃奏授尚書即兼蜀郡大都督府左司馬知節度留後。天寶末元宗幸蜀，特遷蜀郡大都

督府長史劍南節度。圓素懷功名，初聞國難，潛使人探國忠深旨，知有行幸之計，乃增修城池，建置館宇，儲備什器。及乘輿至，殿宇牙帳，咸如宿設，元宗甚嗟賞之，即日拜中書侍郎同中書門下平章事劍南節度，餘如故。

楊國忠雖被殺於馬嵬，未克至蜀，但其狡兔三窟之慮，亦未嘗不周。由此，亦可見明皇實至成都。又其他從幸諸臣傳中，亦明言至成都之事，如《穎王璬傳》：

安禄山反，除蜀郡大都督劍南節度大使……初奉命之藩，卒遽不遑受節，綿州司馬史貴進諫曰：王，帝子也。且爲節度大使。今之藩而不持節，單騎徑進，人何所瞻！請建大槊，蒙之油囊，一爲旌節狀，先驅道路，足以威衆。璬笑曰：但爲真王，何用假旌節乎！將至成都，崔圓迓之，拜於馬前，璬不止之。圓頗怒。元宗至，璬視事兩月，人甚安之。

《崔涣傳》：

天寶末，楊國忠出不附己者，涣出爲劍州騎史。天寶十五載七月，元宗幸蜀，涣迎謁於路……扈從至成都。

《高力士傳》：

力士從幸成都，進封齊國公。

此又皆明言玄宗幸蜀曾至成都者，成都因玄宗行幸之故於肅宗至德二年改爲南京，見《唐書・地理志》，故李白有《上皇西巡南京歌》，又《太平寰宇記》(卷七十二)：

> 十五年(天寶)玄宗幸蜀駐蹕成都，至德二年，十月，駕還西京，改蜀郡爲成都府，長史爲尹。

仝右，華陽縣下：

> 華陽縣本成都縣地，唐貞觀十年，分成都縣之東偏，置蜀縣，在郭下。乾元元年，玄宗狩蜀，駐蹕成都，改爲華陽縣。

由此可見唐時成都之升府，華陽縣名之由興，皆由明皇行幸之故。其他之雜記小説，亦多言駐蹕成都之事，如唐郭提《高力士傳》言："肅宗……即皇帝位於靈武，八月尊太上皇於成都，改元爲至德元年。成都宣赦，上皇謂高公曰：我兒嗣位，應天順人，改元至德，孝乎惟孝。卿之與朕，亦有何憂?"因此言肅宗即位後，玄宗於成都宣赦之事也。並且言玄宗至成都後氣候亦因之而變，有如兩京。"且蜀中風土，有異中原，秋熱冬温，晝晴夜雨，事之常也。及駕出劍門，至巴蜀，氣候都變，不異兩京，九月十九日霜風振厲，朝見之時，皆有寒色，詔即令着袍。二十一日百官皆衣袍立朝，不依舊式。"陰曆九月中旬及。"霜風振厲"，想爲寒流南襲特别爲早，通常則當至十一月以後也，此處所言"朝見"，乃謂於成都朝見上聖也。其最堪尋味者，莫過於唐劉肅《大唐新語》聰敏類所載裴士淹一條。

《大唐新語》(卷八)：

> 玄宗幸成都，給事中裴士淹從。士淹聰悟柔順，頗精歷代史，玄宗甚愛之，馬上偕行，得備顧問。時肅宗在鳳翔，每有大除拜，輒啓聞。房琯爲將，玄宗曰：此不足以破賊也。歷評諸將，並云非滅賊材。又曰：若姚崇在，賊不足滅也。因言崇之宏才遠略。語及宋璟，玄宗不悦曰：彼賣直以沽名耳。歷數十餘人，皆當其目。至張九齡，亦甚重之。及言李林甫，曰：妒賢嫉能，亦無敵也。士淹

因啓曰：既知如此，陛下何用之久耶？玄宗默然不應。

以玄宗之知人，而猶有李林甫、楊國忠之失，幾至於亡國！何則？內懷，色荒，雖明知其奸邪，而不能不用之，藉以遂其慾，此所以默然不對也。玄宗以宋璟爲“賣直沽名”，足見受諫之難，而後之見者，又實有不同，如陸放翁《老學菴筆記》(卷一)載，神宗夜讀《宋璟傳》，賢其爲人，詔訪其後，得於河朔，有裔孫曰宋立，遺像、譜牒、告身皆在。宋立已投軍矣，欲與一武官而其人不願，乃賜四十頃，免徭役雜賦云。”抑何其見之相反，景慕一至於此也。

《神僧傳》載僧一行謂玄宗“萬里當歸”之故事，雖係神話，亦可見玄宗幸成都之遺聞也。其言曰：

唐玄宗問一行國祚幾何？有留難否？對曰：鑾輿有萬里之行。帝驚問其故，不答。退，以小金盒進，署曰：至萬里則開。帝一日發盒視之，蓋當歸少許。及祿山亂，駕幸成都，至萬里橋乃悟，未幾果歸。

又明何宇度《益部談資》(卷中)亦言：

唐史載玄宗狩蜀至萬里橋，問橋名，左右對以萬里。玄宗嘆曰：開元末，僧一行謂更二十年國有難，朕當遠遊至萬里外，此是也。遂駐蹕成都。

一行爲唐僧中之邃於曆法者(見《舊唐書》本傳)，故多所傅會，如唐李石《續博物志》言“明皇在長安，詔一行鑄渾儀及太衍曆。先是，漢洛下閎云，此曆後一千年差一日，有聖人出而正之。至是果一千年。因以一行爲聖人。”此又一附會也。(段成式《酉陽雜俎》中所附會尤多)

此外，明皇幸蜀之遺聞軼事之流傳者尚多，但以近來圖籍多疏散，檢查不易，姑從略。但以上所舉者，亦足以正通志及縣志之失矣。且有詩爲證：

誰道君王行路難，六龍西幸萬人歡，地轉錦江成渭水，天迴玉壘作長安。

九天開出一成都，萬户千門入畫圖，草樹雲山如錦繡，秦川得及此間無？

錦水東流繞錦城，星橋北掛象天星，四海此中朝聖主，峨眉山上列仙庭。

秦開蜀道置金牛，漢水元通星漢流，天子一行留聖蹟，錦城長作帝王州。

——李太白《上皇西巡南京歌十首》録四

（原載《風土什志》一九四六年第一卷第六期，第8~12頁）

成都平原之大石文化遺蹟

成都平原之大石遺蹟，在地方志及繁多著作中，屢見記載。然迄今爲止，尚未對其進行系統之研究。毫無疑問，此乃四川最重要的考古遺蹟之一。大石遺蹟之起源雖久已被人們遺忘，但却成爲無知者迷信崇拜之對象，故得以保存至今，否則不少之大石想必已被毁或被移作他用。其數目雖不甚多[①]，但吾等應知成都爲冲積平原，無可供開採之石層。而今所見之大石，乃古代蜀人千辛萬苦，在幾十以至幾百公里外之山麓開採，而後移運至竪立之處者。再則，在漫長的歷史時期之中，被毁大石必定不少。蓋平原地區石塊乃稀罕之物，稱作其他建築之用的事時有發生，直至數年前仍然如此。今僅存之大石，蓋因迷信而禁毁、禁移之故。吾等實應慶幸此間尚有少數實物作研究古代文化之用。下簡述幾處大石遺蹟之情况。

支機石　支機石在成都西城城墻内側，面對支機石街西端。石呈灰色，乃粗砂岩石，高約 2 米，圍於一小廟院内。支機石之來源及名稱，民間傳説頗多。所有傳説均涉及西漢探險家張騫及神秘星相家嚴君平。嚴氏乃四川人，常在成都爲他人占卜。某次張騫乘木筏探索黄河源頭，竟至銀河，因當時人們相信此兩者是相連的。在回來時他帶了一塊大石，並詢嚴君平此石之由來。嚴告訴他此乃織女星織機下墊石也。騫乃告嚴他如何航至銀河、遇織女，織女送他一石並囑他回來時可向嚴君平詢問其端詳。嚴曰：去歲某夜客星犯織女星座，此必君矣。遂相與詫異。

民間迷信，如果有人欲移動或損壞此石，將會有雷雨驟起[②]。

天涯石　天涯石位於成都東北天涯街。此乃長而平之尖石，爲灰色砂岩，高逾 2 米。或稱天牙石，謂天之牙也，此或因其外形之故[③]。今此石供於一小寺之祭壇上，人們常趨至膜拜。此石之來源無考，然傳説甚多。一説，倘人踐履之或坐其上，則觸處必腫[4]。地方志又稱，天涯石不遠處，另有一石，其形與之略似而較小，稱爲地角石[5]。天涯、地角，係文學上描寫遠處之形容詞。

五塊石 五塊石在成都南郊外半英里武侯祠之後，當地地名亦稱五塊石。係由五塊灰色沙石壘叠而成，高約 3 米。底部一塊已陷入地下，今不可見。各石接縫處侵蝕嚴重。故視之如四塊重叠之略成圓形之石球。石之旁，立小神龕二，乃供奉土地神者。然此與五塊石無必然之聯繫。

相傳，五塊石乃海眼之蓋也。意其下有一井與海相連。又傳，昔有人試欲啓之，風雨驟至，懼而止之[6]。

石筍 石筍乃成都最著名之遺蹟。其記載亦最早。據説南宋時(1127—1267 年)其石猶存。此遺址在成都老西門外約兩百步之石筍街。其石有二，一北一南聳立。文獻記載，石原高約 10 米，惜於公元初已始損壞[7]；唐時(718—905 年)仍約有 4 ~ 5 米高[8]。《華陽國志》卷三謂："時蜀有五丁力士。能移山、舉萬鈞。每王薨，輒立大石，長三丈，重千鈞，爲墓誌，今石筍是也。"此解釋或許是正確的，然其後又有其他解釋出現。其一謂石筍乃海眼之標記，倘移之，則所在處頓成大海。證據之一是每遇夏雨，石旁數英尺處常有小孔出現。如以綫拴一石墜，放入孔中，則將下沉不斷，若無底然。而在雨後，石之周圍必見衆多之小珠[9]。

另一傳説謂，石筍爲神話中之蠶叢氏所留，以紀念蜀國之建立[10]。此説則未必確實。

數歲前，筆者得知石筍尚殘存，是故幾度調查。當地居民相告，有一石筍殘體，落於小溪之中，三十年前冬干水淺時猶可見之，然今已全埋入河底泥淖中矣。又謂，另一大殘塊仍立於某宅後院之井旁，惜覓之未獲。

武丁擔 據《華陽國志》，蜀都城内有一殘破之石，長約 10 米，圍約 2 米。城之北門外 16 公里毗橋處，另有一形狀與之相同之石。此二石乃大力士武丁所用之石擔，使之運土築武擔墩。此即蜀王神妃之墓也。

武丁擔今在成都城之西北角，距石筍不遠。

有人謂石筍、武丁擔乃同一遺蹟，僅記載將之混淆。由於兩石今已無存，自難以評定。然四川博物館收藏有一塊據稱來自武丁墩之石。筆者甚疑此即武丁擔之殘餘。此石乃石灰石質，高約 80 厘米，圍 140 厘米，一端尖狀，另一端殘破，上有文字兩行，約鎸刻於公元十三世紀，文中並未涉及石之來源[11]。由於此石來自武擔墩，自可能爲武丁擔遺物。當然，此僅猜測而已。

上述之大石，均乃獨石(menhirs)也。類似之記載在地方志中尚多，據稱成都附近尚有同樣之巨石。然至今日，大多蕩然無存。筆者對此未及調查，只有留待他日討論。成都平原尚有另一類型之大石，即所謂石行(alignments)者，亦應加以介紹。

飛來石　飛來石在新繁城東北約 4 公里青白江之北岸。石行在一稻田內，排列整齊。筆者曾於 1939 年查訪此遺蹟，憾未製圖、攝影。1943 年冬，筆者重訪該地，而石已無存。詢及當地居民，則謂 1941 年修橋時已被用作原料，當時僅餘若干碎石置於橋邊矣。《新繁縣志》稱，此等列石乃飛來之石也。因此地爲冲積平原，各處皆無較大之石，故有此説。縣誌又云，此石或係流星所化。然未詳述。

八陣圖　成都北約 32 公里之新都城北，緊靠彌牟鎮(今唐家寺)之東，有一遺蹟，由百餘土墩排列而成，此即八陣圖也。每一土墩高約 2 米，墩距亦約 2 米。推測古代當比現在爲高，已有部分被侵蝕。據記載，土墩原有江石(或係大塊卵石)冠其上。然今已無石。或爲當地居民移作他用之故。

所有之記載與傳説，均稱八陣圖乃諸葛亮故壘。云諸葛亮置此土墩練兵，抑或以迷惑進攻之敵。這明顯是後起之傳説，因爲没有任何一種軍隊可以按古代戰争之列陣通過土墩之間窄狹之通道。另一方面，用作練兵場所，亦嫌太小，因其不足 100 平方米之故。用之作迷陣，又失之太疏簡，通過其間，毫無困難。依筆者之見，八陣圖乃四川大石文化組成之一環也。平原不易獲大石，古人乃先建土墩，後以石冠其上。應該説明的是這些土墩並非墳墓，因其中少數已被民衆挖掘。

除新都八陣圖外，至少另有八陣圖兩處。最有名者，乃川東奉節之八陣圖。乃以卵石壘築於河岸上。另一處在成都南約 32 公里之雙流棋盤市，亦係由土墩組成。惜很久以前，已不復存在。此兩處八陣圖，亦謂乃諸葛亮所爲。雖每一八陣圖土墩之數不等，而其排列方法大致雷同。故應視爲同一類型之大石文化。

至於此等大石之原始含義何在，僅能猜測而已。或許即如《華陽國志》之言，此乃墓石。以石筍爲例，僅距武擔墩約半公里，兩者可能有内在聯繫。武擔墩爲人造之墩，極可能乃古墳，是以石筍可能爲墳之墓石。當然，其他竪立大石之原因尚多，諸如立之以紀念重要之社會、政治事件，或充作路標，或爲禁地之標界，等等。每一大石之立意，應由其特殊環境定之。八陣圖之含義不甚了了，然可肯定者，它與諸葛亮之軍事戰術無關，而可能具有宗教意義，爲舉行宗教活動之聖地。

四川大石文化之存在，絶非孤立現象，其分佈幾遍及全世界。從西歐東行，至中亞，經印度，而至阿薩姆、緬甸、雲南、美拉尼西亞、密克羅尼西亞、波利尼西亞，最東至復活島，均有大石文化存在。東北亞，我國之東北、朝鮮亦有之。因之，四川大石文化，僅是分佈極廣之大石綜合文化之一環也。

大石文化之年代，殊難肯定。其中一些，或爲“新石器”文化。然“新石器”之年代僅相對而已。《華陽國志》稱，石筍早在蜀國即有之，此即公元前 500 年左右，但此種習俗無疑起源更早。竪立大石以志重要事件，在中國公元前三世紀即已行之。秦始皇立獨石碑於泰山頂，意在紀念其訪問及統一中國之事迹[12]。在四川，遲至唐朝，仍有此遺風。房琯任漢州刺史，百姓喜之，當他去職，民衆立石以紀念其政績。今房公石仍存廣漢公園内。值得注意的是，居住在阿薩姆、緬甸間山區之那加族，今仍竪大石以紀念社會、生活大事。四川之大石文化，約在新石器時代至東周時期。

【注釋】

〔1〕例如，據馬迪勒 1901 年統計，法國有大石六千一百九十二柱。成都轄區内今僅存大石四柱，它們相距不足 1.6 公里，以此推之，古之大石比今爲多。

〔2〕《蜀中名勝記》(卷 1)引《道教靈驗記》："成都卜肆支機石，即海客携來自天河所得，織女令問嚴君平也。太尉敦煌公孫好奇尚異。命工人鎸取支機一片，欲爲器用。椎琢之際，忽若風瞀墜於右側，如此者三。公知其靈物，乃已之，至今所刻迹在焉。復令穿掘其下，則風雷震驚，咫尺昏曀，遂不敢犯。"

〔3〕某些記載稱，天涯石與天角石相異。陸深《蜀都雜抄》："天涯石在城東門内，寶光寺之東側，有亭覆之……别有一石，則在民居，其高亞於前石，未審何者天涯？何者爲天牙也？"然今僅存一石也。

〔4〕《四川通志》卷 49 引《耆舊傳》云："人坐其上則脚腫不能行，至今不敢踐履及坐。"

〔5〕地角石之形狀及所在處，説法有異。例如，朱秉器《漫録》："地角石在羅城内西北角，高三尺餘。王均之難，爲守城者所壞，今不復有矣。"

〔6〕五塊石之記載，最早見於明朝。王士性《入蜀記》："五塊石磥砢壘綴若累丸然，三面皆方，不測所自始，或云其下海眼也，每人啓之，風雨暴至。余奇之，書'落星'二字，請於中丞亭其上。"

〔7〕《益州耆舊傳》："公孫述時武擔石折，任文公嘆曰，西方智士死，吾當應之。歲中卒。"此處所提及之武擔石，乃石筍也。

〔8〕杜甫《石筍行》："君不見益州城西門，陌上石筍雙高蹲，古來相傳是海眼，苔蘚蝕盡波濤痕。雨多往往得瑟瑟，此事恍惚難明論。"注云：成都子城西金容坊，有石二株，挺然聳峭，高丈餘。

〔9〕《成都記》："距石筍二三尺，夏大雨，往往陷作土穴，泓水湛然，以竹測之，深不可測。及以繩繫石投其下，愈投而愈無窮，故有海眼之説。石筍之地，雨過必有小珠，青黄如粟，亦有小孔可以貫絲。"

〔10〕《蜀中廣記》(卷 2)引《圖經》云："諸葛亮掘之方有篆字，曰蠶叢氏啓國誓蜀之碑。以二石柱横埋之，云接鐵其中，一南一北，無所偏邪。"

〔11〕所刻之字爲"如弦之直，如秤之平"。五代李崧手迹。見《五代史》。

〔12〕文學上所描繪之八陣圖極麗，然未提及其起源，誠可不顧。

〔13〕《史記・秦始皇本紀》："二十八年，始皇東行郡縣，上鄒嶧上，立石，

與魯諸生議刻石頌秦德，議封禪望祭山川之事。乃遂上泰山，立石封祠祀。”立石初並未記述，碑文爲日後所刻。

〔14〕今廣漢公園之房公石，乃一小石也。此與古時描繪極異。如《丹淵集》：“聶侯友仲立漢州學制度，宏侈爲二蜀二冠，當時不知何處得巨石，置講堂之後，質狀怪偉，勢若飛動。”然王士正之《秦蜀驛程記》記之又異：“次漢州西郭，州守濮陽馮達，邀觀房公西湖，已無勺水。入城，宿州署，署中小圃甚潔，花木叢萃可喜。有房公石，舊在池中，今涸矣。馮守云：曾掘地數丈，窮其根不可得，石脈西南行。舊志言尾出於房湖，今湖中乃無片石。”故，房公石乃舊石新立也。

（見《華西邊疆研究學會雜誌》一九三七年第十六卷）

元八思巴蒙文聖旨碑發現記

民國28及29年間(1939—1940年)，成都因空襲嚴重，于是大辟城門，以便城内居民臨時疏散，舊有之四門，亦將其拆除擴大，以免疏散時擁擠。在此種拆毁城垣之中，發現古代之殘碑甚多，甚有發現蜀石經者。以四川大學博物館所收集之殘碑而言，即已不下數十種，其他之未經收集而毁棄者，尚不知有幾許也。因歷代修築城垣，需石甚多，而成都附近，无石礦可供採取，工人爲就地取材計，故凡城垣附近之碑版，當時之被視爲无用，或无價值者，咸輦之以築城，此乃此次辟城門時所以發現殘碑之多也。

民國30年(1941年)春，老南門口，尚餘有拆除城門未運走之石塊數大堆。余一日自其處經過，見一石塊涂滿白堊，其上隱約似有花紋，稍撥而視之，似有文字，但頗奇特，非藏文亦非回文，因成都近康藏，又多回教徒，碑版中頗多刻此二種文字者，故是時有此種猜想也。當命工人輦回舊皇城本館中清理。

在另一石堆中，尚有此碑之碑額，其上亦涂滿白堊，不過“聖旨”二字尚隱隱可見，爲楷書，大約五寸見方。其上所刻之花紋似甚精，因白堊過多，亦不能辨其爲何種花紋也。此額約當此殘碑之三倍，非普通車輛之所能勝，于是轉請南門所駐紮之軍警，代爲保護，俟數日後人夫(約需十餘人方能搬運上車)大車雇齊後，再往搬運。但數日後再至其地時，此碑額已早爲人運走矣。此碑額若爲收藏家聞而運走，或者尚在天壤間，不然其迨已毁于石工斧鑿之下矣。當時曾在各石堆中找尋其他殘段，但未有所發現。

在館中經技工將白堊去盡後，發現其另一面尚有漢文，始知其爲元碑。因其字有類藏文，此時意度其或爲八思巴所造之蒙文國書也。因非研究此道，此時不過爲一種猜測而已。因急拓一本以示韓鴻庵先生，韓君一見大喜，以爲此或爲天壤間僅存之八思巴蒙文碑也，因托其代爲考釋。

此碑現在之所存者，爲其最上一段，高爲六四公分，寬爲一二八公分，厚二九公分，上有長方形孔穴二，寬約八公分，長約十公分，所以受碑額者。自此殘段之形式觀之，此碑原高至少有二公尺以上，故今所存者，不過原碑五之一而已。

碑之另一面爲漢文，僅存四十餘字，均爲每行首三四字，故文義不相聯續。韓君據譯文以爲係青羊宫之碑，實不知漢文中已有“聖朝寵錫青羊宫……制旨謹勒堅珉將以昭……”之語也。又其中有“太上”“玉女”“老子”“西過”等語，似爲述老子之事，而非元文之直接譯文也。此漢文之字體，與四川博物館在老西門所發現之成都萬户府記碑係出一手，書法挺秀，有類北海，但不知出諸何人之手迹也。

此碑係敕立青羊宫之碑，自无疑問。不過此碑係何時被毁以充老南門之建築石料，當爲待考定之問題也。按成都自秦張儀築城以後①，至于隋唐，歷代皆有修葺，但城之範圍均甚小，至唐僖宗時，高駢築羅城堰縻棗，阻錦江繞城東北流，城垣增大爲周二十五里，高二丈六尺，外又繞以高堤二十六里，成都城垣之範圍，始具現在之規模②。至宋程戡③、盧法原、王剛中④、范成大等亦均有修葺。但唐以前之城垣，均係土城，高駢始稍易以磚甓，《新唐書》(卷二二四下)高駢傳：

---

① 按秦城至南宋時尚有存留者，李石《方舟集·學府十咏》自注：“秦城張儀司馬錯所築，自秦惠公乙巳歲至宋紹興壬午一千四百七十八年，雖頹圮所存如崖壁峭立，學舍一奇觀也。”又相傳明藩邸前之照壁(俗稱紅照壁，今有紅照壁街)，即秦城之遺。按紅照壁距學宫不遠。

② 見唐王徽中和四年所作之《創築羅城記》。

③ 《宋史·程戡傳》(卷二九二)：“守益州者，以嫌多不治城堞，戡獨完城浚池自固，不以爲嫌也。”

④ 王剛中帥蜀，有惠政，而史不言其修城事。《宋史·王剛中傳》(卷三八六)：言“成都萬歲池，廣袤十里，溉三鄉田，歲久淤澱。剛中集三鄉夫共疏之。累土爲防，上植榆柳，表以石柱，州人指曰，王公之甘棠也。府學禮殿，東漢興平中建，後又建新學，遭時多故，日就傾圮，屬九縣繕完，悉復其舊。葺諸葛武侯祠，張文定公廟……”剛中既能興建此類不急需之工程，以當時外患之切，其修城，當亦意中事。

> 蜀之土惡，成都城歲壞，騂易以磚甓，陴堞完新，負城丘陵悉墾平之，以便農桑。①

余曾察視現在所辟臨時疏散等缺口，往往于版築土中見有矮小之磚墻，此或係唐城也。雍正修《四川通志》(卷四)言“明趙清始甃以磚石”，似未深考。

元以後，成都城垣之修葺，約可分爲兩時期，一爲明初，再爲清初。明初之修葺，據天啓間所修《成都府志》中《成都記》所載②：

> 洪武十一年封第十一子椿爲蜀王，國成都，都指揮趙祥砌成都磚城。③

其後“宣德三年十月總兵都督陳懷浚修成都隍池”。清康熙二十五年所修《成都府志》所載略同，蓋康熙府志所根據者全爲明志，不過削其中之《成都記》而已，其他則别无可考。

明末張獻忠據蜀，其出走時盡夷成都及附近各縣之城垣，《明史》(卷三〇九)《流寇傳》：

> 獻忠盡焚成都宫殿廬舍，夷其城。

又同治《成都縣志》言：

> 崇禎末，流賊張獻忠亂蜀，王祥曾英合兵討之，賊大懼，决計走保寧，盡夷成都城，隳墻垛。

① 王徽《創築羅城記》中亦有“甃壁涂塈，既麗且堅”之語。
② 此書現藏美國國會圖書館，刊刻至精。
③ 按《明史·蜀王椿傳》(卷一一七)：“洪武十一年封，十八年命駐鳳陽，二十三年就藩成都。”

其他私家記載亂後之成都景象者甚夥，如王沄《蜀遊記略》云：

城中茅舍寥寥，詢其居民，大都秦人矣。

此康熙十年也。方象瑛于康熙二十二年入蜀，而猶未稍復，其《使蜀日記》云：

蜀周五十里，異時人物繁富，號錦城。張獻忠據蜀，己去之秦，盡燒公私廬舍，屠其人凡數十萬，自浣溪至新津，屍山積，水爲不流。今通衢，瓦屋百十所，餘皆誅茅編竹爲之(茅屋皆松潘苗人造，每冬月苗人携妻子至各郡縣，營工給食，婦女能負重，子女帽覆頂，嵌以蚌殼)①。西北隅則頹墉敗礫，蕭然慘人。其民多江楚陝西流寓，土著僅十之二耳。

由此可見成都受禍之烈，及當時之荒凉景象也，故清初收蜀之後，不得不大事修建也。

清初成都城垣之修建，曾有三次，第一次爲康熙初年巡撫張德地，布政使郎廷相等之培修，康熙二十五年《成都府志》(卷五)言：

成都府城池，即會城，大城創于張儀，少城築于楊秀，羅城增于高駢……明趙清甃以磚石，陳懷復浚池隍。明末甲申獻賊毀壞，大清康熙初，巡撫佟鳳彩②，張德地，藩司郎廷相，臬司李翀霄，

① 按此處所言之苗人，乃羌人也。羌人届冬入蜀爲傭，自漢時已然。《後漢書·冉駹夷傳》(卷一一六)："夷人冬則避寒入蜀爲傭，夏則違暑返其落。"又《華陽國志》(卷三)汶山郡"夷人冬則避寒入蜀，傭賃自食，夏則避暑返落，歲以爲常。"是也。蜀中清初以前无苗人，有之亦不爲傭也。

② 據《清史稿·佟鳳彩傳》(卷二七三)：(順治)十七年擢四川巡撫。四川經張獻忠亂，城邑殘破，勸官吏捐輸，修築成都府城。

知府冀應熊，共捐貲，俾華陽成都兩知縣，張行，張暄督築完固。

據《四川通志》所載，此次所修，墻高三丈，厚一丈八尺，周二十二里三分，東西相距九里三分，南北相距七里三分，此則現在成都之規模也。故成都人往往稱“九里三分”之成都，蓋以此地。

是後清雍正五年巡撫憲德亦曾增修，乾隆四十八年總督福康安奏請發帑銀六十萬兩徹底重修，成都城垣之有今日之壯觀者，蓋以最後一次之重修也。

清代之三次修葺，大概均係原來之明城規模，而將城垣加强。如《四川通志·政績(八)》言知府冀應熊，“贊巡撫張德地，定經制，修舉廢厥，氣象蔚然一新”。冀當係王漁洋《蜀道驛程記》中之冀君，該記言：“九月二十五日發成都……巡撫羅中丞祖道萬裏橋前，成都冀君所修，榜曰萬里始此……”冀爲河南舉人，康熙六年任成都府知府，漁洋入蜀，則爲康熙十一年也。

按成都城垣之大事修葺，其可考者，雖在清初，但聖旨碑之被毁以築城，想不致在清初，而當在明初，因明初之毁元代之聖旨碑，亦爲勢有必然者。明趙清之修城已不可考，據雍正《四川通志》(卷三二)職官類言于洪武中任成都都指揮使，其他不詳，《明史》亦无傳①，修城之事亦无其他記載。如曹學佺《蜀中廣記》，于蜀中掌故，匯羅至富，亦无一字及明初修城之事也。

明代成都之城垣如何？現雖无從得知，但以現存之明蜀藩邸推之，亦必甚壯偉。成都蜀王藩邸，踞成都城之中心，面積五百餘畝，方形，而南北略長，建築極爲宏偉，俗所呼爲皇城者是也。皇城城垣于民國7年(1918年)始行拆去，但至今尚有存者，今皇城壩之城洞是也。其他部分之磚石雖已完全拆去，而版築尚多有巍然屹立者。如現殘存之城洞，高幾及十公尺，厚二十二公尺餘，其原來城垣建築之偉大，于此可見也。

明蜀藩邸之城垣，既如此堅實壯偉，其外城之城垣，想亦必相當，

---

① 天啓《成都府志》言“趙祥”，餘均言“趙清”，未知孰是。

其修築之時，需材亦必多，當時之犯忌諱，或視爲无用之碑版，必多聋之以建城①，况元蒙之聖旨碑乎？故以意測之，此聖旨碑之被撲，或當在明初也。

（原載《四川博物館》一九四八年，單刊之二）

① 明初修城時，即南宋以來視爲名貴之蜀石經，亦毁之以填城，清初修城時即有發現。如劉燕庭手批《錢竹汀日記》中自述其爲蜀臬時，聞乾隆四十四年制軍福康安修成都城，什邡令任思仁得蜀石經數十片于土壕中，字尚完好，任貴州人，罷官後，原石携歸黔中。此次辟城門時，于城墻中亦發現有蜀石經，可見明初毁棄碑版之多也。

川康明清土司官印考

1938年夏，由原四川大學西南社會科學研究所資助，本人前往松潘、理縣、茂汶考察羌民族。1939年夏，又擔任舊教育部組織的川康科學考察團社會組組長，至原西康地區作社會調查。往來川康松理茂之間，留心搜訪，遇有明清土司官印，即爲鈐印，集得若干枚。今擇選部分材料，略加考釋，以備研究川康民族史之參考。

1. 明永樂九年(1411年)"火把簇千户所印"此印7.5厘米見方，寬邊，印面鑄九疊篆"火把簇千户所印"七字，背刻"永樂九年十一月□日禮部造"字樣(圖一)。

圖一

按元、明、清于羌族地區各氏族部落悉加"族"字，亦或作"簇"，如《明史》(卷三三〇)，地理志，西番諸衛所云之"岷州西寧溝十五族"、"洮州十八族"及其他文獻記載松潘境内之"静州二十三族""隴木頭二十六族""岳西蓬二十一族"之類，是也。《大明一統志》(卷七十三)"松潘等處軍民指揮使司"謂：松潘"古氏羌地"，唐"廣德初陷于土蕃，至元時始内附。本朝洪武十一年，置松潘衛。二十年，改松潘等處軍民指揮使司，領千户所一，長官司十七，安撫司四：占藏先結簇長官司、蠟匝簇長官司、白馬路簇長官司、山洞簇長官司、阿昔洞簇長官司、北定簇長官司、麥匝簇長官司、者多簇長官司、牟力結簇長官司、班班簇長官司、祈命簇長官司、勒都簇長官司、包藏簇長官司、阿昔簇長官司、思曩兒簇長官司、阿用簇長官司、潘斡寨簇長官司、八郎安撫司、麻兒匝安撫司、阿角寨安撫司、芒兒者安撫司”。是爲“簇”乃“族”字别寫之證。

此處“簇”字之義爲何？火把簇既不見于上述記載松潘境内諸簇中，其地究在何處？查在川、青、藏接壤之金沙江、瀾滄江與潞江三大河流之上源部分，草原遼闊，其牧民久已同化于吐蕃。元代爲和碩特蒙古所役屬。元代爲俺噠汗所征服。清初爲顧實汗屬民。自元代已移置一部分蒙古軍駐牧于此進行管理。吐蕃語稱北方民族爲“霍爾巴”(ཧོར་པ胡人)，包括回紇、吐渾、突厥諸民族。蒙古統治中亞時期，藏人亦呼蒙古人爲霍爾巴，實讀如“霍巴”，亦可單稱爲“霍爾”。故元明以來，此所謂“川藏諸族”中亦有霍爾巴(川藏族見《明史·闡化王傳》)。此輩蒙古人，久已信奉喇嘛教，使用藏文，同化于藏族。至顧實汗時，另委頭領管理，舊統治此牧部之戍軍子孫，遂化爲與本地土著同類之一族。《衛藏通志》(卷十五)載西藏管轄三十九族中，有“夥爾族”，“住牧依絨地方夥爾族”，“夥爾拉賽族”與另一“夥爾族”(與彭他麻族、夥爾拉賽族共住一地)，皆元明管理潞江上遊牧區與金沙江、瀾滄江上游之玉樹二十五族地區之舊酋長子孫族黨夷爲被統治者也。在永樂時此霍爾族酋長應仍爲此地牧部之統治者。其時黄教未興，薩迦已微，此帶牧民部落與衛、康諸部落殆全歸白教統治。白教大德哈立麻，于永樂七年入京朝貢，受封爲大寶法王，六年四月辭歸，明帝“令中官護行”(《明史》(卷三三一)《烏斯藏大寶法王傳》)。同時，白教大德帕木竹巴亦受封爲“灌頂國師闡化王”。永樂十一年，“中官楊三保使烏斯藏還，其王遣從子劄結等隨之入貢。明年，復命三保使其地，令與闡教、護教、贊善三王及川卜、川藏等(族)共修驛站，諸未復者盡復之。自是，道路畢通”(《闡化王傳》)。楊三保亦見《大乘法王傳》，謂永樂十二年，其王辭歸，“後數入貢。帝亦先後命中官喬來喜、楊三保齎賜佛像、法器、袈裟、禪衣、絨錦、採幣諸物”。即謂三保十一年甫還，十二年復使其地，齎賜諸法王土酋也。以當時途程、任務，與一般可考之使節記載推之，楊三保蓋即永樂四年護送哈立麻回藏之中官也。再考其時驛道創建，全在今康藏之間，故所以倚以成功者爲闡教、護教、贊善三王，與川卜、川藏諸族(貢道規定西藏諸法王酋長由川入京，不許經河州)。闡化王住地即今鄧柯縣之靈葱(《明史》作“靈藏”。今靈葱土司尚藏有明代所賜朵甘衛都指揮使印誥，住于此地寺内)。而大寶法王哈立麻，本住拉薩北方之熱振寺(《衛藏通志》作“呼正寺”)，清代白教破滅，乃改黄教，猶保存哈立麻遺物甚多。合此形勢觀之，《明史》所謂驛站，必然建築于通過玉樹二十五族與黑河三十九族地方(西藏管三十九族地方，置黑河總管，故又曰黑河三十九族)。黑河，今云拉曲卡(藏語黑水渡口)，亦即夥爾族分佈之地。其時(永樂時)霍爾巴方爲諸牧族之統治者，已奉白教，而此大寶、闡化、護教、贊善四法王皆白教法王，其“舉元故官”時之當舉此牧部之霍巴酋長可知。其能完成驛站，又必得力于此牧部之霍巴酋長受撫可知。由此諸資料，估計當時地理形勢與社會情俗，結合此印之鑄頒年代與藏文對音，可以肯定“火把”即“夥爾”，即藏文ཧོར་པ舊譯无疑。其酋駐牧地，或即是今黑河也。

明代土司官印和其他官印一樣，大小形制，文字書體，均有嚴格的制度。萬曆年間申時行等編《明會典》(卷七九)，禮部三十七載：“國初設鑄印局，專管鑄造内外諸司印信。其後又有鑄换辨驗……洪武二十六年定，凡開設各處衙印信，劄付鑄印局官依式鑄造給降。其有改鑄銷燬等項，悉領之。弘治……十四年議準，在外大小衙門印記，年久印面平乏，篆文模糊者，方許申知上司驗實具奏，鑄换新印。其舊印送上司，付公差人員繳部，仍發鑄印局看驗。若印記新降未久，捏奏煩擾，雖已鑄换，仍將申奏官吏治罪。”“通政司……並在外……宣慰司，俱從三品，銅印，方二寸七分。”“鴻臚寺……並在外宣撫司，俱從四品，銅印，方二寸五分，厚五分。”“翰林院……並在外……各衙千户所，俱正五品。……並在外招討、司安撫司，俱從五品。銅印，方二寸四分，厚四分五厘。”“吏科等六科……宣撫司、經歷司，俱從七品，銅印，方二寸一分，厚三分。”“户部……宣撫司經歷，以上正、從八品，俱銅印，方二寸，厚二分五厘。”“刑部都察院各司……僧綱司、道紀司及各巡按司，以上正、從九品，俱銅印，方一寸九分，厚二分二厘。”“以上俱直鈕九叠篆文。”明代工部營造尺，一尺約當今 32 厘米。此火把簇千户所印 7.5 厘米，合明代之二寸三分强，與上述文獻記載正五品千户所印方二寸四分的制度相符。

2.“綽司甲布宣撫司印”三方第一方 8.3 厘米見方，邊寬 0.9 厘米，右方之所鑄漢字如上印仍占兩行，而左方之少數民族文字作三行，字形筆畫規整粗細，和通常所見滿漢對照之官印相同(圖二)。第二方 8.1 厘米見方，邊寬 0.9 厘米，印文漢滿對照一如上印。惟印體稍小，而字畫更爲纖秀工整，與上印略有不同(圖三)。

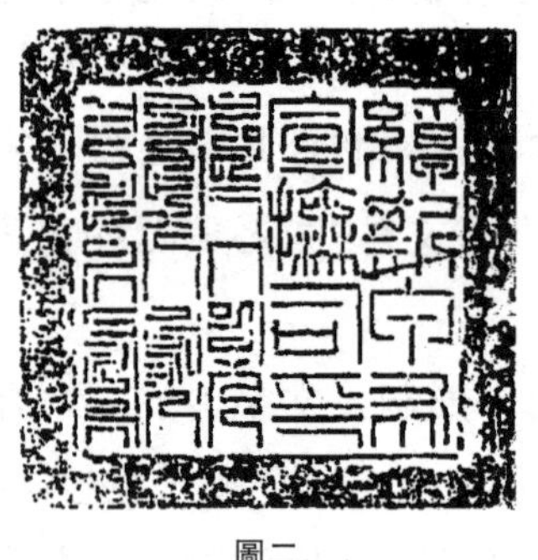
圖二

圖三

此二印雖未著紀年，可以確定爲清代土司官印无疑。清《嘉慶四川通志》(卷九六)，武備志十五，土司一，松茂道提標轄懋功廳協所屬，有“綽司甲布宣撫司諾爾布斯丹臻，始祖資立于康熙三十九年投誠，康熙四十一年頒給安撫司印信號紙。乾隆三十七年，出師金川有功，恩賞戴花翎並二品頂戴。四十一年，頒給宣撫司印信號紙，隨將舊印呈繳。

該土司原係阜和協所管，乾隆五十一年，奉文改隸懋功協管轄，住牧綽司甲，在今金川縣境。其地東至熱六壅滚一百餘里，交黨壩、松岡土司界。南至一百餘里，交惡裹，與打箭爐廳屬革什咱土司界。西至八百餘里，交勒則格爾布，與打箭爐廳屬色爾塔頭人界。北至七百餘里交熱爾谷，與樟蠟營屬阿木思勒格思土司界。四至共一千七百餘里，所管二十九寨番民户口，共一千一百三十户。每三年納貢馬一匹，折徵銀八兩，係由懋功廳衙門徵收。並无認納糧稞"。所管番民主要爲嘉戎。轄地靠近西藏，東至丹蠎司百里，西至雅州八百里，南至革什咱司百里，北至松潘八百里。民國時屬綏靖縣，尚管二十六寨，其時土司名納旺勒耳。此印爲宣撫司印，當係乾隆四十一年(1777年)始授者。

第三方爲5.4厘米見方，邊寬達1厘米，印面雖仍鑄"綽司甲布宣撫司印"字樣，漢文與少數民族文字對照，各占兩行，漢字在右方，少數民族文字在左方，與常見清代官印之字形完全不同，整個鑄字技術顯得比較粗拙，而與上印形制大異其趣(圖四)，似非一般常見之清代土司官印。《嘉慶四川通志》(卷一九二)，《西域志二》，前藏上："元憲宗始于河州置土蕃宣慰司都元帥府，又于四川徼外置碉門、魚通、黎雅、長河西寧等處宣撫司。世祖時復置烏斯藏郡縣其地……明太祖懲唐世吐蕃之亂，思制御之，惟因甚俗。"四川西北康藏之地，其民多藏族，且與西藏相接，土司官印或有使用藏文或其他少數民族文字者。如同上書(卷一一一)，《西域志一》云：類伍齊，"在察木多西北，係由草地進藏徑道，

圖四

原隸西藏。自康熙五十八年大兵進取西藏，該地僧俗人民，投誠歸順，頒給胡土克圖印信。其印係協理黄教那門汗之印，清字、蒙古字、夷字三様篆文”。知清代部分少數民族官印亦有使用蒙古文、藏文或其他當地民族文字者。綽斯甲之嘉戎民族實爲藏族。此印所鑄少數民族文字與蒙古八思巴文頗相似，待考。

以上三印，印文内容相同而不同器，形制亦有不同程度的差異，其鑄頒年代自有先後之别。至其孰先孰後，則一時尚難判定。以下諸印之有類此者，情形亦應相同，不另作説明。

3. 清乾隆十八年“隴木長官司印”印 7 厘米見方，寬邊，印面鑄“隴木長官司印”字様，滿漢對照，漢右滿左，篆體字形方正(圖五)。印背刻有乾隆十八年紀年。

圖五

隴木之稱始于宋代，隴木長官司明代稱爲“隴木頭”。《蜀中廣記》(卷三二)，《邊防記第二》，茂州：“隴木頭長官司，茂之隴木裏也，國初以酋長歸附，授承直郎，世襲長官，歲常貢馬二匹，所屬玉亭、神溪十二寨，有保長統之。”入清之後，清《嘉慶四川通志》(卷九六)，《武備志十五》，土司一，茂州茂州營屬，有“隴木長官司何裳之，其先何文貴，于宋時剿羅打鼓生番有功，授職頒給印信。國朝順治九年(1652 年)投誠，頒給印信號紙，住牧隴木寨。其地東至四十里，交石泉縣界。南至二十里，交州屬馬桑灣界。西至四十里，交静州土司界。北至三十里，交州屬神溪堡界。四至共一百三十里，所管番民户口共二百六十七户，每年折充兵米，司庫兑扣兵餉，認納黄荳三十六石五鬥，黄蠟三十斤，赴營上納”。道光十一年修《茂州志》(卷三)，土司：“隴木長官司何棠之，其先楊文貴于宋時隨剿羅打鼓有功授職。明洪武四年，頒給印信。嘉靖間，土司楊翺隨總兵何卿征白草生番，著有勞績，命改何姓。國朝順治九年投誠，康熙二十四年(1685 年)頒給印信號紙，住隴木東。”所記四至，與上録《嘉慶四川通志》大抵相同，惟言清代給印之始年與《通志》不同，當以州志所載爲準。長官司轄地，東至石泉(今北川)三十里，西至静州土司三十里，南至茂縣二十里，北至松潘三十里，在今茂縣境，所管土民主要爲羌族。由上《茂縣志》記載可知，此印當爲康熙二十四年(1685 年)所鑄頒者。該土司至清代末年尚管一百一十七户，至民國時則完全式微，其土司何九皋已淪爲背夫，1938 年 8 月間曾于茂縣遇之，身帶此印不離。

當時曾出重價購之，不肯售，尚冀將來土司有恢復之日，此則爲其把憑。

4. 清“卓克基長官司印”二方一印 7 厘米見方，邊寬 0.6 厘米，印面鑄“卓克基長官司印”字樣，漢滿對照，漢右滿左(圖六)。另一方 6.7 厘米見方，邊寬 0.5 厘米，與前一印相較，印文内容完全相同，惟形制略小，邊亦稍窄，印文書法，筆畫方折，與上印之往往作圓轉者不完全一樣，整個鑄工亦更加精細(圖七)。

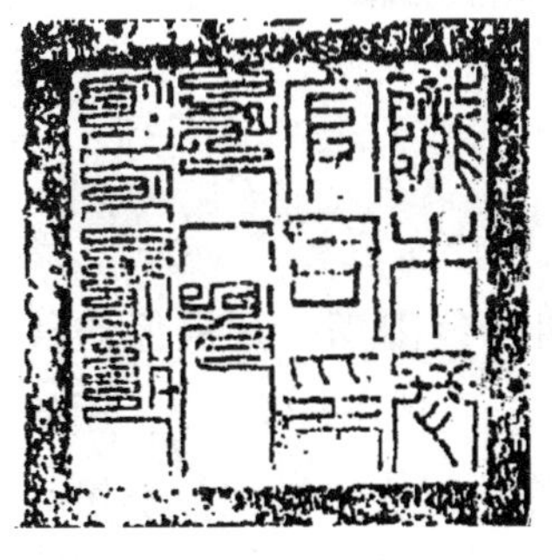

圖六

圖七

清《嘉慶四川通志》(卷九六),《武備志十五》,土司一,雜谷廳維州轄右營屬,載云:“卓克基長官司索朗郎木耳吉,其祖良爾吉係雜谷土舍,乾隆十三年隨征剿大金川有功,十五年頒給長官司印信號紙。住牧卓克基。其地東至梭磨六十里,交麻迷橋界,至維州右營五百里,至維州協五百六十里,至松潘鎮一千零八十里。南至新疆二百一十里,交攢拉界。西至松岡五十里,交八耳康界。又至黨壩一百三十里,交納角溝界。北至郭洛克二百六十里,交草地界。四至共八百一十里,所管番寨十寨,番户共一千五百餘户。每三年輪班朝覲,派土舍頭人代往。貢物鳥槍、腰刀、藏香、哈達、鹿茸、金佛、銀佛、氆氌等類。番民每年與土司納糧,并未認納貢賦。”卓克基一名卓克採,轄地在理番縣境馬爾康之東。此印當爲乾隆十五年(1750年)後所鑄頒。

5. 清乾隆十八年(1753年)“松岡長官司印”印7厘米見方,寬邊,印面鑄“松岡長官司印”字樣,滿漢對照,漢右滿左(圖八)。印背刻楷書漢字“乾隆十八年五月□日禮部造”字樣。

圖八

清《嘉慶四川通志》(卷九六),《武備志十五》,土司一,雜谷廳維州轄右營屬,有“松岡長官司女士司索朗谷色爾滿。其祖係雜谷土目,自唐時安設,並无印信號紙。國朝康熙二十三年(1684年),頒給安撫司印信號紙。乾隆十七年(1752年),土司蒼旺不法伏誅,揀委梭磨土司勒爾悟之胞弟根濯司甲承襲土司。嘉慶五年(1800年),土司納木耳病故,无子，報請以伊妻索朗谷色爾滿頒給號紙，住牧松岡。其地東至卓克基五十里，交八耳康界。由松岡至維州右營五百五十里，至維州協。六百一十里，至松潘鎮。一千一百三十里，南至黨壩。一百三十里，交納角溝界。西至綽司甲百九十里，交也耳日界。北至阿樹郭洛克九百二十里，交草地界。四至共一千九百二十里，所管番寨二十一寨，番户一千餘户。每三年輪班朝覲，派土舍頭人代往。所進貢物，鳥槍、腰刀、藏香、哈達、鹿茸、金佛、銀佛、氆氌等類。番民每年與土司納糧，並未認納貢賦"。松岡長官司，轄地在靖化縣境内馬爾康之西，民國時尚管三十六溝。據印背所刻紀年文字可知，此印當係乾隆十七年(1752年)土司蒼旺伏誅後，由梭磨土司勒爾悟之胞弟根濯司甲承襲土司時另鑄頒給者。

6. 清"黨壩長官司印"6.8厘米見方，印面鑄疊篆"黨壩長官司印"字樣，漢滿對照，漢右滿左(圖九)。

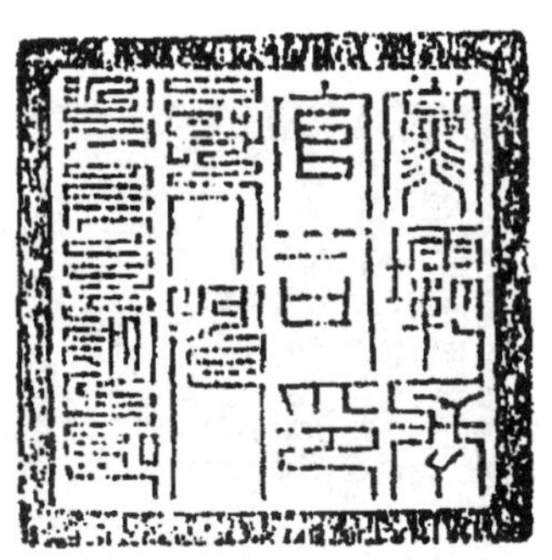

圖九

《嘉慶四川通志》(簡稱《通志》)(卷九六)，《武備志十五》，土司一，雜谷廳維州轄右營屬，有"黨壩長官司。土司更噶斯丹增姜初，其曾祖阿丕，係雜谷土舍。乾隆十三年(1748年)，土舍澤旺隨征剿大金川有功，頒給長官司印信號紙。嘉慶元年(1796年)，土司更噶斯丹增姜初隨征'苗匪'有功，賞戴花翎，住牧黨壩。其地東至卓克基一百三十里，交納角溝界。由黨壩至維州右營六百三十里，至維州協六百九十里。至松潘鎮一千二百一十里。南至新疆三十里，交日旁山界。西至綽斯甲三十里，交格江河界。北至松岡一百三十里，交八凹山界。四至共八百二十里，所管番寨十四寨，番户共二百九十餘户。每三年輪班朝覲，派土舍頭人代往。所進貢物，鳥槍、腰刀、藏香、哈達、鹿茸、金佛、銀佛、氆氌等類。番民每年與土司納糧，並未認納貢賦"。轄地在懋功縣境松岡之南稍西，距馬爾康不遠，民國時尚管五溝，土司名澤郎海。此印當爲乾隆十三年所頒鑄者。

《通志》記載，黨壩、松岡二長官司與瓦寺、梭磨二宣慰使司，皆同爲雜谷廳維州轄右營屬，"以上土司四員，所管番民性情風俗，與瓦寺土司所管番民同"。是皆羌族土司也。

7. 清"四川鐵布上撒路木路惡寨土百户之印"印 6.5 厘米見方，印面鑄"四川鐵布上撒路木路惡寨土百户之印"字樣，漢滿文對照各三行，漢右滿左(圖十)。

圖十

《嘉慶四川通志》(卷九六)，《武備志十五》，土司一，松茂道松潘廳漳蠟營所屬，載云："上撒路木路惡寨土百户阿夏，係西番種類。其先學賴，于雍正二年歸誠授職，頒給號紙印信，住牧上撒路木路惡寨。其地東至五里，交中撒路界。南至二百里，交合壩寨界。西至二百里，交熱當寨界。北至荒山，无里數。四至共四百零五里，所管八寨番民共七十七户，向无認納税銀。每年納青稞七石七鬥，交松潘鎮漳蠟營征收，折充兵米。"其地在理番縣境。此印當係雍正二年(1724年)鑄頒者。

8. 清"下撒路土百户之印"6.5厘米見方，寬邊，鑄漢滿對照之"下撒路土百户之印"字様，漢右滿左(圖十一)。

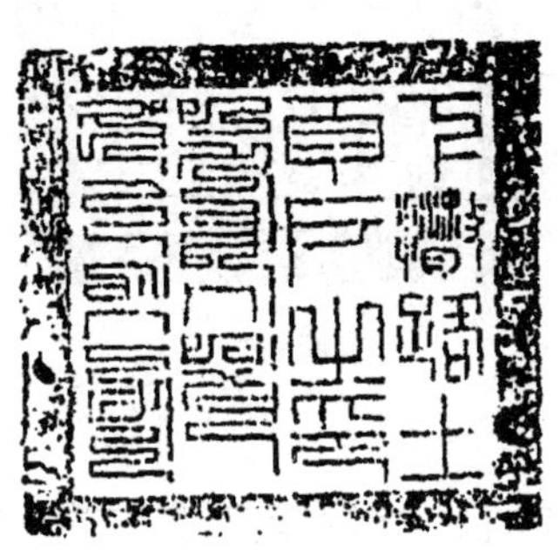

圖十一

下撒路土司，清雍正二年(1729年)年歸附後所置。地屬松潘所轄。《嘉慶四川通志》(卷九六)，《武備志十五》，土司一，松茂道松潘廳漳蠟營所屬，有"下撒路竹弄土百户一旦，係西番種類。其先迫帶，于雍正二年歸誠授職，頒給號紙印信，住竹弄寨。其地東至一百二十里，交洮州所屬楊土司角利羊疆界。南至三百里，交雜谷爾壩寨界。西至十里，交中撒路界。北至十五里，交荒山界。四至共四百五十里，所管十四寨番民共一百七十四户。向无認納税銀，每年納青稞一十七石四鬥，交松潘鎮樟蠟營征收，折充兵米"。《清通考》作雍正四年(1727年)初置，與此稍有出入。其地在今理番縣境。印文无"竹弄寨"三字，與《通志》所載不同，蓋竹弄寨乃土司所住寨名，非土司官名故也。

9. 清"四川穆坪董卜韓胡宣慰司印"印8.6厘米見方，印面鑄漢滿對照之"四川穆坪董卜韓胡宣慰司印"字様，漢右滿左，字各三行，字畫極細而頭尾曲屈，與前述"四川長河西魚通寧遠軍民宣慰使司印"完全一樣(圖十二)。

董卜韓胡爲元明時四川徼外三十六番之一。《明史》(卷三一一)，《四川土司傳·天全六番招討司》云："三十六番者，皆西南諸部落。洪

圖十二

武初，先後至京，授職賜印。立都指揮使二。曰烏斯藏，曰朵甘。爲宣慰司者三，曰朵甘，曰董卜韓胡，曰長河西魚通寧遠。爲招討司者六，爲萬户府者四，爲千户所者十七，是爲三十六種。或三年，或五年一朝貢，其道皆由雅州人，詳《西番傳》。”同書(卷三三一)，《西域傳三》，有《董卜韓胡宣慰司》之專章，云：“董卜韓胡宣慰司，在四川威州之西，其南與天全六番接。永樂九年，酋長南葛遣使奉表入朝，貢方物。……降敕慰諭，使比年一貢，賜金印、冠帶。”前引《大明一統志》(卷八九)，“西蕃”記載明代于歸順吐蕃各族所置三十三指揮司、宣慰使、招討司、萬户府、千户所中，與“長河西魚通寧遠宣慰使司”並列者即有“董卜韓胡宣慰使司”。《蜀中廣記》(卷三二)，《邊防記第二》，川西二，保縣引《保(縣)志》云：“西北生番有孟董十八寨，三國孟獲董卜之裔也，謂之孟董番，亦名董卜韓胡。唐時哥鄰君董卧庭等求内附，處其衆于維壩等州，居小鐵圍山，去縣可七八日程，東抵雜谷八稜碉，摸坡河在東，如卜河在北，即古之孫水也。南流雅州，以牛皮爲船，既渡則曝皮于岸，候干復用焉。永樂八年歸附進貢，授宣慰使司都指揮同知。貢道有三，一由雜谷八稜碉出保縣，一由清溪口出崇慶州，一由靈關出雅州。近與雜谷不睦，故直由雅安。”清《嘉慶四川通志》(卷九七)，《武備志十六》，土司二，天全州黎雅營屬，有“穆坪董卜韓瑚(胡)宣慰使司丹紫江楚，其先于前明世襲土職，至堅參喃喀，于國朝康熙元年歸誠，仍授原職，請領宣慰司印信。乾隆十年，頒給號紙，住牧穆坪。其地東至卧龍關七百餘里，交瓦寺土司界。南至靈關四十餘里，交天全州界。西至廢通蛇勒章谷六百餘里，交洽邊土司界。北至板噶落六百餘里，交新疆沃日土司界。四至共一千九百四十餘里。每年認納貢馬四匹，折征銀三十二兩。又舊管魚通地方草糧五十石，折征銀一兩，共折征銀五十兩，解赴布政司完納"，是康藏土司中規模相當大的一個。俗稱"木坪土司"。至民國18年(1929年)改流，于其地設寶興縣。此印未刻頒鑄紀年，但由印體大小大大超過明代規定的尺寸，故知其爲清代遺物无疑。其與右方漢文對照之左方少數民族文字，當係滿文，合清代官印之常制。其鑄頒時間當不早過康熙元年(1662年)。

10. 清"四川長河西魚通寧遠軍民宣慰使司印"8.6厘米見方，寬邊，印面鑄"四川長河西魚通寧遠軍民宣慰使司印"漢藏(滿)對照各十六字，兩種文字各占印面之半，漢右滿左，字各三行，字畫極細而頭尾曲屈(圖十三)。其形制大小與印文書體風格，與上述"四川穆坪董卜韓胡宣慰司印"完全相同。

圖十三

明清之四川長河西魚通寧遠宣慰司在今之西康康定一帶，元爲碉門魚通黎雅長河西寧遠等處宣撫司。《元史》(卷六十)，地理四，陝西省轄地有"碉門魚通黎雅長河西寧(遠)等處宣撫司"的記載。明襲元置，《大明一統志》(卷八九)《西蕃》載云："西蕃即吐蕃也，其先本羌屬，凡百餘種，散處河、湟、江、岷間。……元憲宗始……又于四川徼外置‘碉門魚通黎雅長河西等處宣撫司’。……本朝洪武六年，詔吐蕃各族酋長舉故有官職者，至京授職。遂置五衙門，建官賜印，俾因俗爲治。……今其地爲指揮司、宣慰司、招討司、萬户府、千户所，凡三十有三。”有“長河西魚通寧遠宣慰使司”列在其下。萬曆年間申時行等修《明會典》(卷一〇八)，朝貢四，西戎下，長河西魚通寧遠等處：“洪武十六年，置長河西等處軍民安撫使司，每年一貢，給與勘合，于四川比號，雅州入境。每貢只許五六十人，多不過一百人，方物該守關官員辯論，申送都、部、按三司審實起送。後改昇宣慰司。弘治以來，人數漸多。嘉靖二年，題用弘治以前例，不許過一千人。隆慶三年，定三年一貢，每貢一千人，内五百人全賞，五百人減賞，于全賞内起送八人赴京，餘留邊聽賞。”《明史》(卷三三一)《西域傳三》有《長河西魚通寧遠宣慰司》專篇載云：“長河西魚通寧遠宣慰司，在四川徼外，地通烏思藏，唐爲吐蕃。元時置碉門、魚通、黎、雅、長河西、寧遠六安撫司，隸土蕃宣尉司。”洪武十六年，“命置長河西等處軍民安撫司”。二十年，“遣惟善招撫長河西、魚通、寧遠諸處”。三十年，“置長河西魚通寧遠宣慰司，自是修貢不絕。初，魚通及寧遠長河西，本各爲部，至是始合爲一”。脱漏一“使”字。明沈德符《萬曆野獲編》(卷三〇)《土司・土酋名號》記載説：“今土司衙門稱號，其字多復叠，非内地州縣一字二字之例。……至于西北番，又有‘長河西魚通定遠宣尉使司’，則俱七字。”有“使”字，與《明一統志》相合而與《明史》不同。至“寧”字作“定”，則與二書皆不合。《蜀中廣記》(卷三五)載：“《志》云：孫水俗謂之長河，天全長河西，以在孫水之西也。”其地在康定(打箭爐)。入清以後，俗稱“明正土司”，康熙五年(1666年)歸附，是時土司名丹怎札克巴。乾隆修《大清一統志》(卷三〇六)，四川，雅州，關隘：“明正長河西魚通寧遠軍民宣慰司，即打箭爐。其地在大渡河外，直黎、雅之西，自古爲荒服地。元置三安撫司，曰長河西，曰魚通，曰寧遠，隸吐蕃宣慰司。明初合爲長河西魚通寧遠宣慰司，世授土職。本朝康熙五年，土酋蛇蠟吒吧歸附，仍授原職，屬雅州。三十九年，藏番昌側集烈等侵據其地，詔遣四川提督唐希順發兵討平之。番族萬二千餘户，相率歸附，仍以故宣慰司蛇蠟吒吧之妻工喀襲職，管轄十五鍋莊番民，并新附各土司，及五十六土千户，三年一貢馬，每年輸納雜糧。自後商賈輻輳，遂成巨鎮。因使官兵駐守，遣監督一員，以榷茶稅。雍正七年，設雅州府同知分駐其地，兼轄番漢。自理塘、巴塘以西，直抵西藏，延袤數千里，悉入版圖。……而打箭爐實爲諸番朝貢互市之要口云。"清代明正土司所轄共四十八部，地方甚大，與德爾格忒並爲關外二主，趙爾豐經營西康時與宣統三年改流，繳印信號紙。

此印大小形制及印文風格，亦與上述清代"四川長河西魚通寧遠軍民宣慰使司印"完全一樣，足證此二印爲清代大抵同時之土司官印，其鑄頒時間當不早過康熙元年(1662 年)。

11. "鹽源縣爪别安撫司印"印二方，一方 7.6 厘米見方，邊寬 0.7 厘米，鑄滿漢對照之"鹽源縣爪别安撫司印"字樣，漢字在右凡二行，滿文在左凡三行，應爲清代土司官印(圖十四)。

圖十四

爪别土司屬麽些族，在今鹽源縣境，清康熙四十九年(1710 年)玉珠珀歸降後授此司之職。乾隆時修《大清一統志》(卷三〇五)，四川，寧遠府，建置沿革："鹽源縣……洪武二十五年，改爲柏興千户所，屬建昌衛。二十七年，改置鹽井衛軍民指揮使司。本朝初，亦曰鹽井衛。雍正六年罷衛，改置鹽源縣，屬寧遠府。”又關隘：“爪别安撫司，在鹽源縣。其地東至小西番，西至喇嘛。本朝康熙四十九年，土酋玉珠珀歸附，授宣撫司。今屬會鹽營。”自玉珠珀以後，其世系爲巳甬補—斯貴—紹先—國當—天錫—廷樑(光緒十五年襲職)。自巳甬補以後，即以巳爲姓。轄地東至小番，西至喇嘛，南至古柏樹，北至水裏，共820里，管民1253户。年納糧銀43兩。民國時土司巳正疆，已極微弱。

另一方7厘米見方，邊寬0.9厘米，印面鑄“鹽源縣爪别安撫司印”漢篆三行九字，筆畫圓轉，與上印之作方折者不同(圖十五)。漢篆而外，别无其他少數民族文字。印體較小而印邊特寬。凡此種種形制特徵，皆與上述一印相異，待考。

此二印均未著紀年，但印文冠有“鹽源縣”字樣。如上引文獻記載所雲，鹽源縣地在清初爲鹽井衛軍民指揮使司，至雍正六年(1728年)始罷衛改置鹽源縣，屬寧遠府轄。故其鑄頒年代，均不能早過雍正六年(1728年)。

12. 清“後所土百户印”印7厘米見方，邊寬1厘米，印面漢文三行“後所土百户印”六年，别无其他民族文字(圖十六)。

圖十五

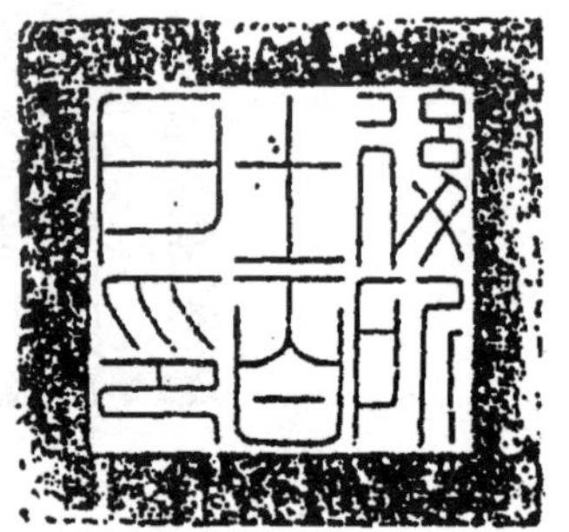

圖十六

清《嘉慶四川通志》(卷九七)，《武備志十六》，土司二，鹽源縣會鹽營屬，除“中所土千户”“左所土千户”“右所土千户”之外，尚有“前所土百户”與“後所土百户”。其“後所土百户”，云：“後所土百户白世榮，係麽些夷人。其先白馬塔于康熙四十九年投誠，世系呈請承襲，頒給印信號紙，住牧後所。其地東至小橋三十里，交會鹽營屬木裏安撫司界。南至喇白洛山頂一百里，交會鹽營屬左所土千户界。西至雅押克山八十里，交會鹽營屬木里安撫司界。北至大河邊十五里，交會鹽營屬木裏安撫司界。四至共二百五十五里，所管各村夷民七十四户，每年認納蕎糧四門二升，赴會鹽營上納，折充兵米。”其地當在鹽源縣境。按土司中之土百户，因級别較低，除給予號紙之外，印信則或有或无，大抵視其轄地範圍大小或地位之重要與否而定。如松潘廳漳蠟營所屬之巴細蛇住壩寨土百户、阿細拓弄寨土首户、上卓爾格寨土百户等，皆“于雍正元年歸誠授職，頒給號紙，无印信”。(見本書卷九六)乃至土千户亦有如此者。據前録文所載，後所土百户轄地二百五十餘里，屬規模較大者，故得有印。但畢竟級别所限，官未入流，印文簡略，漢文之外别无滿文對照，想係與此有關。此印鑄頒時間，當不早過康熙四十九年(1710 年)。

13. 明景泰四年(1453 年)“都綱之印”印 5. 8 厘米見方，印面鑄疊篆“都綱之印”四字(圖十七)。背刻“景泰四年三月□日禮部造”十字。

圖十七

“都綱”乃僧官之號。《萬曆野獲編》(卷二七)，僧道，“僧道異恩”條云：“番僧之號凡數等，最貴曰‘大慈法王’，曰‘西天佛子’。次曰‘大國師’，曰‘國師’，曰‘禪師’，曰‘都綱’，曰‘喇嘛’。”《明史》(卷七五),《職官志四》:“府僧綱司, 都綱一人, (從九品), 副都綱一人。州僧正司, 僧正一人。縣僧會司, 僧會一人。……俱洪武十五年置, 設官不給禄。”萬曆年間申時行等修《明會典》(卷二二六), 僧録司載:“國初置善世院, 洪武十五年改僧録司。……在外僧人, 府屬僧綱司, 州屬僧正司, 縣屬僧會司管領, 皆統于本司。”“凡各處額設寺, 俱有僧人住持, 從各寺僧人保舉有戒行、通經典者, 僧綱等司, 申本司給與劄付。”“凡度僧……在外從僧綱等司造册給批。俱由本司轉申禮部施行。”是“僧綱”乃封建政府正式設立的地方府級僧官, 隸屬于中央之僧録司, 管理本州申報僧人度牒及向僧録司推薦寺廟住持人選等事宜。《蜀中廣記》(卷三一)引《三邊志》云:“(松潘)城西有大悲寺, 唐天寶間僧廣所創也。國初設僧綱司, 以僧惠心爲都綱掌其事。景泰改元, 吐蕃猖獗, 累欲發兵剿討, 嗣都綱智中往撫慰之, 番乃革心嚮化。事聞, 昇智中爲崇化禪師, 賜以銀印、冠帽、袈裟、藏經之屬。智中, 浙之仁和人, 姓姜氏, 别號一天。”此印存于松茂之地, 景泰四年鑄頒, 或與僧智中有關。印大 5.8 厘米見方, 合明代一寸八分强, 與上引《明會典》一寸九分的記載完全吻合。此印雖非土司官印, 然爲明王朝頒給康區土司轄境宗教管理機構之官印, 且有明確紀年, 亦爲研究明代康區土司歷史不可多得之珍貴文物, 故一並附考于此。

“都綱之印”亦有見于其他金石學文獻者。如羅振玉《赫連泉館古印存》即有鈐印一枚, 其大小形制與此全同, 未注有无背刻紀年文字, 亦不云得于何所, 觀此印可定其爲明代遺物。

《明史》(卷三一〇)《土司傳》序稱:“考洪武初, 西南夷來歸者, 即用原官授之。其土官銜號曰宣慰司, 曰宣撫司, 曰招討司, 曰安撫司, 曰長官司。以勞績之多寡, 分尊卑之等差, 而府州縣之名亦往往有之。襲替必奉朝命, 雖在萬里外, 必赴闕受職。天順末, 許土官繳呈勘奏, 則威柄漸弛。成化中, 令納粟備賑, 則規取日陋。孝宗雖發憤釐革, 而因循未改。嘉靖九年始復舊制, 以在州縣官隸驗封, 宣慰、招討等官隸武選。隸驗封者, 布政司領之; 隸武選者, 都指揮領之。于是文武相維,比于中土矣。”清代大承襲明制而略有變化。以上所録土司官印以清代者爲多，明代者較少，以其年代久遠之故，然皆有關明清四川土司歷史不可多得之實物史料，誠可貴也。

整理者説明：原稿无篇題、序號、頁碼，除火把簇等少數印文外，類多簡略，至有僅著十餘字或有鈐印而无考文者。所引古籍文字，往往未經核對，頗有出入未確，係未成篇之草稿。今核查原書，並適當補充資料寫定，加標篇題，以成此文。其撰稿時間約在40年代中，故文中所注土司所在今地，皆屬民國時區劃。如有舛誤之處，責係于己身，與先生无關。

張勛燎

（張勛燎據20世紀40年代手稿整理，見《四川大學考古專業創建四十周年暨馮漢驥教授百年誕辰紀念文集》，四川大學出版社2001年出版）

松理茂汶羌族考察雜記

1938年暑假，余得四川大學西南社會科學研究所的支助，只身前往松潘、理縣、茂汶作羌民族考察，歷時三月。次年夏，又擔任教育部組織的川康科學考察團社會組組長，再次前往調查。現將兩次搜集所得羌人材料若干，結合古代文獻記載的有關歷史情況，整理成文，以供研究羌民族問題之參考。

一、羌民族的歷史

中國歷史上所見之羌，其所占之地域頗廣，北自陝西之南部，甘肅青海之東南，沿川藏邊境，南至雅屬及嘉定，此半月形之山地，均曾爲羌民族居留之所。但二千餘年以來，羌人北受匈奴等民族之侵襲，東南受漢民族之壓迫，西受西藏民族之蹂躪，其未絶滅者，非嚮化于漢人，即變而爲藏人，其所剩餘者只四川西北之松、理、茂、汶數縣之地而已。即此數縣之中，亦非全爲羌人，其沿河及交通便利之處，多爲漢人，其西北，則又多爲西番與嘉戎也(西番、嘉戎均屬藏族)。

“羌”一名詞之最早見者，莫若《竹書》《詩經》及《尚書》。《竹書紀年》：殷商成湯“十九年大旱，氐羌來賓”。又《詩・商頌・殷武》：“自彼氐羌，莫敢不來享，莫敢不來王。”及《周書・牧誓》：“……庸、蜀、羌、髳、微、盧、彭濮人；稱爾干，比爾干，立爾矛，予其誓。”此數處所記載，可相信之程度，自屬可以商榷。其所言氐羌究爲何民族，亦无從考見。不過終宗周之世，氐羌之名，不見于載籍。説者謂周戎，即後來之西羌。此説既難證明，然亦不能否認也。

西漢之世，羌族漸盛，北與匈奴相結，時爲西南之邊患，後經趙充國、馮奉世之討伐，始稍平服，但未能絶也。王莽篡漢，收西羌地，置海西郡(今青海)徙罪人以實之。及莽敗，羌族復據西海，時爲邊亂。

羌與戎，大概有相當之關係。《後漢書·西羌傳》直以戎爲羌，在周時則皆稱之曰戎，或曰西戎。其他種之戎，亦不下十餘種。説者謂周之世不言羌，或其諱言羌，因羌之字爲“羊”與“人”，含有輕視之意。而周人諱之之原因，因周民族之一部分爲羌，又與羌互通婚姻，因周之母族爲姜，姜，即羌也。《後漢書·西羌傳》：“西羌之本，出自三苗，姜姓之别也。”此但可以聊備一解，不足以爲典據也。

《西羌傳》又言，羌之始祖，原出于戎，如“不知爰劍何戎之别也”。又《華陽國志》“有六夷，羌胡，羌虜，白蘭峒，九種之戎”。是皆以羌爲戎者。

按西漢之舊制，益州部置蠻夷騎都尉，梁州部置護羌校尉，幽州部置領烏桓校尉。皆持節領護，理其怨結，歲時循行，問所疾苦，又數遣使驛通動静，使塞外羌爲吏耳目，州郡因此可得警備。東漢初，隗囂利用羌兵，與漢相距。光武平囂，置護羌校尉，以牛邯領之，西方之局稍定。其後馬武平羌，因校尉不職，遂去其官，已而又以羌禍未靖，復立校尉。

東漢爲歷史上羌民族之全盛時期，亦爲當時漢王朝統治最大之患。僅以光武之世而言，據《後漢書·光武紀》記載：建武十年(34 年)十一月，“先零羌寇金城(金城郡故城在今蘭州廣武縣之西南)、隴西，來歙率諸將擊羌于五溪(《續漢書·郡國志》云隴西襄武縣有五谿聚)，大破之”。十一年(35 年)四月，“先零羌寇臨洮”。十月，“因隴西太守馬援擊破先零羌，徙至天水隴西扶鳳”。十二年(36 年)十二月，“金城郡屬隴西郡屬参狼羌寇武都，隴西太守馬援討降之”。十三年(37 年)七月，“廣漢徼外白馬羌豪率種人内屬”。中元元年(56 年)十一月，“参狼羌寇武都，敗郡兵。隴西太守劉盱遣軍救之，及武都郡兵討叛羌，皆破之”。終東漢之世，其禍未嘗稍戢。傾全國之兵，竭府庫之財，經百戰之苦，乃僅能克之，然不能終絶也(其事詳載《後漢書·西羌列傳》，可以詳看)。故范曄嘗嘆“自西戎作逆，未有陵斥上國，若斯其熾也”。

魏晉南北朝之世，羌族仍盛，且有時爲患更烈。因漢人每對于異族歸降之後，每每遷之内地，以爲可以同化于漢族，詎知其患，反及于中國腹地，轉甚于未遷之時也。三國之時，羌人所居之地，接近蜀魏，二國爭欲引爲己援，羌人則坐收其利。司馬氏滅蜀代魏，羌患稍舒，元康以後，賈后與八王之亂，接踵而起，中原板蕩，西北異族，亦乘機而起，變成南北朝一百三十餘年之擾攘局面。即外人所稱爲中國歷史上之黑闇時代，亦即俗所謂五胡亂華者(五胡，匈奴、鮮卑、羯、氐、羌)，氐羌亦各爲其中之一也。

五胡十六國之中，所謂羌氐之族者，一爲仇池之祖之略陽楊氏，一爲前秦之祖之略陽苻氏，一爲後凉之祖之略陽吕氏。以上三者，即歷史上所稱之氐族。氐與羌在史籍中雖屬並稱，而氐與羌之關係，實无從考見。羌之大部，則爲南安姚氏，即後秦之祖也。其事迹均載在史傳，兹不贅(仇池見《魏書・氐傳》《北史・氐傳》，前秦見《晉書・載記》，後凉見《晉書・載記》，後秦見《晉書・姚弋仲載記》)。又《北史》(卷九六)，《列傳八四》，宕昌、鄧至、白羌、黨項等傳，附國傳，亦爲有關氐羌之記載。

氐羌之族，自隋唐而後，則寂焉无聞，大抵其近中原者，多同化于漢族。西方之羌，因吐蕃之興起，亦爲其掩蓋。因吐蕃强盛，征服其周圍民族，中國史籍，乃盡以吐蕃名之，而不復分别之也。

現在之羌人，與歷史上所見之羌人，其關係若何，自爲待考見之問題。不過松理汶茂之羌民，决非完全由他處之羌人，因受漢人之壓迫，而後徙居其地者，自可斷言。現在松理汶茂之羌人，均有同樣之悠久歷史，不過其山嶺阻絶，與漢人之交通較少，故吾人知之較遲耳。但現在之羌人，與歷史上之羌人，自有其相當之關係，此與各地記載中可見之。

《後漢書》以爲秦以後之羌，皆出自无弋爰劍："无弋爰劍者，秦厲公時爲秦所拘執，以爲奴隸，不知爰劍何戎之别也。後得亡歸，而秦追之急，藏于岩穴中，得免。羌人爰劍，初藏穴中，秦人焚之，有景象如虎，爲其蔽火，得以不死。既出，又與劓女遇于野，遂成夫婦。女耻其狀，被髮覆面，羌人因以爲俗。遂俱亡入三河間。諸羌見爰劍不死，怪其神，其畏事之，推以爲豪。河湟間少五穀，多禽獸，以射獵爲事，爰劍教之田畜，遂見敬信，廬落種人，依之者日益衆。羌人謂奴爲无戈，以爰劍嘗爲奴隸，故因名之。其後世世爲豪。至爰劍曾孫忍時，秦獻公初立，欲復穆公之迹，兵臨渭首，滅狄獂戎，忍季父卬畏秦之威，將其種人附落而南，出賜支河曲西數千里，與衆羌絶遠，不復交通，其後子孫分别，各自爲種，任隨所之，或爲氂牛種，越嶲羌是也。或爲白馬種，廣漢羌是也。或爲參狼種，武都羌是也。忍及弟舞，獨留湟中，並多娶妻婦，忍生九子，爲九種。舞生十子，爲十七種。羌之興盛，從此起矣。"又言："自爰劍後，子孫支分，凡百五十種，其九種在賜支河首以西，及在蜀、漢徼北。"關于蜀郡徼外之羌，《後漢書》亦列有數種："氂牛、白馬羌在蜀、漢，其種别名號，皆不可紀知之也。建武十三年(36年)廣漢塞外白馬羌豪樓登等，率種人五千餘户内屬，光武封樓登爲歸義君長。至和帝永元六年(94年)蜀郡徼外大牂夷種羌豪造頭等率種人五十餘萬口内屬，拜造頭爲邑君長，賜印綬。至安帝永初元年(107年)蜀郡徼外羌龍橋等六種萬七千二百八十口内屬。明年蜀郡徼外羌薄申等八種三萬六千九百口，復舉土内屬。冬，廣漢塞外參狼種羌二千四百口復來内屬。"

以上所言蜀郡徼外之羌，其與汶山之羌有别。其所在之地大多在汶山郡之南，或其東北。汶山郡之羌，武帝時，其國名或種名，稱曰冉駹。按《史記》(卷一一六)西南夷傳言："自嶲以東北，君長以十數，徙(音斯，即後來之徙縣)筰都(椊音才各反，即後之沈黎郡)最大。自筰以東北，君長以十數，冉駹(師古曰今夔州開州首領多姓冉者，本皆冉種也，駹音龍)最大。其俗或土著或移徙。在蜀之西，自冉駹以東北，君長以十數，白馬最大(階州茂縣漢白馬氐地)。皆氐類也。此皆巴蜀西南外蠻夷也。"(《漢書》同)

《後漢書》(卷八六)《南蠻西南夷列傳》所言較詳："冉駹夷者，武帝所開，元鼎六年(公元前111年)以爲汶山郡。至地節三年(公元前67

年)，夷人以立郡賦重，宣帝乃省並蜀郡，爲北部都尉。其山有六夷七羌九氐，各有部落，其王侯頗知文書，而法嚴重。貴婦人，黨母族，死者燒其屍。土氣多寒，在盛夏冰猶不釋。故夷人冬則避寒入蜀爲傭，夏則違暑反其邑。衆皆依山居止，累石爲室，高十餘丈爲邛籠。又土地剛鹵，不生谷粟麻菽，惟以麥爲資，而宜畜牧。有牦牛无角，一名童牛，肉重千斤，毛可爲毦(音冒)。出名馬。有靈羊可療毒。又有食藥鹿，鹿麑有胎者，其腸中糞，亦可療毒疾。又有五角羊麝香，輕毛毼鷄牲牲。其人能作旄氈班罽青頓毞毲羊羧之屬，特多雜藥。地有咸土，煮以成鹽。麢羊牛馬食之皆肥。其西又有三河槃于虜，北有黄石，北地盧水胡，其表乃爲徼外。靈帝時復分蜀郡北部，爲汶山郡云。”

此處所言之六夷、七羌、九氐，自然无從考見，而夷又爲普通之名詞，非民族之名詞也。其言“貴婦人，黨母族”，在現在之羌民中，猶有相當痕迹可尋。“死則燒其屍”一層，與過去三十年前，羌民中之埋葬風俗，完全相同，近則多學漢人之穴葬矣。“冬則避寒入蜀爲傭”，羌人至今尚如此。成都市上之羌人，掛牌打井者，到處可見也。至于“累石爲室，高者至十餘丈爲邛籠”語，則爲羌民族居室之特徵，非他民族所有者。故《後漢書》所記，雖已二千餘年，尚可爲現在汶理茂羌人之寫照也。

《華陽國志》所言略同：“汶山郡，本蜀郡北部冉都尉，孝武元封四年置，舊屬縣八，户二十五萬……有六夷羌胡羌虜白半峒九種之戎。牛馬旄氈班罽青頓毞毲羊羧之屬，特多雜藥名香，土地剛鹵，不宜五穀，惟種麥。而冰多寒，盛夏凝凍不釋。故夷人冬則避寒人蜀傭賃自食，夏則避暑反落，歲以爲常。故蜀人謂之作百石子也。”

然汶山郡之羌人，在西漢時，何以稱之曰冉駹？此亦不難索解。冉駹駹之號，或爲其酋豪之姓或名，當時不察，即以之爲其國號或種號。以酋豪之名或姓，爲種名之事，在羌族中，亦頗常見。如范史言：“其(指羌而言)俗世族无定，或以父名母姓爲種號。”又如“研(无弋爰劍之玄孫，忍之子)至豪健，故羌中號其後爲研種”。又如爰劍十三世孫名燒當，“復豪健，其子孫更以燒當爲種號”。冉駹之名，亦不外此例。《後漢書》言：“其山(汶山郡)有六夷七羌九氐。”《華陽國志》亦言：“有六夷羌胡羌虜白蘭峒九種之戎。”其文雖不甚可解，大概此處之“夷”亦係指羌而言。如《華陽國志》言：“汶山曰夷，南中曰昆明，漢嘉越巂曰筰，蜀中曰邛，皆夷種也。”其曰夷、昆明、筰、邛者，其實皆羌類也。

唐以前之各聚落之名，今多不可考。唐以後之名稱，尚有流傳至今者。如理番河(即沱江，又稱雜谷腦河)兩岸之羌人，唐時稱白狗羌，如《唐書》：“武德六年，白蘭白狗羌遣使人貢，七年，以白狗等羌地，置維、恭二州。”維州即現在之威州也。恭州則不甚可考。又如當狗城，以其當白狗羌之路，故名。即廣德二年(764 年)劍南節度嚴武破吐蕃拔當狗城者是也。當狗城之遺址，在于某一地點，今已不可考。大抵總不出維州以西，沱江之下游也。又如籠山城，在唐時爲羌中最强者之一，廣德七年(769 年)，吐蕃陷維州籠山城即此也。今爲籠山寨頗險要。又茂縣城外之静州土司，家藏有唐代敕文，前不久方在 1935 年戰亂中損毁，不勝惋惜。自宋元而後，各羌寨之名，均斑斑可考。因其過詳，不能在此處講述。

二、羌區之地理

羌地之山曰岷山，江曰岷江。岷山即汶山，《史記・封禪書》：“自華以西，名山口瀆山。瀆山者，汶山也。”《漢書》作崏山，岷汶崏，均可通。岷山亦即所謂西山之一部分。“蜀之險在西山，西山之險，州其要領也。”岷江者，即古代地理書中之所謂江源。《禹貢》“岷山導江”，《荀子》“江出于岷山，其源可以濫觴”者，古人不知金沙江，故以岷江爲江源。岷江亦名汶江，亦曰都江，亦曰外水，岷江則通稱也。

羌地之山窮水惡，則罕有其匹。自灌縣而上，即无平地。清末時，有灌縣人董玉書(湘琴)者，以戎馬書生自負，後人松潘總兵夏毓琇幕，作《松游小唱》一詞，詞雖不甚工，而頗能描寫，淋漓盡致。如其中寫岷江沿河風景一段，云“松潘西望路漫漫，風景漸難看，河在中間，山在兩邊，九曲羊腸偏生跨在山腰半。抬頭一綫天，低頭一束練，灘風響似百萬鳴蟬，纏綿不斷。最可厭，一山才斷一山連，面目无更换，總是司空見慣。問蠶叢開國幾經年，這滄桑如何不變”？

岷江水流之急，幾沿河皆灘。其最淺之處，雖僅没脛，然亦不能涉而過也。其惟一交通，則惟縋索與索橋。如隔河僅數十步，有時如欲達彼岸，需繞行一日程或二日程方能達到也。岷江因其水流之急，故爲一種極大之冲刷媒介，河床深至數千尺以上，兩岸多係懸崖，甚少可種植之冲積河階。

自映秀灣而上，石多土少。其岩石多片麻岩（gneiee）、片岩（sshist），其他如花崗岩、石灰岩，亦甚普遍。不過因山勢過陡，土壤均不能沾着，多隨雨水冲刷以去，致成俗所謂“九石一土”之現象，氣候南苦雨，而北苦旱。自娘子嶺以至汶川縣，雨降甚豐，故草木暢茂，山色秀麗。自汶川縣城以上，則童山濯濯，岩石外露，不復見草木青葱之色矣。全年中最高温度爲8月（30.52℃），最低温度爲1月（0.3℃），最多雨者，爲五六兩月。每年落雨平均只38天。故氣候甚佳，不若成都之平原之潮濕，及青甘之乾燥也。其最高之山峰，終年積雪，四時不解，自10月初雪綫開始下降，至1月則降至河谷。至次年三四月時低處之雪，方開始融解。故其農作之時間，由4月起至10月止。其地每日午時後必風，其原因乃由于河谷過深，上下氣壓不同之所致。

羌民族所居留之地，全爲沿岷江河谷，及其支流之河谷。因河谷之地，海拔較低，故可耕種，再高則莊稼不能生長矣。沿岷江正流，近河床水邊便爲大路之地，多爲漢人，或漢化之羌人。羌民所居之地，則爲半山斜坡之上，再上則森林及草原帶，人迹罕到。彼此間之交通極爲不便，故稱溝。

羌民對其環境之應適，可謂十分周到，雖漢民至其地者，亦不能不學羌民之辦法。房屋即其一例也。

三、羌民之體質

羌人之體質，現在幾无所知，華西大學之Morse醫生，曾作不少之測量，但彼則將所測量之絶對數發表，未曾用統計方法，計算其恒數，故不能利用作比較。去年中央研究院曾派人在羌中測量近千人，但尚未能計算其結果。

以余個人之觀測，羌人之體質，大體與漢人相同，而與西番及嘉戎稍異。但其中全无蒙古人式之眼折，亦一異事。羌人之體質，細察之可分爲兩部。即汶川理番爲一部，茂縣至松潘者爲一部。汶川理番之羌人，體較高。但其特别惹人注意者，即爲其勾形之鼻。此陶蘭士所以謂羌人爲東方之猶太人者。此種勾形之鼻，余初見之，頗不得其解。後至嘉戎地界，乃知其鼻形之由來，或者爲如此。嘉戎之鼻高狹而長。羌人原有之鼻（于茂縣松潘羌人中可以見之）低闊而短。若將高長之鼻，加之于低闊之鼻之上，即成勾形之狀。故此種鼻形，並不需假設羌人爲西方民族之遷于此者，而實爲一種混合之鼻形也。

四、羌民族現在之人口

羌民族人口之確數，則毫无統計，茂縣理番編制保甲村時均羌漢不分，混合計之，實不知其中羌人有若干，漢人有若干也。至土司所轄之地帶，估計之數，亦不可得而知。據汶川縣之保甲系統，羌人男 1781 人，女 1721 人，共 3502 人。此數目當然不能視爲可靠。因保甲編制丁口時，多有隱匿之事，藉以避免差役，但无論如何，汶川縣之羌人，至多不能超過 5000 人以上也。余個人之印象及估計，現在所有之羌人，至多不過 60000 人，即茂縣 35000 人，理番縣 20000 人，汶川縣 5000 人。此數目當然極不可靠，不過爲一種猜測而已。

羌人人口，在近百年以來，減少之數，實爲可驚。自經 1935 年戰亂之後，若干羌寨，全被焚毁，其死于兵及瘟病者，又至少在 1/10 以上也。如汶川之蘿葡寨，爲羌人中最富庶之區，據言約百年前，其地有人口 600 餘人，1935 年前約 400 人，以後只 350 餘人而已。又黑虎七族，在明代及清初之時最爲惡蠢，其變叛掠劫，幾无歲无之。歷官其土者，均不能制，其惟一綏靖方法，即爲招撫。《四川通志》所載清康熙中茂縣舉人蔣復嵩所作《招撫黑虎七族記》，可以概見。其中有言："歷代以來，恃其山菁險阻，屢肆猖獗，而茂之黑虎生番尤甚。出没官道，掠擄我人民，□□我牲畜，歲无虛日。守土者議剿議撫，迄无成功，終明之世，未有能攝服者。"又《嘉慶四川通志》(卷九十)，武備志之邊防志引《明史》云，憲宗成化九年，"松潘指揮僉事堯彧志奏：……初黑虎寨最强，相傳有神術，先知官兵，未至即遁去，或潛伏要害竊發，屢敗我衆，按察使龔獨曰：我自不密耳，彼何能知。夜半密勒諸將繞兵進凡三十里，平明抵其寨，蠻大驚潰，斬縛各千人，得其首惡，餘潰死无算，既而大征，破寨二十餘，斬五百級，降者數千，皆編籍輸糧"。(整理者按：此處所引之《明史》，非清代官修之正史，當别是一私家所著書)其丁口之多，可以想見。現在之黑虎寨則如何？一進黑虎溝，則滿目荒涼，斷井頹垣，觸目皆是。即以黑虎之内五寨而言，原有居民600餘户，至1935年之前，尚餘200餘户，以後則只餘160餘户，600餘人而已。此不獨黑虎羌人爲然，七族亦如此。七族最盛時，有200餘屍。今則只餘15户而已。羌人衰落之象可以想見。

羌民族中人口之减少，爲一普遍現象，但此不獨以羌民族爲然。其他之原始民族，與其他高等文化民族接觸時，亦莫不如此。

五、羌人之物質文化

羌人之物質文化，可分下列之數類説明之。

(一)屋宇及室内之用具

羌人之屋宇，其建築之方法及樣式，與漢人者大異。在中國境内之屋宇形式，甚至東亞之屋宇(蒙古人遊牧之帳篷，另爲一種，自當除外)可分爲兩大系：一爲漢式之屋宇，二爲羌藏式之屋宇。漢式之屋宇，大都類能知之，故不贅。羌式之屋宇，除羌人外，藏人西番及嘉戎中均用之。藏番及嘉戎之屋宇，與羌人者，雖不无小異，但皆屬于一類。研究各種建築物，其重要之點，在其樣式，而不在建築之原料。因原料係受自然環境之支配，而建築樣式，則多少受文化及歷史背景之支配也。如羌人之建築，均係石制，因其地片石甚多，俯拾即是，若燒磚爲之，則反事倍而功半矣。他如蘿蔔岩片石甚少，其建築之墻垣，則築土爲之，不過其版築之方法，則與漢人稍異。

羌人之屋宇，幾全爲方形或長方形，通爲二層，下層爲牛羊豕圈，上層住人，再上爲平屋頂，大門開于正中之第一層，而樓梯則置于最後面，故登樓之時，必需經過牛羊圈之全部，其中黑暗穢臭，極爲可怖。全屋无第二門，所有人畜均由此門出入。問其何以如此，則曰“不緊慎”。第二層前面開小窗二，左右各一。故室中極昏暗。室内生火時，此二小窗，亦爲烟囱也。其接近漢人之地，大門則稍爲改良。大門安置于第二層，門左有小平臺一。先由獨木梯上小平臺，再右向而進大門。羌屋前面均有一小院，院與畜圈相通，人畜均由院門出入。院内及畜圈内，入秋時多置青草及小樹枝之類，稱曰“秏子”。厚約二三尺，牛羊豕踐踏之，排泄亦于其中，經冬乃腐，第二年四月中乃出之以爲肥料。對于羌人，此固一舉而兩得，但其穢臭，則實不堪言狀。天晴則穢氣薰人欲嘔，遇雨則糞穢没脛。彼等處之，反泰然若无其事也。

關于大門開于第一層之屋宇，第二層前面爲住宿之所，後面近樓梯處，爲游息炊爨之處，中有一照壁隔開。大門開在第二層者，兩邊爲住宿之處，正中爲廳，後面則爲炊爨之地也。

羌屋之平頂，爲屋宇中最密之處，後面之墻，高起七八尺，上供白石神位。其一旁爲矮平屋，高僅及人，以儲農具及收穫之食糧。屋頂後高前低，向前略斜形而偏于一角，雨水乃由最低處之木澗或石澗流出。周圍(前、左、右)之墻高出屋頂約尺餘，上覆以石板，以作護墻之用。屋頂之建築，其下爲口徑四五寸之樹木，平鋪之，令彼此相接，再上鋪小樹枝、荆棘、竹杪等，最上鋪以黏土，築之令堅實。初建之時，遇大雨則漏，但每下雨一次，即修補一次。人在上面工作，愈久則踐踏堅密，遇雨則不漏矣。但仍需時時填補，不然多次大雨之後，其上之黏土，大半將爲冲刷以去也。再者羌區中之雨降之大且久，故土頂尚可支持也。

室内之陳設，均甚簡單，其受漢化程度較深者，室内陳設多與漢人相同，椅、桌、板凳、床等均備，其他鍋碗筷、陶器等均係由漢地運往。其物質生活，多半已漢化(調查時，需將室内所有之陳設，開一清單)。羌人室中，有一特别設備，即鐵三足是也。其直徑約三尺餘，高二尺餘，重百餘斤。此三足多置于堂屋正中照壁之後，爲室内生活之中心，爲火爐爲炊食物之所，亦爲飲食之處。

三足之分佈，除羌人外，西番藏人，羅羅中均用之。三足在西番藏人羅羅中，爲極尊敬之物，家人及外來之客人在其前不能有不敬之舉動，如烘火時將足踏其上等，羌人中現雖无此種禁忌，想當初時亦有之。如現在羌中以此三足代表火神，如家中无鐵三足，必置三石以代表之。大概原來之三脚爲石，鐵乃後來之代替品也。

(二)農業

羌民爲農業民族，故農作爲其主要工作。其主要農作品爲芋麥，蕎子次之，青稞及麥又次之。芋麥四月種，八九月收穫。此爲其主要食糧，每家之中，倘能收芋麥十餘石，一年生活，即可解决。芋麥之傳入羌中，約在清乾隆以後。不過羌人皆以爲其自祖輩以來均有之。可見民族記憶力之不可靠。其歷來之主要農作，大概爲麥。《後漢書》“惟以麥爲資”是也。青稞爲大麥之一種，其名始見于《北史》，何時傳入羌中，或爲其地原有之變種，則不得而知。麥及青稞，今年十月種，明年六七月收，需時甚久，非宦庶之家，不能種植。麥曲爲敬客之上品，青稞則爲制酒用，種法與麥同。蕎子不知始于何時，爲窮人之主要食品，一年可兩熟，如將早芋麥收後，尚可種蕎麥一季也。

羌人之農作物，除以上者外，尚有麻與菸葉。麻爲其所織麻布之原料，每家必種之。《後漢書》言：“不生谷、粟、麻、菽。”此語實不盡然。不生谷米則有之，至于粟、麻、菽，則盛産之也。煙則全爲自吃之用。煙之傳入羌中，至早亦不過在清初之際，因菸草明末始傳入中國也。粟菽等類，均可種植，但羌人種之者少。蔬菜除辣椒外，亦不種。間有種小白菜秧者。其主要副産爲花椒，爲羌人之 Cash—Crop，每擔可售價五十餘元。

羌人中有一種特别種植方法，彼等稱之曰火地。其法將半山中坡度較平、灌木叢生之地，于夏秋之際，縱火焚之，不耕不鋤，亦不施肥料（火焚後之灰，亦爲一種肥料），將苦蕎種遍撒之，至秋後收穫。此亦前所言之“火種”也。秋後半山中花開似錦者，羌人大地所種之苦蕎也。

羌人之農作方法及農具，亦多與漢人者不同，漢人農人至其地者，亦多襲用羌人之方法。羌人農具中最特别者，則爲耕犁，此犁以雙牛挽之：一人牽牛，一人扶犁，遇有岩石處，則提犁以避之，過石則仍插入土中。其樣式較漢犁爲大，頗近似古代埃及近東等處所用之犁。

（三）手工業

羌人中之手工業，極爲幼稚。所有之木工金工等，均爲漢人入内爲之。其地之各種用具，多係購自市上，或由漢商小販輸入。他如棉布、油、鹽等，均係由外面運入者。羌人惟一之手工業，則爲織麻布。麻四五月種，九十月割，割後曬于屋頂，俟雨水日光浸透後，將麻皮剥下捶洗。在冬季女子无事，則打麻綫，以作織麻布之用。打麻綫不用紡車，而用紡錘，布織成後，必用杵在柱上搗之，制成衣後，每洗必需捶，不然者則不輕不暖。羌寨之中，早晚必聞砧杵之聲，實有“住人理寒服，萬結砧杵勞”之情况也。

（四）副業

背夫，爲羌人男子掙錢之惟一途徑，多于陰曆十月後四月前，農暇之時爲之。羌人不能挑抬，只能背，亦習慣使然也。又羌人不解經商，其地之商業，均由漢人爲之，往其地者，安岳、樂至人爲最多，即其中之土司式微，亦不知經商，如隴木司何九皋，今背于途如齊民也。羌人中之優秀兒童不令之讀書，則令之學端公，亦一副業也。

羌人中最重要之副業，則爲牧畜，因其地山多田少，曠地甚多，最宜于此種副業故也。牧畜以羊爲主要之牲口，牛豕與馬則甚少。羊則山羊綿羊均有，但以山羊爲最多。山羊在羌民之信仰中，極爲重要。如祭禮之犧牲，只能用山羊，不得用綿羊也。每家之羊群，窮者數十頭，富者數百頭。牛則多耕作之用，間亦有用馬者。

羌人雖有牛群及羊群，但彼等從不用乳及乳所制之食品，亦屬可怪之事。今人多以羌人原爲遊牧民族，此説須重加考慮。因未有曾爲牧畜民族，而輕易放棄其飲乳及食乳製品之習慣也。

（五）衣飾

羌人之衣飾，有一種特别習俗，即其色尚白。彼等以白爲上色，他色次之，黑色最下。如《明史》（卷三一一）《四川土司傳》載："正德二年，太監羅籥奏，茂州所轄卜南村、曲山等寨，乞爲白人，願納糧差。其俗以白爲善，以黑爲惡。禮部覆，番人向化，宜令人貢給賞。從之。"可知其尚白，由來已久。故現在羌人中之服色，多用各質料之本色。如麻毛等均用本來之白色，而不加色素，亦祟其原來尚白之遺意也。

羌人内衣，現在幾全用棉質土布，質料愈粗愈佳，至于洋布則非其所喜也。内衣制法，與漢人同，或爲羌婦自製，或爲漢人裁縫入内爲之代制。外衣則爲麻制，極粗厚耐用。衽在右，紐扣或爲麻制，或竟以帶代之。衣長及膝下，腰係帶，外再着羊皮之短背心，或黑羊毛織之對襟長背心。此種長背心，長及膝、極厚重，可御雨。大概背心之用，除禦寒外，多爲背負之用。因背負時，背心厚硬，借可減輕負重之摩擦力故也。女子之外衣，與男子略同。不過前短後長，因女子前面繫圍腰故也。

裹腿爲男女所必用，長五六尺，寬二寸許，麻制或羊毛制，裹法與漢稍異。山上荆棘甚多，故需裹腿以作保護。羌人不戴帽，均裹帕子，羌人原來戴氈帽，帕子乃自漢人中傳入，羌語中无帕子之名，仍以漢語帕子名之，可以概見也。明修《四川通志》曾載一有趣之故事："嘉靖中……風村一十七寨……詣軍門請降……亡何，他寨若番牌大力孫子皆請歸降，效風村故事……兵備使使石泉令李茂元受之。羌俗囚首无冠，茂元具漢冠，易其姓名書冠間，届日啓軍門，鐃吹數部，樅樹鼓大鉦，令諸羌魚鱗入。諸羌聞鼓鉦，望見漢冠，及朱杆彩旗，乃大喜，舉足跳舞，歡呼震天。乃出漢冠冠諸羌，諸羌跪起，各互視其首，踴躍東西走。既而又跪捧其冠以謝……"此可謂深知羌人心理。不過此處言羌俗囚首无冠，不知何所指也。

在清時羌人原蓄辮，現在黑水中尚如此。其他處羌人將髮全行剃去，惟顱頂留髮撮約錢大，長約四五寸。女子髮式如漢女，挽髻，閨女則梳辮，長則盤于頭之周圍。女子亦裹帕。

女子之戒指手鐲，均爲銀制，多仿漢式。現在羌中最時髦之耳環，則爲一緑色之玉石，約銅元大小，中穿小孔，貫以銀環。汶川、理番、茂縣之羌女均如此。至黑虎寨及黑水中，則銀環加大，重約兩餘。

其他之隨身物品，最重要者，則爲煙鬥及銅煙盒，男女必備。幼童自十四五歲後即帶之。女子必帶針筒一只，上綴以穗、珠飾、銅錢等物。

六、羌人之政治組織

羌人之政治組織，歷代以來，均極散漫。事急則彼此相依，事過則互相攻擊，故自秦漢以來，羌民族之人數雖衆，所占之地域雖廣，而從未建立强大之帝國。其中雖不乏杰出之士，如前秦苻氏、後秦姚氏等，但皆竊據一方，較之元人之征服歐亞，滿清之入主中原，則瞠乎其後矣。推原其故，厥爲缺乏組織是也。記載中之所能見者，如《後漢書》所言："不立君臣，无相長一，强則分種爲酋豪，弱則爲人附落，更相抄暴，以力爲雄，殺人償死，无他禁令。其兵常在山谷，短于平地，不能持久，而果于觸突，以戰死爲吉利，病終爲不祥。堪耐寒苦，同之禽獸。"自是以後，莫不如此。如《北史》所載羌之一種名宕昌者，言其"姓别自爲部落，酋帥皆有地分，不相統攝"。至唐時羌種之最强者，如黨項，亦復如是。《舊唐書》："其種每姓别自爲部落，一姓之中，復分爲小部落，大者萬餘騎，小者數千騎，不相統一。"此其所謂原始，不奴役于漢人，即奴役于藏人也。

唐以前之所謂酋帥，即元明之所謂土司，現在羌人土司中，亦有能溯其世系至于唐世者，不過其受中朝封爵多起自元明。故自元明而後，其世系均斑斑可考。清亦沿襲明制，甚少變革。兹將清代之重要土司列于後。

汶川縣：

瓦寺宣慰使司(原爲烏思藏人，明萬曆間平羌人後，駐牧于汶川縣之涂禹山)

理番縣：

梭磨宣慰司

卓克基長官司

松岡長官司(以上皆羌戎西番雜居)

九子屯(清乾隆間征金川後多已戎化而尚保存羌俗)

茂縣：

静州長官司

岳希長官司

隴木長官司

長寧安撫司

水草坪巡檢司(土司蘇朝□家藏有明萬曆敕文)

竹木坎副巡檢司(土司孫振寅現爲聯保主任，住椒子坪)

牟托巡檢土司

實大關副長官司

大定沙壩土千户

松坎土百户

大姓土百户

小姓土百户

小姓黑水土百户

以上不過就其有後裔及衙署可尋者。清代之增減損益尚不止此也。按：土司不一定爲羌人，亦有有功漢人，效莊蹻之王滇者。亦有藏人因征剿羌人，而遂長其地者。如瓦寺土司，原爲烏斯藏人，明萬曆中，因征羌人而駐牧其地。其中尚有原帶來之一部藏人，至今尚保存其一部分之語言。

現在土司制雖已取消，大半之土司，均已衰落，而尚有一部分之土司，雖无其位，尚有莫大之潛在勢力。其一舉一動，均爲羌人所畏服。

其編有保甲之區，土司多爲聯保主任，縣政府亦无如之何。是亦土司之變相也。

羌人性愛自由，尚平等，崇獨立，爲極端之個人主義，此其所以无大規模之政治組織，及明清以來，時常反抗土司制之由來也。因應付流官易，流官之任期亦有限，而土司之剥削，則終身无所逃避故也。土司制爲酋長制之變相，但土司制之功能及其實施之方式，至今尚未有能知其詳者。

七、羌人之社會組織

《西羌傳》言："其俗氏族无定，或以父名母姓爲種號，十二世後，相與婚姻。"《冉駹夷傳》亦言"貴婦人，黨母族"。故有根據此言，以爲羌人原係母系社會，《後漢書》所言爲母系社會之遺留。彼等又列舉羌人中"上門"之風盛行，入贅則女子不出母家，亦可認爲母系組織之遺。其羌人亡後，无論男女，必通知母族，若係女子，除通知母族(彼等名曰母舅)外，亦須通知母族之母族(羌人稱曰母舅)，彼等至時，則舉止傲慢，喪家對之，則極盡恭敬之能事。論者亦認爲此種風俗爲母系之遺。

不過此種解釋于理論上頗有困難。因前者曾以羌人爲遊牧民族，而遊牧民族中，則甚少有母系社會者。故吾人若以羌人原爲母系社會，則不當言其爲遊牧民族矣。《後漢書》中所言，其詞頗爲恍惚，不能知其真意所在。如氏族无定，與貴婦人黨母族等，並不一定爲母系社會之遺留也。

羌人中現在之氏族，則全无組織，但從其文化之他方面觀之，尚可見其氏族制度之痕迹。如同姓不婚(當以羌姓爲準，漢姓不足據)，或爲宗族外婚制之遺。《西羌傳》"十二世後，相與婚姻"之言，實不足爲典據。十二代所經之時間，至少需二三百年，但經如許久之時間後，又誰復能記憶之者。又普通之原始民族中之同族可通婚者，僅三世或五世後即可，不然者，雖百世亦不可也。據余所知，羌人中姨表姊妹可以爲婚，而姑表姊妹，則不能爲婚。詢其意則云，姑與父相似之處太多，而姨母則不然。果如此，則原爲母系民族之問題，亦不能成立。從前羌人火葬時，同族之人，均須到場，母姓則否。在每年十月初一還願之時，如一寨中有數姓居人，則每一姓備羊一頭，由端公祭山神後，每姓各人將羊携至家分食。在此時用羊膊骨所問之吉凶，亦各以每一姓爲分界。

羌人之火墳，亦每姓一座，絶不相混。不過現在因采用穴葬，此習已廢，然可見其爲宗族組織之遺也。

羌人中財産與姓氏之遺傳，均從父傳子，女子除嫁奩外，别无其他權利。即如端公，亦多父子相承，其法器亦傳子而不傳徒。

羌人中之工作及活動之中心，以一寨爲單位，而不以宗族爲單位。每一寨之中，少則一二姓，多則四五姓，而少有一姓一寨者。凡一切經濟活動、社會儀式，均全寨人赴之，而不以一族爲一族之單獨舉動也。如其宗教大典，四月初一之開山，十月初一之還願，均以一寨同雇一端公行之，而不一姓爲一姓之還願也。其神林及山神，均爲一寨所公有，而一寨又有一寨之公山，爲該寨樵蘇之所。他寨之人，不得侵犯。如農作忙時，則寨中人互相幫助，不以宗族而分軒輊也。

每寨之中，並无一定之正式首領，不過有一二人爲衆人公認之領袖，此種領導人物，並非世襲，亦非以家資富有而定，乃全以個人之才能而定。此類人平常爲寨中人所信服，遇有糾紛時，則皆取决之。現在凡編有保甲之區，政府多以之爲保甲長。

八、婚　姻

據典籍所載，羌人之婚俗，多與西北民族相同。《後漢書》："父没則妻後母，兄亡則納釐嫂，故國无鰥寡，種類繁殖。"又如《北史・宕昌羌傳》："父子伯叔兄弟死者，即以繼母、世叔母及嫂弟婦等爲妻。"再如《舊唐書・黨項羌傳》："妻其庶母及伯叔母嫂子弟之婦，淫穢蒸褻，諸夷中最爲甚，然不婚同姓。"其他之例尚多，今不過略舉一二，以明自漢以至唐宋，其婚俗莫不如此。此種收繼婚，爲西北遊牧民族之特徵，因其文化之背景及環境之需要，不得不如此也。但又可爲羌人爲非母系民族之旁證。

整理者説明：此係根據今存之油印稿整理寫定，稿紙每頁版心皆刻印有“西南民族史”字樣，知其爲計劃中系統專著《西南民族史》之部分内容。成稿時間估計大約應在40年代中。

張勛燎

（本文爲張勛燎據20世紀40年代手稿整理，見《四川大學考古專業創建四十周年暨馮漢驥教授百年誕辰紀念文集》，四川大學出版社2001年出版）

英文論文篇

目　　録

CHINESE MYTHOLOGY AND DR. FERGUSON

Before criticizing adversely a scholar's work, two things should be ascertained with reasonable certainty: first, is the work to be criticized of sufficient importance to justify attention; and second, are the errors of the book so misleading as to call for correction.

A series of thirteen volumes, entitled *The Mythology of All Races*, has been issued by the Archaeological Institute of America, under the editorship of Canon J. A. MacCulloch and the late Professor G. F. Moore. Volume Ⅷ, published in 1928, contains *Chinese*, by John C. Ferguson, and *Japanese*, by Masaharu Anesaki. It is with the work of Dr. Ferguson that this article is primarily concerned.

It is evident from the learned society which has issued these volumes, from the reputation of the editors, and from the names of the well known specialists who have written the other volumes, that this series is intended to be authoritative. Both Ferguson and Anesaki are well known scholars. The former has long been considered an authority on Chinese art, and it is generally understood that he is widely read in Chinese literature and has been closely connected with Chinese official and scholarly circles. Under such circumstances, if his work should be shown to contain careless generalizations, faulty classification, and misstatements of fact, it is a very serious matter. Scholars in other fields should have confidence that in relying upon statements made in such a work they are upon firm ground, and sinologists should be able to feel that this ground need not be gone over again.

It may be said at once that from a scholarly standpoint, the work of Ferguson is inferior to that of Anesaki. For example, the latter has provided notes in which he explains etymologies, elaborates difficult points, and gives exact references to his sources. On the other hand, Ferguson refers to an impressive array of Chinese works, but by omitting exact references, makes it practically impossible for a western scholar to check him with any thoroughness.

This is especially clear in his concluding chapter on "Criticism," in which he considers only two men, Wang T'ung and Han Yü. His choice of Wang T'ung and Han Yü is regretable. Wang T'ung has sometimes been regarded as a myth himself, but there are two existing books attributed to him, the *Wên chung tzŭ chung shuo* and the *Yüan ching*. There is nothing in them which can be interpreted as a criticism of Chinese myths, although there is some criticism of older literature on other grounds, and both books have been considered forgeries. Han Yü is mentioned as a critic because of his essays on the bone of the Buddha and to the crocodile. The former has nothing to do with the questions of mythology, simply reflecting the opposition of orthodox Confucians to Buddhism, while the latter is probably a sincere appeal to the crocodile, Such matter is not myth in the sense in which ethnologists use the word.

Dr. Ferguson is also uncritical in his use and selection of sources. Many of the works he cites are simply books of fiction, and no one would consider Frankenstein and Dracula to be myths of the English people. He devotes a chapter to "Theatrical Tales"; but while the Chinese drama does sometimes deal with mythology, the myths are so changed for theatrical purposes as to make the drama of little use in a serious study of mythology.

He does not account for the historical development of his myths. This point may be illustrated by a figure whom Dr. Ferguson treats in some detail (pp. 116-118), Hsi Wang Mu, but as if the conception of the goddess were entirely static. Now in the oldest sections of the *Shan hai ching*, the "Hsi shan ching" and the "Hai nei pei ching," Hsi Wang Mu has a human body with a leopard's tail and tiger's teeth, is fond of whistling, has dishevelled hair, wears jade ornaments, and eats three black-birds. The deity presides over plague, and the sex is not indicated. In the "Ta huang hsi ching," the divinity lives in a cave, and is dreadful in appearance. In a later work, the *Mu t'ien tzŭ chuan*, the goddess has dropped her animal attributes and is an educated Chinese queen.[①] In Huai-nan tzŭ, written about 100 B. C., she no longer presides over pestilence, but has become the goddess possessing the elixir of immortality.[②] Finally, in the *Han Wu Ti nei chuan*[③], the goddess reaches her full state, living in heavenly palaces with courtiers in an establishment modelled on the court of the Han emperors. Dr. Ferguson gives no account whatever of this development, which would be essential in a critical study.

In the "Introduction", Dr. Ferguson over simplifies Chinese culture. That he divides it into Confucian and Taoist spheres is not so bad, even though to do so ignores other important influences. But he goes further and identifies Confucianism with conservatism characterized by ceremonialism, and Taoism with liberalism typified by divination. Such an association is incorrect, because both ceremonialism and divination are characteristic of Confucianism and neither of them is characteristic of Taoism. He says that the Liberal School adhered "to the Eight Diagrams reputed to have been evolved by Fu Hsi from the marks found on the back of a dragon horse," and found its ancient authorization in the *Book of Changes* (p. 8). But the story of the Eight Diagrams of Fu Hsi is the Confucian myth of the invention of writing. Lao Tzŭ does not mention the *Book of*

---

① *Mu t'ien tzŭ chuan*, bk. 3.

② *Huai nan hung lieh chi chieh* (淮南鴻烈集解), Shanghai, c.p., 1922, Bk. 6, p. 16.

③ A forgery attributed to Pan Ku, but the date of its compilation cannot be later than the third and fourth centuries.

Hsi Wang Mu as described in the
Shan hai ching
From the Collection of the Chinese Library,
Harvard University

Changes, but it was spoken of in the highest terms by Confucius.① It is, indeed, one of the most important canons of Confucianism.②

By saying that the Liberal School "provides for changes amidst changing

① "Given a few more years of life to finish my study of the Book of Changes, I may be free from great errors." *Analects*, Ⅶ, 16. This passage is sometimes questioned, but it is the generally accepted version.

② It was the priests of the Taoist religion (which is of much later origin), who utilized the *na-chia* method of the commentators of the Later Han dynasty on the *Book of Changes* in the practice of alchemy and the manufacture of the elixir of life, which has nothing to do with Taoism as a school of philosophy.

Hsi Wang Mu as illustrated in the
Hsien fu ch'i tsung
From the Colleotion of the Chinese Library,
Harvard University

circumstances" (p. 8), Dr. Ferguson misinterprets the positions of *I Yin*, *T'ai Kung*, *Yü Hsiung and Kuan Chung*① (p. 9), and by confusing the adepts and

① Dr. Ferguson alludes (p. 9) to I Yin advising T'ang to plot against Hsia, T'ai Kung and Yü Hsiung advising Wên Wang and Wu Wang against Shang, and Kuan Chung "the first to make a feudal state assume hegemony among other states" as "authoritative examples of the early Tao." But I Yin was one of the most important heroes of Confucianism and is ranked as high as Chou Kung. Ch'êng T'ang, Wên Wang and Wu Wang, whom I Yin, T'ai Kung and Yü Hsiung advised, were the model emperors of Confucianism, and their revolutions against the existing regimes were highly commended and justified by the most orthodox Confucianists. These legendary figures do not prove the liberalism of Taoism, nor do they prove the conservatism of Confucianism. Kuan Chung's writings (those attributed to him) are decidedly legal in nature and they have been classed under the School of Law since the *Han shu i wen chih* (Bibliographical section of the History of the Former Han dynasty).

legalists with the Taoist philosophers①, he calls Ch'in Shih Huang "the greatest supporter of Liberalism..." (p. 9)

The "Introduction" closes with an account of the story of K'ung An-kuo and his labors on the text of the *Analects* and the *Spring and Autumn Annals.*

> "During the Han dynasty, about 150 B. C., the sayings of Confucius were compiled by one of his descendants, K'ung An-kuo. This compilation, called *Lun yü hsün tz'ü*, was based upon the comparison of two texts. One of these was found with other texts, *pi chung shu*, in a wall of the home of Confucius when it was being demolished by Kung Wang, son of the Emperor Ching Ti, who was appointed by his father to be King of the Principality of Lu (modern Shangtung). This text was written in the so-called 'tadpole' characters, *k'o-tou-wên*, and is known as the 'ancient text', *ku wên*. The other text came from the neighbouring principality of Ch'i and, being written in the characters which were used in the last years of the Chow dynasty, is known as the 'modern text', *chin wên*. The compilation of k'ung An-kuo, with some emendations, has remained the standard of the Conservative School for all succeeding generations, and as it includes the *Ch'un Ch'iu*, or 'Spring and Autumn Annals', it carries back the account of China's ancient civilization to a great antiquity." (pp. 10-11)

What evidence is there that K'ung An-kuo made a compilation of two texts of the *Analects* and included in it the *Annals*, which he called the *Lun yü hsün tz'ŭ*?② In what bibliography is this work to be found?③ It is said in a work by Ho Yen④

① The adepts, or magicians, should be sharply distinguished from the Taoist philosophers.

② No such work is known.

③ The *Han shu i wen chih* is the earliest of the Chinese bibliographies existant and is used as a comprehensive checklist of ancient Chinese literature. It says nothing of the compilation of K'ung An-kuo.

④ In the preface of the *Lun yü chi chieh*, a work compiled under the editorship of Ho Yen.

and in *Sui-shu ching chichih* that K'ung An-kuo wrote a commentary on the *Ku lun yü*, but they say nothing of the comparison with the Ch'i text and its inclusion in the *Ch'un ch'iu*. Even these references are considered doubtful. If this is meant to be the compilation of K'ung An-kuo, it did not remain the "standard of the Conservative School for all succeeding generations", because it was said to have been lost by Ho Yen himself. No attempt to combine these two books was ever made, and they cannot carry back the "account of China's ancient civilization to a great antiquity", because the *Lun yü* consists of the sayings of Confucius collected together by his disciples and the *Ch'un Ch'iu* is a history of the period 722-481 B. C. in outline form.

In the chapter on "Taoism" Dr. Ferguson continually confuses Taoism as a philosophy with Taoism as a religion. The latter was founded by Chang Tao-ling and its philosophical foundation was laid by Ko Hung more than a century later. Ko Hung was Confucian in ethics though Taoist in metaphysics, and opposed the naturalism of Lao Tzŭ. Lao Tzŭ was a monistic philosopher with no belief in a personal God, and it is one of the ironies of history that centuries later he was deified, and regarded as the founder of a religion. As an example of the inaccuracy of this chapter it may be noticed that T'ang T'ai Tsung is said first to have claimed descent from Lao Tzŭ (p. 14), and to have given the sage the title of Hsüau Yüan Huang Ti (p. 22). The first of these acts was performed by T'ang Kao Tsu①, and the second by Tang Kao Tsung②, neither being the act of

① According to *Fêng shih Wên-chien chi* (Book 1, first section, Taoist religion), in the third year of Wu Tê (620 A. D.) of the Emperor Kao Tsu, Chi Shan-hsing of Chin-chou saw an old man clad in white on the Yangchio mountains, who called to him and said: "Tell the Emperor of T'ang, that I am Lao Chün and that I am your ancestor. There will be no bandits this year and there will be peace." Kao Tsu immediately sent an envoy who offered a sacrifice to Lao-tzŭ and built a temple to him on the site of the revelation, and changed the name of the district Fu-shan to Shên-shan, "mountain of god." Kao-tsu (618-626 A. D.) was T'ai Tsung's father. T'ai Tsung ruled from 627-649 A. D.

② The canonization of Lao-tzü as Hüan Yüan Huang Ti, according to both the Old and New T'ang Histories, was in the first year of Ch'ien Fêng (666 A. D.) of the Emperor Kao Tsung. This was sixteen years after the death of T'ai Tsung.

T'ai Tsung.

At the end of this chapter (p. 24), Dr. Ferguson says, "The relation of Taoism to the mythological characters of China... is complete. If we were to depend upon the views of the School of Letters (Confucian) we should have scant material." In chapter Ⅲ, the chief characters considered are Yao, Shun, Yü, T'ang, Wĕn and Wu, but far from being connected with Taoism, these men are the heroes of the Confucian canon. Indeed, throughout the whole book Dr. Ferguson quotes more from Confucian than from Taoist works.

As a matter of fact, it would be a mistake to attempt an account of Chinese mythology solely from either Confucian or Taoist sources. In the Confucian canon there are probably many myths, but most of them have been so rationalized that they can be discovered only with the aid of other sources. As for the religious books of Taoism, they are all late, and nearly all their gods are of relatively recent date. Where the Taoist gods are connected with myths, they must be examined very carefully in order to discover the original form. Late Taoist literature is full of legendary inventions, but is not of great value in the study of ancient Chinese folklore and mythology. It would seem as if Dr. Ferguson has made the same mistake as Werner[①], and considered such works as the *Shên hsien t'ung chien*[②] as mythology, whereas they are mainly deliberate inventions.

In the chapter on "Cosmogony", Dr. Ferguson gives an account of the metaphysical speculations of the Taoist philosophers, which are not myths at all. After referring to the story of P'an Ku as an importation from Siam[③], he

---

① E.T.C. Werner, Myths and Legends of China, 1922.

② A book of biographies chiefly of the Taoist gods, saints and sages, and in which is included a short life of Christ which was translated into English by E.T.C. Werner in the *Journal of the Royal Asiatic Society*, *North China Branch*, Vol. LⅡ, pp. 186-191.

③ Perhaps a cosmogonic myth of the south that migrated northward. Where it originated is still undetermined. Dr. Ferguson referred to the book *Shu i chi* of the Sixth century A. D., but the myth was recorded in a much earlier work, the *San wu li chi* by Hsü Chêng, of the third century A. D. It does not say definitely that the myth originated in Siam.

devotes some space to Yü Huang, the "Pearly Emperor." Here (p. 59), Dr. Ferguson says, "This is the first appearance of yü Huang" (and adds that absolutely nothing is known of his origin or life), referring to a story in the *T'ung chien kang mu* of a dream of Sung Chên Tsung, and gives an accoum of his life from the *Sou shên chi.*① Dr. Ferguson has apparently followed Werner② and made the same mistake. The name Yü Huang was much earlier than the time of the Emperor Chĕn Tsung, appearing in the writings of Han Yü (768-824 A. D.) whom Dr. Ferguson has chosen as one of the critics of Chinese myths, in Liu Tsung-yüan (773-819 A. D.) and in Yüan Chen (779-831 A. D.). All these men lived about two centuries before the time of Chên Tsung. It is apparent that the myth of Yü Huang was originated at least two or three centuries before Chên Tsung's time and reached its fullest development in the tenth century, for a vivid celestial court scene of Yü Huang was painted by the famous artist Shih K'o of the Later Shu Kingdom (908-965 A. D.), as recorded in the work of Li Chien, *Tê yü chai hua p'in.*③ Most astonishing of all, Dr. Ferguson says (p. 55), "Liu Hsiang was the author of the *History of the Han*

---

① Whenever only the title *Sou shên chi* is referred to, it is always understood by scholars to be the well known work attributed to Kan Pao of the fourth century A. D. But the life of Yü Huang given by Dr. Ferguson is not to be found there. There is another secondary and obscure work of the same title but of much later compilation (compiled about the end of the sixteenth century A. D.) included in the Tao tsang (道藏). An account of the life of Yü Huang was given in the first book (pp. 9-10) of this work. But the matter is made more confusing in the case of Chiang Tzŭ-wên (p. 65) where Dr. Ferguson also simply referred to the *Sou shên chi*, because this story appears in both of these works. From the nature of the story given by Dr. Ferguson, it was apparently adapted from Kan Pao's work, although Dr. Ferguson's account does not follow either book accurately. But in the case of Yü Huang, it would be entirely wrong to assume the title to be Kan Pao's work because it was compiled at least four centuries before the time of the Sung emperor Chên Tsung, and it would be useless to refer to the work in the *Tao tsang* because it is not original and merely an adaptation from different sources. As a matter of fact, the life of Yü Huang appeared in a much earlier work, the *Kao shang yü huang pên hsing chi ching*, than the Sou shên chi of the *Tao tsang*.

② E.T.C. Werner, *Myths and Legends of China*, pp. 130-131.

③ 宋李廌撰德隅齋畫品,顧氏文房小説本,pp. 7-8.

Dynasty and the founder of the modern style of historical composition." If Dr. Ferguson can produce a history of the Han written by Liu Hsiang, he has made a momentous discovery, but it is more likely that he wrote Liu Hsiang while intending to write Pan Ku. Liu Hsiang was a co-author of a bibliography which was one of the sources of the *Ch'ien han shu.*

The chapter on "Spirits of Nature" ought to be the heart of the book. Yet after mentioning some ceremonials, all taken from Confucian sources, Dr. Ferguson soon passes to the consideration of such deities as the Earth-Gods, the City-Gods, the "T'ien Hou", and other tutelary gods. Unfortunately these gods have little to do with nature myths.

Yet the Chinese possess a rich store of myths concerning the sun, moon, stars, clouds, mountains, rivers, and other natural objects, and one of these, ignored by Dr. Ferguson, may be taken briefly as an example. Hsi Ho was an ancient Chinese sun god, or charioteer of the sun. The earliest appearance of the name is in the "Canon of Yao" of the *History*, where the myth has been rationalized and Hsi Ho, whether a personal name or a title, is a sort of court astrologer. But in the *Shan hai ching* is a different account.

"Between the Southeastern Sea and the 'Sweet Water' is a land called Hsi Ho. There was a woman named Hsi Ho who bathed the sun in Kan Yen. She was the wife of Ti Chün① and gave birth to ten suns." A commentator on this passage② considered that Hsi Ho was the one who took charge of the sun and moon at the beginning of the world. In Chuang Tzŭ③ it is said that on one occasion ten suns appeared at once, which caused a general conflagration. This incident is still further developed in Huai-nan Tzu,④ who places it in the time

① Literally Emperor Chtin. He is an important figure in ancient Chinese mythology, and may be compared with Zeus as the head of the Chinese mythical hierarchy. Dr. Ferguson ignores him entirely.

② Kuo P'o; *Shan hai ching*, bk. 15, "Ta huang nan ching."

③ Chuang tzŭ:昔者十日並出,草木焦枯.

④ *Huai nan hung lieh chi chieh*, bk. 8, "Pên ching hsün", pp. 7-8.

of Yao. Each sun contained a crow.① Yao ordered I to shoot the suns. I shot nine, and the crows in them fell dead②, leaving the one sun which we still possess. This story explains the association of the crow with the sun. It would be interesting to speculate whether this story has any connection with the widely diffused myth of the thunder-bird.

In the *Li sao* there is a hint that Hsi Ho is the charioteer of the sun③, and Huai-nan Tzu says that the sun rides in a chariot drawn by six dragons driven by Hsi Ho. There is an account of the daily journey past different places which correspond to the daylight hours of the Chinese day.④ Some of these names became the nuclei for later legends. The *Shan hai ching* contains legends about worthies who regulated the course of the sun⑤, and Huai-nan Tzŭ ascribes eclipses to the combats of unicorns⑥. The legend of the heavenly dog eating the sun and moon during eclipses is of late origin, and the custom of beating gongs to save them is said to have been introduced from India.

This brief account of the development of a sun myth illustrates the way in which Chinese myths should be treated, as well as the difficulties inherent in the material, for it will be seen that references must be collected from many sources⑦. It should be noticed that the *History* is supposed to be much older than the other sources quoted⑧, and therefore the original form of the myth can hardly be determined. Tradition is very persistent, and the later, cruder versions may really be earlier in their origin. But on the other hand, where such

---

① The *Shan hai ching* says: "There is a crow in the sun."

② See *ch'u tz'ü*, "Tien wên."

③ *Li sao*, tr. by Lira Boon-keng, p. 81, XLVⅢ.

④ *Huai-nan hung lieh chi chieh*, bk. 3, "T'ien wên hsün", pp. 18-19.

⑤ *Shan hai Ching*, Book 14, and 16.

⑥ *Huai-nan hung lieh chi chieh*, bk. 3, "T'ien wên hsün", p. 3.

⑦ Not only do most Chinese myths have a long history and varied forms, but the texts in which they occur require critical examination.

⑧ The date of the compilation of the *Shu ching* is a disputed question which we cannot discuss here.

stories first appear in the late Chou and Han literature, it is often impossible to tell whether they were a part of the old Chinese culture, or represent external influence. The fact that a legend is crude is not necessarily a sign that it is old.

In the instance of this sun myth, we can be fairly sure that we are dealing with a myth of Northern China, where the characteristically Chinese culture arose, because in the *Li sao* of Ch'ü Yüan there is found a different sun myth which represents southern tradition.① In this legend the god of the sun is Tung Chün. The passage runs as follows: "The morning sun, rising from the east, shone through Fusang. The sparkling night dawned gradually as he drove along in his dragon chariot through the thunder. The insignia and flags of cloud floated, and he sighed, hesitated, and looked back. He was clad with a coat of blue cloud and apron of white rainbow. He raised his long arrows and shot the heavenly wolves. After killing them he marched victoriously westward and sank to the depth of darkness, only to rise again in the east next morning."② The long arrows are symbolical of the sun's rays, and the heavenly wolves, of evil and darkness. It is a mistake for Ferguson to group this southern sun god with historical personages like Chang Liang and Kuan Yü, as he does in chapter eight.

Occult practices sometimes find their authorization in myths, and Dr. Ferguson devotes a chapter to the occult, but while he tells stories about divination, alchemy, geomancy, and other interesting subjects, he does not mention any myths in connection with them. And he writes (p. 137) as if he were not sure whether the "transmutation system" and the *Book of Changes* were two things or one. As a matter of fact, the "transmutation system" is the

---

① The *Li sao* is a great repository of myths of Southern China, the modern provinces of Hupei and Hunan. At the time it was written, the third century B. C., there was s sharp contrast in the mode of thinking and in literature between the North and the South. Here *Li sao* is used as a general title for all the works of Ch'ü Yüan as collected in the *Ch'u tz'ü*(楚辭).

② *Ch'u tz'ü*, "Chiu ko", Tung Chün. Not an exact translation, but adapted and abridged.

Book of Changes, and Wên Wang was not the sole author, but only one of those to whom the book is attributed.

Chinese folklore is very rich, and Dr. Ferguson devotes a chapter to it. It is, moreover, a question much discussed in scholarly circles in China at present. Yet such important tales as the *Mêng chiang nü*①, the *Liang shan-po* and the *Chu ying-t'ai* are not mentioned. Instead, Dr. Ferguson has resorted to works of pure fiction shaped for literary purposes.② It would be interesting to know where Dr. Ferguson got his statement that Chung Kuei (p. 152) was a scholar of the Sung period.③ In the story of the "White Serpent" (pp. 158-160) the most important part, dealing with her love affair, the "Thunder Peak Pagoda" under which the serpent spirit is supposed to be imprisoned, and with the "Monastery of the Golden Mountain," the connection with the "Dragon Boat Festival" and with the Buddhist monk Fa Hai, is entirely omitted.

In the chapter on "Buddhistic Myths" Dr. Ferguson has mistaken the *Hsi yu chi* of Li Chih-ch'ang for another book of the same title by Wu Ch'êng-ên. He says: "One of the most noted mythological accounts is that of the adventures of Yüan Chuang, a priest of the Seventh century, who travelled to India in search of Buddhist books. On his return he dictated an account of his travels to Pien Chi, and his narrative is chiefly concerned with a description of the various countries through which he had passed during his journey of sixteen years. This book is called *Ta T'ang Hsi Yu Chi* ('Western travels in the T'ang Dynasty').④ During the Yüan dynasty the noted Taoist Ch'iu Ch'u-chi was sent

① One of the most widely distributed of the Chinese folk-tales. Ku Chieh-kang, the author of the *Ku shih p'ien* has done much work on it.

② *Liao chai ckih i* (Strange stories from a Chinese studio), p. 156. *Chin ku Ch'i kuan* (Curious stories of the past and present), p. 169. *Tung chou lieh kuo chih* (Records of the Eastern Chou dynasty: a historical novel), p. 166.

③ For an authoritative account see, Chao I, *Kai yü ts'ung k'ao*, bk.35.

④ A correct translation would be: "A T'ang record of Western Regions."

by the Emperor Genghis khan to India and was accompanied by his pupil Li Chih-ch'ang. On their return Li wrote the account of their wanderings and of the miraculous events which he had learned to have happened to the priest Yüan Chuang on his earlier visit. The title of Li's book is taken from the earlier one, and it is called *Hsi Yu Chi.*① This later book is full of miraculous events, which, although they are interpreted from a Taoist standpoint, are all connected with the Buddhistic monk Yüan Chuang, and for this reason are classified under the heading of Buddhistic myths. The first part of this book contains an account of the wonderful genealogy of Yüan Chuang."

Li Chih-ch'ang's *Hsi yu chi* is a book of travel recording the journey of Chiu Chu-chi to the camps of Yüan T'ai-Tsu. Ch'iu Ch'uchi was the most famous Taoist of his time, and his Taoist title was Ch'ang Ch'un Tzŭ. So the full title of this little book is called *Ch'ang Ch'un chên jen hsi yu chi.*② As the facts recorded in it are mostly authentic, it is considered a very important book on early geography and travels, and it tells absolutely nothing of the travels of the Buddhistic monk Yüan Chuang and his genealogy. It also had no connection with the *Ta T'ang hsi yü chi*, which records the travels of Yüan Chuang. Dr. Ferguson apparently mistook Li Chih-ch'ang's *Hsi yu chi* for Wu Ch'êng-ên's *Hsi yu chi* because "the wonderful genealogy of Yüan Chuang" which he gives in the next four pages of his book (pp. 190-193), was abridged from the ninth chapter of Wu Ch'êng-ên's book. Li's book and Wu's have no connection with each other except a similarity of titles.

---

① It literally means "Record of Western Wanderings." *Ta T'ang hsi yü chi* and *Hsi yu chi*, although they sound nearly the same when romanized, are quite different in meaning. To regard the latter as a derivation from the former is entirely unwarranted.

② The work has been translated by Arthur Waley into English under the title of *The Travels of an Alchemist, the journey of the Taoist Ch'an-Ch'un from China to the Hindu Kush at the summons of Gingiz Khan, recorded by his disciple Li Chih-ch'ang.* Bretschneider's translation, Waley says, is an inaccurate abridgement of the Russian translation by Palladius.

These points are enough to show the defects of Dr. Ferguson's work. Other errors might be mentioned, such as his mistaking the tortoise for the turtle① as the worst kind of vilification, and the misconception of its origin from the green turban outcast class which he wrongly attributed to the T'ang dynasty.② Other anachronisms occur as on p. 20, "From the time of Chang to that of T'ai Tsung at the opening of the *Han dynasty*, the influence of the conservative School and the Confucian classics was at a low ebb..." and again on pp. 140-1, "The development of the science into the determination of the fortunes of relatives and descendants according to the lucky or unlucky site of the grave of a deceased person, was a development later than the time of *Kuo P'o* in the *Han dynasty*..."③

It is not the purpose of this paper to evaluate Dr. Ferguson's book, but only to point out its mistakes and deficiencies. It must be evident that they are

---

① Pointed out by Sowerby in his review in the *China Journal*, Dec., 1928, pp. 285-286.

② "No worse term of abuse can be employed than to call another man a tortoise. The generally accepted explanation of this use of the term is that the outcast class (*lo hu*) who had no legal status, was obliged during the T'ang dynasty to wear a strip of green cloth tied around the head. The degenerate males of this outcast class lived from the earnings of the prostitution of their wives and daughters. This was the very lowest depth of immorality. As the head of the tortoise is green it became a symbol of the green-beaded outcast; and to call a person a tortoise originally meant to put him in the vilest class of human beings, and also to name him as bastard", p. 101.

This is guess work without any historical foundation. The tabu on the turtle did not begin in the Tang dynasty. We can quote many illustrious names of the T'ang and Sung, and even the Yüan dynasties, named after the term *kuei*. It is only after the Yüan dynasty that such personal names became rare, and at present even words of the same sound are avoided in naming a person. So Chao I in his *Kai yü ts'ang k'ao* (bk.38, pp. 23-24) says that the tabu began in the Yüan dynasty and became prevalent in the Ming period. Although the wearing of a green turban as a sign of disgrace can be traced back as early as the sixth century B. C., it was not officially instituted until the fourteenth century A. D. in the Ming dynasty. (See Lang Ying, *Ch'i hsiu lei kao*, bk.28, pp. 11, 1880 Canton edition; and Chao I: *Kai yü ts'ung k'ao*, bk.38, p. 25). "That the outcast class (*lo hu*)... was obliged in the T'ang dynasty to wear a strip of green cloth tied around the head" is without historical foundation. The use of the term "turtle" in vilification, so far as present evidence goes, has no actual connection with Dr. Ferguson's green turbaned outcast class.

③ Kuo P'o was born in 276 A. D., more than half a century later than the last of the Hans.

serious enough to make the task necessary. A large part of the work does not deal with mythology proper at all. It is as if one were to write on English mythology by giving accounts of Berkeley and Hume, "Mother Goose" "Macbeth" "The Idyls of the King", selections from Lord Dunsany and Bram Stoker, and the *Book of Common Prayer*, with a few pictures of cathedrals and of such celebrities as Guy Fawkes thrown in for local color. Where myths are mentioned, they are not critically dealt with, and there are many misstatements of fact.

No scientific treatment of Chinese mythology exists in English. Probably the task is an impossible one for any westerner at present. Yet it is important for western scholars in other fields to realize that this is the case, and that this work of Dr. Ferguson cannot be considered as adequate or reliable.①

(與 J.K. Shryock 合作, 原載 *Journal of the American Oriental Society*, 1933, Vol. 53, pp. 53-65)

---

① There are many myths which Dr. Fergnson has not considered, such as the Chinese flood myth and the occupational myths. The Chinese flood myth represents a different aspect of this widely distributed story. The other flood myths usually say that God sent the flood to destroy men on account of their wickedness, or merely as a general inundation, but the Chinese myth embodies the idea of controlling the water and the formation of the water-ways by human or supernatural agencies.

THE LOLO OF CHINA: THEIR HISTORY AND CULTURAL RELATIONS

The Lolo are one of the most important and numerous of the nonChinese peoples in the South-west of China. This interesting people long ago attracted the attention of anthropologists and explorers, and a considerable amount of material has been written about them. Most of this information deals with their present state of affairs, or about those who have acquired a large amount of Chinese culture. No serious attempt has been made to correlate these materials with the old Chinese records and the historical peoples who have successively inhabited this area. Such a study is imperative, because without a knowledge of their history, the present amount of information accumulated can hardly be intelligibly interpreted. But such an approach is beset with difficulties from the very beginning. The old Chinese records are sporadic and scattered, and themselves need to be coordinated and worked into a systematic whole.

The Lolo have been in their present habitat for at least more than a thousand years. Being a vigorous and warlike people, they have always constituted the upper stratum of the aboriginal population whereever they went. They occupied the key position in the movements of peoples in this part of China. Although they possess a script they have no history of their own.① The

① The Lolo Script has attracted a great deal of attention among philologists. It is pictographic, some what modelled after the Chinese but lacks the elaborate laws of ideation. According to Chinese sources, it was invented by a Lolo named A-bi about 550 A. D., but the Lolo has three different myths concerning its invention. A-bi called it *Wei-shu*, e. g. "standerd script"; the Chinese called it *Ts'uan Wen*, e. g. "script of the Ts'uan". It is essentially a religious writing only intelligible to the pi-mo (their medicine men). Even the pi-mo of one tribe cannot read the script of the pi-mo of another tribe, as shown by V.K. Ting in his *Man yu san chi* and D' Ollone in his *In Forbidden China*, pp. 106-107.

only source of information available concerning their past comes from the Chinese side. This makes the Chinese sources, although meagre and sometimes inaccurate, especially valuable.

The present study does not attempt to give a full account of the Lolo culture as a whole, but rather to treat specifically those topics from which historical comparisons can be drawn. Not all the materials here used are utilized for the first time, but all of them are examined in a new light, and often times with corrections of older misinterpretations. Special stress is laid on the historical reconstruction of the movements of peoples in Lololand and their connection with the Lolo.

The Origin of the Name "Lolo"

The name Lolo first came into use during the Yuan dynasty (1280-1368 A. D.). It was soon identified with the Lulu, a tribe of the Eastern Tsuan barbarians of the fifth to the ninth centuries A. D., Lolo being a corruption of Lulu.① Whether this identification is correct or not, we have no means of knowing, but the term Lulu has not been used since the Yuan period. The terms used by the Lolo for themselves vary considerably from tribe to tribe at present. The variations of the first syllable usually lie within the phonetic complex where the initial consonant is either *ŋ* or *n* but rarely *l*. The following vowel fluctuates from the range of all the five vowels *a e i o u*. The second syllable is usually *so* or *su* with a few variations, and sometimes omitted altogether.②

---

① *Nan chao yeh shih*, book Ⅱ, pp. 24-25. See also Pelliot, Deux itineraires de chine en inde, BEFEO, Ⅳ, 1904, p. 137.

② Here are some of the variations: No-su, Nou-su, Ngo-su, Ne-su, Nei-su, No-su, No, Na, Lei-su, etc. In Ssuchuan they are called *Man-tzu*, or more courteously *Man-chia*. In south Yunnan the Shahs call them *Myen*.

The earliest interpretation of this term was given by Terrien de Lacouperie. In his *Language of China before the Chinese*[①], he says: "Their name, formerly Lo-kwei in Chinese, altered into Lulu, and now Lolo or Kolo, had become a by-name for many of the mixed tribes which in the south west provinces owe their origin to the intermingling with tribes of the Taic and Mon and other stocks. The variants in their name have come from the influence of the Taic-Shan phonology, which makes *h* or *k* equivalent to *l* in its adaptation of foreign words beginning with the latter consonant." This linguistic interpretation is very misleading, because the nickname Lo-kwei (kwei means ghost in Chinese) is derogatory and of much more recent date than either the name Lulu or Lolo; and the *ko* is a mispronunciation of the Chinese character *lo* by European scholars.[②]

Paul Vial's interpretation is different though naive.[③] He says that the Lolo in Ssuchuan called themselves *No*, and those in Yunnan called themselves *Na*, that the Chinese transcripted it with their nearest character and doubled the sound for the sake of euphony. This can scarcely be the case. If the Lolo called themselves *No* or *Na*, the most probable thing for the Chinese to do was to call them *No-man*, *Na-man*, or *No-yi* or *Na-yi* (*man* and *yi* mean barbarians) as is usually done with all the south-western tribal names. As a matter of fact, in the earlier Chinese records it was actually written *Lulu-man* or *Lolo-man* and later contracted into *Lo-yi*, etc.

Lietard's explanation of the derivation of the term is much more plausible[④], He considered *Lolo* as a corruption of *No-so*, a term most of the Lolo use for themselves. According to Lietard *no* means black and *so* means man

---

① Transactions of the Philological Society, 1885-7, pp. 480-481.

② The Chinese transcription is sometimes differently rendered. 玀玀, 猓猓 sometimes 猓玀. 猓 is often mispronounced as *ko*.

③ *Les Lolos*... 1898.

④ *Au Yunnan*, *les Lo-lo Po*, 1913.

in the Lolo language. So *no-so* means black man. But according to Shirokogoroff[①], the meaning of these syllables do not always agree. For example in the Buš. dialect, the Lolo call themselves *ŋo-so*, whereas black is *no*, and ŋo means five. In the Ni dealect the Lolo call themselves *hi*, and black is *ne*. As to *so*, no such meaning as man is found in the Buš. dialect. Although these syllables are near enough, their variations make the etymological derivation very uncertain.

Furthermore Shirokogoroff conjectured that the name may be of a political origin (like Manchu), or that it may have been given to them by their neighbors (like Tungus), or that it may be a name handed down from great antiquity.[②] He suggested these three possibilities but hesitated to make a decision. To assume a political origin is most improbable. The Lolo were never a close-knit political entity. There is also no ground for assuming that the name was given to them by their neighbors, as the name they used to call themselves is too close to it.

As we know the name was in use nearly eight hundred years ago, we have to make allowance for the variations in the language of this isolated people. We must also remember that *Lolo* is purely a Chinese transcription. For the non-phonetic Chinese characters used phonetically, we must also make allowance for the inconsistencies involved. Taking all these factors into consideration and together with the closeness of the Lolo term they used for themselves, it is fair to assume that the term is not of foreign origin. Its etymological derivation is obscure. Lietard's explanation failed to take into account the fact that most of the Lolo who called themselves *No-so* are not Black Lolo only, but also White Lolo. It has been remarked that the Lolo do not like to be called by this name. This is undoubtedly due to the fact that the term is sometimes used

---

① Phonetic Notes on a Lolo Dialect and Consonant L. Academia Sinica, Bul. Vol. I, pt.2, p. 183.

② Op. cit. p. 184.

contemptuously in the mouth of the Chinese. They do not object to being called *Man-chia* or *Yi-chia* (*man* and *yi* mean barbarians, no better than Lolo in the Chinese sense), because the word *chia* is a courteous term used in address among the dialects of west China.①

Present Distribution of the Lolo

Before going on to give a reconstruction of Lolo history, a few words should be said about the extent of the area they occupy. It is important because it will be the decisive factor in our choice of the descriptions from Chinese sources about the peoples who occupied the Lolo territory successively in history. Only those who have been actually in this region will be examined and comparisons drawn.

The present population of the Lolo is estimated by various writers to be about three millions.② This number is not based on actual count and its reliability is very questionable. They are scattered over the mountainous regions of Yunnan and southwest Ssuchuan. To the west they reach the Burmese border. To the east they have penetrated into the western districts of Kueichou. To the south they have spread into the Ssu-mao districts of Yunnan well below Lat.

---

① E.C. Hicks, a missionary, gives another interpretation of the name Loio. The Lolo used a bamboo basket about the size of a duck's egg in worshipping their ancestors. This ancestral basket is called *Lolo* by the Lolo themselves. So Hicks advanced the theory that the term Lolo, given to the No-so, "is a contemptuous nickname given to them by the Chinese in reference to their peculiar method of venerating their ancestors". This interpretation is followed by other missionary writers, such as S. C. C. Jarke in his *Among the Tribes of South-west China*, Jamieson gives another story by quoting Chang Ying, a Chinese writer of the early 19th century. The Lolo were descended from a Kolo ape, and afterwards turned into Lolo. This is entirely unhistorical. (See C. E. Jamieson, *The Aborigines of Western China*, *China Journal of Arts and Science*. I. p. 376. seq.)

② Terrien de Lacouperie, op. cit. p. 479; Yang Chen-chih. *A Brief Account of the Lolo*, *Ling-nan Journal*, Vol. I, pp. 134-152.

23°. In a northeastern thrust from northern Yunnan along the Ta-liang (great cold) mountain ranges following the northeastern course of the Yangtzu River, they reach as far north as Chia-ting and Ya-chou. This narrow strip of land more than 200 miles long and less than 100 miles broad is extremely rugged and wooded and is known as the home land of the independent Lolo. Geographically the Lolo seem to be intrusive here, because on all three sides they are surrounded by non-Lolo tribes. The Tibetans, Sifan and certain Miao tribes are found on the west, Sifan on the north, and Miao on the southeast. This region from early Han times was known under the name of Chiung-tu, Kung-pu and Yuehsui and inhabited by various tribes which we shall deal with later.

Immediately south of it are the Lolo who are under Chinese control but governed by their own chiefs. This includes the greater part of Yunnan and western parts of Kueichou. It must be understood that the area is not exclusively inhabited by the Lolo. The lower valleys are settled by Chinese immigrants and frequently interspersed with Miao and Shan villages. The Lolo are essentially a mountain people. They dread the lower valleys and especially the humidity and the lassitude of lower altitudes.

Physiographically this whole Lolo region is a southeastern extension of the Tibetan Plateau and the Himalaya ranges. It is traversed by the upper courses of the Mekong river and the Yangtzu with its tributaries. The mountainous nature of the country makes these rivers full of rapids and boulders which renders navigation impossible for any distance. The climate is temperate but quite rigorous in winter.

Early History of Lololand

China has long been in close contact with the part of the country occupied at present by the Lolo, and wars have been incessant with the peoples of the region since the middle of the first millennium B. C. The failure of the ancient records to give any notice to such a vigorous and warlike people as the Lolo is rather striking. This is probably why d'Ollone thought the Lolo only became formidable during the last few centuries.① But one suspects that the Lolo are late comers to their present habitat, for otherwise the silence of the early Chinese records is inexplicable.

The surrounding tribes, which the Chinese called barbarians, have always played a conspicuous part in China's dynastic wars. So in the struggle between the Chou (B. C. 1122-249) and the Shang (B. C. 1766-1121) for the supremacy of China, a part of the aboriginal people of Ssuchuan and Yunnan were used by Wu Wang (B. C. 1122-1114) the actual founder of the Chou dynasty. In the speech at Mu, as recorded in the Canon of History, he says: "... o men of Yung, Shuh, Keang, Maou, Wei, Lu, Peng and P'u, lift up your lances, join your shields, raise your spears, I have a speech to make."② The P'u became well known in early Chinese history and have been identified as inhabitants of Yunnan.③ They were known later under the name Pai P'u, or the Hundred P'u.④ The name P'u is probably a generic name for all the ancient peoples inhabiting this area. In works of the early Christian era,⑤ different tribes of the P'u were described, such as the Ch'iu-liao P'u; the Tailed P'u having tails like the turtle's; the Mu-mien P'u, cultivating the cotton tree (mumien); the Wên-mien P'u, who tatooed their faces; the Chih-kou P'u who

---

① *In Forbidden China.*

② Chinese classics, *Legge's Translation*, vol. Ⅲ, part Ⅱ, pp. 301-302.

③ Ibid., see Commentary.

④ *Yunnan Tung-chih*, *Nan man chih*, Books 172-190. A little information may be found in English in G.E. Gerini, *Researches on Ptolemy's Geography of Eastern Asia*, 1909, AsiaTie Soc Monographs, No. 1, pp. 804-805.

⑤ Such as the *Hua Yang Kuo chih*; and such later works as the *Tung tien*, and others.

pierced their lips, knocked out their teeth and went naked; the Hei-po P'u, who were much like the modern P'o-jên. Some are described as cannibals, others as piercing their breasts or having elongated ears. The tails of the Tailed P'u may be some kind of caudiform appendage like certain tribes of the modern Nagas. These descriptions may be in the main inaccurate, but there is not the slightest indication of Lolo traits. The modern P'u-man of Yunnan are regarded as the remnants of the ancient P'u.①

These peoples were in constant contact with the Chinese border states. In the year 611 B. C., the P'u threatened the powerful state of ch'u and the latter contemplated removing their capital in order to avoid their onslaught.② But as a matter of fact the ch'u always considered this region as their legitimate southern territory.③

Toward the fourth and third centuries B. C. we have more reliable historical data. Chuang Ch'iao of the State of Ch'u led an expeditionary force up the Yangtzu River, finally conquered T'ien (the region surrounding the modern capital of Yunnan province) and annexed it to Ch'u.④ While he was on the expedition its rival state Chin annexed Shu (modern Ssuchuan province) and Pa (modern eastern Ssuchuan and western Hupeh provinces), and Chuang Ch'iao's retreat was cut off.⑤ He was obliged to settle down with his men and made himself king of the barbarians by assuming their garb and adopting their customs. Lietard regarded Chuang Ch'iao as a naturalized Lolo king, but there is no reason for regarding the people Chuang Ch'iao conquered as Lolo.⑥

---

① *Yunna Tung Chih*, op. cit.; and Davies, H.R., *Yunnan*, 1909, p. 375.

② Tso chuan, Legge's tr. p. 273.

③ Ibid., p. 624.

④ Wylie, tr. *JRAI*, Vol. 9, 1880, pp. 53-96.

⑤ Ibid. And also see Chi Li, *Formation of the Chinese People*, pp. 240-241, how Chin annexed Shu and the interesting debate which took place in the Chin court concerning this matter.

⑥ Lietard, *Au Yunnan*, 1913. Rocher mistook Chuang Ch'iao for two different persons as his name mentioned in the *Chien Han shu* and the *Hou Han shu* is slightly difierent. Rocher: TP, X, 1899, p. 15.

During the time of the Former Han dynasty (B. C. 206-A. D. 23), the country conquered by Chuang Ch'iao evolved into the Kingdom of T'ien. To its east rose the Kingdom of Yeh-lang (the modern district of Chu-Chin, e. g. the Northeast of Yunnan province and West of Kueichou province). To the north in the Chien-chang valley was a people called Chiung-tu (the very home of the modern independent Lolo). T'ien and Yeh-lang were kingdoms of considerable size and power. They even asked the Han emperor's envoys such questions as "Whose kingdom is bigger, the Han emperor's or mine?" Intercourse between these kingdoms and the Han emperors was close, and not long later all were annexed to China.① There is nothing to indicate that these peoples were Lolo. The general mass of population seems to be the P'u tribes, organized under Chinese leadership.

A little north of the Chiung-tu tribes (in modern Ya-chou, Ssuchuan province) was a tribe named Bair-lang (in Mandarin P'ailang, means white wolf) during the Later Han dynasty (A. D. 25-220). This tribe submitted to the Chinese and in appreciation of the Han emperors' graces, they offered a song in which the original sounds were transcripted.② In a comparative study of this piece of song, Mr. Wang Ching-ju discovered that it has some bearing on the name of Yeh-lang.③ He reasoned to explain why a tribe in the north was called Bait-lang (white wolf) and a tribe far south of it called Yeh-lang (night groom or man). There must be some connection. So he took Lietard's interpretation of *No-So* as black man and inferred that *yeh* is synonymous with *dark*, and *dark* is synonymous with *black*. *So* or *sou*, according to him, can be evolved from *sian*. *Lang*, in ancient times, could be pronounced *sian*. Proved to his own

---

① Wylie, tr., op. cit.

② *Hou Han shu* (History of Later Han dynasty) in the section *Hsi nan yi chuan* (Southwestern barbarians).

③ *A Comparative Linguistic Study on the Songs of the Bair-lang Tribe*, Academia Sinica, The National Research Institute of History. and Philology, Monographs No. 8, *Hsi Hsia yen chiu*(Tangut studies), pp. 15-54. An English summary may be found in pages 273-274.

satisfaction, so Yeh-lang is easily equated with Lolo. Such a linguistic somersault is entirely unwarrantable, but circumstantially there is some possible connection between Yeh-lang and Lolo. Geographically the Yehlang area was always occupied by tribes of Lolo affinities in later times①, and the arrogant attitude of the Yeh-lang toward the Han emperors also suggests the independent spirit of the modern Lolo. But we shall have to wait for more evidence before such an identification is possible.

The third century. A. D. witnessed the famous campaign into Yunnan by the crafty general and statesman Chu-ko Liang.② He conquered them by force but he won so much affection from them that he is still worshipped among many of the isolated tribes. Legends about him are widespread in this area. Many aboriginal chiefs claimed institution from him. At least we know four famous families of Lolo chiefs, the Cheng, Sha, Lung and An families in Yunnan and Kwei-chow claimed such a beginning.③ Unfortunately Chu-k'o Liang did not leave any record or description of the peoples he conquered.

Soon after this the whole area of T'ien, Yeh-lang and Chiung-tu was consolidated into a kingdom called Ts'uan.④ The Ts-'uan was divided into an Eastern Branch who called themselves Wu-man (black barbarians) occupying eastern Yunnan and extending southeastward into Kuei-chou; and a Western

① Later in the fifth century, it was the home of the Eastern Ts'uan.

② Chen Shou, *San kuo chih* (History of the Three Kingdoms), *Biography of chuk'o Liang*. See also Rocher and Jamieson, op. cit.

③ Jamieson, op. cit. The authenticity of their claims is very hard to ascertain as Chu-k'o Liang has become a culture hero among these aborigines.

④ I, VⅢ. See also *Barbares Ts'ouan*, BEFEO, 8, Nos. 3-4, pp. 334-335. Gerini held that Ts'uan (or Ts'wan) is indentical with Ptolemy's Doanai. "This coincidence in location of the Ts'wan with the Doan, or t'wan, and the Kau of the Annamese historians, coupled with the fact that Ts'wan, or Doan, is the Annamese pronunciation of the Chinese term Ts'wan, is sufficient evidence to show, I think, that they really were the same people. Similar coincidences in names and location also indicate them to be identical with Ptolemy's Doanai. It is therefore pretty certain that in our author's time a conspicuous portion of this people had already advanced into Eastern Laos or Dasama, which they held under sway." op. cit. p. 126. The Difficulty in Gerini's identification is that the Ts'uan did not come into existence during the time of Ptolemy.

Branch who called themselves Pai-man (white barbarians) occupying the region diredtly west of the Wu-man until it reaches the Mekong River. The Eastern Ts'uan (Wu-man) showed strong analogies with the modern Lolo, and one of its tribes, the Lulu, has been regarded as their ancestors. This division into an Eastern and Western or White and Black, branches is not merely a dualistic social distinction because their languages are quite different and each occupies large tracts of distinct areas. Socially there is a wide gulf between them and it also may imply a racial distinction.①

Whence and where the Ts'uan people came and how they destroyed the kingdoms of T'ien and Yeh-lang are questions we are unable to answer at present. During the third and fourth centuries of the Christian era, the Ts'uan were on the move toward this region. Most scholars regarded them as pushing from the north southward.② This was most probably implied by the name of their ruling class, the Ts'uan family. So far as present evidence goes, the founding of the Ts'uan did not involve great racial dislocation.

The term Ts'uan was only a political name derived from the ruling family. The Western Ts'uan claimed that their seventh ancestor was the governor of Chien-ning (in northeastern Yun-nan) during the Ch'in dynasty (265-420 A. D.) and that their original home was in the An-yi district of Shensi.③ This tradition led to the general misconception of the southward invasion of the Ts'uan race. From other sources,④ it seems that the Ts'uan family was a well-known family of Ssuchuan and many of its members rose to high official positions during this period. This seventh ancestor of the Ts'uan, like Chuang Ch'iao, took advantage of the chaotic conditions in China proper and made himself king of the barbarians. Thus the term Ts'uan-man came into use. Although the area was ruled by the Ts'uan family, the great mass of the people

---

① It is especially apparent in the *Man shu*.

② Terrien de Lacouperie, op. cit. pp. 480-481; V.K. Ting, *Man yu san chi*.

③ See VⅢ, I.

④ Such as the *Hua Yang kuo chih*, and *Ssuchuan tung chih* (Gazeteer of Ssuchuan province).

were of different racial stocks, and the modern Lolo is surely one of them.① The Ts'uan maintained their power by acknowledging the suzerainty of China until they were weakened by inter-tribal strife, and finally were conquered by the powerful kingdom of Nan-chao.

Before giving a brief history of Nan-chao, the problem of the origin of the Shan race must be solved, because the Nan-chao has been identified as a Shan Kingdom.② Later writers have followed Terrien de Lacouperie in placing the cradle of the Shan race in Central China, Hupeh and northwestern Ssuchuan provinces.③ This hypothesis was further developed by E. H. Parker.④ Weighty theories about the formation of the Chinese civilization have been put forward based on this hypothesis.⑤

---

① The modern Lolo script is called by Chinese authors *Ts'uan wên*, e. g. Ts'uan script.

② The Nan-chao was identified with the Shans purely on linguistic grounds, such as the word *chao* is a Shan word for *king*, or *kingdom*. The original name of Nan-chao was Mengshê. It was situated on the south of the other five *chao*, so it was called Nan-chao by the Chinese. Among the modern Shans, the first syllable of the son's name is taken from the last syllable of the father's name. This is exactly like the names of the Nan-cho kings, such as: Hsinu-lo, Lo-shen-yen, Shen-lo-pi, Pi-lo-ko, and Ko-lo-feng, etc. (See E. H. Parker, *The Old Thai or Sha Empire of Western Yunnan*, *CR*, Vol. XX, pp. 337 seq.) There are also place names in Yunnan reminiscent of Shan etymology. There are a number of Nan-chao words, especially names of governmental offices and official titles, preserved in the *Man shu* and *Nan-chao yeh shih*, but they have not been scientifically examined.

③ Terrien de Lacouperie, op. cit. pp. 448-452; and his *Cradle of the Shan Race* in A.S. Colquhoun, *Amongst the Shans*, 1885 pp. xxi-lv.

④ op. cit. and in his *Burma*, the first few chapters.

⑤ C. W. Bishop maintains in his *Geographical Factor in the Development of the Chinese Civilization* (Geographical-Review, Vol. 12, 1922, pp. 1941 especially p. 34) how important/apart the Shan-Taic Race contributed to the building of the Chinese civilization, practically all writers have accepted this hypothesis naively. Some have cast doubts on this hypothesis but were unable to examine the Chinese sources. Davies said, in his *Yunnan*: "Whether the Shans ever extended over the provinces of China which lie north of the Yangtze is a question that can probably never be settled. Professor Terrien de Lacouperie is of the opinion that the Shan race was formed in the mountains between Ssuchuan and Shan-hsi out of a mixture of some northern tribe akin to the Chinese with a race of Mon-Khmer stock. This may be so, but M. de Lacouperie does not appear to give any reasons for this opinion." p. 378. A. Henry (1903) who had spent many years among the Shans, postulated a southern origin of the Shans race, but he was unable to utilize the Chinese materials, so his hypothesis remains unheeded by other writers.

Terrien de Lacouperie does not give any evidence to support his theory except the case of Ai-lao.① According to the History of T'ang dynasty (A. D. 618-906), the Nan-chao claimed descent from the Ai-lao. Nan-chao is Shan, so Ai-lao must be Shan. According to the History of Later Han dynasty (A. D. 25-220), the original seat of the Ai-lao was Lao-shan. Lao-shan is situated, according to Terrien de Lacouperie's identification, at the intersection of Honan, Hupeh and An-hui provinces, and extending westward forming the boundaries of Ssu-chuan and Shen-si provinces. In the year A. D. 47, the Ai-lao descended the Chiang and Han on bamboo rafts② and attacked the frontier barbarians Luh-to. In A. D. 51 they surrendered their arms to the governor of Yueh-sui.③ In A. D. 78 they rebelled, but were soon put down. Finally in 629 they established the great state of Nan-chao. This is the supposed origin of the Shan race and its southward migration.④

If we examine the case more carefully we will discover all of Terrien de Lacouperie's evidence is based on false identifications. To place the Lao-shan at the intersection of Honan, An-hui and Hupeh borders is geographically most unlikely.⑤ As Lao-shan may be identified with any place, the most important place name here involved is the well-known district Yueh-sui where the Ai-Lao surrendered. It is too well known to be mistaken, so Terrien de Lacouperie omitted it entirely in his discussions.⑥ Supposing Lao-shan is in the north-eastern Hupeh border, it is at least 1500 miles away from Yueh-sui. For a

---

① See p. 36, Note②.

② Terrien de Lacouperie identified the *Chiang* with the *Yangtzu River*, and the *Han* with the *Han* River, a large tributary of the Yangtzu in northern Hupeh province which takes its source in the Ssuchuan-Shensi border. This identification is entirely unwarranted.

③ Yueh-sui was a well known administrative district in the Han dynasties, situated in the modern districts of northwest Yunnan and southwest Ssuchuan provinces.

④ For a full translation of the Ai-lao myth, see *Si nan man chuan* tr. by A. Wylie, *Revue d'Extreme Orient*, Vol. I, 1892. For Terrien de Lacouperie's interpretation, see the works cited in p. 36, Note ②. The Ai-lao myth given in the *Nan-chao yeh shih* is slightly different.

⑤ See map for Terrien de Lacouperie's identification.

⑥ Terrien de Lacouperie did not mention this place. It would be irreconcilable with his hypothesis.

primitive tribe to migrate 1500 miles in three years with a community of 77 chiefs, 51890 families comprising 553711 persons, fighting their way through hostile tribes, inhospitable mountains and impassable forests, and possibly with Chinese forces pursuing them almost amounts to an impossibility. Terrien de Lacouperie must be misled by the mention of the river Chiang and Han which he identified with the Yangtzu river and its tributary the Han river in Hupeh province. Here the Chiang and Han should be identified with the Mekong river, not the Yangtzu and the Han rivers.①

Lao-shan is expressly stated, in the *Man-shu*, as situated in the Yung-chang area on the upper Mekong river, near the frontier of the district of Yueh-sui in Han dynasty.② According to the commentary of Nan-chao *Yeh-shih*, Lao-shan (sometimes Ai-lao shan) is called Tien-ching shan, situated in the same area.③ The Chiu-lung mountain, which Terrien de Lacouperie placed in the Shensi-Ssuchuan border, is south of the city of Yung-chang according to the same book.

With these place names properly identified, one can clearly see that the original home of the Shan is in Yung-chang, southwest Yunnan (Long. 99° and Lat. 25°), not in north-east Hupeh, Central China (Long. 115° and Lat. 32°). The southward invasion of the Shan is only a misinterpretation and is not substantiated by fact. So far as present evidence goes, the Shan have never been in the Yangtzu valley.④ The aboriginal peoples which the early Chinese came into contact with were chiefly the Miao and Yao (the Pan-hu race claimed

---

① See the Commentary on this passage of the *History of the Later Han Dynasty* by Shen Chin-ban.

② *Man shu*, chapter 3, p. 4. "... Their (the Meng-she Chao, e. g. the Nan-chao) surname is Meng. In the first year of the Chen Yüan, they submitted a letter to the governor of Chien-nan district, Wei Kao. They said originally they were descended from Sha-hu of Yung-chang..." The Sha-hu here is the Sha-yi of the Ai-lao myth, who bore ten sons. The word *hu* 壺 is a misprint of *yi* 壹. because of their close resemblance.

③ That is the Yung-chang area. See IX, Book I, p. 5, *Commentary* by Hu Wei.

④ This view is substantiated by the passage in the *Nan-chao yeh-shih* on the P'o-jên (e. g. one of the Chinese names for the Shah). "P'o-jên is also called Po-yi or Pai-yi.Their natare can stand the heat. Their dwellings are mostly under the bushes (so they are called Po-jên). Originally they were barberians outside of the Lan-tsang chiang (Mekong River)..." Book Ⅱ, p. 24.

to be descended from a dog ancestor) of the Mon-Khmer speaking stock.①

① There is no indication in the Chinese records that any of the early aborigines in the Yangtzu valley can be identified with the Shan. Terrien de Lacouoerie attempts to identify the Shan with Shang (or Yin) dynasty people; it is purely popular etymology. He also identified the state ch' u in Chou dynasty as Shan. (See op. cit. pp. 410411). "In the chronicle of Tso, already mentioned, in 664 B. C, two words are quoted in support of as interesting legend similar to others well known elsewhere. The scene is in Ts'u (i. e. Hupeh, Ts'u is the same as ch'u)"

"A male child was thrown away by his mother's orders in the marsh of Mung: there a tigress suckled him. This was witnessed by the Viscount of Yun, whilst hunting, and when he returned home in terror, his wife (whose son the child was) told him the whole affair, on which he sent for the child and had it cared for. The people of Ts'u called 'suckling' *tou* or nou, and 'a tiger' they called *wu-tu*, hence the child was called 'Tou-wutu', and he became Tze-wên, the chief minister of Ts'u."

"The nearest approximation to these words are found in the Taic-Shan vocabularies, where 'suckle or suckling' is called *dut* (Siamnese), and 'a tiger' is *htso*, *tso*, *su*, etc. The connection here suggested by these vocables is further promoted by this fact that a large proportion of the proper names of that same state of Ts'u are preceded by *tou*, which seems to be a sort of prefixed particle. This is also a peculiarity of the Tchungkia dialect of some tribes still in existence in the southwest of China and formerly in Kiangsi, where they represented the ancient ethnic stock of the state of Ts'u. And this Tchungkia dialect is Tai-Shan to such an extent that Siamese speaking travellers could without much difficulty understand it."

The laws governing the phonetic changes of Chinese and Siamese are still not fully known. Whether *htso*, *tso*, or *su* are derivable from *wu-tu* is still very questionable. The ch'u people at that time (6th Century B. C.) spoke a Chinese dialect. From the literature of this period, the ch'u dialect was not much different from the other dialects spoken in other parts of China. It is most gratuitous to consider the Ch'u dialect as Shah on this flimsy evidence. The proper names of Ch'u prefixed (?) with *tou* are not more than two or three. T. de Lacouperie's statement here is an exaggeration. The Chung-chia (another local Chinese name for the Shan) as we shall show later are everywhere to the south of the Miao-yao groups. Other writers go still further. W. W. Cochrane says that the Shans "actually form one of the chief ingredients that compose the so-called Chinese race". (*Shana*, Vol. I, p, 8) Cochrane also held that "the old name of this region (Ssuchuan) was Shuh, which *looked* suspiciously like the Shan word for 'tiger', and the Shahs of Burma belong to the 'tiger tribe'. This is entirely in ignorance of the meaning and etymology of the Chinese character *shuh*. For a discussion of the language of the Ch'u, see Eduard Erkes: Die Sprache des alten ch'u. *TP*, 1930, XXVⅡ, pp. 1-11.

Dr. Chi Li identifies the ancient states of Wu and Yueh in the lower Yangtzu valley as Shan on the ground that they practiced tattooing. As tattooing is a trait widely distributed, it is very unsafe to use it as a criterion unless it is checked by other traits. The Shans are not the only people in southeastern Asia who practiced tatooing. The moi of Indo-China also tattooed their bodies (see Henry Baudesson: *Indo-China and its Primitive Peoples*, p. 119). The Moi are closely related to the Miao-Yao group of Southern China by possessing the Dog-ancestor myth (see Baudesson, op. cit. pp. 105-107). Linguistically and physically they are also related. The Wu and Yueh did not resist the Chinese advance but the Nan-Chao did, so Dr. Li was troubled with his explanation of this contradictory fact: "After they had reached Yunnan, the Shans evidently determined to make a last stand against the northern invading group, although they kept on their southward migration and give rise to the modern Siamese." (*Formation of the Chinese People*, p. 258) It would be much easier to assume that the Wu and Yueh were not Shans at all.

It may be added that the ancient Wu and Yueh and the modern Shans practiced tattooing to a great extent, but the people of Chu were never reported to have tattooed their bodies. It further weakens the identification of Chu as Shan.

The Chinese only came into contact with the Shan during the early Christian centuries when they came to Yunnan. This point is strongly borne out by the present stratification of aboriginal peoples in south China.① We find everywhere the Miao-yao group is to the north of the Shan group, along the borders of southern Kiangsi, Hunan, Kuangsi and Kueichou. The same is true in Yunnan. The Lolo, Moso and Lisu (they are closely related to each other linguistically) are everywhere found north of the Shan groups.

The formation of the Shan race seems to be quite a recent affair as the homogeniety of their language shows.② Their home is probably in the Yung-chang area, southwestern Yunnan, and by the beginning of the eighth century A. D. they began to spread eastward into southern Kueichou, Kuangsi and even as far east as Kuangtung, and they mingled with the Mon-Khmer peoples. Southward they pushed along the Gekong and Genam valleys driving before them the Gon-Khmer speaking peoples and finally in the thirteenth and fourteenth centuries they reached the sea at what is now Siam. This great southward movement may be due to the downfall of the Nan-chao empire.

The first Nan-Chao king Hsi-nu-lo came to the throne in the year 629 A. D. He was of quite humble origin. In later works he was claimed to be descended from an Indian king, undoubtedly due to Buddhist fabrication.③ Hsi-nu-lo was succeeded by Lo-shen-yen (A. D. 674-713), Lo-shen-yen by Shen-lo-pi (A. D. 714-729), Shen-lo-pi by Pi-lo-ko (A. D. 730-749). In the year A. D. 732 Pi-lo-ko conquered the other five *chao* and consolidated them into one empire. He still acknowledged the suzerainty of China and received his institution from the T'ang Emperor Yuan Tsung (A. D. 713-755) and was given

---

① See map Ⅱ.

② A. Henry, op. cit., p. 97. Cochrane, op. cit., p. 7 and note.

③ See Pelliot, *BEFEO*, IV, 1904, pp. 167-168.

the name Meng-kuei-yi.[①] After him followed two of the most illustrious of the Nan-chao kings: Ko-lo-feng (A. D. 749-779) and Yi-mao-hsun (A. D. 779-809).[②] At this time the Tibetans were the most powerful nation in the west and constantly at war with China. Nan-chao shifted its allegiance, being at one time with the Chinese and at others with the Tibetans, until finally during. the Sung period (A. D. 960-1278) all communication was entirely stopped.

During the reign of Ko-lo-feng, he forced 20000 families of the Western Ts'uan to migrate southward to the Yung-chang area. Some writers regarded this as the southward movement of the Karen, but we have no evidence for such an identification.[③] The Eastern Ts'uan on account of their unintelligible language, all dispersed into the forests and the deep valleys, so they escaped this general forced exodus. Later, the Eastern Ts'uan migrated and occupied the original area of the Western Ts'uan and became powerful again.[④]

Under the Nan-chao were thirty-seven barbarian tribes. Only of the Ts'uan have we had much information. The Western Ts uan were forced out of their territory by Ko-lo-feng, and only the Eastern Ts'uan occupied the Lolo territory at this time. Of all these tribes, it is also the Eastern Ts'uan which show the closest affinities to the present Lolo.

The Eastern Ts'uan were divided into seven tribes: (1) A-yu-lu, (2) A-mang, (3) Kwuei-shan, (4) Pao-man, (5) Lulu-man, (6) Mo-mi-chien and (7) Wu-tun.[⑤] It is the fifth tribe, Lulu-man, that was identified with the Lolo in the Yuan dynasty.[⑥] But the Lulu was not the most important tribe during the

---

① Meaning "returning to righteousness".

② Imousun of E. H. Parker, see op. cit.

③ E. H. Parker, *The Old Thai or Shan Empire of Western Yunnan. China Rev.* XX, pp, 337 seq.

④ See VⅢ, I.

⑤ See I.

⑥ IX, Book 2, pp. 24-25. "Lolo are the descendents of the Lulu of the Ts'uan barbarians. Lolo is a corruption of the sound Lulu."

T'ang period (A. D. 618-906). That position was held by the Wu-tun. According to the *T'ang shuh*, the Wu-tun occupied an area of about one thousand square *li* and were divided into several subtribes, especially the subtribe Chulo, who occupied the area of Chiung-pu and Tai-tun, the area of the Ta-liang mountain range and the Chien-chang valley, it was also at the hands of the Wu-tun tribes in alliance with Chinese armies that the Tibetans suffered their most disastrous defeat.

The Wu-tun and a few other warlike tribes of Lolo affinities around the Ta-liang mountain area were mentioned in the *Sung Shih*, especially as wearing felt cloaks and dressing the hair into a knot on the head. Unfortunately information from this period is very scanty. When the Sung conquered the kingdom of Later Shu (modern Ssuchuan), the general, Wang Chên-pin, drew up a plan for the conquest of Nan-chao and submitted it to Sung Tai-tsu (A. D. 960-976), the founder of the Sung dynasty (A. D. 960-1278). Tai-tsu, aware of the troubles the T'ang had had with the Nan-chao, drew a line with his jade axe along the Ta-tu river and said reluctantly: "Outside this line, the territory is not mine." So all communications with this region were prohibited.①

The kingdom of Nan-chao, after a succession of thirteen kings, was overthrown in the year 902 A. D. and was succeeded by the Ta-li (A. D. 937-1094) of the Tuan fatally. In 1097 A. D. this was succeeded by the Later Ta-li, until the latter was conquered by the Mongols in 1253 A. D. The Mongol conquest was rather a bloodless one.② The most serious strife took place at the beginning of the Ming (A. D. 1368-1644) and Ch'ing (A. D. 1644-1910) dynasties. Most of the Black Lolo fell in these battles and those who remained

① See IX.

② See III, Book 145.

retreated northward. A few accepted the office of Tu-ssu (native chiefs).[1]

During the Ming period the Lolo (formerly Lulu) became prominent, and all the other Eastern Ts'uan tribes seem to have disappeared surreptitiously. They cannot all have become extinct within such a short time. No later Lolo tribal names correspond with the names of the Eastern Ts'uan tribes mentioned in the *T'ang shu* except the Lulu. The only explanation seems to be that these tribal names were names of the ruling families or clans. When the family died out or lost its power, so went with it the name, as in the case of the Ts'uan. The Lolo tribe being the most powerful later, its name became a generic name for them all.

From this brief account the movements of peoples in this part of China can be clearly visualized, The Pai P'u were perhaps the original inhabitants of this region, and later consitituted the bulk of the population of the kingdom of T'ien founded under Chinese leadership, and their remnants are still to be found in Yumnan as the Puman. To the northeast of T' ien, the Yeh-lang showed strong affinities with the Lolo, but their exact relationship can not be ascertained. During the early centuries of the Christian era the Lolo seem to have dispossessed the Pai P'u. Where they came from, it is not known, presumably from the Tibetan-Burman border. At the same time the Miao-Yao group were migrating south-ward on the east in Kueichou and Kuanghsi. The Shan were also beginning to assert themselves and finally consolidated into the kingdom of Nan-chao in the eighth century. During the whole Nan-chao and Ta-li period, the Lolo perhaps constituted the general bulk of the population in the north and the warrior class Lo-chu-tzu of the Nan-chao armies[2] might be chiefly recruited

① See IV, Books 300-319. V, Books 517-522.

② The Nan-chao armies were conscripted from all the aboriginal peoples. The Lo-chutzu were the shock troops selected from the local militia. See *Man sbu*, chap. 9, pp. 2 seq.

from them. After the fall of Ta-li and at the beginning of the Ming and Ch'ing dynasties, there was a general depopulation of the pure Lolo and a more thorough sinicization of the Yunnan area.

Tribal Divisions

The political unit of the Lolo is the tribe. During the T'ang times the Eastern Ts'uan were divided into seven principal tribes, of which only the name Lulu survived. According to the *T'ang Shu* the smallest of these tribes were more than one hundred families each and ruled over by a chief called *Kuei-chu* (Ghost lord). These tribes were constantly at war with each other as the Lolo are at present. Sometimes an able chief of some tribe might attain supremacy and unite them into a loose political unit, as in the case of the Ts'nan. Such unions were of short duration.

As to what had become of the early Lolo tribes, we know nothing. It was not until the Ming period (A. D. 1368-1644), that the name Lolo became well established and their tribes recorded. The *Nan-chao Yeh-shih* gives a list of eleven Lolo tribes subject to the Nan-chao.① They are as follows: *Hei Lolo*, *Pai Lolo*, *Kan Lolo*, *Hai Lolo*, *Sa-mi Lolo*, *Ko Lolo*, *A-che Lolo*, *A-wu Lolo*, *Lu-wu Lolo*, *Lao-wu Lolo* and *Miao Lolo*. At present only the *Hei* (black) *Lolo* and *Pai* (white) *Lolo* are existing names, all the others having vanished. But the *Hei* and *Pai* are no longer tribal names. They are generic names of two types of Lolo and within each contain many tribes. Lietard, who had studied the White Lolo of Yunnan, considered most of these names as inventions of Chinese authors and impossible of identification.② But a closer examination of Lietard's

① Book Ⅱ, pp. 25-27.

② *Au Yunnan*.

tribes will reveal that most of them show close identity. According to Lietard's description of his tribes, the *Na-P'ou* corresponds to the *Hei* (black) *Lolo*, the *Na-P'ou* to the *Pai* (white) *Lolo*, and the *Ko-P'ou* to the *Kan* (dry) *Lolo*. He gives more than twenty other divisional names, and many are nearly the same as these given in the *Nan-chao Yeh-shih*, such as *Sa-m'e*, Lou-ou P'ou A-d'je P'ou, A-tcha P'o, lo-ou P'o, etc.①

Most of the tribal names found in old Chinese records are by no means indicative of racial characteristics. They are given to the natives because of some peculiar features in their dress or customs, occupation, place of their occurrence, and most common of all according to the names of their ruling families. Since all these things have changed, tribes have moved about, and ruling families died out, so their tribal names have changed. A little more fieldwork and study of their history will reveal most of their identities.

Among the independent Lolo of Ssuchuan, Lietard gives the names of twenty-six tribes of Black Lolo, thirty tribes of White Lolo, three tribes of mixed (e. g. black and white) Lolo, and two tribes of slaves. Lietard's information is only secondary and he does not give any further details of their settlements, social usages, etc. d'Ollone, who has travelled through their territory (in 1906-1909), indicated that the tribes occupied well defined territories and trespassing was resented, as he had frequently to change guides and respondents when passing from the territory of one tribe to that of another.② The same condition may have existed from very early times as is shown by the few indications from the early records. As the Lolo are a semi-pastoral people and enjoy hunting, whether they have any rights regarding pasture grounds or hunting territory, we know nothing.

---

① The *Yunnan tung chih* also gives some tribes that are not in the *Nan-chao yeh-shih*, such as: A-hsie Lolo, Pu-la Lolo, Ta- Lolo, Hsiao Lolo, etc.

② D'Ollone, op. cit.

Lietard is more conversant with the tribes of Yunnan. He says that each of the tribes bears the same tribal name, speaks the same dialect, wears the same costume, and is endogamous. Since Lietard is the first investigator to treat this subject, there is no other material for comparison. Tribal endogamy seems to be contrary to the old practice. During the T'ang dynasty, according to *man-shu*, the Black Barbarians intermarried among themselves irrespective of tribal and political divisions. Even the Nan-chao, considered Shan at present but belonging to the category of Black Barbarians, intermarried with the noble families of the Eastern Ts'uan, e. g. the modern Lolo. How the present tribal endogamous system works out we have to wait for more investigation to see.

The Dual Division of Black and White

The designation of black and white is a very common phenomenon among the peoples of southwest China. The term is often used in various shades of meaning and the exact connotation has to be determined in each case. Sometimes it is used to indicate the prevailing color of the costumes the people wear, as in the case of the Black and White Miao.① The term is also employed to convey the idea of the culture status of a people. Certain Miao tribes in southern Hunan province are called black because they are less civilized than their kinsmen near the Chinese towns.② The same is true with the Black and White Lisu, a people related with the Lolo on the Upper Mekong river.③ Sometimes the term *shen* (raw) and *shuh* (cooked or tamed) is used in

① Clark, op. cit. p. 371.

② Jamieson, op. cit. pp. 381-382.

③ Rose, Archibald, and Brown, J. C., *Li-su (Yawyin) Tribes of the Burma-China Frontier*, Memoirs, Asiatic Society of Bengal, Vol. Ⅲ, 1910-1914, pp. 249-276, ix pl.

substitution. But in all these usages, one point is clear. The peoples so far concerned seldom used this term to designate themselves. They are designations applied to them by the Chinese.

The case is different among the Lolo. They actually styled themselves as Black and White.① But the situation is very delicate: and observers often miss this division entirely. It is interesting that d'Ollone passed through the whole span of Lolo territory, and did not notice this division at all. He speaks about the noble families, serfs, slaves, but makes not a single mention of the Black and White distinction. Lietard spent many of his missionary years among the Lolo of Yunnan and considered it as purely a Chinese invention, saying that many of the Lolo in Yunnan do not know of such a distinction. As he got more information from Ssuchuan where the Black Lolo are much more numerous, he found such a division indubitably existed. He was forced to accept it but tried to account for it by a linguistic interpretation.② In Yunnan the Black Lolo only constitute the few ruling families (tu-ssu), so every where one meets are the White Lolo. The situation is somewhat reversed in Ssuchuan, where the majority are Black Bones (as they call themselves) and those recently reduced to serfdom can scarcely be called Lolo on the strict sense of the term.

If we turn to the history of this area, this division is a very old one. At least, it goes back to the ninth century during the T'ang dynasty, when we have documentary evidence. In the *Man-shu* and the *T'ang shu*, whenever a tribe is mentioned, it is invariably appended with the discriminatory term *wu-man*

---

① Jamieson (op. cit. p. 381) says that "they (Lolo) are termed black not because the black Miao are so named, but because of the dark nature of their skin." This is followed by Buxton in his *Peoples of Asia*, p. 156, "they (Lolo) are called 'Black' because of the darkness of their complexions." This is surely not the case. They are certainly fairer than most of the aborigines, as has been noticed by all observers. Some even regard them as fairer than the southern European. If they are so named because of the darkness of their skin, then how should we explain the term "White" Lolo?

② His usual theory, the Lolo called themselves *No-so*, *no means black*, so the Chinese misinterpreted it and called them black.

(black barbarians), or *pai-man* (white barbarians). The following is a table reconstructed from the different sources of this period.

Wu-man Black Barbarians	1. Eastern Ts'uan (Lolo) 2. Ai-lao 3. Nan-chao 4. Tu-ching man 5. Ch'ang-kun man 6. Shih man 7. Shun man 8. Mo man 9. Tu-lao
Pai-man White Barbarians	1. Western Ts'uan 2. Nun-tung man 3. Chins-lin man

This division seems at least to be intended to indicate some racial affinity, as is shown by the manner in which it is used. How far it is accurate, we do not know. A linguistic difference seems to be involved.① If we compare the modern Black and White Lolo, their physical characteristics are quite contrasted. The Black Lolo are characterized by tall stature, sometimes reported taller than Europeans' aquiline nose, well developed brow ridges, and as a whole quite different from the Mongoloid cast in appearance.② The White Lolo are

① *Man shu*, chap. 8, pp. 3-4, "... The language (of the Wu-man) is entirely different from the Pai-man."

② Their fine physical features are noted by all travellers from the time of, Marco Polo down to the present. E. C. Baber remarked that they are taller than any Europeans' but this seems to be exaggerated. D'Ollone (op. cit. p. 51) especially praised their fine features by saying: "There was nothing of the Asiatic; the complexion was not yellow, but swarthy, like that of the inhabitants of Southern Europe; the eyes, neither oblique nor flattened, were large, and protected by fine arched brows; the nose was aquiline, the mouth well cut... 'What superb redskins these men would make, with a plume of feathers or a warbonnet on the head!' "

generally inferior in physique. The cephalic index is also slightly different between the two.① These physical differences at least give us some suggestions about the disentangling of this perplexing question. A careful study of this peculiar institution will undoubtedly reveal some of the secrets of the coalescence and disintegration of the peoples in this part of China.

The Black Lolo every where constitute the ruling chiefs, sometimes even among the Miao in Western Kueichou province.② To be called "black" is an indication of ruling aristocracy. They never intermarry with the White Lolo or with any other people. In Yunnan the Lolo chiefs sometimes marry their daughters to the sons of Chinese officials and distinguished Chinese families,③ but they themselves very rarely marry Chinese wives. Among the independent Lolo of Ssuchuan, endogamy is strictly enforced, d'Ollone wrote that the rule was as strictly observed as in the Indian caste.④

If the division of Black and White among the Lolo has some significance upon the racial question, it will be like the following. The Black Lolo are originally a conquering group representing an uniform racial stock. The White Lolo are people originally representing quite different racial stocks subjugated by the Black Lolo one after another, and having imposed upon them the Lolo language. This process is still going on, in the independent Lolo country. But in Yunnan owing to the advance of the Chinese, the ruling nobility were either fallen in the field or had retreated northward. What is left behind are only those slaves (White Lolo) who do not care whom their masters are. A few ruling

---

① A. F. Legendre, *Far West Chinois*, tableau A-C, T'oung Pao, 1909, T. 10, facing page 642. Subject measured 19. For an analysis, see R. B. Dixon, *Racial History of Man*, p. 281. See also V. K. Ting; *Man Yu san chi.*

② Jamieson, op. cit. p. 381.

③ There is an interesting little book which Dr. J. K. Shryock and I are translating, *The Marriage Customs of the Tu-ssu (native chief) of Yunnan and Kuei-chou*, which tells now the ceremonies of *such* intermarriages are carried out.

④ D'Ollone, op. cit. p. 63.

families have remained and accepted the Chinese office of Tussu (native chiefs). This is the actual condition we find now in Yunnan and the in dependent Lolo country.

The Lolo Cloak and "Horn"

As far as material culture is concerned, the Lolo are much less advanced than their neighbors. They are semi-pastoral, but they do not milk their cows. Agricultural pursuits are left to the slaves, who are hardly Lolo. Their dwelling is a kind of hut made of rammed earth, covered with fir planks and interlaced with bamboo strips. There is nothing that can be called household furniture, no tables, chairs, etc. The only utensils are the few turned wooden bowls, bamboo baskets, and iron pans for boiling purposes. They know no condiments in the preparation of food except the salt which is considered as a great delicacy. The only textile they have is a kind of rough hempen fabric, woven with a method described as the "primitive of the primitives", and the tough felt they use for their cloak. They have no money, weights or measures. They have no pottery. This they shared with other ancient peoples of this region. The Nan-chao, according to the Man-shu, likewise had no pottery. All their containers were made of gold and silver and bamboo.① We may continue to enumerate their negative traits *ad infinitum*, but itwill not help *us* out in our historical deductions. Here we will take two characteristic Lolo traits which are not shared by other peoples in this region at present and trace them to their earliest known origin and draw our conclusions: namely, the Lolo cloak and the Lolo "horn".

---

① *Man sbu*, chap. 8, p. 1, "The culinary utensils of the Nan-chao are made of gold and silver. The officials and generals used bamboo containers. The aristocracy eat with chopsticks, but the ordinary people fetched their food with fingers."

The most characteristic Lolo dress is the felt cloak which both men and women wear as a protection against rain and cold. This garment is usually of deep brown, sometimes blue or of the natural tint of the wool. The texture of the felt is very rough and uneven. This cloak is invaluable to the Lolo. He never doffs it, winter or summer. In sleep, it is his matress, blanket, and even roof. For the Lolo will stretch himself out comfortably in the first hollow he can find among the rocks when night falls, and will slumber peacefully in this wonderful cape. "The true home of the Lolo is his cloak."

This useful and expedient Lolo dress is not used by any other people who now surround them, so it may be considered a national Lolo attire. If we turn to the historical material, we find the ancient Nanchao wore a similar felt cloak. The *Man-shu* says: "All the barbarians (e. g. Nanchao) wear felt cloaks; their other clothes are slightly similar to the Han (Chinese), but their headbags (coiffure) are different. The Nan-chao (e. g. royalties) used red damask (the material cannot be ascertained with certainty), and all others used gray color. Their custom was to use a piece of cloth sewed with the edges of one corner together in the form of a horn. A wooden cone was stuffed into it. It was fixed to the back of the head and the hair twisted around it. Then the rest of the cloth was wrapped around the head. Only the royalties and the high officials were allowed to wear this. The lower officials and the Lo-chu-tzu (warriors) dressed their hair on the forehead into a knot, and they were not allowed to wear the head-bag. All wear felt cloaks and go barefooted. Even the prime ministers and generals are not ashamed of going barefooted."①

The wearing of the felt cloak was evidently a national custom of the Nan-chao. But this raises several interesting questions. The Nan-chao, from the linguistical evidences we possess, were unquestionably Shan. The use of felt

---

① Chapter 8, pp. 1-2.

and especially the cloak is foreign to all the Shans at present. Was this trait lost when they migrated to warmer climates? Or, was this originally a Lolo dress adopted by the Nan-chao from their subjects? These are questions we are unable to answer at present, but as we go further we will find there are still more similarities between the Nan-chao and the modern Lolo.

Another notable one is the peculiar way the Lolo dress their hair, popularly known as the Lolo "horn". The hair is thrown forward, twisted and coiled into the shape of a horn resting on the forehead. In appearance it looks like a horn. It is peculiarly Lolo, and no other people at present in the southwest of China dress their hair in this fashion. The passage just quoted from the *Man-shu* shows that the lower rank officials and the Lo-chu-tzu of the Nan-chao armies wore the same kind of coiffure. This further substantiates our statement that the warrior class of the Nan-chao army were chiefly Lolo.

If we turn,to the Naga tribes of the Manipur, the Marrings have very similar methods of dressing their hair. "The men comb their hair from behind and from the sides, and gather it into a horn-shaped protuberance above the centre of the forehead; round the base of; their horn are usually wound strings of beads of various kinds, and transfixing it crosswise is a steel bodkin–shaped instrument with a sharp point about fifteen inches long and flattened for about a third of its lengfh at the other extremity..."① The ornaments of the coiffure are somewhat different, as may be expected, but the shape and the method of making the coiffure are exactly the same. As there is no other people in Asia known to have dressed their hair in this fashion, the striking coincidence cannot be accidental. The situation is very tempting, especially as the Lolo have a tradition that they came from that direction. It would be rash to speculate now on this single evidence that the Marring Naga and the Lolo are in some way related.

---

① Hodson, T. C., *The Naga*: *Tribes of Manipur*, Macmillan, 1911. pp. 29-30. See also plate facing page 21.

Disposal of the Dead

All peoples are very conservative in the manner of burying their dead. It is a trait that is likely to persist for ages, and can only be changed by radical religious influences from the outside. Since the Lolo have resisted all religious ideas in the past,① their treatment of the dead may be a custom dating back to great antiquity. In contrast to other aboriginal peoples of China, the Lolo practiced cremation. This custom goes back at least to as early as the T'ang dynasty, for the *Man-shu* says: "The Mung-shê and Wu-man do not bury their dead. They burn the corpse three days after death and cover the ashes with soil. They only keep the two ears. The Nan-chao keep the ears in golden vases. The golden vases are put in a silver box and stored in a special room. At every season they are taken out and sacrifices offered to them. The common people use copper and iron vases."② The Wu-man included the Eastern Tsuan, e. g. the progenitors of the modern Lolo. Although the custom of keeping the ears of the dead in metal vases is not present among the modern Lolo, the practice of cremation was corroborated by Marco Polo. He says: "When any of them die, the bodies are burnt, and then they take the bones and put them in little chests. These are carried up the mountains, and placed in great caverns, where they are hung up in such wise that neither man nor beasts can come to them."③ This

---

① The Lolo are surrounded on all sides by Buddhist peoples but they have resisted the advance of Buddhism into their beliefs. Christianity met the same fate in spite of the incessant efforts of the missionaries.

② *Man-shu*, chap. VⅢ, pp. 3-4.

③ Baber, E. C., *China*, *in Some of Its Physical and Social Aspects. Proceedings RGS*, n.s., Vol. V, 1883, pp. 445-448. Baber's identification of the *Coloman* of Marco Polo with the Lolo, I think, is valid.

statement was again substantiated by the Grosvenor expedition in 1876.

"Before reaching Lao-wan-tan we were shown ledges on inaccessible cliffs on which coffins of a very small size were to be seen. I, however, did not observe any. These are supposed to be relics of a bygone barbarous age before the Chinese occupation. When asked how they were ascertained to be coffins, the natives replied that the monkeys, which in summer are very numerous, throw them down the cliffs. It is a source of wonder to the Chinese how they could have been placed in these inaccessible situations."[①] Grosvenor was travelling along the outskirts of the Lolo territory in western Ssuchuan which was occupied by the Lolo in former times. Cremation is an idea abhorrent to the tribes of southwest China. It was never mentioned in the ancient records. Its practice by the Lolo serves as a sure guide for their identification and correlations.

This brings out another question. The Nan-chao were considered Shan, but the present Shan do not cremate their dead. They bury their dead in spite of Buddhist and Hindu influences.[②] This point once more shows that the Nan-chao are more related culturally to the Lolo than to the modern Shan who are considered their direct descendants. The Man-shu further says that "the Pai-man bury their dead like the Chinese and plant trees around the graves". This substantiates the discussion of the dual division of black and white, that they were originally contrasted in culture.

The Ghost Cult of the Tsuan and the Ancestor Cult of the Lolo

Next we may take the ghost cult of the Ts'uan and the ancestor cult of the

① Ibid., p. 446.

② Milne, Leslie, *Shans at Home*, 1910, pp. 89-97.

modern Lolo. It is said in the *T'ang shu* that the barbarians revered their ghost (perhaps ancestors) and had ghost lords (kuei-chu), who ruled over them. Every year each family contributed an ox or goat and sacrificed them at the home of the Kuei-chu, who presided over them. When they summoned the ghosts or sent them away, they carried arms. This is the time they made their raids and revenged their wrongs.①

The most important cult of the modern Lolo is their ancestor cult. We owe our sole knowledge of this to Lietard who gave quite a detailed account.② It appears to be similar to the ancient ghost cult. The chief ceremony takes place in the first or second moon. The families in turn engage a *pi-mo* and invite the villagers to a dance. A pig and a goat are killed. Rice and wine are prepared. They are first offered to the ancestors and then eaten communally. The rituals are quite long and very elaborate. The details of the Ts'uan ghost-cult we have no means of knowing as the information conveyed to us by the *T'ang Shu* is very sketchy, but the essential points seem to be very similar to those of the Lolo ancestor cult. The kuei-chu seemed to be a sort of sacerdotal chief who officiated both at religious ceremonies and in secular affairs. His supersession by a class of priesthood in religious matters is a natural development. The ancestor cult is the most important cult of the Lolo, just as the ghost cult was to the Ts'uan. We are not in a position to say very much on this subject, as our information both on the ancient cult and the modern cult is very scanty. Many writers seem to have overlooked this practice among the Lolo entirely.

---

① See I. The same custom was also present among the Yakuts in ancient times. "During the summer, in olden times, every rich man arranged a kumiss festival, at which all members of the clan assembled and were entertained. Other people, and frequently whole clans, were invited; and during the festival, defensive and offensive leagues were concluded." W. Jochelson: *Kumiss Festivals of the Yakut and the Decoration of the Kumiss Vessels.* Boas Memorial Volume, 1906, p. 263.

② Lietard, *Au Yunnan*, 1913.

The Problem of Lolo Origin

Having made a general review of the history and the probable movements of the Lolo and examined a few of their characteristic cultural traits in comparison with those of the historical peoples who surrounded or related to them, we are now in a position to examine whether they have any bearing on the problem of Lolo origin or not. Before going on, a review of the existing theories concerning this problem will be clarifying.

The earliest one to speculate on this question is perhaps Terrien de Lacouperie, who says: "The Laka Lolos were a southeastern extension of the populations of northeastern Tibet..."① In this, he connects the Lolo with the ancient Jung and Chiang of the Chinese records. As he did not produce any substantial evidence to support his hypothesis, we shall discuss it more fully in connection with V. K. Ting's theory.

In a similar fashion Paul Vial and many other writers connect the Lolo with the Tibetans.② The evidence is primarily linguistical, e. g. by comparison of a very limited number of selected words. The scientific relationship of the so-called Sinitic group of languages is still something to be established, so

---

① Op. cit. pp. 480-481.

② Vial, Paul: *Les Lolos*, 1898.

Deniker, J.: *The Races of Man*, 1900. "The Lolo or Nesus, as they call themselves, of western Sechuen and the north-east of Yunnan, with whom we must connect the Kolo or Golyk or the country of Amdo (east of Tibet), perhaps represent it in its present form, if the portrait of them drawn by Thorel is correct. With slight figure, brownish complexion, they have a straight profile, oval face, high forehead, straight and arched nose, thick beard even on the sides of the face and always frizzy or wavy hair. Their language, however, fixed by a hieroglyphic mode of writing, appears to belong to the Burmese family..." (pp. 381-2)

For H. R. Davies' classification, see op. cit. p. 337. V.K. Ting's classification is somewhat based on Davies', which is adopted by Dr. Chi Li in his book (op. cit.), p. 255.

comments are hardly needed in the present state of our knowledge.

V. K. Ting is the first to establish his hypothesis on a physical and historical basis①, During his prospecting tours in Yunnan, he was able to secure a number of measurements of the Lolo. The cephalic index, as obtained from these measurements, is prevailing dolicocephalic. So he concludes that "historically the Lolos in association with the Chiangs, formed an important people in Northwest Szechuan, Kokonor, and South Turkestan. In the last place they intermarried with the Iranian people known as Yuechi. The Iranian element may have found its way into the Lolos through the Chiangs."② Here Ting is using the term "Iranian" in the same sense as Ripley.

From the details Ting published later in his *Travels in Yunnan*,③ we learn that the subjects he measured are perhaps practically all White Lolo. So, his findings are hardly surprising. The dolichocephalic factor corresponds to the Caspian type, in Dr. R. B. Dixon's terminology, which is the secondary dominant factor among the White Lolo.④ As the White Lolo is a much mixed group subject to the Black Lolo, the dolichocephalic factor may represent a strain of the older population of Mon-Khmer speaking peoples.⑤ If we examine Legendre's measurements, the Brachycephalic factor prevails. Since the number of subjects measured were small in both cases, neither can be considered as conclusive.

---

① Ting, V. K.: *Native Tribes of Yunnan.*, *China Medical Journal*, March, 1921.

② Ibid.

③ Ting, V. K.: *Man yu san chi*, Independent Rev., Nos. 34-36, 1933.

④ Dixon, R. B.: "The Lolo are divided into an aristocracy and a class of common people, and the two groups appear to differ in their physical characteristics. The aristocracy is very similar to the population of Kwangtung, the Palae-Alpine factors being in the majority, with the Alpine type secondary. The common people, on the other hand, show a still stronger dominance of the Palae-Alpine type, the Alpine being displaced as a secondary type by the Caspian." *Racial History of Man*, p. 281. Dixon based his analysis on Legendre's (op. cit.) measurements.

⑤ The Mon-Khmer speaking peoples, the Pnong, Moi, Kha, etc., of S. E. Asia all show a strong dolichocephalic factor. Se Dixon, Ibid., p. 276.

To attribute the long headedness and the supposed Caucasoid features of the Lolo to the infusion of Iranian blood, e. g., the Yuehchi, is too far fetched. First of all, we do not know racially who the Yuehchi were. Were they Iranians, Scythians, Huns, Turks, or Turco Tartars?① From the fragmentary information furnished by the *Chien Han Shu*② the Yuehchi were originally a pastoral nomadic people inhabiting the eastern part of Chinese Turkestan. About the end of the third century B. C. they were defeated by the Hsiung-nu (the Huns) and a large part of them migrated westward and conquered the Tocharians who were responsible for the overthrow of the Greek state of Bactria.③ During the beginning of the present era, they conquered Northwest India, and were known there as the Kushanas, who had much to do with the transmission of Buddhism into China. A small portion of the Yuehchi did not join the western exodus but retreated southward and mixed with the Chiang. They were known later as the Little Yuehchi. when the Chinese drove the Hsiung-nu from Chinese Turkestan, the Little Yuehchi were induced to return to their original place again. This happened about the end of the second century B. C. The Yuehchi hypothesis is too much exploited by recent scholars, and everything in Central Asia is credited to them. Whether the Little Yuehchi had penetrated so far south as

---

① The racial affinity of the Yueh-chi is still a question of much debate. The bibliography is extensive. For the latest discussion see, Sten Konow, *Kharoshthi Inscriotions*, Corpus Inscriptionum Indicarum, Vol. Ⅱ, Pt. I, 1929, pp. xlix-lxxxii. The general opinion seems to be that the Yueh-chi (Kushanas) were Indo-Scythians.

② History of Former Han dynasty.

③ Shortly before the Yueh-chi came to Bactria, the country seemed to have been occupied by a people known to the Greeks as Tocharians (Tukhara of the Indian writers and Tuhuo-lo of the Chinese). They were responsible for the overthrow of the Greek kingdom in Bactria. Where the Tocharians came from, it is not certain-presumably from the same direction as the Yueh-chi, e. g. western Chinese Turkestan. Some identify them with the Chinese Tahsia, and others with the Yueh-chi. Recent discoveries in Chinese Turkestan show that the Tocharians spoke an Indo-European language more related to the Western group, e. g. Greek and Latin, than to the Eastern group, e. g. Iranian and Sanskrit. These discoveries give much color to the theory of the Central Asiatic origin of the Indo-Europeans.

Southwest Ssuchuan or not is very problematical, as we have shown before that the migration of the Lolo since historical times is a northward instead of a southward one. Moreover, if we consider the Yeh-lang as Lolo, they were already an established race during the time when the Yuehchi began to migrate.

The theory of L. H. D. Buxton① is based on Ting's measurements and the information supplied by C. E. Jamieson. Jamieson says that the Lolo came from the Tibetan-Burman border, on the ground that the Lolo are the only people in southwest China frequently associated with the horse.② Buxton connects the Lolo with his Nesiots, who were indirectly related to the longheaded population of Western Asia and the Mediterranean area, corresponding to Elliot Smith's Brown race. The only difference with Ting is that the connection is a southward one around the Himalaya foothills. Both Ting and Buxton seem not to have taken Legendre's measurements into consideration, though they are more important than Ting's. And Buxton seems not to be familiar with the historical facts which are inextricably connected with the problem.

If we now turn to the traditions among the Lolo themselves and see what they say about this problem, we find that according to the various versions recorded, they all point to their coming from the Tibetan-Burman border. How far this tradition may be substantiated, we have no means of knowing. The Lolo, as they were first known to the Chinese, were in the North-east of Yunnan. In this very spot C. E. Hicks made an interesting report. In the Chao-tung area there are many earthen mounds conspicuous on the plains. "Some of these have been opened, and in them have been found rough unhewn stones, apparently placed as door frames, and burned bricks of an unusually large size and marked with a peculiar pattern."③ How much has it any bearing on the

① Op. cit. pp. 156-157.

② Op. cit. p. 381.

③ Hicks, E. C., *The Nou Su*... Chinese Recorder, Vol. 41, p. 211.

question of the origin of the Lolo, it is too early to speculate. According to Hicks, the Lolo in this area have a tradition that these earthen mounds represent a native population, the P'u, whom the Lolo destroyed. Archaeology must have a great part to play in the future.

Nor are the Lolo autochthonous to the Ta-Liang mountains, according to their own tradition. If the stories recorded by Baber① and d'Ollone② contain some truth, they have always regarded themselves as vanquished and deprived of their rich valleys by the Chinese. Their retreat to the mountains continued as late as 1727 in the Ching dynasty. Popular traditions may contain some historical truth, but cannot be taken too seriously as authentic history. One thing seems to be fairly certain-that all their traditions indicate that they are not the original inhabitants of their present habitat.

If we take the few ethnological traits which we have treated before to see whether they have any bearing on the problem, First let us take the dual division of black and white. The use of "black" to indicate orthodox descent or blue-blood was quite prevalent among the older peoples of northeastern Asia. The Western Liao kingdom founded by Yeh-lü Ta-shih called themselves Khara Kitan, e. g. Black Kitan, in order to indicate that they were the original Kitan. The Mongols were also first divided into black and white Tartars. Genghiz Khan and his generals and ministers all belonged to the Black Tartars.③ This cannot be considered as evidence of possible connections, but it may serve as suggestions to the solution of the problem. The use of felt by the Lolo and the practice of the "ghost cult" by the ancient Tsuan are also in accord with the

---

① Baber, E. C., *Travels and Researches in the Interior of China. Royal Geographical Society*, Supplementary papers, Vol. I., p. 121.

② Op. cit. p. 107.

③ See *Mung ta pei lu* (Accounts about the Tartars). What the Black and White Tartar divisions indicated is still a subject of much debate. For a discussion see *Researches on the Wu-liang-haand the Tartars*, 1932, pp. 31-37.

northern nomadic peoples. As to the practice of cremation, no possible suggestions can be made at present. It certainly cannot be attributed to Buddhist or Hindu influence, because the Lolo have never been Buddhists.

There are two other negative traits which point to entirely different directions, namely the lack of pottery and the milking trait. The Lolo are surrounded by pottery making peoples on their south and east, but they have never mastered that art. Most of their pots, bowls, and containers were made of wood. Occasionally they possessed a few pieces of pottery, but they are of Chinese importation. We know very few people in the Old World who lack pottery except a few of the nomads, as the Mongols. Its absence among the Lolo is rather conspicuous, for it cannot be attributed to isolation or to some other cause.

The few ethnological traits mentioned above seem to indicate their connections with the north, but there is one strong negative trait that excludes them from that direction. They are not milk users. The peoples of Asia may be divided into two groups: those who use milk and those who do not, and each occupies a contiguous territory. All the northwestern Asiatics, the Tungus, Mongols, Turks, Tibetans, Hindus, Iranians end all the peoples of the Near East, and the Paleo-Asiatics, constitute the milk using group. The Chinese, Japanese, Shan, Lolo, and most of the Mon-khmer peoples belong to the non-milk using group. Its absence among the Lolo cannot be accidental. Flocks they possess, but milking is unknown. If they were originally pastoral peoples, such an important and essential trait could not be easily and entirely lost.① It cannot be attributed to Chinese influence; as a matter of fact, they have adopted very few Chinese traits. There are also other traits that suggest southern connections,

---

① Such as the Yakuts who retreated to northern Siberian tundras within historical times where the climate is most unfavorable for cattle breeding; but they still retain their cattle under very adverse conditions. See Jochelson, op. cit. pp. 257-271.

such as going barefooted, the use of poison arrow and the Lolo "horn". But the cross-bow is conspicuously lacking although it is a typical weapon in southeastern Asia.

Taking all these facts into consideration, the origin of the Lolo is still a mystery. Most of the theories are based on one set of facts, sometimes with disregard for the others. The question cannot be settled at present, and more field work will be needed in order to put these conflicting facts into their proper settings.

Bibliography

Abbreviations to Periodicals

ASB	Asiatic Society of Bengal
BEFEO	Bulletin de l'Ecole francaise d'Extrême-Orient
BMSAP	Bulletins et Memoires Société d'Anthropologie de Paris
CR	China Review
JRAI	Journal of the Royal Anthropological Institute of Great Britain and Ireland
JRASNCB	Journal of the Royal Asiatic Society, North China Branch
MC	Missions Catholiques
RGS	Royal Geographical Society
TP	T'oung Pao

Baber, E. C.

Travels and Researches in the Interior of China. *RGS*, Supplementary papers, 1882, pp. 1-201.

Bonifacy

Etude sur les coutumes et la langue de Lolo et de La-qua dy Haut Tonkin. *BEFEO*, *V*Ⅲ, 1908, pp. 531-558.

Bonin, Charles-Eude.

Vocabulaires. Mantse de Leang-chan. *TP*, IV, 1903, pp. 124-126.

Bourne, F. S. A.

Report by Mr. F. S. A. Bourne of a Journey to South-western China, presented to both Houses of Parliament by Command of Her Majesty, June 1888. *China*-No. I.

Bridgman, E. C.

Sketches of the Miau-tse. *JRASNCB*, Ⅲ, 1859, pp. 257-286.

Charria, S.

Les Inscriptions Lolo de Lou-k'ian. *BEFEO*, V, 1905, pp. 195-197.

Clark, George.

Translation of a Manuscript Account of the Kwei-chau Miao-tzu, written after the subjugation of the Miao-tzu about 1730. In A. R. Colquhoun, *Across Chrysé*, 1883. Vol. Ⅱ, Appendix, pp. 363-394.

Cordier, Henri.

Les Lolos, etat actuel de la question. *TP*, VⅢ, 1907, pp. 597-688.

Crabouillet, P.

Les Lotos (du Se-tschoun). *MC*, V, 1873, pp. 71-2, 94-5, 105-7.

Davies, H. R.

Yunnan: the link between India and the Yangtze. 1909 Appendix Ⅷ. The Tribes of Yunnan, pp. 332-398.

Deveria, M. B.

Les Lolos et les Miao-tze, a propos d'une brochure de M. P. Vial… *Journal Asiatique*, 1891, pp. 356-369.

Francois, C.

Notes sur les Lo-lo du Kien-tchang. *BMSAP*, V, 1904, pp. 637 -647.

Gutzlaff, C.

Tibet and Sefan. *Journal RGS*, XX, 1850, pp. 191-227.

Henry, A.

The Lolos and other tribes of western China. *JRAI*, XXXⅢ, 1903, pp. 96-107.

Hicks, C. C.

The Nou Su... *Chinese Recorder*, Vol. 41, pp 211-

Hosie, A.

Three Years in Western China. 1890. Chap. VI.

Jamieson, C. E.

The aborigines of Western China. *China Journal of Arts and Science*. Vol. I, 1923, pp 376-

Laufer, B.

The Si-hia Language, a Study in Indo-Chinese Philology. *TP*, XVⅡ, 1916, pp. 1-128.

Legendre, A. F.

Far West Chinois. Races aborigines - les Lolos - etude ethnologic et anthropologie. *TP*, 1909, pp. 340-380, 399-444, 603-665.

The Lolos of Kien-tchang, western China. *Annual Report*, *Smithsonian Institution*, 1911, pp. 569-602.

Liu, C. H.

On a Newly-discovered Lolo MS from Szechuan, China. *Man*. 1932, XXXⅡ, No. 268, OP. 235-6.

Lietard, A.

Le district des Lolos A-chi. *MC*, XXXVI, 1904, pp. 93-96, 105-8, 117-120.

Notions de grammair Lolo (dialects A-hi). *BEFEO*, IX, 1909 pp. 285-314.

Notions de grammaire Lolo (dialects A-hi). *TP*, XⅡ, 1911, pp. 627-663.

Essai de dictionnaire Lolo francais, dialecte A-hi. *TP*, XⅡ, pp. 1-37, 123-156, 316-346, 544-558.

Vocabulaire francaise Lolo. *TP*, XⅢ, 1912, pp. 1-42.

Au Yunnan les Lolo P'o: une tribu des aborigenes de la Chine meridionale. *Bibliotheque Anthropos*, Vol. I, 1913.

Madrolle, C

Quelques peuplades Lo-lo. *TP*, ⅠX, 1908, pp 529-576.

Maire, Henri

La mission des Lolos. *MC*, XⅣ, 1882, pp. 505-7.

Mueller, H.

Beitrag zur Ethnographic de Lolo. *Abessler Archiv*, Ⅲ, pp. 38-68.

Ollone, Vicomte d'

In Forbidden China. 1912.

Ecritures de peuples non chinois de la Chine. 1912.

Playfair, G. M. H.

The Misotzu of Kweichou and Yunnan from Chinese descriptions. *cr*, V, pp. 92-108.

Rocher, Emile

Histoire des princes dy Yunnan et leurs relations avec la Chine d'apres de documents historique chinois, traduits pour la premiere fois. *TP*, X, 1899, pp. 1-32, 115-154, 337-368, 437-458.

Shirokogoroff, S. M.

Phonetic notes on a Lolo dialect and consonant L. Academia Sinica: *Bulletin of the National Research Institute of History and Philology*, Vol. Ⅰ, Part Ⅱ, 1930, pp. 183-225.

Sculie, G., et Tchang Yi-tchou, tr.

Les barbares soumis dy Yunnan Chapitre de Tien hi. *BEFEO*, 1908, Ⅷ, pp. 149-176, 333-379.

Starr, F.

Lolo Objects in the Public Museum, Milwaukee. *Bulletin*, Vol I, 1910-11, pp. 210-220, 8 pl.

Terrien de Lacouperie

On a Lolo MS Written on Satin. *Journal RGS* n. s., Vol. XⅣ, 1882, pp. 119-123.

Lolo not connected with Vei characters. Athenaeum, 23, September, 1882.

The Language of China before the Chinese. *Transactions of the Philological Society*, 1885-7. pp. 394-538.

The beginnings of Writings in Central and Eastern Asia, or, Notes on 450 Embryo-writings and Scripts. 1894.

Ting, V. K.

Native Tribes of Yunnan. *China Medical Journal*, March, 1921.

Vial, Paul

Un tournoi chez les sauvage Lolos. *MC*, XX, 1888, pp. 445-448.

Etude sur l'ecriture des Lolos du Yunnan. *Le Lotus*, IX, 1890, pp. 30-49.

Les Gni ou Gni-pa tribu lolo te du Yunnan. Miscellaneous notes scattered in *MC*, XXV (1893) and XXVI (1894).

Les Lolos-histoire religion moeurs, langue ecriture. Etudes sino-orientales, fascicule A, 1898. (Reviewed in *CR*, XXⅢ, pp. 182-3, by E. H. Parker; and TP, IX, 1898, pp. 413-6). Dictionnaire francaise-lolo, dialecte gni, tribu situe, etc. province du Yunnan. 1909.

Wylie, A., tr.

History of the Southwest Barbarians; tr. from the Tseen Han Shoo (History of Former Han Dynasty) Book 95, by A. Wylie. *JRAI*, IX, 1880, pp. 53-96.

Si nan man chuan, *Hou Han Shu*, book 116 (Section on the south western barbarians in the History of later Han dynasty); tr, by, A Wylie. *Revue d'Extreme Orient*, Vol. I, 1882.

Zaborowski; S.

Les Lolos et les populatians du sud de la Chine d'apres le ouvrages chinois. *Revue de l'Ecole d'Anthropologie de Paris*, XV, 1905, pp. 86-95.

Photqgraphies de femmes Lolo Miao-tse et de natives de la ville de Yunnan, collection de chaussures de sud de la Chine. *BMSAP*, 1901, pp. 140-143.

Roman numbers referred to in the notes are to the following Chinese works

Ⅰ. *Nan man*, *Hsin T'ang shu*, *lieh chüan* 147 (Southern Barbarians, New Official History of the T'ang dynasty).

Ⅱ. *Man i*, *Sung shih*, *lieh chüan* 252-5 (Barbarians, Official History of Sung dynasty).

Ⅲ. *Shin Yuan shih*, *chüan* 145. Barbarians of Yunnan, Hu-kuang and Ssuchuan (New Official History of Yuan dynasty).

Ⅳ. *Tu-ssu*, *Ming shih*, *chüan* 300-319 (Native chiefs, official History of Ming dynasty).

Ⅴ. *Tu-ssu chuan*, *Ching shih kao*, *chüan* 517-522 (Biographies of native chiefs, Draft History of Ching dynasty).

Ⅵ. *Hua Yang Kuo Chih* (History of the country of Hua Yang) Compiled during the 3d century A. D.

Ⅶ. *T'ung Tien* (a cyclopaedia compiled by Tu Yu of the T'ang dynasty) Section on Barbarians.

Ⅷ. *Man Shu* (Book of Barbarians) by Fan Cho (9th Cent. A. D.) See Pelliot, *BEFEO*, IV, Nos. 1-2, p. 132, Note 5.

Ⅸ. *Nan-chao Yeh-shih*, tr. into French by C. Sainson, 1904.

Ⅹ. *Huang Ching chih kung tu* (Atlases of the Tributary Countries of Ching dynasty) compiled during the beginning of the 18th Century.

Ⅺ. *Nan man chih* (Records of Southern Barbarians). Gazetteer of the province of Yunnan, Books 172-190. Comp. during 1826-1835.

Ⅻ. *Nan man chih.* Supplement to the Gazetteer of the province of Yunnan, Books 159-199. Comp. in 1901.

XⅢ. *Man Ssu ho chih*, by Mao Chi-lin (ly23-1716). It is a book about the native chiefs of Kwei-chou, Yunnan, etc. A full supplement to the Official History of the Ming Dynasty.

XⅣ. *Yang Chen-chih*: A Brief Account of the Lolo. Ling-nan Journal, Vol. I, pp. 134-152.

XⅤ. *V.K. Ting*: *Man yu san chi* (Travels in Yunnan and Ssuchuan). *Independent Review*, Nos. 34-56, 42. 1933.

Ancient tribal and place names referred to in the thesis are in red. Those underlined are names in the T'ang period.

Terrien de Lacouperie's identification of Lao-shan. See page 39 .

Actual location of Lao-shan

MAP Ⅰ

YELLOW SEA
Shanghai
Nanking
Hankow
Wenchow
Chungking
Chengtu
Changsha
Canton
Amoy
Swatow
HONG KONG
Vereker Banks
Pratas
GULF OF TONKIN
HAINAN
FRENCH
INDO-CHINA
Paracel Is. and Reefs (China)
Scarborough Shoal
SIAM
Bangkok
Rangoon
Reed Bank
Tizard Bank
Great Coco
Little Coco
Saddle Peak
Middle Andaman
South Andaman
Little Andaman

MAP Ⅱ

YELLOW
SEA
Shanghai
Nanking
Hankow
Hanchung
Wanhsien
Chungking
Changsha
Wenchow
Swatow
Amoy
Canton
HONG KONG
Pratas
GULF OF
TONKIN
HAINAN
Paracels and Reefs
(China)
Scarborough
Shoal
FRENCH
INDO-CHINA
S I A M
Bangkok
Rangoon
MERGUI
ARCHIPELAGO
Middle Andaman
South Andaman

Lolo

Miao-Yao group

Shan

The distribution of these three groups, here represented in the map, is chiefly based on Ryozo Torii's *Geographical dis tribution and present condition of the Miao tribe in China* (in Japanese) J. G. Tokyo, G. S., 1903, pp. 385-400, 465-574; H. R. Davies' *The Tribes of Yunnan*, 1909; C. E. Jamieson, *The Aborigines of Western* China, 1923; *Gazetteer of Upper Burma*; and many of the works given in the Bibliography.

(此爲1934年馮漢驥先生在賓夕法尼亞大學人類學系就讀期間所完成的碩士論文,打印稿今存 Van Pelt Library, University of Pennsylvania)

THE BLACK MAGIC IN CHINA KNOWN AS *KU*[*]

A number of ideas and practices are grouped together under the Chinese term *ku*.② These ideas and practices justify the use of the phrase "Black Magic"; that is, magic whose purpose is to injure someone. In this sense the word is contrasted with *wu*,③ White Magic, or magic whose purpose is beneficial. The phrase "Black Magic" is too general, however, for the Chinese term *ku* refers to certain particular methods of black magic, which are, so far as the authors are aware, peculiar to certain cultures of SouthEastern Asia. In ancient times this specific feature of culture may have been spread over a wider area.

At present, *ku* is used primarily as a means of acquiring wealth; secondarily as a means of revenge. The method is to place poisonous snakes and insects together in a vessel until there is but one survivor, which is called the *ku*. The poison secured from this *ku* is administered to the victim, who becomes sick and dies. The ideas associated with *ku* vary, but the *ku* is generally regarded as a spirit, which secures the wealth of the victim for the sorcerer.

Archaeological evidence indicates that the word *ku* is at least as ancient as the Chinese script itself. The earliest reliable specimens of Chinese writing are

---

* The preparation of this article was made possible by a grant from the Faculty Research Fund of the University of Pennsylvania.

② 蠱; formed by Ch'ung (insects, worms, etc.) 蟲 over min (vessel, dish) 皿.

③ 巫.

inscriptions on the shells of tortoises and on the shoulder-blades of cattle, found in a Yin-Shang site at An-yang, Honan, in 1899. An ancient form of the word *ku* has been identified on these fragments. This form is more pictorial than the present form of the word, and shows clearly two insects in a receptacle.①

This written word therefore has existed in approximately its present form for at least three thousand years. The ideographic nature of Chinese writing and the continuity of Chinese literature have the effect that while a written symbol may acquire new meanings and associations in the course of time, these seldom entirely supersede and eliminate the older meanings, as may happen in phonetic systems. Consequently, while some of the meanings attached to the word *ku* may be older than others, we can be fairly sure that the oldest meaning has not been lost.

The *Shuo* wen, a dictionary of about A. D. 100, says, "Ku is worms in the belly. The commentary on the *Spring and Autumn Annals* (the *Tso chuan*) says, 'Vessel and worms make ku, caused by licentiousness. Those who have died violent deaths are also *ku*.'② The word vessel signifies the utility of the thing." As is indicated by this definition, the Chinese written word is formed by the radical meaning "insects" or "worms" placed above the radical meaning "vessel" or "dish."

In the Pre-Han literature, the word is used in five different ways. It indicates (1) a disease, (2) evil spirits, (3) to cause doubt, or a woman inveigling a man, (4) a worm-eaten vessel, and grain which moulders and is blown away, and (5) a divination symbol. Some of these meanings have become attached to the word by analogy.

The use of *ku* as a disease may be illustrated by a passage from the Tso *chuan*.

---

① 殷墟文字類編 chüan 13. By 羅振玉,商承祚編.

② This passage is later quoted in full.

"In the first year of duke Chao (541 B. C.), the marquis of Chin asked the help of a physician from Ch'in, and the earl of Ch'in sent one named Ho to see him. Ho said, 'The disease cannot be cured. It is said that when women are approached 〔too frequently〕 the result is a disease resembling *ku*. It is not caused by a spirit, nor by food (the methods of magic); it is a delusion which has destroyed the mind.'" When asked what he meant by *ku*, he replied, "'I mean that 〔disease〕 which is produced by excessive sexual indulgence. Consider the word; it is formed by the words for vessel and for insects. It is also used for grain which 〔moulders and〕 flies away. In the *Book of Changes*, a woman deluding a man, and wind throwing down 〔the trees of〕 a mountain, are *ku*. All these have the same signification'".

The fundamental idea of *ku* as a disease is based on an analogy. The human body is regarded as a vessel, into which the disease spirits enter like insects. Many early peoples have regarded disease as due to the possession of the body by an alien spirit. Excessive sexual indulgence causes a man to lose his virility, his soul. This is not *ku*, but the effect is similar to the effect of *ku*. Therefore a woman inveigling a man has come by analogy to be called *ku*.

It will be shown that ancient Chinese ideas associated the wind with the generation of worms. This is applied to mouldering grain, either in the sense that the chaff is blown away by the wind, or that worms generate in the grain, become insects and fly away. It appears that the essential idea behind these meanings of *ku* is a loss of soul.

In the *Shih chi feng ch'an shu*,① it is said that "Duke Teh of Chin instituted the *fou* sacrifice, killing dogs at the four gates of the city to dispel the *ku* plague." The *Ch'in pen chi*② says, "In the second year (of Duke Tek) dogs

① 史記封禪書.

② Chap. 5 of the *Shih chi*. The passage is quoted by De Groot, *Religious System of China*, Vol. V, p. 826.

were killed to ward off *ku*." Dogs have frequently been used in Chinese apotropaic practices, from ancient times until the present.

In the *Shan hai ching*[①] it is said, "Again east 300 Ii, there is the mountain called Ching-chiu, and there is an animal like the fox, having nine tails and the voice of a baby. It eats men, but those who eat it are immune to *ku*." A commentary remarks on this passage,[②] that such men will not "encounter evil atmosphere." This appears to identify *ku* with malignant atmospheric conditions, something like poison gas. But it might also be interpreted as indicating the presence of evil spirits, or something created by black magic.

Cheng Ssu-nung, in his commentary on the *Ta tsung po*[③], said, "At present, people kill dogs in sacrifice to stop the wind." Kuo Pu[④], in his commentary on the *Erh ya*, remarks, "The modern custom of sacrificing dogs in the highways is said to stop the wind." Such customs are very old, and have survived to the present in the belief that the blood of black dogs is an effective antidote to magic. While these latter references are not from pre-Han literature, they probably reflect pre-Han beliefs.

The *Book of Changes* is an ancient work on divination, consisting of the explanations of sixty-four hexagrams, or figures secured in divination. The eighteenth hexagram is formed by the *ken* trigram placed above the *sun* trigram. The *ken* trigram is a symbol of mountains, of resting and stopping, and of the youngest son. The *sun* trigram symbolizes wind or wood, flexibility, penetration, and oldest daughter. The entire hexagram is called *ku*. The text of the *Book of Changes* dealing with the hexagram as a whole, which is probably

---

① 山海經第一南山經.

② *Ibid.*, Commentary by Kuo Pu 郭璞.

③ 周禮注疏 chüan 18,春官大宗伯引鄭司農注.

④ 爾雅釋天第八"祭風曰磔" commentary by Kuo Pu.

the oldest strata of the text, is as follows:

"*Ku* indicates great progress and success. There will be advantage in crossing the great river." ... This means that when a man divined, and secured the hexagram *ku*, the omen was auspicious. It meant that the one who divined would be successful, while his enemies would be injured. Crossing the river was equivalent to an offensive military expedition. The way in which the hexagram *ku* was used in practice may be illustrated by an incident from the *Tso chuan*.

"In the eleventh month of the fifteenth year of Duke He, the marquis of Chin and the earl of Ch'in fought at Han, and the marquis of Chin was taken. Before the expedition, the earl of Ch'in asked his diviner, Tu-fu, to consult the milfoil, and he replied."

"'A lucky response; if they cross the river, the chariots of the marquis will be defeated.'"

"The earl asked to have the matter more fully explained.

"The diviner said, 'It is very lucky. You will defeat his troops three times, and finally capture the marquis of Chin. The figure found is *ku*', of which it is said,"

"The thousand chariots are put to flight three times."

"Then you catch what remains, called the fox."

"That fox in *ku* must be the marquis of Chin. Moreover, the inner symbol of *ku* represents wind, while the outer represents mountains. It is now autumn. We gather the fruit on the hills, and we shake the trees; it is plain we are to be victorious. The fruit falls down, and the trees are all shaken; what can this be but the defeat of Chin?'"

The present text of the *Book of Changes* cannot be older than the Chou period, but the hexagrams are much older. Chinese tradition says that there were different explanations given to the hexagrams in the Hsia and Shang periods. The oracle bones show that the word *ku*, written as insects in a vessel, was in existence during the Shang, period. The authors of this monograph advance the theory that if we had the Shang explanations of the hexagrams, the two trigrams which in the Chou period were held to represent mountains and wind, would be found to represent vessel and insects.

In using eight symbols to represent many things, each symbol must do more than single duty. The written Chinese words for mountains and vessel are very similar. The theory advanced is that the trigram which in the Chou period symbolized mountains, in the Shang period symbolized vessel. This is merely an hypothesis.

But in the case of the other trigram there is very good evidence for the association of insects and wind, Huai-nan Tzu says①:

"Heaven is one. Earth is two. Man is three. Three times three is nine. Two times nine is eighteen. The number eight stands for wind. Wind represents worms, Therefore worms are transformed in eight days." It will be noticed that the number eighteen is the number of the hexagram *ku*.

The *Shuo wen*, in defining the character feng (wind), says, "When the wind blows, worms generate. Therefore worms are transformed in eight days."

A commentator on this passage, Hsü Hao②, says, "The wind has no form that can be pictured, so the character is made from the thing which the wind generates. Therefore the radical 'worm' is the base of the character 'wind.' When the geomancer is searching for a favorable spot in the country, he observes where the wind goes, and he knows that below that spot there are ants. This is the verification of the expression, 'The wind blows, and worms generate.'"

Although the *Huai-nan Tzu* and the *Shuo wen* belong to the Han period, the belief in the connection between the wind and worms must be very old,

---

① 淮南子,墬形訓.

② 説文徐箋.

since the character for wind is written with the radical for worms. The connection appears to have been forgotten, since the *Tso chuan* interprets the hexagram as wind blowing down mountains, an interpretation which does not make sense. The hypothesis advanced here, which does not seem to have occurred to scholars, is that the original meaning of the hexagram was not mountains and wind, but worms in a vessel. This idea is clearly indicated by the written form of *ku* on the oracle bones. And as *ku* was a kind of black magic, the hypothesis explains why the hexagram indicated success to the diviner and injury to his opponent. That was the purpose of black magic.①

The *Chou Ii* says, describing a part of the ancient administration②, "The department consisted of an official and four assistants. They were in charge of the extermination of the poisonous *ku*. They drove it out by spells, and attacked it by efficacious herbs. They directed those who could control *ku*, and watched the effect."③

Cheng K'ang-ch'eng's commentary on this passage in the *Chou li* quotes

---

① European scholars have done little work on the subject of *ku*. It is mentioned by Granet, *Chinese Civilization*, p. 254, and by A. Conrady, "Yih-King-Studien," *Asia Major*, Vol. Ⅶ, 1932, p. 418, who translates the term as "Hexenkessel." The practice of *ku* among the Miao is mentioned by S. R. Clarke, *Among the Tribes of South-west China*, China Inland Mission, 1911, pp. 70, 71. E. T. Williams, "Witchcraft in the Chinese Penal Code," *Jour. North China Branch*, *Royal Asiatic Society*, Vol. XXXⅧ, 1907, pp. 61-96, gives a brief description of *ku*, and of legal efforts to stamp it out. The fullest treatment of *ku* in a European work is in J. J. M. De Groot, Religious System of China, Vol. Ⅴ, pp. 826-69. De Groot devotes a chapter to the subject. But unfortunately half his space is filled with a description of the *Wu-ku* Rebellion under Han Wu Ti. *Wu-ku* was a general term ("White and Black Magic") for any sort of magic, and the rebellion, as well as the conspiracy under the Empress Teng 200 years later, had nothing to do with the peculiar methods of *ku*. De Groot's treatment is unsatisfactory in other respects.

② No attempt is made here to give the various legal enactments against the practice of *ku*. The penal code of the T'ang dynasty on this subject has generally continued in force, and is quoted in later dynastic codes. The practice of *ku* is called an inhuman crime. One who makes *ku*, or instructs in its use, is hanged, his property confiscated, his family and the inmates of his house are banished 3000 li, etc. 唐律疏議 chüan 18.

③ Chap. 37. De Groot quotes this passage, p. 826, but mistranslates the last phrase.

the criminal law of the Han dynasty as saying, "Those who dare to poison people with *ku*, or teach others to do it, will be publicly executed." The law of the Han was based on earlier codes, going back at least to the fourth century B. C., and it is not unlikely that the practice of *ku* was forbidden from the time of the first legal codes in China, perhaps long before. If *ku* always represented a method of injuring others, this is what we would expect, since black magic is usually illegal.

In Ku Yeh-wang's *Yü ti chih*① it is said, "In several provinces south of the Yangtse river, there are people who keep *ku*. The host uses it to kill people. He puts it in food or drink, and the victims do not realize its presence. If the family of the keeper of the *ku* all die, the *ku* flies about without any objective. Any one who encounters it is killed." The *Yü ti chih* is a work of the sixth century A. D., the period of the Six Dynasties, corresponding to the early middle ages in Europe.

In the *Sou shen chi*② of Kan Pao,③ attributed to the fourth century A. D., is the following passage:

"In the province of Yung-yang, there was a family by the name of Liao. For several generations they manufactured *ku*, becoming rich from it. Later one of the family married, but they kept the secret from the bride. On one occasion, everyone went out except the bride, who was left in charge of the house. Suddenly she noticed a large cauldron in the house, and on opening it, perceived a big snake inside. She poured boiling water into the cauldron and killed the snake. When the rest of the family returned she told them what she had done, to their great alarm. Not long after, the entire family died of the

① 輿地志. By 顧野王, A. D. 519-81. A scholar and official.

② 搜神記 chüan 12.

③ 干寶. 4th Cent. A. D. The author flourished under Chin Yüan Ti. His book is a collection of supernatural tales. De Groot quotes these stories (p. 846), but misreads the author's surname as Yü. Giles, *Biog. Dict.*, p. 357, uses the correct form.

plague," Kan Pao also mentions a variety called "dog *ku*" and says that the magic can take the forms of various animals.

"Chao Shou of the P'o-yang district possessed dog *ku*. Once a man named Ch'en Tsen visited Chao, when he was attacked by six or seven large yellow dogs. Yu Hsiang-po①(another man) once ate with Chao's wife. Later he almost died from hemorrhage, and was saved by drinking a medicine prepared from the roots of the orange tree. *Ku* has a strange, ghostly appearance. It can appear in many forms, as dogs, pigs, worms or snakes. It is not recognized by the man himself. All who get it, die."

In the *Sou shen hou chi*②: "Tan Yu was a poor and devout monk There was a family in the district of Yen who manufactured *ku*. Those who ate their food died from hemorrhage. Tan Yu once visited this family, and the host prepared food for him. Tan Yu recited an incantation, and saw a pair of centipedes a foot, long suddenly crawl away from the dish. He then ate the food, and returned home without being harmed."

In the biography of Ku Chi-chih in the Liu Sung history (A. D. 420-479), an instance of *ku* poisoning is recorded. "T'ang Tzu, of the Hsiang district, went to Chu Ch'i's mother P'en's house to drink wine. On returning home he became ill, and vomitted more than ten *ku* worms. Seeing that he was about to die, he directed his wife Chang that after death she should cut open his abdomen in order to get rid of the disease. Later Chang cut open his body, and saw his 'five viscera' completely destroyed."③

These instances from the medieval period of Chinese history indicate a view that *ku* was a kind of poison which was administered in food and drink. A

---

① De Groot translates Yu Hsiang-po as "paternal uncle," but *hsiang* is not a relationship term.

② 搜神後記, chüan 2. Attributed to T'ao Chien 陶潛, a famous poet.

③ The narrative goes on to say that the widow was accused of the crime of mistreating her husband's corpse. The case was brought before Ku Chi-chih, who acquired considerable reputation from the way he handled it.

little later a medical work, the *Tsao shih chu ping yüan hou tsung lun*① of the Sui period (A. D. 589-618) describes how this poison was manufactured.

"There are several kinds of *ku*. All of them are poisonous. People sometimes deliberately prepare *ku*. They take worms, insects, snakes, and other poisonous creatures, and put them together in a vessel. They allow them to eat each other until only one is left, and this survivor is the *ku*. The *ku* can change its appearance and bewitch people. When put in food and drink, it causes disease and calamity (to the one who eats it). There is also 'flying *ku*'. It comes and goes without one's knowledge, and eventually appears somewhat like a ghost. Those who have seen it, die."

This appears to be the earliest account, not later than A. D. 600, of how this magical process was carried out. It gives a reasonable explanation of the formation of the written word, formed of insects and dish. The explanation is still more suitable for the pictograph found on the oracle bones of the Shang period.

The idea behind this practice is quite reasonable. If centipedes and snakes are poisonous individually, the survivor of such a group, who has eaten the others, is considered to combine with himself the collected venom of the group. If a man desires to injure an enemy, no more formidable weapon could be put into his hand. The difficulty is to say when this rational, if mistaken, process becomes pure magic. Action at a distance does not seem to be one of the properties of *ku*. Poisoning and magic are found together in all countries, from the days of Medea. Some of the stories are pure magic, while others indicate no more than a use of poison.

The evidence presented so far may be summarized. The word itself goes back to the oldest written records of the Chinese language. The pictograph

---

① 巢氏諸病源候總論, chüan 25. A medical work of the Sui period.

clearly shows insects, worms, or snakes in a receptable. But in the ancient literature of the Chou period, the word is used in a number of ways, of which the most important and primary appear to be as a diseased condition and as a divination symbol. How far may a magical practice first described clearly about A. D. 600 be ascribed to the period before 500 B. C. ?

The literature which has survived from the Chou period has been carefully edited, for the most part by Confucians, beginning, according to tradition, with Confucius himself. In their desire to idealize the past, and to show, not what really occurred, but what ought to have occurred, they have created great difficulties for the ethnologist.

But it often happens that ideas and practices which are never mentioned in literature, especially in moral, religious, and philosophic literature, survive unchanged in the lives of the people. The explanation that *ku* was originally a magical practice agrees with the pictograph on the oracle bones, with the use of the word to describe a disease, and with its use in divination. The *Tso chuan* indicates that in divination, the symbol indicated that the diviner would be successful in injuring his enemy. In the Han period, the term was used for black magic, and in the medieval period, for a magical method of poisoning an enemy. Therefore it seems reasonable to assume that the term always stood for black magic.

Early Chinese literature describes the culture of the valley of the Yellow River. Later literature indicates that the practice of *ku* extended at one time over the whole area included in China proper. This was probably true long before there is any evidence from the Yangtse valley, or the more southern regions. Even in the medieval period, Chinese observers remarked on the prevalence of the practice in southern China, and from the T'ang period on, the practice appears to have been more and more confined to aboriginal tribes of the south. The policy of repression definitely stated by Cheng K'ang-ch'eng in his commentary on the *Chou li* appears to have been largely effective throughout the more characteristically Chinese areas, and later writers notice the practice of *ku* in the south as a peculiar phenomenon. Nevertheless, the practice of *ku* seems to have been a specific cultural feature which the ancient inhabitants of the Yellow River valley shared with the inhabitants of more southern areas.

The *Ling piao lu i*① of Liu Shun, written about A. D. 900, which is one of the earliest geographic works dealing with Kuangtung and the adjacent southern areas, contains the following passage:

"The mountains and rivers of Ling-piao wind and cluster together. It is not easy to go out or come in. Therefore the district abounds in fogs and mists which become pestilential vapors. People exposed to them are liable to become sick. Their stomachs swell, and they become *ku*. It is popularly said that there are persons who collect poisonous insects in order to make *ku* and poison people. I think that this is due to the humidity of the place, which causes poisonous creatures to flourish there, and not because the people of Ling-piao are cruel by nature."

From the Sung period on (beginning about A. D. 960), all references to *ku* assign its practice to the tribes of the southwest. There is an instance recorded in the *Ling wai tai ta* of Chou ch'u-fei②.

"The *ku* poison of Kuangsi is of two kinds. One kind kills a man quickly, while the other works gradually and does not kill for six months. If a man has a grudge against anyone, he is courteous to him, but poisons him secretly. After half a year, the poison takes effect. The murderer cannot be brought to law, and the poisoning cannot be cured. This is the most cruel form of *ku*. In 1170,

---

① 嶺表録異, chüan 1. A work of the T'ang period, and one of the earliest geographical works now existing about Kuangtung and the adjacent areas.

② 嶺外代答, chünan, 10. By 周去非. The author was assistant sub-prefect of Kueilin, in Kuangsi, during the years A. D. 1174-89. The story is given by De Groot, p. 848.

on the eastern side of Ching-chou, there was a seller of sauce who prepared *ku*. It was discovered, and the man executed. It is said that when his family prepared *ku*, the women, naked and with dishevelled hair, made a nightly sacrifice of a dish of deermeat soup. Grasshoppers, butterflies, and all kinds of insects came down from the roof and ate the soup. That which they emitted was the poison. If anyone wishes to know whether a family keeps *ku* poison, they call tell from the cleanliness of the house. If everything is kept very clean, then the family has *ku*. When the natives of Li-T'ung and Chi-T'ung (in southwestern China) invite guests to a feast, the host must first taste the food in order to convince the guests that there are no grounds for suspicion."

There is a somewhat similar reference in the gazetteer of Yung-fu, a district of Kuangsi.① *Ku* poison is not found generally among the people (i. e, the Chinese), but is used by the Tung② women. It is said that on the fifth day of the fifth month③, they go to a mountain stream and spread new clothes and headgear on the ground, with a bowl of water beside them. The women dance and sing naked, inviting a visit from the King of Medecine (a tutelary spirit). They wait until snakes, lizards, and poisonous insects come to bathe in the bowl. They pour the water out in a shadowy, damp place. Then they gather the fungus (poisonous?) which grows there, which they mash into a paste. They put this into goose-feather tubes, and hide them in their hair. The heat of their bodies causes worms to generate, which resemble newly-hatched silk-worms. Thus *ku* is produced. It is often concealed in a warm, damp place in the kitchen.

"The newly made *ku* is not yet poisonous. It is used as a love potion,

---

① 永福縣誌; quoted by Wang Sen 汪森, in his 粤西叢載, chüan18.

② "獞". The chief aboriginal tribe of Kuangsi.

③ The fifth day of the fifth month is an important day in the Chinese religious calendar, the day of the "Dragon Boat Festival." The story told in connection with it dates from the 3rd Cent. B. C., but the festival is probably much older.

administered in food and drink, and called 'love-medicine.'[①] Gradually the *ku* becomes poisonous. As the poison develops, the woman's body itches until she has poisoned someone. If there is no other opportunity, she will poison even her husband or her sons, but she possesses antidotes."

"It is believed that those who produce *ku* themselves become *ku* after death. The ghosts of those who have died from the poison become their servants. So a majority of the foolish T'ung make this thing. When a man enters a house in a T'ung village, if he sees no ashes on the hearth, and if the faces of the women appear yellow and their eyes red, he knows that there is *Ku* in that house. Bronze chop-sticks are used as a charm against ku. Dipped into poisoned food, they cause it to turn black..."

A similar case is recorded in the *Shuang huai sui ch'ao*.[②] "During the reign of Cheng Tung (1436-1449), Chon Li of the district of Wu-chiang traded in Ssu-eng of Kuangsi, and married a widowed daughter of the Cheng family. He remained there twenty years, until their son was sixteen. One day Chou Li wanted to return home. His wife was unable to dissuade him, but she put *ku* in Chou Li's food without his knowledge. She bade her son follow him, and told the boy secretly that if his father promised to come back, he should cure him. For this purpose she taught him the antidote. When Chou Li reached home the *ku* began to affect him. His belly became swollen, and he drank water excessively. His son asked the date on which he would return to his wife.

"Chou Li replied, 'I also think of your mother, but I am sick. How can I go back? As soon as I get a little better, I shall start.'"

"the son replied, 'I can cure the disease.' He bound his father to a pillar. Chou Li was thirsty and asked for a drink. His son offered him a clay

---

① 和合藥 or 粘食藥.

② 雙槐歲抄, chüan 5. By 黃瑜. 15th Cent. A. D. Chronological records of miscellaneous facts from 1368 (the beginning of the Ming dynasty) to 1487.

bowl filled with water, but when it was almost at his mouth, the boy threw it away. This happened several hundred times. Chou Li became so thirsty that he could hardly bear it. Shortly after, he vomited out a small carp, which was still alive. The swelling soon disappeared, and he was cured. Among the barbarians there are many *ku* poisons so made as to become effective at a certain date. After that date, the case cannot be cured. Widows are called 'ghosts' wives, and men dare not approach them. When strangers marry them, they are usually poisoned."

There is a reference to *ku* in the *shui chi*①. "In Tien (Yun-nan) there are many *ku* sorcerers, especially among the women. They often seduce men. If the beloved was about to go on a long journey, he was always poisoned with *ku*. If the man did not return on the promised date, he died. There was a traveler who went to Tien and loved a woman. When he was leaving the place, the woman said to him, 'I have already poisoned you with *ku*. If you do not return as you have promised, your belly will swell, and then you must come to me as quickly as possible. After a month, it will be incurable.' On that day the man's belly really became swollen. He hesitated to return; then his abdomen burst, and he died. People found in his belly a wooden trough for feeding pigs. It is certainly strange!"

It is significant that in these stories all the practitioners of this love magic are women of the aboriginal tribes of the southwest.

In the *Sui shu ti li chih*② it is recorded that "the inhabitants of these districts (in Kiangsi and some other areas south of the Yangtse) often kept *ku* poison, and the practice was especially prevalent in ICh'un. The method is, on

---

① 述異記, chüan 2. By 東軒主人 (a pen name). The author is unknown. The facts recorded occurred under the Manchu reigns Shun-chih and K'ang-hsi, about the middle of the 17th Cent. It treats of the supernatural, and was published in 1701.

② 隋書地理志, chüan 31. The geographical section of the Sui dynasty history.

the fifth day of the fifth month to collect all kinds of insects and worms, from snakes to lice, putting them together in a vessel, where they devour each other. The survivor is kept. If it should be a snake, it is snake-*ku*. If a louse, then it is louse-*ku*. This *ku* is used to kill people. It is administered through food, and afterwards it consumes the victim's internal organs. When the person dies, his property is moved by the *ku* spirit to the house of the keeper of the *ku*. If for three years the keeper does not kill a man with the *ku*, the keeper himself is killed by it. It is handed down from generation to generation, and is given to a daughter as a dowry. Kan Pao (the author of the *Sou shen chi*) regarded *ku* as a spirit, but this view is mistaken. During the rebellion of Hou Ching, most of the *ku*-keeping families perished. Since the *ku* had no master, it wandered about the roads, and those who met it, died."

Another variety of *ku* is called the "golden caterpillar", or *chintsan. Li Shih-chen in the Pen tsao kang mu*① quotes Ch'en Tsang-chi of the T'ang period as follows: "The ashes of old satin can cure 'the *ku* worms which eat satin.' The commentary says, 'The *worm* crawls like a finger ring. It eats old satin brocade and other silk cloths, just as the silk-worm eats mulberry leaves.' In my opinion, this is the *chin-tsan*." According to Li, the golden caterpillars originated in Szechuan and from there made their way into the Hukuang provinces.

The *T'ieh wei shan tsung hua* of Tsai T'ao② says, "The *chintsa* poison began in Szechuan, but now it has spread to Hu, Kuang, Min and Yueh (Hupeh, Hunan, Kuangtung, Kuangsi, Fukien and Chekiang). There are people who give it away, and this is called 'giving the golden caterpillar a

---

① 本草綱目, chüan 42. By 李時珍. A well known medieal work containing extracts from more than 800 authors, and describing, 1892 medicines. The last half of the 16th Cent. De Groot makes considerable use of the work.

② 鐵圍山叢談, chüan 6. By 蔡絛, First half of the 12th Cent. It treats of events contemporary with the author. The passage is quoted in part by De Groot, p. 850.

husband,' Those who do this place gold, ornaments for dressing the head, satin and brocade with the worm, and put it beside the road for others to find. The magistrate of Yü-lin told me that there was a legal case involving this practice in the district of Fu-Ch'ing. One man brought charge against another, stating that the latter had poisoned his family with *chin-tsan*. The magistrate could not find any evidence of such poison having been used. Then someone suggested bringing hedgehogs to the house of the accused. Since the *chin-tsan* is known to be afraid of hedgehogs, this advice was followed. The *chin-tsan* dared not move, although it hid in a hole under the bed. It was caught and pulled out by the two hedgehogs. It is really astonishing."①

The *Kua i chih*② says, "The *chin-tsan* is a caterpillar the color of gold. It is fed with Shu satin, and its excretions collected, which are then put into food and drink in order to poison people. Those who take it, die. Then the spirit of the worm is glad, and moves the valuables of the deceased to the house of the practitioner, making him suddenly rich. But to get rid of the worm is difficult, because water, fire and swords cannot harm it. The only way is to put gold and silver into a basket with the *chin-tsan*, and then place the basket beside a road. Someone passing by may take it. This is called 'giving the *chin-tsan* a husband'."

The *Fan Tien lu t'an tsung*③ says, "The antidote for those poisoned by the

---

① Williams, "Witchcraft in the Chinese Penal Code", p. 91, quotes the *Hsi yüan lu* 洗冤録, a guide to magistrates in their duties as coroners, as saying that a medicine including two centipedes, one alive, one roasted, was a cure for *ku*. De Groot, pp. 863-69, gives a large number of remedies and antidotes for *ku*, collected from various medical works. They include musk, cinnabar, striped sats, dried centipedes (for snake *ku*), leek, juice, and "thunder stones." These last are prehistoric implements, stone knives and axes, often found in Kuangtung and the island of Hainan. Domestic fowls are said to detect *ku*.

② 括異志, Quoted by De Groot, p. 854. By 魯應龍 of the Sung period. Not to be confused with another book by the same name by 張師正.

③ 梵天廬談叢, chüan 33. By 柴萼. A work of miscellaneous notes, published by the Chung-hua Book Co. of Shanghai in 1926.

chin-tsan is food from the home of one who has kept the *ku*. But it must be given by the keeper of the *ku* personally, for if it is given by anyone else, the antidote will not be effective. Hence if the person knows where he was poisoned, he can go to the man who poisoned him and beg him pitifully for relief. The man will not acknowledge the act at first, but after incessant pleading, he will angrily take a little food and throw it to the patient. On eating it, the victim will be cured instantly. When the appointed time for poisoning arrives and there are no outsiders present, even the keeper's own relatives may become his victims, for otherwise the spirit would cause a calamity of some sort. The spirit is appeased by the poisoning, because the spirits of the victims become his slaves."① There do not seem to be any descriptions of the way in which the *chin-tsan ku* is produced. It is said to be the third stage in the development of *ku*.

Another variety of *ku* poison is called *t'iao-sheng*,② This kind of *ku* is more clearly black magic. It is described in the *Ling wai tai ta*.③"In Kuangsi, those who kill people by *t'iao-sheng* bewitch the food, and invite guests to eat. When eaten, the fish and meat become alive again, living in the victim's stomach, and eventually kill him. It is currently believed that the spirits of those who have met death through *t'iao-sheng* become slaves in the home of the sorcerer. Once a celebrated scholar, while judge of Lei-chou (on the island of Hai-nan), had an experience with t'iao-sheng. He covered some meat with a plate and asked the culprit to bewitch it, in order to test the efficiency of his art. After a while he took up the plate, and hairs were growing out of the meat. What a devil it must be who can do this! Yet undoing the enchantment was quite easy. If you feel that the magic is in your stomach, take *sheng-ma* and

---

① 梵天廬談叢, chüan 33. By 柴萼. A work of miscellaneous notes, published by the Chung-hua Book Co. of Shanghai in 1926.

② 挑生. The phrase may be translated as "to revive", or "to become alive again".

③ 嶺外代答, chün 10.

vomit it out. Then if you feel the magic in your intestines, quickly take *yü-chin* and pass it out. This prescription was printed in Lei-chou for distribution and given to the people after it had been obtained from the culprit."

The *Ch'i hsiu lei kao*① says, "In Yunnan, Kueichou and Kuangsi, what is called *t'iao-sheng* is witchcraft. The sorcerer invites people to eat fish and meat which have been bewitched. When they have eaten them, the animals become alive again in their organs, and then proceed to kill the victims. I (the author) saw recorded in Fan Shih-hu's *Kuei hai yü heng chih*② that there was at that time a man named Li Sou-weng, a judge of Lei-chou. He secured a good prescription... (then follows the prescription, which is similar to that in the preceding paragraph). Officials of the place are often attacked by this magic. The prescription is not readily available, so I publish it here."

The *Nan chung tsa chi*③ says, "The chiefs of Yüan-chiang have handed down the method of producing *ku*. This medicine is not beneficent, but is poisonous. An astonishing fact is that when a new magistrate arrives the people must prepare a feast to welcome him, and they poison him then. The poison does not become effective during his term of office, but the pupils of his eyes turn from black to blue, and his face becomes pale and swollen. Then some months after he leaves office, his whole family die."

Again, in the same work: "The *ku* of the people of Burmah does not make use of medicine, but employs spirits. The spell is handed down from generation to generation. Within forty-nine days, they can bewitch a cow-hide to the size of a mustard seed. They call this 'cowhide *ku*.' They can also bewitch an iron

---

① 七修類稿, chüan 45.事物類. By 郎英. A work of the Ming period.

② 桂海虞衡志, By 范成大. A work of the Sung period. It treated of the geography and natural history of the southern provinces.

③ 南中雜記, By 劉昆. Miscellaneous facts about South China.

ploughshare to the size of a mustard seed, and this they call 'ploughshare *ku*.' The method of applying such *ku* is to conceal the mustard seed under a finger-nail, and shoot it out toward the victim. The poison then enters his stomach. When a Chinese was affected by this poison, tke Burmese would calculate the length of his journey, and chant the incantation. The *ku* poison would affect him on the calculated day. The victim would become thin, his abdomen would swell, and he would die within a few months. There was one man among the native chiefs called Yang Chao-pa, of the district of T'eng-yüeh, who could chant a counter spell which would cause the *ku* poison to leave the Chinese and attack the Burmese."

The *Po yüeh feng tu chi*[①] says, "The *ku* drugs are not of one kind only, and the methods of using them differ. *Ku* sometimes changes the five viscera into earth or wood. Sometimes *ku* is put into chicken or duck meat. When the poison entered the stomach, the chicken or duck would become alive again, with wings and feet. It would compel the victim's soul to become a slave in the house of the sorcerer. When the Chinese caught such a sorcerer, they buried him alive, or burnt him."

The *Tien nan hsin yü*[②] says, "The Pa-yi (Shan) of the mountains (an aboriginal tribe in southwestern China) skin a cow and bewitch its hide to the size of a mustard seed. Those traders who entered the mountains without knowing this fact, sometimes had love affairs with the native girls. When they had sold their merchandise and were about to return home, the natives would invite them to a feast. At the feast, they would promise the girls to return. If they returned as they promised, they would be cured. But if they did not return, the *ku* poison (administered at the feast) became effective, and their

---

① 百越風土記.

② 滇南新語, By 張泓. An account of Yunnan, written in the latter part of the 17th Cent.

bellies burst. The cow-hides came out as if freshly skinned."

The *Ch'ih ya*[①] contains an interesting passage. "On the fifth day of the fifth month collect all those insects and worms that are poisonous, and put them together in a vessel. Let them devour each other, and the one finally remaining is called *ku*. There are snake *ku*, lizard *ku*, and dung- beetle *ku*. The length of time required for the insects to devour each other will be proportionate to the time required for the poisoned victim to die. When the *ku* has been produced, the next step is to put it into food, which will then become a hundred times more delicious, Those who eat this food will die within a few days, or after a year of violent pains in the heart and stomach. The victim's property will imperceptibly be removed to the house of the witch, and his spirit becomes her slave, like the tiger which enslaves its *Ch'ang*. Later the *ku* flies about by night, appearing like a meteor. This variety is called 'flitting *ku*'. When the light grows stronger, a shadow like a living man's is produced. This is then called *t'iao-sheng ku*. When its shadow grows stronger, the *ku* can have intercourse with women. Then it is called *chin-tsan ku*. It can go wherever it desires, and spreads calamity throughout the country-side. The more men it poisons, the more efficient the *ku* becomes, and the richer grows the witch. Among the aborigines, such evils are practiced openly. The native officials called Ti-to became aware of this, and asked a magician to dispel the enchantment. They caught the witch, and buried her alive with her head above the ground. They poured wax on her head and lighted it, in order to call back the poisoned spirits. The ghosts did not dare to approach, and the T'ung women cursed the witch for them. This is the only way to put a witch to death, for otherwise it is impossible to bring her under the law.

"The complexion of those who have been poisoned by *ku* becomes more

① 赤雅, By 鄺露, chüan 2. A description of the Miao country in Southwest China, written about the first part of the 17th Cent. The author was in the service of a native chieftaness for several years.

than ordinarily beautiful. The *Tien chi* (probably leaders among the women) look at them and smile. Then the victim must kowtow to a chieftaness and beg for the antidote. She will give the victim a pill. If the victim takes it, he instantly vomits strange things with human heads and the bodies of snakes, or having eight feet and six wings. These creatures cannot be killed with the sword, or burned. But if alum is placed on them, they die at once. Otherwise they will return to their old place. I lived long among these people, and know the prescription. Use *san-Ch'i* (literally, three seven) powder and water-chestnuts to make pills. Add alum and tea leaves, making them into a powder. Take five *chien* with spring water. If vomiting follows, then stop. An old prescription says to take white *Jang-ho* and drink its juice, then sleep on the roots, after calling aloud the name of the witch. But the effect of this process is very slow."

The *T'ung Chi hsien chih*① says, "If the mat of the victim is burned, he will see for himself who the sorcerer is. The *ku* is a spirit, and goes out in the night to snatch the souls of the dead. The houses of *ku* sorcerers are very clean, because the ghosts of those who have been killed by the *ku* poison act as servants in them. If a man sits in a posture resembling the written word 'woman' (i. e. cross-legged), the *ku* cannot harm him. Or if the witch is enchanting a man, and he buries some of her food secretly under the intersection of two streets, the *ku* spirit will turn on the witch herself. And the *ku* spirit is filled with fear of the hedgehog. If a hedgehog is brought to the house of a witch, the *ku* will be caught immediately. All these prescriptions and methods of detecting *ku* have been tested and shown to be effective, so I publish them here."

The *Tien nan hsin yü*② in another passage remarks, "In Szechuan there

---

① 洞溪纖志, chüan 2. By 陸次雲. The author flourished under K'ang-hsi, 1662-1723. A book about the aboriginal tribes of Southwest China.

② See p. 99, note ②.

are many who keep *ku*, especially the *chin-tsan*, which is the most malignant form. When the owner has become rich, and has the means, he sends it away.... There is no *chin-tsan ku* among the East and West Yi of Yunnan, but the mischief caused by mice, snake, and food *ku* is comparatively greater. On calm nights, when the clouds are heavy, there are things which glitter like meteors, sweeping low over the roofs and flying quickly. The long, luminous tail affects the eye and heart like cold flames. I was very much astonished. When I asked my fellow officials, I began to realize that the lights were due to *ku*, which had been let out by the inhabitants. They also told me that the *ku* was apt to eat children's brains. It also kidnapped spirits. In those families which kept *ku*, the women were always debauched by the *ku*. If the spirit were dissatisfied, it would turn on the keeper and eat his children. Then it could not be sent away until the keeper had become poor, and all his family had perished. For this reason people are often afraid to keep it. Moreover, keeping it is prohibited by law. So the practice is gradually dying out, but it still exists, Those who still supply themselves with ku, do so cretely. In Hsin-hsing and Chien-ch'uan I tried several times to discover who the sorcerers were, in order to put an end to such malevalent things. Sometimes informants appeared, but no evidence could be secured. Hedgehogs are used in detecting *ku*, but without much effect. During the time that the suspects were under arrest, the flitting of the *ku* was noticeably less."

The *Shu yi chi*① says, "When Sun Hsin-yai of Shih-men was magistrate of K'ai-hua (in Yunnan), he was once sitting in the hall when he noticed a kind of light flitting about like a meteor. He asked his servants what it was. They said that it was the flying *ku*, or snake ku. The family who serve the poisonous spirit become rich, but the women and girls of the family are debauched by the snake.

---

① 述異記, chüan 2.

The snake goes out every night, flitting like a meteor. When it comes to a less populous place, it comes down and eats the brains of men. So the inhabitants of K'ai-hua dare not sit outside after dark, being afraid of the *ku*."

The same work remarks again,① "The witch who cultivates *ku* must first take an oath before the spirit that she is willing not to be human in coming transmigrations, and will desire wealth in the present life only. When the victims of the poison die, their property is all removed (by supernatural power) to the house of the witch, and the ghost of the victim becomes her slave. All the work, ploughing, spinning and serving, is done by the enslaved spirit.... Those who have been poisoned by *ku* may cure themselves by jumping into a dung pool. Yu-Chi, Yung,an, Sha-hsien, and other districts of Fukien all have *ku*."

"Recently magistrate Wang, of Yu-Ch'i, bought a load of melons. He opened the melons the next day, and all contained *ku* insects. He accused the man who had sold them, who in turn said that they were bought in a certain shop. The magistrate arrested the shopkeeper and questioned him. He said that he and his family had never been sorcerers. On being beaten, he admitted that there was a sorcerer who had a personal animosity against him. The sorcerer was arrested, and did not deny the accusation. The magistrate had him tortured, but he did not feel the pain. He was put in jail, but escaped during the night. He was followed to his house, but the whole family were gone.

"In recent years there was a strange man who taught others a method for curing *ku*. The man would go to the home of the witch, carrying a chicken. The witch would understand, and give him a dose of medicine. All this must be done silently. The medicine was a sure cure.

"In Fukien, there is toad *ku*, somewhat similar to the *chin-tsan ku*.Those who serve it are mostly covetous of the riches that accompany it. People

---

① 述異記, chüan 2.

sometimes see large sums of money and silks lying beside the road, and they understand that this is someone sending away the *ku*. The *ku* spirit follows anyone who takes the valuables. With the wealth, the sender leaves a book telling the methods of serving the *ku*. The one who picks up the *ku* must clean his house and worship the *ku* spirit only, forsaking all Buddhist and Taoist deities. On the day that belongs to metal, the *ku* spirit will excrete dung like that of white birds, which can be used as poison. Poisons are laid only on the days *keng-hsin* and *sheng-yu*. Those who are poisoned, first sneeze. Then the worms enter the intestines and all the joints. The victim loses consciousness, and his belly swells. When the worms have eaten his bones and entrails, he dies."

"The *ku* poison can be administered in drink as well as in food, or sprinkled on the collars and clothes of the victims. It can be laid on chickens, geese, fish, meat, fruits and vegetables. When a living chicken has been bewitched by *ku*, its legs are eaten by worms, but it can walk and cackle as usual. When meat is bewitched, it will not become soft on being cooked. In all food that has been bewitched, worms will germinate overnight. So the officials in this land will use food presented by others only when it has stood overnight. Food which has no worms on the second day is not bewitched. The spirits of those who have died of *ku* poison become the slaves of the witch. The witches sacrifice eggs to the *ku* spirit on the last night of the year. Husband and wife worship with naked bodies, and thus square their accounts with the *ku* spirit. When a servant of the Yamen is poisoned, the sorcerer gives five ounces of silver to the *ku*; for all official, he gives fifty ounces. Those who poison more people, acquire greater riches. If a sorcerer becomes tired of the *ku*, he doubles the original amount of money he picked up with the *ku* in order to send it away."①

① 述異記, chüan 2.

Yüan Mei[1] says, "Almost all families in Yunnan keep *ku*. It can excrete gold and silver, so they get rich because of it. They let the *ku* out every night, and it darts about like lightning, spreading eastward and westward. A great noise causes it to fall. It may be a snake, toad, or any kind of insect or reptile. People conceal their children because they are afraid of their being eaten by the *ku*. This *ku* is kept in a secret room, and is fed by the women. The *ku* is injured if it is seen by men, because it is formed of pure *Yin* (the female principle of the universe). That *ku* which devours men will excrete gold, while that which devours women will excrete silver. All this was told me by Hua Feng, the general formerly commanding in Yunnan."

Again, in the same work[2]: "Chu Yi-jen was an expert calligraphist, and Ch'en Hsi-fang, the prefect of Ch'ing-yüan in Knangsi, employed him as secretary. One hot summer day, the prefect invited his colleagues to a feast. As they removed their hats on sitting down to the table, they saw a large frog sitting on the top of Chu's head. They brushed it away, when the frog fell to the ground and disappeared. They feasted until night, and again the frog crept to the top of Chu's head, without his being aware of it. They drove it away from him once more, and it fell on the table, spoilt the food, and disappeared."

"When Chu returned to his room, the top of his head itched. The next day his hair fell out, and his head swelled like a red tumour. Suddenly the swelling burst, and a frog stuck its head out. Its forefeet rested on the top of Chu's head, but the lower part of the frog was in the tumour. He picked it with a needle, but could not kill it. He tried to pull it out, but the pain was unbearable. The physicians did not know how to cure it. Finally an old gate-keeper said that it was the *ku*. On his advice they pierced it with a gold hair-pin, and the frog

---

① 袁枚. A. D. 1715-97. A voluminous writer of the Manchu period. This passage is taken from his 子不語, chüan 14. A book recording supernatural events.

② Ibid., ehiian 19. The passage is quoted by De Groot, p. 852.

died. Chu had no further trouble, but the top of his skull sank down like a bowl."

The *Ch'ien chi*① says, "The Miao women who kept *ku* got plenty of money. When the *ku* becomes too strong, it must be sent away. They do this sometimes as often as once a month. Those ignorant of this often pick up money or packages along the mountain paths. The *ku* follows them home. When it gets to the house, it must remain there several days. If its wants are not satisfied, it will cause calamity. During the fall, the Miao women carry pears in cloth bags, selling the pears to children. Many children are poisoned by *ku* in this way. This was discovered by some of the children, and so now, when they buy pears, they ask, 'Do you have *ku* poison in your pears?' If the reply is 'No', the children are safe. Among the women of the Shan, there are many who keep *ku*."

In the *Fan t'ien lu tsung t'an*② is the following passage. "Recently a man named Chiang ch'an-p'o reported that in the district of Lu-an *ku* is used to kill people. The house of the witch is always clean, since the work is done by the *ku*. Many inn-keepers serve the *ku*. If an inn-keeper and his inn are exceptionally clean, those who stay there overnight are poisoned. During one night, several travellers simply disappeared, and all their money and baggage came into the hands of the inn-keeper. There was no sign of the corpses because they were entirely eaten by the *ku* worms."

"Travellers in this district must know whether the inn contains *ku*. They lay their luggage at random on the ground, close the door, and stand outside for a while. If no servants appear, and yet the baggage has [mysteriously] been

① 黔記, chuan 32. By 李宗昉. Written about the beginning of the 19th Cent. It describes the province of Kueichou.

② 梵天廬談叢, chüan 33 By 柴萼. A work of miscellaneous notes published by the Chung-hua Book Co. of shanghai in 1926.

arranged in order, they know that this inn has *ku*. The traveller must not speak of this openly, but pays his fee and goes to some other inn. Such travellers will not be injured by the keeper of the inn, but will be regarded as men with a great destiny."

The *Yi chien chih pu*① says, "In the various districts of Fukien, there are many *Ku* poisoners, but they are especially prevalent in the districts of Ku-T'ien and Ch'ang-Ch'i. There are four kinds, snake *ku*, *chin-tsan ku*, centipede *ku*, and frog *ku*. All can change their forms, and become invisible. All have males and females, which copulate at fixed intervals, varying from two months to once in two years. When the date arrives, the family which keeps the *ku* prepares a ceremony to welcome their coming, and a basin of water is placed before them. The male and female appear in the water and copulate. Then the poison floats on the water, and can be collected with a needle. A person must be poisoned on this date. This is the breath of Yin and Yang (the male and female principles of the universe), and it is infused into people's stomachs, symbolic of the genital functions. It is not effective overnight. When a guest arrives, even a relative, he is poisoned. The poison can be placed in food, drink, or medicine, but it cannot be put into hot soup. When the medium is too hot, the poison is ineffective. If no outsiders come in on that day, a member of the family is selected to be poisoned. When the poison first enters the stomach the victim feels nothing, but gradually the *ku* worms generate and feed on the victim's blood. The worms grow, reproduce, and consume the internal organs. The pain becomes unbearable, and can be relieved only temporarily by drinking water boiled a hundred times. As the pain becomes worse, the victims groan and scratch the bed. When the victim is dying, several hundred worms come out of his eyes, nose, ears and mouth. If they are dried, they can become alive again,

---

① 夷堅志補, chüan 23.

even after a long time. The ghost of the victim is controlled by the *ku*, just as the tiger enslaves the *Ch'ang*①, and becomes a slave of the family. Such [an enslaved] spirit cannot be reincarnated. Even if the corpse of the victim is cremated, the heart and lungs will not burn, but will look like honeycombs."

"In 1175, the mother of Lin Sao-shuan of Ku-T'ien (her surname was Huang) lay dying, apparently from poison. The members of the family said that if she had been poisoned by *ku*, and her matrix was burned so that the light of the fire would shine upon her, she would reveal who had poisoned her. They did this, and she said that on a certain date, she had been poisoned while eating by Huang Ku's wife, Lai Shih. The demon was still in their kitchen. Lin Sao-shuan reported this to the local magistrate, and they went to the house of Huang Ku. In the kitchen they found some pieces of silver, five-colored thread, jewels, and small wooden figures on which were written five "Yi" and five "Shun" (words meaning "opposed" and "favorable"). These were in a box with seven holes. There were also two packs of needles, each fifty in number, and eleven needles were without eyes. All these were not things ordinarily used by people. The man was accused before the magistrate. The magistrate arrested Huang Ku, who feigned death in the court. When released, he became alive again, as if helped by some supernatural power."

"Yü Ch'ing of Kuei-chi was judge at that time, and when the prefect ordered him to examine the case, Huang Ku behaved in the same way. Yü Ch'ing was angry and afraid that the criminal would escape the law, so he came down and cut off Huang's head. He put the head in a basket, and reported the act to the prefect. The prefect reported the case to the emperor and a higher judge, Hsieh Ssu-chi, was asked to investigate the case."

---

① 倀. The spirit of a person who has been eaten by a tiger. It urges the tiger to murder others, in accordance with a common belief that the soul of a murdered man may return to earth if a substitute is provided.

"Hsich accompanied the local officials to the house of Huang Ku, where he saw centipedes of unusual size. Hsieh said, 'This is the evidence.' Lai Shih was arrested, and tried by Hsieh himself. After a three days trial, the death penalty was passed upon her. The figures (she confessed) were used in divination. If the response was favorable, the guest was poisoned; if unfavorable, a member of the family. The eyeless needles were used in gathering the poison, and the number showed that eleven persons had been poisoned. The *ku* likes to eat silk brocade, but if this could not be procured, the five-colored threads were fed to it instead. The silver was to have been used in sending the *ku* away.... Huang Ku's criminal acts really reached Heaven, and Yü Ch'ing obliterated an evil-doer by killing him. Many scholars wrote poems in praise of him."

There are also a number of stories indicating that the virtuous scholar need not fear *ku*. The Chinese have a proverb which says that the heretic cannot overcome the righteous man. Among the Chinese, the educated men have always been the backbone of the moral system. It is natural to find that such men can repel evil influences.

An interesting case is recorded in the *Mu fu yen hsien lu* of Pi Chung-hsün① "In Chih-chou there was a scholar named Tsou Lang, having a *chin-shih* degree. He was poor, but of upright character. One day he was about to start for a nearby town, when on opening his door in the early morning, he saw lying beside it a basket. He opened the basket, and found that it was filled with silver wine-vessels and about a hundred ounces of silver. As it was early morning, no one was watching him. The scholar took it in and said to his wife, 'These things came to me unexpectedly. Are they given to me by Heaven?' He had scarcely finished speaking, when he saw on his left thigh something that

① 幕府燕閑録, extracted in 説郛, chüan 14. By 畢中詢. A lost work of the Sung period.

wiggled in a shimmer of gold. It was a caterpillar. He picked it off with his hand. His hand was hardly turned, when it was back in its old place. He trampled on the worm with his foot and smashed it, but immediately it was again on his body. He threw it into water and into fire, cut it with his sword, and hacked it with an axe, without avail. It followed him everywhere, and never left him. Tsou Lang finally asked the advice of his friends. Those who knew about such matters told him,"

"'You have been betrayed. This thing is the *chin-tsan*. Although it is small, it will cause a great calamity. It can enter the belly and ruin the intestines, after which it will come out unharmed.'"

"Tsou Lang became still more frightened, and told his friend about finding the basket."

"His friend said, 'I knew that already. If you serve this *ku*, you will become rich quickly. This worm eats four inches of Shu satin every day. Collect its excretion, dry it, and grind it to powder. Put a little in food and drink, and give these to others. Anyone who takes it will surely be poisoned. The worm will get what it desires, and it will remove the valuables of its victims to your house.'"

"Tsou Lang laughed and said, 'Am I the man to do this?'"

"His friend said, 'I know surely that you do not desire to do it, but what other thing can you do?'"

"Tsou Lang replied, 'I shall put this worm into the basket with the other things and carry it away. Then there will be no further trouble.'"

"'When a man serves this worm long enough,' the friend said, 'he will become rich. Then he gives several times the amount he originally found with the *ku* away. This is called finding the *chin-tsan* a husband. Then the *ku* worm will go. But if you put in only what you found with the worm, I am sure it will not go. Now you are poor. How can you give several times more than you found?

I am really concerned about you.' "

"Tsou Lang looked at the sky, and replied, 'During my whole life I have tried to be an upright man. I swore not to lose my virtue. It is my misfortune that this thing has happened to me.' He went home and told his wife, saying, 'It is impossible for me to serve the *ku* worm. I am too poor to send it away. The only thing left for me is death. You had better prepare for the future.' "

"He put the worm into his mouth and swallowed it. His family tried to stop him, but it was too late. His wife wept bitterly, thinking that he would surely die. But after a few days he had no further trouble, eating and drinking as usual. A month passed, and still he was not affected. He finally died at a ripe age. And by means of the silver he had found in the basket, he became well to-do. Is it that the sincerity of a man can overcome the most poisonous influences ?"

The following account is taken from the *Yi chien san chih*.①

"In the district of Ch'ang-chou there was a brave scholar of strong character. He often thought that while men were cowardly, there was nothing worthy of being dreaded. He regretted that there were no evil spirits to interfere with him and test his courage. Once he went with a few friends to another village, and saw a parcel covered with silk on the ground. The others dared not even look at it, but he laughed and said, 'I am poor, why should I not take it?' "

"He opened it before them, and found several rolls of silk, three large pieces of silver, and a *ku* frog. He said to the frog, 'You may go where you wish; what I want is the silk and the silver.' He took the things home, where his family wept bitterly, thinking that a calamity would soon occur. The scholar said to them, 'This concerns me, not you'."

---

① 夷堅三志壬, chüan 4. A work of the Sung period.

"That night when he went to bed, there were two frogs, as big as a year old baby, occupying his bed. He killed and ate them both. His family again lamented, but he was delighted to get such good meat. Then he proceeded to get drunk, fell asleep, and passed a peaceful night. The next night there appeared more than ten frogs, though smaller than before. Again he cooked and ate them. The next night there were thirty. Night after night the frogs were increasingly numerous, but their size became ever smaller. At last the whole house was full of frogs, and it was impossible to eat them all. He hired men to bury them in the wilderness. Yet his courage was strengthened still more. Finally the thing stopped after a month, so he laughed and said, 'Is the calamity caused by *ku* no more than this ?' His wife asked him to buy hedgehogs as a precaution but he said, 'I am the hedgehog; what other do you want ?' His family was pacified, and nothing untoward happened. So other people commended his behavior."

The *Yi chien chih pu* contains the following story: ①"In the city of ch'uan-chou, there was a house tenanted by several families. One of the tenants was an under-official named Lin, a native of Ch'in. One night he found an old bamboo basket lying at the street end of an alley. He kicked it playfully, and a small embroidered blanket fell out. On opening it, he discovered silver vessels worth more than two hundred tales. As there was no one around, he took the things home, thinking they had been given to him by Heaven."

"All his neighbors were astonished by this, and the landlord said, 'This is the Ming custom of serving the *chin-tsan*. The original owner has become rich, and wanted to shift the calamity to others. Since you have taken this bait, you must not regret it. Today a demon will appear to you. You had better welcome and serve it. Otherwise, great misfortune will happen to you.' Lin

① 夷堅志補, chüan 23.

remained silent."

"That night a snake, ten feet long, crawled in as if much pleased. Lin caught it and said, 'Are you the demon of the *chin-tsan*? I cannot please you by poisoning people to enrich myself. If I do not, I shall be eaten by you. There is only one death, but I would rather eat you first.' So he bit the snake, and swallowed it from head to tail, not even leaving the bones. Then he called for wine, and drank until he fell asleep. Next morning he rose up well and unharmed, and later he became well-to-do. All admired his courage."

There is an amusing story of this sort in the *Fan T'ien lu t'an tsung*.① "An old man named Tseng, of Lung-yen in Fukien, picked up a box from the road. On opening it, he found about twenty ounces of silver. He took it home. During the night, a handsome young man appeared to him, who tried to compel him to burn incense and take an oath before Heaven that he would administer poison to someone on a certain date. The old man realized that it was the spirit of the *chintsan*. He refused the request, and so the spirit continued to trouble him. Finally worn out, he faithfully promised. On the fatal day, his son-in-law came. The spirit secretely put the poison in the food, and when the son-in-law returned home, he had violent pains in his abdomen. The old man realized that the pains were due to the poison, and relieved him by administering an antidote. The spirit was very angry, and complained to Tseng."

"The old man replied, 'He is my son-in-law, and my daughter has no children. How can I poison him?'"

"The spirit came another time, and exacted a similar promise. This time his sister's son came. The nephew also became violently ill on returning home, and the old man cured him. That night the spirit greatly annoyed Tseng, and the whole family had no sleep."

---

① 梵天廬談叢, chüan 33. By 柴萼. A work of miscellaneous notes, published by the Chung-hua Book Co. of shanghai in 1926.

"The old man Tseng said to the spirit, 'My sister was widowed when she was very young, and this son is her only child. If he dies from poison, my sister's descendants will be cut off. Moreover, I am not willing to do such things. Let us talk the matter over now. Suppose I give you back the original amount of silver, on condition that you go to someone else?'"

"'Since I came to your house,' replied the spirit, 'your farm produce has increased every day, and you forget about this benefit. You have not poisoned anyone yet, and you want me to go. You must add at least thirty per cent interest to the sum you give me. Otherwise I will not spare you.'"

"Then the old man took count, and calculated that he must give the spirit two hundred and more ounces of silver. He got the silver by selling his farm. Then he put it into the box, which he left where he had originally found it."

This ends the collection of illustrations of the practice of *ku*, a collection covering the entire period of Chinese literature. A few generalizations may be made in conclusion.

It must not be supposed, as De Groot implies, that all Chinese believe in these things. On the contrary, the fact that it was extremely difficult to make this collection of passages is in itself evidence of the opposite. The physical symptoms ascribed to magical causes are not imaginary, and the diseases are very real. *ku* figures largely in Chinese medical works, and the term is still used to describe certain conditions caused by internal parasites.

The idea of *ku* is very old. It probably originated in the idea that disease was sometimes caused by black magic. The use of the word as a divination symbol, and in the other ways mentioned in classic literature, are probably later accretions. The concept appears peculiar to Eastern Asia, at least in the method of producing the *Ku* by allowing poisonous things to eat each other. At the same time, all sorts of extraneous notions have been added from time to time.

The practice appears to be a connecting link between Chinese culture and the cultures of Southeastern Asia. However, it was early suppressed in China proper, and survived among the aboriginal tribes of the south.

(與 J. K. Shryock 合作,原載 *Journal of the American Oriental Society*, 1935,Vol. 55, pp. 1-30)

THE ORIGIN OF YÜ HUANG①

Yü Huang, sometimes translated Jade Emperor or Pearly Emperor, is the supreme deity of the Taoist Pantheon. Historically he is a late figure and does not play a prominent rôle in literary sources before the Sung period (A. D. 960-1279), but from the standpoint of popular Chinese mythical lore he is undoubtedly one of the most important deities and his origin should be carefully studied.

The Taoist version of his origin, that he was the son of the king and queen of the country of Kuang-yên-miao-yüeh 光嚴妙樂, a nonexistant utopia, should be repudiated as a late rationalization after the pattern of the life of Buddha.②

On the other hand the statement of some scholars that the god is a fabrication of the Sung emperor Chên-tsung (真宗, A. D. 998-1022) cannot be sustained. This misconception may be due to Wieger③ and has probably been followed by others who have dealt with Chinese mythology, such as Doré,④ Couling,⑤

① The author desires to express his gratitude to Prof. Elisséeff for corrections and suggestions and Dr. J. K. Shryock for improvement in English.

② *Kao-shang Yü Huang Pên Hsing Chi Chine* 高上玉皇本行集經, Commercial *Press ed. Tao tsang* 道藏, 23 chküan 上【盈一】4-6. The date of composition of this work is not definitely known; generally attributed to the Southern Sung (A. D. 1128-1279) or early Yüan (A. D. 1280-1367) periods. For a translation of this legend, see Lewis HODOUS, *Folkways in China* (*London*, 1929), 28-31.

③ Léon WIEGER, *Textes historques*[1] (1902), 1842 and 1846.

④ Henri DORÉ, *Recherches sur les superstitions en Chine*, 1915(9), 468-472.

⑤ Samuel COULING, *The Encyclopaedia Sinica*, 1917, 619.

Werner①, Ferguson②, etc. It is not likely that an emperor who wished to cover up his defeat at the hands of barbarians by some divine ordinance would invent a deity totally unknown to his subject③, Maspero has said that"... with false visions even more than genuine ones it is essential to base them upon well-

---

① E. T. C. WERNER, *Myths and Legends of china* (1922) 130-131; and *A Dictionary of Chinese Mythology* (1932) 598-611.

② J. C. FERGUSON, *Chinese Mythology* (*in Mythology of all Races*, *vol.* 8)(1928) 58-59.

The works of early writers concerning this subject are disregarded in this paper as most of them are so erroneous that they are hardly worth correction, e. g., H. C. DUBOSE, *The Dragon*, *Image*, *and Demon* (1887), 384, says:"As a matter of history, the Emperor Hwéi Tsung in the twelfth century conferred upon a magician, by the name of Chang Ye, the title of Shang te, the Pearly Emperor, and the people, finding one deity so much simpler than an abstract triumvirate, accepted him as their Optimus Maximus."

③ The evidence these authors adduce is very flimsy. The only work they refer to is the *T'ung Chien Kang Mu*, more accurately *T'ung Chien Kang Mu Hsü Pien* 通鑒綱目續编, as the *Kang Mu* proper ends with the year A. D. 959. Doré (*op. cit.*, 471, note 1) refers to Wieger, Couling follows Doré. Werner and Ferguson refer directly to the *T'ung Chien Kang Mu* but do not give any exact reference. Actually they all use Wieger without consulting the *T'ung chien Kang Mu Hsü Pian*, because there is nothing in the text and annotations to justify the statement that Chên-tsung invented Yü Huang.

Wieger says in his *Textes historiques* (p. 1842), "En 1012, date mémorable, invention du dieu le plus populaire de la Chine moderne. Laissons parler l'Histoire...." Then follows a translation of a passage from the *T'ung Chien Kang Mu Hsü Pien* [*cf.* 清嘉慶九年(1804), 蘇州聚文堂刊本 ch. 3, 59b] in which only the name Yü Huang is mentioned and nothing is said of invention. On page 1846 of the same work Wieger remarks again: "A cette occasion, la Grande Histoire renferme la note très importante que voui: 'C'est ici que commence l'histoire du *Pur Auguste*. On ne salt absolument rien de ce personnage, inconnu auparavant. Sa légende, telle que la postédté la débite, fut, selon toute apparence, confectionée à cette date." The original of this passage is given by Wieger as follows: 按祀典之稱玉皇,始此,而本末未詳.近世所奉玉皇本行集經,或始於此時也. This annotation does not occur in the text of the *T'ung Chien Kang Mu Hsü Pien*, nor in the *Sung Shih* 宋史 nor in the *Yü-p'i T'unng Chien Kang Mu Hsu Pien*, nor in the *T'ung Chien Chi Lan*, nor in the *Hsü Tzŭ Chih T'ung Chien*, nor in the *Sung Shih Chi-shih Pên Mo*. I do not know which work is meant by the term 'Grande Histoire.' Nevertheless, Wieger's rendering is inaccurate and misleading. A more literal translation of his text would run as follows: "The use of the title Yü Huang in state sacrificial and worshipping ceremonies 祀典 commences from here but his whole history is not clear. The *Yü Huang Pên Hsing Chi Ching* used nowadays probably dates from this time." It is very clear that this note says nothing about the invention of Yü Huang at this time but only that the state worship of him began from here. Wieger's interpretation that "Le 玉皇 *Pur Auguste*, le dieu le plus populaire de la Chine méridionale moderne, fut bel et bien inventé à cette époque..."(*op. cit.*, 1846, note) is entirely unwarranted.

The recognition of Yü Huang by the state religion was primarily connected with the *T'ien Shu* incident, 天書 'Ecrite C'élestes' of Chén-Tsung's reign. After the conclusion of the truce of Shan Yüan 澶淵 with the Khitan 契丹, which the Emperor later considered humiliating, he conspired to gain prestige among his subjects by some supernatural ordinance. He turned visionary and received the *T'ien Shu* from heaven. This further led the Emperor to perform the *Fêng Shan* 封禪 ceremonies, which could only be performed, theoretically, by founders of dynasties and successful great emperors. The *T'ien Shu Fêng Ssŭ* 天書封祀 was one of the most important and preposterous events during Chên-Tsnng's reign and the documents concerning the whole affair were summarized in CH'ÊN Pangchan 陳邦瞻, *Sung Shih Chi Shih Pên Mo* 宋史紀事本末 22.

established belief... "and" it is evident that, for the Emperor to have so definite a vision of his ancestor bringing him the order from the god, the god must already have ranked as a supreme deity in popular belief."① But Maspero went no farther than the other authors in tracing the early evidence of the development of this myth.

Hodous traced the name of Yü Huang to the *Book of Changes*②. This, however, is a little too imaginative.③ He also cited the *T'ien kung*, heavenly lord, in the *Sou Shên Chi* 搜神記④ and the *T'ien Kung* "venerable old man of heaven," Chang Chien, in the *Yu yang tsa tsu* as possible precursors of *Yü* Huang. As to the *T'ien kung*, it is so vague that it can be interpreted in many ways. The legend of Chang Chien in the *Yu yang tsa tsu*⑤ bears certain

---

① Henri MASPERO, *Mythologie de la Chine moderne*, *Mythologie asiatique illustrée* (Paris, 1928) 239-248. The quotation is from the English translation (London, 1932), pp. 263-271.

'Chen tsong' of the French edition should read 'Tchen tsong' according to the romanization used in Maspero's work. Chen tsong 神宗 (Shên-tsung for us) was the Sung emperor who reigned A. D. 1068-1085. Correspondingly the 'Shên tsung' in the English translation should read 'Chên-tsung'.

I take this occasion to ask M. Maspero on what authority he calls Fig. 10, p. 248 (Fig. 12, p. 272 in the English tr.) "La déesse de la Lune." Chinese artists seldom represent female figures showing their breasts except in obscene scenes. Fig. 10, so far as I can see, is not feminine at all. If the string of "gold cash" 金錢 were not missing, it would be the Liu Hai Hsi Ch'an 劉海戲蟾. 〔EDITORS' NOTE: Cf. V. ALEKSEEV, Les doubles immortels et le taoiste au crapaud d' or auompagnant le dieu de la richesse, *Rscueil du musée d'anthropologle et d'ethno graphic de l'Academic des Sciences* 5 (Petrograd, 1918), 253-318.〕

② Hodous, *op. cit.* 26.

③ 周易・説卦:"干爲天,爲圜,爲君,爲父,爲玉,爲金,爲寒,爲水,爲大赤,爲良馬,爲老馬,爲瘠馬,爲駁馬,爲木果."十三經注疏本, *chüan* 12, pp. 8-9.

Hodous does not give any exact reference, but I suppose this is the passage he referred to. If he interprets "Ch'ien is heaven... ruler... jade..." as Yü Huang, then how would he interpret "Ch'ien is... old horse..."?

④ Hodous, *op. cit.* 27. Hodous did not give any exact reference to the *Sou Shên Chi*. So far as I can find, the term *T'ien kung* 天公 occurs only twice in one place in ch. 10. lb. The term *T'ien ti* 天帝, heavening emperor, also occurs in this work (ch. 19. 2) but it is used with the same vague meaning as in the case of *T'ien kung*.

⑤ 酉陽雜俎,四部叢刊本,14.2.天翁張堅.

resemblances to the myth of Chang Têng-lai which will be given later in this paper, but he also cannot be considered as the precursor of Yü Huang, because the term Yü Huang had already become well known in literary sources almost half a century before the composition of the *Yu yang tsa tsu*.① Thus it is inconceivable that Tuan Ch'êng-shih should use such a vague term as *T'ien wêng*, "venerable old man of heaven," if he meant Yü Huang.

The earliest occurrence of the name Yü Huang is found in the works of the Confucian scholar Han Yü (A. D. 768-824). In a poem admiring the plum blossoms②, he wrote:

"Riding clouds we come together to the home of Yü Huang."

Riding clouds is a mode of locomotion characteristic of Chinese gods and immortals. Liu Tsung-yüan (A. D. 773-819), the great T'ang essayist and poet, in a poem about a waterfall③, wrote:

"Suddenly it is like coming to the presence of Yü Huang,

The jade pendants upon the front of his heavenly crown hanging down?"

The author was comparing the sparkling waterfall to the lustrous jade tassels of Yü Huang's crown. It suggests a well developed myth to which the poet was alluding. More specific was the poet Yüan Chên 元稹 (A. D. 779-831). Bragging about his newly acquired residence to Po Chü-i (A. D. 772-846), he wrote④:

"I am the petty official in charge of Yü Huang's incense table, Although

---

① Hodous says (*op. cit.* 27), "In the *Yu yang tsa tsu*, written at the end of the eighth century..." This date is too early. The author Tuan Ch'êng-shih 段成式 died in the year A. D. 863. His birth date is not known but it cannot be much earlier than A. D. 790 because his father Tuan Wên-ch'ang 段文昌, was born in 773 and died in 831. From his biography in the *Old T'ang History* 舊唐書 167. 9 it would seem that the *Yu yang tsa tsu* was most probably composed during his later years, possibly around the middle oi the ninth century. The *Yu yang tsa tsu* itself records facts as late as 840.

② 昌黎先生集,蟫隱廬影宋世彩堂本, 5.3.

③ 柳河東集,四部備要本,42.14,界圍岩水簾詩."忽如朝玉皇,天冕垂前旒."

④ 元氏長慶集,四部叢刊本,22.2,以州宅夸樂天."我是玉皇香案吏,謫居猶得住蓬來."

banished, I can still live in P'êng-lai."

P'êng-lai was the legendary island of the immortals. All these poetical quotations should be understood in a metaphorical sense. Chinese poetry is noteworthy for its conciseness. From these few lines the picturesque figure of Yü Huang can be clearly visualized. The T'ang dynasty (A. D. 618-907) was the great period of Chinese poetry, and it is natural to find important material embodied in poetic form. The frequent occurrence of Yü Huang in the poetry of this period shows the great popularity of the myth and the poetical nature of the theme.

Some what later there was a well known painting of the imaginary court scene of Yü Huang by the famous artist Shih K'o 石恪 of the Kingdom of Shu 蜀 (A. D. 908-965). The painting has probably been lost, but a full description of it has been handed down to us in the critical catalogue, *Tê Yü chai Hua p'in.*① It says:

"A picture of the court ceremony of Yü Huang by Shih K'o of Shu. The T'ien-hsien, Ling-kuan, Chin-Tung, Yü-nü, San-knan, T'aii, Ch'i-yüan, Ssŭ-shêng, Ching-wei②, gods of stars, wind, rain, thunder, lightning, lords of the mountains and lakes, deities ruling above and below the earth, etc., are all gathered at the court of the Emperor. The great heavenly Emperor Yü Huang sits facing south with all due decorum and dignity. All the deities look up to his pure lustrous countenance with raised heads. Those who see this picture will feel the exaltation and animation. It is like placing oneself in the T'ung Ming Tien.③

---

① 德隅齋畫品 by Li Chai 李廌 of the Sung dynasty.顧氏文房小説本,p. 7-8.玉皇朝會圖.

② 天仙,靈官,金童,玉女,三官,太一,七元,四聖,經緯.

③ 通明殿 Palace of penetrating illumination, i. e. the palace of yü Huang. Cf. *Ishêng Pao-tê Chuan* 翊聖保德傳 by WANG Ch'in-jo 王欽若 (died 1024) of the Sung dynasty (道藏,1006 册,卷中,1a[6]-b[4]):守真嘗朝禮至玉皇大殿,睹共額曰通明殿,不曉其旨.因焚香告曰:通明之誼,竊所未喻,敢祈真教? 真君曰:上帝在無上三天,爲諸天之尊,萬象群仙,無不臣者.常昇金殿,金殿之光明,照於帝身,身之光明,照於金殿.光明通徹,無所不照,故爲通明殿. This is the earliest explanation of the meaning of T'ung Ming Tien.

"Shih K'o's temperament is unrestrained humorous and satirical. Therefore his paintings are unruly and often go beyond the ordinary rules, but they do not lose their unusual beauty. So of the figures he has painted here, some are extraordinarily ugly or mysteriously crabbed in order to insinuate the unusual 〔gathering〕. The deities of the waters have crabs or fishes suspended to their waists 〔a feature he intended〕 to show disdain for the onlookers.... In this painting he dared not blaspheme the figure of Yü Huang, but still it is not free from amusing implications intending to obtain laughter from admirers 〔of the picture〕."

The vividness of the description and the reverent language of the critic toward Yü Huang combine to show his importance as a supreme deity.

All these citations show that Yü Huang was much earlier than the time of the emperor Chên-tsung. He only utilized a well-known, popular deity to further his cause. But through his imperial patronage Yü Huang gained state recognition and became more important in popular religious beliefs than ever before.

Yü Huang as a high god dates back to the eighth and nineth centuries A. D., and his actual genesis may be still a few centuries earlier,① but the actual condition of his origin and the details of the myth are still shrouded in mystery, and as in the case of most popular deities, may never be known. However, there is a popular version of this myth, which does not seem to have been recorded. This version is widely distributed over Central and West China, where the Taoist religion has had its fullest development from the time of Chang Lu.

According to this version, the surname of Yü Huang is Chang, and his

---

① Prof. Elisséeff suggested to me that there might be a connection between Yü Huang and Yü Ching 玉京 mentioned in *Wei Shu* 魏書 114. 24b-25a, and in *Sui Shu* 隋書 35. 27b-28a (The paging is that of the 同文 edition). If this could be proved it would definitely carry the myth farther back three or four centuries. Cf. also J. R. WARE, The *Wei Shu* and the *Sui Shu* on Taoism, *JAOS* 53 (1933), 214 and 243.

first name is Têng-lai.① He is more or less an opportunist, a trickster, and obtained his throne by chance. The story is based on the *Fêng shên Chuan*, a novel describing the canonization of gods. This version continues the *Fêng Shên Chuan*, and since this is a wellknown work, it is not necessary to recapitulate the whole story here②, but only to start from the place where the Yü Huang myth is first mentioned.

Chiang T'ai-kung, standing on the Fêng Shên T'ai, Terrace of Canonization③, appointed all those who lost their lives during the bloody campaign against the Shang as gods to rule over the destinies of man. For a time the procedure was uneventful, but finally only the position of Yü Huang was left vacant, which Chiang T'ai-kung intended to reserve for himself. Some impatient bystander inquired of him who was to become Yü Huang. Half-heartedly, Chiang T'ai-kung replied, "Têng-lai." This literally meant, "I'm coming to that." Standing beside the Fêng Shên T'ai was the opportunist Chang Têng-lai. On hearing his name called, he prostrated himself before the 'Terrace' and thanked Chiang T'ai-kung for creating him Yü Huang. Stupefied by this unexpected turn of events, and unable to retract his words, Chiang T'ai-kung in his intense anger cursed Chang Têng-lai, saying: "Your sons will become thieves and your daughters prostitutes." Chang Têng-lai had, however, to become Yü Huang, because whatever Chiang T'ai-kung says must be fulfilled, for "his mouth is gold and his words jade."

Now there was no place left for Chiang Tai-kung himself; the only shrine

---

① 張等來.

② Those who are not familiar with the *Fêng shên Chuan* 封禪傳 or *Fêng Shên Yen-i* 封神演義, may see WERNER, *A Dictionary of Chiese Mythology* under Chiang Tzŭ-ya. A very brief account is given there. See also DORÉ, *op. cit.* (note 4), Ⅸ, pp. 665-670. This novel is partially translated and resumed by Wilhelm GRUBE and Herbert MUELIER in *Fêng-Shên-Yen-i*, *Die Metamorphosen der Goetter*, Leiden, 1912.

③ 封禪臺.

he could find for himself was the windowsills. Consequently, in present-day China, especially in Central China among the peasants, whenever there is a wedding or a child-birth, or any event that needs protection from malevolent spirits, an inscription is invariably pasted on the window of the room of the bride, or the laboring mother, saying: "Chiang T'ai-kung is here, all gods avoid."① The wedding night and childbirth are critical moments that have to be safeguarded against malevolent spirits. The idea is that, although Chiang T'aikung lost his position as Yü Huang, he still has prestige among the gods because he canonized them, and because he is the only one who hovers around the windows. According to popular belief, evil spirits can only enter the house through the windows because the doors are guarded by door gods whose images are placed there and renewed every new year. If Chiang T'ai-kung guards the windows, the house will be secure against all malevolent spirits.

Although Chang Têng-lai became Yü Huang, he could not annul the curse imposed upon him by Chiang T'ai-kung. So his sons became thieves, and after having committed many minor felonies, they planned a more daring attempt. They went to steal the precious lotus seat of the Buddha. This feat was impossible because they could not escape from the great power of the Buddha, who is omniscient and omnipotent. With a turn of his hand Buddha enslaved them under a pagoda and doomed them to remain there forever. This is why at the foot of every pagoda there are grotesque figures who seem to support it with great exertion. They are the sons of Chang Yü Huang.②

Yü Huang's daughters were doomed to be prostitutes. As their father was Yü Huang, they did not become prostitutes in the ordinary sense of the term,

① 姜太公在此,諸神迴避.

② This explanation is certainly wrong. They are not Yü Huang's sons but guardian deities of the pagoda usually of the Vajrapāni type. For illustration, see G. ECKE and P. DEMIEVILIE, *The Twin Pagodas of Zayton* (Cambridge, Mass., 1935), pis. 12 and 14, fig.5-6, etc. It shows, however, the imagination of the popular mind in seeking to explain what is not understood.

but all married men. There are a wealth of tales about these marriages between immortals and mortals which are too long to be related here. The most dramatic, humorous, and entertaining is the marriage of Yü Huang's seventh daughter Chang Ch'i-chieh, Chang the seventh sister, with the semi-imbecile Ts'ui Wên-jui.[①] Wên-jui was a poor wretch clothed in rags, simple and ignorant. He was a wood-cutter because he was too stupid to earn a living by any other work. Yet he was very filial and obedient to his aged and invalid mother. Every day he went to the woods to chop down a bundle of wood which he sold in the market in order to buy the necessary food for his mother. Day after day he went to the forest and cut the wood and nothing eventful happened. While contented with his lot, he really did not know what contentment meant. One day while he was chopping wood, Chang Ch'i-chieh came to him and offered to marry him. Tsui Wên-jui was so stupid that he did not know what a wife was. The conversation between the two is the most humorous as well as the most ridiculous that anyone can imagine. Finally Wên-jui brought the matter to his mother. She refused on the ground that her son was too stupid to have such a beautiful wife. "It will be a great calamity instead of a great fortune." Chang Ch'i-chieh insisted and she pledged herself to be a good wife and to do all the cooking, weaving and housework. She would not leave unless Wên-jui took her to wife. Finally the old lady yielded and they were married.

Actually Chang Ch'i-chieh proved to be a very good wife. She was industrious and obedient. The cloth she wove was so beautiful and fine that no one would believe it was done with mortal hands. All went on very well. Unfortunately, one day when she was working outside, a rich and handsome young man of the district passed by and saw her. He was so infatuated by her beauty that he was willing to try any means to marry her. The mother-in-law was

① 張七姐下凡嫁崔文瑞.

much perturbed because she was apprehensive of the danger involved, but the wife told her not to worry. She promised to marry this rich young man provided he would pay her husband Wên-jui an exorbitant bride-price to compensate for his loss of a beautiful wife. To this the young man gladly consented, and she went over for the wedding. Being an immortal with supernatural powers she punished him very severely during the wedding night and he promised to repent and never do such a thing again. Then Chang Ch'i-chieh returned to Ts'ui Wên-jui. Wên-jui, on account of the large bride-price he received, became well-to-do. Chang Chi-chieh stayed with him for several years and bore him a son. Then she left him and returned to heaven. She had fulfilled the curse, punished the wicked, and rewarded a filial son.①

This popular version of the origin myth of Yü Huang is entertaining, moral, and exegetical. There may be anachronisms and false explanations in the story but it is certainly a masterpiece of Chinese folk literature. Popular tales without documentary evidence are always very difficult to date. This story is based on the *Fêng shên Chuan* which was probably composed about the period A. D. 1567-1620 by an anonymous author.② There is no way of knowing how much older the story may be. Many of the legends contained in The *Fêng Shên*, *Chuan* are of considerable antiquity, and this compilation may only represent a phase of literary documentation and standardization. Even during the time of Ssŭ-ma Ch'ien, Chiang T'ai-kung was often connected with the supernatural. In the *Fêng Shan Shu* of the *Shih Chi* (ch. 28), it is said that "The eight divine generals existed from antiquity; some say that they were instituted from the time

---

① The legend is often dramatized on the rural stage in Centra land West China. During the late fall when the paddy harvest is in and the nights still warm, an open air stage is erected, and the play given.

② 鲁迅:中國小説史略, 187-191. The *Fêng shên Chuan* was mentioned by Chang Wu-chiu 張无咎 in his preface to the *Ping Yao Chuan* 平妖傳, composed in the year 1620. Thus, the date of composition of the *Fêng shên Chuan* cannot be later than this.

of T'ai-kung." ① The apotheosis of Chiang T'ai-kung may have occurred quite early and culminated in the *Fêng Shên Chuan*. But how and when the origin myth of Yü Huang was grafted to him cannot be definitely determined at the present. To judge from the distribution of the window-sill cult of Chiang T'ai-kung, which is almost universal in China, it may be of considerable antiquity.

（原載 *Harvard Journal of Asiatic Studies*, Vol. I, No. 2(1936), pp. 242-250）

① 史記・封禪書."八神將自古而有之;或曰,太公以來作之." E. CHAVANNES, *Les Mémoires historiques de Se-ma Ts'ien* (3. 432) translates this passage as: "Les huit dieux ont existe dès l'antiquite[2]. D'autres disent que c'està partir de l'Auguste duc qu'on fit (les sacrifices aux huit dieux)." In note 2 of the same page, he says: "Dans l'expression 將自古, le mot 將 a le sens de 'immédiatement, aussitrt.' 'Chavannes' interpretation of the word 將 is rather arbitrary, so he has to omit it in his translation because it does not make sense in French. Such an interpretation, however, does not make sense in Chinese either!

TEKNONYMY AS A FORMATIVE FACTOR IN THE CHINESE KINSHIP SYSTEM①

The Chinese kinship system② is primarily built upon the foundation of the old patronymic sib organization③ and the sharp differentiation of generations. All relatives, both lineal and collateral of the same patronym are classed into one "sib relation" group and all relatives by marriage, including women of the same patronym married out, are classed into the "outside relation" group. The generation principle cuts horizontally through these two groups of relatives and divides them into successive generation strata. These two factors-sib and generation-not only pervade the whole system, but also regulate marriage. A Chinese can marry any one outside his or her patronymic sib; if they are related

---

① The author desires to express his deep gratitude to Prof A. I. Hallowell for his many painstaking corrections and criticisms.

② The earliest study of the Chinese relationship system was made by Lewis H. Morgan in his *Systems of Consanguinity and Affimity of the Human Family* (1870) which gave 196 terms. Subsequently G. Schlegel, A. G. May, G. Jamieson, P. G. von Möllendorff, and Pierre Hoang also dealt with the subject. The more recent and thorough studies are by H. P.Wilkinson, *Chinese Family Nomenclature smd Its Supposed Relation to Primitive Group-marringe* (in Family in Classical China, 1926, Chapter 13, pp. 157-210) and by T. S. Chen and J. K. Sbryock, Chinese Relationship Terms (American Anthropologist, Vol. 34, 1932, pp. 623-64). A. L. Kroeber made a very illuminating analysis of the Chinese system (based on Chen and Shryock's article) in his *Process in the Chinese Kinship System* (American Anthropologist, Vol. 35, 1933, pp. 151-157).

③ There is practically no literature on this important subject in English. For a very generalized conception, the reader may consult L. K. Tao, *Some Chinese Characteristics in the Light of the Chinese Family* (*in Essays Presented to C. G. Seligman*, 1934).

they must be of the same generation irrespective of age. If the kinship system regulates marriage at all, it is only in the derivative sense.

Since generation is an important factor in the Chinese system, we should expect it to be consistently carried through. But there are some notable exceptions in contemporary usage, such as the fact that mother's brothers and wife's brothers are designated by the same term *chiu*, mother's sisters and wife's sisters by the same term *yi*, father' solder brothers and husband's older brothers by the same term *po*, father's younger brothers and husband's younger brothers by the same term shu, father's sisters and husband's sisters by the same term *ku* (as hsiao ku).① These peculiarities are of significance because the Chinese system is not inherently an inconsistent one, but, as Morgan has remarked, it "embodies a well considered plan, which works out its results in a coherent and harmonious manner."② It is still more significant, as we shall show later, that originally the generations of these relatives were clearly differentiated by distinct terms but in the course of time they gradually merged into each other. There must be at work some powerful disruptive force which threw the generation of these relatives into confusion.

There is one advantage in dealing with the Chinese kinship system: the terms are amenable to historical treatment. The changes of every term can be traced from period to period, and the causes of these changes can be, in most cases, ascertained. First we may take the connotations of the term chiu and the terms for the wife's brother during the various periods and arrange them in a table.③

---

① The Chinese characters are not given in this paper. Nearly all the terms used here can be found in the tables in Chen and Shryock's paper cited above, where the Chinese characters are given in full.

② L. H. Morgan, *op. cit.*, p. 421.

③ The chief reference is Liang Chang-chü's *Chêng-wei-lu* (Book of Addresses) in which the first eight books are about kinship terms. This work is a laborious and comprehen sive collection of terms from all periods.

Period	*Connotations of chiu*	*Terms for wife's brother*
I. Before 3rd century B. C.	mother's brother husband's father wife's father	sheng
Ⅱ. 2nd century B. C. to 9th century A. D.	mother's brother	chi hsiung ti
Ⅲ. 10th century A. D. to present	mother's brother wife's brother	chiu

The different connotations of the term chiu in Period I are perfectly intelligible in view of the fact that cross-cousin marriage was undoubtedly in vogue at this time.① In such a marriage the mother's brother and husband's father would be the same person; so also would be mother's brother and wife's father. In Period Ⅱ cross-cousin marriage was dropped, so correspondingly the meaning of *chiu* became confined to mother's brother.②

The terms for the wife's brother were different during each of the three periods. In Period I wife's brother was called *sheng*. *Sheng* also meant at this period father's sister's sons, mother's brother's sons, and sisters' husbands (man speaking).③ This is also explicable by cross-cousin marriage of the bilateral type together perhaps with sister exchange. In Period Ⅱ, because of the disappearance of this type of marriage, sheng was no longer applicable to

① For cross-cousin marriage in ancient China, see Chen and Shryock, *op. cit.*, p. 630.

② The new terms in the modern system for husband's father is kung and for wife's father yo fu.

③ Chen and Shryock, *op. cit*, pp. 630, 657.

any of these relatives and new terms were introduced to take its place. *Chi hsiung ti*① was the term used for wife's brothers.

In Period Ⅲ the term *chiu* (mother's brother) was extended to include wife's brothers. The first use of *chiu* in this new meaning is to be found in the *Hsin T'ang Shu.*② In the Biography of Chu Yenshou, it says: "Yang Hsing-mi's wife is the older sister of Chu Yenshou. Hsing-mi (in ordering Chu Yen-shou to take up an important position) says: 'I am so sick and my sons are too young. Having *chiu* take my place, I shall have no worry'." This is certainly a curious extension of the use of *chiu*. Through all the vicissitudes of the term during the previous periods the generation element was always preserved.③ This blending of generations certainly warrants explanation.

In a strict sociological interpretation the conclusion would be a mariage with the wife's brother's daughter as an extension of the sororate④, because in such a case the wife's brother would be a potential father-in-law. We see in Period I *chiu* also meant father-in-law. Since the wife's brother is a potential father-in-law, so the extension of the term chiu to him is perfectly logical.

---

① It is purely a descriptive term, Chi means wife, hsiung ti means brothers, older and younger, sometimes fu hsiung ti amd nei hsiung ti were used. Both fu and nei mean wife. the new term for father's sister's sister's sons and mother's brother's sons is piao hsiung ti; tzu fu is the term for older sister's husband, and mei fu for younger sister's husband.

② New Annals of the T'ang dynasty (A. D. 618-905), Book 189, p. 10 (Tung-wên edition of the Twenty-four Histories). In this article only the authentic reference of the first occurrence of a new term or the new use of an older term is given. The numerous later references are omitted for the sake of brevity.

③ Indeed the Chinese system does not allow such complete departure from the generation principle, for in modern colloquial usage special modifiers are used to differentiate the generations: such as mother's brothers are called chiu fu; fu indicates they belong to the "father" generation, wife's brothers are called chiu hsiung and chiu ti; hsiung and ti indicate they belong to the "brother" generation.

④ The question of the sororate during the feudal period was discussed in full by Marcel Granet in La polygynie sororale et la sororate dans la Chine féodale (1920). There are many exaggerations and twistings of evidence in this work; however, the discussion is very lively.

However there are several very serious difficulties to this interpretation. In the first place there is absolutely no evidence, either historical or contemporary, to support this hypothesis. In the second place it is contrary to the generation principle. wife's brother's daughter will be one generation lower than ego; so in the Chinese system she is within the incest group. The third is a temporal difficulty. Chiu ceased to mean wife's father at least a thousand years before it was extended to mean wife's brother. In the face of these objections this interpretation is not tenable.

It is significant that Chinese scholars had been employing teknonymy to explain this anomaly long before its introduction into ethnological discussion by E. B. Tylor.① Ch'ien Ta-hsin (1727-1804), one of the most exacting classical scholars of his time, attributed this extension of the meaning of *chiu* to the gradual and imperceptible effect of the practice of teknonymy.② wife's brothers are *chiu* to one's own children. The father adopts the language of his children, so he also calls his wife's brothers *chiu*. This can be clearly seen from the instance of Chu Yen-shou. Yang Hsing-mi called Chu Yen-shou chin together with the mentioning of his own sons. It is inferable that after long teknonymous usage the term *chiu* established itself and displaced the older term.

Whether this hypothesis can be sustained or not depends upon the additional evidences which we can adduce for its support. At this point we may turn to the examination of the terms which the wife uses to address her husband's father's brothers and her husband's brothers. Curiously, a similar mixing of generations occurs.

Po means father's older brothers (both man and woman speaking)

---

① On a Method of Investigating the Development of Institutions, etc. [Journal, (Royal) Anthropological Institute, Vol. 18, pp. 245-69, 1889].

② *Hêng-yen-lu* (Books Ordinary Sayings), Chüan 3.

〔husband's father's older brothers (wife adopting husband's term)〕①

husband's older brothers

Shu means father's younger brothers (both man and woman speaking)

〔husband's father's younger brothers (wife adopting husband's term)〕

husband's younger brothers

So far as I am aware, there is no social or marital usage in China, nor is there any comparable usage that ethnolographic data suggest, which could produce such a terminology. From the historical point of view the terms for these relations were different at different periods. In the *Erh Ya*② the father's older brothers were called *shih fu*.③ From the second century B. C. to the third century A. D. *po fu* was generally used. From the fourth century A. D. and onward only *po* was sometimes used. husband's older brothers were called *hsiung kung* in the *Erh Ya*.④ During the succeeding centuries hsiung chang was commonly employed. About the tenth century A. D. *po* was extended to mean husband's older brothers.⑤ As has been already stated, no possible explanations can be found in marriage forms for this blending of generations: the only possible alternative is teknonymy, husband's older brothers will be *po* to the wife's own children. The mother adopts the terminology of her children, so she also calls them *po*. The term *shu* can be similarly explained.

---

① A man or woman calls his or her father's older brothers po and father's younger brothers shu. The category of the sex of the speaker is usually not distinguished by terms in most cases in the Chinese system. When a woman marries, she adopts her husband's terms in addressing her father-in-law's brothers, e. g., as po and shu. There is no special term used by the wife for her father-in-law's brothers. See Chen and Shryock, *op. cit.*, p. 640.

② The *Erh Ya* is the earliest Chinese dictionary; variously attributed to Chou Kung (B. C. ? -1105) and to the disciples of Confucius (B. C. 551-479). Probably it is not a work by one hand but gradually augmented through many centuries. Its date cannot be much later than the fifth century B. C. The section on relationship terms has been translated by Chen and Shryock, *op. cit*, pp. 654-60.

③ *Erh Ya*, Chen and Shryock translation, p. 655. Both man and woman speaking, wife's term for them being the same.

④ Ibid., p. 659.

⑤ *Chêng-wei-lu*, Chüan 7, p. 6. Most of the chronologies in this paper are based on this work.

Ku in the modern system means:

father's sisters (both man and woman speaking)

[husband's father's sisters (wife adopting husband's term)]

husband's sisters

In Period I *ku* was used to mean father's sisters, husband's mother, and wife's mother (as *wai ku*) due to cross-cousin marriage.① When cross-cousin marriage declined, *ku* was employed only for father's sisters.② husband's older sisters were called *nü kung* in the *Erh Ya*.③ *Nü shu* or *shu mei* were also used a little later for the younger sisters of the husband. During the fourth century A. D. the term *ku* began to be extended to husband's sisters.④ What was the cause of this extension cannot be exactly ascertained although the social history of the period concerned is fairly well known. It cannot be due to marriage with the wife's brother's daughter, in which case the husband's sister would be elevated to the position of the husband's father's sister: the objections to the interpretation of chín by this usage also apply here. Furthermore, other features do not follow either terminologically⑤ or conceptually⑥. Teknonymy remains the best

---

① Chen and Shryock, *op. cit.*, p. 630.

② The modern term for husband's mother is P'o or P'o P'o, literally "old lady." The term for wife's mother is yo mu.

③ *Erh Ya*, *op. cit.*, p. 659.

④ The first occurrence of hsiao *ku* (husband's younger sisters) is in the famous poem *Kung chiao lung nan fei*. The exact date of this poem is disputed but all scholars agree it cannot be later than the fourth Century A. D. Ta *ku* is used for husband's older sisters. Ta means big, senior; hsiao means small, junior.

⑤ As among the Miwok where marriage with the wife's brother's daughter is reflected by twelve terms (E. W. Gifford, Miwok Moieties, University of California Publications in American Archaeology and Ethnology, Vol. 12, 1916, p. 186), but they are all lacking in the Chinese system.

⑥ Among the Omaha marriage with the wife's brother's daughter is reflected by the conceptual identification of the father's sister, the female ego, and the brother's daughter (A. Lesser, Kinship Origins in the Light of Some Distributions, American Anthropologist, Vol. 31, 1929, pp. 711-12) although not indicated by the terminology. In the Chinese system the generations of the father's sisters, husband's father's sister, and the husband's sisters are clearly distinguished conceptually although the terminology fails to differentiate them.

explanation, because husband's sisters will be *ku* of the wife's children.

Correspondingly we find the same peculiarity of blending of generations of mother's sisters with wife's sisters. Both are called *yi*. Originally *yi* was used, as in the *Erh* Ya①, for wife's sisters, mother's sisters were called *tsung mu*.② The first use of *yi* to mean mother's sisters is found in the *Tso Chüan*. In the twenty-third year (B. C. 550) of Duke Hsiang there is a passage: "Yi's daughter of Muchiang."③ By checking the marriages among the feudal lords of this time, it is clear that the term *yi* here does not mean wife's sister, as it ought, but mother's sister. As a matter of fact it ought to say "*tsung mu's* daughter of *Mu-chiang*" not "*yi's* daughter." This passage has perplexed the classical commentators for centuries and it still baffles the modern social anthropologist. Theoretically, a sororate together with a marriage with the father's widows would adequately explain it. In such a marriage, mother's sisters would be equated with wife's sisters. This explanation has certain plausibility, as a man's secondary wives are also called *yi*. That is mother's sisters, wife's sisters, and secondary wives (concubines) are all grouped into one class; a usage usually attributed to the sororate. It is well known that the sororate was practiced among the feudal lords, but as to the inheriting of father's widows there is no evidence. Indeed such a marriage would be abhorrent to the ancient Chinese. We learn from the old writers how they compared the Hsiung-nu, pastoral nomads of the northern steppes, to dogs as they married their father's widows.

The consensus of opinion among the classical commentators about the discarding of *tsung mu* and the extension of *yi* to mean mother's sister is the

---

① *Erh Ya*, *op. cit.*, p. 657.

② Ibid., p. 656.

③ James Legge (The Chinese Classics, etc., Vol. 5, Part 2, p. 503) translated this passage: "A daughter of the younger sister of Muh-Këang (the mother of duke Ching)...." This is certainly a mistranslation. Legge not only did not check up the marriages among the feudal lords, but he did not even read the commentaries carefully.

psychological similarity between these relatives, mother's sisters are yi to one's father just as wife's sisters are *yi* to oneself. The son imitates the language of his father, so he calls his father's yi also yi. In short this case seems to demand a psychological explanation① together with a reverse teknonymy.

The foregoing cases are the only instances in the Chinese system where the generation principle is openly violated. In every case we have tried to explain these exceptions by facts and hypotheses which have proved illuminating in the discussion of analogous phenomena elsewhere. But we found none of them applicable to the Chinese material. Instead, we found teknonymy the only satisfactory explanation. There is no doubt that teknonymy is the determining factor in all these cases, but we may ask, is teknonymy universal in China and of sufficient antiquity that it may have been involved in producing such effects in the kinship terminology? There is no question about the universality of the practice in China; only the frequency of its use might have varied from time to time and from place to place, it is usually of the type that omits the child's name, just as in America a man may call his wife simply "mother."

As to its antiquity, we have to depend upon historical evidence. Skipping the numerous comparatively late references, the earliest instance that can be interpreted as teknonymy is recorded in Kungyang's Comentary of the Spring and Autumn Annals of Confucius. In the sixth year (B. C. 489) of Duke Ai is recorded the instance of Ch'ên Ch'i. Ch'ên Chi in referring to his wife says "Mother of Chang ..." Ch'ang was known to be Chên Ch'i's son. The teknonymous usage here is indubitably clear. The fifth century B. C. is more than a millenium earlier than most of the cases we have just discussed, except the case of yi (B. C. 550) which is more than half a century anterior. On the

① A. L. Kroeber, Classificatory Systems of Relationship (Journal, Royal Anthropological Institute, Vol. 39, 1909, pp. 77-84). Kroeber's views on liuguo-psychological causation of kinship nomenclature have been much attacked by students. For an equitable comment see A. Lesser, *op. cit.*, p. 711.

other hand, if we make allowance for the conservative spirit of the classical writers in recording colloquial language, it is reasonable to infer that teknonymy is much older than this documentary evidence shows.

In the very limited literature on teknonymy, various theories have been put forth to account for its origin①, but no author attempts to use it to explain other social phenomena, Teknonymy as a usage is based on kinship and kinship nomenclature-a circumlocutory way of expressing embarrassing relationships. Through its long and intensive use, why should it not have produced certain peculiarities in kinship terminologies as other social usages are reputed to have done? The Chinese cases are especially illuminating. It would require a series of marital or other special practices to explain the peculiarities of chiu, po, shu, ku, and yi, whereas they can be uniformly explained by a single principle—teknonymy.

[原載 *American Anthropologist*, Vol. 38, No. 1(1936), pp. 59-66]

① R.H. Lowie, Primitive Society (New York, 1920), pp. 107-109, 262.

THE CHINESE KINSHIP SYSTEM[①]

Foreword

Abbreviations

e = ego	h = husband, husband's
f = father, father's	w = wife, wife's
m = mother, mother's	o = older
s = son, son's	y = younger
d - daughter, daughter's	> = older than
b - brother, brother's	< = younger than

---

① It is hard to express the extent of my indebtedness to Professors F. G. Speck, A.I. Hallowell and D.S. Davidson for their guidance, inspiration and interest in my work. My gratitude is especially due to Prof. A.I. Hallowell who has directed my work and examined the manuscript several times, making important corrections and improvements each time. His suggestions were so valuable that it was necessary for me to rewrite and rearrange the first part of the work entirely.

I am also most grateful to Prof. C.K. M. Kluckhohn and Dr. C. M. Arensberg for their careful reading of the manuscript and corrections. For criticism and assistance in the preparation of the manuscript, I am most indebted to my friend Mr. Paul K. Benedict, who has made corrections and improvements practically on every page. To Dr. Leslie Spier, editor of the *American Anthropologist*, I am indebted for permission to incorporate in the section on Teknonymy, material I have contributed to that Journal. I must also thank Prof. Serge Elisse'eff and Prof. J. R. Ware for sponsoring its publication in the *Harvard Journal of Asiatic Studies.* To the Trustees of the Harvard-Yenching Institute, I wish to express my deep gratitude for the fellowship grant which made the completion of the work possible.

si = sister, sister' s

Example: m f b s d > e signifies mother's father's brother's son's daughter older than ego.

Definition of Terms

All terms are used in their customary meanings, as found in anthropological and sociological literature. A few terms are used here with a specialized connotation in connection with the Chinese social system. They are the following:

Family: used always in the sense or the "extended family" of the Gross-Familie, and equivalent to the Chinese term chia 家, or chia ting 家庭.

Sib: a group of people possessing a common sibname (patronym), descended from a common male ancestor, no matter how remote, and characterized by a feeling of relationship. Descent is strictly patrilineal, and the group is strictly exogamous. An organization for the common welfare of all its members, and ancestor worship, may or may not be present. It is equivalent to the Chinese term, *tsung tsu* 宗族.

Sibname: used in the sense of a patronym or surname which all members of a sib possess in common, and equivalent to the Chinese term *hsing* 姓. Descent of the sibname is strictly patrilincal.

Sib relative: relatives who belong to the same sib and possess the same sibname as ego. It is equivalent to the Chinese term *tsung chin* 宗親, or *tsu jên* 族人 "clansmen."

Non-sib relative: relative who belongs to a sib other than ego's and bears a sibname other than ego's. It is equivalent to the Chinese terms *wai chin* 外親 and *nei chin* 内親 combined; or the old legal term *ch'in shu* 親屬. *Wai Chin* refers to relatives through women of the sib married out, and the affinal relatives of father, father's father and ascending *Nei chin* refers to ego's own affinal relatives.

Chronology

The following chronology is given for those who are not familiar with Chinese history since it is impossible to give the Western date in every instance. The tripartite division does not correspond to the traditional Chinese historical divisions but has been adopted here simply with reference to the evolution of the kinship system.

Ancient Period: first millennium B. C., which includes the following dynastic periods:

Chou dynasty, or the feudal period, ca, 1100-249 B. C.

Ch'in dynasty, 248-207 B. C.

Former Han dynasty, 206 B. C.-24 A. D.

Transitional period: first millennium A. D., which includes the following dynastic periods:

Later Han dynasty, 25-220 A. D.

Wei dynasty, 220-264 A. D.

Chin dynasty, 265-420 A. D.

Sung dynasty, 420-479 A. D. Northern Wei dynasty, 399-534 A. D.

Ch'i dynasty, 470-502 A. D. Northern Ch'i dynasty, 550-577 A. D.

Liang dynasty, 502-557 A. D.

Ch'ên dynasty, 557-589 A. D.

Sui dynasty, 581-618 A. D.

T'ang dynasty, 618-907 A. D.

Wu tai, 907-960 A, D.

Modern period: second millennium A. D., which includes the following dynastic periods:

Sung dynasty, 960-1279 A. D.

Yüan dynasty, 1280-1368 A. D.

Ming dynasty, 1368-1644 A. D.

Ch'ing dynasty, 1644-1911 A. D.

(This is the Sung dynasty to which the writer will always refer in the present treatise, not to the one mentioned above under 420-479 A. D.)

[Other contemporary dynastic periods are omitted here since they are not referred to in this work.]

Ancient system: system of the ancient period, i. e., the system in the *Êrh Ya*, supplemented by the *I Li*, the Li Chi. and other contemporary sources.

Modern system: system of the modern period, i. e., the present Chinese system.

Introduction

The interest of the Chinese themselves in problems of kinship was manifested quite early. This interest is primarily a practical one, for the whole Chinese social structure is built upon the basis of the "extended family" organization, which in turn is based upon the systematization of the mutual relationships among its members. If the whole social structure is to function harmoniously, the kinship system, which expresses and defines the rights and obligations of individuals to each other, must first be adjusted. This ideology is further fostered by the teachings of Confucianism, so that kinship becomes a subject of perennial interest.

The systematic recording of relationship terms goes back as far as the

*Êrh Ya*①, a work of the third or second century B. C. (according to the more conservative dating), in which the terms are carefully classified and arranged. Subsequent works of a similar nature all contain special chapters on kinship nomenclature, e. g., the *Shih Ming* [ca. 200 A. D.] and the *Kuang Y'a* [ca. 230 A. D.]—to mention only two of the comparatively earlier ones. These works record later terms which are not present in the *Êrh Ya* and in a sense bring the *Êrh Ya* system up to the date of each compilation. This practice has continued down to the present day.② Even larger encyclopaedic works devote special sections to this subject, e. g., the *T'ai p'ing yü lan* (983 A. D.) has ten chapters③, and the *T'u shu chi ch'eng* 112 chapters④, on kinship nomenclature. Naturally, not all this material is relevant, and much of it belongs to belles lettres. In the ch'ing dynasty a series of special works on kinship terms appeared, the most important and extensive of which are the *Ch'êng wei lu* 稱謂録 of LIANG Chang-chu 梁章鉅 [1775-1849], and the *ch'in shu chi* 親屬記 of CHÊNG Chen 鄭珍 [1806]. Both of these works comprise collections of old terms, and are more or less in the *Êrh Ya* tradition. Of the two, the *ch'eng wei lu* is much wider in scope, but the arrangement of material is rather loose. The *ch'in shu chi* considers only the lineal relatives through father, and the ordering of data

① Tradition has it that the *Êrh Ya* was compiled by Chou Kung (? -1105 B. C.) and augmented by Confucius (551-479 B. C), *Tzŭ* Hsia 子夏 (507-? B. C), Shu-sun T'ung 叔孫通(ca. 200 B. C) and others. It is not the work of one hand, nor of one period, but developed gradually during the first millennium B. C. Cf. B. KARLGREN, BMFEA 3(1931). 44-49. The section on Kinship Terms 釋親 probably dates from ca. 200B. C. Cf.爾雅新研究 by NAITŌ Torajiro. in 先秦經籍考 2. 163-184.

② Most works of the 訓詁 class have a section on kinship terms, e. g., the *P'ien ya* 駢雅(under 5. 釋名稱), *Shih ya* 拾雅, etc., and even works on dialects like the *Hsu fang yen* 續方言 of HANG Shih-chun 杭世駿 (1696-1773), and the *I yu* 異語 of CH'iEN Tien 錢坫 (1744-1806) devote special sections to kinship term variants. Other dictionaries, starting from the *Shuo wên*. contain kinship terms too, but they are not systematically arranged.

③ 太平御覽, 511-521, 宗親部.

④ 圖書集成,明倫匯編:家範典, 1-112.

is more in keeping with the view of orthodox Confucianism.①

By far the most important class of materials is formed by the ritual works, the *Li*. In these works kinship is not treated as a subject by itself but in connection with other subjects ; an exception is the *ch'in shu chi*, a lost section of the *Li*, which dealt primarily with relationship terminology.② These ritual works are important sources for the functional study of the Chinese kinship system because they deal with kinship in action. Such are the *I Li* and the *Li Chi*, works of the second half of the first millenium B. C., that treat kinship in extenso, especially in connection with mourning rites, ancestor "worship", and other aspects of ritual. In all later works on ritualism—too numerous to mention here—kinship is the basic subject of discussion.

In addition, there are numerous miscellaneous works in which discussions on kinship terms occasionally occur. These are among the most important sources from the standpoint of the evolution of the Chinese kinship system, because generally it is here that one finds recorded the newly introduced terms (dialectical or unconventional) which, as a rule, are ignored by the ritual and other formal literature. Very often one finds in them enlightening discussions concerning the introduction and origin of new terminologies.

Thus, the interest in the study of kinship, terminology is not new among Chinese scholars, and actually they sometimes made explanations which might rank with modern sociological interpretations, but the systematic socio-anthropological study began with Lewis H. Morgan.③ Morgan's data were

① Other important works are the *T'ung su pien* 通俗編 (ch. 4:倫常,ch: 18. 稱謂) of CHAI Hao 翟灝,? -1788; the *Hêng yen lu* 恒言録 (ch,3: 親屬稱謂類) of CH'iEN Tahsin 錢大昕, 1727-1804; the *Chêng su wên* 證俗文 (ch. 4) of Ho I-hsing 郝懿行 1757-1825; and the *Kuang shih ch'in* 廣釋親 of CHANG shên-i 張慎儀. There are many other works of a less extensive nature but they rather duplicate each other.

② As quoted in Pai hu tung 8. 19b, the Ch'in shu chi 親屬記 is very similar in nature to the *Êrh Ya*.

③ *Systems of Consanguinity and Affinity of the Human Family*, 1870, Part Ⅲ, ch. Ⅳ.413-437.

supplied by Robert Hart, an Englishman in the employ of the Chinese Maritime Customs. Despite the faulty nature of Hart's material, and notwithstanding Morgan's evolutionistic predilections, which invalidated most of his conclusions, the MorganHart work has remained the basis for most subsequent speculation. Since then has appeared a number of miscellaneous recordings, some in legal treatises or linguistic primers, others in lexicographic works, but, with one exception, none is worthy of serious consideration. This exception is the work of T. S. Chen and J. K. Shryock.① The ChenShryock study is based chiefly on two modern dictionaries, the *Tz'ŭ yüan* and the *Chung hua ta tzŭ tien*. This material, although inadequate and unreliable, has been used to good advantage by the authors. George W. Bounakoff② seems to have made a stupendous attempt to synthesize all the material in European languages in the light of Morgan's hypothesis.

The limitations of all these European works are obvious. First, the terms relied upon have been collected by untrained persons from "uninformed" informants. Secondly, the writers have not made use of the vast amount of easily available Chinese documentary material—indeed, they seem unaware of the existence of such material. Consequently, most of these studies are marred by numerous inconsistencies and errors. The writers could seldom determine the exact nature of a term, because few ever sectioned out the multiple strata of

① "Chinese Relationship Terms," *American Anthropologist* 34 (1932) 623-664.

② *Terms of Reationship in Chinese: An Ethnographical-Linguistic Study* (N. J. Marr Institute of Language and Mentality, Academy of Sciences, USSR. 1936). I have not seen the original work (in Russian) but only the English "Analytical Summary." So far as I can make out, it is mainly based on secondary English sources with the exception of *Êrh Ya*, which is also available in English. Although he has used most of the European sources, he seems to have overlooked the tables of Gustave SCHLEGELn: *Nederlandch-Chinesech woordenboek met de transcriptic der Chi 'ecsche karackters in het Ts'iang-tsiu dialekt*, Leiden, 1886-90, vol. I, p. 1343, *Chineesche GesLachtboon*. The important issue, however, is his methodology which is based upon the Marxian conception of history and the Japhetic theory of language of H. I. Marr. Combining these with the evolutionary stages of L. H. Morgan, he arrives at the "collective beginnings" of Chinese society!

terminology in the Chinese system.①

The present study is based chiefly upon the author's own collection of terms from the primary Chinese sources. All material consulted has been examined critically to insure correctness in terminology and interpretation. The method of approach is primarily historical and linguistic②—partly because it is precisely these aspects which are the most engaging characteristics of the Chinese system and at the same time the least understood, partly because preliminary work of this sort is prerequisite to an understanding of the more implicit aspects of the system. The field of investigation is limited to the historical period, approximately the last twenty-five centuries, within which the system has been fully documented. If kinship system changes occur at all, two thousand years should be long enough for their manifestation.③

Principles of Terminological Composition

The principles governing the composition of terms are both linguistic and sociological. Linguistically, they are formed according to the syntactical principles of the Chinese language; sociologically, their connotations are

---

① Originally the present work included a section called "Critical Review of Early Studies." As it was not in a way constructive and occupied considerable space, it has been deleted.

② By *linguistic*, I mean the usual and the formal approach to the study of kinship systems, i. e., by an examination of the kinship terms themselves, the structural whole they present, and the underlying principles involved.

③ This paper is one of the studies made by the author under a fellowship grant by the Trustees of the Harvard-Yenching Institute, to whom he wishes to express his gratitude. The author is also deeply indebted to Professors A. I. Hallowell, F. G Speck, and D. S. Davidson for constant guidance, suggestions and improvements in this work; to Prof. C.K. M. Kluckhohn and Dr. C. M. Arensberg for their careful examination and corrections of the MS.; to MR. Paul K. Benedict, who has made improvements and corrections on almost every page. The author also wishes to thank Professors S. Elissee' ff and J. R. Ware for suggestions and assistance and especially for sponsoring publication in this Journal.

determined by the relationships which they express and the circumstances under which they are used. The multitude of Chinese relationship terms can be reduced to four fundamental classes, namely, *nuclear terms*, *basic modifiers*, *referential modifiers*, and *vocatives*. Nuclear terms express the nuclear group of relationships and, linguistically, are independent of modifiers. Each nuclear term possesses a primary meaning and one or more secondary meanings. The primary meaning is assumed when the term is used independently, and, when it is used in combination with other elements, the secondary meaning or meanings become paramount. Basic modifiers for the most part express collateral relationship and generation status and can not be used independently as kinship terms. The nuclear terms form the basis for kinship extensions and the basic modifiers locate the exact place of the relative in the total scheme. The combinations and recombinations of these two classes of elements constitute the modern standard system which is the norm of all other terminologies. The referential modifiers modify the standard system into proper forms for referential use in specific applications. Vocatives, aside from their primary usages, transform them into direct forms of address between relatives.

The following is an analysis of these four classes of elements and an exposition of the principles governing their composition and application. In the analysis of the nuclear terms the primary connotations (according to the modern standard system) are given first and then followed by the secondary meanings.

Nuclear Terms

Tsu 祖[2]: father's father. Ancestor. Used in combination with other elements for all ascendants higher than the father's generation.

Sun 孫[3]: son's son. Descendant. Used in combination with other elements for all descendants lower than the son's generation.

Fu 父[4]: Father. Male of higher generation status. Male sex indicator for higher generations. Suffixed to terms of all male relatives of generations higher than ego.

Tzŭ 子[5]: Son. Male of lower generation status. Male sex indicator for lower generations. May be suffixed to terms of male relatives of generations lower than ego, but its use is optional.

Mu 母[6]: Mother. Female of higher generation status. Female sex indicator for higher generations. Suffixed to terms of all married female relatives of generations higher than ego.

Nü 女[7]: Daughter. Female of lower generation status. Female sex indicator for lower generations. Suffixed to terms of all female relatives of generations lower than, ego.

Hsiung 兄[8]: Older brother. Male of the older brother's status. Indicator of seniority within the generation of ego. Used in combination with other elements for male relatives of the generation of, but older than ego.

Ti 弟[9]: Younger brother. Male of younger brother's status, Indicator of juniority for males within the generation of ego. Used in combination with other elements for male relatives of the generation of, but younger than ego.

Tzŭ 姊[10]: Older sister. Female of the older sister's status. Indicator of seniority for females within the same generation of ego. Used in combination with other elements for female relatives of the generation of, but older than ego.

Mei 妹[11]: Younger sister. Female of the younger sister's status. Indicator of juniority for females within the same generation of ego. Used in combination with other elements for female relatives of the generation of, but younger than ego.

Po 伯[12]: Father's older brother. Indicator of seniority. Applicable to terms from ego's generation and ascending, using the direct male lineal line as a standard of comparison.

Husband's older brother. Cannot be extended in this sense.

Shu 叔[13]: Father's younger brother. Indicator of juniority. Applicable to terms from ego's generation and ascending, using the direct lineal line as a standard of comparison.

Husband's younger brother. Cannot be extended in this last sense.

Chih 姪[13a]: Brother's son. Indicator of descent from male collaterals. Used in combination with other elements for descendants of male relatives of the generation of ego.

Shêng 甥[14]: Sister's son. Indicator of descent from female collaterals. Used in combination with other elements for descendants from female relatives of the generation of ego.

Ku 姑[15]: Father's sister. Indicator of relationship comparable with father's sister's. Indicator of descent from father's sister, or from female relatives comparable with father's sister's relationship.

Husband's sister. Cannot be extended in this last sense.

Chiu 舅[16]: Mother's brother. Indicator of relationship comparable with mother's brother's. Indicator of descent from mother's brother, or from male relatives comparable with mother's brother's relationship.

Wife's brother. Cannot be extended in this last sense.

I 姨: Mother's sister. Indicator of relationship comparable with mother's sister's. Indicator of descent from mother's sister, or from female relatives comparable with mother's sister's relationshop. Wife's sister.[17] Indicator of relationship comparable with wife's sister' s. Indicator of descent from wife's sister, or from female relatives comparable with wife's sister's relationship.

Yo 岳[17a]: Wife's parents. Indicator of relationship comparable with wife's parents, such as their cousins.

Hsü 婿[18]: Daughter's husband. Husband. Indicator of connection by marriage with ego's female relatives of the same generation of ego and descending.

Fu 夫[19]: Ego's husband. Husband. Indicator of connection by marriage with ego's female relatives of the same generation of ego.

Ch'i 妻[20]: Ego's wife. Wife.

Sao 嫂[21]: Older brother's wife Female of older brother's wife's status. Indicator of connection by marriage with ego's male relatives of the generation of, but older than ego.

Fu 婦[22]: Son's Wife. Wife. Indicator of connection by marriage with ego's male relatives of the generation of, but younger than, ego and descending generations.

Basic Modifiers

Kao 高: High; revered. Modifying indicator of the fourth ascending generation.

Tsêng 曾: Added; increased Modifying indicator for the third ascending and descending generations.

Hsüan 玄: Far; distant. Modifying indicator for the fourth descending generation.

Tang 堂: Hall; the ancestral hall. Modifying indicator for the second collateral line from the second generation and descending. Ascending vertically, for father's father's brother's children and father's father's father's brother's children, that is, for paternal uncles and aunts once removed and paternal granduneles and aunts once removed. When extended to non-sib relatives, it indicates, in a similar way, the third collateral line.

Ts'ung 從: To follow; through. It is used synonymously with *t'ang*. *t'ang* is a later term and its use is restricted. Wherever *T'ang* is used, *ts'ung* may be substituted, but not vice versa.

Tsai-ts'ung 再從: To follow again, or to follow a second time. Modifying indicator for the third collateral line from ego's generation and descending. Ascendingly, for paternal uncles and aunts twice removed.

Tsu 族: Sib; tribe, Modifying indicator for relationships from the fourth collateral line and beyond.

Piao 表: Outside; external. Indicator of descent from father's sister, mother's brother and mother's sister. Similarly extended to all relatives descended from those whose terms include either *ku* (father's sister), *chiu* (mother's brother) or *i* (mother's sister).

Nei 内: Inside; inner; wife. Indicator of descent from wife's brother, or from relatives comparable with him, e. g., his male sibcousins.

Wai 外: Outside. Reciprocal modifier indicating mother's parents and daughter's children.

The above generalizations are based on the connotations of the modern standard terminology. They are abstracted from the whole range of the nomenclature, with every term taken into consideration. Yet, because of the multitude of possible combinations for every Chinese character, exceptions are inevitable. These exceptions, few and relatively insignificant, will be evident when the whole system is reviewed.

Terminological Composition

In the building of terms, the terminology for the nuclear group of relations is taken as a structural basis, with the exception of parentchild and husband-wife terms, which are used as sex indicators.① All modifying elements

---

① The sex indicators are *fu* 父, *mu* 母 *tzŭ* 子, *nu* 女, *fu* 夫, *fu* 婦, *hsi* 媳, *hsü* 婿. Failure to recognize this set of terms has resulted in much misunderstanding of the system. The first to disspell this misunderslanding was perhaps H. P. WLLKINSON, Chinese Family Nomenclature, *New China Rev.* (1921) 159-191. He writes: The initial error of the writers... was... in taking the sex indicators for male and female appended to varying 'descriptive' appellations of kindred as the name of a class, — that of 'sons' and 'daughters.' "A. L. KROEBER, quite independently, also discovered that" these last four terms (i. e.*fu* 父, *mu* 母, *fu* 夫, *fu* 婦) merely denote the sex of the person referred to, when they are added to other kinship terms.... "Process in the Chinese Kinship System, *American Anthropologist*, 1933, 35, 151-157.

indicating collateral relationship and descent are prefixed①, in succession, to the chosen basis, with the element expressing the nearest relationship nearest the basis and that expressing the farthest relationship furthermost, until the desired relationship is reached. All sex indicators are suffixed. If the generation category of the structural basis is not apparent, as in *chiu* and *i*, the sex indicators also function as generation indicators; here, too, they are always suffixed.

In choosing the structural basis for a term of a relationship, the factors to be considered are, first, generation and second, descent. Take, for example, the term for the father's father's sister's son's daughter's son. This is a complicated one, since the descent has shifted from female to male, and then back to female. Disregarding descent, let us first consider the generation. The individual concerned is of the son's generation. Instantly the basis is reduced to the alternatives *chih or wai shêng*. His immediate relationship with ego is through a female relative of ego's generation; therefore, the term *chih* is eliminated and only *wai shêng* remains. Furthermore, his relationship is a non-sib but consanguineal one, and descent is from father's father's sister, a relationship comparable with father's sister's; therefore, the qualifying elements *ku* and *piao* should be added. He belongs to the third collateral line of non-sib relatives; therefore, the collateral modifier *t'ang* is applicable. Together, these elements form the term *tang ku piao wai shêng*—a term as exact as can be desired. To express a female relationship of the same kind, add *nü* to the above term, making it *t'ang ku piao wai shêng nü* [that is, f f si s d d]. To express a female relationship by marriage, substitute *fu* for *nü*; for a male relationship by

① The terms "prefixing" and "suffixing" are employed here in a loose sense, since there are no true "prefixes" and "suffixes" in Chinese (with the exception, perhaps, of a few elements, notably the nominal suffixes). Here they merely indicate that a certain indivisible element (character) is placed before or after another indivisible element (character) in syntactic relationship.

marriage, substitute *hsü*.

The elements which make up a compound term should always be interpreted in their extended, that is, their secondary, meanings, and should never be understood in their primary meanings. The amalgamation of all the extended meanings makes up the new connotation of the term so compounded. This phenomenon is a feature of Chinese syntax. Failure to understand this has been the source of much misinterpretation.

The following illustrations represent practically the whole range of the structural bases. They are chosen with a view to including the widest variety of combinations, in order to elucidate the nature of terminological formations. The scope, however, is naturally limited, and fuller information must be sought in the tables.

Examples. The *italics* represent the nuclear term used as a structural basis, and the *roman*, the added modifiers:

tsu	f f
po tsu mu	f f o b w
T'ang shu tsu fu	f f f b s < f f
po	f o b
t'ang po fu	f f b s > f
t'ang ku fu	f f b d h
ku piao ku mu	f f si d
chiu	m b
T'ang chiu fu	m f b s
t'ang piao chiu fu	m f f si s s
i	m si
t'ang i fu	m f b d h
tsai Ts'ung i mu	m f f b s d
hsiung	o b

ku piao po fu	f f si s > f
shu	f y b
t'ang shu mu	w of f f b s < f
tsai Ts'ung shu fu	f f f b s s < f
ku	fsi
t'ang i *tzŭ* fu	h of f b d > e
t'ang i piao *tzŭ* fu	h of m f b d d > e
mei	y si
i mei	w y si
t'ang i mei fu	h of w f b d < w
i piao mei fu	h of m si d < e
t'ang i piao mei	m f b d d < e
chih	b s
tsu chih nü	f f f b s s s d

ku piao hsiung	f si s > e	tsai Ts'ung chih hsü	f f b s s d h
t'ang ku piao hsiung	f f si s s > e	wai shêng	si s
sao	o b w	T'ang wai shêng nü	f b d d
chiu piao sao	w of m b s s > e	t'ang ku piao wai shêng	f f si s d s
t'ang chiu piao sao	w of m f b s s > e	sun	s s
ti	y b	chih sun nü	b s d
t'ang ti fu	w of f b s < e	T'ang chih sun	f b s s s
tsai Ts'ung ti	f f b s s < e	wai *shêng* sun hsü	si s d h
tzŭ	o si		

In building terms for the third and fourth ascending and descending generations, the terms of the second ascending and descending generations are used as a basis, generation indicators are added to them. Modifiers of descent are usually added first, before the generation modifiers are prefixed. Examples:

tsu	f f	sun	s s
tsêg tsu mu	f f m	tsêng sun nü	s s d
tsèng po tsu fu	f f f o b	tsêng chih sun fu	b s s s w
kao tsu fu	f f f f	hsüan sun	s s s s

The above represent the compositional principles of the standard system.① The standard terms are universal and form the patterns on which other terms are built or formed. They are for the most part used in formal—i. e., genealogical, legal and ceremonial literature. In ordinary applications, they must be properly qualified by modifiers according to the specific situations under which they are used.

Referential Modifiers

The referential modifiers actually reflect the Chinese social code of

① Some would call it "literary system," in the broad sense of the term.

etiquette, as well as the Chinese psychology concerning the proper attitudes to be assumed in social intercourse. It is a sign of politeness and refinement to pay due respect and compliments to others, and, appropriately but not exaggeratedly, to maintain for oneself a more or less humble position. This is precisely the attitude that conditions the application of kinship terms.

The referential modifiers are also a manifestation of the consciousness of membership in the relational group. The complimentary and depreciatory modifiers cannot be applied indiscriminately; their application is prescribed by the identification with one relational group in contrast with another. Compliments may be applied more loosely, but depreciatives can be used only to those whom one strictly considers members of one's own relational group.

These two attitudes are fundamental in the application and understanding of the whole terminology.

The referential modifiers are governed by definite rules concerning their applications, and are always prefixed to the standard terms. With respect to their nature and usages, all of them can be broadly grouped under the following categories: 1. Complimentary, 2. Depreciatory, 3. Self-reference, 4. Posthumous.

Complimentary. These elements are used in referring to the relatives of the person to Whom one is speaking or writing. They consist of the following three elements: i. Ling 令: Illustrious, worthy, honorable. It may be prefixed to any standard term, except in instances where special stems are provided. ii. Tsun 尊: Honorable, venerable. Used synonymously with *ling*, but restricted in that it refers only to relatives of higher generation or status than that of the person to whom one is speaking, iii. Hsien 賢: Virtuous, worthy. Used alternatively with *ling*, but restricted in that it refers only to relatives of lower generation and status than that of the person to whom one is speaking. There are a few exceptions to this rule, e. g., *hsien shu*, "your virtuous paternal uncle."

Whenever one is in doubt as to whether *tsun* or *hsien* should be prefixed, he uses *ling*. *Ling*, *tsun* and *hsien* have the sense of "your" used in a polite way.

Complimentary modifiers should be prefixed when speaking to persons not related to oneself. They should not be used between sib relatives, except, when speaking to those of lower generations, in reference to their superiors. This latter practice is really teknonymy. The complimentary modifiers should be prefixed when reference is made to the relative of a non-sib relative to whom one is speaking, if that individual is not a connecting relative. If he is a connecting relative and of higher generation than the speaker, the usual standard or vocative kinship term should be used. As a rule, one does not compliment those with whom one has close and direct relationships.

Depreciatory.① These modifiers are prefixed to the standard terms in referring to one's own relatives of the same sibname, when speaking or writing to others. "Depreciatory" is used here in the sense of "modest" or "of one's own." They consist of the following three elements: i. Chia 家: Family, dwelling, household. It is prefixed to the terms of all sib relatives of higher generation and status than ego. ii. Shê 舍: Cottage, shed, household. It is prefixed to the terms of sib relatives of the generation of, but of lower status than, ego (as younger brother); and principally in reference to sib relatives of the first de scending generation, and sometimes all descending generations. It should never be used in reference to relatives in the direct lineal line, e. g., for one's own children, iii. Hsiao 小: Minor, junior, small, diminutive. Prefixed to the terms of sib relatives of lower generation than that of ego, principally in reference to one's own children, grandchildren, etc. With the exception of the lineal descendants, *shê* and *hsiao* can be used synonymously.

Chia, *shê* and *hsiao* have somewhat the sense of "my" used in a modest

① "Depreciatory" is used in contrast to "Complimentary." As the elements *chia* and *shê* show, "depreciatory" is used in the sense of "of my own family" or "of my own sib."

manner. It is important to note that depreciatory modifiers are not applicable to relatives of a different sibname.① They are not even applicable to one's father's married sisters or one ' s own married sisters because these women have adopted their husband's sibnames and are no longer considered as members of one's own family or sib, and therefore they are not to be "depreciated."②

*Self-reference.*③ These modifiers are prefixed to the terms used by ego to refer to himself before another relative, either in speaking or in writing, e. g., a nephew refers to himself before an uncle, or vice versa. They consist of the following two elements: i. Yü 愚: Simple, rude, stupid. It can be prefixed to the terms when used by ego to refer to himself, principally as a relative of higher generation to one of lower generation, ii. Hsiao 小: Junior, minor. It can be prefixed to the terms when used by ego to refer to himself, principally where a relative of lower generation address one of higher generation.

Neither *yü nor hsiao* are applicable to oneself where addressing a relative of the direct lineal line, e. g., father and son, grandfatherand grandson, etc., where special terms are provided for such purposes.

Posthumous. These modifiers are prefixed to—excepting a few special stems for this purpose—the standard terms when used in reference to one's own dead relatives, especially for parents, grandparents, father's brothers, etc. They consist of the following two elements: i. Wang 亡: "Deceased." Prefixed to terms of all relative when dead. ii. Hsien 先 "The late," "the former." Prefixed only to terms of relatives of higher generation or status than ego, when

---

① There is a general term that can be applied to any non-sib relative, i. e., *pi ch'in* 敝親, "my poor (or unworthy) relative."

② *Yen shih chia hsün* 風操篇,2.5a 凡言姑,姊,妹,女子子,已嫁則以夫氏稱之,在室則以次第稱之.言禮成他族,不得云家也.

③ "Self-reference" modifiers are in a certain respect indistinguishable from "deprecatory" except in context. It is especially true of the element *hsiao*. They are separated here for the purpose of exposition.

dead.

When referring to the dead relatives of others the complimentary modifiers must again be prefix to these modifiers. This practice is not common; usually a circumlocutory expression is employed.

There are a number of special stems which are used with the referential modifiers. They will be pointed out in the tables in each connection. For the sake of clarity and brevity, all terms qualified by the referential modifiers, or formed with special words, will be called in later discussion either complimentary, depreciatory, self-reference, or posthumous terminologies.

Vocative Terms

Vocatives are used as forms of addressing relatives direct in person. In literary address, i. e., in writing, the standard terms must be used. Vocatives must not be used together with referential modifiers. The latter can only be prefixed to standard terms.

Vocatives are limited to relatives of higher generations than ego, and to those of the same generation as, but of higher age status than, ego. Relatives of lower generations and age status can be addressed by name, or by using the standard terms as vocatives, if the occasion should arise. All vocatives are formed from three groups of terms: grandparent terms, parent terms, and older sibling terms.

Grandparent terms. The grandparent vocatives vary a great deal with local usage. As they have not been systematically recorded, it is rather difficult to determine the most prevalent ones. *Yeh yeh*, *wêng* or *wêng wêng*, *kung or kung kung*, for paternal grandfather, *P'o or P'o P'o*, *nai nai*, for paternal grandmother, may be considered the most common. No matter which terms are adopted in local usage, the adopted local terms are extended consistently throughout the whole system like these forms. In their extension, they are suffixed to the standard terminology by dropping the *tsu fu* and *tsu mu*, e. g., for *po tsu fu* (f f o b) the vocative is *po wêng*, or *po kung*.

Parent terms. Parent terms are less variable than grandparent terms. *Tieh*, *yeh*, and *pa pa* for father; *ma* and *niang* for mother. *Pa pa* is never, and *niang* is seldom, used in extensions.

Tieh 爹: Vocative for father. Used to form vocative terms for male relatives of the first ascending generation in place of *fu*.

Ma 媽: Vocative for mother. Used to form vocative terms for female relatives of thc first ascending generation in place of *mu*.①

The above rules will not apply in instances where special vocatives are provided. These terms may also be omitted in certain cases where they are unnecessary, just as *fu* and *mu* are sometimes omitted.

Older sibling terms. Ko, or ko ko 哥哥: Vocative for older brother. Used for conjugating vocative terms in place of *hsiung* for male relatives of the generation. of, but older than, ego.

Chieh, or chieh chieh 姐姐: Vocative for older sister. Used for conjugating vocative terms in place of *tzŭ* for female relatives of the generation of, but older than, ego.

It is the vocative nomenclature that varies dialectically. At present, this variability mostly involves the grandparent and parent terms, the older sibling terms showing very little variation. But no matter how variable the dialectical vocatives may be, the above conjugation rules can be applied simply by replacing the given forms with local terms.

The vocative terms are used more loosely, i. e., they are more "classificatory" than the standard terminology. When two relative speak face to face the exact relationship is always understood; it is only in referential usages

① *Ma* and *mu*, in their extensions, indicate a married status, and cannot be applied to unmarried female relatives.

that the more exact terms are needed. The prevalent use of sibnames,① personal names, titles, and numerical order of seniority and juniority② for particularizing each relative in vocative address also makes the accurate system rather too cumbersome.

Supernumerany Terms

There are a few groups of terms which may be called "super numerary"③, viz., the sacrificial, epitaphic, literary and alternative names. These are referred to in the tables.

Sacrificial terms were used in ancient times for the direct lineal ancestors when offering sacrifices to them. There are only a few such terms, but they are now obsolete. Epitaphic terms are used on epiterms, *k'ao* 考 for father and *pi* 妣 for mother. It is only the sons who erect epitaphs for their parents. Sacrificial and epitaphic terms are often confused with terms modified by "posthumous" modifiers. They are frequently used interchangeably, since they all refer to dead relatives, although in slightly different senses. Nevertheless, there are some

---

① Sibnames are used only for particularizing non-sib relatives and women married into the sib.

② The ancient method of denoting seniority and juniority by *po* 伯, *chung* 仲, *shu* 叔, and *chi* 季 has long been obsolete. A purely numerical order is used today. If ego's father is one of six siblings, A, b, C, D, e, and F (capitals indicate males, small letters, females), the numerical order of *ta* 大, *êrh* 二, *san* 三, *ssŭ* 四, *wu* 五 and *liu* 六 will be applied to them, respectively. *Ta* is used in the sense of "eldest." *Jih chih lu*, 23. 38a: 今人兄弟行次,稱一爲大,不知始自何時.漢淮南厲王常謂上大兄,孝文帝行非第一也. If ego's father is D, then ego will call A *ta po*, b *êrh ku*. C *san po*. e *wu ku*, and F *liu shu*. If ego's father is A, then ego will call b *êrh ku*, C *san shu*, D *ssŭ shu*, e *wu ku*, and F *liu shu*. The terms *po* and *shu* change positions in accordance with the relative order of ego's father, but the numerical order remains constant.

There is another method of assigning the numerical order, viz., by separating the male and the female series. As in the above case, A, C, D, and F will be assigned *ta*, *êrh*, *san* and *ssŭ*, respectively, and b, e will be given *ta*. *êrh* respectively. The method used depends upon local custom and family whim.

③ "Supernumerary" is employed here in the sense used by E. W. GIFFORD in his discussion of *California Kinship Terminologies*, UC-PAAE 18, 1922-1926. It is not a happy term, and is adopted here only for want of a better one.

very interesting changes which are of historical significance.

Literary terms are those used only in literary compositions, usually non-vocative and non-referential. Many of them are old obsolete terms but still retained in literary usage. Alternative terms are those that can be used synonymously with the prevalent forms. The adoption of the one or the other depends entirely upon local custom and individual proclivities.

Structural Principles and Terminological Categories

The architectonic structure of the Chinese system is based upon two principles: lineal and collateral differentiation, and generation stratification. The former is a vertical, and the latter a horizontal, segmentation. Through the interlocking of these two principles, every relative is rigidly fixed in the structure of the whole system.

Lineal and Collateral Differentiation

The methods of differentiating collaterals differ in the ancient and the modern systems. In the ancient system, the *Êrh Ya* and *I Li*, each collateral line is differentiated by following the terminology of the kin nearest to the lineal line from whom this line originated; e. g., father's father's father's brother is called *tsu tsêng* wang fu, and his descendants down to ego's generations are differentiated by prefixing the term *tsu* to their respective terms; father's father's brother is called *Ts'ung tsu* wang fu, and all his descendants down to ego's generation are differentiated by prefixing the term *Ts'ung tsu*. This method is also applied to more remote collateral lines.①

① Cf. CHÊNG Chên: 補正爾雅釋親宗族, *Ch'ao ching ch'ao' wên chi*, 1, la-4b.

In the *Êrh Ya* system there is no term for brother's sons and their descendants, nor is there any term for father's brother's son's sons and their descendants, nor for father's father's brother's son's son's sons and their descendants. It seems that the sons of brothers and sib-brothers merge into one another, i. e. brother's sons are one's own sons. On the other hand, the *Êrh Ya* gives the term *ch'u*① for sister's son (man speaking), *li sun*② for sister's son's son (man speaking); chih③ for brother's son (woman speaking), *kuei sun*④ *for brother's son's son* (*woman speaking*). In the strict patrilineal sib organization of the Chou period, even one's own sons are differentiated from one another as regards the order of succession, hence it is difficult to see why there are no terms to differentiate one's own sons from brother's sons and sib-brother's sons, while, on the contrary, terms are provided whereby the man may differentiate his sons from his sister's sons, and the woman may differentiate her sons from her brother's sons.⑤

The differentiating of collaterals in the modern system is far more complete and consistent, but is carried out on a different principle. The generation stratum of ego is used as a basis, and the collateral modifying terminology is extended vertically downward and upward. E. g., father's brother's sons are

---

① *Êrh Ya*:男子謂姊妹之子爲出.

② Ibid.:謂出之子爲離孫.

③ Ibid.:女子謂昆弟之子爲姪.

④ Ibid.:謂姪之子爲歸孫.

⑤ It is very doubtful whether the *Êrh Ya* system is complete. It also has no terms for f si s s, m b s s. and m si s s. By inference, f si s s and m b s s can be called *ch'u*, since sister's husband, f si s, and m b s are called *shêng*, and sister's son is called *ch'u*. But the absence of terms for m si ss is rather disconcerting; these terms cannot all be merged into the terms for ego's own sons. or into any others. For some reason or other the compilers of the *Êrh Ya* seem not to have been interested in the terms for descendants or collaterals of the same generation. On the other hand, the *Êrh Ya* system, as it stands, seems to stress the terms on the matrilineal side of descending generations. Whether or not this is a survival of an earlier matrilineate is a matter of interpretation, since other evidence is inconclusive.

called *T'ang hsiung ti*, their sons and grandsons are called *T'ang chih* and *T'ang chih sun*, respectively. Upwards, *T'ang* is extended to father's father's brother's son, e. g., *t'ang po fu* and *T'ang shu fu*; and to father's father's father's brother's sons, e. g., *T'ang po tsu fu* and *T'ang shu tsu fu*. Other collateral lines, e. g., *tsai-Ts'ung* and *tsu*, are similarly extended.

The development of the modern principle of differentiation began in the Han period. First came the differentiation of one's own sons from brother's sons by employing the terms *yu tzŭ* or *Ts'ung tzŭ*.① During the Chin period the term *chih* was permanently changed from a woman's term for brother's son to a man's term for brother's son. *T'ung t'ang*② was first used during the fifth and sixth centuries for denoting the second collateral line, and was later abbreviated to *T'ang*. *Tsai ts'ung* came into use a little later, and *tsu* is an old term used in a slightly delimited sense. With these important collateral modifying terminologies perfected, the whole process was completed about the end of the first millennium A. D.

---

① Cf. Table I, No. 125.

② Cf. Table I, No. 41.

DIAGRAM I

Ancient System of Collateral Differentiation

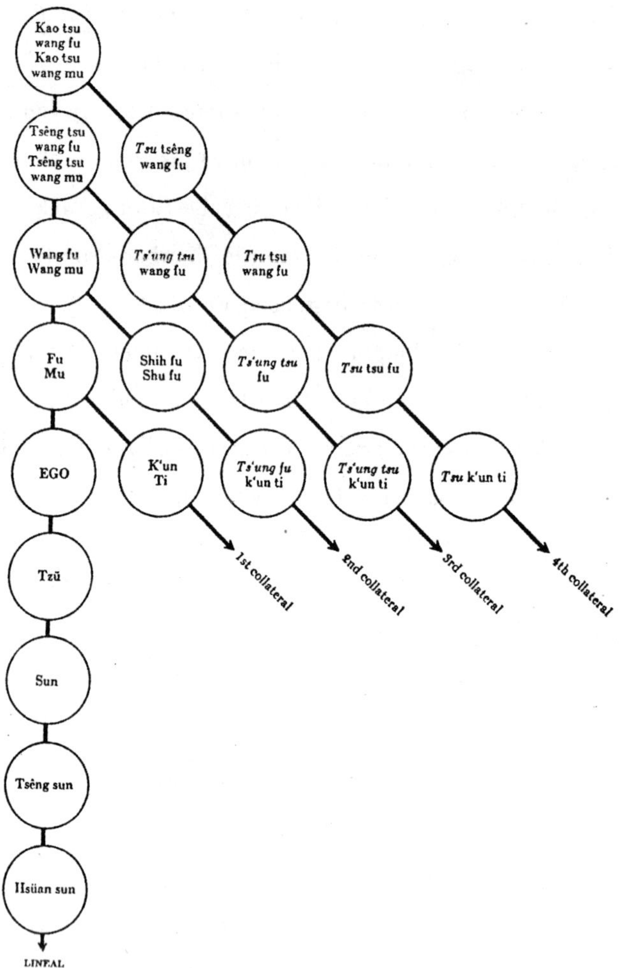

Italics indicate collateral modifiers.

DIAGRAM Ⅱ

Modern System of Collateral Differentiation

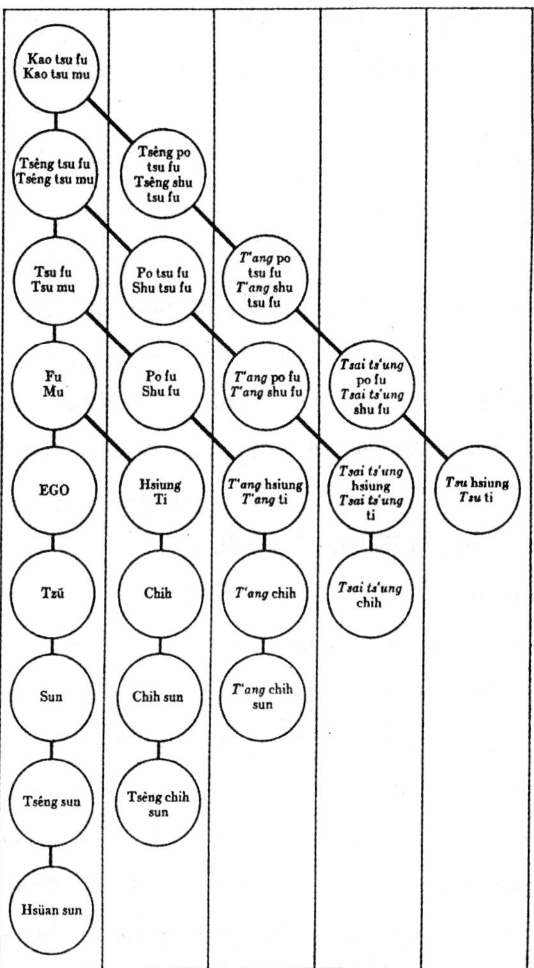

Italics indicate collateral modifiers.

Generation Stratification

All relatives in the system are stratified in successive generation layers. This stratification performs the important function of fixing the exact location of relatives in the system, in conjunction with the principle of collateral differentiation.

In diagram Ⅲ, the vertical columns represent collaterals and the horizontal columns represent generations. When one set of columns is superimpose upon the other, the two afford pigeonholes for every relative in the system. Each relative is then rigidly fixed, and not subject to fluctuations. The generation strata are maintained by the use of generation modifiers. The modifiers are, in most cases, adapted from the nuclear terms from the direct lineal line, since in counting generations the lineal relatives are always used as absolute standards of measure. This adaptation of nuclear kinship terms as generation indicators has been interpreted as partial merging of collaterals and lineals. Given our present knowledge of the system, this interpretation is not tenable.

Since generation is an important structural principle, it must not be disrupted, lest the structure break down. The most serious, if not the only, disruptive factor in this principle is intergeneration marriage. To counteract this influence, generation has become an important factor in the regulation of marital relations. A Chinese is not required to marry any of his or her relatives, but if such marriages do occur between relatives both parties must belong to the same generation stratum. In other words, a Chinese may marry any person outside of his or her own sib; if the parties are related, they must be of the same generation, irrespective of age.

This rule seems to have been less stringent in ancient times. During the Chou period a feudal lord could take his wife's paternal nieces as concubines, or even as wives after his wife's death. The Han emperor, Hui Ti(194-188 B. C.), married his older sister's daughter①, and the T'ang emperor, Chung-tsung (705-710 A. D.), married his paternal grandaunt's daughter.② These instances are severely condemned as incestuous by later historians and moralists③, but they were not so condemned by contemporaries. On the other hand, these instances may have been anomalous; it may be only because the marriages involved emperors that they went unpunished and uncriticized. But, in either case, they do show the laxity of the generation rule during the earlier period.④

There can be no doubt that the generation rule was much stressed even during the Chou period⑤, since the recorded marriages show that the inter-generation type of marriage was the exception rather than the rule.⑥ Its stiffening was gradual, and culminated about the middle of the first millennium A. D. The period of intensive development of the principle seems to have been about the third and fourth centuries A. D., because it is during this period that the generation indicators in personal names became popular. The T'ang Code (ca. 600 A. D.) contains clauses which definitely prohibit marriage between

---

① *Han shu* 外戚列傳,97A5a(孝惠張皇后)宣平侯敖尚帝姊魯元公主,有女,惠帝即位,吕太后欲爲重親,以公主女配後爲皇后……

② *T'ang shu*. 76 19b:中宗和思順聖皇后趙……父環,尚高祖常樂公主,帝爲英王,聘後爲妃.

③ WANG Ming-shêng (1723-1797 A. D.) discussed these instances in his 十七史商榷(廣雅書局本) 86.2a: as the most flagrant violations of the "relationships of humanity", 人倫之極變.

④ The *T'ung tien* discussed two instances of difficulties in mourning obligations arising from inter-generation marriages, 95. 12a: 族父是姨弟爲服議; and the hypothetical case, 95. 5b-6b: 娶同堂姊之女爲妻,姊亡服議. It seems that inter-generation marriage between distant relatives was tolerated during the first half of the first millennium A. D.

⑤ Both the *tsung fa* and the *sang fu* institutions, which were developed during this period, stress the separation of generations. *Sang fu* will be dealt with later. As to *tsung fa*, the subdivisions of *tsung* into minor *tsung* 小宗, for the most part, depends upon the counting of generations.

⑥ The instances of primaty inter-generation marriages can be counted on the fingers. LIANG Yü-shêng (*P'ieh chi*,2.2a) says: 楚成王取文芈二女, (左僖廿二), 晉文公納嬴氏(僖廿四),皆爲甥爲妻者,可謂無别矣.嗣後妻甥者,漢孝惠取張敖女,章帝取竇勛女,吳孫休取朱據女,俱楚録入員額晉重作之俑也.

relatives of different generations.[1] All subsequent codes contain such interdictions, and cite cases. From the end of the first millennium A. D. to the present, not only have inter-generation marriages been rigorously forbidden by law, but popular sentiment against them runs so high that even a teacher marrying his or her pupil, or a person marrying a friend's daughter or son, is condemned.

The underlying concept is the desire to keep constant the generation layers of relatives and to prevent their disruption. If the generation of one relative is disrupted by marriage, then all the positions of the relatives connected with him would also be disrupted, and the system would lose its accuracy of description and thus defeat its own purpose.

Categories

Kroeber's essay on the *Classficatory Systems of Relationship*[2] does not invalidate the use of classificatory and descriptive designations in anthropological discussion; its contribution lies in the establishment of categories that are inherent in all systems. These categories constitute a convenient means for examining the working processes of any system. It is impossible to tabulate the whole Chinese system into one table, but we may take the nuclear terms and tabulate them in the light of the eight categories suggested by Kroeber. It must be understood that these nuclear terms are also used in secondary meanings, qualified by modifiers. In this tabulation only their primary meanings are considered.

Now let us consider the system as a whole, together with the nuclear terms under each category.

---

① *T'ang lü shu* I 户婚 14.2a: 若外姻有服屬，而尊卑共爲婚姻……以姦論 This is followed by expositions of this clause, and by another clause of the same nature but more specific. 尊卑 means "relatives belonging to different generations."

② *Journal*, *Royal Anthropological Institute of Great Britain and Ireland*, 1909, 39, 77-84.

DIAGRAM Ⅲ

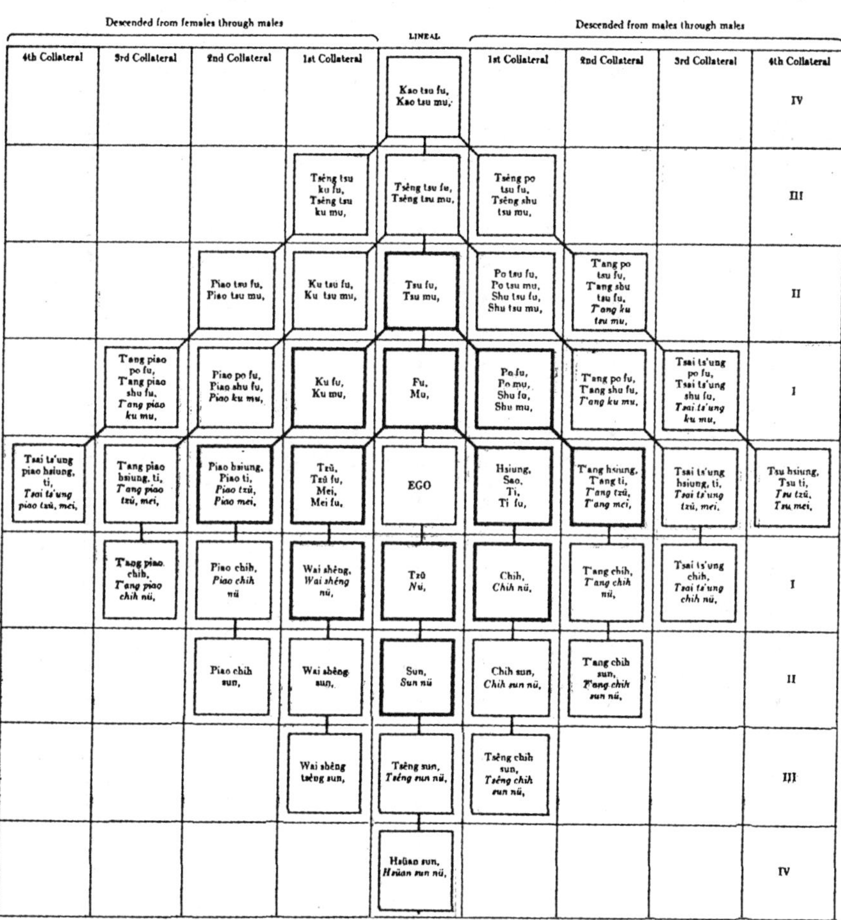

The heavy squares represent the nuclear group of relatives. Those in italics, indicate their descendants have not been carried over into the next generation, e. g., the children of nü are *wai sun and wai sun nü* but not given in the following square. The Roman numerals represent ascending and descending generations.

Categories \ Terms	祖 tsu	孫 sun	父 fu	子 tzŭ	母 mu	女 nü	兄 hsiung	弟 ti	姊 tzŭ	妹 mei	伯 po	叔 shu	姪 chih	甥 shêng	姑 ku	舅 chiu	姨 i	岳 yo	壻 hsü	夫 fu	妻 ch'i	嫂 sao	婦 fu	Total	Percentage
Generation	*	*	*	*	*	*	*	*	*	*			*	*				*	*	*	*	*	*	18	78.27
Blood or marriage	*	*	*	*	*	*	*	*	*	*			*	*				*	*	*	*	*	*	18	78.27
Lineal or collateral	*	*	*	*	*	*	*	*	*	*	*	*	*	*	*	*	*	*	*	*	*	*	*	23	100
Sex of relative	*	*	*	*	*	*	*	*	*	*	*	*	*	*	*	*	*	*	*	*	*	*	*	23	100
Sex of connecting relative	*	*									*	*	*	*	*	*	*	*	*			*	*	13	56.53
Sex of speaker																								0	0
Age in generation							*	*	*	*	*	*										*	*	8	34.78
Condition of connecting relative																								0	0

NUCLEAR RELATIONSHIP TERMS CLASSIFIED ACCORDING TO KROEBER'S CATEGORIES

ⅰ. *The difference between persons of the same and of separate generations.* This category is rigorously observed in the whole system through the use of generation indicators. Generation is not only an important structural principle in the system but is also an important regulator of marriage and a determinator in the application of vocatives. But in the nuclear terminology it is represented by only 78.3 percent of the terms. In the terms po, shu, ku, chiu, i the generation category is overridden. This merging of generations is not inherent in the system, but has been produced through the disruptive force of teknonymy, which will be discussed later.

ⅱ. *The difference between lined and collateral relationships.* This category is strictly fixed in the whole system. Collateral lines are differentiated by special modifiers. Practically all the basic modifiers exist solely for the function of developing this category. In the nuclear nomenclature it is represented by 100 percent of the terms.

ⅲ. *The difference of age within one generation.* This category is only partially represented in the system. It is fully represented in ego's own generation, whether male or female. Among the ascending generations it is operative only among the male relatives, with the exception of the wives of male relatives. Among the descending generations it is not operative at all. In the nuclear terminology it is represented by only 34.8 per cent.

W. H. R. Rivers attributed the differentiation of age within one generation to the practice of tribal initiation, i. e., older brothers will be initiated before younger brothers.① Whether or not this be correct, it is the only general explanation seriously advanced. In ancient China there are vestiges of initiation rites, especially as recorded in the *I Li*② and *Li Chi.*③ Whether or not these

---

① W.H.R. Rivers, *Social Organization*, ed. by W. J. Perry, 1924, p. 189.

② 士冠禮.

③ 冠義.

ancient initiation rites have anything to do with, the expression of this category is by no means certain. Chinese authors usually connect it with the sib organization, *tsung fa*, since in this organization the older brothers have absolute priority over the younger brothers in the transmission of office and property, and special privileges in the sacrificial rites to ancestors and in carrying on the line in general.①

ⅳ. *The sex of the relative.* This category is consistently carried out in the whole system through the employment of sex indicators. In the nuclear terminology the representation is 100 per cent.

ⅴ. *The sex of the speaker.* This category is entirely inoperative. The sex of the speaker is always understood but never expressed. But there are traces of this category in the ancient system. E.g., in the *Êrh Ya* and the *I Li*, the term *chih* is exclusively used as a woman's term for brother's children. A few other terms may have been used only as women's or men's terms, but here we are less certain.

ⅵ. *The sex of the person through whom the relationship exists.* This category is fully expressed in the system through the use of special modifiers. E. g., *piao hsiung ti* may mean father's sister's sons, mother's brother's sons, or mother's sister's sons. But if we say *ku piao hsiung ti*, *chiu piao hsiung ti* and *i piao hsiunq ti*, the terms are exact, and refer to father's sister's sons, mother's brother's sons and mother's sister's sons, respectively. There are lapses in the vocative usages, since the exact status of the connecting relative is always understood and never expressed.

ⅶ. *The distinction of blood relatives, from conecticn by marriage.* With the exception of the terms *chiu* and *i*, this category is consistently expressed. The

---

① Ch'êng Yao-t'ien程瑶田(1725-1814):*Tsung fa hsiao chi* 宗法小記 1.la:宗之道,兄道也.大夫士之家,以兄統弟,而以弟事兄之道也.Ibid.1.1b:尊祖故敬宗,宗之者,兄之也.故曰:宗之道,兄道也.

merging of mother's brother (consanguineal) and wife's brother (affinal) into *chiu*, and of mother's sister (consanguineal) and wife's sister (affineal) into *i*, is due to the influence of teknonymy. In the vocative usages the terminology is looser, because of the mutual adoption of each other's terms by husband and wife.

ⅷ. *The condition of life of the person through whom relationship exists.* This category is present, but usually is not consistently expressed. The most common distinction is between the dead and living relatives, by the application of special modifiers. There are a few distinct terms for this purpose for parents, grandparents, paternal uncles, etc. Other conditions of life of the relative are not expressed, or are indicated only by circumlocutory expressions.

Certain of these categories (ⅱ, ⅳ, ⅵ and possibly ⅶ) are essential to the maintenance of a strict unilateral—patrilineal in Chinese descent. It is also exactly these categories that find their fullest expression in the Chinese system. The great nicety in the distinction of dead and living ancestors (category ⅷ) in the ancient terminology may have been due to ancestor worship, which is less prevalent now.

Reciprocity

In kinship systems there is usually the factor of reciprocity to influence the expression of certain categories. Reciprocity is of three kinds: logical or conceptual reciprocity, verbal reciprocity, and selfreciprocity, i. e., both conceptual and verbal.① It is not, on the whole, a feature of the modern Chinese system, since, to a certain extent, it is incompatible with the consistent expression of certain categories and exactitude in the discrimination of relatives.

---

① Cf. the definition of reciprocity suggested by A. L. *KROEBER*, *California Kinship systems*, UC: *PAAE* 12, 9. 340, note 1; Zuni Kin and Clan, *Anthropolgical Papers*, *AMNH* 18(1919). 78-81.

In the ancient system there are traces of conceptual reciprocity. The *I Li*① *says*, "They call me *ku*, I call them *chih*." Inversely it is also true: "They call me *chih*, I call them *ku*." *Ku*, as used in the *Êrh Ya* and the *I Li*, means father's sister, and *chih* means brother's child (woman speaking), both male and female. In other words, *ku* "indicates the sex of the relative but not of the speaker," whereas *chih* "does not recognize the sex of the relative indicated, but does imply the sex of the speaker."② Therefore, *ku* and *chih* each involve a category which the other does not express. *Ku* and *chih* in their ancient usages are true conceptual reciprocals.

The *Êrh Ya* also states, "They call me *chiu*, I call them *shêng*,"③ *Chiu* is here used in the sense of mother's brother, and *shêng*, sister's child. But the reverse does not hold true. Actually this statement contradicts the other terms recorded in the *Êrh Ya* itself, since *shêng* was used in the sense of father's sister's son, mother's brother's son, sister's husband (man speaking), and wife's brother. The *Êrh Ya* also gives another term, *chu*, for the same relative, sister's child. It is very likely that the above statement is a later interpolation, since *chiu-shêng* was probably reciprocal from the Han to the T'ang periods.④ The whole problem is complicated by the question of cross-cousin marriage and teknonymy, which will be dealt with later. In short, *chiu-shêng* could not have been reciprocal in the ancient system, but *shêng* was itself partially reciprocal, i. e., in the male sex only.⑤

These are the only traces of reciprocity that can be detected in the ancient

---

① 喪服 32. 1b:傳曰:姪者,何也? 謂吾姑者,吾謂之姪.

② A. L. KROEBER: *Classificatory System of Relationship* 81.

③ This statement also occurs in the *I Li*,喪服 33.9a:傳曰:甥者,何也? 謂吾舅者,吾謂之甥.

④ During this period *chiu* was used for mother's brother alone, and *shêng* dropped all its other connotations and became simply a term for sister's child, e. g., *wai-shêng*.

⑤ That is, *shêng* is used reciprocally between mother's brother's son, father's sister's son, sister's husband (M.S.), wife's brother, and male ego. They call male ego *shêng*, and male ego also calls them *shêng*.

system. The tendency toward the consistent use of categories later became so strong that even these few vestiges of ancient reciprocal terms have entirely disappeared from the modern system.

Factors Affecting the System

In the course of development from the ancient to the modern system there has been a slow but persistent tendency toward systematization and more exactly descriptive efficacy in nomenclature. This tendency has to a large extent been conditioned by the sociological lines along which Chinese society is organized, and has to a lesser extent been intentionally fostered by ardent ritualists and framers of etiquette. On the other hand, there are also potent social forces which work against overrationalization and oftentimes throw certain parts of the system out of gear by undermining certain categories. The systematizing forces are the sib-organization and the mourning system. These two factors have supplemented one another in moulding the kinship system to their own pattern. The disrupting forces are the Chinese marriage customs and, most potent of all, teknonymy. The ritualists served as a stabilizing agency in vigilantly conserving the nomenclature① with a view to the exactitude of mourning specifications and the needs for maintaining sib solidarity. But generally they were powerless against the popular tendencies in kinship usages, and very often were forced to accept the already established terms and attempt to harmonize and incorporate them into the whole system.② Thus, in the Chinese system there is a seeming

---

① For example, *chu* and *ku* as terms for the husband's parents have been obsolete since the turn of the first millenium A. D., but they are still used in this sense in ritual works. *Chiu* was extended to include wife's brother ca. 900 A. D., but one never finds *chiu* used in this sense in formal literature.

② E.g., *i* was extended to include mother's sister ca. 500 B. C. During the next seven or eight centuries, the new and old terms were used interchangeably. About 400 A. D. *i* was standardized as term for both mother's sister and wife's sister.

embodiment of a well considered plan while, at the same time, there are many incongruities. No matter how much we may discredit "mock kinship algebra," to borrow a phrase from Malinowski[①], it is pertinent to inquire into the conflicting forces which have moulded, and are today shaping, the Chinese system.

The Sib: Descent and Exogamy

Kinship ties necessarily begin within the family as a procreational unit. These primary ties, as we may call them[②], are biologically the same in all societies[③], though, functionally, they may differ from culture to culture.[④] But kinship ties do not rest within the reproductive family. They are extended to a much wider circle of individuals who are actually or reputedly related to those of the procreational family. In this process of extension certain groups of related individuals are emphasized and certain others minimized, although their degree of relationship may be exactly the same. The basis of this variability in the grouping of kin is the subject of much, perhaps unduly much, anthropological discussion. And naturally so, for it is precisely this variability in kinship patterning that differs so widely among different peoples—particular systems grouping relatives in quite different ways. The character of the kin groups emphasized likewise reflects the wider ranges of the social structure of which the kinship system is part.

In the Chinese kinship system, relatives in the male line receive

---

① Kinship, *Man* 30 (1930). 17. 19-29.

② B. MALINOWSKI would call this "the initial situation of kinship": preface to Raymond FIRTH's *We, The Tikopia* (1936) x.

③ I.e., the divisions into father, mother, son, daughter, brother and sister, members of the strictly procreational family, exist in all kinship systems.

④ E. g., the relationship of "father" to the rest of the procreational group in a patrilineal society may be radically different from that in a matrilineal society.

emphasis; the formalized basis of which is the exogamous patrilineal sib.

Sib organization is called *tsung fa* in Chinese, literally, the "law of kindred." The *tsung fa* was bound up with the feudal system①, which was swept away in the course of the third century B. C. The sib organization, however, has survived to the present day, although in a much attenuated and modified form. The postfeudal development of the sib reached its climax in the third to the eighth centuries A. D., when it is usually termed *Shih tsu* or *tsung tsu*. The causes of this excessive development were many, but primarily it represents a reactionary growth following the abolition of the feudal system. The larger and more prominent sibs took the place of the feudal nobility, both in monopolizing governmental offices and in maintaining social prestige.② Their influence began to decline during the T'ang period. This was, on the one hand, due to the suppressive measures of the T'ang rulers and, on the other hand, to the social upheavals precipitated by the decline of the T'ang dynasty.③ At the present time sib organization, for most people, is less vital than formerly, but its traditions and influences still permeate the whole of Chinese social life.

Tsung fa itself has been well studied, and we need here consider only those two of its characteristics which have direct influence upon the alignment of relatives, viz., patrilineal descent and exogamy. With the *tsung*, the sib, each line of descent is strictly patrilineal, not only in the transmission of the sibname but also in the transmission of office, property, etc. It is also primogenitary:

---

① For the sib organization of the feudal period, cf. WAN Kuang-T'ai 萬光泰, *Tsung fa piao* 宗法表; WAN Ssŭ-ta 萬斯大, *Tsung fa lun* 宗法論; and Ch'êng Yao-T'ien 程瑶田, *Tsung fa hsiao chi* 宗法小記. For a more modern study, cf. Sun Yao 孫曜, *Ch'un Ch'iu shih tai chih shih tsu* 春秋時代之世族(1931).

② Cf. *Kai yü Ts'ung k'ao*, 六朝重世族, 17 1b-9a.

③ Cf. *Tung Chih* 通志:氏族略序, 25.1.

the eldest brother has priority over the younger brothers.① The *tsung* is absolutely exogamous. Marriage within it is impossible, even after a "hundred generations." It is also strictly patrilocal.② Evidence is far from conclusive as to whether or not Chinese society passed through a prior matrilineal phase.③ Exogamy, however, was predominately a Chou institution,④ and its development was rather late. Ancient authorities attest that during the Hsia and Shang [ca. 1700-1100 B. C.] periods members of the same sib could marry after the lapse of five generations.⑤ The institution of strict sib exogamy was traditionally attributed to Chou Kung [ca. 1100 B. C.], who instituted it for the maintenance of sib solidarity. Nevertheless, there is abundant evidence to show that even during the Chou period this interdiction was neither universal nor strictly enforced⑥, It was only after the overthrow of the feudal system and the transformation of the sib organization that absolute sib exogamy gradually prevailed. From the middle of the first millennium A. D. to the present this rule

---

① In the transmission of hereditary titles, the primogenitary principle holds but the property is divided equally among the brothers, although the eldest brother usually receives an extra share. It is only in the ceremonies in the ancestral halls that the primogenitary line has absolute priority over all collateral lines.

② When, for want of male issue, a son-in-law is adopted as son, he adopts the wife's sibname and lives with her parents. He is in every way treated as a son. The children or the third generation revert to his original sibname 三代回宗, but usually one male child is allowed to carry on the wife's line.

③ The existence of an early matrilineal state constitutes the underlying hypotbasis of many recent works on ancient Chinese socicty, e. g., M. GRANET'S *La civilisation chinoiae.* Paris, 1929. and Kuo Mo-jo's 中國古代社會研究, 1931, The evidence they have marshalled is suggestive rather than conclusive.

④ *Li chi* 大傳, 34.7b: 係之以姓而弗别,綴之以食而弗殊,雖百世而婚姻不通者,周道然也. *T' ung Tien*, 96. 2a, cites, 晉范汪祭典:且同姓百代不婚,周道也.

⑤ *T'ai p'ing yü lan* 太平御覽(1808) 鮑氏 ed., 540.7b-8a. citcs 禮外傳. The five generations include the generation or ego. Even then, it is still very doubtful whether the Hsia and yin peoples had any exogamy at all.

⑥ CHAO I says (*Kai yu Ts'ung k'ao*, 31. 2b-3a), 同姓爲婚,莫如春秋時最多 and cites many cases to support his thesis. He concludes, 此皆春秋時亂俗也,漢以後此事漸少.

has been vigorously enforced by law.①

The moulding effect of the exogamous patrilineal sib is seen in the dichotomy of relatives in the system. Relatives are divided, along sib lines, into sib relatives〔tsung Ch'in〕and *non-sib relatives*〔wai Ch'in or nei Ch'in〕. All sib relatives belong to the same sib of ego and possess the same sibname. Paternal relatives descended from females through males or females are non-sib relatives. Maternal and alfinal relatives all belong to the non-sib group.

To maintain this distinction between the sib and non-sib groups, the terminology must be bifurcated in such a way that the paternal relatives descended from males through males are differentiated from those descended from females through males. This is carried out by differentiating the father's brother's sons〔*T'ang hsiung ti*〕and their descendants from father's sister's sons〔*piao hsiung ti*〕and their descendants; brother's sons〔*chih*〕from sister's sons〔*wai shêng*〕; son's sons〔*sun*〕from daughter's sons〔*wai sun*〕; and so on, ascendingly, descendingly, and collaterally This bifurcation is necessary, since father's sister, sister, daughter, or any female sib relative who through sib exogamy has married into other sibs, and their descendants, belong, on account of patrilineal descent, to different sibs from ego.

Nevertheless, the emphasis upon the sib relatives is not so manifest in the whole kinship system as it might be. A partial explanation lies in the minute differentiation in the terminology, which to a certain extent has obscured this grouping. If we look at the application of the depreciatory modifiers, however, this emphasis at once becomes apparent. Only sib relatives are to be depreciated, inasmuch as they are regarded as members of one's own group. Non-sib relatives are not to be depreciated, since they are felt to be outside of one's own group.

---

① E.g., in *T'ang lü*, *shu i* 14. *la*: 諸同姓爲婚者,各徒二年,緦麻以上以姦論.Cf. *Pierre HOANG*: *Le mariage chinois au point de vue Lêgal*, 1898, 43-53.

Conceptually, sib relatives are considered nearer than non-sib relatives, even though their degree of remoteness from ego may be exactly the same. This is best expressed in the mourning obligations. The mourning period for paternal grandparents is one year, but for maternal grandparents only five months; for paternal uncle one year, and for maternal uncle five months; for father's brother's son nine months, and for mother's brother's son only three months. More instructive is the difference in mourning periods for a female sib relative before and after her marriage. The mourning period for father's unmarried sister, ego's unmarried sister, unmarried daughter, and brother's unmarried daughter, is one year; after their marriage, the mourning period is decreased to nine months, i. e., it is lessened by one degree. Therefore, we see that as long as these females remain unmarried they belong to ego's sib, but after marriage they belong to their husband's sibs. This transference through marriage has lessened their bond with the sib and, consequently, with ego.①

The nomenclature of the non-sib relatives is perhaps more expressive of this dual division of relatives. The differentiation between paternal grandparents [*tsu*] and maternal grandparents [*wai tsu*], paternal uncle [*po* and *shu*] and maternal uncle [*chiu*], paternal aunt [*ku*] and maternal aunt [*i*], is, of course, a regular feature of a system based upon exogamous social grouping. But the interesting phenomenon is the merging of the father's sister's, mother's sister's, and mother's brother's descendants in the single term, *piao*.② *Piao*, as a term in itself, means "outside" or "external." The descendants of father's sister, and of mother's sister and brother, although consanguineal relatives of distinct affiliation, are all non-sib relatives, and hence their merging in the

① The mourning obligations of an unmarried female to her paternal relatives are just the same as those of her brother. After marriage, all these obligations are lessened by one degree, and, reciprocally, obligations of these relatives to her are also lessened by one degree.

② The *ku piao*, *chiu piao* and *i piao* are the three first-degree *piao* relationships of the Chinese system.

term piao is understandable.

The introduction and development of *piao* is also of historical interest. In the ancient system of the *Êrh Ya* and the *I Li*, father's sister's sons and mother's brother's sons were merged in the term *shêng*, through cross-cousin marriage.① mother's sister's children, being parallel cousins, stood alone as *ts'ung mu hsiung ti* [for males] and *Ts'ung mu tzŭ mei* [for females]. During the first two centuries A. D., with cross-cousin marriage already long in abeyance, father's sister's sons were designated as *wai* [outside], e. g, *wai hsiung ti*②, and mother's brother's sons as *nei* [inside], e g., *nei hsiung ti.*③ At about the same time④ *chung* and *piao* were used as equivalents of *nei* and *wai*, since *chung* means "middle," "inside" and *piao* means "outside," "external."

During the last few centuries of the first millennium B. C. and the first few centuries A. D., mother's sister's sons were usually designated by the newly extended term *i*, e. g., *i hsiung ti*, although *ts'ung mu hsiung ti* was still permissible.

From the fourth to the seventh centuries A. D. constant confusion was produced through the use of the terms *nei* or *wai* for mother's sister's children, and, consequently, a confusion of relatives involving father's sister's, mother's brother's and mother's sister's descendants.⑤ The reason for this may lie in the fact that these relatives, although of clear affiliation, all belong to the non-sib

---

① See discussion under CROSS-COUSIN MARRIAGE, below, pp. 201-205.

② *I Li* 喪服,33.9b:姑之子.鄭注:外兄弟也.

③ Ibid., 33.10b:舅之子.鄭注:内兄弟也.

④ *Hou-Han shu* 鄭太傳, 100.2-3a:……公業懼,乃詭詞更對曰:……又明公將帥,皆中表腹心.

⑤ E.g., *Tung Tien*, 95.9a-12b:爲内外妹爲兄弟妻服議:(The instance involved is neither mother's brother's daughter, nor father's sister's daughter, who ought to be *nei* or *wai*, respectively, but mother's sister's daughter) 晉徐衆論云:徐恩龍娶姨妹爲婦,婦亡,而諸弟以姨妹爲嫂,嫂叔無服,不復爲姨妹行喪. The 海録碎事 (cited by *Ch'êng wei lu*, 3.20a) states:唐人兩姨之子,相謂爲外兄弟.And 山堂肆考,角集,47b:兩姨之子爲外兄弟,姑舅之子爲内兄弟,一説,⊙子稱姑子爲外兄弟,姑子稱舅子爲内兄弟. The use of *nei* and *wai* is so confusing that even these encyclopaedists do not know which usage is correct.

group and are distinct from the exogamous partilineal sib group. During the T'ang period, the *chung* was dropped and *piao* alone was applied to all these relatives.① Thus *piao* became a general indicator for non-sib consanguineal relations descended from relatives of higher generations than ego.

This conceptual as well as nomenclative dichotomy of relatives is a definitive expression of the exogamous patrilineal sib principle. At the same time, this principle has been modified by another factor-mourning rituals-resulting in the elaborate differentiation of collateral lines in the sib group, rather undermining its original function. But an understanding of this principle is most essential for a grasp of the system as a whole, since it is not only a potent moulding force but is as well a controlling factor in many important kinship usages, i. e., the depreciatory and complimentary terminologies.

Mourning Grades

The Chinese mourning system is based upon the sib organization for its discrimination against non-sib relatives, and on degree of relationships for the assignment of mourning grades. Mourning for sib relatives vanishes at the fourth degree〔fourth collateral〕and at the fourth generation, both ascending and descending from ego.② There is, consequently, in the kinship system a sharp differentiation of the first four collateral lines, and an indefinite grouping of all further collaterals in the *tsu* relationship.

Mourning, *sang fu* in Chinese, is a colossal subject in itself; here we can only touch upon those fundamental aspects that are prerequisite to an

① During the sixth century the subject of *piao* relationships became so popular that even genealogies were compiled for them, e. g., *Wei shu* 高諒傳, 57.5a:諒造親表譜録四十許卷,自五世以下,内外曲盡,覽者服其博記.

② *Li Chi* 大傳, 34. 7b:四世而緦,服之窮也.

elucidation of its influence upon the kinship system. *Chan ts'ui* (three years), *tzŭ ts'ui* (one year), *ta kung* (nine months), *hsiao kung* (five months), and *ssŭ ma* (three months) are, commonly known as the *wu fu*, "five grades of mourning." Actually, the number is greater than five. The specifications of these grades have fluctuated much from period to period; certain grades have been dropped or added in conformity with the excentricities of particular periods. Although the specifications may thus have changed, the fundamental principles which underlie these specifications have remained constant.

All the paraphernalia expressed by the above terms① are mere accessories, the fundamental units of mourning being the "mourning periods." The basic unit is the *year*. All other degrees are either *chia lung* [increased mourning], or *chiang shai* [decreased mourning], relative to the basic unit. These principles are best expounded in the *San nien wên* of the *Li Chi*②, which says: "Why is it that the mourning period for the *nearest kin* is one year? Because the interaction of heaven and earth has run its round; and the four seasons have gone through their changes. All things between heaven and earth begin their processes anew. The rules of mourning are intended to resemble them." "Why should there be three years mourning [for parents]? The reason is to make it more impressive, *chia lung*, by doubling the period, so that it embraces two round years."③"Then why have the mourning of nine months? The reason is to prevent excessive grief." Therefore three years [actually twenty-five months counted as three years] is the highest expression, *lung*, of mourning. Three

---

① The terms *chan ts'ui. tzŭ Ts'ui*, *ta kung*, *hsiao kung*, and *ssŭ ma* specify the kind of apparel to be worn at the mourning for a particular relative.

② 三年問, 58. 3a-4b. For translations in European languages, cf. J. LEGGE, *Li Ki* Sacred Books of the East 28. 393-4; and S. COUVREUR, *Li Ki* (1913), 580-586.

③ Twenty-five months are counted as three years, hence the "three years" mourning is only two years and one month.

months and five months[①] are the lowest, *shai*. One year and nine months are the norms. Heaven above gives an example; earth below, a law; and man between, a pattern. The harmony and unity that should characterize men living in their kinships are hereby completely shown."

Mourning starts from the nearest kin with the basic unit of *ch'i*, one year. The nearest kin have three. According to the *Sang fu chüan*[②], "the relation between father and son is one; between husband and wife is another; and between brothers is a third." With the three nearest kin, with the basic unit of *Ch'i*, and with the principles of *chia lung* and *chiang shai*, the whole system is correlated with the kinship system as in Diagram Ⅳ (see p. 201).

The process is as follows: The mourning period for father is *Ch'i*, one year; for grandfather, *ta kung*, nine months; for great grandfather, *hsiao kung*, five months; and for great great grandfather, *ssŭ*, three months. This is called *shang shai*, "ascending decrease." The mourning period for son is *Ch'i*, one year; for grandson, *ta kung*, nine months; for great grandson, *hsiao kung*, five months; and for great great grandson, *ssŭ* three months. This is called *hsia shai*, "descending decrease." The mourning period for brother is *Ch'i*, one year; for father's brother's son, *ta kung*, nine months; for father's father's brother's son's son, *hsiao kung*, five months; and for father's father's father's brother's son's son's son, *ssŭ* three months. This is called *P'aug shai*, "horizontal decrease."

The *chan ts'ui*, three years, mourning for father is *chia lung*, increased mourning; basically it is only one year. The one year, *Ch'i*, mourning for father's father and father's brothers, is likewise *chia lung*, since basically it is

---

① "Five months" are counted as two seasons, which should be six months. The substitution of five for six reflects an ancient Chinese aversion for even numbers. Thus, the basic periods are: three months (one season), five months (two seasons), nine months (three seasons), and one year (four seasons).

② *I Li* 30. 8b-9a.

the *ta kung* grade, nine months.

All non-sib relatives, whether consanguineal or affinal, are given the last grade of mourning, *ssŭ ma*, three months, no matter how closely related they may be.① They are subject also to the principle of *chia lung*; e. g., in the ancient mourning specifications, the mourning grade for mother's sister is *hsiao kung*, five months, but for the mother's brother it is only *ssŭ ma*, three months②; the former is *chia lung*, and the latter is not. Basically they are all *ssŭ ma*.③

Mourning grades of a simpler kind must have existed long before the Chou period, but their elaboration began only when they fell into the hands of the Confucianists.④ Using the family and sib as the bases for their ideological structure, these literati elaborated the mourning system with a view to the maintenance of sib solidarity. In the course of this elaboration of the mourning system they also standardized its basis, the kinship system, for a carefully graded system of mourning rites requires a highly differential kinship nomenclature, lest an awkward incommen surability ensue. This is especially apparent in the comparison of the *Êrh Ya* and the *I Li* systems. The *Êrh Ya* system, when compared with the system recorded together with the mourning rites〔*Sang fu chuan*〕in the *I Li*, is inconsistent and less differential in many respects. Certain classical scholars naively tried to amend the *Êrh Ya* with the *I Li* system, since they considered the *Êrh Ya* system below the standard of

---

① *I Li* 喪服, 33.2a: 外親之服皆緦也. Cf. *Jih chih lu* 5.35-7.

② In modern mourning specifications mother's brother is increased to five months, *hsiao kung*.

③ For the actual specifications one must consult the ritual works of each period. The above are merelly general statements of principle.

④ Certain scholars believe that the three-year mourning for father was a Shang custom, and that the Ju 儒, who practiced it during the Chou period and later evolved into Confucianists, were descended from the Shang dynasty people. Cf. Hu Shih: 説儒, 胡適論學近著, 第一集, 19-23, 90-94. For an opposite view cf. FÊNG Yu-lan. The Origin of Ju and Mo, *CHHP* 10. 279-310.

Confucian ideals of kinship①. They failed to see that the *Êrh Ya* represents an early state of the system, and the *I Li* a later but rationalized system worked over to conform with the mourning system.

There is no doubt that the *Êrh Ya* system was already to some extent rationalized through Confucian influences, but it is much less so than that in the *I Li*. With the Confucian ideals firmly implanted in the Chinese social structure from the second century B. C. on, the mourning rites were increasingly elaborated and popularized②, and concomitantly the kinship system until both reached their apogée during the T'ang period.

The elaborate mourning rites are a distinctive feature of Chinese ceremonial and social life. Under their influence the Chinese kinship system, through the increasing emphasis laid upon collateral differentiation and generation stratification, was transformed from a classificatory system based upon an exogamous sib organization into one of the descriptive type.③

---

① Cf. 補正爾雅釋親宗族, by 鄭珍: *Ch'ao ch'ing ch'ao* (*wen chi*). 1a-4b.

② Cf. 三年喪服的逐漸的推行, by Hu Shih, *op. cit.*, 95-102.

③ Kingsley DAVIS and W. Lloyd WARNER have made some very pertinent remarks concerning the use of "classificatory" and "descriptive" in connection with kinship analysis [Structural Analysis of Kinship, *American Anthropologist*, 39:2 (1937), 291-315]. They have also formulated a new set of categories for the structural analysis of kinship, with which, I thiak, few students will agree, The present writer disagrees with them in many points on their interpretation of the Chinese system. Since, however, this MS is going to press as their article appears, it is not possible to elaborate this remark.

DIAGRAM Ⅳ①

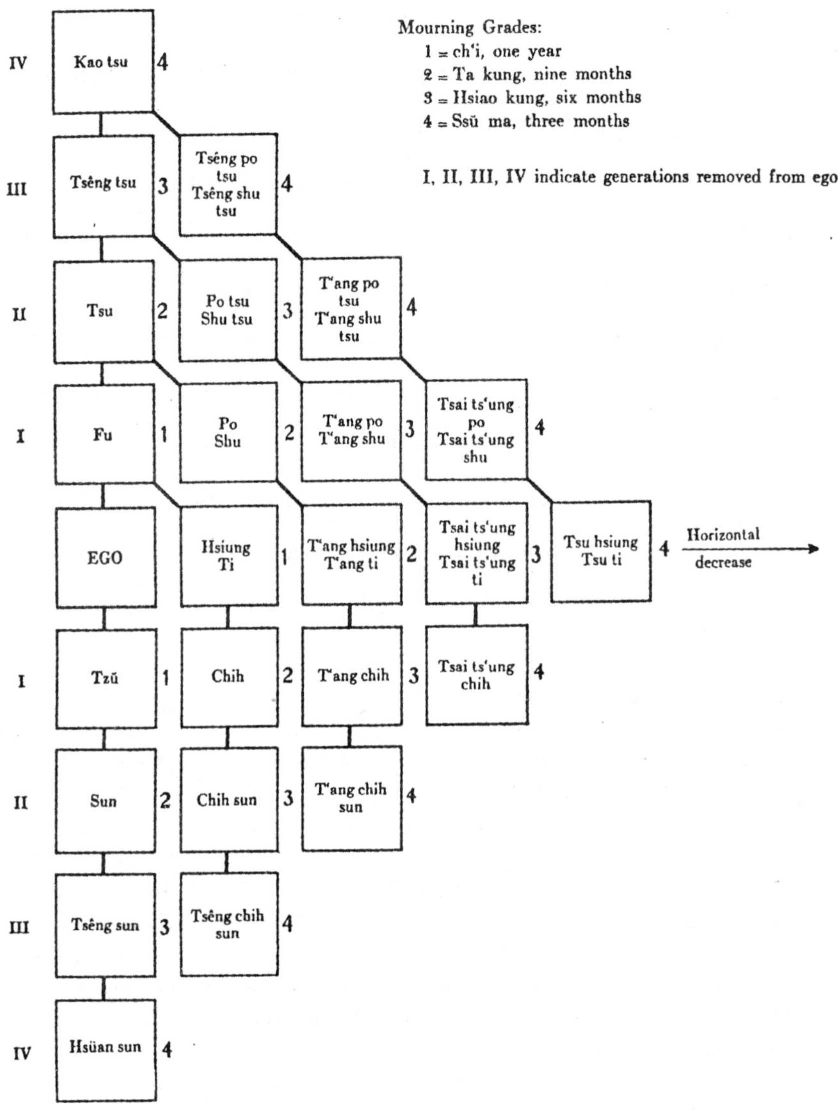

① Since the author is merely outlining the basic mourning system, only the male relatives are given. A complete specification would require eight to twelve diagrams.

Cross-cousin Marriages

Cross-cousin marriage is permitted, but not encouraged, in modern China. Generally, it is discountenanced not on the ground that the blood relationship is too close but on the ground that older relatives might be estranged as a result of difficulties which might arise between the young married couple, or vice versa. On the other hand, however, it is desirable, because it increases the number of relationships and knits the bond more closely.① Theoretically and ritually, it has been disapproved since the beginning of the first century A. D.② Legal prohibition, however, came rather late, the first definite clause being found in the Ming Code.③ Since the enforcement of this law proved rather difficult, in the Ch'ing Code this interdiction was invalidated by another clause, immediately following it, which allowed such marriages.④ It must be noted that in modern China the kinship system is not the primary regulator of marriage;

① As the popular saying goes, 親上加親.

② *Pai hu t'ung*, 10. 16a:外屬小功以上,亦不得娶也.是春秋傳曰,譏娶母黨也.袁準,of the Chin dynasty, says, (*T'ung Tien*, 60. 16b-17a,内表不可爲婚議)曰:今之人内外相婚,禮歟? 曰:中外之親,近於同姓,同姓且猶不可,而况中外之親乎! 古人以爲無疑,故不制也.今以古之不言,因謂之可婚.此不知禮者也. These statements probably read too much into the old ritual works.

③ *Ming lü chi chieh*, 6. 17a: 若娶己之姑舅兩姨姊妹者,杖八十,並離異. The clause in the T'ang Code (*T'ang lü shu* 1.14. 2b), 其父母之姑舅兩姨姊妹……並不得爲婚…… is sometimes expanded to include prohibition against cross-cousin marriage. Cf.*Jung chai sui pi* (*hsü pi*), 8.12. The clause seems to indicate only parents' cross-cousins, not one's own cross-cousins; if so, the interdiction is against inter-generation marriage rather than cross-cousin marriage. But the *T'ung tien* (95. 11 a) seems to show that during the T'ang period marriage with cross-cousins and mother's sister's daughter was actually prohibited.

④ G. JAMIESON: Translations from the *General Code of laws of the Chinese Empire*, Chapter 18: "A man cannot marry the children or his aunt on the father's side, or of his uncle or aunt on the mother's side, because though of the same generation they are within the fifth degree of mourning." But a little later in the *Li*, it reads:"…… In the interest of the people it is permitted to marry with the children of a paternal aunt or of a maternal uncle or aunt." *China Review* 10 (1881-82), 83. Cf. also Sir G. T. STAUNTON, *Ta Tsing Leu Lee* (1810), 115.

the important,factor is sib exogamy supplemented by the generation principle. Thus, not only marriage with cross-cousin, but also with parallel cousin by mother's sister is allowed.① No statistical data for cross-cousin marriage are available at present, but my general impression is that the percentage is very small. In any event, cross-cousin marriage is in no way reflected in the modern kinship system.②

The ancient system as recorded in the *Êrh Ya* and the *I Li* reflects a preferential type of cross-cousin marriage in certain kinship equations.③ The terms concerned are the following④: Chiu 舅:a. mother's brother, b. husband's

---

① The practice of marriage with the mother's sister's daughter began at least as early as the third and fourth centuries A. D. E. g., *T'ung Tien* 95. 9a cites the discussion of 徐衆 of the Chin dynasty concerning the mourning obligations of dual relationship for mother's sister's danghter who married one's own older brother. A great many useless discussions have been lavished on this subject.

② T. S. CHEN and J. K. SHRYOCK in their "Chinese Relationship Terms", *American Anthropologist* 34: 4, 623-669, interpretable in terms of cross-cousin marriage the fact that the father's sister's children and the mother's brother's children are designated by the same terms (see Chen-Shryock Table I. terms 85-92, and Tabe Ⅳ, terms 17-24, and note 33). But I do not see where the marriage element enters. The terms merely indicate crosscousinship and nothing more. In order for these terms to be interpretable in terms of crosscousin marriage, either the mother's brother or father's sister's husband must be addressed by the same term as that used for wife's father, or sister's husband or wife's brother addressed in cross-cousin terminology-in fact, any usage that will bring in the marriage element. Unfortunately, no terminology of this sort exists in the modern system. Hence, the authors' interpretations involving cross-cousin marriage in notes 33, 34,39, 42, 61, 64, 65 and 67, are untenable. Furthermore, these interpretations are based on incomplete and faulty data. E.g., the important modifier piao is omitted from the terms of mother's sister's children, thus making mother's sister's daughters merge with wife's sisters. Mother's sister's children are *piao*, just as mother's brother's children and father's sister's children are *piao*. Not only cross-cousins are designated by *piao*, but also parallel cousins through mother's sister. This consideration completely invalidates the cross-cousin interpretation. Actually, since, as the authors have ably shown, the abandonment of the cross-cousin marriage custom was responsible for the development of the modern system, how can the modern system still be interpreted as indicative of that usage?

③ The first to interpret the *Êrh Ya* system in terms of cross-cousin marriage was M. GRANET, *La civilization chinoise*. 187. The thesis was further developed by sheu and Shryock, *op. cit*. 629-630.

④ In the following notes some of the old Chinese interpretations of the extensions of these terms are given. They are not necessarily correct, but they do serve to show the traditional Chinese conceptions.

father①, c. wife's father, as *wai chiu*.② Ku 姑: a. father's sister, b. husband's mother, c. wife's mother, as *wai ku*. Shêng 甥: a. father's sister's sons, b. mother's brother's sons, c. wife's brother,③ d. sister's husband (man speaking).④ These terms indubitably manifest cross-cousin marriage of the bilateral type, couple with sister exchange, The latter practice is shown especially in the term *shêng*, which means wife's brother and sister's husband.

Indirect evidence can be obtained from the arrangement of the *Êrh Ya*. Here the terms on kinship are arranged into four groups: i. Tsung tsu 宗族, Relatives through father, ii. Mu tang 母黨, Relatives through mother, iii. Ch'i tang 妻黨, Relatives through wife. iv. Hun yin 婚姻, Relatives through husband. It is interesting to note that father's sister's sons, mother's brother's sons, sister's husband (M.S.), and sister's sons are all listed under Group iii, *ch'i tang*. The grouping of these relatives of quite distinct affiliations under *Relatives through wife* clearly demonstrates that the *Êrh Ya* system is built upon

---

① The old interpretation of the extension of *chiu* and *ku* to include husband's father and mother is as follows: The one who is as venerable as father, but who is not the father, is mother's brother, *chiu*. The one to whom one is as attached as much as to mother, but who is not the mother, is father's sister, *ku*. Husband's parents are of similar relationship, hence we call them *chiu* and *ku*. Cf. *Pai hu T'ung*, 8. 20b: 稱夫之父母謂姑舅何? 尊如父而非父者,舅也.親如母而非母者,姑也.故稱夫之父母爲舅姑也.

② Wife's parents are called *wai chiu* (outside *chiu*) and *wai ku* (outside *ku*), that is to say, the wife is an outsider who comes to one's own family and makes it her own family too. She calls the husband's parents *chiu* and *ku*. The husband, in reciprocating, calls her parents *wai chiu* and *wai ku*, as a sign of equality for both parties. *Shih Ming*: 妻之父曰外舅,母曰外姑,言妻從外來,謂至己家爲歸,故反此義以稱之,夫婦匹敵之義也.

③ Wife's brothers are called *wai shêng* (*outside shêng*) because their sister marries ego and becomes ego's wife, hence her male siblings are the *shêng* of an outside sib. *Shih Ming*:妻之昆弟曰外甥,其姊妹女也,來歸己内爲妻,故共男爲外姓之甥.甥者,生也.他姓子本生於外,不得如其女來在己内也.

④ Kuo P'o's commentary on the term *shêng*, in the *Êrh Ya*, says that these four individuals are of equal status, hence they reciprocally call one another *shêng*. 四人體體,故更相爲甥. This conception of 敵體, equal status, between the relationships of *shêng*, has been the basis of most later interpretations; e. g., 姑之子爲甥,舅之子爲甥,妻之昆弟爲甥,姊妹之夫爲甥解, by 俞樾,詁經精舍自課文,春在堂全書本.

the practice of cross-cousin marriage.

Sororate

The sororate was operative during the feudal period, at least among the feudal lords.① The *Êrh Ya* gives the term for sister's husband [woman speaking] as *ssŭ*, literally "private." This is sometimes interpreted as evidence of the sororate, since a woman considers her sister's husband her "private."② The validity of this reasoning is rather dubious, without other terminological corroboration. *Ts'ung mu*, the term in the *Êrh Ya* and the *I Li* for mother's sister, has also been interpreted as a reflection of this usage. *Ts'ung mu* literally means "following mother."③ But the term is best interpreted as a counterpart of *ts'ung fu*, a term for father's brother; hence *ts'ung* indicates the collateral line rather than potential motherhood.

Throughout the historical period, including modern China, the sororate has been practiced, but, since the possibilities are reduced by infant betrothal, its occurrence has been sporadic only. The single reflection in the modern system comes in the term *i*, which means mother's sister, father's concubine, wife's sister, and concubine, This identification seems irrefutable, yet another

---

① Cf. M. GRANET, *La polygynie sororale et le sororat dans la Chine féodale*, 1920. The author overworks his material to arrive at forced conclusions, but most of the relevant data are collected in this little work. The thesis is also incorporated in his later work, *La civilization chinoise*, in which he has utilized the antiquated anthropological theory that the sororate and levirate represent survivals of an early fraternal group marriage.

② Cf. CHEN and SHRYOCK, *op. cit.*, 628. The *Shih Ming* interprets *ssŭ* in quite a different way. Female ego's sister's husband is called *ssŭ*, private, because this man has *private* relations with female ego's sister: 姊妹互相謂夫曰私,言其夫兄弟之中,此人與己姊妹有恩私也. On the basis of this old interpretation, the *ssŭ* does not concern female ego at all, and so is scarcely evidence for the sororate.

③ LIU Hsi (ca. 200 A. D.), in his *Shih Ming*, interprets *tsung mu* in the following manner: mother's sisters come to marry the father as *ti* 娣, hence they are of the status of *tsung mu*. Even if they do not marry the father, the term is still applied to them. This, I believe, is the earliest known sociological interpretation of kinship terminology. Whether or not it is correct is quite another matter.

explanation is possible. A man calls his friends *hsiung*, older brother, and *ti*, younger brother, as a sign of courtesy and intimacy. A woman also calls her female friends *tzŭ*, older sister, and *mei*, younger sister, for the same reason. It is perfectly natural for the wife to call and consider her husband's concubines *mei*, and actually she does. The term *i* may thus be extended without recourse to the actual sororate at all. Similarly, *i* is usually used by children for the father's concubines①, and by servants for the master's concubines, in both instances as a complimentary term.

Where the sororate is practiced extensively, it may be accompanied by marriage with the wife's brother's daughter, because if the wife has no marriageable sister her brother's daughter is a good substitute. There are indications of such a practice in feudal China among the nobility.

When a feudal lord married, his bride was accompanied by eight bridesmaids called yin, who were his future concubines.② The *yin* were recruited in the following manner. The bride and the eight *yin* were divided into three groups, with three women in each group. The first group consisted of the bride, one of her younger sisters or younger half-sisters, *ti*③, and one of her older brother's daughters, *chih*. These three women constituted the principal

---

① The *T'ung su p'ien* (18. 17a-17b) states that the father's concubines are called *i*, because of the old *yin* marriage custom. *I* was originally a term for several sisters who married the same husband. In later times, the *yin* custom was discontinued but concubines are actually equivalent to the *yin*. Therefore, although father's concubines are not mother's sisters, *i* can still be applied to them. This sociological interpretation is rather erroneous. The *yin* marriage custom had nothing to do with the term *i*, and the *yin*'s were never called *i*, but always *chih* 姪 and *ti* 娣.

② *Kung-yang chuan* 莊公十九年,8.1b-2a:媵者何？諸侯娶一國,二國往媵之,以姪娣從.姪者何？兄之子也,娣者何？弟也.

③ Whether *ti* 娣 meant the bride's actual younger sisters, or her younger half-sisters, i. e. her father's *yin*'s daughters, is a matter of speculation. Probably *ti* meant only her younger half-sisters, since there is abundant evidence to show that the daughters of the principal wife, *fu jên*, were always married out as *fu jên*, and *yin*'s daughters always married out as *yin*. In this way the noble-born and low-born were always kept constant 貴賤有常. This interpretation tallies with the uses of *i* and *ti* in the *Êrh Ya*. Cf. 毛際盛: *Shuo wên chieh tzŭ shu i* 說文解字述誼(聚學軒叢書本),2.44a.

group. Two other feudal states of the same sibname as the bride each supplied a principal *yin*, a *ti*, and a *chih*.① Thus there were three groups and nine women in all. The contribution to the *yin* by other states had to be entirely voluntary, and could not be solicited②, for it was not proper to ask children of others to become the dishonorable *yin*.③

This elaborate system for the selection of the yin served to insure a large number of descendants for succession in the feudal lord's office.④ A niece, rather than a second younger sister was included in the *yin* in order to create a difference in the blood, so that if the two sisters failed to bear issue, a niece of different blood might bear a son. Similarly, the two other groups of *yin* were selected from two different states, in order that their blood would be still more dissimilar and the chances of having an heir would thus be tripled.⑤ Sib relatives were selected for the *yin* with a view to preventing jealousy and intrigue within the harem.⑥

The *yin* custom was not strictly what is usually termed "secondary marriages." All the women were married at once, though if a *yin* were too young she could "wait her years in her parental state" until grown up, and was

① *Tso Chuan* 成公十八年, 26.23a:衛人來媵共姬,禮也.凡諸侯嫁女,同姓媵之,異姓則否. This may have been the general role, but there were exceptions.

② *Kung-yang chuan* 莊公十九年,8.2a:何休注:言往媵之者,禮.君不求媵,二國自往媵夫人,所以一夫人之尊.

③ *Pai hu t'ung*,10.12a:所以不聘妾者何? 人有子孫,欲尊之,義不可求人爲賤也……妾雖賢不得爲嫡.

④ Ibid.,10,11a:天子諸侯一娶九女者何? 重國廣繼嗣也.Ibid.,13b,大夫成功受封,得備八妾者,重國廣嗣也.

⑤ *Pai hu t'ung*,10.11b:不娶兩娣何? 博導氣也.娶三國女何? 廣異類也.恐一國血脈相似,以無子也.

⑥ Ibid.,備姪娣從者,爲其必不相嫉妒也.一人有子,三人共之,若己生之也.*Kung-yung chuan*,莊公十九年,8.2a:何休注:必以姪娣從之者,欲使一人有子,二人喜也.所以防嫉妒,令繼重嗣也.因以備尊尊親親也.

then sent to the bridegroom①; but this was rather unusual. In theory, a feudal lord married only once in his life②; if the principal wife, *fu jên*, died a yin might act for the *fu jên* in her ceremonal and social capacities but could not assume the title of *fu jên*.③ Actually, the yin had very little legal status, and were only "legalized mistresses" of the feudal lord.

The ministers, *Ch'ing ta fu*, of the feudal lords could have one wife and two concubines, but could not take the wife's sisters or nieces as yin.④ There are discrepancies in the interpretation of this rule in the classical works, and in a few instances the ministers followed the feudal lords' example and took the wife's younger sister and niece as concubines.⑤ The scholar class, *shih*, i. e., the lower ruling class, were allowed one wife and one concubine.⑥ Opinions differ as to whether or not this one concubine could be the wife's younger sister or niece. According to Ku Yen-wu (1613-1682), a scholar could not take his wife's younger sister or niece as concubine.⑦ All commoners were allowed only one woman, at least in theory.⑧

To judge from the evidence, the yin custom may have been only a kind of "legalized incest", whereby the emperor and feudal lords might assure themselves of an heir. Some of the lower nobility however, might have followed

---

① *Kung-yang chuan* 隱公七年,3.8a:叔姬歸於紀.注:叔姬者,伯姬之媵也.至是乃歸者,待年父母之國也.

② Ibid.,莊公十九年,8.2a:諸侯一聘九女,諸侯不再娶.

③ *Tso Chuan* 隱公元年,2.2b-3a:孟子卒,繼室以聲子.杜注:諸侯始娶,則同姓之國以姪娣媵,元紀死則次妃攝治内事,猶不得稱夫人,謂之繼室. This rule was not absolute, cf. *Pai hu t'ung*, 10-19.

④ *Pai hu t'ung*, 10.17b:卿大夫一妻二妾何? 尊賢重繼嗣也.不備姪娣何? 北面之臣賤,勢不足盡人骨肉之親也.

⑤ E. g., *Tso Chuan*, 35.18*a*:初臧宣叔娶於鑄,生賈及爲而死,繼室以其姪.

⑥ *Pai hu t'ung*, 10. 18a:士一妻一妾何? 下卿大夫禮也.喪服小記曰:士妾有子,則爲之緦.

⑦ *Jih chih lu*, 5.34b: 貴臣貴妾條.

⑧ This is what was called 匹夫匹婦. In fact, under the feudal system, the title to all land was held by the feudal lord, and the common people workad under a "serf" system; no one could afford two women unless he belonged to the ruling class.

suit later. It is not difficult to see why such a highly arbitrary custom could not have become very prevalent even among the nobility; not only was the supply of women limited, but the practice actually ran counter to the generation-principle ideology of this period. For example, a feudal lord was not allowed to marry the noble women of his own estate, because, theoretically, everyone within his feudal state was his subject, and if the lord were married to any woman in his own state her parents would automatically be a generation higher than he and thus could no longer be his subjects. To avoid this contradiction, a feudal lord was required to marry outside his own state.① yin marriage was swept away with the feudal system during the third century B. C. Since the beginning of the Western Han period (B. C. 206-A. D. 8), the practice has never again been recorded, either among the royalty or the nobility.②

When we turn to the ancient kinship system, we find there a peculiarity which seems to reflect the practice of marriage with the wife's brother's daughter. In the *Êrh Ya* sister's sons are called *chu* (M.S.). In a later passage, the same relative is called *shêng*. It has been remarked above, in connection with cross-cousin marriage, that in the *Êrh Ya*, *shêng* is principally used for father's sister's sons, mother's brother's sons, wife's brothers, and sister's hushand (M.S.) This use of *shêng* to mean sister's sons does not comply very well with the generation principle stressed in the *Êrh Ya*.③

There is also a peculiar usage of *shêng* in the works of Mencius [B. C. 373-289]. Mencius used *shêng* to mean daughter's husband.④ It seems that the overriding of the generation principle in the use of *shêng*, was a phenomenon

---

① *Pai hu t'ung*, 10.15a: 諸侯所以不得自娶國中何? 諸侯不得專封,義不臣其父母.春秋傳曰:宋三世無大夫,惡其内娶也.

② Some students have even suspected that the yin marriage custom was a mere invention of the Han scholars.

③ The only other term is the *Êrh Ya* which overrides generations, is *shu* 叔, for father's younger brother and husband's younger brotber.

④ *Mêng tzŭ*, 10A. 10b:舜尚見帝,帝館甥於貳室……

that appeared rather late in the feudal period. *shêng* was applied, during the feudal period, to 1. father's sister's sons; 2. mother's brother's sons; 3. wife's brothers; 4. sister's husband (M.S.); 5. sister's son (M.S.); 6. daughter's husband.

The first four connotations can be interpreted in terms of cross-cousin marriage of the bilateral type, together with sister exchange. The last two meanings seem to demand a cross-cousin marriage of the above type, together with a marriage with the wife's brother's daughter. In a case of this sort, both sister's husband and sister's son can marry ego's daughter, and ego's daughter's husband will he identified with both sister's husband and sister's son. However, in view of the fact that marriage with the wife's brother's daughter was only a "legalized incest" among the nobility and never a prevalent practice, teknonymy is a more plausible, and a simpler, explanation. Both sister's son and daughter's husband will be *shêng* to ego's own son, if cross-cousin marriage is assumed; ego simply adopts the son's term in addressing them.

On the whole, the influence of the sororate, both on the ancient and modern kinship systems, has been rather negligible. Insofar as the evidence goes, the sororate, both in ancient and modern China., is only a permissive type of marriage, that is to say, ego's marriage with one woman does not affect the status of marriage of her sisters, nor does it affect ego's own marriage status.

Levirate①

The junior levirate certainly exists in a few parts of modern China, at least

① Sir James Frazer has insisted upon the intimate co-existence of the sororate and the levitate (*Totemism and Exogamy*, 1910, 4. 139-150). R. H. LOWIE also says: "The connection would undoubtedly appear to be even closer were not much of our information on marriage rules of primitive tribes of rather haphazard character. That is, it may safely be assumed that in not a few' instances it is sheer negligence or defective observation that has made writers report one of the two customs without the other." (*Primitive Society*, 1920, p. 36.) if this correlation is valid, we should find the levirate in China as a correlative institution.

among the poorer classes①, but, even in the few places where it is practiced, it is not considered respectable. A man adopts this only as a last resort in getting a wife. If necessary, he can sell his brother's widow and use the "bride-price" to marry another woman. Legally, marriage with the older brother's or younger brother's widow is stringently prohibited②; the punishment is strangulation for both parties. G. Jamieson has doubted its existence in China at all under such heavy penalties.③

Whether or not the junior levirate existed in ancient China is quite problematical. Granet cites two cases from the *Tso Chuan*, but these can hardly be interpreted as evidence for the levirate.④ Chên and Shryock say that "the

---

① Cf. *China Review*, 10(1881-2), 71, The levirate in China. Also. HUANG Huachieh 黄華節, Shu chieh sao 叔接嫂, *Eastern Miscellany*, 31:7 (1934), 婦 20-21. P. G. Von Möllendorff once remarked, "I have not heen able to find the slightest trace of it (levirate), and it can never be of the same importance with the Chinese as with other people (e. g. to keep the family property), as posthumous adoption, the Chinese substitute for it" fully meets the object. *The Family Law of the Chinese*(1896), 17.

② This law was first explicitly stated in the *Ming lü chi chieh* 6.20, promulgated during the period Hung-wu. 1368-1398 A. D. (latest revision, 1610 A. D.). In all earlier codes the levirate was prohibited under a more general clause, e. g., in the *T'ang lü shu i*, 14, 3a: 諸嘗爲袒免親之妻而嫁娶者,各杖一百.緦麻及舅甥妻,徒一年.小功以上以姦論.妾各減二等,並離之. Under this clause, the levirate is out of the question.

On the other hand, the explicit clause in the Ming Code against the levirate may be a reaction to its introduction into China through the Mongols of the yuan dynasty. Cf.李魯人:元代蒙古收繼婚俗傳入内地之影響.大公報,史地週刊,No. 8,April 10,1936, (Sheet 11),p. 3.

③ *China Review* 10.83 says:"In view of the severe penalty for it, it is scarcely possible that the levirate can be practiced in any part of China."

④ *La civilisation chinoise*, 424-425. The two cases cited are: Pi Wu-Ts'un (LEGGE, *Chinese Classics*, Ⅴ: ⅱ, 773); *Tzŭ Yüan and Hsi Kuei* (Ibid., Ⅴ: ⅰ, 115). In the first case, Pi Wu-Ts'un, who was going to war and intended to marry a woman of better status, refused his father's proposal on the pretext that his father would be able to marry his younger brother to the woman in question. The woman proposed by his father not only cannot he regarded as his wife, but not even as his fiancée. In the second case, Tzŭ Yüan already had the full authority of the state of ch'u, and did not need to marry his older brother's widow in order to acquire his brother's authority, as Granet's theory demands. On the other hand, Hsi Kuei was a noted beauty and Tzŭ Yüan's attempted Seduction was motivated by lust. Unfortunately for Granet's thesis, Tzŭ Yüan did not succeed in seducing her, and was soon killed.

According to the ancient mourning specifications, sister-in-law and brother-in-law are not subject to mourning obligations, hence Granet considers his hypothesis confirmed inasmuch as relatives without mourning obligations may marry. But mere mourning obligations do not prevent marriage, e. g., cross-cousins have mourning obligations to each other but, according to Granet's theory, they are prescribed to marry!

What we need are actual instances of the levirate-not this ambiguous and anomalous kind of material which may he interpreted to support any kind of hypothesis. Granet is laboring to use the sororate and levirate as proof of an earlier fraternal groupmarriage which is in itself a hopeless hypothesis.

relationship terms indicates only the junior levirate, in which an older brother marries his deceased younger brother's wife. A wife calls her husband and her husband's older brother (possible husbands) by the same term, *po*, but uses a different term for his younger brother."① The authors are somewhat confused in this. Where only the older brother can marry the younger brother's widow, the practice is termed the "senior" levirate, not the "junior" levirate. The "senior" levirate alone is not found in Asia. Either both forms of the levirate are practiced by the same people, or the junior levirate alone is practiced, as in India, southeastern Asia, and northeastern Asia. There is also an anachronism in the connotations of *po* cited by the authors. In a few places in the "Book of Odes", *po* is interpreted as meaning husband②, but this usage is not found in literature after 500 B. C. On the other hand, the use of *po* to mean husband's older brother did not begin until the tenth century A. D.③ Thus, *po* meaning husband and *po* meaning husband's older brother not only are not contemporaneous, but are separated by a hiatus of fifteen centuries! Historically minded though the Chinese may be, I do not see how one can interpret this terminology in terms of the levirate.

Chattopadhyay has interpreted the differentiation of older-and younger brothers in India in terms of the junior levirate.④ Such an interpretation is

---

① CHÊN and SHRYOCK, *op. cit.*, 628-629.

② *Shih Ching*, 3C. 7a-8b：伯兮朅兮，邦之桀兮；伯也執殳，爲王前驅.自伯之東，首如飛蓬，豈無膏沐，誰適爲容……The *po* used here is sometimes interpreted as meaning husband, but it is uncertain whether *po* is a relationship term for husband, or a reference to the official title the husband holds, or simply a word meaning "the brave and handsome one." To judge from the context, the last is the preferable interpretation.

③ T'ao Yo 陶岳, *Wu tai shih pu* 五代史補(豫章叢書本),5. 8*a*：(李) 濤爲人不拘補法，與弟澣雖甚雍睦，然聚話之際，不典之言，往往間作.澣娶禮部尚書竇寧固之女，年甲稍高，成婚之名，竇氏出參濤，輒望塵下拜.澣驚曰：大哥風狂耶？新婦參阿伯，豈有答禮儀？濤應曰：我不風，只將是親家母.

④ Chattopadhyay, Levirate and Kinship in India. *Man*, 22 (1922), 25. W. Lloyd WARNER, Kinship Morphology of Forty-one North Australian Tribes, *American Anthropologist* 35. 66 makes a similar interpretation.

extremely weak, unless supported by other terminological corroboration. If the junior levirate explains the differentiation of older and younger brothers, it certainly does not explain the differentiation of older and younger sisters, which is also characteristic of most Indian systems. Whether or not the *tsung fa* adequately explains the expression of the category of age in generation in the Chinese system, as advocated by the old Chinese authors, we do not know; certainly this expression cannot be explained by the junior levirate, which is of so sporadic occurrence in China.

Teknonymy

We have already discussed several types of marriages that are relevant to the determination of minor kinship peculiarities. With the exception of cross-cousin marriage, the influence of the others, both on the ancient and modern systems, has been rather negligible. These problems will be further discussed here in connection with teknonymy and other peculiarities in the system, in order to ascertain the actual determining factor or factors.

As has already been shown, generation is an important structural principle in the Chinese system. It also regulates marriage among relatives, and plays an important rôle in the functioning of Chinese social and ceremonial life as a whole, since the dealings between relatives are in many respects based upon generation differences, so also in the assignment of mourning grades, etc. Since generation is such an important factor in the system, we should expect it to be consistently expressed in terminology. Yet there are some notable exceptions, mother's brother and wife's brother are designated by the same term, *chiu*; mother's sister and wife's sister by the same term, *i*; father's older brother and husband's older brother by the same term, *po*; father's younger brother and husband's younger brother by the same *term*, *shu*; father's sister and husband's sister by the same term, *ku*; etc. These peculiarities are of significance, because originally the generations of these relatives were clearly differentiated by distinct terms, and only in the course of time were they gradually merged into each other.

First, let us take the connotations of the term *chiu*, and the terms for the wife's brother, during the various periods, and arrange them in a single table, as follows:

Period	Connotations of *chiu*	Terms for wife's brother
I 1st Millennium B. C.	mother's brother husband's father wife's father	*shêng*
Ⅱ 1st Millennium A. D.	mother's brother	*fu hsiung ti*
Ⅲ 2nd Millennium A. D.	mother's brother wife's brother	*chiu*

The various connotations of the term *chiu* in Period I are perfectly intelligible from the point of view of cross-cousin marriage, as discussed above. In such a marriage, the mother's brother and husband's father is the same person, so also the mother's brother and wife's father. In Period Ⅱ the cross-cousin marriage was dropped, and consequently the meaning of *chiu* became confined to mother's brother.

The terms for the wife's brother are different for each of the three periods. In Period I wife's brother was called *shêng* 甥. *Shêng* also meant, in this period, father's sister's son, mother's brother's son and sister's husband (man speaking).① This is also explicable in terms of cross-cousin marriage of the

① Cf. *Êrh Ya*.

bilateral type, coupled with sister exchange. In Period Ⅱ, because of the disappearance of this type of marriage, *shêng* was no longer applicable to any of these relatives and new terms were introduced to take its places. *Fu hsiung ti* is the term used for wife's brother.①

In Period Ⅲ the term *chiu* (mother's brother) was extended to include wife's brother. The first use of *chiu* in this new meaning is to be found in the *Hsin T'ang Shu*. In the biography of Chu Yen-shou, we read: "Yang Hsing-mi's wife is the older sister of Chu Yen-shou …… Hsing-mi [luring Chu Yen-shou into a trap] says, 'I have lost my eyesight and my sons are too young. Having *chiu* [meaning Chu Yen-shou] take my place, I shall have no worry.'"② This is certainly a curious extension of the use of *chiu*, for, through all the previous vicissitudes of the term, the generation element had always been preserved. This overriding of the generation principle certainly warrants an explanation.

A strictly sociological interpretation would point to a marriage with the wife's brother's daughter. In Period I *chiu* also meant father-inlaw; since, in this interpretation, the wife's brother is a potential father-in-law, the extension of the term *chiu* to include him would be perfectly logical. However, there are several difficulties in such an interpretation. In the first place, historical evidence does not seem to support this hypothesis, wife's brother's daughter marriage in connection with the yin custom was never a preferred form, nor, as stated above, was it common even among the feudal nobility. Moreover, it disappeared together with the feudal system during the third century B. C., and has never been practiced since. Secondly, *chiu* had ceased to mean wife's father

① The term is purely descriptive. *Fu* 婦 means wife, *hsiung ti* means brother (older and younger). *Pei Ch'i Shu* 崔昂傳, 30.9b-10a: 崔昂直巨, 魏收才士, 婦兄⊙夫, 俱省罪過. Ibid., 鄭元禮傳, 29.6b: 但知⊙夫, 疏於婦弟. *Ch'i hsiung ti* 妻兄弟 and *nei hsiuny ti* 内兄弟 were also permissible at this time. Cf. Table Ⅲ. (From this point the editors have been forced to substitute the symbol ⊙ for some frequently recurring characters. In this instance the missing characters are No. 11 on p. 155.)

② *Hsin T'ang shu* 朱延壽傳, 189.10a: 田頵之附全忠, 延壽陰約曰: 公有所爲, 我願執鞭. 頵喜. 二人謀絶行密. 行密憂甚, 給病目, 行觸柱, 僵. 妻, 延壽姊也, 掖之. 行密泣曰: 吾喪明, 諸子幼, 得⊙代, 我無憂矣. (The missing character is No. 16 on p. 156.)

at least a thousand years before it was extended to mean wife's brother. These two temporal considerations, involving a hiatus of more than a millennium, are irreconcilable with such an interpretation. Thirdly, such a marriage contradicts the generation principle; wife's brother's daughter is one generation lower than ego; and thus, in the Chinese system, is within the incest group. Legally, inter-generation marriage between all relatives became definitely prohibited at least half a millennium before *chiu* was extended to mean wife's brother.① In the face of these objections, the above interpretation is untenable.

It is significant that Chinese scholars had been employing teknonymy to explain this terminological anomaly long before the introduction of the term into anthropological discussion by E. B. Tylor.② Ch'ien Ta-hsin〔1727-1804〕, one of the most penetrating classical scholars of his time, attributed this extension of the meaning of *chiu* to the gradual, imperceptible effect of the practice of teknonymy,③ wife's brothers are *chiu* to one's own children. The father, adopting the language of his children, also calls his wife's brothers *chiu*. This process can clearly be seen in the above-mentioned instance of Chu Yen-shou. Yang Hsingmi called Chu Yen-shou *chiu*, at the same time mentioning his own sons. One can infer that, after long teknonymous usage, the term *chiu* established itself and finally displaced the older term.

Whether or not this hypothesis can be sustained depends upon the additional evidence we can adduce for its support, or, in other words, upon whether or not it can explain all the peculiarities of the same nature in the system. Let us now turn to the examination of those terms by which the wife addresses her husband's brothers: *po* for the husband's older brother, and *shu* for the husband's younger brother. But *po* was originally a term for father's older

---

① The T'ang Code, compiled and promulgated during the period A. D. 627-683, stringently prohibits inter-generation marriage: *T'ang lü shu i* 13.2.

② On a Method of Investigating the Development of Institutions, *Journal*, *Anthropological Institute*, 18 (1889), 245-269.

③ *Hêng yen lu*, 3.13b:予按……後世妻之兄弟獨得舅名,蓋從其子女之稱,遂相沿不覺耳。

brother, and *shu* for father's younger brother. This overriding of generations is quite aberrant, from any point of view. Insofar as I am aware, there is no social or marital usage in China, nor is there any comparable usage that ethnographic data suggest, which could give rise to such a terminology.

From the historical point of view, the terms for these relatives were different at different periods. In the *Êrh Ya* the father's older brother is called *shih fu*. From the second century B. C. down to the present *po fu* has been the standard term, but from the fourth century A. D. on, *po* alone also has been in use.①

In the *Êrh Ya* husband's older brother is called *hsiung kung*.② During the succeeding centuries *hsiung chang* was commonly employed.③ Ca. the tenth century A, D. *po* was extended to include husband's older brother.④

In the *Êrh Ya* the father's younger brother is called *shu fu*. This term has continued in use without any radical change down to the present; as in the case of *po*, above, from the fourth century A. D. on *shu* alone has also been in use. *Shu* is also used in the *Êrh Ya* for husband's younger brother. This usage is rather unusual, inasmuch as it overrides generations and thus contradicts its own statement of principle, that "husband's siblings are affinal siblings."⑤

As has been stated above, no possible explanation for this blending of generations can be found in marriage forms; the only possible alternative is teknonymy. Husband's brother's are *po* and *shu* to female ego's own children. The mother, adopting the terminology of her children, also calls them *po* and *shu*. This case tremendously strengthens our hypothesis, since no other known social factor or form of marital relationship can adequately explain these usages.

---

① *Li Chi* 曾子曰,18.10a:已祭而見伯父叔父.*Yen shih chia hsün* 風操篇 2.6b:古人皆呼伯父叔父,而今世多單呼伯叔.Cf. *Hêng yen lu*, 3.6-7.

② 夫之兄爲兄公.

③ *Shih Ming*. 夫之兄……俗間曰兄章.Cf.Table Ⅳ, term 5.

④ See p. 215, note ②.

⑤ *Êrh Ya*:婦之黨爲婚兄弟,⊙之黨爲姻兄弟.(The missing character is No.18 on p. 156.)

A similar situation exists in the terminology for father's sister and husband's sister, both called *ku*, and mother's sister and wife's sister, called *i*.

As has already been pointed out, *ku* is used in the *Êrh Ya* for father's sister, husband's mother, and wife's mother [e. g., *wai ku*] as a result of cross-cousin marriage. When cross-cousin marriage declined, *ku* was usually employed for father's sister alone. In the *Êrh Ya*, husband's older sister is called *nü kung*, and younger sister *nü mei*.① Somewhat later *shu mei* was used for the husband's younger sister.② In the fourth century A. D. the term *ku* began to be extended to includc husband's sisters.③ The factors behind this extension cannot be exactly ascertained, although the marriage rules and social customs of the period concerned are fairly well known. The extension could not have been due to marriage with the wife's brother's daughter, in which case the husband's sister would be elevated to the position of the husband's father's sister; the above-cited objections to a similar interpretation of *chiu* also apply here. Furthermore, other features do not follow either terminologically④ or conceptually.⑤ Teknonymy remains the best explanation since husband's sisters are *ku* to female ego's own children.

---

① 夫之姊爲女公,夫之女弟爲女⊙.(No. 11 on p. 155.)

② *Hou Han Shu* 曹世叔妻《班昭》傳,114,8b:婦人之得意於夫主,由⊙姑之愛己也;⊙姑之愛己,由叔⊙之譽己也.(First and second are no. 16 on p. 156; last,No. 11 on p. 155.)

③ The earliest occurrence of the term *hsiao ku* for husband's sister is in the famous poem 古詩爲焦仲卿妻作 (*Yü T'ai hsin yung chi*,1.17b):却與小姑别,泪落連珠子.新婦初來時,小姑始扶床,今日被驅遣,小姑如我長. The literature on the dating of this poem has already become enormous. Hu Shih tends to date it earlier than most others, about the middle of the third century A. D., cf. 現代評論, 6:149.9-14:孔雀東南飛的年代. Others tend to date it much later, about the fourth and fifth centuries A. D.

④ E.g., among the Miwok, where marriage with the wife's brother's daughter is reflected in twelve terms (E. W. GIFFORD, *Miwok Moieties*, University of California Publications in American Archaeology and Ethnology, 1916, p. 186), but these are all lacking in the Chinese system.

⑤ Among the Omaha, marriage with the wife's brother's daughter is reflected in the conceptual identification of the father's sister, the female ego, and the brother's daughter [A. LESSER, Kinship Origins in the Light of Some Distributions, *American Anthropologist* 31 (1929), 711-712], but it is not indicated in the terminology. In the Chinese system the generations of father's sister, husband's father's sister, and the husband's sister are clearly distinguished conceptually, although the terminology fails to differentiate them.

Originally *i* was used, as in the *Êrh Ya*, for wife's sisters. In the *Êrh Ya* mother's sisters are called *Ts'ung mu*. The earliest use of *i* to mean mother's sister is found in the *Tso Chuan*. In the twenty-third year (B. C. 550) of Duke Hsiang, a passage reads, "*I*'s daughter of Mu Chiang. "① By checking the relatives connected with Mu Chiang, one finds that the term, *i*, here does not mean wife's sister (or married sister, woman speaking) as it should, but mother's sister. As a matter of fact, the passage should read, "*Ts'ung mu's* daughter of Mu Chiang," *not*, "*i*'s daughter."

Theoretically, the sororate, together with a marriage with the father's widows, would adequately explain the usage. In this combined type of marriage, the father marries mother's sisters and ego marries wife's sisters. Ego again marries father's widows after his decease. Then mother's sisters become equated with wife's sisters. This explanation seems fantastic but has some support, since a man's secondary wives (concubines) may also be called *i*, i. e., mother's sisters, wife's sisters, and secondary wives are all grouped in one class. It is well known that the sororate was practiced among the feudal nobility, but, as regards the inheritance of father's widows, there is no authenticated evidence.② Indeed, such a marriage would have been abhorrent

---

① *Tso chuan* 襄公二十三年, 35.18a.

② M. Granet cites the case of Duke Hsüan (718-700 B. C.) of Wei who married his father's concubine I Chiang (*La civilisation chinoise*, p. 401). Apparently, Granet is not aware of the fact that Ku Tung-kao 顧棟高 (1679-1757) has convincingly shown that I Chiang had not previously been Duke Hsüan's father's concubine (*Ch'un Ch'iu ta shih piao* 春秋大事表,清經解 ed,. 50. 3a-4b: 衛夷姜晉齊姜辨). Even if it be admitted that this is an authentic instance of step-mother and step-son marriage, nothing is proved thereby, since the instance is quite anomalous. Not only are such anomalies recorded in quite a few instances from the Ch'un Ch'iu period, but also examples of incest, involving actual blood relationship, like grandmother and grandson, brother and sister, cf. 王士廉:左淫類記. But Granet has omitted these. Indeed, such anomalies are always cropping up in Chinese history, even in quite recent times, e. g., the T'ang Emperor Kao-tsung (650-684) married his father's concubine Wu Chao 武曌 later known as the notorious Empress Wu of the T'ang dynasty, and the Emperor Hsüan-tsung (712-756) married his son's concubine Yang Yü-huan, well known to Europeans as the foremost beauty of China. One wonders how Granet would interpret these instances.

to the ancient Chinese. We learn that the old writers detested the Hsiung-nu, pastoral nomads of the northern steppes, who married their fathers' widows, and never failed to mention this as an excuse for derision.①

K'ung Ying-ta (A. D. 574-648) explained the extension of *i* to include mother's sister (Ts'ung mu) as due to the psychological similarity between these relatives.② Mother's sister's are *i* to one's father, just as wife's sisters are *i* to oneself. The son, imitating the language of his father, also applies *i* to his father's *i*. In short, this case seems to demand a psychological explanation, together with reverse teknonymy.

The connotations of *shên* are likewise of significance. Father's younger brother's wife and husband's younger brother's wife are both called *shên* in the vocative. In the *Êrh Ya* father's younger brother's wife is called *shu mu*, which is the standard term today. *Shên* first came into use during the Sung period; it is usually regarded as a contracted pronunciation of *shih mu*.③ Its extension to include husband's younger brother's wife was effected about the same period.④ No possible marital relationships could give rise to such an equation of relatives, nor could any other sociological factor. Teknonymy offers the simplest solution. Husband's younger brother's wife is the *shên* of female ego's children.

The origin of the terms *kung*, for husband's father, and *P'o*, for husband's mother, has never been investigated. The old term for husband's father is *chiu*, and for husband's mother, *ku*, both of which reflect cross-cousin marriage, During the first millennium A. D. a large number of terms were introduced for the designation of these two relatives, since *chiu* and *ku* were no longer

---

① *Shih Chi* 匈奴列傳, 110.2a: 父死妻其後母,兄弟死皆取其妻妻之. The Hsiung-Nu customs of marrying father's widows other than one's own mother and the levirate were so well known to the ancient Chinese that they frequently mentioned them as a sign of the moral inferiority of the Hsiung-nu.

② *Tso Chuan* 襄公二十三年, 35. 18 a.

③ *Ming tao tsa chih*, 13b:王聖美嘗言,經傳無嬸字……考其説,嬸字乃世母二字合呼也. *Shih mu*, pronounced as one word, because *shim*, or *shên*.

④ *Tzŭ wei tsa chi* 紫薇雜記, of Lü Tzu-Ch'ien 吕祖謙, 1137-1181 A. D. (*Shuo fu* 説郛,19)2a:吕氏舊俗,母母受嬸房婢拜,以受其主母拜也.嬸見母母房婢妮,即答拜,是亦毋尊尊之義也……母母於嬸處自稱名,或去名不稱新婦,嬸於母處則稱之. *Mu mu* is used in the sense of husband's older brother's wife, and *shên* in the sense of husband's younger brother's wife.

applicable after the discontinuance of that particular type of marriage, but *kung* and *p'o* finally gained prevalence.①

On the other hand, *kung* and *P'o* are prevalent grandparent terms.② Why the wife should apply grandparent terms to the husband's parents is rather perplexing. This terminology is most susceptible to marital irregularities, but we cannot see what marital form, no matter how startling, could be involved here. But if we assume teknonymy, the situation immediately explains itself.

The foregoing cases comprise the most significant terminological anomalies, and constitute about all the instances in the Chinese system, both ancient and modern, where the generation principle is openly violated. In every case we have tried to explain these exceptions by facts and hypotheses which have proved illuminating in the discussion of analogous phenomena elsewhere. But we have found none of them applicable to the Chinese situation; rather, we have found teknonymy the only satisfactory explanation.

There can be no doubt that teknonymy is the determining factor in all these cases, but one may ask whether teknonymy is universal in China and of sufficient antiquity to have been involved in producing such effects in kinship terminology. The universality of this practice in China is unquestionable; the frequency of its use, however, might have varied in time and place. At times the practice was so accentuated that the ordinary forms of address became hardly intelligible.③ In many regions, e. g., Wusih, Kiangsu, the bride ordinarily addresses her husband's relatives as if she were one generation lower. The teknonymy practiced is usually of the type that omits the child's name, just as in English a man may call his wife simply "mother." This type is especially

---

① See Table Ⅳ, terms 1 and 2.

② See Table Ⅰ, terms 13 and 14.

③ E.g., the extreme instance of the practice of teknonymy in South China, as recorded in the *Ch'ing hsiang tsa chi* 青箱雜記, by Wu ch'u-hou 吳處厚 ca. 1080 A. D. (涵芬樓 ed.) 3.2b-3a, of the Sung period, which reads: 嶺南風俗相呼不以行第,唯以各人所生男女小名呼其父母.元豐中(1078-1085),餘任大理丞,斷賓州(modern 賓陽縣 in Kwangsi)奏案,有民韋超,男名首,即呼韋超作父首.韋遨男名滿,即呼韋遨作父滿.韋全【男】女名插娘,即呼韋全爲父插.韋庶女名睡娘,即呼庶作父睡,妻作嬸睡.

efficacious in producing the irregularities just discussed.

As regards the antiquity of teknonymy, we must depend upon historical evidence. The earliest instance that can be interpreted as teknonymy is recorded in Kung-yang's commentary on the *Spring and Autumn Annals* (Ch'un Ch'iu). In the sixth year of Duke Ai (B. C.489) is recorded an instance concerning Ch 'ên Ch'i. He, in referring to his wife, says, "The mother of Ch 'ang...'"① Ch'ang is known to have been Ch'ên Ch'i's son. The teknonymous usage here is indubitably clear. This instance, in the fifth century B. C., is more than a millennium earlier than most of the cases we have discussed above, except those involving *i* and *shêng*, which are about contemporaneous. On the other hand, if we make allowance for the conservative spirit of the classical writers in recording colloquial language, it is reasonable to infer that teknonymy is much older than this documentary evidence would indicate.

The influence of teknonymy on kinship terminology is quite apparent. Gifford, in discussing similar usages in the English and Californian kinship terminologies, has cogently remarked: "There must be, in other kinship systems, many analogous cases (cases analogous to the English teknonymy of calling husband "daddy" and wife "mother"), some of them crystallized into invariable custom like the Luiseňo case, cases which require no startling form of marriage for their explanation, but which could be readily understood as our own, if we were but familiar with the family of the group in question."②

In the very limited literature on teknonymy, various theories have been put

---

① *Kung-yang chuan* 哀公六年,27.12a:諸大夫皆在朝,陳乞曰:常之母,有魚菽之祭,願諸大夫之化我也.

② *Californian Kinship Terminoloyies* 265. In the Chinese instances the situation is so apparent that even so amateur an observer as Hart has been led to remark: "The nomenclature employed in the designation of two brothers-in-law and two sisters-in-law, i. e., by a wife toward the brothers and sisters of her husband, and by a husband toward the brothers and sisters of his wife, seems to have its origin in the names applied to such people by the children (their class children, or nephews and nieces) born of the marriage. Thus an individual's wife's brother is the *kew* 〔= *chiu*〕 of that individual's children, and that individual in speaking of him as his brother-in-law, employs the same word, *kew*, to designate him as such, so with the other." (Morgan, *Systems*..., p. 413.) Morgan, however, engrossed in his evolutionary "stage building," entirely overlooked this pertinent remark.

forth to account for its origin, but no serious attempt has been made to use it in explanation of other social phenomena. Teknonymy as a usage is based on kinship and kinship nomenclature—a circumlocutory way of expressing embarrassing relationships. Through long and intensive use, why should it not have produced certain peculiarities in kinship terminologies, as other social usages are reputed to have done? The Chinese cases are especially illuminating. It would require a series of marital or other special practices to explain the peculiarities of *chiu*, *po*, *shu*, *ku*, *i*, *shên*, *kung*, *p'o* and *shêng*, whereas they can uniformly be explained by the single principle of teknonymy.

Historical Review of Terms

The Chinese method of counting relationships starts with the three nearest kin, i. e., parent-child, husband-wife, and brother-sister, and extends out in all directions. Whenever one comes to the question of Chinese kinship extensions, one always stumbles upon the problem of *chiu tsu* 九族, "nine grades of kindred." This is a much discussed but vague term, which first occurs in the *Book of History*.① Its interpretation comprises two major theories, representing two different schools of classical commentators. The Modern Script School interprets the *chiu tsu* as follows: The four groups of relatives of the father; plus the three groups of relatives of the mother; plus the two groups of relatives of the wife.

The four groups of relatives of the father are: 1. With ego in the center,

① *Shu Ching* 堯典, 2.7b: 以親九族. Whether this is the earliest use of the term or not is very questionable, since the antiquity and authenticity of the 堯典 is much questioned. However this is the focal point of later controversies. 顧頡剛 has a very penetrating discussion of the *Problem of Chiu tsu* 九族問題, in 清華週刊 37: 9-10, 105-111.

counting four generations above, four generations below, and the four collateral lines each counting four generations from the lineal line from males through males. 2. father's sisters, when married, and their descendants. 3. Ego's sisters, when married, and their descendants. 4. Ego's daughters, when married, and their descendants.

The three groups of relatives of the mother are: 5. Mother's father and mother. 6. Mother's brothers. 7. Mother's sisters.

The two groups of relatives of the wife are: 8. Wife's father. 9. Wife's mother.

This interpretation is not followed by the Ancient Script School of classical commentators, who believe the *chiu tsu* includes only the sib relatives but not the non-sib relatives. Therefore, according to their interpretation, the *chiu tsu* takes into account only the first of the above nine groups of relatives. That is, the *chiu tsu* means simply nine "generations," viz., the four ascending and the four descending generations, with *ego* in the middle. Naturally because of the collective responsibility of the individual's social actions, many students tend to narrow down the interpretation in order to lessen the social and legal complications. The *chiu tsu* problem, however, is purely an academic and historical matter.

In the present work the classification of the *Êrh Ya* is generally followed. The actual extent of the terminology listed, however, is entirely dictated by the needs of modern research and by the material available, although all those relatives within the Chinese mourning grades are included. The sib relatives are emphasized, but such emphasis is unavoidable in a system based strictly upon a patrilineal social grouping, where many of the terms for non-sib relatives are merely extended combinations from those for sib relatives.

The relatives are divided into two main groups and subdivided into four tables. The two main divisions are Consanguineal Relatives and Affinal

Relatives. Under Consanguineal, there is a subdivision into Relatives through Father and Relatives through Mother; and under Affinal, into Relatives through Wife and Relatives through Husband. Under each group are also listed persons connected through marriage, that is the "in-law's"; this is a conventional practice.

In the tables the modern standard terminology is given first under each entry; these terms represent the system as it now stands. The slight variant combinations in some of the compounded terms have been carefully collated against one another from contemporary sources. In collating, two criteria were adopted: the statistical and inferential; i. e., if two or more forms are equally common, that form inferentially most in keeping with the working principles of the system is given as the standard form, and the others are given as alternatives. These variations are rather insignificant, and, in view of the number of people using the system and the geographical extent of the system, quite inevitable.

Under each standard term are given the historical terms in their chronological order. Their exact nature, whether alternative, literary, or dialectical① is indicated, together with their modern status.② Following them come the referential and vocative terminologies. If no terms are given, it is understood that they can be formed from previously stated formulae. No stereotyped order is followed, but generally the treatment varies according to the nature of the material and in keeping with special circumstances.

Citations illustrating the use of terms are given in the notes. It is possible only to give citations for the earliest occurrence of a new term, or for an old term used in a new meaning. In some cases, the most typical instances are

---

① Dialectical differences in Chinese kinship terminology have been somewhat exaggerated. Many of them .are mere local variations in pronunciation which do not affect the morphology of the system.

② I.e., the exact connotation and nature of the term in modern usage, if it is still used.

cited. These citations are of importance, since only through them can the exact nature and chronology of a term be determined.

In the tables I have attempted to record as fully as possible the whole range of terms.① Thus, under the father's father no less than twenty terms are given, under various usages and periods, and in some instances the number is still greater. Of course, not all terms can be so treated, especially terms for distant relatives, which are compounded from the basic terminologies, but the slight variations in any possible combinations are given. A full recording of the whole nomenclature and the determination of the exact nature of each term are indispensable conditions for the proper understanding and interpretation of the system, since most of the early misunderstandings are the result of partial and mixed renderings of the system comprising forms from different strata of the terminology.

Consanguineal Relatives

Relatives through Father Table Ⅰ

I. Generation of the father's father's father's father

1. Kao tsu fu 高祖父 f f f f

In the Classics *kao tsu* was sometimes used to mean any ancestor ascending from grand-father.② In the 17th year of Duke Chao (525 B. C.) in the *Tso Chuan*, the first ancestor was called *kao tsu*.③ In another place the ninth

---

① Terms that are idiosyncracies and have no general currency are excluded. E.g., the Emperor Hsüan of the Northern Chou dynasty did not like others to use the term *kao*, so he changed the term *kao tsu* to *chang tsu*, and *tsêng tsu* to *tz'ŭ chang tsu*: *Pei shih* 周宣帝紀, 10.32a: 又不喜聽人有高者, 大者, ……改…… 九族稱高祖者爲長祖, 曾祖爲次長祖. Terms of such nature will not be considered.

② *Jih chih lu*, 24. la:漢儒以曾祖之父爲高祖,考之於傳,高祖者,遠祖之名爾.

③ *Tso chuan* 昭公十七年,48.5a:郯子曰……我高祖少皞摯之立也……

ancestor was referred to as *kao tsu*.① King K'ang (1078-1053 B. C.) called King Wên and King Wu *kao tsu*, but actually they were his great-grand- and grandfathers.② Apparently, during the Chou period, if the actual father's father's father's father is meant, *wang fu* must be added, like the *kao tsu wang fu* used in the *Êrh Ya*. The term *kao tsu* does not occur in the mourning relations of the *I Li*③ and it is surmised that any lineal relative ascending from *tsêng tsu* may be called *tsêng tsu*.④

During the T'ang period *kao mên*⑤ was used, but infrequently; it was most likely a posthumous term. The posthumous and temple term used in the *Li Chi* is *hsien kao*.⑥ The term is no longer used in this sense. Since the Yüan dynasty (1280-1367) *hsien kao* had been used as an epitaphic term for father.

2. Kao tsu mu 高祖母 f f f m

Kao tsu wang mu 高祖王母 is the term used in the *Êrh Ya*.

3. Kao tsu ku mu 高祖姑母 f f f f si

Kao tsu wang ku 高祖王姑 in the *Êrh Ya*.

---

① Ibid.,昭公十五年,47.11b:五曰……且昔而高祖孫伯黶司晉之典籍,以爲大政,故曰籍氏.The term 高祖 is meant for the ninth ancestor of 籍談 It is also used in the same way in the *Shu Ching*, e. g., 盤庚 9. 17a: 肆上帝將復我高祖之德. The term *kao tsu* refers to Ch'êng T'ang (1765-1760 B. C. ?).

② *Shu Ching*, 康王之誥,19,3a:無壞我高祖寡命.

③ In the 喪服傳 of the *I Li*, since there are no mourning specification for f f f f, the term for him does not occur. In the ritual works, the first use of *kao tsu* for f f f f is the 喪服小記 of the *Li Chi*, 32.7b: 有五世而遷之宗,其繼高祖者也.

④ *Mêng Ch'i pi t' an*, 3.3 a: 喪服但有曾祖曾孫,而無高祖玄孫.曾,重也.自祖而上,皆曾祖也;自孫而下,皆曾孫也;雖百世可也. Very probably the use of *kao tsu* for f f f f, and *tsêng tsu* for f f f is due to the development of the sib organization of the Chou period but originally both of them meant simply "distant ancestors". Cf. 丁山:宗法原考, *CYYY*, 4:4 (1934), 399-415, in which he considers that during the Shang and early Chou periods, exact relationships are only counted to two generations both above and below.

⑤ *Chin shih ts'ui pien* 段行琛碑, 101.11b: 高門平原忠武王孝先, *Ch'êng wei lu*, 1.4a, 按高門,高祖也.

⑥ *Li Chi* 祭法,46.8a-9:顯考廟.疏:曰顯考廟者,高祖也.Ibid.,檀弓,9.12a-13:殷主綴重焉.鄭注:綴,猶聯也.殷人作主而聯其重,縣諸廟也;去顯考乃理之.孔疏:顯考,謂高祖也.

4. Kao tsu ku fu 高祖姑父 f f f f si h

No term is given in the *Êrh Ya*. In tracing relationship through women of the father's sib married out, the terms for these women are usually employed; the terms for their husbands, only infrequently.

Ⅱ. Generation of the father's father's father

5. Tsêng tsu fu 曾祖父 f f f

As a form *tsêng tsu* may be used alone. *Tsêng tsu wang fu* is the term used in the *Êrh Ya*. *Tsêng ta fu*①, *ta wang fu*② and *wang ta fu*③ have been common alternative terms since the sixth century A. D. *Tsêng mên*④ was commonly used during the T'ang period. All these terms may be used posthumously. The ancient posthumous term is *huang kao*⑤, as used in the *Li Chi*. *Huang kao* was later used as a posthumous term for father, but has been prohibited since the Yüan dynasty, since *huang* implies "imperial."

The vocative is rather variable. *T'ai wêng*⑥ and *tsêng wêng*⑦ were common from the fourth to the ninth century A. D. *Wêng* means "venerable old man." *T'ai kung* and *t'ai yeh yeh*⑧ are common modern vocatives.

---

① *Shih chi* 夏本紀,2.1b:禹之父鯀,鯀之父帝顓頊,顓頊之父曰昌意……禹之曾大父昌意及⊙鯀,皆不得在帝位. *Ch'ang-li chi* 崔評事墓銘,24.1b:曾大父知道……(Here and in two following notes supply No. 4, on p. 154.)

② *Chü-chiang wên chi* 裴光庭碑,19.3b:大王⊙定……

③ *chin shih yao li* 書祖⊙例,7b:庚承宣爲田布碑,稱曾祖爲王大父.

④ *Hsin t'ang shu* 孝友程袁師傳,195.6b:……改葬曾門以來,閱十二年乃畢.*Chin shih Ts'ui pien* 比邱尼惠源志銘, 82.13a-19b:曾門梁孝明皇帝…… Chien Ta-hsin (*Chien yen T'ang chin shih wên po wei*, 6.13) says: 稱曾祖爲曾門,未詳其義. From what can be deduced from the evidence, *mên* 門 was a very common posthumous term in referring to lineal relatives from the second ascending generation and upward during the fourth to the eighth centuries A. D. Father's father was called 大門中, father's father's father's father was called 高門, so father's father's father was called 曾門. Its origin may be similar to the term 從兄弟門中 as explained by Yen Chih-t'ui. See p. 254, note ③.

⑤ *Li chi* 祭法,46.8a-9:曰皇考廟.孔疏.曰皇考廟者,曾祖也.

⑥ *Nan Shih* 齊廢帝鬱林皇紀,5.1a:太翁.

⑦ 曾翁.Since *wêng* was commonly used as vocative for grandfather, *tsêng wêng* and *T'ai wêng* were used for great grandfather. *Wêng* may also be used for any venerable old man.

⑧ 太公 and 太爺爺. *T'ai* means "great". *Kung* and *yeh yeh* are vocatives for grandfather; *t'ai kung* and *t'ai yeh yeh*, for great grandfather.

6. Tsêng tsu mn 曾祖母 f f m

In the *Êrh Ya*, *tsêng tsu wang mu*. The most common modern vocative is *t 'ai p'o*, or *t'ai p'o p'o*.①

7. Tsêng po tsu fu 曾伯祖父 f f f o b

Tsu tsêng wang fu is used in the *Êrh Ya*, and *tsu tsêng tsu fu* in the *I Li*.② Both these terms also apply to father's father's father's younger brothers.

8. Tsêng po tsu mu 曾伯祖母 f f f o b w

In the *Êrh Ya*, *tsu tsêng wang mu*, and correspondingly *tsu tsêng tsu mu* in the *I Li*. Both these terms also apply to father's father's father's younger brother's wife.

9. Tsêng sbu tsu fu 曾叔祖父 f f f y b

The vocatives of 7 and 9 are similar to 5, but differentiated by prefixing their numerical order or titles.

10. Tsêng shu tsu mu 曾叔祖母 f f f y b w

The vocatives of 8 and 10 are similar to 6, but differentiated by prefixing their sibnames or their husband's numerical order.

11. Tsêng tsu ku mu 曾祖姑母 f f f si

Tsêng tsu wang ku is the term used in the *Êrh Ya*. Modern vocative, *ku t'ai p'o*.

12. Tsêng tsu ku fu 曾祖姑父 f f f si h

Modern vocative, *ku t'ai kung* 姑太公 or *ku t'ai yeh* 姑太爺.

Ⅲ. Generation of the father's father

13. Tsu fu 祖父 f f

Tsu may be used alone to mean father's father, but it may mean any

---

① 太婆 or 太婆婆. *p'o* or *p'o p'o* are vocatives for grandmother; *t'ai p'o*, for great grandmother. K'ung p'ing-chung 孔平仲, ca. 1080 A. D., 朝散集,豫章叢書 ed., 2.19a:代小子廣孫寄翁翁.太婆八十五,寢膳近何似?

② *I Li* 喪服, 33.6a:族曾祖⊙母.鄭注:族曾祖父母者,曾祖昆弟之親也.

ancestor.① In the *Êrh Ya*, *tsu* was used synonymously with *wang fu*②, but *wang fu is now more often used in the posthumous sense. Since the Han period ta fu*③ has been frequently used. Other early alternative terms, like *tsu chün*④, *tsu wang fu*⑤ and *tsu wêng*⑥, are commonly met in literature. Another common early term is *kung*⑦, which in many localities is still used as a vocative.⑧ Since *kung* is a common complimentary term for any older man, its connotation as a relationship term is indefinite. It is used to mean father, husband's father, etc. *T'ai kung*⑨ is used in the *Hou Hun Shu* to mean father's father, but is now used as a vocative for father's father's father.

The most common modern vocatives are *yeh yeh* 爺爺, *kung kung* 公公, *a wêng* 阿翁, *wêng wêng* 翁翁.⑩ Their usage depends upon local custom.

The depreciatory term is *chia tsu* or, uncommonly, *chia kung*. The prefixing of *chia* to *tsu* to refer to one's own father's father dates from the Han period. It is sometimes condemned as incorrect and vulgar⑪, but is nevertheless in universal usage today.

The complimentary term is *tsun tsu fu*.⑫ *Ta mên chung*⑬ was used as a

---

① *Jih chih lu*, 24.1a：自父而上，皆曰祖.書微子之命曰，乃祖成湯是也.

② *Êrh Ya*：祖，王⊙也.

③ *Shih Chi* 留侯世家, 55.1a：留侯張良者，其先韓人也.大父開地……Ibid.鄭當時傳, 120.6*b*：然其知交皆其大⊙行.

④ *K'ung ts'ung tzŭ* 居衛篇, 2.45b：子思既免，曰……祖君屈於陳蔡作春秋.

⑤ *Chin shih Ts'ui pien* 王文干墓誌, 113.62a：奉天定難南朝元從功臣諱英進，公之祖王父也.

⑥ 樂清縣白鶴寺鐘款識有祖翁祖婆之稱.Cf.*Ch'êng wei lu*, 1.7*a*.

⑦ *Lü shih ch'un ch'iu*, 10.10a：孔子之弟子從遠方來者，孔子荷杖而問之曰：子之公不有恙乎？

⑧ Cf. *Ch'êng wei Lu*, 1.8a.

⑨ *Hou Han Shu* 李固傳, 93.14b：姊文姬【固女】……見二兄歸……曰：李氏滅矣！自太公以來，積德累仁，何以遇此？During the Han period, *kung* was sometimes used for father; *t'ai kung*, for father's father.

⑩ *Shih shuo hsin yü*, 3B. 10a.

⑪ Cf. *Yen shih chia hsün* 風操篇, 2. 4b-5b.

⑫ Ibid., 2.5a-b：凡與人言，稱彼祖⊙母，世⊙母，⊙母及長姑，皆加尊字.自叔以下，則加賢字，尊卑之差也.(Supply No. 4, p. 154)

⑬ Ibid., 2.6a：大門中.

complimentary term during the fifth or sixth century A. D. It was most probably a posthumous term, and is not used today.

The ancient posthumous terms were *wang kao*① and *huang tsu kao*.② The former was probably more often used in connection with ancestral temples, and the latter, with sacrifices. This minute distinction might be due to the important rôle of ancestral worship and sacrifices in the sib organization during the feudal period. During the fifth century A. D. *hsien wang chang jên*③ was commonly used. None of these terms is used today. The modern posthumous terms are *hsien tsu* 先祖 or *wang tsu* 亡祖.

14. Tsu mu 祖母 f m

The term in the *Êrh Ya* is *wang mu* 王母, which corresponds to *wang fu*. Later terms, like *ta mu*④ and *tsu p'o*⑤, more or less correspond to the terms for father's father. The depreciatory term is *chia tsu mu*, and the complimentary term, *tsun tsu mu*. The ancient posthumous term is *huang tsu pi*⑥, and the modern term, *hsien tsu mu*. *T'ai P'o* was once used as a vocative for father's mother but it is now used for father's father's mother. The most common modern vocatives are *p'o p'o* 婆婆⑦ and *nai nai* 奶奶.⑧

15. Po tsu fu 伯祖父 f f o b

Both the *Êrh Ya* and *I Li* give the term *ts'ung tsu tsu fu*.⑨ It applies to both

---

① *Li Chi* 祭法,46.8a-9b:曰王考廟.孔疏:曰王考廟者,祖廟也.

② *Ibid.* 曲禮,3.22*a*:祭王⊙曰皇祖考,王母曰皇祖妣.

③ *Yen shih chia hsün* 書證篇,6.15b:今世俗呼其祖考爲先亡丈人,又疑丈當作大.

④ *Hsin shu* 俗激篇,3.1b:今其甚者,到大⊙矣,賊大母矣.*Han shu* 文三王傳,47.5b:共王母曰李太后,李太后清平王之大祖也.顔師古注:大母,祖母也.

⑤ 祖婆;see p. 237, note ⑥.

⑥ *Li Chi* 曲禮,3.22a:王母曰皇⊙妣.

⑦ K'ung p'ing-chung 朝散集, *op. cit.*, 代小子廣森寄翁翁,2.19a:婆婆到輦下,翁翁在省裏.

⑧ *Ch'in shu chi* 1.6b: 嬭,按今讀奴蟹切,曰嬭嬭.或以呼母,或以呼⊙母,或似呼伯叔母.嬭, is also written 奶. It originally meant mother and was read *ni*, as in the *Kuang yün*, 嬭,楚人呼母.

⑨ *I Li* 喪服,33.1a:從⊙⊙⊙母.

older and younger brothers of father's father.

*Po wêng*① is a modern vocative. The vocatives of 13 may also be applied here by prefixing the numerical order or title.

16. Po tsu mu 伯祖母 f f o b w

Ts'ung tsu tsu mu is the term both in the *Êrh Ya* and the *I Li*.② Since the *Êrh Ya* also gives the term *ts'ung tsu wang mu* 從祖王母, in can be inferred that during the Chou period father's father's brothers may also have been called *ts'ung tsu wang fu*. During the Han period it was abbreviated to *ts'ung tsu mu*.③ *po p'o*④ is a more modern term, and may be used vocatively.

17. Shu tsu fu 叔祖父 f f y b

Compare 15. In the *Kuo Yü* the term *ts'ung tsu shu mu*⑤ is used for father's father's younger brother's wife. It can be inferred that in ancient times *Ts'ung tsu sbu fu* may also have been used for father's father's younger brother and *ts'ung tsu shih fu* for father's father's older brother, but this inference is by no means certain. Since the T'ang period *shu wêng*⑥ has been a common alternative term, and may be used in the vocative. The vocatives of 13 may also be applied here, according to local usage, by prefixing the numerical order.

18. Shu tsu mu 叔祖母 f f y b w

Compare 16 and 17. In the Han dynasties *chi tsu mu*⑦ seems to have been used. According to another interpretation, *chi tsu mu* means father's father's

---

① 伯翁, cf., 龔大雅, 義井題記 in *Pa Ch'iung shih chin pu chêng*, 117.12a-14b.

② Cf. p. 240, note ③.

③ *Li Chi* 檀弓, 9.25b: 敬姜曰: 婦人不飾. 鄭注: 敬姜者, 康子從⊙⊙.

④ 伯婆.

⑤ *Kuo yü* 鲁語, 5.12a: 公⊙文伯之母, 季康子之從⊙叔母也. (First missing character is No. 4, p. 154.)

⑥ *Ch'ang-li chi*, 23., 13a: 祭李氏二十九娘子文. Han Yü refers to himself as 十八叔翁 and to his wife as 十八叔婆. Ibid. 23. 12b: 祭滂文, where he refers to himself as 十八翁 and to his wife as 十八婆. They were offering sacrifice to his brother s grandchildren.

⑦ *Chin shih Ts'ui pien* 18. 1 *b*: 收養季⊙母.

brother's secondary wives[①], but there is no means of checking this. Since the T'ang period *shu p'o* seems to have been a common vocative. *P'o p'o* may be used in the vocative for 16 and 18 by prefixing the numerical order of their husbands, or their own sibnames.[②]

19. Ku tsu mu 姑祖母 f f si

Wang ku 王姑 is the term given in the *Êrh Ya*.

20. Ku tsu fu 姑祖父 f f si h

21. Chiu tsu fu 舅祖父 f m b

Chiu tsu[③] may be used alone. The inverted form *tsu chiu*[④] was used quite early; and *ta chiu*[⑤] was used during the Later Han period.

22. Chiu tsu mu ○○母 f m b w

23. I tsu mu 姨祖母 f m si

24. I tsu fu ○○父 f m si h

The vocatives for the above can be constructed from the vocatives for grandparents, whatever forms are used, by prefixing *ku*, *chiu* and *i*.

25. T'ang po tsu fu 堂伯祖父 s of 7 or 9 > f f

26. T'ang po tsu mu ○○○母 w of 25

27. T'ang shu tsu fu 堂叔祖父 s of 7 or 9> f f

28. T'ang shu tsu mu ○○○母 w of 27

No term is given for 25 and 27 in the *Êrh Ya*, but *tsu tsu wang mu* 族祖王母 is used for 26 and 28. It is inferred that *tsu tsu wang fu* may have been used

---

① Ch'ien Ta-hsin says (*Ch'ien yen T'ang chin shih wên po wei*, 1. 26b) that 其稱季⊙母,猶言庶⊙母也.(Supply *tsu*, ancestor.)

② *Yen shih chia hsün* 風操篇, 2.7b:⊙母之世叔母,皆當加其姓以別之.

③ *Lêng lu tsa shih* 冷廬雜識, by Lu I-t'ien 陸以湉, ca. 1850 A. D. 筆記小説大觀 ed. 2.25b:今之稱謂……稱⊙之⊙爲⊙⊙.(Supply *fu*……*chiu*……*chiu-tsu*.)

④ *Chin shu* 應詹傳, 70. 1b:鎮南大將軍劉弘,詹之⊙⊙也.

⑤ *Hou Han Shu* 張禹傳,74.2a:⊙⊙況,族姊爲皇祖考夫人……況……見光武,光武大喜曰:今乃得我大⊙乎!(Supply tsu-fu.)

for 25 and 27. In the *I Li*, *tsu tsu fu* is used for 25 and 27, and *tsu tsu mu* for 26 and 28[①], whereas in the *Êrh Ya* these terms are used for the son and the son's wife of either 25 or 27. The *I Li* is simply using an abbreviated form.

Vocatives of 15-18 may be applied here, respectively.

29. T'ang ku tsu mu 堂姑祖母 d of 7 or 29

In the *Êrh Ya*, *tsu tsu ku*. This term is rather inconsistent with the whole *Êrh Ya* system, since logically it should be *tst*, *tsu wang ku*. Perhaps the *Êrh Ya* was already beginning to use abbreviated forms.

30. T'ang ku tsu fu 堂姑祖父 h of z

Vocatives can be built up by prefixing grandparent vocatives with *ku*, and can further be differentiated by prefixing the numerical order of 29, or the sibname of 30.

31. Piao tsu fu 表祖父 f f f si s

32. Piao tsu mu ○○母 w of 31

The above two terms can be further differentiated by prefixing *ku*, *chiu* and *i*, e. g., *ku piao tsu fu* for f f f si s, *chiu piao tsu fu* for f f m b s, *i piao tsu fu* for f f m si s. Ordinarily, *piao tsu fu* is applied to them all. Usually these relationships are not continued socially after the death of the f f f si and f f m, unless it be that either of the parties strongly wishes to maintain them. Terms for their descendants will not be given in this table. If the relationships are maintained, terms could easily be constructed, e. g., the sons of 31 will be called *t'ang piao po fu* and *t'ang piao shu fu*, etc.

Ⅳ. Generation of the father

33. Fu 父 father

Fu is primarily a standard literary term throughout, and is seldom used

---

① *I Li*, 33. 6a.

alone as a vocative. *Wêng*① was an old vocative. *A kung*② and *tsun*③ were prevalent from the third to the sixth centuries A. D. About the fifth century A. D. members of some of the royal families called father *hsiung hsiung*④, a term for older brother. During the T'ang dynasty the royal family called father *ko*⑤, nowadays a universal vocative for older brother. Before this, *ko* had never been used in either of these senses.⑥ It might be that *ko* was an old dialectical term for father, and that during this period it became confused with *hsiung*, thereupon losing its original meaning of father and acquiring the connotation of "older brother," but the matter is most perplexing.

Yeh 耶 is a vocative used from the sixth century A. D. on⑦; it is also written 爺⑧, *Tieh* 爹⑨, which may be a later variant pronunciation of *t'o* 爹⑩, a dialectical form of western Hupeh of about the same period, is now a common vocative. *Pa pa* is almost as commonly used as *tieh*; it first occurred in the

---

① *Shih chi* 項羽本紀,7.26a:漢王曰……吾翁即若翁.

② *Nan Shih* 顔延之傳, 34.4b: ……又非君家阿公. According to 王念孫 (*Kuang ya shu chêng*) 公 and 翁 are very similar in sound and may be dialectical renderings of a same term.

③ *Sung shu* 謝靈運傳,67.30a:阿連才悟如此,而尊作常兒遇之.*Shih shuo hsin yü* 品藻篇,2B.30a:劉尹至王長史許清言,時苟子年十三,倚床邊聽.既去,問⊙曰,劉尹語何如尊? Ibid.9b:謝太傅未冠,始出西詣王長史清言,良久,去後苟子問曰:向客何如尊? (Supply *fu*.)

④ *Pei Ch'i shu* 南陽王綽傳,12.6b:兄兄.

⑤ *Chiu T'ang shu* 王琚傳,106.16b:元宗泣曰:四哥仁孝. The *ko* is meant for the Emperor 睿宗.*Ibid.* 棣王琰傳,107.5a:惟三哥辯其罪.The 三哥 is here used by 琰 in referring to his father, Emperor Hsüan-tsung. *Ko* was also used by the royal family of the T'ang dynasty to refer to oneself before the son. *Chêng wei lu*, 1.15a: states: 淳化閣帖有唐太宗與高宗書稱哥哥敕.⊙對子自稱哥哥.蓋唐代家法如是.(Supply *fu*.)

⑥ 哥 is defined in the *Shuo wên* as "to sing," or "a song."

⑦ *Yen shih chia hsün* 文章篇,4.10b.

⑧ *Nan shih* 侯景傳,80.22b:王偉勸立七廟……並請七世諱……景曰:前世吾不復憶,惟阿爺名標. The original form is 耶,and 爺 is a later form with classifier No.88 added.For discussion cf. *Kai yü ts'ung k'ao*,37.15; *Hêng yen lu*, 3.2; *and Ch'êng wei lu*, 1.15-16.

⑨ *Ch'ang-li chi* 祭女挐女文,23.14a:阿爹阿八,使汝妳……祭於第四小娘子之靈.Cf.*Shu P'o*,1.2b-3a,呼⊙爲爹.

⑩ *Kuang ya*:爹……⊙也,pronounced t'o. *Nan shih* 始興忠武王憺傳,52.15b:詔征以本號還朝,人歌之曰:始興王,人之爹【徒我反】赴人急,如水火,何時復來哺乳我.荆土方言謂⊙爲爹,故云. For discussion cf. *Kai yü Ts'ung k'ao*, 37.15.

Kuang Ya, which reads, "*pa……is father.*"① The *Cheng tzŭ T'ung* considers *pa a term of the southern aborigines*②, and states that the aborigines call their elders *pa pa* 八八, or *pa pa* 巴巴, and that the: Chinese lexicographers added the classifier 父 to form 爸. On the other hand, *pa* is also considered a later variant pronunciation of *fu* 父.③

The dialectical difference, insofar as the evidence goes, seems to indicate that *tieh* is predominantly a northern usage④, and *pa*, a southern⑤; but this explanation is,by no means certaia.

The *Kuang Yün* states that the people of Wu call father *chê*⑥, but according to the *T'ung Ya* father was called *lao hsiang* in Wu.⑦ None of these terms seem to be in use today. The inhabitants of Fuchow,call father *lang pa* 郎罷⑧; this usage dates from the T'ang period. Before that, *lang* alone also had the meaning of father⑨; hence *lang pa* may be combination variant of *lang* and *pa*. In modern usage in that place, however, *lang pa* is always.used in the referential and never in the vocative.

Fu Ch'in 父親⑩ may be used as a literary vocative by the son in

① 爸……⊙也.

② *Chêng tzŭ T'ung*:爸.The Miao and Yao tribes of southwest China still call father *pa*, or its slight variants.Cf.*Miao fang pei lan* 苗防備覽 by Yen Ju-i 嚴如熤(1843 紹義堂 ed.)8.6a,9.2b, and 9.10a; *Ling piao chi man* 嶺表紀蠻 by Liu Hsi-fan 劉錫藩(1932, Shanghai,Commercial Press) 137.

③ Chêng Chên (*Ch'in shu chi*, 1.1b) says that 古讀巴如逋,即⊙之重唇音,遂作巴加⊙.今俗呼⊙或爲巴巴,或爲耙耙,或爲八八,並此字.

④ *Kuang yün*:爹,北人呼⊙.

⑤ *Chi Yün*:爸,(部可切,又必駕切)吳人呼⊙.The *Ch'êng wei lu*, 1.27a: also states that 吳俗稱⊙爲阿伯.*Po* 伯 may be a different rendering of *pa* 爸.

⑥ 奢(正奢切),吳人呼⊙. The modern pronunciation is the same of *yeh* 爺.

⑦ *T'ung Ya* 稱謂,19.4b.

⑧ *Hua yang chi*,1.13a:囝,哀閩也.自注:囝,音蹇,閩俗呼子爲囝,呼⊙爲郎罷.郎罷别囝,吾悔汝生……

⑨ *Shu I*,1.9b:古人謂⊙爲阿郎.*Pei shih* 汲固傳,85.4a:【李】憲即爲固長育,至十餘歲.恒呼固夫婦爲郎婆.According to 朱⊙(cited by *Ch'êng wei lu*,1.26a)蓋北朝稱⊙⊙郎也.

⑩ *Ch'in* 親 means "relative","parent".

addressing his father, as in a letter. In this connection, *ta jên* 大人① and *Ch'i hsia* 膝下② must be appended, making the term *fu ch'in ta jên Ch'i hsia*, a stereotyped form of literary address. In addressing letters, *Ch'i hsia* is used for either parent, whereas *ta jên* may be appended to any term for relatives of higher generations, *ch'i hsia* is primarily a literary parent term; its literal meaning is "like a child at your knees."

The father, in referring to himself before his children, may use *nai kung* 乃公③, *nai wêng* 乃翁④ and the more colloquial and modern terms a *tieh*, *a pa*, or *lao tzŭ* 老子. In certain localities *lao tzŭ* may also be used for father in general.⑤

The depreciatory term is *chia fu*, or *chia yen*.⑥ *Yen* literally means "the stern and respected one." *Chia chün*⑦ is also fairly common. *Chia kung*⑧ is a rather uncommon old term.

The complimentary term is *tsun ta jen* 尊大人. *Tsun chün*⑨, *tsunhung*⑩, *tsun hou*⑪, *fêng wêng*, *fêng chün*,⑫ in modern times are literary rather than

---

① 大人 literally means "big man", that is "senior". It is frequently used alone as a vocative, e. g., *Shih Chi* 越世家,41.11b; Ibid.,高祖本紀 8.32a.

② *Hsiao Ching* 聖治章,5.4b:故親生之膝下以養⊙母……注:膝下,謂孩幼之時也.

③ *Han Shu* 陳萬年傳,66.17a:萬年嘗病,命咸教戒於床下.語至夜半,咸睡,頭觸屏風.萬年大怒,欲杖之,曰:乃公教戒汝,汝反睡不聽吾言,何也?

④ 乃翁 is somewhat equivalent to 乃公. *Nai* 乃 is used in the sense of "your."

⑤ *Chêng tzŭ t'ung*: *s.v. fu*, fahter.

⑥ *I Ching*, 4.16a:家人有嚴君焉,⊙⊙之謂也.*Hsiao Ching* 聖治章,5.1a:孝莫大於嚴⊙.

⑦ *Shih shuo hsin yü*, 1A. 3a: 家君. Here the term *chia chün* is used both as a complimentary and depreciatory term. (From this point in Dr. Fêng's article the editors have been forced to revert to their usual practice of providing only indispensable citations from the Chinese.)

⑧ *Chin shu* 43.6b. *Chia kung* is no longer used in this sense; it is now used for mother s father.

⑨ *Shih shuo hsin yü*, 2A. 1a; *Chin shu*, 75.5a. Sometimes *chün chia tsun* is used, e. g., *Shih Shuo hsin yü*, 2B. 34a.

⑩ *Chin Shu*, 82. 1b; Ibid., 92.23b.

⑪ *Shih shuo hsin yü*, 1A. 28b: 尊侯.

⑫ 封翁 and 封君 were used originally for those who received titles through sons who had risen to high official positions. Later they became common complimentary terms.

vocative.

K'ao 考 is a posthumous term. In ancient literature it was also used for the living father, being synonymous *with fu*.① At present, however, it is primarily an epitaphic term. At different periods *k'ao* was used with various modifiers to express special circumstances. In the *Chü Li* of the *Li Chi*, *huang k'ao*② is used as a posthumous term for father, but in the *Chi Fa* of the same work it is used as a temple term for father's father's father.③ *Wang k'ao* is a temple term in the *Li Chi* for father's father in connection with sacrifices④, but during the T'ang period it was occasionally used as a posthumous term for father.⑤ *Huang k'ao* and *wang k'ao* have been prohibited for common use since the Yüan dynasty, being reserved only for the imperial family.⑥ Thereafter the term *hsien k'ao* came into use as a universal epitaphic form.⑦ But this term sharply contradicts the old usage, since in the *Li Chi*, *hsien k'ao* is used as a temple term for father's father's father' s father.⑧

Fu chün 府君 is another popular epitaphic term. Originally, i. e., in the Han dynasty, only those who had been governors (*t'ai shou* 太守) could be called *fu chün* by their sons, but since the T'ang period the term has been used indiscriminately.⑨ The ordinary posthumous terms are *hsien fu* 先父, *wang fu*

---

① According to the *Shuo Wên*, *k'ao* means "old." Thus it could be applied to any old man. Its application to mean father is a later development and its use as a posthumous term is a still later specialization. Cf. *Ch'in shu chi* 1.5.

② *Li Chi*, 5.22a.

③ *Ibid*. 46.8b-9a:皇考.

④ *Ibid*. 46.8-9: 王考.

⑤ *Ch'ang-li chi* 24. 10a.

⑥ This prohibition is best illustrated in the *Yüan tien chang* 元典章, 1908 edition,31. 16a-b.

⑦ The term *hsien k'ao* 顯考 was used for father much earlier than the Yüan period, e. g., *Shu Ching* (K'ang kao), 14.3a. It continued to be used down to the fourth and fifth centuries A. D. for parents both living and dead. *Hsien* means "great", "illustrious", etc. Down to the Sung period, *hsien* is predominantly used in the posthumous sense. Cf. also the *Chin Shih Li*, 5. 55b.

⑧ 鄭珍(*Ch'in sbu chi*, 2. 3a) rather bemoans such contradiction.

⑨ Cf. *Hêng yen lu*, 3.3b-5b; Ch'êng wei lu, 1. 21a-b.

亡父, *hsien ta fu* 先大夫, *hsien chün* 先君, *hsien tzŭ* 先子, *hsien chün tzŭ* 先君子①, *hsien kung* 先公②, etc. The complimentary posthumous terms are *tsun hsien chün* 尊先君 and *tsun fu* 尊府.③

The ancient temple term for father is *ni* 禰.④

34. Mu 母 mother

Mu, like *fu*, is primarily a standard term and is seldom used in the vocative. Other ancient alternative terms are *yü*⑤ and *wên*⑥, but these terms can be applied to any old woman. During the T'ang period, *niang tzŭ*⑦ was used for mother but at the same time it was also used for any young woman. This usage seemed to be northern. *Niang tzŭ* is used in modern terminology sometimes as a husband's term for wife, sometimes for any young woman.

The most peculiar variant of the term for mother is *tzŭ tzŭ* 姊姊 which was used by the royalty of the Northern Ch'i dynasty⑧; *tzŭ* being a term for older sister. According to the *Shuo Wên*, the people of Shu call mother *chieh* and the people of Huai nan call mother *Shê*.⑨ The older form of *chieh* 姐, according to the *Yü P' ien*, is written 毑. In the 說山訓 of the *Huai nan tzŭ*, shê is used for mother and Kao Yu comments that it is a Chiang Huai practice.⑩ The *Shuo Wên also states* that *shih* 媞 was used for mother in Chiang Huai. Kuo P'o (267-324

① *Hsien chün* and *hsien tzŭ* originally were terms used during the feudal period by the nobility in referring to their deceased fathers. They became common terms at about the end of the period.

② *Hou Han Shu* 93. 15a.

③ *Ch'ang-li chi* 21.6b.

④ *Tso Chuan* 32. 4b. *Ni* means "near", "closer", i. e., the father is nearer than the father's father, etc. It is the same as 昵. Cf. also *Shu Ching* 10. 11 a.

⑤ 嫗, *Shuo wên*; *Hsin Shu* 3. 1b.

⑥ 媪, *Shuo wên*; *Kuang ya*; *Han fei tzŭ* 10b, Also read *ao*.

⑦ 娘子, *Shu I*, 1.9b-10a; for its uses during the various periods, cf. *Kai yü ts'ung kao*, 38.1 a-3a.

⑧ *Pei Ch'i shu* 9.4a.

⑨ Hsü Shên seems to consider 社 a variant of 姐.

⑩ *Huai nan tzŭ* 16. 12a-b. Chiang Huai is the area between the Yangtze and Huai Rivers.

A. D.) said that the people of Chiang Tung① called mother *shih* 㑊, also pronounced *chih*, or *ch'ih*. *Shê*, *shih*, *chih* and *Ch'ih* all seem to have been derived from the same root and probably represent Variants of *chieh*.② Apparently, from the third century B. C. to the fourth century A. D., *chieh*, with its variant forms, was a very prevalent vocative for mother throughout, the Yangtze valley. Even down to the thirteenth century A. D. mother was sometimes called *chieh chieh*.③ On the other hand, from Han to T'ang times *chia chia* was frequently used for mother and might be another variant transcription of *chieh chieh*.④

Perhaps due to the close similarity of these two sounds—*tzŭ* and *chieh*—and to the vagaries of transcription, for a time *tzŭ* was used for *chieh*. *Tzŭ*, being the older and more literary term, triumphed over *chieh*, and the latter lost its original meaning and acquired the meaning of older sister, like *tzŭ*. This seems the only reasonable explanation, and, if true, means that we have here an exact parallel with *hsiung* and *ko*, as discussed above. Apparently, no marital relations are involved.

The universal modern vocative is *ma* 媽 or *ma ma*.⑤ *Niang* 娘⑥, or *niang niang*, are also very commonly used in many localities. The *Kuang Yün* says that the people of ch'u called mother *ni*.⑦ The *Chi Yün states that the people of*

① Chiang Tung is a vague geographical term, approximately the lower Yangtze delta.

② According to Chêng Chên (*Ch'in shu chi*, 1.6b) the ancient pronunciation of *chieh* 姐 and *shê* 社 was about the same and both were in the rhymes 魚, 虞, 模 which are very close. Hence he considers *shê* to be a dialectical variant of *chieh*.

③ *Ssŭ Ch'ao wên chien lu* 四朝聞見録,己集, by YEH Shao-wêng 葉紹翁, ca, 1220 A. D. (知齋不足叢書 edition) 16a.

④ *Pei Ch'i shu* 12.8b: 家家.

⑤ But cf. *Hsi shang fu t'an* 席上腐談, by Yü Yen 俞琰(寶顔堂秘笈 edition) 1.2a.

⑥ As explained before, *niang* can be used in various designations sometimes overriding generations. Used as a vocative for mother, it was first noticed during the fourth and fifth centuries A. D. *Nan Shih* 44.5a-b; *Pei Shih* 64.13b-14a.

⑦ 奶 (嬭); cf. *Ch'in shu chi*, 1.6. ch'u 楚 is the ancient term for the middle Yangtze valley and at present approximately the modern Hupeh and Hunan provinces.

Ch'i called mother mi①, and the people of Wu called mother *mi*.② *Ni* and *mi* may be early dialectical variants of *ma*. The Miao, Yao and Tung tribes of Southwest China still call mother *mi* or *ma*.③ Whether the aboriginal terms influenced the Chinese, or vice versa, or whether they both have been derived from a common earlier form, we at present have no way to determine. Certainly *ma* is only a slightly differing version of *mu*.④

Mu ch'in 母親 is sometimes used as a vocative, but more commonly in addressing one's mother in a letter; in the latter case, *ta jên* and *ch'i hsia* must be suffixed.

The depreciatory term is *chia mu*⑤, or *chia tz'ŭ*.⑥ Tz'ŭ literally means "the affectionate one." *Tsun lao*⑦ was used around the fifth century A. D., and *chia fu jên* was allowable during the Later Han times. ⑧

Ling mu 令母⑨, *ling tz'ŭ* 令慈, *ling t'ang* 令堂, and *tsun t'ang* 尊堂⑩, are the most common complimentary terms. *Tsun shang*⑪ and *tsun fu jên*⑫ were used from the fifth to the eighth centuries A. D. At present *tsun fu jên* is used as a complimentary term for another's wife. *T'ai fu jên*⑬ may be used for anther's mother when the father is dead. *An jên* 安人 and *kung jên* 恭人, originally

---

① 嫛. Cf. also the *Yü p'ien*. Ch'i is the old name for the modern province of Shantung.

② 媄. Wu is the ancient name for roughly the southern part of Kiangsu province.

③ *Miao fang pei lan*, *op. cit.*, 8.6a, and 9.10a. *Ling piao chi man*, *op. cit.*, 137.

④ *Ch'in shu chi*, 1.7a.

⑤ *Yen shih chia hsün*, 2.4b-5a. It seems that the prefixing of *chia* (house) to the terms of lineal ascendants to form depreciatory terms was not prevalent during Yen's time.

⑥ This is the opposite of the term *chia yen*, "the stern one," for father. The mother is supposed to be affectionate and the father, stern.

⑦ *Sung Shu* 91.15 a: 尊老.

⑧ *Hou Han Shu* 78.9a: 家夫人.

⑨ *Ts'ai chung-lang chi* 6.7b.

⑩ *Lu shih-lung wên chi* 10. 10a. *T'ang* 堂 is derived from *Pei T'ang* 北堂, a non-vocative, non-referential literary term for mother. Cf. *T'ung su pien*, 18.5a-5b.

⑪ *Sung shu* 91.15a:尊上.

⑫ *Ch'ang-li chi* 29. 3b: 尊夫人.

⑬ This was originally used for a titled woman, e. g., *Han Shu* 4.12a-b: 太夫人.

terms for a titled woman, may be used loosely, if incorrectly, as complimentary terms.

The posthumous term is *pi*①, as defined by the *Shuo Wên*. Yet this view is sometimes disputed, since in classical literature the term was often used indiscriminately for both living and dead mother. The modern usage follows the interpretation of the *Li Chi*, that *mu* is used when the mother is living, and *pi* when she is dead.② *Huang pi*③ was an old sacrificial term but has been forbidden since the Yüan period. *Hsien pi*④ is exclusively an epitaphic term.

35. Po fu 伯父 f o b

The old term in the *Êrh Ya* and *I Li* is *shih fu*.⑤ In the *Li Chi*, *po fu*⑥ is sometimes used in place of *shih fu*. *Po* itself means oldest, e. g., an oldest brother may be called *po hsiung*, and an oldest sister, *po tzŭ*. Since the Wei and Chin periods, *po* alone has been used as a vocative for father's older brother.⑦ From the Sung period down to modern times, *po po* has been the most prevalent vocative. The posthumous term is *wang po* 亡伯. *Ts'ung hsiung ti mên chung*⑧ is an old term used *circa* the fifth century A. D. but seldom heard today.

36. Po mu 伯母 f o b w

Shih mu is the old term used in the *Êrh Ya*. *I Li*⑨ and *Li Chi*. ⑩ *Po mu* is

---

① 妣. The *Êrh Ya* uses *mu* and *pi* synonymously.

② *Li Chi* 5. 22b.

③ Ibid. 5.22a.

④ *Wang shih chung chi* 38a: 顯⊙This is, perhaps, the first use of *hsien pi*, but it is used for the living mother. Now *hsien pi* is used exclusively as a corresponding term to *hsien k'ao*.

⑤ *I Li* 30.8b. *Shih* means "generation". That is, the father's older brother is the one in the father's "generation" to succeed to the grandfather.

⑥ *Li Chi* 18.10a: 伯.

⑦ See p. 221, note ①.

⑧ *Yen shih chia hsün* 2. 6a: 從兄弟門中. It literally means "within the gate of father's brother's sons", a circumlocution for expressing a moumful situation.

⑨ *I Li* 30, 9b-10a.

⑩ *Li Chi* 18, 15a.

also used in the *Li Chi*. ①

37. *shu fu* 叔父 f y b

Circa the latter half of the first millennium B. C., *chu fu*②, *ts'ung fu*③, and *yu fu*④ were used for father's brothers, both older and younger. They are still used today as alternative terms but are primarily literary forms. *Ts'ung fu*, a contraction of *ts'ung tsu fu*, was also used for father's father's brother's sons.

Shu fu also was used in another sense in early times. The father's first younger brother was called *chung fu*, the second younger brother, *shu fu*, and the youngest, *chi fu*.⑤ This usage was never common. *Chi fu* was also used for father's younger brothers in general, not necessarily his youngest brother.⑥ *Ts'ung wêng* is a relatively late and uncommon term.⑦

Since the third century A. D. *shu*, *a shu*, or *shu shu* have been used as common vocatives.

Among the royal families of the Northern Ch'i and T'ang dynasties, father's brothers were called *a hsiung*; this may be a family peculiarity.

The depreciatory term is *chia shu fu*, or simply *chia shu*. Yen's *Family Instructions* states that it is incorrect to use *chia po* for father's older brother, since he is an elder of father and one dare not use *chia*.⑧ This is somewhat over-rationalistic; *chia po* is the most common form today. The complimentary term for another's father's younger brother is *hsien shu*, or *ling shu*.

---

① Ibid., 43.2b.

② *Shih Ching* 9C. 2a: 諸⊙. *Chu fu* is a very vague term, literally "the fathers".

③ *I Li* 31.17a: 從⊙昆弟. Since father's brother's sons can be called *ts'ung fu k'un ti*, father's brothers can be called *Ts'ung fu*. *Pei shih* 22.8.

④ *Li Chi* 8.4b-5a: 猶⊙. Since brother's sons can be called *yu tzŭ*, it is inferred that father's brother can be called *yu fu*, "like father."

⑤ *Shih Ming*: 季⊙.

⑥ *Shih chi* 7.1 b; *Ch'ang-li Chi* 23.9b; Han Yü refers to himself as *chi fu*.

⑦ *T'ang chih yen*, 3.1a: 從翁.

⑧ *Yen shih chia hsün* 2.5a.

The posthumous tern is *wang shu*. *Ts'ung hsiung ti mên chung* is an old term both for father's older and younger brothers.

38. Shu mu 叔母 f y b w

This is also the term used in the *Êrh Ya*. *Chi mu*① was used during the Han period, but rarely. The vocative *shên*② dates from the Sung dynasty. This term is not found in the classical literature, and is thought to be a contraction of *shih mu*. In modern times *shên shên*, *shên mu*, or *shên niang* have been commonly used as vocatives. Another common usage is by prefixing her sibname, or the numerical order of her husband, to *ma*. This also applies to 36.

39. Ku mu 姑母 f si

"Father's sisters are ku," defines the *Êrh Ya*. *Ku* is also used in the *I Li*.③

The vocative for father's unmarried sister is *ku*, or *ku ku* prefixed by her name or numerical order. When she is married, *ku ma* is the most prevalent form.

Chia ku mu is sometimes used as a depreciatory term. Yen's *Family Instructions* considered this usage incorrect, for when a woman was married out she was no longer a member of the family, so that *chia* could not be applied.④

40. Ku fu 姑父 f si h

*Ku hsü*⑤ and *ku fu*⑥ are used as alternative terms, mostly from the third to

---

① *Hou Han Shu* 118.20*a*.

② *Ming tao tsa chih*, 13b：嬸.

③ *I Li* 31.16b-17a. LIANG Ch'ang-chü (*Chêng wei lu*, 8.13a-14b) considers *ku tzŭ mei* a term for father's sister. As far as its use in the *I Li* is concerned, it should be interpreted as *ku* (father's sister), and *tzŭ* and *mei* (ego's own sisters). The other instances which Liang cites in support of the use of *ku tzŭ* for father's older sister, and *ku mei* for father's younger sister, are very questionable.

④ *Yen shih chia hsün* 2.5a.

⑤ *Pei Ch'i Shu* 18.3 b：婿.

⑥ *San Kuo Chih* 13.3a；*Nan Shih* 57.14a.

the sixth centuries A. D.

41. T'ang po fu 堂伯父 f f b s > f

Êrh Ya gives the term *ts'ung tsu fu* for father's father's brother's sons, both older and younger than father. By inference from other usages, *ts'ung tsu shih fu* may be used for the former. Since the Han period, *ts'ung po*, or *ts'ung po fu* have been used.① During the fifth and sixth centuries A. D. the term *t'ung t'ang* was introduced, since agnate relatives of the same paternal grandfather offer sacrifices in the same ancestral hall. *T'ung t'ang* literally means "the same hall." During the T'ang period the *t'ung* was dropped and only *t'ang* was used.② Later the term was extended to other collateral lines.

42. T'ang po mu 堂伯母 w of 41

As can be inferred from *ts'ung tsu fu* and *ts'ung tsu shih fu*, the older term would be *ts'ung tsu mu* or *ts'ung tsu shih mu*. Since the Han period *ts'ung po mu* or simply *ts'ung mu* have been used.

43. T'ang shu fu 堂叔父 f f b s < f

Compare 41. *Ts'ung tsu shu fu* may, by inference, be the older term. Since the Han period *ts'ung shu* or *ts'ung shu fu*③ have been used as alternative terms.

In the vocatives of 41 and 43 the modifier *t'ang* is usually dropped, i. e., the vocatives of 35 and 37 may be applied here, respectively, modified by their names or numerical order.

44. T'ang shu mu 堂叔母 w of 43

Ts'ung tsu shu mu may be the older form. The later abbreviated form *ts'ung shu mu* may be used alternatively with *t'ang shu mu*. *T'ang shên* is a vocative extension of *shên*.

---

① *Chin Shu* 80. la.

② Ch'iEN Ta-hsin〔*Hêng yen lu*, 3.9a-b.〕

③ *Sung Shu* 52.5a.

45. T'ang ku mu 堂姑母 f f b d

The term in the *Êrh Ya* is *ts'ung tsu ku*, later abbreviated to *ts'ung ku*.① *Ts'ung* and *t'ang* are synonymous. The vocative for father's sister may be used here, modified by her name or numerical order.

46. T'ang ku fu 堂姑父 f f b d h

The vocative, for father's sister's husband may be used here, modified by his sibname.

47. Tsai ts'ung po fu 再從伯父 s of 25 or 27 > f

Tsu fu is the term used in the *Êrh Ya* and *I Li*.② *Tsu po fu* may be used for this relation, but it can be applied to any male sib relative of the father's generation older than father, from the fourth collateral line onward-so it is a rather loose term.

48. Tsai ts'ung po mu 再從伯母 w of 47

49. Tsai ts'ung shu fu 再從叔父 s of 25 or 27 < f

Tsu fu is used in the *Êrh Ya*, *Tsu shu*③ and *tsung shu*④ are later alternatives, but used rather loosely. In the vocatives of 47 and 49, *tsai ts'ung* is usually dropped, leaving only *po* and *shu* modified by their names or numerical order.

50. Tsai ts'ung shu mu 再從叔母 w of 49

The vocatives of 36 and 38 may be applied to 48 and 50, respectively, modified by their sibnames or their husbands' numerical order, or by both.

51. Tsai ts'ung ku mu 再從姑母 d of 25 or 27

In the *Êrh Ya*, *tsu tsu ku* 族祖姑. In modern times, *tsu ku* 族姑 has been used alternatively, but in a rather loose fashion.

---

① *Chin Shu* 51.2b.

② *I Li* 33.6a: 族.

③ *Chin Shu* 83. 1a.

④ *Yin hua lu*, 2.2a: 宗叔.

52. Tsai ts'ung ku fu 再從姑父 h of 51

53. Ku piao po fu 姑表伯父 f f si s > f

Chung wai chang jên[①] was used during the fifth and sixth centuries A. D. During the Sung dynasty *piao chang jên*[②] and *wai po fu*[③] were frequently used. Before the Tang period, *chang jên* was used as a polite term for any old man; but since then it has been used as a synonym for *yo fu*, wife's father.

54. Ku piao po mu 姑表伯母 w of 53

Chang mu[④] was used during the fifth and sixth centuries A. D., but is now used exclusively for wife's mother.

55. Ku piao shu fu 姑表叔父 f f si s < f

56. Ku piao shu mu ○○叔母 w of 55

57. Ku piao ku mu ○○姑母 f f si d

58. Ku piao ku fu ○○姑父 f f si d h

59. Chiu piao po fu 舅表伯父 f m b s < f

60. Chiu piao po mu ○○伯母 w of 59

61. Chiu piao shu fu 舅表叔父 f m b s < f

62. Chiu piao shu mu ○○叔母 w of 61

63. Chiu piao ku mu ○○姑母 f m b d

64. Chiu piao ku fu ○○姑父 h of 63

65. I piao po fu 姨表伯父 f m si s > f

66. I piao po mu ○○伯母 w of 65

67. I piao shu fu ○○叔父 f m si s < f

68. I piao shu mu ○○叔母 h of 67

69. I piao ku mu ○○姑母 f m si d

---

① 中外丈人, cf. *Yen shih chia hsün* 2.8*b*. *Chung-wai* is synonymous with *chung-piao*.

② *T'ai p'ing kuang chi* 太平廣記 (1934, Peiping, 文友堂 ed.) 148. 4a.

③ Cf. 東觀餘論附録(學津討原 ed.) 5a.

④ *Yen Shih Chia hsün* 2.8b. The use of *wang* 王 *mu* and *hsieh* 謝 *mu* is no longer intelligible. Perhaps their use is based on the most well-known sibnames of the time, Wang and Hsieh.

70. I piao ku fu ○○姑父 w of 69

The terms listed under 53 are applicable to 55, 58, 59, 61, 64, 65, 67 and 70 respectively, during the period mentioned above. In ordinary modern usage the modifiers *ku*, *chiu* and *i* are usually omitted, so that terminologically these relatives are not distinguished from one another. Conceptually, the exact relationship is always assumed.

Ⅴ. Generation of the speaker

71. Pên shên 本身 ego, a male.

A female would use the same terms, except for those provided in Table Ⅳ and certain terms in Table Ⅲ.

72. Ch'i 妻 wife

*Ch'i tzŭ*① 妻子 is commonly used, but it may also mean "wife and children". In certain cases *fu*② is used synonymously with *Ch'i*, but it may be used to mean "woman" in general. In kinship usage *fu* is principally used for the wives of those who are of lower generations and age status.

*Fei*③ is a very old term and so also is *nei chu*,④ but the latter is rather uncommon. *Nei shê*⑤ and *ju jên*⑥ were commonly employed during the first half of the first millennium A. D. *Shih*⑦, *chia*⑧, and *shih chia*⑨ are also very old

---

① *Jih Chih lu*, 24. 5a.

② *I Ching*. 1. 33a:婦.

③ 妃 *Êrh Ya*; *Shuo Wên*; *Shih Ming*. *Tso chuan* 5.19a; *Chan kuo ts'ê* 3.83 a. *Fei*, as used before the Han period, is a term for "wife" in general. It is only during the Han period and since that *fei* is reserved for the wives of nobility and the Emperor's secondary wives. Cf. *ch'in shu chi*, 2.5b-6b.

④ *Tso Chuan* 42. 9b: 内主. *Nei chu* literally means "inside lord".

⑤ 陳琳:飲馬長城窟行(*Yü T'ai hsin yung chi*,1.13a):内舍.

⑥ *Chiang wên-T'ung chih* 1.1 b: 孺人. *Ju jên* was originally a term for titled women during the feudal period, e. g., *Li Chi* 5.11 b. It became a common term for wife during the third and fourth centuries A. D. Since then, it has reverted to its old connotation.

⑦ *I Li* 6.8b: 室. *Li Chi* 28.20b.

⑧ *Shih Ching* 7B. 5b:樂子之無家. *Tso chuan* 14. 10b.

⑨ *Shih Ching* 4A. 6b: 室家.

terms, but are still commonly employed as literary forms.

Chieh fa[①] and *chung k'uei*[②] are primarily literary terms. *Chieh fa* is applied only to the first marriage principal wife; *chung k'uei* is also used as a literary complimentary term.

The wife, when speaking to the husband, calls herself *Ch'ieh* 妾, "your concubine"; or, *chi chou Ch'ieh*.[③] These abject terms are seldom, if ever, used except in literature. During the feudal period, a noble woman could on formal occasions, call herself *pei tzŭ*[④], or *hsiao tung*[⑤], according to rank. These terms are now entirely obsolete. *Chün fu*[⑥] is a common form, but mostly used in poetry.

The husband calls the wife *hsien Ch'i*[⑦], or *niang tzŭ*[⑧], and, more anciently, *hsi chün*.[⑨] These highly complimentary terms are rarely used in daily life, and are rather mere literary forms. *Ch'ing* is a reciprocal term, i. e., used alike both by husband and wife, and is now a predominately literary form of address. Husband and wife may call each other by name, or they may use no term at all and just refer to each other as "you," "he," and "she." After issue, teknonymy is the most common practice.

The depreciatory term is *nei*.[⑩] *Nei tzŭ* 内子, *nei jên* 内人 and *pi nei* 敝内 *are its derivatives. Cho ching*[⑪] and *shih jên*[⑫] are more literary. The above terms

---

① *Wên Hsüan*, 29. l4b:結髪.

② *I Ching* 4.17a: 中饋. *Chung k'uei* literally means "the family larder" and is used metaphorically.

③ *Shih Chi* 8.4a: 箕帚妾; i. e., a female with broom and dust-basket ready to serve.

④ *Tso Chuan* 15.2a: 婢子.

⑤ *Lun Yü*, 16. 10*a*: 小童; *Li Chi* 5.12a.

⑥ *Shih Ching* 13B. 6a: 君婦.

⑦ 賢妻 literally "virtuous wife."

⑧ *Pei Ch'i Shu* 39. 5a: 娘子.

⑨ *Han shu* 65.5 a: 細君.

⑩ It is also a general term used for wife and concubine together, e. g., *Tso Chuan* 14.18b. Cf. *Hêng yen lu*, 3.9b-10a and *Ch'êng wei lu*, 5.12b-13b.

⑪ 拙荆 is derived from the 荆釵布裙 of Mêng Kuang 孟光, wife of Liang Hung 梁鴻 of the Later Han dynasty. The variants are *shan ching* 山荆, *ching fu* 荆婦 and *ching jên* 荆人.

⑫ *Shih Ching* 2C. 6a: 室人.

are used mostly in refined society. *Chia li*[1] and *hsiang li*[2] are vulgar terms. *Hun chia*[3], *hun shê*[4], *lao P'o*[5], and *chia chu P'o*[6] are vulgar and dialectical forms used mostly in the referential, and are not necessarily depreciatory.

The complimentary term is *fu jên* 夫人, originally a term for the wife of a man of rank. More intimately, *sao fu jên* 嫂夫人 may be used. *T'ai T'ai* is more colloquial.[7] *Ling shih*[8] and *ling Ch'i*[9] are literary in nature. In ancient times *nei tzŭ*[10] was used as a complimentary term, but is now exclusively used as a depreciatory term. *k'ang li*[11] is a literary form used to refer to another's wife, and, more commonly, to refer to both husband and wife as *hsien kang li*.

Pin[12] and *ling jên*[13] are posthumous terms for wife. *Tê pei*[14] is a posthumous complimentary term. It is also used as a literary form for the wife in the case of an aged couple.

---

① "In the home." Cf. YAO k'uan 姚寬? -1161 A. D., 西溪叢話, 學津討原 ed., 2.19b.

② 鄉里, "in the country." *Nan Shih* 64. 16a: 謂妻楊, 呼爲鄉里, 曰: 我不忍令鄉里落他處, 今當先殺鄉里.

③ *Nan T'ang chin shih* 南唐近事 of Chêng Wên-pao 鄭文寶, 953-1013 A. D. (寶顔堂秘笈 ed.) 3a-4b: 渾家; also *Liang Ch'i i kao* 梁溪遺稿, 詩鈔 of Yu Mou 尤袤 1127-1194 A. D., (錫山尤氏叢刊 ed.) 淮民謡, 11b.

④ 渾舍 is a variant of *hun-chia*.

⑤ 老婆 "old woman." Cf. *Ch'êng wei lu*, 5.10a. This is the most common modern term.

⑥ *Hêng yen lu*, 3. 13b-14a: 家主婆.

⑦ Ho Liang-chün 何良俊, *Ssŭ yu chai Ts'ung shuo* 四友齋叢説(紀録匯编 ed.) 6.52b-53a: 太太. Cf. also *T'ung su pien*, 18. 8a. During the Ming period, *t'ai t'ai* was a term for the wives of officials of the 中丞 rank and higher.

⑧ 令室.

⑨ *Shih Ching* 20B, 8b: 令妻.

⑩ *Yen tzŭ Ch'un Ch'iu*, 6.9a: 内子. *Nei tzŭ* was used during the feudal period as a term for the wife of ministers of the feudal lords, e. g., *Li Chi* 44.16a. and *Shih ming*. Hence it is sometimes used as a complimentary term.

⑪ *Tso Chuan* 27. 2b: 伉儷.

⑫ *Li Chi* 5. 22b: 嬪.

⑬ *Chu tzŭ nien P'u* 朱子年譜 by Wang Mu-hung 王懋竑 1668-1764 A. D. (粤雅堂叢書本) 2A. 13a: 令人.

⑭ *Ch'êng wei lu*, 5.14a: 德配.

73. Hsiung 兄 o b

The *Êrh Ya* used *hsiung* to explain *k'un.*① The two terms apparently were synonymous in ancient times. Kuo P'o's (276-324 A. D.) commentary on the *Êrh Ya* states that the people of Chiang Tung called older brother k'un. The *Shuo Wên* does not give the character 罤, but gives the character 翼罤, and states that the Chou people used this term for older brother. 翼 is probably its original form and 罤 and 晜, its variants. 昆 is a later borrowed form.② In the *Shih Ching*, only *the Wang Fêng* (4A. 9a) uses the term *k'un*, all others using *hsiung*. This fact is regarded as evidence that *k'un* is a Chou term.

In the *I Li* all male paternal cousins of the same sibname of ego and within the *Ta Kung* degree of mourning are given as *k'un ti*, and all male paternal cousins of the same sibname but beyond the *Ta Kung* degree of mourning, and all male cousins of different sibnames from ego are given as *hsiung ti*③, This illustrates the intentional differentiation and standardization of the degrees of relationship adopted by the ritual books in employing terms in other than their original connotation. *k'un* is entirely obsolete at present.④

The vocative is *ko*⑤哥 or *ko ko* a euphonic duplication. *Ko*, as given in the *Shuo wên*, does not mean older brother at all; it means "to sing," or "a song." *Ko* was first used from the sixth to the eighth centuries A. D., to mean father and then in the ninth and tenth centuries A. D. it became a vocative for older brother.⑥

---

① *Êrh Ya*: 罤.

② The *Shuo wên* lists the character 昆 but not with the meaning "older brother." The *Yü p'ien* gives 罤 and states that it is the same as 昆. Huang k'an 皇侃 (488-545 A. D.) says, that *k'un* 昆 means "bright", "brilliant". Out of reverence the older brother is called *k'un* (論語義疏, 6.2b-3a 古經解匯函 edition). This is rather a rationalization.

③ *Ch'êng wei lu*, 4.2b.

④ For a most complete and classical study of the difference between these characters, cf. 昆弟兄弟釋異 by Tsang Yung 臧庸, 1767-1811, 拜經堂文集 (1930), 1.

⑤ *Kuang yün*.

⑥ *Kai yü Ts'ung k'ao*, 37.25b.

According to the *Fang Yên*, the people of Chin and Yang called older brother *po* or *pò*①, The *Shih Ming* says that the people of Ch'ing and Hsü used the term *huang* 荒. Until the fourteenth to the seventeenth centuries A. D. the peoples of the lower Yangtze delta still called older brother 況 *huang*.②況 and 荒 are pronounced about the same. The ancient pronunciation of *hsiung* 兄 may have been *huang* 況, as the two characters are often used interchangeably.③ The *Pai hu T'ung* uses 況 to explain 兄.

74. Sao 嫂 o b w

The *Êrh Ya* reads, "Woman calls older brother's wife *sao*," but it does not give the man's term. Whether or not *sao* was exclusively a woman's term we have no means of knowing. The *Shuo Wên* defines *sao* as "older brother's wife" but does not specify man or woman; it was most probably a term for both man and woman.④

75. Ti 弟 y b

The younger brother, when speaking to the older brother or sister, calls himself *pi ti*⑤, or *hsiao ti*.⑥ The older brother or sister calls the younger brother *hsien ti*.⑦, These were old usages; at present simply *ti* is used.

*Chia ti*⑧ was used as a depreciative from the third to the eighth centuries A. D. It is now incorrect to use this term. The present term is *shê ti*, and the complimentary term, *ling ti* or *hsien ti*.

76. Ti fu 弟婦 y b w

Ti hsi 弟媳, is an alternative term. *Fu* and *hsi* are synonymous in

---

① *Fang Yen*, 10. 4a: 䄒 Its pronunciation is very uncertain.

② *Yen pei tsa chih* 研北雜誌, by Lu Yu 陸友, ca. 1330 A. D. (得月簃 edition) 49a.

③ *Shih Ching*, 3A. 7a; Ibid., 18B. 1a: *Han shu*. 76. 6a. with YEN Shih-Ku's note.

④ For example, *Chan kuo ts'ê* 3.6a.

⑤ *San kuo chih* 29. 26a (commentary): 鄙弟.

⑥ 木蘭詩:小弟.

⑦ *Shih Chi* 86. 9a: 賢弟.

⑧ *Ts'ao tzŭ* Ch'ien chi 釋思賦序, 1.5b; *T'ang shu* 162. 22b.

relationship terminology. The older brother usually avoids the younger brother's wife, and vice versa. Conversation can be only formal, and a proper distance must be maintained.

77. Tzŭ 姊 o si

Tzŭ is now used chiefly in standard and literary contexts. It may be doubled as *tzŭ tzŭ*. The universal vocative is *chieh* or *chieh chieh*. Compare 34 for changes of *chieh*. *Chieh* may also be used for any young woman, e. g., *hsiao chieh*, which is equivalent to "Miss."

*Hsü*① was an ancient term for older sister, used in the state of ch'u; *shao*② was used in Ch'i. *Mêng*③ was an old term for father's concubine's daughter older than father's principal wife's daughter. Later, in certain regions, it was used to mean older sister in general.④ *Nü hsiung*⑤ may be used as a literary alternative for *tzŭ*.

78. Tzŭ fu 姊夫 o si h

The term in the *Êrh Ya* is *shêng*—a reflection of cross-cousin marriage. *Tzŭ chang* and *tzŭ hsü*⑥ are modern ltern atives. *Chieh fu* is more colloquial. Teknonymy is the most common practice as regards the vocative. If there is no child, brother terms are usually used.

The *Êrh Ya* says that sisters call each other's husband *ssŭ*⑦, "private"; this is considered evidence of the sororate. It has long been obsolete. In modern times, brother and sister use the same term.

79. Mei 妹, y si

---

① *Li Sao* (*Wên Hsüan*, 32.9b) 嫛; also *Shuo Wên*.

② *Kuang yün* 嫈.

③ *Tso chuan* 2.2a: 孟.

④ *Fang yen*, 12. la.

⑤ *Shuo wên*: 女兄.

⑥ *Hou Han Shu* 49. 12b: ⊙; *Chin Shu* 39. 8a-b. (No. 18 on p. 157.)

⑦ 私. *Shih Ching* 3B. 9a. The *Shih ming* gives the traditional, but rationalistic, explanation.

*Ti*① is said to be a woman's term for younger sister but this is by no means certain. During the feudal period *ti* had a special connotation in connection with the yin marriage. *Nü ti*② is a literary alternative term for *mei*. The *Shuo Wên* states that the people of ch'u called younger sister *wei*③, which may be a variant of *mei*.

The depreciatory term *chia tzŭ* is used for older sister, and *shê mei* for younger sister. This use of these terms is continued even after the sisters are married, although theoretically this should not be done.

80. Mei fu 妹夫 y si h

In the *Êrh Ya* the term is *shêng*—a reflection of cross-cousin ma-riage. The *Êrh Ya* also says that sisters call one another's husbands *ssŭ*—a supposed reflection of the sororate. *Mei chang* and *mei hsü* are modern ahematives. For other usages, compare 78.

81. T'ang hsiung 堂兄 f b s > e

Ts'ung fu k'un ti is the term in the *Êrh Ya* and *I Li*④ for the first male paternal cousins. Later it was abbreviated to *Ts'ung hsiung*⑤ for the father's brother's sons older than speaker, and *ts'ung ti*⑥ for those younger than the speaker. *Kung k'un ti* was used in the *Shih Chi*.⑦ During the fifth and sixth centuries A. D. *T'ung T'ang* was substituted for *Ts'ung*, e. g., *T'ung T'ang hsiung* and *T'ung T'ang ti*. During the latter part of the T'ang dynasty the *T'ung*

① *Shih Ming*: 娣. This interpretation is followed by Chêng Chên in his *Ch'ao ching ch'ao wên chi*, 1. 17b-18a. This view is hardly justifiable, however, on the basis of the *Êrh Ya's* use of *mei* and *ti*. The former is used both by man and woman; the latter, in reference to the yin costom of the feudal period, refers to younger sisters who have married the same man. Thus *ti* can also be applied to husband's younger brother's wife, as in the *Êrh Ya*.

② *Shuo wên*: 女弟.

③ 媦. Cf. also *Kung-yang chuan* 4.7b.

④ *I Li* 31. 17a.

⑤ *Liang Shu* 31.1a.

⑥ *San kuo chih* 8.1a.

⑦ Shih Chi 49.6a: 公.

was dropped, only *T'ang hsiung* and *T'ang ti* being used. *T'ang and Ts'ung* can still be used alternatively.

82. T'ang sao 堂嫂 w of 81

83. T'ang ti 堂弟 f b s < e

84. T'ang ti fu 堂弟婦 w of 83

85. T'ang tzŭ 堂姊 f b d > e

The older term is *Ts'ung fu tzŭ mei* for father's brother's daughters, both older and younger than speaker. The development is exactly parallel with that of 81, *T'ang hsiung*.

86. T'ang tzŭ fu ○○夫 h of 85

87. T'ang mei 堂妹 f b d < e

88. T'ang mei fu ○○夫 h of 87

89. Tsai Ts'ung hsiung 再從兄 f f b s s > e

The older term is *Ts'ung tsu k'un ti*, as used in the *Êrh Ya* and the *I Li*.[1] *Tsai Ts'ung* was substituted later. *Tsai* means "once again" or "a second time." *Ts'ung* is synonymous with the later term *T'ang*, which indicates the second collateral line. Hence *tsai Ts'ung* indicated the third collateral line.

90. Tsai Ts'ung sao 再從嫂 w of 89

91. Tsai Ts'ung ti 再從弟 f f b s s < e

92. Tsai Ts'ung ti fu 再從弟婦 w of 91

93. Tsai Ts'ung tzŭ 再從姊 f f b s d > e

94. Tsai Ts'ung tzŭ fu 再從姊夫 h of 93

95. Tsai Ts'ung mei 再從妹 f f b s d < e

96. Tsai Ts'ung mei fu 再從妹夫 h of 95

97. Tsu hsiung 族兄 f f f b s s s > e

The alternative and more exact term is *san Ts'ung hsiung* 三從兄. *San*

---

① *I Li* 33.1b：祖.

means "third", and *Ts'ung* signifies second collateral. Hence *san Ts'ung* means the fourth collateral line, since *Ts 'ung* begins the count from the second collateral line. This principle can be extended and the terms formed, e. g., *ssŭ Ts'ung*, *wu Ts'ung*, *liu Ts'ung*, indicating the fifth, sixth, seventh collateral lines, respectively. *Tsu* 族 is a vague term applied to all sib relatives from the fourth collateral line and beyond, without further discrimination. *Tsung hsiung*[1] is a modern alternative. *Tsung* 宗 is in a certain sense synonymous with *tsu* 族. *Ts'ung tsêng tsu k'un ti*[2] was used during the Han period; it is a rather clumsy device involving the enumeration of ancestors.

Ch'in T'ung hsing[3] is the term given in the *Êrh Ya* for male paternal cousins of the same sibname, of the fifth collateral line. It is obsolete now; generally *tsu hsiung ti* is used, or, more exactly, *ssŭ Ts'ung hsiung ti*.

98. Tsu sao 族嫂 w of 97

99. Tsu ti 族弟 f f f b s s s < e

100. Tsu ti fu 族弟婦 w of 99

101. Tsu tzŭ 族姊 f f f b s s d > e

102. Tsu tzŭ fu 族姊夫 h of 101

103. Tsu mei 族妹 f f f b s s d < e

104. Tsu mei fu 族妹夫 h of 103

The vocatives for brothers and sisters, brothers' wives and sisters' husbands can be correspondingly applied to 81-104, individualized by their names, numerical order, or sibnames. Depreciatory and complimentary forms can be formed in the regular way.

105. Ku piao hsiung 姑表兄 f si s > e

---

① 宗兄 is just as indefinite as *tsu hsiung*, and can be applied to any older sibbrother from the fourth collateral line and beyond. But *tsung hsiung* was used during the feudal period by younger brothers to refer to the primogenitary eldest brother. *Li Chi* 19. 10b-11a.

② *Hsin Shu* 8.6a-b.

③ 親同姓.

The old term in the *Êrh Ya* is *shêng*—a reflection of crosscousin marriage. During the Han period *wai hsiung ti*[1] and *Ts'ung nei hsiung ti*[2] were used for both the older and the younger. The term *piao* also dates from this period. *Shêng*, *wai hsiung ti* and *Ts'ung nei hsiung ti* are all obsolete now.

In the vocative *ku* is always dropped, leaving only *piao hsiung* or *piao ko*. *Piao hsiung* is more literary and formal, *piao ko* is strictly vocative. In certain localities *lao piao* 老表 is used.

106. Ku piao sao 姑表嫂 w of 105

Vocative *piao sao*.

107. Ku piao ti 姑表弟 f si s < e

108. Ku piao ti fu ○○弟婦 w of 107

109. Ku piao tzŭ ○○姊 f si d < e

Vocative *piao chieh*.

110. Ku piao tzŭ fu ○○姊夫 h of 109

111. Ku piao mei ○○妹 f si d < e

112. Ku piao mei fu ○○妹夫 h of 111

113. T'ang ku piao hsiung 堂姑表兄 f f si s s > e

114. T'ang ku piao sao ○○表嫂 w of 113

115. T'ang ku piao ti ○○表弟 f fsi s s < e

116. T'ang ku piao ti fu ○○○弟婦 w of 115

117. T'ang ku piao tzŭ ○○○姊 f f si s d > e

118. T'ang ku piao tzŭ fu ○○○姊夫 h of 117

119. T'ang ku piao mei ○○○妹 f f si s d < e

120. T'ang ku piao mei fu ○○○妹夫 h of 119

Terms 113-120 may also be applied to the children of father's father's brother's daughter. This is by inference only; no documentary usage has been

① *I Li* 33. 9b.

② *Wên Hsüan*, 25.1*a*.

noted.

Ⅵ. Generation of the son

121. Tzŭ 子 son

Tzŭ, in ancient times, was used to mean child, either male or female. Thus it was often compounded with other elements to signify son, e. g., *chang fu tzŭ*.① *Êrh*② is synonymous with *tzŭ*; it is now used mostly as a diminutive, with no sex connotation, so that it has to be combined with other elements to express son, as in the modern term *êrh tzŭ*.③ *Hsi*④ is an old term for son, but also has thc indefinite meaning of child; consequently, the forms *hsi nan*⑤ for son and *hsi nü* for daughters are used. *Ssŭ* 嗣⑥ means "descendant," and is also used for son. During the feudal period *ssŭ tzŭ*⑦ referred to the eldest succeeding son, but in modern terminology is used for the adopted son. *Hsing*⑧, in ancient times, may be used for son but it may mean any descendant, being synonymous with *shêng*⑨, "to bear." *Nu*⑩ is another old term.

Ku and *ni*⑪ were uncommon old, perhaps local, terms for son. *Tsai* 崽⑫, and *tsai* 囝⑬ are modern dialectical forms, apparently derivatives from *tzŭ*. 囝

---

① *Shih Chi* 67. 19a-b: 夫子丈; literally, "male child."

② *Kuang ya*:兒.

③ *Shih Chi* 52. 2a.

④ 息 means "to reproduce", or "to bear". Hence it is used both for male and female children. See p. 275, note⑤, and p. 278, note ①.

⑤ *Ts'ao tzŭ-chien chi* 8. 1.

⑥ *Shu Ching* 4.7a.

⑦ *Li Chi* 4.5a.

⑧ *Shih Ching* 1C. 7a: 姓; and *Tso Chuan* 42. 32a.

⑨ Since the ancient pronunciation of *hsing* is about the same as 生, they are used interchangeably. *Shih Ching* 20D. 7b.

⑩ *Shih Ching* 9B. 10b: 帑.

⑪ *Kuang Ya*:㝅,婗. Cf. 王念孫,廣雅疏證,6B.4.

⑫ *Fang Yen*, 10. 1b.

⑬ *Chêng tzŭ tung*, *s.v.*

may also be pronounced *chien*.①

Tzŭ can be combined with various modifiers to express the more exact and complicated relationships of sonship resulting from ancestor worship, inheritance, concubinage, divorce and remarriage, adoption, etc.

The son, in speaking to the father, calls himself *nan* 男, "a male issue." *Êrh tzŭ* 兒子 is more vocative, and *nan* is principally a literary form of address. During the mourning period the son refers to himself as *ku tzŭ*②, *ai tzŭ*③, *ku ai tzŭ*④, *pu hsiao nan*⑤, or *chi jên*.⑥

The father calls the son *êrh tzŭ* both in the vocative and in writing. In speaking, usually only the name is used. In writing, the relationship term is used together with the name, as "*êrh tzŭ* so and so." This rule applies to relatives of all descending generations.

The complimentary term is *ling lang*.⑦ Other combinations are *lang chün*⑧, or *hsien lang*⑨. *Hsien tzŭ*⑩, *ling tzŭ*⑪, and *ling ssŭ*⑫ are alternative terms, somewhat more literary. *Kung tzŭ*⑬ was originally a term for the sons of

---

① Chêng Chên (Ch'in shu chi, 2. 12b) says that the *Chi Yün* gives the pronunciation 九件切. This is incorrect and probably a confusion with 孨. But *chien* may be a T'ang pronunciation, e. g., in *Hua yang chi*, 1. 13a. However, at present the character is pronounced differently in different localities. In Fukien, it is pronounced "chan", in Chekiang and Kiangsu. "lan", and in Kiangsi, Kwangtung, Hupeh and Hunan, 'tsai'.

② 孤, "orphaned son", used when mourning for the father when the mother is living.

③ 哀, "grieving son", used when mourning for the mother when the father is chungpiao.

④ This is used in mourning for either parent when both of them are dead. The differentiation began during the T'ang dynasty. Cf. *Kai yü Ts'ung kao*, 37. 8a-9b.

⑤ 不孝男 "unfilial son".

⑥ *Shih Ching* 7B. 3b: 棘人.

⑦ 郎 is originally a title of office. During the Han period, high officials could appoint their sons *lang*. Thus *lang* became a complimentary term. *Cf Ch'êng wei lu*, 6.3a.

⑧ *Yü t'ai hsin yung chi*, 1.18b.

⑨ 古文苑, *Ssŭ pu Ts'ung kan* ed., 10. 17a.

⑩ *Wei Wu-ti chih* 43a-b.

⑪ *Nan Shih* 59. 6a.

⑫ *Mo Chi*, 2.12b.

⑬ *Shih Shing* 1C. 6b; Ibid. 13A. 5a.

the feudal nobility and later for the sons of men of high official positions. But now it has become a general complimentary term almost as prevalent as *ling lang*. Another very common, rather vulgar, term is *shao yêh* 少爺, which also originally referred to the son of a man of rank or of an official, e. g., as used by the servants in referring to the master's son.

The depreciatory term is hsiao tzŭ, or *hsiao êrh*. More vulgarly *hsiao Ch'üan* 小犬, "a little dog." *Chien hsi*① and *jo hsi*② are obsolete literary terms.

122. Tzŭ fu 子婦 s w

Hsi fu 媳婦 is a more colloquial term. *Hsi* 媳 was originally written 息, which means "son" or "child." During the Sung period the female classifier was added, forming 媳.③ Thus it became a distinct term for daughter-in-law. *Hsi fu* may be used for the wives of all the relatives of descending generations.

Son's wife is usually addressed with this name by her parents-inlaw. The father-in-law sees her only on formal occasions, and usually maintains a proper distance. When the daughter-in-law gets older and has children, the parents-in-law may even use the grandchildren's term in referring to her—extreme extension of teknonymy.

123. Nü 女 daughter

*Nü tzŭ tzŭ*④ and *fu jên tzŭ*⑤ are used in the *Li Chi* and *I Li* for daughter, in distinction to *chang fu tzŭ* for male child. *Ying*⑥ is said to have been an ancient term for daughter, but this is by no means certain.

Nü êrh is more colloquial. It is used both by parents and daughter, and is a general term as well. When the daughter writes to her parents only *nü* is used

---

① *Shih Chi* 43.32b:賤息.

② *Nan Shih* 46. 10a: 弱息.

③ Cf. *Ch'êng wei lu*, 8.17b-18a.

④ *I Li* 31.16b-17a. *Li Chi* 2.13b.

⑤ *I Li* 32.4a.

⑥ *Yü p'ien*: 嬰. It is usually a term for infant.

in referring to herself.

The complimentary terms are *ling yüan*①, *ling ai*②, *nü kung tzŭ* 女公子 and, more colloquially, *Ch'ien chin*③ and *hsiao chieh*.④ *Yü nü*⑤ was used during the feudal period, but is no longer used in this sense. *Hsiao niang tzŭ* was commonly used during the T'ang and Sung periods.⑥

The depreciatory terms are *hsiao nü*, more vulgarly, *hsiao ya t'ou* 小丫頭, "little handmaid." *Hsi nü*⑦ is an old obsolete term, which could be used as a literary form. *Chia tzŭ*⑧ was admissible during the Han period, but was never used in this sense in later times and nowadays is used as a depreciatory term for older sister.

124. Nü hsü 女婿 d h

Mencius uses the term *shêng*. The *Êrh Ya* uses the term *hsü*, which may also mean "husband" in general.⑨ *Hsü* is combined with a variety of qualifiers to signify daughter's husband, e. g., *tzŭ hsü*⑩, *lang hsü*, and *hsü shêng*.⑪ Other alternative terms are *nü fu*⑫ and *pan tzŭ*⑬. *Chiao K'o*⑭, *tung ch'uang*⑮, *t'an*

---

① 令媛 *yüan* is a term for a beautiful girl and *ling yüan* is probably derived from *Shih Ching*, 3A. 5a.

② 令愛, your beloved one.

③ 千金, "a thousand tales of gold," that is precious. *Yin p'ao sui pi* 音匏隨筆, by TSAO Mou-chien 曹楙堅(乙亥叢編 edition.) 8a.

④ 小姐 was used during the Sung period as a term for young maid servants, or prostitutes. Cf. *Kai yü Ts 'ung k'ao*, 38.12. At present it is used as a complimentary term for the daughter of another and for any young woman.

⑤ *Li Chi*, 49.3 a: 玉女.

⑥ Cf. *Kai yü Ts'ung k'ao*, 38.1a.

⑦ *Shih Chi*, 8.4a: 息女.

⑧ *Yen shih chia hsün*, 2.5a: 家⊙. (No. 10, p. 155.)

⑨ Originally, it was a complimentary term for an able scholar.

⑩ *Shih Chi* 89.10a.

⑪ ⊙(*Ch'êng wei lu*, 8. 21b).(No. 14, p. 156.)

⑫ *Chin Shu* 34. 8a.

⑬ 半子, half son. *Liu pin-K'o wên chi*, 外集,祭虢州楊庶子文,10.7.

⑭ 嬌客 literally, "delicate" or "graceful guest". It is non-vocative and non-referential.

⑮ 東床 "the one who occupies the bed in the eastern chamber", is based on the anecdote of 王羲之, 東床坦腹, *Chin Shu* 80.1b. Cf. *Shih ch'ang T'an*, 1.3b.

ch'uang①, *k'uai hsü*, *chia hsü*②, and *mi Ch'in*③ are mostly literary forms, used more or less in a complimentary way.

*Ch'ing*④ was originally a dialectical form (Shantung) for daughter's husband, and later was commonly used as a literary term. The forms *tsu pien* 卒便 and *p'ing shih* 平使 are erroneous derivatives of *ch'ing*.⑤ *Ch'ing* is also used to mean "husband" in general. *Ch'ing* and *hsü* were originally complimentary terms for a man of ability.

The complimentary terms are *ling hsü* and *ling T'an*. *Ling T'an* is derived from *T'an ch'uang*, and is rather uncommon.

Depreciatory term, *hsiao hsü*.

125. Chih 姪 b s

The *Êrh Ya* gives no term for brother's son, man speaking. It is conjectured that brother's sons (man speaking) could be called sons, *tzŭ*. The *Li Chi* uses the term *yu tzŭ*, "like son,"⑥ but whether or not it is an established term is quite uncertain. During the Han dynasty the term *ts'ung tzŭ*⑦ was commonly employed, but more commonly the purely descriptive forms *hsiung tzŭ* and *ti tzŭ* were used. There is evidence that brother's sons were simply called *tzŭ*.⑧

Chih, as used in the *Êrh Ya*, was a woman's term for brother's son. It is similarly used in the *I Li* (32.1b). The use of *chih* as a man's term for brother's

---

① 坦床.

② 快⊙ and 佳⊙ mean practically the same thing. *Pei Shih* 34. 16b-17a.

③ *Chiu T'ang Shu* 159. 7a:密親.

④ *Fang Yen* 3.1a: 倩.

⑤ *Fang Yen*, *loc. cit.*, commentary. *Kuang Ya*, *loc. cit.*

⑥ *Li Chi* 8. 4a.

⑦ *Shih shuo hsin yü*, 1*A*. 21*b* (*commentary*): 從子.

⑧ *Han shu* 71.4a-b; *Hou Han Shu* 90B. 18b: Tsai Yung refers to his father's younger brother and himself as *fu tzŭ*. It also must be understood that whenever one is referring to well-known relationships, or in the vocative, the more inclusive terms *fu tzŭ* are usually used, otherwise the more exact terms.

son dates from the Chin period (265-420). This usage originated in north China and then became general.① The woman's term for brother's son was then prefixed with *nei*, thus forming nei chih, in contra-distinction to *chih*.

Chih nan is mostly a self-reference term. *Yüan*② is a complimentary term, not commonly used. The common complimentary term is *ling chih*.

126. Chih fu 姪婦 b s w

Chih hsi fu is more colloquial. As remarked above, *hsi fu* applies to the wives of all relatives of descending generations.

127. Chih nü 姪女 b d

Chih as used in the *Êrh Ya* and *I Li* is devoid of sex connotation, a feature characteristic of one of a pair of reciprocal terms. *Ku* and *chih* are conceptual reciprocals. When *chih* was transformed into a man's term. it ceased to be reciprocal and the sex indicator was suffixed, e. g., chih nü for brother's daughter. The inverted form *nü chih* may also be used. *Yu nü* and *Ts'ung nü* are the terms corresponding to *yu tzŭ* and *Ts'ung tzŭ*. *Hsiung nü* and *ti nü* are descriptive terms corresponding to *hsiung tzŭ* and *ti tzŭ*.

128. Chih hsü 姪婿 b d h

*I hsing*③ is an unconmmon ancient term, rarely understood today. *Hsiung hsü*, "older brother's *hsü*," and *ti hsü*, "younger brother's *hsü*," are descriptive alternatives. *Chih nü hsü* is more colloquial.

129. Wai shêng 外甥 si s

The *Êrh Ya* gives the term *ch'u* and, in a later passage, *shêng*. *ch'u* is probably an older term than *shêng*, since *shêng*, but not *ch'u*, is used in the *I Li*.④

---

① *Yeh shih chia hsün* 2.7a.

② 阮 as a complimentary term was based on the uncle-nephew relationship of 阮籍 and 阮咸. Cf. *Shih shuo hsin yü*, 3A. 38a.

③ *Ta tai li chi*, 6. 7a: 異姓.

④ *I Li* 33. 9a.

Wai shêng came into use during the Chin dynasty; it is also written 外生.①
*Chai hsiang*② is a term used, probably rarely, *circa* the first half of the first millennium A. D.

130. Wai shêng fu 外甥婦 si s w
131. Wai shêng nü 外甥女 si d
132. Wai shêng hsü ○○婿 si d h
133. T'ang chih 堂姪 f b s s
134. T'ang chih fu ○○婦 f b s s w
135. T'ang chih nii ○○女 f b s d
136. T'ang chih hsü ○○婿 f b s d h
137. T'ang wai shêng 堂外甥 f b d s
138. T'ang wai shêng fu ○○甥婦 f b d s w
139. T'ang wai shêng nü ○○甥女 f b d d
140. T'ang wai shêng hsü ○○甥婿 f b d d h
141. Ku piao chih 姑表姪 f si s s
142. Ku piao chih fu ○○○婦 w of 141
143. Ku piao chih nü ○○○女 f si s d
144. Ku piao chih hsü ○○○婿 h of 143
145. Ku piao wai shêng ○○外甥 f si d s
146. Ku piao wai shêng fu ○○外甥婦 w of 145
147. Ku piao wai shêng nü ○○○○女 f si d d
148. Ku piao wai shêng hsü ○○○○婿 h of 147

① *Shih shuo hsin yü*, 3A. 3a (commentary).

② 宅相, "house site," is of interesting origin. *Chin shu* 41.1a: Wei Shu was an orphan reared in his maternal grandmother's home, the Ning family. When the Ning's built a house, a geomancer prophecied that this house site, *Chai hsiang*, would have a daughter's son who would be great. Wei Shu's maternal grandmother considered this prophecy had been fulfilled, when Wei Shu, although young, was brilliant and precocious. Wei Shu then said, "I will fulfill the prophecy of this good house site, chai hsiang." *Pei Ch'i Shu* 29. 2b; *Shih ch'ang T'an*, 1.3a.

149. Tsai Ts'ung chih 再從姪 s of 89 or 91

150. Tsai Ts'ung chih fu ○○姪婦 w of 149

151. Tsai Ts'ung chih nü ○○○女 d of 89 or 91

152. Tsai Ts'ung chih hsü ○○○婿 h of 151

153. Tsu chih 族姪 s of 97 or 99

154. Tsu chih fu ○○婦 w of 153

155. Tsu chih nü ○○女 d of 97 or 99

156. Tsu chih hsü ○○婿 h of 155

Ⅶ. Generation of the son's son

157. Sun 孫 s s

*Tzŭ hsing*① is an old obsolete term. During the Chin period *wan shêng* 晚生, "late born," was used for son, likewise, *hsiao wan shêng*, "little late born," for son's son.② *Wên sun* is a literary form derived from the Book of History③; it originally referred to King Wên's son's son. *Sun êrh* and *sun tzŭ* are more colloquial, *êrh* and *tzŭ* being diminutives.

*Chia sun*④ was used as a depreciatory term during the Han period, but has never been used since and is now considered incorrect. The correct depreciatory term is *hsiao sun*.

Sun may be combined with various modifiers to express the exact relationships, e. g., *chang sun* for the oldest son's son, *shih sun* or *Ch'êng chung sun*⑤ for the eldest son's eldest son, who must carry the three years mourning obligations in his father's place in the event that the father has died before the grandfather.

158. Sun fu 孫婦 s s w

---

① *Shih Ching* 1C. 7a; *I Li* 44.2b; *Shih Chi* 49. 2a.

② *Chin shu* 69. 7b; *p'ieh chi*, 4.2a.

③ Shu Ching 17. 35a: 文孫.

④ *Yen shih chia hsün* 2.5a.

⑤ *I Li* 30.12a:其適孫承重者.

159. Sun nü 孫女 s d

Sun, as in the *I Li*, may be used to mean grandchild or any descendant from the second descending generation and down. In modern usage *sun nü* is employed in contra-distinction to *sun*. The inverted form, *nü sun*, is also permissible.

160. Sun hsü 孫婿 s d h

161. Wai sun 外孫 d s

162. Wai sun fu ○○婦 d s w

163. Wai sun nü ○○女 d d

164. Wai sun hsü ○○婿 d d h

165. Chih sun 姪孫 b s s

Ts'ung sun is a term found in the *Kuo Yü*.① *Yu sun*② was occasionally used during the T'ang period, and earlier, but is seldom used today, except as a literary form.

166. Chih sun fu ○○婦 b s s w

167. Chih sun nü ○○女 b s d

168. Chih sun hsü ○○婿 b s d h

169. Wai chih sun 外姪孫 b d s

170. Wai chih sun fu ○○○婦 b d s w

171. Wai chih sun nü ○○○女 b d d

172. Wai chih sun hsü ○○○婿 b d d h

In local variations, *chih wai sun* 姪外孫 and *T'ang wai sun* 堂外孫 may be used for 169-172.

173. Wai shêng sun 外甥孫 si s s

The term in the *Êrh Ya* is *li sun* 離孫, literally "departing grandson." Whether or not there is any significance in this term one cannot say. Other

① *Kuo yü* 3.7a.

② *Yüan shih Chang-Ch'ing chi* 54.4b.

ancient alternative terms are *Ts'ung sun shêng*[①] and *mi sun*.[②]

174. Wai shêng sun fu 外甥孫婦 si s s w

175. Wai shêng sun nü ○○孫女 si s d

176. Wai shêng sun hsü ○○孫婿 si s d h

177. T'ang chih sun 堂姪孫 f b s s s

178. T'ang chih sun fu ○○○婦 w of 177

179. T'ang chih sun nü ○○○女 f b s s d

180. T'ang chih sun hsü ○○○婿 h of 179

181. Ku piao chih sun 姑表姪孫 f si s s s

182. Ku piao chih sun fu ○○○○婦 w of 181

183. Ku piao chih sun nü ○○○○女 f si s s d

184. Ku piao chih sun hsü ○○○○婿 h of 183

185. Tsai Ts'ung chih sun 再從姪孫 s of 149

186. Tsai Ts'ung chih sun fu ○○○○婦 w of 185

187. Tsai Ts'ung chih sun nü ○○○○女 d of 149

188. Tsai Ts'ung chih sun hsü ○○○○婿 h of 187

189. Tsu sun 族孫 s of 153

190. Tsu sun fu ○○婦 w of 189

191. Tsu sun nü ○○女 d of 153

192. Tsu sun hsü ○○婿 h of 191

Tsu chih sun 族姪孫 may be used in substitution for *tsu sun* in terms 189-192, but the *chih* is not necessary.

Ⅷ. Generation of the son's son's son

193. Tsêng sun 曾孫 s s s

According to old usages all descendants from the son's son's son and

① *Tso Chuan* 60.20b.

② Ibid 60. 17b:彌.

descending can be called *tsêng sun*, or *hsi sun*.① During the Han period *êrh sun* was probally used synonymously with *tsêng sun*.②

Ch'ung sun 重孫 is the modern colloquial term.

194. Tsêng sun fu 曾孫婦 s s s w

195. Tsêng sun nü 曾孫女 s s d

196. Tsêng sun hsü ○○婿 s s d h

197. Wai sun tsêng sun 外孫曾孫 d s s, or s d s

198. Wai sun tsêng sun nü ○○○○女 d s d, or s d d

199. Tsêng chih sun 曾姪孫 b s s s

200. Tsêng chih sun nü ○○○女 b s s d

201. Wai shêng tsêng sun 外甥曾孫 si s s s

202. Wai shêng tsêng sun nü ○○○○女 si s s d

Ⅸ. Generation of the son's son's son's son

203. Hsüan sun 玄孫③ s s s s

204. Hsüan sun fu ○○婦 s s s s w

205. Hsüan sun nü ○○女 s s s d

206. Hsüan sun hsü ○○婿 s s s d h

The following terms are found in the *Êrh Ya*; although of no practical use, they are given here because of their theoretical interest:

207. Lai sun 來孫 s s s s s

208. K'un sun 昆○ s s s s s s

209. Jêng sun 仍○ s s s s s s s

210. Yün sun 雲○ s s s s s s s s

Relalives through Mother-Table Ⅱ

---

① *Chiu T'ang shu* 160. 19b.

② *Han Shu* 2. 2b. The interpretations of the term *êrh sun* 耳孫 are quite divergent. Perhaps the interpretation of 李裴 is the more prevalent usage in the Han period but it by no means precludes its use in the other connotations. Cf. *Hsüeh Lin* 3. 10-11.

③ *Jih Chih lu*, 5. 32b.

Ⅰ. Generation of the mother's father's father

1. Wai tsêng tsu fu 外曾祖父 m f f

In the *Êrh Ya* the term is *wai tsêng wang fu* ○ ○○王父.

2. Wai tsêng tsu mu ○○祖母 m f m

Wai tsêng wang mu ○○王母, as used in the *Êrh Ya*. Vocatives of the above two terms vary locally; they are largely based on the vocatives of 3 and 4, with generation modifiers.

Ⅱ. Generation of the mother's father

3. Wai tsu fu 外祖父 m f

Wai tsu may be used alone. The term in the *Êrh Ya* is *wai wang fu* 外王父. *Wai ta fu*① and *wai wêng*② are modern alternatives. The modern vocatives *chia kung*③, also pronounced *ka kung*, and *wai kung* were used as early as the fifth century A. D.

4. Wai tsu mu 外祖母 m m

Wai wang mu is used in the *Êrh Ya*. *Wai P'o*④ is the most common modern vocative; likewise common is *chia P'o*, also pronounced *ka P'o*. *Chia mu*⑤ was used during the fifth and sixth centuries A. D. Since *chia* at that time meant "mother," *chia mu* meant mother's mother. *Chia mu* is now used as a depreciatory term for mother. *Liao liao*⑥ is a dialectical form used in certain parts of North China.

5. Wai po tsu fu 外伯祖父 m f o b

---

① *Chang Yu-shih wên chi* 張右史文集, collected works of CHANG Lei 張耒(1052-1112 A. D.), *Ssŭ pu Ts'ung k'an* edition, 17.9b.

② *Yüan shih chang-Ch'ing chi* 9.5b.

③ *Yen shih chia hsün* 2.8a.

④ *Jung chai sui pi*, *ssŭ pi* 2.11*a*.

⑤ *Yen shih chia hsün* 2.8a.

⑥ *K'ang-hsi tzŭ tien* 嫽. *Liao* is also read *lao*, and is synonymous with *ao*. YEN Chih-T'ui (*Yen shih chia hsün* 2.7b) says that during his time the uncultured people called mother's parents by the same term as father's parents when the latter were all dead.

6. Wai po tsu mu ○○○母 m f o b w

7. Wai shu tsu fu 外叔祖父 m f y b

8. Wai shu tsu mu ○○○母 m f y b w

Ku wai tsu mu may be used for the mother's father's sister, *chiu wai tsu fu* for the mother's mother's brother, and *i wai tsu mu* for the mother's mother's sister. These relationships are not maintained socially, but the terms show how they can be handled. Practically, there are many ways of solving this terminological problem, e. g., if the necessity for addressing these relatives should arise, one may adopt the terms.of the mother's brother's son, who is the nearest relative of the same generation of ego on the mother's side.

Ⅲ. Generation of the mother

9. Chiu fu 舅父 m b

Or simply *chiu*, as used in the *Êrh Ya*. Since in modern usage, *chiu* also means wife's brother, the generation and sex indicator *fu* is necessary. *Po chiu* 伯舅 may be used for the mother's older brother, and *shu chiu* 叔舅 for the younger brother. These terms are now mainly literary. The mother's brothers and their family may be vaguely referred to as *wai shih* or *wai chia*.①

Vocatives are *chiu chiu*, *a chiu*, or *chiu tieh*. *Chia chiu*② was used as a depreciatory term during the fourth and fifth centuries A. D., but is not used today and is considered incorrect. *Ling chiu* and *tsun chiu* are complimentary terms.

10. Chiu mu 舅母 m b w

*Chin*③ is an old vocative used during the Sung period, and is now rather uncommon. The modern vocative is *chiu ma*.

11. I mu 姨母 m si

In the *Êrh Ya* and the *I Li* the term is *Ts'ung mu*.④ *I* originally meant "wife's sister." The first use of *i* for mother's sister is found in the *Tso Chuan*,

---

① Literally "outer family". *Chin Shu* 41.1a.

② *Shih shuo hsin yü*, 3B. 32a.

③ *Shu I*, 1.9b: 妗. *Ming t'ao tsa chih*, 13b.

④ *I Li* 33. 2a.

the 23rd year (B. C. 550) of Duke Hsiang.① This extension is attributed to the psychological similarity of these two relatives and to reverse teknonymy. Since the Han period *i* has entirely displaced the older verm *ts'ung mu*. *I* is also used for concubines a usage attributed to the sororate. The inverted form *mu i* may also be used.

Vocatives are *a i* or *i ma*.

12. I fu 姨父 m si h

*I fu*②, *i chang jên*③, or *i Chang*, were used during the first millennium A. D., but are uncommon today.

13. t'ang chiu fu 堂舅父 m f b s

Ts'ung chiu is used in the *Êrh Ya* and can still be used today, but more as a literary form.

14. T'ang chiu mu 堂舅母 w of 13

15. T'ang i mu 堂姨母 m f b d

16. T'ang i fu 堂姨父 h of 15

Ⅳ. Generation of the speaker

17. Chiu piao hsiung 舅表兄 m b s > e

Shêng is the term in the *Êrh Ya*-a reflection of cross-cousin marriage. *Nei hsiung*④ was a substitute used during the Han period; later it became confused with *wai hsiung*⑤, a term for father's sister's son. Today these terms are not used with the same meanings. *Nei hsiung* is now used for the wife's older brother, and *wai hsiung* for half brothers, by the same mother, older than ego. *Chiu tzŭ*⑥ and *chiu ti*⑦ are purely descriptive terms which were used *circa* 500

---

① *Tso Chuan* 35, 18a.

② *Yen shih chia hsün* 3.23a.

③ *Pei Shih* 47.7b-8a. *I chang jên* is now used to mean wife's mother's sister's husband.

④ *I Li* 33.10a.

⑤ *Sung Shu* 93. 4b-5a.

⑥ *Chin Shu* 34.8b.

⑦ *Ch'ang-li Chi* 32.7b.

A. D.; at present they both mean "wife's brothers."

Piao was first introduced during the latter part of the Han period, after cross-cousin marriage had long ceased to be preferential, *Piao*, or *chung piao*[1], was first used for mother's brother's and father's sister's children, and later was extended to include mother's sister's children.

In the vocative *chiu* is always dropped, leaving simply *piao hsiung* or *piao ko*, and, in certain localities, *lao piao*.

18. Chiu piao sao 舅表嫂 w of 17
19. Chiu piao ti ○○弟 m b s< e
20. Chiu piao ti fu ○○弟婦 w of 19
21. Chiu piao tzŭ ○○姊 m b d > e
22. Chiu piao tzŭ fu ○○姊夫 h of 21
23. Chiu piao mei ○○妹 m b d < e
24. Chiu piao mei fu ○○妹夫 h of 23
25. I piao hsiung 姨表兄 m si s > e

Ts'ung mu k'un ti is used in the *Êrh Ya* and *I Li* (33.9a). *I hsiung ti* was used during the last few centuries of the first millennium B. C. and approximately the first half of the first millennium A. D.[2] It can still today be used as an alternative term.[3] *Wai hsiung ti* was sometimes used during the T'ang period[4], having resulted from a confusion with the term for mother's brother's sons and father's sister's sons, which finally led to the extension of the term *piao* and the partial merging of the three relationships.

26. I piao sao 姨表嫂 w of 25
27. I piao ti ○○弟 m si s < e

---

① *San kuo chih* 11.20. *Chung piao* is equivalent to *nei wai*.

② See discussion, pp. 192-193. *Nan shih* 57.17a.

③ Cf. LIANG Chang-chü, *Ch'êng wei lu*, 3.20b. WANG Shih-han 汪師韓, 1707-? A. D., considers *i hsiung ti* a northern peculiarity: *t'an shu lu* 談書録,(昭代叢書 ed.) 45a.

④ 海録碎事 (cited by *Ch'êng wei lu*, 3.20a).

28. I piao ti fu ○○弟婦 w of 27

29. I piao tzŭ ○○姊 m si d > e

30. I piao tzŭ fu ○○姊夫 h of 29

31. I piao mei ○○妹 m si d < e

32. I piao mei fu ○○妹夫 h of 31

33. T‘ang chiu piao hsiung 堂舅表兄 m f b s s > e

34. T‘ang chiu piao sao ○○○嫂 w of 33

35. T‘ang chiu piao ti ○○○弟 m f b s s < e

36. T‘ang chiu piao ti fu ○○○弟婦 w of 35

37. T‘ang chiu piao tzŭ 堂舅表姊 m f b s d > e

38. T‘ang chiu piao tzŭ fu ○○○○夫 h of 37

39. T‘ang chiu piao mei 堂舅表妹 m f b s d < e

40. T‘ang chiu piao mei fu ○○○○夫 h of 39

Terms 3340 may also be applied to the children of father's mother's brother's sons, i. e., the children of 59-62 in table Ⅰ, hence these terms are not given there. This extension is inferred only from popular usage, there being insufficient documentary evidence for collation. At any rate, when one considers non-sib relatives on the third collateral line in as far as the third generation descending, the terminology becomes vague, and, indeed, an accurate system is not necessary here, since in almost all cases these relationships are not maintained socially.

41. T‘ang i piao hsiung 堂姨表兄 m f b d s > e

42. T‘ang i piao sao ○○表嫂 w of 41

43. T‘ang i piao ti ○○表弟 m f b d s < e

44. T‘ang i piao ti fu ○○表弟婦 w of 43

45. T‘ang i piao tzŭ 堂姨表姊 m f b d d > e

46. T‘ang i piao tzŭ fu ○○表姊夫 h of 45

47. T‘ang i piao mei ○○表妹 m f b d d < e

48. T'ang i piao mei fu ○○表妹夫 h of 47

Ⅴ. Generation of the son

49. Chiu piao chih 舅表姪 m b s s

50. Chiu piao chih fu ○○○婦 m b s s w

51. Chiu piao chih nü ○○○女 m b s d

52. Chiu piao chih hsü ○○○○婿 m b s d h

53. Chiu piao wai-shêng 舅表外甥 m b d s

54. Chiu piao wai-shêng fu ○○○○婦 m b d s w

55. Chiu piao wai-shêng-nü ○○○○女 m b d d

56. Chiu piao wai-shêng hsü ○○○○婿 m b d d h

57. I piao chih 姨表姪 m si s s

58. I piao chih fu ○○○婦 m si s s w

59. I piao chih nü ○○○女 m si s d

60. I piao chih hsü ○○○婿 m si s d h

61. I piao wai shêng ○○外甥 m si d s

62. I piao wai-shêng fu ○○○○婦 m si d s w

63. I piao wai-shêng nü 舅表外甥女 m si d d

64. I piao wai-shêng hsü ○○○○婿 m si d d h

65. T'ang chiu piao chih 堂舅表姪 s of 33 or 35

66. T'ang chiu piao chih fu ○○○○婦 w of 65

67. T'ang chiu piao chih nü ○○○○女 d of 33 or 35

68. T'ang chiu piao chih hsü ○○○○婿 h of 67

69. T'ang i piao chih 堂姨表姪 s of 41 or 43

70. T'ang i piao chih fu ○○○○婦 w of 69

71. T'ang i piao chih nü ○○○○女 d of 41 or 43

72. T'ang i piao chih hsü ○○○○婿 h of 71

Ⅵ. Generation of the son's son

73. Chiu piao chih sun 舅表姪孫 m b s s s

74. Chiu piao chih sun fu ○○○○婦 m b s s s w

75. Chiu piao chih sun nü ○○○○女 m b s s d

76. Chiu piao chih sun hsü ○○○○婿 m b s s d h

77. I piao chih sun 姨表姪孫 m si s s s

78. I piao chih sun fu ○○○○婦 m si s s s w

79. I piao chih sun nü ○○○○女 m si s s d

80. I piao chih sun hsü ○○○○婿 m si s s d h

Since most of these terms are extensions from table Ⅰ, their historical development, vocative and complimentary usages can be inferred from there.

Affinal Relatives

Relatives through Wife-Table Ⅲ

Ⅰ. Generation of the wife's father

1. Yo fu 岳父 w f

The term in the *Êrh Ya* is *wai chiu*, and in the *Li Chi* (52.27b), *chiu* is used alone for this relationship. As *chiu* also meant mother's brother during this period, the terminology reflects *cross-cousin marriage*. During the Later Han period *fu kung*① and *fu wêng*② were prevailingly used, as purely descriptive terms. Whether or not *chang jên* 丈人 was used for wife's father during the Han period is by no means clear③; it became the prevailing term during the T'ang dynasty.④ *Yo fu* and *chang jên* are the universal modern terms, and the use of the one or the other depends upon local custom. *Yo fu* is more formal and literary, *chang jên* is more colloquial. Sometimes the combined and abbreviated

① *Hou Han Shu* 71.11a.

② *San Kuo Chih* 1.22b-23a.

③ *Han Shu* 94A. 25b-26a. In the *Nêng kai chia man lu*, 2.28, this erroneously considered to be the origin of *chang jên* for wife's father. The term *chang jên* used here merely means any older man; cf. Yen Shih-Ku's commentary on this passage.

④ *Chiu T'ang Shu*. 147.1b.

form *yo chang* is used. Another very common but non-vocative and non-referential term is *T'ai shan*, name of the eastern sacred mountain of the old Chinese Empire. There are many interpretations of the origin of the terms *yo fu*, *chang jên* and *T'ai shan*, of interest to those who are concerned with the origin of individual terms.

One interpretation of the origin of the term *yo* is that found in the *Chiao ssŭ chih* of the *Han Shu* (25A.13a), viz., large mountains are called *yo shan*, and small mountains, *yo hsü*. Since mountains can be called both *yo* and *hsü*, and since *hsü* also means daughter's husband, the meaning of *yo* was transferred and *yo* became a term for wife's father.① Another interpretation goes thus: Yo Kuang of the Chin dynasty was the father of the wife of Wei Chieh; since these two men were the best-known personages of their time, and since their relationship as father-in-law and son-in-law was much admired by the people, it is possible that *yo chang* 岳丈 is a corruption of *Yo chang* 樂丈.②

The story of the origin of the term *T'ai shan* is as follows: In the year 725 A. D. the Emperor Hsüan-tsung offered sacrifices to T'ai Shan, "Mount T'ai." According to precedence, all those officials who participated in it, with the exception of the San Kung 三公, were promoted one rank. Chang Yüeh, the premier, was the marshal of ceremonies. This son-in-law, Chêng I, was promoted from the ninth rank to the fifth rank and was accorded the privilege of wearing purple robes. In the banquet of celebration the Emperor was surprised by his quick advancement. The professional court jester, Huang Fa-cho, remarked: "This is the influence of T'ai Shan!" This is popularly considered the explanation of the origin of the term.③ But *T'ai shan* must already have had the meaning of father-in-law, since this joke is a *pun*, *T'ai shan* being

---

① *Jih sun chai pi chi* 日損齋筆記 by 黄溍 (1277-1357 A. D.) (墨海金壺 edition) 10b.

② *Chin Shu* 36. 13b; *Kai yü Ts'ung k'ao* 37.20a.

③ Cf. *Shih ch'ang T'an* 1.2b.

interpreted both as wife's father and as Mount T'ai; i. e., Chêng I's unprecedented promotion was due to his participation in the sacrifices to T'ai Shan, or, in a satirical sense, to the influence of his father-in-law, Chang Yüeh.

Still another version of the origin of the terms *T'ai Shan* and *yo* relates that Mount T'ai, also called Eastern Yo, has a peak named Chang Jên. Since *chang jên* means wife's father, and Chang Jên is one of the peaks of T'ai Shan, *T'ai shan* has become a term for wife's father—a kind of punning and semantic transference. Furthermore, T'ai Shan is also called Yo, whence the term *yo* is derived.①

These are interesting speculations, any one of which is just as reasonable as any other. One point seems to be certain, viz., that no sociological factors or marital implications are involved. First, from the linguistic point of view, both *yo* and *T'ai shan* have never been used in any sense other than "venerable high mountain" and "Mount T'ai." Second, as relationship terms, both of them are late introductions, not earlier than the T'ang period. If there were any sociological implications, they should be easily detectable.

The application of *chang jên* to wife's father, as remarked above, first became prevalent during the T'ang period. Before and during the Han periods it could be applied to any old man to whom one might wish to pay respect. From the fourth to the sixth centuries A. D. *chang jên* was used for mother's brother, mother's sister's husband and father's sister's husband, e. g., *chung wai chang jên*. Hence, its use for wife's father may be an alternative extension from the term *chiu*, which was used during this period for mother's brother and sometimes for wife's father. If this idea is correct, the use of *chang jên* may be an indirect survival from cross-cousin marriage.

---

① *Kai yü Ts'ung k'ao* 37.20a.

*Wai fu*①, *ping sou*②, and *ping wêng*③, were alternative terms used during the Sung period. *Fu t'o*④ is an old dialectal term used in southwest China during the Han period.

Chia yo is used as a depreciatory term, but theoretically it may be incorrect.

2. Yo mu 岳母 w m

Wai ku or *ku* alone are used in the *Êrh Ya* and *Li Chi-a* reflection of cross-cousin marriage. *Chang mu* and *T'ai shui*⑤ are terms corresponding to *chang jên* and *T'ai shan*. Before the T'ang period, *chang mu* could be applied to father's and mother's married sisters, mother's brother's wife, or the wife of any person whom one addressed as *chang jên*. *Mu t'o*⑥ was a dialectal form corresponding to *fu t'o*.

Yo fu and *yo mu* may be used voeatively, but generally the husband adopts the wife's terms, addressing her parents with parent terms. Post-issue, teknonymy is the most common practice.

In referring to wife's father's parents, circumlocution by enumeration of relations is common, In certain localities *lao chang jên* and *lao chang mu* are used in the referential. Inferentially and logically, *yo tsu fu* and *yo tsu mu* would be correct, but they are not used. In the vocative, one usually adopts the wife's terms.

---

① Cf. *Ch'ien chü lu* 潜居録 (*Shuo Fu* 說郛, 32) 1b.

② *Tung P'o Ch'üan chi* 東坡全集, *Ssŭ pu pei yao* ed., 13. 7: 冰叟.

③ *Yu huan chi wên* 遊宦紀聞, by CHANG Shih-nan 張世南 (ca. 1200 A. D.), 知不足齋叢書本 6. 2b. On *ping sou* and *ping wêng* see p. 303, note ②.

④ *Fang Yen*, 6.7a: ⊙女多.

⑤ 合璧事類 (cited by the *Ch'êng wei lu*, 7.13a): 泰水. The term *T'ai shui* is really interesting. The opposite of *shan*, mountain, is *shui*, water. Water is here used in the sense of "rivers" or "lakes". Since wife's father is called *T'ai shan*. so *T'ai shui* is used for wife's mother. The *Ho pi shih lei* being a cyclopaedia compiled during the Sung period, the term must have been quite common during that time. At present it is not a very good term and employed mostly on non-vocative and non-referential occasions.

⑥ Cf. *Fang yen* 6.7a.

3. Po yo fu 伯岳父 w f o b

4. Po yo mu 伯岳母 w f o b w

5. Shu yo fu 叔岳父 w f y b

6. Shu yo mu 叔岳母 w f y b w

Alternatively and more commonly, *po chang jên* is used for 3, *po chang mu* for 4, *shu chang jên* for 5, and *shu chang mu* for 6. *Lieh yo*① is an uncommon complimentary term for 3 and 5.

wife's father's sister and her husband are called *ku chang mu* and *ku chang jên*, wife's mother's sister and her husband are called *i chang mu* and *i chang jên*, and wife's mother's brother and his wife, *chiu chang jên* and *chiu chang mu*, respectively.

Ⅱ. Generation of the wife

7. Chiu hsiung 舅兄 w o b

Shêng, which is used in the *Êrh Ya*, reflects cross-cousin, marriage. The *Êrh Ya* also gives the term *hun hsiung ti*, "brothers by marriage" a purely descriptive term. The *Li Chi*② gives the term *ssŭ Ch'in hsiung ti*, also more or less descriptive, since *ssŭ Ch'in* literally means "private relations." *Fu hsiung ti*③ and *nei hsiung ti*④ were in use from the Chin to the T'ang dynasties, and can still be used as alternative terms. *Fu* and *nei* both mean "wife." *Chiu* was first applied during the tenth century A. D., through teknonymy.⑤

8. Chiu sao 舅嫂 w o b w

*Ch'i sao*⑥ may be used, but is a purely descriptive term.

9. Chin ti 舅弟 w y b

---

① *Ho pi shih lei* (cited by *Ch'êng wei Lu* 7.13a), 列岳.

② *Li Chi* 27. 11b.

③ See p. 218, note ②.

④ *Liang Shu* 12. 4a; *Chin shih Ts'ui pien* 101.26a. The use of *nei hsiung ti* for wife's brothers was confused with that for mother's brother's sons. It may be due to the influence of earlier cross-cousin marriage terminology from which the new nomenclature still could not extricate itself.

⑤ See discussion pp. 216-220.

⑥ *Nan shih* 45. 13b.

10. Chiu ti fu 舅弟婦 w y b w

11. I *tzŭ* 姨姊 w o si

12. I *tzŭ* fu 姨姊夫 w o si h

The term in the *Êrh Ya* for wife's sisters' husbands is *ya*① or *yin ya as used in the Shih Ching*.② *Yu bsü*③ was used during the Han period and T'ung mên a little later.④ *Liao hsü* originated as a local term in eastern China. *Lien mei* and *lien chin*⑤ were first used during the Sung period. *Lien chin* is the most commonly used term at present; it probably originated as a local form in North China. *I fu*⑥, as a term, is as old as any of those above, but more descriptive. These terms are used reciprocally, i. e., ego refers to his wife's sisters' husbands by any of these terms, according to local usage, and they refer to him by precisely the same term. These terms are only used in the referential. Vocatively, brother terms are usually adopted, or teknonymy is practiced.

13. I mei 姨妹 w y si

*Ch'i mei*⑦ and *nei mei*⑧ are alternative and principally descriptive terms. *I*, as used in the *Êrh Ya*, is interpreted as meaning the wife's sisters who have married different men, and most probably it was originally a man's term.⑨ *Ti* 娣 is used to mean sisters who have married the same man in connection with the yin marriage custom, and is more likely to be a woman's term.⑩ *Hsiao i* is a

① 亞.

② *Shih Ching* 12A. 3b: 姻亞.

③ *Han Shu* 64A. 10b: 友婿.

④ *Êrh Ya*: 同門,僚⊙.

⑤ *Luan chên tzŭ lu*, 懶真子録, by MA Yung-Ch'ing 馬永卿, ca. 1110 A. D. (1920, Commercial Press ed.) 2.5b: 連袂,連襟.

⑥ *Ho pi shih lei* (cited by *Ch'êng wei Lu* 7. 17a-b).

⑦ *San kuo chih* 22. 1b.

⑧ Ibid. 9. 6a.

⑨ *Shih Ching* 3B. 9a; *Tso Chuan* 8.24a.

⑩ *Shih Ching* 18D. 5a. Cf. the *Shih ming*. It seems the term *ti* cannot be separated from the yin marriage custom. Accordingly, when the yin marriage ceased to be practiced, *ti* also ceased to function.

modern colloquial expression.

14. I mei fu 姨妹夫 w y si h

15. T'ang chiu hsiung 堂舅兄 s of 3 or 5 > w

16. T'ang chiu sao ○○嫂 w of 15

17. T'ang chiu ti ○○弟 s of 3 or 5 < w

18. T'ang chiu ti fu ○○弟婦 w of 17

19. T'ang i tzŭ 堂姨姊 d of 3 or 5 > w

20. T'ang i tzŭ fu ○○姊夫 h of 19

21. T'ang i mei ○○妹 d of 3 or 5 < w

22. T'ang i mei fu ○○妹夫 h of 21

wife's father's sister's children, wife's mother's sister's and brother's children are called *nei piao hsiung ti* for males, and *nei piao tzŭ mei* for females. It could be further differentiated by adding *ku*, *i* and chiu, e. g., *nei ku piao hsiung* for wife's father's sister's son older than wife.

Ⅲ. Generation of the son

23. Nei chih 内姪 w b s

Chih was originally a woman's term for brother's child, being reciprocal with *ku*. Since the Chin period it has been used more as a man's term for brother's son, hence *nei* is prefixed, in contradistinction with *chih* alone. See Table Ⅰ, 125. In contemporary usage, female ego would use *chih* for brother's son before marriage, but after marriage she would use *chih* for husband's brother's son and *nei chih* for her own brother's son.

24. Nei chih fu ○○婦 w b s w

25. Nei chih nü ○○女 w b d

26. Nei chih hsü ○○婿 w b d h

27. I wai shêng 姨外甥 w si s

*Ch'i shêng*① was used *circa* sixth century A. D. It is more or less descriptive, i. e., wife's *shêng*.

---

① *Liang Shu* 28. 2a.

28. I wai shêng fu ○○甥婦 w si s w

29. I wai shêng nü ○○甥女 w si d

30. I wai shêng hsü ○○甥婿 w si d h

In certain local usages *i chih* may be substituted for *i wai shêng* in terms 27-30. Although illogical, it is permitted locally.

Ⅳ. Generation of the son's son

31. Nei chih sun 内姪孫 w b s s

The *Êrh Ya* uses the term *kuei sun*, which literally means "returning grandson." *Kuci sun* was probably a woman's term, since the *Êrh Ya* says that chih's sons are called *kuei sun*, and *chih* is primarily a woman s term in the *Êrh Ya*.

32. Ne chih sun fu ○○○婦 w b s s w

33. Nei chih sun nü ○○○女 w b s d

34. Nei chih sun hsü ○○○婿 w b s d h

35. I wai shêng sun: w si s s[①]

36. I wai shêng sun fu: w si s s w

37. I wai shêng sun nü: w si s d

38. I wai shêng sun hsü: w si s d h

In some local usages *i chih sun* may be substituted for *i wai shêng sun*. Terms 23 to 38 are used by husband and female ego alike.

Affinal Relatives

Relatives through Husband-Table Ⅳ

Ⅰ. Generation of the husband's father

1. Kung 公 h f

In the *Êrh Ya* the general term is *chiu*; when he is living, *chün chiu*[②] is

① For characters, see Nos. 24-30 above.

② *Êrh Ya*: 君舅.

used—a reflection of cross-cousin marriage. In modern ritual works, the compilers still use *chiu* for husband's father and refuse to employ the modern term *kung*. If they are afraid lest the term be misunderstood, they employ the descriptive nomenclature, e. g., *fu* of *fu* 夫之父 "father of husband" or *mu* of *fu* 夫之母 "mother of husband."

*Chang*① and *chung*② were used during and somewhat before the Han period. *Kuan*③ was a local term in the lower Yangtze valley *circa* the end of the T'ang dynasty. All these terms seem to have been more or less local, and their degree of prevalence is uncertain. The modern term *kung* dates from about the fourth and fifth centuries A. D.④; it is also used in the doubled form *kung kung*.

*Hsien chiu*⑤, *huang chiu*⑥, and *hsien tzŭ*⑦ are old posthumous terms no longer used today.

2. P'o 婆 h m

Ku, and *chün ku* only when she is living, are the terms used in the *Êrh Ya*-a reflection of cross-cousin marriage. *Wei*⑧ was used during the Han Period, and *wei ku*⑨ is equivalent to *chün ku* of the *Êrh Ya*. *Chia*, or *a chia*⑩, are terms used *circa* the fourth and fifth centuries A. D. and surviving quite late as dialectal forms. *Mu*⑪ was also used *circa* 500 A. D. *P'o* in ancient usage may mean any old woman; its use for husband's mother dates from the T'ang period.

---

① *Shih Ming*: 章.

② *Lü Shih Ch'un Ch'iu* 14.17 a: 妐.

③ *Nan T'ang Shu* (by MA Ling) 25.2a: 官.

④ Yü T'ai hsin yung chi 1. 16a-21a.

⑤ Êrh Ya: 君舅.

⑥ *I Li* 6. 1a-2b.

⑦ *Kuo Yü* 5. 9b: 先子.

⑧ *Shuo wên*: 威.

⑨ Wang Nien-Sun (*Kuang ya su chêng* 6B. 5): 威姑.

⑩ *Pei Ch'i Shu* 30.4b. *Nan shih* 33. 9a. The *chia* may be a different rendering of *ku*, as they may be pronounced about the same. Cf. *Yen shih chia hsün* 1.14a.

⑪ 姥 read 木五切 mu.

The use of *kung* and *P'o* for husband's parents might also be due to teknonymy, since from quite early times *kung* and *P'o* have commonly been used as grandparents' terms.

Huang ku and *hsien ku* are ancient posthumous terms.

Ⅱ. Generation of the husband

3. Pên shên 本身 ego, a female

Ego, a female, might, in speaking to the husband's relatives, refer to herself as *hsin fu*, during the fourth and fifth centuries A. D.① This custom seems to have been in vogue as late as the twelfth century A. D.② At present, the proper relationship term should be used.

4. Fu 夫 husband

Chang fu 丈夫 and *fu hsü* are alternative terms. *Hsü* may be used alone for husband. *Lao kung*③ and *nan jên*④ are colloquial rather vulgar, terms.

Whether or not *shih*⑤, *po*⑥, *tzŭ*⑦, *chün tzŭ*⑧, *fu tzŭ*⑨, and *chia*⑩ are actually ancient relationship terms for husband cannot be determined. They might be merely general complimentary terms for man used in the sense of "husband", or simply circumlocutory expressions. *T'ien*⑪, *so T'ien*⑫, and *kao*

---

① *Shih shuo hsin yü* 2B. 40b-41a：王平子年十四五,見王夷甫婦郭氏貪,欲令婢路上儋糞,平子諫之,並言不可.郭大怒,謂平子曰:昔夫人臨終,以小郎囑新婦,不以新婦囑小郎. *Hsin fu* literally means "the bride".

② *Shu I* 1. 12a.

③ This is used chiefly in southeast China, as in Kiangsu, Kwangtung, etc. It literally means "the old male".

④ A very common term used in the sense of "husband"; literally, "male".

⑤ *Shih ching* 3C. 3a：士.

⑥ 伯;see p. 215, note ①.

⑦ *Shih ching* 4C. 2b：子.

⑧ Ibid. 7A. 5a.

⑨ *Mêng Tzŭ* 6A. 4a; *Hou Han Shu* 113. 9.

⑩ *Kuo Yü* 6.8b; *Mêng Tzŭ* 6A. 6a.

⑪ *I Li* 30. 15b. *T'ien* (heaven) is used in the sense of the "positive" or "male" principle.

⑫ 所天 is based on the above, employed only in literary usages, i. e., non-vocative and non-referential, chên[1] are primarily literary forms; *kao chên* is used almost exclusively in poetry.

The wife calls the husband *liang*[2], *liang jên*[3], *lang*[4], and ch'ing.[5] *Ch'in* is a common reciprocal term. All these words are old forms, now chiefly retained in literary usage and seldom, if ever, used in the vocative. The wife may call the husband by his personal name, or just "you"[6], and most prevalently she employs teknonymy.

The depreciatory terms are *wai tzŭ*[7], and *cho fu* 拙夫 or *yü fu* 愚夫. These terms are employed only in refined society. Ordinarily, the wife refers to her husband as *t'a* 他, meaning "he" or "him," or by teknonymous and circumlocutory expressions.

Huang p'i[8] is an ancient and now obsolete posthumous term.

5. Po 伯 h o b

Hsiung kung is used in the *Êrh Ya*. *Kung* 公 is often written 伀 or 妐, *and is sometimes pronounced chung*.[9] *Hsiung chang*[10] was commonly used during the Han period. *Chang* is written 傽 or 嫜.

Po means principally father's older brother. Its extension to husband's older brother first occurred at about the end of the T'ang period.[11] This change can be explained on the basis of teknonymy. *Po po* is more colloquial.

---

① 古絶句四首〔*Yü T'ai hsin yung chi* 10.6a〕:藁砧.

② *I Li* 5. 8a.

③ *Shih ching* 6C. 8a; *Mêng Tzŭ* 8B. 11b-12a.

④ *Chin shu* 96, 9b.

⑤ *Shih shuo hsin yü* 3B. 48b-49a:卿.

⑥ *Yen shih chia hsün* 1.13b:倡和之禮,或爾汝之.

⑦ Wife calls husband *wai* and husband calls wife *nei*; this practice dates from the middle of the first millennium A. D. Cf. *Hêng Yen Lu* 3.11a.

⑧ *Li Chi* 5.22a:皇辟.

⑨ *Êrh Ya* commentary.

⑩ *Shih Ming*:兄章.

⑪ See p. 215, note ②.

6. Mu mu 母母 h o b w

Ssŭ fu is the ancient term used in the *Êrh Ya*①, and is scarcely known today. *Mu mu* first came into use during the Sung period.② It is sometimes written 姆姆; the pronunciation differs slightly in different localities.

7. Shu 叔 h y b

*Hsiao shu*③, *shu lang*④, and *hsiao lang*⑤ are alternative terms that date from the fourth and fifth centuries A. D. *Hsiao shu* is more colloquial, *shu lang* and *hsiao lang* are more literary. *Shu* is used in the *Êrh Ya*.

In the lower strata of present-day society, the younger brother-inlaw can usually "play jokes" with the older sister-in-law. This circumstance is primarily based on the popular assumption that the younger brother-in-law is always a minor and that the older sister-in-law assumes a kind of maternal attitude.

8. Shên shên 嬸嬸 h y b w

Ti fu is an ancient term.⑥ *Ssŭ* and *ti* are also used in the *Êrh Ya* to mean sisters who married the same man; the younger calls the older *ssŭ*, and the older calls the younger *ti*.⑦ This usage is probably connected with the yin marriage. When used for husband's brother's wives, the *fu* should be appended as it is in the *Êrh Ya* and *I Li* (33.2a-b).

Shên shên was first used during the Sung period.⑧ *Shên* was originally a term for father's younger brother's wife, and its extension to husband's younger brother's wife is certainly teknonymous.

Female ego and husband's brothers wives may refer to each other as *ti ssŭ*,

---

① 姒婦.

② See p. 225, note ③.

③ *Shih Chi* 69.15b-16a.

④ *Wên Hsüan* 40. 6b.

⑤ *Chin Shu* 96. 9b.

⑥ Cf. *Êrh Ya*.

⑦ 姒,娣.

⑧ See p. 225, notes ②, ③.

as recorded in the *Êrh Ya*, and as *hsien hou*[①] and *chou li*[②], as used during the Han period. *Ti ssŭ* and *hsien hou* are now obsolete. *Chu li* is the prevailing term at present; it is reciprocal and used only in the referential.

9. Ku 姑 h si

Ta ku 大姑 may be used for the older sister, and *hsiao ku* 小姑 for the younger sister, of the husband. On the other hand, *ta ku* need not necessarily indicate that the sister is actually older than the husband, since the female siblings may be counted in a separate numerical series. Hence *ta* and *hsiao* may only indicate the seniority and juniority among the husband's female siblings. In fact, *ta ku* and *hsiao ku* may be both younger than the husband. These terms are mainly used for the husband's unmarried sisters, but they may continue to be used after their marriage, though rarely.

In the *Êrh Ya*, husband's older sister is called *nü kung* 女公, and the younger, *nü mei* 女妹. *Shu mei* was used during the Han period.[③] *Hsiao ku* was first applied ca. the fifth century A. D. Since *ku* originally meant father's sister, its extension is attributable to teknonymy.

10. Ku fu 姑夫 h si h

Ku fu also means father's sister's husband, and its application to husband's sister's husband is undoubtedly teknonymous.

Conclusions

Having discussed the system in its morphological and historical aspects, I shall here venture upon a few concluding remarks. It may safely be asserted that

---

① *Han Shu* 25A. 18b: 先後.

② *Fang Yen* 12. 1a: 築娌. *Chu* is a synonym of 妯.

③ Cf. *Hou Han Shu* 114.8.

during the last two thousand years the system has undergone a series of changes both in its structural principles and terminological categories, yet has retained many features of the old system. The latter stability seems to be related to the continuity of Chinese civilization as a whole. As regards the changes, there is, generally speaking, a broad historical correlation with the changes in the development of Chinese society. One notes that practically all the kinship changes occurred during the last two centuries of the first millennium B. C. and the whole of the first millennium A. D. During this period the system was in a state of flux. Many old terms were dropped, changed, or delimited in connotation. New terms were introduced, as if by way of experiment; some were incorporated into the system, others fell into oblivion. Almost all the new terms used in the modern system originated at this time. The whole system was finally stabilized during the T'ang period, after a thousand years of constant transformation and confusion.

This millennium likewise was a period of civil and social strife, the aftermath of the dissolution of the old feudal system. To be sure, the entire social structure was not suddenly transformed; many of the old social institutions lingered on, though in slightly modified forms.① Nevertheless, the evolution of the new social order was begun. It was a slow and gigantic process, accompanied by periods of alternating political and social tranquillity and chaos, of reactionary and progressive thought. This was an age of widening contacts with outside influences, especially from the third to the sixth centuries A. D., the "Dark Ages" of Chinese history, when nearly all the territory north of the Yangtze was overrun by less civilized peoples from the northern steppes; the resultant large waves of Chinese migration southward resulted in the efflorescence of the *shih tsu* 世族 organization and its excrescent manifestation

---

① There are students who would even consider present China a fundamentally feudal society. This is somewhat an exaggeration and depends on one s definition of "feudalism".

in the *mên fa* 門閥① system of official recruitment. The entire process is too complex a subject to be dealt with here, but it shows a general chronological correlation with the development of the kinship system. When the kinship system crystalized toward the end of the first millennium A. D., Chinese society still continued to evolve. The kinship system, being a more conservative institution and in some ways a stabilizing mechanism for other social institutions, has remained essentially the same as it was during the T'ang period.

The individual parts of the system have exhibited varying amounts and rates of change, i. e., the changes have been differential. The nomenclature for sib relatives has experienced relatively little alteration, although there have been refinements in the degrees of differentiation and, for some terms, changed connotations. This may be due to the fact that, although the old sib system, *tsung fa*, has been transformed into the modern sib organization, *shih tsu*, the sib principle has remained the basis of kinship evolution. The increased descriptive efficacy represents merely refinements of superficial features of the system, correlated with the elaboration of the mourning ritualism.

Most remarkable changes have occurred in the terminology for nonsib relatives, especially in the nomenclature for affinal relatives, which Aginsky calls "basic terminology"②. A glance at Tables Ⅲ and Ⅳ will show how radical and complete the changes are. It is a generally accepted fact among social anthropologists that the affinal terminology is extremely sensitive to variations in marital relationships. But have the Chinese marriage regulations radically changed during this period? This question finds a simple answer in

① *Mên fa*, as a system of official recruitment, is based on sib connections. Cf. 楊筠如:九品中正與六朝門閥(1931).

② B. W. Aginsky. Kinship systems and the forms of marriage, *Memoirs*, *American Anthropological Association*, 45 (1935), 14.

history. The most important factor in the regulation of marriage in China, from the first millennium B. C. down to the present, has been sib-exogamy supplemented by the generation principle. It has been pointed out above that as time went on a gradual stiffening of this rule took place, but there was little actual change. In general, the effect of marriage regulations upon the kinship system has been so small that we are justified in ignoring it. We can also, in the manner employed before, dispose of the sororate and the levirate as moulding influences on the system.

Cross-cousin marriage, however, presents a very different problem, for it is upon this that the affinal terminology of the old system was undoubtedly based. If we assume that the decline in the frequency of this form of marriage resulted in the breakdown of the old affinal nomenclature, we must still explain the origin of the new terminology. These new terms are, in my opinion, not the products of new forms of marriage, but are the result of the operation of teknonymy. Marital relationships as a whole have had little influence upon the modern system. The reason for this may lie in the fact that the Chinese marriage regulations are purely restrictive, not prescriptive, i. e., aside from certain restrictions connected with sib-exogamy and generation, there is complete freedom of choice.

The morphological configuration of the Chinese system has puzzled many a student. Morgan, in generalizing on the system, vacillated between his Malayan and Turanian, saying that "it falls below the highest type of the Turanian form, and affiliates wherever it diverges with the Malayan."① Lowie, apparently using the same material, considered the Chinese system either a "generation" or a "bifurcate merging" system②—which is equivalent to saying that it is either Malayan or Turanian. T. S. Chen and J. K. Shryock, using Lowie's

---

① Morgan, *System... op. cit.*, 413.

② R. H. Lowie, Relationship Terms, *Encyclopa edia Britannica*.

system of classification, call the Chinese system "bifurcate collateral."① Kroeber is of the same opinion, but says, "the Chinese system appears to consist of a 'classificatory', that is non-descriptive, base, which has been made over by additions into a 'descriptive' system similar in its working to the English one, in fact is more precisely and successfully descriptive than this."② Compare this with Morgan's remark that the Chinese system "has accomplished the difficult task of maintaining a principle of classification which confronts the natural distinctions in the relationships of consanguinity, and, at the same time, of separating those relationships from each other in a precise and definite manner."③

Actually, the Chinese system is not one that lends itself to any simple characterization in terms such as "classificatory" or "descriptive." It must first be understood in the light of its own morphological principles and historical development. In Morgan's definition of the terms, the Chinese system is both classificatory and descriptive. This is not an "inconsistency" from the point of view of Morgan's system, but a characteristic of a system moulded by diverse factors of a counteracting nature. It is the elucidation of these underlying factors that is of scientific import rather than any particular characterization. This problem has been approached through a detailed analysis of the changes which the Chinese system has undergone during the documentary period of its history. Insofar as the data have permitted, correlative sociological facts have been evaluated with reference to these changes and the nature of possible dynamic factors indicated.

---

① *Op. cit.*, 627.

② Process in the Chinese Kinship, *op. cit.*, 151.

③ Morgan, *Systems*..., 413.

Chinese Works Frequently Cited

The following list has been prepared for the sole purpose of avoiding the constant repetition of bibliographical information in the text. The works are arranged alphabetically according to the romanized brief title as used in the text and notes. Since full bibliographical information is usually given in the notes for Chinese works cited only once or twice and for European works referred to, they are not given here.

Chan kuo ts'ê 戰國策校注:commentaries by Pao Piao 鮑彪, *circa* 1150 A. D., and Wu Shih-tao 吳師道,1283-1344 A. D.; Ssŭ pu Ts'ung k'an 四部叢刊.

Ch'ang li chi 昌黎先生集:Collected works of Han Yü 韓愈,768-824 A. D.; Ssŭ pu pei yao 四部備要.

ch'ao ching ch'ao wên chi 巢經巢文集:Collected works of Chêng Chên 鄭珍,1806-1864 A. D.;清代學術叢書 edition.

Ch'êng wei lu 稱謂録:by Liang Chang-chü 梁章鉅,1775-1849 A. D.; 1875 edition.

Chêng tzŭ t'ung 正字通:compiled *circa* 1670 A. D. by Liao Wênying 廖文英;1670 edition.

Chi yün 集韵:compiled by Ting Tu 丁度,990-1053 A. D., and others; *Ssŭ pu pei yao* edition.

Chiang Wên-t'ung chi 江文通集:Collected works of Chiang Yen 江淹, 444-505 A. D.; *Ssŭ pu Ts'ung k'an* edition.

Ch'ien yen t'ang chin shih wên pa wei 潛研堂金石文跋尾:by Ch'ien Tahsin 錢大昕,1727-1804 A. D.;1884 潛研堂全書 edition.

Chin shih li 金石例:by P'an Ang-hsiao 潘昂霄,*circa* 1300 A. D.;徐氏隨庵叢書 edition.

Chin shih Ts'ui pien 金石萃編:compiled by Wang Ch'ang 王昶,1727-1806 A. D.;經訓堂 edition.

Chin shih yao li 金石要例:by Huang Tsung-hsi 黄宗羲,1609-1695 A. D.;借月山房匯鈔 edition.

Chin shu 晉書:by Fang Chiao 房喬,*circa* 630 A. D., and others; 1894,同文書局 edition.

Ch'in shu chi 親屬記:by Chêng Chên 鄭珍,1806-1864 A. D.;廣雅叢書 edition.

Chiu T'ang shu 舊唐書:by Liu Hsü 劉昫,887-946 A. D., and others; 1894.同文書局 edition.

Ch'ü-chiang wên chi 曲江文集:Collected works Of Chang Chiu-ling 張九齡,673-740 A. D.; *Ssŭ pu Ts'ung k'an* edition.

Êrh ya 爾雅義疏:Commentary by Ho I-hsing 郝懿行,1757-1825 A. D.; *Ssŭ pu pei yao* edition. Since the section referred to is the short *Shih Ch'in* 釋親,Relationship Terms, no page reference is given in the notes.

Fang yen 方言:by Yang Hsiung 揚雄,53 B. C.-18 A. D.; commentary by Kuo P'o 郭璞,276-324 A. D.;*Ssŭ pu Ts'ung k'an* edition.

Han fe tzŭ 韓非子:by Han Fei 韓非,? -324 B. C.;*Ssŭ pu pei yao* edition.

Han shu 漢書: by Pan Ku 班固,32-92 A. D.;1894,同文書局 edition.

Hêng yen lu 恒言録:by Ch'ien Ta-hsin 錢大昕,1727-1804 A. D.; 1884,潛研堂全書 edition.

Hou Han shu 後漢書:by Fan Yer 范曄,? -445 A. D.;1894,同文書局 edition.

Hsiao ching 孝經注疏:115,阮刻十三經注疏 edition.

Hsin shu 新書:by Chia I 賈誼,*circa* second century B. C.; *Ssŭ pu pei yao* edition.

Hsin T'ang shu 新唐書:by Ou-yang Hsiu 歐陽修,1007-1072 A. D., and Sung Ch'i 宋祁,998-1061 A. D.;1894,同文書局 edition.

Hsüen lin 學林:by Wang Kuan-kuo 王觀國,*cirea*1140 A. D.;武英殿聚珍版 edition.

Hua yang chi 華陽集:by Ku k'uang 顧況,*circa* 8th and 9th centuries A. D.;1855 雙峰堂 edition.

Huai nan tzŭ 淮南子:attributed to Liu An 劉安,? -122 B. C.;1876 浙江書局 edition.

I ching 周易注疏:1815 阮刻十三經注疏 edition.

I Li 儀禮注疏:1815 阮刻十三經注疏 edition.

Jih chih lu 日知録集釋:by Ku Yen-wu 顧炎武,1612-1681 A. D., commentary by Huang Ju-Ch'êng 黄汝成;1872 湖北崇文書局 edition.

Jung chai sui pi 容齋隨筆:by Huny Mai 洪邁,1123-1202 A. D.; *Ssŭ pu Ts'ung k'an* 續編 edition.

Kai yü Ts'ung k'ao 陔餘叢考:by Chao I 趙翼,1727-1814 A. D.; 1790, 壽考堂甌北全書 edition.

Kuang shih Ch'in 廣釋親:by Chang Shên-i 張慎儀,based on 錢塘梁氏殘稿.夢園叢書 edition.

Kuang ya 廣雅疏證:by Chang I 張揖,*circa* 230 A. D., commentary by Wang Nien-sun 王念孫,1744-1832 A. D.; 1879, 淮南書局 edition. Since the section referred to is the *Shih Ch'in* 釋親,Relationship Terms, 6. 1-6, no page reference is given in the notes.

Kuang yün 廣韵:revised by Ch'ên P'êng-nien 陳彭年,961-1017 A. D., and others; *Ssŭ pu Ts'ung k'an* edition.

Kung-yang chuan 公羊注疏:1815,阮刻十三經注疏 edition.

K'ung Ts'ung tzŭ 孔叢子:attributed to K'ung Fu 孔鮒,*circa* 200 B. C.; *Ssŭ pu Ts'ung k'an* edition.

Kuo yü 國語:commentary by Wei Chao 韋昭,204-273 A. D.; *Ssŭ pu*

Ts'ung k'an edition.

Li chi 禮記注疏:1815,阮刻十三經注疏 edition.

Liang shu 梁書:by Yao Ssŭ-lien 姚思廉,? -637 A. D.;1894,同文書局 edition.

Liu Pin-k'o wên chi 劉賓客文集:Collected works of Liu Yü-hsi 劉禹錫, 772-842 A. D.;*Ssŭ pu pei yao* edition.

Lu Shih-lung wên chi 陸士龍文集:Collected works of Lu Yün 陸雲,262-305 A. D.; *Ssŭ pu Ts'ung k'an* edition.

Lun yü 論語注疏:1815,阮刻十三經注疏 edition.

Lü shih Ch'un Ch'iu 吕氏春秋:attributed to Lü Pu-wei 吕不韋,? -235 B. C.; *Ssŭ pu pei yao* edition.

Mêng Ch'i pi t'an 夢溪筆談:by Shên Kua 沈括,1030-1094 A. D.;津逮秘書 edition.

Mêng tzŭ 孟子注疏:1815,阮刻十三經注疏 edition.

Ming lü chi chieh fu li 明律集解附例:compilation of 1585 A. D.,萬曆十三年;1908,修定法律館 edition.

Ming tao tsa chih 明道雜誌:by Chang Lei 張耒,1052-1112 A. D.; 顧氏文房小説 edition.

Mo chi 默記:by Wang Chih 王铚,*circa* 1120 A. D.;1918 涵芬樓 edition.

Nan shih 南史:by Li Yen-shou 李延壽,*circa* seventh century A. D.;1894 同文書局 edition.

Nan T'ang shu 南唐書:by Ma Ling 馬令 *circa* 1100 A. D.; *Ssŭ pu Ts'ung k'an* 續編 edition.

Nêng kai chai man lu 能改齋漫録:by Wu Tsêng 吴曾,*circa* 1150 A. D.; 武英殿聚珍版 edition.

Pa Ch'iung shih chin shih pu chêng 八瓊室金石補正:compiled by Lu Tsêng-hsiang 陸增祥,*circa* 1850 A. D.;吳興劉氏希古樓 edition.

Pai ching T'ang wên chi 拜經堂文集:by Tsang Yung 臧庸,1767-1811

A. D.;1920 上元宗氏石印 edition.

Pai hu T'ung白虎通疏證:attributed to Pan Ku 班固,32-92 A. D., and others; commentary by Ch'ên Li 陳立, 1809-1869 A. D.; 1875 淮南書局 edition.

Pei Ch'i shu 北齊書:by Li Pai-yao 李百藥,565-648 A. D.;1894 同文書局 edition.

Pei mêng so yen 北夢瑣言:by Sun Kuang-hsien 孫光憲,? -968 A. D.;雅雨堂叢書 edition.

Pei shih 北史:by Li Yen-shou 李延壽, *circa* 7th century A. D.; 1894 同文書局 edition.

P'ieh chi 瞥記:by Liang Yü-shêng 梁玉繩,*circa* 1780 A. D.;清白士集 edition.

San kuo chih 三國志:by Ch'ên Shou 陳壽,233-297 A. D.;1894 同文書局 edition.

Shih Ch'ang t'an 釋常談:anonymous;*circa* 1100 A. D.;百川學海 edition.

Shih chi 史記:by Ssŭ-ma Ch'ien 司馬遷,? 145-74? B. C.;1894 同文書局 edition.

Shih ching 毛詩注疏:*Ssŭ pu pei yao* edition.

Shih ming 釋名疏證:by Liu Hsi 劉熙,*circa* 200 A. D., commentary by Pi Yüan 畢沅, 1730-1797 A. D.; 廣雅叢書 edition. The part referred to is the Section Ⅱ:*Shih Ch'in Shu* 釋親屬, Relationship Terms. No page reference is given in the notes.

Shih shuo hsin yü 世說新語: by Liu I-Ch'ing 劉義慶, 403-444 A. D., commentary by Liu Hsiao-piao 劉孝標, *circa* 530 A. D.; *Ssŭ pu Ts'ung k'an* edition.

Shu ching 尚書注疏:1815,阮刻十三經注疏 edition.

Shu i 書儀: by Ssŭ-ma Kuang 司馬光, 1019-1086 A. D.; 學津討原 edition.

Shu Po 鼠璞:by Tai Shih 戴埴,*circa* 1220 A. D.;學津討原 edition.

Shuo wên 説文解字:by Hsü Shên 許慎,*circa* 200 A. D.,commentary by Hsü Hsüan 徐鉉,916-991 A. D.;*Ssŭ pu Ts'ung k'an* editon.

Sung shu 宋書:by Shên Yo 沈約,441-513 A. D.;1894 同文書局 edition.

Ta Tai li chi 大戴禮記:by Tai Tê 戴德,*circa* 100 B. C.; *Ssŭ pu Ts'ung k'an* edition.

T'ang chih yen 唐摭言:by Wang Ting-pao 王定保,870-954(?) A. D.;雨雅堂叢書 edition.

T'ang lü su i 故唐律疏議:codified by Chang-sun Wu-chi 長孫無忌,? -659 A. D. and others. *Ssŭ pu Ts'ung k'an* 三編 edition.

Ts'ai Chung-lang chi 蔡中郎集:Collected works of ts'ai Yung 蔡邕,133-192 A. D.; *Ssŭ pu Ts'ung k'an* edition.

Ts'ao Tzŭ-chien chi 曹子建集:Collected works of Ts'ao Chih 曹植,192-232 A. D.; *Ssŭ pu Ts'ung k'an* edition.

Tso chuan 左傳注疏:1815 阮刻十三經注疏 edition.

Tsung fa hsiao chi 宗法小記:by Ch'êng Yao-T'ien 程瑶田,1725-1814 A. D.;清經解 edition.

T'ung su p'ien 通俗篇:by Chai Hao 翟灝,? -1788 A. D.; 無不宜齋 edition.

T'ung tien 通典:compiled by Tu Yu 杜佑,735-812 A. D.;1896,浙江書局 edition.

T'ung ya 通雅:by Fang I-chih 方以智,*circa* 1650 A. D.; 立教館 edition.

Wang Shih-chung chi 王侍中集:Collected works of Wang Ts'an 王粲,177-217 A. D.;漢魏六朝百三名家集 edition.

Wei Wu-ti chi 魏武帝集:Collected works of Ts'ao Ts'ao 曹操, 155-220 A. D.;漢魏六朝百三名家集 edition.

Wên hsüan 六臣注文選:compiled by Hsiao T'ung蕭統,501-531 A. D., commentary by Li Shan 李善,? -688 A. D. and others. *Ssŭ pu Ts'ung k'an* edition.

Yen shih chia hsün 顔氏家訓:by Yen Chih-T'ui 顔之推,531-591 A. D.; *Ssŭ pu pei yao* edition.

Yen tzŭ Ch'un Ch'iu 晏子春秋: attributed by Yen Ying 晏嬰,? -493 B. C.;*Ssŭ pu pei yao* edition.

Yin hua lu 因話録:by Chao Lin 趙璘,*circa* 840 A. D.; 稗海 edition.

Yü p'ien 玉篇:compiled in 543 A. D. by Ku Yeh-wang 顧野王 augmented in 760 A. D. by Sun Ch'iang 孫强,revised in 1008 A. D. by Ch'ên P'êng-nien 陳彭年,and others; *Ssŭ pu Ts'ung k'an* edition.

Yü T'ai hsin yung chi 玉臺新咏集:compiled by Hsü Ling 徐陵,507-583 A. D.;*Ssŭ pu Ts'ung k'an* edition.

Yüan shih chang-Ch'ing chi 元氏長慶集:Collected works of Yüan Chên 元稹,779-831 A. D.; *Ssŭ pu Ts'ung k'an* edition.

(原載 *Harvard Journal of Asiatic Studies*, 1937, Vol. 2, No. 2, pp. 141-275)

DISCOVERY AND EXCAVATION OF THE YONG LING: THE ROYAL TOMB OF WANG CHIEN

As one travels along the Chengtu plain, he will notice hundreds of artificial mounds breaking the monotony of a featureless landscape. Some of these mounds are of tremendous size amounting to fifteen or more meters in height and hundreds of meters in circumference. Except a very few, all of them are burial tumuli ranging from the fifth or fourth centuries B. C. down to modern times. As no other monumental vestiges survive the ravages of human and natural agencies outside the tombs, their identity is as a rule entirely lost. The local people simply call them hillocks or royal tombs. Many of them are considered to be important *feng-shui* 風水① to the locality and people are forbidden to move earth from them. The Yung Ling is only one of these mounds.

In historical records and local tradition the Yung Ling is called the Chin-Tai 琴臺 and supposed to be the site of the house of the celebrated poet Ssuma Hsiang-ju 司馬相如 (200-118 B. C.) of the Former Han dynasty, a native of Chengtu, Chin-T'ai means literally "lute-platform". i. e., a place for playing the lute, and, in an extended sense, the site of the residence of the poet. It began to be mentioned in historical records around the fifth century A. D., and became a place of great poetical interest from the Tang dynasty onwards, perhaps because of the romantic episodes in the life of the poet. But how the

---

① Literally, wind and water, i. e., geomancy.

Yung Ling lost its identity and was mistaken for the Chin-T'ai is a question still waiting to be solved. The two places were distinct during the Southern Sung dynasty (1127-1279 A. D.) as the historical records clearly show. After the Yuan dynasty only the Chin-T'ai was mentioned in most cases, but not the Yung Ling. The reason is probably the proximity of the two places, as both are in the western suburb of Chengtu. As the Chin-T'ai was apparently a smaller mound and may be leveled to the ground and entirely lost, people gradually began to point to the much higher and bigger Yung Ling mound as the Chin-T'ai.

Before describing the discovery and excavation of the royal tomb, it would be proper to give a short biography of the emperor himself as a historical introduction. Wang Chien was a native of Hsiang-ch'eng 項城 in modern Honan province.① He was of humble ancestry and born in 847 A. D. He was tall in stature with a commanding appearance. As a young man, he became a desperado. Once a monk remonstrated with him saying: "A young man of your noble appearance, why not do something worthwhile instead of being a scourge to the land!" He was much moved by the rebuke and enlisted in the army. Owing to his gallantry and ability, he won quick promotions. When the notorious rebel Huang Chao 黄巢 sacked the T'ang capital in 880 A. D., the Emperor Hsi-tsung 僖宗(874-888) fled to Chengtu, and Wang Chien and four others led a small army to his protection. The emperor was much pleased and made him one of the commanders of the imperial guards. When Hsi-tsung fled again from his capital in 885 A. D., Wang Chien led him through the flames of the burning suspension paths 棧道 to Hsing yuan 興元 (modern Han-chung in southern Shensi). On this account he was made the governor of Pi-chow 壁州刺史 and later the commissioner for defence of Li-chow 利州防禦使 both in northern Szechwan. At this time the great T'ang dynasty was drawing to its end

① Some records state that he was a native of Wu-yang 舞陽, which is not far from 項城.

and the local warlords were fighting among each other, while the T'ang emperor was powerless to do anything about it. Within a period of twenty years, Wang Chien conquered the whole of Szechwan and parts of Shensi, Kansu, and Kweichow for himself. In 903 A. D. the T'ang emperor Chao-tsung 昭宗(889-904) made him King of Shu 蜀王. When Chu Wen 朱温(907-912), founder of the short Liang dynasty (907-922), murdered Chao-tsung in 904 A. D., practically ending the T'ang dynasty, Wang Chien declared himself Emperor of Shu (Szechwan) in 907 A. D.

China proper was in great turmoil during this time, but Szechwan prospered and enjoyed considerable peace under Wang chien's able administration. Many people from other parts of China fled to Szechwan as a place of refuge. Although Wang Chien had practically no education himself, he was a great patron of literature and art. He was also a great admirer of T'ang court life and remained loyal to the T'ang regime until its very end. Most of the men he used and trusted were old officials from the T'ang court who came to him from North China. Wang Chien ruled as emperor of Szechwan for twelve years and died in 918 A. D. at the age of seventy-two. He was succeeded by his son Wang Yen 王衍, who was conquered by the Later T'ang dynasty in 925 A. D. From the date of Wang chien's first entry into Szechwan in 887 A. D. down to 925 A. D., the kingdom which he founded lasted only thirty- seven years.

The Yung Ling is only about half a mile outside the old west gate of the present city wall of Chengtu. The mound is about fifteen meters high at present, but originally it might have been a little higher as there has been a considerable amount of erosion during the last thousand years. The diameter is about seventy-five meters and it is circumscribed with stone blocks about two meters high. It is situated between two rivulets and is orientated directly to the south. The rivulet at the front curves in toward the royal tomb to form a semicircle, which is of great geomantic significance. Originally there were stone obelisks, horses, lions, tigers and a med guards standing in front of the tomb. But none of these are in existence today. According to the records, there were temples dedicated to the emperor beside the royal tomb and they were still standing during the Southern Sung period. On the walls were mural paintings executed by well-known artists of the time.

The writer first made a rough reconnaisance of the site during the winter of 1937. At that time nearly one-third of the mound-earth bad been removed by the road builders of Chengtu. A little examination led him to believe that it was not the Chin-Tai at all but a large tomb. Pottery sherds of the corded type, stamp-ornamented bricks, ornamented tile fronts were found in abundance in the exposed parts of the tumulus. Even well glazed pottery of the Liu-li-Ch'ang 琉璃廠 and Chiung-yao 邛窑 types, reputed wares of the T'ang and Sung periods, were also found among them. It was quite evident that the date of the site could not be earlier than the Tang dynasty.

During the fall of 1939, the Paochi-Tienshui Railway Construction Office began to build a large air-raid dugout under the mound. At the west end of this dugout the workers struck a brick wall. After being informed about its discovery, the writer went immediately to examine it. The bricks were of very large size without any decoration or inscription. Although the exposed part of the wall was only two square meters, it further convinced the writer that it was a tomb. The writer explained the importance of the discovery to the engineer in charge of the work, and asked him to fill up the pit again until we are ready to make further excavations.

After the establishment of the Szechwan Museum in the spring of 1941 by the Szechwan Provincial Government in cooperation with the National Szechwan University, preliminary preparations were made for the excavation of the site. During this interval, prominent archaeologists were invited to examine the site, such as Dr. Li Chi 李濟 Chief of the Archaeological Division of the Institute of History and Philology, Academic Sinca, and Dr. G.D. Wu 吳金鼎 of the same institution. After preliminary explorations, full excavation work was started on September 15, 1942, first with the help of Dr. T. K. Cheng 鄭德坤 and Mr. M. C. Lin 林名均 of the West China Union University Museum. Later with the assistance accorded by the Academia Sinica and the National Central Museum, excavation work was expanded during the spring of 1943. Dr. G. D. Wu was fnvited to serve as field director. The whole excavation work was finished by the end of September, 1943.

The royal tomb is roughly rectangular in shape and divided into three chambers with the anterior and posterior chambers slightly smaller than the central one. The whole structure is formed by a series of thirteen double arches of red sand stone and covered with stone slabs between. The anterior chamber is 5.4m by 4.4m and 5.8m high at the key-stone. At the entrance is a huge red lacquered wooden door, lavishly ornamented with gilded bronze work. Outside the door was sealed with red sandstone blocks weighing hundreds of pounds each. Outside the stone sealing is another sealing of large burned bricks. The whole sealing is about three meters in thickness.

About three meters behind the front door in the anterior chamber are three steps leading to the main floor. Then there is another door partitioning the anterior and central chambers. The door is somewhat similar to the front door. There were perhaps ornamental fittings in the anterior chamber, presumably wood carvings and draperies, as the traces of these fittings are clearly visible on the two side walls. There is now nothing left in this chamber except a few gilded bronze and iron rings presumably handles of a large box. Other things were either removed by the tomb robbers or decayed.

The central chamber is the burial chamber. It is 11 meters by 6 meters and 6.35 meters at the highest point of the arches. The pedestal for the coffin is built approximately in the middle of the floor but slightly to the rear. It is 7.45 meters by 3.35 meters and. 84 meters in height and carried by twelve gold armour-clad guards. Only the trunks of the guards are above the floor as if they are carrying the whole weight. The guards are about two-thirds life-size. They are arranged six on the east side and six on the west but not in symmetrical groups.

The lower edge of the pedestal walls are carved in lotus flowers and the upper edge in dragon designs. The edges protrude out slightly from the walls. The central row of the pedestal walls are panels of female musicians sculptured in deep relief except the rear wall which is carved in large lotus flowers. There are ten musicians on the east and ten on the west walls, two musicians and two dancers on the front wall, making altogether twenty-four panels.

The top of the pedestal is surfaced with fine white marble but in the centre it is intersticed with green marble to make an agreeable design. The coffin is placed immediately on the top. What the coffin was exactly like, it is now impossible to tell as it was made of wood and has entirely decayed. What now remains are only the large gilded bronze rings and corner plates attached to the different layers of the coffin and sometimes the lacquer surface. From all the available evidence it seems that the coffin rested on another wooden platform of four successive series of balustrades, one higher than the other. The outer coffin, which is called *kuo* 椁 was in the form of a pavilion, with doors on the two long ends. These two small doors are elaborately, decorated with gilded bronze plates and bosses, just as on the two large chamber doors. Inside this outer coffin is placed the coffin itself, which is approximately 2.82 meters by 0. 84 meter.

Immediately behind the pedestal is a large grey sandstone basin 1. 13 meters in diameter and 0.44 meter deep placed on a brick pedestal of irregular shape. It ls plain and of rough workmanship. Inside the basin is placed a red sandstone disc 0.36 meter in diameter and 0.17 meter thick. On this stone disc is placed a large brown glazed pottery basin. In it are placed two green glazed porcelaneous lamps.

Behind the stone basin is the third door partitioning the central and posterior chambers. Its construction and ornamentation are similar to the other two doors. The posterior chamber is 5.8 meters by 4.4 meters and 5.5 meters high. The rear wall of the chamber is formed by the rear sealing of stone blocks which are more than three meters thick. The rear part of the chamber rose to a platform extending to the whole width of the chamber, 4.4 meters by 2.6 meters and 0.78 meter high. The frontal of the platform is divided into three panels. The central panel shows a circling dragon, the other two panels are carved with a lion in each. The upper edge of the frontal shows two dragons playing with a pearl. All are in relief.

At the outer edge of the platform are placed the two sets of Jade Tablets 玉册, dedicated to the emperor. They are placed end to end and extending the whole width of the platform. Each set consists of fifty-three tablets 簡. The first and last tablets of each set are 330mm long, 105mm wide and 15mm thick, with polychrome painting of a warrior clad in gold armour. These are really a few of the earliest Chinese polychrome paintings extant. The other tablets are of uniform size, 330mm long, 32mm wide and 20mm thick. Each tablet is perforated horizontally at each end, and silver threads put through them connect the whole set. On the first set of fifty-three tablets is inscribed the imperial eulogical essay 哀册; on the second set is inscribed the essay offering the posthumous title 謚册. The inscribed characters are gilded and of very fine calligraphy. Each set is placed in a long black lacquered wooden box. The covers of the boxes are elaborately ornamented with phoenix and lion designs of silver and gold plates.

At the rear of the platform and right in the center is placed the sitting statue of the emperor. It is about two-thirds life-size and sculptured in fine red sandstone. The emperor is seated on a stool of semilunar shape with legs hanging down, i. e., just like us moderns. This is quite unconventional of the time as chairs and stools had not come into common use during the T'ang period. He should have been sitted on the floor as the other musicians. This shows that the adoption of the use of chairs in China may first have come as an aristocratic custom. There may have been a wooden shrine with curtains over the statue, but they were all decayed except for a few brass and iron nails left. Originally the statue was painted, perhaps with dragon designs on the robes, but only a few traces of the colors (white, red, green) are left.

Before the statue is placed a double box holding the great jade seal bearing the posthumous title 高祖神武聖文孝德明惠皇帝謚寶, the jade disc 璧, and other things emblematic of the emperor. The outer box is 67cm square and 20cm high. The inner box is 60cm square and 15cm high. These measurements can only be taken as approximate as the boxes have been disturbed and the wooden parts entirely decayed. They are mostly taken from the edge and corner plate fittings, silver decorations, and from lacquer traces on the mud. There may be warpings and distortions.

The boxes are varnished with black lacquer and lavishly decorated with gilded silver engravings. Take, for example, the cover of the outer box. On the center is a gilded silver plate with phoenixes finely engraved on it. On the two sides are two warriors each holding an axe. They are also engraved on gilded silver plate. Other parts of the box are also fully studded with decorations.

The seal, the jade disc and other things are put in the inner box. The seal is 119×118mm and 35mm thick. The handle is of animal design and 73mm high. The seal belt 綬 has been rotted away with only the jade tips and silver buckles remaining. The jade disc is 95mm in diameter and engraved in dragon and phoenix designs. Other things are still under study. As the box and its contents bad been originally disturbed, their exact relative positions cannot be exactly ascertained.

In all three chambers the ceiling and arches were painted sky blue and the walls were painted crimson. In the central chamber and directly above the coffin was hung a great canopy. The frames of the canopy were made of wood and at certain parts reenforced with iron and with an iron cross top. The whole thing was covered with fine fabric, lacquered, painted and gilded. It can be seen from the impressions made by certain fallen parts preserved in the mud. The hanging chain and hook are still in position on the ceiling.

When the tomb was first opened, four-fifths of it was filled with mud which flowed in annually from the crevices in the front during the summer rains. These crevices are vestiges of the holes opened by the early robbers and not properly sealed later. The strata in the mud are clearly visible. Each stratum represents a big rain but not an annum.

The foregoing is a brief description of the inside of the tomb as it was first uncovered. It is evident that the construction of the tomb as a whole is rather simple and the grave furnitures scanty. The poverty of grave furniture may be explained by robbery. All those considered valuable at that time, such as golds, silver, pearls, precious stones, porcelains, and even bronzes must have been removed from the tomb. However, a few valuables are left over, including among them a large jade belt (consisting of seven large jade plaques finely carved in dragon designs), a large silver pot weighing about a pound and finely engraved, two small embossed silver boxes probably for holding cosmetics, a small silver pig, embossed and finely engraved a large silver scratcher, a silver bowl, etc. All these must have been taken from the coffin and left by the robbers.

When was the tomb robbed? We can only conjecture. Most probably not more than ten years after it was first buried, i. e., between 925 to 933 A. D. The founder of the succeeding local kingdom, Meng Chih-hsiang 孟知祥 of

Later Shu 後蜀, issued an order to repair the tomb in 933 A. D. which showed that the tomb had already been pilfered by that time.

There is another perplexing problem which cannot be solved at present, i. e., no skeletal remains have been found in the coffin or in other parts of the tomb. So certain people suspect that this tomb was only a dummy. But from the other finds (such as the jade tablets, seals, disc, etc.) it cannot simply be a dummy and must be a real tomb. Moreover, more than thirty pounds of mercury were found in the coffin which tallies exactly with the ancient traditions. The skeleton might have been entirely decayed, as it is our experience that most Han and T'ang and even Ming tombs are without any skeletal remains in them in the Chengtu plain. As it had been robbed not long after it had been buried, the body might have been removed by the robbers.

Before we close, it would be appropriate to discuss a few points about the significance of the excavation. There are hundreds of imperial tombs in China but none of them has been scientifically opened (except the Yin tombs in Anyang excavated by the Academia Sinica, which really belong to a different category). This excavation is really the first of its kind ever undertaken in Chinese archaeology. So it is beset with many difficulties as well as with possibilities.

It is well known that all emperors were buried with a very elaborate ritual but what was inside the tomb is profound secret which had never been revealed. This was especially true of the T'ang emperors.① Now this excavation at last reveals some of the secrets of the burial customs of the T'ang emperors. There are several reasons for us to take this position. First, since Wang Chien declared

---

① The T'ang emperors' burial ceremonies were forbidden to be discussed at the time so very little was recorded about them. 唐書,禮志:李義府許敬宗以爲凶事非臣子所宜言,遂去其國恤一篇,由是天子凶禮闕焉,至國有大故,則皆臨時采掇附比以從事,事已則諱而不傳,故後世無考焉.

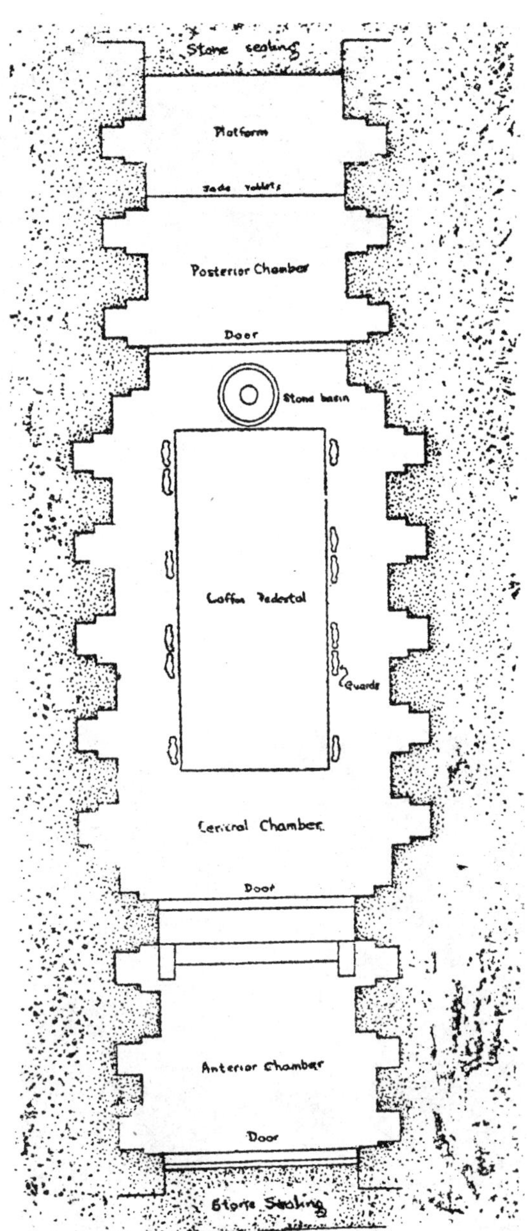

Sketch plan of the interior of the tomb (Drawn by Mr.Yang Yu-Jen Szechwan Museum).

1.The frontal of the coffin pedestal.The dancers and musicans and two of the guards carrying the pedestal can be seen. From this picture one can get a general view of the tomb.

2.Statue of the Emperor.

3. One of the musicians playing the drum.

4.One of the armour-clad guards.

The above photographs were taken by Mr.Mo Chung-chiang, Society for Research in Chinese Architecture.

himself emperor, his successor and subjects must bury him as an emperor when he died. Secondly, the men whom Wang Chien used were mostly officials of the old T'ang regime who came to Szechwan as refugees. These people were familiar with T 'ang court ritualism. So in Wang Chien's burial, the use of T 'ang ritualism was to be expected. Thirdly, what have been recovered tally perfectly well with the meagre notices occasionally noted down in the historical records, e. g., the jade tablets and the seal. From these facts, we think it is reasonable to infer that the tomb was built probably according to the T'ang imperial tombs. Although it was robbed and disturbed, only the movable things, especially the valuable objects, were affected. As to its historical value and its structure as a whole, its value is still very great.

The most important finds are the jade tablets, the jade seal and the sculptures. We know the *tsie* 册 and the *pao* 寶① are inseparable paraphernalia of all imperial burial ceremonies since Han times, but no one had ever seen them except those very fortunate few who were actually present at these ceremonies. So what they look like and how they are made, no one actually knows. The present finds serve as the only specimens scienticaIly recovered.

Historically and artistically, the sculptures are of greater value. We know that practically ninety-nine percent of all the sculptures found in Szechwan are Buddhistic. The earliest ones date from fifth century A. D. These sculptures show essentially the Gandhara influence and as circumscribed by their subject matter, they exhibit very little artistic creative quality. The sculptures in the tomb are different. They are really the only non-religious sculptures ever discovered in Szechwan and have even no peer in other parts of China. The female musicians and dancers are executed in the most lively and realistic way, i. e., the artist can bring his imagination and ability into full play. The same

① Means the seal bearing the posthumous title.

can also be said of the armoured guards. Even the statue of the emperor, although a portraiture of a realistic, austere and formal kind, exhibits the artist's superb ability in execution. It tallies very well with the description in the historical records, with heavy brows, deep set eyes, straight nose, high malars and thin lips.

Many of the other finds are still under study. The results cannot be stated exactly at present. For example, the structure of the tomb itself is a monumental piece of architecture and it is now under expert study at the Society for Research in Chinese Architecture.

〔原載 *Szechwan Museum*, Chengtu, Occasional paper, 1(四川省博物館單刊之一),1944〕

荆楚文庫編纂出版委員會
武漢大學出版社

中國親屬稱謂指南

目　　録

導　論

中國人對親屬關係很早就發生了興趣。這種興趣主要是實用性的。因爲中國的整個社會結構都建立在“擴大家庭”組織的基礎之上，而擴大家庭又建立在其内部成員系統化了的相互聯繫的基礎之上。如果整個社會的結構要協調地發揮作用，那么，表述和規定個人之間的權利和義務的親屬制度必須首先得到調整。這種觀念後來被儒學進一步加以發展。因此，親屬關係就成了各個時代都感興趣的課題。

對親屬名詞的系統的記録可以追溯到《爾雅》——一本出現于公元前2或3世紀的書(根據較保守的估計)①。在這本書裏，對親屬稱謂進行了認真的分類和編排。後起的《爾雅》類著作都用了專章來記録親屬稱謂詞。例如《釋名》和《廣雅》就是這樣——在此僅提及這類著作中較早的兩種。這類著作記録了後來産生的而在《爾雅》里未見的稱謂，在某種意義上説這使每個時代都有一個《爾雅》系統。這種做法一直沿襲至今②。甚至大型的類書也有專門章節談親屬稱謂。比如，《太平御覽》中有十卷③，《圖書集成》中有一百一十二卷④。當然，這些書的内容不全都與親屬稱

---

① 按傳統説法，《爾雅》是周公(？—公元前1105年)所編，由孔子(公元前551—前479年)、子夏(公元前507—?)、叔孫通(約公元前200年)等人修訂。它不是由一人所寫，也非一時之作，而是在公元前1000年間逐步完成的。參見B. 卡格雷:《遠東古代博物館學報》第3卷，1931年，44~49頁。《爾雅》中的“釋親”部分很可能完成于約公元前200年。參看《爾雅新研究》，刊《先秦經籍考》第2卷，163-184頁。

② 訓詁學的大部分著作都有親屬稱謂内容。例如《駢雅》(卷五《釋名稱》)、《拾雅》等。甚至方言著作，像杭世駿(1696—1773)的《續方言》、錢坫(1744—1806)的《異語》等，都有專章談親屬稱謂的各種變體。其他以《説文》爲首的字詞典也收録親屬稱謂，不過没有把它們系統編排起來。

③ 《太平御覽》卷五百一十一至卷五百二十一《宗親部》。

④ 《圖書集成·明倫匯編》“家範典”。

謂有關，其大部分還是屬于純文學的范疇。清代産生了一大批關于親屬稱謂的專著，其中影響最大、最有價值的是梁章鉅的《稱謂録》和鄭珍的《親屬記》。這兩本書都收録舊有的稱謂，都或多或少地保持了《爾雅》的傳統。《親屬記》僅僅包括父系直系親屬，較多地按儒家的正統觀點來安排處理材料①。

對親屬材料的最重要的劃分體現在禮儀著作《禮》中間。在這類著作中，不僅把親屬看成親屬本身，而且還把他們與其他事物聯繫起來。《親屬記》則不是這樣，它主要論述親屬關係名詞，而缺少《禮》的内容②。要研究中國親屬制的功能，禮儀著作是最重要的資料來源，因爲它們都注重實際的社會生活中的親屬關係。《儀禮》和《禮記》便是如此。這兩本書産生于公元前1—5世紀，在廣大的背景中來看待親屬關係；尤其是把親屬關係與喪服、"敬祖"以及禮的其他方面相聯繫。在後來的所有禮儀著作中(數量太大，在此無法一一列舉)，親屬關係都是基本的論題。

除此之外，大量的雜記著作也常常涉及親屬稱謂。從中國親屬制演變的角度講，這些是最重要的資料來源。一般説來，正是在此可以找到新産生的稱謂(包括方言的或不大通行的)。作爲一種慣例，禮儀著作和其他文學著作是不理會這些稱謂的。在雜記著作中，人們常常可以發現有關新稱謂産生和發展情況的精辟論述。

所以，對親屬稱謂的研究在中國學者中早已不是新鮮事，事實上，他們曾做過的某些解釋甚至可以跟現代社會學理論相媲美；然而，對中國親屬稱謂的系統的社會人類學的研究卻是從摩爾根開始的③。摩爾根的材料是由羅伯特·哈特——一個受雇于中國海關的英國人所提供的。

---

① 重要的著作還有翟灝(？—1788)的《通俗編》(卷四《倫常》和卷十八《稱謂》)，錢大昕(1727—1804)的《恒言録》(卷三《親屬稱謂類》)，鄭懿行(1757—1825)的《證俗文》，以及張慎儀的《廣釋親》。除此之外，還有許多毫無特色的、僅僅是互相重複的著作。

② 從《白虎通》中的引文來看，《親屬記》在性質上十分接近《爾雅》。

③《人類家族的血親和姻親制度》第3部分，第4章，1870年，413-437頁。

儘管哈特提供的材料不夠真實，儘管他深受摩爾根進化論的影響，以致他的大部分推論没有意義，但摩爾根-哈特的工作卻仍爲後來的研究奠定了基礎。自那以後，涌現了不少雜録，一些包含在法律文獻中或語言學入門書中，另一些包含在詞匯著作中。然而，除了一本以外，没有哪一本值得重視。這就是 T. S. 切恩和 J. K. 施賴奥克的著作①。施賴奥克的研究主要根據兩本現代詞典：《中華大字典》和《辭源》。雖然這樣的材料不夠翔實，不大可靠，但兩位作者卻能很好地利用。而喬治 · W. 邦納柯夫的嘗試卻似乎有點糟糕②，他試圖像處理歐洲語言那樣按摩爾根的假説把這些材料綜合起來。

這些歐洲人的著作顯然有局限性。首先，這些稱謂詞是通過未受過專門訓練的非正式合作人收集的。其次，作者都没有利用中國豐富的早期文獻材料——看來，他們真的不知道有這些材料。結果，這些研究大部分有不少錯誤和遺漏。由于這些研究者没有把中國的親屬稱謂系統作多層次劃分，所以他們幾乎不能確定稱謂的確切性質③。

現在這本書，主要以筆者從基本的中文文獻里收集到的稱謂詞爲依據。全部材料都以批判的眼光加以驗證，以保證準確地使用和闡釋各個稱謂。研究方法主要是歷史的和語言學的④方法。這一方面是因爲歷史的和語言學的方法最能揭示中國親屬制的特點，儘管它不好理解；另一

---

① 《中國的關係名詞》，刊《美國人類學家》34 卷，1932 年，623-664 頁。

② 《漢語中的關係名詞：人種語言學研究》（N. J. 馬爾，蘇聯科學院語言與心理研究所，1936 年）。我没有看到該書的俄文原著，只見到該書的英文摘要；所以，我只能指出一點：邦納柯夫主要用的是第二手的英語材料，只有《爾雅》除外，雖然《爾雅》也有英文譯本。他儘管利用了大量的歐洲人的研究成果，但似乎没有注意到古斯塔夫 · 施萊戈的“中國的親族關係表”（見《附有吳方言漢字轉寫的荷漢詞典》，萊頓，1886—1890 年，第 1 卷，1343 頁）。不過，最值得注意的還是他的建立在馬克思的歷史觀和 H. I. 馬爾的印歐語言理論基礎之上的方法論。他把這二者與摩爾根的進化階段論結合起來，竟然就發現了中國社會的“共同起源”。

③ 原計劃寫一節“早期研究述評”，但由于在結構上不好安排，而且將占很大篇幅，後來便放棄了。

④ 此處“語言學的”，指研究親屬制通常正式采用的方法，也就是考察親屬稱謂本身，親屬稱謂的整個結構，以及其體現的原則。

方面是因爲這種預備工作是深刻理解中國親屬制的各個方面的必要前提。考察的時期限于近二十五個世紀，這一時期的親屬制的文獻保存完備。如果説親屬制到現在發生了變化，那么兩千年的歷史對于這種變化來説已經是夠長的了。

第一章　稱謂的構成原則

決定稱謂的構成的原則是語言學的和社會學的原則。從語言學來看，親屬稱謂是按漢語的句法規則組成的；從社會學看，親屬稱謂的語義是由其反映的親屬關係以及所處的語境來決定的。中國的複雜而多樣的親屬關係名詞可以概括爲四種基本類型，即核心稱謂、基本修飾語、敘稱修飾語和面稱稱謂。核心稱謂表示核心的親屬關係，可以不帶修飾語。每個核心稱謂都包含一種主要意義，一種或多種次要意義。當它單獨使用時，主要意義起作用；當它與其他語素聯合使用時，次要意義就變成主要的了。大部分基本修飾語都是表示旁系親屬關係以及輩分的，不能獨立作爲親屬稱謂使用。核心稱謂構成擴大的親屬關係的基礎，基本修飾語則規定每個親屬在總的格局中的確切位置。這兩種類型的稱謂語素通過一次組合和二次組合就形成了現代的標準稱謂系統，這個系統是所有其他稱謂的樣板。敘稱修飾語在特定語境中把標準系統改變爲適當的敘稱形式。面稱，除了主要用法以外，還把稱謂變成親屬之間使用的直接稱呼形式。

下面，就是對這四種類型的稱謂的分析，以及對支配其構成和應用原則的説明。在分析核心稱謂時，首先給出主要意義，然後給出次要意義。

一　核心稱謂

祖：父之父。祖先。與别的語素連用指所有高於父親一輩的上輩親屬。

孫：子之子。下輩。與别的語素連用指所有低於兒子一輩的下輩親屬。

父：父親。上輩男性。上輩男性的標誌，加在所有比“己身”(ego)輩分高的上輩男性親屬的稱謂後面。

子：兒子。下輩男性。下輩男性的標誌，可以加在比“己身”輩分低的男性親屬的稱謂後面，但其用法是自由的。

母：母親。上輩女性。上輩女性的標誌，加在所有比“己身”輩分高的女性上輩親屬的稱謂後面。

女：女兒。下輩女性。下輩女性的標誌，加在所有比“己身”輩分低的女性親屬的稱謂後面作後綴。

兄：兄弟中的年長者。男性兄長一輩。與“己身”平輩的年齡較長者的標誌，與其他語素連用表示長於“己身”的平輩男性親屬。

弟：弟弟。與弟弟同輩的男性。與“己身”平輩的年齡較幼者的標誌，與其他語素連用表示幼於“己身”的平輩男性親屬。

姊：姐姐。與姐姐同輩的女性。爲“己身”同輩中較年長的女性親屬的標誌，與别的語素連用表示比“己身”年長的平輩女性親屬。

妹：妹妹。與妹妹同輩的女性。比“己身”年幼的平輩女性，與别的語素連用表示年幼於己的平輩女性親屬。

伯：父之兄。年較長者的標誌。把直系男性親屬系統作爲參照系，“伯”可以用作從己輩算起向上推溯的親屬的稱謂。又指夫之兄。

叔：父之弟。年較幼者的標誌，把直系男性親屬系統作爲參照系，可以用作從己輩算起向上推溯的親屬稱謂。

姪：兄弟之子。男性旁系的世系標誌。與其他語素連用指與“己身”同輩的男性親屬的後代。

姑：父之姊妹可與父之姊妹相比的親屬的標誌。表示血緣關係起自父之姐妹，或起自可與父之姐妹相比擬的女性親屬。又指夫之姐妹。

甥：姐妹之子。女性旁系的世系標誌。與其他語素連用指與“己身”平輩的女性親屬的後代。

舅：母之兄弟可與母之兄弟相比的親屬的標誌。表示血緣關係起自母之兄弟，或起自可與母之兄弟相比擬的親屬。又指妻之兄弟。

姨：母之姊妹。可與母之姊妹相比的親屬的標誌。表示血緣關係來自母之姐妹或來自可與母之姐妹相比擬的女性親屬。又指妻之姐妹可與妻之姐妹相比的親屬的標誌。表示血緣關係來自妻之姐妹，或來自可與妻之姐妹相比照的女性親屬。

岳：妻之父母。可與妻之父母相比的親屬，如他們的表哥表姐的標誌。

二　基本修飾語

高：第四代上輩親屬的修飾性標誌。

曾：補充，增加。對第三代上輩和下輩親屬的修飾性標誌。

玄：遥遠、深奥。第四代下輩親屬的修飾性標誌。

堂：廳堂。表示第二旁系的標誌。垂直向上推溯，它指父之父之兄弟之子和父之父之父之兄弟之子。也就是指堂伯父、堂叔父和堂姑母，以及堂伯祖父、堂叔祖父和堂姑祖母。

從：跟從。它在使用上與“堂”同義。“堂”是後起的稱謂，其使用範圍有限。在用“堂”的地方，“從”就可能被替换。

再從：再次跟從。表示第三旁系的標誌。向上推，指再從伯父叔父和再從姑母。

族：宗族、家族。表示第四旁系及更遠的親屬關係的標誌。

表：在外；外部。是父之姊妹、母之姊妹和母之兄弟的子女的標誌。同時，它也用來表示以“姑”(父之姊妹)、“舅”(母之兄弟)或“姨”(母之姊妹)等稱謂相稱呼的那些人的一切後代子女。

内：在内；内部。妻子。是妻之兄弟或可與之相比的親屬的後代子女的標誌。

外：在外。表示母之父母和女之子女的修飾語。

以上是根據現代標準稱謂所作的概括分析，是從全部稱謂中抽象出來的，對每一稱謂都進行了考察。但是，對於每一個中國人來説，在使用稱謂時都存在多種可能的組合，因此，例外現象是不可避免的。在以歷史角度來考察整個系統時，這些例外現象(它們不僅數量少而且相對而言無代表性)，就可以清楚地顯示出來。

三　稱謂的構成

在構成各種稱謂時，表示核心親屬關係的稱謂是作爲結構的基礎來使用的；只有表示父母和子女、妻子和丈夫的關係的稱謂例外，這些稱謂被用作性别標誌①。所有表示旁系關係和下輩的修飾性語素都依次作所選的結構基礎——核心稱謂——的前綴②，表示最近的親屬關係的語素離核心稱謂最近，表示最遠的親屬關係的語素離核心稱謂最遠，以這樣的方式來構成所需的稱謂。所有的性别標誌都作後綴。假如結構基礎中的"輩分"範疇不明顯，如"舅"和"姨"，那麼這時的性别標誌就同時也是輩分標誌。這時，它們也總是作後綴。

① 性别標誌爲：父、母、子、女、夫、婦、媳、婿。在理解中國親屬制時由於没有認識到這套稱謂的性質，已經引起了極大的誤解。第一個注意到這種誤解的可能要算 H. P. 威金斯。他在《中國的家族稱謂》(《新中國評論》，1921 年，159-191 頁)中寫道："這些研究者的第一個錯誤……是……把附加在各種'描寫性'親屬名稱上的表示男女性别的標誌當成了一類親屬——'兒子'和'女兒'的總稱。"A. L. 克魯伯也獨立地發現，"這最後四個稱謂(指父、母、夫、婦)在附於别的親屬稱謂上面時，僅僅表示被指稱者的性别。"(《中國親屬系統的形成過程》，《美國人類學家》35 卷，1933 年，151-157 頁)

② 術語"前綴"和"後綴"是在不嚴格的意義上用的，因爲在漢語裏無真正意義上的"前綴"和"後綴"(也許個别語素例外，特别是那些貌似後綴的語素)。"前綴""後綴"在此只表示：在句法關係中某個不可分的語素(漢字)置於另一個不可分的語素(漢字)之前或之後。

在選擇一種親屬關係的稱謂的結構基礎時，首先要考慮的因素是輩分，其次是世系。讓我們拿父之父之姊妹之子之女之子的稱謂來作例子。這是一個複雜稱謂，因爲世系已從女系變成了男系，後來又變回到女系。我們先來看看輩分，暫不説世系。這裏所指的這個人屬於兒子一輩，因此，立即可以把結構基礎縮小到兩個可替換的稱謂上："姪"和"甥"。他與"己身"(ego)的關係是通過與"己身"平輩的女性親屬而建立的，因此，可以排除稱謂"姪"。剩下的是"甥"。進一步看，他與"己身"的關係不是宗親關係，而是血親關係。此世系是經由父之父之姊妹傳遞下來的，其關係可與"己身"父之姊妹的關係相比照，因此，應加上限定性語素"姑"和"表"。他屬於非宗親的第三旁系親屬，因此，可以用限定語"堂"。把以上這些語素組合起來，就構成了稱謂"堂姑表外甥"——一個表達十分精確的稱謂。在後面加個"女"字就構成了與上述關係相同的女性親屬的稱謂"堂姑表外甥女"。要表示與堂姑表外甥結婚的女性親屬的關係，就把"女"換成"婦"；若要表示與堂姑表外甥女結婚的男性親屬的關係，則用"婿"替換"女"。

複雜稱謂的各種構成要素一般應該按其擴大的意義即次要意義來理解，決不應按主要意義來理解。全部擴大的意義的綜合就形成了稱謂的新的含義。這種現象是漢語句法的一個特徵，不了解這點將造成絶大的誤解。

下面的表代表了這些結構基礎的實際範圍。這裏的範圍還是有限的，充分的討論留待後面第四章的各表裏詳細展開。

例解　黑體字代表用作結構基礎的稱謂，一般字體爲附加修飾語。

祖	父之父
伯**祖**母	父之父之兄之妻
堂叔**祖**父	父之父之父之兄弟之子幼於祖父者
伯	父之兄
堂**伯**父	父之父之兄弟之子長於父者

姑表伯父	父之父之姊妹之子長於父者
叔	父之弟
堂叔母	父之父之父之兄弟之子幼於父者之妻
再從叔父	父之父之父之兄弟之子之子幼於父者
姑	父之姊妹
堂姑父	父之父之兄弟之女之夫
姑表姑母	父之父之姊妹之女
舅	母之兄弟
堂舅父	母之父之兄弟之子
堂表舅父	母之父之父之姊妹之子之子
姨	母之姊妹
堂姨父	母之父之兄弟之女之夫
再從姨母	母之父之父之兄弟之子之女
兄	兄
姑表兄	父之姊妹之子長於己者
堂姑表兄	父之父之姊妹之子之子長於己者
嫂	兄之妻
舅表嫂	母之兄弟之子長於己者之妻
堂舅表嫂	母之父之兄弟之子之子長於己者之妻
弟	弟
堂弟婦	父之兄弟之子幼於己者之妻
再從弟	父之父之兄弟之子之子幼於己者
姊	姊
堂姊夫	父之兄弟之女長於己者之妻
妹	妹
姨妹	妻之妹
堂姨妹夫	妻之父之兄弟之女幼於妻者之夫
姨表妹夫	母之姊妹之女幼於己者之夫

堂姨表**妹**	母之父之兄弟之女之女幼於己者
姪	兄弟之子
族**姪**女	父之父之父之兄弟之子之子之女
再從**姪**婿	父之父之兄弟之子之子之女之夫
外甥	姊妹之子
堂**外甥**女	父之兄弟之女之女
堂姑表**外甥**	父之父之姊妹之子之女之子
孫	子之子
姪**孫**女	兄弟之子之女
堂姪**孫**	父之兄弟之子之子之子
外甥**女**婿	姊妹之女之夫

在構成上三輩、上四輩親屬和下三輩、下四輩親屬的稱謂時，以上二輩親屬和下二輩親屬的稱謂作基礎，另以輩分標誌附加其上。世系標誌通常放在最前端，在作前綴的輩分標誌之前。例如：

祖	父之父
曾**祖**母	父之父之母
曾伯**祖**父	父之父之父之兄
高**祖**父	父之父之父之父
孫	子之子
曾**孫**女	子之子之女
曾姪**孫**婦	兄弟之子之子之子之妻
玄**孫**	子之子之子之子

上述內容便是中國親屬稱謂的標準系統①的構成原則。標準稱謂具有普遍意義，是其他稱謂所據以建立的模式。因此，在正式文獻——即家譜、法律條文和禮儀作品裏，大多使用標準稱謂，在日常應用中，標準稱謂必須配上適合特定語境的修飾語。

---

① 如果從廣義上説，可能有人會稱這爲“書面語系統”。

四 敘稱修飾語

敘稱修飾語實際上不僅反映中國人對社會地位的態度，而且反映中國人的社會禮儀準則。它是講禮貌、舉止文雅的表現：對他人純粹表示尊敬和贊美，對自己則表示謙卑。這態度精確地支配着親屬稱謂的使用規則。

敘稱修飾語還是親屬内部成員集團意識的表現形式。表敬意的修飾語和表謙卑的修飾語不能不加選擇地使用，其使用規則是由一親屬集團與另一親屬集團之間不同的身份認同決定的。表敬意的修飾語隨意使用也無妨，但表謙卑的修飾語却只能用於那些絶對屬於“自己”這一親屬集團的人。

這兩種態度便是使用和理解所有中國親屬稱謂的基礎。

敘稱修飾語有嚴格的用法規則，總是加在標準稱謂前面。依性質和用法的不同，可以把它們分成四大類：(1)敬稱修飾語；(2)謙稱修飾語；(3)自稱；(4)謚稱修飾語。

敬稱修飾語 這些修飾語用來指聽話人或收信人的親屬，包括下述三種：(1)令：美好的，可尊敬的。它可加在任何標準稱謂前面，除了標準稱謂具有特殊語素時例外。(2)尊：可尊敬的，尊貴的。與“令”的意思相同。但嚴格地説它僅適用於比聽話人的輩分或身份高的親屬。(3)賢：賢德，可敬的。與“令”替换使用。但嚴格地説它僅用於稱那些聽話人的親屬中比他輩分或身份低的人。不過這一規則也有例外，如“賢叔”便是。“賢叔”意爲“你的賢德的叔父”。

當一個人不好確定是用“尊”還是“令”作前綴時，可以用“令”。“令”“尊”“賢”都含有禮貌性的“您的”的意思。

當聽話人爲非親屬時，稱呼其親屬應該用表敬修飾語作前綴。在與下輩親屬談話提到其長輩親屬時用表敬修飾語，除此之外，宗親之間不用表敬修飾語。這實際上是從兒稱呼的用法。當敘稱中提到某位非宗親親屬的親屬時，如果他不是一個與自己有關係的親屬，對他的稱謂應前加表敬修飾語；如果他是一個與自己有關係的比己輩分高的親屬，那麼應該使用一般的標準稱謂或面稱稱謂。作爲慣例，人們對那些與自己關係緊密的直系親屬不用敬稱。

謙稱修飾語① 當向旁人談話或寫信提稱到自己的與己同姓的親屬時，在其標準稱謂前加上表謙修飾語。這裏的"表謙修飾語"按"自己的"或"謙虛的"的意義來用，包括三種語素：(1)家：家庭，居家，家務。用在所有比己輩分身份高的宗親的稱謂前面。(2)舍：農舍，房屋，住處。用在比己輩分身份低的宗親的稱謂前面，主要用於對第一旁系下輩宗親的敘稱，有時可稱所有下輩親屬，但不能用於對直系親屬的敘稱，如不能用來敘稱自己的兒女。(3)小：微小。加在比己輩分低的宗親的稱謂前面，主要用來稱自己的兒女和孫兒孫女等。"舍"除了不用於直系下輩親屬之外，與"小"可以換用。

"家""舍""小"都有某種自我謙卑的意味。值得重視的是：表謙性修飾語不用於稱呼不同姓的親屬②，甚至不能用來稱呼己之父親的已婚的姐妹或己之已婚的姐妹。因爲她們已經采用丈夫的姓，不再屬於自己這個家庭或家族，所以不能以謙稱來稱呼他們③。

自稱④ 在別的親屬面前稱呼自己時(口語或書信形式)，稱謂前面

① "謙稱"是與"敬稱"相對應使用的。如"家""舍"所示，謙稱暗含有"我本人的家庭"或"我本人的家族"的意思。

② 有一個通稱——"敝親"(我的窮親戚)，可以用於任何非宗親。

③ 《顔氏家訓·風操篇》："凡言姑、姊妹、女子子，已嫁則以夫氏稱之，在室則以次第稱之。言禮成他族，不得云家也。"

④ 如果不是在一定的語境中，自稱與謙稱在某些方面很難區分，尤其是語素"小"。這裏爲了論述起見，特地把二者區分開來。

加上自稱。例如一個姪兒在伯父面前稱呼他自己時就用自稱。它們包括兩種語素：(1)愚：簡單，愚笨，魯莽。它可以加在自己稱呼自己所用的稱謂前，主要用於聽話人爲下輩親屬、説話人爲上輩親屬時的情境。(2)小：微小。它可加在自己稱呼自己所用的稱謂前，主要用於下輩親屬與上輩親屬説話的情境。

當“自己”跟直系親屬如父親、兒子、祖父、孫子等説話時，“愚”和“小”都不適合於稱呼“自己”本人。這時，需要以專門的稱謂來稱呼“自己”。

謚稱修飾語 這部分修飾語——除了幾個特殊的詞根以外——放在對已死的親屬的稱謂前面，對已故的父母、祖父母和伯叔父等尤其是這樣。它們包括兩種語素：(1)亡：已故的。加在所有已死的親屬的稱謂前。(2)先：在先的，原先的，從前的。僅僅加在比己輩分或地位高的已死親屬的稱謂前面。在稱呼别人的已死的親屬時，表敬修飾語必須加在上述修飾語的前面。但這種用法不常用，一般是用委婉詞語來指稱。

還有一些用作敍稱修飾語的特殊的詞根，這些將在第四章相關的表裏列出。爲簡潔明瞭起見，所有受敍稱修飾語限定的，或者由特殊的詞根構成的稱謂，將在後面以敬稱、謙稱、自稱或謚稱等形式來展開討論。

五 面稱稱謂

面稱是對個别的具體的親屬的直接稱呼形式。在文學作品，即書面語作品中，必須使用標準稱謂作面稱。面稱不能與敍稱修飾語連用。敍稱修飾語只能與標準稱謂連用。

面稱只限於稱呼比己輩分高的或與己同輩但比己年長的親屬，對輩分低的或年齡小的親屬可以直接用名字來稱呼，或者用標準稱謂作面稱。

祖父母的面稱　對祖父母的面稱形式依地域的不同有多種。由於這些稱謂未系統記録過，所以要確定哪一種是最流行的很難。下列幾種也許是最通用的：稱呼祖父的“爺爺”、“翁”或“翁翁”、“公”或“公公”，稱呼祖母的“婆”“婆婆”“奶奶”。不論各地采用哪一種稱謂，它們在擴展用於系統裹的其他親屬方面則是一致的。在擴展使用時，將上述稱謂與標準稱謂中的“祖父、祖母”相替换，作標準稱謂的後綴。例如，將“翁”或“公”替换標準稱謂“伯祖父”中的“祖父”，就構成了面稱形式“伯翁”或“伯公”。

父母的面稱　對父母的面稱比對祖父母的面稱變體少。稱呼父親的有“爹”“爺”“爸爸”，稱呼母親的有“媽”和“娘”。“爸爸”决不擴展，使用“娘”也很少擴展。

爹：對父親的面稱，並用於構成上一輩男性親屬的面稱，代替“父”。

媽：對母親的面稱，並用於構成上一輩女性親屬的面稱，代替“母”①。

在存在特殊面稱的場合，上述規則將不適用。在某些不必用稱謂的場合，上述稱謂可以略去，就像有時略去“父”“母”這樣的稱謂一樣。

兄和姊的面稱　“哥”或“哥哥”：稱呼兄，並用於構成對長於己的男性平輩親屬的面稱，代替“兄”。

“姐”或“姐姐”：對姊的面稱，並用於構成對長於己的女性平輩親屬的面稱，代替“姊”。

正是面稱稱謂形成了衆多的地方變體。在現代，面稱變體主要集中在祖父母和父母的稱謂上。兄和姊的面稱變體很少。但不論各地的面稱形式如何不同，上述的構造規則仍然適用，只要用各地的稱謂來替换標

① “媽”和“母”在外延上是指已婚者，因此不能用於未婚的女性親屬。

準稱謂中的特定部分即可。

面稱的使用較隨便，也就是説，它們比標準稱謂系統更具有“類分”性質。當兩個親屬面對面説話時，他們總知道對方的確切的親屬關係，因此，只是在敘稱情況下才需要使用較精確的親屬稱謂。姓氏①、名字、頭銜和排行②也廣泛用作對每個親屬的面稱，這使精密的稱謂系統更加複雜化了。

六 其他次要性稱謂

另有幾組稱謂可以稱爲次要性稱謂，即祭祀稱謂、碑銘稱謂、書面語稱謂和替代性稱謂。這些稱謂在後面的第四章裏將論及。

祭祀稱謂在古代用於祭祀時稱説直系祖先。這類稱謂僅有幾個，現在已經停用。碑銘稱謂用於基碑和紀念碑的碑文。嚴格講這類稱謂只有兩個，一個是“考”，指父親，一個是“妣”，指母親。只有兒子才給父母立碑。祭祀稱謂和碑銘稱謂常常與由謚稱修飾語所構成的稱謂相混淆，二者常常互換使用，因爲它們都是指已死的親屬，雖然在意義上有細微差別。不過，仍有一些很有趣的變化發生。這些變化反映了歷史的發展進程。

---

① 姓氏僅僅用於稱述非宗親以及嫁入本族的婦女。

② 古代表示長幼用“伯、仲、叔、季”，它們早已停用。現代完全以排行來表示。如果己身的父親是六個同胞兄弟姊妹 A、b、C、D、e、F 中的一個（大寫體代表男性，小寫體代表女性），那麽他們相應的排行就是大、二、三、四、五、六。“大”意爲“最年長的”。《日知録》卷二十三：今人兄弟行次，稱一爲大，不知始自何時。漢淮南厲王常謂上大兄，孝文帝行非第一也。”如果己身的父親是 D，己身就稱呼 A“大伯”，稱呼 b“二姑”，稱呼 C“三伯”，稱呼 e“五姑”，稱呼 F“六叔”。如果己身的父親是 A，己身就稱呼 b“二姑”，稱呼 C“三叔”，稱呼 D“四叔”，稱呼 e“五姑”，稱呼 F“六叔”。稱謂“伯”和“叔”調换了位置，使之與己身父親的排行相一致，但整個排行的順序依然不變。

還有另一種表示排行的方式，即把男性和女性分開。如上例中，把 A、C、D、F 分别表示爲大、二、三、四，把 b、e 分别表示爲大、二。使用哪種方式依各地風俗和各個家庭的習慣而定。

書面語稱謂是僅用於書面文獻的稱謂，通常没有面稱與敘稱之分。它們大部分是已過時的古詞，但在書面語中仍在使用。替代性稱謂是指那些可與通用的稱謂形式同義使用的稱謂。是采用這種或那種稱謂，完全取决於地方習俗以及個人的喜好。

第二章　結構原則與稱謂範疇

中國親屬制的構成結構依據兩個原則：直系親屬與旁系親屬的劃分，輩分的分層。前者是垂直劃分，後者是水平劃分。通過這兩個原則的結合，每一種親屬就被牢牢地固定在整個系統結構中。

一　直系與旁系的分别

區分旁系親屬的方式在古代親屬制和現代親屬制中是不相同的。古代親屬制中，如《爾雅》和《儀禮》中，每支旁系的區分，是通過共用與該旁系所源出的直系親屬最接近的那一親屬的稱謂而實現的。例如：父之父之父之兄弟稱爲“族曾王父”，其後代直到與“己身”同輩的各代旁系親屬，就在各自的稱謂前加上“族”字，以示區别。父之父之兄弟稱爲“從祖王父”，其後代直到與“己身”同輩的所有各代旁系親屬，都在稱謂前加上“從祖”，以示區别。這種方式也適用於更遥遠的旁系親屬①。

在《爾雅》系統，對兄弟之子及其後代無稱謂，對父之兄弟之子之子及其後代也無稱謂。好像兄弟之子和族兄弟之子無分别，意即兄弟之子也就是自己之子。另一方面，《爾雅》又給了姊妹之子的稱謂“出”（男子用）②，姊妹之子之子的稱謂“離孫”（男子用）③；以及兄弟之子的稱謂

---

① 參見鄭珍《補正爾雅釋親宗族》，刊《巢經巢文集》卷一。
② 《爾雅》：“男子謂姊妹之子爲出。”
③ 《爾雅》：“謂出之子爲離孫。”

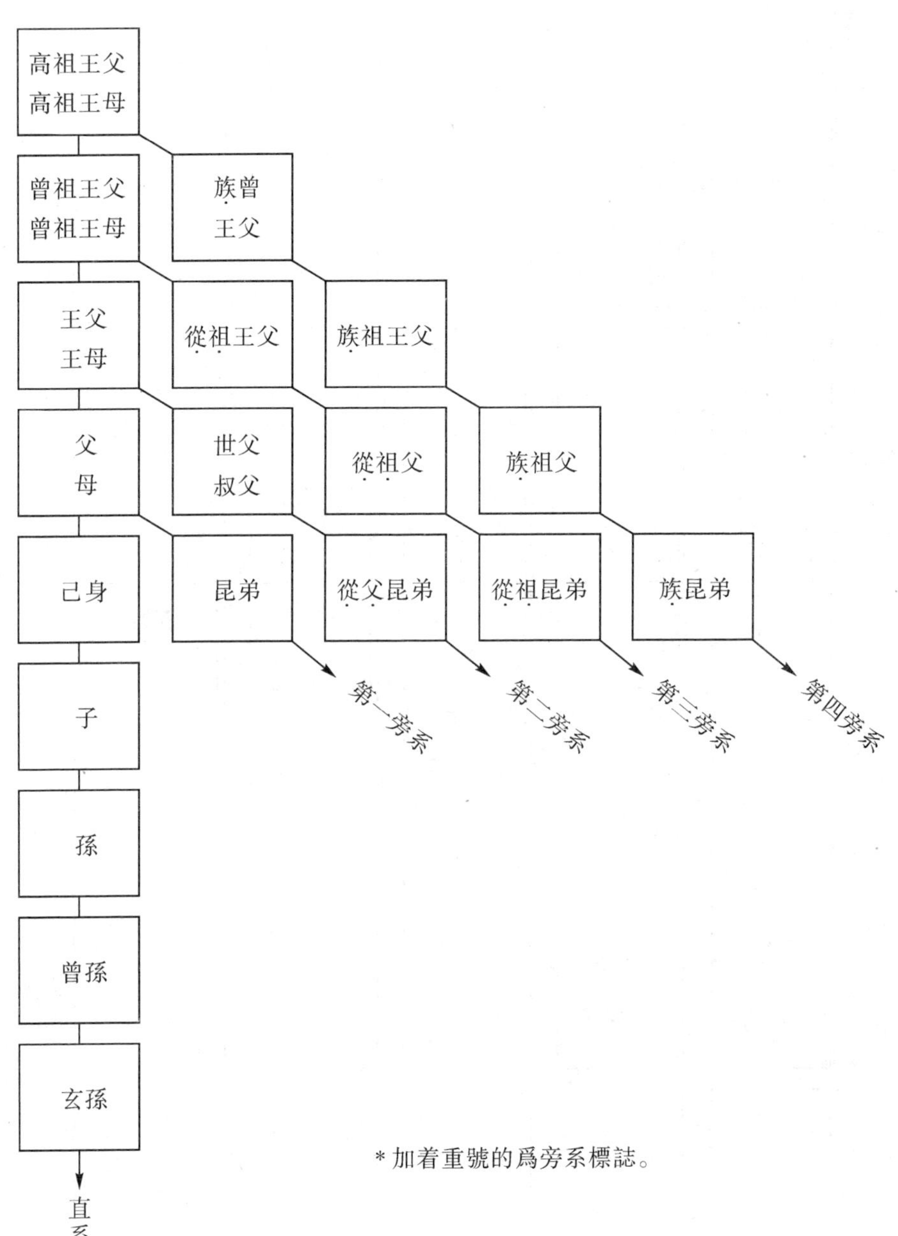

圖1 古代親屬制的旁系劃分

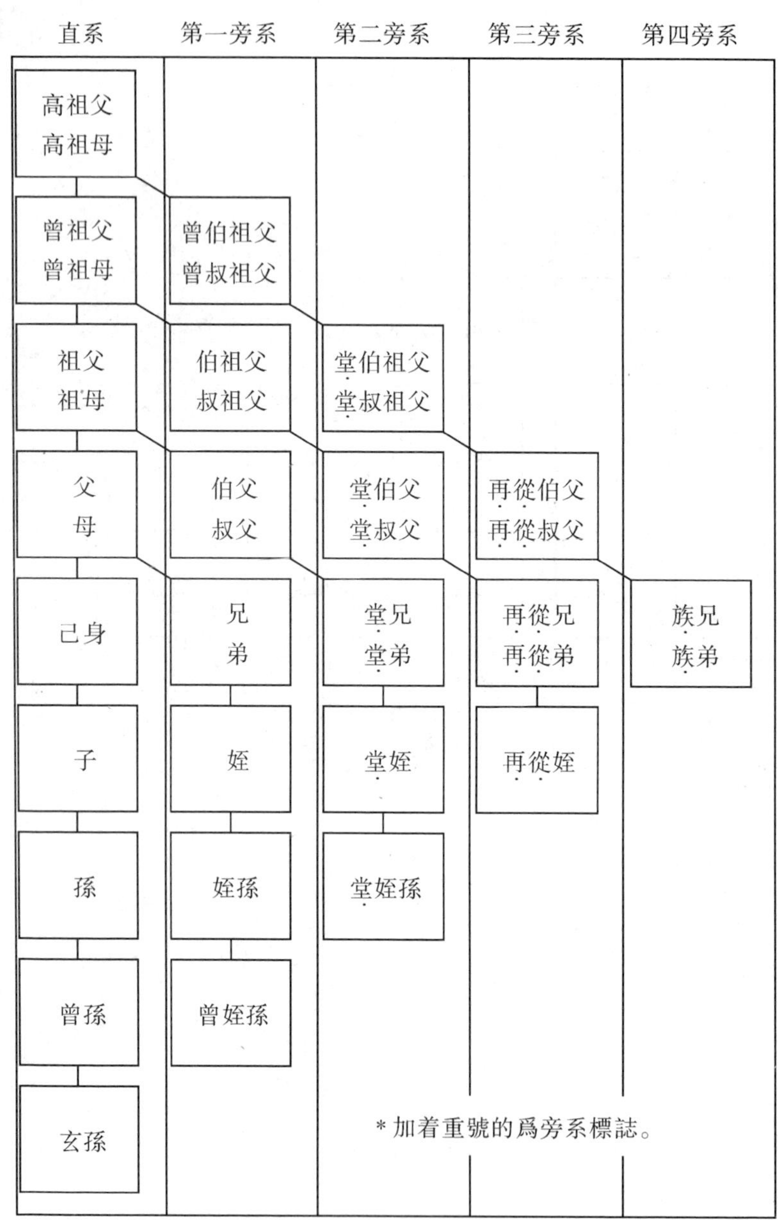

圖 2　現代親屬制的旁系劃分

“姪”(女子用)[①]，兄弟之子之子的稱謂“歸孫”(女子用)[②]。在周代嚴格的父系宗族社會裏，甚至自己的兒子也是按繼承權的次第而相互分別開來的。因此很難理解爲什麼没有稱謂把己之子與兄弟之子區分開來。與此相反，却存在男子用來把己之子與姊妹之子區别開來的稱謂，以及女子用來把己之子與兄弟之子區别開來的稱謂[③]。

在現代親屬制裏，旁系的區分更完善更統一。但實現的原則却有所不同。表示旁系的修飾語，以“己身”這一輩分層作基礎，朝上輩和下輩垂直擴展。例如，父之兄弟之子稱作“堂兄弟”，堂兄弟之子、孫相應地被稱作“堂姪”和“堂姪孫”。朝上輩推，“堂”擴及父之父之兄弟之子，如“堂伯父”和“堂叔父”，擴及父之父之父之兄弟之子，如“堂伯祖父”和“堂叔祖父”。其他的旁系親屬如“再從”和“族”這兩支旁系，也依此擴展。

現代的旁系劃分原則起源於漢代。最初，以“從子”或“猶子”這樣的稱謂來區分己之子和兄弟之子[④]。在晉代，“姪”這個稱謂開始從女子對其兄弟之子的稱呼變成了男子對其兄弟之子的固定稱謂。“同堂”最早使用是在五六世紀[⑤]，表示第二旁系親屬，後來簡稱爲“堂”。“再從”的使用要稍晚一點。“族”是一個古老的略含界定意義的稱謂。隨着這些重要的旁系稱謂的完善，大約在公元 10 世紀時，全部旁系劃分原則的演變就完成了。

---

① 《爾雅》：“女子謂晜弟之子爲姪。”

② 《爾雅》：“謂姪之子爲歸孫。”

③ 《爾雅》系統是否完整，很值得懷疑。對父之姊妹之子之子和母之姊妹之子之子也没有稱謂。既然姊妹之夫、父之姊妹之子、母之兄弟之子被稱作“甥”，姊妹之子被稱作“出”，照此推斷，父之姊妹之子之子和母之兄弟之子之子也當稱作“出”。但是，母之姊妹之子之子無稱謂也不好解釋，這類稱謂不可能全部都與己身之子或别的親屬的稱謂合流了。出於某種原因，《爾雅》的編者對與己身平輩的旁系親屬的子女的稱謂似乎不感興趣。另一方面，《爾雅》系統似乎重視母系的後輩子女的稱謂。這是不是母系制的遺蹟還有待研究，因爲尚無其他有説服力的證據可證明。

④ 參見第四章第 1 表 125 號稱謂。

⑤ 參見第四章第 1 表 41 號稱謂。

二 輩分層

在圖 3 裏，竪軸綫表示旁系，橫軸綫表示輩分。當一條軸綫與另一條軸綫相交時，就給系統裏的一個親屬規定了一個位置框。每個親屬都被嚴格地固定起來，不受變動的影響。輩分層由於輩分標誌的使用而得到保留。這種標誌大部分是取自直系親屬的核心稱謂，因爲在計算輩分時，直系親屬總是無條件地作爲衡量的標準。這種以核心親屬稱謂作爲輩分標誌的做法歷來被解釋爲旁系和直系的部分融合。但按我們現在對中國親屬制的分析，這一解釋是站不住脚的。

輩分是一個重要的結構原則，它不能被打亂，以免使整個結構受到破壞。對這個原則最嚴重的破壞因素（如果算不上唯一的因素的話），是不同輩分的親屬之間的通婚。爲了抵制這種影響，輩分就成了婚姻關係準則中最重要的因素。在中國，不提倡某個人與其任何親屬結婚，但如果親屬間一定要通婚，則通婚雙方必須屬於同一個輩分。换言之，中國人可以與本宗族以外的任何人結婚，若結親雙方有親屬關係，那麼他們必須屬於同一輩分，而年齡的大小可以不論。

這個輩分原則在古代看來是不太嚴格的。在周代，一個封建諸侯可以以他的妻子的姪女爲妾，在妻子死後甚至可以把她立爲正妻。漢代，惠帝（公元前 194—前 188 年在位）娶其姊之女①。唐中宗（公元 705—710 年在位）娶其姑婆之女②。這些事例都被後代的歷史學家和道學家嚴厲地斥責爲亂倫③，但是當事人所處的那些時代的人却未對他們進行如此嚴厲

① 《漢書·外戚列傳》："（孝惠張皇后）宣平侯敖尚帝姊魯元公主，有女，惠帝即位，吕太后欲爲重親，以公主女配帝爲皇后……"

② 《唐書》卷七十六："中宗和思順聖皇后趙……父環，尚高祖常樂公主，帝爲英王，聘後爲妃。"

③ 王鳴盛（1723—1797）在其《十七史商榷》（卷八十六）（廣雅書局本）中討論了這些事例："人倫之極變"。

的抨擊。也許因爲這是個别現象，也許因爲當事人是帝王，所以才未受到責難和懲罰。但不管是哪種情況，都確實表明了上古時代輩分原則的不嚴格性①。

源自父系女性亲屬之世系				直 系	源自父系男性亲屬之世系			
第四旁系	第三旁系	第二旁系	第一旁系	**高祖父 高祖母**	第一旁系	第二旁系	第三旁系	第四旁系 4
			曾祖姑父 曾祖姑母	**曾祖父 曾祖母**	曾伯祖父 曾叔祖父			3
		表祖父 表祖母	姑祖父 姑祖母	**祖父 祖母**	伯祖父 伯祖母 叔祖父 叔祖母	堂伯祖父 堂叔祖父 堂姑祖母		2
	堂表伯父 堂表叔父 堂表姑母	表伯父 表叔父 表姑母	姑父 姑母	**父 母**	伯父伯母 叔父叔母	堂伯父 堂叔父 堂姑母	再從伯父 再從叔父 再從姑母	1
再從表兄、弟 再從表姊、妹	堂表兄、弟 堂表姊、妹	表兄 表弟 表姊 表妹	姊 姊夫 妹 妹夫	**己身**	兄、嫂 弟、弟妇	堂兄堂弟 堂姊堂妹	再從兄、弟 再從姊、妹	族兄 族弟 族姊 族妹
	堂表姪 堂表姪女	表姪 表姪女	外甥 外甥女	**子 女**	姪 姪女	堂姪 堂姪女	再從姪 再從姪女	1
		表姪孫	外甥孫	**孫 孫女**	姪孫 姪孫女	堂姪孫 堂姪孫女		2
			外甥曾孫	**曾孫 曾孫女**	曾姪孫 曾姪孫女			3
				玄孫 玄孫女				4

圖 3

＊黑體代表核心親屬集團。着重號表示：這種親屬的子女不再往下傳遞世系。例如，“女”的子女爲“外孫”和“外孫女”，但在“女”下面的方框却不列“外孫”和“外孫女”。阿拉伯數字代表上輩和下輩的輩分。

① 《通典》討論了不同輩分間通婚引起的喪服等級的提高帶來麻煩的兩個事例，見卷九十五“族父是姨弟爲服議”；還討論了假設的例子，見卷九十五“娶同堂姊之女爲妻，姊亡服議”。在公元1—5世紀時，不同輩分的遠親之間通婚似乎是可以容忍的。

當然，毋庸置疑，就是在周代也是很重視輩分原則的①。根據有記載的婚姻資料來看，不同輩分之間的通婚是個别現象，而不是一種通例②。對輩分原則的强調是逐步進行的，大約在五六世紀達到高潮。這一原則似乎在3—4世紀得到大發展。《唐律》(約制訂於600年)制訂了嚴禁不同輩分之間通婚的條文③。後來的所有律例都包含這種禁令以及引證的案例。從公元10世紀到現在，不同輩分之間的通婚不僅受到法律嚴厲禁止，而且引起民衆的强烈反感，以至於一個教師與其學生或一個人與其朋友的兒女結婚，都將被認爲是大逆不道。

這種根深蒂固的觀念就是想使親屬的輩分永遠保持不變，不遭到破壞。假如一個親屬的輩分被婚姻所打亂，那麼所有與他有關係的親屬的位置都將被打亂，親屬制就會失去對親屬關係的正確反映，從而不能發揮自身應有的功能。

三　範　　疇

克魯伯的論文《親屬關係的類分制》④並未使人類學的兩個術語“類分”和“描寫”失去意義。該文的貢獻在於提出了存在於各種親屬制中的範疇。這些範疇爲測試一種親屬制的工作過程提供了一個便利的工具。把中國親屬制的所有内容都納入一個表裏是不可能的，但我們可以根據克魯伯提出的八個範疇，把其中的核心稱謂納進一個表裏。必須注意的

① 在周代發展起來的宗法制和喪服制强調輩分的區分。喪服在後面將詳細討論。至於説宗法，其大宗分爲小宗在多數情況下由輩分的計算來決定。

② 不同輩分間通婚的早期事例屈指可數。梁玉繩説：“楚成王取文芈二女(《左傳・僖公二十二年》)，晉文公納嬴氏(《僖公二十四年》)，皆以恒爲妻者，可謂無别矣。嗣後妻甥者，漢孝惠取張敖女，章帝取竇勳女，吴孫休取朱據女，俱楚覩、晉重作之俑也。”(《瞥記》卷二)

③《唐律疏議・户婚》：“若外姻有服屬，而尊卑共爲婚姻……以姦論。”緊接在這段引文後面的是對這一條款的解釋，以及另一條性質相同但更特别的條款。“尊卑”是指屬於不同輩分的親屬。

④《大不列顛及愛爾蘭皇家人類學學報》39卷，1909年，77-84頁。

是：這些核心稱謂加上修飾語後也可以在次要意義上來使用，在下表中只考慮了其主要意義。

下面讓我們把中國親屬制作爲一個整體，看看核心稱謂在每一範疇中的分佈。

(1)同輩與不同輩之别。這一範疇可從整個親屬制的輩分標誌的使用中準確地觀察到。輩分不僅是親屬制中重要的結構原則，而且還是婚姻關係中重要的調節因素，以及面稱稱謂使用中的决定因素。但在全部核心稱謂中，它僅占 78.3%。在“伯、叔、姑、舅、姨”這些稱謂中，輩分範疇受到壓制而未能顯示出來。這種不同輩分的混淆不是親屬制本身固有的，而是由從兒稱引起的混亂造成的。

(2)直系與旁系之别。這一範疇在整個親屬制中受到嚴格限定。旁系由特殊標誌來區分。實際上，所有基礎修飾語的功能都是爲了發展這一範疇。在核心稱謂中所有稱謂都能表示這一範疇。

(3)平輩的年齡之别。這一範疇在親屬制中僅有部分代表。在“己身”這一輩，不論男性還是女性都有年齡之别。在上輩親屬中，只有男性親屬及其妻子有此分别，在下輩親屬中，無此分别。

稱謂 範疇	祖	孫	父	子	母	女	兄	弟	姊	妹	伯	叔	姪	甥	姑	舅	姨	岳	婿	夫	妻	嫂	婦	總計	百分比
輩分	+	+	+	+	+	+	+	+	+	+			+	+				+	+	+	+	+	+	18	78.27
血緣或婚姻	+	+	+	+	+	+	+	+	+	+			+	+				+	+	+	+	+	+	18	78.27
直系或旁系	+	+	+	+	+	+	+	+	+	+	+	+	+	+	+	+	+	+	+	+	+	+	+	23	100
親屬的性别	+	+	+	+	+	+	+	+	+	+	+	+	+	+	+	+	+	+	+	+	+	+	+	23	100
所從出的親屬的性别	+	+									+	+	+	+	+	+	+	+	+			+	+	13	56.53
説話人的性别																							0	0	
同輩中的年齡長幼							+	+	+	+	+	+										+	+	8	34.78
所從出的親屬的生命狀况																							0	0	

＊根據克魯伯提出的範疇對核心稱謂進行的分類。

里佛斯把平輩中年齡的區分歸之於部落的啓蒙禮儀，即哥哥將比弟弟先接受啓蒙①。不管這正確與否，這還是認真提出來的唯一解釋。在古代中國，存在着各種啓蒙禮儀，大部分記録在《儀禮》②和《禮記》③裏。這些古代的啓蒙禮儀與平輩的年齡分别這一範疇有無關係，尚不能肯定。中國學者一般把這一範疇與宗族組織"宗法"相聯繫，因爲在宗族組織裏，在爵位和財産的繼承上以及在祭祀祖先和繼承世系的特權上，兄長都具有絶對的優先權④。

(4)親屬的性别。這一範疇在中國親屬制裏通過性别標誌的普遍使用來實現，在核心稱謂中它占100%。

(5)稱呼人的性别。這種範疇完全没有反映。因稱呼人的性别總是可知的，所以不需要表示。但在古代親屬制裏有這一範疇留下的痕迹。例如，在《爾雅》和《儀禮》裏，稱謂"姪"僅爲女子使用，稱呼其兄弟之子。也許，還有另一些稱謂也僅爲女性使用或僅爲男性使用，但我們無法肯定是不是這樣。

(6)某親屬關係所從出的那一親屬的性别。這一範疇在中國親屬制裏通過特殊標誌的使用得到充分的表述。例如，"表兄弟"這個稱謂可能包含幾種親屬關係：父之姊妹之子、母之兄弟之子、母之姊妹之子。但假如我們把父之姊妹之子稱作"姑表兄弟"，把母之兄弟之子稱作"舅表兄弟"，把母之姊妹之子稱作"姨表兄弟"，那麽這幾個稱謂就分别準確地反映了相應的親屬關係。在面稱中没有做這種精確的劃分，因爲稱呼人與被稱呼人之間的確切親屬關係總是很明顯的，不需要表述出來。

(7)血親與姻親之别。這一範疇得到全面的反映，只有"舅、姨"兩個稱謂例外。母之兄弟(血親)和妻之兄弟(姻親)都稱作"舅"，母之姊妹和妻之姊妹都稱作"姨"，這是從兒稱呼的影響所致。面稱中的從兒稱

---

① W. H. R. 里佛斯《社會組織》(W. J. 佩里編，1924年)189頁。

② 《儀禮・士冠禮》。

③ 《禮記・冠義》。

④ 程瑶田(1725—1814)《宗法小記》："宗之道，兄道也。大夫、士之家，以兄統弟，而以弟事兄之道也。"又："尊祖故敬宗，宗之者，兄之也。故曰：家之道，兄道也。"

呼比較隨便，丈夫和妻子可以互稱對方“爸爸”或“媽媽”。

(8)某親屬關係所從出的那一親屬的生命狀況。這種範疇是存在的，但一般並未得到全面的反映。最常見的區別方式是用特殊標誌來區分已故親屬和健在的親屬。對已故的和健在的父母、祖父母、伯父叔父等，分別存在不同的稱謂。對親屬的其他生命狀況未加以反映，或僅用委婉語來表示。

上述這些範疇(第 2，第 4，第 6，第 7 也可能)對於保持一種嚴格的單係——在中國爲父系——世系是必要的。準確地講，正是在中國親屬制裏，這些範疇得到了充分的表述。

要求區分已故或健在的祖先的做法也許可以歸因於祖先崇拜——這在現代已不流行。

四　相　關　性

在各種親屬制中，一般都存在影響某些範疇的表達的相關性因素。相關性有三種：邏輯或概念相關、言語相關以及自我相關——即在概念和言語兩方面都相關①。從總體上看，相關性不是中國現代親屬制中的一個特徵，因爲從某種程度上講，它與全面地表達某些範疇、準確地區分各種親屬是不相容的。

在古代親屬制裏存在概念相關的遺蹟。《儀禮》説：“謂吾姑者，吾謂之姪。”②反過來説也是正確的：“謂吾姪者，吾謂之姑。”“姑”，如《爾雅》和《儀禮》所用，意指父之姊妹，“姪”意指兄弟之子女(女子用)。換言之，“姑”“標記的是被稱呼的親屬的性別，非稱呼人的性別”；而“姪”

---

① 參見 A. L. 克魯伯對“相關性”下的定義。見《加利福尼亞親屬制》(《加利福尼亞大學美國考古學和人種學文集》第 12 卷第 9 部分 340 頁，注釋 1)和《祖尼人的親族穌氏族》(《美國自然博物館人類學論集》第 18 卷，1919 年，78-81 頁)。

② 《儀禮・喪服》：“傳曰：‘姪者，何也？謂吾姑者，吾謂之姪。’”

“不表示被指稱的親屬的性别，僅暗示稱呼人的性别”①。所以，“姑”和“姪”都包含一個對方所没有表述的範疇。在古代用法中，“姑”“姪”確實是概念相關。

《爾雅》又説：“謂吾舅者，吾謂之甥。”②“舅”在此處用來指母之兄弟，“甥”指姊妹之子女。但，反之却不能成立。實際上，這種説法與《爾雅》中記録的“甥”的另一些含義是相矛盾的。在那裏，“甥”指父之姊妹之子，母之兄弟之子、姊妹之夫(男子用)及妻之兄弟。《爾雅》還用了另一個稱謂“出”來指稱這同一種親屬關係——姊妹之子女。上引《爾雅》那句話很可能是後人加進去的，因爲“舅”“甥”很可能是在漢代至唐代這段時期才發生相關關係的③。交表婚和從兒稱(它們將在後面加以討論)的影響使這個問題複雜化了。因此，在古代親屬制裏“舅、甥”很可能没有相關性，但“甥”有部分相關，即“甥”僅用在男性親屬之間④。

這些便是在中國古代親屬系統裏能找到的僅有的相關性遺蹟。後來，普遍應用各種範疇的趨向變得非常强大，以致這些殘存的古代相關性稱謂在現代親屬制度中便完全消失了。

---

① A. L. 克魯伯《親屬關係的類分制》81 頁。

② 這種説法在《儀禮·喪服》中也可見：“傳曰：‘甥者何也？謂吾舅者，吾謂之甥。’”

③ 在這一時期，“舅”僅用於指母之兄弟，“甥”的其他含義消失，成了僅指姊妹之子女的稱謂，如“外甥”。

④ 意即，“甥”用於己身(男性)與母之兄弟之子、父之姊妹之子、姊妹之夫和妻之兄弟之間。他們稱己身爲“甥”，己身也稱他們爲“甥”。

第三章　影響親屬制的因素

中國的古代親屬制在向現代親屬制發展演變的過程中，存在着一種緩慢的然而却很頑强的趨勢：向系統化發展，向更有效更精確的描寫式稱謂發展。這種趨勢在很大程度上是由中國社會據以組織起來的基礎——社會家系決定的，在較小程度上則是由狂熱的禮學家和禮儀執行者人爲促成的。然而，在另一方面又存在着一些潛在的抵制過分系統化的力量。這些力量時常暗地裏破壞着親屬制的某些範疇，使親屬制的某些部分失靈。促進系統化的力量是宗族組織和喪服制，二者對親屬制産生互補性的影響。削弱系統化的力量是中國的婚俗和從兒稱。禮學家在保持宗族的穩固發展和喪服規則的準確使用方面是一支穩定的力量，他們頑强地維護稱謂的傳統規範①。但是總的來説，他們無法抗拒稱謂使用中的普遍趨勢，常常不得不接受已經廣爲流行的稱謂，然而却時常試圖將這些稱謂納入原有的系統，並使之協調一致②。因此，無論我們多麽不相信“模擬親屬代數學”——借自馬林諾夫斯基的用語③，但是我們對影響中國親屬制（它現在正處於解體的境地）的這幾種相互衝突的力量進行研究探索還是很應當的。

---

① 例如，自公元1世紀起，“舅”“姑”就不再指夫之父母，但是，在禮儀著作中仍然按這個意義來使用。“男”大約在公元900年的時候擴展到指妻之兄弟，但我們在正式的書面文獻中從未發現過這樣的用法。

② 例如，大約在公元前500年“姨”擴展到指母之姊妹。在其後的七八百年裏，指母之姊妹的新舊稱謂交替使用。到了大約公元400年，“姨”被確立爲指母之姊妹和妻之姊妹的標準稱謂。

③《親屬》，刊《人類》雜志第30卷，1930年第7期，19-20頁。

一　宗族：世系與族外婚

在家庭内部，親屬關係必然首先作爲一種生育單位出現。如我們上面所述，各個社會中的家庭内部的這些主要親屬關係，從生物學角度講都是相同的①，可是從功能上講却是依文化的不同而有所差異②。親屬關係不僅僅局限於具有生育功能的家庭内部，而且還擴大到廣大的個人圈子裏，這些個人在事實上或名義上與具有生育功能的家庭的成員有聯繫。在擴大的過程中，一些有聯繫的個人集團受到重視，另一些則受到冷落，即使這兩類人的親等關係可能完全一樣。人類學非常重視(也可説是過分重視)在親屬分類中存在的這種變異的基礎。從現實來看它也是值得重視的，因爲這種親屬分類模式在各民族中存在着變異，極不相同，每一特定親屬制各以完全不同的方式來劃分親屬。受到强調的親屬集團的特徵也同樣反映了社會結構的廣大範圍，親屬制是這社會結構的一部分。

在中國親屬制裏，男系親屬受到强調，其形成的基礎是族外婚下的父系宗族組織。宗族組織在中國稱爲“宗法”，照字面講就是“宗族之法”。宗法與封建制有密切聯繫③。封建制在公元前3世紀崩潰④，然而宗族組織却保存到現代，儘管在形式上有了相當的改變。封建制結束以後，到公元3—8世紀時，宗族組織發展到了頂點。這時它通常被稱爲“世族”或“宗族”。引起這種大發展的原因很多，但主要是由封建制

① 即父、母、子、女、兄弟、姊妹這些嚴格的生育家庭的成員在任何親屬制中都是存在的。

② 例如，在父系社會中父親和生育家庭組織的其他成員的關係同在母系社會中的這種關係可能完全不同。

③ 對封建時期宗族組織的研究，可參看萬光泰的《宗法表》，萬斯大的《宗法論》，以及程瑶田的《宗法小記》。至於現代人的研究，可參孫曜的《春秋時代之世族》(1931年)。

④ 此處所言“封建制”是按舊史的觀點，指盛行於上古的封王侯建國的制度。此制相傳於黄帝建國始，至周代達到完善，秦統一全國後開始崩潰。以下的“封建時代”“封建時期”也是在這個意義上來使用的。——譯者注。

消亡後其對立的社會力量的發展造成的。顯赫的大家族取代了封建貴族在國家政權中和社會等級體系中的位置①。到了唐代，豪門世族的影響開始下降。這一方面是因爲唐統治者采取了壓制政策，另一方面是因爲唐的衰落加速了社會的動亂②。到現代，宗族組織對於大多數人來説已不如從前那麽重要，但它的傳統影響仍滲透於中國社會生活的每一個角落。

宗法已經有人很好地研究過了。這裏我們只需要考察那些直接影響親屬集團的劃分的兩個因素：父系世系和族外婚。就"宗"——"宗族"來説，每一世系不僅在姓氏的繼承上，而且在財産、爵位等等的繼承上，都是嚴格的父系氏族繼承制。同時，每一世系都遵循長子優先的原則：長兄對其他弟兄有優先權③。在"宗"内部實行絶對的族外婚制。屬於同一個宗族的人不能通婚，即使一百代以後也不行。同時，在"宗"内部實行嚴格的居夫家制④。在中國歷史上究竟存不存在過一個母系社會階段，現在還不能充分證明⑤。但族外婚則明顯地是周代的風俗⑥。族外婚在中國出現較晚。據古代經典文獻證實：在夏、商時代(約公元前1700—前1100年)，同宗者間隔五代以後纔可互相通婚⑦。依照傳統説法，嚴格的宗族外婚制是由周公(約公元前1100年)建立的。他設此制旨在保證宗

① 參見《陔餘叢考·六朝重世族》。

② 《通志·氏族略序》。

③ 在繼承爵號時是實行長子世襲的原則，但是財産却是在各兄弟之間平均分配的，雖然長兄通常能得到額外的份額。只有在祭祖的時候，長兄長子長孫纔對所有的次兄次子次孫有絶對的優先權。

④ 由於想得到一個兒子，便把女婿視爲兒子。這時這個男子要用妻子的姓，居住在妻家，在各個方面他都被作爲兒子來看待。他的第三代子女又用他原來的姓，即"三代回宗"，但通常允許其中一位男孩兒繼承這個男子的妻子的世系。

⑤ 關於遠古時代存在母系社會一説，已成了近來許多研究中國古代社會的著作提出假説的依據。例如M. 格蘭特的《中國之文明》(巴黎，1929年)，郭沫若的《中國古代社會研究》(1931年)。他們提出的論據多是聯想性的，而不是推理性的。

⑥ 《禮記·大傳》："繫之以姓而弗别，綴之以食而弗殊，雖百世而婚姻不通者，周道然也。"《通典·晉范汪祭典》："且同姓百代不婚，周道也。"

⑦ 《太平御覽》(鮑刻本)卷五百四十引《禮外傳》。"五代"包括己身一代。即使這樣，夏殷時代的人是否實行族外婚仍大可懷疑。

族的穩固發展。但是仍有充分的證據表明：就是在周代，族外婚也是既不普遍也不强制推行的①。只是在封建制被推翻、宗法組織發生變化以後，絶對的族外婚制才開始逐步流行。從公元五六世紀到現在，同族不婚的原則都一直受到各個朝代的法律的强有力支持②。

族外婚下的父系宗族的影響從中國親屬制的親屬二分方式中可見。所有親屬依據族係被分成“宗親”和“非宗親”(稱爲“外親”或“内親”)。所有宗親都屬於“己身”這個家族，擁有同樣的姓氏；而父系親屬中的女性親屬及其後代子孫則爲“外親”，母系親屬和姻親也都屬“外親”。

爲了保持宗親和外親的分别，稱謂就必須相應地一分爲二：把父系親屬中自男系而出的男性親屬與自女系而出的男性親屬區分開來。即把父之兄弟之子(堂兄弟)及其後代與父之姊妹之子(表兄弟)及其後代區分開，把兄弟之子(姪)與姊妹之子(外甥)區分開，把兒子之子(孫)與女兒之子(外孫)區分開，把其他的上輩、下輩和旁輩親屬中的宗親和非宗親區分開，通過這種“二分”來保持宗親與非宗親的差别。這種“二分”是必要的，因爲父之姊妹、己之姊妹、己之女兒，或者任何在族外婚制下嫁到别的家族去的女性宗親及其後代子孫，按父系世系的原則，都不屬於“自己”這個家族。

可是，從整個親屬制來看，對宗親的重視並不像上面所説的那樣明顯。其原因，部分是由於稱謂的精細區别在一定程度上阻礙了親屬的分類。但是，當我們把視綫轉向表謙的修飾語的使用時，這種重視程度就會立即明顯起來。表謙性稱謂只能用於指稱宗親，因爲他們是“自己”這個親屬集團的成員；而對非宗親則不能使用表謙性稱謂，因爲他們是屬於“自己”親屬集團以外的人。

---

① 趙翼在《陔餘叢考》(卷三十一)中説“同姓爲婚，莫如春秋時最多”，並引用了許多例子來證實他的觀點。他推斷：“此皆春秋時亂俗也，漢以後此事漸少。”

② 如《唐律疏議》卷十四：“諸同姓爲婚者，各徒二年，緦麻以上以姦論。”參見皮埃爾·霍格《從法律角度考察中國的婚姻》，1898年，43-53頁。

在觀念上，宗親與“自己”的關係被認爲比非宗親近，即使他們的親等是完全一樣的。這一點在喪服制中得到最充分的體現。對祖父祖母的服喪期是一年，但對外祖父外祖母的服喪期則僅爲五個月；對伯父叔父的服喪期是一年，對舅父的服喪期則僅爲五個月；對父之兄弟之子服喪期是九個月，對母之兄弟之子服喪期僅爲三個月。更富啓發意味的是，未婚女性宗親和已婚女性宗親在服喪期上的差别。對父之未婚姊妹、己之未婚姊妹、己之未婚的女兒以及兄弟之未婚的女兒，服喪期均爲一年。但如果她們是已婚的，服喪期就降爲九個月，即降低一個等級。因此我們發現，這些女性親屬只要没有結婚，她們就依然屬於“自己”這個家族，一旦結婚她們就屬於丈夫的那個家族。這種由婚姻關係發生的世系的改變，減少了她們與原有家族的聯繫，其結果自然也減少了與“自己”的聯繫①。

對非宗親的稱謂也許更能表達這種親屬的二分。把祖父母與外祖父母區分開，伯父叔父與舅父區分開，姑母與姨母區分開，這自然是建立在外婚性社會組織之上的親屬制的一個普遍特徵。但有趣的是，父之姊妹的後代、母之姊妹的後代和母之兄弟的後代都合用一個單一的稱謂：“表”②。“表”，就字面講是“外”“外部”的意思。父之姊妹的後代和母之姊妹及兄弟的後代，雖然從血親關係看屬於不同的系屬，但他們全都屬於非宗親。因此，他們合用一個稱謂“表”便是可以理解的了。

“表”的引入和普遍使用也是由歷史造成的。在《爾雅》和《儀禮》的古代系統中，在交表婚的影響下，父之姊妹之子與母之兄弟之子的稱謂發生合流，都用一個“甥”③。而母之姊妹之子女則仍然用“從母兄弟”(指其子)和“從母姊妹”(指其女)來表示。在公元1—2世紀時，交表婚已長期廢除，對父之姊妹之子女便以“外”相稱，例如“外兄弟”④；對母

① 婦女未婚時對父系親屬的服喪期與對兄弟們的服喪期相同。結婚後她對這些親屬的服喪期降一等，相應地，這些親屬對她的服喪期也降一等。

② “姑表”“舅表”“姨表”是中國親制中的三個第一等表親。

③ 參見後面的“交表婚”一節。

④ 《儀禮・喪服》“姑之子”鄭玄注：“外兄弟也。”

之兄弟之子女便以“内”相稱，例如“内兄弟”①。大約在其同時②，“從”和“表”也作爲“内”和“外”的同義詞來使用。“從”意爲“中間，内部”，“表”意爲“外面，外部”。

在公元前最後幾個世紀和公元最初幾個世紀，“從母兄弟”雖然還可以使用，但通常却以新起的稱謂“姨”來稱呼母之姊妹之子女。

從公元4—7世紀，對母之姊妹之子女使用“外”或“内”導致了長期混亂，這種混亂後來擴大到父之姊妹的後代、母之兄弟的後代和母之姊妹的後代身上③。究其原因可能在於這一事實：這些親屬雖然系屬不同，但都屬於非宗親，都與外婚制下的父系宗族組織有區别。到了唐代“從”消失，“表”便獨自用於上述那些親屬④，這樣“表”就成了對血親中輩分比己高的非宗親親屬的後代子女的通稱。

這種在稱謂上和觀念上對親屬進行的二分，是族外婚制下的父系宗族制原則的特定表現。同時這一原則又受到另一因素——喪服的制約，導致對宗族組織中的旁系親屬作精細劃分，因此大大地破壞了該原則原來的功能。然而，對這一原則的理解又是從總體上把握中國親屬制的最根本的要求，因爲它不僅是一個潛在的影響力量，而且在許多重要的親屬稱謂——即謙稱和敬稱的使用中還是一個鉗制力量。

二 喪服等級

中國喪服制不僅以父系宗族組織爲基礎，使宗親與非宗親互相區别，

① 《儀禮·喪服》“舅之子”鄭玄注：“内兄弟也。”

② 《後漢書·鄭太傳》：“公業懼，乃詭詞更對曰：‘……又明公將帥，皆中表腹心。’”

③ 例如《通典》卷九十五“爲内外妹爲兄弟妻服議”：“晉徐衆論云：‘徐恩龍娶姨妹爲婦，婦亡，而諸弟以姨妹爲嫂，嫂叔無服，不復爲姨妹行喪。”《海録碎事》(引自《稱謂録》說：“唐人兩姨之子，相謂爲外兄弟。”《山堂肆考》(角集卷四)：“兩姨之子爲外兄弟，姑舅之子爲内兄弟。一説舅子稱姑子爲外兄弟，姑子稱舅子爲内兄弟。”“内”和“外”的使用十分混亂，連這類書的編者也不知哪種用法是正確的。

④ 第六世紀時表親關係變得如此普遍，就連家譜中也有其一席之地。如《魏書·高諒傳》：“諒造親表譜録四十許卷，自五世以下，内外曲盡，覽者服其博記。”

而且還以親屬關係的等級爲基礎，以此確立喪服等級。對於宗親施行喪服的範圍爲：旁系到第四旁系爲止，直系到上四輩和下四輩爲止①。其結果，在中國親屬制中，第 1~4 旁系與其他統稱爲“族”的更遠的旁系之間便存在根本的區别。“喪服”本身就是一個大題目，在這裏我們只能涉及它的一些主要方面，這些方面對於闡釋喪服對中國親屬制的影響是很有必要的。喪服的五個等級爲：斬衰(三年)、齊衰(一年)、大功(九個月)、小功(五個月)和緦麻(三個月)，這些一般被稱爲“五服”。實際上其種類不止這五種。這些喪服等級的規格在不同時期有很大不同，在每一特定時期，喪服等級隨着中間值上升或下降。雖然喪服規格可能發生變化，但決定這些規格的基本原則仍然不變。

上述“斬衰”等術語表述的僅僅是附屬性單位②，而喪服的基本單位是“期”，期的基本單位是“年”。喪服的其他等級規格一是“加隆”(提高喪服等級)，二是“降殺”(降低喪服等級)，二者都以基本單位“年”爲基點。《禮記・三年問》對喪服規則做了詳盡論述③，其曰：“至親以期斷，是何也？曰：天地則已易矣，四時則已變矣；其在天地之中者，莫不更始焉。以是象之也。”“然則何以三年也？曰：加隆焉爾也，焉使倍之，故再期也。”④“由九月以下，何也？曰：焉使弗及也。故三年以爲隆，緦小功以爲殺⑤，期九月以爲間。上取象於天，下取法於地，中取則於人。人之所以群居和壹之理盡矣。”

爲親屬服喪從最親近的親屬始，以“期”——“一年”爲其基本單位。最親近的親屬有三種。《儀禮・喪服傳》説：“父子一體也，夫妻一體也，昆弟一體也。”⑥有了三種最親近的親屬，有了基本單位“期”，再加上“加隆”和“降殺”規則，全部喪服制就與親屬制聯繫起來了，如圖 4 所示。

---

① 《禮記・大傳》：“四世而緦，服之窮也。”

② 斬衰、齊衰、大功、小功、緦麻這些術語規定了爲某一親屬居喪時穿的衣服。

③ 有關歐洲語的譯本，可參看 J. 萊格的《禮記》(《東方的聖書》第二十八卷，393-394 頁)，S. 庫里渥《禮記》(1913 年，580-586 頁)。

④ 二十五個月算作三年，因此服期三年實則只有兩年零一個月。

⑤ 五個月算作兩季六個月。以五替换六反映了古代中國人不喜歡雙數。因此，基本服期是：三月(一季)、五月(兩季)、九個月(三季)和一年(四季)。

⑥ 《儀禮》卷三十。

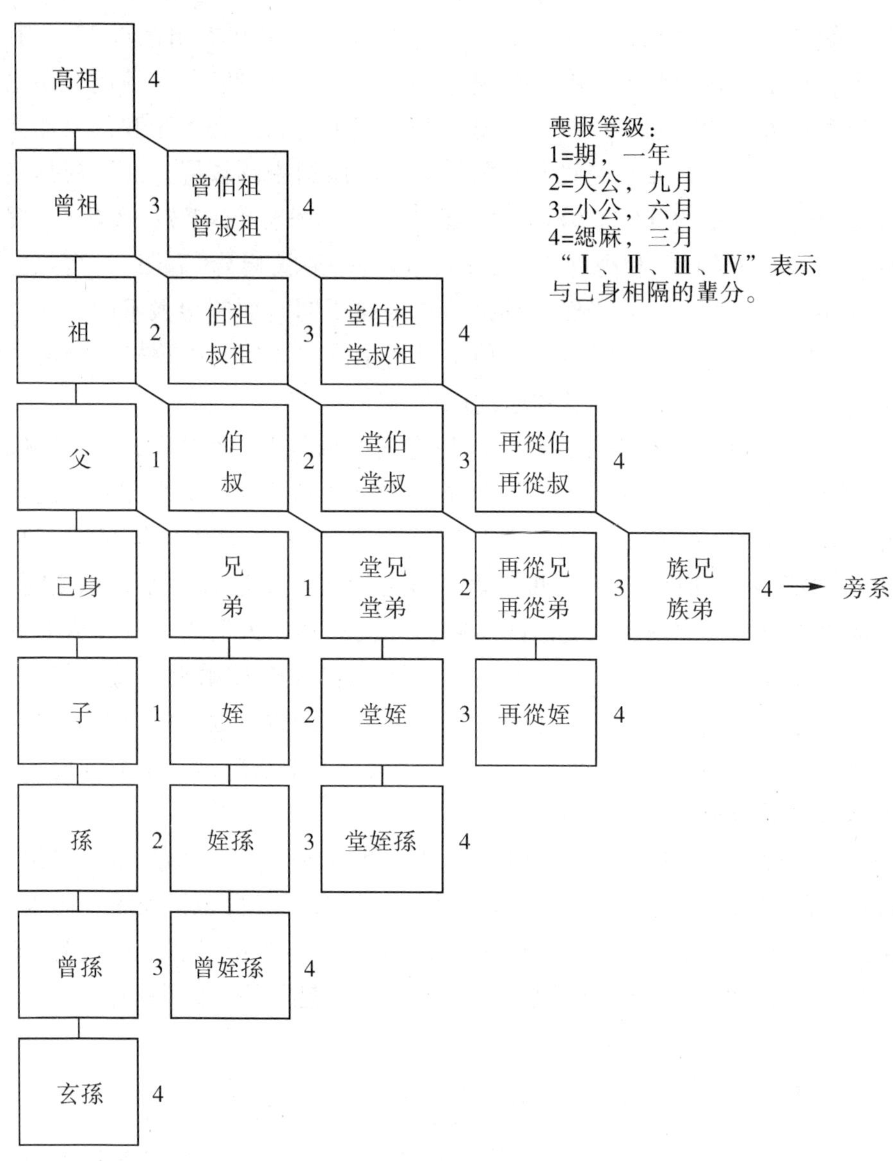

圖 4

＊作者僅勾勒了喪服制的基本面貌，因此只舉了男性親屬。全部喪服規格需要 8 至 12 張圖表才能表述。

喪服的具體内容如下：爲父服“期”，一年；爲父之父服“大功”，九個月；爲父之父之父服“小功”，五個月；爲父之父之父之父服“緦”，三個月。以上爲“上殺”(即往上遞減)。爲子服“期”，一年；爲孫服“大功”，九個月；爲曾孫服“小功”，五個月；爲玄孫服“緦”，三個月。以上爲“下殺”(即往下遞減)。爲兄弟服“期”，一年；爲父之兄弟之子服“大功”，九個月；爲父之父之兄弟之子之子(祖父之兄弟之孫)服“小功”，五個月；爲父之父之父兄弟之子之子之子(曾祖父之兄弟之曾孫)服“緦”，三個月。以上爲“旁殺”(即平行遞減)。

爲父服“斬衰”三年，是喪服的升級，屬於“加隆”。按基本規則，爲父只服“期”一年。爲祖父和伯父叔父服“期”一年也同樣屬於“加隆”，它們原來只屬於“大功”那一級——九個月。

所有的非宗親，不管跟“己身”的關係是親近還是疏遠，不管是血親還是姻親，都只適用最後一級喪服“緦麻”(三個月)①。他們也受“加隆”規則的制約。例如，在古代喪服制中，母之姊妹的喪服級别是“小功”，五個月；而母之兄弟的喪服級别却是“緦麻”，三個月②。前者是“加隆”，後者不是。按基本規則，它們都屬於“緦麻”③。

簡單的喪服制早在周代以前可能就産生了。只是到了儒家手中，喪服制才開始複雜起來④。儒家以家庭和家族爲其思想體系的基礎，爲了保持家族的穩固，他們把喪服制複雜化了。在這喪服制的複雜化過程中，他們也對喪服制的基礎——親屬制進行了規範化。因爲有嚴格的等級分别的喪服制要求具有區别性强的親屬稱謂系統，以避免喪服等級與親屬身份不符的情况發生。把《爾雅》系統與《儀禮》系統相對比，這一點就顯得特别明顯。與《儀禮·喪服傳》記録的系統相比，《爾雅》系統在許多方面都是前後矛盾的。一些古代學者天真地試圖以《儀禮》系統來修正《爾

① 《儀禮·喪服》:“外服之親皆緦也。”參看《日知録》卷五。

② 在近代喪服制中，對母之兄弟的服期提高到五個月，“小功”。

③ 此處論述的僅僅是一般原理。要想確知現實的喪服規則，人們必須查閲所處時代的禮儀著作。

④ 一些學者認爲，爲父服喪三年是商代的習俗；在商代實行此俗而後來演變成了儒家的。“儒”是商代人的後裔。參見胡適《説儒》(《胡適論學近著》第一集，19-23頁，90-94頁)。與此相反的觀點請參看馮友蘭《墨家和儒家之起源》(CHHP 10卷，279-310頁)。

雅》，他們認爲《爾雅》系統與儒家劃分親屬的標準不符①。他們没有看到，《爾雅》實際上代表的是中國早期的親屬制，而《儀禮》代表的則是後期的親屬制。爲使《儀禮》系統與喪服制保持一致，對它已經進行過訂正，使之趨於合理。

毋庸置疑，在儒家思想的影響下，對《爾雅》系統已進行了一定程度的人工處理，但其人工處理的程度遠不如《儀禮》。從公元前 2 世紀起，隨着儒家思想頑强地滲透於中國的社會結構，喪服制便逐漸變得複雜化、大衆化了②。相應地，中國的親屬制也隨之複雜化、大衆化了。這兩種趨向到唐代發展到高潮。

複雜的喪服制是中國的禮俗和社會生活的代表性特徵。在其影響下，中國親屬制漸漸重視旁系的劃分和輩分的分層，從一種以族外婚下的宗族組織爲基礎的類分式親屬制逐步轉變成描寫式親屬制③。

三 交表婚

在現代中國，交表婚是允許的，但並不提倡。一般來説，交表婚不被支持，不是由於血緣關係太近，而是由於年輕的表兄妹結婚可能産生糾紛，而這糾紛將影響老一輩親屬之間的親近關係，使他們疏遠開來。然而，另一方面，人們又想實施交表婚，因爲交表婚可以增加親屬集團的人數，把親屬集團網織得更密，使結親雙方“親上加親”。從公元 1 世紀起，交表婚就開始遭到社會禮俗和理論學説的反對④。但從法律上加

---

① 參見鄭珍《補正爾雅釋親宗族》，刊《巢經巢文集》卷一。

② 參見胡適《三年喪服的逐漸的推行》，見前引著作 95-102 頁。

③ 金斯利·戴維斯和 W. 勞埃德·沃納在分析親屬關係時已經對“類分式”和“描寫式”這兩個術語的使用做了中肯的論述(見《親屬關係的結構分析》，刊《美國人類學家》39 卷 2 期，1937 年，291-315 頁)。他們還建立了一套有關親屬關係結構分析的新的範疇。我認爲，不會有多少學者會贊同這套範疇。他們對中國親屬制所做的許多解釋，我個人是不同意的。但由於我的這篇文稿即將付印，來不及在此展開我的觀點。

④《白虎通》卷十：“外屬小功以上，亦不得娶也。是《春秋傳》曰譏娶母黨也。”晉代的袁準説：“今之人内外相婚，禮與？曰：‘中外之親，近於同姓，同姓且猶不可，而況中外之親乎！古人以爲無疑，故不制也。今以古之不言，因謂之可婚，此不知禮者也。’”(《通典》卷六十“内表不可爲婚議”)

以明文禁止則是較晚的事情，在《明律》裏，才第一次發現明令禁止交表婚的條文①。由於以法律手段禁止非常困難，所以，在《清律》裏這一禁令就爲另一條文所取代，這條文允許實行交表婚②。必須提到的是，在現代中國，影響婚姻的主要因素不是親屬制，而是族外婚和輩分原則。因此，不僅交表兄妹之間通婚得到許可，而且平表兄妹之間通婚(即與母之姊妹之子女通婚)也得到許可③。雖然我没有關於現代中國交表婚方面的確切的調查材料，但總的印象是交表婚所占比重甚小。總之，在現代中國親屬制裏，交表婚没有得到反映④。

---

① 《明律集解》卷六："若娶己之姑舅兩姨姊妹者，杖八十並離異。"《唐律》中的條款"其父母之姑舅兩姨姊妹……並不得爲婚……"(《唐律疏議》卷十四)有時是擴大化的禁止交表婚的條文。參見《容齋隨筆》卷八。這些條文似乎僅僅針對父母的交表兄弟姊妹，而不是針對己身的交表兄弟姊妹。如果真是如此，那麼這種禁令反對的是不同輩分之間的婚姻，而不是交表兄弟姊妹之間的婚姻。但《通典》似乎表明，在唐代實際上是禁止與交表親以及母之姊妹之女通婚的。

② G. 杰米森《中國皇朝法律通典》第 18 章："一個人不能與其姑母的子女或舅父和姨母的子女結婚，雖然輩分相同，但他們都是五服以内的親屬。"但後來在談到《禮》時，他又説："人們從功利目的出發，則允許與姑母的子女或舅父和姨母的子女結婚。"(《中國評論》10 卷，1881—1882 年，83 頁)另見斯湯頓《大清律例》，1810 年，115 頁。

③ 與母之姊妹之女結婚的事實至少在公元 3—4 世紀就已經存在了。例如，《通典》(卷九十五)就引用了晉代徐衆對下述問題——當某人之母之姊妹之女嫁與某人之兄後出現的雙重身份的服制——的議論。不過，對這一問題的討論大部分可以説是無價值的。

④ T. S. 切恩和 J. K. 施賴奥克在《中國的親屬關係名詞》(《美國人類學家》34 卷 4 期，623-669 頁)一文中，根據交表婚來解釋父之姊妹之子女和母之兄弟之子女使用同樣的稱謂的現象(見切恩-施賴奥克文章中的第Ⅰ表，85-92 號稱謂；第Ⅳ表，17-24 號稱謂；以及注釋 33)。但是，我不認爲這與交表婚有關。這些稱謂除了表示這些親屬之間具有交表關係以外，不表示别的任何東西。如果要按交表婚來理解這些稱謂的話，母之兄弟就必須用稱呼妻之父親的稱謂來稱呼，或者父之姊妹之夫必須用稱呼姊妹之夫或妻之兄弟的稱謂來稱呼。可惜的是，在現代親屬制裏不存在這樣的稱謂。因此，這兩位先生在注釋 33、34、39、42、61、64、65、67 裏對交表婚所作的解釋是靠不住的。此外，這些解釋所依據的材料也是不完整、不可靠的。例如，重要的修飾性語素"表"在母之姊妹之子女的稱謂中省掉了，使得母之姊妹之子女與妻之姊妹的稱謂混同。母之姊妹之子女稱爲"表"，猶如母之兄弟之子女和父之姊妹之子女稱爲"表"一樣。不僅交表親用"表"來表示，而且源自母之姊妹的平表親也用"表"表示。這樣的認識便使上述對交表親稱謂所作的解釋變得毫無意義。實際上，正如二位先生已經指出過的，交表婚俗的廢止對現代親屬制的發展有重大影響，那麼怎麼還能把現代親屬制理解爲是交表婚的反映呢?

《爾雅》和《儀禮》等所記録的古代系統反映了在某些親屬範圍中優先實行交表婚的傾向①。下述稱謂就是例證②：

"舅"；a. 指母之兄弟；b. 指夫之父親③；c. 指妻之父親，如"外舅"④。

"姑"：a. 指父之姊妹；b. 指夫之母親；c. 指妻之母親，如"外姑"。

"甥"：a. 指父之姊妹之子；b. 指母之兄弟之子；c. 指妻之兄弟⑤；d. 指姊妹之夫(男子使用)⑥。

這些稱謂不容懷疑地顯示了雙向的與姊妹互換婚姻相結合的交表婚。這種姊妹互换婚尤其體現在稱謂"甥"上面。"甥"既指妻之兄弟，又指姊妹之夫。

間接例證可從《爾雅》的編排中獲得。在那裏，親屬稱謂分爲四組來編排：(1)宗族——父系親屬；(2)母黨——母系親屬；(3)妻黨——妻系親屬；(4)婚姻——夫系親屬。有趣的是，父之姊妹之子，母之姊妹之子，姊妹之夫以及姊妹之子都歸入第三組"妻黨"。把這些不屬於姻親的親屬都歸爲"妻系親屬"，這樣的編排方式很清楚地表明，《爾雅》系統是以現實的交表婚爲基礎的。

---

① 第一個以交表婚來解釋《爾雅》系統的是 M. 格蘭特，見《中國之文明》187 頁。這一觀點後來由切恩和施賴奥克加以進一步發展，見上引著作 629-630 頁。

② 在以下的注釋中，列舉了中國古代對這些稱謂語義擴大所作的一些解釋。這些解釋不一定正確，但確實反映了中國的傳統觀點。

③ 古代對"舅""姑"的語義擴大到夫之父母所作的解釋如下："稱夫之父母謂姑舅何？尊如父而非父者，舅也。親如母而非母者，姑也。故稱夫之父母爲舅姑也。"(《白虎通》卷八)

④《釋名》："妻之父曰外舅，母曰外姑，言妻從外來，謂至己家爲歸，故反此義以稱之，夫婦匹敵之義也。"

⑤《釋名》："妻之昆弟曰外甥，其姊妹女也，來歸己内爲妻，故其男爲外姓之甥。甥者，生也。他姓子本生於外，不得如其女來在己内也。"

⑥ 郭璞對《爾雅》的"甥"注爲："四人體敵，故更相爲甥。"後來的解釋大多以"敵體"這個概念爲基礎。例如，"姑之子爲甥，舅之子爲甥，妻之昆弟爲甥，姊妹之夫爲甥解。"(俞樾《詁經精舍自課文》,《春在堂全書》本)

四　姊妹同婚

姊妹同婚在封建時代很流行，至少在封建貴族中是如此①。《爾雅》給出了對姊妹之夫的稱謂(女子用)，如“私”，字面意義爲“私人的”。這意味着女子把姊妹的丈夫看作是自己“私人的”②，因此，我們在一定程度上可以把這視爲姊妹同婚的證據。當然，如果没有别的稱謂進一步證明，單憑這一個例子是没有多少説服力的。《爾雅》和《儀禮》中稱母之姊妹的稱謂“從母”也可看作是姊妹同婚的反映。“從母”從字面講是“隨之而來的母親”的意思③。其中的“從”表示旁系，而不是表示潛在的母親，因此，“從母”最好看成是與父之兄弟的稱謂——“從父”相對應的一個稱謂。

在中國歷史上，包括現代，都存在姊妹同婚，但是，幼年訂婚的風俗降低了發生姊妹同婚的可能性，所以姊妹同婚一直只是一種個别現象。在現代親屬制裏，唯一反映這一現象的是稱謂“姨”，它指母之姊妹、父之妾、妻之姊妹以及己之妾。雖然下面的論證似乎無可辯駁，但其他解釋也是可能的。作爲一種禮貌而親密的表示，男子稱呼其朋友爲“兄”或“弟”。出於同樣目的，女子也稱其女性朋友爲“姊”或“妹”。自然地，妻子也把丈夫之妾看作自己的“妹妹”，並以“妹”相稱。在現實生活中，妻子正是這樣做的。如果不是受到現實的姊妹同婚的制約，“姨”這一稱謂

---

① 參見 M. 格蘭特《共夫的姊妹同婚與中國封建時代的姊妹同婚》(1920 年)。本書作者雖然是在充分利用材料的基礎上做出的有力論斷，但這本小書仍然包括了大部分相關材料。他後來的著作《中國之文明》也利用了這些材料，在《中國之文明》裏作者運用了已經過時的人類學理論——姊妹同婚和收繼婚是遠古時代親密關係的集團婚的反映。

② 參見前引切恩和施賴奥克的論文(628 頁)。《釋名》對“私”的解釋有所不同，其曰：“姊妹互相謂夫曰私，言其夫兄弟之中，此人與己姊妹有恩私也。”按照這個古代的解釋，“私”與女性己身完全無關，就很難成爲姊妹同婚的證據。

③ 劉熙(約公元 200 年)在他的《釋名》中是這樣解釋的：母之姊妹嫁與己之父作“娣”，便具有“從母”的身份；但即使她們不嫁給己之父系，她們還是可以稱作“從母”的。我相信，這是已知最早的對親屬稱謂所作的社會學解釋。這一解釋正確與否，那又是另一回事。

也許會擴展開來。同樣地，“姨”常常被兒童用來稱呼父之妾[①]，被僕人用來稱呼主人之妻。在這兩種用法中“姨”都作敬稱。

在姊妹同婚盛行之處，往往存在娶妻之兄弟之女的婚姻形式。因爲假如妻子没有可以出嫁的姊妹，那麽妻子的兄弟的女兒便是最好的代替人。在中國封建社會的貴族集團中，存在過這種婚姻形式。

封建諸侯結婚時，新娘有八名隨嫁女郎，稱爲“媵”，這些“媵”便是未來的妾[②]。封建諸侯以下述方式來接收這些媵：新娘和八名媵被分成三組，每組三人；第一組包括新娘、新娘的一位妹妹或同父異母的妹妹——“娣”[③]，以及新娘哥哥的一位女兒“姪”，這三位女子構成最基本的一組；與新娘同姓的另外兩個封建諸侯國各提供一名“媵”、一名“娣”和一名“姪”[④]，因此總共爲三組九位女子。同姓的諸侯國提供媵必須完全是自願的，不能向她們提出這種要求[⑤]，因爲要求别人的女兒做不太體面的媵是不合適的。[⑥]

實行這種複雜的媵婚制，旨在確保有衆多的子嗣繼承爵位[⑦]。選新

① 《通俗編》説父之妾稱作“姨”是因爲古老的媵婚制的緣故。“姨”最初是對同嫁給一個丈夫的几位姊妹的共有稱謂。到後世媵婚制雖然廢除了，但妾實際上就相當於媵。因此，儘管父之妾不再是母之姊妹，“姨”還是可以用於父之妾的。這種社會學意義上的解釋很不正確。媵婚制與“姨”無任何聯繫，媵從未被稱作“姨”，而總是被稱作“姪”和“娣”。

② 《公羊傳·莊公十九年》：“媵者何？諸侯一國，二國往媵之，以姪、娣從。姪者何？兄之子也。娣者何？弟也。”

③ 説“娣”是指新娘的同母妹妹，或者説是指新娘的異母妹妹（即她的父親的媵的女兒），都只是一種猜測。很可能“娣”僅僅指新娘的異母妹妹，因爲有充分證據表明：正妻（夫人）的女兒總是嫁出去做“夫人”，而媵的女兒總是嫁出去做“媵”。這樣，高貴者，其後代也高貴，卑賤者，其後代也卑賤。這種解釋與《爾雅》中“姨”和“娣”的用法相吻合。參見毛際盛《説文解字述誼》（《聚學軒叢書》本）。

④ 《左傳·成公十八年》：“衛人來媵共姬，禮也。凡諸侯嫁女，同姓媵之，異姓則否。”這可能是一般通則，也有例外。

⑤ 《公羊傳·莊公十九年》何休注：“言往媵之者，禮。君不求媵，二國自往媵夫人，所以一夫之尊。”

⑥ 《白虎通》卷十二：“所以不聘妾者何？人有之孫，欲尊之，義不可求人爲賤也……妾雖賢不得爲嫡。”

⑦ 《白虎通》卷十：“天子諸侯一娶九女者何？重國廣繼嗣也。”又：“大夫功成受封，得備八妾者，重國家廣繼嗣也。”

娘的姪女爲媵，而不選新娘的第二個妹妹，其目的是爲了製造出血緣上的差異。當新娘和其妹妹兩人都無後嗣的時候，血緣不相同的姪女便可以生一個兒子。同樣地，另外兩組媵分别從不同的諸侯國選出，也是爲了使媵的血緣關係更加遥遠，獲得子嗣的機會便可增加三倍①。選本族親屬爲媵，是爲了防止妻妾之間産生妒忌，搞陰謀詭計②。

嫁媵之俗嚴格講不等於一般所説的“重婚”。所有女子成年後都很快要結婚。選做媵的女子如果年紀太小，可以“待年父母之國”，直到長大成人以後再出嫁③，但這不大常見。從理論上講，一個封建諸侯一生只能結一次婚④；假如他的正妻——“夫人”死了，他的一位媵就可接替夫人的位置，但不可享受夫人的尊號⑤。實際上，這樣的媵合法地位很低，只能算封建諸侯的“被認可的女主人”。

封建貴族中的“卿大夫”，可以有一個正妻、兩個妾，但不能以妻子的姊妹或姪女爲媵⑥。在經典文獻中，對這一規則的解釋有分歧。有一些例子證明，卿大夫也同封建諸侯一樣娶妻之姊妹和姪女爲妾⑦。知識分子階層——“士”(即下層統治階級)允許有一個正妻、一個妾⑧。至於這個妾可不可以是妻子的姊妹或姪女，學者們的觀點尚不一致。顧炎武

① 《白虎通》卷十：“不娶兩娣何？博異氣也。娶三國女何？廣異類也。恐一國血脈相似，以無子也。”

② 《白虎通》卷十：“備姪娣從者，爲其不必相嫉妒也。一人有子，三人共之，若己生之也。”《公羊傳·莊公十九年》何休注：“必以姪娣從之者，欲使一人有子，二人喜也。所以防嫉妒，令重繼嗣也。因以備尊尊親親也。”

③ 《公羊傳·隱公七年》：“叔姬歸於紀。”注：“叔姬者，伯姬之媵也。至是乃歸者，待年父母之國也。”

④ 同上《莊公十九年》：“諸侯一聘九女，諸侯不再娶。”

⑤ 《左傳·隱公元年》：“孟子卒，繼室以聲子。”杜注：“諸侯始娶，則同姓之國以姪娣媵，元妃死則次妃攝治内事，猶不得稱夫人，謂之繼室。”但這一規則不是絶對的，參看《白虎通》卷十。

⑥ 《白虎通》卷十：“卿一妻二妾何？尊賢重繼嗣也。不備姪娣何？北面之臣賤，勢不足盡人骨肉之親也。”

⑦ 如《左傳》卷三十五：“初臧宣叔娶於鑄，生賈及爲而死，繼室以其姪。”

⑧ 《白虎通》卷十：“士一妻一妾何？下卿大夫禮也。《喪服小記》曰：‘士妾有子，則爲之緦。’”

(1613—1682)認爲，士不能娶妻之妹妹或姪女爲妾①。平民百姓則只能有一個女人，至少在理論上是如此②。

從上面的事例來判斷，媵婚之俗也許僅僅是一種“被法律認可的亂倫”，借助此俗封建王侯可以確保自己有後嗣。不過，某些下層貴族也可以步其後塵。不難理解，爲什麽這麽一種高度專制的婚俗甚至在貴族中間也没有流行開，因爲它限制了可提供的婦女的數量，而且實際違反了封建時期的輩分原則思想。例如，封建諸侯不可以娶其領地内的貴族婦女。從理論上講，他的封建領地内的每一個人都是他的財産，如果他與領地内的某位女子結婚，這位女子的父母就自動成爲他的長輩，就不再是他的財産了。爲了避免這一矛盾，就要求封建諸侯娶他的領地之外的女子爲妻③。到公元前 3 世紀，媵婚制隨着封建制的崩潰而消失。從西漢初年起，就没有再發現這方面的記載，無論是皇室中的媵婚還是貴族中的媵婚都没有④。

當我們再回過頭來看古代親屬制時，我們發現了一個特例，它似乎反映了娶妻之兄弟之女爲妻的婚姻。在《爾雅》中，把姊妹之子稱爲“出”，後來又把他們稱爲“甥”。這在上面論及交表婚時已談過了。《爾雅》中“甥”主要用來指父之姊妹之子、母之兄弟之子、妻之兄弟以及姊妹之夫。“甥”指姊妹之子的用法没有恪守《爾雅》所强調的輩分原則⑤。

在孟子(公元前 373—前 289)的著作裏，“甥”還有一種特殊的用法。孟子用“甥”來表示女兒的丈夫⑥。輩分原則對“甥”失去影響，似乎是在封建後期才發生的。在封建時期，“甥”用來指：(1)父之姊妹之子；(2)母之兄弟之子；(3)妻之兄弟；(4)姊妹之夫；(5)姊妹之子；(6)女兒

① 《日知録》卷五“貴臣貴妾”條。

② 這就是所謂的“匹夫匹婦”。在封建制下，實際上全部土地都爲封建主所有；老百姓是在農奴制下面干活，誰也没有能力娶兩個老婆，除非他是統治階級的一員。

③ 《白虎通》卷十：“諸侯所以不得娶國中何？諸侯不得專封，義不臣其父母。《春秋傳》曰：‘宋三世無大夫，惡其内娶也。’”

④ 有些學者懷疑媵婚制僅僅是漢代的文人臆造出來的。

⑤ 《爾雅》中另一個不區分輩分關係的稱謂是“叔”，指父之弟，也指夫之弟。

⑥ 《孟子》卷十(一)：“舜尚見帝，帝館甥於貳室……”

之夫。

上述前四種意義可以從雙向型的與姊妹互換婚相伴隨的交表婚中得到解釋，後兩種意義大概要根據雙向型的與娶兄弟之女相聯的交表婚來解釋。在這裏，姊妹之夫和姊妹之子都能够娶“己身”之女；而“己身”之女之夫將具有雙重身份：既是女兒的丈夫，又是姊妹的兒子。然而，如果我們考慮到這一事實：與妻之兄之女發生的婚姻僅僅是一種在貴族中間存在的“合法的亂倫”，它從未發展成爲普遍實行的婚姻形式；那麽我們用“從兒稱呼”來解釋“甥”的後兩種用法就顯得較爲合理、較爲簡便。在交表婚存在的條件下，姊妹之子和女兒之夫都將是“己身”之子之甥，而“己身”只不過借用了兒子所用的稱謂來稱呼他們罷了。

總之，不論在古代還是在現代，姊妹同婚對中國親屬制的影響都是微乎其微的。就以上的例證來看，姊妹同婚在古代中國和現代中國都僅僅是一種可允許的婚姻，也就是説，“己身”和某位女子的婚姻不影響該女子的姊妹的婚姻，也不影響“己身”本人的婚姻。

五 收 繼 婚[1]

弟收兄妻的收繼婚在現代中國的某些地區肯定存在，至少在貧困階級中存在[2]。但是，即使在存在收繼婚的地方，收繼婚也是不受歡迎的。男子實施收繼婚僅僅是以此作爲娶妻的最後手段。如有必要，他可以賣

① 詹姆斯·弗雷澤爵士堅持認爲姊妹同婚和收繼婚有密切的并存關係(《圖騰崇拜和族外婚》第4卷，1910年，139-150頁)。R. H. 羅維也認爲：“倘使不因爲我們關於初民婚俗的報告不怎麽頂詳確，這個關係還要見得更密切。那就是説，我們可以假定，在不少的案例中，完全是疏忽將事觀察不道地，使那些著作者報告這個制度而不提及那個制度。”(《初民社會》中譯本，商務印書館1935年版，43頁)

② 參見《中國的收繼婚》，刊《中國評論》第10卷，1881—1882年，71頁。還可參看黃節華《叔接嫂》，刊《東方雜論》31卷第7期，1934年。馮·默倫多夫曾經説過：“我還没有發現過收繼婚的些微遺蹟。收繼婚對其他民族來説非常重要，但對中國人則不然。對中國人來説，收繼婚的重要性遠比不上謚稱。”(《中國人的家族之法》，1896年，17頁)

掉他的兄弟的遺孀，用賣新娘所得的錢去另娶一個女人。在法律上，與兄或弟的遺孀結婚是嚴格禁止的①，違反的雙方將被處以極刑。G. 賈米森因此懷疑，在如此嚴厲的刑罰下中國會有收繼婚存在②。

中國古代存不存在收繼婚，目前仍大有爭議。格蘭特雖然從《左傳》裏找到兩個例證，但還是不能以此證明存在收繼婚③。切恩和施賴奧克認爲，“親屬關係名詞僅僅反映‘弟收兄妻’的收繼婚，在此婚姻形式中，兄娶其亡弟的妻子爲妻。妻子對丈夫和丈夫之兄(潛在的丈夫)都以同一稱謂‘伯’相稱，但對丈夫之弟却用另外的稱謂來稱呼。”④這兩位先生對收繼婚的認識有點模糊。兄娶弟妻的婚姻應是“兄收弟妻”的收繼婚，而不是“弟收兄妻”的收繼婚。“兄收弟妻”的收繼婚在亞洲還没有單獨發現。在一個民族中間，這兩種收繼婚要麽是同時存在，要麽是僅僅存在“弟收兄妻”的收繼婚，如印度、東南亞和東北亞就是這樣。另外，他們在轉引“伯”的語義時没有注意語義的時代性。“伯”在《尚書》裏有幾處

---

① 這條法律在洪武年間(1368—1398)頒佈的《明律集解》(1610年重新修訂)中第一次得到明確表述。在所有早期法典中收繼婚都是遭到禁止的。例如，《唐律疏議》卷十四：“諸嘗爲袒免親之妻而嫁娶者，各杖一百。緦麻及舅甥妻，徒一年。小功以上以姦論。妾各減二等，並離之。”按照這一條款，收繼婚是根本不可能的。另一方面，《明律》明確規定禁止收繼婚可能是對在元統治下收繼婚傳入中國的一種逆反行爲。參見李魯人《元代蒙古收繼婚俗傳入内地之影響》，刊《大公報·史地週刊》第8期，1936年4月10日第3版。

② 見《中國評論》10卷，83頁：“考慮到刑罰是這樣殘酷，因此在中國任何地方出現收繼婚都是不可能的。”

③ 見《中國之文明》424-425頁。引用的兩個例子是：敝無存(萊格《中國古籍》5卷第2部分，773頁)、子淵(譯音)和息嬀(同前引書5卷第1部分，115頁)。在第一例裏，敝無存將去打仗，他想榮立戰功歸來後娶一位身份較高的女子。於是便以可把提到的那位女子嫁給他弟弟爲由，拒絶了父親給他提的親。這位他所拒絶的女子不僅不是他的妻子，甚至連未婚妻都不是。在第二例裏，子淵在楚國已經握有充分的權力，不需要通過娶其兄的遺孀的方式來獲取權力。從另一方面看，息嬀是一個美貌的女子，子淵是由於性慾衝動才企圖誘姦她的。子淵没能把她弄到手，很快就把她殺掉了。這些事實對格蘭特的論點是很不利的。

根據古代喪服制度的規定，姻姊妹和姻兄弟無服，而無服的親屬是可以通婚的，因此格蘭特認爲他的假説無懈可擊。但是，親屬之間的婚姻並不是僅僅由喪服來決定的。例如，交表親雖然都是有服的親屬，可是，根據格蘭特的理論，他們却是可以相互通婚的！

我們需要的是收繼婚的實際事例，而不是那種可以用來支持任何假説的模棱兩可的特殊例子。格蘭特竭力想用姊妹同婚和收繼婚來證明遠古時代存在過一種親密關係的集團婚，這本身就是一種毫無希望證明的假説。

④ 前引切恩和施賴奧克的論文，628-629頁。

可以理解爲指丈夫①，但這種用法在公元前500年以後的文獻裏就沒有再出現。此外，“伯”指丈夫之兄也是直到公元10世紀時才出現的②。因此，“伯”指丈夫和“伯”指丈夫之兄不僅不是同時產生的，而且還整整間隔了15個世紀！在歷史上，儘管中國人可能善於聯想，但我仍然不明白怎麽能用收繼婚來解釋“伯”的意義。

曾以“弟收兄妻”的婚姻來解釋在印度兄和弟之間的區别③，這種解釋除非在稱謂上得到證實，否則是相當脆弱的。即便“弟收兄妻”的婚姻可以解釋兄和弟的區别，它却肯定不能解釋姊和妹的區别，而這一區别也是印度大多數親屬制度的特徵。宗法能不能圓滿解釋中國親屬制中同輩親屬年齡範疇的表述方式，我們不知道；但是可以肯定，用“弟收兄妻婚”是不能解釋的，因爲“弟收兄妻婚”在中國僅僅是一種個别現象。

六 從兒稱

我們討論了與決定少數親屬的特徵有關的幾種婚姻形式，除了交表婚以外，婚姻對中國親屬制的影響不論在古代還是在現代都是微不足道的。在此，我們將聯繫從兒稱和親屬制的其他特點來進一步討論這類問題，以發現真正起作用的決定因素。

---

① 《詩經》卷三(三)：“伯兮朅兮，邦之桀兮；伯也執殳，爲王前驅。自伯之東，首如飛蓬，豈無膏沐，誰適爲容……”此處的“伯”有時被人理解爲指丈夫。但是，“伯”是對丈夫的稱謂，還是指丈夫所享有的官銜，或者僅僅表示勇敢英俊的丈夫，這都還不能肯定。從上下文來看，最後一種解釋較爲合理。

② 陶岳《五代史補》(《豫章叢書》本)卷五：“(李)濤爲人不拘禮法，與弟澣雖甚雍睦，然聚話之際，不典之言，往往同作。澣娶禮部尚書竇寧固之女，年甲稍高，成婚之夕，竇氏出參濤，輒望塵下拜。澣驚曰：‘大哥風狂耶？新婦參阿伯，豈有答禮儀？’濤應曰：‘我不風，只將是親家母。”

③ 查特帕德海《印度的親屬與收繼婚》，刊《人類》雜志第22卷，1922年，25頁。W. 勞埃德·沃納在《北澳大利亞41個部族的親屬關係形態研究》(刊《美國人類學家》第35卷，66頁)中也提出了類似的解釋。

如前文所述，輩分是中國親屬制中的一個重要的結構原則。輩分因素制約着親屬的婚姻，在中國的社會生活和禮儀活動中起着重要的作用。親屬内部的活動在許多方面都以輩分的區分爲先決條件，在喪服等級的確立等方面也是這樣。既然輩分在中國親屬制中是如此重要的因素，我們就可以預料到輩分原則在稱謂上也將得到相應的體現。但是，仍有一些例外現象值得注意。比如，母之兄弟和妻之兄弟用同一個稱謂“舅”表示，母之姊妹和妻之姊妹用同一個稱謂“姨”表示，父之兄和夫之兄用同一個稱謂“伯”表示，父之弟和夫之弟用同一個稱謂“叔”表示，父之姊妹和夫之姊妹用同一個稱謂“姑”表示，等等。這些例外現象是很重要的。按理説，對這些輩分不同的親屬應該用不同的稱謂加以明確區分。只是隨着時間的推移，它們才逐漸混同起來了。

我們首先看看稱謂“舅”的語義的演變，以及各個時期對妻之兄弟使用的稱謂。我們把它們列表如下：

時期	“舅”的語義	對妻之兄弟使用的稱謂
1 （公元前 1000 年間）	母之兄弟 夫之父 妻之父	甥
2 （公元後 1000 年間）	母之兄弟	婦兄弟
3 （公元 11—20 世紀）	母之兄弟 妻之兄弟	舅

在第 1 時期，稱謂“舅”的各種意義可以從上面討論過的交表婚中得到合理的解釋。在交表婚條件下，母之兄弟和夫之父親爲同一個人，母之兄弟和妻之父親也爲同一個人。在第 2 時期交表婚消失，於是，“舅”的語義就限定在母之兄弟上面。

妻之兄弟的稱謂在三個時期中各有不同。第 1 時期，妻之兄弟稱爲“甥”。這一時期“甥”同時又指父之姊妹之子、母之兄弟之子和姊妹之夫

(男子用)①。這也可根據雙向的與姊妹互換婚相聯繫的交表婚來解釋。在第2時期，由於交表婚的消失，“甥”便不再應用於上述親屬，新的稱謂便開始産生並取代了“甥”。“婦兄弟”成了對妻之兄弟的稱謂②。

在第3時期，稱謂“舅”(母之兄弟)的使用範圍擴大到妻之兄弟。這一新義的使用在《新唐書》裏首次發現。我們在《新唐書·朱延壽傳》裏讀到：“(楊行密)妻，延壽姊也……行密泣曰：‘吾喪明，諸子幼，得舅(指朱延壽)代，我無憂矣。’”③“舅”在使用中的這種擴展確實令人費解，因爲在此之前不論如何變化，“舅”的輩分特徵總是保留的。在這裏，輩分原則不起作用了，這肯定是“舅”得以擴展使用的原因之一。社會學的解釋則將這種現象完全歸結於娶妻之兄弟之女的婚姻。在第1時期，“舅”也指岳父。在存在娶妻之兄之女的婚姻的社會中，妻之兄弟便是潛在的岳父；因此，“舅”擴展到岳父上面便是順理成章的事。但是，這樣的解釋仍有不少疑點。首先，這種解釋看來不符合事實。以妻之兄弟之女爲媵的婚姻從未占據主要地位。如上所述，它也不是普遍的形式，即使在封建貴族中也是如此；并且，它在公元前3世紀便同封建制一起消失了，從此没有再恢復過。其次，早在擴展到妻之兄弟以前至少一千年，“舅”就已經停止用來指妻之父親了。因此，這兩種前後相隔一千多年的存在短暫的概念與上述解釋不相符。再次，娶妻之兄弟之女的婚姻與輩分原則相衝突。妻之兄弟之女比己身低一輩，因此，這種婚姻在中國親屬制裏屬於亂倫。在法律上，不同輩分親屬之間的婚姻早在“舅”擴展到妻之兄弟之前五百年就已被嚴格禁止了④。所以，從這幾點來看，上面

---

① 參見《爾雅》。

② “婦兄弟”純粹是一個表謙性稱謂。“婦”意爲妻子，“兄弟”是兄和弟的合稱。《北齊書·崔昂傳》：“崔昂直臣，魏收才士，婦兄妹夫，俱省罪過。”又《鄭元禮傳》：“但知婦夫，疏於婦弟。”在這個時期也可使用“妻兄弟”和“内兄弟”。

③ 《新唐書·朱延壽傳》：“田頵之附全忠，延壽陰約曰：‘公有所爲，我願執鞭。’頵喜。二人謀絶行密。行密憂甚，紿病目，行觸柱，僵。妻，延壽姊也，掖之。行密泣曰：‘吾喪明，諸子幼，得舅代，我無憂矣。’”

④ 公元627—683年編纂並頒布的《唐律》嚴厲禁止不同輩分之間的通婚(見《唐律疏議》卷十三)。

的解釋是不能令人信服的。

值得提到的是：在 E. B. 泰勒把這種稱謂納入人類學的視野之前，中國學者就一直用從兒稱來解釋上述稱謂不可思議的長期存在性①。錢大昕(1727—1804)，他是那個時代目光最敏鋭的學者之一，將“舅”的語義擴展歸因於從兒稱。“舅”用作從兒稱引起其語義發生了緩慢的難以覺察的變化，最終導致語義擴展②。“己身”的妻子的兄弟對於己身的兒女來説是舅，“己身”對於兒女來説是父親，因此，“己身”可以用兒女用的稱謂“舅”來稱呼妻子的兄弟。這一過程在上面所提到的朱延壽的例子中可以清楚地看到。楊行密在談到自己兒子的同時，稱朱延壽爲“舅”。我們可以推想，“舅”在長期用作從兒稱以後，便固定下來並最終取代了原來的稱謂。

這一假説能否成立，有賴於我們能否再找到些充分的證據，或者换句話説，有賴於該假説能否解釋中國親屬制中的所有特殊現象。下面，讓我們來考察妻子稱呼丈夫的兄弟所用的稱謂。“伯”用來稱夫之兄，“叔”稱夫之弟。但“伯”最早是用於稱父之兄的，“叔”是稱父之弟的。這種背離輩分原則的現象，無論從什麽角度來看，都是很不正常的。據我所知，在中國還没有哪種社會的或婚姻的行爲能導致這種稱謂的産生。從人類學提供的材料來看，在其他民族中也没有相類似的現象存在。

從歷史的觀點看，對這些親屬所用的稱謂在各個不同時期是各不相同的。《爾雅》裏，父之兄稱爲“世父”。從公元前 2 世紀到現在，“伯父”一直是標準稱謂，但是從第 4 世紀起的一段時期内，僅僅單用“伯”③。

《爾雅》稱夫之兄爲“兄公”④，在其後幾個世紀，夫之兄常稱爲“兄

① 《論調查風俗演變的方法》，刊《人類學學會會刊》第 18 卷，1889 年，245-269 頁。

② 《恒言録》卷三：“予按……後世妻之兄弟獨得舅名，蓋從其子女之稱，遂相沿不覺耳。”

③ 《禮記・曾子問》：“已祭而見伯父叔父。”《顔氏家訓・風操篇》：“古人皆呼伯父叔父，而今世多單呼伯叔。”參見《恒言録》卷三。

④ 夫之兄爲兄公。

章"①。到大約第10世紀時，"伯"擴大到了夫之兄上面。

《爾雅》稱父之弟爲"叔父"，一直沿用至今而未發生大的變化。與"伯"相同，從第4世紀起也僅僅單用"叔"。《爾雅》也用"叔"來指夫之弟。這種用法是很不尋常的，它混淆了不同的輩分，與《爾雅》本身表達的原則——"婿之黨爲姻兄弟"——是矛盾的②。

因此，如上所述，這種輩分的混同從婚姻形式上不可能找到答案，只有用從兒稱纔可能加以解釋。夫之兄弟對於己身(女性)的兒女來説是"伯"和"叔"，"己身"對於兒女來説是母親，因此，這個作母親的"己身"可以采用兒女用的稱謂"伯""叔"來稱呼夫之兄弟。這種情形有力地支持了我們的假説，而别的已知的社會因素或婚姻形式都不能完滿地解釋上述用法。

同樣的情形在以下親屬的稱謂中也存在：稱父之姊妹和夫之姊妹的"姑"，稱母之姊妹和妻之姊妹的"姨"。

如上文已經提出的，由於交表婚的影響，在《爾雅》裏"姑"指父之姊妹、夫之母親和妻之母親(如"外姑")。當交表婚消失以後，"姑"一般就僅指父之姊妹。《爾雅》裏，夫之姊稱作"女公"，夫之妹稱作"女妹"③。後來還偶爾用過"淑妹"來稱夫之妹④。到第4世紀，"姑"開始擴展到夫之姊妹上面⑤。儘管這一時期的婚姻規則和社會風俗已經爲人熟知，但是引起這種擴展的因素仍然無法確切肯定。這種擴展不可能歸因於娶妻之兄弟之女的婚姻，因爲在這種婚姻裏，夫之姊妹將被提高到夫之父親

---

① 《釋名》："夫之兄……俗間曰兄章。"參見第四章第4表，第5號稱謂。

② 《爾雅》："婦之黨爲婚兄弟，婿之黨爲姻兄弟。"

③ 夫之姊爲女公，夫之女弟爲女妹。

④ 《後漢書·曹世叔妻(班昭)傳》："婦人之得意於夫主，由舅姑之愛己也；舅姑之愛己，由叔妹之譽己也。"

⑤ "小姑"指夫之姊妹最早出現在名詩《古詩爲焦仲卿妻作》(見《玉臺新咏集》卷一)裏："却與小姑别，泪落連珠子。新婦初來時，小姑始扶床。今日被驅遣，小姑如我長。"有關這首詩的年代已有很多文章討論過。胡適傾向於認爲它産生的時間比其他同時代的詩歌早，約産生於3世紀中葉。參見《孔雀東南飛的年代》，刊《現代評論》第6卷149期，9-14頁。其他人認爲它産生的時間較晚，約産生於4—5世紀。

的姊妹的地位。上面所引的解釋"舅"的例子在此也適用。另外，從稱謂上①或觀念上②也找不出别的可供解釋的綫索。因此，既然夫之姊妹是"己身"的兒女的姑，那麼用從兒稱來解釋是再好不過了。

"姨"最早是用來指妻之姊妹，如《爾雅》。《爾雅》稱母之姊妹爲"從母"。"姨"指母之姊妹最早見於《左傳》。《左傳·襄公二十三年》(公元前550年)寫道："穆姜姨之女。"③我們查考了與穆姜有關係的親屬，發現本該指妻之姊妹的稱謂"姨"在此並不是指妻之姊妹(或已婚的姊妹，女性用)，而是指母之姊妹。因此，上面那句話應理解爲"穆姜的從母的女兒"，而不應理解爲"穆姜的姨的女兒"。

從理論上講，與娶父之遺孀相伴隨的收繼婚將充分解釋這種用法。在這種婚姻裏，父親娶母親的姊妹，己身娶妻子的姊妹。當父親病故後，己身又娶父親的遺孀。這時，母之姊妹就變得與妻之姊妹相等同了。這種解釋聽起來有點離奇，但還是有依據的。因爲男子的第二個妻子(妾)也可被稱作"姨"，即母之姊妹、妻之姊妹和第二個妻子都劃在一個類别裏。衆所周知，收繼婚在封建貴族中流行過，至於説收繼父之遺孀的婚姻還没有得到可靠的證明④。確實，這種婚姻本來不大適應於古代中國

---

① 例如，在米沃克人中間，與妻之兄弟發生的婚姻有12個稱謂來反映(E. W. 吉福德《米沃克部族的各個分支》，《加利福尼亞大學考古學和人種學文集》，1916年，186頁)。

② 在奥馬哈人中間，與妻之兄弟發生的婚姻在觀念上有所反映，即反映在對父之姊妹、女性己身和兄弟之女的認識同上，但是在稱謂上却無所表示。在中國親屬制中，父之姊妹、夫之父之姊妹以及夫之姊妹雖然在稱謂上没有加以區分，但在觀念上仍是可以明顯區分的。

③ 《左傳·襄公二十三年》。

④ M. 格蘭特引用了衛國的宣公(公元前718—前700年)娶其父之親夷姜的例子(《中國之文明》，401頁)。然而，格蘭特顯然不知道顧棟高(1679—1757)已經令人信服地證明，夷姜從前不是宣公父親的妾(見《春秋大事表·衛夷姜晉齊姜辨》，刊《皇清經解》)。退一步説，即使承認這種繼母與繼子結婚的事是有根據的，它也不能證明什麼，因爲這種事例是相當特殊的。從春秋時代起，不僅這類待殊例子可以找到許多，就連涉及直系血親關係，如祖母與孫子、兄弟與姊妹之間亂倫的例子也可以找到不少。(參見王士廉《左淫類記》)但格蘭特避而不談這些。説實在的，上述這種特例在中國歷史上總是存在的，即使在稍後的朝代裏也是如此。例如，唐高宗(650—684年在位)娶其父之妾武曌，武曌後來成了臭名昭著的武后。唐玄宗(712—756年在位)娶其父之妾楊貴妃，歐洲人都知道她是中國的絶代佳人。我們不知道格蘭特將如何看待這些事情。

人。我們知道，從前的文人學士都憎惡娶父之遺孀的匈奴人，歷來就把這作爲嘲笑他們的笑料①。

孔穎達(574—648)把“姨”由指妻之姊妹向指母之姊妹的擴展，歸結爲這兩種親屬之間存在的心理共性②。母親的姊妹對於“己身”的父親來説是姨，如同妻子的姊妹對於“己身”來説是姨一樣。因此，兒子如果跟着父親稱呼，就可以稱母親的姊妹爲“姨”。總之，這一現象看來不僅需要用心理學來解釋，而且還需要用逆從兒稱(即子從父稱)來解釋。

“嬸”的演變同樣是有意義的。面稱時，父之弟之妻和夫之弟之妻都稱作“嬸”。《爾雅》裏，父之弟之妻稱作“叔母”，這在今天是標準稱謂。“嬸”的最初使用是在宋代。通常認爲它是“世母”二字的合音③。大約在這一時期，“嬸”的使用擴展到了夫之弟之妻④。没有哪一種婚姻關係可能造成這種均衡的親屬關係，别的社會因素也不可能。但是，若以從兒稱來解釋就非常簡單：夫之弟之妻是己身(女性)的孩子的嬸。

表示夫之父親的“公”和表示夫之母親的“婆”，其語源還未考察過。古老的稱夫之父親的稱謂是“舅”，稱夫之母親的稱謂是“姑”，二者都反映着交表婚。在公元1—10世紀期間，在交表婚中止以後，雖然涌現出了大量的指稱這兩種親屬的稱謂，但最終流行開的只有“公”和“婆”⑤。

另一方面，“公”和“婆”又是稱呼祖父母的最常用的稱謂⑥。妻子爲什麽會用稱呼祖父母的稱謂來稱夫之父母，這是很不好理解的。用不合規範的婚姻來解釋是最容易的，但我們不知道是什麽樣的婚姻形式(不

---

① 《史記·匈奴列傳》：“父死，妻其後母；兄弟死，皆取其妻妻之。”匈奴人娶父之遺孀而不娶己之母親的婚俗以及收繼婚對古代中國人是如此熟悉，因此他們把這視爲匈奴人道德敗壞的標誌。

② 《左傳·襄公二十三年》。

③ 《明道雜志》：“王聖美嘗言經傳無嬸字……考其説，嬸字乃世母二字合呼也。”“世母”連讀成一個字就成了 Sbim 成 Shen。

④ 吕祖謙(1137—1181)《紫薇雜記》(《説郛》卷十九)：“吕氏舊俗，母母受嬸房婢拜，似受其主母拜也。嬸見母母房婢跪，即答拜。是母母亦尊尊之義也……母母於嬸處自稱名，或去名不稱新婦，嬸於母母處則稱之。”“母母”意爲夫之兄之妻，“嬸”意爲夫之弟之妻。

⑤ 見第四章第4表1、2號稱謂。

⑥ 見第四章第1表13、14號稱謂。

管它多麼令人驚奇)在其中起作用。可是如果我們假定是從兒稱造成的,那麼就可以立即做出解釋。

上述這些例子包括了稱謂上最值得注意的特殊現象,概括了中國古代和現代親屬制中輩分原則受到公開破壞的全部情况。對每一種情况,我們都力圖用事實和假説來解釋其中的例外現象,每種假説都對别的例外現象的考察具有啓發意義。但是,我們没有發現哪一種假説適合於中國的情况,反之,只有用從兒稱才能做出滿意的解釋。

因此,毋庸置疑,從兒稱是上述這些情况的决定因素。也許有人會問,在中國從兒稱是否普遍存在,是否大部分古代中國人都運用從兒稱。從兒稱在中國的流行範圍很難劃定,不過,它的使用程度很可能依時代和地域而有所不同。在有些朝代,從兒稱受到特别重視,以致一般的稱呼形式都變得微不足道了①。在有些地方,如江蘇無錫,新娘通常以對長輩的態度來稱呼自己丈夫的親屬,仿佛她比他們低一輩。在實際運用中,從兒稱一般屬於這一類型:省去兒女的姓名,就像英國人直接稱呼妻子爲"媽媽"那樣。從兒稱對上述那些不規範稱謂的産生起着特殊的作用。

關於古代的從兒稱,我們必須從歷史材料中去尋找。可以看作是從兒稱的最早例證見於《春秋公羊傳》。該書卷二十七《哀公六年》記載了一段有關陳乞的史料,陳在談到其妻時説:"常之母……"②已知常是陳乞的兒子,顯然這裏是一種從兒稱。這一公元前5世紀的史料與我們上面所討論的大部分實例相比要早一千多年,只有"姨"和"嬸"的情况例外,它們差不多發生於同一個時期。另一方面,如果我們考慮到古代學者在

① 在中國南方存在着極端的從兒稱例子,如宋代吳處厚(約1080年)《青箱雜記》(涵芬樓本)記載:"嶺南風俗相呼不以行第,唯以各人所生男女小名呼其父母。元豐中(1078—1085),余任大理丞,斷賓州(今廣西賓陽縣)奏案,有民韋超,男名首,即呼韋超作父首。韋遨男名滿,即呼韋遨作父滿。韋全(男)女名插娘,即呼韋全作父插。韋庶女名睡娘,即呼庶作父睡,妻作嬸睡。"

② 《公羊傳·哀公六年》:"諸大夫皆在朝,陳乞曰:'常之母,有魚菽之祭,願諸大夫之化我也。'"

記録民間口語方面的保守態度，那麼就有理由推斷，從兒稱的實際發生年代要比文獻記載的早得多。

從兒稱對親屬稱謂的影響是非常明顯的。吉福德在討論英語中的類似的用法，以及加利福尼亞人的親屬稱謂時，已經令人信服地指出："在其他的親屬制中，一定存在許多與之相類似的用法（即類似於英國人稱呼丈夫爲'爸爸'、稱呼妻子爲'媽媽'的從兒稱那樣的用法），其中一些用法演變成了固定不變的習俗；一定存在許多不需要用令人驚訝的婚姻形式來加以解釋的稱謂的使用情況。但如果我們對所要討論的家族組織很熟悉，那麼這些稱謂的使用就能很容易理解，如同理解我們自己的稱謂一樣。"①

在關於從兒稱的有限的論著中，已經有若干種探尋其起源的理論，但是還没有哪一種理論試圖用從兒稱來認真地解釋别的社會現象。

從兒稱作爲一種習慣用法，是建立在親屬關係和親屬稱謂之上的，是對那些不好稱呼的親屬使用的委婉的稱呼方式。經過長期的頻繁的使用，從兒稱這一稱呼方式爲什麼不能使親屬稱謂産生某些新的特殊的意義呢？就像别的社會習慣行爲那樣。中國的從兒稱是特别富有啓發性的。對"舅、伯、叔、姑、姨、嬸、公、婆、甥"的特殊含義需要用一系列的婚姻或其他社會因素來解釋，而這些特殊含義又全都可以用從兒稱這一個原則來解釋。

---

① 見《加利福尼亞人的親屬稱謂》，265 頁。中國的情形非常明顯，因此，即使像哈特這樣的非專業工作者也能觀察到："用來指稱兩姻兄弟和兩姻姊妹的稱謂，即妻子用來指稱夫之兄弟和姊妹以及丈夫用來指稱妻之兄弟和姊妹的稱謂，似乎來源於子女（或者説是被稱呼者的姪兒姪女）對這些人所用的稱謂。所以，如果某個人妻子的兄弟是某個人的子女的'舅'，那麼這個人在談到其妻子的兄弟時就用同一個稱謂'舅'來指稱，對另外幾種親屬的稱謂也同此理。"（摩爾根《人類家族血親與姻親的制度》，413 頁）。然而，當摩爾根沉溺於構建他的進化階段論時，却完全忽略了這一中肯的意見。

第四章　稱謂詞的歷史考察

中國人計算親等的方法是從最近的三種親屬算起，即從父子、夫妻和姊妹算起，然後擴展到其他親屬。如果要討論中國的親屬的範圍，一般總要涉及"九族"——一個被廣泛討論過却仍很模糊的術語，它的首次使用見於《書經》①。對它的解釋主要有兩種，分別代表了兩種不同的古典學派。今文經學派的解釋是：父系四族，外加母系三族和妻系兩族。

父系親屬的四族是：1. 以"己身"爲中心，上推四代，下推四代。對於四支旁系親屬，從源自男性直系親屬的男性旁系親屬起，每一支數四代。2. 父之姊妹，若已婚則包括其後代。3. "己身"之姊妹，已婚則包括其後代。4. "己身"之女，已婚則包括其後代。

母系親屬的三族是：5. 母之父母。6. 母之兄弟。7. 母之姊妹。

妻系親屬的三族是：8. 妻之父。9. 妻之母。

古文經學派的解釋則與此不同。他們認爲"九族"僅僅包括宗親，而不包括非宗親。因此，在他們看來，"九族"僅僅指上述九類親屬中的第一類。也就是說，"九族"僅僅指九代，即上輩四代、下輩四代，加上中間的"己身"一代。自然地，由於對個人的社會行爲抱有集體責任感，許多學者都傾向於對"九族"作狹義的理解，以減少社會生活和法律方面的複雜性。不過，無論怎麽解釋，"九族"問題都僅僅是一個純學術性的歷史問題。

---

① 《書經・堯典》："以親九族"。這到底是不是"九族"的最早使用還大可懷疑，因爲《堯典》是否真是古人所作還很難說，不過，這正是近來人們争論的焦點。顧頡剛已經對"九族"問題做過深入的分析。見《清華週刊》第37卷，9、10期合刊，105-111頁。

在今人的著作裏，一般都沿用《爾雅》的分類法。然而，實際引述的親屬稱謂的範圍却完全由現代研究的需要和可用的材料所决定，雖然在喪服等級裏包括了所有這些親屬。宗親受到特別重視，這在一個以嚴格的父系社會組織爲基礎的親屬制裏是不可避免的。在這樣的親屬制裏，很多表示非宗親的稱謂不過是擴展了的宗親稱謂。

所有親屬分成兩大類，在此之下又分爲四個小類。兩個大類是血親親屬和姻親親屬。在血親親屬中有兩個支系：父系親屬和母系親屬；在姻親親屬有兩個支系：妻系親屬和夫系親屬。每一類親屬中都包括那些與這些親屬有婚姻關係的人，這是一種慣例。

在下面的各個稱謂表裏，每一項首先列出現代的標準稱謂，這些稱謂代表現代的親屬制。對一些複合稱謂的變體根據現在的資料逐個進行了仔細核對。核對時采用了兩種標準：統計標準和邏輯標準。即，如果兩個(或兩個以上)形式都同爲通用形式，那麼就以與親屬制的内在原則最一致的那個形式爲標準形式，而以另一個爲替换形式。這些變體不很重要。在中國，親屬稱謂通行地域廣，使用人口多，産生變體是必然的。

在每一標準稱謂下面按時間順序寫出歷史上出現過的稱謂。指出這些稱謂的性質以及在現代的狀况①，而不管它們是替换性稱謂，是書面語稱謂，還是地方性稱謂②。接下來是敘稱稱謂和面稱稱謂。如果没有列出敘稱和面稱，那麼應該知道，它們是可以按照先前提到的公式來構成的。雖然這中間無規律可循，但一般來説，每種面稱和敘稱都要依據構成成分的不同而有所不同，都要適合各種特殊的環境。

説明各種稱謂的用法的引文放在注釋裏。正文中只列出那些能表明某個新稱謂的最早用法或者能表明舊稱謂的新義的引文。在有些情况下，引用了最典型的例子。這些引文是非常重要的，因爲只有從這裏面才能

① 即某個稱謂在現代的準確含義和性質，如果這個稱謂仍在使用的話。

② 中國親屬稱謂的方言差異被過分夸大了。很多方言稱謂僅僅在語音上有所不同，但並不影響親屬稱謂系統的外部形態。

確定一個稱謂的準確性質和使用年代。

在以下各表中，我力圖盡可能全面地列出每種稱謂的不同的形式①。因此，在“父之父”項下，就出現了將近20個稱謂，分别代表不同的用法、不同的時期。在有些情况下，列出的稱謂數量比這還要多。當然，並不是對每種稱謂都是這樣處理的，特别是對那些用基本稱謂組合而成的遠親稱謂就不是這樣處理；但複合稱謂如有可能的變體則一律列出。在對中國親屬制的早期研究中産生的錯誤，大部分是由對層次不同的親屬稱謂構成的中國親屬制所作的片面而混亂的解釋所致。因此，要正確理解和解釋中國親屬制，就必須詳細地描述全部親屬稱謂以及每一稱謂的確切性質。

一　血親親屬——第1表：父系親屬

Ⅰ. 高祖輩

1. 高祖父(父之父之父之父)②

在古代經典中，“高祖”有時用於指祖父以上的任何祖先③。《左傳·昭公十年(公元前525年)》稱始祖爲“高祖”④，在該書另一處第九代祖先也被稱爲“高祖”⑤。康王(公元前1078—前1053)稱文王和武王爲“高

① 不包括那些性質特殊的或流行面很窄的稱謂。例如，北周宣帝不喜歡别人使用稱謂“高”，於是就把“高祖”改成“長祖”，把“曾祖”改成“次長祖”。《北史·周宣帝紀》：“又不喜聽人有高者、大者……改……九族稱高祖者爲長祖，曾祖爲次長祖。”像這種類型的稱謂將不涉及。

② 原文中親屬關係以英語字母的組合來表示，如父之父之父之父＝ffff，父之母＝fm，現一律改用漢語來表示。——譯者注。

③《日知録》卷二十四：“漢儒以曾祖之父爲高祖，考之於傳，高祖者，遠祖之名爾。”

④《左傳·昭公十七年》：“郯子曰……我高祖少皞摯之立也……”

⑤ 同上《昭公十五年》：“王曰……且昔而高祖孫伯黶司晉之典籍，以爲大政，故曰籍氏。”“高祖”指籍談的第九世祖。《書經》也以同樣的方式使用了“高祖”。例如《書經·盤庚》：“肆上帝將復我高祖之德。”“高祖”指“成湯”。

祖”，但實際上他們是他的曾祖父和祖父[①]。很明顯，在周代如果被指稱者確實是父之父之父之父，就要加“王父”二字，如《爾雅》所用的“高祖王父”那樣。“高祖”在《儀禮》記載的喪服關係中没有出現[②]。可以推想，曾祖以上的任何直系親屬都可稱作“曾祖”[③]。

唐代使用“高門”來指高祖父[④]，但不大常見。這很可能是一種謚稱。《禮記》裏，這樣的謚稱叫“顯考”[⑤]。現在“顯考”已經不在這個意義上來使用了，因爲從元代(1280—1367)起，它就一直作爲對父親用的碑銘稱謂。

2. 高祖母(父之父之父之母)

《爾雅》使用“高祖王母”。

3. 高祖姑母(父之父之父之父之姊妹)

《爾雅》使用“高祖王姑”。

4. 高祖姑父(父之父之父之父之姊妹之夫)

該親屬關係在《爾雅》中無稱謂。對父族中已嫁出去的女性親屬一般有稱謂，而對她們的丈夫則很少有稱謂。

Ⅱ. 曾祖輩

5. 曾祖父(父之父之父)

稱謂形式“曾祖”可以單獨使用。《爾雅》裏用的稱謂是“曾祖王父”。

---

① 《書經・康王之誥》：“無壞我高祖寡命。”

② 《儀禮・喪服傳》對父之父之父之父没有規定服制，所以該書没有這一親屬的稱謂。禮儀著作裏最早用“高祖”來指父之父之父之父的是《禮記・喪服小記》：“有五世而遷之宗，其繼高祖者也。”

③ 《夢溪筆談》卷三：“喪服但有曾祖曾孫，而無高祖玄孫。曾，重也。自祖而上，皆曾祖也；自孫而下，皆曾孫也；雖百世可也。”“高祖”用於指父之父之父之父、“曾祖”用於指父之父之父很可能是由周代宗法組織的發展造成的。而這兩個稱謂原來只指遠親。

④ 《金石萃編・段行琛碑》：“……高門平原忠武王孝先。”《稱謂録》卷一：“按：高門，高祖也。”

⑤ 《禮記・祭法》“顯考廟。”疏：“曰顯考廟者，高祖也。”《禮記・檀弓》：“殷主綴重焉。”鄭注：“‘綴’猶聯也。殷人作主而聯其重，縣諸廟也；去顯考乃埋之。”孔疏：“顯考，謂高祖也。”

從6世紀以來，“曾大父”①“大王父”②“王大父”③就一直是常見的替换性稱謂。“曾門”④在唐代普遍使用。這幾個稱謂都可作謚稱。如《禮記》所載，古代對父之父之父的謚稱是“皇考”⑤。後來“皇考”成了對父親的謚稱，元代以後被禁用，因爲“皇”暗含“皇帝”之意。

面稱有多種。在4—9世紀時常常使用“太翁”⑥和“曾翁”⑦。“翁”意爲“德高望重的老人”。現代常用的面稱是“太公”和“太爺爺”⑧。

6. 曾祖母(父之父之母)

《爾雅》用的是“曾祖王母”。現代在面稱時最常用的是“太婆”或“太婆婆”⑨。

7. 曾伯祖父(父之父之父之兄)

《爾雅》使用“族曾王父”，《儀禮》使用“族曾祖父”⑩。二者也可用於指父之父之父之弟。

8. 曾伯祖母(父之父之父之兄之妻)

《爾雅》裏用“族曾王母”，相應地，《儀禮》裏用“族曾祖母”。二者也都可用於指父之父之父之弟之妻。

9. 曾叔祖父(父之父之父之弟)

---

① 《史記·夏本紀》：“禹之父鯀，鯀之父帝顓頊，顓頊之父曰昌意……禹之曾大父昌意及父鯀，皆不得在帝位。”《昌黎先生集·崔評事墓銘》：“曾大父知道……”

② 《曲江文集·裴光庭碑》：“大王父定……”

③ 《金石要例·書祖父例》：“庾承宣爲田布碑，稱曾祖爲王大父。”

④ 《新唐書·孝友程袁師傳》：“改葬曾門以來，閱十二年乃畢。”《金石萃編·比邱尼惠源志銘》：“曾門梁孝明皇帝……”錢大昕説：“稱曾祖爲曾門，未詳其義。”(見《潛研堂金石文跋尾》卷六)從已有材料看，“門”是4—8世紀時很常見的稱謂，用於指自上二輩起的已故的長輩直系親屬。父之父被稱爲“大門中”，父之父之父之父被稱作“高門”，因此“曾門”便是稱父之父之父。顔之推認爲“曾門”的原義與“從兄弟門中”同。

⑤ 《禮記·祭法》：“曰皇考廟。”孔疏：“曰皇考廟者，曾祖也。”

⑥ 《南史·齊廢帝鬱林王紀》：“太翁”。

⑦ 由於“翁”常用作對祖父的面稱，因此“曾翁”和“太翁”便用作對曾祖父的面稱。“翁”也可用於稱呼任何德高望重的老年男子。

⑧ “太”意爲“大”，“公”和“爺爺”是對祖父的面稱，“太公和“太爺爺”用來稱呼曾祖父。

⑨ “婆”或“婆婆”用於面稱稱呼祖母，“太婆”用於面稱稱呼曾祖母。孔平仲(約1080年)《朝散集》(《豫章叢書》本)卷二“代小子廣孫寄翁翁”：“太婆八十五，寢膳近何似?”

⑩ 《儀禮·喪服》：“族曾祖父母。”鄭注：“族曾祖父母者，曾祖昆弟之親也。”

7 和 9 的面稱與 5 同，只是在前面須加上各自的排行或名號以互相區別。

10. 曾叔祖母(父之父之父之弟之妻)

8 和 10 的面稱與 6 同，只是須在前面加上各自的姓氏或丈夫的排行以互相區別。

11. 曾祖姑母(父之父之父之姊妹)

《爾雅》使用“曾祖王姑”。現代面稱爲“姑太婆”。

12. 曾祖姑父(父之父之父之姊妹之夫)

現代的面稱爲“姑太公”或“姑太爺”。

Ⅲ. 祖輩

13. 祖父(父之父)

“祖”可以單獨使用，表示父之父，但也可以表示任何先祖[①]。《爾雅》裏，“祖”用作“王父”的同義語[②]，但“王父”現在常用作謚稱。自漢代起，“大父”常常被使用[③]。其他的早期替換性稱謂，如“祖君”[④]“祖王父”[⑤]和“祖翁”[⑥]，在文獻裏也時常可見。另一個早期的常用稱謂是“公”[⑦]，現在很多地方仍用它來作面稱[⑧]。“公”是一個常見的對老年人的尊稱，因此當它作爲親屬稱謂使用時意義是不太固定的，它可以用於指父親、夫之父，等等。《後漢書》裏“太公”用於指父之父[⑨]，但現在“太公”却是對父之父之父的面稱。

---

① 《日知録》卷二十四：“自父而上，皆曰祖。《書・微子之命》曰乃祖成湯是也。”

② 《爾雅》：“祖，王父也。”

③ 《史記・留侯世家》：“留侯張良者，其先韓人也。大父開地……”《史記・鄭當時傳》：“然其知交皆其大父行。”

④ 《孔叢子・居衛篇》：“子思既免，曰……祖君屈於陳、蔡，作《春秋》。”

⑤ 《金石萃編・王文干墓志》：“奉天定難南朝元從功臣諱英進，公之祖王父也。”

⑥ 樂清縣白鶴寺鐘款識有祖翁祖婆之稱。參見《稱謂録》卷一。

⑦ 《吕氏春秋》卷十：“孔子之弟子從遠方來者，孔子荷杖而問曰：‘子之公不有恙乎？”

⑧ 參見《稱謂録》卷一。

⑨ 《後漢書・李固傳》：“姊文姬(固女)……見二兄歸……曰：‘李氏滅矣！自太公以來，積德累仁，何以遇此？’”在漢代“公”有時表示父，“大公”有時表示父之父。

現代對父之父最常用的面稱是“爺爺”公公”“阿翁”“翁翁”①。它們的具體用法受到各地風俗的支配。

對父之父的謙稱是“家祖”或“家公”(不太常用)。“家”加在“祖”前面指稱己之父之父是從漢代開始的。在有一段時期“家”被指責爲是一種粗鄙的不正確的稱謂②，然而在今天它仍在廣泛使用。

對父之父的尊稱是“尊祖父”③。5 或 6 世紀時，用“大門中”作尊稱④，這很可能是一種謚稱，在今天已經停用。

古代對父之父的謚稱是“王考”⑤和“皇祖考”⑥。前者可能多用於宗廟，後者可能多用於祭祀。這種細小的分別大概導源於祖先崇拜和祭祀在封建時期家族組織中的重要作用。5 世紀時，最常用的是“先亡丈人”⑦。這些稱謂在今天都已經停用。現代的謚稱是“先祖”或“亡祖”。

14. 祖母(父之母)

《爾雅》的稱謂是“王母”，與“王父”對應。後世使用的稱謂，如“大母”⑧和“祖婆”，都或多或少地與稱父之父的稱謂相對應。謙稱是“家祖母”，尊稱是“尊祖母”。古代的謚稱是“皇祖妣”⑨，現代的謚稱是“先祖母”。“太婆”過去曾用作對父之母的面稱，但現在是用作對父之父之母的面稱。現在對父之母最常用的面稱是“婆婆”⑩和“奶奶”⑪。

15. 伯祖父(父之父之兄)

---

① 《世説新語》。

② 參見《顔氏家訓·風操篇》。

③ 同上《風操篇》:“凡與人言，稱彼祖父母、世父母、父母及長姑，皆加尊字。自叔以下，則加賢字，尊卑之差也。”

④ 同上《風操篇》:“大門中”。

⑤ 《禮記·祭法》:“曰王考廟。”孔疏:“曰王考廟者，祖廟也。”

⑥ 同上《曲禮》:“祭王父曰皇祖考，王母曰皇祖妣。”

⑦ 《顔氏家訓·書證篇》:“今世俗呼其祖考爲先亡丈人，又疑丈當作大。”

⑧ 《新書·俗激篇》:“今其甚者，到大父矣，刖大母矣。”《漢書·文三王傳》:“共王母曰李太后，李太后清平王之大母也。”顔師古注:“大母，祖母也。”

⑨ 《禮記·曲禮》:“王母曰皇祖妣。”

⑩ 孔平仲《朝散集》卷二“代小子廣森寄翁翁”:“婆婆到輦下，翁翁在省裏。”

⑪ 《親屬記》卷一:“妳，按今讀奴蟹切，曰妳妳。或以呼母，或以呼祖母，或以呼伯叔母。”“妳”也寫作“奶”，原指母親，讀作 ni。《廣韵》:“妳，楚人呼母。”

對這一親屬關係，《爾雅》和《儀禮》所給的稱謂是“從祖祖父”①，它既可指父之父之兄，也可指父之父之弟。

現代的面稱是“伯翁”②。13 的面稱在前面加上一定的排行或名號也可用於 15。

16. 伯祖母(父之父之兄之妻)

《爾雅》和《儀禮》用“從祖祖母”③。《爾雅》還用了另一個稱謂“從祖王母”，由此推測，在周代父之父之兄弟也可稱作“從祖王父”。到了漢代，“從祖王母”略作“從祖母”④。“伯婆”是近代以來產生的稱謂，可作面稱用。

17. 叔祖父(父之父之弟)

請與 15 比較。《國語》用稱謂“從祖叔母”來表示父之父之弟之妻⑤。由此推測，在古代“從祖叔父”也許可用於指父之父之弟，“從祖世父”也許可用於指父之父之兄。但這種推測尚未得到證實。從唐代起，“叔翁”成了常見的替換性稱謂⑥，並可作面稱。各地的 13 的面稱也可用於 17，但前面須加排行。

18. 叔祖母(父之父之弟之妻)

請與 16 和 17 比較。漢代似乎使用過“季祖母”⑦。另一種觀點認爲，“季祖母”是指父之父之兄弟的第二個妻子⑧，但無例可以證明。唐代起，常用的面稱大約是“叔婆”。“婆婆”可以用作 16 和 18 的面稱，但應在前面加上她們丈夫的排行或她們自己的姓氏⑨。

---

① 《儀禮・喪服》：“從祖祖父母。”

② 參見龔大雅《義井題記》，刊《八瓊室金石補正》卷一百一十七。

③ 參見《儀禮・喪服》：“從祖祖父母。”

④ 《儀禮・檀弓》：“敬姜曰：‘婦人不飾。’”鄭注：“敬姜者，康子從祖母。”

⑤ 《國語・魯語》：“公父文伯之母，季康子之從祖叔母也。”

⑥ 見《昌黎先生集・祭李氏二十九娘子文》。韓愈在此文裏稱自己爲“十八叔翁”，稱自己的妻子爲“十八叔婆”。同前《祭滂文》，韓愈在此稱自己爲“十八翁”，稱妻子爲“十八婆”。這幾個稱謂都是在祭祀韓愈的兄弟的孫子時使用的。

⑦ 《金石萃編》卷十八：“收養季祖母。”

⑧ 錢大昕說：“其稱季祖母，猶言庶祖母也。”(見《潛研堂金石文跋尾》卷一)

⑨ 《顔氏家訓・風操篇》：“父母之世叔母，皆當加其姓以別之。”

19. 姑祖母(父之父之姊妹)

“王姑”是《爾雅》用的稱謂。

20. 姑祖父(父之父之姊妹之夫)

21. 舅祖父(父之母之兄弟)

“舅祖”可以單獨使用①，其相反的形式“祖舅”用得很早②。“大舅”用於後漢③。

22. 舅祖母(父之母之兄弟之妻)

23. 姨祖母(父之母之姊妹)

24. 姨祖父(父之母之姊妹之夫)

對上述19~24的面稱可根據對祖父母的面稱來仿造。但不管用何種形式，前面都須加“姑”或“舅”或“姨”。

25. 堂伯祖父(7或9之子長於父之父者)

26. 堂伯祖母(25之妻)

27. 堂叔祖父(7或9之子幼於父之父者)

28. 堂叔祖母(27之妻)

《爾雅》對25和27無稱謂，但26和28却用了“從祖王母”來表示。由此推想，“從祖王父”也可用於25和27。《儀禮》對25和27用“族祖父”，對26和28用“族祖母”④；但在《爾雅》裏這兩個稱謂却是指25或27的兒子及其妻子。《儀禮》用的只是“族祖王父”和“族祖王母”的縮略形式。

15~18的面稱可分别用於25~28。

29. 堂姑祖母(7或9之女)

《爾雅》使用“族祖姑”。這個稱謂與整個《爾雅》系統很不一致。按邏輯推理，對29的稱謂應爲“族祖王姑”才對。也許，《爾雅》當時已經開始運用縮略形式了。

30. 堂姑祖父(29之夫)

---

① 陸以湉《冷廬雜識》(刊於《筆記小説大觀》)卷二：“今之稱謂……稱父之舅爲舅祖。”

② 《晉書·應詹傳》：“鎮南大將軍劉弘，詹之祖舅也。”

③ 《後漢書·張禹傳》：”祖父況，族姊爲皇祖考夫人……況……見光武，光武大喜，曰：‘乃今得我大舅乎！’”

④ 見《儀禮》卷三十三。

在祖父母的面稱前加上“姑”，即可構成30的面稱。若要進一步區分，可加上29的排行或30的姓氏。

31. 表祖父(父之父之父之姊妹之子)

32. 表祖母(31之妻)

在以上兩個稱謂前加上“姑”或“舅”或“姨”，可對這類親屬關係進行細緻的劃分。例如，用“姑表祖父”表示父之父之父之姊妹之子，用“舅表祖父”表示父之父之母之兄弟之子，用“姨表祖父”表示父之父之母之姊妹之子。一般地説，“表祖父”對這些親屬全都適用。從社會一般情況來講，父之父之父之姊妹或父之父之母死了以後，上述這些親屬關係通常不再往下延續，除非這些有親屬聯繫的雙方强烈地希望保持這種關係。這裏不再列出對這些親屬的後代的稱謂。如果這些親屬關係保持下來，其稱謂不難構造。例如，31的兒子可稱作“堂表伯父”和“堂表叔父”。其餘的不再一一列舉。

Ⅵ. 父輩

33. 父(父)

“父”主要是作爲標準的書面稱謂來使用的，極少單獨作面稱稱謂。“翁”是一個古老的面稱稱謂①。3—6世紀時很流行的是“阿公”②和“尊”③。約5世紀時，皇室的一些成員稱父親爲“兄兄”④——一個本指兄的稱謂。唐代時，皇室成員稱父親爲“哥”⑤——現代廣泛用於稱呼兄

---

① 《史記·項羽本紀》：“漢王曰：‘……吾翁即若翁。’”

② 《南史·顔延之傳》：“……又非君家阿公。”據王念孫《廣雅疏證》，“公”和“翁”在讀音上非常相近，很可能是同一個詞所形成的兩個不同的方言變體。

③ 《宋書·謝靈運傳》：“阿連才悟如此，而尊作常兒遇之。”《世説新語·品藻篇》：“劉尹至王長史許清言，時苟子年十三，倚床邊聽。既去，問父曰：劉尹語何如尊？”又《世説新語·賞譽》：“謝太傅未冠，始出西詣王長史清言，良久。去後苟子問曰：‘向客何如尊？’”

④ 《北齊書·南陽王綽傳》：“兄兄”。

⑤ 《舊唐書·王琚傳》：“玄宗泣曰：‘四哥仁孝。’”此處“哥”指睿宗。同前《棣王琰傳》：“惟三哥辯其罪。”用“三哥”來稱他父親玄宗。在唐代皇室成員中，父親也用“哥”來稱呼自己。《稱謂録》卷一説：“《淳化閣帖·唐太宗與高宗書》稱‘哥哥’敕。父對子自稱‘哥哥’，蓋唐代家法如是。”

的面稱。在此之前，“哥”從未用於稱呼兄，也從未用於稱呼父親①。情況也許是這樣：“哥”是一個古老的在方言中用來指父親的稱謂，在隋唐時代與“兄”發生了混同，從而失去了原來的指父親的意義，獲得了指兄的意義。然而，事實却遠比這複雜得多。

“耶”是 6 世紀起開始使用的一個面稱稱謂②，也寫作“爺”③。“爹”④(讀 die⑤)可能是較早的“爹”⑥(讀 tuo)的變體，“爹”(tuo)是當時湖北西部的一個方言稱謂。“爹”(die)現在是一個常見的面稱形式。“爸爸”與“爹”差不多同樣常見，它首見於《廣雅》，其曰：“爸……父也。”《正字通》説“爸爸”是南方少數民族用的稱謂⑦，他們稱年長者爲“八八”，或“巴巴”。字典編纂家們給它添了一個義符“父”，便形成了“爸”。另外，“爸”還被認爲是“父”的音變的結果⑧。

就已有的例證而言，這種方言的差異似乎表明，“爹”主要用於北方⑨，“爸”主要用於南方⑩。但這種假設尚未證實。

---

① “哥”在《説文》裏釋爲“歌唱”或“歌曲”。

② 《顏氏家訓·文章篇》。

③ 《南史·侯景傳》：“王偉勸立七廟……並請七世諱……景曰：‘前世吾不復憶，惟阿爺名標。’”“耶”是原始形式，“爺”是後起的形式。詳細討論請參見《陔餘叢考》卷三十七、《恒言録》卷三和《稱謂録》卷一。

④ 《昌黎先生集·祭女挐女文》卷二十三：“阿爹阿八，使汝妳……祭於第四小娘子之靈。”參見《鼠璞》卷一：“呼父爲爹。”

⑤ 原文爲威妥瑪式拼法，現改爲漢語拼音。以下各例與此同。——譯者注。

⑥ 《廣雅》：“爹……父也”，讀 tuo。《南史·始興忠武王憺傳》：“詔徵以本號還朝，人歌之曰：‘始興王，人之爹(徒我反)，赴人急，如水火，何時復來哺乳我。’荆土方言謂父爲爹，故云。”參見《陔餘叢考》卷三十七。

⑦ 見《正字通》：“爸”。中國西南地區的苗族和瑤族至今仍稱父親爲“爸”，或與“爸”稍有不同的變體。參見嚴如熤《苗防備覽》(紹義堂本，1843 年)卷八、卷九，劉錫蕃《嶺表紀蠻》(上海，商務印書館，1932 年)137 頁。

⑧ 鄭珍説：“古讀巴如逋，即父之重唇音，遂作巴加父。今俗呼父爲巴巴，或爲耙耙，或爲八八，並此字。”(《親屬記》卷一)

⑨ 《廣韵》：“爹，北人呼父。”

⑩ 《集韻》：“爸(部可切，又必駕切)，吳人呼父。”《稱謂録》卷一也説：“吳俗稱父爲阿伯。”“伯”也許是“爸”的另一變體。

《廣韵》説吳人稱父親爲“箸”[①]，而《通雅》説吳人稱父親爲“老兄”[②]，這兩個稱謂看來在今天已經停用。福州人稱父親爲“郎罷”[③]，這始於唐代。在此以前，“郎”也有表示父親之意[④]，因此，“郎罷”可能是“郎”和“爸”相結合而産生的一個變體。在現代，福州人總是用“郎罷”作敘稱，决不作面稱。

“父親”可以在書面語(如書信)中使用[⑤]。同時，在“父親”前面必須加“大人”[⑥]和“膝下”[⑦]，構成“父親大人膝下”——一種程式化的書面語稱謂。在書信稱呼中，“膝下”用於指父母雙方，而“大人”則可以附加在任何長輩親屬稱謂上面。“膝下”主要是一個稱呼父母的書面語稱謂，其字面意義爲“像孩子一樣圍繞在膝旁”。

父親在子女面前可以自稱“乃公”[⑧]“乃翁”[⑨]以及更口語化、更有現代色彩的“爹”“爸”或“老子”。在一些地方，一般用“老子”來指父親[⑩]。

對父親的謙稱是“家父”或“家嚴”[⑪]。“嚴”的字面意義是“嚴厲而受尊敬的人”。“家君”也很常見[⑫]，“家公”則是不太常見的古老稱謂[⑬]。

---

① 《廣韻》：“箸(正奢切)，吳人呼父。”“箸”的現代讀音與“爺”同。

② 《通雅·稱謂》。

③ 《華陽集》卷一：“‘囝，哀閩也。’自注：囝，音蹇，閩俗呼子爲囝，呼父爲郎罷。……郎罷別囝，吾悔生汝……”

④ 《書儀》卷一：“古人謂父爲阿郎。”《北史·汲固傳》：“(李)憲即爲固長育，至十餘歲。恒呼固夫婦爲郎婆。”

⑤ “親”意爲“親屬”或“雙親”。

⑥ “大人”常常單獨用來作面稱。詳見《史記·越世家》《史記·高祖本紀》。

⑦ 《孝經·聖治章》：“故親生之膝下以養父母……”注：“膝下，謂孩幼之時也。”

⑧ 《漢書·陳萬年傳》：“萬年嘗病，命咸教戒於床下。語至夜半，咸睡，頭觸屏風。萬年大怒，欲杖之，曰：“乃公教戒汝，汝反睡不聽吾言，何也?’”

⑨ “乃翁”相當於“乃公”。“乃”意爲“你的”。

⑩ 參見《正字通》：“父”。

⑪ 《易經》卷四：“家人有嚴君焉，父母之謂也。”《孝經·聖治章》：“孝莫大於嚴父。”

⑫ 《世説新語》卷一(一)：“家君”。“家君”在此既作尊稱又作謙稱。

⑬ 見《晉書》卷四十三。“家公”早已不在這個意義上使用，現在它指母之父親。

對父親的尊稱是“尊大人”。“尊君①，尊公②，尊侯③、封翁、封君④”在近代以來僅用於書面語而不用於口語。

“考”是謚稱。在古代文獻裏，“考”也指在世的父親，作“父”的同義語⑤。現在它主要作碑銘稱謂。在不同的時期，“考”與不同的修飾成分連用以表示特定的環境。“皇考”在《禮記・曲禮》中用作對父親的謚稱⑥，但在該書《祭法》中却用作在宗廟的神主牌位中對父之父之父的稱謂⑦。“王考”在《禮記》裏是指在宗廟的神主牌位中對父之父的稱謂⑧，但在唐代它有時却用作對父親的謚稱⑨。從元代起，“皇考”和“王考”就被禁止在民間使用，而僅僅保留在皇室中間⑩。元代以後，“顯考”成了一個廣泛使用的指父親的碑銘稱謂⑪，但這與古代用法嚴重衝突，因爲在《禮記》裏，“顯考”是用在宗廟的神主牌位中指父之父之父之父的⑫。

“府君”是另一個使用面廣的碑銘稱謂。最初，也就是漢代，只有那些地方行政官(太守)可以被其兒女稱爲“府君”，但從唐代開始，各種人都可以使用這稱謂了⑬。常見的對父親的謚稱是“先父、亡父、先大夫、

① 《世説新語》卷二(一)，《晉書》卷七十五。有時也用“尊家君”，如《世説新語》卷二(二)。

② 《晉書》卷八十二、卷九十二。

③ 《世説新語》卷一(一)：“尊侯”。

④ “封翁”和“封君”原來是指那些依靠身居高位的兒子而獲得封號的人，後來它們成了常見的尊稱。

⑤ 按《説文》的解釋，“考”意思是“老”，因此它可用於指任何老年人。“考”用於指父親是後來産生的，它成爲專門的謚稱也是後來的事。參見《親屬記》卷一。

⑥ 《禮記》卷五：“祭王父曰皇祖考……父曰皇考。”

⑦ 同上《祭法》：“曰皇考廟。”孔疏：“曰皇考廟者，曾祖也。”

⑧ 同上《祭法》：“曰王考廟。”孔疏：“曰王考廟者，祖廟也。”

⑨ 見《昌黎先生集》卷二十四。

⑩ 這一禁忌在《元典章》(卷三十一，1908年版)裏有很好的論述。

⑪ “顯考”早在元代以前就已經用來指父親了，如《書經》卷十四《康誥》。它一直用到4—5世紀，指父母，包括在世的和已故的。“顯”意爲“顯赫”“顯著”。到宋代時“顯”主要用於謚稱。另見《金石例》卷五。

⑫ 鄭珍對這種背離傳統的用法深感痛惜(見《親屬記》卷二)。

⑬ 參見《恒言録》卷三、《稱謂録》卷一。

先君、先子、先君子①、先公②”，等等。尊敬性的謚稱是“尊先君”和“尊府”③。

父親在古代宗廟中稱作“禰”④。

34. 母(母)

與“父”一樣，“母”主要是一個標準稱謂，很少用於面稱。古代的另一些替換性稱謂是“嫗”⑤和“媪”⑥，但這兩個稱謂可用於指任何老年婦女。唐代時，用“娘子”指母親⑦，但它同時又指任何年輕的女子。這個稱謂似乎流行於北方。在近代稱謂系統中，“娘子”有時用作丈夫稱呼妻子的稱謂，有時又用作對任何年輕女子的稱謂。

對母親的稱謂最特殊的要算“姊姊”，它用於北齊時代的皇室之中⑧。“姊”本指“比己年長的姊妹”。《説文》説，蜀人稱母親爲“姐”，淮南人稱母親爲“社”⑨。《玉篇》説“姐”的古字是“毑”。《淮南子·説山訓》用“社”來指母親。高郵認爲這是江淮一帶的用法⑩。《説文》也説在江淮一帶用“媞”來指母親。郭璞(276—324)説，江東⑪人士稱母親爲“㑵”。“社”“媞”“㑵”似乎是同源字，可能是“姐”的不同變體⑫。從公元前3世紀到公元4世紀，“姐”同其變體顯然是流行於長江流域的對母親所用的

① “先君”和“先子”原是封建時代的貴族用來指稱其父親的稱謂，到封建末期它們已經可以爲一般人使用。

② 《後漢書》卷九十三。

③ 《昌黎先生集》卷二十一。

④ 《左傳》卷三十二。“禰”意爲“接近、靠近”，即表示父親比父親的父親等更親近，它與“昵”同義。另見《書經》卷十。

⑤ “嫗”，見《説文》《新書》卷三。

⑥ “媪”，見《説文》《廣雅》《韓非子》。“媪”又讀 ɑo。

⑦ “娘子”，見《書儀》卷一。它在各個時期的用法請參看《陔餘叢考》卷三十八。

⑧ 《北齊書》卷四。

⑨ 許慎似乎認爲“社”是“姐”的一個變體。

⑩ 《淮南子》卷十六。江淮指長江和淮河之間的地區。

⑪ 江東是一個含義不明的地理概念，差不多等於長江下游的三角洲。

⑫ 在鄭珍看來，“姐”和“社”的古代讀音基本相同，二者都屬於魚韻、虞韵和模韵，這幾個韻都十分接近。因此他認爲“社”是“姐”的方言變體。見《親屬記》卷一。

面稱形式。甚至到13世紀時，母親有時仍被稱作“姐姐”①。另一方面，從漢至唐，“家家”常用於指母親，它大概是“姐姐”的另一書寫形式②。

在一段時期内“姊”用來代替了“姐”。這也許是由於這兩個字的讀音相近，或者是由於書寫時産生的聯想。但不管是哪種原因，“姊”作爲一個更古老、更常用於書面的稱謂而最終戰勝了“姐”，“姐”則失去了本義，取得了與“姊”一樣的意義：比已年長的姊妹。這似乎是唯一合理的解釋。如果事實真是如此，這就意味着這種情况與上面討論過的“兄”和“哥”的情况是完全對應的。很明顯，婚姻關係在此没有起作用。

現代對母親普遍使用的面稱是“媽”或“媽媽”③。“娘”④或“娘娘”在許多地方也很常見。《廣韻》説楚人稱母親爲“妳”⑤。《集韻》説齊人稱母親爲“㜷”⑥，吴人稱母親爲“媎”⑦。“妳”和“㜷”也許是“媽”早期的地方變體。中國西南地區的苗族、瑶族和侗族至今仍稱母親爲mi或mɑ⑧。現在我們無法確定：是這些少數民族稱謂影響了漢族稱謂，還是漢族稱謂影響了少數民族稱謂；或者是二者都源於同一個更古老的形式。能够肯定的是：“媽”是稍稍變化了的“母”的口語形式⑨。

“母親”有時用作面稱，但更常見的則是用作書信稱謂。作書信稱謂時，後面必須加“大人”和“膝下”。

謙稱是“家母”⑩或“家慈”⑪。“慈”從字面上講是“慈愛的人”的意

---

① 葉紹翁(約1220年)《四朝聞見録》己集(《知齋不足叢書》本)。
② 《北齊書》卷十二：“家家”。
③ 參見俞琰《席上腐談》卷一(《寶顔堂秘笈》本)。
④ 如前所釋，“娘”有時可在各種稱呼裏使用，而不管輩分因素。“娘”用作對母親的面稱最早見於4—5世紀。詳見《南史》卷四十四、《北史》卷六十四。
⑤ “妳”，參見《親屬記》卷一。“楚”在古代指長江中游地區，相當於現在的湖北、湖南兩省。
⑥ “㜷”，可另見《玉篇》。“齊”是一個古代用語，指現在的山東一帶。
⑦ “吴”是古代用語，大致指蘇南地區。
⑧ 上引《苗防備覽》卷八、卷九。上引《嶺表紀蠻》137頁。
⑨ 《親屬記》卷一。
⑩ 《顔氏家訓》卷二。“家”加在直系長輩親屬的稱謂前以構成謙稱，這在顔之推所處的時代似乎不大流行。
⑪ “家慈”是“家嚴”的對應詞。母親被認爲是慈祥的，而父親則是嚴厲的。

思。“尊老”約用於公元5世紀[①]，後漢時也可用“家夫人”[②]。

“令母”[③]“令慈”“令堂”“尊堂”[④]是最常見的尊稱。“尊上”[⑤]和“尊夫人”[⑥]用於5世紀至8世紀。現在“尊夫人”是用作對別人妻子的尊稱。“大夫人”[⑦]可用於指某位死了父親的人的母親。“安人”和“恭人”原指有封號的婦女，也可不受限制地用作對母親的尊稱。

謚稱是“妣”[⑧]，如《説文》所釋。但這一説法仍有争議，因爲在古代文獻裏，這個稱謂時常無區别地既用於指已故的母親，也用於指在世的母親。現代的用法沿襲《禮記》：母親在世時稱“母”，去世後稱“妣”[⑨]。“皇妣”是古老的祭祀稱謂[⑩]，但元代以後被禁止使用。“先妣”是唯一的碑銘稱謂[⑪]。

35. 伯父(父之兄)

在《爾雅》《儀禮》中的古老稱謂是“世父”[⑫]。《禮記》有時以“伯父”[⑬]來代替“世父”。“伯”意爲“年齡最大的”。例如，兄弟中年齡最大的可稱爲“伯兄”，姊妹中年齡最大的可稱爲“伯姊”。從魏晉以來，“伯”單獨用作對父之兄的面稱。從宋代到現代，“伯伯”是最流行的面稱。謚稱是“亡伯”。“從兄弟門中”是使用於5世紀的古老稱謂[⑭]，今天已很少聽到。

---

① 《宋書》卷九十一：“尊老”。

② 《後漢書》卷七十八：“家夫人”。

③ 《蔡中郎集》卷六。

④ 《陸士龍文集》卷十。“堂”源出於“北堂”。“北堂”不是面稱，也不是書面的敘稱。參見《通俗編》卷十八。

⑤ 《宋書》卷九十一：“尊上”。

⑥ 《昌黎先生集》卷二十九：“尊夫人”。

⑦ “太夫人”原指有封號的婦女，如《漢書》卷四：“太夫人”。

⑧ 《爾雅》裏“母”和“妣”爲同義詞。

⑨ 《禮記》卷五。

⑩ 同上。

⑪ 《王侍中集》：“顯妣”。這也許是“顯妣”的最早使用，但它在此文中指在世的母親。現在“顯妣”却是與“顯考”相對應的一個專門性稱謂。

⑫ 《儀禮》卷三十。“世”意爲“輩”“代”。意即，父之兄是承襲了祖父血統的父親那輩的人。

⑬ 《禮記》卷十八：“伯”。

⑭ 《顔氏家訓》卷二：“從兄弟門中”。它在字面上意爲“在父之兄弟之子的家門中”，是居喪時用的一種委婉表達式。

36. 伯母(父之兄之妻)

“世母”是《爾雅》《儀禮》①和《禮記》②中使用的古老稱謂。《禮記》中還用了“伯母”③。

37. 叔父(父之弟)

大約在公元前最後五百年,“諸父”④“從父”⑤和“猶父”⑥被用來指父之兄弟,包括父之兄和父之弟。它們至今仍是替换性稱謂,但主要作書面稱謂。“從父”又是“從祖父”的縮略形式,也用來指父之父之兄弟之子。

“叔父”在上古還有另一種意義。父親的第一個弟弟被稱作“仲父”,第二個弟弟被稱作“叔父”,最小的弟弟被稱作“季父”⑦。這種用法不很常見。“季父”也用來泛指父親的弟弟,但不一定是其最小的弟弟⑧。“從翁”用得相對要晚一些,而且不常見⑨。

從第3世紀起,“叔”“阿叔”或“叔叔”就一直是常用的稱謂。

在北齊和唐代的皇室成員中間,父之兄弟被稱作“兄”,這也許是家庭内部的特殊用法。

謙稱是“家叔父”,或者就叫“家叔”。《顔氏家訓》認爲,用“家伯”稱父之兄是不對的,因爲他比父親年長,不敢以“家”來稱呼他⑩。這種論斷過分理性化,而在今天“家伯”還是最常見的。對父之弟的尊稱是“賢叔”或“令叔”。

---

① 《儀禮》卷三十。
② 《禮記》卷十八。
③ 同上卷四十三。
④ 《詩經》卷九(三):“諸父”。“諸父”是個含義不明確的稱謂,字面意思是“各位父親”。
⑤ 《儀禮》卷三十一:“從父昆弟”。既然父之兄弟之子可以稱爲“從父昆弟”,那麽父之兄弟就可以稱爲“從父”。另見《北史》卷二十二。
⑥ 《禮記》卷八:“猶父”。兄弟之子可以稱爲“猶子”,照此推斷,父之兄弟就可以稱爲“猶父”。
⑦ 《釋名》:“季父”。
⑧ 《史記》卷七。《昌黎先生集》卷二十三,韓愈自稱“季父”。
⑨ 《唐摭言》卷三:“從翁”。
⑩ 《顔氏家訓》卷二。

謚稱是“亡叔”。“從兄弟門中”是對父之兄和父之弟都適用的古代稱謂。

38. 叔母(父之弟之妻)

這也是《爾雅》所用的稱謂。“季母”用於漢代①，但很罕見。面稱用的“嬸”産生於宋代②。“嬸”在古代文獻裹没有發現，被看成是“世母”的縮略形式。在現代，最常見的面稱是“嬸嬸”“嬸母”或“嬸娘”。另一種常見的稱謂構成方式是：以叔母的姓加上“媽”，或以叔母丈夫的姓加上“媽”。這種構成方式對36也適用。

39. 姑母(父之姊妹)

《爾雅》對“姑”的定義是：“父之姊妹爲姑。”在《儀禮》裹也用“姑”③。

對父之未婚姊妹的面稱是“姑”或“姑姑”，前面須加上她們的名或排行。對父之已婚姊妹，“姑媽”是最流行的稱謂。

“家姑母”有時用作謙稱。《顔氏家訓》認爲這種用法不正確，因爲一個女子出嫁以後就不再是家庭的成員，所以對她不能以“家”相稱④。

40. 姑父(父之姊妹之夫)

“姑婿”⑤和“姑父”⑥同義，主要用於3—6世紀。

41. 堂伯父(父之父之兄弟之子長於父者)

《爾雅》用“從祖父”來指父之父之兄弟之子，既包括長於父者也包括幼於父者。從其他用法推斷，對父之父之兄弟之子中長於父者可用“從祖世父”來稱呼。漢代起一直使用“從伯”或“從伯父”⑦。因爲同祖父的

---

① 《後漢書》卷一百一十八。

② 《明道雜志》：“嬸”。

③ 《儀禮》卷三十一。梁章鉅認爲“姑姊妹”是指父之姊妹的稱謂(見《稱謂録》卷八)。按《儀禮》的用法，“姑姊妹”應理解爲“姑”(指父之姊妹)和“姊”“妹”(指己身的姊和妹)。梁引用了其他一些材料來證明“姑姊”指父之姊，“姑妹”指父之妹，這些材料都很不可靠。

④ 《顔氏家訓》卷二。

⑤ 《北齊書》卷十八：“婿”。

⑥ 《三國志》卷十三，《南史》卷五十七。

⑦ 《晉書》卷八十。

男系親屬在同一個祠堂裏祭祀祖先，所以到 5、6 世紀時産生了稱謂“同堂”。唐代時，“同”脱落，只保留“堂”①。後來，“堂”這個稱謂擴大到其他的旁系親屬上面。

42. 堂伯母(41 之妻)

如果根據“從祖父”和“從祖世父”來推斷，那麽對 41 之妻的較古老的稱謂應是“從祖母”或“從祖世母”。漢代起一直用“從伯母”或直接用“從母”。

43. 堂叔父(父之父之兄弟之子幼於父者)

請比較 41。根據 41 的稱謂來看，對 43 的較古老的稱謂可能是“從祖叔父”。漢代起“從叔”或“從叔父”②用作替换性稱謂。

當面稱呼 41 和 43 時不用“堂”，也就是説，可以用 35 和 37 的面稱來分别稱呼他們，前面加上他們的姓氏或排行作修飾語。

44. 堂叔母(43 之妻)

“從母叔母”可能是較古老的稱謂。後來的縮略形式“從叔母”可以與“堂叔母”换用。“堂嬸”是“嬸”在面稱中的擴展。

45. 堂姑母(父之父之兄弟之女)

《爾雅》的稱謂是“從祖姑”，後來簡縮爲“從姑”③。“從”和“堂”同義。父之姊妹的面稱可以用於 45，前面加姓氏或排行。

46. 堂姑父(父之父之兄弟之女之夫)

對 46 當面稱呼時可以用父之姊妹之夫的面稱，以姓氏作修飾語。

47. 再從伯父(25 或 27 之子長於父者)

《爾雅》和《儀禮》用的稱謂是“族父”④。“族伯父”可用來表示這種親屬關係，但它還可用來指從第四旁系開始的與父同輩但比父年長的任何男性宗親，因此它是一個内涵相當寬泛的稱謂。

---

① 錢大昕《恒言録》卷三。

② 《宋書》卷五十二。

③ 《晉書》卷五十一。

④ 《儀禮》卷三十三：“族”。

48. 再從伯母(47 之妻)

49. 再從叔父(25 或 27 之子幼於父者)

《爾雅》裏使用“族父”。“族叔”①和“宗叔”②是後起的可替換性稱謂，但所指對象不固定。在當面稱呼 47 和 49 時，一般省去“再從”，只保留“伯”和“叔”，前面加姓氏或排行作修飾語。

50. 再從叔母(49 之妻)

36 和 38 的面稱可以分別用於 48 和 50，以她們的姓氏或她們丈夫的排行做修飾語，或者同時以這二者作修飾語。

51. 再從姑母(25 或 27 之女)

《爾雅》裏使用“族祖姑”。上古以後，用“族姑”作替換性稱謂，但所指範圍不嚴格。

52. 再從姑父(51 之夫)

53. 姑表伯父(父之父之姊妹之子長於父者)

5 世紀和 6 世紀時使用“中外丈人”③。在宋代經常使用“表丈人”④和“外伯父”⑤。唐代以前，“丈人”是對老年男子的敬稱，但是自唐代起，“丈人”却成了“岳父”(妻之父)的同義詞。

54. 姑表伯母(53 之妻)

5 世紀和 6 世紀時用“丈母”⑥指 54。但是現在“丈母”却是表示妻之母親的專有稱謂。

55. 姑表叔父(父之父之姊妹之子幼於父者)

56. 姑表叔母(55 之妻)

57. 姑表姑母(父之父之姊妹之女)

---

① 《晉書》卷八十三。

② 《因話録》卷二：“宗叔”。

③ 參見《顔氏家訓》卷二，“中外”義同“中表”。

④ 《太平廣記》(文友堂本，1934，北平)卷一百四十八。

⑤ 參見《東觀餘論附録》(刊《學津討原》)。

⑥ 《顔氏家訓》卷二。“王母”和“謝母”的使用不好理解，也許這是因爲“王”“謝”是當時的兩個顯赫的姓氏。

58. 姑表姑父(父之父之姊妹之女之夫)

59. 舅表伯父(父之母之兄弟之子長於父者)

60. 舅表伯母(59 之妻)

61. 舅表叔父(父之母之兄弟之子幼於父者)

62. 舅表叔母(61 之妻)

63. 舅表姑母(父之母之兄弟之女)

64. 舅表姑父(63 之夫)

65. 姨表伯父(父之母之姊妹之子長於父者)

66. 姨表伯母(65 之妻)

67. 姨表叔父(父之母之姊妹之子幼於父者)

68. 姨表叔母(67 之夫)

69. 姨表姑母(父之母之姊妹之女)

70. 姨表姑父(69 之妻)

上面 53 所列的各個時期的稱謂，可分别應用於 55、58、59、61、64、65、67、70。在現代一般用法中，通常省去修飾語“姑”“舅”“姨”。因此，在稱謂上這些親屬是無區别的，但在觀念上，這些確切的親屬關係則總是可以確認的。

V．己輩

71. 本身(“己身”，男性)

女性將用同樣的稱謂，第 4 表所列的那些親屬和第 3 表所列的部分親屬除外。

72. 妻(妻)

“妻子”①是普遍使用的稱謂，但它也可以指妻子和兒女。在某些情況下，“婦”②在用法上與“妻”同義，但“婦”也可以用作對婦女的通稱。在作親屬稱謂時，“婦”主要用來指那些輩分、地位較低的親屬的

① 《日知録》卷二十四。

② 《易經》卷一：“婦”。

妻子。

“妃”①和“内主”②是很古老的稱謂，但後者很罕見。1 至 5 世紀時，“内舍”③“孺人”④用得很普遍。“室”⑤“家”⑥“室家”⑦也是很古老的稱謂，但至今仍常作書面稱謂用。

“結髮”⑧“中饋”⑨主要用作書面語稱謂，“結髮”僅僅用於指元配妻子，“中饋”還用於書面語作敬稱。

妻子與丈夫説話時，自稱“妾”或“箕帚妾”⑩。除了作書面語稱謂以外，這些卑下的稱謂很少被使用。封建時代，貴族婦女在正式場合依據各自的等級，自稱“婢子”⑪或“小童”⑫。這些稱謂現在已完全廢除了。“君婦”⑬是常見的形式，但主要用在詩歌裏。

丈夫稱呼妻子爲“賢妻”⑭或“娘子”⑮，較早稱爲“細君”⑯。這些高雅的敬稱很少用於日常交際，而僅僅作書面稱謂用。“卿”是一個相關性稱謂，也就是説，它用於夫妻之間互相對稱，現在主要作書面語稱謂。夫妻之間可以互稱名字，或者什麽都不稱，只稱一個“你”“他”“她”。有了子女以後，夫妻之間的稱呼最常用的是從兒稱。

---

① “妃”，見《爾雅》《説文》《詩經》《左傳》卷五、《戰國策》卷三。“妃”在漢代以前是對妻子的通稱，在漢代和漢代以後，則用來專指貴族和皇帝的妾。參見《親屬記》卷二。

② 《左傳》卷四十二：“内主”。“内主”字面上意爲“内部的主人”。

③ 陳琳《飲馬長城窟行》(《玉臺新咏集》卷一)：“内舍”。

④ 《江文通集》卷一：“孺人”。“孺人”原指封建時代有封號的婦女，如《禮記》卷五。在 3—4 世紀時，它成了對妻子的通稱，自那以後仍然在最初的意義上使用。

⑤ 《儀禮》卷六：“室”。《禮記》卷二十八。

⑥ 《詩經》卷七(二)：“樂子之無家”。《左傳》卷十四。

⑦ 《詩經》卷四(一)：”室家”。

⑧ 《文苑》卷二十九：“結髮”。

⑨ 《易經》卷四：“中饋”。“中饋”字面意義爲“家中的食品”，此處用作比喻。

⑩ 《史記》卷八：“箕帚妾”。

⑪ 《左傳》卷十五：“婢子”。

⑫ 《論語》卷十六：“小童”。《禮記》卷五。

⑬ 《詩經》卷十三(三)：“君婦”。

⑭ “賢妻”字面上指“賢慧的妻子”。

⑮ 《北齊書》卷三十九：“娘子”。

⑯ 《漢書》卷六十五：“細君”。

謙稱用“内”[1]。“内子”“内人”“敝内”是其派生形式。

“拙荆”[2]和“室人”[3]多用於書面。這幾個稱謂主要在上流社會中使用。“家裏”[4]和“鄉里”[5]是民間用的稱謂。“渾家”[6]“渾舍”[7]“老婆”[8]“家主婆”[9]是方言中的粗俗稱謂，主要用於敘稱，但不一定是謙稱。

尊稱是“夫人”，原指有爵位的人的妻子，關係比較親近的，可以用“嫂夫人”。“太太”多用於口語[10]，“令室”和“令妻”[11]是書面稱謂。古代用“内子”作尊稱[12]，但現在它專門用作謙稱。“伉儷”是書面語稱謂，用於敘稱别人的妻子[13]。更常見的，則是用“賢伉儷”來敘稱别人的丈夫和妻子。

“嬪”[14]和“令人”[15]是對妻子的謚稱。“德配”[16]是表敬的謚稱，書面語裏還用作對老年妻子的稱謂。

73. 兄(兄)

《爾雅》用“兄”來釋“晜”[17]。這兩個稱謂在古代顯然是同義的。郭璞(276—324)在《爾雅注》裏説，江東人稱兄爲“晜”。《説文》没有收“晜”，

---

① “内”也是對妻子和妾的通稱，如《左傳》卷十四。參看《恒言録》卷三和《稱謂録》卷五。

② “拙荆”源於後漢時梁鴻之妻孟光的“荆釵布裙”。其變體有：“山荆”“荆婦”和“荆人”。

③ 《詩經》卷二(三)：“室人。”

④ 參看姚寬(？—1161)《西溪叢話》(刊《學津討原》)卷二。

⑤ 《南史》卷六十四：“謂妻楊，呼爲鄉里，曰：‘我不忍令鄉里落佗處，今當先殺鄉里。’”

⑥ 鄭文寶(953—1013)《南唐近事》(刊《寶顔堂秘笈》)：“渾家”。也見尤袤(1127—1194)《梁谿遺稿・詩鈔》(刊《錫山尤氏叢刊)“淮民謡”。

⑦ “渾舍”是“渾家”的變體。

⑧ 參見《稱謂録》卷五。“老婆”是現代最常見的稱謂。

⑨ 《恒言録》卷三：“家主婆”。

⑩ 何良俊《四友齋叢説》(刊《紀録匯編》)卷六：“太太”。另見《通俗編》卷八。在明代“太太”是中丞和更高級别的官員妻子的稱謂。

⑪ 《詩經》卷二十(二)：“令妻”。

⑫ 《晏子春秋》卷六：“内子”。“内子”在封建時代用作對卿大夫的妻子的稱謂，如《禮記》卷四十四和《釋名》所用。因此，它有時作爲尊稱使用。

⑬ 《左傳》卷二十七：“伉儷”。

⑭ 《禮記》卷五：“嬪”。

⑮ 王懋竑(1668—1764)《朱子年譜》(《粤雅堂叢書》本)卷二(一)：“令人”。

⑯ 《稱謂録》卷五：“德配”。

⑰ 《爾雅》：“晜，兄也。”

但收了“翼”，並説周人用它來指兄。“翼”很可能是本字，“罤”是它的變體。“昆”是後起的假借字①。在《詩經》裏只有《王風》用了稱謂“罤”，其他的仍用“兄”。這個事例可看作“罤”是周代的稱謂的根據。

在《儀禮》中，所有與己身同姓的在喪服制裏屬於“大功”等級的父系男性族兄弟都被稱作“罤弟”；所有與己身同姓但不屬於“大功”等級的父系男性族兄弟，以及所有與己身不同姓的男性表兄弟都被稱作“兄弟”②。這反映了禮儀著作對親屬等級實行的人爲區分和規範化，這些稱謂不是在原來的意義上而是在别的意義上來使用的。“罤”在現代完全棄用了③。

面稱是“哥”④，或聲音和諧雙音節的“哥哥”。“哥”，在《説文》裏根本不表示兄，而是表示“歌唱”或“歌曲”。“哥”最早用來指父親是在6—8世紀，後來到9、10世紀時演變成了對兄的面稱⑤。

據《方言》記載，荆州人和揚州人稱兄爲“膊”（念bo或po）⑥。《釋名》説，青州人和徐州人以“荒”稱兄。直到14—17世紀，長江下游三角洲的人還稱兄爲“况”⑦。“况”和“荒”讀音相近。在古代“兄”可能與“况”讀音相同，因這兩個字在古代經常换用⑧。《白虎通》以“况”釋“兄”。

74. 嫂（兄之妻）

《爾雅》寫道：“女子謂兄之妻爲嫂。”然而男子稱呼兄之妻用什麽稱謂，《爾雅》没有指明。“嫂”究竟是不是女子專用的稱謂，我們無從知曉。《説文》給“嫂”下的定義爲“兄之妻”，但並没有規定使用者的性别。

---

① 《説文》列了“昆”字，但没有説“昆”有“兄”之意。《玉篇》收了“罤”，説它同“昆”。皇侃（488—545）説“昆”意爲“光明、明亮”，出於尊敬便稱兄爲“昆”（見《論語義疏》卷六，《古經解匯函》本）。這種説法不無道理。

② 《稱謂録》卷四。

③ 對“昆弟”和“兄弟”的區别最詳盡的研究，請看臧庸（1767—1811）的《昆弟兄弟釋異》，刊《拜經堂文集》（1930年）卷一。

④ 見《廣韻》。

⑤ 《陔餘叢考》卷三十七。

⑥ 《方言》卷十：“膊”。其讀音很難確定。

⑦ 陸友（約1330年）《研北雜志》（刊《得月簃》本）49頁。

⑧ 《詩經》卷三（一）、卷十八（二）。《漢書》卷七十六及顔師古的注。

很可能“嫂”這個稱謂男女都可使用①。

75. 弟(弟)

弟在跟兄或姊説話時，自稱“鄙弟”②或“小弟”③，兄或姊稱弟爲“賢弟”④。這都是從前的用法，現在只簡單地稱“弟”。

從3至8世紀，用“家弟”作謙稱⑤，現在用“家弟”已經不合適。現在用的謙稱是“舍弟”。尊稱是“令弟”或“賢弟”。

76. 弟婦(弟之妻)

“弟媳”是可替换性稱謂。“婦”和“媳”在作親屬稱謂時是同義的。兄對弟之妻一般要回避，反之亦然。他們在談話時只能談正事，并且要保持一定的距離。

77. 姊(姊)

“姊”現在主要用在標準書面語裏，可以有雙音節形式“姊姊”。最普遍的面稱是“姐”或“姐姐”。請比較34中“姐”的演變。“姐”也可用來指任何年輕女子，例如稱呼“小姐”，這與英語的“Miss”相當。

“嬃”(xu)是古代對姊的稱謂⑥，用於楚國。“㜷”用於齊國⑦。“孟”是古老的對父之妾之女長於父之正妻之女者的稱謂⑧，後來在一些地區又用來專指姊⑨。“女兄”在書面語裏可與“姊”换用⑩。

78. 姊夫(姊之夫)

《爾雅》裏的稱謂是“甥”——交表婚的一種反映。“姊丈”和“姊婿”⑪是上古以後的替换性稱謂。“姐夫”是更爲口語化的稱謂。在面稱中，從

① 另見《戰國策》卷三。
② 《三國志注》卷二十九：“鄙弟”。
③ 《木蘭詩》：“小弟”。
④ 《詩經》卷八十六：“賢弟”。
⑤ 《曹子建集·釋思賦序》卷一。《唐書》卷一百六十二。
⑥ 《離騷》(《文苑》卷三十二)：“嬃”。也見《説文》。
⑦ 《廣韵》：“㜷”。
⑧ 《左傳》卷二：“孟”。
⑨ 《方言》卷十二。
⑩ 《説文》：“女兄”。
⑪ 《後漢書》卷四十九：“婿”。《晉書》卷三十九。

兒稱是最常見的。如果没有子女，就常常比照兄弟的稱謂來稱呼。

《爾雅》説，姊妹互稱對方丈夫爲“私”①。這被視爲姊妹同婚的證據。“私”很久以前就已停止使用了。在現代，兄弟和姊妹對姊夫用的稱謂都是相同的。

79. 妹(妹)

“娣”據説是女子用來稱呼妹妹的稱謂②，但尚未得到證實。在封建時代，“娣”與媵婚制相聯繫，有特殊的含義。“女娣”是“妹”的替换性書面稱謂③。《説文》認爲，楚人稱妹妹爲“媦”④，這可能是“妹”的變體。

謙稱“家姊”用於指姊姊，“舍妹”指妹妹。在姊妹結婚後仍用“家姊”“舍妹”相稱，從理論上講，這是不正確的。

80. 妹夫(妹之夫)

《爾雅》裏的稱謂是“甥”——交表婚的一種反映。《爾雅》還説，姊妹互稱對方丈夫爲“私”——據認爲是姊妹同婚的反映。“妹丈”和“妹婿”是上古以後的替换性稱謂。其他用法參閲 78。

81. 堂兄(父之兄弟之子長於“己身”者)

“從父昆弟”是《爾雅》和《儀禮》⑤用來指父系第二旁系平輩兄弟的稱謂。後來縮略爲“從兄”和“從弟”，前者指父之兄弟之子比説話人年長者⑥，後者指父之兄弟之子比説話人年幼者⑦。“公昆弟”，用於《史記》⑧。在 5—6 世紀期間，“同堂”與“從”替换，如“同堂兄”和“同堂

---

① 《詩經》卷三(三)。《釋名》對“私”作了傳統的合理性解釋。

② 《釋名》：“娣”。鄭珍在他的《巢經巢文集》(卷一)中也持這種觀點。然而，根據《爾雅》中“妹”“娣”的用法來看，這種觀點很難説是正確的。“妹”可被男子使用，也可被女子使用；“娣”，與封建時代的媵婚制有關，指嫁給同一個男子的姊妹中較年輕者。因此，“娣”也可用於指夫之弟之妻，如《爾雅》那樣。

③ 《説文》：“女弟”。

④ 另見《公羊傳》卷七。

⑤ 《儀禮》卷三十一。

⑥ 《梁書》卷三十一。

⑦ 《三國志》卷八。

⑧ 《史記》卷四十：“公”。

弟”。到唐代後期，“同”脱落，只使用“堂兄”和“堂弟”。“堂”和“從”至今仍可互换。

82. 堂嫂(81 之妻)

83. 堂弟(父之兄弟之子幼於“己身”者)

84. 堂弟婦(83 之妻)

85. 堂姊(父之兄弟之女長於“己身”者)

對父之兄弟之女較古老的稱謂是“從父姊妹”，既指長於“己身”者，也指幼於“己身”者。堂姊的稱謂的演變與 81“堂兄”的演變完全一致。

86. 堂姊夫(85 之夫)

87. 堂妹(父之兄弟之女幼於“己身”者)

88. 堂妹夫(87 之夫)

89. 再從兄(父之父之兄弟之子之子長於“己身”者)

較古老的稱謂是“從祖昆弟”，用在《爾雅》和《儀禮》裏①。後來“從祖”换成“再從”。“再”意思是“再一次”或“第二次”。“從”與後起的表示第二旁系的稱謂“堂”意義相同。因此，“再從”就表示第三旁系。

90. 再從嫂(89 之妻)

91. 再從弟(父之父之兄弟之子之子幼於“己身”者)

92. 再從弟婦(91 之妻)

93. 再從姊(父之父之兄弟之子之女長於“己身”者)

94. 再從姊夫(93 之夫)

95. 再從妹(父之父之兄弟之子之女幼於“己身”者)

96. 再從妹夫(95 之夫)

97. 族兄(父之父之父之兄弟之子之子之子大於“己身”者)

“三從兄”是更爲準確的替换性稱謂。“三”意爲“第三”，“從”表示第二旁系，“三從”就表示第四旁系。這個規則可以擴展，以此來構成稱謂。例如，“四從、五從、六從”分别表示第五、第六、第七旁系。“族”

---

① 《儀禮》卷三十三：“祖”。

是一個概念模糊的稱謂，如果不作進一步界定，它可用來指第四旁系及更遠的旁系。“宗兄”是上古以後的替換性稱謂①。“宗”在某種意義上與“族”同義。“從曾祖昆弟”用於漢代②，這是一個涉及了祖先輩數的笨拙的稱謂。

“親同姓”是《爾雅》所列的稱謂，指第五旁系的同姓宗兄弟，現已停用。一般用“族兄”，或者更準確地，用“四從兄弟”來表示。

98. 族嫂(97 之妻)

99. 族弟(父之父之父之兄弟之子之子之子幼於己身者)

100. 族弟婦(99 之妻)

101. 族姊(父之父之父之兄弟之子之子之女長於“己身”者)

102. 族姊夫(101 之夫)

103. 族妹(父之父之父之兄弟之子之子之女幼於“己身”者)

104. 族妹夫(103 之夫)

兄弟、姊妹、兄弟之妻、姊妹之夫的面稱可以相應地用於 81～104。對每個具體的親屬，再加上他們的名、排行或姓氏。81～104 的謙稱和尊稱按一般規則來構成。

105. 姑表兄(父之姊妹之子長於“己身”者)

《爾雅》用的古代稱謂是“甥”——交表婚的一種反映。漢代用“外兄弟”③和“從内兄弟”④來指其長於己者和幼於己者。“表”也起源於這一時期。“甥”“外兄弟”“從内兄弟”現在都已停止使用。

面稱時一般省去“姑”，只稱“表兄”或“表哥”。“表兄”書面意較濃，且較正式。“表哥”只能作面稱。有些地方用“老表”來稱呼。

106. 姑表嫂(105 之妻)

面稱爲“表嫂”。

---

① “宗兄”同“族兄”一樣不是確指性稱謂，可用於比己身年長的第四旁系或更遠旁系的男性平輩親屬。但是在封建時代，“宗兄”却是弟弟們用來指稱長兄的稱謂。見《儀禮》卷十九。

② 《新書》卷八。

③ 《儀禮》卷三十三。

④ 《文苑》卷二十五。

107. 姑表弟(父之姊妹之子幼於"己身"者)
108. 姑表弟婦(107 之妻)
109. 姑表姊(父之姊妹之女長於"己身"者)
面稱爲"表姐"。
110. 姑表姊夫(109 之夫)
111. 姑表妹(父之姊妹之女幼於"己身"者)
112. 姑表妹夫(111 之夫)
113. 堂姑表兄(父之父之姊妹之子之子長於"己身"者)
114. 堂姑表嫂(113 之妻)
115. 堂姑表弟(父之父之姊妹之子之子幼於"己身"者)
116. 堂姑表弟婦(115 之妻)
117. 堂姑表姊(父之父之姊妹之子之女長於"己身"者)
118. 堂姑表姊夫(117 之夫)
119. 堂姑表妹(父之父之姊妹之子之女幼於"己身"者)
120. 堂姑表妹夫(119 之夫)

113~120 的稱謂也許可用來稱呼父之父之兄弟之女之子女。但這僅僅是推測，尚無文獻可證。

Ⅵ. 子輩

121. 子(子)

"子"在上古用於指兒女，包括兒子和女兒；因此常常把它與別的語素組合起來專指兒子，例如"丈夫子"[①]。"兒"與"子"同義[②]，現在主要作愛稱，對兒子和女兒均可使用。因此，"兒"要專指兒子必須與其他語素相結合，如現代用的稱謂"兒子"。[③] "息"是表示兒子的古代稱謂[④]，

---

① 《史記》卷六十七："丈夫子"，其字面意義爲"男孩子"。

② 《廣雅》："兒"。

③ 《史記》卷五十二。

④ "息"意爲"生育"。因此它既可表示男孩，也可表示女孩。

但也含有不確定的指子女的意思。因此，用“息男”來指兒子①，“息女”指女兒。“子嗣”意爲後代②，也用來指兒子。在封建時期“嗣子”指年齡最大的繼子③，而在現代則指養子。“姓”在上古可用來表示兒子④，但也可用來表示所生養的任何後代子孫，與“生”⑤同義。“孥”是古代使用的另一個稱謂⑥。

“㝅”和“婗”⑦是不常見的表示兒子的古代稱謂，可能是地方性稱謂。“崽”⑧和“囝”⑨是現代的地方性稱謂，很明顯是“子”的派生詞。“囝”也可讀 jian⑩。

“子”可與各種修飾語合用，以準確地表示各種較複雜的具有兒子身份的親屬關係，這些關係産生於祖先崇拜、過繼、同居、再婚、收養，等等。

兒子在跟父親説話時，自稱“男”。“兒子”是較常見的口語稱謂，“男”則主要是書面語稱謂。在舉喪期間，兒子稱自己爲“孤子”⑪“哀子”⑫“孤哀子”⑬“不孝男”或“棘人”⑭。

父親在書面語和口語中都稱兒子爲“兒子”。在口語中，一般僅稱呼名字；在書面語中，稱謂與名字合用，如“兒子某某”。這一規則也適用

---

① 《曹子建集》卷八。

② 《書經》卷四。

③ 《禮記》卷四。

④ 《詩經》卷一(三)：“姓”。《左傳》卷四十二。

⑤ “兄”在古代的讀音與“生”相近，因此二者可替换使用。見《詩經》卷二十(四)。

⑥ 《詩經》卷九(二)：“孥”。

⑦ 《廣雅》：“㝅”“婗”。參見王念孫《廣雅疏證》卷六(二)。

⑧ 《方言》卷十。

⑨ 參見《正字通》。

⑩ 鄭珍説，《集韻》給“囝”註音爲“九件切”。這是不正確的，可能是與“𡥅”混淆了。在唐代時“囝”也許讀 jian，如《華陽集》卷一。但是現在“囝”的讀音在各地却是各不相同的。它在福建讀作 zhan，在江蘇和浙江讀作 lan，在江西、廣東、湖北、湖南讀作 zai。

⑪ 當母在父亡時用“孤子”。

⑫ 當母亡，父爲中表時用“哀子”。

⑬ 當父母雙亡時用“孤哀子”。對這幾個稱謂的區别使用始於唐代。參見《陔餘叢考》卷三十七。

⑭ 《詩經》卷七(二)：“棘人”。

於所有晚輩親屬。

尊稱是“令郎”[①]。其他的有：“郎君”[②]“賢郎”[③]“賢子”[④]“令子”[⑤]“令嗣”[⑥]。“公子”原爲封建貴族的兒子的稱謂[⑦]，後來成了達官貴人的兒子的稱謂，但是現在它已成了一個通用的尊稱，差不多與“令郎”一樣流行。另一個民間常見的稱謂是“少爺”，它原指有地位有官銜的人的兒子，如僕人用“少爺”來稱呼主人的兒子。

謙稱是“小子”或“小兒”，較粗俗的是“小犬”。“賤息”[⑧]和“弱息”[⑨]是已經棄用的書面語稱謂。

122. 子婦(子之妻)

“媳婦”較口語化。“媳”原寫作“息”，指“兒子”或“子女”。到宋代，加了個“女”旁，構成了“媳”[⑩]。這樣它就成了專指兒子之妻的稱謂。“媳婦”可用來表示所有晚輩親屬的妻子。

兒子的父母對兒子的妻子一般以名字相稱。兒子的父親只在正式場合才與兒子的妻子相遇，并且一般要保持適當的距離。當兒子的妻子年齡增長有了孩子以後，兒子的父母甚至可以以孫子的稱謂來稱呼她——一種典型的從兒稱。

123. 女(女)

《禮記》和《儀禮》用“女子子”[⑪]和“婦人子”[⑫]來指女兒，區别於指兒

---

① “郎”原是一種官名。漢代時高級官員可以任命他們的兒子爲“郎”。因此，“郎”就成了一種尊稱。參見《稱謂録》卷六。

② 《玉臺新咏集》卷一。

③ 《古文苑》卷十，《四部叢刊》本。

④ 《魏武帝集》卷四十三。

⑤ 《南史》卷五十九。

⑥ 《默記》卷十二。

⑦ 《詩經》卷一(三)、卷十三(一)。

⑧ 《史記》卷四十三：“賤息”。

⑨ 《南史》卷四十六：“弱息”。

⑩ 參見《稱謂録》卷八。

⑪ 《儀禮》卷三十一。《禮記》卷二。

⑫ 《儀禮》卷三十二。

子的“丈夫子”。“嬰”據説是上古用來指女兒的稱謂[①]，但尚未證實。

“女兒”是較口語化的稱謂，父母和女兒本人都可使用。同時它還是一個泛稱。女兒給父母寫信時，自稱“女”。

尊稱是“令媛”[②]“令愛”“女公子”，以及較口語化的“千金”[③]“小姐”[④]。封建時期用“玉女”[⑤]作尊稱，但“玉女”現已不在這個意義上使用。“小娘子”是唐宋時代常見的尊稱[⑥]。

謙稱是“小女”，通俗一點的謙稱是“小丫頭”。“息女”用於古代[⑦]，作書面語稱謂，現已停用。“家姊”在漢代可用作對女兒的謙稱[⑧]，但後來不再在這個意義上使用。“家姊”在現代是對姊的謙稱。

124. 女婿(女之夫)

孟子用“甥”指女兒的丈夫，《爾雅》用“婿”，“婿”也可作丈夫的通稱[⑨]。“婿”專指女兒的丈夫時須與一些修飾語連用，如“子婿”[⑩]“郎婿”和“婿甥”。其餘一些可選用的稱謂是“女夫”[⑪]“半子”[⑫]。“嬌客”[⑬]“東床”[⑭]“坦床”“快婿”“佳婿”[⑮]“密親”[⑯]是主要的書面語稱謂，多少含有尊稱意味。

---

① 《玉篇》：“嬰”。它通常指嬰兒。

② “令媛”是指美女的稱謂，可能源出於《詩經》卷三(一)。

③ “千金”意爲珍貴之物。參見曹楙堅《音匏隨筆》(刊《乙亥叢編》)。

④ “小姐”在宋代用於稱年輕女僕或妓女。(《參見《陔餘叢考》卷三十八)現在它用作尊稱，稱別人的女兒或稱任何年輕女子。

⑤ 《禮記》卷四十九：“玉女”。

⑥ 參見《陔餘叢考》卷三十八。

⑦ 《史記》卷八：“息女”。

⑧ 《顔氏家訓》卷二：“家姊”。

⑨ “婿”原是對有才華的學者的尊稱。

⑩ 《史記》卷八十九。

⑪ 《晉書》卷三十四。

⑫ 《劉賓客文集・外集》：“祭虢州楊庶子文”。

⑬ “嬌客”字面意義爲“柔弱的或嬌美的客人”，它不作面稱或敘稱。

⑭ “東床”源出於王羲之的“東床坦腹”的佚事，見《晉書》卷八十。另見《釋常談》卷一。

⑮ “快婿”和“佳婿”實際上所指相同。見《北史》卷三十四。

⑯ 《舊唐書》卷一百五十九：“密親”。

“倩”原是一個方言稱謂(山東話)①，指女兒的丈夫，後來成了常見的書面語稱謂。“卒便”和“平使”是“倩”的錯誤的派生形式。“倩”也用來泛指丈夫。“倩”和“婿”都用於尊稱有本事的人。

對女兒的丈夫的尊稱是“令婿”和“令坦”。“令坦”派生於“坦床”，不大常見。

謙稱是“小婿”。

125. 姪(兄弟之子)

《爾雅》没有列出男子稱呼兄弟之子所用的稱謂。我們推測，男子對兄弟之子稱“子”。《禮記》使用“猶子”(即猶如兒子)②，但這是不是一個爲社會公認的稱謂，還不能肯定。漢代時，“從子”用得相當普遍③，但更普遍的是純描寫性稱謂“兄子”和“弟子”。有證據表明，當時對兄弟之子就稱“子”④。

“姪”，如《爾雅》所用，是女子稱呼兄弟之子的稱謂，《儀禮》中的用法(卷三十二)與此同。“姪”用作男子稱兄弟之子的稱謂始於晉代(265—420)，最早起源於中國北方，隨後擴展開來⑤。當時女子稱兄弟之子的稱謂前面要加一個“内”字，構成“内姪”，以與男子用的“姪”相區别。

“姪男”主要用於自稱。“阮”是尊稱，但不大常見⑥。常見的尊稱是“令姪”。

126. 姪婦(兄弟之子之妻)

“姪媳婦”是較口語化的稱謂。如上所述，“媳婦”適用於所有晚輩親屬的妻子。

127. 姪女(兄弟之女)

---

① 《方言》卷三：“倩”。

② 《禮記》卷八。

③ 《世説新語》卷一(一)注：“從子”。

④ 《漢書》卷七十一。《後漢書》卷九十(二)：蔡邕稱他父親的弟弟和他本人爲“父子”。也可以這樣來理解，如果稱呼的是較熟悉的親屬，就用籠統的稱謂“父子”，否則就用較精確的稱謂。

⑤ 《顔氏家訓》卷二。

⑥ “阮”作尊稱是根據阮籍和阮咸的叔姪關係而來的。參見《世説新語》卷三(一)。

“姪”，如《爾雅》和《儀禮》所用，不顯示被稱呼人的性别，這是一個稱謂與另一個稱謂之間具有相關關係的特徵之一。“姪”和另一個稱謂“姑”存在概念相關的關係。當“姪”成了男子使用的稱謂以後，其相關性便消失了，這時可在“姪”的後面加上性别標誌，如“姪女”(指兄弟之女)，也許其相反形式“女姪”也可以使用。“猶女”和“從女”是與“猶子”和“從子”相對應的，“兄女”和“弟女”是描寫性稱謂，與“兄子”“弟子”相對應。

128. 姪婿(兄弟之女之夫)

“異姓”是上古時不很常見的稱謂①，今天已很難理解。“兄婿”(兄之女婿)和“弟婿”(弟之女婿)是描寫性稱謂，可替换“姪婿”。“姪女婿”較爲口語化。

129. 外甥(姊妹之子)

《爾雅》列了稱謂“出”，在後文又列了“甥”。“出”可能比“甥”古老，因爲在《儀禮》裏只用了“甥”，而未用“出”②。“外甥”是從晉代開始使用的，也寫作“外生”③。“宅相”是大約公元頭五個世紀時使用的稱謂④，可能用得極少。

130. 外甥婦(姊妹之子之妻)

131. 外甥女(姊妹之女)

132. 外甥婿(姊妹之女之夫)

133. 堂姪(父之兄弟之子之子)

134. 堂姪婦(父之兄弟之子之子之妻)

135. 堂姪女(父之兄弟之子之女)

136. 堂姪婿(父之兄弟之子之女之夫)

---

① 《大戴禮記》卷六：“異姓”。

② 《儀禮》卷三十三。

③ 《世説新語》卷三(一)注。

④ “宅相”(屋基)的來源很有意思。據《晉書》卷四十一記載：“魏舒，少孤，爲外家寧氏所養。寧氏起宅，相宅者云：‘當出貴甥。’外祖母以魏氏甥小而慧，意謂應之。舒曰：‘當爲外氏成此宅相。’”

137. 堂外甥(父之兄弟之女之子)

138. 堂外甥婦(父之兄弟之女之子之妻)

139. 堂外甥女(父之兄弟之女之女)

140. 堂外甥婿(父之兄弟之女之女之夫)

141. 姑表姪(父之姊妹之子之子)

142. 姑表姪婦(141 之妻)

143. 姑表姪女(父之姊妹之子之女)

144. 姑表姪婿(父之姊妹之子之女之夫)

145. 姑表外甥(父之姊妹之女之子)

146. 姑表外甥婦(145 之妻)

147. 姑表外甥女(父之姊妹之女之女)

148. 姑表外甥婿(147 之夫)

149. 再從姪(89 或 91 之子)

150. 再從姪婦(149 之妻)

151. 再從姪女(89 或 91 之女)

152. 再從姪婿(151 之夫)

153. 族姪(97 或 99 之子)

154. 族姪婦(153 之妻)

155. 族姪女(97 或 99 之女)

156. 族姪婿(155 之夫)

Ⅶ. 孫輩

157. 孫(子之子)

"子姓"是古老的早已棄用的稱謂①。晉代用"晚生"指兒子，相應地，用"小晚生"指兒子之子②。"文孫"是書面稱謂，出自於《書經》③，

① 《詩經》卷一(三)。《儀禮》卷四十四。《史記》卷四十九。

② 《晉書》卷六十九。《瞥記》卷四。

③ 《書經》卷十七："文孫"。

原來是指文王的兒子之子。“孫兒”和“孫子”較爲口語化，“兒”和“子”是愛稱。

在漢代用“家孫”作謙稱①，但漢以後不這樣使用。現在不以“家孫”作謙稱，而以“小孫”作謙稱。

“孫”可與各種修飾語連用，以表達確切的親屬關係。例如，以“長孫”指長子之子，以“適孫”或“承重孫”指長子之長子②。當長子之長子的父親死在祖父之先時，長子之長子必須爲父親服喪三年。

158. 孫婦(子之子之妻)

159. 孫女(子之女)

“孫”，如《儀禮》所示，可用於指孫子和孫女或從下二輩起的任何晚輩親屬。在現代“孫女”用作與“孫”相對的稱謂。其相反形式“女孫”也允許使用。

160. 孫婿(子之女之夫)

161. 外孫(女之子)

162. 外孫婦(女之子之妻)

163. 外孫女(女之女)

164. 外孫婿(女之女之夫)

165. 姪孫(兄弟之子之子)

“從孫”是《國語》裏可見的稱謂③。“猶孫”在唐代及唐代以前時常可見④，但現在除了書面語以外很少使用。

166. 姪孫婦(兄弟之子之子之妻)

167. 姪孫女(兄弟之子之女)

168. 姪孫婿(兄弟之子之女之夫)

169. 外姪孫(兄弟之女之子)

---

① 《顔氏家訓》卷二。

② 《儀禮》卷三十：“其適孫承重者”。

③ 《國語》卷三。

④ 《元氏長慶集》卷五十四。

170. 外姪孫婦(兄弟之女之子之妻)

171. 外姪孫女(兄弟之女之女)

172. 外姪孫婿(兄弟之女之女之夫)

在方言裏，可用“姪外孫”和“堂外孫”來指169~172。

173. 外甥孫(姊妹之子之子)

《爾雅》裏的稱謂是“離孫”，字面意思是“分離之孫”。這個稱謂有無重要意義，還不能斷定。古代的其他替換性稱謂是“從孫甥”①和“彌孫”②。

174. 外甥孫婦(姊妹之子之子之妻)

175. 外甥孫女(姊妹之子之女)

176. 外甥孫婿(姊妹之子之女之夫)

177. 堂姪孫(父之兄弟之子之子之子)

178. 堂姪孫婦(177之妻)

179. 堂姪孫女(父之兄弟之子之子之女)

180. 堂姪孫婿(179之夫)

181. 姑表姪孫(父之姊妹之子之子之子)

182. 姑表姪孫婦(181之妻)

183. 姑表姪孫女(父之姊妹之子之子之女)

184. 姑表姪孫婿(183之夫)

185. 再從姪孫(149之子)

186. 再從姪孫婦(185之妻)

187. 再從姪孫女(149之女)

188. 再從姪孫婿(187之夫)

189. 族孫(153之子)

190. 族孫婦(189之妻)

191. 族孫女(153之女)

---

① 《左傳》卷六十。

② 同上，卷六十：“彌”。

192. 族孫婿(191之夫)

"族姪孫"可替换189~192中的"族孫"，但"姪"不是非用不可。

Ⅷ. 曾孫輩

193. 曾孫(子之子之子)

按古代的用法，從子之子之子算起的所有下輩後代親屬都可稱作"曾孫"或"細孫"①。漢代時"耳孫"可能與"曾孫"同義②。

"重孫"是現代的口語稱謂。

194. 曾孔婦(子之子之子之妻)

195. 曾孫女(子之子之女)

196. 曾孫婿(子之子之女之夫)

197. 外孫曾孫(女之子之子，或子之女之子)

198. 外孫曾孫女(女之女，或子之女之女)

199. 曾姪孫(兄弟之子之子之子)

200. 曾姪孫女(兄弟之子之子之女)

201. 外甥曾孫(姊妹之子之子之子)

202. 外甥曾孫女(姊妹之子之子之女)

Ⅸ. 玄孫輩

203. 玄孫③(子之子之子之子)

204. 玄孫婦(子之子之子之子之妻)

205. 玄孫女(子之子之子之女)

206. 玄孫婿(子之子之子之女之夫)

下列稱謂在《爾雅》裏可以見到，雖然實際上不會用到這些稱謂，但

---

① 《舊唐書》卷一百六十。

② 《漢書》卷二。對"耳孫"的解釋有多種。可能李裴的解釋反映了漢代的普遍用法，但也不排除"耳孫"還有其他意義。參見《學林》卷三。

③ 《日知録》卷五。

爲了理論的需要還是把它們列在這裏。

207. 來孫(子之子之子之子之子)

208. 昆孫(子之子之子之子之子之子)

209. 仍孫(子之子之子之子之子之子之子)

210. 雲孫(子之子之子之子之子之子之子之子)

二　血親親屬——第2表：母系親屬

Ⅰ. 外曾祖輩

1. 外曾祖父(母之父之父)

《爾雅》的稱謂是“外曾王父”。

2. 外曾祖母(母之父之母)

《爾雅》使用“外曾王母”。1和2的面稱在各地有很大差異，它們大部分以3和4的面稱爲基礎，再加上輩分標誌。

Ⅱ. 外祖輩

3. 外祖父(母之父)

“外祖”可獨立使用。《爾雅》的稱謂是“外王父”。“外大父”①和“外翁”②是上古以後的替換性稱謂。現代面稱是“家公”③(“家”也念作ga)和“外公”，它們早在5世紀時就開始使用了。

4. 外祖母(母之母)

“外王母”用於《爾雅》。“外婆”是現在最常見的面稱④，同樣地，“家婆”(“家”也念ga)也很常見。“家母”用於5世紀和6世紀。當時

① 《張右史文集》卷十七，《四部叢刊》本。

② 《元氏長慶集》卷九。

③ 《顔氏家訓》卷二。

④ 《容齋隨筆》卷二。

“家”指母親，所以“家母”就指母親的母親。“家母”現在則是對母親的謙稱。“嫽嫽”是方言稱謂①，流行於中國北方某些地區。

5. 外伯祖父(母之父之兄)

6. 外伯祖母(母之父之兄之妻)

7. 外叔祖父(母之父之弟)

8. 外叔祖母(母之父之弟之妻)

可以用“姑外祖母”來指母之父之姊妹，用“舅外祖父”指母之母之兄弟，用“姨外祖母”指母之母之姊妹。這些親屬關係在社會裏没有保留，不過，上述稱謂却顯示了在稱謂上對這些親屬關係應該如何對待。其實，處理這種稱謂問題可以有許多方式。例如，當需要稱呼這些親屬的時候，可以用母之兄弟之子使用的稱謂來稱呼。母之兄弟之子是母系平輩親屬中與“己身”關係最接近的親屬。

Ⅲ. 母輩

9. 舅父(母之兄弟)

對母之兄弟可以簡單地稱“舅”，就像《爾雅》那樣。在現代，由於“舅”也指妻之兄弟，因此，輩分和性别標誌“父”必須得到保留。“伯舅”可用於指母之兄，“叔舅”可指母之弟。這些稱謂現在主要用於書面語。母之兄弟以及他們的家庭可以籠統地稱爲“外室”或“外家”②。

面稱是“舅舅”“舅”或“舅爹”。“家舅”在4世紀和5世紀時用作謙稱③，但這種用法在今天被認爲是不正確的，已經停用。“令舅”和“尊舅”是尊稱。

10. 舅母(母之兄弟之妻)

---

① 《康熙字典》：“嫽”。“嫽”(liao)也讀lao，與“媼”同義。顔之推説，在他那個時代，未受過教育的人在其父之父母去世以後，對其母之父母用的稱謂與父之父母同(見《顔氏家訓》卷二)。

② 《晉書》卷四十一。

③ 《世説新語》卷三(二)。

“妗”是古代的面稱[①]，用於宋代，現在已很少見。現在的面稱是“舅媽”。

11. 姨母(母之姊妹)

在《爾雅》和《儀禮》裏這個稱謂是“從母”[②]。“姨”原指妻之姊妹。“姨”指母之姊妹最早見於《左傳・襄公二十三年》(公元前550年)[③]。這種語義擴展一方面可歸因於這二種親屬之間存在的心理共性，另一方面可歸因於逆從兒稱。自漢代起“姨”完全取代了較老的稱謂“從母”。“姨”還用於指妾——這是姊妹同婚的結果。相反形式“母姨”也可以使用。

面稱是“姨”或“姨媽”。

12. 姨父(母之姊妹之夫)

“姨父”[④]“姨丈人”[⑤]或“姨丈”使用於公元後一千年間，但今天已不常見。

13. 堂舅父(母之父之兄弟之子)

“從舅”用於《爾雅》，今天還在使用，但多用作書面稱謂。

14. 堂舅母(13之妻)

15. 堂姨母(母之父之兄弟之女)

16. 堂姨父(15之夫)

Ⅳ. 己輩

17. 舅表兄(母之兄弟之子長於“己身”者)

“甥”是《爾雅》裏的稱謂，是交表婚的一種反映。“内兄”在漢代時用作替换稱謂[⑥]，後來與“外兄”[⑦]——指父之姊妹之子的稱謂相混淆。

---

① 《書儀》卷一：“妗”。《明道雜志》卷三。

② 《儀禮》卷三十三。

③ 《左傳》卷三十五。

④ 《顔氏家訓》卷三。

⑤ 《北史》卷四十七。“姨丈人”現在用來指妻之母之姊妹之夫。

⑥ 《儀禮》卷三十三。

⑦ 《宋書》卷九十三。

今天這兩個稱謂在使用時意義不同。“内兄”現在用來指妻之兄，“外兄”指比“己身”年長的同母異父兄弟。“舅子”[①]和“舅弟”[②]是純描寫性稱謂，大約用於 5—6 世紀。現在這兩個稱謂都指妻之兄弟。

“表”産生於交表婚優先制已經廢止了很久以後的後漢時期。“表”或“中表”[③]最初是用於指母之兄弟之子女和父之姊妹之子女，後來才擴展到母之姊妹之子女。

面稱時“舅”總是脱落的，只稱“表兄”或“表哥”，在某些地方則稱“老表”。

18. 舅表嫂(17 之妻)

19. 舅表弟(母之兄弟之子幼於己身者)

20. 舅表弟婦(19 之妻)

21. 舅表姊(母之兄弟之女長於己身者)

22. 舅表姊夫(21 之夫)

23. 舅表妹(母之兄弟之女幼於己身者)

24. 舅表妹夫(23 之夫)

25. 姨表兄(母之姊妹之子長於己身者)

“從母昆弟”用在《爾雅》和《儀禮》(卷三十三)裏。“姨兄弟”用於公元前 1、2 世紀和公元 1—5 世紀[④]。在今天它還能作爲替换性稱謂使用[⑤]。“外兄弟”用於唐代某些時期[⑥]，它是母之兄弟之子的稱謂和父之姊妹之子的稱謂相混同的結果。這種混同最終導致了稱謂“表”的擴大使用，以及這三種親屬關係(父之姊妹之子、母之兄弟之子、母之姊妹之子)的部分合併。

---

① 《晉書》卷三十四。

② 《昌黎先生集》卷三十二。

③ 《三國志》卷十一。“中表”等於“内外”。

④ 《南史》卷五十七。

⑤ 參見梁章鉅《稱謂録》卷三。江師韓(1707—?)認爲“姨兄弟”是北方稱謂。見《談書録》，刊《昭代叢書》45 頁。

⑥ 《海録碎事》(引自《稱謂録》卷三)。

26. 姨表嫂(25 之妻)

27. 姨表弟(母之姊妹之子幼於“己身”者)

28. 姨表弟婦(27 之妻)

29. 姨表姊(母之姊妹之女長於“己身”者)

30. 姨表姊夫(29 之夫)

31. 姨表妹(母之姊妹之女幼於“己身”者)

32. 姨表妹夫(31 之夫)

33. 堂舅表兄(母之父之兄弟之子之子長於“己身”者)

34. 堂舅表嫂(33 之妻)

35. 堂舅表弟(母之父之兄弟之子之子幼於“己身”者)

36. 堂舅表弟婦(35 之妻)

37. 堂舅表姊(母之父之兄弟之子之女長於“己身”者)

38. 堂舅表姊夫(37 之夫)

39. 堂舅表妹(母之父之兄弟之子之女幼於“己身”者)

40. 堂舅表妹夫(39 之夫)

33~40 的稱謂還可用於指父之母之兄弟之子之子女，即第 1 表中 59~62 的子女。因此，在上面第 1 表中就没有列出這些親屬的稱謂。不過，這種擴大用法是僅僅根據一般的用法推斷出來的，尚無翔實的文獻材料以供核實。總之，當人們把第三旁系非宗親親屬看成與下三輩(即曾孫輩)親屬的關係一樣疏遠時，稱謂就變得模糊了。事實上，準確的稱謂系統在這裏是不必要的，因爲差不多在多數情況下，這樣的親屬關係在社會裏都没有保留。

41. 堂姨表兄(母之父之兄弟之女之子長於“己身”者)

42. 堂姨表嫂(41 之妻)

43. 堂姨表弟(母之父之兄弟之女之子幼於“己身”者)

44. 堂姨表弟婦(43 之妻)

45. 堂姨表姊(母之父之兄弟之女之女長於“己身”者)

46. 堂姨表姊夫(45 之夫)

47. 堂姨表妹(母之父之兄弟之女之女幼於“己身”者)
48. 堂姨表妹夫(47 之夫)

V. 子輩
49. 舅表姪(母之兄弟之子之子)
50. 舅表姪婦(母之兄弟之子之子之妻)
51. 舅表姪女(母之兄弟之子之女)
52. 舅表姪女婿(母之兄弟之子之女之夫)
53. 舅表外甥(母之兄弟之女之子)
54. 舅表外甥婦(母之兄弟之女之子之妻)
55. 舅表外甥女(母之兄弟之女之女)
56. 舅表外甥婿(母之兄弟之女之女之夫)
57. 姨表姪(母之姊妹之子之子)
58. 姨表姪婦(母之姊妹之子之子之妻)
59. 姨表姪女(母之姊妹之子之女)
60. 姨表姪婿(母之姊妹之子之女之夫)
61. 姨表外甥(母之姊妹之女之子)
62. 姨表外甥婦(母之姊妹之女之子之妻)
63. 舅表外甥女(母之姊妹之女之女)
64. 舅表外甥婿(母之姊妹之女之女之夫)
65. 堂舅表姪(33 或 35 之子)
66. 堂舅表姪婦(65 之妻)
67. 堂舅表姪女(33 或 35 之女)
68. 堂舅表姪婿(67 之夫)
69. 堂姨表姪(41 或 43 之子)
70. 堂姨表姪婦(69 之妻)
71. 堂姨表姪女(41 或 43 之女)
72. 堂姨表姪婿(71 之夫)

Ⅵ. 孫輩

73. 舅表姪孫(母之兄弟之子之子之子)
74. 舅表姪孫婦(母之兄弟之子之子之子之妻)
75. 舅表姪孫女(母之兄弟之子之子之女)
76. 舅表姪孫婿(母之兄弟之子之子之女之夫)
77. 姨表姪孫(母之姊妹之子之子之子)
78. 姨表姪孫婦(母之姊妹之子之子之子之妻)
79. 姨表姪孫女(母之姊妹之子之子之女)
80. 姨表姪孫婿(母之姊妹之子之子之女之夫)

上述稱謂的大部分是從父系親屬部分的稱謂中擴展而來的，因此，這些稱謂在歷史上的演變以及這些稱謂的面稱形式和尊稱形式都可根據父系親屬部分的稱謂來推斷。

三　姻親親屬——第3表：妻系親屬

Ⅰ. 妻之父輩

1. 岳父(妻之父)

《爾雅》的稱謂是“外舅”，《儀禮》(卷五十二)單以“舅”來稱妻之父。“舅”在這一時期還指母之兄弟，因此“舅”這個稱謂反映着交表婚。後漢時“夫公”①和“夫翁”②用得很普遍，這是兩個純描寫性的稱謂。在漢代“丈人”是否指妻之父親還不太清楚③，但是到唐代時它已是指妻之父親的一個很流行的稱謂了④。“岳父”和“丈人”在現代用得很普遍；在稱呼時是用“岳父”還是用“丈人”，這取決於各地的習慣。“岳父”較爲正式

① 《後漢書》卷七十一。

② 《三國志》卷一。

③ 《漢書》卷九十四(一)。《能改齋漫録》(卷二)錯誤地認爲“丈人”指妻之父親起源於《漢書》。其實，這裏的“丈人”是指任何老年男子。參見顔師古對《漢書》這段文字的注釋。

④ 《舊唐書》卷一百四十七。

和書卷意，“丈人”則較爲口語化。有時也使用這兩個稱謂組合後的縮略式“岳丈”。另一個很常見但不同於面稱和敘稱的稱謂是“泰山”。很多關心個人稱謂起源的人都對“岳父”“丈人”“泰山”發生了興趣，他們對這三個稱謂的來源作了各種各樣的解釋。

對“岳”的來源的一種解釋見於《漢書》，該書稱大山爲“岳山”，稱小山爲“岳婿”。既然山被稱爲“岳”和“婿”，而“婿”又指女兒之夫，那“岳”的語義便可以發生轉移，成爲指妻之父親的稱謂①。另一種解釋是：晉代的名士樂廣爲另一位名士衛玠的妻子的父親，他們這種妻父與女婿的關係受到人們很大的尊敬，因此，很可能“岳丈”就來源於“樂丈”的訛稱②。

“泰山”的來源則是這樣的：公元 725 年，唐玄宗前往泰山祭天地，按照慣例，參加祭祀的人除了三公以外全都晉升一級。宰相張説當時任祭祀使，其女婿鄭鎰因此由九品官升到五品官，獲得穿紫色官服的特權。在歡慶的宴會上，唐玄宗對鄭鎰提升如此之快大爲驚訝。伶人黄幡綽便説：“此乃泰山之力也。”這個説法被很多人看成是對稱謂“泰山”的來源的解釋③。但是，“泰山”在當時很可能已經有妻之父親的意義，因爲伶人黄幡綽説的話是一個雙關語，他説的“泰山”既可理解爲妻之父親，也可理解爲山的名字——泰山。也就是説，鄭鎰的破格提升既可看作是他參加泰山祭祀的結果，也可看作是他岳父張説施加影響的結果。

關於稱謂“泰山”和“岳”還有另一種説法：泰山又稱“東嶽”，其山峰之一爲丈人峰。由於“丈人”既是妻之父親的稱謂，又是泰山的一座山峰名，所以“泰山”也成了妻之父親的稱謂——這是雙關語引起的語義轉移。另外，泰山還可稱作“岳”，稱謂“岳”即由此而來。④

這些説法都是一些有趣的主觀想象，每種想象都像别的想象那樣有

---

① 黄溍（1277—1357）《日損齋筆記》（《墨海金壺》本）。

② 《晉書》卷三十六。《陔餘叢考》卷三十七。

③ 參見《釋常談》。

④ 《陔餘叢考》卷三十七。

道理。有一點似乎可以肯定，這就是，這裏没有涉及任何社會因素或婚姻關係。第一，從語言學觀點看，“岳”和“泰山”這兩個詞在此之前除了表示“高大的山”和“山東境内的泰山”以外，没有在任何别的意義上使用過。第二，“岳”和“泰山”作爲親屬稱謂使用是較晚的事，不會早於唐代。因此，如果“岳”和“泰山”有什麼社會性含義的話，應當很早就已經被人注意到了。

“丈人”指妻之父親，最早流行於唐代。在唐代和唐代以前，“丈人”可用來指人們想對之表示尊敬的任何老年男子。從 4 世紀到 6 世紀，“丈人”用來指母之兄弟、母之姊妹之夫和父之姊妹之夫，如“中外丈人”。因此，“丈人”用於指妻之父親可能是“舅”語義擴展的結果以及“丈人”與“舅”互相替换的結果。“舅”在這個時期用於指母之兄弟，有時指妻之父親。假如這種觀點成立，那麽“丈人”的使用可能是關於交表婚的間接證據。

“外父”①“冰叟”②和“冰翁”③是替换性稱謂，用於宋代。“父姼”④是漢代時使用於中國西南地區的一個古老的方言稱謂。

“家岳”用作謙稱，但從理論上講，這也許是不正確的。

2. 岳母(妻之母)

“外姑”或“姑”用於《爾雅》和《儀禮》——這是交表婚的一種反映。“丈母”和“泰水”⑤是與“丈人”“泰山”相對應的兩個稱謂。在唐代以前，“丈母”可用來指父親和母親的已婚姊妹、母親的兄弟的妻子，或任何被稱作“丈人”的人的妻子。“母姼”是方言稱謂⑥，與“父姼”相對應。

“岳父”和“岳母”可作面稱，但在面稱時丈夫一般都從妻子稱，用父

---

① 《潜居録》(刊《説郛》卷三十二)。

② 《東坡全集》卷十三：“冰叟”。《四部備要》本。

③ 張世南(約 1200 年)《遊宧紀聞》卷六(《知不足齋叢書》本)。

④ 《方言》卷六：“父姼”。

⑤ 《合璧事類》(引自《稱謂録》卷七)：“泰水”。泰水”這個稱謂的確有意思。“山”的反義是“水”，“水”在這裏意指江河湖泊。既然妻之父被稱作“泰山”，妻之母就自然被稱作“泰水”。《合璧事類》是編於宋代的一部類書，“泰水“這個稱謂看來在宋代很常用。但現在“泰水”是不太適宜的稱謂，主要用在非面稱和非敘稱的場合。

⑥ 參見《方言》卷六。

母稱謂來稱呼妻子的父母。有了子女以後，從兒稱是最常見的稱呼方式。

在敘稱妻之父之父母時，通常是用冗長的語言把這種關係表述出來。在某些地區，用“老丈人”和“老丈母”來作敘稱。從邏輯上來推斷，也許可以用“岳祖父”和“岳祖母”，但在實際稱呼中没有這樣用過。在面稱時，人們通常采用妻子所用的稱謂來稱呼。

3. 伯岳父(妻之父之兄)

4. 伯岳母(妻之父之兄之妻)

5. 叔岳父(妻之父之弟)

6. 叔岳母(妻之父之弟之妻)

較常見的可替换稱謂是：“伯丈人”(表示 3)、“伯丈母”(表示 4)、“叔丈人”(表示 5)、“叔丈母”(表示 6)。“列岳”是對 3 和 5 的尊稱①，不常見。

妻之父之姊妹及其丈夫稱爲“姑丈母”和“姑丈人”，妻之母之姊妹及其丈夫稱爲“姨丈母”和“姨丈人”，妻之母之兄弟及其妻子稱爲“舅丈人”和“舅丈母”。

Ⅱ. 妻輩

7. 舅兄(妻之兄)

“甥”，用在《爾雅》裏，反映着交表婚。《爾雅》還用了另一個稱謂“婚兄弟”(經婚姻關係而成的兄弟)——這是一個純描寫性稱謂。《禮記》用了“私親兄弟”②，這也多少帶點描寫性質。“私親”在字面上意爲“私人的親屬”。“婦兄弟”和“内兄弟”③用於晉至唐代，到現在仍可作爲替换性稱謂使用。“婦”和“内”都指妻子。“舅”在作爲從兒稱使用的過程中，從 10 世紀起開始成爲對妻之兄的固定稱謂。

---

① 《合璧事類》(引自《稱謂録》卷七)：“列岳”。

② 《禮記》卷二十七。

③ 《梁書》卷十二。《金石萃編》卷一百零一。“内兄弟”指妻之兄弟的用法與“内兄弟”指母之兄弟之子的用法相混淆。這可能是由於受到上古的反映交表婚的稱謂的影響，新産生的稱謂没能從這種稱謂的影響中擺脱出來。

8. 舅嫂(妻之兄之妻)

“妻嫂”也可使用①，但這是一個純描寫性稱謂。

9. 舅弟(妻之弟)

10. 舅弟婦(妻之弟之妻)

11. 姨姊(妻之姊)

12. 姨姊夫(妻之姊之夫)

《爾雅》裏指妻之姊妹之夫的稱謂是“亞”或“婭亞”，《詩經》使用了這個稱謂②。“友婿”用於漢代③，漢以後不久，使用“同門”④。“僚婿”原是中國東部的方言稱謂。“連袂”和“連襟”最早用於宋代⑤，現代最常用的是“連襟”。“姨夫”同上述稱謂一樣古老⑥，但具有明顯的描寫性質。這些稱謂在用法上都有相關關係，即“己身”在談到妻之姊妹之夫時采用上述稱謂之一來稱呼，而妻之姊妹之夫在談到“己身”時也一點不差地用同樣的稱謂來稱呼。這些稱謂都僅用於敘稱。在面稱中通常采用對兄弟用的稱謂，或采用從兒稱。

13. 姨妹(妻之妹)

“姨妹”⑦和“内妹”⑧可以互換，它們主要是描寫性的。“姨”，《爾雅》用了這個稱謂，可理解爲是指分別嫁給不同男子的妻子的姊妹，原來很可能只爲男子所用⑨。“娣”用於指嫁給同一個男子的姊妹，它與媵婚婚俗相關，很可能只爲女子所用⑩。“小姨”是現代口語中使用的稱呼形式。

14. 姨妹夫(妻之妹之夫)

---

① 《南史》卷四十五。

② 《詩經》卷十二(一)：“婭亞”。

③ 《漢書》卷六十四(一)：“友婿”。

④ 《爾雅》：“同門”“僚婿”。

⑤ 馬永卿(約公元1110年)《嬾真子録》(1920年，商務印書館出版)卷二：“連袂”“連襟”。

⑥ 《合璧事類》(引自《稱謂録》卷七)。

⑦ 《三國志》卷二十二。

⑧ 同上卷九。

⑨ 《詩經》卷三。《左傳》卷八。

⑩ 《詩經》卷十八(四)。參見《釋名》。“娣”似乎與媵婚婚俗有關。因此，媵婚制廢止以後，“娣”也就不再使用了。

15. 堂舅兄(3 或 5 之子長於妻者)
16. 堂舅嫂(15 之妻)
17. 堂舅弟(3 或 5 之子幼於妻者)
18. 堂舅弟婦(17 之妻)
19. 堂姨姊(3 或 5 之女長於妻者)
20. 堂姨姊夫(19 之夫)
21. 堂姨妹(3 或 5 之女幼於妻者)
22. 堂姨妹夫(21 之夫)

妻之父之姊妹之子女、妻之母之姊妹之子之子女和妻之母之兄弟之子女被稱作“内表兄弟”(男性)和“内表姊妹”(女性)。若要進一步區分,可加上“姨”“姑”或“舅”。例如,妻之父之姊妹之子長於妻者可稱作“内姑表兄”。

Ⅲ. 子輩

23. 内姪(妻之兄弟之子)

“姪”原爲女子用的稱謂,指兄弟之子女,與“姑”有相關關係。晉代以來,“姪”更多地爲男子使用,指兄弟之子。因此,指妻之兄弟之子時“姪”前面應加“内”,以區别於單用的“姪”。請參見父系親屬部分第 125 號稱謂。在現代,女性己身在結婚前用“姪”稱呼己之兄弟之子,結婚後却用“姪”稱呼夫之兄弟之子,對己之兄弟之子則稱“内姪”。

24. 内姪婦(妻之兄弟之子之妻)
25. 内姪女(妻之兄弟之女)
26. 内姪婿(妻之兄弟之女之夫)
27. 姨外甥(妻之姊妹之子)

“妻甥”大約用於 6 世紀①,或多或少帶有描寫性質,也就是説,它表示“妻子之甥”。

28. 姨外甥婦(妻之姊妹之子之妻)

① 《梁書》卷二十八。

29. 姨外甥女(妻之姊妹之女)

30. 姨外甥婿(妻之姊妹之女之夫)

在某些地方可以用“姨姪”替换 27~30 中的“姨外甥”。雖然這在邏輯上講不通，但在實際用法中却是許可的。

Ⅳ. 孫輩

31. 内姪孫(妻之兄弟之子之子)

《爾雅》用稱謂“歸孫”，意爲“歸來之孫”。“歸孫”可能是女子用稱謂，因《爾雅》説“姪之子爲歸孫”，而“姪”在《爾雅》裏主要爲女子使用。

32. 内姪孫婦(妻之兄弟之子之子之妻)

33. 内姪孫女(妻之兄弟之子之女)

34. 内姪孫婿(妻之兄弟之子之女之夫)

35. 姨外甥孫(妻之姊妹之子之子》

36. 姨外甥孫婦(妻之姊妹之子之子之妻)

37. 姨外甥孫女(妻之姊妹之子之女)

38. 姨外甥孫婿(妻之姊妹之子之女之夫)

在某些地方可以用“姨姪孫”替换“姨外甥孫”。23~28 的稱謂丈夫可以使用，女性己身也同樣可以使用。

四　姻親親屬——第 4 表：夫系親屬

Ⅰ. 夫之父輩

1. 公(夫之父)

《爾雅》裏對夫之父的通稱是“舅”，當夫之父在世時稱爲“君舅”①——交表婚的一種反映。在近現代的禮儀著作中，編纂者們仍采用“舅”來指夫之父，而不采用現代的稱謂“公”。如果使用“舅”可能發生歧義，他們

① 《爾雅》：“君舅”。

就使用“夫之父”“夫之母”一類的描寫性稱謂。

“章”①和“妐”②用於漢代和漢代以前。“官”③是出現在長江下游流域的地方稱謂，大約用於唐代末年。這幾個稱謂似乎都或多或少地帶有方言色彩，其流行的範圍不好確定。現代的稱謂“公”產生於 4—6 世紀④，其雙音節形式“公公”也可以使用。

“先舅”“皇舅”⑤“先子”⑥是古老的謚稱稱謂，今天不再使用。

2. 婆(夫之母)

“姑”以及“君姑”(稱在世的夫之母)是《爾雅》使用的稱謂——這是交表婚的一種反映。“威”用於漢代⑦，“威姑”與《爾雅》的“君姑”意義相同⑧。“家”或“阿家”是大約 4—5 世紀所用的稱謂⑨，在方言里長期使用。“姥”用於 5 世紀左右⑩。“婆”在古代可指任何老年婦女，它指夫之母是從唐代開始的。“公”“婆”指夫之父母的用法大概也要歸之於從兒稱，因爲“公”“婆”很早就是稱祖父母的常用的稱謂。

Ⅱ. 夫輩

3. 本身(己身，女性)

在 4—5 世紀時，己身(女性)在跟丈夫的親屬説話時可能稱自己爲“新婦”⑪。這種習俗一直流行到 12 世紀⑫。現在則根據己身跟聽話人的

---

① 《釋名》：“章”。
② 《吕氏春秋》卷十四：“妐”。
③ 馬令《南唐史》卷二十五：“官”。
④ 《玉臺新詠集》卷一。
⑤ 《儀禮》卷六。
⑥ 《國語》卷五：“先子”。
⑦ 《説文》：“威”。
⑧ 王念孫《廣雅疏證》卷六(二)：“威姑”。
⑨ 《北齊書》卷三十。《南史》卷三十三。“家”可能是“姑”的變體，因爲二者讀音相近。參見《顔氏家訓》卷一。
⑩ “姥”讀作 mu(木五切)。
⑪ 《世説新語》卷二(二)：“王平子年十四五，見王夷甫婦郭氏貪，欲令婢路上儋糞。平子諫之，並言不可。郭大怒，謂平子曰：‘昔夫人臨終，以小郎囑新婦，不以新婦囑小郎。’”“新婦”意爲“新娘”。
⑫ 《書儀》卷一。

關係而選用適當的稱謂。

4. 夫(夫)

"丈夫"和"夫婿"是替换性稱謂。"婿"可以單獨使用，表示丈夫。"老公"①和"男人"②是口語中使用的較粗俗的稱謂。

"士③、伯、子④、君子⑤、夫子⑥、家⑦"是不是古代實際存在的指丈夫的親屬稱謂，還不能確定。它們可能只是對男子的一般的尊稱，但又可在丈夫的意義上來使用，或者它們是對丈夫的委婉的稱呼。"天"⑧"所天"⑨和"藁砧"⑩主要用於書面語，"藁砧"基本上只用於詩歌裹。

妻子稱丈夫爲"良"⑪"良人"⑫"郎"⑬和"卿"⑭。"卿"是常見的相關性稱謂。所有這些稱謂都是古代稱謂，現在主要保留在書面語裹，在面稱中極少使用。妻子對丈夫可以稱名字，或者就只稱"你"⑮，但用得最多的還是從兒稱。

謙稱是"外子"⑯"拙夫"或"愚夫"。這些僅用於上流社會。一般情況下，妻子對旁人稱自己的丈夫爲"他"，或者從兒稱，或者用親屬關係的描寫形式來表示。

"皇辟"是古代的謚稱稱謂⑰，現已棄用。

---

① 這主要用於中國南方，如江蘇、廣東等地。其字面意義爲"老年男子"。
② "男人"常常用於指稱丈夫，字面意義爲"男子"。
③ 《詩經》卷三(三)："士"。
④ 《詩經》卷四(三)："子"。
⑤ 同上卷七(一)。
⑥ 《孟子》卷六(一)。《後漢書》卷一百一十三。
⑦ 《國語》卷六。《孟子》卷六(一)。
⑧ 《儀禮》卷三十。
⑨ "所天"僅用於書面，即不用於口語中的面稱和敘稱。
⑩ 《古絶句四首》(《玉臺新咏集》卷十)："藁砧"。
⑪ 《儀禮》卷五。
⑫ 《詩經》卷六(三)。《孟子》卷八(二)。
⑬ 《晉書》卷九十六。
⑭ 《世説新語》卷三(二)："卿"。
⑮ 《顔氏家訓》卷一："倡和之體，或爾汝之。"
⑯ 妻子稱丈夫爲"外"和丈夫稱妻子爲"内"産生於五、六世紀。參見《恒言録》卷三。
⑰ 《禮記》卷五："皇辟"。

5. 伯(夫之兄)

“兄公”用於《爾雅》。“公”常寫作“伀”或“妐”，有時讀作“鐘”[1]。漢代常用“兄章”[2]。“章”寫作“偉”或“嫜”。

“伯”主要指父之兄。“伯”擴大到夫之兄最早大約發生在唐代末年。這種演變可以用從兒稱來解釋。“伯伯”多用在口語中。

6. 母母(夫之兄之妻)

“姒婦”是《爾雅》用的古代稱謂，今天已鮮爲人知。“母母”的最早使用是在宋代。它有時寫作“姆姆”，讀音在各地稍有不同。

7. 叔(夫之弟)

“小叔”[3]“叔郎”[4]和“小郎”[5]是替换性稱謂，産生於 4—5 世紀。“小叔”較口語化，“叔郎”和“小郎”則書面意較濃。“叔”用於《爾雅》。

在現代的下層社會裏，小叔(夫之弟)一般可以與嫂子(兄之妻)開玩笑。這主要是因爲社會上普遍存在這樣的假定：小叔一般都尚未成年，而嫂子又可看作是具有母親身份的人。

8. 嬸嬸(夫之弟之妻)

“娣婦”是古代稱謂[6]。《爾雅》也用“姒”和“娣”來指嫁給同一個男子的姊妹，妹稱姊爲“姒”，姊稱妹爲“娣”。這種稱謂很可能與媵婚制有關。當“婦”用來指夫之兄弟之妻時，應該加前綴，如《爾雅》和《儀禮》(卷三十三)那樣。

“嬸嬸”最早使用是在宋代。“嬸”原指父之弟之妻，它擴大到夫之兄弟之妻肯定是從兒稱所致。

女性己身和夫之兄弟之妻在敘稱時可互稱“娣姒”，如《爾雅》那樣，

---

① 《爾雅注》。
② 《釋名》：“兄章”。
③ 《史記》卷六十九。
④ 《文苑》卷四十。
⑤ 《晉書》卷九十六。
⑥ 參見《爾雅》。

或者稱“先後”①和“築娌”②(這兩個稱謂用於漢代)。“娣姒”和“先後”現已棄用。現在流行的敘稱是“妯娌”，它有相關性，僅用於敘稱。

9. 姑(夫之姊妹)

“大姑”用於指夫之姊，“小姑”指夫之妹。但是在實際使用時，“大姑”指稱的夫之姊妹不一定比丈夫年長，因爲同胞姊妹之間的長幼順序是單獨排列的；因此“大”和“小”僅僅表示夫之姊妹之間的長幼順序。在現實生活中，比丈夫年幼的大姑和小姑都是可能存在的。“大姑”和“小姑”主要用於指夫之未婚姊妹，對夫之已婚姊妹也可使用，但很少見。

《爾雅》裏夫之姊稱爲“女公”，夫之妹稱爲“女妹”。漢代使用“叔妹”③。“小姑”最早使用約在5世紀。“姑”原指父之姊妹，因此，從兒稱是造成這種擴展的原因。

10. 姑夫(夫之姊妹之夫)

“姑夫”還可指父之姊妹之夫，它用於指夫之姊妹之夫無疑是從兒稱的結果。

---

① 《漢書》卷二十五(一)：“先後”。

② 《方言》卷十二：“築娌”。“築”與“妯”同義。

③ 參見《後漢書》卷一百一十四。

結　　論

討論完了中國親屬制的形態及歷史以後，現在我們可以來簡單總結一下。這種説法可能比較有把握：在近兩千年間中國親屬制在結構原則和稱謂範疇方面都發生了一系列變化，但是在其他很多方面仍保留着古代親屬制的特徵。古代親屬制的這種頑固性似乎是與整個中國文明的連續性相關聯的。一般地説，這些變化與中國社會的發展變化之間存在廣泛的對應關係。人們注意到，親屬制的所有變化實際上都發生在公元前2世紀至公元10世紀期間。在整個這段時期内，中國親屬制都在不斷地變化。許多舊稱謂退出了使用，或改變了形式，或限定了指稱範圍。經過小規模使用，新稱謂開始涌現，其中一些被納入親屬制内，另一些則自行消亡。現在使用的每一個新稱謂差不多都是在這一時期産生的。在經歷了一千年連續不斷的變化和混亂之後，整個親屬制便終於穩定下來。

封建制消亡後的這一千年也是内戰連綿、社會動亂的時期。可以肯定，社會的整個結構不是突然改變的，許多舊的社會習俗稍加改頭換面又繼續保存下來①。但不管怎麽樣，新的社會秩序的演進畢竟開始了。這是一個緩慢而艱巨的過程，安定的社會政治局面與混亂的局面交替出現，進步的思想和反動的思想并存。這是一個與外界擴大影響和接觸的時期，尤其是3至6世紀——中國的"黑暗年代"時期，長江以北地區幾乎都遭到北方少數民族的騷擾。漢人向南方大規模移民的浪潮使世族組織達到鼎盛時期，另一方面，又使它在官方的募兵制度的"門閥制"中成爲多餘的社會組織②。這個移民過程相當複雜，在此無法詳述，但是它

① 有學者甚至認爲現代中國仍基本上是一個封建社會。這種觀點有點言過其實，過份拘泥於"封建制"的定義。

② "門閥制"，作爲官方的一種募兵制度，是以宗族關係爲基礎的。

却顯示了與親屬制的發展之間存在的總的年代順序關係。10 世紀左右，中國親屬制已經定型，而中國社會却仍在繼續演變。親屬制是一種較保守的制度，在某些方面具有比别的社會制度更穩定的機制。中國現代親屬制在基本方面與唐代親屬制相同。

親屬制的個人系統部分表現在各種不同程度的變異上。對宗親稱謂來説，雖然對不同程度的變異有所處理，一些稱謂的語義有所變化，但宗親稱謂相對來説變異很小。這也許是由於雖然舊的宗族制度——“宗法”轉變成了新的宗族組織——“世族”，但宗族原則仍是親屬關係變化的基礎。有效的描寫性稱謂的增加僅僅表示與喪服禮教相關聯的親屬制的表面特徵的變化。

最顯著的變化發生在非宗親稱謂上面，特别是姻親稱謂——阿金斯基稱之爲“基礎稱謂”①。只要看一看第四章第 3 表和第 4 表就可知道，這種變化是多麼巨大！社會人類學家一般都承認，姻親稱謂對姻親關係的變動十分敏感。但是，在這一時期中國的婚姻制度有没有發生根本性的變化呢？這個問題要讓歷史事實來回答。從公元前 10 世紀到現在，中國婚姻規則中最重要的因素是族外婚原則以及輩分原則。前面我們已經指出，這種原則隨着時間的推移逐漸受到强調，但現實的婚姻生活却没有起什麼變化。因此，總的説來婚姻規則對親屬制影響很小，以致可以不加考慮。我們也可這樣來看待姊妹同婚和收繼婚對中國親屬制所産生的影響。

不過，交表婚却是另一碼事，因爲舊的親屬制中的姻親稱謂無疑地正是以交表婚爲基礎的。如果我們假設，交表婚數量的減少將引起舊的姻親稱謂的減少以致消失，那麼我們就可以解釋新的稱謂是如何産生的。在我看來，這些新稱謂不是新的婚姻形式的産物，而是從兒稱運用的結果。從總體上看，婚姻關係對現代親屬制影響甚微。其原因在於：中國的婚姻規則是限制性的，而不是規定性的——即除了要受族外婚和輩分

---

① B. W. 阿金斯基《親屬制與婚姻形式》，刊《美國人類學學會論文集》第 45 卷，1935 年，14 頁。

原則的限制以外，完全有選擇的自由。

中國親屬制的形態構造曾迷惑了許多學者。摩爾根在評價中國親屬制時拿不準它應屬於馬來亞式還是屬於土蘭式，説“中國親屬制落後於最高形態的土蘭式，并且不管有什麽差異，中國親屬制都與馬來亞式有關”。① 羅維顯然利用了摩爾根的成果，認爲中國親屬制要麽是一種“輩分式”親屬制，要麽是一種“二分混合型”親屬制②——等於説要麽是馬來亞式，要麽是土蘭式。T. S. 切恩和 J. K. 施賴奥克運用了羅維的分類系統，稱中國親屬制是“二分旁系型”的親屬制③。克魯伯也持這種觀點，但他説，“中國親屬制看來是由一種類分的非描寫性的基礎所構成，這個基礎通過增添新成分被改造成了一種‘描寫性’系統，它在功能上近似於英國的系統，但事實上比之更精確更優越。”④請將這一點與摩爾根的下面的話相比較：中國親屬制“完成了保存類分原則的艱巨任務，這種類分原則抗拒着血親關係的自然劃分，同時又要以準確而固定的方式把這些關係相互區分開來”。⑤

實際上，中國親屬制不能簡單地歸爲“類分式”，或歸爲“描寫式”；而必須首先根據它本身的構造原則和在歷史上的發展來理解它。按摩爾根對“描寫式“類分式”下的定義來看，中國親屬制既是類分的又是描寫的。根據摩爾根的親屬制理論，這種説法並非自相矛盾，而是體現了包含相反性質的不同因素的親屬制所具有的特點。對這些基本因素作出解釋比起解釋任何别的特徵更有科學意義。我們在具體分析文字産生以來中國親屬制的變化時已經討論了這一問題。在資料允許的範圍内，我們考察了與中國親屬制的變化有關的歷史事實，以及影響各種可能有生命力的因素的性質的歷史事實。

---

① 前引摩爾根的著作《人類家族的血親和姻親制度》413 頁。

② R. H. 羅維《關係名詞》，《不列顛百科全書》第 12 卷。

③ 前引論著 627 頁。

④ 前引《中國親屬系統的形成過程》151 頁。

⑤ 摩爾根《人類家族的血親和姻親制度》413 頁。

參考文獻舉要

鮑彪(約1150年)、吳師道(1283—1344)《戰國策校注》,《四部叢刊》本。

韓愈(768—824)《昌黎先生集》,《四部備要》本。

鄭珍(1806—1864)《巢經巢文集》,《清代學術叢書》本。

梁章鉅(1775—1849)《稱謂録》,1875年本。

廖文英《正字通》,1670年本。

丁度等《集韵》,《四部備要》本。

江淹(444—505)《江文通集》,《四部叢刊》本。

錢大昕(1727—1804)《潜研堂金石文跋尾》,《潜研堂全書》本,1884年。

潘昂霄(約1300年)《金石例》,《隨庵徐氏叢書》本。

王昶(1727—1806)《金石萃編》,經訓堂本。

黄宗羲(1609—1695)《金石要例》,《借月山房彙鈔》本。

房喬(約630年)等《晉書》,同文書局本,1894年。

鄭珍《親屬記》,《廣雅叢書)》本。

劉昫(887—946)等《舊唐書》,同文書局本,1894年。

張九齡(673—740)《曲江文集》,《四部叢刊》本。

郝懿行(1757—1825)《爾雅義疏》,《四部備要》本。因爲有關的只是很短一節"釋親",所以注釋裏没有提到這本書。

揚雄(公元前53—公元18)著、郭璞(276—324)注《方言》,《四部叢刊》本。

韓非(?—公元前324)《韓非子》,《四部備要》本。

班固(32—92)《漢書》,同文書局本,1894年。

錢大昕《恒言録》，《潛研堂全書》本。

范曄(？—445)《後漢書》，同文書局本，1894年。

《孝經注疏》，阮刻《十三經注疏》本，1815年。

賈誼(約公元前2世紀)《新書》，《四部備要》本。

歐陽修(1007—1072)、宋祁(998—1061)《新唐書》，同文書局本，1894年。

王觀國(約1140年)《學林》，武英殿聚珍版。

顧況(約8—9世紀)《華陽集》，雙峰堂本，1855年。

劉安(？—公元前122)《淮南子》，浙江書局本，1876年。

《周易注疏》，阮刻《十三經注疏》本，1815年。

《儀禮注疏》，阮刻《十三經注疏》本，1815年。

顧炎武(1612—1681)《日知録》(黄汝成集釋)，湖北崇文書局本，1872年。

洪邁(1123—1202)《容齋隨筆》，《四部叢刊續編》本。

趙翼(1727—1814)《陔餘叢考》，壽考堂《甌北全書》本，1790年。

張慎儀《廣釋親》，據錢塘梁氏殘藁，《愛園叢書》本。

王念孫(1744—1832)《廣雅疏證》(《廣雅》爲張揖所作)，淮南書局，1879年。因爲有關的只是"釋親"一節中的親屬稱謂，所以注釋裏没有涉及這本書。

陳彭年(961—1017)等《廣韵》，《四部叢刊》本。

《公羊注疏》，阮刻《十三經注疏》本，1815年。

孔鮒(約公元前200年)《孔叢子》，《四部叢刊》本。

《國語》，韋昭(204—273)注，《四部叢刊》本。

《禮記注疏》，阮刻《十三經注疏》本，1815年。

姚思廉(？—637)《梁書》，同文書局本，1894年。

劉禹錫(772—842)《劉賓客文集》，《四部備要》本。

陸雲(262—305)《陸士龍文集》，《四部叢刊》本。

《論語注疏》，阮刻《十三經注疏)本，1815年。

呂不韋(？—235)《呂氏春秋》,《四部備要》本。

沈括(1030—1094)《夢溪筆談》,《津逮秘書》本。

《孟子注疏》,阮刻《十三經注疏》本,1815年。

《明律集解附例》(編於公元1585年,萬曆十三年),修定法律館本,1908年。

張耒(1052—1112)《明道雜志》,《顧氏文房小説》本。

王銍(約1120年)《默記》,涵芬樓本,1918年。

李延壽(約7世紀)《南史》,同文書局本,1894年。

馬令(約1100年)《南唐書》,《四部叢刊續編》本。

吳曾(約1150年)《能改齋漫録》,武英殿聚珍版。

陸增祥(約1850年)《八瓊室金石補正》,吳興劉氏希古樓本。

臧庸(1767—1811)《拜經堂文集》,上元宗氏石印本,1920年。

陳立(1809—1869)《白虎通疏證》(《白虎通》一般認爲是班固等人所著),淮南書局本,1875年。

李百藥(565—648)《北齊書》,同文書局本,1894年。

孫光憲(？—968)《北夢瑣言》,《雅雨堂叢書》本。

李延壽《北史》,同文書局本,1894年。

梁玉繩《瞥記》,《清白士集》本。

陳壽(233—297)《三國志》,同文書局本,1894年。

《釋常談》(無名氏著,約1100年),《百川學海》本。

司馬遷(公元前？145—74？),同文書局本,1894年。

《毛詩注疏》,《四部備要》本。

畢沅(1730—1797)《釋名疏證》[《釋名》爲劉熙(約200年)所著],《廣雅叢書》本。該書可參考的是卷二"釋親屬"。注釋裏未提及此書。

劉義慶(403—444)著、劉孝標(約530年)注《世説新語》,《四部叢刊》本。

《尚書注疏》,阮刻《十三經注疏》本,1815年。

司馬光(1019—1086)《書儀》,《學津討原)本。

戴埴(約 1220 年)《鼠璞》,《學津討原》本。

許慎(約 200 年)《説文解字》[徐鉉(916—991)注],《四部叢刊》本。

沈約(441—513)《宋書》,同文書局本,1894 年。

戴德(約公元前 100 年)《大戴禮記》,《四部叢刊》本。

王定保(870—954?)《唐摭言)》,《雅雨堂叢書》本。

《唐律疏議》[長孫無忌(?—659)等人編纂],《四部叢刊三編》本。

蔡邕(133—192)《蔡中郎集》,《四部叢刊》本。

曹植(192—232)《曹子建集》,《四部叢刊》)本。

《左傳注疏》,阮刻《十三經注疏》本,1815 年。

程瑶田(1725—1814)《宗法小記》,《皇清經解》本。

翟灝(?—1788)《通俗編》,無不宜齋本。

杜佑(735—812)《通典》,浙江書局本,1896 年。

方以智(約 1650 年)《通雅》,立教館本。

王粲(177—217)《王侍中集》,《漢魏六朝百三名家集》本。

蕭統(501—531)著、李善(?—688)注《六臣注文選》,《四部叢刊》本。

顔之推(531—591)《顔氏家訓》,《四部叢刊》本。

《晏子春秋》[一般認爲是晏嬰(公元前?—493)所作],《四部備要》本。

趙璘(約 840 年)《因話録》,《稗海》本。

《玉篇》(543 年顧野王編,760 年孫强增補,1008 年陳彭年等人修訂),《四部叢刊》本。

徐陵(507—583)編《玉臺新咏集》,《四部叢刊》本。

元稹(779—831)《元氏長慶集》,《四部叢刊》本。

譯 後 記

馮漢驥先生(1899—1977)是我國著名的人類學家和考古學家。他早年留學美國，就學於哈佛大學和賓夕法尼亞大學，獲人類學博士學位。回國後在四川大學史學係和華西大學社會學係任教。中華人民共和國成立後出任四川省博物館館長，主持四川和西南地區的考古工作。

馮漢驥先生在人類學和考古學上建樹卓著，著述頗豐。《中國親屬稱謂指南》(原名《中國親屬制度》)是他在人類學方面的代表作，寫於三十年代，以英文發表在《哈佛亞洲研究學報》上，此後一直没有譯成中文。

對中國親屬制的研究在中國早已有之，但是現代科學意義上的研究則是從摩爾根的《人類家族的血親和姻親制度》開始的；馮漢驥先生在繼承摩爾根研究成果的基礎上進一步發展了關於中國親屬制的理論。除了《中國親屬稱謂指南》以外，他還寫有《由中國親屬名詞上所見之中國古代親屬制》《作爲中國親屬制構成部分的從子女稱》等。在《中國親屬制度》中，他運用現代人類學把親屬制分爲“描寫式親屬制”和“類分式親屬制”的原理，通過分析親屬制的表層結構——親屬稱謂入手，探討了中國親屬制與婚姻制、宗法制的關係，描述了中國親屬制的發展軌迹，在當時的學術界産生了較大影響。

中國是一個重人倫的國家，親屬關係及其網絡盤根錯節，親屬稱謂紛繁複雜。要想把握中國的社會結構，有必要首先把握中國的親屬結構。然而，由於歷史的原因，對親屬問題的研究在我國三十多年來幾乎是個空白，以致這部舊著至今仍然是此項研究中最系統、最深入的一部。因此，它的出版到現在仍然具有重要意義。

這部著作寫於五十多年前，作者是按當時的觀點，是利用當時的材料來寫的。有些術語跟現在的含義已經大相徑庭，有些觀點現在看來已經過時，有些材料現在又有了新的考證，但是爲了保持原作的風貌，譯者一般没有一一注解(個别可能引起誤解的除外)，讀者想必自會歷史地看待這些問題。

在此書的翻譯過程中，曾得到北京師範大學中文系伍鐵平教授的熱情幫助，上海文藝出版社民間文學讀物編輯室對本書中文本的出版也給予了大力支持，謹在此向他們一並致謝。

譯者

1989年3月於成都

湖北省圖書館
圖書目録
第一期

目　録

序

湖北省立圖書館藏書僅萬餘本而種類項目尚未分列清楚，好學之士惜焉。今年春，予奉令來長教育，命孫君述萬爲館長，從事整理。九月，孫君去職，馮君漢驥繼任。馮君學有專長，經驗宏富，任職以來，計劃擴充暨整理事甚詳，並仍督同館員編製目録至本月工始竣。

現該館圖書目録業已印成，行將公諸世。從此到館閲覽者一披目録即可知藏書之種類及其數目，而館内管書人員亦可按册索書有如探囊之便舉。歷年來，棼亂錯雜之典籍一旦清理就緒，牙籤鄴架琳琅滿目亦一快意事也。今當目録第一期出版之始，特弁數言於首，以誌馮君及諸館員之勤兼爲湖北圖書館前途慶。

民國十七年十二月蒲圻劉樹杞識

借書規則

1 本館書借書時間規定上午九時至十二時，下午二時至五時。

2 借書人欲借書時須至本館圖書出納處填寫保單，請本市妥實商店擔保，由本館發給借書證，以後每次借書之時須將此借書證繳驗。

3 尚無商店擔保者須隨時按照全書之價格繳納押金，還書之時即將押金全數退還。

4 本館所發出借書證適用時間以六個月爲限，過期作廢。

5 尚閱者將借書證遺失須即時到本館申明作廢，否則他人以此證所借之書仍歸原人負責，再補發借書證須繳洋一角。

6 借書人借書之時須於目録中檢出，將者碼著名書名填於借書券上(可向圖書出納處索取)簽名蓋章及連同借書證交與本館圖書收發處即可將書籍借出，圖書借出以三種爲限(洋裝每種不得過五册，線裝書每種不得過十册)，在前書未還以前不得再借他書。

7 圖書借閱時間以二星期爲限，若未閱完時可再續借一星期，但遇必要時本館得隨時通知取還。

8 圖書借出逾期不還者以逾期之日起算每日納銅元四枚，逾一月仍不還者則通知其保證人責其賠償或於借書人押金内扣除。

9 圖書借出如有失落損壞圈點批塗評改等情借書人須照全書價賠償。

10 倘借書人欲借之書已爲他人借出者可在本館圖書出納處預訂。

11 本館後列各種書籍概不借出：(1)貴重書籍及大部書籍；(2)參考書籍字典類書等；(3)新聞紙及雜誌；(4)各種圖表地圖碑帖；(5)展覽橱内之展覽書籍。

12 倘一書之索閲者甚多而本館只有一二部者，本館爲大多數閲者之便利計得保留或限時間借閲之。

13　十六歲以下之幼童欲借書時須有家長或所進學效教員之擔保，至借書手續仍照前訂規則辦理之。

14　圖書借出時借書人應仔細證明書中有無損壞塗污圈點等情向本館辦事人員申明以免誤會。

學校及機關領取特許證規則

15　凡學校及機關借閲圖書者本館得給特許借書證。

16　特許證發出日期以每年一月至五月爲第一期，八月至十二月爲第二期。

17　特許期滿之時須將所借書籍全部送還。

18　以特許證所借各書如有遺失污損圈點等情該特許學校或關機負有完全賠償責任。

19　補領特許借書證時須繳洋五洋。

20　凡以特許證借書時借書券上須由該特許證之學校或機關蓋章。

21　以特許證借書只以本館通常圖書爲限。

參觀藏書室規則

22　參觀人須記載姓名籍貫住址職業於題名簿内。

23　參觀人須由本館職員導引。

24　參觀人到館時未得職員導引之前請在會客室暫待。

25　參觀時請勿携帶幼孩及僕從。

26　參觀時請勿吸煙及吐痰。

27　參觀人在藏書室内欲檢視書籍行欵版本者可囑導引人取閲。

28 参觀人對於本館如有意見得面告函達或記於批評簿上。

29 有精神或傳染病者謝絶参觀。

30 参觀時間以星期一至星期六上午九時至十二時，下午一時至四時爲限。

本目録之用法

1. 本編所收各書均照杜法按類排列。閲者如欲閲《心理學》書籍，則可於分類大綱内檢閲，知《心理學》分類號碼爲「150」再檢目録「150」内號碼内，則《心理學》之書籍皆在。

2. 本編後面附有類目索引，每字均按王雲五氏之四角號碼檢字法排列。例如《心理學》之《心》字檢字號碼爲「3300」，則於「3300」號碼下亦可檢得《心理學》之分類號碼類「150」。—「四角號碼檢字法之用法詳後」

3. 本編著録各書之後均附有《書碼》，閲者將書檢得之後，可將《著者》《書名》《書碼》寫於借書券上（借書券可在本館圖書出納處索取）交本館辦事人員，本館人員即可按碼取書，極爲敏捷。

編輯弁言

本館藏書泰半皆係經每次變亂後收集各機關及各學校之餘燼而成，故殘缺者居半。計其總數，共約十萬餘本。民國十三年間，曾經一次之整理編印有目録數册。但數年以還，書籍之佚失者什居二三，又以編法不善，書籍之排列，與目録之次第不相連貫，故書籍之凌亂與檢查之不易，依然如故。雖有目録，實等於無目録也。今年春，又得省政府教育廳撥發之時中書局及前武昌中央軍事政治學校圖書館書籍數千册，均未編目。檢閲之時，多感不便，乃以數月之工，將全館書館盡行加以整理，依現代圖書館之方法，分類編目，而先以是編付印，爲本館目録之第一期。

整理圖書，其重要工具，則爲分類。有分類則可統馭一切，各書均依類相次，不致凌亂。當本館編目之初，即擬自撰分類法。曾採各種科學分類法，爲其系統之建設；及各種圖書分類法，以成其子目，而謀合乎書籍之應用。其大綱爲：

0	總類	Generalities
1	中國經籍	Chinese Classics
2	哲學及宗教	Philosphy and Religion
3	史地	History and Geography
4	社會科學	Social Sciences
5	物理科學	Physical Sciences
6	生物科學	Biological Sciences
7	應用科學	Applied Sciences
8	美術	Fine Arts

9　語言及文學　　　　Language and Literature

等十大類。而以 Classification Decimale, Institute Internationalede Brexelle 之改定杜威分類法十進符號以孳衍之，爲數千子目。但以時間短促，一時未能寫定，編目在即，迫不及待。故經考慮之後，乃採杜威分類法(以下簡稱杜法)原本，共由有四：

(一)案我國圖書目録之學，創自劉向父子之七略别録，班氏删之，而成藝文一志。魏鄭獻校中秘之書而制中經。晉荀勖又因中經，更著新簿。始定四部之分，標甲乙之名。但其書已佚，其體例已不可見。其後流至江左，作者乃各出新裁，自爲部類，以王儉之七志，阮孝緒之七録爲最著。至唐長孫無忌等修隋書經籍志，乃裒集諸家，纂定經史子集之名。而後之言目録者，雖於其中子目，各有增減，要皆不甚相遠。迨至清乾隆間，開四庫館刊提要成，其法始大備，而世之言目録者，鮮不以此爲圭臬，駸駸乎有定一尊之勢。但自海通以還，每年出版之書，往往軼出四部之外，於是乃羣起而非之，以爲四部法不足概括書籍之全體，而應時而起者，則有吾師沈胡二氏之仿杜威十進分類法，及杜定友氏之圖書分類法。杜氏之書較爲晚出，其部類亦略爲詳備。

四庫法不足供現代圖書館之應用，固無論矣，而仿杜威十進分類法，及圖書分類法，亦皆不過將杜法原本，加以改纂。其改良之處固甚多，而凌亂之處，亦不減於杜法，且還不如其詳備。

(二)自編分類，本可因事制宜，自爲部類，但分類之事，言人人殊，所編者亦未必盡如人意，而於用者方面反增其類難。反不如採用一公認之分類法之較爲便利也。

(三)杜法之編纂，在五十餘年前，而此五十年間，各種科學之進步，一日千里，而杜法不免落後。然其足能成爲歐美圖書館界四大分類之一，而採用之爭先恐後者，良以其部屬及符號之簡明易記，有以致之。且又富於間展性，無論何種新科學之發明，均可依類附入，如一爐冶成，不生痕迹。

(四)當杜法出版之初，不過四十餘面之小册，今已至第十二版，内容增至一千二百餘面之多。其與時共進，及其部屬之詳備，於此可知。且國内大圖書館如北平清華學校圖書館，天津南開大學圖書館，上海東方圖書館，厦門大學圖書館等處，皆曾經採用，而得良好之結果。良以採用既多，知之者必衆。故於閲者之檢閲上，亦較爲便利。

本編採用杜法之理由，已如上所述。但採用之後，即將其子目中有不合乎我國書籍之應用者，則略爲變通，但以不失其本來面目爲原則。至其分類之理論及類例，原書俱在，可備檢查，兹不贅。

書籍之著録，自劉略而後，詳簡二體並行。詳者可以參稽彼此之異同，簡者可供檢閲之便利，前者流爲四庫總目，後者降爲文淵閣書目。皆各有體裁，不可偏廢。本編之著録各書，以書名爲主，而附以著者，出版處，出版家，出版年，全書之面數或本數，以及叢書之種類等等。使閲者於各書應有之概念，可一目瞭然。既不失之繁，亦不失之簡。

本編所收，皆係本館舊藏及新購補充之現代書籍四千餘種。至於館内所藏之借籍五千餘種(六萬餘册)，現已編成書名卡片目録，可備參考。其分類目録，不日亦可編成，俟財力充裕之時，即可付印，爲本館目録之第二期。

本編自編纂以至殺青，共歷時約二月。良以時間短促，編輯不易，錯謬之處，在所不免。而尤以文學類爲最凌亂，因付印過急，未遑糾正。至於校對，尤爲草率。希閲者時加指正。

中華民國十七年十二月馮漢驥謹識

分類大綱

000　總類

010　目録學
020　圖書館學
030　百科全書
040　普通論文總集
070　新聞學
080　叢書

100　哲學

100　哲學總論
　109　哲學史
110　形而上學
130　心靈學
　131　精神衛生學
　133　巫卜星
　134　催眠術
　136・7　兒童學
　137　睡眠　　夢

138 相術
140 哲學派別
150 心理學
160 邏輯
170 倫理學
171 原理
172 國家倫理
173 家庭倫理
174 職業倫理
175 遊戲倫理
176 性道德
177 社會倫理
178 各種刺激物「如烟酒問題等」
179 其餘倫理問題
180 中國哲學
181·1 印度哲學
182 西臘哲學
190 歐美哲學

200 宗教

220 基督教
221 基督教經典
267·3 基督教青年會
290 比較宗教學
291 神話學
294 佛教

299·5　道教

300　社會科學

310　統計學

312　人口論　生育節制論

320　政治學

321　政體論

323　人民國家之關係

324　選舉

325　殖民

327　外交

327·51——中國

328　立法

329　政黨

330　經濟學

331　勞動

332·1　銀行

332·4　貨幣

334　合作社

335　社會主義

336　財政

336·2　稅則　關稅

337　生産

339　消耗

340　法律

341　國際公法

341·1 國際會議
341·2 國際條約
341·3 戰時國際公法
341·4 國際刑法
341·5 國際私法
341·8 制外法權
342 憲法
342·51 中國憲法
343 刑法
345 中國法典
347·1 ——民法
347·7 ——商法
347·9 ——司法 法庭 訴訟 審判
349 外國法
350 政府行政
351 中央行政
335 地方行政
355 軍事學
354 社會 慈善事業
364 罪犯學
366 秘密會社
368 保險
369·4 童子軍
370 教育
371 教授法
372 初等教育 幼稚園
373 中學教育
374 課外教育

375　課程
376　婦女教育
377　大學教育　專門教育
379　義務教育　各國教育狀況
380　商業　交通
380・8　商業地理
382　國際貿易
383　郵政
385　鐵道　航業
390　禮俗
392　家庭問題　婚姻問題
395　禮節
396　婦女問題
398　諺語　歌謡

400　語言學

410　比較語言學
419　世界語
420—480　歐美各國語言
495　中國語言
495・11　國語
495・12　國音
495・121　註音字母
495・13　字典
495・15　文法

500　自然科學

510　數學

　511　算學

　512　代數

　513　幾何

　514　三角學

　156　解析幾何

　517　微積分

520　天文學

530　物理學

540　化學

549　鑛物學

550　地質學

570　生物學

　512　人類學

　575　進化論

580　植物學

590　動物學

600　應用科學

610　醫學

　611　解剖學

　612　生理學

612·6　性教育
613　衛生
614　公共衛生
615　藥物學
616　病理學　治療學
617　外科
618　婦孺科
619　獸醫
620　工程學
621　機械工程
625　土木工程
630　農業
633　作物學
634　果木及森林
635　園藝
636　牧蓄
638　蠶蜂
639　水産
640　家政
650　商業管理
657　簿記
658　商業經營
659·1　廣告
660　化學工藝
670　製造
680　手工
690　實用建築學

700 美術

701 美術概論
730 畫論 畫册 幾何畫
770 攝影術
780 音樂
790 遊藝 運動 田徑賽

800 文學

810 中國文學
  811 詩詞
  812 戲劇
  814 散文
  816 書牘
  818 詩文總集
  819 雜體詩文
820 英國文學
930 德國文學
840 法國文學
850 意大利文學
895·2 日本文學

900　歷史

930　古代史

940　歐洲史

　940・3　歐戰史

　942　英國史

　943　德國史

　944　法國史

　947　俄國史

950　東洋史

　951　中國史

　952　日本史

　954　印度史

000 總　　類

010 目録學

漢書藝文志講疏；顧實著· 015·51—K252
上海，商務，民十四年·再版·262面·「東南大學叢書」

漢書藝文志姚氏學；姚明輝著· 015·51—Y162
南京，共和書局，民十三年·

梁任公胡適之先生審定研究國學書目；梁啓超，胡適合著· 016·51—L251
上海，亞洲書局·35面·

三訂國學用書撰要；李笠著· 016·51—L189
北京，樸社出版經理部，民十六年·140面·

國學用書類述；支偉成著· 016·51—C62
上海，泰東，民十六年·

政治書報指南；北京清華學校政治學研究會編· 016·61—P223
北京，公記書局·150面·

020 圖書館學

現代圖書館序説；馬宗榮著· 020—M112
上海，商務，民十七年·63面·「學藝叢刊」

現代圖書館經營論；馬宗榮著· 020—M112
上海，商務，民十七年·206面·「學藝叢刊」

圖書館簡説；蔡瑩著· 020—T417

上海，中華，民十三年·3版·43面·

圖書館學概論；杜定友著· 020—T768

上海，商務，民十六年·初版·136面·「百科小叢書第一百五十四種」

圖書館通論；杜定友著· 020—T768

上海，商務，民十四年·53面·「上海圖書館協會叢書」

圖書館學；楊昭哲著· 020—y122

上海，商務，民十五年·2册·「尚志學會叢書」

兒童圖書館之研究；(日)今澤慈海，竹貫宜人合著，陳逸譯· 022·58—C675

上海，商務，民十三年·初版·108面·

圖書館管理法，(日)文部省編· 025—W262

東京，金港堂書籍株式會社，民元年·2册·

圖書館管理法；朱元善編· 370·8—C544

上海，商務，民六年·179面·「教育叢書」

圖書選擇法；杜定友著· 025·21—T768

上海，商務，民十五年·46面·「上海圖書館協會叢書」

美國圖書館事情；(日)文部省編· 027—W262

東京，金港堂書籍株洲式會社，民九年·283面·

028·6　讀書法

古書讀校法；陳鐘凡著· 028·6—C270

上海，商務，民十四年·147面·「東南大學叢書」

讀書的方法；胡適講演· 028·8—H414

武昌大學，民十四年·24面·

讀書法；鄒德謹，蔣正陸合著· 028·8—T697

上海，商務，民十六年·6版·42面·「通俗教育叢書」

讀書法；叟霍康原著，包懷白譯· 028·8—K824

上海，出版合作社，民十六年·初版·80面·

030 百科全書

少年百科全書；王昌謨等編· 030—W136
上海，商務，民十五年·20册

日用百科全書；王言綸等編· R
上海，商務，民十三年·13版·2册· 039·511—E140

日用百科全書補編；王岫盧等編· R
上海，商務，民十五年·再版·1515面· 039·511—E140

日用須知；商務印書館編· 039·51—S162
上海，商務，民十二年·278面·

040 普通論文彙集

現代論文叢刊；朱毓魁輯· 040—C839
上海，文明，民十四年·再版·4册·

常識文範；中華書局編譯所編· 040—C976
上海，中華，民五年·4册·

小學國文成績選粹；方瀏生輯· 040—F167
上海，中華，民十二年·13版·4册·乙編 丙編 丁編

世界知識新文庫；陸羽輯· 040—L425
上海，廣文，民十三年·3版·20册合訂·

國學概論；章炳麟講演，曹聚仁編· 040—C189
上海，泰東，民十四年·9版·162面·

中國學術討論；中國學術討論社編· 040—C976
上海，羣眾圖書公司，民十六年·第一集·

國故論叢；中華學藝社編· 040—C976

上海，商務，民十五年・171 面・「學藝叢刊」

二千五百年來之國學；范皕誨著・　040—F136

上海，世界學會，民十六年・31 面・「世界學會國學小叢書」

國故學討論集；許嘯天著・　040—H376

上海，羣學社，民十六年・3 册・

國故探新；唐鉞著・　404—T215

上海，商務，民十五年・309 面・

國學必讀；錢基博輯・　040—T601

上海，中華，民十三年・2 册・

新文學叢書；聞野鶴輯・　040—W241

上海，新文化書社，民十二年・444 面・

070　新聞學

新聞學撮要；戈公振著・　070—K127

上海，新聞記者聯歡會，民十四年・284 面・

應用新聞學；任白濤著・　070—J127

上海，亞東，民十五年・再版・208 面・「中國新聞學社叢書第一種」

新聞學總論；邵飄萍著・　070—S171

北京，京報館，民十三年・254 面・

實際應用新聞學；邵飄萍著・　070—S171

北京，京報館，民十二年・232 面・

實用新聞學；(美)休曼原著，史青譯・　070—Sh92

上海，廣學會，民二年・172 面・

新聞事業；東方雜誌社編・　080—T860—30

上海，商務，民十四年・3 版・92 面・「東方文庫」

新聞學大綱；伍超著・　070—W308

上海，商務，民十四年・222 面・

中國報學史；戈公振著・　079・51—K436

上海，商務，民十六年·初版·183面·

最近之五十年；上海申報館編· 079·51—S195

上海，申報館，民十二年·

中國新聞發達史；蔣國珍著· 079·51—T566

上海，世界，民十六年·74面·

080 叢書

百科小叢書· 080—P225

民十二年至十七年·細目分見各類·

表解叢書六十三種；上海科學書局編· 080—S155′

清光緒三十二年至民三年·細目分見各類·

中學世界百科全書；世界書局編· 080—S271

上海，世界·一函九册·

東方文庫八十一種；東方雜誌編· 080—T60

上海，商務，民十四年·內缺7，9，12，24，25，五種·細目分見各類·

100 哲學

100 哲學

東西文化批評；東方雜誌社編· 080—T860—311
　上海，商務，民十四年·3版·2册·「東方文庫第三十一種」

東西文化及其哲學；梁漱溟著· 100—L263
　上海，商務，民十一年·3版·384面·

泰西哲學説一臠；梁啓超著· 100—L251
　上海，商務·「飲冰室叢著第八種」

哲學入門；華文祺譯· 100—T221
　上海，商務，民十一年·3版·205面·

哲學研究；曾昭鐸著· 101—T521
　上海，羣學社，民十七年·142面·

哲學概論；陳大齊著· 102—C288
　北京大學出版部，民十一年·178面·

哲學概論；劉以鍾著· 102—L258
　上海，商務，民十三年·5版·122面·

哲學要領；蔡元培譯· 102—K211
　上海，商務，民十年·9版·83面·

哲學大綱；蔡元培著· 102—T417
　上海，商務，民十年·7版·81面·

簡易哲學綱要；蔡元培著· 102—T417
　上海，商務，民十三年·142面·

哲學問題；東方雜誌社編· 080—T860—33
上海，商務，民十四年·3版·90面·「東方文庫」

哲學問題；(英)羅素原著，黄凌霜譯· 104—R911

科學與哲學；張東蓀著· 104—C171
上海，商務，民十三年·90面·

哲學大辭書；(日)百科辭書編輯所編· R
東京，株式會社，大正四年·5版·4册· 103—P225

109 哲學史

哲學史；(美)杜威講，劉伯明譯· 109—D515
上海，泰東，民十年·3版·80面·

西洋哲學史；瞿世英譯· 109—C964
上海，商務，民十一年·2册·「通俗叢書」

西洋哲學史；黄懺華著· 109—H471
上海，商務，民十二年·287面·

西洋古代中世哲學史大綱；劉伯明著· 108—L372
上海，中華，民十一年·再版·224面·「新文化叢書」

近代西洋哲學史大綱；劉伯明著· 109—L372
上海，商務，民十一年·3版·138面·「新文化叢書」

現代思潮；(日)桑本巖翼原著，南庶熙譯· 109—S126
上海，商務，民十一年·147面·「時代叢書」

歐洲思想大觀；(日)金子築水原著，林科棠譯· 109—C669
上海，商務，民十三年·204面·「新智識叢書」

歐洲思想大觀；(日)金子築水原著，蔣桑漢譯· 109—C669
上海，泰東，民十五年·252面·

110 形而上學

形而上學序論；(法)柏格森原著，楊正宇譯· 110—B454

上海，商務，民十年·再版·10面·「尚志學會書」

宇宙與物質；東方雜誌社編·　080—T860

上海，商務，民十四年·3版·83面·「東方文庫」　47

創化論；張東蓀譯·　113—B454

上海，商務，民十一年·4版·2册·「尚志學會叢書」

羅素思想自由；(英)B. Russell原著，朱枕薪譯·　110—R911

上海，民智，民十五年·再版·38面·「新中國叢書」

思想自由史；(英)伯利原著，宋桂煌譯·　110—B959

上海，民智，民十六年·216面·

近世我之自覺史：一名新理想哲學及其背景；　110—C222

(日)朝永三十郎原著，蔣方震譯·

上海，商務，民十三年·再版·153面·

人生觀之論戰；郭夢良編·　120—K425

上海，泰東，民十五年·再版·

科學與人生觀；亞東圖書館編·　120—Y116

上海，亞東，民十六年·5版·2册·

吳稚暉的人生觀；吳稚暉著·　110—W281

上海，羣眾圖書公司，民十五年·114面·

批評吳稚暉的一個新信仰的宇宙觀及人生觀；張亦鏡著·　110—C158

廣州，美華浸會印書局，民十四年·96面·

人生觀的科學；釋太虛著·　110—T139

上海，泰東，民十五年·3版·97面·

西洋哲學概論；五平陵著·　109—W153

上海，泰東，民十三年·312面·

近代思想解剖；商務印書館譯·　109—T880

上海，商務，民十年·再版·「新智識叢書」

近代思想；過耀根著·　109—S435

上海，商務，民十四年·7版·2册·「尚志學會叢書」

現代哲學一臠；東方雜誌社編·　080—T860

上海，商務，民十四年·3版·90面·「東方文庫」　34

近代哲學家；東方雜誌社編· 080—T860
上海，商務，民十三年·再版·73面·「東方文庫」 38

一個唯情論者的宇宙觀及人生觀；朱謙之著· 113—C821
上海，泰東，民十三年·178面·

唯情哲學；袁家驊著· 120—Y416
上海，泰東，民十三年·288面·

認識論淺説；范壽康著· 080—P225
上海，商務，民十六年·61面·「百科小叢書」 145

112 哲學方法論

哲學中之科學方法；(英)羅素原著，王星拱譯· 192·9—R911
上海，商務，民十一年·再版·343面·

130 心身鍛練法

心理療法；(日)井上圓了原著，盧謙譯· 610·8—T347
上海，醫學書局，民九年·再版·67面·「丁氏醫學叢書」 131

静坐三年；(日)本能武太原著，華文祺譯· 131—A147
上海，商務，民十四年·7版·244面·

心身鍛練法；(日)江閒俊一網野靈峯原著，雲鶴譯· 131—C495
上海，商務，民九年·3版·76面·

因是子静坐法；蔣維喬著· 131—C524
上海，商務，民十三年·20版·54面·

静坐心理；雷通羣譯· 131—C550
上海，商務，民十一年，再版·93面·

長壽哲學；(日)鈴木美山原著，蔣維喬譯· 131—L346
上海，商務，民九年·3版·273面·

樂天却病法；劉仁航著· 131—L364
上海，商務，民十一年·8版·2冊·

心身强健秘訣；劉仁航著· 131—T277
上海，商務，民十四年·6版·170面·

身心調和法；(日)藤田靈齊原著，劉仁航譯· 613—T278
上海，商務，民十三年·6版·69面·

精神衛生論；秦同培譯· 131—T649
上海，商務，民九年·3版·152面·

精神與身體神經健全法；鄒德謹譯· 131—T697
上海，商務，民六年·33面·「通俗教育叢書」

强健身心法；董蘭伊著· 131—T854
上海，商務，民十五年·12面·「衛生叢書之一」

岡田式静坐法；吴德亮譯· 131—W296
上海，商務，民十五年·4版·72面·

133　巫卜星

妖怪學講義總論；(日)井上圓了原著，蔡元培譯· 133—T664
上海，商務，民十一年·8版·198面·

穿透真傳；張鳳藻著· 133·3—C152
上海，文明，民十五年·70面·

六壬尋原；張純照著· 133·3—C152
上海，文明，民十四年·3冊·

神峯通考；張楠著· 133·3—C161
上海，文明，民十五年·2冊·

煙波釣叟歌；(宋)趙普著· 133·3—C21
上海，文明，民十四年·88面·

六壬指南；陳良謨著· 133·3—C279
上海，文明，民十四年·2冊·

河洛理數；陳摶著· 133·3—C288

上海，文明，民十五年·4 册·

六壬鬼撮脚；誠意伯著· 133·3—C362

上海，文明，民十四年·42 面·

奇門遁甲統宗；(漢)諸葛亮著· 133·3—C811

上海，文明，民十四年·4 册·

乾坤法竅；范宜賓著· 133·3—F1432

上海，文明，民十五年·2 册·

羅經解定；胡國楨著· 133·3—H405

上海，文明，民十五年·2 册·

陽宅大全；壑居士著· 133·3—I135

上海，文明，民十五年·3 册·

選擇正宗；顧鍾秀著· 133·3—K246

上海，文明，民十五年·2 册·

奇門五總龜；郭子晟著· 133·3—K421

上海，文明，民十四年·240 面·

滴天髓窮寶鑑；劉基著· 133·3—L356

上海，文明，民十五年·152 面·

張星果宗；陸生著· 133·3—L434

上海，文明，民十五年·4 册·

星平會海；霞陽水中龍著· 133·3—P382

上海，文明，民十五年·4 册·

梅花易數；邵雍著· 133·2—S171

上海，文明，民十四年·2 册·

五行大義；蕭吉著， 133·3—S386

上海，文明，民十五年·112 面·

淵海子平，子平真銓；徐升著· 133·3—S481

上海，文明，民十五年·2 册·

地理知本金鎖秘；鄧恭著· 133·3—T264

上海，文明，民十五年·2 册·

地理録要；蔣平階著· 133·3—T570

上海，文明，民十五年・2 册・

董公選要覽；董潛著・　133・3—T857

上海，文明，民十五年・62 面・

靈棋經；東方朔著・　133・3—T860

上海，文明，民十四年・102 面・

三命通會；萬民英著・　133・3—W125

上海，文明，民十五年・4 册・

太清神鑑；王朴著・　133・3—W158

上海，文明，民十五年・106 面・

羅經透解；王道亨著・　133・3—W153

上海，文明，民十五年・2 册・

陰陽二宅全書；姚廷鑾輯・　133・3—Y167

上海，文明，民十五年・4 册・

增删卜易；野鶴老人著・　133・3—Y19

上海，文明，民十四年・3 册・

牙牌神數；岳慶著・　133・3—Y310

上海，文明，民十四年・54 面・

神骨冰鑑；白鶴山人著・　133・6—P226

上海，文明，民十四年・52 面・

地理末學；紀大奎著・　133・8—C379

上海，文明，民十五年・2 册・

郭璞葬經水龍經；郭璞著・　133・8—K426

上海，文明，民十五年・230 面・

平沙玉尺經；劉秉忠著・　133・8—L372

上海，文明，民十五年・166 面・

陽宅紫府寶鑑；劉文淵著・　133・8—L377

上海，文明，民十五年・100 面・

地理正宗；蔣平階著・　133・8—T570

上海，文明，民十五年・2 册・

134 催眠術

催眠術與心靈現象；東方雜誌社編· 080—T860
上海，商務，民十四年·3版·87面·「東方文庫」 53

近世催眠術；(日)熊代彥太郎原著，華文祺，丁福保合譯· 610·8—T347
上海，醫學書局，民八年·3版·110面·「丁氏醫學叢書」 134

實用催眠術；龐靖編· 134—P177
上海，中華，民十二年·再版·84面·

千里眼研究法；鮑方洲著· 134—P185ce
上海，商務，民十二年·73面·

催眠新法；鮑方洲著· 134—P185cm
上海，中華，民十一年·6版·82面·

135 夢的研究

笑與夢；東方雜誌社編· 080—T860
上海，商務，民十四年 3版·80面·「東方文庫」 52

夢；舒新城編· 135—S313
上海，中華，民十六年·114面·「常識叢書」

136·7 兒童學

兒童性向的測驗報告；教育雜誌社編· 370·8—C544
上海，商務，民十四年·92面·「教育叢書」 62

兒童研究；朱元善編· 370·8—C541
上海，商務，民十一年·再版·108面·「教育叢書第二集第四編」 2·4

兒童心理之研究；陳鶴琴著· 136·7—C275
上海，商務，民十四年·2冊·「師範叢書」

兒童心理學；(德)R. Gaupp原著，陳大齊譯· 136·7—C236
上海，商務，民十五年·214面·「學藝叢書」

兒童學；(日)關寬之原著，朱孟遷，邵人模合譯· 136·7—K296
上海，商務，民十一年·355 面·

兒童學概論；(日)關寬一原著，程王雪莩譯· 136·7—K296
上海，公民書局，民十一年·129 面·「公民叢書」

兒童學概論；凌冰著· 136·7—L341
上海，商務，民十一年·3 版·156 面·

兒童論；(美)密魯原著，余家菊譯· 136·7—M615
上海，商務，民十一年·3 版·78 面·

兒童心理學綱要；艾華著· 136·7—N137
上海，商務，民十二年·94 面·

兒童的新觀念；曾展謨譯· 136·7—T521
上海，商務，民十六年·324 面·「師範叢書」

青春期的心理學；斐立特屈雷西原著，湯子庸譯· 136·7—T674
上海，商務，民十五年·再版·259 面·「新智識叢書」

幼稺之意義；(美)John Fiske 原著，王克仁譯· 136·72—F547
上海，中華，民十一年·26 面·

138　相術

相理衡真；陳淡埜著· 138—C288
上海，文明，民十四年·4 册·

神相全编；陳搏著· 138—C288
上海，文明，民十四年·6 册·

神相水鏡集；范文元著· 138—F134
上海，文明，民十四年·2 册·

柳莊相法；袁柳莊著· 138—L380
上海，文明，民十四年·2 册·

麻衣相法； 138—M125
上海，文明，民十四年·2 册·

演禽三世相法；袁天綱選· 138—Y422

上海，文明，民十四年・2冊・

神相鐵關刀；破納雲谷山人著・ 138—P465

上海，文明，民十四年・112面・

140 哲學派別

赫克爾一元哲學；馬君武譯・ 147—H118

上海，中華，民十年・4版・2冊・「新文化叢書」

無元哲學；朱謙之著・ 149—C821

上海，泰東，民十一年・161面・

現實主義哲學研究；(日)金子筑水原著，蔣徑三譯・ 149・2—C661

上海，商務，民十七年・98面・

實用主義；(美)乾姆斯著・孟憲承譯・ 149・9—J237

上海，商務，民十三年，203面・「尚志學會叢書」

實驗主義；(英)莫越原著，方東美譯・ 149・9—W962

上海，中華，民十一年・3版・100面・「哲學叢書」

150 心理學

心理學表解；上海科學書局編・ 080—S155

上海，科學書局，清光緒三十二年・38面・「表解叢書」 150

心理學大綱；陳大齊著・ 150—C288

上海，商務，民十三年・9版・216面・「北京大學叢書」

迷信與心理；陳大齊著・ 150—C288

北京大學出版部，民十一年・19面・「新潮叢書」

心理學概論；(丹)海甫定原著，(英)龍特士原譯，王國維譯・ 150—H675

上海，商務，民十五年・8版・484面・「哲學叢書」

心理學；陸志韋編· 150—L425
上海，商務，民十四年·258 面·

心理學初步；舒新城編· 150—S313
上海，中華，民十二年·205 面·「青年叢書」

心理學大意；舒新城編· 150—S313
上海，中華，民十五年·106 面·「常識叢書」

心理學導言；吳頌臯譯· 150—W961
上海，商務，民十二年·123 面·「通俗叢書」

心理學之哲學的研究；教育雜誌社編· 370·8—C544
上海，商務，民十四年·78 面·「教育叢書」 80

心理學；杜定友，王引民合編· 150—T768
上海，中華，民十四年·再版·154 面·

心理學原理；吳康著· 150—W287
上海，商務，民十一年·再版·154 面·

心理學各方面之研究；教育雜誌社編· 370·8—C544
上海，商務，民十四年·82 面·「教育叢書」 81

心理學論叢；東方雜誌社編· 080—T860
上海，商務，民十三年·84 面·「東方文庫」 36

郭任遠心理學論叢；郭任遠，吳頌臯等合譯· 150—K123
上海，開明，民十七年·286 面·「黎明學社叢書」

實用心理學要義；鄭康明編· 150—C354
上海，亞東，民十三年·64 面·

教育心理學大意；廖世承譯· 150—C725
上海，中華，民十四年·9 版·254 面·「教育叢書」

藝術鑑賞的心理；管容德譯· 150—F882
上海，梁溪圖書館，民十五年·93 面·

心理學論文集；高覺敷著· 150—K166
上海，商務，民十五年·432 面·「民譯叢書第二種」

人類的行爲；郭任遠著· 150—K423
上海，商務，民十二年·292 面·

現代心理學之趨勢；舒新城譯． 150—M784
上海，中華，民十四年．再版．266 面．「新文化叢書」

商業心理學；(日)大野辰見原著，高書田譯． 150—T134
上海，商務，民十三年．278 面．「現代教育名著」

心的初現；李小峯譯． 150—T38
北京，北新書局．78 面．

現代心理；陶孟和編． 150—T248
北京，太人出版部，民十二年．再版．194 面．「新潮叢書」

心理學講義；(日)長尾植太郎原著，蔣維喬譯． 150—I568
上海，商務，民元年．104 面．

行爲主義心理學；臧玉淦譯． 150—W334
上海，商務，民十五年．再版．390 面．「心理學叢書」

動的心理學；(美)烏特窪原著，潘梓年譯． 150—W879
上海，商務，民十三年．295 面．「尚志學會叢書」

吳偉士心理學；謝循初譯． 150—W879m
上海，中華，民十三年．「少年中國學會叢書」

女子心理學；楊鄂聯，朱賜鈞合編． 150—Y134
上海，商務，民十三年．5 版．179 面．

感覺之分析；馬黑原著，張庭英譯． 152—M118
上海，商務，民十三年．286 面．「哲學叢書」

思維術；(美)杜威原著，劉伯明譯． 153—D515
上海，中華，民十一年．5 版．229 面．「新文化叢書」

實用記憶法；郭烋著． 154—K427
上海，大東，民十三年．3 版．40 面．

笑之研究；(法)H. Bergson 原著，張聞天譯． 157—B454
上海，商務，民十二年．201 面．「尚志學會叢書」

戀愛心理研究；斯丹大爾原著，任伯濤譯． 157—S589
上海，亞東，民十五年．再版．24 面．

變態心理學概論；教育雜誌社編． 370．8—C544
上海，商務，民十四年．78 面．「教育叢書」 82

犯罪心理學；(日)寺田精一原著，張廷健譯· 080—P225
上海，商務，民十六年·126 面·「百科小叢書」 124

瘋狂心理；(英)哈臧原著，李小峯，潘梓年合譯· 158—H103
上海，北新，民十六年·再版·200 面·「北新叢書之一」

本能論；趙演著· 158—C220
民十六年·「民鑑叢書第三種」

柯爾文氏本能及習慣説；樊炳清著· 370，8—C544
上海，商務，民十一年·3 版·71 面·「教育叢書第一彙」 1·7

意志修養法；鄒德謹，蔣正陸合著· 159—T697
上海，商務，民十二年·5 版·66 面·「通俗教育叢書」

160　邏輯

名學稽古；東方雜誌社編· 080—T860
上海，商務，民十四年·3 版·85 面·「東方文庫」 37

邏輯概論；枯雷頓原著，劉奇譯· 160—C862
上海，商務，民十五年·555 面·「哲學叢書」

名學淺説；(英)耶方斯原著，嚴復譯· 160—J351
上海，商務，民十四年·13 版·141 面·

穆勒名學；(英)穆勒納翰原著，嚴復譯· 160—W61
上海，商務，民十二年·3 册·

名學綱要；屠孝實著· 160—T793
上海，商務，民十四年·再版·240 面·「學藝叢書」

論理學；王熾昌，洪鋆合著· 160—W136
上海，中華·民十五年·7 版·107 面·

論理學；王振瑄編· 160—W136
上海，商務，民十四年·108 面·

科學方法論；王星拱著· 160—W156
北京，北京大學出版部，民九年·324 面·「新潮叢書第一種」

邏輯與數學邏輯論；汪奠基著・ 160—W175
　上海，商務，民十六年・268 面・「科學叢書」
意見及信仰；(法)黎明原著，馮承鈞譯・ 163—L492
　上海，商務，民十一年・395 面・「尚地學會叢書」

170　倫理學

哲學與倫理；教育雜誌社編・ 370・8—C544
　上海，商務，民十四年・113 面・「教育叢書」 79
倫理學表解；上海科學書局編譯所編・ 080—S155
　上海，科學，清光緒三十三年・51 面・ 170
倫理學淺説；余家菊著・ 080—P225
　上海，商務，民十六年・40 面・「百科小叢書」 133
倫理學；(日)法貴慶次郎講義，胡庸誥等合編・ 170—H419
　湖北官書處，清光緒三十一年・164 面・「教科叢編」
倫理學導言；(美)薛蕾原著，朱進譯・ 170—S412
　上海，商務，民十一年・3 版・232 面・
倫理學；孫貴定編・ 170—S518
　上海，商務，民十二年・64 面・
道德的將來；(英)C. E. M. Jad 原著，張東民譯・ 080—J57
　上海，北新書局・90 面・「明日叢書」 170

170.9　倫理學史

西洋倫理學史；楊昌濟譯・ 170・9—C395
　北京，北京大學，民九年・再版・271 面・
西洋倫理學小史；賈豐臻著・ 170・9—C476
　上海，商務，民十四年・116 面・「新智識叢書」
西洋倫理學史；(日)三浦籐原著，謝晉青譯・ 170・9—S121
　上海，商務，民十四年・411 面・「哲學叢書」

中國倫理學史；（日）三浦藤原著，張宗元等合譯·　170·9—Z121
　上海，商務，民十五年·489 面·「哲學叢書」
中國倫理學史；蔡元培著·　170·9—T417
　上海，商務，民十三年·9 版·200 面·

171　倫理學原理

倫理學原理；蔡元培譯·　170—P285
　上海，商務，民十三年·7 版·218 面·
西洋倫理主義述評；東方雜誌社編·　080—T860
　上海，商務，民十三年·再版·84 面·「東方文庫」　35
近世倫理學説；朱元善著·　370·8—C544
　上海，商務，民十一年·3 版·82 面·「教育叢書第一集第三篇」　1·3
現代思想與倫理問題；（德）倭鑑原著·鄭次川譯·　171—W226
　上海，公民書局，民十年·84 面·「公民叢書」
中國先哲人性論；江恒源著·　171—C501
　上海，商務，民十五年·253 面·「哲學叢書」
人生哲學；李石琴著·　170—L196
　上海，商務，民十六年·再版·上卷·
人生哲學；舒新城編·　171—S313
　上海，中華，民十五年·7 版·
人生哲學；張墨池著·　170—C164
　上海，愛智學社，民十六年·3 版·107 面·
人生哲學與唯物史觀；徐六幾，郭夢良等合譯·　170—K168
　上海，商務，民十一年·172 面·
倫理與唯物史觀；（德）考次原著，董亦湘譯·　171—K168
　教育研究社，民十六年·190 面·
自然道德；（法）戴森柏原著，王岫盧譯·　171—D459
　上海，公民書局，民十年·120 面·「公民叢書」
德育問題；王克仁，邵爽秋合譯·　170—P182

上海，中華，民十一年·3版·62面·「教育小叢書」

德育鑑；梁啓超著· 170—L251

上海，商務·170面·「飲冰室叢著第二種」

人生之意義與價值；(德)倭鑑原著，余家菊譯· 171—EU22

上海，中華，民十五年·6版·156面·

德育原理；(美)杜威原著，元尚仁譯· 170—D515

上海，中華，民十年·再版·60面·「教育小叢書」

新道德論；(日)浮田和民原著，周宏業，羅普合譯· 170—F231

上海，商務，民十四年·7版·87面·「尚志學會叢書」

實驗主義倫理學；周谷城編· 170—C778

上海，商務，民十三年·再版·136面·

品性論；秦同培著· 170—T648

上海，中華，民九年·3版·296面·

勤儉論；中華書局編譯所編· 171—SM44

上海，中華，民七年·6版·116面·

職分論；(英)斯邁爾原著，蔣方震譯· 170—SM43

上海，商務，民十六年·232面·

職分論；葉農生著· 170—Y186

上海，中華，民九年·3版·182面·

處世哲學；東方雜誌社編· 086—T860—43

上海，商務，民十四年·3版·62面·「東方文庫」

人鏡；于傳林著· 170—Y360

上海，中華，民十二年·4版·

一種人生觀；馮友蘭著· 080—P225

上海，商務，民十年·48面·「百科小叢書第七二種」 72

青年之人生觀；蔣維喬著· 171—T568

上海，商務，民十三年·3版·37面·

172　國家倫理

廉潔問題；劉湛恩著· 172—L356

上海，青年協會書局，民十六年·76面·「公民教育叢刊第二十二種」

法國公民教育；華南圭譯· 172·1—B461

上海，商務，民二年·513面·

歐美列強國民性之訓練；陳壽凡著· 172·1—C287

上海，商務，民十二年·266面·

公民學課程大綱；周之淦等合譯· 172·1—C771

上海，商務，民十二年·再版·168面·「中華教育改進社叢書」

公民學教科書；周鯁生著· 172·1—C778

上海，商務，民十二年·2册·

公民常識；黄祖度著· 172·1—H486

長沙，中華，民十一年·再版·

公民道德；高陽，陶彙曾合著· 172·1—K179

上海，商務，民十四年·再版·第一册·

胆汁録；李警眾著· 172·1—L182

上海，泰東，民九年·74面·

新民説；梁啓超著· 172·1—L251

上海，商務·2册·「飲冰室叢書第一種」

國民之修養；陸費逵著· 172·1—L426

上海，中華，民十一年·再版·40面·

公民鑑；(美)馬維克，斯密司原著，蘇錫元譯· 172·1—M118

上海，商務，民五年·再版·272面·

國民立身訓；謝无量編· 171—S125

上海，中華，民六年·222面·

自助論；商務印書館編譯所編· 172·1—SM43

上海，商務，民二年·3版·

公民教育論；朱元善編· 372·1—C5443·9

上海，商務，民六年·54面·「教育叢書第三集第九篇」

公民教育；(美)D. snedden原著，陶履恭譯· 172·1—SN22

上海，商務，民十二年·347面·「現代教育名著」

公民學；戴厚培著· 172·1—T23

上海，中華，民十年·178 面·

公民模範；翁長鐘著· 172·1—W271

上海，中華·266 面·

172·4 戰時倫理

戰爭哲學；東方雜誌社編· 080—T860

上海，商務，民十三年·再版·77 面·「東方文庫」

將來之大戰；杭立武著· 172·4—Ir9

上海，商務，民十二年·再版·157 面·「新智識叢書之十九」

戰爭與進化；過耀根著· 172·4—K433

上海，商務，民十四年·4 版·75 面·「新智識叢書」

戰爭的原因結果及其防止法；青年協會書報部譯· 172·4—P143

上海，青年協會書局，民十四年·118 面·「非戰小叢刊」

戰時之正義；(英)羅素原著，太朴譯· 172·4—R911

上海，商務，民十二年·再版·150 面·「共學社羅素叢書」

173 家庭倫理

私生子問題；曹雪松著· 173—T182

上海，羣眾圖書公司，民十七年·54 面·

母道；歐陽溥存譯· 173·5—L136

上海，中華，民十年，8 版·118 面·「女學叢書之一」

中國婦女美談；盧壽籛著· 173·5—N406

上海，中華，民十年·3 版·300 面·「女學叢書」

174 職業倫理

商業道德；盛在珦著· 174—C322

上海，商務，民五年·3 版·88 面·

少年弦韋；范褘著· 174—F134S

上海，青年協會書局，民十三年·四版·212面·

他山石語；范褘著· 174—F434t

上海，青年協會書報部，民十年·88面·「皕誨叢著之一」

工業主義之倫理；(美)華德演講，簡又文譯· 174—H442

上海，北新書局·138面·

177　社會倫理

交際術；鄒德謹著· 177—T697

上海，商務，民九年·6版·58面·

177·6　戀愛論

新性道德討論集；章錫琛輯· 176—C190

上海，開明，民十五年·再版·217面·「婦女問題叢書」

近代戀愛觀；(日)厨川白村原著，夏丏尊譯· 177·6—C863

上海，開明，民十七年·207面·

戀愛論；(日)厨川白村原著，任白濤譯· 177·6—C863

上海，學術研究會總會，民十三年·3版·82面·「學術研究會叢書」

革命與戀愛；洪瑞釗著· 177·6—H522

上海，民智，民十七年·90面·

近代戀愛名論；任白濤輯· 177·6—J127

上海，亞東，民十六年·268面·

三角戀愛解決法；曹雪松輯· 177·6—T474

上海，羣眾，民十七年·54面·

178　其餘倫理問題

青年修養録；趙鉦鐸輯· 178—C201

上海，商務，民十四年·11版·

青年之友；江蘇第一師範學校編· 178—C514

上海，天一書局，民十二年·186面·「江蘇第一師範叢書」

生活系統；周谷城著· 178—C778

上海，商務，民十三年·184面·「新智識叢書」

淑世新語；胡貽穀著· 178—H406

上海，青年協會書報部·民七年·3版·34面·

克已論；葉農生譯· 178—Y186

上海，中華，民八年·4版·90面·

生活藝術化之是非；徐蔚南著· 179·7—S483

上海，世界書局，民十七年·再版·59面·

畜德録；席啓圖輯· 170—S368

上海，掃葉山房·一函六册·

人格修養法，獨立自尊；鄒德謹，蔣正陸合著· 170—T697

上海，商務，民十二年·7版·58面·「通俗教育叢書」

181·1 中國哲學

東方文化；唐大圓輯· 181·1—T213

上海，泰東，民十五年·12面·

中國哲學史；趙蘭坪輯· 181·1—C209

上海暨南學校出版部，民十四年·3册·

中國哲學史；謝无量著· 181·1—S425

上海，中華，民十七年·再版·458面·

中國哲學史大綱；胡適著· 181·1—H414

上海，商務，民十一年·8版·「北京大學叢書」

中國古代學術思想變遷史；梁啓超著· 181·1—251

上海，羣眾，民十五年·再版·

清代學術概論；梁啓超著· 181·18—L251

上海，商務，民十一年·3版·183面·「共學社史學叢書」

周易哲學；朱謙之著· 181·1—C821

上海，學術研究會，民十五年·3版·「學術研究會叢書」

古學巵言；朱謙之著·　181·1—C821

上海，泰東，民十三年·3版·282面·

理學常識；徐敬修輯·　181·1—S476

上海，大東，民十四年·再版·118面·

子學常識；徐敬修輯·　181·1—S476

上海，大東，民十四年·再版·158面·

孔子與釋迦；蔣維喬著·　181·1—T573

上海，商務，民十四年·再版·33面·

儒道兩家關係論；(日)津田左右吉原著，李繼煌譯·　181·1—T644

上海，商務，民十五年·95面·「國學小叢書」

儒教與現代思潮；鄭子雅著·　181·101—C351

上海，商務，民十五年·再版·「國學小叢書」

孟子研究；王治心著·　181·102—W136

上海，羣學社，民十七年·225面·

老子集訓；陳柱輯·　181·1031—C270

上海，商務，民十七年·132面·

老子哲學的研究和批評；程辟金著·　181·104—C244

上海，民智，民十五年·

莊子；莊周著·　181·1034—C916

上海，商務，民十五年·108面·「學生國學叢書」

墨子十論；陳柱著·　181·104—C270

上海，商務，民十七年·238面·

楊墨哲學；蔣竹莊著·　181·104—T561

上海，商務，民十七年·202面·

墨子學案；梁啓超著·　181·1041—L251

上海，商務，民十五年·4版·177面·「共學社哲人傳記叢書」

墨經校釋；梁啓超著·　181·1041—L251

上海，商務，民十三年·3版·163面·

墨學微；梁啓超著·　181·1041—L251

上海，商務·104 面·「飲冰室叢著第三種」

韓非予法意；夏忠道著· 181·1066—H256

上海，静協會書局，民十六年·122 面·

標點註解管子通釋；管仲著· 181·1061—K311

上海，泰東，民十三年·234 面·

王充哲學；王充著· 181·12—W137

上海，中華，民十七年·再版·230 面·「學生叢書之一」

傳習録；王守仁著· 181·171—W155

上海，商務，民十六年·178 面·「學生國學叢書」

陽明學派；謝无量著· 181·172—S426

上海，商務，民七年·再版·196 面·「學生叢書之一」

謙之文存；朱謙之著· 181·19—C821C

上海，泰東，民十五年·二册合訂·

自由史觀；太虛法師著· 181·19—T139

上海，羣眾圖書公司，民十七年·98 面·

李石岑論文集；李石岑著· 181·1—196

上海，商務，民十三年·226 面·

181·4 印度哲學

印度哲學概論；梁漱溟著· 181·4—263

上海，商務，民十一年·3 版·313 面·「北京大學叢書之五」

塔果爾及其森林哲學；馮飛譯· 181·4—T129

上海，商務，民十一年·223 面·「時代叢書」

人生之實現；(印)太戈爾著· 181·4—T129

上海，泰東，162 面·

182 西臘哲學

希臘哲學史；何子恒著· 182—H199

上海，光華，民十五年·26 面·

柏拉圖之理想圖；吳獻書著· 184·1—P697
上海，商務，民九年·再版·2册·「尚志學會叢書」

亞理斯多德；(英)鐵聶耳原著，劉衡如譯· 185·1—T212
上海，中華，民十一年·3版·182面·「哲學叢書」

193　德國哲學

倭伊鑑哲；(德)Meyrick Booth 原著，瞿世英譯· 193·9—B644
上海，商務，民十四年·159面·「尚志學會叢書」

杜里舒及其學説；費鴻年著· 193·9—F186
上海，商務，民十三年·140面·「學藝書刊」

杜里舒講演録；講學社編· 193·9—D831
上海，商務，民十二年·

實生論大旨；(德)杜里舒原著，江紹原譯· 193·9—D831
上海，亞東，民十二年·234面·

194　法國哲學

法蘭西學術史略；(法)柏爾格森原著，李璜譯· 194—B454
上海，亞東，民十年·118面·

柏格森；(法)格柏森著，湯澈，葉芬可譯· 194·9—B454
上海，泰東，民十一年·102面·

柏格森之哲學；劉延陵譯· 194·9—B454P
上海，商務，民十二年·110面·「新智識叢書」

物質與記憶；(法)柏格森原著，張東蓀譯· 194·9—B454W
上海，商務，民十三年·再版·「尚志學會叢書」

心力；(法)柏格森原著，胡國鈺譯· 194·9—B454S
上海，商務，民十三年·222面·

197・9 俄國哲學

托爾斯泰學說；愛爾伯原著，謝晉青譯・ 197・9—T588

上海，新文化書社，民十四年・13版・80面・

200　宗教

200　宗教

宗教問題；(日)安島健原著，甘浩澤譯· 200—A141
上海，商務，民十四年·109 面·「百科問題小叢書」

諸教參考；(美)赫士譯，于漢清筆記· 200—K294
上海，廣學會，民十五年·6 版·88 面·

宗教基礎；S. A. soob 原著，陳楚譯· 201—C773
上海，商務，民十四年·98 面·「新智識叢書」

新宗教觀；簡又文著· 201—M422
上海，青年協會書局，民十二年·再版·180 面·「宗教研究叢書」

神的哲學；袁定安著· 201—Y422
上海，履學會，民十三年·180 面·

四教考略；格然特著· 204—G767
上海，廣學會，民十五年·

宗教教學法大綱；彭長琳著· 207—P271
上海，廣學會，民十四年·160 面·

迷信與科學；東方雜誌社編· 080—T860—51
上海，商務，民十四年·3 版·70 面·「東方文庫」

210-280　基督教

基督教與進化；(美)富司迪原著，王善治譯· 215—F786

上海，美以美會全國書報部，民十二年·135面·

科學與基督教信仰；胡貽穀著· 215—H419

上海，青年協會書局，民十四年·再版·52面·「基督教叢書」

科學的基督化思想；(美)張好美原著，謝頌羔，米星如合譯· 215—J643

上海，中國主日學合會，民十四年·101面·

舊新約間之宗教；(美)查理原著，郁孟高，黄葉秋合譯· 220—C38

北京，聖公書局室，民十五年·110面·

舊約歷史；陳金，勵德厚合著· 220·9—W632

上海，廣學會，民十五年·4版·194面·

太初；潘志蓉· 222·1—M259

上海，廣學會，民二年·168面·

以色列諸先知；力戈登原著，莊霜根譯· 224—P544

上海，廣學會，民十三年·166面·

舊約聖經婦女；狄珍珠原編，張仲温譯· 225—M414C

上海，廣學會，民十三年·152面·

新約婦女；狄珍珠原編，張仲温譯· 225—M414S

上海，廣學會，民十三年·107面·

訓十二使徒真詮；(英)司密氏原著，(英)季理斐譯· 226—B83

上海，廣學會，民十三年·230面·

使徒保羅言行録；(英)司密氏原著，(英)季理斐譯· 226—Sm54

上海，廣學會，民十三年·224面·

國外佈道英雄集李提摩太傳；(英)蘇爾特原著，梅益盛譯· 226—S064

上海，廣學會，民十三年·100面·

耶穌比喻講義；太樂爾原著，門愛蘭譯· 226·8—T219

上海，廣學會，民十四年·再版·86面·

闢基督抹殺論；(英)殷雅各原著，聶紹經譯· 230—Iu4

上海，廣學會，民十四年·86面·

現代教基督思想與中國文化；胡貽穀著· 230—H419

上海，青年協會書會，民十四年·72面·

基督抹殺論；(日)幸德秋水原著，貍弔疋譯· 230—H440

上海，東亞，民十三年·114 面·

近代基督教思潮；李志實著· 230—L199

上海，廣學會，77 面·

基督教與新中國；羅運炎著· 230—L399

上海，美以美會全國書報部，民十二年·二版·106 面

安慰人的妙訣；（英）米路爾原著，（英）季理斐譯· 230—M615

上海，廣學會，民十二年·再版·69 面·

基督與現代問題；如雅德著· 230—R843

上海，青年協會書局，民十四年·62 面·

評基督抹殺論；洗嗣莊等合著· 230—S211

上海，青年協會書局，民十六年·148 面·

歷史上之基督；（英）顧樂偉原著，（英）莫安仁譯· 232—G518

上海，廣學會，民十二年·4 版·165 面·

耶穌基督；（英）馬克策原著，（英）季理斐譯· 232—M199

上海，廣學會，民十三年·再版·119 面·

基督與戰斗；（英）韋理生原著，（英）梅益盛譯· 232—W699

上海，廣學會，民五年，92 面·

新時代的信仰；謝扶稚著· 234·2—S417

上海，青年協年書局，民十四年·30 面·

實用講道學；（美）萬應遠編，徐松百譯· 251—B84

廣州，東山，美華浸會印書局，民十四年·200 面·

近代宣道學大綱；（美）霍德原著，謝頌羔，米星如合譯·

上海，美以美會書報部，民十三年·116 面· 251—S423

傳道經驗譚；楊道榮著· 251—Y139

漢口，信義書局，民十四年·34 面·

267·3 基督教青年會

學校青年會會務之研究；陳鐘聲著· 267·3—C270

上海，青年協會書報部，民十年·100 面·

青年會事業之設計訓練法；克樂愷原著· 267·3—C548

上海，青年協會書局，民十五年 · 116 面 ·

青年會教育事業概要；劉湛恩著 · 267 · 3—L356

上海，青年協會書局，民十三年 · 156 面 ·

青年會與教會之關係；謝洪賚著 · 267 · 3—S418

上海，青年會書報發行所，民五年 · 162 面 ·

青年會創立者；謝洪賚著 · 267 · 3—S418

上海，青年會書報發行所，民三年 · 112 面 ·

青年與中國前途；青年協會書報部編 · 267 · 3—T665

上海，青年協會書局，民十五年 · 130 面 ·

270 教會史

教會歷史；(美)赫士原著 · 270—H329

上海，廣學會，民十五年 · 6 版 · 2 册 ·

280 反基督教問題

最近反基督教運動的紀評；張亦鏡著 · 280—C158

廣州，美華浸會印書局，民十四年 · 112 面 ·

教會覺悟與非基督教運動 · 280—H419

上海，青年協會，民十四年 · 66 面 ·

290 比較宗教學

比較宗教學；F，B，Tebens 原著，嚴既澄譯 · 290—T348

上海，商務，民十四年 · 142 面 ·「新知識叢書」

神話研究；黄石著· 291—H485
上海，開明，民十六年·233 面·

294　佛教

學佛淺説；王博謙輯· 294—W154
民十三年·42 面·

中國佛教小史；陳彬龢著· 294—c285
上海，世界，民十六年·65 面·

究元決疑論；東方雜誌社編· 080—T86—045
上海，商務，民十四年·3 版·73 面·「東方文庫」

大乘起信論考證；梁啓超著· 294—L251
上海，商務，民十三年·108 面·

廬山學；太虛著· 294—T139
上海，泰東，民十五年·379 面·

大乘與人間兩般文化；太虛著· 294—T139
上海，泰東，民十四年·54 面·

心筏；蔡慎鳴著· 294—T414
涅盤學社，民十二年·138 面·「佛學叢書」

基督教之佛學研究；王治心著· 294—W136
上海，廣學會，民十三年·118 面·

其餘各教

開封一賜樂業教考；東方雜誌社編· 080—T860—72
上海，商務，民十四年·3 版·69 面·「東方文庫」

元也里可温考；東方雜誌社編· 080—T860—73
上海，商務，民十四年·3 版·79 面·「東方文庫」

道教源流；傅代言譯· 299·5—S410
上海，中華，民十六年·130 面·「常識叢書」

300 社會科學

301 社會學

社會學表解；上海科學書局編· 080—S155—302
上海，科學書局，民三年·101 面·「表解叢書」

美的社會組織法；張競生著· 300—C153
北京，北新，民十五年·240 面·「審美叢書之一」

社會學概論；(美)E·S·Bogurdus 原著，瞿世英譯· 300—B633
上海，商務，民十四年·175 面·

社會學大綱；朱聚仁，曹源文著· 300—C821
上海，民智，民十五年·3 版·190 面·

社會學方法論；(法)E. Durheim 原著，許德珩譯· 300—D935
上海，商務，民十四年·191 面·

現代社會學；李達著· 300—L198
上海，現代，民十五年·304 面·

社會學問答；(日)納武津原著，甘浩澤譯· 300—N450
上海，商務，民十四年·120 面·「百科問答小叢書」

社會學；歐陽鈞輯· 300—O131
上海，商務，民十一年·8 版·146 面·

羣學肄言；(英)斯賓塞爾原著，嚴復譯· 300—S33
上海，商務，民十年·12 版·352 面·

社會學大綱；王平陵著· 300—W153
上海，泰東，民十五年·170 面·

近世社會學；(日)遠藤隆吉原著，覃壽公譯・　300—Y430
上海，泰東，民十三年・4 版・414 面・

社會論；劉延陵著・　080—P225—38
上海，商務，民十五年・再版・58 面・「百科小叢書第三十八種」

社會論；COIE 原著，張東蓀，吳獻書合譯・　301—C674
上海，商務，民十一年・173 面・「今人會叢書」

社會觀；陳安仁著・　301—C268
上海，泰東，民十五年・3 版・97 面・

社會學及現代社會問題；(美)愛爾烏德原著，趙作雄譯・　301—E59
上海，商務，民十四年・7 版・360 面・「世界叢書」

易卜生社會哲學；袁振英譯・　301—Ib7
上海，泰東，民十七年・194 面・

社會哲學原論；(英)馬肯底原著，鄒敬方譯・　301—M111
上海，學術研究會，民十二年・252 面・「學術研究會叢書」

社會改造原理；(英)羅素原著，王岫廬譯・　301—R911
上海，公民，民十年・270 面・「公民叢書」

社會學原理；朱亦松著・　301—C825
上海，商務，民十七年，284 面・

社會進化論；薩瑞譯・　301—S15
上海，商務，民十五年・3 版・175 面・

社會進化史；蔡和森著・　301—T405
上海，民智，民十六年・4 版・230 面・

中國社會文化；東方雜誌社編・　080—T860—32
上海，商務，民十四年・3 版・89 面・「東方文庫」

社會問題

主要社會問題；(美)拜得原著，楊廉譯・　301—B511
上海，商務，民十七年・363 面・

社會問題；(美)愛爾烏德原著；王造石，趙廷爲合譯・　301—E159
上海，商務，民十五年・3 版・209 面・「世界叢書」

社會問題；熊得山著· 301—K363

上海，北新，民十六年，再版·144面·

社會問題詳解；(日)高鼻素之原著，盟西譯· 301—K165

上海，商務，民十一年·再版·2册·「社會叢書」

社會問題概觀；(日)生田等原著，周佛海譯· 301—226

上海，中華，民十五年·2册·「新文化叢書」

社會問題概論；王首春著· 080—P225—127

上海，商務，民十六年·52面·「百科小叢書」

301 社會心理學

社會心理學；(美)愛爾烏特著，金本基，解壽晉合譯· 301—EL88

上海，商務，民十二年·再版·311面·「共學社社會經濟叢書」

社會心理學新論；陸志韋編· 301—L425

上海，商務，民十四年·再版·155面·

羣眾；(法)魯滂著，鐘健閎譯· 301—L492

上海，泰東，民十五年·「205」面·

社會心理之分析；(英)倭拉士原著，梁仲策譯· 301—W155

上海，商務，民十二年·233面·「社會叢書」

304 社會問題討論集

内國問題討論大綱第一二輯；陳白華輯· 304—C285

上海，青年協會，民十四年·2册·「公民教科叢書第十三種」

社會問題講演録；江亢虎講演· 304—C504

上海，商務，民十四年·再版·158面·「東南大學叢書」

社會問題概觀；周佛海譯· 304—C774

上海，商務，民十五年·6版·

狄雷博士講演録；徐松石譯· 204—D342

上海，商務，民十三年·再版·130面·

社會結構學；(英)羅素講；伏盧筆記· 304—R911
上海，商務，民十五年·再版·98面·「羅素講演録之四」

羅素論文集；東方雜誌社編· 080—T860—44
上海，商務，民十四年·2册·「東方文庫」

社會問題；陶孟和著· 304—T218
上海，商務，民十五年·3版·191面·

社會鑑；王立謙著· 304—W47
上海，商務，民十二年·3版·158面·

楊杏佛講演集· 304—y126
上海，商務，民十六年·369面·

社會科學季刊；北京大學社會科學季刊編輯會編· R—305—P223
北京大學出版部，民十三年·第一，二卷·

307　社會教育

社會教育概論；馬宗榮著· 307—M121
上海，商務，民十四年·116面·「學藝叢刊」

社會教育；余寄輯· 307—Y346
上海，中華，民六年·89面·「少年中國學會叢會」

教育社會學

應用教育社會學；(美)Smith原著，陳啓天譯· 307—S51
上海，中華，民十四年·80面·「少年中國會書叢書」

309　社會學史

歐洲社會思想史；黄新民譯· 309—H485
上海，光華，民十六年·164面·

社會學史要；易家鉞著· 309—I112

上海，商務，民十三年·121面·「共學社通俗叢書」

社會通詮；(美)甄克思原著，嚴復譯· 309—J422

上海，商務，民十四年·10版·208面·

社會調查

社會調查；張鏡予著· 309·1—C152

上海，商務，民十三年·172面·

社會調查方法；樊弘著· 309·1—F127

上海，商務，民十六年·184面·「社會研究叢刊」

310 統計學

統計學表解；上海科學書局編輯所編· 080—S155—310

上海，科學書局，民二年·2冊·「表解叢書」

應用統計淺説；壽毅咸著· 080—P225—28

上海，商務，民十二年·72面·「百科小叢書第二十八種」

統計學；陳其鹿著· 311—C270

上海，商務，民十五年·再版·300面·「新文化叢書」

統計新論；金國寶著· 311—K665

上海，中華，民十三年·再版·165面·「新文化叢書」

統計學原著；(英)倍林等原著，趙文鋭譯· 311—P176

上海，商務，民十三年·61面·「經濟叢書」

311 人口論

馬爾薩斯人口論；林騤編· 080—P225—106

上海，商務，民十五年·66面·「百科小叢書第一百零六種」

人口問題；吳應圖著· 312—W299

上海，中華，民十四年·130 面·「常識叢書」

人口問題；(美)柯克斯原著，武堉幹譯·　312—C839

上海，商務，民十四年·201 面·「新智識叢書」

歷代户口通論；黎世衡著·　312—L217

上海，世界，民十一年·128 面·

中國人口論；陳長衡著·　312—C270

上海，商務，民十三年·6 版·150 面·「尚志學會叢書」

312　人口限制論

產兒限制論；(日)安部磯雄原著，李達譯·　312—A141

上海，商務，民十一年·141 面·「新時代叢書第六種」

節制生育問題；程浩著·　312—C335

上海，亞東，民十五年·3 版·212 面·

生育節制論；徐傅霖譯·　312—S477

上海，中華，民十二年·129 面·三版·

節育主義；(美)山額爾夫人原著，陳海澄譯·　312—Sa58

上海，商務，民十四年·156 面·

民生主義與人口問題；王警濤著·　312—W137

上海，民智，民十六年·118 面·

313　統計

經濟統計；上海銀行週報社編·　R—330·2—y275

上海，該社，民十二至十四年·三册·

中國年鑑；阮湘編·　R—310·51—C976

上海，商務，民十五年·3 版·2123 面·

民國元年工商統計概要；黄炎培編·　313—H489

上海，商務，民四年·89 面·

物價指數號，統計彙刊；廣東省政府農工廳統計科編·　313—K322

廣東省政府，民十五年・26 面・

日本帝國第十四統計年鑑；（日）内閣書記官室統計課編・ R—310—N270

東京，八尾商店，明治二十八年・1099 面・

320 政治學

政治學表解；上海科學書局編・ 080—S155—320

上海，科學書局，民元年・4 册・「表解叢書」

政治概論；張慰慈著・ 320—C172

上海，商務，民十三年・240 面・

政治學大綱；張慰慈著・ 320—C172

上海，商務，民十五年・517 面・「北京大學叢書之七」

政治學；陳敬第輯・ 320—S289

民元年・258 面・「見法政講義第二册」

政治學；（日）小野塚原著，鄭篪譯・ 320—S410

上海，商務，民二年・7 版・281 面・

公民與民治；劉湛恩著・ 320—L356

上海，青年協會，民十五年・43 面・「公民教育叢刊第十一種」

民眾政治與英國的政治；蔣國珍著・ 320—T566

上海，世界，民十七年・再版・53 面・

政治泛論；（美）威爾遜原著，（日）高田譯，章起謂重譯・ 320—W699

上海，商務，民二年・2 册・

320・1 政治哲學

物理與政治；W・B・Opchen 原著，鐘建閎譯・ 320・1—B146

上海，商務，民十三年・168 面・

孟子政治哲學；陳顧遠著・ 320・1—C278m

上海，泰東，民十一年・再版・120 面・

墨子政治哲學；陳顧遠著・ 320・1—C278me

上海，泰東，民十五年・3 版・126 面・

政治哲學導言；范用餘譯・ 320・1—F247

上海，商務，民十二年・再版・249 面・

政治心理；(法)勒明原著，馮承鈞譯・ 320・1—L46

上海，商務，民十一年・再版・371 面・「共學社時代叢書」

平民政治的基本原理；(美)芮恩施原著，羅志希譯・ 320・1—R276

上海，商務，民十一年・再版・173 面・

政治理想；(英)羅素原著，劉衡如，吳蔚人合譯・ 320・1—R911

上海，中華，民十一年・6 版・128 面・

政治思想；(英)羅素原著，程振基譯・ 320・1—R911

上海，商務，民十三年・3 版・99 面・

古代政治思想研究；謝无量著・ 320・1—S425

上海，商務，民十三年・再版・63 面・「國學小叢書」

柏拉圖政治教育學說今解；(德)K. Stemberg 原著，俞頌華譯・ 320・1—ST45

上海，商務，民十三年・51 面・「新智識叢書」

政治中之人性；(英)儒倭拉士原著，鍾建閎譯・ 320・1—W155

上海，商務，民十三年・231 面・

經濟的政治基礎；俾爾特查理士原著，董時譯・ 320・1—B38

上海，商務，民十三年・81 面・「新智識叢書」

主權論；張奚若著・ 080—P225—79

上海，商務，民十四年・51 面・「百科小叢書第七十九種」

320・4　政治論文集

政聞時言；梁啓超著・ 320・4—L251c

上海，商務・2 册・「飲冰室叢著第十種」

飲冰室自由書；梁啓超著・ 320・4—L251

上海，商務・143 面・「飲冰室叢著第十一種」

杜威羅素講演録合刊；張靜廬輯・ 320・4—D515

上海，泰東，民十五年・5 版・164 面・

杜威五大演講；胡適譯・ 320・4—D515h

北京，晨報社，民十一年・14 版・2 冊・
民政發展精義；(英)馬司特曼演講，(英)梅益盛，蔣茂森合譯・ 320・4—M393
上海，廣學會，民五年・58 面・
經濟狀況與政治思想；(英)羅素演講，伏廬記・ 320・4—R911
上海，商務，民十一年・84 面・
甲寅雜誌存稿；章士釗輯・ 320・5—C190
上海，商務，民十五年・4 版・2 冊・

320・9 政治思想史

先秦政治思想史；梁啓超著・ 320・9—L251
上海，商務，民十二年・316 面・
歐洲政治思想史；高一涵著・ 320・9—K168
上海，商務，民十五年・「北京大學叢書」
歐洲政治思想小史；高一涵著・ 320・9—K168s
上海，中華，民十一年・4 版・250 面・「新文化叢書」
近時國際政治小史；周鯁生著・ 080—P225—6
上海，商務，民十二年・再版・93 面・「百科小叢書」

321 政體論

國家主義論文集；少年中國學會編・ 321—S172
上海，中華，民十五年・5 版・177 面・
國家主義；(印度)太戈爾原著，
(法)喬治巴西勒原譯，樓桐孫重譯・ 321—T129
上海，商務，民十四年・121 面・
聯邦政治概要；吳漢章著・ 080—P225—77
上海，商務，民十四年・150 面・「百科小叢書第七十七種」
聯邦政治；陳茹玄著・ 321・021—C277
上海，商務，民十四年・212 面・「政法叢書」
西洋氏族制度研究；易家鉞著・ 321・2—I112

上海，商務，民十五年·再版·284面·「社會叢書」

平民主義；李守常著· 080—P225—15

上海，商務，民十四年·3版·35面·「百科小叢書第十五種」

現代民治政體；(英)蒲徠斯原著，梅祖芬譯· 321·8—B843

上海，商務，民十二年·220面·「世界叢書」

公共意見與平民政治；(美)羅偉爾原著，范用餘譯· 321·8—L251

上海，商務，民十三年·295面·

平民政治； 321·8—P230

上海，民友社，民二年·4冊·

現代民立政治；(英)蒲徠士原著，楊永泰譯· 321·8—P414

上海，泰東，民十三年·

近世民主政治論；(日)森口繁治原著，薩孟武譯· 321·8—S202

上海，商務，民十四年·191面·「政法叢書」

全民政治；(美)威爾確斯原著，廖仲愷譯· 321·8—W64

上海，民智，民十四年·再版·256面·

323　人民與國家之關係

國内戰争六講；張君勱講· 323·2—C152

上海國立自治學院，民十三年·107面·「國立自治學院叢書第一種」

革命概説；凌其翰著· 323·2—L340

上海，世界，民十六年·43面·

革命心理；(法)黎朋原著，杜師業譯· 333·2—L492

上海，商務，民十年·4版·2冊·「尚志學會叢書」

羣已權界；(英)穆勒約翰原著，嚴復譯· 323·44—M61

上海，商務，民十三年·8版·168面·

日本民權發達史；(日)植原悦二郎著，黄文中譯· 323·4—C629

上海，商務，民十五年·435面·

增訂公民綱要；青年協會書報部編· 323·6—T665

上海，青年協會，民十五年·60面·「公民教育叢刊」

324 選舉

英國選舉制度；張慰慈著· 324·42—C172
上海，商務，民十二年·148 面·

女子参政之研究；王世杰著· 324·3—W155
北京，新知識書社，民十年·56 面·「學術叢書第一種」

325 殖民政策

殖民；阮湘著· 080—P224—69
上海，商務，民十三年·81 面·「百科小叢書第六十八種」

殖民政策；吳應圖著· 325—W299
上海，中華，民十五年·170 面·「常識叢書」

華僑志；密亨原著，岑德影譯· 325·51—M231
上海，商務，民十七年·153 面·

旅美華僑實録；屠汝凍輯· 325·73—T792
杭縣，屠汝棟，民十三年·120 面·

327 外交

外交史表解；上海科學書局編輯所編· 080—S155—327
上海，科學書局，民三年·2 册·「表解叢書」

國際關係論；（英）J. Bryce 原著，鍾建閎譯· 327—B843
上海，商務，民十三年·26 面·

外交 A·B·C·；常書林著· 327—C196
上海，世界，民十六年·110 面·

外交新紀元；陳榮廣，王幾道合著· 327—C293
上海，泰東，民六年·180 面·

太平洋問題；陳立廷輯・　327—C279
上海，青年協會，民十六年・112 面・「國際問題叢書」

戰後太平洋問題；(美)各學者合著，
(日)阿部豐治原譯，姚伯麟譯・　327—N168
上海，泰東，民十年・252 面・

國際問題；謝扶雅著・　327—S417
上海，青年協會，民十五年・202 面・「公民教育叢刊第三種」

最近世界外交史；戴鑫修著・　327—T130
民十五年・下册・

外交政策；(日)稻田周之助原著，楊水泰譯・　327—T220
上海，泰東，民四年・210 面・「政治叢書」

國民外交常識；錢基博著・　327—T601
上海，商務，民十五年・76 面・

最近外交史；作新社編・　327—T684
上海，該社，清光緒二十八年・57 面・

英帝國之將來；郭闕居譯・　327・42—P392
廣州，民聲社，民十七年・42 面・

大亞細亞主義論；(日)小寺謙吉原著，(日)中國百城書合譯・　327・5—S410
東京，日清印刷株式會社，民十年・796 面・

327・51　外交—中國

國民外交小叢書；國民外交叢書社編・
上海，中華，民十四年・5 册・細目見各項

革命的外交；周鯁生著・　327・51—C778
上海，太平洋，民十七年・174 面・

解放運動中之對外問題；周鯁生著・　327・51—C778
上海，太平洋，民十六年・394 面・

被侵害之中國：即中國主幹之不平等條約；劉彦著・　327・51—L379
上海，太平洋，民十七年・294 面・

中國近時外交史；劉彦著・　327・51—L379C

上海，商務，民十年·3版·636面·

帝國主義壓迫中國史；劉彥著· 327·51—L379t

上海，太平洋，民十七年·2册·

中國外交史；曾友豪著· 327·51—T533

上海，商務，民十五年·467面·

國民會議國際問題草案；汪精衛編· 327·51—W175

北京，國際問題研究會，民十四年·3版·120面·

經濟侵略下之中國；漆樹芬著· 327·51—T555

著者自印，民十五年·454面·

國立武昌商科大學講演集；周鯁生編· 327·51—C778

武昌，時中合作書社，民十四年·48面·

帝國主義與中國；常書林著· 327·51—C196

上海，世界，民十六年·63面·

門户開放之今昔觀；國民外交叢書社編· 327·51—K105

上海，中華，民十五年·4版·50面·「國民外交小叢書」

對華門户開放主義；陶彙曾著· 080—P225—87

上海，商務，民十五年·81面·「百科小叢書第八十七種」

歐洲列強武力對華的開端；陳儒平譯· 327·4—R275

上海，北新，民十六年·再版·34面·

近時國際問題與中國；楊幼炯著· 327·51—Y144

上海，泰東，民十七年·242面·

帝國主義侵畧中國史；于樹德講演· 327·51—y36

上海，國光，民十六年·62面·

國恥史

國恥痛史· 327·51—K434

237面·

國恥小史；吕思勉著· 327·51—L453

上海，中華，民十一年·9版·2册·「通俗教育叢書」

增訂國恥小史；沈文濬編· 327·51—S218

上海，中國圖書公司，民十六年・13 版・72 面・

國恥小史續編；趙玉森編・　327・51—C220

上海，中國圖書公司，民十五年・5 版・77 面・

中國喪地史；謝彬編・　327・51—S415

上海，中華，民十五年・148 面・「常識叢書」

新編國恥小史；曹增美，黄孝先合編・　327・51—T471

上海，商務，民十七年・249 面・

外交思痛録；莊病骸編・　327・51—C918

上海，交通圖書館，民七年・再版・272 面・

327・51　不平等條約

各國對中國不平等條約；程中行編・　327・51—C332

上海，世界，民十七年・229 面・

中國國際商約論；鄭斌著・　327・51—C358

上海，商務，民十四年・223 面・「政法叢書」

中國國際條約義務論；刁敏謙著・　327・51—T311

上海，商務，民十四年・「274」面・

中外訂約失權論；邱祖銘著・　080—P225—85

上海，商務，民十五年・90 面・「百科小叢書第八十五種」

不平等條約的研究；張廷灝著・　327・51—C173

上海，光華，民十五年・156 面・

取消不平等條約之方法及步驟；朱世全著　327・51—C823

上海，泰東，民十七年・116 面・

不平等約討論大綱；孫祖基編・　327・51—S530

上海，青年協會，民十四年・153 面・「公民教育叢刊」

中日關係

二十年來之中日關係；中華書局編譯所編・　327・51—C976

上海，中華，民十四年・6 版・170 面・「學生叢書之一」

日本人之支那問題；中華書局編輯所編・　329・51—C976

上海，中華，民八年·「196」面·

近代中日關係略史；國民外交叢書社編· 327·51—K405

上海，中華，民十五年·49面·「國民外交小叢書」

歐戰期間中日交涉史；劉彥編· 327·51—L379

上海，商務，民十年·3版·「382」面·

日本新滿蒙政策·日本對華最近野心之暴露；

(日)山田原著，周佩嵐譯· 327·51—S149

上海，民智，民十七年·再版·106面·

山東問題彙刊；張一志輯· 327·51—C158

上海，歐美同學會，民十年·2册·

青島潮；龔振黄編· 327·51—K381

上海，泰東，民八年·79面·

日本出兵山東濟南慘案；無袈和尚編· 327·51—W300

山東駐滬慘案編輯社，民十七年·58面·

中俄關係

中俄關係略史；國民外交叢書社編· 327·51—K405

上海，中華，民十五年·63面·「國民外交小叢書」

蘇俄的東方政策；布施勝治原著，半粟譯· 327·47—P384

上海，太平洋，民十六年·396面·

最近十年中俄之交涉；遠東外交研究會編· 327·51—Y430

哈爾濱，該會，民十二年·252面·

中英關係

英日侵略及對策；陳震異著· 327·51—C270

北京，著者，民十四年·128面·

八十五年之中英；顧器重編· 327·51—K246

上海，國民圖書館，民十六年·278面·

英帝國主義與中國；楊幼炯著· 327·42—Y144

北京，反帝國主義同盟會，民十五年·再版·104面·

西藏問題；謝彬著· 080—P225—88
上海，商務，民十五年·105面·「百科小叢書第八十八種」

327·52　日本外交政策

日本外交史；松平基則著· 327·52—L121
東京，交盛館，明治三十九年·946面·

328　立法　議會

代議立法與直接立法；董修甲著· 080—P225—94
上海，商務，民十五年·95面·「百科小叢書第九十四種」
代議政治；東方雜誌社編· 080—T860—36
上海，商務，民十四年·3版·72面·「東方文庫」
萬國比較政府議院之權限；吳昆吾，戴修駿合編· 328—C398
上海，商務，民六年·148面·
會場必携；費培傑著· 328·1—F187
上海，商務，民十三年·3版·119面·
議會通詮；孔昭焱著· 328·2—K411
上海，商務，民二年·62面·
日本議會紀事本末；畢厚編· 328·52—P290
民元年·
日本議會法規；商務印書館編譯所編· 328·52—S62
上海，該館，民元年·4版·143面·
首領論；E·B，Gowin原著，鐘建閎譯· 328·362—G748
上海，泰東，民十二年·143面·

329　政黨

政黨政治論；劉文島著· 329—L377

上海，商務，民十二年·65面·

歐美政黨政治；(日)田中萃一郎原著，畢厚譯· 329—T332

上海，商務，民二年·84面·

汎繫主義；劉秉麟編· 080—P225—131

上海，商務，民十六年·65面·「百科小叢書第一三一種」

近十年來世界上兩大怪物；劉公度著· 329·94—L365

上海，世界，民十六年·70面·

330 經濟學

經濟原論表解；上海科學書局編輯所編· 080—S155—330

上海，該局，民元年·94面·「表解叢書」

經濟科學概論；周佛海譯· 330—B633

民十六年·

經濟學；李佐庭輯· 340—C289

民元年·331面·「見法政講義第二册」

富之研究；(英)E. Cannan原著，史維煥，陶因合譯· 330—C164

上海，商務，民十三年·260面·「經濟名著」

社會之經濟基礎；陳震異譯· 330—C270

上海，商務，民十一年·418面·「社會經濟叢書」

法國之產業政策；陳彬龢編· 330·C285

上海，世界，民十六年·61面·

社會經濟學；陳家瓚譯· 330—C662

上海，羣益，民二年·517面·

經濟原論· 330—C690

371面·

國際經濟總論；(日)堀江歸一原著，王首春譯· 330—C928

上海，商務，民十六年·247面·「經濟叢書」

傅克思氏經濟學；宋任譯· 330—F951

上海，泰東，民十七年·4版·186面·

政治經濟學；(法)李特原著，陶樂勤譯· 330—G361
上海，泰東，民十二年·3冊·

經濟學要旨；季特原著，李橫譯· 330—G361e
上海，中華，民十五年·132面·「少年中國學會叢書」

協力主義政治經濟學；(法)季特原著，陶樂勤譯· 330—G361S
上海，泰東，民十二年·4版·3冊·

經濟學大要；賀紹章編· 330—H187
上海，商務，民九年·16版·67面·

國際經濟政策；何思原著· 330—H210
上海，商務，民十六年·553面·

資本主義經濟學之史的發展；林植夫譯· 330—H414
上海，商務，民十七年·391面·「經濟叢書」

經濟概要；胡祖同編· 330—H416
上海，商務，民九年·7版·162面·

商業經濟概論；(日)户田海市原著，周佛海，郭心崧合譯· 320—H420
上海，商務，民十七年·412面·「現代商業叢書」

商業經濟；柳準著· 330—L380
上海，商務，民一年·56面·

經濟學；李佐庭著· 330—L190
上海，羣益，民九年·330面·「法政講義第一集第六册」

公民經濟；劉秉麟著· 330—L372
上海，商務，民十四年·再版·第三册·

經濟學原理；劉秉麟著· 330—L372
上海，商務，民十年·3版·197面·

李士特經濟學與傳記；劉秉麟著· 330—L3721
上海，商務，民十四年·126面·「經濟叢書社叢書之十一」

經濟學大意；歐陽溥存編· 330—C136
上海，中華，民十五年·110面·

經濟科學大綱；(俄)格達諾夫原著，施存統譯· 330—P414
漢口，長江書店，民十六年·566面·「新青年社叢書」

經濟史觀；(美)塞利格曼原著，陳石孚譯· 330—Se48
上海，商務，民十年·167面·「世界叢書」

經濟學研究；孫同康著· 330—S529
武昌，時中，民十四年·146面·

國民經濟原論；(日)津村秀松原著，馬凌甫譯· 330—T643
上海，源記書莊，民十五年·2冊·

經濟學大意；(日)津村秀松原著，彭耕譯· 330—T644
上海，羣益，民六年·再版·129面·

經濟學各論；(日)監谷廉等原著，王我藏譯· 330—Y208
上海，商務，民二年·168面·

馬寅初演講集· 330·4—M122
上海，商務，民十四年·「經濟叢書社叢書」

經濟叢編；國務院編· 330·8—T571
該院，民十年·8冊·

經濟大辭書；(日)百科辭書編輯部編· B—330·2—P225
東京，同文館，明治四十三年·9冊·「日本百科辭書」

支那經濟全書；(日)東亞同文會編· R—330·3—T861
東京，該會，明治四十二年·3版·12冊·

330·9 經濟學史

經濟思想小史；(法)季特原著，李澤彰譯· 080—P225—19
上海，商務，民十二年·40面·「百科小叢書第十九種」

人類經濟進化史略；(美)ELY and Wieker原著，邵光謨譯· 330·9—EL91
上海，泰東，民十五年·104面·「黎民學會叢書」

近世經濟政策之思潮；(奥)非利波伊基原著，土恒重譯· 330·9—F181
上海，學術研究會，民十二年·154面·「學術研究會叢書第九册」

經濟學史；(法)基特里斯脱原著，王廷祖譯· 330·8—G361
上海，商務，民十四年·285面·「經濟名著之一」

近世經濟思想史論；(日)河上肇原著，李天培譯· 330·9—H214
上海，學術研究會，民十六年·188面·「學術研究會叢書第一册」

經濟思想史；(美)L. H. Hansy原著，藏啓芳譯． 330·9—H193
上海，商務，民十四年·再版·791面·

近世歐洲經濟發達史；(美)阿格原著，李光忠譯· 330·9—993
上海，商務，民十四年·3版·728面·

經濟學史概論；(日)北澤新次郎原著，周佛海譯· 330·9—P223
上海，商務，民十三年·162面·

331 勞工問題

社會政策；東方雜誌社編· 080—T860—21
上海，商務，民十四年·3版·98面·「東方文庫」

勞工問題研究；鄭行巽著· 331—C351
上海，世界，民十七年·118面·

世界各國新社會政策；鄭斌著· 331—C358
上海，商務，民十七年·181面·「新時代史地叢書」

中國罷工史；賀嶽僧著· 331—H189
上海，世界，民十六年·65面·

中國社會政策；何海鳴著· 331—H202
北京，華星印書社，民九年·186面·「附録」144面·

社會政策；胡鈞著· 331—H401
上海，商務，民九年·224面·

工業政策；(日)關一原著· 331—K296
上海，商務，民十五年·2册·「經濟名著之一」

工業政策；(奥)菲里波維原著，馬君武譯· 331—P538
上海，中華，民十一年·332面·

實業革命史；林子英著· 831—L316
上海，商務，民十七年·184面·「新時代史地叢書」

薩樊事件；盧劍波著· 331—L405
上海，泰東，民十七年·153面·

失業問題研究；魯竹書著· 331—L415

上海，中央圖書局，民十六年·151面·

分配論；(英)馬沙原著，劉秉麟譯· 331—M399

上海，商務，民十四年·再版·200面·「社會經濟叢書」

勞動經濟論；(日)北澤新次郎原著，宋應祺，朱應會合譯· 331—P223

上海，泰東，民十七年·276面·

資本問題；吳應圖編· 331—W285

上海，中華，民十五年·110面·「常識叢書第十三種」

工會組織研究；殷壽光著· 331—y272

上海，世界，民十六年·81面·

童工；沈丹泥著· 331·3—S222

上海，世界，民十六年·78面·

勞動之改造；(法)錫亞魯爾季特原著，姚伯麟譯· 331·8—G361

上海，學術研究會，民十五年·276面·「學術研究會叢書」

失業人民及貧民救濟政策；馬君武編· 080—F225—81

上海，商務，民十四年·98面·「百科小叢書第八十一種」

收入及恤貧政策；(德)Philipperich 原著，馬君武譯· 331·8—P538

上海，中華，民十四年·345面·「新文化叢書」

工業中的人道觀；羅屈里原著，沈星若，仇子同合譯· 331·8—R371

上海，青年協會，民十六年·172面·

失業者問題；邵振青著· 331·8—S170

上海，泰東，民十年·再版·62面·「社會小叢書」

332·1 銀行學

銀行學表解；上海科學書局編輯所編· 080—S155—332

上海，該局，民三年·105面·「表解叢書」

銀行實務表解；上海科學書局編輯所編· 080—S155—332

上海，該局，民三年·2冊·「表解叢書」

銀行營業法解表；上海科學書局編輯所編· 080—S155—332

上海，該局，96面·「表解叢書」

銀行要義；楊端六著· 080—P225—8

上海，商務，民十二年·41 面·「百科小叢書第三種」

銀行原論；陳家瓚著·　332·1—C270

上海，羣益，民十四年·806 面·

銀行學；陳其鹿著·　332·1—C270S

上海，商務，民十三年·219 面·

銀行攬要；孫德全編·　332·1—529

上海，商務，民八年·2 册·

銀行計算法；李徵，謝霖合編·　332·1—L181

上海，中國圖書公司，民五年·215 面

銀行服務論；謝菊曾著·　332·1—S420

上海，商務，民十三年·再版·218 面·

銀行制度論；謝霖，李徵合著·　332·1—S420

上海，中國圖書公司，民五年·247 面·

中華銀行史；周葆鑾編·　332·1—C789

上海，商務，民十二年·3 版·439 面·

上海銀行公會事業史；徐滄水編·　332·1—S476

上海，銀行週報社，民十四年·140 面·

銀行公會聯合會議彙紀；上海銀行週報社編·　332·1—Y275

上海，該社·125 面·「經濟類鈔第二輯」

法蘭西銀行史；楊德森編·　332·1—Y139

上海，商務，民十五年·74 面·

英格蘭銀行史；楊德森編·　332·1—Y139e

上海，商務，民十五年·120 面·

意大利銀行史；楊德森編·　332·1—Y139i

上海，商務，民十四年·68 面·

美國聯合準備銀行制述要；吳宗壽譯·　332·1—W281

上海，商務，民十三年·51 面·「經濟叢書社叢書之八」

銀行年鑑·　B—332·1—Y275

上海，銀行週報社，民十一年·

332·14 信託公司

依託研究；潘士浩著· 332·14—P159
上海，商務，民十年·148 面·

依託及信託公司論；（日）細失祐治原著，資耀華譯· 332·14—S366
民十七年·174 面·「經濟叢書」

各國信託公司法理論；（日）佐野善原著，范況譯· 332·14—T684
南通，翰聖林書局，民十年·198 面·

信託公司概論；楊端六著· 332·14—Y132
上海，商務，民十一年·57 面·

332·4 貨幣學

貨幣學表解；上海科學書局編輯所編· 080—S155—332
上海，該局，民二年·49 面·

貨幣淺說；楊端六著· 080—P225—16
上海，商務，民十二年·46 面·「百科小叢書第十六種」

貨幣制度；東方雜誌社編· 080—T860—20
上海，商務，民十四年·3 版·84 面·「東方文庫」

貨幣學；（美）肯列原著，王怡柯譯· 332·4—K261
上海，商務，民十三年·386 面·「經濟叢書社叢書之六」

貨幣膨漲各國公債略史；ScLigmam 原著；吳東初譯· 332·1—S48
上海，商務，民十三年·89 面·

貨幣概論；王恒編· 332·4—W141
上海，中華，民十三年·106 面·「常識叢書第九種」

貨幣論；王效文編· 332·4—W151
上海，商務，民十三年·273 面·

理論實用外國匯兑；吳宗熹著· 332·4—W297
上海，商務，民十六年·上卷·

銀價之研究；邵金鐸譯· 332·41—S170
上海，學術研究會，民十年·再版·120 面·「學術研究會叢書」

國際匯兑與貿易；丘漢平，傅文楷合編· 332·45—C736

上海，民智，民十五年·2 册·

外國匯兑原理；(英)高申原著，劉濬川譯· 332·45—G691

上海，商務，民十年·148 面·

中國國外匯兑；馬寅初著· 332·45—M122

上海，商務，民十四年·229 面·

外國匯兑詳解；吳應圖編· 332·45—W299

上海，泰東，民九年·122 面·

外國匯兑論；(英)Hartley Withers 原著，梁雲池譯· 332·45—W776

上海，商務，民十二年·120 面·

匯兑論；俞希稷編· 332·45—y371

上海，商務，民十四年·248 面·

倫敦貨幣市場概要；史保定原著，金國寶譯· 332·4942—SP19

上海，商務，民十四年·223 面·「經濟叢書社叢書之十」

中國幣制問題；金國寶著· 332·4—C665

上海，商務，民十七年·289 面·

中國今日之貨幣問題；徐滄水輯· 332·4—S476

長沙，輯者自印，民十年·330 面·

支那貨幣論；楊端六譯· 332·4—Y132

上海，泰東，民十一年·114 面·

上海金融市場論；銀行週報社編· 332·5—Y275

上海，該社，民十二年·145 面·「經濟類鈔」

取締外鈔問題；金侶琴著· 332·5—C666

上海，光華，民十六年·28 面·「經濟小叢書」

民國鈔券史；徐滄水編· 332·5—S476

銀行週報社，民十三年·107 面·

332·6 交易所

票據交换所研究；徐滄水著· 332·6—S476

上海，銀行週報社，民十一年·140 面·

各國交易所法制論；(日)佐野善原著，范況譯· 332·6—T683

南通，翰墨林書局，民十年・186 面・

交易所大全；吳叔田等輯・ 332・6—W13

上海，交易所所員養成所，民十年・198 面・

332・8 利息問題

國際投資淺説；周佛海著・ 080—P225—147

上海，商務，民十六年・59 面・「百科小叢書」

投資常識；韋伯勝著・ 332・8—W198

上海，商務，民十三年・再版・59 面・「商業叢書第七種」

利息問題；吳應圖編・ 332・8—W285

上海，中華，民十五年・116 面・「常職叢書第十九種」

334 合作主義

合作制度；東方雜誌社編・ 080—T860—22

上海，商務，民十四年・88 面・「東方文庫」

合作論；Clayton 原著，徐謂津譯・ 334—C579

上海，商務，民十三年・121 面・「新智識叢書之一」

勞動組合；J. Clayton 原著，黄兆升譯・ 334—C5791

上海，商務，民十三年・91 面・「新智識叢書」

協作論；(法)季特原著，樓桐孫譯・ 334—G361

上海，商務，民十四年・392 面・「經濟名著第五種」

消費合作運動；(日)位田祥易原著，林騤，唐敬果合譯・ 324—P261

上海，商務，民十三年・255 面・

合作主義；孫錫麒著・ 334—S527

上海，商務，民十三年・2 册・

協作社的效用；戴傳賢著・ 334—T121

上海，民智，民十五年・4 版・70 面・「國民黨叢刊之五」

信用合作社經營論；于樹德著・ 334—Y363

上海，中華，民十二年・654 面・「新中學會經濟叢書」

消費合作社；王效文譯· 080—P225—37
上海，商務，民十三年·77面·「面科小叢書第三十七種」
合作銀行通論；吳頌臯著· 080—P227—27
上海，商務，民十二年·42面·「面科小叢書」

335　社會主義

社會主義史；(德)俺伯亞原著，胡漢民譯· 335—B38
上海，民智，民十六年·150面·
社會主義史；趙蘭坪編· 335—C209
上海，商務，民十七年·133面·「新時代史地叢書」
社會主義與社會改良；(美)Rely原著，何飛雄譯· 335—E91
上海，商務，民十三年·再版·322面·
社會主義與進化；夏化尊，李繼楨譯· 335—K165
上海，商務，民十五年·4版·151面·「新時代叢書」
各國社會運動史；劉秉麟編· 335—L372
上海，商務，民十六年·197面·「現代社會科學叢書」
近世社會思想史；徐文亮譯· 335—P233
上海，開明，民十七年·217面·
綜合研究各國社會思潮；邵振青著· 335—S170
上海，商務，民十年·150面·
大同共産主義；朱謙之著· 335—C281
上海，泰東，民十六年·190面·
鮑爾希維克之分析；(法)Pierre Charles原著，唐誦莽譯· 335—C386
上海，民智，民十七年·54面·
共産主義批評；室伏高信原著，沈茹秋譯· 335—S273
上海，開明，民十五年·230面·
布爾什維主義底心理；(美)施羅戈原著，陳國榘譯· 335—SP2
上海，商務，民十五年·3版·149面·「時代叢書」
社會主義與個人主義；(英)王爾德原著，袁振英譯· 335—W645

香港，受匡出版部，民十七年·54 面·

財產起原論；(英)列文斯基原著，陳適譯· 335·01—L291

上海，公民，民十年·90 面·「公民叢書經濟類第三種」

馬克思主義與社會史觀；社會主義研究社譯· 335·4—W67

上海，民智，民十六年·

反科學的馬克思主義；郭任遠著· 335·5—K423

上海，民智，民十六年·180 面·

唯物史觀與倫理之研究；胡漢民著· 335—H405

上海，民智，民十六年·3 版·306 面·

新經濟學；(德)羅撒盧森堡原著，陳壽僧譯· 335·5—L979

中國新聞社，民十六年·314 面·

336 財政學

財政詮要；壽景偉著· 080—P225—60

上海，商務，民十三年·68 面·「百科小叢書第六十種」

財政學大綱；(美)亞當士原著，劉秉麟譯· 336—Ad17

上海，商務，民十四年·4 版·154 面·

最新財政學；張家驪著· 336—C152

上海，商務，民十七年·314 面·

財政學總論；陳啓修著· 336—C270

上海，商務，民十四年·再版·186 面·

財政學；黄可權輯· 340—C289

民元年·282 面·「見法政講義第二册」

財政學；孟森著· 336—M121

上海，商務，民五年·221 面·

財政學；壽景偉編· 336—362

上海，商務，民十四年·210 面·

財政總論；(日)小川鄉太郎原著，何崧齡譯· 336—S410

上海，商務，民十六年·206 面·「經濟叢書」

社會問題與財政；(日)小川鄉太郎原著，甘浩澤等譯· 336—S410
上海，商務，民十三年·387 面·「新智識叢書」

比較財政學；(日)小林亞三郎原著，宋教仁譯· 336—S110
上海，商務，民六年·4 版·2 册·

豫算决算論表解；上海科學書局編譯所編· 080—S155—336
上海，該局，民二年·72 面·「表解叢書」

各國豫算制度論；(日)工藤重義原著，李猶龍譯· 336—K389
上海，羣益，民元年·255 面·

豫算决算論；(日)工藤重義原著，易應湘譯 336—K389
上海，羣益，清宣統三年·248 面·

張文襄公電稿加税免釐部分；李景銘摘鈔· 336·2—C152
北京，經濟學會·「176」面·

最近各省金融商况調查録；桂紹熙編 336—K344
民五年·66 面·

336·2　税則

關税與國權；賈士毅著· 336·2—C478
財政部滬調查貨價處，民十六年·650 面·

租税；王首春著· 080—P225—129
上海，商務，民十六年·61 面·「百科小叢書第一二九種」

日本收回關税權之經過；盛俊譯· 336·2—C320
財政部駐滬調查貨價處，民十四年·52 面·

海關權與民國前途；金葆光編· 336·2—C668
上海，商務，民十七年·「238」面·

中國關税制度論；(日)高柳松一郎原著，李達譯· 336·2—L370
上海，商務，民十三年·250 面·「經濟叢書社叢書」

修改税則始末記；李景銘編· 336·2—L181
北京，經濟學會，民八年·2 册·

關税問題；陳立廷著· 336·2—C279
上海，青年協會，民十七年·3 版·160 面·「公民教育叢刊」

關税問題討論大綱；陳立廷編 · 336 · 2—C279
上海，青年協會 · 90 面 ·

中國關税問題；北京銀行月刊社編 · 336 · 2—P223
北京，該社，民十二年 ·「263」面 ·

中國關税問題 · 336 · 2—P249
嚮導週報社，民十四年 · 74 面 ·「嚮導叢書第二種」

中國關税問題；馬寅初著 · 080—P225—4
上海，商務，民十二年 · 再版 · 40 面 ·「百科小叢書第四種」

中國海關制度沿革；湯德森輯 · 336 · 2—y139
上海，商務，民十四年 · 136 面 ·

中國陸路關税史；童蒙正編 · 080—P225—89
上海，商務，民十五年 · 115 面 ·「百科小叢書第八十六種」

中國厘金問題；王振光著 · 336 · 2—W136
上海，商務，民十四年 · 再版 · 115 面 ·

中國鹽政小史；歐宗佑編 · 080—P225—336
上海，商務，民十六年 · 84 面 ·「百科小叢書第一百三十種」

膠州灣鹽業調査録；景本白編 · 336 · 261—C698
北京，鹽政雜誌社，民十一年 · 38 面 ·

川鹽紀要；林振翰編 · 336 · 261—L316
上海，商務，民八年 · 618 面 ·

浙鹽紀要；林振翰編 · 336 · 261—L316C
上海，商務，民十四年 · 396 面 ·

粤鹽紀實；鄒琳編 · 336 · 261—T694
上海，商務，民十一年 · 294 面 ·

336 · 24　所得税

英國所得税；金國實著 · 080—P225—66
上海，商務，民十三年 · 104 面 ·「百科小叢書第六十六種」

所得税論；(美)施理曼原著，王官彦，王官鼎合譯 · 336 · 24—S246
中華經濟學會，民十年 · 136 面 ·

336・3　公債

公債論表解；蔣筠編・　080—S155—336

上海，科學書局，民三年・86 面・「表解叢書」

公債；何公敢著・　080—P225—59

上海，商務，民十三年・80 面・「百科小叢書第五十九種」

内國公債史；徐滄水編・　336・3—S47C

上海，商務，民十二年・172 面・

中華民國公債法規；徐滄水著・　336・3—S476C

上海，銀行週報社，民十一年・100 面・

公債論；（日）田中穗積原著，陳與年譯・　336・3—T332

上海，商務，民二年・3 版・181 面・

整理中國外債問題；萬籟鳴著・　336・3—W124

上海，光華，民十六年・103 面・

内國公債彙覽；中國銀行總司庫編・　336・3—y275

北京，銀行週報社，182 面・

336・4　歐洲財政史

歐戰財政紀要；陳燦編・　336・4—C270

上海，商務，民十一年・139 面・

德意志之戰時經濟；（瑞）嘉塞爾原著，陳燦譯・　336・43—C480

北京大學，民七年・90 面・

336・51　中國財政史

民國財政史；賈士毅編・　336・51—C478

上海，商務，民十三年・2 册・

中國財政史；胡鈞編・　336・51—H401

上海，商務，民九年・408 面・

中國財政史略；徐式莊編・　336・51—S481

上海，商務，民十五年・105 面・「學藝叢刊」

民國財政論；楊汝梅著· 336·51—y14
上海，商務，民十七年·再版·372面·

革命後之江西財政；張靜廬編· 336·51—C171
上海，光華，民十六年·94面·

338 物價問題

物價問題；周佛海著· 080—P225—64
上海，商務，民十三年·115面·「百科小叢書第六十四種」

物價指數淺説；金國寶著· 080—P225—103
上海，商務，民十五年·124面·「百科小叢書第一百零三種」

編制上海物價指數論叢；盛俊編· 338·5—C320
財政部駐滬調查貨價處，民十四年·75面·

上海市場；潘忠甲著· 338·4—P151
財政部駐滬調查貨價處，民十四年·96面·

股份公司經濟論；(日)上田曾次郎原著，周沉剛譯· 338·7—S156
上海，商務，民十二年·「258」面·

338·9 勞動法

勞動法；孫紹康編· 338·9—S527
上海，商務，民十六年·118面·

339 貧乏

救貧叢談；(日)河上肇原著，楊山木譯· 339—H214
上海，商務，民十六年·96面·

貧乏論；(日)河上肇原著，止止譯· 339—H214P
上海，泰東，民十二年·54面·「新人叢書第一種」

340　法律

法律；周鯁生著· 080—P225—13
　上海，商務，民十四年·38 面·「百科小叢書第十三種」
法學通論；陳敬第著· 340—C270
　上海，羣益，民二年·4 版·186 面·「法政講義第一集第一册」
法學通論表解總論；上海科學書局編譯所編· 080—S155—310
　上海，該局，民元年·46 面·「表解叢書」
法學通論表解各論；上海科學書局編譯所編· 080—S155—340
　上海，該局，民元年·2 册·「表解叢書」
法政講義；陳崇基輯· 340—C289
　上海，羣益，民元年·3 版·10 册·
法政彙刊； 340—L178
　24 册·
法學通論；孟森著· 340—M211
　上海，商務，民三年·97 面·
法意；(法)孟德斯鳩原著，嚴復譯· 340—M212
　上海，商務，民四年·再版·「611」面·
公民；法制；陶彙曾著· 340—T247
　上海，商務，民十四年·第二册·
法制概要；陶保霖編· 340—T248
　上海，商務，民九年·再版·80 面·
大陸近代法律思想小史；方孝嶽編· 340·1—F174
　上海，商務，民十四年·2 册·「世界叢書」
中國古代法理學；王振先著· 340·1—W136
　上海，商務，民十四年·65 面·「國學小叢書」
法律經濟辭典；(日)清水澄原著，郭開文等譯· R—310·3—T668
　上海，羣益，民三年·567 面·

法律大辭書；(日)百科辭書編輯部編· R—310·3—P225
東京，同文館，明治四十二年·9冊·「日本百科辭書」

漢譯日本法律經濟辭典；(日)田邊慶彌原著，王我藏譯· R—340·3—T336
上海，商務，民二年·14版·148面·

341 國際公法

國際公法要覽；羣益書社編· 341—C956
上海，該社，民三年·168面·

平時國際公法表解；王達善編· 080—S155—341
上海，科學書局，民二年·78面·

平時國際公法；(日)中村進午原著，陳時夏譯· 341—C978
上海，商務，民四年·5版·333面·

平時國際公法；金保康輯· 340—C289
民二年·234面·「見法政講義第四冊」

二十世紀國際公法；(法)福偶原著，朱文黼譯· 341—F257
上海，民友社，民二年·496面·

現行國際法；甯協萬著· 341—N242
上海，商務，民十六年·751面·

國際公法之將來；何本海原著，陳宋熙譯· 341—OP5
上海，泰東，民十七年·100面·

春秋國際公法；張心徵著· 341—C170
北京，張仲清，民十三年·「364」面·

341·1 國際會議

萬國聯合論；(美)陀留布勒原著，(英)梅益盛，陸詠笙合譯· 341·1—T766
上海，廣學會，民五年·104面·

國際同盟論；(英)羅仁斯原著，(英)莫安仁，王官鼎合譯· 341·1—L435
上海，廣學會，民八年·80面·

國際聯盟概況；鄭毓秀譯· 341·1—C359

上海，商務，民十五年 · 261 面 ·

萬國聯盟；周鯁生著 · 341 · 1—C778

上海，商務，民十一年 · 260 面 ·

國際聯盟；夏渠著 · 341 · 1—H256

上海，商務，民十七年 · 96 面 ·「新時代史地叢書」

國際聯盟講評；(日)信夫淳平著，王岫盧譯 · 341 · 1—S437

上海，公民，民十年 · 156 面 ·「公民叢書」

國際聯盟及其趨勢；吳品今著 · 341 · 1—w293

上海，商務，民十四年 · 再版 · 2 册 ·「時代叢書」

國際紛争與國際聯盟；信夫淳平原著，薩孟武譯 · 341 · 1—437S

上海，商務，民十七年 · 418 面 ·

巴黎和議後之世界與中國；汪兆銘編 · 341 · 1—w166

上海，民智，民十五年 · 206 面 ·

華盛頓會議小史；周守一編 · 241 · 1—C785

上海，中華，民十二年 · 4 版 · 354 面 ·「新世紀叢書」

華會見聞録；賈士毅編 · 341 · 1—C478

上海，商務，民十二年 · 再版 · 320 面 ·

日内瓦三國海軍會議始末記；張繼煦編 · 341 · 1—C112

民十七年 · 84 面 ·

341 · 2　國際條約

國際條約大全；商務印書館編譯所編 · R341 · 211—S162

上海，該館，民十四年 · 4 版 · 970 面 ·

協商及參戰國與德國之和平條約；新學會社編 · 341 · 2—S155z

上海，該社，民九年 ·「346」面 ·

國際條約要義；竇田來編 · 341 · 2—T383

上海，中華，民三年 · 136 面 ·

341 · 3　戰時國際公法

戰時國際公法表解；上海科學書局編 · 080—S155—341

上海，該局，民二年·65面·「表解叢書」

戰時國際公法；金保康輯· 340—C289

民二年·再版·149面·「見法政講義第四册」

戰時國際公法；(日)中村進成午原著，陳時夏譯· 341·3—C978

上海，商務，民四年·159面·

局外中立精義；(英)羅倫原著，王肇焜等合譯· 341·3—L438

上海，商務，民三年·150面·

341·5 國際私法

中國國際法論；(日)今井嘉幸原著，張森知譯· 341·5—C676

上海，商務，民四年·317面·

國際私法表解；張誠一編· 080—S155—341

上海，科學書局，民二年·84面·「表解叢書」

國際私法；傅疆輯· 340—C289

民二年·再版·298面·見法政講義第四册

國際私法；(日)山田三良原著，李倬譯· 341·5—S149

上海，商務，民四年·3版·253面·

341·8 領事裁判權—中國

法權恢復運動；新時代教育社編·

民十年·8面·「新時代民眾叢書」

領事裁判權；東方雜誌社編· 080—T860—18

上海，商務，民十四年·3版·86面·「東方文庫」

領事裁判權與中國；國民外交叢書社編· 341·8—K105

領事裁判權問題；郝立輿編· 080—B225—78

上海，商務，民十四年·125面·「百科小叢書第七十八種」

領事裁判權討論大綱；黄秩庸編· 341·8—H471

上海，青年協會，民十五年·89面·

天津租界及特區；南開大學政治學會編· 341·8—N120

上海，商務，民十五年·114面·「市政叢書」

上海洋涇濱北首租界章程· 341·8—S155
上海，商務，民十五年·46面·
租借地；金保康著· 080—P225—128
上海，商務，民十六年·53面·「百科小叢書」
上海公共租界收回問題；王世杰編· 341·8—W155
上海，太平洋，民十六年·16面·

342　憲法　憲法史

憲法汎論表解；上海科學書局編· 080—S155—342
上海，該局，民二年·92面·「表解叢書」
比較憲法表解；上海科學書局編· 080—S155—342
上海，該局，民二年·5面·「表解叢書」
國法學；熊範與著· 340—C289
民二年·四版·226面·「見法政講義第一册」
歐美憲政真相；陳壽凡著· 342—G287
上海，商務，民六年·310面·
憲法論綱；(日)法曹閣原著，陳文中譯· 342—F111
上海，羣益，清宣統三年·再版·537面·
憲法研究書；(日)富岡康郎原著，吳興讓譯· 342—F256
上海，商務，清宣統三年·223面·
治法；盧信著· 342—L406
上海，泰東，民十三年·78面·
憲法學原理；(日)美濃部達吉原著，歐宗祐，何作霖合譯· 342—M180
上海，商務，民十四年·316面·「政法叢書」
政治學及比較憲法論；(美)巴路捷斯原著，(日)高田譯· 342—P118
上海，商務，民十五年·7版·2册·
新國家論；薩孟武編· 342—S115
上海，商務，民十七年·219面·「政法叢書」
世界新憲法；商務印書館編譯所編· 342—S162

上海，該館，民十一年·「282」面·

世界現行憲法；商務印書館編譯所編· 342—S162

上海，該館，民五年·再版·860面·

世界聯邦共和國憲法；泰東圖書局編譯所編· 342—T135

上海，泰東，民十一年·4冊·

憲法；(日)清永澄原著，盧弼，黃炳言譯· 342—T668

上海，昌明公司，清光緒三十二年·443面·

比較憲法；王世杰著· 342—W155

上海，商務，民十六年·822面·「現代社會科叢書」

法美憲政正文；商務印書館編譯所編· 342—S162F

上海，該館，民元年·101面·

美法英德四國憲法比較；(英)温澤爾原著，楊錦森等譯· 342—W245

上海，中華，民二年·60面·

歐洲新憲法述評；東方雜誌社編· 080—T860—17

上海，商務，民十四年·3版·99面·「東方文庫」

英國立憲鑑；(英)莫安仁著· 242·42—M821

上海，廣學會·民元年·80面·

英制綱要；錢文選著· 342·42—T616

上海，商務，民九年·134面·

英國憲政叢書；汪大燮著· 342·42—W175

上海，商務，清宣統三年·3冊·

德國憲法；朱和中譯· 332·43—H824

上海，民智，民十二年·196面·

新德國社會民主政象記；張嘉森著· 342·43—C152

上海，商務，民十一年·397面·

法國憲法釋義；金季譯· 342·44—C662

上海，商務，民二年·再版·94面·

法國政府大綱；趙蕴琦著· 342·44—C219

上海，商務，民十一年·198面·「世界叢書」

法國民主政治；朱文著· 342·44—C830

上海，民友社，民二年・5 版・280 面・

瑞士民主政治；Boujour 原著，許同華譯・　342・194—B642

上海，商務，民十二年・155 面・

瑞士的政府和政治；布魯克原著，趙蘊綺譯・　342・494—B791

上海，商務，民十三年・344 面・「世界叢書」

美國憲法釋義；(美)卜布爾原著，沈允昌譯・　342・73—P385

上海，商務，民五年・再版・87 面・

美國政府大綱；趙蘊琦著・　342・73—C219

上海，商務，民十年・344 面・「世界叢書」

美國政治精義；沈步洲譯・　342・73—S220

上海，中華，民四年・3 册・

美國共和政鑑；(美)特韋斯原著，錢智修譯・　342・73—T258

上海，商務，民元年・88 面・

342・51　中國憲法

中國民治論；鮑明鈐著・　342・51—B323

上海，商務，民十四年・「412」面・

國憲議；張君勱著・　342・51—C152

著者自印，民十一年・「168」面・

憲法芻議；陳國綱著・　342・51—C278

唯一研究所，民十一年・再版・52 面・

中國比較憲法論；鄭毓秀著・　342・51—C359

上海，世界，民十六年・122 面・

中華民國根本法及草案；商務印書館編譯所編・　342・51—S162

上海，商務，民十一年・81 面・

中華民國政府大綱；曾友豪著・　342・51—T533

上海，商務，民十五年・「350」面・

中華民國法統遞嬗史；王景濂，唐乃霈合編・　342・51—W136

無錫，民視社，民十一年・224 面・

中華憲法平議；(美)偉羅璧原著，萬兆之譯・　342・51—W684

上海，中華，民八年·152 面·

343 刑法

刑法總論；李維鈺輯· 340—2C89
民二年·383 面·「見法政講義第三册」

刑法各論；袁永廉輯· 340—C289
民二年·「392」面·「見法政講義第二册」

刑法各論表解；王毓炳著· 080—S155—343
上海，科學書局，民元年·192 面·「表解叢書」

中華民國暫行刑律釋義；陳承澤著· 343·51—C270
上海，商務，民十四年·6 版·183 面·

中華現行刑律要義；陳承澤著· 343·51—C270
上海，中華，民二年·99 面·

新刑律釋義；秦瑞玠著· 343·51—T648
上海，商務，民十四年·6 版·322 面·

獨逸監獄法；柳大謐輯· 340—C289
民四年·331 面·「見法政講義第三册」

345 法典—中國

中華民國法令大令三編；商務印書館編譯所編· P—345·1—163
上海，該館，民十二年·四版·

中華六法；商務印書館編譯所編· 345·1—S162
上海，該館，民十一年·6 册·

現行中華新六法；丁澄編· 345·1—T546
上海，文明，民十三年·12 册·

現行律民事有效部分集解；鄭爱諏編· 345·1—D359
上海，世界，民十七年·251 面·

大理院判例解釋現行六法集解；周東白輯· 345·1—C787

上海，世界，民十七年・3 册・

大理院法律解釋分輯；王世裕著・　345・1—W156

上海，商務，民十一年・4 版・164 面・

最新司法判詞；商務印書館編譯所編・　345・1—S162

上海，商務，民十年・4 册・

國民政府最高法院解釋法律文件彙編第一集；郭衛編・　345・1—K429

上海，法學編譯社，民十七年・80 面・

國民政府現行法令大全六法全書合編；郭衛等編・　345・1—K429w

上海，法學編譯社，民十七年・2 册・

347・1　民法

民法總則；周大烈；陳國祥輯・　340—C289

民二年・754 面・「見法政講義第七册」

民法總則表解；上海科學書局編・　080—S155—347・1

上海，該局，清宣統三年・22 面・「表解叢書」

民法要義；(日)梅謙次郎原著，陳承澤，陳時夏合譯・　347・1—M184

上海，商務，民二年・5 册・「法學名著」

民法原論；(日)富井政章原著，陳海瀛，陳海起合譯・　347・1—F256

上海，商務，民二年・5 版・459 面・

民法財產；壬許著・　347・1—J129

上海，羣益，民二年・4 版・3 册・「法政講義第一集第 22—24 册」

民法相續法表解；上海科學書局編・　080—S155—347

上海，該局，民二年・64 面・「表解叢書」

民法財產物權；姚華輯・　40—S289

民二年・363 面・見法政講義第八册

民法物權表解；趙國材著・　080—S155—347

上海，科學書局，民元年・22 面・「表解叢書」

民法財產債權擔保；壬許輯・　310—S280

民二年・831 面・見法政講義第八册

民法債權表解；趙國材著・　080—S155—347

上海，科學書局，民元年·36面·「表解叢書」

親屬法大綱；陶彙曾著· 347·6—T247

上海，商務，民十七年·457面·「政法叢書」

民法親屬法表解；上海科學書局編· 080—S155—347

上海，該局，民二年·70面·「表解叢書」

347·7 商法

商法總則；陳漢第輯· 340—S289

民二年·285面·「見法政講義第九册」

中國商業法令；鄭希陶譯· 347·7—C359

民十五年·86面·

大理院判例解釋現行商法大全；周東白輯· 347·7—C783

上海，世界，民十三年·「472」面·

比較商法論；王家駒著· 347·7—W137

上海，中華，民六年·248面·

商法總則表解；上海科學書局編· 080—S155—347

上海，該局，民元年·28面·「表解叢書」

商法海法商表解；上海科學書局編· 080—S155—347

上海，該局，民二年·78面·「表解叢書」

商法商行爲；雷光宇輯· 340—C289

民二年·352面·「見法政講義第十册」

商法商行爲表解；上海科學書局編· 080—S155—347

上海，該局，民二年·96面·「表解叢書」

商法保險法表解；上海科學書局編· 080—S155—347

上海，該局，民三年·76面·「表解叢書」

商法手形法；方表輯· 340—C289

民二年·340面·見法政講義第十册

商法手形法表解；上海科學書局編· 080—S155—347

上海，該局·民二年·6面·「表解叢書」

破產法表解；上海科學書局編· 080—S155—347

上海，該局，民二年・70 面・

改訂商標法要義；章圭琢著・　349—C189

上海，商務，民十四年・再版・42 面・

新商法商人通例公司條例釋義；民友社編・　347・7—M239

上海，該社，民三年・「913」面・

公司條例釋義；姚成瀚編・　347・7—y152

上海，商務，民十年・4 版・「260」面・

票據法研究續編；徐滄水輯・　347・7—S476

上海，銀行周報報社，民十四年・「274」面・

票據法原理；王敦黨編・　347・7—W158

上海，商務，民十一年・9 面・

票據法研究；銀行週報社輯・　347・7—y275

上海，該社，民十一年・244 面・

海商法；陳鴻慈輯・　340—C289

民二年・四版・314 面・見法政講義第十册

著作權律釋義；秦瑞玠著・　347・7—T648

上海，商務，民三年・再版・62 面・

商法會社；陳時夏輯・　340—C289

民二年・387 面・見法政講義第九册

商會法通釋；歐陽瀚存著・　347・7—0133

上海，商務，民十三年・89 面・

商法調查案理由書；上海總會等編・　347・7—S162

上海，民友社，民元年・816 面・

347・9　訴訟法

訴訟常識；胡暇著・　347・9—H405

上海，商務，民十一年・82 面・

民事訴訟法論綱；（日）高木豐三原著，陳與年譯・　47・9—K177

上海，商務，民十二年・4 版・2 册・「法學名著」

民刑事訴訟須知；周鳳彝編・　343—C774

湖北高等審判廳，民七年・203 面・

民事訴訟法；季祖虞輯・ 340—C289

民二年・233 面・見法政講義第五册

民事訴訟法；李穆輯・ 340—C289

民二年・151 面・見法政講義第五册

民事訴訟法；黄祖治・ 340—C289

民二年・222 面・「見法政講義第五册」

民事訴訟法；李穆輯・ 340—C289

民二年・471 面・見法政講義第六册

民事訴訟法要論表解；上海科學書局編・ 080—S155—47

上海，該局，民元年・60 面・「表解叢書」

民事訴訟法各論表解；上海科學書局編・ 080—S155—374

上海，該局，民元年・2 册・「表解叢書」

刑事訴訟法；張一鵬著・ 340—C289

民二年・10 面・見法政講義第七册

刑事訴訟法要論表解；上海科學書局編・ 080—S155—347

上海，該局，民元年・48 面・「表解叢書」

華洋訴訟例案彙編；姚之鶴著・ 341・5—y151

上海，商務，民四年・2 册・

347・9 法院 審判 法庭

法院編制法表解；上海科學書局編・ 080—S155—347

上海，該局，民三年・2 册・「表解叢書」

各國法庭制度；青年協會書報部編・ 347・9—T665

上海，該會，民十五年・55 面・「公民教育叢刊」

審判心理學大意；（德）馬勃原著，陳大齊譯・ 347・91—M328

上海，商務，民十四年・194 面・「尚志學會叢書」

349 外國法

英律摘要；（英）羅賓生原著，張爾雲譯・ 349・42—R56

上海，商務，民九年·97 面·

德國六法；商務印書館編譯所譯·　349·43—S162

上海，商務，民二年·再版·877 面·

小本日本六法全書；商務印書館編譯所譯·　349·52—S162

上海，該館，民三年·「524」面·

民法要義；(日)梅謙次郎原著，孟森譯·　349·527—M184

上海，商務，民二年·2 册·

民法要義；(日)梅謙次郎原著，金泯瀾譯·　349·527—M184

上海，商務，民二年·258 面·

民法要義；(日)梅謙次郎原著，陳與燊譯·　349·527—M184

上海，商務，民二年·317 面·

民法要義；(日)梅謙次郎原著，陳承澤，陳時夏合譯·　349·527—M184

上海，商務，民二年·311 面·

刑事訴訟法論；(日)松室致原著，陳時夏譯·　349·527—S573

上海，商務，民二年·330 面·

商法論；(日)松波仁一郎原著，秦瑞玠譯·　349·527—S573S

上海，商務，民二年·3 册·

日本商法論；(日)松波仁一郎原著，秦瑞玠譯·　349·5277—S573

上海，商務，民二年·3 版·222 面·「法學名著」

350　行政法

行政法總論；白鵬飛著·　350—P227

上海，商務，民十六年·316 面·「學藝叢書」

行政法總論；熊範輿輯·　349—C289

民元年·28 面·見法政講義第一册

行政法總論表解·　080—S155—350

上海，科學，民元年·56 面·「表解叢書」

比較行政法；(美)葛德奈原著，民友社譯·　350—G62

上海，民友社，民二年·544 面·

比較行政法表解；上海科學書局編輯所編· 080—S155—350

上海，科學，民二年·2 册·「表解叢書」

行政法讯論；(日)清水澄原著，金泯瀾譯· 350—T668

上海，商務，民二年·6 版·「271」面·

行政法各論；陳崇基著· 340—C289

民元年·202 面·見法政講義第一册

行政法各論；(日)清水澄原著，商務印書館編譯所譯· 350—T668S

上海，商務，民六年·7 版·152 面·

法國行政法；(法)裴埒德彌原著，項方等譯· 350—P225

上海，商務，民元年·186 面·

351 中央政府

政府論；(美)黎卡克原著，梁同譯· 351—L315

上海，科學會，民三年·200 面·「政治學第二編」

列國政治異同考；(美)Roib 原著· 351—R271

上海，商務，清光緒三十三年·再版·322 面·

世界共和國政要；商務印書館編譯所編· 351—S162

上海，商務，民二年·3 版·226 面·

各國近時政況；(日)小野塚喜平次原著，林覺民譯· 351—S410

上海，商務，民元年·318 面·

352 地方政府

省制條議；張嘉森著· 352—C152

上海，商務，民五年·再版·84 面·

省憲輯覽；愚厂輯· 352—y357

上海，德記，民十年·「299」面·

湖南省憲法草案· 352—H432

上海，泰東，民十年 · 38 面 ·

地方自治通論；陳顧遠著 · 352—C278

上海，泰東，民十一年 · 228 面 ·

地方自治講義；甘鵬雲編 · 352—C760

湖北地方自治研究社，清光緒三十四年 · 214 面 ·

地方自治制度表解；上海科學書局編輯所編 · 080—S155—352

上海，科學，民二年 · 2 册 ·「表解叢書」

地方自治精義；(日)織田萬原著，泰東圖書局譯 · 352—C625

上海，泰東，民十二年 · 72 面 ·

各國地方自治綱要講義；中國内務部編 · 352—C976K

上海，泰東 · 211 面 ·「地方自治講義第一種」

地方自治講義；(日)水野練太郎原著，商務印書館編譯所譯 · 352—S162

上海，商務，清宣統三年 · 66 面 ·

地方自治討論大綱；孫祖基著 · 342—S511

上海，青年協會書局，民十五年 · 250 面 ·「公民教育叢刊十六種」

自治論；(日)獨逸學協會原譯，謝冰重譯 · 352—1773

上海，商務，清宣統二年 · 5 版 · 159 面 ·

地方行政要義；王倬編 · 352—W136

上海，商務，民三年 · 2 册 ·

352 · 1　市政

市政制度；張慰慈著 · 352 · 1—C172

上海，亞東，民十四年 · 370 面 ·

市政指南；李宗黄著 · 352 · 1—L181

上海，商務，民十六年 · 54 面 ·

市町村自治行政論；孟繼旦編 · 352 · 1—M210

東京，東華書局，清光緒三十四年 · 242 面 ·

市政述要；白敦庸著 · 352 · 1—P227

上海，商務，民十七年 · 153 面 ·

市政經營論；(日)矢田匕太郎原著，吴劍秋譯 · 352 · 1—S259

上海，商務，民十四年 · 212 面 ·「都市叢書」

市政新論；董修甲著 · 352 · 1—T856

上海，商務，民十六年 · 3 版 · 210 面 ·

市組織法；董修甲著 · 352 · 1—T856

上海，商務，民十七年 · 185 面 ·「市政叢書」

美的市政；楊哲明者 · 352 · 1—y121

上海，世界，民十六年 · 70 面 ·

都市問題之研究；(日)枥内吉胤原著，楊名遂譯 · 352 · 1—y132

雲南，昆明市政公所，民十三年 · 146 面 ·「市政叢刊之二」

市政府論；阮毅存著 · 352—y427

上海，世界，民十六年 · 88 面 ·

現代歐美市制大綱；顧彭年著 · 080—P225—13

上海，商務，民十二年 · 再版 ·「百科小叢書第十八種」

新村市；東方雜誌社編 · 080—T860—19

上海，商務，民十四年 · 3 版 · 100 面 ·「東方文庫」

352 · 11 市政府—法令

現行地方自治法令講義；中國内務部編 · 352 · 101—C976n

上海，泰東 · 222 面 ·「地方自治講義第二種」

現行關係地方自治各項法規；中國内務部編 · 352 · 101—C976

上海，泰東，民十四年 · 9 版 · 162 面 ·「地方自治講義第三種」

縣自治法要義；劉世長著 · 352 · 101—L374

上海，商務，民十三年 · 再版 · 116 面 ·

縣自治法釋義；潘上礬著 · 352 · 101—P1549

杭州，潘上礬律師事務所，民十年 ·「122」面 ·

中華民國現行地方自治法令；商務印書館編譯所譯編 · 352 · 101—S162

上海，商務，民十三年 · 再版 · 64 面 ·

352 · 15 市政府—各地

山西地方自治綱要；中國内務部編 · 352 · 15—C9762S

上海，泰東・476 面・「地方自治講義第十二種」

廣東地方自治；中國内務部編・　352・15—C976Kw

上海，泰東・295 面・「地方自治講義第十一種」

一歲之廣州市；黄炎培著・　352・15—H489

上海，商務，民十五年・3 版・109 面・

膠州行政；(德)沙美原著，朱和中譯・　352・15—S141

上海，民智書局，民十六年・226 面・

湖南自治運動史上編；王無爲著・　352・15—W162

上海，泰東，民九年・179 面・

352・19　世界各國

東京市之市政；李謨著・　352・19—L192

上海，民智，民十二年・212 面・

英德法美比較都市自治論；(美)門羅氏原著，朱毓芬譯・　352・19—M926

上海，中華，民十年・「186」面・

美國市政府；(美)孟洛原著，臧啓芳譯・　352・19—M926

上海，商務，民十四年・500 面・「政法名著」

英國田園市；(日)弓家七鄉原著，張維翰譯・　352・19—M164

上海，商務，民十六年・81 面・「市政叢書」

352・2　警察

警界必攜；郭公闕編・　351・74—K424

上海，商務，民十年・5 版・2 册・

違警罰法要義；吳源瀚編・　351・74—W299

内務部編譯處，民七年・120 面・

警察實務表解；上海科學書局編輯所編・　080—S155—352

上海，科學書局，民二年・2 册・「表解叢書」

警察法表解；上海科學書局編輯所編・　080—S155—352

上海，科學書局，民二年・96 面・「表解叢書」

352 · 4 衛生(參見 614 公共衛生)

衛生行政講義；中國内務部編· 352 · 051—C976w
上海，泰東 · 210 面 ·「地方自治講義第七種」

城市衛生學；G. Jewett 原著，李耀東譯· 352 · 41—L552
上海，廣學會，民十二年 · 66 頁 ·

市衛生論；宋介著· 352 · 4—S554
上海，商務，民十五年 · 61 面 ·「市政譯書」

352 · 5 工程(參見 625 土木工程)

都市計畫法制要論；(日)池田宏原著，蔣紹封譯· 352 · 5—C655
雲南，昆明市政公所，民十三年 · 222 面 ·「市政叢刊之一」

道路水利及土木行政講義；中國内務部編· 352 · 051—C976t
上海，泰東 · 130 面 ·「地方自治講義第九種」

市政工程學；凌鴻勛著· 352 · 5—L340
上海，商務，民十三年 · 234 面 ·

352 · 9 其餘市政問題(參見所屬各項如教育行政)

教育行政，警察行政；張則川，劉遠駒合著· 352 · 9—C171
湖北地方自治研究社，清光緒三十四年 · 263 面 ·

教育行政講義；中國内務部編· 352 · 9—C976C
上海，泰東 · 210 面 ·「地方自治講義第六種」

勸業及公共營業講義；中國内務部編· 352 · 9—C976h
上海，泰東 · 300 面 ·「地方自治講義第八種」

地方財政學要義講義；中國内務部編· 352 · 9—C976d
上海，泰東 · 344 面 ·「地方自治講義第五種」

户籍法講義；中國内務部編· 352 · 9—C976h
上海，泰東 · 409 面 ·「地方自治講義第四種」

慈善行政講義；中國内務部編· 352 · 9—C976tE
上海，泰東 · 137 面 ·「地方自治講義第十種」

都市居住問題；(德)Pohle 原著，陳迪光譯· 352—P754

上海，商務，民十三年 · 210 面 ·「新智識叢書」

355　軍事學

軍事常識；蔣方震著 · 355—T563

上海，商務，民六年 · 2 册 ·

孫子兵法史証；支偉成編 · 355 · 01—C624

上海，泰東，民十五年 · 171 面 ·「諸子研究之八」

七子兵略；陳益標點 · 355 · 01—C270

上海，掃葉山房，民十五年 · 268 面 ·

兵的改造與其心理；朱執信著 · 355 · 05—C821

上海，民智，民十五年 · 6 版 · 72 面 ·「國民叢書第一種」

行軍指要；(英)哈密原著，(布)金楷理口譯，趙元益重譯 · 355 · 01—H105

上海，江南製造局 · 6 册 ·

新軍論；(法)卓來原著，劉文島，廖世劭合譯 · 355 · 01—J327

上海，商務，民十五年 · 3 版 · 418 面 ·「共學社時代叢書」

精神講話一斑；林修梅著 · 355 · 01—L326

上海，國光，民十五年 · 再版 · 58 面 ·

曾胡治兵語録；蔡鍔輯 · 355 · 01—T416

上海，商務，民十五年 · 7 版 · 45 頁 ·

增補曾胡治兵語録；蔣中正增輯 355 · 01—T561

中國國民黨陸軍軍官學校，民十三年 · 116 面 ·

軍語 · 355 · 06—C955

310 面 ·

列强青年之軍事預備教育；中央陸軍軍官學校編 · 355 · 07—C979

國民革命軍軍事雜誌社地，民十七年 · 302 面 ·

軍事教育全書；鄒明倫著 · 355 · 08—C781

著者刊，清光緒三十三年 · 481 面 ·

德國練兵要書；(德)康貝原著，李丹崖譯 · 355 · 08—K153

清光緒甲申年 · 2 册 ·

軍事學大全；崔作模著． 355．68—T736

上海，商務．244 面．

歐戰最新改良軍事叢編；端木善孚著． 355．08—T820

民十三年．第一册．

兵工問題；陸世益著． 355．11—L432

上海，商務，民十五年．再版．「114」面．

裁兵計畫書；蔣方震著． 355．11—T563

上海，商務，民十一年．「207」面．

陣中要務令草案． 355．3—C297

陸軍軍隊符號；陸軍軍學編輯局編． 355．3—L425

北京，陸軍部纂譯官處，民十三年．50 面．

應用戰法命令正篇． 355．3—y285

上海，漢武社，清宣統三年．55 頁．

戰術學． 355．4—C141

3 册．

歐洲發明新戰術；黄海泉著． 355．4—H475

武昌，著易堂，民十四年．112 面．

戰術學教程；日本士官學校編． 355．4—J141

上海，漢武社，民元年．3 册．

前敵須知；(英)克利賴原著，舒高第，鄭昌棪合譯． 355．4—K205

上海，江南製造局．4 册．

戰法新書；顧臧，馮寅賓合譯． 355．4—K253

上海，均益圖書公司，清光緒三十三年．305 面．

實兵指揮之參考；廣州軍事研究社編． 355．4—K320

該社，民十五年．260 面．

歐戰發明小部隊攻擊法；(法)白丹原著，黄海泉譯． 355．4—P227

武昌，永盛，民十二年．76 面．

臨陣管見；(布)斯拉弗斯原著，金楷理口譯，趙元益重譯． 355．4—S589

上海，江南製造局．4 册．

最新應用戰術；王作新著． 355．4—W136

北京，武學書館，民十二年・再版・315 面・

兵要地理；軍學編輯局編・ 355・47—C954

三册合一・

古今戰事圖説：平定粤匪之部；陳曾壽著・ 395・4—C289

上海，商務，序清光緒廿五年・5 册・

新兵器之研究；鄒燮斌著・ 355・8—T696

湖北軍警周刊社，民十四年・128 面・

步兵前哨；賀忠良著・ 356—H180C

上海，漢武社，民元年・55 頁・

步隊行軍篇；賀忠良著・ 356—H180d

上海，漢武社，民元年・50 頁・

步兵偵探；賀忠良著・ 356—H180s

上海，漢武社・四版・66 頁・

步兵射擊教範解説；李蒙滋譯・ 356—L191

保定，墨花齋，民六年・242 面・

步兵操典草案・ 356—P409

274 面・

步兵操典；文明書局編・ 356—W259

上海，中華，民十五年・248 面・

礮法畫譜；丁友雲著・ 358—T354

上海，江南製造局，清光緒十四年・25 頁・

野戰礮兵射擊教範解義・ 358—y197

228 面・

360　紅十字會

紅十字會之歷史；(美)莫約西原著・ 360—N178

上海，商務，民八年・37 面・

364 盜匪問題

中國盜匪問題之研究；何西亞著· 364—H210
上海，泰東，民十四年·再版·102 面·

364 犯罪學

犯罪學；朗伯羅梭民原著，劉麟生譯· 364—L838
上海，商務，民十一年·431 面·「共學社社會經濟叢書」

監獄官練習要書；田荊華等合著· 365—C598
監獄研究社，清光緒三十四年·29 面·

感化録；金兆鑾等合著 365—C662
上海，商務，民十二年·59 面·

監獄服務；(日)山田虎一郎講授，劉元績，李明經合編· 365—S122
東京，伊藤幸吉，清光緒三十三年·137 面·

日本監獄制度；(日)小河滋次郎講述，王八鑑譯· 365—S410
赤城，法政研究會，清光緒三十三年·31 面·

監獄學；(日)小河滋次郎，印南於菟吉講授，田慶臧等合編· 365—S410
東京，伊藤幸吉，清光緒三十三年·166 面·

366 秘密會社

中國秘密社會史；商務印書館編譯所編· 366—S162
上海，商務，民十二年·5 版·169 面·

世界之秘密結社；東方雜誌社著· 080—T86012
上海，商務，民十四年·3 版·76 面·「東方文庫第十二種」

368 保險學

保險學；王效文著· 368—W155

上海，商務，民十四年・2 册・

人壽保險學；S・S・Huebner 原著，徐兆蓀譯・　368・3—H87

上海，商務，民十四年・269 面・「經濟叢書社叢書之九」

369・4　童子軍

少年中國運動；王光祈著・　369・4—W146

上海，中華，民十四年・2 版・230 面・「少年中國學會小叢書」

童子軍追踪術；張亞良著・　369・43—C173

上海，商務，民九年・再版・93 面・

童子軍結繩法；張亞良著・　369・43—C173C

上海，商務，民十四年・6 版・85 面・

童子軍自由車隊訓練法；張亞良著・　369・43—C173t

上海，商務，民十一年・4 版・102 面・

童子軍引擎使用法；張亞良著・　369・43—C173y

上海，商務，民十一年・3 版・94 面・

參與萬國童子軍大會報告；章駿著・　369・43—C177

上海，商務，民十四年・128 面・

幼童軍教練法；程季枚著・　369・43—C331

上海，商務，民十年・再版・96 面・

童子軍中國旗語；程季枚著・　369・43—C331t

上海，商務，民十三年・69 面・

童子軍專論；治永清著・　369・43—C658

上海，商務，民十五年・184 面・「北京師範大學叢書」

英國少年義勇團；(日)今西嘉藏原著，朱元善譯・　369・43—C676

上海，商務，民八年・3 版・162 面・

童子軍徽章；朱樸著・　369・43—C833

上海，商務，民十年・再版・66 面・

童子軍斥候必携；瞿同慶譯・　369・43—C874

上海，務商，民十三年・5 版・57 面・

童子軍初步；中國童子軍協會著・　369・43—C976

上海，商務，民十一年·6版·155面·

童子軍規律；中華全國童子軍協會編· 369·43—C976K

上海，商務，民十四年·6版·116面·

英國幼兒團；(英)貝登堡原著，汪仁侯譯· 369·43—P251

上海，商務，民十一年·97面·

童子軍烹調法；蔣千，吕雲彪合著· 369·43—T561p

上海，商務，民十一年·3版·60面·

童子軍游戲法；蔣千，吕雲彪合著· 369·43—T561y

上海，商務，民十年·3版·52面·

童子軍日記；杜定友著· 369·43—T768

上海，商務，民八年·3版·94面·

童子軍體操；魏鼎勳著· 369·43—W207

上海，商務，民十三年·5版·70面·

童子軍露營須知；吳銘之著· 369·43—W290

上海，商務，民九年·3版·70面·

童子軍橋梁建築法；嚴家麟著· 369·43—y211c

上海，商務，民十三年·3版·59面·

童子軍營舍建筑法；嚴家麟著· 369·43—y211y

上海，商務，民十三年·再版·54面·

女童軍教練法；周起鵬著· 369·43—C771

上海，商務，民十一年·109面·

初級女童子軍；汪仁侯著· 369·46—W169

上海，商務，民十二年·65面·

370 教育學

教育入門；沈子善等合著· 370—C771

上海，中華，民十五年·148面·

教育論；斯賓塞爾原著，任鴻雋譯· 370—S33

上海，商務，民十二年·127 面·

教育的理法問題；蘇儒善著· 370—S460

上海，亞東，民十五年·148 面·

教育學原理；孫貴定著· 370—S518

上海，商務，民十三年·138 面·

教育學講義；蔣維喬著· 370—T568

上海，商務，民元年·116 面·

教育學；楊嘉椿著· 370—y121

上海，商務，民十一年·56 面·

教育之改造；(日)中島半次郎原著，陳適譯· 370·1—C978

上海，公民，民十年·44 面·「公民叢書教育類第五種」

教育哲學大綱；范壽康著· 370·1—F132C

上海，商務，民十四年·再版·79 面·「學藝彙刊」

教育哲學；(美)杜威原著，沈振聲筆述，劉伯明譯· 370·1—D515C

上海，泰東，民十四年·5 版·151 面·

孔子教育哲學；葛琨著· 370·1—K423

民十四年·170 面·

教育哲學大意；波特原著，孟憲承譯· 370·1—R614

上海，商務，民十三年·160 面·

現代教育思潮；樊炳清著· 370·8—C544—1·2

上海，商務，民十一年·3 版·143 面·「教育叢書一集一編」

教育思潮概説；鄭次川編· 080—P225—73

上海，商務，民十四年·35 面·「百科小叢書第七十三種」

現代教育思潮；鄭次川，林科棠合譯· 370·1—C359

上海，商務，民十二年·109 面·

教育思潮大觀；(日)中島半郎原著，鄭次川譯· 370·1—c978

上海，商務，民十一年·260 面·「新智識叢書之十六」

近代教育思想；劉炳藜著· 370·1—L372

上海，北新，民十四年·118 面·

輓近教育學説概論；王駿聲著· 370·1—W158

上海，商務，民十三年·再版·124 面·

司丹烈霍爾氏教育學説；樊炳清著· 370·8—C544—1·5

上海，商務，民十一年·3 版·36 面·「教育叢書一集五編」

凱善西台奈氏教育學説；樊炳清著· 370·8—C544—1·6

上海，商務，民十一年·3 版·85 面·「教育叢書一集六編」

杜威教育學説之研究；(日)永野芳夫原著，林科棠譯· 370·1—D515

上海，商務，民十三年·160 面·

杜威教育哲學；(美)杜威講演，金海觀等合記· 370·1—D515d

上海，商務，民十一年·再版·111 面·「南京高等師範叢書第四種」

教育上興味與努力；(美)杜威原著，張裕卿，楊偉文合譯· 370·1—D515c

上海，商務，民十二年·38 面·

明日之學校；(美)杜威原著，朱經農，潘梓年合譯· 370·1—D515m

上海，商務，民十二年·285 面·

民本主義與教育；(美)杜威原著，鄒恩潤譯· 370·1—D515m

上海，商務，民十七年·653 面·「現代教育名著」

平民主義與教育；(美)杜威講著，常道直譯· 370·1—D515P

上海，商務，民十四年·4 版·368 面·「共學社教育叢書」

全民教育論發凡；常乃德著· 370·1—c195

上海，商務，民十五年·235 面·「民鐸叢書第一種」

教育研究實用主義；朱元善著· 370·1—c839

上海，商務，民三年·178 面·

個性與教育；教育雜誌社編· 370·8—C544—60

上海，商務·民十四年·106 面·「教育叢書第六十種」

個性教育；范壽康著· 370·1—F132

上海，商務，民十三年·120 面·「師範小叢書」

個性論；(美)桑代克原著，舒新城譯· 370·1—T393

上海，中華，民十一年·43 面·「教育叢書」

學校與社會；(美)杜威原著，劉衡如譯· 370·1—D515S

上海，中華，民十一年·146 面·「教育小叢書」

社會學與教育；教育雜誌社編· 370·8—C544—45

上海，商務，民十四年・94 面・「教育叢書」

教育之社會原理述要；教育雜誌社編・　370・8—C544—46

上海，商務，民十四年・91 面・「教育叢書第四十六種」

社會與教育；陶孟和著・　370・1—T248

上海，商務，民十二年・3 版・262 面・「北大叢書之六」

密勒氏人生教育；鄭宗海，俞子夷合譯・　370・1—M612

上海，商務，民十三年・4 版・266 面・「北京高師叢書第三種」

教育與人生；(英)羅素原著，李大年譯・　370・1—R911

上海，啓智，民十七年・206 面・

教育之改造；(日)中島半次郎原著，陳適譯・　370・1—c978

上海，公民，民十年・44 面・「公民叢書教育類第五種」

實效教育論；錢智修編・　370・8—C544—5・10

上海，商務，民六年・30 面・「教育叢書第三集第十編」

教育學與各科學；朱元善著・　370・8—C544—1・2

上海，商務，民十一年・3 版・55 面・「教育叢書第一集第二編」

教育之科學的研究；(美)吉特氏原著，鄭宗海譯・　370・1—J881

上海，商務，民十三年・332 面・

370・15　教育心理學

教育心理學大要；教育雜誌社編・　370・8—c544—61

上海，商務，民十四年・81 面・「教育叢書第六十一種」

學習之心理；朱元善編・　370・8—c544—3・4

上海，商務，民六年・84 面・「教育叢書第三集第四編」

學習之基本原理；愛德華原著，錢希乃，祝其樂合譯・　370・15—Eb95

上海，商務，民十三年・292 面・「師範叢書」

心智使用法；(美)基脱遜原著，俞人元譯・　370・15—K658

上海，商務，民十五年・120 面・「新智識叢書」

學習心理學；派爾原著，朱定鈞，夏承楓合譯・　370・15—P993

上海，中華，民十四年・3 版・202 面・「教育叢書」

教育心理學綱要；舒新城編・　370・15—S313

上海，商務，民十二年·再版·122面·

心理原理實用教育學；舒新城著· 370·15—S313

上海，商務，民十四年·7版·192面·「尚志學會叢書」

教育心理學；(日)松本亦太郎，橋山崎淺次郎合著，

朱兆萃，邱陵合譯· 370·15—S573

上海，商務，民十三年·再版·271面·

教育心理學；吳致覺著· 370·15—W281

上海，商務，民十二年·79面·

370·2 教育統計學

教育統計學大綱；薛鴻志著· 370·2—S411

北京高等師範編譯部，民十一年·148面·「北京高師教育叢書」

370·3 教育辭典

中國教育辭典；王尚等合編· R—370·3—W155

上海，中華，民十七年·

370·4 教育論文集

教育短評；教育雜誌社編· 370·8—544—34

上海，商務，民十四年·126面·「教育叢書第八十四種」

戰後教育論；(英)巴德雷原著，陸懋德譯· 370·4—B143

上海，商務，民十一年·66面·

杜威三大演講；(美)杜威講演，劉伯明，沈振聲合譯· 370·4—D515

上海，泰東，民十年·3版·300面·

教育叢稿；李廷翰著· 370·4 L189

上海，中華，民十年·382面·

教育文存；陸費逵著· 370·4—L426

上海，中華，民十一年·再版·414面·

英美教育近著摘要；衛士生等合著· 370·4—W221

上海，商務，民十三年·430面·

世界教育會議之經過；殷芝齡著・　370・63—y270
上海，商務，民十二年・72 面・

370・72　師範教育

師範學校論；賈豐臻著・　370・8—C544—1・8
上海，商務，民十一年・3 版・87 面・「教育叢書第一集第八編」

師範生的良友；張化工著・　370・72—C172
上海，商務，民十三年・54 面・

370・8　教育叢書

教育叢書三集；「缺第二集第三編，第三彙第十一編」　370・8—S544
上海，商務，民四年至六年，細目分見各類・

教育叢著；教育雜誌社編・八十六種，缺 1，4—4 種・　370・8—S545
上海，商務，民十四年，細目分見各類・

370・9　教育史

教育史；范壽康著・　370・9—F132
上海，商務，民十二年・426 面・

教育史；李步青著・　370・9—L195
上海，中華，民十一年・14 版・100 面・

教育史；楊游著・　370・9—y127
上海，商務，民十一年・10 版・79 面・

西洋教育小史；王誨初著・　080—P225—93
上海，商務，民十五年・43 面・「百科小叢書第九十三種」

西洋教育史大綱；姜琦著・　370・9—C521
上海，商務，民十一年・再版・496 面・

西洋教育制度的演進及其背景；莊澤宣著・　370・9—c916
上海，民智，民十七年・266 面・

西洋教育史綱要；王鳳喈著・　370・9—W140
上海，商務，民十一年・143 面・

近三世紀西洋大教育家；(美)格萊夫斯原著，莊澤宣譯· 370·9—G784
上海，商務，民十四年·180面·「現代教育名著」

近代教育史；(美)格萊夫斯原著，吳康譯· 370·9—G784d
上海，商務，民十二年·再版·「463」面·「世界叢書」

中國教育史；陳青之著· 370·951—c270
北京師大心理室，民十五年·290面·「北京師大教育叢書之五」

中國教育制度沿革史；郭秉文著· 370·951—K426
上海，商務，民十一年·164面·

中國教育史大綱；王鳳喈著· 370·951—W140
上海，商務，民十七年·395面·「北京師大叢書」

371 教授法 管理 行政 教員

教授法概要；俞子夷編· 370·8—c544—3·1
上海，商務，民六年·112面·「教育叢書」

科學教授之我見；祈天錫原著，程湘帆譯· 371·3—c417
上海，伊文思，民十三年·18面·

新教授法原論；入澤宗壽原著，羅迪先譯· 371·3—J154
上海，商務，民十三年·234面·

教育方法原論；(美)克伯屈原著，孟憲承，愈慶棠合譯· 371·3—K559
上海，商務，民十六年·464面·「現代教育名著」

教授指導；程湘帆著· 371·3—c345
上海，商務，民十五年·189面·

修學指導；鄭宗海著· 375—c351
上海，商務，民十三年·再版·84面·「東南大學叢書」

教授時間之研究；朱元善編· 370·8—c544—2·2
上海，商務，民十一年·58面·「教育叢書」

協動教學法

協動教學法的嘗試；教育雜誌社編· 370·8—C544—58

上海，商務，民十四年·90 面·「教育叢書第五十八種」

試行協動教學法的成績報告；教育雜誌社編·　370·8—c544—59

上海，商務，民十四年·110 面·「教育叢書第五十九種」

實驗各科動的教育法；吕雲彪等合著·　371·3—L4533

上海，商務，民十二年·124 面·

動的教育學；繆序賓，吕雲彪合編·　370·1—M261

上海，商務，民十年·100 面·

分團教授

分團教授之實際；朱元善編·　370·8—c544—3·2

上海，商務，民六年·47 面·「教育叢書第三集第二編」

實驗分團教授法；陳文鍾等合著·　371·3—c282

上海，商務，民八年·237 面·

分團教授精義；吕雲彪等合著·　371·3—L453

上海，商務，民八年·104 面·

設計教學法

實驗設計教學法；芮佳瑞著·　080—P225—0

上海，商務，民十二年·70 面·「百科小叢書第九種」

設計教學法輯要；康紹言，薛鴻志合著·　371·3—K153

上海，商務，民十二年·196 面·「北京師範大學叢書」

設計教學試驗實況；沈百英著·　371·3—8220

上海，商務，民十一年·78 面·

設計教學法；(美)克拉可韋瑞原著·沈有乾譯·　371·3—K855

上海，中華，民十二年·138 面·

設計教育大全；(日)松清泰嚴原著，林本等合譯·　371·3—S474

上海，商務，民十二年·188 面·

單級教授　復試教授

軍級教師之友；陳子仁著·　371·3—C289

上海，商務，民十五年·143面·

革新單級教育；李曉農，辛曾燦合著· 371·3—L185

上海，商務，民十三年·111面·

複試教授法；范祥善著· 371·3—F132d

上海，商務，民四年·170面·

道爾頓制

道爾頓制原理；芮佳瑞著· 080—P225—34

上海，商務，民十二年·86面·「百科小叢書第三十四種」

柏克赫司特女士與道爾頓制；中華教育改進社編· 371·88—C976

上海，商務，民十四年·38面·

道爾頓式教育的研究；林本譯· 371·38—L325

上海，商務，民十三年·58面·

柏女士講演討論集；許興凱輯· 371·38—P221

北京晨報社出版部，民十四年·230面·

道爾頓研究室制；(美)杜威原著，錢希乃，諸葛龍合譯· 371·8—D515

上海，商務，民十四年·4版·104面·

道爾頓制實驗報告；廖世承著· 731·38—L282

上海，商務，民十四年·188面·「東南大學教育科叢書」

道爾頓制教育；柏克赫司特女士原著，趙廷爲，曾作忠合譯· 371·38—P228

上海，商務，民十三年·183面·

道爾頓制概觀；舒新城著· 371·38—S313

上海，中華，民十二年·216面·

道爾頓制淺説；舒新城著· 371·38—S313C

上海，中華，民十三年·112面·

湖北省立模範小學校試行道爾制一年的經過；王義周編· 371·38—W143

湖北省立模範小學校勤業商社，民十三年·70面·

371·39 其餘各種教學法

英語教學法；張士一講演· 371·39—C170

上海，中華，民十二年・再版・41 面・

葛雷學校之組織；江蘇省立第一師範學校編・　371・39—C514

上海，商務，民十三年・再版・67 面・

教育的發問答；朱元善著・　371・39—C839

上海，商務，民十一年・57 面・「教育叢書第二集第三編」

各科教授法；范壽康著・　371・39—F132

上海，商務，民十二年・144 面・

生活教育設施法；顧樹森著・　371・39—K252

上海，中華，民三年・114 面・

新制各科教授法；李步青著・　371・39—L195

上海，中華，民四年・100 面・

修學效能增進法；(美)韋伯爾博士原著，鄭宗海譯・　371・39—W769

上海，商務，民十三年・36 面・

各科教授法精義；(日)森岡常藏原著，白作霖譯・　371・39—S202

上海，商務，民三年・337 面・

自然研究校外教授實施法；蔡松筠著・　371・39—T414

上海，商務，民十一年・196 面・「理科叢刊」

校外教授實施法；蔡松筠著・　371・39—T414S

上海，商務，民十一年・196 面・

371・42　職業教育

職業教育概論；莊譯宣著・　080—P225—92

上海，商務，民十五年・2 面・「百科小叢書第九十二種」

職業教育之理論及職業之調查；教育雜誌社編・　370・8—C544—65

上海，商務，民十四年・8 面・「教育叢著第六十五種」

工藝科教學法；教育雜誌社編・　370・8—C544—5

上海，商務，民十四年・77 面・「教育叢著五十五種」

手工教授法；趙傳璧編・　370・8—C544—3

上海，商務，民六年・54 面・「教育全著三集七編」

職業教育論；朱景寬譯・　370・8—C544—2・10

上海，商務，民十一年·44 面·「教育叢書二集十編」

手工教育論；朱元善編· 370·8—C544—1·9

上海，商務，民十一年·165 面·「教育叢書第一集第九編」

青年職業指導；(美)卜龍飛原著，王文培譯· 371·42—B623

上海，中華，民十三年·

職業教育真義；朱元善著· 371·42—C838

上海，商務，民六年·258 面·

職業指導實驗；莊澤宣著· 371·42—c916

上海，商務，民十四年·207 面·

職業教育概論；莊澤宣著· 371·42—c916

上海，商務，民十五年·72 面·「百科小叢書第九十二種」

職業心理學；(美)古力非此原著，鄒恩潤譯· 371·12—G875

上海，商務，民十五年·176 面·「職業教育叢刊」

職業指導大綱；郎擎霄著· 371·12—L140

上海，泰東，民十六年·2 册·

小學職業陶冶；(美)勒維特氏布朗氏原著，楊聯鄂，彭望芬合譯· 371·44—L489

上海，商務，民十四年·66 面·「職業教育叢刊第六種」

職業技師養成法；(日)秋保治安原著，熊崇煦譯· 371·12—T676

上海，商務，民八年·165 面·

職業教育研究；鄒恩潤著· 371·42—T692

上海，商務，民十二年·再版·116 面·「職業教育叢刊第一種」

社會的國民教育；(日)田中義一原著，董瑞椿譯· 371·43—T332

通俗教育研究會，民六年·73 面·

371·5 學校行政

教育行政效率問題一部分的研究；教育雜誌社編· 370·8—c544—36

上海，商務，民十四年·83 面·

學校管理法；郭秉文著· 370·8—C544—2·6

上海，商務，民十一年·34 面·「教育叢書第二集第六編」

大學校管理法；(美)W. E. Chartes 原著，何炳松譯· 371·5—C38

上海，公民，民十一年·66面·「公民叢書教育類第六種」
學校管理法；范壽康著·　371·5—F132
上海，商務，民十二年·95面·
學校庶務之研究；蔣世剛著·　371·5—T571
上海，商務，民十三年·160面·
實驗簡易理化器械製造法；蔡文森著·　370·8—C544—2·9
上海，商務，民十一年·180面·「教育叢書第二集第九編」

371·7　學校衛生

小學校救急法；朱傑編·　370·8C544—2·7
上海，商務，民十一年·再版·63面·「教育叢書二集七編」
體育之進行與改造；教育雜誌社編·　370·8—C544—68
上海，商務，民十四年·80面·「教育叢著第六十八種」
小學體育教學法；教育雜誌社編·　370·8—C544—69
上海，商務，民十四年·70面·「教育叢著第六十九種」
學校健康之保護；丁福保著·　610·8—T347—371·7
上海，譯書公會，清宣統三年·127面·「丁民醫學叢書」
衛生科教學法大綱；愛博敦原著，朱有光譯·　371·7—A653
上海，伊文思，民十四年·126面·
袖珍學校衛生；薛德焴著·　371·7—S413
江陰，華通印書館，民十一年·80面·
學生衛生寶鑑；吳傳紱譯·　371·7—W281
上海，中華，民八年·再版·192面·「衛生叢書之一」
學校衛生學；印有模著·　371·7—y288
上海，商務，民四年·7版·78面·
初級體育教練法；(美)葛雷原著，錢江春，戴昌鳳合譯·　371·73—G793
上海，中華，民十三年·3版·122面·
體育教材；麥克樂，沈重威合著·　371·73—M123
上海，商務，民十七年·328面·
衛生故事和教學法；沈百英著·　371·73—S220

上海，商務，民十二年・56 面・

371・8 學校課外運動

學校劇；范壽康著・ 080—P225—36
上海，商務，民十二年・68 面・「百科小叢書第三十六種」

學校風潮的研究；教育雜誌社編・ 370・8—C544—74
上海，商務，民十四年・81 面・「教育叢著第七十四種」

學潮研究；顧倬著・ 371—K246
上海，中華，民十一年・117 面・

訓育之理論與實際；教育雜誌社編・ 370・8—C544—73
上海，商務，民十四年・95 面・「教育叢著第七十三種」

學校生活指導法；朱元善編・ 370・8—C544—3・6
上海，商務，民六年・58 面・「教育叢書第三集第六編」

學校之社會的訓練；朱元善編・ 370・8—C544—3・5
上海，商務，民六年・65 面・「教育叢書三集第五編」

學生社會服務之研究；(美)朝慕儒著・ 371・8—H439
上海，青年會組合，民三年・106 面・

中國學生運動小史；查良鑑著・ 371・8—C110
上海，世界，民十六年・84 面・

學生自治須知；芮佳瑞著・ 371・5—j161
上海，商務，民十一年・3 版・59 面・

學生與政治；高爾松，高爾柏合著・ 371・8—K167
上海，新文化書社，民十四年・234 面・

371・9 特殊教育

特殊教育之實施；教育雜誌社編・ 370・8—C544—42
上海，商務，民十四年・94 面・「教育叢書第三十四種」

天才教育論；朱元善編・ 370・8—C544—2・11
上海，商務，民十一年・33 面・「教叢書二集第十一編」

特別教育；周維城著・ 371・9—C781

上海，商務，民六年·128 面·

372　小學教育

優良小學事彙第一輯；教育部普通司輯· 372—C544
上海，商務，民八年·294 面·

兒童的教育；(美)愛倫凱原著，譯沈澤民· 372—K52
上海，商務，民十四年·92 面·

兒童與教材；(美)杜威原著，鄭宗海譯· 372—D515
上海，中華，民十一年·28 面·「教育叢書」

小學校與家庭；顧旭侯著· 372—K248
上海，商務，民十一年·56 面·

小學教師必携；商務印書館編譯所編· 371—S162
上海，商務，民三年·35 面·

兒童之訓練；G. Smher 原著，陳鴻璧譯· 372—sh62
上海，商務，民十三年·107 面·「新智識叢書之二十一」

兒童矯幣論；葉農生譯· 372—y188
上海，中華，民六年·94 面·

小學教育參考書；教育雜誌社編· 370·8—C544—85
上海，商務，民十四年·3 册·「教育叢著第八十五種」

兒童自治施行實況；教育雜誌社編· 370·8—G544—75
上海，商務，民十四年·3 册·「教育叢著第七十五種」

372·01　小學教學法

小學教學法概要；教育雜誌社編· 370·8—C544—47
上海，商務，民十四年·74 面·「教育叢著第四十七種」

現代小學教學法綱要；朱鼎元著· 372·01—C837
上海，商務，民十四年·219 面·

小學實施設計教學法；崔唐卿著·372·01—T735
北京師大附小，民十四年·3 版·236 面·

設計組織小學課程論；(美)龐錫爾原著，鄭宗海，沈子善合譯· 372·01—B644
上海，商務，民十四年·416面·「現代教育名著」

372·102 心理測驗

學齡兒童智力測驗法；程浩譯· 080—P225—41
上海，商務，民十三年·87面·「百科小叢書第四十一種」

比奈氏智能發達診斷法；樊炳清著· 370·8—C544—2·5
上海，商務，民十一年·35面·「教育叢書二集第五編」

教育測量；(美)愛里斯等原著，張秉潔，胡國鈺合譯· 372·102—Ay74
北京高等師範，民十一年·350面·「北京高師叢書」

兒童心智發達測驗法；(法)賓尼特原著，費培傑譯· 372·102—B512
上海，商務，民十二年·128面·「教育叢書」

智力測驗法；陳鶴琴，廖世承合著· 372·102—C275
上海，商務，民十一年·再版·250面·「南京高師叢書」

智慧測量；許興凱著· 372·102—H376
北京，農報社，民十二年·202面·「農報社叢書第十二種」

麥柯爾教育測量法撮要；(美)麥柯爾原著，柯佐周譯· 372·102—M124
武昌，中山大學出版部，民十六年·202面·

比納西蒙智力測驗；推孟原著，華超譯· 372·102—T273
上海，商務，民十三年·2冊·「世界叢書」

測驗統計法概要；俞子夷著· 372·102—Y370
上海，商務，民十四年·再版·75面·

372·2 幼稚園

幼稚教育及日美之幼稚園；教育雜誌社編· 370·8—C544—72
上海，商務，民十四年·72面·「教育叢著第七十二種」

蒙鐵梭利教育之兒童；裴雷女史原著，顧樹森等合譯· 372·2—P255
上海，中華，民六年·84面·「教育叢書之一」

小學游技；譚競公著· 372·2—T102
上海，商務，民五年·再版·109面·

幼稚園課程研究；唐穀譯．　372・2—T206
上海，中華，民十二年・91面・

孩子們的音樂；(日)田邊尚雄原著，豐子愷譯・　372・2—T336
上海，開明，民十七年・128面・

幼稚園教育；王駿聲著・　372・2—W136
上海，商務，民十六年・169面・「師範叢書」

設計的兒童游戲；楊彬如著・　372・2—Y136
上海，商務，民十一年・84面・

實用主義兒童訓練法；沈鏡清著・　372・207—S211
上海，商務，民五年・再版・122面・

小學各科教學法

小學自然科教學法；教育雜誌社編・　370・8—C544—54
上海，商務，民十四年・90面・「教育叢著第五十四種」

作文及文學教學法；教育雜誌社編・　370・8—C544—49
上海，商務，民十四年・107面・「教育叢著第四十九種」

小學國語教學法概要；教育雜誌社編・　370・8—C544—48
上海，商務，民十四年・89面・「教育叢著第四十八種」

外國語教學法；教育雜誌社編・　370・8—C544—57
上海，商務，民十四年・102面・「教育叢著第五十七種」

小學校商業科教授法；朱元善編・　370・8—C544—3・12
上海，商務，民六年・53面・「教育叢書三集第十二編」

小學算術教學法及練習法；教育雜誌社編・　370・8—C544—51
上海，商務，民十四年・90面・「教育叢著第五十一種」

初級算術教授法；陳友松，廖榮善合著・　372・7—C292
上海，伊文思，民十四年・38面・

小學公民教育及教學法；教育雜誌社編・　370・8—C544—52
上海，商務，民十四年・94面・「教育叢書」

小學校的公民教育；趙宗預著・　372・80—C201
上海，商務，民十七年・155面・

小學公民科教學法；唐湛聲著· 372·83—T201
上海，中華，民十四年·2版·109面·「教育小叢書」

小學史地教學法；教育雜誌社編· 370·8—C544—53
上海，商務，民十四年·80面·「教育叢著第五十三種」

小學地理教學法；薛鍾泰著· 372·8—S411
上海，中華，民十一年·3版·80面·「教育小叢書」

373 中學教育

中學訓練問題；陳啓天著· 373—C270
上海，中華，民十一年·48面·「師範叢書」

中學教育；廖世承著· 373—L282
上海，商務，民十三年·444面·「師範叢書」

初級中等教育；曾作忠著· 373—T331
上海，中華，民十三年·268面·「北京師大叢書」

中學校之博物學教學法；教育雜誌社編· 373—C544—40
上海，商務，民十四年·90面·「教育叢著第五十種」

374 家庭教育 自動教育

勤勞教育論；朱元善編· 370·8—C544—3·8
上海，商務，民六年·133面·「教育叢書三集第八編」

自習主義教學法；陳達著· 374—C288
上海，商務，民十年·3版·247面·

家庭教育；陳鶴琴著· 374—C275
上海，商務，民十五年·160面·「東南大學教育科叢書」

美國家事教育；莊澤言著· 374—C916
上海，商務，民十年·再版·173面·

家庭教育與學校；熊翥高著· 374—H356
上海，商務，民十二年·71面·

常識修養法；鄒德謹著· 374—J697
上海，商務，民十一年·5版·54面·「通俗教育叢書」

各科常識問答；湖南五育勵進會編· 374—H432
長沙，荷花池，南華書社·民十五年·再版·2册·

常識講義；上海交通大學學生會義務學校編· 374—M152
上海，民智，民十二年·70面·

實務才幹養成法；鄒德謹，蔣正陪合編· 374—T697
上海，商務，民六年·再版·37面·「通俗教育叢書」

自學自習法；朱元善編 370·8—C544—2·1
上海，商務，民十一年·再版·92面·「教育叢書二集一編」

學校團；秦同培著· 370·8—C544—1·10
上海，商務，民十一年·53面·「教育叢書一集第十編」

成人教育；教育雜誌社著· 370·8—C544—66
上海，商務，民十四年·93面·「教育叢著第六十六種」

實用主義科外教育設施法；楊祥麐著· 374—Y121
上海，商務，民十四年·3版·240面·

375　課程

小學的新課程；教育雜誌社編· 370·8—C544—3
上海，商務，民十四年·2册·「教育叢書」

小學課程概論；程湘帆叢· 375—S345
上海，商務，民十二年·268面·「中華教育改進社叢書之一」

新學制中學的課程；教育雜誌社編· 370·8—C544—2
上海，商務，民十四年·75面·「教育叢書」

教材之研究；教育雜誌社編· 370·8—C544—76
上海，商務，民十四年·94面·「教育叢書」

社會化的學程；德爾滿原著，鄭國粱譯· 375—T273
上海，商務，民十二年·3册·「燕京大學叢書」

新學制課程標準綱要；全國教育聯合會編· 375—T720

上海，商務，民十四年・再版・135 面・

376 女子教育(參見 396 婦女問題)

女子教育之問題及現狀；教育雜誌社編・ 370・8—C544—71
上海，商務，民十四年・74 面・「教育叢著第七十一種」

新女子職業教育；段碧江著・ 376—T816
上海，中華，民十二年・72 面・

378 專門及大學教育

國立北京大學廿周年紀念册 378・511—P223
北京大學，民六年・438 面・

學校指南；商務印書館編輯所編・ 378・51—S162
上海，商務，民十二年・

379 公共及義務教育

平等教育計畫；張崇玖著・ 379—C152
上海，泰東，民十一年・98 面・

各國教育談；陳其昌等合著・ 379—C278
上海，商務，民十三年・155 面・

視察教育世界一周記；賈豐臻著・ 379—C475
上海，商務，民十一年・再版・256 面・

通俗教育談；顧倬著・ 379—K246
上海，中國圖書公司，光緒三十三年・63 面・

平民教育實施法；顧旭侯等合著・ 379—K248
上海，商務，民十四年・106 面・

露天學校；李乃得汝耶斯原著，黃光斗譯・ 379—L189

上海，泰東，民十一年·94 面·

貧民教育譚；李廷翰編·　379—L198

上海，教育雜誌社，民二年·3 版·99 面·

教育問題；(日)淺野馴三郎原著，甘浩澤譯·　379—T629

上海，商務，民十四年·98 面·「百科問答叢書」

二百兆平民大問題；吳敬恒著·　379—W281

上海，商務，民十三年·73 面·

國家主義的教育；余家菊，李璜合著·　379—y346

上海，中華，民十二年·3 版·162 面·「少年中國學會叢書」

義務教育之研究及討論；教育雜誌社編·　370·8—C544—63

上海，商務，民十四年·78 面·「教育叢著第六十三種」

歐美之義務實習教育；教育雜誌社編·　370·8—C544—64

上海，商務，民十四年·90 面·「教育叢著第六十四種」

各地方實施義務教育彙刊；　379—K201

北京教育部，普通教育司·110 面·

義務教育之商榷；袁希濤編·　379—y421

上海，商務，民十年·57 面·

平民學校教學法；賴成鑲著·　379·1—L20

上海，商務，民十六年·80 面·「城市平民教育叢刊」

平民學校管理法；殷祖赫著·　379·1—y270

上海，商務，民十六年·32 面·「城市平民教育叢刊」

世界各國學制考；吳家鎮·　379·1—W281

上海，商務，民十三年·493 面·「人文叢書」

庚子賠款與教育；教育雜誌社編·　370·8—C544—83

上海，商務，民十四年·3 册·「教育叢著第八十三種」

美國退還庚子賠欵餘額經過情形；章之汝等合譯·　379·11—C177

上海，商務，民十四年·175 面·「中華教育改進社叢刊之二」

379·14　教育法令

教育法令選；教育雜誌社編·　370·8—C544—86

上海，商務，民十四年·3 册·「教育叢著第八十六種」

教育新法令；中國教育部編· 379·14—C976

上海，商務，民八部·8 版·4 册·

新編普通教育法令；丁督盦著· 379·14—T346

上海，中華，民十一年·再版·215 面·

379·15 學校視察法

教育視察與視察後的感想；教育雜誌社編· 370·8—C544—78

上海，商務，民十四年·92 面·「教育叢著第七十八種」

學校調查綱要；張裕卿著· 379·152—C173

上海，商務，民十二年·36 面·

視學綱要；王光樽著· 379·152—W145

上海，商務，民九年·3 版·88 面·

學校參觀法；湯中，蔡文森合著· 379·152—T190

上海，商務，民十四年·4 版·210 面·

379·173 鄉村教育

鄉村教育研究及研究法；教育雜誌社編· 370·8—C544—44

上海，商務，民十二年·70 面·「教育叢著第四十四種」

農村教育；顧復著· 379·172—K247

上海，商務，民十五年·5 版·79 面·

鄉村教育；喻謨烈著· 379·173—y382

上海，商務，民十六年·168 面·「師範叢書」

379·4—9 世界各國教育狀況

世界教育狀況；陸費達著· 379·4—L426

上海，商務，清宣統三年·訂正再版·

歐戰後各國教育之改革；教育雜誌社編· 370·8—C544—77

上海，商務，民十四年·96 面·「教育叢著第七十七種」

德法英美國民比較論；余寄譯· 379·4—C978

上海，中華，民六年·188面·

歐洲新教育·　379·4—R661

上海，商務，民十四年·369面·「師範叢書」

八年歐美考察教育團報告；袁希濤等合編·　379·4—y421

上海，商務，民九年·354面·

英國教育要覽；余家菊著·　379·42—y346

上海，中華，民十四年·212面·

德國教育之精神；(日)吉田熊次原著，華文祺等合譯·　379·43—C395

上海，商務，民五年·230面·

德國教育之實况；陸規亮著·　379·43—L420

上海，中國圖書公司，民五年·172面·

德國工商補習學校；(德)培倫子原著，陸振邦譯·　379·43—P258

上海，商務，民十四年·88面·「職業教育叢刊」

蘇俄之教育；(俄)司各脱尼林原著，許崇清譯·　379·47—N27

上海，商務，民十七年·226面·「現代教育名著」

比利時之新學校；(法)利葉原著，陳能慮譯·　379·493—F416

上海，商務，民十一年·141面·

教育獨立問題之討論；教育雜誌社編·　370·8—C544—35

上海，商務，民十四年·101面·「教育叢著第三十五種」

孟禄的中國教育討論；陳寶泉等合著·　379·51—C285

上海，中華，民十二年·再版·168面·

中國教育統計概覽；中華教育改進社編·　379·51—C976

上海，商務，民十三年·60面·「中華教育改進社叢書」

中國教育問題的討論；劉廷芳著·　379·51—L375

上海，中華基督教青年會全國協會書報部，民十一年·56面·

中國教育一瞥録；王卓然著·　371·51—W137

上海，商務，民十二年·392面·

江蘇教育行政概況；蔣維喬著·　379·514—T568

上海，商務，民十三年·88面·

吉林近三年間教育概况；吉林教育廳編·　379·516—C694

吉林，該廳，民十年·54 面·

考察日本菲律賓教育團記實；陳寶泉等譯· 379·52—C285

上海，商務，民六年·212 面·

日本留學指掌；崇文書局編· 379·52—C986

東京，大葉久吉，明治三十八年·597 面·

考察日本實業補習教育記要；李步青，路孝植合著· 379·52—L195

上海，商務，民七年·103 面·

調查日本教育紀要；唐碧譯· 379·52—T211

通俗教育研究會，民五年·92 面·

新大陸之教育；黄炎培著· 379·7—H489

上海，商務，民六年·256 面·

美國鄉村教育概觀；古楳著· 379·7—K265

上海，中華，民十五年·3 版·100 面·「教育叢書」

美國教育徵覽；汪懋祖著· 379·73—W172

上海，中華，民十一年·再版·232 面·「教育叢書」

東南洋之新教育；黄炎培著· 379·91—H189

上海，商務，民十一年·2 册·

380 商業 交通

380·3 商業政策

商業學表解；上海科學書局編輯所編· 080—S155—380

上海，科學書局，清宣統元年·66 面·「表解叢書」

國際商業政策；(美)菲士克原著，周佛海譯· 080·3—F541

上海，商務，民十三年·147 面·

商業政策；(奥)菲里波誰原著，馬君武譯· 380·3—P538S

上海，中華，民十三年·2 册·「新文化叢書之一」

商業政策；(日)井土辰九郎原著，吳譯· 380·3—T664

上海，泰東，民四年·328 面·「政法叢書之一」

380·6　交通

交通政策；(奥)菲里波維原著，馬君武譯·　380·6—P538
上海，中華，民十三年·186 面·

交通史；王倬著·　380·6—W136
上海，商務，民十二年·152 面·

中國近世道路交通史；楊得任著·　380·6—y139
吉林，永衛印書局，民十七年·230 面·「站員教育叢書第十種」

交通救國論：一名交通事業治標策；葉恭綽著·　380·6—y185
上海，商務，民十三年·111 面·

380·8　商業地理

商業地理；蘇繼廎著·　380·8—S460
上海，商務，民十三年·再版·2 册·

商業地理；曾牖著·　380·8—T533
上海，商務，民九年·3 版·2 册·

380·9　商業史

世界商業史；(日)和田垣謙三原著，徐崇釋，周葆鑾合譯·　380·9—H216
上海，商務，民元年·199 面·

近世商業史；趙文鋭著·　380·9—C218
上海，商務，民十七年·238 面·「新智識叢書」

中國商業史；王孝通著·　080—P225—22
上海，商務，民十四年·3 版·112 面·「百科小叢書」

中國商戰失敗史；黄炎培，龐三松合著·　380·951—H489
上海，商務，民六年·220 面·

中國商業史；陳燦著·　380·951—C270
上海，商務，民十四年·187 面·

上海通商史；(英)裘普司著，程灝譯·　380·951—C742

上海，商務，民十五年·三版·91 面·

382 國際貿易

國際貿易；吳應圖著· 382—W299
上海，中華，民十三年·115 面·「常識叢書第八種」

中國國際貿易；殷壽光著· 382—y272
上海，世界書局，民十六年·125 面·

今世中國貿易通志；陳重民著· R382—C270
上海，商務，民十三年·633 面·

383 郵政

郵政章程；中國—交通部—郵政總局· 383—C976
郵政總局，民十五年·270 面·

中華民國十三年郵政儲金事務總論；
中國—交通部—郵政總局編· 383—C976C
郵政總局·41 面·

中華民國十四年郵政事務總論；中國—交通部—郵政總局編· 383—C976C
郵政總局·70 面·

郵政辦事手續；奚楚明著· 383—H249
上海，郵政海關英文專校，民十四年·84 面·

日本郵政全書；郵政研究社編· 383—y324
東京，秀光社，清光緒三十三年·824 面·

385 鐵道 航業

鐵道學表解；上海科學書局編輯所編· 089—S155—385
上海，科學書局，民二年·3 冊·「表解叢書」

美國鐵路管理法；湯震龍著· 385—T198

上海，商務，民十二年 · 231 面 ·

中國鐵道要鑑；劉馥易，振乾合著 · 385—T814

上海，昌明公司，清宣統元年 · 再版 · 520 面 ·

中國鐵道外債論；吳鼎昌著 · 385—W296

奉天，圖書發行所，清宣統二年 · 90 面 ·

鐵道常識；嚴曾壽著 · 385—y211

武昌，共進書社，民十二年 · 52 面 ·

各國航業競爭；國民外交叢書社編 · 327 · 51—K405

上海，中華，民十五年 · 55 面 ·「國民外交小叢書」

389　度量

中外度量衡幣比較表；杜亞泉等合著 · 389—T769

上海，商務，民六年 · 七版 · 147 面 ·

390　風俗　禮節

世界風俗談；東方雜誌社編 · 080—T860—13

上海，商務，民十四年 · 3 版 · 79 面 ·「東方文庫」

中國風俗史；張亮采著 · 390—C162

上海，商務，民十五年 · 11 版 · 222 面 ·

392 · 3　家庭問題

新家庭；姜繼襄著 · 392 · 3—C521

民十二年 · 156 面 ·

家庭問題；易家鉞著 · 392 · 3—E188

上海，商務，民十一年 · 4 版 · 177 面 ·「時代叢書」

家庭改進運動辦法大綱；傅若愚著 · 392 · 3—F247

上海，青年協會，民十四年・27 面・「家庭改進叢書第一種」

中國家庭問題；易家鉞，羅敦偉合著・ 392・3—I112

上海，泰東，民十五年・178 面・「家庭研究社叢書」

家庭新論；沈鈞儒著・ 392・3—S211

上海，商務，民十四年・再版・70 面・

家庭的研究；謝頌羔著・ 392・3—S423

上海，美以美會，民十四年・113 面・

家庭進化論；嚴恩椿著・ 392・3—Y211

上海，商務，民十二年・4 版・90 面・

392・5 婚姻問題

中國古代婚姻史；陳顧遠著・ 392・5—C278

上海，商務，民十四年・148 面・「國學小叢書」

家庭與婚姻；東方雜誌社編・ 080—F860—29

上海，商務，民十四年・3 版・127 版・「東方文庫」

社交與性愛；黃粱譯・ 392・5—H478

上海，出版合作社，民十五年・118 面・

戀愛與結婚；(瑞典)愛倫凱原著，朱舜琴譯・ 392・5—K52

上海，光華書局，民十五年・再版・302 面・

婚姻訓；盧壽錢著・ 392・5—L400

上海，中華，民八年・80 面・「婦女叢書之一」

結婚論；宋喜釗，費保彦合譯・ 392・5—S554

上海，中華，民八年・4 版・60 面・

德國人之婚姻問題；王光祈著・ 392・5—W145

上海，中華，民十四年・2 版・85 面・「少年中國學會小叢書」

395 交際禮節

交際全書正續補；鐵冷著・ 395—T319

上海，中原書局，民十六年・13 版・2 冊・

396　婦女問題

婦女將來與將來的婦女；張友松譯・　080—L966—396

上海，北新書局・120 面・「明日叢書」

婦女之過去與將來；李漢俊譯・　396—L185

上海，商務，民十一年・再版・206 面・「新智識叢書之三」

婦女運動；東方雜誌社編・　080—T861—27

上海，商務，民十四年・3 版・2 册・「東方文庫」

女子自殺的解剖・　396—C152

南京，中山，民十七年・146 面・「知行叢書之二」

婦女問題；張佩芬著・　396—C68

上海，商務，民十五年・4 版・112 面・「新智識叢書」

日本婦女運動考察紀略；陳維輯・　396—C290

上海，商務，民十七年・266 面・「現代婦女叢書」

女性論；馮飛著・　396—F204

上海，中華，民十五年・108 面・「新文化叢書」

婦女與經濟；(美)紀爾曼原叢，鄒敬芳譯・　396—G42

上海，學術研究會，民十三年・316 面・「學術研究會叢書」

自由女性；(美)高德曼女士原著，盧劍波譯・　396—G569

上海，開明，民十六年・186 面・「婦女問題研究會叢書」

性的故事；(英)赫勃脱夫人原著，松濤譯・　396—G415

上海，開明，民十六年・145 面・「婦女問題研究會叢書」

婦女職業問題；易家越著，　396—I112

上海，泰東，民十五年・4 版・138 面・「家庭研究社叢書」

婦女職業與母性論；東方雜誌社編・　080—T860—28

上海，商務，民十四年・3 版・94 面・「東方文庫」

母性復興論；(瑞典)愛倫凱原著，黄石譯・　396—K52

上海，民智，民十五年・124 面・

婦女之天職；季理斐著・　396—M175

上海，廣學會，民十二年・44 面・

女性問題研究集；梅生著・ 396—M185

上海，新文化，民十七年・4 册・

中國婦女問題討論集；梅生著・ 396—M185C

上海，新文化，民十五年・6 册・

婦女年鑑；梅生編・ 396—M185F

上海，新文化，民十三年・2 册・

婦女與社會；(法)倍信爾原著，沈端先譯・ 396—P123

上海，開明，民十六年・758 面・「婦女問題研究會叢書」

婦女問題十講增訂；(日)本間久雄原著，姚伯麟譯・ 396—P260

上海，學術研究會，民十三年・2 册・「學術研究會叢書」

婦女問題十講；(日)本間久雄原著，章錫琛譯・ 396—P260

上海，開明，民十五年・316 面・「婦女問題叢書第一種」

婦女修養談；謝旡量著・ 396—s425

上海，中華，民九年・235 面・「女學叢書之一」

女性中心説；(日)堺利彥編，李達譯・ 396—S199

上海，商務，民十五年・134 面・「新時代叢書」

女性中心説；(日)堺利彥編，夏丏尊漢譯・ 396—W34

上海，民智，民十四年・再版・182 面・

中國婦女戀愛觀；王平陵著・ 396—W153

上海，光華，民十五年・再版・73 面・

與謝野晶子論文集；張嫻譯・ 396—Y356

上海，開明，民十五年・162 面・

中國婦女在法律上之地位；趙鳳喈著・ 396・2—c204

上海，商務，民十七年・152 面・「社會研究叢刊第二種」

女性與文學；輝羣女士著・ 396・8—H503

上海，啓智書局，民十七年・102 面・「表現小叢書之一」

女人的故事；(英)喬治原著，胡學勤譯・ 396・9—G293

上海，開明，民十六年・226 面・「婦女問題研究會叢書」

婦女實鑑；中華書局編・ R—396—C926

上海，中華，民九年·

398　諺語　歌謡

諺語的研究；小説月報社編·　808—sh41—15
上海，商務，民十四年·56面·「小説月報叢刊第十五種」

歌謡論集；鐘敬文著·　398—C959
上海，北新書局，民十七年·436面·

民間文學；徐蔚南著·　398—S483
上海，世界，民十七年·再版·65面·

希臘神話；沈雁冰著·　398·4—S224
上海，商務，民十四年·112面·「兒童世界叢刊」

民謡集；何中孚輯·　398·8—H199
上海，泰東，民十三年·80面·

中國民歌研究；胡懷琛著·　398·8—H405
上海，商務，民十四年·121面·

歌謡；吳啓瑞等合輯·　398·8—W287
上海，中華，民十三年·8册·「平民文學叢書」

分類標點中英對照名言大辭典；許啃天著·　398·903—H371
上海，羣學社，民十五年·1082面·

400 語學

400 語言學

世界語概要；後覺著． 080—P225—96
上海，商務，民十五年．134 面．「百科小叢書第九十六種」

國際語運動；東方雜誌編． 080—T860—70
上海，商務，民十四年．92 面．「東方文庫」

德國學校近世語教授法；周越然譯． 407—P226
上海，商務，民五年．162 面．

世界語講義；盛國成著． 408．9—C320
上海，民智，民十一年．286 面．

萬國語音學大意；沈彬著． 414—S220
上海，中華，民十一年．再版．52 面．

英文典表解；上海科學書局所輯編． 080—S155—425
上海，科學書局，清光緒三十二年．54 面．「表解叢書」

東文典學表解；上海科學書局編輯所編． 080—S155—495
上海，科學書局，清光緒三十二年．47 面．「表解叢書」

495．1 中國語言學

小學常識；徐敬修著． 495．1—S476
上海，大東，民十四年．114 面．「國學常識之一」

字義類例；陳獨秀著． 495．1—C289
上海，亞東，民十四年．115 面．

文字源流；張之純，莊慶祥合著． 495・12—C152
上海，商務，民十五年・25 版・60 面・
文字源流參考書；張之純編． 495・12—C152
上海，商務，民十四年・6 版・97 面・
文始；章炳麟著． 495・12—C189
中國文字學大綱；何仲英著． 495・12—H199
上海，商務，民十二年・3 版・104 面・

495・11　國語

小學國語話教學法；張士一著． 495・11—C170
上海，中華，民十一年・81 面・「國語叢書」
國語學草創；胡以魯著． 495・11—H406
上海，商務，民十二年・147 面・
新學制國語教科書；顧頡剛，葉紹鈞，合輯． 495・11—K246
上海，商務，民十三年・6 册・
國語教學法；黎錦熙著． 495・11—L215K
上海，商務，民十三年・264 面・
國語教學法講義；劉儒著． 495・11—L379
上海，商務，民十一年・124 面・
國語常識會話；陸衣言著． 495・11—L427K
上海，中華，民十二年・5 版・24 面・
黎錦熙的國語講壇；陸衣言著． 495・11—L427K
上海，中華，民十年・
國語文；馬國英著． 495・11—M116K
上海，中華，民十二年・54 面・「國語講義第七種」
國際交際會話；馬國英著． 495・11—M166K
上海，中華，民十一年・33 面・
王璞的國語會話；王璞著． 495・11—W154
上海，中華，民十二年・232 面・
實用國語會話；王璞著． 495・11—W154s

上海，商務，民十一年·5版·58面·

國語話；炳樂嗣著· 495·411—y269K

上海，中華，民十五年·40面·「國語講義第六種」

國語概論；樂嗣炳著· 495·11—y269K

上海，中華，民十二年·30面·「國語講義第一種」

國語旗語；樂嗣炳著· 495·11—y269K3

上海，中華，民十二年·再版·44面·「國語講義第十二種」

495·12 國音

國語發音學；後覺著· 495·12—H243

上海，中華，民十一年·74面·「國語講義第三種」

國音學；高元著· 495·12—K179

上海，商務，民十一年·145面·

增補訂正國音易解；黎均荃，陸衣言合著· 495·12—L215

上海，中華，民十一年·48面·

國音字母排列法；劉善薰著· 495·12—L373

上海，中華，民十五年·45面·

國語發音學大意；陸衣言著· 495·12—L427

上海，中華，民十一年·3版·68面·

中華國音留聲機片課本；陸衣言等合著· 495·12—L427c

上海，中華，民十一年·7版·72面·

國音入聲字指南；馬國英著· 495·12—M116y

上海，中華，民十五年·77面·

國音獨習法；馬國音著· 495·12—M116y1

上海，中華，民十二年·29面·

國音；蔣鏡芙著· 495·12—T561

上海，中華，民十二年·4版·45面·「國語講義第二種」

比較實驗國語正音法；秦鳳翔著· 495·12—T645

上海，中華，民十一年·72面·

國語發音學；汪怡著· 495·12—W200

上海，商務，民十三年・325 面・

聲韻沿革大綱；樂嗣炳著・　495・12—y269s

上海，中華，民十五年・34 面・「國語講義第五種」

國語辨音；樂嗣炳著・　495・12—y269K

上海，中華，民十五年・46 面・「國語講義第四種」

495・121　注音字母

國音字母書法體式；中華書局編譯所編・　495・121—C976

上海，中華，民十二年・再版・10 面・

注音字母教授法；陸衣言著・　495・121—L427

上海，中華，民十年・3 版・146 面・

495・13　中國字典

康熙字典；凌紹雯編・　R—495・13—K151

14 册・

辭源；陸爾奎等合編・　R—495・131—L425

上海，商務，民九年・6 版・4 册・

中華大字典；徐元誥等合編・　R—495・13—Su484

上海，中華，民四年・4 册・

國文成語辭典；莊適著・　R—495・13—C918

上海，中國圖書公司和記，民十五年・7 版・「1030」面・

注音新辭典；中華書局編譯所編・　R—495・113—C976

上海，中華，民十年・603 面・

中華民國最新字典；葛天爵等合編・　495・13—K428

上海，會文堂，民十七年・14 版・

虚助詞典；施括乾著・　495・13—S425

上海，亞東，民十二年・84 面・

495・15　中國文法

馬氏文通；馬建忠著・　495・15—M112

上海，商務，清光緒三十一年·2冊·

中等國文典；章士釗著· 495·15—C190

上海，商務，民十一年·302面·

國文法草創；陳承澤著· 495·15—C270

上海，商務，民十一年·119面·

國文法之研究；金兆梓著· 495·15—C662

上海，中華，民十一年·140面·

文法要略；莊慶祥著· 495·15—C916

上海，商務，民十一年·2冊·

國語聲調研究；侯覺著· 495·15—H243

上海，中華，民十五年·109面·「國語小叢書」

國語文法四講；易作霖著· 495·15—H124

上海，中華，民十三年·224面·

國文作法；高語罕著· 495·15—K179

上海，亞東，民十二年·再版·452面·

漢文典；來格恂著· 495·15—L127

上海，商務，民九年·2冊·

語體文法；李適著· 495·15—L181

上海，中華，民九年·90面·

國語文法綱要六講；黎錦熙著· 495·15—L215

上海，中華，民十四年·72面·

國語文法；黎明著· 495·1—L216

上海，中華，民十二年·33面·

中國語法講義；孫俍工著· 495·15—S519

上海，亞東，民十二年·3版·168面·

文法津梁；宋文蔚著· 495·15—S568

上海，商務，民十一年·11版·3冊·

白話文速成法；達文社著· 495·15—T119

上海，中華，民十二年·5版·66面·

白話文做法；戴渭清等合著· 495·15—T132

上海，新文化，民十二年·210 面·

國語虛字用法；戴渭清著·　495·15—T433

上海，商務，民十二年·108 面·

國語文法概要；崔唐卿著·　495·15—T735

北京師範大學附屬小學，民十三年·64 面·

中國語法綱要；楊樹達著·　495·15—y137

上海，商務，民十年·4 版·78 面·

500 自然科學

500 自然科學

科學與將來；(英)J·B·S·Halbane 原著，張東民譯· 080—H129—501
上海，北新，民十七年·70 面·「明日叢書」

科學的將來；(英)羅素原著，李元譯· 080—R911—501
上海，北新，民十七年·47 面·「明日叢書」

科學基礎；東方雜誌社編· 080—T860—46
上海，商務，民十四年·3 版·82 面·「東方文庫第四十六種」

科學分類論；阮毅成著· 501—y426

世界科學新譚；孟壽椿著· 500—M211
上海，亞東，民十七年·2 册·

科學與未來之人生；(英)羅素原著，趙文鋭譯· 500—R911
上海，中華，民十五年·38 面·

科學叢談；(美)斯洛孫原著，尤佳章譯· 500—S155
上海，商務，民十七年·289 面·「新智識叢書」

最近自然科學概觀；(日)大町文衛原著，劉文藝譯· 500—T134
上海，商務，民十五年·

自然科學之革命思潮；中華學藝社編· 501—C976
上海，商務，民十五年·139 面·「學藝彙刊 14」

科學方法；胡寄南著· 501—H401
上海，世界，民十六年·51 面·

科學的改造世界；李元著· 501—L202

上海，北新，民十七年・238 面・「科學叢書之一」

科學原理；(日)平林初之輔原著，周梵公譯・　501—P367

上海，商務，民十三年・「新智識叢書」

最近自然科學；(日)田邊元原著，周昌壽譯・　501—T336

上海，商務，民十五年・165 面・

理科大要；學務公所圖書課編・　502—H386

天津學務公所，清光緒三十三年・172 面・

大塊文章；潘梓年譯・　504—B957

上海，北新，民十六年・268 面・

蘭氏科學常談續編；(英)蘭克司得原著，伍周甫譯・　501—L247

上海，商務，民十七年・215 面・「新智識叢書」

科學雜俎；東方雜誌社編・　080—T860—58

上海，商務，民十四年・3 版・4 册・「東方文庫」

科學教育之原理及其教授法；教育雜誌社編・　370・8—C544—67

上海，商務，民十四年・92 面・「育叢著第六十七種」

理化新教授法；朱元善編・　370・8—C544—2・8

上海，商務，民十一年・45 面・「教育叢書」

理科淺説；丁錫華編・　507—T351

上海，中華，民八年・再版・28 面・「通俗教育叢書」

少年自然科學叢書；鄭貞文，胡嘉詔合編・　508—C351

上海，商務，民十四年・10 册・

先秦自然學概論；陳文濤著・　509—C290

上海，商務，民十七年・172 面・「國學小叢書」

510　數學

羅素算理哲學；傅種孫，張邦銘合譯・　510・1—R911

上海，商務，民十一年・349 面・「羅素叢書」

初級混合數學；程廷熙，傅種孫合編・　510—C346

上海，中華，民十二年·第一册·

混合算學教員準備書；段育華校· 510—T819

上海，商務，民十五年·第一册·

數學辭典；趙繚編· R—510·3—C209

上海，羣益，民十二年·再版·「990」面·

數學遊戲大觀；陳懷書等合編· 510·7—C275

上海，商務，民十五年·312面·

蓋氏對數表；F·G·Gauss原著，杜亞原，壽孝天合譯· 510·8—G237

上海，商務，民十三年·101面·

511 算學

算術學表解；上海科學書局編輯所編· 080—S155—511

上海，科學書局，清光緒三十三年·52面·「表解叢書」

新的算術；龔實善著· 511—K383

上海，泰東，民十五年·288面·

算術，現代初級中學教科書；嚴濟慈著· 511—y212

上海，商務，民十二年·291面·

珠算入門；達文社編· 511·2—T119

上海，中華，民九年·138面·

512 代數

代數習題詳解；張鵬飛，華襄治合著· 512—C168

上海，中華，民十五年·4版·285面·

代數學教科書；陳文著· 512—C290

上海，商務，民九年·333面·

二次方程式詳論；何魯著· 512—H205e

上海，商務，民十四年·125面·「算學叢書第七種」

代數學；何魯著· 512—H205t

上海，商務，民十三年・208 面・

初學代數學；胡桂聲著・　512—H405c

上海，商務，民十三年・335 面・「大同大學叢書」

藤澤博士續初等代數學教科書；黄際遇譯・　512—H471

武昌國立高等師範學校，民六年・286 面・

大代數學講義；(日)上野清原著，五家炎，張廷華合譯・　512—S516

上海，商務，民九年・83 面・

查理斯密初等代數學；王家炎譯・　512—SW53

上海，商務，民十一年・「449」面・

代數學，現代初中教科書；吳在淵著・　512—W297

上海，商務，民十二年・上册・

方程式論；Fleran Cajori 原著・　512・2—C124

上海，中華，民十四年・「294」面・

最小二乘式；李協著・　512・2—L185

上海，商務，民十三年・117 面・「算學叢書第一種」

虛數詳論；何魯，段子燮合著・　512・24—H205

上海，商務，民十六年・102 面・

代數學問題解法指導；匡文濤著・　512・9—K336

上海，中華，民十四年・193 面・

513　幾何

立體幾何學表解；上海科學書局編輯所編・　080—S155—513

上海，科學書局，民元年・46 面・「表解叢書」

幾何學講義；(日)上野清原著，張廷華譯・　513—S156

上海，商務，民十一年・657 面・

非歐几里得幾何學；武崇經譯・　513—W302

上海，商務，民八年・79 面・

温德華士幾何學；張彝，周藩合譯・　513—W488

上海，商務，民十一年·466 面·

平面幾何學教科書；(日)菊池大麓原著，黄元吉譯· 513·1—C885

上海，商務，民元年·256 面·

幾何學教科書；(日)樺正董原著，曾鈞譯· 513·1—H450

上海，中國圖書公司，清光緒三十三年·197 面·

近世平面幾何學；郭鳳藻，武崇經合著· 513·1—K422

上海，商務，民八年·178 面·

何崇禮平面幾何學問題解法；王醉六著· 513·1—W159

上海，科學會編譯部，民三年·303 面·

平行綫論；羅巴曲斯奇原著，齊汝璜譯· 513·13—L781

上海，商務，民十七年·50 面·

立體幾何學教科書；(日)菊池大麓原著，胡豫譯· 513·3—C885

上海，商務，民元年·98 面·

幾何學教科書：立體；(日)椿正董原著，曾鈞譯· 513·3—H450

上海，中國圖書公司，清光緒三十三年·95 面·

幾何學講義；(日)上野清原著，張廷華譯· 513·3—S156

上海，商務，民五年·170 面·

幾何學：立體部；謝洪賚編· 513·3—S418

上海，商務，1906 年·222 面·

定量問題；王邦珍著· 513·9—W153

上海，商務，民十七年·230 面·「學藝叢書」

514 三角學

三角法表解；上海科學書局編輯所編· 080—S155—514

上海，科學書局，清光緒三十二年·42 面·「表解叢書」

三角術；趙修乾著· 514—C205

上海，商務，民十三年·「287」面·

温德華士三角法；顧裕魁譯· 514—W488

上海，商務，民十一年·「284」面·

新中學平面三角法教科書；胡仁源著· 514·5—H407

上海，中華，民十二年·74 面·

平面三角法講義；匡文濤著· 514·5—K336

上海，商務，民八年·526 面·

球面三角法講義；匡文濤著· 514·6—K336

上海，商務，民八年·233 面·

516　解析幾何

解析幾何學表解；上海科學書局編輯所編· 080—S155—516

上海，科學書局，民二年·41 面·「表解叢書」

解析幾何學講義；匡文濤編· 516—K336

上海，商務，民七年·340 面·

斯密氏及改勒解析幾何學原理；龔文凱譯· 516—m65

上海，科學會編譯部，民二年·636 面·

温特渥斯解析幾何學；鄭家斌譯· 516—W488

上海，商務，民六年·330 面·

517　微積分學

微分學表解；上海科學書局編輯所編 080—S155—517

上海，科學書局，民二年·38 面·「表解叢書」

微分積分學；(日)長澤龜之助原著，馬瀛譯· 517—C198

上海，商務，民三年·350 面·

微積分學講義；匡文濤編· 517—K336

上海，商務，民十一年·再版·394 面·

級數概論；(日)林鶴一，小倉金之助合著，歐陽祖綸譯· 517—L315

上海，商務，民十七年·695 面·「算學叢書」

微分積分學；彭世鵬著． 517—P278
上海，中華，民四年．2册．

520 天文學

宇宙；（日）石井重美原著，黄家金譯． 520—S250
武昌，時中，民十四年．68面．「地學小叢書」

天空現象談；丁錫華著． 520—T351tk
上海，中華，民十四年．40面．「通俗教育叢書之一」

談天；丁錫華著． 520—T351tt
上海，中華，民十四年．146面．「學生叢書之一」

宇宙論；周昌壽著． 080—P225—89
上海，商務，民五年．71面．「百科小叢書第八十九種」

526．9 測量法

實地測量法；工家炎著． 526．9—W136
上海，商務，民十一年．86面．

實用測量法；衛梓松著． 526．9—W222
上海，商務，民八年．164面．

529 歷法

曆法；林炯著． 080—P225—21
上海，商務，民十二年．再版．53面．「百科小叢書第二十一種」

新曆法；東方雜誌社編． 080—T860—49
上海，商務，民十四年．3版．74面．「東方文庫」

二十世紀陰陽合曆；中華書局編譯所編． 529．3—C976
上海，中華，民十三年．214面．

530　物理

物理學原理及其應用；郭察理，謝玉銘合著，于樹樟譯·　530—C81
上海，商務，民十七年·323 面·

物理學；周昌壽著·　530—C771
上海，商務，民十四年·241 面·

實用物理學；Milikan and Gale 原著，周昌壽，高銛合譯·　530—M621
上海，商務，民十三年·529 面·

物理學；王兼善著·　530—W136
上海，商務，民十一年·412 面·

物理學問題精解；王枚生著·　530—W149
上海，商務，民十四年·456 面·

物理學問答；楊壽桐著·　530—y138
上海，文明，清光緒三十一年·174 面·

以太；周昌壽著·　080—P225—83
上海，商務，民十四年·60 面·「百科小叢書第八十三種」

通俗相對論大意；費祥編·　080—P225—17
上海，商務，民十二年·69 面·「百科小叢書第十七種」

相對性原理；東方雜誌社編·　080—T860—48
上海，商務，民十三年·再版·90 面·「東方文庫」

相對律之由來及其概念；周昌壽著·　530·1—C771
上海，商務，民十二年·90 面·「學藝彙刊之一」

愛因斯坦氏相對論及其批評；(德)杜里舒原著，張君勱譯·　530·1—D831
上海，商務，民十三年·40 面·

相對原理及其推論；文元模譯·　530·1—E163
上海，商務，民十四年·89 面·「尚志學會叢書」

相對論淺釋；(德)愛因斯坦原著，夏元瑮譯·　530·1—E168
上海，商務，民十二年·「122」面·「通俗叢書」

從牛頓到愛因斯坦；(美)哈樓原著，文元模譯· 530·1—H249
上海，商務，民十二年·60面·

愛因斯坦和相對性原理；(日)石原純原著,周昌壽,鄭貞文合譯· 530·1—S252
上海，商務，民十二年·180面·

相對論與宇宙觀；聞齊譯· 530·1—W240
上海，商務，民十二年·115面·「通俗叢書」

最近物理學概觀；(日)日下部原著，鄭貞文譯· 530·2—J441
上海，商務，民十五年·3版·230面·

理化詞典；陳英才等合編· 530·3—C202
上海，中華，民九年·「324」面·

物的分析；(英)羅素演講，任鴻雋譯記· 530·4—R911
上海，商務，民十一年·64面·

理化簡易器械製作及實驗法；馬紹良著· 530·7—M124
上海，商務，民十一年·192面·

物理遊戲；V·E·Johnson原著，錢嘉集，朱夢梅合譯· 530·7—J638
上海，商務，民十四年·106面·

物理學實驗教程；(美)密爾根，蓋爾原著· 530·7—M621
上海，商務，民十二年·132面·

機械學大意；陳其文著· 531—C270
上海，商務，民十一年·57面·

機械學；劉振華著· 531—L356
上海，商務，民十年·210面·

放射淺説；程瀛章著· 680—P255—26
上海，商務，民十三年·69面·「百科小叢書第二十六種」

鐳錠；東方雜誌社編· 080—T860—56
上海，商務，民十四年·3版·78面·「東方文庫」

540 化學

化學表解；上海科學書局編輯所編· 080—S155—540

上海，科學書局，清光緒三十三年・2冊・「表解叢書」

化學；鄭貞文著・　540—C351

上海，商務，民十二年・614面・

化學；鄭貞文，鄭尊法合著・　540—C351

上海，商務，民十二年・20面・

化學；鍾衡臧著・　540—C962

上海，中華，民十四年・123面・

化學集成；孔慶萊著・　540—K411

上海，商務，民十二年・2冊・

化學概論；(美)麥費生，罕迭生原著・　540—M241

上海，商務，民十五年・635面・

漢譯麥費孫；罕迭生化學；(美)極白重訂，許傳音譯・　540—M241

上海，商務，民十一年・412面・

化學；王兼善著・　540—W136

上海，商務，民十一年・465面・

化學教科書；閻玉振，王鶴清合著・　540—y244

北京，文化學社，民十五年・528面・

化學小史；程瀛章等合編・　080—P225—82

上海，商務，民十四年・74面・「百科小叢書第八十二」

化學史通考；丁緒賢著・　540・9—T346

北京大學出版部，民十四年・420面・「國立北京大學叢書之十一」

化學計算法解脱；(日)近藤清次郎，池田清原著，

尤金鏞，尤金緘合譯・　541—C677

南通州，翰墨林書局，清光緒三十四年・279面・

原子論淺説；李書華著・　080—P225—29

上海，商務，民十二年・46面・「百科小叢書第二十九種」

原子構造概論；(日)竹内潔原著，陸志鴻譯・　541・2—C818

上海，商務，民十六年・133面・「學藝彙刊」

原子新論；(英)羅素原著，何道生譯・　541・2—R911

北京樸社出版經理部，民十六年・150面・

原子說發凡；(英)羅素原著，鄭貞文譯· 541·2—R911
上海，商務，民十六年·140面·

化學方程式；(日)藤井鄉三原著，尤金鏞譯· 541·9—T77
南通州，翰墨林書局，清光緒三十四年·149面·

化學實驗教程；(美)麥費孫，罕迭生原著，徐善祥譯· 542—S481
上海，商務，民十一年·90面·

自學輔導化學實驗法；蔡松筠編· 542—T414
上海，中華，民十六年·168面·

分析化學實驗書；(英)克勞氏原著，項鎮方譯· 543—C626
上海，商務，民四年·4版·431面·

定性分析；陳世璋著· 544—C286
上海，商務，民十三年·274面·

定性分析化學；顧樹森著· 544—K252
上海，商務，民二年·205面·

無機化學教科書；任元，林先民合編· 546—J128
上海，中國圖書公司和記，民三年·486面·

實驗無機化學；(美)斯密原著，鄭恂立譯· 546—Sn51
上海，商務，民十五年·259面·

實用有機化學教科書；馬君武著· 547—M112
上海，商務，民十一年·「421」面·

549 物學

高等鑛物學講義；張錫田著· 549—C170Kt
上海，商務，民十一年·614面·

鑛物鑑識法；張錫田著· 549—C170KW
上海，商務，民十一年·225面·

地質鑛物學；張資平著· 549—C171
上海，商務，民十三年·409面·

新式鑛物學；鍾觀誥著· 549—C963

上海，商務，民三年・74 面・

鑛物學；宋崇義著・　549—S554

上海，中華，民十二年・116 面・

鑛物學；杜若城著・　549—T769

上海，商務，民十二年・112 面・

鑛物學；杜亞泉著・　549—T769

上海，商務，民二年・「180」面・

鑛物學講義；杜亞泉著・　549—T769

上海，商務，民元年・92 面・

實用教科書鑛物學；吳冰心著・　549—W293

上海，商務，民十一年・206 面・

550　地質學

地文學表解；上海科學書局編輯所編・　080—S155—551

上海，科學書局，清光緒三十三年・41 面・「表解叢書」

自然地理學；張資平著・　080—P225—25

上海，商務，民十二年・76 面・「百科小叢書第二十五種」

普通地質學；張資平著・　550—C152P

上海，商務，民十五年・287 面・「學藝叢書」

石雅；章鴻釗著・　550—C181

農商部地質調查所，民十年・348 面・「地質專報乙種第二號」

通俗地質學；趙國賓著・　550—C208

上海，商務，民十三年・200 面・「新智識叢書」

地質學；(美)賴康忒原著，包光鏞，張逢辰合譯・　550—C767

上海，商務，民四年・「479」面・

地文學問答；(日)富山房原著，陳大稜譯・　550—F256

上海，新民，清光緒二十九年・124 面・

地質學；謝家榮著・　550—S416

上海，商務，民十三年·244 面·「中國科學社叢書之一」

自然地理；傅運森著· 550—F247

上海，商務，民十三年·14 版·81 面·

最新自然地理學；余維濤著· 550—y350

上海，昌明公司，清光緒三十一年·184 面·

地質學者達爾文；張資平著· 550·9—C152t

上海，商務，民十五年·140 面·「學藝叢刊」

地球的年齡；李仲揆著· 080—P225—153

上海，商務，民十六年·90 面·「百科小叢書」

談地；史禮綬著· 551—S256

上海，中華，民十五年·184 面·「學生叢書之一」

火山；章鴻釗著· 080—P225—33

上海，商務，民十三年·68 面·「百科小叢書第三十三種」

地震；翁文灝著· 080—P225—3

上海，商務，民十三年·90 面·「百科小叢書第三十二種」

氣象學；竺可楨著· 080—P225—1

上海，商務，民十二年·再版·71 面·「百科小叢書第一種」

地層測算術；劉季辰著· 551·7—L353

農商部地質調查所，民八年·44 面·

巖石通論；周則岳譯· 080—P225—53

上海，商務，民十三年·89 面·「百科小叢書第五十三種」

中國鑛產；黄著勳著· 553—H471

上海，商務，民十五年·「306」面·

中國鑛業紀要；丁文江，翁文灝合著· 553—T353

農商部地質調查所，民十年·46 面·「地貿專報丙種第一號」

煤；謝家榮著· 080—P225—10

上海，商務，民十二年·再版·87 面·「百科小叢書第十種」

煤業概論；王寵佑著· 080—P225—101

上海，商務，民十五年·144 面·「百科小叢書第一百零一種」

石炭；東方雜誌社編· 080—T860—55

上海，商務，民十四年·3版·78面·「東方文庫」

鐵；彭維基著·　080—P225—100

上海，商務，民十五年·153面·「百科小叢書第一百種」

中國鐵鑛誌；丁格蘭原著，謝家榮譯·　553·3—T231

農商部地質調查所，民十二年·2册·

中國地勢變遷小史；李仲揆著·　080—P225—2

上海，商務，民十五年·4版·48面·「百科小叢書第二種」

中國地質圖説明書；譚錫疇譯·　555—T161

上海，商務，民十四年·「120」面·

560　石生物學

古動物學；（法）補勒教授原著，周太玄譯·　560—3664

上海，商務，民十一年·124面·

化石；張作人著·　080—P225—125

上海，商務，民十一年·93面·「百科小叢書」

570　生物學

普通生物學；陳櫝著·　570—C270

上海，商務，民十五年·4版·296面·

生物學；（日）丘淺次郎原著，薛德焴等合譯·　570—C736

上海，商務，民十三年·342面·「高等教育理科叢書」

近世生物學；王其樹著·　570—W136

上海，商務，民十七年·3版·「201」面·

生物之世界；（英）窪勒斯原著，尚志學會譯·　570—W155

上海，商務，民九年·2册·「尚志學會叢書」

生物學與長壽；周太玄著． 080—P225—152
上海，商務，民十六年．64 面．「百科小叢書」

生物學的人生觀；庫利斯帖恩愛哈特原著，張修爵譯． 570．1—H44
上海，商務，民十三年．351 面．「尚志學會叢書」

博物詞典；王烈等合編． H—570．3—P278
上海，中華，民十年．「632」面．

博物學實驗教程；懷桂琛著． 570．7—H455
上海，商務，民九年．188 面．

博物講義；李約著． 570．7—L202
上海，商務，民十一年．192 面．

科學小叢書；上海中華書局編譯所編． 570．8—T696
上海，中華，民十三至十五年．8 册．

572 人類學

人類學大意；顧壽白著． 080—P225—57
上海，商務，民十三年．78 面．「百科小叢書第七十五種」

人類之過去現在及未來；（日）丘淺次郎原著，上官垚登譯． 080—P225—42
上海，商務，民十三年．95 面．「百科小叢書第四十二種」

人類進化論；張資平著． 080—P225—74
上海，商務，民十四年．96 面．「百科小叢書第七十四種」

人類進化觀；陳安仁著． 572—C269
上海，泰東，民十五年．再版．152 面．

人類學；陳映璜著． 572—C292
上海，商務，民十二年．257 面．「北京大學叢書之四」

人類進化之研究；過耀根著． 572—K432
上海，商務，民十四年．163 面．「新智識叢書」

原人；（英）湯姆遜原著，伍況甫譯． 572—T384
上海，商務，民十六年．「科學叢書」

蠻性的遺留；（美）摩耳原著，李小峯譯． 572．7—M784

北京，北新，民十四年・182 面・

人的研究；法佛利野德原著，周太玄譯・ 573—F912

上海，中華，民十四年・再版・149 面・

上古的人；(法)房龍原著，任冬譯・ 573—v896

上海，亞東，民十七年・140 面・

人與自然；(美)吕諾士原著，李小峯譯・ 573・1—L451

北京晨報社，民十三年・186 面・「晨報社叢書」

人文地理學；張資平著・ 080—P225—71

上海，商務，民十三年・88 面・「百科小叢書第七十一種」

575　演化論

進化淺説；王謞初著・ 080—P225—70

上海，商務，民十三年・42 面・「百科小叢書第七十種」

進化論與善種學；東方雜誌社編・ 080—T860—50

上海，商務，民十四年・3 版・78 面・「東方文庫」

進化與人生；(日)丘淺治郎原著，劉文典譯・ 575—C736

上海，商務，民十四年・5 版・286 面・

達爾文物種原始；馬君武譯・ 575—D259

上海，中華，民十四年・5 版・5 册・「新文化叢書」

地球與其生物之進化；(美)葛拉普博士講演，

趙國斌，楊鍾建筆記・ 575—G751

上海，商務，民十三年・2 册・「新智識叢書」

天演論；(英)赫胥黎原著，嚴復譯・ 575—H982

上海，商務，民十五年・23 版・「114」面・

互助論；(俄)克魯泡特金原著，周佛海譯・ 575—K927

上海，商務，民十五年・「403」面・「社會經濟叢書」

進化；太朴譯・ 575—M123

上海，商務，民十二年・131 面・「新時代叢書」

進化——從星雲到人類；(英)麥開柏原著，太朴譯・ 575—M123

上海，商務，民十三年·131 面·「新時代叢書第七種」

通俗進化論；薛德清著· 575—S413

上海，商務，民五年·100 面·

575·1 優生學 遺傳學

遺傳學淺説；陳益善編· 575·1—C270

上海，中華，民十五年·151 面·「常識叢書」

遺傳論；(英)唐凱司德原著，周建人譯· 575·1—D715

上海，商務，民十三年·「154」面·「新時代叢書第五種」

遺傳學；李積新著· 575·1—L181

上海，商務，民十二年·112 面·

遺傳學概論；王其樹著· 575·1—W137

上海，商務，民十五年·「105」面·「學藝叢書」

遺傳與優生；劉雄著· 080—P225—43

上海，商務，民十三年·85 面·「百科小叢書第四十三種」

575—577 性論 細胞學 生命起原論

男女特性比較論；(德)發爾亭原著，余志遠譯· 575·5—y155

上海，商務，民十五年·264 面·「新智識叢書」

性論；中華學藝社編· 575·9—C976

上海，商務，民十七年·136 面·「學藝叢刊 17」

性之原理；(日)丁田次郎原著，汪厥明譯· 575·9—T352

上海，商務，民十五年·188 面·「新知識叢書」

人類性源論；費鴻年著· 080—P225—132

上海，商務，民十六年·92 面·「百科小叢書」

生物之起源；費鴻年著· 080—P225—95

上海，商務，民十五年·70 面·「百科小叢書第九十五種」

新生命論；費鴻年著· 080—P225—44

上海，商務，民十三年·75 面·「百科小叢書第四十四種」

原生；(法)派茄姆原著，蔣丙然譯· 576—P217
上海，商務，民十一年·121 面·「新智識叢書」

生命論；永井潛原著，胡步蟾譯· 576—y475
上海，商務，民十七年·275 面·「科學叢書」

細胞學大意；薛德焴著· 080—P225—31
上海，商務，民十二年·56 面·「百科小叢書第三十一種」

細胞與生命之起源；沙爾多利原著，周太玄譯· 576·3—Sa77
上海，商務，民十六年·199 面·「科學叢書」

生與死；(法)達司脱原著，蔣丙然譯· 577·2—D262
上海，商務，民十六年·322 面·「科學叢書」

生命之不可思議；(德)海凱爾原著，劉文典譯· 577·2—H118
上海，商務，民十四年·再版·508 面·「哲學叢書」

死之研究；華文祺著· 577·7—C235
上海，商務，民十二年·2 册·

580　植物學

植物學表解；上海科學書局編輯所編· 080—S155—580
上海，科學書局，清光緒三十三年·43 面·「表解叢書」

實用植物表解；上海科學書局編輯所編· 080—S155—580
上海，科學書局，民元年·65 面·「表解叢書」

植物學教科書；(美)胡爾德原著，奚若，蔣維喬合譯· 580—C832
上海，商務，民二年·430 面·

植物學；(美)甘惠德編，杜亞泉譯· 580—K120
上海，商務，民四年·260 面·

植物學；凌昌煥譯· 580—L340
上海，商務，民十五年·114 面·

植物教科書；馬君武著· 580—M112
上海，商務，民九年·「439」面·

三好學植物學講義；黃以仁等合譯· 680—M699
上海，商務，民十一年·上中二册·

實驗植物學教科書；(日)三奸學原著，杜亞泉譯· 580—M699
上海，商務，清宣統三年·128面·

高等植物學；鄒秉文等著· 580—T695
上海，商務，民十二年·「470」面·

新撰植物學教科書；(日)三好學原著，杜亞泉譯· 580—T760
上海，商務，宣統三年·200面·

實驗植物學教科書；杜亞泉著· 580—T769
上海，商務，民二年·128面·

植物名實圖考；吳其濬著· R—580·3—W282
上海，商務，清道光二十八年·854面·

植物名實圖考長編；吳其濬著· R—580·3—W282
上海，商務，民八年·1129面·

植物學大辭典；孔慶萊等合編· R—580·3—K411
上海，商務，民七年·再版·「1638」面·

植物解剖學與生理學；(法)畢宋原著，李亮恭譯· 581—P689
上海，商務，民十四年·「348」面·

590 動物學

動物學表解；上海科學書局編輯所編· 080—S155—590
上海，科學書局，清光緒三十三年·55面·「表解叢書」

實用動物學表解；上海科學書局編輯所編· 080—S155—590
上海，科學書局，民二年·94面·「表解叢書」

動物與人生；陳大榕譯· 590—C288
上海，商務，民十三年·183面·「新智識叢書之五」

動物新論；(日)箕作佳吉原著，杜就田譯· 590—G387
上海，商務，民二年·270面·

水產動物學；江蘇省立水產學校編· 590—C514
上海，商務，民十五年·248面·

動物學教科書；馬君武著· 590—M112
上海，商務，民十年·「484」面·

動物實驗指南；薛德焴著· 590—S453
上海，商務，民七年·5册·

動物學；丁文江著· 590—T353
上海，商務，民十一年·「354」面·

動物學；杜就田著· 590—T761
上海，商務，民十二年·106面·

動物學大辭典；杜亞泉等編· R—590·3—T769
上海，商務，民十一年·4版·「3050」面·

動物採集保存法；許家慶著· 590·7—H389
上海，商務，民四年·110面·

昆蟲故事；(法)法布爾原著，杜蘭女士譯· 595—F112
上海，北新，民十六年·136面·「通俗科學叢書」

昆蟲研究法；鄒盛文著· 570·8—T696
上海，中華，民十三年·26面·「科學小叢書」

美麗的蝴蝶；施乃普著· 570·8—T696
上海，中華，民十三年·27面·「科學小叢書」

昆蟲採集製作法；許家慶著· 595·7—H369
上海，商務，民元年·90面·

蟻；(日)松村年原著，祝枕江譯· 080—P225—76
上海，商務，民十四年·38面·「百科小叢書第七十六種」

世界上爬行的動物；鄒盛文著· 570·8—T696
上海，商務，民十三年·34面·「科學小叢書」

四季禽類；W·P·Westal原著，周則岳譯· 080—P225—58
上海，商務，民十三年·79面·「百科小叢書第五十八種」

600 應用科學

600 應用科學

工業常識；(日)中村康之助原著，白鵬飛譯· 606—C978
上海，商務，民十四年·「121」面·

實業致富新書；盧壽錢著· 606—L406
上海，中華，民五年·2冊·

巴拿馬太平洋萬國博覽會要覽；李宣龔著· 606—L196
上海，商務，民三年·251面·

上海總商會商品陳列所報告書；上海總商會商品陳列所編· 606—S155
上海，商會商品陳列所，民十一年·417面·

上海總商會商品陳列所第二次報告書；
上海總商會商品陳列所編· 606—S155e
上海，總商會商品陳列所，民十二年·232面·

新法事物發明史；趙宗預著· 608—C201
上海，商務，民十二年·3版·4冊·

發明與文明；黄土恒著· 608—H485
上海，商務，民五年·3版·154面·「新智識叢書之二」

近世之新發明；葛綏成著· 608—K427
上海，中華，民十五年·144面·

近世世界商工業史；(日)桐生政次原著，人演社譯· 609—T885
上海，文明，清光緒二十九年·126面·

英國實業史；(英)吉賓斯原著，丁雄譯· 609—G352

上海，廣學會，清光緒三十三年・160 面・

德國實業發達史；(美)哈渥原著，吳之椿譯・ 609—H105

上海，商務，民十二年・183 面・「新智識叢書之一」

美國工商發達史；葉建伯著・ 609—y181

上海，商務，民十四年・3 版・333 面・

經濟改造中之中國工業問題；陳銘勛著・ 609—C281

新時代教育社，民十七年・202 面・

中國實業要論；金廷蔚著・ 609—C669

上海，商務，民十四年・183 面・

中國工業史；陳家錕著・ 609—C270

上海，中國圖書公司和記，民六年・134 面・

中國工藝沿革史略；許衍灼著・ 609—H370

上海，商務，民七年・134 面・

通州興辦實業章程；翰墨林編譯印書局編・ 609—H134

南通，翰墨林編譯印書局，清宣統二年・三版・「382」面・

提倡國貨論，陳震異著・ 609—C270

上海，太平洋，民十七年・122 面・

610　醫學

醫學通論；陳無咎著・ 610—C291

上海，民智，民十二年・80 面・

醫學常識；洪武間，鮑鑑清合編・ 610—H522

上海，商務，民十六年・255 面・

普通醫學新智識；丁福保著・ 610・8—T347—610

上海，文明，民二年・2 版・104 面・「丁氏醫學叢書」

醫學綱要；丁福保著・ 610・8—T347—610・2

上海，醫學書局，民四年・3 版・「264」面・「丁氏醫學叢書」

簡明醫學教書・ 610・8—T347—610・4

上海，醫學書局・224 面・「丁氏醫學叢書」

醫學指南；丁福保著・ 610・8—T347—610・42

上海，醫學書局，民十一年・4 版・「丁氏醫學叢書」

丁氏一家言；丁福保著・ 610・8—T347—610・8

上海，醫學書局，民九年・「307」面・「丁氏醫學叢書」

醫學日記十種；戴麒等合編・ 610・8—T347—610・83

上海，醫學書局・「丁氏醫學叢書」

醫學小叢書四種；孫祖烈等合編・ 610・8—T347—610・8

上海，醫學書局・126 面・「丁氏醫學叢書」

醫話叢存；丁福保著・ 610・8—T347—610・81

上海，文明，清宣統二年・138 面・「丁氏醫學叢書」

醫學文庫；吳宗等合編・ 610・8—T347—610・82

上海，醫學書局・「丁氏醫學叢書」

醫海一滴；達觀等合編・ 610・8—T344—614・5

上海，醫學書局・「154」面・「丁氏醫學叢書」

醫界之鐵椎；丁福保著・ 610・8—T347—610・07

上海，醫學書局，民六年・2 版・158 面・

新醫學六種；丁福保著・ 610・8—T347—610・07

上海，譯書公會，清宣統三年・「138」面・

醫師開業術；(日)立神正夫原著，萬鈞譯・ 610・8—T347—614・24

上海，醫學書局，民四年・120 面・「丁氏醫學叢書」

中外醫通；丁福保著・ 610・8—T347—615

上海，醫學書局，民三年・2 版・428 面・「丁氏醫學叢書」

中西醫學三十種；盧謙等合編・ 610・8—T347—616

上海，學醫書局・5 册・「丁氏醫學叢書」

漢法醫典；(日)野津猛男著・ 610・8—T347—615・5

上海，醫學書局，民五年・72 面・「丁氏醫學叢書」

醫學新名詞解釋；萬鈞著・ 610・8—T347—611・0114

上海，醫學書局，民七年・98 面・「丁氏醫學叢書」

中國醫學史；陳邦賢著・ 610・8—T347—610・95

上海，醫學書局・74 面・「丁氏醫學叢書」

西洋醫學史；丁福保著・ 610・8—T347—610・94

上海，丁氏醫院，民三年・102 面・「丁氏醫學叢書」

醫學大辭書；(日)百科辭書編輯局編・ R—610・8—P225

東京，同文館，明治四十三年・4 册・「日本百科辭書」

中國醫學大辭典；謝觀編・ R—610・8—S119

上海，商務，民十五年・4 版・2 册・

南洋醫科考試問題答案；丁福保著・ 610・8—T347—610・41

上海，醫學書局，民二年・2 版・「48」面・

太醫局程文・ 610・8—T347—610・1

上海，醫學書局，「丁氏醫學叢書」

611 解剖學

人體解剖賓習法；(日)石川喜直原著，萬鈞等合譯・ 610・8—T347—611

上海，醫學書局，民四年・196 面・「丁氏醫學叢書」

新撰解剖學講義；丁福保譯・ 610・8—T347—611・01

上海，醫學書局，民元年・4 册・「丁氏醫學叢書」

組織學總論；(日)二村領次郎原著・晉陵下工譯・ 610・8—T347—612・014

上海，丁氏醫院，民二年・203 面・「丁氏醫學叢書」

612 生理衛生學

生理衛生學表解；上海科學書局編輯所編・ 080—S155—612

上海，科學書局，(清)宣統三年・43 面・「表解叢書」

生理學中外名詞對照表；孫祖烈著・ 610・8—T347—612・0114

上海，醫學書局，民六年・40 面・

生理衛生學；顧壽白著・ 612—K252

上海，商務，民十五年・188 面・

生理衛生新教科書；(日)三島通良原著，杜亞泉，杜就田合譯・ 612—S144

上海，商務，清光緒三十三年·155 面·

生理衛生教科書；(日)高橋本吉，山内繁雄原著，丁福保譯· 610·8—T347—613

上海，醫學書局，民三年·2 版·118 面·「丁氏醫學叢書」

生理學講義；丁福保譯· 610·8—T347—612·01

上海，醫學書局，民五年·2 册·「丁氏醫學叢書」

最新解剖生理衛生學；商務印書館編譯所譯· 612—S163

上海，商務，民十一年·472 面·

人體生理衛生學提要；薛德焴著· 612—S413

上海，商務，民十三年·3 版·324 面·「武昌高等師範理科叢書之一」

生理衛生學；宋崇義著· 612—S554

上海，中華，民十五年·114 面·

生理學；(美)史砥爾原著，謝洪賚譯· 612—St32

上海，商務，民三年·「274」面·

生理及衛生學；王兼善著· 612—W136

上海，商務，民十年·「292」面·

實用教科書生理衛生學；吳冰心著· 612—W293

上海，商務，民十一年·164 面·

生埋學講義；嚴保誠著· 612—y225

上海，商務，民元年·104 面·

胃腸機能保養法；王羲龢著· 612—W15

上海，商務，民八年·93 面·「通俗醫書」

實驗深呼級練習法；王懷琪編· 612·2—W141

上海，商務，民十五年·3 版·「99」面·

内分泌；顧壽白著· 080—P225—30

上海，商務，民十三年·52 面·「百科小叢書第三十種」

612·6 性教育

性教育與學校課程；教育雜誌社編· 370·8—C544—39

上海，商務，民十四年·100 面·「教育叢書」

性教育的理論；教育雜誌社編· 370·8—C544—38

上海，商務，民十四年·89 面·「教育叢書」

性教育概論；教育雜誌社編· 370·8—C544—37

上海，商務，民十四年·89 面·「教育叢書」

巴哥羅底兩性教育觀；教育雜誌社編· 370·8—C544—42

上海，商務，民十四年·76 面·「教育叢書」

青年期之性的衛生及道德；教育雜誌社編· 370·8—C544—41

上海，商務，民十四年·114 面·「教育叢書」

男女性之分析；教育雜誌社編· 370·8—C544—40

上海，商務，民十四年·72 面·「教育叢書」

性教育；柴福沅著· 612·6—C128

上海，世界，民十六年·82 面·

性與人生；周建人著· 612·6—C771

上海，開明，民十六年·129 面·「婦女問題研究會叢書」

世界性的風俗譚；胡仲持譯· 612·6—H201

上海，光華，民十五年·64 面·

性的知識；(美)魯濱遜原著，方可譯· 612·6—R568

上海，開明，民十七年·279 面·

家庭性教育實施法；(美)珊格爾夫人原著，封熙卿譯· 612·6—s558

上海，商務，民十一年·57 面·「婦女叢書第一集第六編」

結婚的愛；(英)司托撥著· 612·6—St73

上海，北新，民十六年·183 面·

性教育；施多惠著· 612·6—St79

上海，北新，民十七年·283 面·

性之生理與衛生；R，T，Trall 原著，任厂譯· 612·6—T663

上海，北新，民十六年·再版·239 面·

性欲衛生篇；俞鳳賓著· 612·6—y370

上海，商務，民十四年·84 面·「衛生學要義之一」

性的危機；袁振英著· 612·6—y421

廣州，受匡出版部，民十七年·165 面·

生殖譚；華文祺，丁福保合譯· 610·8—T347—612·6

上海，醫學書局，民十年·4版·96面·「丁氏醫學叢書」

髮鬚瓜；江紹原著· 612·799—J13

上海，開明，民十七年·21面·

脊椎動物的化學感覺；帕刻原著，臧玉海譯· 612·86—P225

上海，商務，民十七年·156面·

痛饑懼怒時的身體變化；卡儂原著，臧玉淦譯· 612·821—C164

上海，商務，民十七年·234面·

613 衛生學

實驗衛生學講本；丁福保著· 610·8—T347—613·01

上海，醫學書局，民七年·2版·211面·「丁氏醫學叢書」

衛生碎金録；谷君等合編· 610·8—T347—613·02

上海，醫學書局·「211」面·「丁氏醫學叢書」

衛生文庫；伍廷芳等合編· 610·8—T347—613·04

上海，醫學書局·「丁氏醫學叢書」

衛生學問答；丁福保著· 610·8—T347—613·07

上海，丁氏醫院，民二年·13版·196面·「丁氏醫學叢書」

氣候與健康；顧壽白著· 080—P225—39

上海，商務，民十三年·64面·「百科小叢書第三十九種」

衛生勉學法；朱元善，華文祺合編· 613—C839

上海，商務，民十二年·126面·

人生二百年；顧實著· 613—K252

上海，商務，民十二年·232面·

長生不老法；顧實著· 613—K252c

上海，商務，民九年·137面·

攝身論；胡宣明，杭海合編· 613—s414

上海，商務，民十二年·2册·

衛生新論；吳兗著· 613—W287

上海，中國圖書公司和記，民十一年·46面·

運動生理；程瀚章著·　613·17—C275
上海，商務，民十三年·286 面·「新智識叢書」

斷食治病法；（日）西川光次郎原著，王義龢譯·　613·2—S370
上海，商務，民九年·再版·92 面·

日用衛生；孫佐著·　613·2—S530
上海，商務，民十二年·103 面·「通俗教育叢書」

健康不老廢止朝食論；蔣維喬著·　613·2—T568
上海，商務，民十三年·8 版·138 面·

營養化學；鄭貞文著·　080—P225—40
上海，商務，民十三年·82 面·「百科小叢書第四十種」

食物論；鄒德謹著·　613·2—T697
上海，商務，民十一年·93 面·「通俗教育叢書」

食物與衛生；東方雜誌社編·　080—T860—54
上海，商務，民十四年·3 版·104 面·「東方文庫」

素食養生論；楊章父，孫重沓公合編·　613·2—y121
上海，中華，民十二年·64 面·

冷水浴；劉仁航著·　613·43—L364
上海，商務，民十六年·69 面·

衣服論；鄒德謹著·　613·43—T697
上海，商務，民十二年·73 面·「通俗教育叢書」

陸軍衛生學；趙士法，陳捷合編·　613·67—C214
上海，商務，民九年·再版·223 面·

軍隊衛生學；楊鶴慶著·　613·67—y126
上海，商務，民十四年·37 面·「醫學小叢書」

旅行衛生；莊適著·　613·69—C918
上海，商務，民十年·76 面·「通俗教育叢書」

普通衛生救急治療法；（日）金澤嚴原著，盧謙譯·　610·8—T347—613·6
上海，醫學書局·60 面·

實驗却病法；丁福保著· 610·8—T347—613·061

上海，醫學書局，民九年·5版·「74」面·「丁氏醫學叢書」

無藥療病法；(日)系左近原著，華文祺譯· 610·8—T347—613·08

上海，醫學書局，民八年·5版·76面·

簡易療病法；朱夢梅著· 613·8—C830

上海，商務，民六年·再版·139面·「婦女叢書」

萬病自然療法；顧實著· 613·8—K252

上海，商務，民十一年·4版·136面·

通俗自療病法；蘇儀貞著· 613·8—S460

上海，中華，民十二年·3版·74面·

613·7 體操

仿效體操；趙光紹著· 613·7—C208

上海，商務，民十三年·51面·

體育學；羅一東著· 613·7—L393

上海，中華，民十五年·147面·

實驗五分鍾呼吸運動法；陸師通著· 613·7—L432

上海，中華，民十五年·22面·

體育之理論及實際；徐福生著· 613·7—S477

上海，商務，民四年·再版·「298」面·

德國室内體操；吳欽泰著· 613·7—T300—1·12

上海，商務，民十四年·70面·「體育叢書第一集第十二編」

設計的模仿操；楊彬如著· 613·7—y136

上海，商務，民十二年·「83」面·

保哲氏啞鈴體操；李培藻譯· 613·71—B637

上海，商務，民十四年·195面·

教室柔輭體操；(美)C·R·Borben原著，李浮夢譯· 613·71—B644

上海，商務，民十四年·55面·「體育叢書第一集第十編」

設計式游戲操；崔唐卿著· 613·71—T735

北京，師大附屬小學校，民十三年·「88」面·

布蘭島成組木棍體操；(美)布蘭島原著，李培藻譯· 613·72—B733
上海，商務，民十四年·75面·

初級體育教練法；(美)葛雷原著，錢江春，戴昌鳳合譯· 613·72—G793
上海，中華，民十五年·5版·122面·

發達肌肉法；(美)邱力克原著，張壽仁譯· 613·72—G951
上海，商務，民十四年·3版·91面·「體育叢書第一集第七編」

棍棒；國民體育社譯· 613·72—K435
上海，商務，民十一年·60面·「體育叢書第一集第四編」

米勒氏十五分鐘體操；張諤譯· 613·72—M914
上海，商務，民十四年·7版·99面·

業餘運動法；王懷琪著· 613·72—W142
上海，商務，民十五年·3版·82面·

神經衰弱養療法；盧壽錢著· 613·8—L406
上海，中華，民九年·68面·

神經衰弱自療法；王義龢著· 613·8—W155
上海，商務，民十年·79面·「通俗叢書」

神經衰弱之大研究；華文祺，丁福保合編· 613·8—T347—616·8
上海，醫學書局，民八年·2版·63面·「丁氏醫學叢書」

腦髓與生殖之大研究；黄章森著· 613·8—T347—612·82
上海，醫學書局，清宣統元年·2版·62面·

人種改良學；陳壽凡著· 613·9—C287
上海，商務，民十五年·4版·3册·「新智識叢書」

優生問題；(美)Havlaock Ellis原著，王新命譯· 613·9—EL59
上海，商務，民十三年·72面·「新智識叢書」

優生學與婚姻；(美)威廉魯濱生原著，高方譯· 613·9—R568
上海，亞東，民十七年·156面·

賢明的父母；(英)司托潑原著，水宵人譯· 613·9—St73
上海，北新，民十六年·58面·

胎教；宋嘉釗著．　613・8—S554
　上海，中華，民十五年・78 面・「女學叢書之一」
胎教；陳兼善著．　080—P225—75
　上海，商務，民十四年・60 面・「百科小叢書第七十五種」
强種須知；丁林女士原著，沈駿英譯．　613・9—T439
　上海，廣學會，民十五年・3 版・68 面・

614　公共衛生

衛生叢書；中華衛生教育會編．　614—C976
　上海，商務，民十一年・3 版・152 面・
公民衛生；程瀚章著．　614—C335
　上海，商務，民十三年・172 面・「新智識叢書」
中國衛生實用教科書；愛博敦著．　614—N147
　上海，伊文思，民十二年・162 面・
近世法醫學；（日）田中祐吉原著，徐雲，丁福保合譯．　610・8—T347—614
　上海，醫學書局，清宣統三年・276 面・「丁氏醫學叢書」
法醫學；（日）石川清忠纂著，王佑，楊鴻通合譯．　614・2—S250
　上海，商務，民十年・「741」面・
蚊蠅消滅法；陳家祥著．　614・43—C270
　上海，商務，民十六年・45 面・「平民叢書」
治蠅要覽；費耕雨著．　614・43—F187
　上海，商務，民十一年・46 面・
痘及種痘；錢守山，斯秀紹合編．　614・473—T613
　上海，商務，民十一年・48 面・「醫學小叢書」
鼠疫要覽；陳繼武著．　614・49—C270
　上海，商務，民七年・再版・134 面・
學校傳染病處理法；高鏡郎著．　614・5—K166
　上海，商務，民十四年・120 面・
國民必讀防疫須知；顧鳴盛著．　614・5—K250

上海，文明，民七年 · 62 面 ·

預防傳染病之大研究；丁福保著 · 610 · 8—T347—614 · 5

上海，文明，清宣統三年 · 128 面 ·「丁氏醫學叢書」

霍亂預防法；朱夢梅著 · 614 · 514—C830

上海，商務，民八年 · 46 面 ·

實用急救法；趙士法著 · 614 · 8—C214

上海，商務，民十一年 · 再版 · 66 面 ·「南京高等師範叢刊第一理」

急症救治法；姚昶緒著 · 614 · 8—y151

上海，大東，民九年 · 114 面 ·

軍隊救急簡法 · 614 · 8—C955

上海，商務 · 33 面 ·

家庭侍疾法；丁福保著 · 610 · 8—T347—614 · 5

上海，醫學書局，民五年 · 2 版 · 226 面 ·「丁氏醫學叢書」

家庭防病救險法；(美)凌騏原著，中華衛生教育會譯 · 614 · 5—L340

上海，商務，民十四年 · 5 版 · 45 面 ·

家庭新醫學講本；丁福保著 · 610 · 8—T347—614 · 5

上海，醫學書局，民五年 · 3 版 · 76 面 ·「丁氏醫學叢書」

615 · 1　藥物學

藥理學；余雲岫著 · 615 · 1—y354

上海，商務，民十一年 · 2 册 ·

普通藥物教科書；丁福保著 · 610 · 8—T347—615 · 1

上海，醫學書局 · 104 面 ·「丁氏醫學叢書」

續編 · 上海，醫學書局，民九年 ·

增訂藥物學綱要；丁福保著 · 610 · 8—T347—615 · 1

上海，醫學書局，民九年 · 2 版 · 422 面 ·

拉德法英美日藥物名彙；華鴻編 · 615 · 1—H410

上海，商務，民十一年 · 50 面 ·

藥物要義；姚昶緒著 · 615 · 1—y151

上海，商務，民十一年 · 2 册 ·「醫學小叢書」

藥物學大成；丁福保譯· 610·8—T347—165·01
上海，醫學書局，民十一年·3版·2册·「丁氏醫學叢書」

漢藥實驗談；(日)小泉榮次郎原著，晉陵下工譯· 610·8—T347—615·1
上海，醫學書局，民七年·再版·318面·「丁氏醫學叢書」

西藥實驗談；丁福保著· 610·8—T347—615·1
上海，醫學書局，民九年·3版·481面·「丁氏醫學叢書」

實用經驗治療學；葉祖章著· 610·8—T347—615·1
上海，醫學書局，民九年·306面·「丁氏醫學叢書」

化學實驗新本草；丁福保著· 610·8—T347—615·1
上海，醫學書局，民十一年·6版·272面·「丁氏醫學叢書」

家庭新本草；丁福保等合編· 610·8—T347—615·1
上海，醫學書局，民六年·5版·「160」面·「丁氏醫學叢書」

毒物淺説；葉牖著· 080—P225—144
上海，商務，民十六年·82面·「百科小叢書」

615·4 藥方

實用經驗良方，兒科經驗良方；丁福保，李祥麟合編· 610·8—T347—515·4
上海，醫學書局，民七年·3版·113面·「丁氏醫學叢書」

醫科大學病院經驗方；(日)湏子太原編，萬鈞譯· 610·8—T347—515·4
上海，醫學書局，民三年·217面·「丁氏醫學叢書」

新萬國藥方；丁福保著· 610·8—T347—515·4
上海，醫學書局，民十一年·4版·659面·「丁氏醫學叢書」

中國經驗良方；葉瑗著· 610·8—T347—515·4
上海，醫學書局，民六年·39面·「丁氏醫學叢書」

簡明調劑學；(日)鈴木梅藏原著，張彭年譯· 610·8—T347—515·4
上海，醫學書局，民九年·2版·122面·「丁氏醫學叢書」

中西醫方會通；丁福保著· 610·8—T347—515·4
上海，醫學書局，民九年·235面·「丁氏醫學叢書」

中西驗方新編；陳繼武著· 615·4—C270
上海，商務，民十四年·5版·520面·

良方彙選；中華書局編譯所編· 615·4—C976

上海，中華，民十一年·再版·132 面·

湯頭歌訣；汪昂著· 615·5—W172

上海，商務·2 册·

616·01　微生物學

微生物；余雲岫著· 616·01—y354

上海，商務，民十年·再版·45 面·

實用細菌學；姜白民著· 616·01—C523

上海，商務，民十四年·再版·「289」面·

細菌；胡先驌著· 080—P225—5

上海，商務，民十二年·再版·99 面·「百科小叢書第五種」

616·07　診斷學

新脈學一夕談，或，發熱之原理； 610·8—T347—616·07

上海，醫學書局，民三年·2 版·「55」面·「丁氏醫學叢書」

診斷學實地練習法；丁福保等合編· 610·8—T347—616·07

上海，醫學書局，民七年·3 版·「259」面·「丁氏醫學叢書」

診斷學大成；丁福保著· 610·8—T347—616·07

上海，醫學書局，民七年·2 版·2 册·「丁氏醫學叢書」

斷診一夕談；丁福保著· 610·8—T347—616·07

上海，醫學書局，民三年·2 版·「52」面·「丁氏醫學叢書」

初等診斷學教科書；丁福保著· 610·8—T347—616·07

上海，醫學書局，民九年·4 版·「99」面·「丁氏醫學叢書」

内科分類審症法；丁福保著· 610·8—T347—616·07

上海，醫學書局，民八年·2 版·96 面·「丁氏醫學叢書」

臨牀病理學；丁福保著· 610·8—T347—616·07

上海，醫學書局，民十一年·2 版·394 面·「丁氏醫學叢書」

醫量；陳无咎著· 616·07—C291

上海，民智，民十七年·再版·「54」面·

616 内科

最新内科治療；(日)橋本節齊原著，姚鑫振譯· 616—C550
陝西，和濟書局，民三年·614面·

内科學一夕談；顧鳴盛譯· 616—K250
上海，醫學書局，民五年·107面·「丁氏醫學叢書」

内科全書；汪尊美等合編· 616—W176
上海，商務，民十二年·3版·2册·

内科學綱要；(日)安藤重次郎著· 610·8—T347—616
上海，文明，民元年·2版·374面·「丁氏醫學叢書」

維納内科學；丁福保著· 610·8—T347—616
上海，醫學書局，民七年·2版·148面·「丁氏醫學叢書」

近世内科全書；丁福保譯· 610·8—T347—616
上海，醫學書局，民九年·2版·2册·「丁氏醫學叢書」

内科全書；(日)河内龍若原著，丁福保譯· 610·8—T347—616
上海，醫學書局，民三年·3版·384面·「丁氏醫學叢書」

内科録要；侯光迪等合編· 610·8—T347—616
上海，醫學書局·

内科看護學；楊鶴慶著· 616—y126
上海，商務，民十四年·129面·

新内經；丁福保著· 610·8—T347—616
上海，醫學書局，民三年·4版·2册·「丁氏醫學叢書」

616 病理及治療學

新撰病理學講義；丁福保著· 610·8—T347—616
上海，醫學書局，民七年·2版·3册·「丁氏醫學叢書」

頓死論；丁福保著· 610·8—T347—616·1
上海，醫學書局，民六年·32面·「丁氏醫學叢書」

實扶垤里亞血清療法；(日)馬島珪之助原著，李祥麟譯· 610·8—T347—616·15
上海，文明，清宣統元年·46面·

喉痧新論；丁福保著· 610·8—T347—616·32
上海，醫學書局，民十一年·3版·48面·「丁氏醫學叢書」

赤痢新論；(日)志賀潔原著，華文祺，丁福保合譯· 610·8—T347—616·34
上海，醫學書局，民九年·2版·91面·「丁氏醫學叢書」

赤痢實驗談；丁福保著· 610·8—T347—616·34
上海，醫學書局，民六年·「45」面·「丁氏醫學叢書」

皮膚病學美容法；(日)山田弘倫原著，丁福保譯· 610·8—T347—616·5
上海，醫學書局，民七年·88面·「丁氏醫學叢書」

皮膚病學；(日)簡井八百珠原著，丁福保譯· 610·8—T347—616·5
上海，醫學書局，民七年·2版·368面·「丁氏醫學叢書」

寄生蟲病；姚昶緒著· 616·57—Y151
上海，商務，民十年·47面·「醫學小叢書」

中風之原因及治法；丁福保著· 610·8—T347—616·81
上海，醫學書局，民二年·96面·「丁氏醫學叢書」

傳染病；余雲岫著· 616·91—Y353
上海，商務，民十年·再版·46面·「醫學小叢書」

急性傳染病講義；丁福保著· 610·8—T347—616·91
上海，醫學書局，民九年·2版·294面·「丁氏醫學叢書」

麻疹療治法；李天佐，孫重沓合編· 616·912—L198
上海，中華，民十四年·152面·

可怕的猩紅熱；胡定安著· 616·917—H415
上海，商務，民十一年·41面·

删定傷寒論；南涯古益著· 610·8—T347—616·2
上海，醫學書局，民五年·2版·25面·「丁氏醫學叢書」

新傷寒論；(日)宮本叔原著，丁福保譯· 610·8—T347—616·927
上海，醫學書局，民四年·3版·74面·「丁氏醫學叢書」

霍亂新論瘧疾新論合編；丁福保著· 610·8—T347—616·93
上海，醫學書局，民九年·46面·「丁氏醫學叢書」

616·95 花柳病

生殖器病學；(日)佐藤進原著，李祥麟譯· 610·8—T347—616·95
上海，醫學書局，民三年·「62」面·

伍氏泌尿器病學，諸氏花柳病學；丁福保編· 610·8—T347—616·95
上海，醫學書局，民七年·88面·「丁氏醫學叢書」

淋病一夕話；李振軒著· 616·95—L199
上海，李振軒診所，民四年·16面·

花柳病學叢刊；萬鈞著· 610·8—T347—616·95
上海，醫學書局，民九年·再版·76面·

花柳病；姚昶緒著· 616·95—L376
上海，商務，民十一年·再版·2冊·「醫學小叢書」

最新花柳醫治法；顧鳴盛著· 616·95—K250
上海，文明，民八年·再版·152面·

花柳易知；中華書局編譯所編· 616·95—C976
上海，中華，民十一年·再版·38面·

樓麻質斯彙編；孫祖烈著· 610·8—T347—616·991
上海，醫學書局，民六年·100面·「丁氏醫學叢書」

新撰虛勞講義；丁福保著· 610·8—T347—616·995
上海，醫學書局，民五年·2版·162面·

虛癆精義；李振軒著· 610·8—T347—616·995
上海，李振軒診所，民六年·2版·74面·

癆蟲戰爭記；丁福保著· 610·8—T347—616·995
上海，醫學書局，民五年·2版·「98」面·「丁氏醫學叢書」

肺癆病預防法；(日)竹中成憲原著，丁福保譯· 610·8—T347—616·995
上海，醫學書局，民六年·4版·95面·「丁氏醫學叢書」

肺癆病一夕談；丁福保著· 610·8—T347—616·995
上海，醫學書局，民三年·3版·48面·「丁氏醫學叢書」

肺結核症再發之預防；(德)Lomisch原著，洪百容譯· 616·995—L838
上海，商務，民十一年·57面·

最新癆病治療法；劉求是著·　616·995—L356
漢口，求是醫院，民十一年·88面·

617　外科

安氏外科學，皮氏外科學；丁福保編·　610·8—T347—617
上海，醫學書局，民七年·「24」面·「丁氏醫學叢書」

外科總論；(日)下平用彩原著，徐雲，萬鈞合譯·　610·8—T347—617
上海，醫學書局，民四年·3冊·「丁氏醫學叢書」

實用外科手術；汪于岡著·　617—W178
上海，商務，民九年·269面·

外科療法；余雲岫著·　617—y354
上海，商務，民十一年·再版·48面·「醫學小叢書」

創傷療法；丁福保著·　610·8—T347—617·1
上海，醫學書局，民五年·2版·180面·「丁氏醫學叢書」

脚氣病之原因及治法；丁福保著·　610·8—T347—617·58
上海，文明，清宣統二年·119面·「丁氏醫學叢書」

瘰癧之原因及治法；丁福保著·　610·8—T347—617·5
上海，醫學書局，民六年·2版·138面·「丁氏醫學叢書」

司氏眼科學，克氏眼科學；丁福保編·　610·8—T347—617·7
上海，醫學書局，民十一年·2版·「48」面·「丁氏醫學叢書」

眼科易知；中華書局編譯所編·　617·7—C976
上海，中華，民十一年·3版·26面·

沙眼；孫祖烈著·　617·77—S530
上海，泰東，民十一年·41面·

618　婦孺科

近世婦人科全書；丁福保著·　610·8—T347—618

上海，譯書公會，民元年·3冊·

女性養生鑑；郭人驥，酈人麟合著· 618—K423

上海，商務，民十四年·再版·169面·「醫林叢刊」

婦女衛生新論；(英)莎利勃原著，景遜譯· 618—S14

上海，商務，民十四年·291面·

婦女生育論；蘇儀貞著· 618—S460

上海，中華，民十三年·4版·65面·

女性衛生常識；蘇儀貞著· 618—S461

上海，中華，民十四年·57面·

女子應有的智識；(美)珊格夫人原著，趙元任夫人譯· 618—S58

上海，商務，民十五年·再版·104面·「新智識叢書」

不姙症及治法；(日)宮田權之烝原著，周藩譯· 610·8—T347—618·17

上海，醫學書局，民五年·64面·「丁氏醫學叢書」

子之有無法；(日)田村化三郎原著，丁福保譯· 610·8—T347—618·17

上海，醫學書局，民八年·「66」面·「丁氏醫學叢書」

胎生學；(日)大澤岳太郎原著，丁福保譯· 610·8—T347—618·21

上海，丁氏醫院，民二年·110面·「丁氏醫學叢書」

胎產常識；劉无諍編· 618·2—W310

長沙，泰東，民十七年·126面·

胎產病防護法；姚昶緒著· 618·2—y151F

上海，商務，民十年·再版·48面·「醫學小叢書」

胎產須知；姚昶緒著· 618·2—y151

上海，商務，民十年·再版·48面·「醫學小叢書」

姙娠生理篇；(日)今淵恒壽原著，丁福保譯· 610·8—T347—612·21

上海，醫學書局，民四年·2版·108面·「丁氏醫學叢書」

分娩生理學；(日)今淵恒壽原著，華文祺，丁福保合譯· 610·8—T347—618·41

上海，醫學書局，民七年·2版·112面·「丁氏醫學叢書」

竹氏產婆學；(日)竹中成憲原著，丁福保譯· 610·8—T347—618·4

上海，醫學書局，民九年·4版·104面·「丁氏醫學叢書」

姙婦疹察法；丁福保著· 610·8—T347—618·3

上海，醫學書局，民五年·2版·53面·「丁氏醫學叢書」

產科學初步；丁福保著·　610·8—T347—618·2

上海，醫學書局，民四年·2版·136面·「丁氏醫學叢書」

618·9　小兒科

兒科叢刊；東埜等合編·　610·8—T347—618·9

上海，醫學書局·「114」面·「丁氏醫學叢書」

新篡兒科學；(日)伊藤龜治郎原著，丁福保譯·　610·8—T347—618·9

上海，醫學書局，民三年·2版·245面·「丁氏醫學叢書」

莫氏小兒科學，惠氏兒科學；丁福保編·　610·8—T347—618·9

上海，醫學書局，民七年·「256」面·「丁氏醫學叢書」

近世小兒科學；(日)齋藤秀雄原著，程瀚章譯·　618·9—C120

上海，商務，民十六年·「720」面·

小兒病療治法；蘇儀貞著·　618·9—S460

上海，中華，民十三年·78面·

小兒病指南；姚昶緒著·　618·9—Y151

上海，商務，民九年·48面·「醫學小叢書」

619　獸醫學

獸醫學大意；關鵬高著·　619—K297

上海，商務，民九年·3版·60面·

獸醫易知；中華書局編譯所編·　619—C976

上海，中華，民十一年·3版·60頁·

621　機械學及電氣工程

氣機發達簡明史；孔祥鵝著·　080—P225—23

上海，商務，民十五年·3版·66面·「百科小叢書第二十三種」

蒸氣機；劉振華著． 621·1—L356
上海，商務，民十六年·再版·217面·「學藝叢書」

發電機電動機構造法；(英)A. H. Avery原著，馬紹良譯． 621·313—Av37
上海，商務，民十二年·151面·

電機鐵路；陳章著． 080—P225—156
上海，商務，民十六年·59面·「百科小叢書」

無線電原理；王錫恩著． 080—P225—84
上海，商務，民十四年·128面·「百科小叢書第八十四種」

無線電學；王錫恩著． 621·3842—W155
上海，商務，民十四年·3版·158面·

無線電話原理；(美)累馬丁原著，嵇觀譯． 080—P225—56
上海，商務，民十三年·52面·「百科小叢書第五十六種」

内燃機關；劉振華著． 621·4—L356
上海，商務，民十四年·56面·「學藝彙刊」

工廠設備，一名，工廠保安及衛生設備法；
(日)勝田一原著，方漢城譯． 621·7—S230
上海，商務，民十三年·159面·

622 礦業

礦物採集鑑定法；陳學郢，孫佐合編． 622—C275
上海，商務，民三年·4版·104面·

中國十大礦廠調查記；顧瑣著． 622—K249
上海，商務，民五年·497面·

礦業條例通釋；歐陽瀚存著． 622·007—C133
上海，商務，民十三年·97面·

625 土木工程

道路；劉友惠著． 080—P225—67

上海，商務，民十三年 · 95 面 ·「百科小叢書第六十七種」

道路叢刊第一集；中華全國道路建設協會編 ·　625—C976

上海，道路月刊發行部，民十四年 ·「1522」面 ·

道路計畫書；易榮膺著 ·　625 · 7—I126

上海，商務，民十四年 · 再版 · 113 面 ·

歐美水利調查録；宋希尚編 ·　627—S566

南京，河海工程專門學校，民十三年 · 334 面 ·「河海叢刊」

行道樹；張福仁編 ·　628 · 48—C154

上海，商務，民十七年 · 101 面 ·「市政叢書」

629　航空

飛行學要義；東方雜誌社編 ·　080—T860—57

上海，商務，民十三年 · 3 版 · 88 面 ·「東方文庫」

航空論；黄璧著 ·　629 · 13—H484

上海，商務，民十四年 · 131 面 ·

航空戰術；軍學編輯局編 ·　629 · 13—C955

18 面 ·

629 · 2　汽車

汽車學；裴元嗣著 ·　629 · 2—P256

上海，商務，民十六年 · 再版 · 178 面 ·

摩托車與道路；吳山著 ·　629 · 2—W294

上海，中華，民十三年 · 191 面 ·「常識叢書第五種」

630　農業

農業學表解；上海科學書局編輯所編 ·　080—S155—630

上海，科學書局，清宣統元年·2冊·「表解叢書」

農業政策綱要；(日)橋本傳左衛門原著，黄通譯· 630—C550

上海，商務，民十六年·179面·

農業政策；(奥)菲里波維原著，馬君武譯· 630—P538

上海，中華，民十五年·280面·「新文化叢書之一」

農業淺説；丁錫華著· 630—T350

上海，中華，民八年·36面·「通俗教育叢書之一」

農林學問答；萬鴻慶著· 630—W123

上海，商務，民十一年·45頁·

教育中心中國新農村之建設；王駿聲著· 630·1—W136

上海，商務，民十七年·160面·「師範叢書」

農村社會學；顧復著· 630·1—K247

上海，商務，民十三年·114面·

中等農業經濟學；顏綸譯· 630·1—y233

上海，中華，民十四年·113面·

中等農藝化學；蔣繼尹著· 630·24—T561

上海，中華，民十四年·64面·

新體農業講義；唐昌治著· 630·4—T201

上海，商務，民十一年·5版·111面·

改進中國農業與農業教育意見書；

(美)白德斐原著，傅焕光譯· 630·7—B982

北京，教育部，民十一年·28面·

丹麥之農業及其合作；顧樹森· 630—K232

上海，中華，民十六年·78面·「歐游叢刊第三集」

美國之農業教育；徐正鑑著· 630·7—S482

上海，商務，民十三年·235面·

中國農業教育問題；鄒秉文著· 630·7—T695

上海，商務，民十二年·69面·

大中華農業史；張援著· 630·951—C173

上海，商務，民十年·161面·

中國農業之經濟觀；凌道揚著· 630·951—L341
上海，商務，民十四年·再版·89 面·

農荒預防策；東方雜誌社編· 080—T860—23
上海，商務，民十四年·3 版·95 面·「東方文庫」

土壤學；何術曾著· 631—H210
上海，商務，民八年·修訂再版·128 面·

中等農業氣象學；倪慰農著· 631·11—N192
上海，中華，民十五年·124 面·

中等農具學；顔綸譯· 631·3—y234
上海，中華，民十五年·125 面·

農具學；顔綸譯· 631·3—y234L
上海，商務，民八年·127 面·

肥料學表解；上海科學書局編輯所編· 080—S155—631
上海，科學書局，清宣統三年·84 面·「表解叢書」

肥料學；陸旋著· 631·8—L432
上海，商務，民八年·再版·124 面·

中等肥料學；蔣繼尹著· 631·8—T561
上海，中華，民十四年·77 面·

蟲害學；謝申圖著· 632—S423
上海，商務，民九年·156 面·

633　作物學

作物學；賈樹模著· 633—C478
上海，商務，民二年·6 版·76 面·

蘇俄農民政策述評；吳義田著· 630—W285
共和書局，民十六年·39 面·

中等作物學；周汝沆著· 633—C777
上海，中華，民十四年·121 面·

中等稻作學；周汝沆著・ 633—C777da
上海，中華，民十四年・再版・78 面・

四十五大作物論；顏綸譯・ 633—y234
上海，商務，民十三年・2 册・

中國作物論；原頌周著・ 633—y413
上海，商務，民十三年・407 面・

麥；顧復著・ 080—P225—98
上海，商務，民十五年・55 面・「百科小叢書第九十八種」

稻；孫繩武著・ 080—P225—97
上海，商務，民十五年・121 面・「百科小叢書第九十七種」

稻草的方法；鄒盛文著・ 570・8—T696
上海，中華，民十四年・31 面・「科學小叢書」

棉；過探先著・ 080—P225—8
上海，商務，民十二年・再版・92 面・「百科小叢書第一集第八種」

殖棉學；章之汶著・ 633・51—C177
上海，商務，民十五年・221 面・「中國科學社叢書」

中等棉作學；馮澤芳著・ 633・51—F203
上海，中華，民十四年・80 面・

634 果木及森林

果樹盆栽法；吳瑜著・ 634—W299
上海，中華，民十四年・2 版・92 面・

桑樹栽培教科書；鄭辟疆著・ 634・38—C358
上海，商務，民八年・4 版・131 面・

葡萄譜；劉德藩著・ 634・8—L375
漢口，中華印務公司，民十一年・22 面・

林學大意；林骙著・ 080—P225—54
上海，商務，民十五年・再版・90 面・「百科小叢書第五十四種」

林業淺説；林騤著・ 080—P225—35

上海，商務，民十三年・41 面・「百科小叢書第三十五種」

造林要義；陳植著・　080—P225—141

上海，商務，民十六年・「88」面・「百科小叢書」

種樹的淺説；丁錫華著・　634・9—T351

上海，中華，民十一年・5 版・38 面・「通俗教育叢書之一」

種樹的方法；鄒盛文著・　570・8—T696

上海，中華，民十五年・3 版・31 面・「科學小叢書」

森林學大意；凌道揚著・　634・9—L341

上海，商務，民六年・再版・129 面・

廣種白銀樹利益説；劉德藩著・　634・9—L375

漢口，中華印務公司，民十一年・「30」面・

中等林學大意；殷良弼著・　634・9—Y271

上海，中華，民十四年・112 面・

635　園藝

種菜的方法；鄒盛文著・　570・8—T696

上海，中華，民十四年・22 面・「科學小叢書」

盆栽花木實驗法；花好月圓人壽室編・　635—H148

上海，國華，民九年・「110」面・

園藝學；劉大紳著・　635—L375

上海，商務，民八年・117 面・

園藝一斑；盧壽籛著・　635—L406

上海，中華，民十一年・56 面・「女學叢書之一」

園作須知農作物篇；陸紹曾著・　635—L432

上海，中國圖書公司，民四年・106 面・

最新園藝法；孟昭昇著・　635—M210

上海，文明，民十三年・再版・42 面・

簡明園藝學；丁錫華著・　635—T351

上海，中華，民十一年・59 面・

藝蘭秘訣；清芬室主人編· 635—T667
上海，國華，民九年·76 面·

花卉盆栽法；吳君瑜著· 635—W281
上海，中華，民十五年·106 面·

種花的方法；鄒盛文著· 570·8—T696
上海，中華，民十四年·32 面·「科學小叢書」

姣艷的薔薇；鄒盛文著· 570·8—T696
上海，中華，民十三年·31 面·「科學小叢書」

636 畜牧

養畜學表解；上學科學書局編· 080—S145—636
上海，科學書局，清宣統二年·92 面·「表解叢書」

畜產學；關鵬萬著· 636—K297
上海，商務，民七年·114 面·

家畜飼養汎論；(日)八鍬儀七郎，石崎芳吉合著，西師意譯· 636—P111
東京，大橋新太郎，清光緒三十三年·160 面·

養鷄淺説，盧壽籛著· 636—L406
上海，中華，民十年·38 面·「通俗教育叢書之一」

農業動物飼養法；吳劍心著· 636—W281
上海，商務，民十三年·67 面·

最新養鷄法；王言綸，劉大綸合編· 636·5—W163
上海，商務，民十三年·126 面·

638 蠶蜂

製絲新法；張青選著· 636—C152
上海，宋兆信，清宣統元年·116 面·

製絲教科書；鄭辟疆著・　638—C358

上海，商務，民七年・114 面・

蠶體生理教科書；鄭辟疆著・　638—C358e1

上海，商務，民六年・110 面・

蠶體解剖教科書；鄭辟疆著・　638—C358e2

上海，商務，民七年・86 面・

蠶體病理教科書；鄭辟疆著・　638—C358e3

上海，商務，民七年・116 面・

養蠶法教科書；鄭辟疆著・　638—C358y

上海，商務，民九年・158 面・

中國蠶業概況；萬國鼎著・　638—W132

上海，商務，民十三年・65 面・

最新養蜂法；劉大綸著・　638・1—L375

上海，商務，民十三年・68 面・

實地養蜂法；王歷農著・　638・1—W147

上海，中華，民十四年・89 面・

養蜂采蜜管理法；張品南著・　638・1—T665

上海，新學會社，民十二年・152 面・

639　水產

水產學大意；闞鵬萬著・　639—K297

上海，商務，民八年・91 面・

中等水產學；周監殷，魚華仙合編・　639—C771

上海，中華，民十七年・156 面・

金魚養育法；(德)赫德各莫臘透原著，照士，嘯翁合譯・　639—H176

上海，商務，民六年・99 面・

640 家政

家政學表解；上海科學書局編輯所編． 080—S155—640
上海，科學書局，清宣統元年．65 面．「表解叢書」

家政學；（日）下田歌子原著，單士釐譯． 640—H279

實用一家經濟法；邵飄萍著． 640—S171
上海，商務，民十一年．5 版．164 面．「婦女叢書第一集第一編」

衣食住；沈德鴻編． 640—S222
上海，商務，民十一年．4 版．3 册．「新智識叢書」

居住論；鄒德謹等合編． 640—T697
上海，商務，民十四年．159 面．「通俗教育叢書」

家事實習寶鑑；王言綸著． 640—W163
上海，商務，民十五年．3 版．215 面．

家政淺説；姚銘思著． 640—y162
上海，中華，民八年．4 版．34 面．「通俗教育叢書之一」

641 烹飪

人類的食；張伯倫著． 641—C355
上海，商務，民十七年．150 面．「兒童史地叢書」

家庭食譜；李公耳著． 641—L188
上海，中華，民八年．190 面．

家庭食譜三編；時希聖著． 641—S236
上海，中華，民十四年．214 面．

家庭食譜四編；時希聖著． 641—S236
上海，中華，民十五年．344 面．

素食譜；時希聖著·　641—S236s
上海，中華，民十四年·254 面·

食物新本草；丁福保譯·　610·8—T347—641·1
上海，醫學書局，民六年·3 版·151 面·「丁氏醫學叢書」

烹飪一斑；盧壽籛著·　641·5—L406
上海，中華，民十一年·56 面·「女學叢書之一」

649　兒童養育法　看護學

看護學；丁福保著·　610·8—T347—610·73
上海，醫學書局，民七年·3 版·168 面·「丁氏醫學叢書」

病人看護法；姚昶緒著·　649—
上海，商務，民十一年·48 面·「醫學小叢書」

育兒問答；瞿宣穎著·　649—C873
上海，商務，民十一年·163 面·

育兒談；丁福保譯·　610·8—T347—649·1
上海，醫學書局，民六年·4 版·66 面·「丁氏醫學叢書」

育兒之模範；孫祖烈著·　610·8—T347—649·1
上海，醫學書局，民六年·204 面·

幼兒保育法；顧倬著·　649·1—K253
上海，商務，民十年·44 面·

育兒；盧壽錢譯·　649·1—L406
上海，中華，民十一年·156 面·

育兒一斑；盧壽籛著·　649·1—L406e
上海，中華，民九年·128 面·「女學叢書之一」

育兒法；姚昶緒著·　649·1—y151
上海，商務，民十年·46 面·「醫學小叢書」

玩具圖説；施詠湘著·　619·5—S247
上海，商務，民十年·3 册·「手工叢書」

650 商業

經商要素；張慰中著． 650—C173
上海，泰東，民九年．2 册．

新體商業講義；盛在瑜著． 650—C322
上海，商務，民八年．44 面．

商業指南；中華書局編譯所編． 650—C976
上海，中華，民十五年．「272」面．

能率增進法；黄士恒，薩君陸合編． 650—H485
上海，商務，民十年．75 面．「商業叢書第六種」

上海商業名録；徐珂著． 650．03—S478
上海，商務，民十年．594 面．

現代商業經營法；過耀根著． 651—K433
上海，商務，民十一年．189 面．

商店組織管理法；汪筱謝著． 651—W174
上海，商務，民十一年．2 册．「商業叢書第四種」

654 電報

明密電報新書． 654—M251
上海，文明．90 面．

明密碼電報書；商務印書館編譯所編． 654—S162
上海，商務，民十六年．90 面．

實驗電報學；曾清鑑編譯． 654—T521
上海，商務，民十四年．「97」面．

655．19 雕版術

中國雕版源流考；留菴著． 655．1951—L389

上海，商務，民十三年・4 版・68 面・「文藝叢刻乙集」

656　鐵路管理

鐵路車務實驗談；鄭乃文著・　656—C355
上海，中華，民十二年・87 面・

鐵路職務攬要；韋燕著・　656—W199
上海，商務，民七年・98 面・

657　簿記

查賬要義；徐廣德著・　080—P225—65
上海，商務，民十三年・73 面・「百科小叢書第六十五種」

成本會計概要；楊肇遇著・　080—P225—47
上海，商務，民十三年・66 面・「百科小叢書第四十七種」

銀行簿記法表解；上海科學書局編輯所編・　080—S155—657
上海，科學編輯所，民三年・82 面・「表解叢書」

複式商業簿記；章祖源著・　657—C192
上海，中華，民十二年・185 面・

工業簿記；(日)吉田良三原著，陳家瓚譯・　657—C359
上海，商務，民十三年・再版・136 面・

會計學；(日)吉田良三原著，張永宣譯・　657—C359
上海，中華，民六年・248 面・

會計監查；韓秋白著・　657—H123
北京，銀行周報社，民十三年・62 面・

工業會計攬要；李謨著・　657—L192
上海，中華，民十五年・69 面・「常識叢書第十七種」

鐵路會計學；李懋勛著・　657—L192t
上海，商務，民十三年・333 面・

商業簿記；李宣韓著・　657—L196

上海，商務，民十一年·8 版·2 册·

近世會計學；劉葆儒譯· 657—L372

上海，商務，民十三年·「348」面·

銀行簿記法；謝霖，李徵合著· 657—S420

上海，中國圖書公司和記，民十六年·13 版·318 面·

英美會計師事業；徐永祥著· 657—S484

上海，銀行周報社，民十四年·305 面·「會計叢書第二種」

會計師制度之調查及研究；徐永祥著· 657—S484k

上海，銀行周報社，民十二年·142 面·「會計叢書第一種」

銀行會計科目名辭· 657—T627

上海，銀行周報社，民十三年·50 面·

近世簿記法大綱；(日)東奭五郎原著，陳掖神譯· 657—T861

上海，商務，民十三年·132 面·

審計學；吳應圖著· 657—W299

上海，商務，民十六年·再版·295 面·

新式商業簿記；楊汝梅著· 657—Y130

上海，中華，民十五年·5 版·254 面·

最新商業簿記教科書；楊汝梅著· 657—Y130t

日本，錦堂，清宣統元年·增訂再版·377 面·

記賬單位論；楊冕著· 657—Y132

上海，商務，民十一年·77 面·

商業簿記；楊端六著· 657—Y132s

上海，商務，民十二年·226 面·

銀行成本會計論；銀行周報社編· 657—Y275

上海，銀行周報社，民十四年·77 面·

財政商業高等利息計算法；吳宗燾著· 658—W281

上海，商務，民十二年·164 面·「經濟叢書社叢書之二」

財政商業高等利息計算法練習問題解法；吳宗燾著· 658—W281

上海，商務，民十二年·94 面·「經濟叢書社叢書之二」

658　商業經營法

分業商品學；潘昑閣輯．　658—P162
上海，商務，民十七年．142 面．「商業叢書第十三種」

商學研究；北京民國大學商學研究會編．　658—P223
北京，民國大學商學研究會，民十五年．121 面．

進貨學；吳東初著．　658—Y132
上海，商務，民十二年．210 面．「商業概要第二卷」

商品學；盛在瑜著．　658—C322
上海，商務，民十三年．9 版．72 面．

店友須知；陳銘勳著．　658—C281
上海，商務，民十四年．6 版．92 面．

新式販賣術；華文祺著．　658—H442
上海，商務，民十一年．176 面．「商業叢書第二種」

銷貨法五百種；蔡文森著．　658—T664
上海，商務，民十年．164 面．「商業叢書第五種」

零售學；吳東初著．　658—W296
上海，商務，民十二年．113 面．「商業概要第一卷」

中國商業習慣大全；吳桂辰等合編．　658—W287
上海，世界，民十二年．「276」面．

科學的工廠管理法；張廷金譯．　658—C171
上海，商務，民十四年．再版．70 面．

工廠適用學理的管理法；(美)戴樂爾原著，穆湘玥譯．　658—T213
上海，中華，民十四年．再版．80 面．

659．1　廣告學

廣告須知；甘永龍著．　659．1—K122
上海，商務，民十四年．7 版．105 面．「商業叢書第一種」

廣告心理學；(美)史可德原著，吳應圖譯．　659．1—SC086
上海，商務，民十五年．187 面．

實用廣告學；蔣裕泉著．　659．1—T594

上海，商務，民十五年·再版·61面·

廣告心理學；(日)井關十二郎原著，唐開斌譯· 659·1—T664

上海，商務，民十四年·125面·「商業叢書第十種」

660 化學工藝

無機化學工業；程瀛章，李續祖合著· 660—C383

上海，商務，民十四年·615面·

理論實驗日用化學；(日)近藤耕藏原著，石鳴球譯· 660—C677

上海，商務，民十七年·289面·

工業製造法；奚楚明著· 660—H249

上海，商務，民十一年·525面·

實驗小工藝；奚楚明著· 660—H249s

上海，泰東，民十一年·2册·

工業藥品大全；胡超然著· 660—H401

上海，商務，民十六年·7版·653面·

實用工業知識；韓守藩著· 660—K411

上海，公民書局，民十年·207面·「工業叢書第二種」

最新化粧品製造法；郭本瀾著· 660—K426

上海，商務，民十三年·203面·

日用工藝品製造法；毛福全著· 660—M137

上海，商務，民十一年·165面·

日用品製造法；博撲民著· 666—P231

上海，中華，民十一年·4版·182面·

化學工藝寶鑑；杜亞泉著· 660—T769

上海，商務，民十年·398面·

工業化學實驗法；羅哲斯原著，韓組康譯· 660·7—R631

上海，中華，民十五年·525面·

鹽；鄭尊法著· 080—P225—99

上海，商務，民十五年·125 面·「百科小叢書第九十九種」

食品化學；劉倫編·　664—L367

上海，商務，民十六年·229 面·

糖；鄭尊法著·　080—P225—142

上海，商務，民十六年·80 面·「百科小叢書」

珐瑯器製造法；王言綸著·　666·2—W163

上海，商務，民十年·再版·89 面·

陶瓷學；何應樞著·　666·3—H213

上海，商務，民十三年·149 面·

染色學；沈覲寅著·　667—S211

上海，商務，民十六年·321 面·

新編染色術；楊時中著·　667·2—y137

上海，商務，民十二年·63 面·

煤膏；張輔良著·　080—P225—143

上海，商務，民十六年·94 面·「百科小叢書」

669　冶金學

冶金學；王本治著·　669—W153

上海，商務，民十六年·551 面·

鐵冶金學；胡庶華著·　669·1—H414

上海，商務，民十五年·189 面·「學藝叢書」

中國冶業紀要；洪彦亮著·　080—P225—15

上海，商務，民十六年·71 面·「百科小叢書」

670　工藝製造

車床木工；M·J·Glben 原著，郭元梁譯·　674—G565

上海，商務，民十三年·55 面·

造紙概論；方漢城著・ 080—P225—62
上海，商務，民十三年・70 面・「百科小叢書第六十二種」

紡織工業大要；陳文著・ 677—C290
上海，商務，民七年・66 面・「職業教育叢書」

江蘇省紡織業狀況；江蘇實業廳第三科編・ 677—C514
上海，商務，民九年・225 面・

橡皮；方漢城著・ 080—P225—55
上海，商務，民十三年・58 面・「百科小叢書第五十五種」

馬來半島之橡皮事業；周國鈞著・ 678—C778
上海，國立暨南大學出版課，民十六年・260 面・

680 手工業

編物圖說；張叔平著・ 680—C170
上海，商務，民六年・55 面・

實用手工參考書；熊翥高著・ 680—H356
上海，商務，民十年・4 版・3 册・

摺紙圖說；桂紹烈著・ 680—K344
上海，商務，民十一年・4 版・66 面・「手工叢書第一編」

手工教材：小學適用；李彤文，蕭連牖合編・ 680—L199
上海，商務，民十一年・2 册・

剪紙圖說；施詠湖著・ 680—S247
上海，商務，民十一年・4 版・94 面・「手工叢書」

續摺紙圖說；施詠湖著・ 680—S247
上海，商務，民十年・再版・66 面・

手工圖畫聯絡教材；孫捷著・ 680—S511
上海，商務，民十年・126 面・

麥稈辮圖說；汪祖原著・ 680—W176
上海，商務，民九年・2 版・84 面・「手工叢書」

手工平面物標本；趙傳璧著· 680·7—C261
上海，商務，民四年·37面·
金木工及玻璃細工；陳文著· 680—C290
上海，商務，民七年·56面·
實用木工學· 680—L503
上海，商務，民七年·282面·

700 美術

700 美術

美術概論；黃懺華著· 080—P225—134
上海，商務，民十六年·98·「百科小叢書」

輓近美學思潮；吕徵著· 080—P225—19
上海，商務，民十三年·114面·「百科小叢書第四十九種」

美學淺説；吕澂著· 080—P225—11
上海，商務，民十二年·再版·54面·「百科小叢書第十一種」

美與人生；東方雜誌社編· 080—T860—67
上海，商務，民十四年·3版·100面·「東方文庫」

藝術談概；東方雜誌社編· 080—T860—68
上海，商務，民十四年·3版·81面·「東方文庫」

美的人生觀；張競生著· 701—C152
北京，北新，民十四年·2版·212面·

藝術概論；(日)黑田鵬信原著，豐子愷澤· 701—H215
上海，開明，民十七年·101面·

藝術思潮，華林著· 701—H441
上海，出版合作社，民十五年·再版·76面·

近代美術思潮；黃懺華著· 701—H471
上海，商務，民十一年·71面·

美學原理；(英)馬霞爾原著，肅石君譯· 701—M356
上海，泰東，民十三年·3版·164面·

美的哲學；徐慶譽著· 701—S476
　民十七年·
藝術論；(俄)托爾斯泰原著，耿濟之譯· 701—T588
　上海，商務，民十年·269面·
美學綱要；(日)墨田鵬信原著，俞寄凡譯· 702—2H15
　上海，商務，民十一年·82面·
美學綱要；(德)耶魯撒冷原著，王平陵譯· 702—J487
　上海，泰東，民十五年·再版·56面·
美術及音樂教學法；教育雜誌社編· 370·8—C544—56
　上海，商務，民十四年·105面·「教育叢著第五十六種」
藝術教育之原理；朱元善編· 370·8—C544—1·4
　上海，商務，民十一年·3版·149面·「教育叢書第一集第四編」
藝術教育學；雷家駿著· 707—L471
　上海，商務，民十四年·162面·「師範叢書」

709　美術史

美學略史；黄懺華著· 080—P225—50
　上海，商務，民十三年·36面·「百科小叢書第五十種」
近世美學；(日)高小林次郎原著，劉仁航譯· 709—K175
　上海，商務，民十一年·243面·
西洋美術史；豐子愷著· 709—F224
　上海，開明，民十七年·246面·
西洋美術史；吕徵著· 709—L450
　上海，商務，民十一年·163面·
中國美術史；(日)大村西崖原著，陳彬和譯· 709·51—T134
　上海，商務，民十七年·262面·「歷史叢書」
中國美術小史；滕固著· 080—P225—90
　上海，商務，民十五年·51面·「百科小叢書第九十種」
日本美術的新印象；劉海粟著· 709·52—L362

上海，商務，民十一年・191 面・

730—750 造形 畫論 畫册 幾何畫

造形美術；(德)The dor Volbehr 原著，錢稻孫譯・ 080—P225—45
上海，商務，民十三年・「百科小叢書第四十五種」

新繪學；伍聯德，陳炳洪合編・ 740—W308
上海，商務，民十二年・2 册・

子愷漫畫；豐子愷著・ 740—F224
上海，開明，民十五年・再版・96 面・「文學週報社叢書」

子愷畫集；豐子愷著・ 740—F224h
上海，開明，民十六年・再版・96 面・「文學週報社叢書」

文農諷刺畫集；黄文農著・ 740—H188
上海，光華，民十六年・76 面・「漫畫會叢書第一種」

北遊漫畫；魯飛著・ 740—L416
上海，光華，民十七年・45 面・

百石齋叢畫・ 741—P225
上海，拾葉山房，民十二年・8 册・

停雲閣叢畫・ 741—T369
上海，商餘協會，民十二年・4 册・

大觀樓叢畫・ 741—W178
上海，泰華，民十年・4 册・

平面幾何畫法；求是學社編・ 744—C744
上海，求是學社，清光緒三十三年・6 册・

用器畫法圖式；(日)平瀨作五郎原著・ 744—S367
東京，九善株式會社，明治四十一年・3 册・

袖珍製圖便覽；童世享編・ 740—T908
上海，商務，民十四年・75 面・

平面立體幾何畫法；王濟仁著・ 741—W136

上海，暨南大學出版課，民十七年・196 面・「國立暨南大學叢書」

最新圖案法；俞劍華著・ 745—y370

上海，商務，民十五年・171 面・

讀畫輯略；玉卿老人著・ 750—C279

上海，商務，民十四年・126 面・「文藝叢刊甲集」

書畫大觀；俞丹林，陳牧林合編・ 745—y373

上海，中華，民十二年・4 册・

750 繪畫

四畫概要；吳夢非著・ 080—P225—91

上海，商務，民十五年・76 面・「百科小叢書第九十一種」

近代西洋繪畫；東方雜誌社編・ 080—T860—69

上海，商務，民十四年・3 版・2 册・「東方文庫」

水彩畫概論；倪貽德著・ 752—N192

上海，光華，民十五年・117 面・

770 攝影

照相學；陳思義編・ 770—287

上海，商務，民十五年・再版・234 面・

照相鏤板印圖法；(美)頁列尼原著，衛理，王汝騆合譯・ 770—p250

白朗尼照相鏡用法；商務印書館編譯所編・ 770—S162

上海，商務，民十年・24 面・

簡明照相法；商務印書館編譯所編・ 770—S162

上海，商務，民十二年·19 面·

新篇攝影術；杜就田著· 770—T760

上海，商務，民十年·188 面·

民十三之故宮；陳萬里著· 779—C2901

上海，開明，民十七年·

780 音樂

音樂的常識；豐子愷著· 780—F224

上海，亞東，民十四年·396 面·

普通樂學：高級中學適用；蕭友梅著· 780—S399

上海，商務，民十七年·189 面·

各國國歌評述；王光祈著· 780—W146

上海，中華，民十五年·130 面·「音樂叢刊之一」

歐洲音樂進化論；王光祈著· 780—W146O

上海，中華，民十三年·55 面·「音樂叢刊之一」

西洋音樂史綱；俞寄凡著· 080—P225—138

上海，商務，民十六年·114 面·「百科小叢書」

東西樂制之研究；王光祈著· 780·9—W145

上海，中華，民十五年·232 面·「音樂叢刊之一」

霓裳羽衣：學校歌舞劇；凌純聲，童之絃合編· 782—L340

上海，商務，民十七年·123 面·

中外學校唱歌集；A·J·Anderson 原著· 784—An23

上海，商務，民十二年·83 面·

790 遊藝　運動

民間遊戲；嵇字經輯· 790—C388

上海，商務，民十七年·134 面·

遊戲專論；治永清著·　790—C658

上海，商務，民十三年·147 面·「北京師範大學叢書」

正反遊戲法；王懷琪著·　790—W142

上海，商務，民十二年·29 面·

中國體育史；郭希汾著·　790·9—K432

上海，商務，民九年·133 面·

劇院的將來；Bouamy Robret 原著，徐霞村譯·　080—R575—792

上海，北新，民十七年·46 面·「明日叢書」

舞蹈術；張英穀著·　793—C173

上海，新民圖書館，民十二年·「144」面·

舞蹈遊戲；王季粱，孫淡合著·　793—W137

上海，商務，民十年·「98」面·

行進遊技法；汪應鈞著·　793—W178

上海，商務，民十三年·150 面·

上海，商務，民十六年·7 版·115 面·

七巧八分圖；錢蕓吉著·　794—T618

上海，商務，民十二年·4 版·2 册·

益智圖；童葉庚著·　794—T879

上海，商務，民十三年·7 版·6 册·

田徑游泳競技運動法；教育雜誌社編·　3T0·8—C544—70

上海，商務，民十四年·106 面·「教育叢著第七十種」

田徑賽的理論與實際；謝似顔著·　796—S423

上海，開明，民十六年·212 面·

劍術基本教練法；周烈著·　796—C799

上海，中華，民十五年·三版·52面·

游泳術；顧極來著· 796—K246
上海，商務，民十四年·
踢毽術；沙濤著· 796—S141
上海，商務，民十一年·42面·

作戰遊技法；孫撲編· 796—S527
上海，商務，民十三年·5版·106面·
拳術學教範；陸師凱，陸師通合著· 796·6—L432
上海，商務，民十五年·5版·258面·
十二潭腿新教授法；王懷琪著· 796·6—W142s
上海，中華，民十三年·106面·
雙人潭腿；吳琦，楊煥章合著· 796·6—W281
上海，商務，民十七年·25面·
潭腿；精武體育會編· 796·6—T656
上海，商務，民十五年·8版·109面·「技擊叢刊第二種」
易筋經廿四式圖説；王懷琪著· 796·6—W142
上海，商務，民十一年·7版·42面·
訂正八段錦；王懷琪著· 796·6—W142d
上海，商務，民十五年·11版·28面·

籃球；國民體育社編· 797—E435
上海，商務，民十五年·5版·93面·「體育叢書」
臺球；劉大紳編· 797—L375
上海，商務，民十一年·259面·「體育叢書」
杖球；潘知本譯· 797—P151
上海，商務，民十二年·94面·「體育叢書」
棒球；潘知本編· 797—P151P
上海，商務，民十一年·46面·「體育叢書」

槌球運動法；倪灝森譯．　797—N191
上海，商務，民十三年．再版．84 面．

網球術；孫撲編．　797—S527
上海，中國圖書公司，民六年．59 面．

圈球遊戲；王小峯編．　797—W156
上海，商務，民十二年．3 版．22 面．

籃球遊戲法；殷黎樵編．　797—y271
共進中學校，民十二年．22 面．

800 文學

800 文學

文藝思潮論；(日)厨川白村原著，樊從予譯· 801—C863
上海，商務，民十三年·131面·「文學研究會叢書」

近代文學思潮；黄懺華著· 801—H471
上海，商務，民十五年·144面·「新智識叢書」

歐洲最近文藝思潮；憶秋生著· 801—I127
上海，商務，民十三年·163面·「小説世界叢刊」

歐洲近代文藝思潮概論；(日)本間久雄原著，沈端先譯· 801—I260
上海，開明，民十七年·362面·

新文學概論；(日)本間久雄原著，汪馥泉譯· 801—P260
上海，商務，民十四年·146面·

新文學概論；(日)本間久雄原著，章錫琛譯· 801—P260
上海，商務，民十五年·134面·「文化研究會叢書」

新文藝評論；孫俍工輯· 801—S519
上海，民智，民十二年·460面·

近代文學概觀；東方雜誌社編· 080—T860—59
上海，商務，民十四年·3版·2册·「東方文庫」

801 文學批評

文藝批評淺説；周全平著· 080—P225—136

上海，商務，民十六年·78 面·「百科小叢書」

文學批評與批評家；東方雜誌社編· 080—T860—60

上海，商務，民十四年·3 版·90 面·「東方文庫」

社會的文學批評論；(美)蒲克女士原著，傅東華譯· 801—B855

上海，商務，民十一年·75 面·「文學研究會叢書」

近代文學叢談；趙景深著· 801—C201

上海，新文化，民十四年·145 面·

學術叢話；黄懺華著· 801—H471

上海，泰東，民十五年·4 版·140 面·

近代文學與社會改造；東方雜誌社編· 080—T860—62

上海，商務，民十四年·3 版·77 面·「東方文庫」

文學革命；張天花著· 801—C171

上海，民智，民十七年·236 面·

自己的園地；周作人著· 801—C771

北京，晨報社，民十二年·348 面·

近代文學十講；(日)厨川白村原著，羅迪先譯· 801—C863

上海，學術研究會，民十六年·3 版·2 册·「學術研究會叢書之四」

表現的鑑賞；胡夢華，吳淑貞合著· 801—H410

上海，現代，民十七年·280 面·

浪漫的與古典的；梁實秋著· 801—L263

上海，新月，民十六年·174 面·

近代文藝的背景；(日)内崎作三郎原著，王璧如譯· 801—N270

北平，北新，民十七年·172 面·

文學的科學化；徐蔚南著· 801—s483

上海，世界，民十六年·59 面·

唯美派的文學；滕固著· 801—T275

上海，光華，民十六年·144 面·

寫實主義與浪漫主義；東方雜誌社編· 080—T860—61

上海，商務，民十四年·3 版·74 面·

給志在文藝者；任白濤譯· 801—J127

上海，亞東，民十七年·261·

對于少年作家的暗示；(美)馬爾騰原著，范存忠譯· 801—M334

上海，新文化，民十四年·82面·「新文化小叢書」

文藝辭典；孫俍工編· 803—S519

上海，民智，民十七年·

808·1 詩學研究(普通)

詩學；(希臘)亞里斯多德原著，傅東華譯· 808·1—Ar46

上海，商務，民十五年·120面·「文學研究會叢書」

詩歌原理；汪静之著· 080—O225—139

上海，商務，民十六年·69面·「百科小叢書」

詩的原理；小説月報社編· 800—Sh41—49

上海，商務，民十四年·78面·「小説月報叢刊第四十九種」

詩學原理；王希和著· 800·1—W155

上海，商務，民十三年·142面·

浪花；C. F. 譯· 808·1—W142

北京大學新潮社，民十三年·再版·117面·「陽光社文藝小叢書」

808·2 戲劇研究(普通)

近代戲劇家論；東方雜誌社編· 080—T860—63

上海，商務，民十四年·3版·86面·「東方文庫」

現代獨幕劇；東方雜誌社編· 080—T860—82

上海，商務，民十四年·3版·3册·「東方文庫」

愛美的戲劇；陳大悲著· 800·2—C288

北京，晨報社，民十三年·262面·「晨報社叢書」

劇本的登場；谷劍塵著· 808·2—K255

東南劇學編譯社，民十四年·100面·「戲劇叢書」

戲劇短論；徐公美著· 808·2—S478

上海，光華，民十五年·241面·

戲劇作法講義；孫俍工著· 808·2—S519

上海，亞東，民十四年·178 面·

戲曲論；余心著·　808·2—y351

上海，光華，民十六年·90 面·

808·3　小説研究

短篇小説作法研究；張志澄著·　808·3—C152

上海，商務，民十七年·188 面·「文學叢書」

小説法程；(美)哈米頓著，華林一譯·　808·3—H48

上海，商務，民十二年·19 面·「文學叢書」

小説通論；沈蘇約著·　808·3—S221

上海，梁溪圖書館，民十五年·再版·100 面·

小説論；郁達夫著·　808·3—y376

上海，光華，民十五年·100 面·

小説作文講義；孫俍工著·　808·3—S519

上海，中華，民十三年·28 面·

創作討論；小説月報社編·　808·3—S41—13

上海，商務，民十四年·80 面·「小説月報叢刊第十三種」

説部常識；徐敬修著·　808·3—S476

上海，大東，民十四年·108 面·「國學常識之十」

小説考證；蔣端藻著·　808·3—T571

上海，商務，民十二年·3 版·3 册·「文藝叢刻乙集」……續編·二册·

小説考證拾遺；蔣瑞藻編·　808·3—T571

上海，商務，民十一年·113 面·

小説話；解著·　808·3—C565

上海，中華，民八年·120 面·

中國小説史大綱；張靜廬著·　808·3—C191

上海，泰東，民十年·再版·60 面·

中國小説史略；郭希汾著·　808·3—K427

上海，新文化·94 面·

中國小説史略；魯迅著·　808·3—L416

上海，北新，民十六年・四版・318 面・

小説舊聞鈔；魯迅著・ 808・3—L416

北京，北新，民十五年・156 面・

歐美小説叢談；孫毓修著・ 808・3—S35

上海，商務，民五年・177 面・「文藝叢刻甲集」

西洋小説發達史；謝六逸著・ 808・3—S20

上海，商務，民十二年・160 面・

歐美近代小説史；鄭次川著・ 808—P225—135

上海，商務，民十六年・110 面・「百科小叢書」

808・5　演説術

小演説家；張九如，周翥青合著・ 808・5—C152

上海，中華，民十五年・148 面・「兒童課餘眼務叢書第一種」

演説與辯論；高葆真著・ 808・5—C814

上海，廣學會，民三年・357 面・

講演法的研究；李寓一著・ 808・5—L202

上海，現代，民十七年・122 面・

演説術；M. Lewis 原著，殷凱譯・ 808・5—L585

上海，太平洋，民十五年・再版・92 面・

演説學大綱；楊炳乾著・ 808・5—Y139

上海，商務，民十七年・16 面・

演説；袁澤民著・ 808・5—Y416

上海，商務，民十一年・7 版・98 面・

808・6　書信作法　公文程式

書信構造法；嚴渭漁著・ 808・6—Y228

上海，中華，民十一年・3 版・72 面・

酬世文柬指南；徐珂輯・ 808・6—S478

上海，商務，民九年・10 版・179 面・

國民政府軍用公文程式；精誠書店編・ 808・6—T656

上海，精誠書店，民十七年・290 面・

國民政府現行公文程式詳解；王尹孚輯・ 808・6—W163

上海，法學編譯社，民十七年・426 面・

書信彙集(普通)

歐洲近二百年名人情書；霍甫曼編，魏蘭譯・ 808・6—H675

上海，亞東，民十七年・274 面・

詩文彙集(普通)

陀螺：詩歌小品集；周作人譯・ 808・8—C771

上海，新潮社，民十四年・277 面・「新潮社文藝叢書」

緑湖；凌夢痕輯， 808—L241

上海，民智，民十三年・482 面・

國外民歌譯；劉復譯・ 808・8—L372

上海，北新，民十六年・再版・158 面・

屠蘇；白水等合著・ 808—P227

上海，光華，民十五年・193 面・「獅吼社同人叢著第一輯」

小説月報叢刊；小説月報社編・ 808—Sh41

上海，商務，民十三至十四年・51 册・

星海；文學研究會編・ 808—W255

上海，商務，民十三年・上册・「文學研究會會刊」

809　文學史

文藝史概要；張資平著・ 809—C152

武昌，時中合作書社，民十四年・162 面・

文學大綱；鄭振鐸編・ 809—C351

上海，商務，民十六年・10 册・

歐洲文學史；周作人著・ 809—C771

上海，商務，民十三年・6 版・209 面・「北京大學叢書之三」

歐洲文學入門；(法)法格原著，顧鍾序譯· 809—F139
上海，商務，民十三年·160面·「文學叢書」

810 中國文學

文學常識；傅東華著· 080—P225—L23
上海，商務，民十六年·54面·「百科小叢書」

文學常識；劉哲盧輯· 810—L356
上海，源記，民十五年·108面·

文學論；劉永濟著· 810—L379
上海，太平洋，民十五年·4版·260面·

新文學研究法；載渭清，吕雲彪合著· 810—T132
上海，大東，民九年·2册·

新文學淺説；胡懷琛著· 810·1—H405
上海，泰東，民十一年·162面·

新文學評論；王世輯· 810·1—W155
上海，新文化書社，民十五年·2册·

文學論略；章太炎著· 81C—C189
上海，羣衆，民十五年·再版·64面·

中國文學研究；鄭振鐸輯· 810·2—C387
上海，商務，民十六年·「小説月報十七卷號外」

中國文學概論；(日)監谷温原著，陳彬龢譯· 810·2—y208
北京，樸社，民十五年·10面·

走到出版界；高長虹著· 810·4—K166
上東，泰東，民十七年·210面·「狂飈叢書第二集第九種」

現代文學作家；錢杏邨著· 810·1—T612
上海，泰東，民十七年·106面·

中國文學雜論；楊鴻烈著· 810·1—Y125
上海，亞東，民十七年·22面·

810・7　文學讀本

模範文選；程演生輯・　　810・7—C349
北京，國立北京大學，民十二年・3 版・320 面・

國文讀本評注；許國英輯・　　810・7—H371
上海，商務，民十三年・4 册・

白話文範；何仲英輯・　　810・7—H522
上海，商務，民九年・3 册・

初級古文讀本；沈星一輯・　　810・7—S221
上海，中華，民十二年・2 册・

新制國文教本評註；謝无量輯・　　810・7—S425
上海，中華，民十一年・4 册・

國文故事選讀；陶孟和選・　　810・70T248
上海，亞東，民十五年・154 面・

810・8　中國修辭學

中國修辭學；張弓著・　　810・8—C160
天津，華英，民十五年・143 面・

作文法講義；陳望道著・　　810・8—C290
上海，民智，民十一年・182 面・

作文研究；胡懷琛著・　　810・8—H105
上海，商務，民十五年・107 面・

國語文作法；黄正厂著・　　810・8—H171
上海，中華，民十三年・84 面・「國語小叢書」

實用文章義法；謝无量著・　　810・8—425
上海，中華，民十三年・2 册・

論説文作法講義；孫俍工著・　　810・8—S519
上海，商務，民十四年・121 面・

記敘文作法講義；孫俍工著・　　810・8—S519
上海，民智，民十五年・4 版・356 面・

修辭學講義；董魯安著· 810·8—T854
北京，文化學社，民十五年·2冊·

810·9 中國文學史

中國文學小史；趙景深編· 810·9—C201
上海，文華書局，民十七年·211面·

中國文學史略；胡懷琛著· 810·9—H105
上海，梁溪圖書館，民十五年·4版·200面·

中國文學源流；胡毓寰著· S10·9—H419
上海，商務，民十三年·338面·

國語文學史；凌獨見著· 810·9—L311
上海，商務，民十二年·359面·

中國大文學史；謝无量著· 810·9—S125
上海，中華，民十六年·636面·

中國婦女文學史；謝无量著· 810·9—S125
上海，中華，民十三年·346面·

中國文學史；曾毅著· 810·9—T524
上海，泰東，民十一年·336面·

中國文學變遷史；劉真晦，沈雁冰合著· 810·9—L356
上海，新文化，民十七年·9版·「114」上·

中古文學史；劉師培著· 810·9—L373
北京，國立大學，民十二年·128面·

中古文學概論；徐嘉瑞著· 810·9—S476
上海，亞東，民十三年·上冊·

中國六大文豪；謝无量著· 810·9—S425
上海，中華，民十三年·349面·

平民文學之兩大文豪；謝无量著· 810·9—S425
上海，商務，民十三年·114面·

白話文學史；胡適著· 810·9—H414
上海，新月書局，民十七年·上冊·

五十年來之中國文學；胡適輯·　810·9—H414

上海，申報館，民十三年·94面·「申報五十周年紀念刊之一種」

811　詩——研究

詩品注；鍾嶸著·　811—c979

上海，開明，民十六年·132面·

詩人性格；周服著·　811—C774

上海，商務，民十三年·110面·

詩式；朱寶瑩著·　811—C833

上海，中華，民十三年·四版·286面·

小詩研究；胡懷琛著·　811—G405

上海，商務，民十三年·94面·

漢詩研究；古層冰著·　811—K265

上海，啓智，民十七年·150面·

漢詩評釋；(H)桂胡村，高橋豹軒合著·　811—K345

詩論；潘大道著·　811—P160

上海，商務，民十三年·100面·「學藝彙刊」

詩學常識；徐敬修著·　811—S476

上海，大東，民十四年·190面·「國學常識之八」

新詩概説；胡懷琛著·　811—H405

上海，商務，民十三年·再版·54面

新詩法講義；孫俍工著·　811—S519

上海，商務，民十四年·250面·

811·08　詩一總集

古詩源；沈德潛輯·　811·08—S222

上海，泰東，民十六年·309面·

白話唐詩五絶百首；凌善清輯·　811·08—L341

上海，中華，民十一年·再版·100面·

白話唐人七絶百首；浦薛鳳輯· 811·08—P415
上海，中華，民十一年·4版·100面·

白話宋詩七絶百首；凌善清輯· 811·08—L341
上海，中華，民十一年·4版·98面·

近代詩鈔；陳衍輯· 811·08—C293
上海，商務，民十二年·6册·

雲朝；朱自清等合著· 811—08—C835y
上海，商務，民十三年·4版·157面·「文學研究會叢書」

春雲；绿波社社員編· 811·08—L438
天津，教育書社，民十二年·175面·

時代新聲；盧冀野著· 811·08—L405
上海，泰東，民十七年·176面·

新詩年選；北社編· 811·08—P223
上海，亞東，民十二年·251面·

歧路：新詩集；小説月報社編· 808—Sh41—3
上海，商務，民十三年·63面·「小説月報叢刊第八種」

眷顧；小説月報社編· 88s—h41—53
上海，商務，民十四年·109面·「小説月報叢刊第五十八種」

海嘯；小説月報社編· 803—sh41—27
上海，商務，民十四年·66面·「小説月報叢刊第二十七種」

良夜；小説月報社編· 808—sh41—17
上海，商務，民十四年·68面·「小説月報叢刊第十七種」

811·1 楚詞

屈原；陸侃如著· 811·1—428
上海，亞東，民十二年·332面·

楚詞新論；謝无量著· 811·1—S425
上海，商務，民十三年·再版·76面·「國學小叢書」

楚詞概論；游國恩著· 811·1—y323
北京，述學社，民十五年·366面·

811・9　詩—別集

嘗試集；胡適著・　811・9—H414
上海，亞東，民十二年・5 版・193 面・

深誓；章衣萍著・　811・9—C182
北京，北新，民十四年・90 面・「交藝小叢書」

荷花；趙景深著・　811・9—C201
上海，開明，民十七年・74 面・

芳屋；陳志莘著・　811・9—C287
上海，新文化書社，民十三年・74 面・

草莽集；朱湘著・　811・9—C834
上海，開明，民十六年・187 面・「新文叢書第一種」

踪跡；朱自清著・　811・9—C835c
上海，亞東，民十三年・174 面・

胡思永的遺詩；胡思永著・　811・9—H414
上海，亞東，民十三年・152 面・

草兒在前集；康洪章著・　811・9—K151
上海，亞東，民十三年・236 面・

河上集；康洪章著・　811・9—K151
上海，亞東，民十三年・100 面・

草兒；康白情著・　811・9—k153
上海，亞東，民十二年・384 面・

精神與愛的女神；高長虹著・　811・9—K166
北京，平民藝術國，民十四年・86 面・「狂飈小叢書」

獻給自然的女兒；高長虹著・　811・9—k1663
上海，泰東，民十七年・80 面・「狂飈叢書第二第三種」

卷耳集；創造社編・　811・9—K125
上海，泰東，民十三年・4 版・148 面・「創造社辛夷小叢書第二種」

食客與凶年；李金髪著・　811・9—L181
上海，北新，民十六年・235 面・

晚禱；梁宗岱著． 811·9—L251

上海，商務，民十四年·63面·「文學研究會叢書」

揚鞭集；劉半農著． 811·9—L360

北京，北新，民九年·上册·

郵吻；劉大白著． 811·9—L375

上海，開明，民十五年·99面·「黎明社叢書」

舊夢；劉大白著． 811·9—L375C

上海，商務，民十三年·449面·「文學研究會叢書」

渡河；陸志韋著． 811·9—L425

上海，亞東，民十二年·215面·

春深了；閔之寅著． 811·9—M248

上海，羣衆圖書公司，民十五年·44面·「新詩集」

夜風；沐鴻著． 811·9—M351

上海，泰東，民十七年·210面·

繁星；冰心女士著． 811·9—P372

上海，商務，民十五年·90面·「文學研究會叢書」

天堂與五月；邵洵美著． 811·9—S171

上海，光華，民十六年·168面·「獅吼社叢書」

花一般的罪惡；邵洵美著． 811·9—S171h

上海，金屋，民十七年·55面·

飛霞：原名自己的花園；沈秀鵑著． 811·9—S221

上海，羣衆，民十六年·72面·

將來之花園；徐玉諾著． 811·9—S484

上海，商務，民十三年·3版·134面·「文學研究會叢書」

微痕；曹唯非著． 811·9—T478

上海，泰東，民十五年·292面·

戀歌；曹雪松，丁丁合輯． 811·9—T482

上海，泰東，民十五年·111面·

新夢；蔣光赤著． 811·9—T566

上海，書店，民十四年·172面·

流雲；宗白華著·　811·9—T752
　上海，亞東，民十二年·71面·
流雲小詩；宗白華著·　811·9—T752
　上海，亞東，民十七年·再版·61面·
斜坡：曼尼的詩集；曼尼著·　811·9—W134
　上海，新文化書社，民十三年·95面·
童心；王統照著·　811·9—W159T
　上海，商務，民十四年·260面·「文學研究會叢書」
蕙的風；汪静之著·　811·9—W166
　上海，亞東，民十二年·再版·242面·
君山；韋業蕪著·　811·9—W195
　北京，未名社，民十六年·140面·「未名新集之一」
死水；聞一多著·　811·9—W240
　上海，新月，民十七年·91面·
我倆的心；雅風，丁丁合著·　811·9—y111
　北京，海音，民十六年·60面·「海音叢書之四」
西還；俞平伯著·　811·9—y372
　上海，亞東，民十三年·182面·
冬夜；俞平伯著·　811·9—y372
　上海，亞東，民十二年·246面·

812　詞

詩學指南；謝无量著·　811—S425
　上海，中華，民十一年·5版·97面·
詞餘講義；吳梅著·　811—W920
　北京大學出版部，民十二年·再版·124面·
詞選；胡適輯·　811—H414
　上海，商務，民十七年·403面·

813 戲曲

宋元戲曲史；王國維著· 812·09—w145
上海，商務，民十五年·5版·199面·「文藝叢刊甲集」

戲劇短論；徐公美著· 812—S478
上海，光華，民十五年·241面·

中國戲曲概評；向培良著· 812—H286
上海，泰東，民十七年·164面·

戲學彙考；凌善清·許志豪合著· 812—L341
上海，大東，民十五年·再版·十册·

梨園佳話；王夢生著· 812—w149
上海，商務，民四年·160面·「文藝叢刻甲集」

李笠翁曲話；李漁著· 812·8—L202
上海，梁溪圖書館，民十四年·135面·「文藝叢書」

繪像增批第六才子書；金聖歎批· 822·7—T290

元曲選；臧晉叔輯· 82·17—T415
上海，商務，民七年·影博古堂本·48面·

元曲別裁集；盧前編· 812·7—L405
上海，開明，民十七年·47頁·

劇本彙刊第一集第二集；歐陽予倩等合編· 812·9—S155
上海，商務，民十四年·再版·193面·

死後之勝利；小說月報社編· 808—Sh41—7
上海，商務，民十三年·62面·「小說月報叢刊第七種」

孤鴻；小說月報社編· 808—Sh41—48
上海，商務，民十四年·60面·「小說月報叢刊第四十八種」

懇親會；小說月報社編· 808—Sh41—35
上海，商務，民十四年·67面·「小說月報叢刊第三十五種」

青春的夢；天著· 812·9—C172
上海，中華，民十三年·147面·「少年中國學會小叢書」

幽蘭女士；陳大悲著· 812·9—o288

上海，現代，民十七年・120面・「現代戲劇叢書」

棄婦；侯曜著・ 812・9—H242c

上海，商務，民十四年・72面・「文學研究會通俗戲劇叢書」

復活的玫瑰；侯曜著・ 812・9—H242F

上海，商務，民十五年・145面・「文學研究會通俗戲劇叢書第二種」

山河淚；侯曜著・ 812・9—H242S

上海，商務，民十五年・再版・81面・「文學研究會通俗戲劇叢書」

沉悶的戲曲；向培良著・ 812・9—H286

上海，光華，民十六年・78面・「狂飆叢書第三第四種」

青春底悲哀；熊佛西著・ 812・9—H357

上海，商務，民十三年・137面・「文學研究會通俗戲劇叢書」

西冷橋畔；胡雲翼著・ 812・9—H419

上海，北新，民十六年・146面・

新婚的夢；胡雲翼著・ 812・9—H4193

上海，啓智，民十七年・108面・「天風社叢書」

斷鴻零雁；黄嘉謨著・ 812・9—H471

上海，第一線書店，民十七年・108面・

還未過去的現在；黄鵬基著・ 812・9—H481

上海，光華，民十七年・123面・

蘭溪女士；谷鳳田著・ 812・9—K255

上海，羣衆，民十六年・136面・「文學社叢書之一」

聶嫈；郭沫若著・ 812・9—K425n

上海，光華，民十四年・98面・「創造社叢書」

三個叛逆的女性；郭沫若著・ 812・9—K425s

上海，光華，民十五年・261面・

星空；郭沫若著・ 812・9—K425s

上海，泰東，民十三年・198面・

女神：戲曲詩歌集；郭沫若著・ 812・9—K425y

上海，泰東，民十五年・8版・238面・「創造社叢書第一種」

紅玫瑰；李鴻梁著・ 812・9—L185

上海，梁溪圖書館，民十四年·46 面·

琳麗；白薇著· 812·9—P227

上海，商務，民十六年·208 面·

人間的樂園；濮舜卿著· 812·9—P397

上海，商務，民十七年·98 面·

闊人的孝道；蒲伯英著· 812·9—P415K

北京，晨報社，民十三年·114 面·「晨報社叢書第十七種」

道義之交；蒲伯英著· 812·9—P415t

北京，晨報社，民十二年·94 面·「晨報叢書戲劇集第一種」

宇宙之謎；星北著· 812·9—S445

上海，泰東，民十五年·84 面·

咖啡店之一夜；田漢著· 812·9—T334

上海，中華，民十四年·265 面·

女健者；左幹臣著· 812·9—T681

上海，啓智，民十七年·118 面·

蔓羅姑娘；王新命著· 812·9—W155

上海，泰東，民十三年·3 版·109 面·「孤芳集第一輯」

814 散文—別集

章太炎先生所著書；章炳麟著· 814·9—C189

上海，古書流通處，民十三年·4 册·

精刊章譚合鈔；章炳麟，譚嗣同合著· 814·9—C189

285 面

飲冰室全集；梁啓超著· 814·9—L251

上海，中華，民五年·8 册·

梁任公近著第一輯；梁啓超著· 814·9—L251

上海，商務，民十五年·3 版·2 册·

梁任公學術講演集；梁啓超著· 814·9—L251

上海，商務，民十五年·4 版·第一集 第三集·

吴盧文録；吴盧著．　814．9—W299
上海，亞東，民十四年．4 版．207 面．

胡適文存一二集；胡適著．　814．9—H414
上海，亞東，民十六年．4 版．

漱冥三十前文録；梁漱冥著．　814．9—L263
上海，商務，民十三年．再版．252 面．

大圓文存；唐大圓著．　814．9—T213
上海，泰東，民十六年．287 面．

唐鉞文存；唐鉞著．　814．9—T215
上海，商務，民十四年．274 面．

朱執信集；朱執信著．　814．9—C821
上海，建設社，民十年．2 册．

朱執信文鈔；朱執信著．　814．9—C821
上海，民智，民十五年．448 面．

吴稚暉學術論著；吴稚輝著．　814．9—W281
上海，出版合作社，民十五年．3 版．430 面．

吴稚暉學術論著續編；吴稚輝著．　814．9—W281
上海，出版合作社，民十六年．154 面．

吴稚暉學術論著第三篇；吴稚輝著．　814．9—W281
上海，出版合作社，民十六年．164 面．

吴稚暉先生文粹；吴稚暉著．　814．9—W281
上海，全民，民十七年．4 册．

汪精衛文存；汪精衛著．　814．9—W166
廣州，民智，民十五年．258 面．

談虎集；周作人著．　814．9—C771
上海，開明，民十七年．再版．310 面．

雨天的書；周作人著．　814．9—C771
上海，北新，民十六年．再版．302 面．

華蓋集；魯迅著．　814．9—L416
北京，北新，民十五年．190 面．

華蓋集續編；魯迅著· 814·9—L416

上海，民新，民十五年·26面·「魯迅雜感集第三」

關于魯迅及其著作；台静農著· 814·9—L416

北京，未名社刊物經舊處，民十五年·122面·

遠生遺著；黄遠庸著· 814·9—H489

上海，商務，民十五年·3版·4册·

文學生活；張若谷著· 814·9—C159

民十七年·

寸草心；陳學昭著· 814·9—C275

民十七年·

雨珠；朱樂人著· 814·9—C839

回音社，民十一年·132面·

苦酒集；芳草著· 814·9—F131

上海，北新，民十七年·236面·

枯葉集；華林著· 814·9—H441

上海，泰東，民十三年·86面·

文藝論集；郭沫若著· 814·9—K425

上海，光華，民十六年·3版·344面·

青年的煩悶及其他；劉時民著· 814·9—L373

上海，革新，民十七年·246面·

兩種力；毛翰哥著· 814·9—M138

上海，泰東，民十七年·214面·

火與肉；邵洵美著· 814·9—S171

上海，金屋，民十七年·76面·

紅葉；薛伯賢著· 814·9—S412

上海，羣衆，民十七年·149面·「紅暉文社叢書之二」

自剖文集；徐志摩著· 814·9—S476

上海，新月，民十七年·210面·

巴黎的鱗爪；徐志摩著· 814·9—S514

上海，新月，民十七年·再版·182面·

北京乎；孫福熙著· 814·9—S514
上海，開明，民十六年·224面·
死人之嘆息；滕固著· 814·9—T275
上海，泰東，民十四年·133面·
雜拌儿；俞平伯著· 814·9—Y372
上海，開明，民十七年·222面·
達夫全集；郁達夫著· 814·9—Y376
上海，創造社，民十七年·「創造社叢書第十七種」

816　書牘

鄭板橋家書；鄭燮著· 816·8—C359
上海，羣衆圖書公司，民十五年·3版·35面·
秋水軒尺牘；許思湄著· 816·8—H376
上海，羣學社，民十七年·3版·
雪鴻軒尺牘；龔未齋著· 816·8—K382
上海，羣學社，民十七年·706面·
曾國藩家書，家訓，日記；曾國藩，著陶樂勤標點· 816·8—T526
上海，源記書莊，民十二年·4册·
俞曲園書信；俞樾著· 816·9—y374
上海，羣衆圖書公司，民十五年·再版·45面·
曙；高長虹著· 816·9—K166
上海，泰東，民十七年·136面·「狂飆風叢書第二第四種」
寄小讀者；冰心女士著· 816·9—P372
上海，北新，民十七年·5版·242面·
三葉集；田壽昌等合著· 816·9—T337
上海，亞東，民十四年·4版·166面·

818　詩文—總集

當代八家文鈔；胡君復輯· 818—H402

上海，中國圖書公司，民五年・4 册・

開明文選・ 818—K111

上海，開明・「第一輯至第七輯」

國語文選；沈鎔輯・ 818—S224

上海，大東，民十五年・998 面・

近世文選；沈鎔輯・ 818—S224

上海，大東，民十五年・570 面・

學生文藝叢刊彙編；沈鎔輯・ 818—S224

上海，大東，民十四年・再版・2 册・

通俗文類鈔；新文學社輯・ 818—S436

上海，中華，民十一年，3 册・

新文選；王石京輯・ 818—W155

上海，文明，民十三年・4 册・

文藝全書；王蘊章等合著・ 818—W160

上海，中原，民十五年・4 版・808 面・

彩虹；彩虹社編・ 818・9—T433

上海，泰東，民十七年・154 面・「彩虹文學社社刊之一」

彌灑社創作集；錢江春等合著・ 818・9—T601

上海，商務，民十四年・2 册・「彌灑社叢書」

近人白話文選；吴遁生，鄭次川合著・ 818・9—W296

上海，商務，民十三年・再版・2 册・

819 雜體詩文

庸盦筆記；薛福成著・ 819・08—s411

上海，掃葉山房，民六年・3 册・

茶餘客話；阮蔡生著・ 819・08—Y425

上海，商務・71 面・

增廣智囊補；馮夢龍輯・ 819・08—F209

上海，商務・38 面・

近五千年見聞録・　819・08—K400
上海，進步，民五年・188 面・

嘯亭雜録；汲修主人著・　819・8—C397
上海，商務・

勁草筆記；姜繼襄著・　819・08—c521
湘鄂印書館，民十二年・338 面・

梵天廬業録；柴萼著・　819・08—C128
上海，中華，民十五年・再版・

古今怪異集成；中華書局編輯所編・　819・08—C976
上海，中華，民八年・4 册・

古今格言；江畲經編・　819—C293
上海，商務，民十一年・11 版・169 面・

中國寓言初編；沈德鴻編・　819—S222
上海，商務，民八年・三三版・48 面・

東西南北；王夫凡著・　819—W140
上海，現代，民十七年・105 面・

西瀅間話；陳源著・　819・9—C293
上海，新月，民十七年・388 面・

空山靈雨；落華生著・　819・9—L165
上海，商務，民十五年・再版・120 面・「文學研究會叢書」

山野掇拾；孫福熙著・　819・9—S514
上海，北新，民十六年・301 面・

楹聯新話；陳方鏞輯・　819・06—C274
上海，中華，民十一年・再版・114 面・

古今聯語彙選初集；胡君復緝・　819・06—K265
上海，商務，民十五年・12 版・4 册・

朝花夕拾；魯迅著・　819・9—L416
北平，未名社，民十七年・176 面・

胐盦客座談話；吳稚暉著・　819・9—W281
上海，泰東，民十一年・2 册・

820 英美文學

英國文學史；歐陽蘭著· 820·9—O134
北京，京師大學文科出版部，民十六年·204面·

長子；(英)高斯倭綏原著，鄧演存譯· 822—G139
上海，商務，民十一年·115面·「文學研究會叢書」

法綱；(英)高爾斯華綏原著，郭沫若譯· 822—K175
上海，創造社，民十六年·138面·「世界名著選第四種」

戀愛之果；(英)包爾原著，朱枕薪譯· 822—P284
上海，民智，民十六年·再版·68面·「新中國叢書」

譚格瑞的續絃夫人；(英)阿作爾平内羅原著，程希孟譯· 822—P653
上海，商務，民十二年·166面·「文學叢書」

沙樂美；(英)王爾德原著，田漢譯· 822—W644s
上海，中華，民十二年·84面·「少年中國學會叢書」

同名異娶；(英)王爾德原著，王靖，孔襄我合譯· 822—W644t
上海，泰東，民十年·110面·「新人叢書」

温德米爾夫人的扇子；(英)王爾德原著，潘家詢譯· 822—W644w
北京，北新，民十五年·152面·

獄中記；(英)王爾德原著，張聞天等合譯· 822—W644y
上海，商務，民十三年·再版·「214」面·「文學研究會叢書」

哈孟雷特；(英)莎士比亞原著，田漢譯· 822·33—Sh15h
上海，中華，民十一年·172面·「莎翁傑作集第一種少年中國學會叢書」

亨利第六遺事；(英)莎士比亞原著，林紓譯· 822·33—Sh15h
上海，商務，民五年·102面·

羅密歐與朱麗葉；(英)莎士比亞原著，田漢譯· 822·33—Sh15c
上海，中華，民十四年·再版·137面·「莎翁傑作集第六種少年中國叢學會書」

威尼斯的商人；(英)莎士比亞原著，曾廣勛譯· 822·33—Sh15w
上海，新文化，民十三年·110面·「青年文藝社叢書」

如願；(英)莎士比亞原著，張采真譯· 822·33—Sh15y
上海，北新，民十六年·220面·「莎士比亞名劇之一」
鴿與輕夢；(英)高爾斯華綏原著，席滌塵，趙宋慶合譯· 822·9—K167
上海，開明，民十六年·168面·
華倫夫人之職業；(英)蕭伯納原著，潘家洵譯· 822·91—Sh26
上海，商務，民十二年·120面·「文學研究會叢書」
不快意的戲劇；(英)蕭伯納原著，金法基，袁弼合譯· 822·91—Sh26
上海，商務，民十二年·35面·「文學叢書」
美國的模範家庭；派克耳夫人原著，陸退川譯· 829—P134
上海，北新，民十六年·319面·

830　德國文學

德國文學概論；劉大杰編· 80·2—L375
上海，北新，民十七年·376面·
近代德國文學主潮；小説月報社編· 808—Sh41—11
上海，商務，民十三年·65面·「小説月報叢刊第十一種」
德國文學史大綱；張傳普著· 830·9—C152
上海，中華，民十五年·133面·
費德利克小組；楊丙辰譯· 832—D139
上海，商務，民十二年·177面·「德國名劇世界叢書」
織工；(德)霍脱邁原著，陳家駒譯· 832—H294
上海，商務，民十三年·139面·「文學研究會叢書」
强盜；(德)釋勒原著，楊丙辰譯· 832—Sch33
上海，北新，民十五年·284面·
威廉退爾；(德)許雷原著，馬君武譯· 832—Sch33
上海，中華，民十五年·144面·
雪萊詩選；郭沫若譯· 832·6—Sh44
上海，泰東；民十五年·75面·

颶運動；小説月報社編· 808—Sh41—24
上海，商務，民十四年·76 面·「小説月報叢刊第二十四種」
長生訣；(捷克)加貝克原著，余上沅譯· 832·9—C17
上海，北新，民十五年·170 面·
北歐文學一臠；小説月報社編· 808—Sh41—29
上海，商務，民十四年·78 面·「小説月報叢刊第二十九種」
萊森寓言；鄭振鐸譯· 838—L566
上海，商務，民十四年·41 面·「文學研究叢書」
史特林堡戲劇集；張毓桂譯· 839·72—S257
上海，商務，民十一年·163 面·
近代丹麥文學一臠；小説月報社編· 89·8—Sh41—31
上海，商務，民十四年·59 面·「小説月報叢刊第三十一種」
野鴨；易卜生原著，徐鴣荻譯· 839·826—Ib7
民十七年·
易卜生集；易卜生原著，潘家洵譯· 859·826—Ib71
上海，商務，民十年·3 册一本·「世界叢書」
海上夫人；易卜生原著，楊熙初譯· 880·86—Ib7h
上海，商務，民十一年·3 版·194 面·「文學叢書」
傀儡家庭；易卜生原著，陳嘏譯· r—S353—3·51
上海，商務，民九年·再版·130 面·「説部叢書三集五十一編」
梅孽；易卜生原著，林紓譯· r—35—4·13
上海，商務，民十年·100 面·「説部叢書四集十三種」

840 法國文學

法國文學史；李璜著· 840·9—L185
上海，中華，民十二年·再版·290 面·
法國文學史；(法)Panlhiol 原著，王維克譯· 810·9—P288
上海，泰東，民十四年·215 面·「青年社叢書之一」

路曼尼亞民歌一班；朱湘譯· 841—V131
上海，商務，1921·64 面·「文學研究會叢書」

紅衣記；(法)E·Brieux 原著，陳良猷譯· 842—B767
上海，東泰，民十年·188 面·「新智識叢書」

茶花女劇本；(法)小仲馬原著，劉復譯· 842—D891
上海，北新，民十六年·3 版·270 面·

吕克蘭斯鮑夏；(法)嚣俄原著，東亞病夫譯· 842—H875
上海，真善美書店，民十六年·172 面·

吕伯蘭；(法)嚣俄原著，東亞病夫譯· 842—H876
上海，真善美書店，民十六年·257 面·

愛與死；夢茵譯· 812—M215
上海，泰東，民十七年·141 面·

法朗士集；小説月報社編· 808—Sh41—39
上海，商務，民十四年·93 面·「小説月報叢刊第三十九種」

婦人書簡；(法)卜勒浮斯特原著，李劼人譯· 846—P929
上海，中華，民十三年·三版·20 面·「少年中國學會叢書」

磨坊文札；(法)都德原著，成紹宗，張人權合譯· 848—T771
上海，創造社，民十六年·「世界名著選第二種」

850　意大利文學

神曲一臠； 808—Sh41—10
上海，商務，民十三年·93 面·「小説月報叢刊第十種」

陶康珴琪；(意)D，Annunzi 原著，張聞天譯· 852—An78
上海，中華，民十三年·120 面·「少年中國學會叢書」

倍那文德戲曲集；沈雁冰，張聞天合譯· 862·5—B431
上海，商務，民十四年·292 面·「文學研究會叢書」

891・4 印度文學

太戈爾詩；小説月報社編・ 808—Sh41—26
上海，商務，民十四年・108 面・「小説月報叢刊第二十六種」

詩人的宗教；小説月報社編・ 808—Sh41—5
上海，商務，民十三年・84 面・「小説月報叢刊第五種」

謙屈拉；(印度)太戈爾原著，吳致覺譯・ 891・42—T129
上海，商務，民十二年・45 面・

春之循環；(印度)太戈爾原著，瞿世英譯・ 891・42—T126
上海，商務，民十一年・再版・92 面・

新月集；(印度)太戈爾原著，鄭振鐸譯・ 891・42—T129
上海，商務，民十三年・再版・53 面・「文學研究會叢書」

太戈爾戲曲集；瞿世英，鄧演存合譯・ 891・42—T129
上海，商務，民十二年・79 面・「文學研究會叢書」

太戈爾戲曲集；高滋譯・ 891・42—T129
上海，商務，民十三年・78 面・「文學研究會叢書」

飛鳥集；(印度)太戈爾原著，鄭振鐸譯・ 891・41—T129
上海，商務，民十二年・再版・88 面・

印度寓言；鄭振鐸編・ 891・4—C351
上海，商務，民十四年・87 面・「文學研究會叢書」

魯拜集；創造社編・ 891・55—C925
上海，泰東，民十五年・3 版・112 面・「辛夷小叢書第四種」

阿富汗的戀歌；小説月報社編・ 808—Sk41—44
上海，商務，民十四年・85 面・「小説月報叢刊第四十四種」

891・7 俄國文學

蘇俄的文藝論戰；(俄)Chujak 原著，任國楨譯・ 891・7—C471
北京，北新，1925・103 面・「未名叢書」

俄羅斯名著；(俄)克魯洛夫等合著，李秉之譯・ 891・7—K205
上海，亞東，民十四年・第一集・

俄國文學史略；鄭振鐸編・ 891・709—C351

上海，商務，民十三年・204 面・「文學研究會叢書」

俄國詩壇的昨日今日和明日；小説月報社編・　808—Sh41—57

上海，商務，民十四年・88 面・「小説月報叢刊第五十七種」

近代俄國文學家論；東方雜誌社編・　080—T860—64

上海，商務，民十四年・3 版・71 面・「東方文庫」

十二個；(俄)亞歷山大勃洛克原著，胡斅譯・　891・71—P230

北京，北新，1926・74 面・「未名叢刊」

安那斯瑪；(俄)安東列夫原著，郭協邦譯・　891・72—An25a

上海，新文化，民十二年・157 面・

人之一生；(俄)安特列夫原著，耿濟之譯・　891・72—An25j

上海，商務，民十三年・再版・167 面・「文學研究會叢書」

狗的跳舞；(俄)安特列夫原著，張聞天譯・　891・72—An25K

上海，商務，民十二年・110 面・「文學研究會叢書」

桃色的雲；(俄)愛羅先珂原著，魯迅譯・　891・72—Er69

上海，北新，民十六年・3 版・285 面・「文藝叢書」

貧非罪；(俄)Ostrovsky 原著・鄭振鐸譯・　891・72—Os7P

上海，商務，民十三年・再版・119 面・「俄羅斯文學叢書」

罪與愁；(俄)Ostrovsky 原著，柯一岑譯・　891・72—Cs7t

上海，商務，民十一年・126 面・「俄羅斯文學叢書」

蘇俄獨幕劇集；曹靖華譯・　891・72—B136

北京，未名社，民十六年・168 面・「未名叢刊之一」

俄國戲曲集；(俄)史拉美克原著，鄭振鐸等譯・　891・72—Sr13

上海，商務，民十年・10 面・「俄羅斯文學叢書」

三姊妹；(俄)柴霍甫原著，曹靖華譯・　891・72—T117

上海，商務，民十四年・162 面・「文學研究會叢書」

兒童的智慧；(俄)托爾斯泰原著，常惠譯・　891・72—T588

上海，北新，1926・120 面・

黑暗之光；(俄)托爾斯泰原著，鄧演存譯・　891・72—T588b

上海，商務，民十二年・再版・130 面・「文學叢書」

活屍；(俄)托泰爾斯原著，文範邨譯・　891・72—T88h

上海，商務，民十二年·再版·88 面·「文學叢書」

我的生涯；(俄)托爾斯泰編，李藤譯· 891·79—T588

上海，商務，民十五年·再版·128 面·「文學研究會叢書」

朵思退夫斯基；(俄)科捷連斯基原輯英譯，李偉森重譯· 891·79—C742

上海，北新，民十七年·401 面·

891 其餘各國文學

波蘭文學一臠；小説月報社編· 808—sh41—43

上海，商務，民十四年·2 册·「小説月報叢刊第四十二四十三種」

新猶太文學一臠；小説月報社編· 808—Sh41—53

上海，商務，民十四年·77 面·「小説月報叢刊第五十三種」

聖書與中國文學；小説月報社編· 808—Sh41—25

上海，商務，民十四年·65 面·「小説月報叢刊第二十五種」

新猶太小説集；小説月報社編· 808—Sh41—54

上海，商務，民十四年·75 面·「小説月報叢刊第五十四種」

芬蘭文學一臠；小説月報社編· 808—Sh4—36

上海，商務，民十四年·115 面·「小説月報叢刊第三十六種」

阿那托爾；(奥)顯尼志勞原著，郭紹虞譯· 894·362—Soh59

上海，商務，民十一年·122 面·「文學研究會叢書」

比利時的悲哀；(俄)Anlreyev 原著，沈琳譯· 894·93—An25

上海，商務，民十一年·117 面·「文學叢書」

婀拉亭與巴羅米德· 808—Sh41—56

上海，商務，民十四年·64 面·「小説月報叢刊第五十六種」

青鳥；(比)梅脱靈原著，傅東華譯· 894·932—M269

上海，商務，民十三年·再版·181 面·「文學研究會叢書」

梅脱靈戲曲集；湯澄波譯· 894·932—M269

上海，商務，民十二年·170 面·「文學研究會叢書」

愛的遺留；(比)梅脱靈原著，谷鳳田譯· 894·932—M269

北京，海音，民十六年·129 面·

895·2　日本文學

兩條血痕；周作人著·　895·2—C771
上海，開明，民十七年·再版·196面·「日本小説集」

走向十字街頭；（日）厨川白村原著，緑蕉，大杰合譯·　895·2—C863
上海，啓智，民十七年·234面·「表現社叢書」

出了象牙之塔；（日）厨川白村原著，魯迅譯·　895·2—C863c
民十四年·「未名叢刊之一」

文藝思潮論；（日）厨川白村原著，樊從予譯·　895·2—C863W
上海，商務，民十三年·131面·「文學研究會叢書」

一束古典的情書；（日）林房雄原著，林伯修譯·　895·2—L318
上海，現代，民十七年·131面·

日本的詩歌；小説月報社編·　808—Sh41—4
上海，商務，民十三年·93面·「小説月報叢刊第四種」

武者小路實篤集；小説月報社編·　808—h41—46
上海，商務，民十四年·79面·「小説月報叢刊第四十六種」

狂言十番：日本古代小喜劇集；周作人譯·　895·22—C771
北京，北新，民十五年·再版·173面·

日本現代劇選：菊池寬劇選；田漢譯·　895·22—C885
上海，中華，民十四年·再版·104面·「少年中國學會叢書」

戀愛患病者；（日）菊池寬原著，劉大杰譯·　895·22—C885c
上海，北新，民十六年·146面·

學校劇本集；（日）神田豐穗原著，徐傳霖譯·　895·2—S199
上海，商務，民十三年·316面·

出家及其弟子；（日）倉田百三原著，孫百剛譯·　895·22—T448
上海，創造社，民十六年·254面·

一個青年的夢；（日）武者小路原著，魯迅譯·　895·22—W303
北京，北新，民十六年·314面·

一個青年的夢；（日）武者小路實篤原著，魯迅譯·　895·22—W303i
上海，商務，民十二年·232面·「文學研究會叢書」

妹妹；(日)武者小路實篤原著，周日棣譯· 895·22—W303m
上海，中華，民十四年·220面·

苦悶的象徵；(日)厨川白村原著·魯迅譯· 895·24—C863
上海，北新，民十五年·147面·

思想，山水，人物；(日)鶴見祐輔原著，魯迅譯· 895·24—H217
上海，北新，民十七年·278面·

落葉；郭沫若著· 895·26—K55
上海，創造社，民十五年·154面·

蘇曼殊全集；柳亞子編· 895·2—S461
上海，北新，民十七年·3册·

曼殊逸著爾種；柳無忌編· 895·29—L382
上海，北新，民十六年·86面·

波斯故事；章鐵民譯· 895·5—c172
上海，北新，民十七年·237面·

F 小説

北方奇俠傳；趙焕亭著· F—C205P
上海，世界，民十七年·246面·

奇俠精忠傳；趙焕亭著· F—C2050
上海，益新，民十六年·4版·8册·
……續編·6册·

三國志；許嘯天校· F—C664
上海，羣學社，民十五年·五版·2册·

連環圖畫三國志；劉再蘇校· F—L356
上海，世界，民十六年·再版·三集·24册·

標本宋人評話京本通俗小説· F—C693
上海，商務·民十四年·104面·

增圖忠烈小俠五義· F—C98C
上海，商務·408面·

列國志；許嘯天校・　F—H371
上海，羣學社，民十四年・再版・2 册・

來生福彈詞・　F—H430
上海，商務・2 册・

花月痕・　F—H148
上海，商務，清咸豐八年・2 册・

秦漢演義；黄士恒著・　F—H485
上海，商務，民十二年・5 版・4 册・

前漢演義上編・　F—H485
上海，商務，民十二年・4 版・5 册・

前漢演義中編・　F—H485
上海，商務，民十二年・4 版・5 册・

前漢演義下編・　F—H485
上海，商務，民十二年・再版・6 册・

鏡花緣；李汝珍著・　F—L187
上海，亞東，民十二年・2 册・

官場現行記；李伯元著・　F—L195
上海，亞東，民十六年・2 册・

白話淺註聊齋志異；商務印書館編譯所註釋・　F—L283
上海，商務，民十五年・4 册・

老殘遊記；劉鄂著・　F—L370
上海，亞東，民十五年・再版・328 面・

唐宋傳奇集；魯迅輯・　F—L416t
上海，北新，民十七年・2 册・

太平天國演義；龍潭居士，(别名)著・　F—L508
上海，尚文，民九年・6 册・

今古奇觀；鮑廣生標點・　F—p186
上海，新文化，民十七年・4 版・2 册・

清代演義；王炳成著・　1—F153t
上海，商務・4 册・

清代演義；商務印書館編輯所編． F—S62tt
上海，商務，民十七年．5版．1函8册．

浮生六記；沈復著． F—S221
上海，樸社，民十四年．154面．「霜楓之一」

隋唐演義． F—S503
上海，商務，清康熙二十二年．

檮杌閒評． F—T251
自由書報社．355面．

繪圖元史通俗演義；蔡東凡編． F—T415
上海，會文堂，民九年．6册．

紅樓夢；曹雪芹著． F—T474
上海，東亞，民十一年．3版．3册．

紅樓夢；曹雪芹著，抱恨生校． F—T474a
上海，新文化書社，民十六年．3册．

紅樓夢本事辯證；壽鵬飛著． F—S302
上海，商務，民十六年．58面．「文藝叢刊一集」

南史演義；杜綱著． F—T763n
上海，商務，民九年．4册．

北史演義；杜綱著． F—T763p
上海，商務．6册．

水滸；施耐庵著． F—S216
上海，羣學社，民十六年．4版．2册．

連環圖畫水滸；王劍星編． F—W136
上海，世界，民十七年．二集．2册．

三俠五義；問竹主人(别名)著． F—W247
上海，亞東，民十四年．2册．

兒女英雄傳；文鐵仙著． F—W264
上海，亞東，民十四年．2册．

儒林外史；吴敬梓著． F—w281
齊省堂，民三年．6册．

儒林外史；吳敬梓著，許嘯天句讀· F—w281y
上海，羣學社，民十三年·再版·80 面·

西遊記；吳承恩著· F—w281Sy
上海，亞東，民十四年·4 版·2 册·

舊小說；吳曾祺輯· F—w297
上海，商務，民十三年·6 版·1 函 20 册·

二十年目覩之怪現狀；吳研人著，魏冰心標點· F—w299
上海，世界，民十五年·4 册·

新華春夢記；楊塵因著· F—y121s
上海，泰東，民九年·3 版·5 册·

岳飛全傳；通俗小說社編· F—y310
民十三年·

東方創作集；東方雜誌社編· 080—860—74
上海北，商務，民十四年·3 版·2 册·「東方文庫」

枯葉雜記；東方雜誌社編· 080—860—81
上海，商務，民十四年·3 版·92 面·「東方文庫」

彷徨；小說月報社編· 808—Sh41—40
上海，商務，民十四年·82 面·「小說月報叢刊第四十種」

笑的歷史；朱自清著· 808—Sh41
上海，商務，民十四年·87 面·「小說月報叢刊」

校長；小說月報社編· 808—Sh41—45
上海，商務，民十四年·93 面·「小說月報叢刊第四十五種」

技藝；小說月報社編· 808—Sh41—60
上海，商務，民十四年·96 面·「小說月報叢刊第六十種」

瘋人日記；小說月報社編· 808—Sh41—20
上海，商務，民十四年·90 面·「小說月報叢刊第二十種」

牧羊兒；小說月報社編· 808—Sh41—52
上海，商務，民十四年·92 面·「小說月報叢刊第五十二種」

垣白；小說月報社編· 808—Sh41—50
上海，商務，民十四年·89 面·「小說月報叢刊第五十種」

曼殊斐兒；小説月報社編· 808—Sh41—3

上海，商務，民十三年·71 面·「小説月報叢刊第三種」

世界的火災；小説月報社編· 808—Sh41—2

上海，商務，民十三年·93 面·「小説月報叢刊第二種」

社戲；小説月報社編· 808—Sh41—9

上海，商務，民十三年·78 面·「小説月報叢刊第九種」

換巢鸞鳳；小説月報社編· 808—Sh01—1

上海，商務，民十三年·84 面·「小説月報叢刊第一種」

鄰人之愛；小説月報社編· 808—Sh41—16

上海，商務，民十四年·53 面·「小説月報叢刊第十六種」

商人婦；小説月報社編· 808—Sh41—14

上海，商務，民十四年·88 面·「小説月報叢刊第十四種」

犯罪；小説月報社編· 808—8h41—12

上海，商務，民十三年·78 面·「小説月報叢刊第十二種」

三天；小説月報社編· 808—hs1—33

上海，商務，民十四年·00 面·「小説月報叢刊第三十三種」

冲積期化石；張資平著· F—c152c

上海，泰東，民十一年·204 面·「創造社叢書第四種」

模範父母；張九如著· F—c152m

上海，新文化，民十五年·三版·202 面·

植樹節；張資平著· F—I52CS

上海，新宇宙，民十七年·186 面·

壓迫；張資平譯· F—C152i

上海，新宇宙，民十七年·203 面·

梅雪争芳記；張秋蟲著· F—c152ms

上海，世界，民十五年·3 册·

白話短篇寫實小説；張九如著· F—c152P

上海，新文化，民十三年·3 版·109 面·

我與他：夫妻；張静盧著· F—c152w

上海，羣衆，民十七年·82 面·

何典；張南莊著· F—c166

上海，卿雲圖書公司，民十七年·3版·100面·

雪的除夕；張資平著· F—c171

上海，商務，民十四年·254面·「文學叢書」

不等衡的偶力；張資平著· f—C171

上海，商務，民十六年·再版·327面·「文藝叢書」

最後的幸福；張資平著· F—C171t

民十七年·

致死者；張維祺著· F—C172

上海，亞東，民十六年·再版·112面·

偵探新語；昌明公司編· F—C197

上海，昌明公司，清光緒三十年·68面·

情書一束；章衣萍著· F—C182

北京，北新，民十五年·264面·

名家小説；章行嚴選· F—C190

上海，亞東，民十五年·4版·4册·

説苑導遊録；常覺等合著· F—C195

上海，時還，民十五年·5版·138面·「文學指南號外增刊之一」

滑稽世界；趙苕狂著· F—C201h

上海，世界，民十三年·再版·4册·

神怪鬥法記；趙苕狂著· F—C210S

上海，世界，民十五年·3册·

畸人；趙伯顔著· F—C213

上海，新宇宙，民十七年·110面·「文藝叢書第一種」

婦女奇冤録；趙苕狂輯· F—C216

上海，大東，民九年·154面·

小雪；超超著· F—C229

上海，亞東，民十五年·170面·

雅士；澤人著· F—C247

上海，現代，民十七年·134面·

小雨點；陳衡哲著· F—C275
上海，新月，民十七年·156面·

東遊記；陳霨蘢著· F—C283
上海，世界，民十五年·3冊·

不安定的靈魂；陳翔鶴著· F—c286
上海，北新，民十六年·314面·「沉鐘叢刊」

倦旅；陳月昭著· F—C296
上海，梁溪圖書館，民十四年·122面·「婦女問題研究會叢書」

新舊家庭；程瞻盧著· F—C331
上海，商務，民十二年·再版·2冊·

中國短篇小説集；鄭振鐸輯· F—C351
上海，商務，民十五年·2冊·

胡蝶；許欽文著· F—C369
上海，北新，民十七年·104面·

北伐從軍雜記；金聲著· F—C669
民十六年·

瑪麗；敬隱漁著· F—C699
上海，商務，民十六年·再版·84面·「文學研究會叢書」

留西外史；陳春隨著· F—C270
上海，新月，民十六年·143面·

禮拜六；周瘦鵑，王鈍根合編· F—C785
上海，中華，民十三年·10冊·

煩惱的網；周全平著· F—C787
上海，泰東，民十四年·150面·「創造社叢書第八種」

離別之夜；鍾紹虞著· F—C969
上海，泰東，民十七年·再版·170面·「待名叢書」

管他呢；芳草著· F—F178
上海，北新，民十七年·224面·

竹林的故事；馮文炳著· F—F217
民十四年·

十六年之雜碎；傳彦長著· F—F247
民十四年·

海上花列傳；韓子雲著· F—H223
上海，亞東，民十五年·3册·

留東新史；向愷然著· F—H183
上海，世界，民十四年·再版·3册·

飄渺的夢及其他；向培良著· F—H286
民十五年·「烏合叢書之一」

慕春；許傑著· F—H369
上海，光華，民十七年·再版·140面·

故鄉；許欽文著· F—H369K
上海，北新，民十六年·3版·331面·「烏合叢書之一」

毛線襪及其他；許欽文著· F—H369m
北京，北新，民十五年·272面·

鼻涕阿二；許欽文著· F—H369p
上海，北新，民十六年·129面·

中秋月；胡雲翼著· F—H119
上海，光華，民十七年·122面·

往何處去；胡也頻著· F—H419
上海，第一綫書店，民十七年·128面·

聖徒；胡也頻著· F—H119s
上海，北新，民十六年·154面·

妖媚的眼睛；黄中著· F—H471
上海，金屋，民十七年·181面·

古畫微；黄賓虹著· F—H484
上海，商務，民十四年·68面·「小説世界叢刊」

罪惡；黄心真著· F—H485c
上海，新宇宙，民十七年·199面·

轉變；洪靈菲著· F—H522c
上海，亞東，民十七年·240面·

處女夢；火雪明著． F—H531

上海，羣衆，民十七年．再版．134 面．

西子湖邊；易家鉞著． F—I112

上海，泰東，民十四年．166 面．

談異；伊園主人著． F—I130

上海，掃葉山房，民三年．4 册．

冶工軼事；朱樹人著． F—K157

上海，中華，民七年．50 頁．

實生活；高長虹著． F—K196S

上海，現代書局，民十七年．93 面．「狂飆出版物之一」

清晨起來；高歌著． F—K169

上海，泰東，民十七年．第一集．「狂飆叢書第二」

昨夜及其他；顧仲雍著． F—K264

北京，北新，民十四年．70 面．

新婚瑣記；苦海餘生著． F—K267

上海，國民圖書館．56 面．

覆舟夢；狂生著． F—K339

上海，啓智印務公司，民十六年．260 面．

橄欖；郭沫若著． F—K425

上海，創造社出版部，民十五年．25 面．「創造社叢書」

犧牲者；戈魯陽著． F—K436

上海，亞東，民十七年．212 面．

趙子曰，老舍著． F—L155

上海，商務，民十七年．348 面．「文學研究會叢書」

綴網勞蛛；落華生著． F—L165

上海，商務，民十四年．再版．230 面．「文學研究會叢書」

雷雨之夜；李耕著． F—L181

上海，新文化，民十年．再版．96 面．

彷徨；魯迅著． F—L416

北京，北新，民十五年．256 面．「烏合叢書之一」

自由花範；李涵秋著· F—L185
上海，世界，民十二年·4 册·

馬大少爺的奇蹟；黎錦明著· F—L215
上海，現代，民十七年·125 面·

花之寺；凌叔華著· F—L341
上海，新月，民十七年·182 面·

碎錦；劉冠悮輯· F—L365
民十七年·

支那女兒；劉大杰著· F—L375
上海，北新，民十七年·221 面·

蓮蓉月；羅西著· F—L379
上海，現代，民十七年·155 面·

醉裹；羅黑芷著· F—L393
上海，商務，民十七年·218 面·「文學研究會叢書」

挣扎；樓建南著· F—L400
上海，現代，民十七年·150 面·

三絃；盧冀野著· F—L405
上海，泰東，民十六年·再版·100 面

或人的悲哀；盧隱女士著· F—L408
上海，商務，民十四年·67 面·「小説月報叢刊」

吶喊；魯迅著· F—L416
新潮社，民十二年·再版·272 面·「文藝叢書」

深春的落葉；龍實秀著· F—L507
香港受匡出版部，民十七年·184 面·

週年；馬仲殊著· F—M112
上海，創造社，民十六年·129 面·

幻滅；茅盾著· F—M153
上海，商務，民十七年·147 面·「交學研究會叢書」

中國創作小説選；梅生輯· F—M185
上海，新文化，民十三年·2 册·

然犀録；猛盦老人著． F—M214

上海，商務，民十一年．3 册．

青年的花；夢葦著． F—M215

上海，新文社，民十三年．156 面．「青年文藝社叢書」

紅日；沐鴻著． F—M215

上海，泰東，民十七年．2142 面．「狂飆叢書第二」

曙光底微笑；倪家祥著． F—N190

上海，羣衆圖書公司，民十六年．128 面．「紅暉文化叢書之一」

雌蝶影；包柚斧著． F—P160

時報館，清光緒三十四年．136 面．

二青年；包天笑著． F—P192e

上海，商務，民六年．2 册．

埋石棄石記；包天笑著． F—P1921

上海，商務，民元年．120 面．

馨兒就學記：教育小説；包天笑著． F—F192S

上海，商務，民元年．再版．169 面．

我離開十字街頭；向培良著． F—P258

上海，光華，民十五年．42 面．「狂飆叢書第三」

皮克的情書；彭家煌著． F—P271P

上海，現代，民十七年．102 面．

茶杯裏的風波；彭家煌著． F—P271t

上海，現代，民十七年．171 面．

超人；冰心女士著． F—P372

上海，商務，民十五年．149 面．「文學研究會叢書」

近代俠義英雄傳；不肖生著． F—P395

上海，世界，民十七年．8 册．

斧背；尚鉞著． F—S158

上海，泰東，民十七年．180 面．「狂飆叢書第二第七種」

病；尚鉞著． F—S158P

上海，泰東，民十七年．208 面「狂飆叢書第二第一種」

泰西歷史演義；商務印書館編譯所編·　F—S162ts
上海，商務，民四年·3版·210面

好管閒事的人；沈從文著·　F—S211L
上海，新月，民十七年·258面·

老實人；沈從文著·　F—S211fr
上海，現代，民十七年·199面·

入伍後；沈從文著·　F—S222
上海，北新，民十七年·200面·

美人磁：言情小説；商務印書館編譯所編·　F—S353—2·70
上海，商務，民四年·3版·170面·「説部叢書二集第七十編」

海外拾遺：筆記小説；商務印書館編譯所編·　F—S35—2·72
上海，商務，民四年·再版·116面·「説部叢書二集第七十二編」

錯中錯：言情小説；商務印書館編譯所編·　F—S353—2·75
上海，商務，民四年·3版·2册·「説部叢書二集第七十五編·」

墮淚碑：哀情小説；商務印書館編譯所編·　F—S353—2·77
上海，商務，民四年·4版·2册·「説部叢書二集第七十七編·

外交秘事；商務印書館編譯所編·　F—S353—2·90
上海，商務，民四年·135面·「説部叢書二集第九十編」

時諧：短篇小説；商務印書館編譯所編·　F—S353—2·92
上海，商務，民四年·2册·「説部叢書二集第九十二編·」

後不如歸：言情小説；黄翼雲著·　F—S353—2·97
上海，商務，民四年·再版·114面·「説部書二集第九十七編·」

壁上血書：偵探小説；徐大著·　F—S353—2·99
上海，商務，民四年·57面·「説部叢書二集第九十九編·」

海天情孽；黄士洪著·　F—S353—3·4
上海，商務，民五年·51面·「説部叢書三集第四編」

冰原探險記；王無爲著·　F—s353—3·14
上海，商務，民十三年·三版·87面·「説部叢書三集第十四編·」

古國幽情記；寒蕾著·　F—s353—3·32
上海，商務，民六年·3册·「説部叢書三集第三十二編·」

科學家庭；包天笑著· F—S353·3·58

上海，商務，民九年·再版·2冊·「説部叢書三集第五十八編·」

四字獄；徐慧公著· F—s353—3·81

上海，商務，民十年·再版·94面·「説部叢書三集第八十一編·」

白羽記初編；沈步洲著· F—S353—3·74

上海，商務，民十年·再版·2冊·「説部叢書三集第七十四編·」

白羽記續編；沈步洲著· F—S353—3·83

上海，商務，民十一年·再版·2冊·「説部叢書三集第八十三編·」

白羽記三編；沈步洲著· F—S353—3·96

上海，商務，民十年·再版·2冊·「説部叢書三集第九十六編」

菱鏡秋痕；庶鳥諳著· F—S353—3·85

上海，商務，民十年·再版·2冊·「説部叢書三集第八十五編」

童子偵探隊；包天笑著· F—S35—3·90

上海，商務，民十年·再版·2冊·「説部叢書三集第九十編」

隅屋；瞿官穎著· F—S353—3·98

上海，商務，民十一年·再版·2冊·「説部叢書三集第九十八編·」

恩怨；王卓民著· F—S353—3·99

上海，商務，民十一年·再版·113面·「説部叢書三集第九十九編·」

瞻廬小説集；程瞻廬著· F—S410C

上海，世界，民十五年·再版·104面·

從軍日記；謝文翰著· F—S425

北京，北新，民十四年·70面·「北新小叢書之三」

白話小説文範；新文學社編· F—s436

上海，中華，民十年·5版·190面·

心羣月；心羣文藝社編· F—s439

上海，羣衆圖書公司，民十五年·50面·

悲惨世界；蘇曼殊著· F—s461

上海，泰東，民十年·再版·106面·

毁去的序文；徐雌著· F—s476hC

上海，新文化書社，民十四年·104面·「綠波社小叢書」

紅粉地獄；徐恥痕著．　F—s476hf

上海，世界，民十五年．3 册．

清朝官場奇報録；孫劍秋著．　F—s511

望雲山房，民九年．134 面．

雨後及其他；沈從文著．　F—212

上海，春潮書局，民十七年．141 面．

大西洋之濱；孫福熙著．　F—s514

北京，北新，民十四年．92 面．

海的謳暮者；孫俍工著．　F—s519

上海，民智，民十三年．248 面．

英蘭的一生；孫夢雷著．　F—s521

上海，開明，民十六年．362 面．

新説書；孫毓修著．　F—s354

上海，商務，民三至五年．3 册．

癡華鬘；斯那著．　F—s589c

上海，北新，序民十五年．「92」面．

平凡的死；滕固著．　F—T275

上海，金屋，民十七年．102 面．

最後的微笑；蔣光慈著．　F—T569

上海，現代，民十七年．190 面．

少年飄泊者；蔣光赤著．　F—T566

上海，亞東，民十五年．再版．126 面．

義塚；錢杏邨著．　F—T612

上海，東亞，民十七年．180 面．

觀樂的舞蹈；錢杏邨著．　F—T612

上海，現代書局，民十七年．170 面．

悵惘及其他；錢公俠著．　F—T613

上海，春潮書局，民十七年．181 面．

情人；左幹臣著．　F—T683

上海，亞細亞書局，民十七年．134 面．

創痕；左幹臣著· F—T684

上海，亞細亞書局，民十七年·

征鴻；左幹臣著· F—T684

上海，泰東，民十七年·108 面·

淡霞與落葉；萬曼著· F—w125

上海，新文化，民十三年·132 面·「緑波社小叢書」

孤雁；王以仁著· F—w143

上海，商務，民十五年·178 面·「文學研究會叢書」

柚子；汪魯彦著· F—w148

上海，北新，民十五年·236 面·

拘史；王新命著· F—w156

上海，泰東，民十三年·117 面·「孤芳集第二輯」

一葉；王統照著· F—w159

上海，商務，民十一年·154 面·「文學研究會叢書」

雪夜；汪敬熙著· F—w166s

上海，亞東，民十五年·再版·96 面·

耶蘇的吩咐；汪静之著· F—w166y

上海，開明，民十五年·75 面·

翠英及其夫的故事；汪静之著· F—w175

上海，亞東，民十六年·168 面·

列那孤的歷史；王巷譯· F—w251

上海，開明，民十五年·113 面·「文學社週報叢書」

革命外史；翁仲著· F—w271

吳越書店，民十七年·112 面·

紫滕花下；吳江冷著· F—w281c

上海，民智，民十二年·108 面·

上下古今談；吳敬恒著· F—w281ss

上海，文明，民十五年·10 版·4 册·

九命奇寃；吳研人著· F—w299C

上海，世界，民十五年·

玉君；楊振聲著·　F—Y121yu
北京，橫社，民十六年·3版·167面·

失蹤；楊邨人著·　F—Y141·
上海，亞東，民十七年·132面·

午夜角聲；葉勁風著·　F—Y181
上海，商務，民十四年·130面·「小説世界叢刊·」

小説彙刊；葉紹鈞等合著·　F—Y191
上海，商務，民十一年·142面·

前輩先生；葉小鳳著·　F—Y192
上海，光華，民十六年·174面·

城中；葉紹鈞著·　F—Y191c
上海，開明，民十六年·再版·157面·

劍鞘；葉紹鈞，俞平伯合著·　F—Y191
上海，樸社，民十三年·238面·「霖風之四」

火災；葉紹鈞著·　F—Y191h
上海，商務，民十三年·再版·197面·「學文研究會叢書」

隔膜；葉紹鈞著·　F—Y191k
上海，商務，民十三年·160面·「文學研究會叢書」

線下；葉紹鈞著·　F—Y191s
上海，商務，民十四年·235面·「文學研究會叢書」

稻草人；葉紹鈞著·　F—Y191t
上海，商務，民十四年·三版·312面·「文學研究會叢書」

鳥稚；葉鼎洛著·　F—Y103
上海，現代，民十七年·159面·

鐵手；羽仙著·　F—Y358
上海，交通，民九年·158面·

迷羊；郁達夫著·　F—Y376
上海，北新，民十七年·164面·

西湖三光；員子沙著·　F—Y414
上海，泰東，民十七年·176面·

趙先生底煩惱；許欽文著· F—H669
上海，北新，民十七年·3版·160面·

新仔婚的故事；林蘭著· F—L323
上海，北新，民十七年·180面·(民間故事之一)

巧舌婦的故事；林蘭編· F—L342
上海，北新，民十七年·203面·

近代法國小説集；東方雜誌社編· 08—F810—76
上海，商務，民十四年·3版·3册·「東方文庫」

大荒歸客記；(法)曲特拉痕脱原著，梁禾青，趙尊嶽合繹· F—D667
上海，商務，民十三年·3版·2册·「説部叢書」

小物件；(法)都德原著，李劼人譯· F—D264s
上海，中華，民十四年·3版·375面·

達哈士孔的狒狒；(法)都德原著，李劼人譯· F—D611h
上海，中華，民十三年·164面·

法蘭西短篇傑作集；水沫社譯· F—C793
上海，現代，民十七年·186面·

茶花女遺事；(法)小仲馬原著，曉齋主人，冷紅生合譯· F—D891e
上海，商務，民十五年·117面·

法宫秘史前編；(法)大仲馬原著，君朔譯· F—D891f
上海，商務，民四年·再版·2册·

玉樓花劫續編；(法)大仲馬原著，林紓譯· F—D891y
上海，商務，民二年·再版·2册·

十二姊妹及其他；(法)愛華爾特原著，袁嘉華譯· F—Ew14s
上海，北新，民十七年·217面·

馬丹波娃利；(法)G. Lanbert原著，李劼人譯· F—F616
上海，中華，民十四年·578面·「少年中國學會叢書」

紅百合；(法)法郎士原著，金満成譯· F—F844h
上海，現代，民十七年·392面·

堪克賓；(法)法郎士原著，曾仲鳴譯· F—F844k
上海，創造社，民十六年·100面·

黛絲；(法)法郎斯原著，杜衡譯·　F—F844t
上海，開明，民十七年·239面·「水沫社彳亍叢書」

友人之書；(法)法郎士原著，金满成譯·　F—F844y
上海，北新，1926年·316面·

活冤孽；(法)Victor Hugo原著，俞忽譯·　F—H874
上海，商務，民十二年·3册·「文學叢書」

穡者傳；(法)麥爾香原著，朱樹人譯·　F—M155s
上海，文明，民十五年·80面·

髭須及其他；(法)莫泊桑原著，李青崖譯·　F—M445C
上海，樸社，民十三年·78面·「霜楓之三」

一生；(法)莫泊三原著，徐蔚南譯·　F—M445i
上海，商務，民十五年·2册·「文學研究會叢書」

人心；(法)莫泊桑原著，李劼人譯·　F—M445j
上海，中華，民十二年·再版·286面·

莫泊桑短篇小説集；(法)莫泊桑原著，李青崖譯·　F—M445m
上海，民十五年·3版·3册·「文學研究會叢書」

歐兒拉；(法)莫泊桑原著，張秀中譯·　F—M4450
上海，海音，民十五年·66面·

水上；(法)莫泊桑原著，章克標譯·　F—M445s
上海，開明，民十七年·177面·

田家女；(法)莫泊桑原著，顧希聖譯·　F—M445t
上海，光華，民十七年·88面·「世界名著選」

遺産；(法)莫泊桑原著，耿濟之譯·　F—M445y
上海，商務，民十三年·再版·116面·「文學研究會叢書·」

嘉爾曼；(法)梅禮美原著，樊仲雲譯·　F—M544
上海，商務，民十五年·138面·「文學研究會叢書·」

毒蛇圈；(法)鮑福原著，知新室主人譯·　F—P185
上海，廣智，清光緒三十二年·234面·

漫郎攝實戈；(法)伯雷華斯德原著，商務印書館譯·　F—P229
上海，商務，清光緒三十三年·

白利與露西；(法)羅曼・羅蘭原著，葉靈鳳譯・ F—R647
上海，現代，民十七年・139 面・

銷金窟；時報館記者譯・ F—S235
上海，時報館，清光緒三十四年・188 面・

毒藥罇；(法)嘉波留原著，商務印書館譯・ F—s353—1・68
上海，商務，民三年・再版・130 面・「説部叢書初集六十八編」

愛國二童子傳；(法)沛那原著，林紓，李世中合譯・ F—s353—1・82
上海，商務，民三年・再版・「説部叢書初集八十二編」

離恨天；(法)森彼得原著，林紓，王慶驥合譯・ F—s353—2・16
上海，商務，民四年・3 版・99 面・「説部叢書二集十六編」

玉樓花刼前編；(法)大仲馬原著，林紓，李世中合譯・ F—s353—2・31
上海，商務，民四年・3 版・2 册・「説部叢書二集三十一編」

大俠紅繫蕗傳；(法)阿克西原著，林紓，魏易合譯・ F—s353—2・33
上海，商務，民四年・再版・140 面・「説部叢書二集三三編」

蟹蓮郡主傳；(法)大仲馬原著，林紓，王慶通合譯， F—s353—2・37
上海，商務，民四年・再版・2 册・「説書叢書二集三七編」

溷中花；(法)爽稜阿過伯原著，林紓，王慶通合譯・ F—s353—2・38
上海，商務，民四年・2 册・「説部叢書二集三八編」

魚海淚波；(法)辟尼略坻原著，林紓，王慶通合譯・ F—s353—2・41
上海，商務，民四年・115 面・「説部叢書二集第四十一編」

哀吹録；(法)巴魯隆原著，林紓，陳家麟合譯・ F—s353—2・45
上海，商務，民四年・再版・71 面・「説部叢書二集四三編」

義黑；(法)德羅尼原著，林紓，陳家麟合譯・ F—s353—2・45
上海，商務，民四年・再版・66 面・「説部叢書二集四十五編」

八十日；(法)裘爾俾奴原著，叔子譯・ F—s353—2・50
上海，商務，民四年・再版・60 册・「説部叢書二集五十三編」

孤星淚：勵志小説；商務印書館編譯所編・ F—s333—2・53
上海，商務，民四年・再版・2 册・「説部叢書二集 53 編」

苦兒流浪記；(法)受克脱麥羅原著，包公毅譯・ F—s353—2・79
上海，商務，民四年・三版・3 册・「説部叢書二集第七十九編」

法宫秘史前编；(法)大仲馬原著，君朔譯· F—S353—2·83
上海，商務，民四年·再版·2冊·「説部叢書二集83編」

冰蘖餘生記；(法)勒東路易原著，雙石軒譯· F—s353—3·2
上海，商務，民五年·再版·2冊·「説部叢書三集二編」

香鈎情眼；(法)小仲馬原著，林紓，王慶通合譯· F—s353—3·5
上海，商務，民十三年·4版·2冊「説部叢書三集五編」

巴黎繁華記；商務印書館譯· F—s353—3·5
上海，商務，清光緒三十一年·「説部叢書」

大荒歸客記；(法)曲特拉痕脱原著，梁禾青，趙尊嶽合譯· F—s353—3·8
上海，商務，民十三年·3版·2冊·「説部叢書三集八編」

銅圜雪恨録；(法)余增史原著，雙石軒譯· F—s353—3·12
上海，商務，民五年·2冊·「説部叢書三集第十二編」

鸚鵡緣；(法)小仲馬原著，林紓，王慶通合譯· F—s353—3·41
上海，商務，民十年·3版·2冊·「説部叢書三集四一編」

鸚鵡緣三編；(法)小仲馬原著，林紓，王慶通合譯· F—s353—3·44
上海，商務，民十年·3版·2冊·「説部叢書三集四四編」

金臺春夢録；(法)丹米安，(俄)華伊爾原著，林紓，王慶通合譯 F—S353—3·50
上海，商務，民十年·3版·2冊·「説部叢書三集50編」

情天異彩；(法)周魯倭原著，林紓，陳家麟合譯· F—s353—3·75
上海，商務，民十年·再版·109面·「説部叢書三集75編」

賂史；(法)亞波倭得原著，林紓，陳家麟合譯· F—s353—3·84
上海，商務，民十年·再版·2冊·「説部叢書三集八十四編」

近代英美小説集；東方雜誌社編· 080—T860—75
上海，商務，民十四年·3版·102面·(東方文庫)

歐陸縱横秘史；劉丰儂譯， F—L372
上海，中華，民九年·3版·112面·

歐戰演義初集；陸士諤輯· F—L432
上海，文明，民六年·98面·

歐洲大陸小説集；東方雜誌社編· 080—T800—78
上海，商務，民十四年·3版·2冊·(東方文庫)

列地狐歷險記；(英)T·W·Burgess 原著，李善通譯· F—B912
上海，商務，民十四年·93 面·「兒童世界叢刊」

約瑟安得路傳；(英)斐勒丁原著，伍光健譯· F—F46
上海，商務，民十七年·353 面·(世界文學名著)

渦堤孩；(英)E. Gosse 原著，徐志摩譯· F—G695
上海，商務，民十三年·再版·111 面·(文學叢書)

秘密女子；(英)哈葛德原著，貢少芹譯· F—H105
上海，文明，民十四年·8 版·124 面·

二義同囚録；甘永龍，朱炳勳合譯· F—H236
上海，中國國圖書公司，民五年·4 册·

斯芬克斯之美人；(英)甘縻倫夫人原著，無悶居士譯· F—k120
上海，廣智，清光緒三十四年·3 册·

贗爵案；(英)柯楠李登原著，張舍我譯· F—k195
上海，商務，民九年·2 册·

女首領；倫媚姿原著，(日)支那井蛙譯· F—L490
上海，小説林，清光緒廿年·2 册·

劇場奇案；(英)福爾奇斯林母原著，商務印書館譯· F—S353—1·2
上海，商務，民三年·再版·172 面·「説部叢書初集二編」

案中案；偵探小説；(英)屠哀爾士原著，商務印書館譯· F—S353—1·6
上海，商務，民三年·再版·83 面·「説部叢書初集六編」

吟邊燕語：神怪小説；(英)沙士比亞原著，林紓，魏易合譯· F—S353—1·8
上海，商務，民三年·再版·156 面·「説部叢書初集八編」

美洲童子萬里尋親記：倫理小説；(英)亞丁原著，林紓等合譯·
F—S353—1·9
上海，商務，民三年·再版·96 面·

金銀島：冒險小説；(英)司的反生原著，商務印書館譯· F—S353—1·11
上海，商務，民三年·再版·85 面·「説部叢書初集十一編」

迦茵小傳：言情小説；(英)哈葛德原著，林紓，魏易合譯· F—S353—1·13
上海，商務，民三年·再版·2 册·「説部叢書初集十三編」

埃及金塔剖記：神怪小説；(英)哈葛德原著· F—S353—1·17

上海，商務，民三年・3 版・3 册・「説部叢書初集十七編」

英孝子火山報仇録：倫理小説；

(英)哈葛德原著，林紓，魏易，合譯・ F—S353—1・20

上海，商務，民三年・再版・2 册・「説部叢初集廿編」

鬼山狠俠傳：神怪小説；(英)哈葛原著，林紓，曾宗鞏合譯・ F—S353—1・22

上海，商務，民三年・再版・2 册・「説部叢書初集廿二編」

斐洲烟火愁城録：冒險小説；林紓，曾宗鞏合譯・ F—S353—1・26

上海，商務，民三年・再版・2 册・「説部叢書初集廿六編」

刼後英雄略；(英)司各德原著，林紓，魏易合譯・ F—S353—1・27

上海，商務，民三年・再版・2 册・「説部叢書初集二十七編」

一柬録：道德小説；(英)孛來姆原著，商務印書館譯・ F—S353—1・29

上海，商務，民三年・再版・108 面・「説部叢書初集廿九編」

孝女耐兒傳；(英)卻而司迭更司原著，林紓，魏易合譯・ F—S353—1・31

上海，商務，民三年・「説叢書初集世一編」

玉雪留痕：言情小説；(英)哈葛德原著，林紓，魏易合譯・ F—s353—1・32

上海，商務，民三年・再版・132 面・「説部叢書初集世二編」

魯濱孫飄流記；(英)達孚原著，林紓，曾宗鞏合譯・ F—S353—1・33

上海，商務，民三年・再版・2 册・「説部叢書初集世三編」

洪罕女郎傳：言情小説；(英)哈葛德原著，林紓，魏易合譯・ F—S353—1・35

上海，商務，民三年・再版・2 册・「説部叢書初集世五編」

白巾人：偵探小説；(英)歇復克原著，商務印書館譯・ F—S353—1・36

上海，商務，民三年・再版・2 册・「説部叢書初集世六編」

蠻荒志異：神怪小説；(英)哈葛德原著，林紓，曾宗鞏合譯・ F—S353—1・39

上海，商務，民三年・再版・158 面・「説部叢書初集世九面」

阱中花：言情小説；(英)巴爾勒斯原著，商務印書館譯・ F—S353—1・40

上海，商務，民三年・再版・2 册・「説部叢書初集四十編」

香囊記；(英)斯且來威門原著，商務印書館譯・ F—S353—1・42

上海，商務，民三年・再版・100 面・「説部叢書初集四十二編」

三字獄：言情小説；(英)赫穆原著，商務印書館譯・ F—S353—1・45

上海，商務，民三年・再版・82 面・「説部叢書初集四十三編」

紅礁畫槳録：言情小説；(英)哈葛德原著，林紓，魏益合譯· F—s353—1·45
上海，商務，民三年·再版·2 册·「説部叢書初集四十五編」

海外軒渠録：寓情小説；
(英)狂生斯威佛特原著，林紓，陳家麟合譯· F—S353—1·46
上海，商務，民三年·再版·120 面·「説部叢書初集四十六編」

簾外人：偵探小説；(英)格利吾原著，商務印書館譯· F—s353—1·47
上海，商務，民三年·再版·154 面·「説部叢書初集四十七編」

煉才爐：政治小説；(英)亞力杜梅原著，甘永龍譯· F—s353—1·48
上海，商務，民三年·再版·78 面·「説部叢書初集四十八編」

七星寶石：偵探小説；(英)勃藍姆司道格原著，商務印書館譯· F—s353—1·49
上海，商務，民三年·再版·86 面·「説部叢書初集四十九編」

鐵錨手；(英)般福德倫納原著，商務印書館譯· F—s353—1·55
上海，商務，民三年·再版·94 面·「説部叢書初集五十五編」

露中人；(英)哈葛德原著，林紓，陳家麟合譯· F—s353—1·56
上海，商務，民三年·再版·3 册·「説部叢書初集五十六編」

蠻陬奮跡記：冒險小説；(英)特來生原著，商務印書館譯· F—s353—1·57
上海，商務，民三年·再版·94 面·「説部叢書初集五十七編」

橡湖仙影：社會小説；(英)哈葛德原著，林紓，魏易合譯· F—s353—1·58
上海，商務，民三年·再版·3 册·「説部叢書初集五十八編」

波乃茵傳：寫情小説；(英)赫拉原著，商務印書館譯· F—s353—1·59
上海，商務，民三年·再版·「説部叢書初集五九編」

二俑案：偵探小説；(英)許復古原著，商務印書館譯· F—s353—1·61
上海，商務，民三年·再版·106 面·「説部叢書初集六十一編」

空谷佳人：愛情小説；(英)博蘭克巴勒原著，商務印書館譯· F—s353—1·63
上海，商務，民三年·再版·84 面·「説部叢書初集六十三編」

秘密地窟：義俠小説；(英)華司原著，商務印書館譯· F—s353—1·64
上海，商務，民三年·再版·72 面·「説部叢書初集六十四編」

雙孝子噀血酬恩記：倫理小説；
(英)大隈克力司蒂穩雷原著，林紓等合譯· F—s353—1·65
上海，商務，民三年·再版·2 版「説部叢書初集六十五編」

真偶然：言情小説；(英)伯爾原著，商務印書館譯・　F—s353—1・67
上海，商務，民三年・再版・133 面・「説部叢書初集六十七編」
指中秘録：偵探小説；(英)麥區蘭拜原著，商務印書館譯・　F—S353—1・70
上海，商務，民三年・再版・2 册・「説部叢書初集七十編」
寶石城：偵探小説；(英)白髭拜原著，商務印書館譯・　F—S353—1・72
上海，商務，民三年・再版・131 面・「説部叢書初集七十二編」
雙冠璽：歷史小説；(英)特渴不厄拔佇原著，何心川，林黻楨合譯・
F—S353—1・73
上海，商務，民三年・再版・103 面・「説部叢書初集七十三編」
畫靈：言情小説；(英)曉公偉原著，商務印書館譯・　F—S353—1・74
上海，商務，民三年・再版・84 面・「説部叢書初集七十四編」
多那文包探案：偵探小説；(英)狄克多那文原著，商務印書館譯・
F—S353—1・76
上海，商務，民三年・再版・135 面・「説部叢書初集七十六編」
一萬九千磅：偵探小説；(英)般福德倫納原著，商務印書館譯・
F—S353—1・77
上海，商務，民三年・再版・102 面・「説部叢書初集七十七編」
紅星佚史：神怪小説；(英)羅達哈葛德原著，周逴譯・　F—S353—1・78
上海，商務，民三年・再版・221 面・「説部叢書初集七十八編」
塚中人：言情小説；(英)密羅原著，黄序譯・　F—S353—1・81
上海，商務，民三年・再版・113 面・「説部叢書初集八十一編」
盜窟奇緣：言情小説；(英)蒲斯培原著，商務印書館譯・　F—S353—1・83
上海，商務，民三年・再版・18 面・「説部叢書初集八十三編」
苦海餘生録：警世小説；(英)白來登女士原著，商務印書館譯・
上海，商務，民三年・再版・166 面・「説部叢書初集八十六編」
復國軼聞：航海小説；(英)波士俾原著，商務印書館譯・　F—S353—1・87
上海，商務，民三年・再版・93 面・「説部叢書初集八十七編」
情俠：義俠小説；(英)譚偉原著，商務印書館譯・　F—S353—1・88
上海，商務，民三年・再版・134 面・「説部叢書初集八十八編」
媒孽奇譚：婚事小説；(英)白朗脱原著，商務印書館譯・　F—S353—1・89

上海，商務，民三年・再版・95面・「説部叢書初集八十九編」

冰天漁樂記：冒險小説；(英)可頓原著，商務印書館譯・ F—S353—1・92

上海，商務，民十三年・再版・2册・「説部叢書初集九十五編」

鐵血痕；倍來原著，商務印書館譯・ F—S353—1・95

上海，商務，民三年・再版・2册・「説部叢書初集九十五編」

新天方夜談：社會小説；(英)路易斯地文，佛尼司地文原著・ F—S353—3・97

上海，商務，民三年・再版・143面・「説部叢書初集九十七編」

雙鴛侶：義俠小説；(英)格得史密斯原著，商務印書館譯・ F—S353—1・99

上海，商務，民三年・再版・109面・「説部叢書初集九十九編」

孝女耐兒傳：倫理小説；(英)卻而司迭更司原著，林紓，魏易合譯・ F—S353—2・1

上海，商務，民三年・4版・3册・「説部叢書二集一編」

塊肉餘生述前編：社會小説；(英)卻而司迭更司原著，林紓，魏易合譯・ F—S353—2・2

上海，商務，民四年・3版・2册・「説部叢書二集二編」

電影樓臺：社會小説；(英)柯南達利原著，林紓等合譯・ F—S353—2・6

上海，商務，民四年・3版・83面・「説部叢書二集六編」

冰雪因緣：社會小説；(英)卻而司迭更司原著，林紓等合譯・ F—S353—2・6

上海，商務，民四年・3版・6册・「説部叢書二集六編」

蛇女士傳：社會小説；(英)柯南達利原著，林紓等合譯・ F—S353—2・7

上海，商務，民四年・再版・103面・「説部叢書二集七編」

蘆花餘孽：社會小説；(英)色東麥里曼原著，林紓，魏易合譯・ F—S353—2・8

上海，商務，民四年・再版・80面・「説部叢書二集八編」

髯刺客傳：歷史小説；(英)柯南達利原著，林紓等合譯・ F—S353—2・10

上海，商務，民四年・再版・129面・「説部叢書二集十編」

黑太子南征録：軍事小説；(英)柯南利達原著，林紓等合譯・ F—s353—2・12

上海，商務，民四年・再版・2册・「説部叢書二集十二編」

金風鐵雨録：軍事小説；(英)柯南利達原著，林紓等合譯・ F—s353—2・13

上海，商務，民四年・3版・3册・「説部叢書二集十三編」

西奴林那小傳：言情小説；(英)安東尼賀迫原著，林紓等合譯·

F—S353—2·14

上海，商務，民四年·3版·8面·「説部叢書二集十四編」

賊史：社會小説；(英)卻而司迭更司原著，林紓等合譯· F—s353—2·19

上海，商務，民四年·再版·2册·「説部叢書二集十五編」

璣司刺虎記：言情小説；(英)哈葛德原著，林紓等合譯· F—s353—2·19

上海，商務，民四年·再版·2册·「説部叢書二集十九編」

劍底鴛鴦：言情小説；(英)司各德原著，林紓等合譯· F—s353—2·20

上海，商務，民四年·4版·2册·「説部叢書二集二十二編」

三千艷尸記：神怪小説；(英)哈葛德原著，林紓等合譯· F—s353—2·21

上海，商務，民四年·再版·2册·「説部叢書二集二十一編」

滑稽外史：滑稽小説；(英)卻而司迭更司原者，林紓等合譯· F—s353—2·22

上海，商務，民四年·再版·6册·「説部叢書二集二十二編」

天囚懺悔録：社會小説；(英)約翰沃克森罕原著，林紓等合譯·

F—s353—2·24

上海，商務，民四年·再版·15面·「説部叢書二集二十四編」

脂粉議員：社會小説；(英)司丢阿忒原著，林紓等合譯· F—s353—2·25

上海，商務，民四年·再版·150面·「説部叢書二集二十五編」

貝克偵探談初編：偵探小説；(英)馬克丹諾等原著，林紓等合譯·

F—s353—2·27

上海，商務，民四年·再版·9面·「説部叢書二集二十七編」

十字軍英雄記：軍事小説；(英)司各德原著，林紓等合譯· F—s353—2·29

上海，商務，民四年·3版·2册·「説部叢書二集二十九編」

恨綺愁羅記：歷史小説；(英)柯南達利原著，林紓等合譯· F—s353—2·30

上海，商務，民四年·4版·2册·「説部叢書二集三十編」

慧星奪壻録：社會小説；卻洛得倭康等原著，林紓等合譯· F—s353—2·34

上海，商務，民四年·再版·182面·「説部叢書二集三十四編」

雙雄較劍録：言情小説；(英)哈葛德原著，林紓等合譯· F—s353—2·35

上海，商務，民四年·再版·2册·「説部叢書二集三十五編」

薄倖郎：言情小説；(英)銷司倭司女士原著，林紓等合譯· F—s353—2·36

上海，商務，民四年・再版・2 册・「説部叢書二集三十六編」

殘蟬曳聲録：政治小説；(英)測欠希洛原著，林紓等合譯・　F—s353—2・40

上海，商務，民四年・再版・145 面・「説部叢書二集四十編」

羅刹雌風：偵探小説；(英)希洛原著，林紓等合譯・　F—s353—2・44

上海，商務，民四年・再版・122 面・「説部叢書二集四十四編」

假跛人；江德偉著・　F—s353—2・46

上海，商務，民四年・再版・49 面・「説部叢書二集四十六編」

血泊鴛鴦：言情小説；(英)哈葛德原著，林紓等合譯・　F—s353—2・52

上海，商務，民四年・再版・155 面・「説部叢書二集五十二編」

露惜傳：哀情小説；(英)司各德原著，陳大登等合譯・　F—s353—2・54

上海，商務，民四年・再版・2 册・「説部叢書二集五十四編」

亞媚女士別傳：言情小説；(英)卻而司迭更司原著，薛一諾等合譯・　F—s353—2・55

上海，商務，民四年・再版・2 册・「説部叢書二集五十五編」

笑裏刀；(英)司提文生原著，薛一諤等合譯・　F—s353—2・56

上海，商務，民四年・3 版・141 面・「説部叢書二集五十六編」

續笑裏刀；枕流譯・　F—s353—2・57

上海，商務，民四年・2 册・「説部叢書二集五十七編」

黑樓情孽：哀情小説；(英)馬尺芒忒原著，林紓等合譯・　F—s353—2・58

上海，商務，民四年・再版・2 册・「説部叢書二集五十八編」

博徒別傳：社會小説；(英)柯南達利原著，陳大登等合譯・　F—s353—2・59

上海，商務，民四年・再版・89 面・「説部叢書二集五十九編」

遮那德自伐八事：俠義小説；(英)柯南達利原著，陳大燈等合譯・　F—s353—2・61

上海，商務，民四年・再版・2 册・「説部叢書二集六十一編」

鍾乳髑髏：冒險小説；(英)哈葛德原著，林紓等合譯・　F—s353—2・64

上海，商務，民四年・3 版・10 面・「説部叢書二集六十四編」

廬宮祕史：歷史小説；(英)恩蘇霍伯原著，甘永龍等合譯・　F—s353—2・65

上海，商務，民四年・再版・2 册・「説部叢書二集六十五編」

劫花小影：言情小説；(英)勃雷登原著，王蘊章譯・　F—s353—2・66

上海，商務，民四年·再版·2册·「説部叢書二集六十六編」

白頭少年：社會小説；(英)蓋婆賽原著，陳家麟譯·　F—s353—2·68

上海，商務，民四年·再版·136面·「説部叢書二集六十八編」

青藜影：言情小説；(英)布斯俾原著，薛一諤等合譯·　F—s353—2·71

上海，商務，民四年·3版·89面·「説部叢書二集七十一編」

洪荒鳥獸記：科學小説；(英)柯南達利原著，李薇香譯·　F—s353—2·73

上海，商務，民四年·再版·2册·「説部叢書二集七十三編」

雪市孤踪：言情小説；天行譯·　F—s353—2·76

上海，商務，民四年·60面·「説部叢書二集七十六編」

飛將軍：理想小説；(英)葛利裴史原著，天游譯·　F—s353—2·89

上海，商務，民四年·2册·「説部叢書二集八十九編」

斷雁哀絃記：哀情小説；包天笑譯·　F—s353—2·91

上海，商務，民四年·2册·「説部叢書二集九十一編」

合歡草：言情小説；(英)偉烈原著，衛聽濤等合譯·　F—s353—2·93

上海，商務，民四年·2册·「説部叢書二集九十三編」

玉樓慘語：哀情小説；(英)威連格勒克司原著，胡克等合譯·　F—s353—2·94

上海，商務，民四年·再版·164面·「説部叢書二集九十四編」

俠母破奸記：社會小説；(英)加倫湯姆原著，劉幼新譯·　F—s353—2·96

上海，商務，民四年·再版·85面·「説部叢書二集九十六編」

亨利第六遺事；(英)莎士比亞原著，林紓等合譯·　F—s353—3·1

上海，商務，民五年·102面·「説部叢書三集一編」

情窩；(英)威利遜原著，林紓等合譯·　F—s353—3·3

上海，商務，民五年·2册·「説部叢書三集三編」

奇女格露枝小傳；(英)克拉克原著，林紓等合譯·　F—s353—3·7

上海，商務，民五年·63面·「説部叢書三集七編」

車中毒針；(英)勃拉錫克原著，吴檮譯·　F—s353—3·10

上海，商務，情光緒三十二年·142面·「説部叢書三集十編」

樹穴金；東鳳鳴譯·　F—s353—3·11

上海，商務，民五年·101面·「説部叢書」

詩人解頤語；(英)倩伯司原著，林紓等合譯·　F—s353—3·17

上海，商務，民十年·三版·2冊·「說部叢書三集十七編」

慧劫；(英)可林克洛悌原著，劉澤沛等合譯· F—s353—3·19

上海，商務，民十一年·再版·2冊·「說部叢書三集十九編」

天女離魂記；(英)哈葛德原著，林紓等合譯· F—s353—3·20

上海，商務，民六年·3冊·「說部叢書三集二十編」

煙火馬；(英)哈葛德原著，林紓等合譯· F—s353—3·23

上海，商務，民十年·再版·3冊·「說部叢書三集二十三編」

毒菌學者；(英)惠霖勞克原著，朱有畇譯· F—s353—3·24

上海，商務，民十二年·再版·2冊·「說部叢書三集廿四編」

蓬門畫眉録；(英)亨利瓦特女士原著，惲懺樵譯· F—s353—3·25

上海，商務，民十一年·再版·2冊·「說部叢書三集廿五編」

女師飲劍記；(英)布白原著，林紓等合譯· F—s353—3·29

上海，商務，民九年·再版·138面·「說部叢書三集廿九編」

歷刼思仇；(英)華特生原著，王女荃等合譯· F—s353—3·31

上海，商務，民十年·再版·2冊·「說部叢書三集三十一編」

黑沼疑雲録；(英)洛平華拉原著，陸秋心譯· F—s353—3·36

上海，商務，民十一年·3版·2冊·「說部叢書三集卅六編」

圍爐瑣談；(英)柯南達里原著，劉延陵等合譯· F—s353—3·38

上海，商務，民九年·再版·141面·「說部叢書三集三十八編」

綠光；Garvsis原著，張毅漢譯· F—s353—3·45

上海，商務，民十一年·3版·2冊·「說部叢書三集四十五編」

賊博士；Aunon原著，無我生譯· F—s353—3·46

上海，商務，民十二年·3版·77面·「說部叢書三集四十六編」

孤露佳人；(英)亨利瓦特夫人原著，范彥矧譯· F—s353—3·47

上海，商務，民十一年·3版·2冊·「說部叢書三集四十七編」

孤露佳人續編；(英)亨利瓦特夫人原著，范況等合譯· F—s353—3·56

上海，商務，民七年·2冊·「說部叢書三集五十六編」

癡郎幻影；(英)賴共堂原著，林紓等合譯· F—s353—3·52

上海，商務，民十年·3版·4冊·「說部叢書三集五十二編」

模範家庭；(英)Mrs. H. Wood原著，陳觀奕譯· F—s353—3·54

上海，商務，民十三年・4 版・141 面・「説部叢書三集五十四編」

牝賊情絲記；(英)陳施利原著，林紓等合譯・　F—s353—3・55

上海，商務，民十年・3 版・2 册・「説部叢書三集五十五編」

桃大王因果録；(英)参恩女士原著，林紓等合譯・　F—s353—3・57

上海，商務，民十年・3 版・2 册・「説部叢書三集五十七編」

玫瑰花；(英)巴克雷原著，林紓等合譯・　F—s353—3・59

上海，商務，民十年・3 版・2 册・「説部叢書三集五十九編」

再世爲人；(英)湯姆格倫原著，何故枚譯・　F—s353—3・61

上海，商務，民八年・2 册・「説部叢書三集六十一編」

贗爵案；(英)柯南李登原著，張舍我譯・　F—s353—3・63

上海，商務，民十三年・3 版・2 册・「説部叢書三集六十三編」

鬼窟藏嬌；(英)武英尼原著，林紓等合譯・　F—s353—3・64

上海，商務，民十年・3 版・2 册・「説部叢書三集六十四編」

模範家庭續編；(英)亨利凡特原著，陳觀弈譯・　F—s353—3・66

上海，商務，民八年・2 册・「説部叢書三集六十六編」

西樓鬼語；(英)約克魁迭斯原著，林紓等合譯・　F—s353—3・69

上海，商務，民十年・3 版・2 册・「説部叢書三集六十九編」

蓮心藕縷緣；(英)卡叩登原著，林紓等合譯・　F—s353—3・71

上海，商務，民十年・3 版・2 册・「説部叢書三集七十一編」

鐵匣頭顱；(英)哈葛德原著，林紓等合譯・　F—S353—3・73

上海，商務，民十年・3 版・2 册・「説部叢書三集七十三編」

重臣傾國記；(英)勒格克斯原著，趙尊嶽合譯・　F—S353—3・78

上海，商務，民十二年・3 版・2 册・「説部叢書三集七十八編」

鐵匣頭顱續編；(英)哈葛德原著，林紓等合譯・　F—s353—3・82

上海，商務，民八年・2 册・「説部叢書三集八十二編」

金梭神女再生緣；(英)哈葛德原著，林紓等合譯・　F—s353—3・86

上海，商務，民十年・3 版・2 册・「説部叢書三集八十六編」

戎馬书生；(英)楊支原著，林紓等合譯・　F—s353—3・89

上海，商務，民十年・3 版・107 面・「説部叢書三集八十九編」

泰西古劇；(英)達威生原著，林紓等合譯・　F—s353—3・91

上海，商務，民十年·再版·3冊·「説部叢書三集九十一編」

鸇巢記上編；林紓等合譯· F—s353—3·92

上海，商務，民十年·再版·2冊·「説部叢書三集九十二編」

妄言妄聽；林紓等合譯· F—s353—3·93

上海，商務，民十年·再版·2冊·「説部叢書三集九十三編」

焦頭亂額；林紓等合譯· F—s353—3·94

上海，商務，民十年·再版·2冊·「説部叢書三集九十四編」

歐戰春閨夢；(英)高桑斯原著，林紓等合譯· F—s353—3·87

上海，商務，民十年·再版·2冊·「説部叢書三集八十七編」

歐戰春閨夢續編；(英)高桑斯原著，林紓等合譯· F—s353—3·97

上海，商務，民十一年·2冊·「説部叢書三集九十七編」

玉雪留痕；(英)哈葛德原著，林紓等合譯· F—s353—4·2

上海，商務，清光緒三十二年·再版·132面·「説部叢書」

紅礁畫槳録；(英)哈葛德原德，林紓等合譯· F—s353—5·5

上海，商務，清光緒三十三年·再版·2冊·「説部叢書」

橡湖仙影；(英)哈葛德原著，林紓等合譯· F—s353—6·4

上海，商務，清光緒三十三年·3冊·「説部叢書」

秘密地窟；(英)華司原著，商務印書館譯· F—s353—7·4

上海，商務，清光緒三十三年·「説部叢書」

畫靈；(英)曉公偉原著，商務印書館譯· F—s353—8·4

上海，商務，清光緒三十三年·「説部叢書」

金絲髪；(英)格離痕原著，商務印書館譯· F—s353—8·9

上海，商務，清光緒三十三年·「説部叢書」

盗窟奇緣；(英)蒲斯培原著，商務印書館譯· F—s353—9·3

上海，商務，民元年·再版·184面·「説部叢書」

冰天漁樂記；(英)經斯頓原著，商務印書館譯· F—s353—10·3

上海，商務，清光緒三十四年·2冊·「説部叢書」

奇獄一；(美)麥枯滑特爾原著，林蓋天譯· F—M155c

上海，小説林，清光緒二十年·54面·

歐戰從軍記；(美)馬恩堵原著，趙開譯· F—N159

上海，商務，民十四年·2冊·「小説世界叢刊」

黄金血：偵探小説；(美)樂林司郎治原著，商務印書館譯·　F—s353—1·10

上海，商務，民三年·再版·130面·「説部叢書初集第十編」

回頭看：理志小説；(美)威士原著，商務印書館譯·　F—s353—1·12

上海，商務，民三年·再版·144面·「説部叢書初集第十二編」

紅柳娃；(美)柏拉蒙原著，商務印書館譯·　F—s353—1·44

上海，商務，民三年·再版·99面·「説部叢書初集第四十四編」

舊金山：冒險小説；(美)諾阿布羅克士原著，金石褚嘉猷合譯·F—s353—1·51

上海，商務，民三年·再版·118面·「説部叢書初集第五十一編」

一仇三怨：婚事小説；(美)沙斯惠夫人原著，商務印書館譯·　F—s353—1·90

上海，商務，民三年·再版·166面·「説部叢書初集第九十編」

三人影：偵探小説；(美)樂林司朗治原著，商務印書館譯·　F—s353—1·93

上海，商務，民三年·再版·20面·「説部叢書初集第九十三編」

雙喬記；言情小説；(美)杜伯原著，商務印書館譯·　F—s353—1·98

上海，商務，民三年·再版·86面·「説部叢書初集第九十八編」

拊掌録：滑稽小説；(美)華盛頓歐文原著，林紓，魏易合譯·　F—s353—2·4

上海，商務，民四年·4版·76面·「説部叢書二集第四編」

大食故宫餘載：歷史小説；

(美)華盛頓歐文原著，林紓，魏易合譯·　F—s353—2·11

上海，商務，民四年·3版·208面·「説部叢書二集第十一編」

旅行述異；(美)華盛頓歐文原著，林紓，魏易合譯·　F—s353—2·17

上海，商務，民四年·3版·2冊·「説部叢書二集第十七編」

西利郡主别傳：言情小説；

(美)馬支孟德原著，林紓，魏益合譯·　F—s353—2·18

上海，商務，民四年·3版·2冊·「説部叢書二集十八編」

藕孔避兵録：偵探小説；(美)蜚立伯倭本翰原著，林紓，魏益合譯·

F—s353—2·26

上海，商務，民四年·3版·183面·「説部叢書二集二十六編」

希臘興亡記：歷史小説；(美)彼得巴利原著，曾宗鞏譯·　F—s353—2·73

上海，商務，民四年·再版·86面·「説部叢書二集七十八編」

城中鬼域記：社會小説；(美)愛娜温飛爾原著，汪德禕譯· F—s353—2·82
上海，商務，民四年·再版·119面·「説部叢書二集八十二編」

孤士影：言情小説；(美)馬林克羅福原著，詩廬譯· F—s353—2·86
上海，商務，民四年·再版·2册·「説部叢書二集八十六編」

稗苑琳瑯；社會小説；(美)美林孟原著，詩廬譯· F—s353—2·87
上海，商務，民四年·「説部叢書二集八十七編」

橄欖仙；(美)巴蘇謹原著，林紓，陳家麟合譯· F—s353—3·13
上海，商務，民十年·3版·2册·「説部叢書三集第十三編」

庵冠浪影；(美)C. C. Andrews原著，丁宗一，陳堅合譯· F—s353—3·18
上海，商務，民七年·再版·98面·「説部叢書三集第十八編」

鄉里善人；(美)伊几羌甯原著，胡君復，惲鐵樵合譯· F—s353—3·27
上海，商務，民十一年·再版·2册·「説部叢書三集二十七編」

怪手印；丁宗一，陳堅合譯· F—s353—3·21
上海，商務，民十一年·4版·2册·「説部叢書二集二十一編」

蛇首黨；(美)奥琴黎夫原著，范況，張逢辰合譯· F—s353—3·33
上海，商務，民十二年·3版·113面·「説部叢書三集三十三編」

黑偉人；博嘉華盛頓原著，孟憲成譯· F—s353—3·60
上海，商務，民九年·再版·2册·「説部叢書」

荒村奇遇；(美)佛老尉佗原著，李澄宇譯· F—s353—3·67
上海，商務，民八年·2册·「説部叢書三集六十七編」

明眼人；(英)H. G. Wells原著，孟憲成譯· F—s353—3·70
上海，商務，民十三年·3版·114面·「説部叢書三集七十編」

還珠曲豔史；(美)堪伯路原著，林紓，陳家麟合譯· F—s353—3·76
上海，商務，民九年·2册·「説部叢書三集七十九編」

黑奴籲天録；(美)斯浩原著，林紓譯· F—s5·9h
上海，文明書局，民九年·2册·

焦頭爛額；(美)尼可拉斯原著，林紓，陳家麟合譯· F—s353—3·94
上海，商務·2册·「説部叢書」

紅柳娃；(美)柏拉蒙原著，商務印書館譯· F—s353—5·4
上海，商務，清光緒三十二年·再版·96面·「説部叢書」

撒克遜劫後英辦略；W. Scott 原著，林紓，魏易合譯．　F—sc84
上海，商務，民十三年．288 面．

瑪麗瑪麗；(英)司蒂芬士原著，徐志摩，沈性仁合譯．　F—st4
民十七年．

金銀島；(英)司堤反生原著，商務印書館譯．　F—st48
上海，商務，清光緒三十年．94 面．

格裏佛遊記；(英)斯偉夫特原著，韋叢蕪譯．　F—sW55
上海，商務，民十七年．卷一

蠻陬奮跡記；(英)特來生原著，商務印書館譯．　F—T2584
上海，商務，清光緒三十二年．94 面．

道連格雷畫像；(英)王爾德原著，杜衡譯．　F—W644
上海，金屋，民十七年．420 面．

獄中記；(英)王爾德原著，張聞天等合譯．　F—W644
上海，商務，民十一年．217 面．「文學研究會叢書」

膺梯小豪傑；(英)楊支原著，林紓等合譯．　F—Y121
上海，商務，民五年．9 面．

天囚懺悔録：社會小説；(英)約翰沃克森罕原著，林紓等合譯．
F—Y447
上海，商務，清光緒三十四年．157 面．

夢遊二十一世紀：科學小説；(荷)達愛斯克洛提斯原著，楊德森譯．
F—353—I．3
上海，商務，民三年．再版，64 面．「説部叢書初集三編」

天方夜譚；奚若譯．　F—Ar11
上海，商務，民十三年．2 册．

兩條腿；(丹)愛華耳特原著，李小峯譯．　F—EW141
北京，北新，民十四年．126 面．

猶太小説集；魯彦譯．　F—L416y
上海，開明，民十五年．136 面．

無畫的畫帖；(丹)安徒生原著，趙景生譯．　F—An23w
上海，新文化，民十二年．94 面．

愛的教育；(意)亞米契斯原著，夏丏尊譯· F—An51
上海，開明，民十七年·4版·420面·

愛彌兒：教育小説；(法)盧梭原著，魏肇基譯· F—I762
上海，商務，民十二年·283面·

炭畫；(波蘭)顯克微支原著，周作人譯· F—s116
上海，北新書局·再版·117面·

雪人；(匈牙利)莫爾納等原著，沈雁冰譯· F—M280
上海，開明，民十七年·403面·「文學週報社叢書」

西班牙宫闈瑣語：歷史小説；商務印書館譯· F—s35—2·80
上海，商務，民四年·再版·80面·「説部叢書二集八十編」

孝友鏡；(比)恩海斯翁士原著，林紓，王慶通合譯· F—s353—3·48
上海，商務，民十年·3版·2册·「説部叢書三集四十八編」

高加索民間故事；(德)狄爾原著，鄭振鐸譯· F—D33
上海，商務，民十七年·240面·

少年維特之煩惱；(德)歌德原著，郭沫若譯· F—G554
上海，創造社，民十七年·221面·「創造社世界名著選第一種」

德國大秘密；陸澹譯· F—L433
上海，交通圖書館，民九年·2册·

少年歌德之創造；西譯· F—M447
上海，新新，民七年·124面·

茵夢湖；(德)施篤模原著，郭沫若，錢君胥合譯· F—St74
上海，泰東，民十年·再版·72面·

意門湖；(德)斯托爾姆原著，唐性天譯· F—St74
上海，商務，民十二年·3版·73面·「文學研究會叢書」

憂愁夫人；(德)蘇臺爾曼原著，胡仲持譯· F—Su22
上海，商務，民十三年·354面·「文學研究會叢書」

浮士德；梁遇春，顧綬昌合譯· F—T690
上海，北新，民十七年·195面·

伊索寓言演義；孫毓修譯· 888·6—Ae88
上海，商務，民十一年·168面·「演義叢書第一種」

希臘名士伊索寓言；林紓等合譯．　888．6—Ae88S
上海，商務，民十三年．十九版．68頁．

近代俄國小説集；東方雜誌社編．　080—L860—77
上海，商務，民十四年．3版．5册．「東方文庫」

小人物的懺悔；(俄)安特立夫原著，耿式之譯．　F—Am25
上海，商務，民十二年．再版．155面．「文學研究會叢書」

現代小説譯叢；(俄)安特立夫原著，周作人譯．　F—An25
上海，商務，民十二年．再版．380面．「世界叢書」

工人綏惠略夫；(俄)阿志跋綏夫原著，魯迅譯．　F—Ay79
上海，商務，民十一年．202面．「文學研究會叢書」

窮人；(俄)陀思妥耶夫斯基原著，韋叢蕪譯．　F—D742
民十七年．「未名叢刊之一」

外套；(俄)果戈裹原著，章漱園譯．　F—G557
北京，未名社，民十五年．71面．「未名叢刊之一」

育樂師；(俄)克羅連科原著，張亞權譯．　F—K459
上海，商務，民十五年．240面．「文學研究會叢書」

貧非罪；(俄)阿使特洛夫斯基原著，鄭振鐸譯．　F—Os7
上海，商務，民十一年．119面．「俄羅斯文學叢書」

甲必丹之女；(俄)普希金原著，安壽頤譯．　F—P419C
上海，商務，民十一年．再版．226面．「俄羅斯文學叢書」

普希金小説集；趙城之譯．　F—P419P
上海，亞東，民十三年．418面．

曇花夢；(俄)薩拉斯奇夫原著，商務印書館譯．　F—S353—1．23
上海，商務，民十三年．再版．80面．「説部叢書初集二十三編」

羅刹因果録；(俄)託爾斯泰原著，林紓，陳家麟合譯．　F—S353—2．39
上海，商務，民四年．再版．89面．「説部叢書二集三十九編」

雪花園：醒世小説；(俄)託爾斯泰原著，雪生譯．　F—S353—2．63
上海，商務，民四年．54面．「説部叢書二集六十三編」

驃騎父子：義俠小説；(俄)託爾斯泰原著，朱東潤譯．　F—S353—2．81
上海，商務，民四年．60面．「説部叢書二集八十一編」

不測之威；(俄)託爾斯泰原著，商務印書館譯． F—S353—2·95
上海，商務，民四年·再版·2冊·「説部叢書二集第九十五編」

社會聲影録；(俄)託爾斯泰原著，林紓，陳家麟合譯． F—S353—3·22
上海，商務，民六年·117面·「説部叢書三集二十二編」

現身説法；(俄)託爾斯泰原著，林紓，陳家麟合譯． F—S353—3·53
上海，商務，民十年·3版·3冊·「説部叢書三集五十三編」

恨縷情絲；(俄)託爾斯泰原著，林紓，陳家麟合譯． F—S353—3·62
上海，商務，民九年·再版·2冊·「説部叢書三集六十二編」

俄羅斯宫闈秘記；張叔嚴編． F—S353—3·72
上海，商務，民十三年·3版·2冊·「説部叢書三集七十二編」

悒鬱；(俄)柴霍甫原著，趙景深譯． F—T117
上海，開明，民十六年·206面．

三年；(俄)契訶夫原著，張友松譯． F—T117s
上海，北新，民十六年·再版·227面·「近代世界名家小説之一」

柴霍甫短篇小説集；(俄)Tchehov原著，耿濟之，耿勉之合譯． F—T117t
上海，商務，民十三年·再版·241面·「俄羅斯文學叢書」

托爾斯泰小説集；(俄)托爾斯泰原著，新人社譯． F—T588
上海，泰東，民十二年·2冊．

復活；(俄)托爾斯泰原著，耿濟之譯． F—T588
上海，商務，民十五年·3版·3冊·「俄羅斯文學叢書」

九封書；浮司德屠格涅夫原著，沈穎譯． F—T844
上海，自由社·76面·「自由叢刊」

畸零人日記；(俄)屠格涅夫原著，樊仲雲譯． F—T844
上海，開明，民十七年·198面．

父與子；(俄)屠格涅甫原著，耿濟之譯． F—T844
上海，商務，民十一年·「俄羅斯文學叢書」

薄命女；(俄)都介涅夫原著，張友松譯． F—T844P
北京，北新，民十六年·176面·「歐美名家小説叢刊之一」

勝利戀歌；(俄)屠格涅夫原著，李傑三譯． F—T844Se
上海，光華·75面．

新時代；(俄)屠格涅甫原著，郭沫若譯· F—T844ss
上海，商務，民十四年·560面·

前夜；(俄)屠格涅甫原著，沈穎譯· F—T814t
上海，商務，民十一年·再版·311面·「俄羅斯文學叢書」

近代日本小説集；東方雜誌社編· 080—T860—7
上海，商務，民十四年·3版·112面·「東方文庫」

日本小説集；小説月報社編· 808—Sh41—47
上海，商務，民十四年·95面·「小説月報叢刊第四十七種」

芥川龍之介集；(日)芥川龍之介原著，魯迅等合譯· F—C56
上海，開明，民十六年·200面·

現代日本小説集；周作人譯· F—C771
上海，商務，民十四年·3版·383面·「世界叢書」

月夜；(日)川島原著· F—c901
北大，新潮社，民十三年·98面·

一捻紅；包天笑譯· F—P192
上海，小説林，清光緒二十年·178面·

色情文化：日本小説集；吶吶·，(别名)譯· F—S13
上海，第一線書店，民十七年·175面·

天際落花：言情小説；(日)墨岩周六著· F—S353—1·1
上海，商務，民三年·再版·119面·「説部叢書初集一編」

珊瑚美人：言情小説；(日)三宅彦爾原譯，商務印書館編· F—S353—1·15
上海，商務，民三年·再版·133面·「説部叢書初集十五編」

賣國奴：軍事小説；(日)登張竹風原譯，吳檮譯· F—S353—1·16
上海，商務，民三年·再版·188面·「説部叢書初集十六編」

懺情記：言情小説；(日)黑巖淚香原著，商務印書館譯· F—S353—1·18
上海，商務，民三年·再版·2册·「説部叢書初集三十一編」

寒桃記：偵探小説；(日)黑巖淚香原者，吳檮譯· F—S353—1·31
上海，商務，民三年·再版·2册·「説部叢書初集十八編」

澳洲歷險記：冒險小説；(日)櫻井彦一郎原著，金石，褚嘉猷合譯·
F—S353—1·37

上海，商務，民三年・再版・70 面・「説部叢書初集三十七編」

秘密電光艇：科學小説；(日)押川春浪原著，金石，褚嘉猷合譯・ F—S353—1・38

上海，商務，民三年・140 面・「説部叢書初集第三十八編」

寒牡丹：哀情小説；(日)尾崎紅葉原著，吳檮譯・ F—S353—1・41

上海，商務，民三年・再版・2 册・「説部叢書初集四十一編」

血蓑衣：義俠小説；(日)村井弦齋原著，商務印書館譯・ F—S353—1・50

上海，商務，民三年・再版・「説部叢書初集五十編」

俠黑奴；(日)尾崎德太郎原著，吳檮譯・ F—S353—1・52

上海，商務，民三年・再版・54 面・「説部叢書初集五十二編」

美人煙草；(日)尾崎德太郎原著，吳檮譯・ F—s353—1・53

上海，商務，民三年・再版・68 面・「説部叢書初集五十三編」

世界一周；(日)渡邊氏原著，商務印書館譯・ F—s353—1・66

上海，商務，民三年・再版・87 面・「説部叢書初集六十六編」

航海少年：冒險小説；(日)櫻井彦一郎原著，商務印書館譯・ F—S353—1・75

上海，商務，民三年・再版・92 面・「説部叢書初集七十五編」

朽木舟：冒險小説；(日)櫻井彦一郎原著，商務印書館譯・ F—S353—1・80

上海，商務，民三年・再版・101 面・「説部叢書初集八十編」

鬼士官：寫情小説；(日)少栗風葉原著，商務印書館譯・ F—S353—1・84

上海，商務，民三年・再版・178 面・「説部叢書初集八十四編」

鴛盟離合記：言情小説；(日)黑巖淚香原著，湯爾和譯・ F—S353—1・85

上海，商務，民三年・再版・2 册・「説部叢書初集八十五編」

橘英男：偵探小説；(日)楓村居士原著，商務印書館譯・ F—S351—1・94

上海，商務，民三年・再版・175 面・「説部叢書初集九十四編」

不如歸：哀情小説；(日)德富健次郎原著，林紓，魏益合譯・ F—S353—2・23

上海，商務，民四年・4 版・「説部叢書二集二十三編」

俠如郎：冒險小説；(日)押川春郎原著，吳檮譯・ F—s353—2・74

上海，商務，民四年・再版・75 面・「説部叢書二集四十七編」

模範町村；(日)横井時敬原著，唐人傑，徐鳳書合譯・ F—S353—2・67

上海，商務，民四年・再版・120 面・「説部叢書二集六十七編」

秘密怪洞：社會小說；(日)曉風山原著，郭家聲，孟文翰合譯· F—s353—2·88

上海，商務，民四年·99面·「説部叢書二集八十八編」

空虛；(日)細田源吉原著，鄭佐蒼，張資平合譯· F—s366

上海，新宇宙，民十七年·74面·「文藝叢書二種」

外交秘事；(日)千葉紫草纂譯，商務印書館重譯· F—T630

上海，商務，民三年·3版·128面·

妹妹；(日)武者小路實篤原著，周伯棣譯· F—w303

上海，中華，民四年·220面·

母與子；(日)武者小路實篤原著，瞿萬秋譯· F—w3C4

上海，真美善書店，民十七年·742面·

短編小說；胡適譯· F—D264

上海，亞東，民十四年·8版·第一集·

愛的藝術；藹理斯著· F—EL59

上海，北新，民十六年·再版·134面·

這便宜人生；樊仲雲譯· F—F136

上海，新宇宙，民十七年·177面·

處女的心；果爾蒙原著，蓬子譯·北京，晨報社，民十三年· F—F743

上海，北新，民十六年·再版·224面·

貍奴角：偵探小說；果盤原著，飯囊譯· F—K438

上海，小説林，清光緒三十一年·「小説林言情小說之一」

義賊畢加林；蘭原著，楊敬慈譯· F—L134

北京，晨報社，民十三年·「北京晨報社叢書十四種偵探小說一集」

星火；胡愈之譯· F—P232

上海，現代，民十七年·216面·

小仙源：冒險小說；商務印書館譯· F—S353—1·5

上海，商務，民三年·再版·81面·「説部叢書初集五編」

環遊月球：科學小說；商務印書館譯· F—S353—1·7

上海，商務，民三年·再版·128面·「説部叢書初集七編」

降妖記：偵探小說；陸康華，黃大鈞合譯· F—s353—1·14

上海，商務，民三年・111 面・「説部叢書初集十四編」

奪嫡奇冤：偵探小説；商務印書館譯・ F—s353—1・19

上海，商務，民三年・再版・254 面・「説部叢書初集十九編」

雙指印：偵探小説；商務印書館譯・ F—S353—1・2

上海，商務，民三年・再版・100 面・「説部叢書初集二十一編」

指環黨；商務印書館譯・ F—s353—1・24

上海，商務，民三年・再版・120 面・

桑伯勤包探案：偵探小説；商務印書館譯・ F—s353—1・28

上海，商務，民三年・再版・104 面・「説部叢書初集二十八編」

希臘神話：神怪小説；巴德文原著，商務印書館譯・ F—s353—1・69

上海，商務，民三年・再版・90 面・「説部叢書初集六十九編」

新飛艇：科學小説；尾楷忒星期報社原著，商務印書館譯・ F—s353—1・91

上海，商務，民三年・再版・156 面・「説部叢書初集九十一編」

漫郎攝實戈：言情小説；商務印書館譯・ F—s353—2・42

上海，商務，民四年・三版・140 面・「説部叢書二集四十二編」

匈奴奇士録；周逴譯・ F—s353—2・51

上海，商務，民四年・再版・180 面・「説部叢書二集五十一編」

清宮二年記：歷史小説；德菱原著，東方雜誌社譯・ F—S353—2・60

上海，商務，民四年・再版・127 面・「説部叢書二集六十編」

青衣記：言情小説；商務印書館譯・ F—S353—2・69

上海，商務，民四年・3 版・2 册・「説部叢書二集六十九編」

愛兒小傳：艷情小説；陶祝年，莊孟英合譯・ F—S353—2・98

上海，商務，民四年・144 面・「説部叢書二集九十八編」

娜蘭小傳：言情小説；蔡爾𫊼維斯原著，夢癡，耕者合譯・ F—s353—2・100

上海，商務，民四年・再版・2 册・「説部叢書二集一百編」

名優遇盜記；郭演公譯・ F—S353—3・6

上海，商務，民五年・83 面・「説部叢書三集 6 編」

真愛情；蓮心，雛燕合譯・ F—S353—3・9

上海，商務，民十一年・再版・95 面・「説部叢書三集九編」

戰場情話；史久成譯・ F—s353—3・10

上海，商務，民十三年·再版·2 册·「説部叢書三集十編」

血痕；生可譯·　F—s353—3·15

上海，商務，民十三年·4 版·78 面·「説部叢書三集十五編」

戀花情果；王卓民譯·　F—s353—3·16

上海，商務，民十年·3 版·2 册·「説部叢書三集十六編」

奇婚記；劉幼新編·　F—s353—3·28

上海，商務，民六年·101 面·「説部叢書三集二十八編」

地獄礁；卓呆譯·　F—s353—3·30

上海，商務，民十三年·再版·2 册·「説部叢書三集三十編」

秘密軍港；范況，張逢辰合譯·　F—s353—3·35

上海，商務，民十一年·4 版·112 面·「説部叢書三集三十四編」

紅粉殲仇記；李拜蘭譯·　F—s353—3·35

上海，商務，民十一年·4 版·81 面·「説部叢書三集三十五編」

賢妮小傳；丁宗一，陳堅合譯·　F—s353—3·36

上海，商務，民十一年·再版·2 册·「説部叢書三集二十六編」

續賢妮小傳；丁宗一，陳堅合譯·　F—S352—3·37

上海，商務，民九年·再版·「説部叢書三集三十七編」

再續賢妮小傳；丁宗一，陳堅合譯·　F—S353—3·39

上海，商務，民十一年·3 版·2 册·「説部叢書三集三十九編」

妒婦遺毒記；黄静英譯·　F—S353—3·40

上海，商務，民十一年·3 版·118 面·「説部叢書三集四十編」

拉哥比在校記；商務印書館譯·　F—S353—3·43

上海，商務，民十三年·3 版·2 册·「説部叢書三集四十三編」

雙鄒淚；包天笑譯·　F—S353—3·6

上海，商務，民九年·再版·86 面·「説部叢書三集六十九編」

風島女傑；羅文亮譯·　F—S353—3·76

上海，商務，民十三年·3 版·57 面·「説部叢書三集七十六編」

蜘蛛毒；徐慧公譯·　F—S353—3·77

上海，商務，民九年·再版·102 面·「説部叢書三集七十七編」

碧玉串；尤玄甫譯·　F—S353—3·80

上海，商務，民十年·115 面·「説部叢書三集八十編」

苦海雙星；蔣炳然，廖鳴韶合譯· F—S353—3·89

上海，商務，民十年·再版·2 册·「説部叢書三集八十九編」

紅鴛艷牒；陳大悲譯· F—S353—3·95

上海，商務，民十年·再版·2 册·「説部叢書三集九十五編」

鸝巢記續编；林紓，陳家麟合譯· F—S353—3·100

上海，商務，民十一年·再版·2 册·「説部叢書三集一百編」

荒服鴻飛記續编；G. C. Sheld 原著，天游譯· F—Sh34

上海，商務，民十四年·5 册·「小説世界叢刊」

獄中記；A. A. Sotto 原著，徽明學社編· F—S023

上海，開明，民十六年·257 面·

前夜；沈潁譯· F—T98

民十年

婚後；得利賽原著，張友松譯· F—T257

上海，北新，民十七年·156 面·

域外小説集；周作人譯· F—W644

上海，羣益，民九年·328 面·

他們的兒子；E. Zamacois 原著，沈餘譯· F—Z15

上海，商務，民十七年·10 面·「文學研究會叢書」

貓的天堂；左拉原著，劉復譯· F—Z074m

上海，北新，民十六年·20 面·「北京孔德學校小叢書之一」

失業；左拉原著，劉復譯· F—Z074s

上海，北新，民十六年·再版·20 面·「北京孔德學校小叢書之二」

900 歷史

史學常識；徐敬修著· 901—s476

上海，泰東，民十四年·再版·68 面·「國學常識之五」

新史學；(美)魯濱孫原著，何炳松譯· 900—R563

上海，商務，民十四年·3版·271面·「北京大學叢書之十」

歷史哲學；朱謙之著·　901—C821

上海，泰東，民十五年·389面·

史學要論；李守常著·　080—P225

上海，商務，民十三年·88面·「科學小叢書第五十一種」

歷史研究法；何炳松著·　080—P125—122

上海，商務，民十六年·100面·「百科小叢書」

史學新論；楊鴻烈著·　901—Y126

北京，晨報社，民十三年·242面·「晨報社叢書第二十種」

歷史教學法；(美)約翰生亨利原著，何炳松譯·　907—H396

上海，商務，民十五年·452面·「現代教育名著」

西洋文化史綱；劉炳榮著·　901—L372

上海，太平洋書店，民十五年·206面·

文化之出路；Soott Nearing 原著，周谷城譯·　901—N27

上海，現代書局，民十七年·145面·

二十世紀之母；P. Y. 著·　901—P1

上海，出版合作社，民十五年·160面·

逝世文化史；謝劻之著·　901—S118

上海，光華，民十五年·244面·

中國民族與世界文化；徐慶譽著·　901—S476

上海，世界學會，民十七年·84面·「世界學會新思想叢書」

世界大事年表；傅運森編·　902—F247

上海，商務，民三年·356面·

世界史表解；上海科學書局編輯所編·　080—S155—902

上海，科學書局，清宣統三年·33面·「表解叢書」

909　世界史

初級世界史；金兆梓著·　909—C662

上海，中華，民十四年·139面·

世界史；周傳儒著． 上海，商務，民十四年．2 册．	909—C771
世界史；傅運森著． 上海，商務，民十二年．71 面．	909—F247s
世界史；傅運森，王鍾麒合著． 上海，商務，民十三年．4 版．2 版．	909—F247s
世界史；李泰棻著． 上海，商務，民十五年．10 版．273 面．	909—LI98
人類的行爲；(法)房龍原著，沈性仁譯． 上海，商務，民十五年．再版．下册．「少年史地叢書」	909—V26
漢譯世界史綱；(英)韋爾斯原著，向達等合譯． 上海，商務，民十七年．3 版．2 册．	909—W458
萬國史綱；(日)元良勇次郎，家永豐吉合著，邵希雍譯． 上海，商務，民三年．258 面．	909—Y428
歷史教科書，新學制；傅運森著． 上海，商務，民十二年．2 册．	909—F247s
政法類典：歷史之部． 上海，作新社，清光緒二十九年．168 面．	909—T684
現代五大強國；許士毅著． 上海，中華，民十三年．148 面．「常識叢書第四種」	
世界亡國稗史；楊南邨著． 上海，交通圖書館，民七年．92 面．	909—Y130

910—916 地理

世界地理學表解；上海科學書局編輯所編． 上海，科學書局，清光緒三十二年．3 册．「表解叢書」	080—S155—910
政治地理表解；蔣筠著． 上海，科學書局，民三年．2 册．「表解叢書」	080—S155—910

瀛寰全志，重訂本；謝洪賚著· 910—S118
上海，商務，民十三年·2冊·

世界地理志；徐大煜著· 910—s482
競南學社，清光緒三十一年·352面·

初級世界地理；丁詧盦著· 910—T346
上海，中華，民十五年·220面·

新制世界地理；曾慶錫著· 910—T521sc
武昌，中華大學，民十三年·90面·

世界地理參證；曾慶錫著· 910—T521sh
武昌，中華大學，民十三年·62面·

新學制地理教科書；王鍾麒著· 910—w136s
上海，商務，民十二年·2冊·

地理教科書；王鍾麒著· 910—W136t
上海，商務，民十五年·45版·2冊·

白話地理教本；(美)衛雅各原著，李榮春譯· 910—W222
上海，自由社，民二年·58面·

戰後新興國研究；東方雜誌社編· 080—T860—16
上海，商務，民十四年·3版·2冊·「東方文庫」

戰後世界新形勢紀要；王華隆著· 911—W142
上海，商務，民十一年·再版·82面·

東洋史要地圖；商務印書館編譯所編· 911·52—S162
上海，商務，民二年·2版·44面·

中外地理大全；陶履恭，楊文洵合著· 910—T247
上海，中華，民十年·5版·2冊·

外國地理；謝觀著· 910—S419
上海，商務，民十三年·重訂18版·2冊·

外國地理講義；孫毓修，朱元善合著· 910—S535
上海，商務，民元年·132面·

經濟地理學原理· 910—W164
上海，商務，民十五年·172面·「新智識叢書」

人生地理教科書，制新學；張其昀著· 910—C152
上海，商務，民十五年·3冊·

人文地理；傳運森著· 910—F247
上海，商務，民十年·8版·73面·

人文地理學；王華隆著· 910—W142
上海，商務，民十四年·206面·

地理教本甲編：歐羅巴洲；(美)謙本圖原著，孫毓修譯· 914—C225
上海，商務，民四年·4版·382面·

亞細亞洲，地理讀本已編；(美)謙本圖著，孫毓修譯· 915—C225
上海，商務，民元年·再版·332面·

中國地理大勢；吕思勉著· 915·4—C225
上海，中華，民十四年·5版·2冊·

中學地參考書；馬晉義著· 915·1—M112
湖南，作民社，清光緒三十三年·388面·

本國地理；繆育南著· 915·1—M262
上海，商務，民十四年·3版·2冊·

本國地理；謝觀著· 915·1—S419
上海，商務，民十三年·24版·2冊·

初級本國地理；丁詧盦著· 915·1—T346
上海，中華，民十五年·19版·2冊·

初級本國地理參考書；丁詧盦著· 915·1—T346
上海，中華，民十五年·2冊·

新體中國地理；藏勵龢著· 915·1—T446
上海，商務，民元年·

近編中華地理分誌；王金紱著· 915·1—W136
北京，求知學社，民十三年·2冊·「西北大學叢書之一」

中國境界變遷大勢考附圖；蘇演存著· 915·1—S462
上海，商務·

中國境界變遷大勞考· 915·1—s462

上海，商務，民五年·再版·218面·

中國海疆之變遷及南北天然之區劃；李仲揆講演· 915·1—L181c

武昌，中華大學，民十二年·8面·「暑校講演録第一集之七」

各省區域沿革一覽表；謝觀著· 915·1—s419k

上海，商務，民三年·223面·

現行行政區劃一覽表；陳鎬基著· 915·1—C278

上海，商務，民五年·再版·33面·

世界最新地圖華英地名表；陳鎬基著· R—910·2—0278

上海，商務，民十四年·6版·23面·

英華華英地名檢查表；中華書局編譯所編· R—910·2—0976

上海，中華，民九年·再版·99面·

大中華江西省地理志；林傳甲著· 915·133—L316

南昌，裕成刷印公司，民七年·324面·

大中華湖北省地理志；林傳甲著· 915·131—L316

京師，中國地學會，民八年·322面·

北亞美利加，地理讀本乙編；(美)謙本圖原著，孫毓修譯· 917—C225

上海，商務，民二年·3版·213面·

910·2 遊覽指南

中國旅行指南；商務印書館編譯所編· 910·2—s462

上海，商務，民十二年·10版·405面·

北京便覽；姚祝萱著· 910·2—P223

上海，中華，民十二年·再版·471面·

實用北京指南；商務印書館編譯所編· 910·2—P223

上海，商務，民十五年·4版·

實用北京指南；徐珂編· 910·2—P223

上海，商務，民十二年·3版·

上海指南；商務印書館編譯所編· 910·2—s155

上海，商務，民十五年·22版·566面·

廣州快覽；劉再蘇著· 910·2—K320
上海，世界書局，民十五年·152面·

天津快覽；劉再蘇編· 910·2—T342
上海，世界書局，民十五年·185面·

青島概要；葉春墀編· 910·2—Y181
日照，葉春墀，民十一年·126面·

鷄公山指南；徐珂編· 910·2—C392
上海，商務，民十一年·再版·37面·

廬山指南；徐珂編· 910·2—L408
上海，商務，民十一年·再版·

莫干山指南；徐珂纂· 910·2—M771
上海，商務，民十一年·再版·38面·

北戴河指南；徐珂編· 910·2—P223
上海，商務，民十一年·再版·87面·

泰山指南；胡君復編· 910·2—T135
上海，商務，民十二年·

西湖遊覽表指南；徐珂編· 910·2—S370
上海，商務，民十二年·14版·168面·

910·3 地名辭典

中外地名辭典；丁詧盦，葛綏成合編· R—910·3—T346
上海，中華，民十三年·再版·307面·

外國地名人名辭典；(日)坂本健一著，新學社譯· R—910·3—s345
寧波，新學會社，清光緒三十二年·3版·「634」面·

外國人名地名表；何松齡等合譯· R—910·3—H210
上海，商務，民十三年·再版·719面·

912 地圖

世界新輿圖；奚若著· 912—sh238

上海，商務，民七年·

世界改造分國地圖；丁詧盦著· 912—T345

上海，商務，民十年·

表解説明世界新形勢一覽圖； 912—T793

上海，世界輿地學社，民十三年·32頁

袖珍世界新輿圖；童世亨著· 912—T901

上海，商務，民九年·

世界形勢一覽圖；童世亨著· 912—T902

上海，商務，民十四年·

世界改造後環球列國地圖；華英對照；亞新地學社編· 912—Y114

武昌，亞新地學社，民十六年·

最新中華形勢圖；洪懋熙著· 912·51—H521

上海，東方輿地學社，民十六年·

湖北分縣詳圖；亞新地學社編· 912·51—Y114

武昌，亞新地學社，民十六年

913　考古學

考古學零簡；東方雜誌社編· 080—T860—71

上海，商務，民十四年·3版·102面·「東放支庫」

東北亞洲搜訪記；湯爾和譯· 913—N200

上海，商務，民十五年·265面·「地理叢書」

910—919　遊記

環球周遊記；景憝著· 910—C693

上海，中華，民十五年·3版·356面·

環球日記；錢文選著 91c—T616

上海，商務，民九年·164面·

國外遊記彙刊；姚祝萱輯． 910—Y151
上海，中華，民十四年．再版．8 册．

戰後歐遊見聞記； 914—C916
上海，商務，民十二年．再版．549 面．

英國一瞥；顧彭年譯． 914．2—K251
上海，商務，民十三年．135 面．「少年史地叢書」

德意志一瞥；鄭次川著． 9143．—C351
上海，商務，民十二年．13 面．「少年史地叢書」

德國一週；莊君著． 914．3—C916
上海，商務，民十四年．125 面．

法蘭西一瞥；顧德隆譯． 914．4—K253
上海，商務，民十五年．102 面．「少年史地叢書」

意大利一瞥；Feuuenore 原著，鄭次川譯． 914．5—F362
上海，商務，民十三年．99 面．「少年史地叢書」

新俄遊記；江亢虎著． 914．7—C504
上海，商務，民十四年．4 版．175 面．

俄羅斯一瞥；鄭次川譯． 914．7—W171
上海，商務，民十二年．124 面．

瑞典一瞥；汪今鸞譯． 914．85—W166
上海，商務，民十四年．98 面．「少年史地叢書」

比利時一瞥；陳濟芸譯． 914．93—C273
上海，商務，民十四年．107 面．「少年史地叢書」

瑞士一瞥；顧德隆譯． 914．94—K253
上海，商務，民十四年．96 面．「少年史地叢書」

希臘一瞥；Edith A. Browne 原著，周育民譯． 914．95—B816
上海，商務，民十二年．118 面．

古今遊記叢鈔；勞亦安輯． 915．1—L152
上海，中華，民十三年．12 册．

木國新遊記；張英輯． 915．1—C173
上海，商務，民九年．3 版．160 面．

新遊記彙刊；中華書局編譯所譯・　915・1—C976
上海，中華，民十五年・四版・8冊・

新遊記彙刊續編；姚祝萱輯・　915・1—Y151
上海，中華，民十四年・2版・6冊・

天下名山勝景記；王泰來著・　915・1—W158
上海，會文堂，民十七年・178面・

續天下名山勝景記；琴石山人著・　915・1—C686
上海，會文堂，民十七年・2冊・

徐霞客遊記；(明)徐宏祖著・　915・1—s478
上海，羣衆圖書公司，民十七年・4冊・

伏園遊記；孫伏園著・　915・1—s135
北京，北新，民十五年・122面・

丁格爾步行中國記；陳曾穀譯・　915・1—T348
上海，商務，民九年・188面・

直隸風土調查録；直録省視學編・　915・111—C627
上海，商務，民五年・再版・208面・

山東省一瞥；陳博文編・　915・112—C285
上海，商務，民十四年・92面・「少年史地叢書」

二十年來之膠州灣；謝開勳編・　915・112—s419
上海，中華，民九年・150面

湖北省一瞥；陳博文編・　915・131—C285
上海，商務，民十七年・64面・「少年史地叢書」

建筑漢口商場計畫書；湯震龍著・　915・131—T190
督辦漢口建筑場事宜處民十三年・126面・

蒲圻鄉土志；宋衍綿著・　915・131—s569
蒲圻教育局，民十二年・128面・

四川省一瞥；周傳儒著・　915・155—C771
上海，商務，民十五年・168面・「少年史地叢書」

雅安歷史；賈鴻基著・　915・155—C476
日新工業社，民十四年・2冊・

甘肅省一瞥；陳博文著· 915·122—C285

上海，商務，民十五年·80面·「少年史地叢書」

東三省一瞥；陳博文著· 915·16—C285

上海，商務，民十四年·再版·87面·「少年史地叢書」

東三省紀略；徐日義著· 915·16—s481

上海，商務，民四年·546面·

新廣東觀察記；李宗黄著· 915·1—L181s

上海，商務，民十一年·214面·

雲南遊記；謝彬著· 915·153—s422

上海，中華，民十五年·3版·310面·「新世紀叢書」

新疆遊記；謝彬著· 915·18—s422

上海，中華，民十二年·420面·「新世紀叢書」

黑龍江鄉土志；林傳甲著· 915·163—L316

私立奎垣學校，民二年·再版·56面·

燕晉察哈爾旅行記；侯鴻鑑著· 915·182—H241

無錫競志女學校，民十年·109面·

蒙古調查記；東方雜誌社編· 080—T860—10

上海，商務，民十四年·3版·94面·「東方文庫」

西藏調察記；東方雜誌社編· 080—T860—11

上海，商務，民十四年·3版·82面·「東方文庫」

高麗一瞥；鄭次川著· 915·2—C351

上海，商務，民十三年·64面·「少年史地叢書」

臺灣：汪洋著· 915·2—W178

上海，中華，民六年·196面·

日本一瞥；俞松笠著· 915·2—Y373

上海，商務，民十五年·106面·「少年史地叢書」

土耳其一瞥；(英)密林根原著，孟琇瑋譯· 915·6—M622

上海，商務，民十五年·132面·「少年史地叢書」

緬甸一瞥；R. J. Kely原著，汪今鸞譯· 915·92—K298

上海，商務，民十四年·111面·「少年史地叢書」

南非洲一瞥；汪今鸞著·　916·8—K537
上海，商務，民十四年·116 面·「少年史地叢書」

留美採風録；徐正鏗著·　917—s476
上海，商務，民十五年·358 面·

新大陸遊記；梁啓超著·　917·3—L251
296 面·「飲冰室叢著第十二種」

美國視察記；伍廷芳著·　917·3—W308
上海，中華，民四年·154 面·

江亢虎南遊迴想記；江亢虎著·　919·14—C504
上海，中華，民十四年·3 版·105 面·

馬來鴻雪録；黄强著·　919·1—H471
上海，商務，民十七年·上册·

菲律賓；鄭民編·　919·14—C356
上海，商務，民十四年·192 面·

南洋；夏思痛著·　919·14—H265
上海，泰東，民四年·222 面·

南洋；黄栩園著·　919·14—H475
上海，中華，民十三年·171 面·「常識叢著」

南洋旅行漫記；梁紹文著·　919·14—L163
上海，中華，民十五年·4 版·283 面·「少年中國學會叢書」

澳洲一瞥；F. Fox 原著，吴艮培譯·　919·4—F831
上海，商務，民十二年·109 面·「少年史地叢書」

南美洲一瞥；E. A. Browne 原著，周傳儒譯·　918—B816
上海，商務，民十二年·95 面·「少年史地叢書」

兩極探險記；勃魯斯原著，劉虎如譯·　919·8—B83
上海，商務，民十六年·170 面·「地理叢書」

920　傳記

中國人名大辭典；陸爾奎，方賓觀等合編·　R—920—L425

上海，商務，民十年・再版・

史傳今義；梁啓超著・ 920—L251

上海，商務，2 册・「飲冰室叢著第四種」

歷代名臣言行録；朱桓著・ 920—C824

上海，會文堂，序清嘉慶十二年・8 册・

蘇秦張儀；吕思勉著・ 920—L452

上海，中華，民十五年・八版・106 册・「學生叢書」

李白與杜甫；傳東華著・ 06・—P225—151

上海，商務，民十六年・85 面・「百科小叢書」

中國八大詩人；胡懷琛著・ 920—H405

上海，商務，民十四年・再版・106 面・「國學小叢書」

模範軍人；孫毓修著・ 920—s535

上海，商務，民十四年・4 版・6 册・

清代樸學大師列傳；支偉成著・ 980—C624

上海，泰東，民十四年・2 册・

紅花岡四烈士傳；革命紀念會編・ 920—K271

上海，民智，民十六年・54 面・

黄克强蔡松坡軼事；天懺生，冬山合編・ 960—T341

文藝編譯社、民十三年・8 版・130 面・

歷代名醫列傳；丁福保著・ 610・8—T347—920

上海，醫學書局，民二年・2 版・111 面・「丁氏醫學叢書」

科學名人傳；中國科學社編・ 610・8—T347—920

上海，中國科學社，民十三年・247 面・

世界十大成功人傳；劉麟生著・ 920—L366

上海，商務，民十五年・3 版・54 面・「職業教育叢書」

世界實業大王；董瑞椿譯・ 921—T856

上海，中華，民十三年・3 版・292 面・

近世秦西列女傳；高君珊著・ 920—B639

上海，商務，民七年・3 册・

社會改造之八大思想家；

(日)生田長江，本間久雄原著，林木等合譯·　920—s226
上海，商務，民十五年·5版·280面·「新智識叢書」
世界文學家列傳；孫俍工著·　920—s519
上海，中華，民十五年·336面·
俄國四大文學家；小説月報社編·　808—sh41—19
上海，商務，民十四年·85面·「小説月報叢刊第十九種」
但底與歌德；東方雜誌社編·　080—T860—65
上海，商務，民十四年·3版·96面·「東方文庫」
柏格森與歐根；東方雜誌社編·　080—T860—39
上海，商務，民十四年·3版·102面·「東方文庫」
美國十大富豪；盧壽籛著·　920—L406
上海，中華，民十一年·6版·76面·
愛倫該女史傳蒙臺梭利女史傳；朱元善編·　370·8—054—1·12
上海，商務，民十一年·3版·27面·「教育叢書一集十二篇」
近代名人與近代思想；司各脱原著，鍾建閎譯·　920—s083
上海，商務，民十七年·316面·「歷史叢書」

921　傳記(個人)

玄奘；孫毓修著·　921—H381
上海，商務，民十四年·7版·55面·「少年叢書」
李義山戀愛事跡考；雪林女士著·　921—H186
上海，北新，民十六年·140面·
東坡逸事續編；沈宗元著·　921—S41
上海，商務，民十五年·4版·65面·
巖嵩歷史；金嘯梅著·　921—Y226
上海，新華書局，民十二年·66面·
多爾袞軼事；楊公道著·　921—T370
中華圖書館，民八年·100面·
吳三桂軼事；楊公道著·　921—W294

中華圖書館，民八年·96 面·

年羹堯全史；上海世界書局編· 921—W220

上海，世界書局，民十年·64 面·

雍正軼事；楊公道著· 921—Y129

中華圖書館，民八年·再版·104 面·

慈禧寫照記；(美)卡爾女士原著，陳霆鋭譯· 921—T910

上海，中華，民五年·3 版·214 面·

戴東原：二百年生日論文集；梁啓超等合編· 921—T131

北京，晨報社出版部，民十三年·20 面·「晨報社叢書十三種」

龍峯老人年譜；唐廷愷著· 921—T213

民十五年·56 面·「唐園叢書」

李鴻章軼事；楊公道著· 921—L185

中華圖書館，民八年·再版·98 面·

西學東漸記；容閎原著，徐鳳石，惲鐵樵合譯· 921—Y80

上海，商務，民四年·118 面·

袁世凱全傳； 921—Y421

上海，文藝編譯社，130 面·

蘇曼殊年譜及其他；柳亞子，柳無忘合編· 921—s462

民十七年·

李純；隱廬編· 921—L181

北京，國民圖書館，民九年·再版·109 面·

吳佩孚歷史；東魯逸民著· 921—W293

上海，新民，民九年·再版·109 面·

回憶；朱謙之著· 921—C821

上海，現代書局，民十七年·86 面·

伊略脱傳；朱元善編· 370·8—C544—1·11

上海，商務，民十一年·3 版·46 面·「教育叢書一集十一編」

理嘉圖；劉秉麟編· 080—P225—105

上海，商務，民十五年·70 面·「百科小叢書第一百零五種」

哥倫布；劉麟生編· 080—P225—20

上海，商務，民十二年・再版・43 面・「百科小叢書第二十種」

荷馬；王希和編・ 080—P225—46

上海，商務，民十三年・52 面・「百科小叢書第四十六種」

盧梭；范壽康編・ 080—P225—102

上海，商務，民十五年・60 面・「百科小叢書第一百零二種」

亞丹斯密；劉秉麟編・ 080—P225—104

上海，商務，民十五年・126 面・「百科小叢書第一百零四種」

柏拉圖；范壽康編・ 080—P225—109

上海，商務，民十五年・58 面・「百科小叢書第一百零九種」

包以爾；小説月報社編・ 809—sn41—34

上海，商務，民十四年・59 面・「小説月報叢刊第三十四種」

梭羅古勃；小説月報社編・ 800—sh41—28

上海，商務，民十四年・101 面・「小説月報叢刊第二十八種」

瑞典詩人赫滕斯頓；小説月報社編・ 800—sh41—23

上海，商務，民十四年・64 面・「小説月報叢刊第二十三種」

法朗士傳；小説月報社編・ 808—h41—38

上海，商務，民十四年・76 面・「小説月報叢刊第三十八種」

莫泊三傳；東方雜誌社編・ 080—T860—66

上海，商務，民十四年・3 版・76 面・「東方文庫」

克魯泡特金；東方雜誌社編・ 080—T860—40

上海，商務，民十四年・3 版・61 面・「東方文庫」

郁根傳：德國大哲學家；錢智修編・ 3708・8—C544—3・12

上海，商務，民六年・84 面・「教育叢書第三集十二篇」

裴斯泰洛齊傳；朱元善編・ 370・8—C544—2・12

上海，商務，民十一年・再版・41 面・「教育叢書二集十二篇」

安徒生傳；顧均正編・ 921—An23

上海，開明，民十七年・221 面・

畢斯麥；林萬里編・ 921—B542

上海，商務，民十五年・19 版・59 面・「少年叢書」

克林威爾；錢智修編・ 921—C88

上海，商務，民十四年·6版·57面·「少年叢書」

達爾文；錢智修編· 921—D259

上海，商務，民十四年·6版·58面·「少年叢書」

富蘭克林；孫毓修編· 921—F854

上海，商務，民十四年·8版·42面·「少年叢書」

甘地小傳；Romain Rolland 原著，謝頌羔，米星如合譯· 921—G151

上海，美以美會全國書報部，民十四年·73面·

加里波的；林萬裏編· 921—G182

上海，商務，民十五年·12版·58面·「少年叢書」

華盛頓；林萬里編· 921—W277

上海，商務，民十二年·17版·58面·「少年叢書」

托爾斯泰傳；(英)Charles Sarolea 原著，張邦銘等合譯· 951—T588

上海，泰東，民十二年·3版·143面·

前德皇威廉二世自傳；王揖唐譯· 921—W649

上海，商務，民十三年·再版·214面·

太戈爾；楊甸葛，鍾餘蔭合譯· 921—T129

上海，新文化，民十三年·　面·

太戈爾傳；鄭振鐸譯編· 921—T129

上海，商務，民十四年·152面·「文學研究會叢書」

易卜生研究；劉大杰編· 921—I67

上海，商務，民十七年·146面·「文學叢書」

唐德傳；(德)卡爾弗爾崙德原著，商承祖，羅　階合譯· 921—K135

上海，中華，民十一年·288面·「哲學叢書」

林肯；錢智修編· 921—L638

上海，商務，民十四年·9版·46面·「少年叢書」

雕刻家米西盎則羅；李金髮編· 921—M582

上海，商務，民十五年·69面·「文學研究會叢書」

拿破崙本紀；(英)洛加德原著，林紓，魏易合譯· 921—N162

上海，商務，民十二年·3版·380面·

大彼得；林萬里編· 921—P441

上海，商務，民十四年・15 版・60 面・「少年叢書」
興登堡成敗鑑；(法)蒲哈德原著，林紓，林騶合譯・　921—s438
上海，商務，民十一年・125 面・
蘇格拉底；錢智修編・　921—S014
上海，商務，民十四年・6 版・43 面・「少年叢書」

930　古代史

埃及小史；James Boikie 原著，高仲洽譯・　932—B149
上海，商務，民十四年・116 面・「少年史地叢書」
羅馬小史；高仲洽編・　937—K366
上海，商務，民十四年・108 面・「少年史地叢書」
羅馬社會史；喜渥恩編・　937—H252
上海，商務，民十三年・81 面・「少年史地叢書」
希臘小史；高君韋編・　938—K166
上海，商務，民十四年・104 面・「少年史地叢書」

940　歐洲史

西洋表解；上海科學書局編輯所編・　080—s155—940
上海，科學書局，清光緒三十二年・72 面・「表解叢書」
增訂西洋史表解；上海科學書局編輯所編・　080—s155—940
上海，科學書局，清宣統三年・2 册・「表解叢書」
西洋史；陳衡哲編・　940—C275
上海，商務，民十四年・4 版・2 册・
西洋史要；(日)小川銀次郎原著，樊炳清，薩端合譯・　940—s410
上海，商務，民三年・再版・179 面・

西史紀要；伍光建編· 940—W308
上海，商務，民七年·2册·

近世歐洲史；何炳松編· 940·2—H209
上海，商務，民十五年·再版·417面·

西洋近百年史；李泰棻編· 940·2—L198
上海，商務，民十五年·5版·2册·

外史鱗爪；梁啓超編· 940—L251
上海，商務，民三年·3册·「飲冰室叢書」

歐洲文藝復興史；蔣方震編· 940·21—T563
上海，商務，民十一年·149面·「共學社史學叢書」

文藝復興大史；陳衡哲編· 080—225—107
上海，商務，民十五年·60面·「百科小叢書第一百零七種」

歐戰發生史；東方雜誌社編· 080—T35—1
上海，商務，民十四年·3版·96面·「東方文庫」

大戰雜話；東方雜誌社編· 080—T860—5
上海，商務，民十四年·3版·112面·「東方文庫」

世界大戰全史；張乃燕編· 940·3—C166
上海，商務，民十五年·「686」面·

歐洲和議後之經濟；(英)坎斯原著，陶孟和沈性仁合譯· 940·3—K522
上海，新年青社，民九年·219面·「新青年叢書」

世界最近之局勢，世界大戰；孟憲章編· 940·3—M211
北京師範大學史地學社，民十四年·254面·

世界最近之局勢，巴黎和會；孟憲章編· 940·2—M211
北京師範大學，民十五年·172面·

美國總統威爾遜參戰演説；蔣夢麟譯· 940·3—M699m
上海，商務，民八年·5版·63面·

美國總統威爾遜和議演説；錢智修譯· 940·3—W699m
上海，商務，民八年·94面·

英漢合璧威爾遜和議演説；錢智修譯· 940·4—w699Y
上海，商務，民八年·204面·

凡爾登戰記；(英)太晤士報社編，張庭英譯· 940·3—M482
上海，商務，民十二年·再版·195面·「時代叢書」

蘇格蘭小史；(英)密頓原著，顧德隆譯· 941—M698
上海，商務，民十五年·105面·「少年史地叢書」

英國現代史；賀昌羣編· 942—H181
上海，商務，民十七年·100面·「新時代史地叢書」

戰後的德國；陳彬龢編· 940—G285
上海，世界，民十六年·88面·

德國富强之由來；朱章寶編· 943—s821
上海，商務，民十四年·6版·46面·「新智識叢書」

開戰時之德意志；(英)陶安原著，黄理中譯· 943—T245
上海，商務，民五年·再版·138面·「新智識叢書之三」

德皇作戰計畫書；黄中譯· 943·08—W67
上海，中華，民五年·182面·

德皇外妾自述記；陳仲子，黄中合譯· 943·08—C270
上海，開明社，民六年·130面·

法國現代史；金兆梓編· 944—C662
上海，商務，民十七年·131面·「新時代史地叢書」

法蘭西小史；馬紹良譯· 944—M121
上海，商務，民十四年·86面·「少年史地叢書」

法國革命史；徐壽齡編· 944—S481
上海，商務，民十五年·再版·129面·「少年史地叢書」

法蘭西新史；左舜生編· 944—T682
上海，啓智，民十七年·214面·

俄羅斯經濟狀況；劉炳麟編· 080—P225—80
上海，商務，民十四年·55面·「百科小叢書第八十種」

俄國大革命紀略；東方雜誌社編· 080—T860—S
上海，商務，民十四年·3版·82面·「東方文庫」

蘇俄改建論；章淵若編· 947—C194

上海，泰東，民十七年・227 面・「社會叢書之二」

新俄羅斯；(日)川上後彦原著，王揖唐譯・ 949—C901

上海，商務，民十二年・139 面・

俄宮見聞記；(瑞士)伊里雅原著，李秉之譯・ 947—TI129

上海，亞東，民十四年・168 面・

新俄回想録；・ 947—S089

序民十三年・284 面・

俄羅斯的革命經過；蘇格羅夫原著，朱應會譯・ 947・08—S460

上海，太平洋，民十七年・532 面・

新土耳其；柳克述編・ 949・6—L381

上海，商務，民十六年・44 面・

土耳其革命史；柳克述編・ 949・6—L381

上海，商務，民十七年・146 面・「新時代史地叢書」

950 東亞史

東洋史表解；上海科學書局編輯所編・ 080—S155—950

上海科學書局，清光緒三十二年・60 面・「表解叢書」

中國與暹羅；稽翥青編・ 950—C388

上海，商務，民十三年・277 面・

東亞各國史，中學教科書；傅運森編・ 950—F247

上海，商務，民十三年・19 版・70 面・

東亞各國史參考書；傅運森，丁桂英合編・ 950—I247

上海，商務，民十一年・4 版・255 面・

中國史乘中未詳諸國考證；希勒格原著，馮承鈞譯・ 950—SCh36

上海，商務，民十七年・196 面・「尚志學會叢書」

東洋史；王桐齡編・ 950—W15

上海，商務，民十五年・3 版・2 冊・

951　本國歷史

中國歷史研究法；梁啓超編·　951—L251
上海，商務，民十五年·229面·

本國史；趙玉森編·　951—C220P
上海，商務，民十一年·

新著本國史；趙玉森編·　951—C220s
上海，商務，民十四年·4版·2册·

初級本國歷史；金兆梓編·　951—C662
上海，中華，民十五年·18版·2册·

本國史，現代初中教科書；顧頡剛，王鍾麒合編·　951—K248
上海，商務，民十四年·4版·3册·

本國史；陸光宇編·　951—L428
上海，商務，民十四年·216面·

白話本國史；吕思勉編·　951—L452Ph
上海，商務，民十二年·4册·

本國史，高級中學教科書；吕思勉編·　951—L452Ph
上海，商務，民十四年·3版·313面·

本國史；吕思勉編·　951—L452Ph
上海，商務，民十三年·2版·313面·

本國史；王桐齡編·　951—W159
北京，文化書社，民十五年·3册·

近代史讀本；印水心編·　951—Y288
上海，世界，民十五年·3册·

歷史講義；上海交通大學學生會義務學校編·　951—Y472
上海，民智，民十二年·24面·

中國文化史；顧康伯編·　951·001—K249
上海，泰東，民十三年·2册·

湖西遺事；彭孫貽編· 951·072—P278

上海，商務，民六年·16頁「痛史第二十二種」

明季稗史初編 951·072—W262

上海，商務，民元年·6册·

明季稗史續編； 951·072—T699

上海，商務，民五年·3册·

甲申朝事小紀；抱陽生編· 951·08—P194

上海，商務，民五年·10册·「痛史第二十一種」

清史要略；陳懷編· 951·08—C275

鉛印本

清史纂要；劉法曾編· 951408—L359

上海，中華，民四年·3版·202面·

清代通史；蕭一山編· 951·08—S388

北京，國立北京大學，民十二年·2册·

清朝全史；(日)稻葉君山原著，但燾譯· 951·088—T222

上海，中華，民十三年·4册·

清史講義；汪榮寶，許國英合編· 951·08—W178

上海，商務，民十二年·5版·2册·

中國近百年史資料；左舜生輯· 951·08—T682

上海，中華，民十五年·3版·2册·

乾隆英使覲見記；(英)馬戛爾原著，劉半農譯· 951·081—M112

上海，中華，民六年·209面·「清外史叢刊」

清室外紀；(英)濮蘭德，白克好原著，陳冷汰，陳詔先合譯· 951·08—P397

太平天國史科第一集；程演生編· 951·083—C349

北京大學出版部，民十五年·119面·

太平天國外紀；(英)林利原著，孟憲承譯· 951·03—L323

上海，商務，民四年·3册·

太平天國野史；凌善清編· 951·083—L341

上海，中華，民十五年·3版·

太平軍軼事；楊公道編・ 951・083—Y129
中華圖書館，民七年・再版・88 面・
庚子使館被圍記；
(英)樸笛南姆威爾原著，陳冷汰，陳詒先合譯・ 951・087—P399
上海，中華，民六年・268 面・「清外史叢刊」
新中國；H. B. Grapbill 原著，朱有光譯・ 951—G795
上海，商務，民十七年・344 面・
中國改造問題；東方雜誌社編・ 080—T860—15
上海，商務，民十四年・3 版・95 面・「東方文庫」
民國十週紀事本末；許指嚴編・ 951・09—H376
上海，交通圖書館，民十一年・679 面・
中華民國開國史；谷鍾秀編・ 951・09—K255
上海，泰東，民十五年・5 版・208 面・
共和關鍵録；觀渡廬編・ 951・09—K296
上海，著易堂，民元年・400 面・
辛亥革命史；東方雜誌社編・ 080—T860—1
上海，商務，民十四年・3 版・74 面・「東方文庫」
帝制運動始末記；東方雜誌社編・ 080—T860—2
上海，商務，民十四年・3 版・114 面・「東方文庫」
壬戌政變記；東方雜誌社編・ 080—T860—3
上海，商務，民十四年・3 版・104 面・「東方文庫」
軍務院攷實；兩廣都司令部參謀聽編・ 951・09—L268
上海，商務，民五年・再版・
癸亥政變紀略；劉楚湘編・ 951・09—L356
上海，泰東，民十三年・3 版・268 面・
新編民國史；劉炳榮編・ 951・09—L372
上海，太平洋書店，民十五年・
歐戰後之中國；徐世昌編・ 951・09—S481
上海，中華，民十年・62 頁・
外蒙古近世史；陳崇祖編・ 951・7—C270

上海，商務，民十一年·230面·

蒙古鑑；卓宏謀編· 951·7—C763

北京，卓宅，民十二年·3版·466面·

蒙古志；姚明輝著· 951·7—Y162

上海，圖書公司，清光緒三十三年·348面·

日本研究叢書提要；陳德徵著· 952—C263

上海，世界書局，民十七年·

日本研究叢書；陳德徵主編· 952—C269

上海，世界書局，民十七年·4册·

日本民族性研究；東方雜誌社編· 080—T860—14

上海，商務，民十四年·3版·80面·「東方文庫」

日本小史；滕柱譯· 952—F497

上海，商務，民十四年·90面·「少年史地叢書」

日本論；戴季陶編· 952—T121

上海，民智，民十七年·再版·176面·

臺灣革命史；漢人編· 952—H130

上海，泰東，民十五年·169面·

甘地主義；東方雜誌社編· 080—T860—41

上海，商務，民十四年·3版·68面·「東方文庫」

印度史綱；劉炳榮編· 954—L372

上海，太平洋，民十五年·172面·

印度小史；滕柱譯· 954—T275

上海，商務，民十四年·10面·「少年史地叢書」

波斯問題；(日)憲籐原治原著，鄭次川合譯· 955—H22

北京，公民書局，民十年·112面·「公民叢書」

猶太人與猶太主義；吳義田編· 956·3—W285

上海，世界，民十六年·68面·

暹羅；(日)山口武原著，陳清泉譯· 959·3—s148

上海，商務，民十三年·再版·227面·

鐵蹄下之新嘉波；陳柏年編· 959·5—C285

中國經濟研究會，民十五年・118 面・

加拿大小史；滕柱譯・　971—T275

上海，商務，民十五年・117 面・「少年史地叢書」

菲利濱獨立戰史；商務印書館編譯所編・　991・4—s162

上海，商務，民二年・3 版・142 面・

補 編

（自本編付印後未及印成之前一月之中，本館復購到現代書籍六百餘種，因附于此）

000 總記

崔東壁集；許嘯天句讀． 001·86—T735
上海，羣學社，民十七年·2冊·

四庫全書問答；任啓珊著． 010—J—17
上海，啓智印務公司，民十七年·334面·

圖書館組織與管理；洪有豐著． 020—H523
上海，商務，民十五年·260面·

圖書館學ABC；沈學植著． 020—S214
上海，世界，民十七年·130面·

學校圖書館學；杜定友著． 020—T768
上海，商務，民十七年·173面·

童話論集；趙景深著． 028·5—C201
上海，開明，民十六年·186面·「文學週報社叢書」

風先生和兩太太；（法）保羅繆塞原者，顧均正譯． 028·5—M976
上海，開明，民十六年·144面·「世界少年文學叢刊」

國語文類選；朱毓魁輯． 039·51—C839
上海，中華，民十年·6版·4冊·

古史辨；顧頡剛著． 040—K248

北京，樸社出版經理部，民十五年・3版・286面・

國學月報彙刊第一集；北京述學社編・　040—P223

北京，樸社出版經理部，民十七年・274面・

100　哲學

法蘭西學術史略第一集；李璜譯・　100—B454

上海，亞東，民十九年・118面・「少年中國學會叢書」

西洋哲學ABC；謝頌羔著・　100—S423

上海，世界，民十七年・86面・

新主義評論；陳本文輯・　104—C285

上海，民治，民十七年・2册・

海天集，北大一九二五哲學系畢業同學紀念刊；楊廉輯・　105—Y130

上海，北新，民十五年・342面・

人格；(印)太谷爾原著，景梅九，張墨池合譯・　126—T129

上海，光明，民十六年・3版・150面・

精神與身體神經健全法；鄒德謹譯・　131—T697

上海，商務，民六年・再版・33面・「通俗教育叢書」

强健身心法；董蘭伊譯・　131—T854

上海，中華，民十五年・10版・128面・「衛生叢書之一」

150　心理學

心理學ABC；郭任遠著・　150—K423

上海，世界，民十七年・97面・

行爲心理學大意；(美)華村原著，謝循初譯・　150—W334

上海，中華書報流通處，民十七年・149面・

變態心理學 ABC；黄維榮著· 158—H481
上海·世界，民十七年·110面·

170 倫理學

人生底開端；陳德徵著· 170—C288
上海，民智，民十六年·再版·250面·

新論；劉彦和著· 170—L397
上海，泰東，民十六年·133面·

國民之修養；陸費達輯· 170—L426
上海，中華，民十一年·再版·40面·

人生勝利術彙編；(美)波臨登原著，青年協會書報部譯· 170—P974
上海，青年協會書報部，民十一年·3版·82面·

人生哲學；舒新城著· 170—S313
上海，中華，民十四年·3版·405面·

曾文正公學案；龍夢蓀編· 170—T526
上海，商務，民十四年·454面·

俟解；王船山著· 170—W136
上海，泰東，民十一年·50面·

國民必讀；王鳳喈等合編· 170—W140
上海，商務，民十一年·65面·

人生觀 ABC；張東蓀著· 171—C171
上海，世界，民十七年·117面·

顔氏家訓；費有容著· 173—Y233
上海，羣學社，民十四年·225面

中國婦女美談；盧壽籛著· 173·5—L406
上海，中華，民十年·3版·300面·「女學叢書之一」

實業家之修養；陸費逵著· 174—L426
上海，中華，民十年·5版·46面·

181・1　中國哲學

節本明儒家案；姚宗義著・　181・17—H471
上海，商務・2冊・「飲冰室業著第六種」

高似孫子略；高似孫著・　181・1—K175
北平，樸社出版經理部，民十七年・初版・100面・

李石岑講演集；李石岑著・　181・1—L196
上海，商務・民三年・

諸子辨；(明)宋濂著・　181・1—S561
北京，樸社出版經理部・民十五年・48面・

新序説苑；莊適注・　181・102—L361
上海，商務・民十六年・140面・「學生國學叢書」

孟子事實録；崔東壁著・　181・102—T735
北京，文化學社，民十七年・53面・

朱子學派；謝无量著・　181・163—S425
上海，中華・民七年・202面・「學生叢書之一」

人的生活；(日)武者小路實篤原著，毛詠棠，毛宗武合譯・　181・2—W302
上海，中華・民十四年・4版・194面・「新文化叢書」

人生之實現；(印度)太谷兒著・　181・4—T129
上海，泰東・162面・「新人叢書」

200　宗教

宗教學ABC；謝頌羔著・　200—S423
上海，世界，民十七年・111面・

青年會幹事養成實習計劃第一二　267・3—T665

現代佛教；(日)山崎精華編・　294—S148
東京，大雄閣，昭和三年・188面・

300 社會科學

人類的歷史；陳翰笙著· 300—C275
上海，北新，民十六年·再版·76 面·

社會學的基本知識；陳毅夫著· 300—C276
南京，南京印書館，民十七年·124 面·

社會科學概論；郭任遠書· 308—K423
上海，商務，民十七年·297 面·

社約論考；張奚若著· 080—P225—108
上海，商務，民十五年·80 面·「百科小叢書第 108 種」

社會學 ABC；孫本文著· 301—S526
上海，世界，民十七年·122 面·

文化與社會；孫本文著 301—S526W
上海，啓智書局，民十七年·150 面·

人道；盧信著· 304—L306
上海，泰東，民十五年·14 版·97 面·

社會結構學五講；羅素講演· 304—R911
北京，晨報社，民十年·104 面·

學術演講録第一二期；松江暑期講習會編· 304—S571
上海，新文化書社，民十三年·180 面·

中華民國拒毒會第一年度報告；中華民國拒毒會編· 306—C976
民十三年·156 面·

生育節制法；(美) Mrs Margaret Sanger 原著，中華節育研究社譯· 312—Sa58
民十一年·26 面·

320 政治學

商君書之研究；支偉成編· 320—S162

上海，泰東，民十四年·78 面·

建國銓真；徐樹錚著·　320—S481

上海，公民，民十四年·103 面·

英漢合璧平民政治的基本原理；(美)芮恩施原著，羅志希譯·　320·1—R276

上海，商務，民十四年·4 版·341 面·

現代中國政治；王恒著·　320·951—W142

上海，啓智，民十七年·256 面·

現代三大帝國主義；(法)布立厄耳原著，丁作韶譯·　080—P225—126

上海，商務，民十六年·50 面·「百科小叢書第一百二十六種」

霸術；(意)馬加維理原著，伍光建譯·　321·03—M184

上海，商務，民十四年·64 面·

世界共和國政要；商務印書館編譯所譯·　321·8—S162

上海，商務，民元年·再版·216 面·

革命與進化；邵可侶原著，袁振英譯·　323·2—F531

香港，受匡出版部，民十七年·84 面·

和平運動討論大綱；劉恩等合輯·　323·2—L356

上海，青年協會，民十五年·130 面·

327　外交

戰後列國大勢與世界外交；張介石編·　327—C160

上海，中華，民十六年·136 面·

國民外交常識；陳耀東著·　327—C292

上海，新月書店，民十七年·266 面·

近百年國際政治史略；馮節著·　327—F216

上海，商務，民十七年·67 面·

327·51　外交—中國

怎樣取消不平等條約；浙江省黨務指導委員會宣傳部編·　327·51—C252

浙江省黨務指導委員會宣傳部印·56 面·「宣傳部叢書之六」

中日外交史；陳博文著· 327·51—C285

上海，商務，民十七年·初版·166面·「新時代史地叢書」

經濟侵略與中國；高爾松，高爾柏合著· 327·51—K167

中國經濟研究會·328面·

列强在中國之勢力；李長傳著· 327·51—L182

上海，大東，民十七年·94面·

不平等條約概論；柳克述著· 327·51—L381

上海，泰東，民十五年·235面·

日本併吞滿蒙論；細野繁勝原著，王慕甯譯· 327·51—S366

上海，太平洋書店，民十七年·218面·

山東問題與國際聯盟；徐東藩著· 327·51—S182

山東外交協會，民九年·32面·

中國存亡問題；孫文著· 327·51—S532

上海，民智，民十七年·120面·

日本蹂躪山東痛史；唐巨川著· 327·51—T201

上海，大東，民十七年·62面·

帝國主義侵略中國的趨勢和變遷概論；汪精衛著· 327·51—W175

上海，青年愛國書店，民十四年·116面·

中國外交關係史；(英)懷德原著，王峨孫譯· 327·51—W624

上海，商務，民十七年·154面·

民國政黨史；謝彬著· 329·09—S422

上海，學術研究會總會，民十六年·242面·「學術研究會叢書之十二」

330 經濟學

商業理財學；(英)揭　原著，商務印書館譯· 330—G352

上海，商務，清光緒三十三年·83面·

馬克思主義經濟學；(日)河上肇原著，温盛光譯· 330—H214

上海，啓智，民十七年·132面·「社會科學叢書第二編」

資本論解説；(德)考茨基原著，戴季陶譯·　330—K168
上海，民智，民十六年·308面·

經濟學ABC；李權時著·　330—L182
上海，世界，民十七年·123面·

經濟學，新學制高級中學教科書；劉秉麟編·　330—L372
上海，商務，民十七年·385面·

新經濟學；(德)羅撒盧森堡原著，陳壽僧譯·　330—L979
中國新文社，民十七年·再版·314面·

資本主義與戰爭；(日)松下芳男原著，徐文亮譯·　330—S571
上海，啓智，民十七年·160面·「社會科學叢書第三編」

原富；(英)斯密亞丹原著，嚴復譯·　330—M51
清光緒二十八年·258頁

經濟地理與國際問題；韓亮仙編·　30·1—H122
上海，民智，民十七年·390面·

經濟統計；上海銀行週報社編·　330·2—Y275
民十二，三，四，年份·3册·

經濟狀況與政治思想；伏廬筆記·　330·4—R911
上海，商務，民十五年·再版·84面·「羅素演講録之二」

馬克斯經濟概念；朱應琪，朱應會合譯·　330·5—C945
上海，泰東，民十七年·96面·

先秦政治經濟思想史；甘乃光著·　330·9—K120
上海，商務，民十五年·138面·「國學小叢書」

現代世界經濟大勢；(俄)庫里塞爾原著，耿濟之譯·
上海，中華，民十五年·再版·234面·「新文化叢書」

民眾世界史要；劉叔琴編·　330·9—L373
上海，開明，民十七年·初版·145面·

331　勞工問題

蘇俄治下的勞働反對派；陳彬龢著·　331—C285

上海，共和，民十六年 · 71 面 ·

生產論；李權時著 · 331—L182

上海，東南書店，民十七年 · 152 面 ·「經濟叢書」

消費論；李權時著 · 331—L182

上海，東南書店，民十七年 · 138 面 ·「經濟叢書」

英美勞働運動史；李大年編 · 331—L199

上海，學術研究會總會，民十六年 · 初版 · 298 面 ·「該會叢書之十五」

工業政策；菲里波維原著，馬君武譯 · 33—P538

上海，中華，民十一年 · 332 面 ·

經濟論集；姚仲拔著 · 332 · 1—Y151

上海，銀行週報社，民十一年 · 170 面 ·

銀行年鑑；銀行週報社編 · 332 · 1—Y275

上海，銀行週報社，民十一年 · 再版 · 266 面 ·

鑛業條例通釋；歐陽瀚存編 · 332 · 41—S170

上海，商務，民十三年 · 97 面 ·

耕者要有其田；嚴仲達著 · 333—Y212

上海，民智，民十七年 · 86 面 ·

334　合作主義

各國合作事業概況；朱樸著 · 334—C833

上海，中國合作學社，民十七年 · 初版 · 26 面 ·「合作小叢書歷史之部二」

世界合作運動鳥瞰；（法）CharLes Gie 原著，王世穎譯 · 334—G361

上海，合作學社，民十七年 · 初版 · 17 面 ·「合作小叢書歷史之部一」

合作原理；壽勉成著 · 334—S302

上海，中國合作學社，民十七年 · 初版 · 28 面 ·「合作小叢書總論之部一」

合作法規；壽勉成著 · 334—S302

上海，中國合作學社，民十七年 · 80 面 ·

合作主義通論；王世穎著 · 334—W155

上海，世界，民十六年 · 62 面 ·

合作商店實施法；王世穎著· 334·6—W157
上海，中國合作學社，民十七年·初版·48面·「合作小叢書實施之部一」

世界社會主義運動概況；陳宗熙編· 335—C287
上海，北新，民十七年·98面·

336　財政學

歐戰財政經要；陳燦編· 336—C289
上海，商務，民十一年·139面·

財政學；黄可權輯· 336—H477
上海，羣益，民元年·3版·282面·

財政學新論；(日)馬場鍈一原著，李祚輝譯· 336—M112
上海，太平洋，民十七年·24面·

340　法律

法學通論；(日)織田萬原著，劉崇佑譯· 340—C625
上海，商務，民二年·12版·251面·

法制淺説；許企謙編· 310—H369
上海，中華，民八年·再版·44面·「通俗教育叢書之一」

法制經濟通論；(日)户水寛人等原著，阿燏時等合譯· 310—H369
上海，商務，民二年·8版·887面·

法制問答；(日)岡松參太郎著· 343—K156
東京，吉川弘文館，明治三十七年·122面·

國際關係論；(英)勃萊士原著，鍾建閎譯· 341—B843
上海，商務，民十三年·270面·

國際條約大全；商務印書館編譯所編· 341·2—S162
上海，商務，民十四年·4版·970面

新譯國際私法；(日)中村進午原著，袁希鐮譯· 341·5—C978
上海，中國圖書公司，清光緒三十三年·292面·

法學通論表解總論；胡顧生著· 080—S155—432
上海，科學書局，民元年·46面·「表解叢書」
……各論前一册·
……各論後一册·

中華民國憲法；民十二年· S42·51—C976

刑法學總論；鄭衛元覺著· 343—K429
上海，會文堂書局，民十七年·再版·2册·「法學叢書之一」

罪與罰；(美)胡黛蓮女士原著，袁振英譯· 343·2—D357
香港，受匡出版部，民十七年·38面·

中華民國刑法；王寵惠編· 343·51—W137
上海，民智，民十七年·174面·

國民政府現行法規；國民政府法制局編· 345·1—K435
法政學社，民十七年·再版·4册·

遺產之廢除；(美)黎特原著，潘公展譯· 347·6—R22
上海，中華，民十四年·312面·「新文化叢書」

惺存遺著；陶保霖著· 347·01—T248
上海，商務，民十一年·2册·

中國古代法理學；王振先著· 347·09—W137
上海，商務，民十四年·65面·「國學小叢書」

九朝律考；程樹德著· 347·09—C345
上海，商務，民十六年·2册·

國民政府修正民刑事訴訟律大全；張恒編· 347·9—C155
上海，校經山房，民十七年·4册·

法國六法；商務印書館編譯所譯· 349·44—S162
上海，商務，民二年·897面·

中華民國的內閣；章熊著· 350·951—C181
古城書社編譯所，民十七年·初版·134面·

352　地方行政

地方自治講義：廣東地方自治；中國一内務部編·　352—C771
上海，泰東，176 面·

地方自治講義：第二種市町村制，第三種憲法訊論；
朱德權，陳登山合譯·　352—C837
湖北地方自治研究社，清光緒三十四年·313 面·

官幕必攜縣政全書；許天醉等合輯·　352—H377
上海，政藝合作社，民十七年·5 版·12 册·

地方自治制講義；雷奮編·　352—L472
上海，中國圖書公司，清宣統元年·再版·36 面·
「江蘇教育總會附設法政講習所講義之一」

地方自治講義：第一種府縣郡制；沈澤生編·　352—S211
湖北地方自治研究社，清光緒三十四年·241 面·

新廣東觀察記；李宗黄著·　352·051—L181
上海，商務，民十一年·214 面·

市政全書；陸丹林編·　352·1—L433
上海，道路月刊社，民十七年·再版·1410 面·

市政學綱要；董修甲著·　352·1—T856
上海，商務，民十六年·524 面·「政法叢書」

都市論 ABC；楊哲明著·　352·1—Y121
上海，世界，民十七年·112 面·

市憲議；董修甲著·　352·11—T856
上海，新月書店，民十七年·172 面·

建筑漢口新村計劃大綱；　352·15—C601
民十七年·14 面·

漢口新村合作章程；武漢市社會局編·　352·15—H130
民十七年·30 面·

新俄羅斯；(日)川上俊彦原著，王揖唐譯·　354·47—C907

上海，商務，民十二年·139面·

軍隊應用數量之參考；劉繼屏編· 355—L352

漢口，民智書局，民十七年·160面·

孫子十家註：袁韜壺標點；孫濱著· 355·01—S319

上海，掃葉山房，民十五年·下册·

列强青年之軍事預備教育；中央陸軍軍官學校教授部編· 355·07—C975

軍事雜誌社，民十七年·302面·

軍事學術大全；劉炎編· 355·08—L379

上海，真美書社，民十七年·2册·

野戰砲兵射擊問答；民四年·120面· 358—Y197

日本赤十字社發達史；(日)川侯馨一著· 361—C900

日本赤十字社，大正六年·5版·680面·

童子軍良伴；杜定友編· 369·43—T768

上海，商務，民十七年·158面·

370 教育學

學習心理；(美)科爾文原著，黄公覺譯· 370·15—C725

北京高等師範出版社，民十一年·334面·

教育心理學；廖世承編· 370·15—L282

上海，中華，民十四年·3版·494面·「教育叢書」

教育心理的實驗；(美)斯達奇原著；戴應觀譯· 370·15—St28

上海，商務，民十一年·210面·「尚志學會叢書」

教育心理學導言；(美)史屈朗原著，朱定鈞，張繩祖合譯· 370·15—St88

上海，商務，民十四年·279面·「師範叢書」

教育論；斯賓塞原著，任鴻雋譯· 370·4—Sp33

上海，商務，民十二年·127面·

全國教育會議報告；中華民國大學院編· 370·63—c976

上海，商務，民十七年·782面

近代中國留學史；舒新城編· 370·951—S313
上海，商務，民十六年·300面·「教育叢書」

改良私塾法；方瀏生著· 371·3—F167
上海，中華，民五年·再版·62面·

個别作業與道爾頓制；(英)林勤原著，舒新城譯· 371·3—L989
上海，中華，民十五年·236面·「教育叢書」

青年與職業；王志莘編· 371·42—W137
上海，商務，民十三年·再版·56面·「職業修養叢書」

兒女教育貯金法；(日)赤川菊村原著，王駿聲譯· 37·6—s641
上海，商務，民十一年·再版·125面·

測驗概要；廖世承，陳鶴琴合編· 372·102—L282
上海，商務，民十四年·348面·「師範叢書」

兒童游戲；王伍，屠元禮合編· 372·2—w16
上海，商務，民五年·再版·70面·

各種常識問答；湖南五育勵進協會編· 374—H4321
長沙，荷花池南華書社，民十五年·再版·2册·

時間經濟法；蕭子昇著· 374—s386
上海，商務，民十四年·再版·97面·「通俗教育叢書」

婦女修養談；謝无量著· 376—s425
上海，中華，民九年·3版·206面·「女學叢書之一」

道德教育論；蔣拙誠編· 377—T561
上海，商務，民八年·90面·

大學之行政；(美)伊利亞原著，謝冰譯· 378·1—EL42
上海，商務，民十七年·96面·

留英須知；農勁公譯· 378·42—F811
上海，别發洋行，民十年·51面·

全民教育制度的演進；(美)吉德原著，王克仁譯· 379—J884
上海，民智，民十七年·再版·130面·

社會教育概説；馬宗榮著· 379—M119
上海，商務，民十四年·116面·「學術彙刊」

英美教育近著摘要；官廉等合編． 379—w226
上海，商務，民十三年．430 面

黃炎培考察教育日記；黃炎培著． 979．51—H189
上海，商務，民十一年．3 版．

收回教育權運動；舒新城著． 379．51—s313
上海，中華，民十六年．116 面．

中國教育改造；陶知行著． 379．51—T245
上海，亞東圖書館，民十七年．214 面．

一個小學十年努力紀；中央大學實驗小學校編． 379．514—c979

上海求學指南；王永禮，柴福　合編． 379．514—W163
上海，天一，民十一年．3 册．

商人寶鑑；張士傑編． R—380．3—C170
上海，商務，民十一年．5 版．865 面．

中國商戰失敗史；黃炎培，龐淞合編． 380．951—H489
上海，商務，民六年．220 面．

390　風俗禮節

婚喪禮雜説；張鴻來著． 390—C156
北京，文化學社，民十七年．初版．74 面．

392．3　家庭問題

中國過渡時代的家庭；李兆民著． 392．3—L181
上海，廣學會，民十四年．122 面．

中國之家庭問題；潘光旦著． 392．3—P154
上海，新月書店；民十七年．324 面．

392．5　婚姻問題

最新結婚學；蟾儕著． 392．5—C142

上海，中國圖書公司和記，民五年·

新性道德討論集；章錫琛編·　392·5—c190

上海，開明，民十五年·再版·217面·「婦女問題叢書」

夫婦之性的生活；(日)田中香涯原著，葉癸譯·　392·5—T312

上海，民智，民十五年·3版·

396　婦女問題

婦人與社會；(德)倍倍爾原著，沈端先譯·　399—P123

上海，開明，民十六年·758面·「婦女問題研究會叢書」

現代思潮與婦女問題；(日)本間久雄原著，張佩芬女士譯·　396—P200

上海，泰東，民十七年·132面·

婦女論集；文娜女士著·　396—W260

北京，北新，民十六年·再版·138面·

新婦女解放；天喬，劍波合著·　396·1—T342

上海，泰東，民十七年·133面·

398　諺語歌謡

神話學ABC；謝六逸著·　398·4—s420

上海，世界，民十七年·127面·

希臘神話ABC；汪倜然著·　398·4—W175

上海，世界，民十七年·118面·

400　語言學

世界語全程；盛國成編·　408·9—C320

上海，開明，民十七年·264面·

英漢雙解詳注略語辭典；倪灝森編· 423·51—N190
上海，商務，民十二年·224面·

495·1 中國語言學

國文測驗舉例；周廷珍，歐濟甫合編· 495·1—C786
上海，中華，民十一年·124面·

文字學形義篇；朱宗萊著· 495·—C821
國立北京大學出版部，民十二年·4版·32面·

中國韻文通論；陳鐘凡著· 495·12—C270
上海，中華，民十六年·418面·「文學叢書」

四角號碼學生字典；陸爾奎，方毅合編· 495·12—L425
上海，商務，民十七年·632面·

四角號碼檢字法：第二次改訂；王雲五著· 495·13—W163
上海，商務，民十七年·9　面·

笑之圖解；黎錦熙編· 495·15—L215
北京，文化學社，民十五年·17面·「國語文法例題詳解之一」

國語典；馬繼貞著· 495·15—M112
上海，泰東，民十四年·152面·

詞論；楊樹達著· 495·15—Y137
上海，商務，民十七年·618面

音韻常識；徐敬修編· 495·16—s476
上海，商務，民十四年·再版·136面·

歷代白話文範；江蔭香著· 495·18—c519
上海，世界，民十三年·3版·2冊·

國語教學法講義；劉儒編· 495·18—L379
上海，商務，民十一年·120面·

古白話文選；吳遁生，鄭次川合編· 495·18—w296
上海，商務，民十三年·再版·2冊·

500　自然科學

科學談話；(日)日日新聞社原編，韓守藩譯・　500—H140
上海，公民，民十一年・2冊・「常識叢書第三種」

科學概論；黄昌穀講・　501—H471
上海，民智，民十五年・4版・180面・

漢譯科學大綱；(英)湯姆生原著，王岫廬等合譯・　502—T74
上海，商務，民十三年・4冊・

自然科學教科書；鄭貞文等合編・　507—C351
上海，商務，民十二年・3冊・

自然科學常識講義；侯紹裘著・　507—H242
上海，民智，民十一年・46面・

理科實驗法；(美)梅佩禮，(中)徐作和合著・　507—M185
上海，伊文思，民十四年・132面・

博物學教授指南；(日)山内繁雄，野原茂六原著，嚴保誠等合譯・
507—s121
上海，商務，民三年・再版・123面・

510　數學

混合算學教科書；段育華著・　510—T819
上海，商務，民十三年・6版・8冊・

數學遊戲；周永謨著・　510・7—C789
上海，科學會編譯部，民二年・226面・

蓋氏對數表；F. C. Gauss 原著，
(日)宮本藤吉爾原譯，杜亞泉，壽孝大合譯・　510・8—G237
上海，商務，民十一年・17版・101面・

實用主義中學新算術；陳文編· 511—C290
上海，商務，民十一年·11版·319面·

中等算術教科書；黄際遇編· 511—H471
上海，商務，民十一年·8版·274面·

新制算術教本；王永靈，胡樹楷合編· 511—W163
上海，中華，民十一年·18版·2册·

加減乘除；翁爲著· 511—W274
上海，商務，民十三年·86面·

新中學算術教科書；吳在淵，胡敦復合編· 511—W296
上海，商務，民十二年·6版·282面·

珠算全書；馬駿鈞編· 511·3—M112
上海，中華，民十一年·再版·2册·

財政商業高等利息計算法；吳宗壽編· 511·8—W297
上海，商務，民十二年·164面·「經濟叢書社叢書之二」

算術習題解答，現代初中教科書；余介石，陳伯琴合編· 511·9—Y318
上海，商務，民十四年·241面·

近世初等代數學；吳在淵編· 512—W296
上海，商務，民十一年·754面·

温德華士代數學；屠坤華譯· 512—W488
上海，商務，民十一年·15版·461面

平面幾何學要覽；匡文濤編· 513·1—K336
上海，商務，民十三年·5版·2册·

極大極小問題；王邦珍編· 513·19—W153
上海，商務，民十五年·271面·「學藝叢書」

平面立體幾何畫法；王濟仁編· 515—w136
暨南大學出版課，民十七年·196面·「國立暨南大學叢書」

530 物理學

物理學講義；陳學郢編· 530—C275

上海，商務，民八年·3 册·

最近物理學概觀；鄭貞文編·　530—C351

上海，商務，民十一年·224 面·

科學常識講議；義務學校編·　530—H242

上海，民智，民十二年·28 面·

無機化學；彬湼兒原著，蕭湘譯·　546—P357

上海，時中書局，清光緒三十一年·739 面·

鑛物學：民國新教科書；徐善祥編·　549—s181

上海，商務，民四年·3 版·260 面·

地震淺説；楊宗健，王恭睦合編·　551·22—Y121

上海，中華，民十五年·3 版·92 面·

570　生物學

進化論 ABC；張慰宗著·　575—C172

上海，世界，民十七年·111 面·

人種改良學；陳壽凡譯·　575—C187

上海，商務，民十二年，3 版·2 册·「新智識叢書之十一」

人文生物學論叢；潘光旦著·　575·1—P154

上海，新月書店，民十七年·308 面·

優生學與婚姻；威廉魯濱生原著，高方譯·　575·1—R568

上海，東亞圖書館，民十七年·156 面·

610　醫學

實用法醫學大全；(日)石川清忠原著，王佑，楊鴻通合譯·　610—C250

中國各書局，清光緒三十四年·740 面·

臨證秘典；張卿黻編·　60·3—C154

上海，商務，民十一年・再版・456 面・

生理衛生學表解；上海科書局編・ 080—S155—612

上海，學局局，清宣統三年・43 面・「表解叢書」

紙塑人體符號解説； 612・03—C633

東京，島津製作所標本部・172 面・

612・6 性學

性學 ABC；柴福沅著・ 612・6—C128

上海，世界，民十七年・117 面・

兒童的性生活；莫爾原著，夏斧心譯・ 612・6—M735

上海，商務，民十七年・408 面・

婦女生育論；蘇儀貞編・ 612・6—S4

上海，中華，民十三年・4 版・65 面・

性愛的研究與初夜的知識；羽太鋭治原著，黄孤飄譯・ 612・6—Y358

上海，啓智，民十七年・

613 衛生學

衛生學 ABC；沈齊春著・ 613—S222

上海，世界，民十七年・135 面・

健康學；(美)沙井特原著，江孝賢等合譯・ 613—Sa73

上海，中華，民十一年・再版・188 面・

萬病自療全書；鍾尚友編・ 613・8—C969

上海，大陸圖書公司，民九年・191 面・

中國公共衛生之建設；胡明宣著・ 614—S414

上海，亞東，民十七年・130 面・

616 病理及治療學

診斷學；(日)下平用彩編，湯爾和譯・ 616・07—H279

上海，商務，民八年・2 冊・

麻疹新編；黄政修著· 616·912—H471
民十七年·66頁·
麻疹療治法；李天佐著· 616·912—L198
上海，中華，民十四年·152面·
淋病一夕話；李振軒著· 616·95—L199
上海，李振軒診所，民四年·16面·
最新助産婦學；(日)楠田謙藏原著，姚昶緒譯· 618·2—N124
上海，大東，民十四年·2册·

623　軍事工程

新兵器特刊；鄒燮斌編· 623·4—T696
湖北軍警週刊社，民十四年·128面·
潛水艇；徐燕謀編· 623·9—S484
上海，商務，民六年·再版·92面·

630　農業

中國農業改造問題叢著；唐啓宇著· 630—T201
上海，民智，民十七年·188面
農業合作ABC；王世穎著· 630—W156
上海，世界，民十七年·102面·
中國重要農産物之對外貿易概況；中央農民運動講習所編· 633—C97
中國國民黨中央農民運動講習所，民十六年·22面·
中國之主要農産物；中央農民運動講習所編· 633—C976
中央農民運動講習所，民十六年·46面·
作物學實驗教程；黄紹緒編· 633—H480
上海，商務，民十七年·118面

640 家政

家庭萬寶全書；魯雲奇著· 640—L465
上海，中華圖書集成公司，民七年·再版·6册·

650 商業

進貨學：商業概要第二卷；吳東初編· 610—W297
上海，商務，民十二年·210面·
中國郵電航空史；謝彬著· 650·09—s415
上海，中華，民十七年·212面·「史地叢書」
增訂交通必攜；商務印書館編譯所編· 656—s162
上海，商務，民十一年·3版·90面·
新式官廳簿記及會計；楊汝梅編· 657—Y130
上海，商務，民十七年·4版·339面·
商店學業指南；大東書局編· 618—T131
上海，大東，民十四年·5版·212面「青年商業叢書之一」
廣告學ABC；蒯世勛著· 659·1—K291
上海，世界，民十七年·101面·

700 美術

藝術家的難關；鄧以蟄著· 701—T263
北京，古城書社，民十七年·100面·

藝術教育 ABC；豐子愷著·　707—F224
上海，世界，民十七年·111 面·

築城學教程；　721·2—C819
民十五年改訂·124 面·

構圖法 ABC；豐子愷著·　740—F224
上海，世界，民十七年·118 面·

半農談影；劉半農著·　770—L372
上海，開明，民十七年·65 面·

故宫攝影集；　770—T668
清宫善後委員會，民十四年·53 圖

攝影學 ABC；吳静山著·　770—W297
上海，世界，民十七年·131 面·

音樂界：十期彙刊；上海音樂學校編·　780—s155
上海，民智，民十二年·421 面

名利網；沈醉了，陳雪鵠合著·　780—s222
上海，開明，民十七年·再版·86 面·

中國名歌選；錢君匋編·　780—T601
上海，開明，民十七年·62 面·

784　唱歌

名家唱歌集；章世葜，王季綸合編·　784—C10
中國博文館編輯社，清光緒三十二年·128 面·

教育唱歌；黄子繩等合編·　78—H486
湖北官書處，清光緒三十一年·2 册·

唱歌游戲；王季梁編·　784—W137
上海，商務，清光緒三十一年·80 面

790 遊藝　運動

中國影戲大觀；徐耻痕編· 792—s155
上海，明月，民十七年·再版·「80 面」

達摩劍；趙連和著· 796—S209
上海，商務，民十四年·145 面·「持擊叢刊第一種」

女子手巾體操；克羅克威廉原著，王懷琪譯· 796—X205
上海，商務，民十一年·42 面·

課外運動法；李憂聲著· 796—L182
上海，商務，民十三年·99 面·

運動員指南；李培藻著· 796—L195
上海，商務，民十四年·106 面·

游泳新術；李石岑著· 796—L196
上海，商務，民十四年·3 版·136 面·

中華新武術；馬良著· 796—M117
上海，商務，民九年·2 冊·

田徑賽運動；(美)麥克樂原著，李德晉譯· 796—M155
上海，商務，民十一年·4 版·220 面·「體育叢書」

體操遊戲；沈鏡清，奚萃光合編· 796—S211
上海，商務，民十年·142 面·

日本柔術；徐桌呆譯· 796—S476
上海，中華，民九年·138 面·

四川西北軍學聯合秋季運動會紀事； 796—S585
運動會編纂處，民十六年·144 面·

田徑賽規則；中華基督教青年會遠東運動會編· 796—T665
上海，青年協會書局，1926—1927·101 面·

徒手疊羅漢；王懷琪，吳洪興合編· 796—W142
上海，商務，民十二年·53 面·

西湖風景疊羅漢；王懷琪編· 796—W142
上海，商務，民十二年·57 面·

運動技術概要；遠東運動會中國委員會編· 796—Y430
上海，商務，民八年·222 面·

西洋拳術；陳霆鋭編· 796·6—C288
上海，中華，民七年·96 面·

拳藝學初步；朱鴻壽著· 796·6—C824
上海，商務，民九年·123 面·

拳藝學進階；朱鴻壽著· 796·6—C824
上海，商務，民六年·165 面·

石頭拳術秘訣；郭粹亞，金一明合編· 796·6—K433
上海，中華，民十一年·94 面·

好拳法；滕學琴編· 796·6—T276
上海，中華，民七年·再版·126 面·

少林拳術秘訣；尊我齋主人編· 796·6—T737
上海，中華，民十年·134 面·

易筋經十二勢圖説；王懷琪編· 796·6—W142
上海，商務，民十一年·44 面·

女子籃球規則；黄斌生譯· 797—Am35
上海，女青年會全國協會書報部，民十三年·62 面

足球規例；(美)維乃氏原著，朱樹蒸譯· 797—C834
上海，中華，民四年·37 面·

女子籃球；潘知本編· 797—P151
上海，商務，民十四年·107 面·「體育叢書」

籃球規則；中華基督教青年會遠東運動會編· 797—T665
上海，青年協會書局，1926—1927·122 面·

足球規則；中華基督教青年會遠東運動會編· 797—T665
上海，青年協會書局，民十五年·30 面·

手球規則；中華基督教青年會遠東運動會編· 797—T665
上海，青年協會書局，民十五年·15 面·

壘球規則；中華基督教青年會全球協會編． 797—T665

上海，青年協會書局，民十四年．51 面．

800 文學

文學概論；沈天葆著． 800—S222

上海，梁溪，民十五年．161 面．

801 文學批評

法蘭西文學；楊袁昌英著． 080—P225—12

上海，商務，民十二年，再版．51 面．「百科小叢書第十二種」

意大利文學；王希和著． 080—P225—69

上海，商務，民十三年．58 面．「百科小叢書第六十九種」

文學生活；張若谷著． 801—c159

上海，金屋書店，民十七年．初版．180 面．

文學講話；趙景深著． 801—c201

上海，亞細亞書局，民十七年．208 面．

文藝批評 ABC；傅東華著． 801—F244

上海，世界，民十七年．96 面．

文學的紀律；梁實秋著． 801—L263

上海，新月，民十七年．158 面．

表現主義的文學；劉大杰著． 801—L375

上海，北新，民十七年．192 面．

歐洲大戰與文學；沈雁冰著． 801—S224

上海，開明，民十七年．初版．125 面．

農民文學 abc；謝六逸著． 801—S420

上海，世界，民十七年．112 面．

文藝與性愛；(日)松村武雄原著，謝六逸譯・　801—S574
上海，開明，民十七年・再版・83 面・

法國的浪漫主義；曾仲鳴著・　801—T521
上海，開明，民十七年・初版・91 面・

一家言；曾孟樸編・　901—T223
上海，真善書店，民十七年・240 面・

近代文學 ABC；吳雲著・　801—W299
上海，世界，民十七年・125 面・

文藝辭典；孫良工編・　R—803—S519
上海，民智，民十七年・980 面・

808　文學叢書

最近的世界文學；趙景深編・　808—C201
上海，遠東圖書公司，民十七年・177 面・

真美善月刊；真美善雜誌編輯所編・　808—C296
上海，真美善書店，民十七年・「第一卷合刊一册，第二卷一號至六號」

莽原，合平第二卷；下册：二卷十三至二十四期・　808—M133
北平，未名社出版部，民十七年・

馬來情歌集；鐘敬文編・　808・1—C960
上海，遠東圖書公司，民十七年・88 面・

詩歌原理 ABC；傅東華著・　808・1—F245
上海，世界，民十七年・125 面・

西洋詩學淺説；王希和著・　088—P225—52
上海，商務，民十三年・103 面・「百科小叢書第五十二種」

西洋之神劇及歌劇；俞寄凡著・　080—P225—140
上海，商務，民十六年・72 面・「百科小叢書第一百四十種」

辨論術 ABC；陸東平著・　808・5—L433
上海，世界，民十七年・129 面・

演説學 ABC；余楠秋著・　808・5—Y349

上海，世界，民十七年·80 面·

810 中國文學

童話評論；趙景深輯· 810—C201

上海，新文化書社，民十三年·250 面·

兒童文學概論；魏壽鏞，周候于合著· 810—W206

上海，商務，民十二年·85 面·

中國文學研究；鄭振鐸編纂· 010·2—C387

上海，商務，民十六年·

名家漢文評釋；久保得著· 810·4—C270

早稻田大學，321 面·

梁任公學術演講集；梁啓超著· 810·4—L251

上海，商務，民十五年·「第一集二册，第三集一册」

文心雕龍雜記；黃侃著· 810·8—H477

北京，文化學社，民十六年·274 面·

新文學作法入門；廣文書局編輯所編· 810·8—K322

上海，世界書局，民十年·66 面·「學生門經叢一書」

作文論；葉紹鈞著· 080—P225—48

上海，商務，民十三年·68 面·「百科小叢書第四十八種」

修辭格；唐鉞著· 080—P225—14

上海，商務，民十三年·89 面·「百科小叢書第十二種」

國語文學史；胡適著· 810·9—H414

北京，文化學社，民十六年·240 面·

白話文學史；胡適著· 810·9—H414

上海，新月書店，1928·上册·

文學常識；徐敬修編· 810·9—S476

上海，大東，民十四年·140 面·再版·

811　詩詞

鐘嶸詩品之研究；張陳卿著・　811—C152
北京，文化學社，民十五年・114 面・

人間詞話箋証；靳德峻編・　811—c673
北京，文化，學社，民十七年・初版・56 面・

詩品注；陳延傑，鍾嶸著・　811—c979
上海，開明，民十六年・132 面・

嘗試集批評與討論；胡懷琛著・　811—H405
上海，泰東，民十一年・139 面・

詞選；胡適選註・　811—H114
上海，商務，民十七年・381 面・

古戀歌；愛絲女士輯・　811—N147
上海，亞細亞書局，民十七年・109 面・

英漢三昧集；蘇曼殊著・　811—S461
上海，泰東，民十二年・再版・120 面・

讀風偶識；崔東壁著・　811—T735
北京，文化學社，民十七年・初版・208 面・

人間詞話；王國維著・　811—W145
北京，樸社，民十五年・32 面・

陶淵明詩；陶淵明著・　811・3—T250
上海，商務，民十六年・95 面・「學生國學叢書」

雪壓軒集；賀雙卿著・　811・8—H187
北京，文化學社，民十六年・35 面・

811・9　詩一別集

鮫人；裘柱常著・　811・9—C740
上海，現代，民十七年・103 面・「畸形小集第二種」

春夏秋冬；郭子雄著・　811・9—K428

上海，金屋，民十七年·82面·

絶俗樓我輩語；白采著· 811·9—P227

上海，開明書店·105面·

志摩的詩；徐志摩著· 811·9—s476

上海，新月書店，民十七年·148面·

寂寞的國；汪静之著· 811·9—W175

上海，開明，民十六年·171面·「文學週報社叢書」

受難者的短曲；楊騷著· 811·9—Y37

上海，開明書店，民十七年·127面·

骷髏上的薔薇；于賡虞著· 811·9—Y361

北京，古城書社，民十六年·77面·

812 戲曲

顧曲塵談；吳梅編· 812—W290

上海，商務，民十四年·3版，2册·「文藝叢刻甲集」

元曲選；臧晉叔輯· 812·7—T445

上海，商務，民七年·影博古堂本·48面·

上海，商務，民十三年·71面·「林氏選評名家文集」

黄梨洲集；黄梨洲著· 814·—H418

上海，羣學社，民十五年·422面·

明夷待訪録；黄梨洲著· 814·8—H478

上海，梁溪圖書館，民十四年·102面·

櫻花集；衣萍著· 814·9—c182

上海，北新，民十七年·226面·

談龍集；周作人著· 814·9—C771

上海，開明，民十七年·310面·

天鵝集；朱溪著· 814·9—c821

上海，人間書店，民十七年·108面·

北影；朱自清著· 814·9—c837

上海，開明，民十七年·初版·129面·

獻心；黄天石著·　814·9—H487

香港，受匡出版部，民十七年·57面·

國學蠡酌；梁啓超著·　814·9—L251

上海，商務，311面·「飲冰室叢著第五種」

而已集；魯迅著·　814·9—L416

上海，北新，民十七年·216面·

時代在暴風雨裹；毛一波著·　814·9—M139

上海，現代，民十七年·236面·

我們的七月；O·M·輯·　814·9—N67

上海，亞東，民十七年·206面·

師復文存；師復著·　814·9—s260

廣州革新書局，1927年·382面·

花環；孫席珍著·　814·9—s527

上海，亞細亞書局，民十七年·132面·

孟和文存；陶孟和著·　814·9—T248

上海，亞東，民十四年·152面·

淡霞和落葉；萬曼著·　814·9—w128

上海，新文化書社，民十三年·132面·「緑波社小叢書」

佛西戲劇第一集；熊佛西著·　812·9—H357

北京，古城書社，民十六年·207面·

愛的革命；胡春冰著·　812·9—H101

上海，現代，民十七年·97面·「現代戲劇叢書」

芙蓉花淚：拒毒劇本；黄嘉謨著·　812·9—H471

上海，中華國民拒毒會，民十七年·108面·

洪深劇本創作集；洪深著·　812·9—H522

上海，東南書店，民十七年·170面·

白薔薇；劉大杰著·　812·9—L375

上海，東南書店，民十七年·114面·

潘金蓮；歐陽予倩著·　812·9—0140

上海，東方書店，民十七年・103 面・

卡昆岡；徐志摩，陸小曼合著・ 812・9—s476

上海，新月書店，民十七年・89 面・

814 散文一別集

模範文選；程演生編・ 814—C292

北京，國立大學出版部，民十二年・3 版・320 面・

劉子政集；林紓輯・ 8112—L372

上海，商務，民十三年・63 面・「林氏選評名家文集」

柳河東集；林紓輯・ 814・5—L308

上海，商務，民十三年・113 面・「林氏選評名家文集」

歸震川集；林紓輯・ 814・7—K347

上海，商務，民十三年・129 面・「林氏選評名家文集」

唐荆川集；唐順之著・ 814・7—T212

上海，商務，76 面・「林氏選評名家文集」

顔習齋集；顔習齋著・ 814・7—Y236

上海，羣學社，民十五年・360 面・

虞道園集；林紓選評，虞集・ 814・7—Y378

上海，商務，民十三年・79 面・「林氏選評名家文集」

方望溪集；林紓輯・ 814・8—F173

化外的文學；王夫凡編・ 814・9—w139

上海，現代，民十七年・133 面・「藍皮小書」

雜拌儿：一名梅什兒；俞平伯著・ 814・9—Y372

上海，開明，民十七年・222 面・初版・

國學演講録；章炳麟著・ 815・9—C189

上海，梁溪圖書館，民十五年・176 面・3 版・

816　書牘

分類尺牘全書；袁韜壼編· 816—Y422
上海，羣學書社，民八年·12 册·

無法投遞之郵件；落華生著· 816·9—L165
北平，文化學社，民十七年·4 面·

給小朋友的信；徐學文著· 816·9—s478
上海，開明，民十七年·112 面·

緑箋；蔣逸霄著· 816·9—T56
北京，古城書社，民十七年·114 面·

818　詩文—總集

後山文集；林紓著· 818·7—C286
上海，商務，民十三年·52 面·「林氏選評名家文集」

盾鼻集；梁啓超著· 818·9—L251
上海，商務，民十二年·2 册·7 版·

秋雁集；藝林社編· 818·9—N187
上海，亞細亞書局，民十七年·164 面·「藝林叢刊第三輯」

819　雜體詩文

寤語拾存；顔啓芳著· 819—Y231
北京，文化學社，民十六年·44 面·

北京俚曲；殷凱輯· 819—Y271
上海，太平洋，民十六年·430 面·

邃漢齊謎話；薛鳳昌編· 819·06—s411

文苑導游録；常覺等合輯· 89·9—c195
上海，時還，民十七年·10 册·

魯迅在廣東；鍾敬文編· 819·9—c960
上海，北新，民十六年·121面·

流離；寒星著· 819·9—H146
上海，亞東圖書館，民十七年·186面·

不死日記；沈從文著· 819·9—s222
上海，人間書店，民十七年·123面·

篁君日記；沈從文著· 819·9—s222
北平，文化學社，民十七年·134面·

日記九種；郁達夫著· 819·9—Y376
上海，北新，民十七年·250面·3版·

820 英美文學

一朶紅的紅的玫瑰；白爾痕斯原著·程鶴西譯· 821—B937
北平，文化學社，民十七年·100面·

林肯；(德)林凡脱原著·沈性仁譯· 822—D832
上海，商務，民十二年·80面·「世界叢書」

相鼠有皮；顧德隆譯· 822—G39
上海，商務，民十四年·142面·「文學研究會通俗戲劇叢書第五種」

一個理想的丈夫；(英)王爾德原著，徐培仁譯· 822—w646
上海，金屋書店，民十七年·277面·

拊掌録；(美)華盛頓歐文原著，林紓，魏易合譯· 827·24—108
上海，商務，民十四年·77面·

史推拉；哥德原著，湯元吉譯· 832—G555
上海，商務，民十四年·77面·「文藝叢刻乙集」

840 法國文學

吕克蘭斯鮑夏；(法)嚣俄原著，東亞病夫譯· 842—H875

上海，真美善書店，民十六年 · 172 面 ·「俄嚣戲劇全集第六種」

吕伯蘭；(法)嚣俄原著，東亞病夫譯 · 842—H876

上海，真美善書店，民十六年 · 257 面 ·「嚣俄戲劇全集第九種」

夫人學堂：穆理哀喜劇；東亞病夫譯 · 842—M733

上海，真美善書店，民十六年 · 136 面 ·

890　其餘各國文學

黑假面人；(俄)安特列夫原著，李霽野譯 · 891 · 72—An26

上海，未名社，民十七年 · 112 面 ·「未名叢刊之一」

亂婚裁判；蘇俄性生活的真相；(蘇俄)德美朶委奇原著，温盛光譯 · 891 · 72—T255

上海，啓智書局，民十七年 · 78 面 ·

日本文學；謝文逸著 · 895 · 2—s420

上海，開明，民十六年 · 176 面 · 上册 ·「世界文學叢書」

曼殊全集；柳亞子編 · 895 · 2—s461

上海，北新，民十七年 · 436 面 ·

日本現代劇三種；(日)山平有三等原著，田漢譯 · 895 · 22—s149

上海，東南書店，民十七年 · 123 面 ·

900　歷史

歷史哲學概論；Robert Flint 原著，郭斌佳譯 · 901—F647

上海，新月書店，民十七年 · 296 面 ·

歷史學與社會科學；李璜著 · 901—L185

上海，啓智書局，民十七年 · 111 面 ·

文化評價 ABC；葉法無著 · 901—Y182

上海，世界，民十七年 · 91 面 ·

世界史表解；上海科學書局編· 080—S155—900
上海，科學書局，宣統三年·前後2册·

史學通論；(日)浮田和民講述，李浩生譯· 904—F231
杭州，合衆譯書局，清光緒二十九年·103面·

910—919 地理，遊記

世界地理表解，上海科學書局編· 080—s155—910
上海，科學書局，清宣統三年，中下2册·「表解叢書」

新都遊覽指南；方繼之編· 910·2—F161
上海，大東，民十七年·184面·

華英地名表；陳鎬基編· 910·3—c278
上海，商務，民十四年·6版·23面·

912 地圖

東洋歷史地圖；(日)石澤發身編· 912—s250
東京，弘文館，明治三十九年·15版·21圖

最近改正漢文萬國地圖；(日)松邑孫吉編· 912—s572
東京，三松堂，明治三十九年·36面·

世界新輿圖；奚若著· 912—sh23
上海，商務，民七年·

世界改造分國地圖；丁詧盦著· 912—T345
上海，商務，民十年·

袖珍世界新輿圖；童世亨著· 912—T901
上海，商務，民九年·

世界形勢一覽圖；童世亨著· 912—T901
上海，商務，民十四年·

世界改造後環球列國地圖華英對照；　912—Y114
武昌，亞新地學社，民十六年·

最新中華形勢圖；洪懋熙著·　912·51—H521
上海，東方輿地學社，民十六年·

支那古今沿革地圖；(日)小島彦七著·　912·51—s410
東京，三松堂，明治三十八年·66面·

挪威一瞥；Mockler Farrgman 原著，汪今鸞譯·　914·81—M717
上海，商務，民十五年·135面·「少年史地叢書」

中原的蠻族；鄭飛卿記·　915·113—c352
上海，開明，民十六年·115面·

陝西旅行記；王桐齡著·　915·12—w159
北京，文化學社，民十七年·144面·

大中華山西地理志；林傳甲著·　915·122—L316
山西，文廟圖書館，民八年·324面·

漢口小志；徐焕斗著·　915·131—H130
漢口，商務，民四年·2册·

廬山遊記；胡適著·　915·133—H414
上海，新月書店，民十七年·74面·

江浙旅行記；王桐齡著·　915·14—W159
北京，文化學社，民十七年·136面·

上海軼事；陳伯熙編·　915·141—C285
上海，泰東，上中2册·

上海閒話；姚公鶴編·　915·141—Y159
上海，商務，民十四年·再版·2册·

日本視察記；王桐齡著·　915·2—W159
北京，文化學社，民十七年·242面·

920　傳記

清儒學案；許嘯天編·　920—H376

上海，羣學社，民十七年 · 224 面

辯士舌；孫毓修編 · 920—S534

上海，商務，民十三年 · 再版 · 73 面 ·

921 列傳

三十三年落花夢；宮崎寅藏著 · 921—K395

上海，出版合作社，民十五年 · 4 版 · 140 面 ·

陶淵明；梁啓超編 · 921—L251

上海，商務，民十三年 · 119 面 ·「國學小叢書」

鮑羅庭之罪惡；(俄)尤其皮克原著，朱毓原譯 · 921—p585

廣州平社，民十七年 · 76 面 ·

東坡逸事；沈宗元編 · 921—S211

上海，商務，民十四年 · 6 版 · 93 面 ·

東坡逸事續編；沈宗元編 · 921—S211

上海，商務，民十五年 · 4 版 · 66 面 ·

英國海軍秘史；(英)施格鉄原著，秦翰才譯 · 921—SC085

上海，文明，民十二年 · 2 册 ·

崔東壁先生年譜；崔東壁著 · 921—T705

民十七年 · 104 面 ·

晏子春秋；支偉成編 · 9121—Y248

上海，泰東，民十二年 · 15 面 ·

袁世凱全傳軼事；野史氏編 · 921—Y421

文藝編譯社，民十四年 · 12 版 · 3 册 ·

袁世凱軼事；野史氏編 · 921—Y421

上海，文藝編譯社，民十四年 · 12 版 · 90 面 ·

……續録 · 1 册 ·

英俄與猶太人；丁作韶著 · 933—T352

上海，世界，民十六年 · 17 面 ·

940　歐洲史

西史綱要；張仲和著· 910—C152
北京，文化學社，民十五年·2册·
法國十八世紀的思想史；彭基相著· 944—P271
上海，新月書店，民十七年·204面·

947　俄國史

戰後世界政治之關鍵；(英)亞諾得原著，周谷城譯· 947—Ar63
上海，春潮書局，民十七年·初版·184面·
俄國革命運動史；山内封介原著，衛仁山譯· 947·08—s148
上海，太平洋書店，民十七年·494面·
新俄國之研究；邵飄萍著· 947·09—s171
日本，大阪東瀛編譯社，民十六年·3版·140面
俄國革命史；楊幼炯編· 947·09—Y144
上海，民智，民十七年·「432面」·

951　中國史

中山出世後中國六十年大事記；半票編· 951—P144
上海，太平洋，民十七年·「674面」·
漢書補注補正；楊樹達著· 951·02—Y137
上海，商務，民十四年·「203面」·「北京師範大學叢書」
明代軼聞；林慧如著· 951·02—L319
上海，中華，民八年·「205面」·
清代軼聞；裘毓麐編· 951·08—c742

上海，中華，民六年・5版・4册・

清朝野史大觀；小横香室主人編・ 951・08—s410f

上海，中華，民十年・12册・

清稗類鈔；徐珂著・ 951・08—S478

上海，商務，民九年・4版・48册・

太平天國有趣文件十六種；劉復輯・ 951・083—L359

上海，北新，25頁。

太平天國軼聞；進步書局編輯所編・ 951・083—T652

上海，文明，民十一年・4版・4册・「稗史叢書」

庚子聊軍統帥瓦德西拳亂筆記；王光祈譯・ 951・087—W144

上海，中華，民十七年・270面・

李鴻章遊俄紀事；王光祈著・ 951・087—W784

上海，東南書店，民十七年・100面・

奉直戰史；上海宏文圖書館編・ 951・09—s155f

上海，宏文，民十三年・七版・2册・

江浙戰史；上海宏文圖書館編・ 951・09—s155c

上海，宏文，民十三年・再版・4册・

西康疆域溯古録；胡吉廬編・ 951・5—H401

上海，商務，民十七年・163面・

952 日本史

日本研究叢書；陳德徵編・ 952—c289

上海，世界書局・4册・

日本研究叢書提要；陳德徵著・ 952—C289

上海，世界，民十七年・416面・

日俄戰争；吕思勉編・ 952—L452

上海，商務，民十七年・144面・「新時代史地叢書」

菲律賓；鄭民編・ 991・4—356

上海，商務，民十四年・192面・

小説

西奴娜小傳；(英)安東尼賀殂原著，林紓，魏易合譯· F—A141
上海，商務，民元年·81 面·

美洲童子萬里尋親記；(英)亞丁原著，林紓譯· F—Ad35
上海，商務，民九年·4 版·86 面·

安徒生童話集；趙景深譯· F—An23n
上海，新文化，民十三年·112 面·「緑波社叢書第一種」

歐美小說；(俄)安特劉夫等原著，虛白，萬孚合譯· F—An15
上海，真美善書店，民十七年·「216 面」

三公主；阿斯皮爾孫原著，顧均正譯· F—AS16
上海，開明書店，民十七年·155 面·

山梯尼克頓學校；(英)比亞生原著，張墨池譯· F—B18
上海，公民，民十年·58 面·「公民叢書教育類第四種」

藍花；趙景深，洪北平合譯· F—C201
上海，新宇宙書店，民十七年·初版·112 面·

梔子花球；趙景深著· F—C210
上海，北新，民十七年·246 面·

阿麗思漫遊奇境記；(英)Dowis Catroee 原著，趙元任譯· F—C236
上海，商務，民十二年·再版·223 面·

印度寓言；鄭振鐸編· F—C351
上海，商務，民十四年·87 面·「文學研究會叢書」

漩渦；陳白塵著· F—C285
上海，金屋，民十七年·188 面·

天問；陳銓著· F—C299
上海，新月書店，民十七年·2 册·

福爾摩斯探案大全集；種小青等合編· F—C345
上海，世界，民十六年·12 册·

少女之誓；(法)Frncois Rene de Chateaubriand，原著，戴望舒譯· F—C391
上海，開明書店，民十七年·156 面·

芥川龍之介小説集；湯鶴逸譯· F—c569
北平，文化學社，民十七年·143 面·

林娟娟；金滿成著· F—c667
上海，現代，民十七年·135 面·

殘燼集；金溟若著· F—c667
上海，北新，民十七年·122 面·

木偶奇遇記；科羅狄原著，徐調孚譯· F—c698
上海，開明，民十七年·381 面·

飄蕩的衣裙；周樂山著· F—c789
上海，遠東圖書公司，民十七年·128 面·

兵；周毓英著· F—C789
上海，創造社，民十五年·153 面·

龍華道上；朱扶湘著· F—C823
上海，新東方書店，民十七年·166 面·

月夜；川島著· F—C901
北大新潮社，民十七年·3 版·76 面·

海上迷宫：春蘭生著· F—C944
上海，民治書店，民十七年·4 册·

孽海春潮；春蘭生著· F—C944
上海，好青年圖書館，民十七年·2 册·

白話魯濱孫飄流記；(英)達夫原者，嚴叔平譯· F—D262
上海，中華，民十五年·4 版·「362」面·

魯濱孫飄流續記；(英)達孚原著，林紓，曾宗鞏合譯· F—D262
上海，商務，民九年·2 册·「小説叢書第十一篇」

清宫二年記；德菱女士原著，東方雜誌社譯· F—D446
上海，商務，民十三年·5 版·177 面·

塊肉餘生述前編；(英)卻而司迭更司原著，林紓，魏易合譯· F—D555
上海，商務，民三年·2 册·「小説叢書第二十二種」

孝女耐兒傳；(英)郤而司迭更司原著，林紓，魏易合譯· F—D555
上海，商務，民三年·3 册·「小説叢書第三十一種」

後期穴居人；(美)杜柏原著，何其寬合譯· F—D722h
上海，商務，民十三年·210面·「兒童史地叢書」

樹居人；(美)杜柏原著，鄭振鐸，何共寬合譯· F—D722s
上海，商務，民十三年·122面·「兒童史地叢書」

前期穴居人；(美)杜柏原著，沈志堅，何其寬譯· F—D722s
上海，商務，民十三年·137面·「兒童史地叢書」

前期海濱人；(美)杜柏原著，何其寬譯· F—D722t
上海，商務，民十四年·288面·「兒童史地叢書」

法蘭西小説；(法)大仲馬等原著，夏萊蒂等合譯· F—D89t
上海，真美善書局，民十七年·139面·

玉樓花刼；(法)大仲馬原著，林紓，李世中合譯· F—n891
上海，商務，民元年·再版·2册·

愛羅先珂童話集；(俄)愛羅先珂原著，魯迅譯· F—Er69
上海，商務，民十六年·227面·「文學研究會叢書」

桃園；馮文炳著· F—F217
上海，開明，民十七年·再版·247面·

深淵；(德)Jan Forge原著，鍾憲民譯· F—F763
上海，現代書局，民十七年·215面·

蜜蜂；(法)Anatof France原著，穆木天譯· F—F844
上海，泰東，民十三年·122面·「世界兒童文學選集第三種」

色的熱情；(法)葛爾孟原著，虛白譯· F—G68
上海，真美善書店，民十七年·141面·

草原上；(俄)高爾基原著，朱溪譯· F—G677
上海，人間書店，民十七年·146面·

魯森堡之一夜；(法)古爾孟原著，鄭伯奇譯· F—G743
上海，泰東，民十一年·136面·「世界名家小説第三種」

德國童話集；(德)格利姆原著，劉海峯，楊鐘鍵合譯· F—G883a
北京，文化學社，民十七年·57面·

歐洲童話集；張昭民譯· F—G8830
上海，北新，民十七年·245面·

窄門；(法)安得烈紀得原著，穆木天譯· F—G361
上海，北新，民十七年·244 面·

鍾乳髑髏；(英)哈葛德原著，陳家麟，林紓合譯· F—H122
上海，商務，清光緒三十四年·187 面·

璣司刺虎記；(英)哈葛德原著，曾宗鞏，林紓合譯· F—H122
上海，商務，清宣統元年·2 册·

人生小諷刺；(英)哈代原著，虚白，仲彝合譯· F—H216
上海，真美善書店，民十七年·「316」面·

若有其事；許欽文著· F—H369
上海，北新，民十七年·193 面·

孤星淚；(法)囂俄原著，商務印書館譯· F—H307
上海，商務，民三年·2 册·

子卿先生；許傑著· F—H371
上海，開明，民十七年·200 面·

虚白小説；虚白著· F—H380
上海，真美善書店，230 面·

德妹；虚白著· F—H380
上海，真美善書局，民十七年·150 面·

紅花； F—H513
上海，芳草書店，民十七年·150 面·

做父親去；洪爲法著· F—H323
上海，金屋書店，民十七年·81 面·

拊掌録；(美)華盛頓歐文原著，林紓，魏易合譯· F— 7
上海，商務，清光緒三十三年·76 面·

天鵝；高君箴，鄭振鐸合譯· F—K166t
上海，商務，民十四年·361 面·「文學研究會叢書」

金風鐵雨録；(英)柯南達利原著，林紓，曾宗鞏合譯· F—K195
上海，商務，清光緒三十四年·再版·3 册·

電影樓臺；(英)柯南達利原著，林紓，魏易合譯· F—K195
上海，商務，民二年·83 面·

博徒别傳；(英)柯南達利原著，陳大燈，陳家麟合譯· F—K195
上海，商務，清光緒三十四年，102 面·

清慈禧太后　　記；喀南宗著，健公譯· F—K218
上海，商務，民六年·再版·124 面·

芝蘭與茉莉；顧一樵著· F—K248
上海，商務，民十六年·4 版·130 面·「文學研究會叢書」

女屍；谷劍塵著· F—K255
上海，真美善書店，民十七年·138 面·

凄咽；蒯斯曛著· F—K291
上海，泰東，民十七年·216 面·

紅墳；廣州文學會編· F—K320h
香港，受匡出版部，民十六年·82 面·

仙宫；廣州文學會編· F—K320s
香港，受匡出版部，民十六年·67 面·

嬰屍；廣州文學會編· F—K320s
香港，受匡出版部，民十七年·148 面·

塔；郭沫若著· F—K425
上海，商務，民十六年·再版·325 面·「文藝叢書」

戀愛之路；(俄)柯倫泰夫人原著，沈端先譯· F—K834
上海，作新書社，民十七年·114 面·

歧路燈；李緑園著· F—L190
北京，樸社出版經理部，民十六年·412 面·

夢幻的陶醉；李自珍著· F—L129
北京，文化學社，民十六年·136 面·

烈火；黎錦明著· F—L215
上海，開明書店，民十六年·175 面·

小説零簡；梁啓超著· F—L251
上海，商務，民十三年·3 版·174 面·「飲冰室叢著第十三種」

太平天國外記；(英)林利原著，孟憲承譯· F—L323
上海，商務，民十五年·3 版·2 册·

義黑；(法)德羅尼原著，林紓，廖琇崑合譯· F—L390
上海，商務，民四年·66面·

阿串姐；盧夢殊著· F—L406
上海，真美善書店，民十七年·228面·

曼麗；廬隱女士著· F—L408
北京，古城書社，民十七年·166面· F—L432s

順治太后外紀；陸士諤著·
上海，中華，民十二年·4版·108面·「清秘史之一」

愛美生學畫記；雷家駿編· F—L471
上海，商務，民十二年·43面·「兒童藝術叢書」

愛的幻滅；曼陀羅著· F—M133
上海，真美善書店，民十七年·148面·

三國演義；毛宗崗著· F—M133
上海，亞東，民十一年·2册·

曼殊斐爾小説集；(英)曼殊斐爾原著，徐志摩譯· F—M318
上海，北新，民十六年·

海鷗集；藝林社編· F—N187
上海，亞細亞書局，民十七年·128面·「藝林叢刊第二輯」

盜窟奇緣；(英)蒲斯培原著，商務印書館譯· F—P114
上海，商務，民元年·2册·

三寶太監下西洋記通俗演義； F—S121
上海，商務，4册·

天堂與五月；邵洵美著· F—S171
上海，光華，民十六年·158面·「獅吼社叢書」

雨後與其他；沈從文著· F—S222
上海，春潮書局，民十七年·141面·

阿麗思中國遊記；沈從文著· F—S2220
上海，新月書店，民十七年·278面·

華生包探案；商務印書館編譯所譯· F—S353—1·4
上海，商務，民三年·再版·120面·「説部叢書初集第四編」

回頭看；(美)威士原著，商務印書館編譯所譯· F—S353—1·12

上海，商務，民三年·再版·144册·「説部叢書初集第十二編」

巴黎繁華記；商務印書館編譯所譯· F—S353—1·25

上海，商務，民三年·再版·2册·「説部叢書初集第二十五編」

魯濱孫飄流續記；(英)達夫原著，林紓，曾宗鞏合譯· F—S353—1·34

上海，商務，民三年·再版·2册·「説部叢書初集第三十四編」

尸櫝記；(英)華爾登原著，商務印書館譯· F—S353—1·50

上海，商務，民三年·再版·20面·「説部叢書初集第六十編」

化身奇談；(英)安頓原著，商務印書館譯· F—S353—1·96

上海，商務，民三年·再版·100面·「説部叢書初集九十六編」

俠隱記；(法)大仲馬原著，君朔譯· F—S353—2·48

上海，商務，民四年·3版·4册·「説部叢書二集四十八編」

當罏女；王卓民編· F—S353—3·40

上海，商務，民三年·再版·2册·「説部叢書三集第四十編」

玫瑰花續編；(英)巴克雷原著，林紓，陳家駒合譯· F—S353—3·65

上海，商務，民三年·再版·12面·「説部叢書三集第六十五編」

媒孽奇談；商務印書館譯· F—S353—9·9

上海，商務，95面·「説部叢書九集九編」

歷代名人奇聞趣史；新華書局編· F—S435

上海，新華，民十一年·72面·

毁去的序文；徐雉著· F—S476

上海，新文化書社，民十四年·104面·「緑波社小叢書」

小説季報； F—S476

上海，清華書局·V1—V4，民七年至九年·

奔波；徐蔚南著· F—S484

上海，北新，民十七年·133面·

到大連去及其他；孫席珍著· F—S527

上海，春潮書局，民十七年·123面·

强盗；(德)釋勒原著，楊丙辰譯· F—SCh33

上海，北新，民十五年·284面·

你往何處去；(波蘭)顯克微克原著，徐炳昶，喬曾劬合譯· F—S116
上海，商務，民十一年·388面·

地中海濱；(波蘭)顯克微支原著，張友松譯· F—116a
上海，春潮，民十七年·143面·

旅行述異；(美)華盛頓歐文原著，林紓，魏易合譯· F—Ir8
上海，商務，民十三年·2冊·

格里佛遊記；(英)斯偉夫特原著，韋叢蕪譯· F—SW54
北平，北新，民十七年·卷一·「未名叢刊」

大唐三藏取經詩話；黎烈文著· F—T131
上海，商務，民十四年·75面·

大宋宣和遺事；黎烈文著· F—S131
上海，商務，民十三年·144面·

地之子；臺靜農著· F—T13
北平，未名社，民十七年·256面·「未名新集之一」

僕人；汪原放譯· F—W137
上海，亞東圖書館，民十七年·10面·

俄國童話集；唐小圃著· F—T212
上海，商務，民十三年·6冊·

天雨花；陶貞懷著· F—T245
上海，商務，4冊·

在黑暗中；丁玲著· F—T349
上海，開明書店，民十七年·270面·

孽海花；曾孟樸著· F—T528
上海，真美善書店，民十七年·再版·「第一，二編」

魯男子；曾孟樸著· F—T328
上海，真美善書店，179面·

夜談隨録；霽園主人閒齊氏編· F—T545
上海，商務，序民二年·187面·

假利券；(俄)托爾斯泰原著，楊明齋譯· F—T588
上海，商務，民十一年·130面·「文藝叢刻乙集」

我的生涯；一個俄國農婦自述；(俄)托爾斯泰編，李藻譯· F—T
上海，商務，民十四年·18面·「文學研究會叢書」

懺悔；(俄)托爾斯泰原著，張墨池，景梅九合譯·
南京，樂天，民十一年·再版·100面·

空大鼓；(俄)托爾斯泰原著，周作人譯·
上海，開明，民十七年· 面·

克利米戰血録；(俄)托爾斯泰原著，朱世溱譯· F—T58h8
上海，中華，民六年·104面·

故事；(俄)托爾斯泰原著，唐小圃譯· F—T588
上海，商務，民十二年·67面·

物語；(俄)托爾斯泰原著，唐小圃譯· F—T588
上海，商務，民十二年·74面·

寓言；(俄)托爾斯泰原著，唐小圃譯· F—T588
上海，商務，民十二年·27面·

民話；(俄)托爾斯泰原著，唐小圃譯· F—T588
上海，商務，民十二年·2册·

小説；(俄)托爾斯泰原著，唐小圃譯· F—T588
上海，商務，民十二年·124面·

托爾斯泰短篇小説集；(俄)托爾斯泰原著，瞿秋白，耿濟之合鐸·
F—T588t
上海，商務，民十三年·4版·244面·

履園叢話；錢梅溪輯· F—T608
上海，商務，序同治九年·2册·

歡樂的舞蹈；錢杏邨著· F—T612
上海，現代，民十七年·170面·

悵惘及其他；錢公俠著· F—T613
上海，春潮書局，民十七年·131面·

左公平回記；嚴庭樾編· F—T680
上海，中國圖書公司和記，民五年·2册·

情人；左幹臣著· F—T683

上海，亞細亞書局，民十七年・131 面・

創痕；左幹臣著・ F—T684

上海，亞細亞書局，民十七年・126 面・

石榴花；杜衡著・ F—T763

上海，一線書店，民十七年・132 面・

羅亭；屠格涅夫原著，趙景深譯・ F—T845

上海，商務，民十七年・229 面・「文學研究會叢書」

標點宋人平話新編五代史評話；董大理編・ F—T857

上海，商務，民十四年・198 面・

小約翰；(荷蘭)望藹覃原著，魯迅譯・ F—A289

北平，未名社，民十七年・260 面・「未名叢刊之一」

贛第德；(法)凡爾太原著，徐志摩譯・ F—V889

上海，北新，民十六年・196 面・

愛的犧牲；王誌之著・ F—W136

北平，文化學社，民十七年・234 面・「荒島社叢書」

死綫上；王任叔著・ F—W144

上海，金屋書店，民十七年・198 面・

黄金；王魯彥著・ F—W148

上海，人間書店，民十七年・186 面・

虞初支志；王葆心著・ F—W156Y

上海，商務，民十五年・136 面・

憔悴的杯；王茨蓀著・ F—W159

北京，北新，民十七年・368 面・

翠英及其夫的故事；汪静之著・ F—w175

上海，亞東圖書館，民十七年・再版・168 面・

七封書信的自傳；魏金枝著・ F—w201

上海，人間書店，民十七年・116 面・

生之細流；聞國新著・ F—w240

北京，文化學社，民十七年・156 面・

上下古今談；吳敬恒著・ F—w281ss

上海，文明，民十五年・10版・4册・

母與子；(日)武者小路實篤原著，崔萬秋譯・　F—w304

上海，真美善書店，民十七年・756面・

王爾德童話；(英)王爾德原著，穆木天譯・　F—w644w

上海，泰東，民十一年・112面・「世界兒童文學選集第一種」

鬼；(英)王爾德原著，虛白譯・　F—w646

上海，真美善書店，民十七年・114面

鷹梯小豪傑；(英)楊支原著，林紓，陳家麟合譯・　F—Y121

半夜角聲；葉勁風著・　F—Y181

上海，商務，民十四年・130面・「小説世界叢刊」

九月的玫瑰；葉靈風譯・　F—Y186

上海，現代書局，民十七年・134面

天竹；葉靈鳳著・　f—Y86t

上海，現代，民十七年・126面・

未亡人；葉鼎洛著・　F—Y193

上海，新宇宙書店，民十七年・310面・

白癡；葉鼎洛著・　F—Y193

上海，真美善書店，民十七年・178面

南北戰爭趣談；剡淡老叟輯・　F—Y255

民七年・

增圖七俠五義傳；石玉昆原著，俞樾重編・　F—Y374

上海，商務，序清光緒己丑年・525面

南丹及奈儂夫人；佐拉原著，東亞病夫譯・　F—N075

上海，真美善書店，民十七年・136面

洗澡；(法)左拉原著，徐霞村譯・　F—N075

上海，開明，民十七年・108面・「文學週報社叢書」

類目索引

0024	度量	389
0028	廣告學	559・1
0033	意大利文學	850
	戲劇	852
	遊記	914・5
	烹飪	641・5
0040	文學	800
	文學史	809
	文學批評	801
	文學讀本	810・7
0040	文字學(見語言學)	400
	交通	380・6
	交易所	332・6
	交際術	177
	交際禮節	395
0060	音樂	780
0062	諺語	393
0166	語言學	400
0260	訓育	371・8
0263	訴訟法	347・9
0292	新詩	811
	新文學	810・1
	新聞學	070
0366	識字運動	379
0464	詩文一總集	818
	詩文彙集(普通)	808・8
	詩學研究(普通)	808・1
0468	讀書法	028・6

0669	課程	375
0761	記憶	154
0762	詞	811
0764	設計教學法	371・3
0862	診斷學	616・07
	論理學(見邏輯)	
0865	議院	328
1000	一元論	147
1010	三角學	514
	工業政策	331
	工會	331
	工業史	609
	工程學	620
	工藝製造	670
1010	亞裏斯多德	185・1
	巫	133・4
1040	平民教育	379
	平民政治	321・8
	平民主義	321・4
	平面三角	514・5
	平面幾何	513・1
1043	天文學	520
1060	西臘哲學	182
	西洋畫	750
	百科全書	030
1064	礮兵	358
1068	礦業	622
	礦物學	540

1071	電報	654
1090	不平等條約	327・51
	票據法	347・7
1128	預算决算	336
1217	聯語	819・06
	聯邦政治	321・021
1223	水產	639
	水產動物學	590
	水彩畫	752
1240	刑法	343
	刑事訴訟法	347・9
1241	孔子	181・1
1212	形而上學	110
1315	職業指導	371・42
	職業教育	371・42
	職業倫理	174
1421	殖民政策	325
1519	珠算	511・2
1710	孟子	181・102
1768	歌謡	398
	歌舞	782
1814	政治學	320
	政體論	321
	政治哲學	320・1
	政治史	320・9
	政黨	329
2026	信託公司	332・14
2041	航空	629

2290	利息	332・8
2291	種花	635・9
2297	稻	633・1
2299	絲	638
2300	卜	133・3
2320	外科	617
	外國匯兑	332・45
	外交	327
	外交—中國	327・51
2324	代數	512
2325	俄國史	947
	哲學	197・9
	文學	891・7
	戲劇	891・72
	戲劇研究(普通)	808・2
2390	秘密會社	366
2412	動物學	590
2421	化學	540
	化學實驗	542
	化學工藝	660
2423	德國	
	戲劇	832
	文學	830
	歷史	943
	哲學	193
2454	特殊教育	371・9
2472	幼稚園	372・2
2480	貨幣學	332・4

2792	網球	797
2821	作物學	633
2821	作文法	810・8
2822	倫理學	170
	倫理學史	170・9
	人生哲學	171
	國家倫理	172
	公民倫理	172・1
	戰時倫理	172・4
	家庭倫理	173
	職業倫理	174
	社會倫理	177
	倫理學原理	171
2824	微積分學	517
	微生物學	616・01
2891	税則	336・2
3011	注音字母	495・121
3028	家政	640
	家庭問題	392・3
	家庭教育	374
	家庭倫理	173
3030	進化論	575
3033	憲法　憲法史	342
3040	宇宙論	113
3012	寓言	819
3060	審判	347・9
3080	實驗主義	149・9
3090	宗教	200

	宗教與科學	215
3210	測量法	526・9
3214	叢書	080
3310	心理學	150
	教育心理學	370・15
	心理測驗	371・102
	心身鍛煉法	130
3316	治療學	616
	冶金學	669
3318	演説術	808・5
3410	法律	310
	法典—中國	315
	法院	347・0
3413	法庭	347・9
	法令	352・11
	法國哲學	194
	歷史	944
	戲劇	842
	文學	840
3421	社會科學	300
	社會學	301
	社會問題	301
	社會心理學	301
	社會學史	309
	社會教育	307
	社會倫理	177
	社會調查	309・1
	社會主義	335

3430	造紙	676
	造型美術	730
3490	染色學	667
3516	油畫	750
3520	神話	398 · 4
3530	遺傳學	575 · 1
3611	混合算學	510
3630	邏輯	160
3710	盜匪問題	364
3730	運動	790
	選舉	324
3750	軍火	355 · 82
	軍事學	355
3780	資本問題	331
3811	汽車	629 · 2
3814	游泳	796
3815	海商法	347 · 7
3824	複式教授	371 · 3
3830	道路	625
	道教	299 · 5
	道爾頓制	371 · 38
	遊記	910—919
	遊覽指南	910 · 2
	遊藝	790
3912	消費合作社	334 · 5
4003	太平洋問題	327
4010	土壤學	631
	土木工程	625

	科孺婦	618
4762	劃市計都	352・5
4793	橡皮	678
4796	格言	819
4844	教育學	370
	市教育	352・9
	教育社會學	307
	教育史	370・9
	教授法	371
	教育哲學	370・1
	教育辭典	370・3
	教育統計	370・2
	教育法令	379・14
	教育測驗	372・102
	教育心理學	370・15
	教會史	270
4860	警察	352・2
5000	中國哲學	181・1
	財政史	335・51
	憲法	342・51
	教育史	370・951
	教育問題	379・51
	教育統計	379・51
	商業史	380・951
	家庭問題	392・3
	語言學	495・1
	字典	495・13
	文法	495・15

	工業史	609
	醫學史	610・9
	農業史	630・951
	體育史	790・9
	小説史	808・3
	文學	810
	文學史	810・9
	修辭學	810・8
	戲曲	812
	詩一研究	811
	總統	811・08
	别集	811・9
	歷史	951
	中日關係	327・51
	中英關係	327・51
	中俄關係	327・51
	中央行政	351
	中央政府	351
	中學教育	373
5010	畫論	740
5013	蟲害學	632
5023	本能	158
5034	專門及大學教育	378
5060	書牘	816
	書信彙集(普通)	808・6
	書信作法	808・6
5090	東亞史	950
	東方哲學	181・1

6015	國際匯兑	332・45
	國際關係	327
	國際條約	341・2
	國際貿易	382
	國際會議	341・1
	國際聯盟	341・1
6022	易卜生	839・826
6033	思想(心理)	153
6040	田徑賽	796
6060	圖案	745
	圖書館學	020
6071	昆蟲學	595
6073	園藝	635
6080	足球	797
6090	果木	634
6211	跳舞	793
6299	縣自治	352・101
6355	戰術學	355・4
	戰時倫理	172・4
	戰時國際公法	341・3
6363	獸醫學	619
6480	財政學	336・4
	財政史	33
6650	單級教授	371・3
6703	眼科	617・7
6733	照相學	770
7021	雕版術	655・19
7022	肺癆病	616・995

7750	母性	396
7760	醫學	610
	醫方	615・4
7771	巴黎和會	341・4
7772	印度哲學	181・4
	文學	891・4
	歷史	954
7774	民法	347・1
	民權	323・4
	民治政體	321・8
	民事訟訴法	347・9
7777	關係問題	336・2
7778	歐洲史	910
	歐戰	940・3
	歐洲財政史	336・4
7810	監獄學	365
8000	人類學	572
	人生觀	120
	人生哲學	171
	人口論	312
	人口限制論	312
	人民與國家之關係	323
	人類進化	572
8010	金工	680
8018	鑛產	553
8022	分析化學	514
	分團教授法	371・3
8033	無線電學	621・3842

8810	藍煤	799
8814	簿記	657
8844	算學	511
9872	節慾論	178
9000	小説	F
9000	小説考証	808・3
	小學教育	372
	小學教學法	372・01
	小學各科教學法	372
	小兒科	618・9
9050	拳術	796・6
9060	省憲	352
9489	煤鑛	553・2
9501	性論	575・9
	性教育	612・6
9502	情感	157
9822	幣制問題	332・4
9942	勞資問題	331
	勞動法	338・9

黨 義 書 籍

（本編採用國立廣東中山大學圖書館革命文庫分類法）

分類大綱

S00	總類
S10	孫文主編
S12	原著
S13	三民主義的討論和研究
S14	建國大綱及方略的討論和研究
S15	五權憲法的討論和研究
S16	政策及宣言策
S17	講演集　函牘
S18	叢書
S19	孫中山歷史
S20	中國國民黨
S28・3	黨員論文集
S28・4	黨員演講集
S29	黨史
S29・9	黨員傳記
S30	黨化教育
S40	國民政府
S50	中國革命問題

S59　中國革命史
S60　世界革命問題
S70　反革命運動

S00　總載

革命哲學；朱謙之著·　s01—C821
上海，泰東，民十年·236 面·「創造社叢書第二種」
革命原理；郎擎霄著·　s01—L140
廣州，丁卜圖書社，民十六年·227 面·

S10　孫文主義

孫文主義總論；邵元冲講演·　s10—s171
上海，民智，民十五年·初版·5 面·「中山學院叢刊第一種」
中山主義表解；王祖佑編·　S10·2—W159
對於孫文主義之哲學的基礎之商榷；孫鏡亞著·　S11—S511
上海，三民公司，民十五年·3 版·39 面·
孫文主義之哲學的基礎；戴季陶著·　s11—T121
上海，民智，民十五年·4 版·68 面·
孫中山生平及其主義大綱；文莊著·　s11—W251
上海，光華，民十五年·77 面·

S12　原著

孫中山先生遺教；黄昌穀編·　s12·3—H471
上海，民智，民十五年·798 面·

三民主義；孫文演講． s12·3—s511
上海，太平洋書店，民十六年·6版·274面·

民族主義；孫文講演． S12·31—s511
上海，民智，民十三年·142面·

民權主義；孫文著． S12·32—s511
上海，民智，民十四年·202面·

建國方略；孫文著． s12·4—s511
上海，民智，民十一年·464面·

孫文學説；孫文著． S12·41—s511
上海，民智，民十三年·3版·215面·

軍人精神教育；孫文著． s12·41—s511
上海，民智，民十六年·5版·84面·

民權初步；孫文著． s12·43—S511
上海，民智，民十六年·124面·

五權憲法；孫文演講． s12·5—s511
上海，民智，民十五年·5版·28面·

中山先生文集；飛俠輯． s12·8—s511
明明書局，民十五年·初版·126面·

S13 三民主義的討論和研究

三民主義精義；三民公司編． s13—s511
上海，三民公司，民十七年·5版·560面·

到大同的路；朱謙之著． s13—C821
上海，泰東，民十七年·175面·

中山政治淺説；韓德光編． s13—H123
上海，中央圖書局，民十六年·再版·120面·

三民主義之認識；胡漢民著． s13—H405
上海，進一書局，民十七年·76面·

三民主義的連環性；胡漢民著． s13—H405
上海，民智，民十七年·110面·

三民主義者之使命；胡漢民著·　s13—H405
上海，民智，民十六年·158 面·

孫公紀念週課本；甘乃光編輯·　s13·1—K121
上海，三民公司，民十五年·再版·36 面·

三民主義討論大綱；劉湛恩編·　s13·1—L306
上海，青年協會，民十六年·45 面·「公民教育叢刊」

三民主義要畧；民智書局編·　s13·1—M238
上海，民智，民十七年·3 版·30 面·

三民主義常識；孫中山講演·　s13·1—s
上海，三民公司，民十六年·106 面·

三民主義概論；楊幼炯著·　s13·1—Y144

三民主義考試問答一百條；　s13·2—c601
上海，建國書局，民十七年·4 版·62 面·
上海，民智，民十七年·134 面·「革命叢書」

全民政治問答；魏冰心輯·　s13·4—W205
上海，中央圖書局，民十六年·67 面·

民生主義討論大綱；李權時編·　s13·5—L181
上海，青年協會，民十六年·62 面·

民生主義與人口問題；王警濤著·　s13·5—W136
上海，民智，民十六年·118 面·

三民主義與中國及世界；羅敦偉著·　s13·6—L398
上海，民義書局，民十六年·47 面·

三民主義與共産主義；張冰淇著·　s13·61—C152
上海，民生書店，民十七年·49 面·

S14　建國大綱及方畧的討論和研究

革命與權術；洪瑞釗著·　s14—H523
上海，民智，民十七年·74 面·「革命叢書」

革命與腐化；任中敏著·　s14—J126
上海，民智，民十七年·177 面·「革命叢書」

建國大綱釋義；魏冰心輯． s14・1—W205

上海，中央圖書局，民十七年・再版・74 面・

訓政；嚴思椿著・ s14・32—Y213

上海，各大書店，民十七年・282 面・

訓政時期調查户口之意見；許崇　著・ s14・33—H369

上海，民智，民十七年・再版・24 面・

訓政大綱提案説明書；胡漢民著・ s14・32—H405

中國國民黨湖北省黨務指導委員會宣傳部，民十七年・16 面・

訓政時期地方行政計劃；邵元冲著・ s14・32—171

上海，民智，民十五年・再版・44 面・

建國方略淺説；魏冰心編・ s14・4—W205

上海，中央圖書局，民十六年・　面・

中山主義淺説；魏冰心輯・ S14・41—w200

上海，中央圖書局，民十六年・3 版・51 面・

建國方略問答；印維　輯・ s14・4—Y288

上海，中央圖書局，民十七年・4 版・164 面・

中國國民黨實業講演集；中國國民黨中央執行委員會實業部編・ s14・42—C976

上海，民智，民十五年・4 版・94 面・

中山實業淺説；萬扶風編・ s14・42—w122

上海，中央圖書局，民十六年・129 面・

S15　五權憲法的討論和研究

五權憲法論；陳顧遠著・ s15—C278

上海，光明書局，民十六年・34 面・

五權憲法大綱；謝瀛洲編・ s15—s426

上海，遠東書局，民十七年・再版・214 面・

五權憲法釋義；魏冰心編・ s15—w205

上海，中央圖書局，民十七年・3 版・104 面・

中山先生之革命政策；黎照寰編・ s16—L215

上海，民智，民十七年・78 面・

中同先生對於關國民會議及廢除不平等條約的主張；孫中山演講・　s19・1—s511

上海，三民書店・　面・

S17　講演集　函牘

中山演義；許慕・　s17・1—H373

廣州，國民書店，民十六年・再版・4 册・

中山主義講演集；馬　山輯・　s17・11—M117

上海，三民公司，民十五年・再版・86 面・

孫中山先生演講録；孫文演講・　s17・1—s511

上海，民智，民十二年・122 面・

孫總理講演集；孫文演講・　s17・1—s511

國民革命軍中央軍事政治學校政治部，民十五年・123 面・

孫中山演講集；孫中山演講・　s57・1—s511

220 面・

孫中山先生十講；孫文演講・　s17・1—s511

上海，民智，民十五年・5 版・122 面・

中山演講集；孫文演講・　s17・1—S511

上海，太平洋書店，民十五年・4 版・436 面・

孫中山先生由上海過日本之言論；　s17・1—s511

廣州，民智，民十五年・5 版・136 面・

中山社會主義談；三民公司編・　s17・12—s121

上海，三民公司，民十六年・3 版・38 面・「三民叢書第二種」

孫中山先生對農民之訓詞；孫文講演・　s17・12—s511

中國國民黨中央農民運動講習所，民十六年・22 面・

S18　叢書

孫中山先生遺言；　s18—S155

上海書店，民十四年・再版・34面・

中山叢書； s18—s511

上海，太平洋書店，民十五年・4版・3册・

S19 孫中山歷史

中山先生之生與死；范體仁編・ s19—F133

上海，光明書局，民十六年・再版・100面・

孫逸仙傳記；(美)林百克愿著，徐植仁譯・ s19—511

上海，三民公司，民十五年・338面・

孫逸仙倫敦被難記；孫文著・ s19・2—s511

上海，新民社，民十六年・84面・

孫中山榮哀録；中華革新學社編・ S19・3—C976

中華革新學社，民十四年・115面・

孫中山先生北上與逝世後詳情；黄昌穀講演・ S19・3—H471

上海，民智，民十五年・再版・52面・

孫中山評論集第一編；三民公司編・ s19・3—s121

上海，三民公司，民十五年・3版・104面・

中山先生思想概觀；周佛海著・ s19・4—C774

上海，民智，民十六年・5版・50面・

中山思想問答；朱亮基輯・ s19・4—C828

上海，中央圖書局，民十五年・再版・124面・

中山先生思想概要；新覺編・ s19・4—s435

上海，光明，民十六年・5版・142面・

孫中山先生之生活；黄昌穀講演・ s19・5—H471

上海，民智，民十五年・初版・52面・

孫中山先生與中國；高爾柏，高爾松合編・ s19・71—K167

上海，民智，民十五年・5版・84面・

中山故事；馬眉伯編・ s19・8—M118

上海，商務，民十七年・116面・「新時代少年叢書」

孫中山軼事集；三民公司編· s19·8—s121
上海，三民公司，民十五年·再版·220 面·

孫中山年年譜；賀嶽僧編· s19·92—s511
上海，世界書局，民十七年·再版·73 面·

中山嘉言鈔；周潤寰輯· s19·93—C777
上海，中央圖書局，民十六年·再版·70 面·

孫中山先生陵墓圖案；孫中山先生葬事籌備處編· s19·97—s511
上海，民智，民十四年·30 面·

S20 中國國民黨

國民革命與中國國民黨上編；戴季陶著· S20—T121
廣州，平社，民十七年·再版·

中國國民黨問答；魏冰心輯· S20—W05
上海，中央圖書局，民十六年·再版·71 面·

S21 規程

中國國民黨總章； S21—C976
國民政府軍事委員會總政治部，民十六年·15 面·

中國國民黨黨務；上海法學編譯社編· S21—s155
上海，會文堂，民十七年·46 面

中國國民黨中央執行委員各省區代表聯席會議宣言及決議案； s21·4—c976
國民革命軍總司令部政治部，民十六年·70 面·

中國國民黨第二屆中央執行委員第三屆全體會議宣言訓令及決議案； s21·4—c976
中央軍事委員會總政治部，民十六年·59 面·

中國國民黨第一次全國代表大會宣言； s21·4—c976

25 面．

中國國民黨第一二次全國代表大會宣言； s21．4—c976
漢口特別市黨部執行委員會，民十五年．56 面．

中國國民黨第一二次全國代表大會宣言及議決案； s21．4—c976

中國國民黨中央各省區聯席會議宣言及議決案； s21．4—c976
中國國民黨湖北省黨部．174 面．

中國國民黨第二次全國代表大會宣言及決議案； s21．4—c976
國民革命軍總司令部政治部，民十五年．104 面．

中國國民黨第二次全國代表大會及宣言決議案； s21．4—c976
長沙，民治書局，民十六年．98 面．

中國國民黨第二次全國代表大會宣言； s21．4—c976
上海，三民公司．民十六年．5 版．30 面．

中國國民黨重要宣言訓令集；陸軍軍官學校政治部編． s21．4—L425
民十三年．212 面．

汪陳甘願出席問題； s22—w165
民十七年．79 面．

國民政府五中會議；國民政府委員編． s22．1—K435
中國統一書局，民十七年．182 面．

開國民會議的基礎；曾傑著． s22．1—T521
廣州，人民的建設雜誌社，民十五年．24 面

中國國民黨黨員須知；中央圖書局編． s23—c979
民十六年．

中國國民黨政策；黎照寰輯． s24—L215
上海，商務，民十七年．246 面．

中國國民黨政治主張；陳毅夫著． s24—c276
南京，中山書局，1928．216 面．

S28 刊物

浙江；中國國民黨浙江省黨部． s28—c．52

民十四年·128面·

湖北省漢口特別市黨務訓練所攷試特刊·　s28—C976

中國國民黨湖北省漢口特別市黨務訓練所，114面·

S28·3　黨員論文集

血花集；張天化編·　s28·3—C171

上海，民智，民十七年·88面·「革命文庫第三種」

算舊賬；老朽輯·　s28·3—L155

上海，泰東，民十七年·198面·

建設碎金；民智書局編　s28·3—M238

上海，民智，民十六年·

天討；民報特刊編·　s28·3—M239

上海，民智，民十七年·156面·「革命文庫第二種」

黨國要人最近的幾封信集；大東書局輯·　s28·3—T134

上海，大東，民十七年·94面·

中山主義名人書信集；秦同培輯·　s28·3—T649

上海，中央圖書局，民十六年·

革命軍；鄒容著·　s28·3—T699

上海，民智，民十七年·80面·

汪精衛文存初集；汪精衛著·　s28·3—w175

廣州，民智，民十五年·258面·

吳稚暉與汪精衛；　s28·3—w281

上海，革新，民十七年·78面·

吳稚暉與汪精衛之商榷；吳稚暉汪精衛合著·　s28·3—w281

上海，中山書店，民十六年·88面·

吳稚暉先生最近對於黨國之意見；吳稚暉著·　s28·3—w281

廣州平社，民十六年·60面·

吳稚暉言論集；泰同培編·　s28·3—w281

上海，中央圖書局，民十六年·2册·

吳稚暉論政及其他；吳敬恒著·　s28·3—W281

上海，出版合作社，民十七年·

吳稚暉近著；吳稚暉著· s28·3—w281

北京，北新，民十五年·270面·

汪精衛與吳稚暉的論文集；嚴朂哉編· s28·3—Y226

上海，新時代，民十七年·153面·

吳稚暉最近言論集； s28·3—W281w

上海，大東，民十七年·2册·

S28·4 黨員演講集

演講録(第一集)；中國國民黨湖北省市黨務訓練所編· s28·4—c976

民十七年·144面·

破除迷信與革命；馮玉祥講演· s28·4—K218

河南省政府宣傳部·16面·「馮總司令講演之一」

何應欽陳銘樞最近言論集；大東書局輯· s28·4—H213

上海，大東，民十七年·58面·

胡漢民最近言論集；大東書局輯·s28·4—H405

上海，大東，民十七年·2册·

胡漢民在俄演講録第一集；胡漢民演講· s28·4—H405

廣州，民智，民十五年·再版·34面·

胡漢民先生演講集；胡漢民演講· s28·4—H405

上海，民智，民十六年·3册·

過之翰演講集；過之翰演講· s28·4—K430

陝西，財政廳徵收人員訓練班，民十七年·109面·

謬斌最近言論集；大東書局輯· s28·4—M261

上海，大東，民十七年·48面·

戴季陶講演集；戴季陶講演· s28·4—T121

上海，新民，民十七年·170面·

邵元冲先生演講集第一輯；邵元冲演講· s28·4—s171

上海，商務，民十七年·119面·

青年之路；戴季陶著· s28·4—T121

上海，民智，民十七年·3版·262面·

蔣介石言論集；朱亮基編·　s28·4—T561

上海，中央圖書局，民十六年·320面·

中山主義名人演講集；秦同培編·　s28·4—T648

上海，中央圖書局，民十六年·2册·

汪精衛先生講演集；汪精衛講演·　s28·4—w175

上海，文華書局，民十五年·130面·

S29　黨史

中國國民黨史；華林一著·　s29—H441

上海，商務，民十七年·13面·「新時代史地叢書」

中國國民黨概論；汪精衛著·　s29—w175

上海，光明，民十六年·再版·46面·

中國國民黨史概論；汪精衛著·　s29—w175

中央軍事政治學校，民十六年·3版·24面·

孫大總統廣州蒙難記；蔣介石著·　s29·4—T561

上海，民智，民十五年·5版·70面·

彈劾共產黨兩大要案；中國國民黨中央監察委員會輯·　s29·6—C976

中國國民黨中央監察委員會，民十六年·30面·

革命與清黨；黄昌穀著·　s29·6—H741

民十七年·初版·44面·

廣州事變與上海會議；廣州平社編·　s29·9—K320

民十七年·

革命與反革命；郎醒石編·　s29·6—L141

上海，民智，民十七年·611面·

清黨運動；清黨運動急進會編·　s29·6—T667

清黨運動急進會，民十六年·302面·

吳稚暉反共文匯；吳稚暉著·　s29·6—w281

上海，待旦書社，民十七年·222面·

S29·9 黨員傳記

紅花岡四烈士傳；革命紀念會輯· s29·9—K217
上海，民智，民十六年·54 面·

陳英士先生革命小史；邵元冲編· s29·9—s171
上海，民智，民十四年·22 面·

蔣介石先生歷史及北伐之言論；新中國社編· s29·9—s435
新中國社，民十六年·再版·92 面·

蔣介石的革命工作；文砥編· s29·9—T561
上海，太平洋，民十七年·再版·2 册·

S30 黨化教育

三民主義教育學；張九如編· s30—C152
上海，新時代教育社，民十七年·196 面·「新時代黨代教育叢書」

黨化教育概論；陳德徵著· s30—C288
上海，光華，民十六年·59 面·

黨化教育淺説；朱成碧編· s30—C834
上海，中央圖書局，民十六年·75 面·

實施三民主義化教育宣傳大綱；湖北省黨務指導委員會宣傳部編·
s30—C976

黨化教育輯要；中央圖書局編· s30—C979
上海，中央圖書局，民十六年·再版·135 面·

黨化教育實施法；顧詩靈編· s30—K252
上海，大東，民十七年·4 版·92 面·

黨化教育；徐蔚南著· s30—s483
上海，世界，民十六年·3 版·55 面·

黨化教育概論；王克仁著· s30—W145
上海，民智，民十六年·106 面·

孫中山主義讀本；三民公司編． s33．4—s121
上海，三民公司，民十六年．6版．61面．

中山主義婦女淺説；朱成碧編． s33．67—C834
上海，中央圖書局，民十六年．73面．

中山主義軍人淺説；韓德光編． s33．8—H123
上海，中央圖書局，民十六年．112面．

軍人必讀；中央圖書局編． s36．1—C99
上海，中央圖書局，民十六年．129面

軍事政治工作；黄鍾編． s36．1—H471
上海，泰東，民十七年．再版．241面．

革命軍刑事條例，革命軍連坐法； s36．1—K217

革命軍人四字讀本；國民革命軍中央軍事政治學校編． S36．1—K329
民十五年．36面．

總理逝世三週紀念； s38．4—H130
42面．「漢口中山日報特刊」

近代革命紀念日；張廷休編． s39—G171
上海，民智，民十七年．160面．

革命史上的重要紀念日；謝振鐸編． s39—s416
廣州黄浦中央軍事政治學校政治部發行股，民十六年．442面．
「黄浦叢書之九」

S40　國民政府

現代法制常識問答；戴季陶輯． s40—T121
上海，中央圖書局，民十六年．100面．

黨治考察記；吳潤東編． s40—w281
上海，泰東，民十七年．335面．

國民政府五院組織法合刊；中國國民黨中央黨部編． s41—K435
上海，東方圖書公司，民十七年．40面．

國民政府法規彙集：第一集；民智書局編譯所編． s41．1—M238

上海，民智，民十七年．52 面．

公安警察問答；李萬里輯． s14．3—L20C

上海，中央圖書局，民十七年．再版．118 面．

S50　中國革命問題

國民革命問題；朱劍芒輯． s50—C821

上海，中央圖書局，民十七年．再版．63 面．

中國國民革命之使命；一名世界改造之原理；范錡著． s50—F121

上海，民智，民十七年．352 面．

今日之革命與革命者．徐天一著． s50—s482

上海，民智，民十七年．82 面．「革命叢書第五種」

國民革命之兩大使命；曹雪松著． s50—T474

上海，大東，民十七年．3 版．90 面．

現今革命之意義；李石曾著． s51—L196

吳越書店，第 1 版．37 面．「國民小叢書」

中國之革命運動及其背景；邵元冲講演． s51—s171

上海，民智，民十六年．再版．32 面．「中山學院叢書第二種」

國民革命與世界大同；朱謙之編． s53．1—C821

上海，泰東，民十六年．145 面．

打倒帝國主義； s55—w175

國民革命軍總司令部政治部．236 面．

省港罷工中之中英談判；鄧中夏著． s57．2—T261

中華全國總工會省港龍工委員會宣傳部，民十五年．「86 面」．

農工小資產階級革命同盟論的分析和糾正；羅什著． s57—L397

上海，再造社，民十七年．40 面．「再造社叢書之一」

省港罷工概觀；鄧中夏著． s57．2—T261

中華全國總工會省港罷工委員會宣傳部，民十五年．92 面．

中國學生運動小史；查良鑑輯· s57·4—C110
上海，世界書局，民十六年·81面·

五世兇手之供狀； s57·51—W309

沙面慘殺案；高爾松，高爾柏合編· s57·9—k167
青年政治宣傳會，民十四年·134面·

漢口慘殺案；高爾松，高爾柏合編· s57·9—K167
青年政治宣傳會，民十四年·78面·

中國獨立運動的基點；戴季陶著· s57·9—T121
廣州，民智，民十四年·88面·

S59　中國革命史

中國民族革命運動史；建國書店編· s59—C601
上海，泰東，民十七年·再版·13面·

中國革命史；貝華編· s59—P250
上海，光明，民十六年·3版·225面·

國民革命要覽；師鄭編· s59—s260
新時代教育社，民十六年·4版·227面·

中國的革命運動；蔣國珍著· s59—T566
上海，世界書局，民十七年·再版·48面·

中國革命實地見聞録；斷永樓主人原著，樂嗣炳譯· s59—T824
上海，三民公司，民十六年·218面·

中國革命史；印維廉著· s59—Y288
上海，世界書局，民十七年·212面·

革命日誌；志光編· s59·1—C631
上海，新宇宙書店，民十七年·103面·

廣州三月二十九革命史；革命紀念會編· s59·1—K217
上海，民智，民十五年·初版·186面·

孫大元帥東征日記；古應芬記録· s59·1—K265
上海，民智，民十五年·初版·38面·

S60 世界革命問題

世界弱小民族問題；李作華著・ s60—L1971

漢口，白鶴印刷公司，民十七年・190 面・

各國革命史略；邵元冲講演・ s69—s171

上海，民智，民十五年・5 版・146 面・

近代革命史概要；張廷休編・ s69・2—C171

上海，民智，民十七年・170 面・

近十年來世界上兩大怪物；劉公度著・ s70—L365

上海，世界，民十六年・170 面・

帝國主義問答；張百天輯・ s71・4—C171

上海，中央圖書局，民十七年・再版・74 面・

帝國主義與中國；高爾松，高爾柏合編・ s71・4—K167

青年政治宣傳會，民十五年・再版・328 面・

附録　馮漢驥論著係年書目

1929 年

《湖北省立圖書館圖書目録》第一期(附類目索引、黨義書籍)，湖北官紙印刷局印

1933 年

Chinese Mythology and Dr. Ferguson (與 J. K. Shryock 合作)，Journal of the American Oriental Society Vol. 53，pp. 53-65.

1934 年

The Lolo of China：Their History and Cultural Relations，賓夕法尼亞大學碩士論文。手稿今存美國賓夕法尼亞大學範佩特圖書館(Van Pelt Library，University of Pennsylvania)

1935 年

The Black Magic in China Known as Ku (與 J. K. Shryock 合作)，Journal of the American Oriental Society Vol. 55，pp. 1-30；抽印本見 Philadelphia，Pa.，American Oriental Society，Offprint Series，No. 5

1936 年

The Origin of Yu Huang，Harvard Journal of Asiatic Studies，Vol. I，No. 2，pp. 242-250

Teknonymy as a Formative Factor in the Chinese Kinship System，American Anthropologist，Vol. 38，No. 1，pp. 59-66

1937 年

The Chinese Kinship System，Harvard Journal of Asiatic Studies，Vol. 2，No. 2，pp. 141-275。抽印本見 Philadelphia：University of Pennsylvania，141-275 頁。重印本見 Cambridge：Published for the Harvard-Yehching Institute by the Harvard University Press，1948。又見：Harvard-Yehching Institute studies XXII，Cambridge：Harvard University，1967。該書中譯本見《中國親屬稱謂指南》(徐志誠譯)，上海文藝出版社，1989

1938 年

The Historical Origins of the Lolo (與 J. K. Shryock 合作)，Harvard

Journal of Asiatic Studies, Vol. 3, No. 2, pp. 103-127。中譯本《彝族的歷史起源》見《馮漢驥考古學論文集》, 文物出版社, 1985

1941 年

《由中國親屬名詞上所見之中國古代婚姻制》,《齊魯學報》1 期

1942 年

《倮儸與東爨》,《雜説月刊》1 期

1943 年

《中國文化發展的南向與北向説的新論》,《學思》3 卷 6 期

《漢和圖書分類法》(A Classification Scheme for Chinese and Japanese Books), (與裘開明、於震寰合作), Committees on Far Eastern Studies, American Council of Learned Societies, Washington, D. C.

War Excavation Reveals Tomb, El Palacio, Vol. L, No. 11, pp. 265-266

1944 年

The Discovery and Excavation of the Royal Tomb of Wang Chien, Quarterly Bulletin of Chinese Bibliography, N. S. Vol. 4, Nos. 1-2, pp. 1-11; Szechwan Museum, Chengtu, Occasional paper. 1(四川省博物館單刊之一), 9 頁; 抽印本見 Archives of the Chinese Art Society of America (New York), Vol. Ⅱ, 1947

《禹生石紐辨》,《説文月刊》第 4 卷合刊本

1945 年

The Megalithic Remains of the Chengtu Plain, Journal of the West China Border Research Society Vlo. XVI Series A, pp. 15-22; 中譯本《成都平原之大石文化遺蹟》見《馮漢驥考古學論文集》, 文物出版社, 1985

1948 年

《元八思巴蒙文聖旨碑發現記》,《四川博物館》單刊之二

《川康明清土司官印考》(張勛燎據 20 世紀 40 年代手稿整理), 四川大學歷史文化學院考古學係編《四川大學考古專業創建四十週年暨馮漢

驥教授百年誕辰紀念文集》，四川大學出版社，2001

《鬆理茂汶羌族考察雜記》（張勛燎據 20 世紀 40 年代手稿整理），四川大學歷史文化學院考古學係編《四川大學考古專業創建四十週年暨馮漢驥教授百年誕辰紀念文集》，四川大學出版社，2001

1950 年

Marriage Customs in the Vicinity of I-Ch'ang（與 J. K. Shryock 合作），Harvard Journal of Asiatic Studies，Vol. 13，No. 3-4，pp. 362-430

1951 年

《岷江上游的石棺葬文化》，成都《工商導報》1951 年 5 月 20 日，《學林》副刊

《評張仲實譯本恩格斯〈家庭、私有財產及國家的起源〉》，成都《工商導報》1951 年 1 月 21 日，《學林》副刊 2 期

1954 年

《成都萬佛寺石刻造像》，《文物參考資料》9 期；日文譯本見《成都萬佛寺の石刻造像》，《美術史》一七册（美術史學會編，日本京都，便利堂）昭和 30 年 10 月（1955）

《關於資陽人頭骨化石出土的地層問題》（童恩正據 1954 年手稿整理），《馮漢驥考古學論文集》，文物出版社，1985

《關於資陽人頭骨化石問題》（張勛燎據 1954 年手稿整理），四川大學歷史文化學院考古學係編《四川大學考古專業創建四十週年暨馮漢驥教授百年誕辰紀念年文集》，四川大學出版社，2001

1956 年

《相如琴臺與王建永陵》，《史學論叢》（四川大學歷史係編）

《駕頭考》，《史學論叢》（四川大學歷史係編）

《跋吳三桂周五年曆書》，《史學論叢》（四川大學歷史係編）

1957 年

《前蜀王建墓内石刻伎樂考》，《四川大學學報》1 期

《記唐印本陀羅尼經咒的發現》，《文物參考資料》5 期

《論盤舞》,《文物參考資料》8 期

(美)莫爾根著《古代社會》(譯著,與楊東蓀、張栗原合作),北京:生活、讀書、新知三聯書店;商務印書館 1971 年重印(馮漢驥撰寫的"譯校後記"已收入《川大史學·馮漢驥卷》,四川大學出版社,2006)

《論南唐二陵中的玉册》,《考古通訊》9 期

1959 年

《四川古代的船棺葬》(與楊有潤、王家祐合作),《考古學報》2 期

《王建墓内出土"大帶"考》,《考古》8 期

1960 年

《四川船棺葬發掘報告》(主編),文物出版社

1961 年

《雲南晉寧石塞山出土文物的族屬問題試探》,《考古》9 期

《前蜀王建墓出土的金銀平脱漆器及銀錯胎漆器》,《關於"楚公豪戈的真僞並略論四川"巴蜀"時期的兵器》,《文物》11 期。徐中舒主編《巴蜀考古論文集》,文物出版社,1987

《四川的畫像磚墓及畫像磚》,《文物》11 期

1963 年

《雲南晉寧石塞山出土銅器研究——若干主要人物活動圖像試釋》,《考古》6 期

Unearthing an Unknown Culture, China Reconstructs, Vol. 12, No. 9, pp. 38-41

1964 年

《前蜀王建墓發掘報告》(專著),文物出版社;文物出版社 2002 年再版

《略論玉蜀黍、番薯的起源及其在我國的傳播》(張勛燎據"文革"以前手稿整理),《馮漢驥考古學論文集》,文物出版社,1985

1973 年

《岷江上游的石棺葬》，《考古學報》2 期

1974 年

《雲南晉寧出土銅鼓研究》，《文物》1 期

1979 年

《記廣漢出土的玉石器》(與童恩正合作)，《四川大學學報》(哲學社會科學版) 1 期；《文物》2 期

1980 年

《西南古奴隸王國》，《歷史知識》4 期；徐中舒主編《巴蜀考古論文集》，文物出版社，1987

《四川彭縣出土的銅器》，《文物》12 期

編後記

本集按照《荆楚文庫》規範編輯，有關編寫特此説明之：

一、本集共兩卷，分論文篇和著作篇。

論文篇分中文論文篇和英文論文篇。中文論文篇以文物出版社 1985 年出版的簡體版本《馮漢驥考古學論文集》和四川大學出版社 2006 年出版的簡體版本《川大史學 馮漢驥卷》爲底本，而爲盡量選全，增加《〈藏書絶句〉的著者》《中國文化發展的南向與北向説的新論》《明皇幸蜀與天回鎮》等篇，均以初版原稿爲底本。英文論文篇以四川大學出版社 2015 年出版的《川大史學・馮漢驥英文卷》爲底本，收録 1949 年前馮漢驥所著的英文論文 7 篇。

著作篇收録徐志誠譯《中國親屬稱謂指南》和馮漢驥主持編撰的《湖北省圖書館圖書目録(第一期)》。《中國親屬稱謂指南》是馮漢驥在人類學方面的代表作，寫于 20 世紀 30 年代，以英文發表在《哈佛亞洲研究學報》，1989 年由徐志誠翻譯，上海文藝出版社出版簡體版本。本書以此版爲底本。《湖北省圖書館圖書目録(第一期)》以初版爲底本。

在此，感謝馮士美先生、張勛燎先生、四川大學出版社和武漢大學圖書館的協助。同時，向徐志誠先生致謝。

二、馮漢驥先生“論著係年書目”附録於集後，展示馮漢驥先生學術成就，以饗讀者。

三、本集所收各篇著述，均不作任何删節。文本由編者審讀，字句殘缺或難以辨認者用□表示。

本書編輯從前人成果中獲益良多。限於學識，編輯之錯漏在所難免，敬祈識者指謬。

编者